Civil Proce

Commentary and Materials

Fifth Edition

Civil Procedure

Commentary and Materials

Fifth Edition

Stephen Colbran

B Com (Hons), LLB (Hons) (UQ), LLM (Hons), Grad Cert (Higher Ed) (QUT), PhD (UQ)
Solicitor, Queensland
Professor of Law, School of Commerce and Law Central Queensland University

Peta Spender

BA, LLB (Hons equiv) (NSW), LLM (Syd)
Barrister and Solicitor, Australian Capital Territory; Solicitor, New South Wales
Professor, College of Law, Australian National University
Presidential Member, ACT Civil and Administrative Tribunal

Sheryl Jackson

LLB (Hons) QIT, LLM (UQ)
Associate Professor, Faculty of Law, Queensland University of Technology

Roger Douglas

BA (Hons), LLB (Hons) (Melb), MPhil (Yale), PhD (La Trobe)
Barrister and Solicitor, Victoria
Professor of Law, La Trobe University

Tania Penovic

BA, LLB (Hons) (Melb), MSt (Oxon), Grad Cert (Law Teaching) (Monash)
Deputy Director, Castan Centre for Human Rights Law, Monash University

LexisNexis Butterworths
Australia
2012

LexisNexis

AUSTRALIA	LexisNexis Butterworths
	475–495 Victoria Avenue, Chatswood NSW 2067
	On the internet at: www.lexisnexis.com.au
ARGENTINA	LexisNexis Argentina, BUENOS AIRES
AUSTRIA	LexisNexis Verlag ARD Orac GmbH & Co KG, VIENNA
BRAZIL	LexisNexis Latin America, SAO PAULO
CANADA	LexisNexis Canada, Markham, ONTARIO
CHILE	LexisNexis Chile, SANTIAGO
CHINA	LexisNexis China, BEIJING, SHANGHAI
CZECH REPUBLIC	Nakladatelství Orac sro, PRAGUE
FRANCE	LexisNexis SA, PARIS
GERMANY	LexisNexis Germany, FRANKFURT
HONG KONG	LexisNexis Hong Kong, HONG KONG
HUNGARY	HVG-Orac, BUDAPEST
INDIA	LexisNexis, NEW DELHI
ITALY	Dott A Giuffrè Editore SpA, MILAN
JAPAN	LexisNexis Japan KK, TOKYO
KOREA	LexisNexis, SEOUL
MALAYSIA	LexisNexis Malaysia Sdn Bhd, PETALING JAYA, SELANGOR
NEW ZEALAND	LexisNexis, WELLINGTON
POLAND	Wydawnictwo Prawnicze LexisNexis, WARSAW
SINGAPORE	LexisNexis, SINGAPORE
SOUTH AFRICA	LexisNexis Butterworths, DURBAN
SWITZERLAND	Staempfli Verlag AG, BERNE
TAIWAN	LexisNexis, TAIWAN
UNITED KINGDOM	LexisNexis UK, LONDON, EDINBURGH
USA	LexisNexis Group, New York, NEW YORK
	LexisNexis, Miamisburg, OHIO

National Library of Australia Cataloguing-in-Publication entry

Author:	Colbran, Stephen.
Title:	Civil Procedure: Commentary and Procedures.
Edition:	5th edition.
ISBN:	9780409331943 (pbk).
	9780409331950 (ebook).
Notes:	Includes index.
Subjects:	Civil procedure — Australia.
Dewey Number:	347.9405.

© 2012 Reed International Books Australia Pty Limited trading as LexisNexis.

First edition 1998; Second edition 2002 (reprinted 2003, 2004, 2005); Third edition 2005 (reprinted 2006); Fourth edition 2009 (reprinted 2012).

Inquiries should be addressed to the publishers.

Typeset in Adobe Caslon Pro and Trade Gothic.

Printed in China.

Visit LexisNexis Butterworths at www.lexisnexis.com.au

Contents

Contents

Contents

Preface

Since the dawn of civilisation, humankind has settled disputes by warfare and diplomacy. While alternative dispute resolution may be a form of diplomacy, modern litigation is perceived by some as a sanctioned form of warfare. Using Sun Tsu's, *The Art of War* as an analogy — the parties are the disputants wishing to gain territory or reclaim lost rights; their barristers are the generals and their solicitors are foot soldiers assisting in the battle; the Rules of Court and legislation are akin to terrain; the judge is all-powerful nature (presiding over weather, environmental conditions, skirmishes, and the rules of the game); discovery, inspection, subpoenas and private detectives are the means of spying; and costs are represented by rapid consumption of wealth and mental strength. In such an environment, strategy and tactics often dominate rational solutions. Parties' and societies' resources are consumed at an astonishing rate, and community perception moves against the system seeking alternatives.

But warfare is not the only solution. Diplomacy and what some perceive as 'alternative dispute resolution' have always had their place. The categories of alternative dispute resolution have enlarged in recent times to encompass negotiation, mediation, case appraisal, mini-trial etc. These forms of dispute resolution have played their part in modifying the development of the rules of civil procedure and tactics of the game.

Problems of Australian civil procedural law include:

- defects in the way in which witnesses give evidence — namely varying performance, time delays, memory lapse, tutoring, advocates for particular parties and points of view;
- focus on the procedure and personalities, not the problem;
- impact of technology;
- managing large cases and class actions;
- inordinate delays;
- how to manage off-shore outsourcing and quality issues;
- too much emphasis on an adjudicated solution at the risk of ignoring earlier dispute resolution alternatives;
- increasing numbers of ill-prepared self-litigants;
- perceived unfairness and evident frustration among litigants;
- absence of procedures to exchange evidence at the earliest available opportunity;
- the court as a hostile environment, including foreign rules, jargon and pressure;
- parties sanctioning delay;
- leaving the litigation to the parties' devices results in unnecessary expenditure of both time and money with the potential of unfairness;
- excessive cost;

- non-supervision of cost rules;

- frustration of witnesses who are cut short when they want to tell their story;

- the rich being able to afford better lawyers, producing an unfair result and power imbalances;

- inconsistent taxation treatment of corporations and individuals; and

- pressures on judges to perform to meet the pressure of a relentless workload.

Politicians and the press blame lawyers: too much delay and restrictive practices, which inflate costs. Lawyers blame the government: appoint more judges and throw more money at the problem.

Since the fourth edition of this text, there have been numerous changes in the Rules of Court in most jurisdictions. Most of these changes represent a rationalisation of the litigation system in an attempt to manage cost, delay and access to justice. The focus of law reform has been to address some of the problems previously identified, including:

- enabling and encouraging resolution of disputes by agreement rather than adjudication;

- encouraging access to justice;

- providing cheaper, less labour-intensive, and quicker means of adjudication;

- establishing mechanisms to assist with the use of technology;

- frank exchange of real contentions and relevant information through enlarging discovery and refining the scope of pleadings;

- continual development of case management regimes; and

- movement towards uniformity of court rules within and between jurisdictions.

For such reforms to succeed, there needs to be a fundamental recognition of Australian procedural law and a change of mindset for all involved in dispute resolution. It is our aim in this work to help achieve these reforms through educating future generations of lawyers.

This book is an attempt to capture these realities to present a coherent exposition of civil litigation in all Australian jurisdictions. We have summarised Australian procedural law, compiled a useful set of materials, and created what we feel is an appropriate national approach to the teaching of this subject.

The size of the task has required the workload to be distributed among the authors, as follows:

- Stephen Colbran (general editor): Chapters 3, 8, 9, 15, 16, 19;

- Peta Spender: Chapters 1, 2, 6, 7, 12;

- Roger Douglas: Chapters 10, 17, 18, 20, 21;

- Sheryl Jackson: Chapters 4, 11, 13, 14; and

- Tania Penovic: Chapter 5.

The law is up-to-date on materials available to the authors as at May 2012.

Our debt to other writers is evident in the numerous excerpts from cases, journal articles and other sources. We are grateful for their assistance.

The authors wish to express their gratitude to the LexisNexis Butterworths team for their assistance with production of this book, particularly Catherine Britton.

This work is dedicated to the families of all the authors involved, without whose assistance it would never have been written, in particular: for Peta Spender (Walt, Grace, Euey and Gabe);

for Sheryl Jackson (Royce, Dean, Stacey and Nathan); for Roger Douglas (Robin Burns); for Tania Penovic (Scott, Anna, Zara, Richard and Elizabeth) and for myself (Angela, Elizabeth, Rachel and Sam). We are also indebted to Professor Greg Reinhart and Ms Molly O'Brien for their contributions to earlier editions of this work.

Stephen Colbran
Central Queensland University
School of Commerce and Law
August 2012

Acknowledgments

The authors and publishers are grateful to the holders of copyright in material from which extracts appear in this work, particularly to the following:

- The Hon J C Campbell and *The Australian Bar Review* for permission to reproduce material from J C Campbell, 'The Purpose of Pleadings' (2004) 25 *Aust Bar Rev* 116;

- Commonwealth of Australia — All legislative material herein is reproduced by permission but does not purport to be the official or authorised version. It is subject to Commonwealth of Australia copyright;

- © Commonwealth of Australia 2011 for permission to reproduce material from <www.nadrac.gov.au>;

- Extracts from cases included in *The Law Reports* and *The Weekly Law Reports* are reproduced by permission of The Incorporated Council of Law Reporting for England and Wales, Megarry House, 119 Chancery Lane, London WC2A 1PP, England, <http://www.iclr.co.uk>;

- LEADR — Association of Dispute Resolvers, <http://www.leadr.com.au>, leadr@leadr.com.au for the LEADR Model of Mediation;

- Louis Schetzer and the Alternative Law Journal for permission to reproduce material from L Schetzer, 'Consumer Debt-related Legal Problems' (2010) 35(2) *Alt LJ* 107;

- The State of Western Australia, the copyright owner of Western Australian case law and legislative materials which are reproduced with permission;

- Sir Laurence Street for permission to reproduce material from <http://www.laurencestreet.com.au>;

- Thomson Reuters for material from the *Australasian Dispute Resolution Journal* and the *Building and Construction Law Journal*; and

- Christopher Wood and 13 Wentworth Selbourne Chambers for permission to reproduce material from *Pleading in Commercial Cases*, 29 November 2007.

While every care has been taken to establish and acknowledge copyright, the publishers tender their apologies for any accidental infringement. The publishers would be pleased to come to a suitable arrangement with the rightful owners in each case.

Statutes

References are to paragraph numbers

Uniform Civil Procedure Rules (Amendment No 51) 2011

Vexatious Proceedings Act 2008

Workers Compensation Act 1987

Workplace Injury Management and Workers Compensation Act 1998

NORTHERN TERRITORY

Building Act 1993

Choice of Law (Limitation Periods) Act 1994

Competition Code

Consumer Affairs and Fair Trading Act

Defamation Act 2006

Evidence Act 1939

Evidence Act 2011

Juries Act

Jurisdiction of Courts (Cross-vesting) Act

VICTORIA

Supreme Court (General Civil Procedure)
Rules 2005 .... 1.4.2, 10.5.1E, 10.5.8E,
   10.10.5E, 11.2.2E, 11.2.20E, 11.4.1E,
   11.4.15E, 11.5.1E, 11.7.1E, 11.7.11E,
   11.7.13E, 13.1.37E, 13.3.2E, 13.3.11E,
   14.1.2E, 14.2.1E, 16.7.2E, 20.7.2E, 21.7.16E
O 6 .... 8.3.2E
O 7 .... 4.2.5, 8.9.9
O 9–11 .... 10.1.3
O 9 .... 10.4.3E, 10.5.1E
O 10 .... 10.5.5
O 11 .... 10.10.5E
O 12 .... 21.7.19, 21.8.13
O 13 .... 11.2.2E, 11.2.20E, 11.5.1E, 11.7.1E,
   11.7.11E, 11.7.13E
O 14 .... 11.3.1, 11.4.1E, 12.5.1
O 15 .... 10.7.2
O 16 .... 10.7.7
O 17 .... 10.7.5
O 18 .... 10.9.2
O 18A 10.9.9
O 21 .... 12.2.2
O 22 .... 12.4.3, 12.5.1
O 23 .... 12.4.3
O 26 .... 17.3.27
O 29 .... 13.1.2, 13.1.37E
O 30 .... 13.3.2E, 13.3.11E
O 31 .... 13.4.1
O 32 .... 12.2.8E
O 33 .... 14.2.1E, 14.2.12
O 36 .... 5.2.23E, 5.2.25C
O 37 .... 14.1.2E
O 37A 16.5.8, 21.4.2
O 37B 15.4.12
O 44 .... 14.3.9
O 48 .... 18.2.9
O 59 .... 11.4.15E
O 60 .... 18.7.12
O 61 .... 21.1.7
O 62 .... 16.7.2E
O 63 .... 20.2.1, 20.4.6C
O 63, Pts 4, 5 .... 20.7.7
O 64 .... 19.1.1
O 67 .... 21.5.1
O 69 .... 21.1.7, 21.7.14
O 70 .... 21.1.7
O 71 .... 21.1.7
O 72 .... 21.1.7
O 73 .... 21.1.7, 21.9.1
O 74 .... 21.1.7, 21.10.1
O 75 .... 21.1.7
O 76 .... 21.1.7
O 80 .... 8.9.33
r 1.14 .... 2.5.5
rr 2.01–2.03 .... 5.1.3
r 2.03 .... 9.8.12

r 2.04 .... 5.1.4
r 3.01 .... 5.5.7E, 5.5.8, 8.2.11
r 3.01(4) 8.2.11
r 3.01(5) 8.2.11
r 3.02 .... 5.5.10E, 7.7.9, 8.2.11
r 3.04 .... 5.5.8
r 3.05 .... 8.2.11
r 3.05(2) 8.2.11
r 4.01 .... 7.5.1
r 4.04 .... 7.5.1
r 4.05 .... 7.6.1
r 5.04 .... 7.5.3, 11.4.1E, 11.4.2
r 5.11 .... 7.4.7, 7.5.8
r 5.11(1A)(a) 7.4.7
r 5.11(3) 7.4.7
r 5.12 .... 7.7.1, 8.2.11
r 5.12(2) 7.7.8
r 5.12(3) 7.7.9
r 6.02 .... 8.2.1, 9.10.1
r 6.03 .... 8.2.2
r 6.04(a) 8.4.2, 8.4.6, 8.4.7
r 6.04(b) 8.4.14
r 6.04(c) 8.4.15
r 6.04(d) 8.4.16
r 6.04(e) 8.4.16
r 6.05 .... 8.5.3
r 6.06 .... 8.3.3
r 6.07 .... 8.3.1, 8.3.2E, 8.3.3, 8.3.9, 16.2.4
r 6.07(1) 9.5.1
r 6.07(1)(d) 8.3.13
r 6.07(1)(e) 8.3.7
r 6.07(2.1) 8.3.7
r 6.07(5) 8.3.9
r 6.07(5)(b) 8.3.13
r 6.07(6) 8.3.13
r 6.08 .... 8.7.1
r 6.09 .... 8.2.9, 8.3.1
r 6.10 .... 8.8.1, 8.8.3
r 6.10(3) 8.8.12
r 6.11 .... 8.3.6
r 6.12(1) 8.3.4
r 6.13 .... 8.4.10
r 6.14 .... 8.2.7, 8.9.10, 8.9.17
r 6.15 .... 8.5.2
r 6.16 .... 8.3.5
r 6.17 .... 8.7.1
r 6.30.1 .... 20.3.1
r 7.01 .... 8.9.9
r 7.01(1)(a) 8.9.15, 8.9.26
r 7.01(1)(b) 8.9.18
r 7.01(1)(c) 8.9.19
r 7.01(1)(d) 8.9.20
r 7.01(1)(e) 8.9.20
r 7.01(1)(f)–(h) 8.9.16
r 7.01(1)(f)(ii) 8.9.21
r 7.01(1)(h) 8.9.10, 8.9.17

NATIONAL SCHEME LAW

IMPERIAL

INTERNATIONAL

Table of Practice Directions

Abbreviations and Bibliographical References

ACT	Australian Capital Territory
ALRC	Australian Law Reform Commission
CL	Common Law
Div	Division
F	Form
FCR	Federal Court Rules
HCR	High Court Rules
NSW	New South Wales
NT	Northern Territory
O	Order
PC	Practice case
PN	Practice note
Pt	Part
Qld	Queensland
r	rule
rr	rules
s	section
ss	sections
SA	South Australia
SC	Supreme Court
Tas	Tasmania
UCPR	Uniform Civil Procedure Rules
Vic	Victoria
WA	Western Australia
Astor	H Astor, 'Rethinking Neutrality: A Theory to Inform Practice — Part 1' (2000) 11 *ADRJ* 73.
Astor and Chinkin	H Astor and C Chinkin, *Dispute Resolution in Australia*, 2nd ed, LexisNexis Butterworths, Sydney, 2002.
Auerbach	J Auerbach, *Justice Without Law*, OUP, New York, 1983.

Baker	J Baker, *Who Settles and Why?*, Civil Justice Research Centre, Sydney, 1994.
Bamford	D Bamford, *Principles of Civil Litigation*, Thomson Reuters, Sydney, 2010.
Banks	R Banks, 'Alternative Dispute Resolution: A Return to Basics' (1987) 61 *ALJ* 569.
Black	The Honourable Justice M Black, 'The Courts, Tribunals and ADR: Assisted Dispute Resolution in the Federal Court of Australia' (1996) 7 *ADRJ* 138.
Boniface et al	D Boniface, M Kumar and M Legg, *Principles of Civil Procedure in New South Wales*, 2nd ed, Thomson Reuters, Sydney, 2012.
Boulle	L Boulle, *Mediation: Principles, Process, Practice*, Butterworths, Sydney, 1996.
Boulle and Mack	L Boulle and K Mack, *Laws of Australia*, 'Dispute Resolution', Law Book Co, looseleaf, 1997.
Boulle and Nesic	L Boulle and M Nesic, *Mediation: Principles, Process and Practice*, Butterworths, London, 2001.
Brown and Marriott	H Brown and A Marriott, 'Negotiation' in *ADR: Principles and Practice*, Sweet & Maxwell, London, 1999.
Cairns	B Cairns, 'Practice and Procedure', *Halsbury's Laws of Australia*, Butterworths, Sydney, looseleaf, vol 20.
Cairns (2011)	B Cairns, *Australian Civil Procedure*, 9th ed, Thomson Reuters, Sydney, 2011.
Charlton and Dewdney	R Charlton and M Dewdney, *The Mediator's Handbook: Skills and Strategies for Practitioners*, 2nd ed, Law Book Co, Sydney, 2004.
Chinkin and Dewdney	C Chinkin and M Dewdney, 'Settlement Week in New South Wales: An Evaluation' (1992) 3 *ADRJ* 93.
Flemming	R Flemming, 'Review Essay: Ordinary Litigation in America's Civil Courts: Images of Lawyers and Bargaining' (1992) 26 *Law and Society Rev* 669.
Fisher and Ury	R Fisher and W Ury, *Getting to Yes*, 2nd ed, Arrow Books Ltd, London, 1997.
Fiss	O Fiss, 'Against Settlement' (1984) 93 *Yale LJ* 1073.
Fulton	M Fulton, *Commercial Dispute Resolution*, Law Book Co, 1989.
Galanter	M Galanter 'Why the "Have" Come Out Ahead: Speculations on Limits of Legal Change' (1974) 9 *Law and Society Rev* 95.
Genn	H Genn, *Hard Bargaining: Out of Court Settlement in Personal Injury Actions*, Clarendon Press, Oxford, 1987.

Hamilton et al	J Hamilton, G Lindsay, M Morahan and C Webster, *NSW Civil Procedure Handbook*, Thomson Reuters, Sydney, 2011.
Handford	P Handford, *Limitations of Actions The Laws of Australia*, 3rd ed, Thomson Reuters, Sydney, 2012.
Harman	I Harman, 'Confidentiality in Mediation', in *Cases for Mediation*, G Raftesath and S Thaler, (eds) LBC Information Services in association with LEADR.
Ingleby	R Ingleby, *In the Ball Park. Alternative Dispute Resolution and the Courts*, Australian Institute of Judicial Administration, Melbourne, 1991.
Legg	M Legg, *Regulation, Litigation and Enforcement*, Thomson Reuters, Sydney, 2011.
Mack	K Mack, *Laws of Australia*, 'Dispute Resolution', Law Book Co, looseleaf, 1997, Vol 13.1, Ch 5.
Mandikos	B Mandikos, *Civil Procedure*, 2nd ed, Thomson Reuters, Sydney, 2009.
McEwan et al	C McEwan, L Mather and R Maiman, 'Lawyers, Mediation, and the Management of Divorce Practice' (1994) 28 *Law and Society Rev* 149.
Miller and Sarat	R Miller and A Sarat, 'Grievances, Claims and Disputes: Assessing the Adversary Culture' (1980–81) 14 *Law and Society Rev* 525.
Noone	M Noone, 'Mediation' in the *Essential Legal Skills Series*, Cavendish Publishing Ltd, 1996.
Pickering	M Pickering, 'The Art of Settlement and Negotiation' (1988) 10 *Law Society Bulletin* 197.
Ross	H Ross, *Settled Out of Court. The Social Process of Insurance Claims Adjustment*, Aldine, Chicago, 1970.
Sampford et al	C Sampford, S Blencowe and S Condlin, *Educating Lawyers for a Less Adversarial System*, The Federation Press, Sydney, 1999.
Schoenfield	M Schoenfield, 'Strategies and Techniques for Successful Negotiation' (1983) 69 *American Bar Assoc J* 1226.
Singer	R Singer, 'The Rolling Stones Revisited: Exploring the Concept of User Satisfaction as a Measure of Success in Alternative Dispute Resolution' (1995) 6 *ADJR* 77.
Spencer	D Spencer, 'Mandatory Mediation and Neutral Evaluation: A Reality in New South Wales' (2000) 11 *ADRJ* 237.
Worthington and Baker	D Worthington and J Baker, *The Costs of Civil Litigation*, Civil Justice Research Centre, Sydney, 1993.

Court Adjudication in the Civil Justice System

CHAPTER 1

OVERVIEW

This chapter will explore the changing nature of court adjudication within the broader adversarial and inquisitorial models of litigation. The chapter will also examine the broad concept of procedural law and explore its relationship to substantive law. The experiences of individuals whose disputes are processed by civil processes will be illustrated and the juridical basis of the inherent jurisdiction of superior courts considered. Other important issues such as the concept of open justice and the emerging human right to a fair hearing which is now part of state and territory law will be discussed.

While Australian civil procedure is still predominantly modelled upon the adversarial system, the last two decades have been characterised by an increasing interest in mitigating party control of litigation. The chapter will consider the flaws in the civil justice system which led to a desire for reform while **Chapter 2** will examine the development of the concept of overriding purpose, which is now well established in legislation and court rules in all jurisdictions and its use in case management systems and strategies.

INTRODUCTION

1.1.1   Our book is about Australian civil procedure. It examines the procedures which are available to litigate civil disputes in the superior courts of Australian jurisdictions. We will examine these procedures through:

- the Supreme Courts of the Australian Capital Territory, New South Wales, Northern Territory, Queensland, South Australia, Tasmania, Victoria and Western Australia;
- the High Court; and
- the Federal Court.

However, jurisdiction is exercised in many arenas; for example, specialist courts and tribunals and intermediate courts. Most Australian jurisdictions have a three-tiered court system. There are lower level courts in the federal court system and the state and territory court systems. For example, in 1999 the Federal Magistrates Court was established by the Commonwealth Parliament as an independent federal court under the Australian Constitution. The lower courts

1

in the states and territories are known as Magistrates Courts, Courts of Petty Sessions or Local Courts. Intermediate courts are known as District or County Courts. However, Tasmania, the Australian Capital Territory and the Northern Territory do not possess the intermediate jurisdiction.

The underlying structure of each Supreme Court is similar. Each is a single superior court which is the intermediate appeal court and the body primarily entrusted with the supervision of state and territory law, state and territory legal institutions and the local legal institutions: J Crawford and B Opeskin, *Australian Courts of Law*, 4th ed, Oxford University Press, London, 2004, p 127. The Supreme Courts possess general jurisdiction and are thereby distinguishable from the High Court and Federal Court. The latter courts have a defined or statutory jurisdiction, even though they are both superior courts.

There are a number of important consequences that generally attach to the classification of 'superior court'. For example, the court has power to regulate its own procedure and may punish summarily for contempt. The decisions of superior courts are not generally amenable to the writs of certiorari, prohibition or mandamus by which decisions of inferior courts and tribunals may be reviewed, although the decisions of statutory superior courts are reviewable under s 75(v) of the Constitution: M Aronson, B Dyer and M Groves, *Judicial Review of Administrative Action*, Lawbook Co, Pyrmont, NSW, 2004.

The focus of our discussion of civil procedure will be the rules of the state and territory Supreme Courts, High Court and Federal Court as supplemented by enactments, case law, practice directions and practice notes. Although there are significant differences in the regulation of civil disputes in these jurisdictions, it is possible to unify the approaches of the jurisdictions in order to discern the principles of civil procedure.

Before examining the sources of procedural law, it is worth considering what is meant by the term 'civil procedure'.

WHAT IS CIVIL PROCEDURE?

1.2.1   Procedural law is the law which governs the conduct of proceedings before the court; that is, 'the mode of proceeding by which a legal right is enforced, as distinguished from the law which gives or defines the right': *Poyser v Minors* (1881) LR 7 QBD 329 at 333 per Lush J.

Civil procedure is seen primarily as a process for the resolution of civil disputes. Although our book generally deals with the rules and practices which regulate formal adjudication of civil disputes in a court, it is important to realise that such adjudication is quite atypical. Galanter reminds us of this in the following extract.

1.2.2E	**Justice in Many Rooms**
	M Galanter in Cappelletti (ed), *Access to Justice and the Welfare State*,
	European University Institute, Florence, 1981, pp 149–50

The Centrifugal Perspective: Access 'In the Shadow of the Law'

Most disputes that, under the current rules, could be brought to a court are in fact never placed on the agenda of any court … This is true of criminal as well as civil matters. Many of these disputes are 'resolved' by resignation, 'lumping it', or 'exit' by one party.

Of those disputes pursued, a large portion are resolved by negotiation between the parties, or by resort to some 'forum' that is part of (and embedded within) the social setting within which the dispute arose, including the school principal, the shop steward, the administrator, etc. Negotiation ranges from adjustments which are indistinguishable from the everyday accommodations that constitute the relationship to those which are 'bracketed' as disruptions or emergencies. Similarly, embedded forums range from those which are hardly distinguishable from the everyday decision-making within an institution to those which are specially constituted to handle disputes which cannot be resolved by everyday processes.

Of those disputes taken to a court (official forum), the vast majority are disposed of (by abandonment, withdrawal, or settlement) [150] without full-blown adjudication, and often without any authoritative disposition by the court. Of those cases that do reach full authoritative adjudication by a court, a large portion do not involve a contest. They are uncontested either because the dispute has already been resolved (as often in divorce) or because only one party appears.

1.2.3 Further reading

M Cain, 'Where are the Disputes? A Study of a First Instance Civil Court in the UK' in M Cain and K Kulcsar (eds), *Disputes and the Law*, Akademiai Kiado, Budapest, 1983.

R Cranston, *Law, Government and Public Policy*, Oxford University Press, Melbourne, 1987, p 63ff.

W Felstiner, R Abel and A Sarat, 'The Emergence and Transformation of Disputes: Naming, Blaming and Claiming' (1980) 15 *Law & Soc'y Rev* 631.

H Genn and S Beinart, *Paths to Justice: What People Do and Think about Going to Law*, Hart Publishing, 1999.

P Pleasence, *Causes of Action: Civil Law and Social Justice*, 2nd ed, The Stationery Office, Norwich, 2006.

1.2.4 But there is more to the formal law of civil procedure than individual dispute resolution, and the purpose of procedural law is not only to provide institutions and rules which facilitate dispute resolution, but also to perpetuate the rule of law. J A Jolowicz states that the purposes of procedural law are restricted to the provision of the institutions and rules of procedure best fitted to the fair, economical and expeditious adjudication of disputes which the parties choose to submit to the court: 'On the Nature and Purposes of Civil Procedural Law' (1990) *CJQ* 262 at 271. This idea focuses upon individual disputes; however, the process of litigation as a whole has two other distinct but connected purposes. He states:

> First, civil proceedings serve to demonstrate the effectiveness of the law; secondly they provide the opportunity for the judges to perform their functions of interpreting, clarifying, developing and, of course, applying the law.

Galanter observes that 'courts produce not only decisions but also messages. These messages are resources which parties use in envisioning, devising, negotiating and vindicating claims (and in avoiding, defending and defeating them)': M Galanter, 'Justice in Many Rooms', above, p 158. If the messages are too discouraging, justice will be denied and the law will be ineffective. If the messages are too encouraging the courts will become overloaded, leading to delay.

One significant message conveyed by the litigation system is the prospect of success for an individual litigant. This is a matter of substantive law.

THE INTERDEPENDENCE OF SUBSTANCE AND PROCEDURE

1.3.1 The rules of procedure are often referred to as 'adjectival' rules in the sense that they qualify substantive rights. They are meant to regulate the way in which substantive rights and obligations are claimed, proved and enforced, without impacting on the definition of those rights. So, procedure is not about the law that *creates* the legal right or status, it relies upon a distinction between substantive and procedural law.

A discussion of the rules of procedure presupposes that it is meaningful to consider process rules and principles apart from particular substantive objects. Robert Cover states that the rules of procedure are intended to be 'trans-substantive' in effect; that is, they are intended to be equally or similarly relevant to many different sorts of substantive disputes: R M Cover, 'For James Wm. Moore: Some Reflections on a Reading of the Rules' (1975) 84 *Yale LJ* 718. Certainly in some contexts the courts classify rules as procedural or not; for example, where the validity of a rule made under the general rule-making power of the court is under challenge: see *Schutt Flying Academy v Mobil* (2000) 1 VR 545, and (on appeal) *Mobil v Victoria* (2002) 189 ALR 161; *State Bank of South Australia v Hellaby* (1992) 59 SASR 304 or when deciding which laws applies under the principles of conflicts of laws: *John Pfeiffer Pty Ltd v Rogerson* (2000) 203 CLR 503 at [99] per Gleeson CJ, Gaudron, McHugh, Gummow and Hayne JJ.

However, there are differing views about the relationship between substantive and procedural law. For instance, Collins MR considered that 'the relation of rules of practice to the work of justice is intended to be that of handmaid rather than mistress': *Re Coles and Ravenshear* [1907] 1 KB 1 at 4, whereas Main argues that the construction of substantive law entails assumptions about the procedures that will apply when that substantive law is ultimately enforced: 'The Procedural Foundation of Substantive Law' (2010) 87 *Washington University Law Review* 801.

Jolowicz ('On the Nature and Purposes of Civil Procedural Law' (1990) *CJQ* 262 at 266–70) highlights two important distinctions between the operation of substantive and procedural law:

- subjection to substantive law is involuntary, whereas recourse to procedural law is voluntary. In the overwhelming majority of cases, the person who supposes or knows himself or herself to be possessed of a substantive right is not compelled to enforce it by litigation; and

- substantive law is self-executing, whereas procedural law creates choices for the parties. Generally speaking, even where a procedural rule is mandatory in form, if the opponent chooses to do nothing about it, nothing will happen.

1.3.2 The capacity of some procedural forms to transform the requirements of the substantive law has been observed by some commentators. Certainly in some areas of law, the procedural forms of action which preceded the Judicature Acts led to the development of particular doctrinal categories of substantive law. For example, the development of the procedure of *indebitatus assumpsit* allowed for the development of the modern law of contract based on the consensual exchange of promises: see N C Seddon and M P Ellinghaus, *Cheshire and Fifoot's Law of Contract*, 9th ed, LexisNexis Butterworths, Sydney, 2008, pp 1212–1213. For a more modern example, Scott has traced changes in United States securities law due to judicial concern to accommodate the class action: H S Scott, 'The Impact of Class Actions on Rule 10b-5' (1971) 38 *Uni of Chicago* LR 337.

1.3.3 Questions

1. How has the increased availability of alternative dispute resolution affected Jolowicz's first argument about the voluntary nature of procedural law?
2. Does your answer to Question 1 differ where the court has mandated that the parties participate in alternative dispute resolution procedures?
3. How has the increased use of case management techniques by Australian courts (see **Chapter 2**) affected Jolowicz's argument about the choices created for the parties by the rules of procedure?

1.3.4 Further reading

M Bayles, 'Principles for Legal Procedure' (1986) 5 *L & Phil* 33.

R Bone, 'Making Effective Rules: The Need for Procedure Theory' (2008) 61 *Okla LR* 319.

J Jacobs, 'The Vanishing Substance — Procedure Distinction in Contemporary Corporate Litigation: An Essay' (2007) 41 *Suffolk University Law Review* 1.

J Mashaw, 'Administrative Due Process: The Quest for a Dignitary Theory' (1981) 61 *Buffalo LR* 885.

S Roberts, 'Alternative Dispute Resolution and Civil Justice: An Unresolved Relationship' (1993) 56 *MLR* 452.

L Solum, 'Procedural Justice' (2004) 78 *S Cal LR* 181.

R Summers, 'Evaluating and Improving Legal Process A Plea for "Process Values"' (1974) 60 *Corn LR* 1.

SOURCES OF CIVIL PROCEDURAL LAW

Statutory jurisdiction

1.4.1 The rules of civil procedure in superior courts are made by the legislature, the executive and the courts themselves. The legislative source of civil procedure in the states and territories is the Supreme Court Act or its equivalents. Each jurisdiction has a statute which sets up the relevant Supreme Court and the parameters for its procedures: Supreme Court Act 1933 (ACT); Court Procedures Act 2004 (ACT); Supreme Court Act 1970 (NSW); Civil Procedure Act 2005 (NSW); Supreme Court Act (NT); Supreme Court Act 1995 (Qld) (which will be repealed by the Civil Proceedings Act 2011 (Qld) once it enters into force); Supreme Court of Queensland Act 1991 (Qld); Supreme Court Act 1935 (SA); Supreme Court Civil Procedure Act 1932 (Tas); Supreme Court Act 1986 (Vic); Civil Procedure Act 2010 (Vic); Supreme Court Act 1935 (WA). The Federal Court and the High Court possess similar legislation: Judiciary Act 1903 (Cth); Federal Court of Australia Act 1976 (Cth). Among other things, this legislation establishes the court, its composition, administration and statutory powers.

1.4.2   These Acts provide that procedural rules may be made by delegated legislation. The Rules of Court were originally made by the legislature, but are now subject to extensive alteration by the judges, to whom the legislature has granted wide-ranging powers to make delegated legislation relevant to the court's own procedures. The rules are devised by rules committees, which are composed of judicial officers and representatives of the government and the legal profession. The Rules of Court which will be examined in this book are as follows: Court Procedures Rules 2006 (ACT); Federal Court Rules 2011 (Cth); High Court Rules 2004 (Cth); Uniform Civil Procedure Rules 2005 (NSW); Supreme Court Rules (NT); Uniform Civil Procedure Rules 1999 (Qld); Supreme Court Civil Rules 2006 (SA); Supreme Court Rules 2000 (Tas); Supreme Court (General Civil Procedure) Rules 2005 (Vic); Rules of the Supreme Court 1971 (WA). In most jurisdictions there are committees of review, which are authorised to review the rules. In addition, because the rules are delegated legislation, they are subject to parliamentary disallowance after being tabled. In most jurisdictions, either house of parliament may disallow the rules within a prescribed time period.

While the Rules of Court are an important source of civil procedure, they are not a code, and they complement the inherent jurisdiction of the court: see discussion at 1.4.4 below. The inherent jurisdiction entitles the court to issue practice notes and directions. Practice notes and directions are usually commentaries, which are issued by an officer of the court, to assist parties in preparing litigation. While practice notes and directions are not legally binding, courts may ensure they are complied with by exercising their inherent power to make an order against a party, such as a stay on proceedings or an order for costs. Any such order, however, is subject to the Rules of Court: see *Gittins v WHC Stacy and Son Pty Ltd* [1964–5] NSWR 1793.

1.4.3   Further reading

E Campbell, *Rules of Court: A Study of Rule-making Powers and Procedures*, Law Book Co, Sydney, 1985, pp 1–11.

J Crawford and B Opeskin, *Australian Courts of Law*, 4th ed, Oxford University Press, Melbourne, 2004.

Inherent jurisdiction

1.4.4   Supreme Courts have an inherent jurisdiction deriving from their status as superior courts of record. The inherent power, as an incident of judicial power, provides superior courts with such power as is necessary to ensure that their procedures are capable of producing just outcomes. The overall purpose of the inherent jurisdiction is to allow the courts to regulate their process and to prevent abuse of process: *Riley McKay Pty Ltd v McKay* [1982] 1 NSWLR 264.

Mason points to four general purposes of the inherent jurisdiction: ensuring convenience and fairness in legal proceedings; preventing steps being taken that would render judicial proceedings ineffective; preventing abuse of process; acting in aid of superior courts; and aiding or controlling inferior courts and tribunals: K Mason, 'The Inherent Jurisdiction of the Court' (1983) 57 *ALJ* 449. Although the inherent jurisdiction is a 'somewhat metaphysical concept' (Mason above at 458), it is the source of many court procedures (e.g. the practice notes) and orders: e.g. Mareva and Anton Piller orders. Mason describes these inherent powers as a 'vast armoury of remedies' that judges have developed to respond to the 'limitless ways in which the due administration of justice can be delayed, impeded or frustrated': at 449. In the following extract, Dockray explores the nature of the inherent jurisdiction.

1.4.5E	**The Inherent Jurisdiction to Regulate Civil Proceedings**
	M S Dockray
	(1997) 113 *LQR* 120

[120] The phrase 'the inherent jurisdiction of the court' is in constant use today ... Clearly this is an important idea, and not just in terms of frequency of use. It is the foundation for a whole armoury of judicial powers, many of which are significant and some of which are quite extraordinary ... They include power to deny a litigant a full hearing; to make orders without listening to the party affected; to decline to hear an advocate; to exclude a party or the public from the courtroom; ... to order a party to speak or to keep silent; to require parties to surrender their property before judgment or to submit to a search and seizure.

[121] The phrase seems to have been in regular use before 1875 only in the law of contempt of court. It began to be used regularly in relation to procedural powers, costs and control of solicitors about 1880 ... while routine use of the phrase in law reports and textbooks ... began only after 1945.

[122] The phrase has been used in English cases in at least three different ways: (i) it has been used to describe the general powers of the old superior courts which the Supreme Court inherited on its creation; (ii) the phrase has also been used to mean powers which a court possesses simply by virtue of being a court, or perhaps by virtue of being a court of a specific kind. In this sense, inherent powers are intrinsic features of a body which is constituted as a court. Finally (iii) inherent powers have also been said to be incidental powers which arise either out of or because of the work which the court undertakes.

Theories
[124] Despite the constant use of the phrase 'inherent jurisdiction' in modern practice, English cases do not contain much of an explanation of what it means. 'Jurisdiction' means power or source of powers. But in what way precisely do powers inhere? The fullest exposition of the theory that inherent powers are powers which are intrinsic in a court is contained in an influential article, first published in 1970, ['The Inherent Jurisdiction of the Court', (1970) *Current Legal Problems* 23] when Sir Jack H. Jacob said that:

[125] the jurisdiction to exercise these powers was derived, not from any statute or rule of law, but from the very nature of the court as a superior court of law, and for this reason such jurisdiction has been called 'inherent' ... the essential character of a superior court of law necessarily involves that it should be invested with a power to maintain its authority and to prevent its process being obstructed and abused. Such a power is intrinsic in a superior court;

it is its very life-blood, its very essence, its immanent attribute ... The jurisdiction which is inherent in a superior court of law is that which enables it to fulfil itself as a court of law. The juridical basis of this jurisdiction is therefore the authority of the judiciary to uphold, to protect and to fulfil the judicial function of administering justice according to law in a regular, orderly and effective manner.

This article ... contains two central propositions, which are connected ... First, that inherent jurisdiction is a feature only of superior courts. Second, that the examples of inherent jurisdiction which the article collects are just that; they are not simply a ragbag of special cases, but make up a class of powers (including the power to punish contempt) all of which have as their common source an immanent attribute which is part of the intrinsic nature or the essential character of a superior court.

Is inherent jurisdiction confined to superior courts? Admittedly at common law the inherent power to punish certain types of contempt was confined to courts of record, a category which it could be argued broadly matches the contemporary idea of a superior court. It is also the case that at the time when Sir Jack's paper was written, the phrase inherent jurisdiction was almost always used in connection with the superior courts. But there is no reason to insist on this restriction ... today. On the contrary, ... a substantial number of ... cases recognise that inferior courts or tribunals may possess at least some inherent powers or jurisdiction. All courts, it has been said, have inherent power to regulate their own procedure, to make practice directions, to [126] control abuse of process; 'to exclude the public if it becomes necessary for the administration of justice' and to refuse to hear advocates who misconduct themselves ...

An alternative explanation of the nature of inherent jurisdiction can be found in *Connelly v DPP* in the judgment of Lord Morris of Borth-y-Gest, who said that:

> There can be no doubt that a court which is endowed with a particular jurisdiction has powers which are necessary to enable it to act effectively within such jurisdiction. I would regard them as powers which are inherent in its jurisdiction. A court must enjoy such powers in order to enforce its rules of practice and to suppress any abuses of its process ...

On this view, inherent powers exist because they are necessary if the court in question is to manage the work which has been assigned to it in an appropriate fashion. The second sentence in Lord Morris's statement appears to suggest that inherent powers to control procedure are incidents of substantive jurisdiction rather than features which are part of the character of a court. On this view, it seems that inherent powers do not grow out of substantive jurisdiction, but rather arise at common law as the [127] legal incidents of that jurisdiction. The point arose in *R v Norwich Crown Court, ex parte Belsham*, where the Queen's Bench Divisional Court was asked to consider the origin and nature of the inherent power of the Crown Court to control abuse of process. It was argued that the jurisdiction of the Crown Court is derived from statute and that powers 'which are inherent in its jurisdiction' must inevitably stem from statute. In a unanimous judgment, the Divisional Court indicated (*obiter*) that it preferred the theory that inherent powers arise at common law and independently of the statutes which create the substantive jurisdiction of a court.

There are advantages in this theory that inherent powers arise at common law when they are necessary if the court or tribunal in question is to be able to manage its activities appropriately. The theory is consistent with the cases and it explains why not all inherent powers are possessed by all courts and tribunals. It also avoids metaphysical debate about the immanent attributes of superior courts and concentrates attention instead on what is necessary and appropriate if a particular court is to be able to undertake its work effectively. These are important advantages. Nonetheless, like the competing theories, this version describes rather than defines inherent powers. It leaves the crucial question of the limits of the jurisdiction unanswered.

Limits

[128] [I]t has been said that where a situation is the subject of detailed and precise legislation, the court will rarely choose to exercise its inherent powers, which are then regarded as residual and principally confined to dealing with cases which have not been contemplated.

The relationship between inherent powers to control proceedings and the Rules of the Supreme Court is a special application of the same ideas, so that the [Rules] may also limit inherent powers in some cases. This conclusion does not depend, of course, on the legislative force or status of the rules themselves. Since inherent powers are the creation of the common law, it is in general correct to say that the Rules of the Supreme Court, being no more than delegated legislation, cannot widen, or take away the court's inherent common law powers, unless this is authorised by primary legislation ...

Apart from statute and mandatory rules, are there other limits to the inherent powers of the court to regulate its business? Some extravagant general claims have been made from time to time. For example, it has been argued that the court has inherent jurisdiction to order anything it thinks necessary to do justice in pending proceedings. Such a rule is too vague [129] and unpredictable to be treated as having the quality of law. Taken literally, this claim is an invitation to the court to assume virtually despotic powers; it was unequivocally rejected by Lord Hailsham in *The Siskina*, by Ackner LJ in *A J Bekhor & Co Ltd v Bilton*.

[T]he cases do not contain any definition which unifies and fixes the limits of the inherent [130] jurisdiction. In these circumstances, the most reliable general guide to the ambit and nature of inherent jurisdiction, it is suggested, is a notable group of recent decisions in which the court has denied that it has inherent power to make a procedural order of some particular sort; these cases include judgments which deny that the court has inherent jurisdiction to recast the law of discovery; to award security for costs against a defendant; ... to detain a party or witness in order to coerce another to comply with a court order; ... to order compensation to be paid to someone who has suffered by the implementation of an order of the court; to order production of hospital records on terms that disclosure is not made to the applicant (or to his legal advisers); [or] to backdate orders. ...

These decisions are quite inconsistent with the idea that the inherent jurisdiction is an unlimited reservoir from which new powers can be fashioned at will. ...

Factors which have been treated as influential in novel cases include the contribution which the proposed power could make to the effective administration of justice in the substantive and procedural context in which the rule would be applied — 'reasonable necessity' seems to be a popular standard in this context; the impact which the proposed power would have on persons subject to it; the importance of the rights thereby affected [131] and the extent to which those rights could be protected by the provisions of an express order by the court; the degree of confidence with which the court can determine where the balance of fairness lies; the implications to be drawn from limitations in existing statutes or rules in the field; the scale and complexity of the proposed regulation and the practical difficulty which would be experienced by the court in question in applying it; and the degree to which the proposed power represents a deviation from established practice.

> The cautious approach adopted in these cases has much to be said for it ... Major innovations in procedural law should ... be recognised as an institutional responsibility, not a matter on which individual judges should respond to the pleas of particular litigants. Procedural revolutions should appear first in statutes or in the Rules of Court, not in the law reports.

1.4.6   Notes and questions

1. Dockray argues at [132] that 'we should not treat the inherent jurisdiction as a kind of ubiquitous judicial prerogative originating in the ineffable spirit of the court'. In the extract above, Dockray quotes an influential earlier article by Jacob: 'The Inherent Jurisdiction of the Court' (1970) *Current Legal Problems* 23. Does Jacob treat the inherent jurisdiction in the manner criticised by Dockray?

2. An important distinction has traditionally been drawn between the inherent jurisdiction of the court and the jurisdiction conferred by statute; for example, the Federal Court and the Family Court. Consider the following comments of the High Court in *DJL v Central Authority* (2000) 201 CLR 226 at 240:

   > The Family Court is thus not a common law court as were the three common law courts at Westminster. Accordingly, it is 'unable to draw upon the well of undefined powers' which were available to those courts as part of their 'inherent jurisdiction'. The Family Court is a statutory court, being a federal court created by the Parliament within the meaning of s 71 of the Constitution. A court exercising jurisdiction or powers conferred by statute 'has powers expressly or by implication conferred by the legislation which governs it' and '[t]his is a matter of statutory construction'; it also has 'in addition such powers as are incidental and necessary to the exercise of the jurisdiction or the powers so conferred'. It would be inaccurate to use the term 'inherent jurisdiction' here and the term should be avoided as an identification of the incidental and necessary power of a statutory court.

   See also *Jackson v Sterling Industries Ltd* (1987) 162 CLR 612; (1987) 71 ALR 457 (extracted at **16.5.4C**) and *Cardile v LED Builders Pty Ltd* (1999) 198 CLR 380; (1999) 162 ALR 294; regarding the powers of the Federal Court and *Taylor v Taylor* (1979) 25 ALR 418 regarding the Family Court.

3. Is there a distinction between an inherent and an implied or incidental jurisdiction in this context? See *Watson v Clarke* [1990] 1 NZLR 715.

4. Is Dockray asserting at [127] that tribunals have inherent powers? Would such powers be analogous to the implied or incidental jurisdiction of the Federal and Family Courts? If not, why not?

5. Dockray at [132] emphasises the capacity of procedural rules to affect human rights and urges that the powers exercised under the inherent jurisdiction should take second place to statutes and mandatory procedural rules. Do you agree with this approach?

1.4.7   Further reading

P De Jersey, 'The Inherent Jurisdiction of the Supreme Court' (1985) 15 *Q Law Soc J* 325.

J Donnelly, 'Inherent Jurisdiction and Inherent Powers of Irish Courts' (2009) 2 *Judicial Studies Institute* 122.

ACCESS TO CIVIL JUSTICE — THE CONTEXT

1.5.1   Another important facet of the operation of procedure is the experience of individuals whose disputes are processed by the system of civil procedure. We are told by Cover and Fiss that particular roles are assigned to participants in the procedural system and that the concept of role introduces an element of impersonality into a procedural system: *The Structure of Procedure*, Foundation Press, New York, 1979, p 168. The doctrine of precedent in the common law system encourages the removal of the personal characteristics of participants in defining the rights and duties defined by the substantive law. However, during litigation the personal circumstances of participants shape their potential access to justice and the role they play in the litigation. In the following extract, John Noonan describes the participants in a famous American tort case. His work is important to an understanding of the context of the procedural system.

1.5.2E   **Persons and Masks of the Law**
Chapter 4 'The Passengers of the Palsgraf'
John T Noonan Jr, 1976

[111] The most famous tort case of modern times is ... *Palsgraf v Long Island Railroad Company*, [248 NY 339] decided in 1928 by the most excellent state court in the United States with an opinion by the most justly celebrated of American common-law judges, Benjamin N Cardozo. The facts of the case as stated by Cardozo were these:

Plaintiff was standing on a platform of defendant's railroad after buying a ticket to go to Rockaway Beach. A train stopped at the station bound for another place. Two men ran forward to catch it. One of the men reached the platform of the car without mishap, though the train was already moving. The other man, carrying a package, jumped aboard the car, but seemed unsteady as if about to fall. A guard on the car, who had held the door open, reached forward to help him in, and another guard on the platform pushed from behind. In this act, the package was dislodged, and fell upon the rails. It was a package of small size, about fifteen inches long, and was covered by a newspaper. In fact it contained fireworks, but there was nothing in its appearance to give notice of its contents. The fireworks when they fell exploded. The shock of the explosion threw down some scales at the other end of the platform [112] many feet away. The scales struck the plaintiff, causing injuries for which she sues.

Cardozo held that the plaintiff could not recover. No negligence to her by the railroad had been shown. 'The risk reasonably to be perceived,' Cardozo wrote, 'defines the risk to be avoided, and risk imports relation; it is risk to another or others within the range of apprehension.' When the guard pushed the passenger with a package, he could not have apprehended that the plaintiff was endangered by his action. In his action he did not relate to her. As to her he could not have been negligent.

William S Andrews, who wrote an opinion in the case no less eloquent than Cardozo's, saw negligence as a breach of duty of a man to observe care toward 'his fellows,' not toward specific persons he should have seen as endangered by what he did ...

Both summaries of fact were wonderfully laconic. Andrews was the superior in impersonality, eliminating even [113] the sex of 'plaintiff.' Compelled by grammatical necessity to use a personal pronoun, Cardozo did disclose that the plaintiff was female. Otherwise, neither judge said anything about her age, marital status, maternal responsibilities, employment, or income. What injuries she had suffered ... could not be learned from either opinion.

What compensation she had sought or what compensation she had been awarded — a jury had decided in her favour — was unmentioned.

No greater information was given about the defendant, except that it was a railroad .... The income and expenses, assets and liabilities, owners and directors of the defendant were unstated. Its officers and its guards or 'servants' were anonymous. ...

Cardozo and Andrews made no reference of any kind to the lawyers who had conducted the litigation ... The judges made no comment upon their training, their competence, their presentation of the evidence, their relationship to their clients ... Nothing was said as to negotiations they might have conducted with each other. Their remuneration and the bearing of the decision upon it were not touched upon.

[114] A fortiori, the judges said nothing of themselves — their own income and investments, their marital and parental status, their professional experience, their personal experience of New York commuter trains, their own study or debate over the case. The authors of the opinion and the dissent were, if possible, less visible than the plaintiff, the defendant, and the three lawyers. Who they were was not a fact of the case. Ignoring the lawyers and themselves, stripping the litigants to their status of plaintiff and defendant, Cardozo and Andrews had performed the standard operations of opinion writers announcing the rules of law which governed their conclusions ...

The Participants
[122] *Counsel* ... The railroad was represented by Joseph F Keany and William McNamara, who gave their addresses as 'Pennsylvania Station'. Keany, the senior man, had the title of General Solicitor of the Long Island Railroad and was listed as an officer of the company ...

The actual trial was conducted by Keany's junior, McNamara. He was a recent graduate of New York Law School, a proprietary institution not to be confused with New York University Law School. McNamara introduced no witnesses, [123] cross-examined the plaintiff and her witnesses with moderate spirit but not exhaustively, and sought to bring out that a lot of people on the platform were carrying bundles. His summation to the jury, unreported, could not have taken more than fifteen minutes ... McNamara's performance was that of a workmanlike lawyer earning his salary with an economy of motion. He spent part of an afternoon and a morning trying the case and had given, perhaps, half a day to preparing it. If his salary, which would not have been above $6,000 a year, is prorated to this time, the railroad had spent no more than $16 in defending itself.

Opposing him was Matthew W Wood, a solo practitioner who had an office in the tallest building then in New York, the Woolworth Building on lower Broadway. He was from Middleburgh, a small town in upstate New York. ... [H]e had studied law at New York Law School but had graduated from Yale Law School. He had been admitted to the bar when he was twenty-eight, and he had been in practice twenty-one years when he took Mrs Palsgraf as a client. His biography gives the outline of a boy from the country, making with diligence a modest legal career ...

Operating by himself, he was in the least prosperous category of urban practitioners and had to resort to stratagems to dig up business ... [124] How he and Mrs Palsgraf had come to each other's attention and why she thought he would be a good torts lawyer are not evident. He became her lawyer two months after the accident.

Wood's preparation of the case was not elaborate. He presented the plaintiff; her two daughters, Elizabeth and Lilian; her local doctor, Karl Parshall; an engraver and his wife, the Gerhardts, who had been on the platform too; and a neurologist, Graeme M Hammond, for thirty years professor of nervous and mental diseases and chief of clinic at the Post Graduate, with a war service record of examining 68,000 soldiers, close to eighty years old at time of the trial ... On the critical question of the plaintiff's injuries, Dr Parshall, the local physician, thought they were permanent, but McNamara brought out on cross-examination that he had never treated a similar case; the jury could have taken his name as a significant pun. The testimony of the specialist, Dr Hammond, that his patient was suffering from 'traumatic hysteria' was vital. Hammond's services were obtained the day before the trial. Wood's case, like Keany's, was an economical one, sparely presented and sparely financed ...

[125] Filing costs and the clerk's fee in the lower court came to $142. Dr Hammond charged $125. Mrs Palsgraf made $416 a year. At the time of trial, she had not yet paid Dr Parshall's bill of $70, now three years due. It is improbable to the point of implausibility that she would have had the cash on hand to pay the court and Dr Hammond a total of $267. It is unequally implausible that she would have had the cash to pay Wood. It is not inconceivable that her relatives could have funded the case, but it seems more probable that Wood had a fee contingent on his success and that he financed the litigation. It would not have been unusual if his contingent interest was one half the recovery after a trial — one third if a settlement was made before trial.

Wood asked for $50,000 in his complaint on her behalf. The discrepancy between this amount and any injuries he was able to show suggest strongly that he planned to bargain. As he did not get any expert medical until the day before the trial, it may be inferred that Keany and McNamara were not interested in negotiating seriously short of what professional jargon denominates as 'the courthouse steps' ...

[126] *Clients.* 'Plaintiff,' 'Palsgraf,' 'Mrs Palsgraf' bore the Christian name of Helen. She was forty-three and the mother of three children, of whom the younger two, then fifteen and twelve, were with her at the time of the accident. She was married, but neither side judged it desirable to ask who her husband was or where he was. It may be inferred that they had separated. She testified that she paid the rent, that she had always worked, and that she was 'all alone.'

At the time of the accident Helen Palsgraf lived in a basement flat at 238 Irving Avenue in Ridgewood, performing janitorial work in the apartment building, for which she was allowed ten dollars a month on her rent. She did day work outside the apartment, earning two dollars a day or about eight dollars a week. She spoke English intelligibly but not with complete grammatical correctness ...

[During the accident] Helen Palsgraf had been hit by the scales on the arm, hip, and thigh. The chief perceptible effect of the accident, according to the doctors, was a stammer. Dr Parshall said that she began to stutter and stammer about a week after the event. Dr Hammond declared that 'it was with difficulty that she could talk at all' ...

[127] The two most important facts of the case from Helen Palsgraf's perspective must have been the time it took to be heard and the size of the verdict she won. The accident took place August 24, 1924. The summons beginning her suit was [128] served on October 2, 1924. The trial took place on May 25 and 26, 1927. For anyone who has been injured and is awaiting compensation, two years and nine months is a very long time to wait ... When the trial was finally held, she won a verdict fourteen times her annual income. Even if she could keep only half for herself, she had a fortune in prospect. She was able to enjoy the thought of disposing of it for a whole year before the Court of Appeals took it from her, and she could nurse a faint hope for another five months until, on October 9, 1928, the Court of Appeals denied Wood's motion for reargument.

[Defendant] ... In 1924 the [defendant's] ... [n]et income from railroad operations was just over $4 million, ... [and] [o]ver 60 percent of the operating income was from passenger traffic ...

[129] In 1924 the railroads of the United States killed 6,617 persons and injured 143,739 persons. A substantial number of those killed and injured were the railroads' own employees and another large fraction were classified as 'trespassers,' those who had no business on railroad property. Helen Palsgraf fell in the classification neither of employees nor of trespassers but of passengers, of whom 204 were killed and 6,822 were injured in 1924 ...

[130] *Judges*. Burt Jay Humphrey presided. ... When he conducted the *Palsgraf* trial, he was sixty-four; he had been on the bench twenty-five years and a judge of the New York Supreme Court for three ...

[131] The jury was drawn from Brooklyn, where Mrs Palsgraf lived, where the accident had occurred, and where the trial took place. It would be too much to say that they were Mrs Palsgraf's neighbours, but it may be guessed from the result that they were persons used to travelling on the Long Island and not overly sympathetic to railroads. They retired at 11:55 am and returned with their verdict at 2:30 pm — time enough to eat lunch at the expense of the state of New York and to discuss liability and damages for at least an hour, and perhaps longer.

The case went from Judge Humphrey's court to the appellate division in Brooklyn [which upheld the award]. Keany and McNamara then took the railroad's case [to the Court of Appeals] ... Its members were exclusively white, male, and over fifty ... [132] In age they ranged from Andrews, seventy, to Crane and O'Brien, fifty-four; Cardozo, Lehman, and Kellogg were in the later fifties, Pound in his middle sixties. Two had not gone to a regular day law school — O'Brien had gone nights to New York Law School, while holding a job in the office of the Corporation Counsel of New York City; Pound had read law with his father in Lockport. Cardozo was technically a dropout, having studied only two years at Columbia Law School at a time when three years had just become the requirement. Andrews, Crane, and Lehman [133] were all actual law graduates of Columbia, as was Kellogg of Harvard ...

The court was an elected body ... All [the judges] were members of the upper middle class, the sons of prosperous fathers, ... three were the sons of judges ... All, save O'Brien, had been in private practice. All, save O'Brien, had been first elected to the Supreme Court before promotion to the higher level. All now received a salary of $22,000 ($500 more for the Chief Judge) and $3000 in lieu of expenses. The richest was Lehman, the son of Mayer Lehman, founding partner of the investment bankers, Lehman Brothers ...

[Noonan discusses the judgment of the Court of Appeals here, which was adverse to Helen Palsgraf.]

[144] Severe impartiality led in Palsgraf to the aspect of the decision which seemed least humane: the imposition by Cardozo of 'costs in all courts' upon Helen Palsgraf. Under the New York rules of practice, costs were, in general, discretionary with the court. An old rule, laid down in 1828, was that when the question was 'a doubtful one and fairly raised, no costs will be allowed'. In practice, the Court of Appeals tended to award costs mechanically to the party successful on appeal. Costs here amounted to $142.45 in the trial court and $100.28 in the appellate division. When the bill of the Court of Appeals was added, it is probable that costs in all courts amounted to $350, not quite a year's income for Helen Palsgraf. She had a case which the majority of judges who heard it — Humphrey, Seeger, Andrews, Crane, and O'Brien — thought to constitute a cause of action. By a margin of one, her case had been pronounced unreasonable ... The effect of the judgment was to leave the plaintiff, four years after her case had begun, the debtor of her doctor, who was still unpaid; her lawyer, who must have advanced her the trial court fees at least, and her adversary, who was now owed reimbursement for expenditure in the courts on appeal.

1.5.3   Notes and questions

1. Mrs Palsgraf's experience raises many questions about access to justice and the content of this expression in particular contexts: see generally, R Cranston, *How Law Works: The Machinery and Impact of Civil Justice*, Oxford University Press, Oxford, 2006, Ch 5.

2. Access to justice is often regarded as synonymous with the ideals of due process. A Sarat, 'Access to Justice: Citizen Participation and the American Legal Order' in L Lipson and S Wheeler (eds), *Law and the Social Sciences*, Russell Sage Foundation, New York, 1986 describes 'due process' as follows (p 527):

    The right to one's day in court, the right to be heard, the right to take part in procedures through which one's fate is determined all provide the basic substance of due process, which is, in turn, at the heart of our conceptions of fairness and justice.

    However, there are considerable differences among commentators on how the ideals should be interpreted and protected, and which of them is to be regarded as more significant.

3. To what extent do the views of the commentators on due process accord with those of the litigants? The Justice Research Centre conducted a study of Australian plaintiffs' satisfaction with dispute resolution processes in 1997. In the study, personal injury plaintiffs evaluated their experiences of the civil process in disputes that were resolved by four different procedures — trial, arbitration, pre-trial conference and mediation. The first two procedures are adjudicative and the last two are non-adjudicative. The study found that the plaintiffs whose disputes were resolved by consensual processes (here pre-trial conference and mediation) were more satisfied with the process than those who used adjudicative processes (here trial and arbitration): M Delaney and T Wright, *Plaintiffs' Satisfaction with Dispute Resolution Processes: Trial, Arbitration, Pre-Trial Conference and Mediation*, Justice Research Centre Report, January 1997.

    Compare that result with the report of RAND Institute for Civil Justice in 1989, which studied tort litigants over several jurisdictions in the United States. Although the samples were of a similar size (255 and 286 tort litigants respectively), the RAND study found greater satisfaction with the adjudicative procedures. The plaintiffs' perceptions of fairness were strongly correlated with perceptions that the procedures were 'dignified, careful and unbiased'. Interestingly, the study found that the trial engendered high levels of perceived control and comprehension: Lind et al, *The Perception of Justice. Tort Litigants' Views of Trial, Court-Annexed Arbitration, and Judicial Settlement Conferences*, RAND Institute, 1989.

To what extent might these findings be reconciled?

4. Which ideals of due process do you regard as fundamental to civil litigation? Do they differ from those that you would assign to the criminal justice system?

1.5.4   Further reading

Access to Justice Advisory Committee, *Access to Justice: An Action Plan*, Report to the Commonwealth Attorney-General and Minister for Justice, May 1994.

C Parker *Just Lawyers: Regulation and Access to Justice*, Oxford University Press, New York, 1999.

R Sackville, 'The Access to Justice Report: Change and Accountability in the Justice System' (1994) 4 *Journal of Judicial Administration* 65.

T Tyler, *Why People Obey the Law*, Princeton University Press, Princeton, 2006.

THE ADVERSARIAL AND INQUISITORIAL MODELS OF LITIGATION

1.6.1   Traditionally civil procedure systems have been classified along a dichotomy between adversarial and inquisitorial procedural models. Under the adversarial model, 'two adversaries generally take charge of the procedural action', while under an inquisitorial system, 'officials perform most of the activities': D Maleshin, 'The Russian Style of Civil Procedure' (2007) 21 *Emory Int'l L Rev* 543. Maleshin continues:

> The main attributes of the classic [adversarial] procedural system are: [1] pretrial conferences and party-controlled, pre-trial investigations, [2] trials designed as 'concentrated courtroom drama …' [3] passive judges, [4] class actions, and [5] party-selected and paid experts.

> [544] On the other hand, the main attributes of the [inquisitorial] procedural system are: [1] a lack of distinction between the pre-trial and trial phases, [2] active judges, [3] judicial proof taking and fact gathering, [4] judicial examination of witnesses, and [5] court-selected experts.

However, the type of civil procedure adopted in a particular legal system is a manifestation of broader influences which shape that legal system. In the following extract, the Australian Law Reform Commission describes the characteristics of the adversarial and inquisitorial models as 'legal families' derived respectively from the common law and civil systems.

1.6.2E	**Review of the Adversarial System of Litigation: Rethinking the Federal Civil Litigation System** Australian Law Reform Commission (ALRC) Issues Paper 20, April 1997, pp 17–19 (footnotes omitted)

Legal 'families'

2.2 There are a number of dominant legal families that distinguish the various legal systems of the world ... These families are not rigidly distinguished from each other but there are sufficiently significant differences between them to define them, based on the following basic characteristics:

- objectives of the legal system.
- source of law.
- legal method.

The 'adversarial'/'inquisitorial' dichotomy

2.3 The two legal families that have dominated, and continue to dominate, 'western' legal systems are the civil law and common law systems. The origins of the first lie in Roman Law and the *code civil* of nineteenth century France, while the common law derives from medieval English civil society. The transplantation of both legal families throughout the western world and beyond was assured by the French and British empires.

2.4 Many of the cardinal features of the two legal families are different: their separate developments spanned many centuries. However, even as 'ideal types' they are far from polar opposites. Both have as their overall objective the establishment of systems for the just resolution of disputes and the maintenance of social order. It is their means of achieving such ends which differ.

2.5 In the legal systems of today there is no pure example of either the civil law or common law system. All relevant legal systems in the western world are to greater or lesser degrees hybrids of these two models or of other legal families. Nonetheless in order to be able accurately to characterise the legal system that presently operates in Australia it is useful to outline some of the features that distinguish the common law and civil law families.

2.6 The essential features of the common law family include:
- A concern to determine legal disputes according to their individual circumstances and related judge-made case law, rather than applying general statements of legal principle.
- Common law orthodoxy dictates that the source of law is to be found in the texts of individual judgments. Modern common law legal systems however have substantial bodies of highly detailed legislation which comprise the primary source of law.
- Common law applies to all legal persons including the state. Traditionally there is no division between public and private law.
- An inductive form of legal reasoning is adopted whereby legal principle derives from the texts of many single judgments.
- In the litigation system the trial is the distinct and separate climax to the litigation process.
- Court-room practice may be subject to rigid and technical rules.
- Proceedings are essentially controlled by the parties to the dispute and there is an emphasis on the presentation of oral argument by counsel. The role of the judiciary is more reactive

than proactive. Given the parties' opportunity and responsibility for mounting their own case the system is more participatory.

- The judiciary possesses an inherent and separate power to adjudicate.
- The expense and effort of determination of disputes through litigation falls largely on the parties.

2.7 The essential features of the civil law family include:

- A concern to determine legal disputes according to predetermined legal principles established to maintain social order.
- The source of law is to be found in authoritative statements of basic legal principles for example, the Civil and Criminal Codes — issued by the state and propounded upon by legal scholars.
- There is a separation of public law (concerning relations between the individual and the state) and private law (between individuals).
- A deductive form of legal reasoning is adopted whereby pre-existing general statements of legal principle are applied to the specific circumstances of individual cases.
- In litigation no rigid separation exists between the stages of the trial and pre-trial in court cases. Legal proceedings are viewed as a continuous series of meetings, hearings and written communications during which evidence is introduced, witnesses heard and motions made.
- Rules relating to court-room practice are intended to be minimal and uncomplicated.
- The role played by lawyers is less conspicuous with an emphasis on written submissions rather than oral argument. The role of the judiciary is both proactive and inquisitive. The greater directorial role of the judiciary allows less room for the parties to direct their own case. In this sense the system is more hierarchical than participatory.

1.6.3 Bentham considered that an ideal system of procedure would cut across the standard distinctions between 'inquisitorial' and 'adversarial' systems. He favoured active questioning by the judge, which is generally associated with the former model. However, he also valued confrontation of parties and witnesses face to face in oral proceedings and regarded cross-examination as the redeeming feature of the English tradition: J Bentham, *Principles of Judicial Procedure*, ii Works 47, ed Bowring.

Bentham's views accord with the strong reliance on orality which characterises the adversarial system. Under this system, cross-examination has traditionally occupied hallowed ground as a device for finding the truth. By contrast, inquisitorial systems have developed a tradition of documentary proof. G Downes, 'The Roles of Practitioners in Adversarial and Inquisitorial Systems from the Point of View of Australian Practitioners: Changing Roles and Skills for Advocates', *Beyond the Adversarial System Conference*, Brisbane, 10–11 July 1997, p 3 describes this tradition as follows:

> The file (dossier) is all important. The process is directed to developing this file. It bears similarities to our own court file. It is compiled in an adversarial manner in that it is primarily composed of the documents presented by the opposing parties. It contains evidence (both documents and witness statements). It contains submissions. The process of adjudication is primarily concerned with an assessment of this file. The hearing focuses on the file. Cross-examination, as we know it, is virtually unknown. Questions are asked by the court. At best, some questions asked by the court are prompted by submissions from the advocates.

1.6.4 While both the adversarial and inquisitorial systems have particular characteristics, it is axiomatic that any procedural system has hybrid features in practice. The approach of the

ALRC Issues Paper 20, extracted at **1.6.2E** above, recognises this. It is often stated in procedural scholarship that it is misleading to equate Anglo-American procedure with the notion of adversarial 'contest' or systems influenced by Roman law with notions of 'inquest', when most procedural systems are actually hybrids. M Damaska argues that it is preferable to distinguish these categories in terms of their purpose rather than treating them as different means to shared ends: *The Faces of Justice and State Authority*, Yale University Press, New Haven, 1986, pp 3–6, 10–12, 69. He argues that the purpose of an 'inquest' is implementation of state policy in order to solve a problem; the purpose of a 'contest' is the legitimated resolution of a single dispute between identifiable parties. Damaska further states that it would be surprising to find any modern state which had only one kind of procedural arrangement, and indeed, that examples of particular institutional arrangements which fit the 'ideal types' exactly are quite exceptional. Nevertheless, these concepts, if used precisely, have considerable explanatory power: pp 224–5.

1.6.5 Notes and questions

1. Fact-finding is generally the most time-consuming and costly aspect of the preparation of a civil matter for hearing. Consider the different ways in which fact-finding is undertaken in the adversarial and inquisitorial systems. Which fact-finding system is the most efficient? What criteria have you adopted in determining efficiency? See S Shavell, 'The Social Versus the Private Incentive to Bring Suit in a Costly Legal System' (1982) 11 *J of Legal Studies* 333.

2. Should orality play a central role in civil litigation? Lord Eldon in *Ex parte Lloyd* (1822) Mont 70 at 72 stated that the truth is best discovered by 'powerful statements on both sides of the question'. Can these 'powerful statements' be made in writing, or does oral presentation facilitate the discovery of 'truth'?

3. The procedure adopted by most Australian tribunals is said to be inquisitorial. To what extent does tribunal procedure conform to the inquisitorial archetype discussed by Maleshin at **1.6.1** above? For commentary by the courts on this model, see *Bushell v Repatriation Commission* (1992) 175 CLR 408 at 424–5 per Brennan J, and *Paramananthan v Minister for Immigration and Multicultural Affairs* (1998) 160 ALR 24 at 56ff per Merkel J.

1.6.6 Further reading

R Hulbert, 'Comment on French Civil Procedure' (1997) 45 *Am J Comp* 747.

J Langbein, 'The German Advantage in Civil Procedure', (1985) 52 U Chi L Rev 823.

R Marcus, 'Putting American Procedural Exceptionalism into a Globalized Context' (2005) 53 *Am J Comp* L 709.

F Nagorcka, M Stanton and M Wilson, 'Stranded between Partisanship and the Truth? A Comparative Analysis of Legal Ethics in the Adversarial and Inquisitorial Systems of Justice' (2005) 29 *MULR* 448.

P Underwood, 'The Trial Process: Does One Size Fit All?' (2006) 15 *J of Judicial Administration* 165.

THE OPERATION OF THE AUSTRALIAN CIVIL JUSTICE SYSTEM

1.7.1 This section will discuss overarching issues that impact upon the operation of the Australian civil justice system. Entrenched norms, such as the principle of open justice, inform the operation of civil procedure generally. However, emerging human rights, such as the right to fair hearing, may challenge both entrenched norms and established procedures.

Certain flaws in the civil justice system, such as delay, have prompted calls for greater efficiency, leading ultimately to profound systemic change by the development of the overriding purpose and case management, which will be discussed in **Chapter 2**.

THE PRINCIPLE OF OPEN JUSTICE

Introduction

1.7.2 The principle of open justice is a fundamental aspect of the system of justice (both civil and criminal) in Australia and the conduct of proceedings in public is an essential quality of an Australian court of justice. As stated by Spigelman:

> The principle that justice must be seen to be done ... is one of the most pervasive axioms of the administration of justice in our legal system. It informs and energises the most fundamental aspects of our procedure. ('Seen to be Done: The Principle of Open Justice — Part 1' (2000) 74 *ALJ* 290)

As a fundamental principle of the common law, the principle of open justice confers particular benefits on the administration of justice; e.g., by acting as a bastion against the exercise of arbitrary power by judges, improving judicial performance, acting as a check on the veracity of witnesses, and allowing parties to litigation to publicly vindicate their rights: D Butler and S Rodrick, *Australian Media Law*, 4th ed, Thomson Reuters, Sydney, 2012, p 206.

The open justice principle has been adopted and expounded in many cases, perhaps most importantly in *Scott v Scott* [1913] AC 417, discussed in the extract of *Rinehart v Welker*, at **1.7.7E** below. It is also protected by Art 14 of the International Covenant on Civil and Political Rights (ICCPR), to which Australia is a party. Two Australian jurisdictions — Australian Capital Territory and Victoria — have passed legislation incorporating Art 14 of the ICCPR into their domestic laws, as elaborated below at **1.8.1ff**.

The phrase 'open court' refers to a place where the public has a right of admission and where an interested member of the public has a right of free access to the matter being heard there: *Dando v Anastassiou* [1951] VLR 235 at 237–8. The distinction between open court and the chambers jurisdiction is discussed at **1.7.9** below.

EXCEPTIONS TO THE PRINCIPLE OF OPEN JUSTICE

1.7.3 There is no inherent power of the court to exclude the public: *John Fairfax Publications Pty Ltd v District Court of NSW* (2004) 61 NSWLR 344 (CA) per Spigelman CJ at [18]. However, there are many common law and statutory exceptions to the principle of open justice that allow courts to make suppression orders or non-publication orders or to close the court if the pre-conditions to the exercise of the power are satisfied. The common law exceptions are discussed in the extract of *Rinehart v Welker*, at 1.7.7E below; the statutory exceptions are addressed in the following paragraph.

There are both general and specific statutory provisions that modify the principle of open justice. The general provisions are as follows: Federal Court of Australia Act 1976 (Cth), s 17(4); Judiciary Act 1903 (Cth) ss 15, 16; Court Procedures Act 2004 (ACT), ss 41, 50; Human Rights Act 2004 (ACT) s 21(2), (3); Civil Procedure Act 2005 (NSW) s 71; Evidence Act (NT) ss 57, 59; Supreme Court Act (NT) s 17; Civil Proceedings Act 2011 (Qld) s 126; Supreme Court of Queensland Act 1991 (Qld) s 128; Evidence Act 1929 (SA) Pt 8 Div 2; Evidence Act 2001 (Tas) s 194J; Charter of Human Rights and Responsibilities Act 2006 (Vic) s 24(2), (3); Supreme Court Act 1986 (Vic) ss 18, 19.

Further, there is a 'plethora' of specific statutory provisions that empower a court to close the court or to make non-publication orders in respect of a proceeding e.g. family law proceedings (Family Law Act 1975 (Cth) ss 97, 121), coronial inquests, adoption proceedings, proceedings involving children and proceedings that concern terrorist activities or matters of national security: for details, see D Butler and S Rodrick, *Australian Media Law*, 4th ed, Thomson Reuters, Sydney, 2012, pp 244–5.

1.7.4 As stated above, the principle of open justice is an important democratic ideal, which is zealously safeguarded by the media. Recently attempts have been made to harmonise the grounds upon which suppression and non-publication orders may be made across state, territory and federal jurisdictions, resulting in draft model provisions endorsed by the Standing Committee of Attorneys-General in May 2010. New South Wales is the first jurisdiction to adopt the model provisions in the Court Suppression and Non-publication Orders Act 2010 (NSW) (the CSPO Act).

At the time of writing, no other state or territory has adopted the model provisions, although the Commonwealth has introduced the Access to Justice (Federal Jurisdiction) Amendment Bill 2011 which, if passed, will insert the model provisions into legislation including the Federal Court of Australia Act 1976 (Cth) and the Judiciary Act 1903 (Cth).

1.7.5E   **Court Suppression and Non-publication Orders Act 2010 (NSW)**

3 Definitions

…

"non-publication order" means an order that prohibits or restricts the publication of information (but that does not otherwise prohibit or restrict the disclosure of information).

…

"suppression order" means an order that prohibits or restricts the disclosure of information (by publication or otherwise).

4 Inherent jurisdiction and powers of courts not affected

This Act does not limit or otherwise affect any inherent jurisdiction or any powers that a court has apart from this Act to regulate its proceedings or to deal with a contempt of the court.

…

6 Safeguarding public interest in open justice

In deciding whether to make a suppression order or non-publication order, a court must take into account that a primary objective of the administration of justice is to safeguard the public interest in open justice.

---

7 Power to make orders

A court may, by making a suppression order or non-publication order on grounds permitted by this Act, prohibit or restrict the publication or other disclosure of:

    (a)   information tending to reveal the identity of or otherwise concerning any party to or witness in proceedings before the court or any person who is related to or otherwise associated with any party to or witness in proceedings before the court, or

    (b)   information that comprises evidence, or information about evidence, given in proceedings before the court.

8 Grounds for making an order

    (1)   A court may make a suppression order or non-publication order on one or more of the following grounds:

        (a)   the order is necessary to prevent prejudice to the proper administration of justice,

        (b)   the order is necessary to prevent prejudice to the interests of the Commonwealth or a State or Territory in relation to national or international security,

        (c)   the order is necessary to protect the safety of any person,

        (d)   the order is necessary to avoid causing undue distress or embarrassment to a party to or witness in criminal proceedings involving an offence of a sexual nature (including an act of indecency),

        (e)   it is otherwise necessary in the public interest for the order to be made and that public interest significantly outweighs the public interest in open justice.

    (2)   A suppression order or non-publication order must specify the ground or grounds on which the order is made.

1.7.6   These provisions were subjected to intense scrutiny during the *Rinehart v Welker* litigation, which resulted in 14 written judgments and many more *ex tempore* decisions in the New South Wales courts and the High Court during 2011–12. The following is an extract from a New South Wales Court of Appeal judgment which discusses the litigation and the broader issues regarding open justice.

1.7.7E   **Rinehart v Welker**

[2011] NSWCA 403

Court of Appeal New South Wales

19 December 2011

[A dispute arose about a family trust and certain children who were beneficiaries under the trust commenced proceedings to seek a restructure of the trust and removal of their mother (Rinehart) as trustee. Rinehart sought a suppression and non-publication order in reliance on a deed entered into by members of the family in April 2007 whereby the parties agreed to resolve disputes confidentially — initially by mediation, then arbitration. Rinehart argued that the dispute should be resolved in accordance with the deed and therefore a suppression order was necessary to preserve the confidentiality of the dispute prior to the conduct of any mediation and arbitration. There were several first instance and appellate judgments in these proceedings but the judgment below concerns an application to set aside the decision of Tobias AJA acting as a single judge of the New South Wales Court of Appeal in *Rinehart v Welker* [2011] NSWCA 345.]

Bathurst CJ and McColl JA (at [25]): Underlying the enactment of the CSPO Act [i.e. the Court Suppression and Non-publication Orders Act 2010 (NSW)] was, in part, a concern to resolve the question whether a court's inherent or implied power to make orders restricting the publication of any aspect of proceedings before it extended to orders purporting to bind the world at large: see *Hogan v Hinch* [2011] HCA 4; (2011) 85 ALJR 398 (at [23]–[27], [46]) per French CJ; *Attorney-General (NSW) v Mayas Pty Ltd* (1988) 14 NSWLR 342 (at 355) per McHugh JA, Hope JA agreeing; Second Reading Speech, Court Suppression and Non-publication Orders Bill, New South Wales Legislative Council, *Parliamentary Debates* (Hansard) 23 November 2010.

[26] The principle of legality favours a construction of legislation such as the CSPO Act which, consistently with the statutory scheme, has the least adverse impact upon the open justice principle and common law freedom of speech and, where constructional choices are open, so as to minimise its intrusion upon that principle: *Hogan v Hinch* (at [5], [27]) per French CJ; see also *Raybos Australia Pty Ltd v Jones* (1985) 2 NSWLR 47 (at 55) per Kirby P. ...

[32] [Section] 6 of the CSPO Act requires the court when considering whether to make an order under the Act to "take into account that a primary objective of the administration of justice is to safeguard the public interest in open justice". The principle of open justice is one of the most fundamental aspects of the system of justice in Australia: *John Fairfax Publications Pty Ltd v District Court of NSW* [2004] NSWCA 324; (2004) 61 NSWLR 344 (at [18]) per Spigelman CJ (Handley JA and Campbell AJA agreeing). Open justice ensures public confidence in the administration of justice: see *Moti v R* [2011] HCA 50 (at [100]) per Heydon J; *Hogan v Hinch* (at [20]) per French CJ; *R v Tait* (1979) 46 FLR 386 (at 401–403) per Brennan, Deane and Gallop JJ. It is unnecessary to add to the large body of judicial opinions discussing the concept. It is sufficient, in our view, to illustrate the proposition embedded in s 6 by referring to Lord Atkinson's statement in *Scott v Scott* [1913] AC 417 (at 463), that "in public trial is [to be] found, on the whole, the best security for the pure, impartial, and efficient administration of justice, the best means of winning for it public confidence and respect."

[33] "The entitlement of the media to report on court proceedings is a corollary of the right of access to the court by members of the public": *John Fairfax Publications Pty Ltd v District Court of NSW* (at [20]). Media interests had standing at common law to be heard on the making of orders affecting the publication of court proceedings (see generally *John Fairfax Group Pty Ltd (Receivers and Managers appointed) v Local Court of New South Wales* (1992) 26 NSWLR 131) a position now enshrined in s 9(2)(d), CSPO Act at least insofar as a "news media organisation" is concerned.

[34] A number of exceptions to the principle of open justice are recognised. Viscount Haldane VC referred to two in *Scott v Scott* (at 437) as being "cases of wards of Court and of lunatics [where] the Court is really sitting primarily to guard the interests of the ward or the lunatic [and] [i]ts jurisdiction is ... parental and administrative, and the disposal of controverted questions is an incident only in the jurisdiction" and "litigation as to a secret process, where the effect of publicity would be to destroy the subject-matter ... which stands on a different footing [and] [t]here it may well be that justice could not be done at all if it had to be done in public". (See also the Earl of Halsbury (at 441–443); Earl Loreburn (at 446); Lord Atkinson

(at 450–451, 462); Lord Shaw of Dunfermline (at 482–483). His Lordship then said (at 437–438):

> As the paramount object must always be to do justice, the general rule as to publicity, after all only the means to an end, must accordingly yield. *But the burden lies on those seeking to displace its application in the particular case to make out that the ordinary rule must as of necessity be superseded by this paramount consideration.*
>
> *... [H]e must make out his case strictly, and bring it up to the standard which the underlying principle requires* [and] *... he must satisfy the Court that by nothing short of the exclusion of the public can justice be done. The mere consideration that the evidence is of an unsavoury character is not enough, any more than it would be in a criminal Court, and still less is it enough that the parties agree in being reluctant to have their case tried with open doors.*

(Emphasis added)

[35] Lord Loreburn said (at 446):

> ... in all cases where the public has been excluded with admitted propriety the underlying principle, as it seems to me, is that the administration of justice would be rendered impracticable by their presence, whether because the case could not be effectively tried, or the parties entitled to justice would be reasonably deterred from seeking it at the hands of the Court.

Lord Loreburn's statement was regarded as indicating the general approach by Viscount Dilhorne in *Attorney General v Leveller Magazine Ltd* [1979] AC 440 (at 457).

[36] As Brereton J said (Suppression Order decision (at [11]), referring *to John Fairfax Group Pty Ltd (Receivers and Managers Appointed) and Another v Local Court of New South Wales* (1991) 26 NSWLR 131 (at 141) per Kirby P), another "well-established illustration was in blackmail and extortion cases", where:

> If the very openness of court proceedings would destroy the attainment of justice in the particular case (as by vindicating the activities of the blackmailer) or discourage its attainment in cases generally (as by frightening off blackmail victims or informers) or would derogate from even more urgent considerations of public interest (as by endangering national security) the rule of openness must be modified to meet the exigencies of the particular case.

[37] A further exception is where disclosure of the information would seriously affect its commercial value: *Australian Broadcasting Commission v Parish* (1980) 43 FLR 129 at 133; *Hogan v Crime Commission* (at [42]).

[38] None of these exceptions apply in the present case.

The administration of justice

[39] The concept of the administration of justice is multi-faceted. We doubt whether a single statement can capture the connotation it carries in a range of contexts. As Young JA has said (at [86]) as used in s 50 of the *Federal Court of Australia Act*, "it is, ... a reference to the

public interest that the court should endeavour to achieve effectively the object for which it was appointed to do justice between the parties": *Australian Broadcasting Commission v Parish* (at 133) per Bowen CJ.

[40] Mahoney JA (with whom Hope AJA agreed) captured the concept in *John Fairfax Group Pty Ltd v Local Court of New South Wales* (1991) 26 NSWLR 131 (at 161), when (after referring to McHugh JA's statement in *John Fairfax & Sons Ltd v Police Tribunal (NSW)* (at 355)) he said:

> This leads to the consideration of what is meant by "necessary to secure the proper administration of justice" in this context. The phrase does not mean that if the relevant order is not made, the proceedings will not be able to continue. Plainly they can. If the name of an informer is not hidden under a pseudonym, the proceedings will go on: at least the instant proceeding will. ... *The basis of the implication is that if the kind of order proposed is not made, the result will be — or at least will be assumed to be — that particular consequences will flow, that those consequences are unacceptable, and that therefore the power to make orders which will prevent them is to be implied as necessary to the proper function of the court. ...*

The effect of parties' agreements

[41] The parties to the proceedings entered into a Deed pursuant to cl 20 of which they agreed that "disputes arising under this deed" should be dealt with first by confidential mediation and, if that failed, by confidential arbitration. It also contained cl 20.8.

[42] Party autonomy is said to be "fundamental in modern arbitration law" and, to find reflection in legislative recognition of parties' right "to agree about how their commercial disputes are to be resolved subject to, inter alia such safeguards as are necessary in the public interest": s 1C, *Commercial Arbitration Act 2010*; s 1 *Arbitration Act 1996* (UK). "[P]arties value English arbitration for its privacy and confidentiality": *Department of Economics, Policy and Development of the City of Moscow v Bankers Trust Co* [2004] EWCA Civ 314; [2005] QB 207 (at [1], [30]) per Mance LJ (Carnwath LJ agreeing); see also *Fiona Trust & Holding Corp v Privalov* [2007] UKHL 40; [2008] 1 Lloyd's Rep 254 (at [6]) per Lord Hoffman; *Thoroughvision Pty Ltd v Sky Channel Pty Ltd* [2010] VSC 139 (at [16]–[17]).

[43] The private character of the arbitration hearing is "something that inheres in the subject matter of the agreement to submit disputes to arbitration". It is said that "[t]he efficacy of a private arbitration will be damaged, even defeated, if proceedings in the arbitration are made public by the disclosure of documents relating to the arbitration": *Esso Australia Resources Ltd v Plowman (Minister for Energy & Minerals)* [1995] HCA 19; (1995) 183 CLR 10 (at 26, 27) per Mason CJ, Brennan and McHugh J agreeing.

[44] However, as Mason CJ explained in *Esso Australia Resources Ltd v Plowman (Minister for Energy & Minerals)* (at 27ff) in rejecting the view that confidentiality is an essential characteristic of a private arbitration, privacy is not synonymous with confidentiality. To secure confidentiality an express provision may be necessary, although even that may not bind persons such as witnesses not parties to the arbitration agreement. It is no doubt for that reason that cl 20.8 appears in the Trust Deed.

[45] According respect to party autonomy does not mean that everything associated with a private arbitration wears a mantle of confidentiality. Even where an arbitration hearing has been conducted in private pursuant to a court order and even recognising that "[p]arty

autonomy requires the court so far as possible to respect the parties' choice of arbitration", once a court's supervisory jurisdiction is invoked, the fact the arbitration was held in private is only a factor relevant to the question whether the proceedings should be heard in open court: *Department of Economics, Policy and Development of the City of Moscow v Bankers Trust Co* (at [28], [30], [34]–[36]). ...

Conclusion

... [49] In our view, with respect, Tobias AJA relevantly erred. His Honour failed to approach the question whether a suppression order should be granted on a basis which has the least adverse impact upon the open justice principle: see [26] above.

[50] Tobias AJA made the order under s 8, at least in part, to give effect to the maxim *pacta sunt servanda* (agreements are to be kept). He also held that publication would render any appeal nugatory presumably on the basis set out in pars [32] and [33] of his judgment that if a stay was granted the trustee's response and the ultimate resolution of the proceedings would be confidential and there would be significant pressure on Mrs Rinehart to make public her response and the ultimate resolution of the proceedings.

[51] It is well accepted that the Court will, in appropriate circumstances, give effect to agreements to arbitrate by ordering a stay of proceedings brought in breach of the arbitration agreement. That jurisdiction recognises the party autonomy to which we have referred. However, as is apparent from the foregoing discussion, that is not determinative of the question whether, on an application for such a stay, it is necessary for the proper administration of justice for the Court to make a suppression order to give effect to a provision such as cl 20.8 prohibiting disclosure of the nature of the dispute both before, during and after the arbitration proceedings. Tobias AJA, with respect, appears to have treated it as such. In our view, his Honour erred (at [19]) in treating the fact that the parties had agreed to the cl 20.8 clause as effectively determining the question whether a suppression order should be made.

[52] His Honour, with respect, was somewhat dismissive (at [30]) of the plaintiff beneficiaries' submission about the public interest in the determination of a dispute involving the alleged misconduct of a trustee. As we have said, the plaintiff beneficiaries make allegations of breach of trust and seek that the Court invoke its statutory power to remove a trustee. It is not suggested that proceedings were brought for a collateral purpose or that the disclosure of the materials would have any effect on the value of the assets of the trust or other assets of the parties. The proper conduct of trustees is a matter which warrants close public scrutiny. It was a proper factor to take into account in determining whether a suppression order was necessary. ...

[55] In our view, having regard to the nature of the proceedings it was neither "necessary to prevent prejudice to the administration of justice" and, further contrary to the requirement to treat open justice as "a primary objective" referred to in s 6 of the Act for the Court to exercise its power under s 8 to suppress information of the nature of that caught by Tobias AJA's orders. Suppression of such information would undermine, rather than ensure, public confidence in the administration of justice.

[Young JA delivered a separate concurring judgment discharging the suppression order.]

1.7.8 This case may be located at (viewed 20 July 2012) <http://www.caselaw.nsw.gov.au>. For a description of the Rinehart litigation, see W Bonython, 'The Welker v Rinehart Litigation', (2012) 8(5) *Privacy Law Bulletin* 88.

Open justice and the chambers jurisdiction

1.7.9 Traditionally minor interlocutory matters were dealt with in chambers: *Medical Board of Victoria v Meyer* (1937) 58 CLR 62 at 93–6. Now most interlocutory proceedings are conducted in open court and the chamber jurisdiction is used when the proceedings are not open to the public or where the statute conferring jurisdiction upon a court allows that jurisdiction to be exercised by a judge sitting in chambers (e.g. Federal Court Act 1976 (Cth) s 17(2)) or if the practice is for such powers or those of an analogous nature to be exercised in chambers: *Smeeton v Collier* (1847) 1 Exch 457; 154 ER 194; *Parkin v James* (1905) 2 CLR 315; 11 ALR 142 at 149 per Griffith CJ.

Some jurisdictions retain the distinction between the exercise of jurisdiction by the court, (that is in open court), and individual judges sitting in chambers exercising the jurisdiction of the court i.e. the High Court of Australia (Judiciary Act 1903 (Cth) s 16), the Supreme Court of Tasmania (Supreme Court Civil Procedure Act 1932 (Tas) s 16) and Western Australia: Supreme Court Act 1935 (WA) s 41(3).

See generally *Halsbury's Laws of Australia*, 'Courts and Judicial System', LexisNexis Butterworths, [125-125].

1.7.10   Further reading

C Davis, 'The Injustice of Open Justice' (2001) 8 *James Cook UL Rev* 92.

Judicial Commission of NSW, 'Closed Court, Suppression and Non-publication Orders' *Civil Trials Bench Book*, viewed 18 June 2012, <http://www.judcom.nsw.gov.au/>.

A Kenyon, 'Not Seeing Justice Done: Suppression Orders in Australian Law and Practice', (2006) 27 *Adelaide Law Review* 279.

J Spigelman, 'Seen to be Done: The Principle of Open Justice — Part I' (2000) 74 *ALJ* 290.

J Spigelman, 'Seen to be Done: The Principle of Open Justice — Part II' (2000) 74 *ALJ* 378.

HUMAN RIGHTS CHALLENGES TO THE CIVIL JUSTICE SYSTEM

The right to a fair hearing

1.8.1 In 1980, Australia ratified the International Covenant on Civil and Political Rights (ICCPR). Article 14 of the ICCPR relevantly states as follows:

> All persons shall be equal before the courts and tribunals. In the determination of … his rights and obligations in a suit at law, everyone shall be entitled to a fair and public hearing by a competent, independent and impartial tribunal established by law.

Two Australian jurisdictions — Australian Capital Territory and Victoria — have incorporated Art 14 of the ICCPR into their domestic laws by passing Human Rights Acts which are based on the dialogue model of rights exemplified by the Human Rights 1998 (UK).

1.8.2E   **Human Rights Act 2004 (ACT)**

Fair trial

21 (1) Everyone has the right to have criminal charges, and rights and obligations recognised by law, decided by a competent, independent and impartial court or tribunal after a fair and public hearing.

1.8.3E   **Charter of Human Rights and Responsibilities Act 2006 (Vic)**

Fair hearing

24 (1) A person charged with a criminal offence or a party to a civil proceeding has the right to have the charge or proceeding decided by a competent, independent and impartial court or tribunal after a fair and public hearing.

1.8.4   When argued, the right to fair hearing may operate as a counterbalance to traditional or evolving civil procedures, particularly where judicial discretion is involved.

1.8.5C   **Hodgson v Amcor Ltd; Amcor Ltd v Barnes (No 3)**
[2011] VSC 272
Supreme Court of Victoria — Common Law Division

[The Amcor parties, in the course of the trial, sought to call and rely upon the evidence of a witness, Mr Conn.]

Vickery J
Case Management Ground
[26] By way of background:
    (a)   Mr Conn's witness statement was served without the leave of the court and without consent on 29 April 2011. This was some 19 days before the commencement of the trial;
    (b)   ... [Pursuant to case management orders] [t]he Amcor Parties were directed to file their witness statements by 18 February 2011. This date was the culmination of a number of extensions granted to Amcor to file its witness statements;
    (c)   Amcor filed and served its witness statements by 18 February 2011 in compliance with the order of the court. These witness statements however did not include statements from either Mr Conn or Mr Reid.

[27] Case management orders such as those made [in this case] were made pursuant to s 47(1) Civil Procedure Act 2010. However, case management orders designed to serve the interests of justice in the course of a trial, particularly a long and complex matter such as

the present case are not immutable. The procedures set in place for the management of the trial must be capable of reasonable adaptation to ensure that the trial is in fact conducted in accordance with the interests of justice as the case proceeds to judgment.

[28] Further, it is axiomatic that a just determination of a proceeding is the product of a trial, which must be conducted fairly and in accordance with the principles of natural justice and procedural fairness. Nothing in the *Civil Procedure Act 2010* (Vic) detracts from these principles. Indeed they are supported by its terms. The overarching purpose of the Act defined in s 7(1) provides:

> The overarching purpose of this Act and the rules of court in relation to civil proceedings is to facilitate *the just*, efficient, timely and cost effective resolution of the real issues in dispute. [Emphasis added]

[29] Further, s 6 of the Civil Procedure Act provides that nothing contained in it is intended to override the Charter of Human Rights and Responsibilities Act 2006. ...

[30] ... The reference to the Charter in the Civil Procedure Act serves to underpin the importance of maintaining the right to a fair trial ... in the application of the powers provided.

[31] Natural justice or procedural fairness in the curial sense includes the right of a party to present relevant evidence in support of its case both oral and documentary.

[32] The provisions of the Civil Procedure Act therefore call for a balance to be applied between the case management requirements of achieving an efficient, timely and cost effective resolution of the real issues in dispute, and the requirements for a fair hearing to achieve a just outcome on the other.

[33] In this case Mr Conn's witness statement was served on 29 April 2011, 19 days before the commencement of the trial. In the course of opening the case for Amcor senior counsel referred to the evidence proposed to be called through Mr Conn.

[34] The trial is now at the end of the third week. The defendant parties have not been taken by surprise in relation to the evidence of Mr Conn, and do not advance any procedural prejudice resulting from having him called now.

[35] In this case the balance between case management considerations and the dictates of a fair trial falls squarely in favour of permitting Mr Conn to be called by the Amcor parties.

[Vickery J found that the evidence in the witness statement was admissible and ought to be admitted.]

1.8.6 Certain judgments in the Australian Capital Territory Supreme Court have adopted a similar approach and found that the right to fair hearing may modify the approach to interlocutory decision-making. For example, in determining the principles to be applied to a grant of leave to appeal against an interlocutory decision in *Capital Property Projects (ACT) Pty Ltd v Planning and Land Authority* [2008] ACTCA 9, Refshauge J opined that the principles should be applied more liberally in the light of s 21 of the Human Rights Act 2004 (ACT) 'since an error in the interlocutory decision may have the effect of derogating from the fairness of the trial': at [29]. Similarly, in interpreting the interaction between the traditional approach to summary judgment, which emphasises 'exceptional caution' *(General Steel Industries Inc v Commissioner for Railways (NSW)* (1964) 112 CLR 125 at 129) and the overriding purpose in r 21 of the

Court Procedures Rules 2006 (ACT), the late Connolly J of the Australian Capital Territory Supreme Court found that the 'traditional common law approach is consistent with the statutory recognition by way of s 21 of the Human Rights Act 2004 of the right to a fair trial': *West v New South Wales* [2007] ACTSC 43 at [21].

1.8.7   Notes

1. Compare the approach discussed above with that taken by the Victorian Court of Appeal in *De Simone v Benvol Constructions & Developments Pty Ltd* [2010] VSCA 231 and the Victorian Supreme Court in *Russell v Yarra Ranges Shire Council* [2009] VSC 486.

2. For an analysis of the Human Rights Act (ACT) and the Victorian Charter generally, see *R v Momcilovic* (2011) 280 ALR 221; (2011) 85 ALJR 957; *Director of Housing v Sudi* [2011] VSCA 266, *Hakimi v Legal Aid Commission (ACT)* (2009) 227 FLR 462; *R v Fearnside* (2009) 165 ACTR 22 and *Re Application for Bail by Islam* (2010) 175 ACTR 30. A valuable resource is the Human Rights Law Centre, viewed 18 June 2012, <http://www.hrlc.org.au>.

FLAWS IN, AND REFORM OF, THE CIVIL JUSTICE SYSTEM

Delay

1.9.1 The combination of high costs and endemic delays in the Australian civil justice during the 1980s deterred people from pursuing claims and thereby reduced access to justice. At that time, party control of litigation was accompanied by a policy of 'doing justice on the merits'; that is, the court decided the case on the basis of true facts and the correct law and not on procedural grounds. This 'justice on the merits' approach was taken to override procedural arrangements, therefore where there was non-compliance with the procedural rules, the court would forgive the defect in order to decide the case on its merits.

The response to this crisis led to major reforms which began in the early 1990s and are analysed in The Hon Robert French CJ, 'The Future of Litigation: Dispute Resolution in Jurassic Park?', *Bar Association of Queensland Annual Conference*, 7 March 2009, p 9ff. These initiatives led to the development of case management, which will be discussed in **Chapter 2**. See also A Zuckerman, 'Justice in Crisis: Comparative Dimensions of Civil Procedure', *Civil Justice in Crisis: Comparative Perspectives of Civil Procedure*, Oxford University Press, New York, 1999, p 16ff.

Western Australia has expressly stated the goal of elimination of delay in its Supreme Court Rules.

1.9.2E	**Rules of the Supreme Court 1971 (WA)**
	Order 1 — Application, Elimination of Delay and Forms

Elimination of delays

4A The practice, procedure and interlocutory processes of the Court shall have as their goal the elimination of any lapse of time from the date of initiation of proceedings to their final determination beyond that reasonably required for interlocutory activities essential to the fair and just determination of the issues bona fide in contention between the parties and the preparation of the case for trial.

Efficiency

1.9.3   Zuckerman has argued for simplified procedures which can be invoked by both plaintiffs and defendants in order to obtain a speedy resolution of disputes: 'Quality and Economy in Civil Procedure: The Case for Commuting Correct Judgments for Timely Judgments' (1994) 14 *Oxford J of Legal Studies* 353. By foregoing some existing procedural devices, such an approach might lead to less accurate judgments. However, he argues that it makes sense to trade some quality for speed and economy, in view of the expense and delay involved in the present process of the law. He states (at 354) that:

> … the needs of the community may be better served by faster and simpler proceedings, albeit at some cost to accuracy, than by a highly accurate procedure in which delays can rob judgments of their utility and in which expense places the protection of the law beyond the reach of the great majority.

In the following excerpt, Zuckerman elaborates this argument through an analysis of the requirements of civil justice.

1.9.4E	**Quality and Economy in Civil Procedure: The Case for Commuting Correct Judgments for Timely Judgments**
	A A S Zuckerman
	(1994) 14 *Oxford J of Legal Studies* 353
	(footnotes omitted)

Correct Decisions and Just Procedures

[354] According to Bentham the direct end of procedure is rectitude of decision, that is, the correct application of the substantive law to the true facts. Rectitude of decision should, according to Bentham, be attained without unnecessary delay, vexation or expense. However, any attempt to construct a procedure designed to achieve this goal inevitably comes against the constraints that delay, vexation and expense impose on the practical attainability of rectitude of decision or, as we may refer to it, a correct or accurate resolution of disputes. The attainment of correct resolutions is, at least in part, a function of the resources that we are prepared to invest in the civil process. Up to a point, the more we invest in the investigation of an issue of fact, the more likely we are to get to the truth. Similarly, with questions of law. The more professional and judicial effort is devoted to them, the more likely it is that we would get the correct answer.

Does this mean that citizens may reasonably [355] demand from the State to be provided with the most accurate procedure? It is clearly counter-intuitive to suggest that the State ought to design the most accurate civil procedure regardless of cost, when the State need not provide, regardless of cost, the most effective health service or, indeed almost any other public benefit. Yet it is equally unreasonable to suppose that the civil trial need not achieve any level of accuracy to satisfy the demands of justice. Dworkin has suggested that citizens do nevertheless have some legitimate claims in this regard. They have a right to demand 'procedures justified by the correct assignment of importance to the moral harm the procedures risk'. By moral harm Dworkin means simply the injustice caused to a litigant whose claim or defence, as the case may be, is rejected when the litigant is in the right, over and above the material loss or emotional pain suffered as a result of such decision. We may agree, then, that in devising a system of civil procedure, the legislature should take reasonable steps to prevent the injustice that ensues from erroneous decisions, which deny litigants their due. Yet, since the legislature need not strive to take all possible steps to ensure that judgments are factually and legally correct, this leaves a very considerable scope for choice between different procedures and for decisions about the allocation of resources to procedure. Notwithstanding this wide choice, the legislature, according to Dworkin, is bound by certain principles of justice when it comes to devising a civil procedure. Prominent amongst them is the principle that citizens should be treated as equals.

We shall have occasion to discuss further the dictate of treating litigants as equals. Here we need only observe that the preceding discussion has brought out an important feature of procedure. As the institutional means for enforcing rights, the legal procedure must be just. A procedure which does not even attempt to give citizens what is theirs by right cannot be regarded as a just procedure. However, a procedure may be just even though it does not always give citizens what is theirs by right; namely, even though its results are sometimes erroneous and therefore unjust. We are distinguishing therefore between a just procedure and a just or correct result. A just result (or judgment or decision) is one which follows from the correct application of the law to the true facts and therefore give the parties what is theirs. An unjust or incorrect result is one which does not achieve this end, which does not correctly apply the law or does not accurately determine the facts. An unjust judgment is one where the plaintiff's rightful claim is denied or the defendant's rightful defence is rejected.

This conception of a just judgment throws into relief a practical problem. For although the criterion for a just result is clear, it may be difficult to determine whether any particular judgment is just. 'The characteristic mark of imperfect procedural justice', Rawls writes, 'is that while there is an independent criterion for the correct outcome, there is no feasible procedure which is sure to lead to it'. Where the issue in dispute is a factual one, the criterion of what is true or false, of whether it was the plaintiff's car or the defendant's car, that demolished the garden fence, is of course independent of the legal procedure. But unfortunately we do not have a super-test for judging the conformity of judgments to the truth. All we possess is the legal procedure that we have devised. It follows that our confidence in the justice of any given decision, and its conformity with [356] fact and law, is a function of our confidence in the procedure that has produced the particular result or of our acceptance of the procedure, as distinguished from the particular result, as just procedure.

The concept of just procedure is very difficult to unravel, as we have already seen. A just procedure must aim at achieving correct results, but it need not always achieve this aim in order to remain a just procedure. Nor does it have to secure any particular level of accuracy or quality in its overall product. This does not, however, mean that we can have no conception of what is a just procedure. For, as we have seen, we can consider whether we are satisfied with the measures adopted to promote just results. Further, we may ask whether the procedure adopted is consistent with, or sufficiently promotes, some other aims or principles that we wish procedure to attain.

1.9.5 Notes and questions

1. Zuckerman subsequently argues that judges should be more prepared to use summary procedures, particularly summary judgment, to dispose of matters. For a discussion of summary judgment see **Chapter 12**.

2. Tyler's work indicates that the major criteria used by people to assess process fairness are ethicality, honesty and the effort to be fair. In response to Zuckerman's final point in this extract, are these criteria 'aims or principles' that procedure ought to attain? See T Tyler, 'What is Procedural Justice? Criteria Used by Citizens to Assess the Fairness of Legal Procedures' (1998) 22 *L & Soc Rev* 103 at 128.

1.9.6 Zuckerman's arguments are based on a notion of distributive justice and Parker makes a similar point by asking why, in a world of finite resources, justice should be seen as more important than health or a basic standard of living. He concludes that '[j]ustice, it seems, must always be rationed to some extent': S Parker, *Islands of Civic Virtue? Lawyers and Civil Justice Reform*, Inaugural Professorial Lecture, Griffith University, 5 December 1996.

In the extract below, Leubsdorf is critical of an approach to procedural reform which is based on the 'fairly trite criteria' of cheapness, speed and accuracy.

1.9.7E | **The Myth of Civil Procedure Reform**
John Leubsdorf
in A Zuckerman (ed), *Civil Justice in Crisis: Comparative Perspectives of Civil Procedure*
Oxford University Press, New York, 1999, pp 53–67
(footnotes omitted)

What is the Goal?

[54] How could we decide whether today's civil procedure is an improvement on the common law system? We can try to assess the relative fairness of any given part of the systems ... although our judgment of what is fair will inevitably arise from our own culture, including our own procedural system. Judging the relative fairness of systems taken as a whole is still more problematic: what constitutes procedural fairness is by no means obvious. Should the standard be enforced of the substantive law, convenient dispute resolution, litigant satisfaction, social cohesion, controlled exercise of state power, or some combination of these factors? ...

[55] Bypassing for the moment the debate about goals, we might fix on three fairly trite criteria for appraising a procedural system: the cost of litigation; the time needed to resolve disputes; and the accuracy with which the system finds the facts and applies the law. As we have seen, some will question these criteria: those, for example, who see litigation less as law enforcement and more as dispute resolution might replace accuracy with litigant satisfaction.

And the three criteria sometimes conflict. Making procedure speedier and cheaper might well make it less accurate even though keeping it slower and more expensive will not necessarily make it more accurate ...

Unfortunately, even granted the willingness to appraise a system in its typical working, it is virtually impossible to assess accuracy, short of readjudicating a sample of cases with enough thoroughness to guarantee almost total correctness. [56] Deleting the accuracy criterion leaves us with speed and cheapness which are relatively measurable but tell us only part of what we would like to know. ... [67] Ultimately, our judgment of a procedural system should go beyond its average speed, cheapness, and accuracy ... The most firmly implanted myth of procedural reform may be that we can talk usefully about it as simply an effort to increase judicial efficiency without talking about our visions about procedural and social justice.

1.9.8   Note and question

1. How much weight should be given to issues of social justice in debating procedural reform?

2. Chapter 2 examines case management and the overriding purpose which have become the prevailing instruments of civil procedural reform in Australia in the last decade. Consider the debates canvassed in this chapter when analysing the material in Chapter 2.

Further reading

1.10.1   Articles, books and papers

G Brouwer, 'Inquisitorial and Adversary Procedures — A Comparative Analysis' (1981) 55 *ALJ* 207.

G Certoma, 'The Accusatory System v the Inquisitorial System: Procedural Truth v Fact?' (1982) 56 *ALJ* 288.

A Clarke, 'Civil Justice: The Importance of the Rule of Law' (2009) *International Lawyer* 39.

P Connolly, 'The Adversary System — Is it Any Longer Appropriate?' (1975) 49 *ALJ* 439.

G Davies, 'Justice Reform: A Personal Perspective' (1997) 15 *Aust Bar Rev* 109.

G Davies, 'The Reality of Civil Justice Reform: Why We Must Abandon the Essential Elements of Our System' (2003) 12 *Journal of Judicial Administration* 155.

G Davies and S A Sheldon, 'Some Proposed Changes in Civil Procedure: Their Practical Benefits and Ethical Rationale' (1993) 3 *Journal of Judicial Administration* 111.

O Fiss, 'Against Settlement' (1984) 93 *Yale LJ* 1073.

M Galanter and M Cahill, '"Most Cases Settle": Judicial Promotion and Regulation of Settlements' (1994) 46 *Stanford LR* 1339.

H Genn, *Judging Civil Justice*, Cambridge University Press, London, 2010.

R Gilson and R Mnookin, 'Disputing Through Agents: Cooperation and Conflict Between Lawyers and Litigation' (1994) 94 *Columbia LR* 509.

R Kagan, 'Do Lawyers Cause Adversarial Legalism? A Preliminary Inquiry', 1994 19(1) *Law and Social Inquiry* 1.

A Marfording and A Eyland, 'Civil Litigation in New South Wales: Empirical and Analytical Comparisons with Germany' (2010) *University of New South Wales Faculty of Law Research Series* 28.

R McGarvie, 'Judicial Responsibility for the Operation of the Court System' (1989) 63 *ALJ* 79.

C Pincus, 'Court Involvement in Pre-trial Procedures' (1987) 61 *ALJ* 471.

R Posner, 'An Economic Approach to Legal Procedure and Judicial Administration' (1973) 2 *J of Legal Studies* 399.

R Sackville, 'The Access to Justice Report: Change and Accountability in the Judicial System' (1994) 4 *J of Judicial Administration* 65.

G Samuels, 'The Economics of Justice' (1991) 1 *J of Judicial Administration* 114.

S Shavell, 'The Fundamental Divergence Between the Private and the Social Motive to Use the Legal System' (1997) 26 *J of Legal Studies* 575.

H Stacey and M Lavarch (eds), *Beyond the Adversarial System*, Federation Press, Sydney, 1999.

G Thwaite and A Reuter, 'Civil Litigation in the German Legal System' (1994) 12 *Aust Bar Rev* 41.

C Tobias, 'More Modern Civil Process' (1995) 56 *University of Pittsburgh LR* 801.

W Twining, 'Alternative to What: Theories of Litigation, Procedure and Dispute Settlement in Anglo–American Jurisprudence: Some Neglected Classics' (1993) 56 *Modern LR* 380.

B Wolski, 'Reform of the Civil Justice System Two Decades Past — Implications for the Legal Profession and for Law Teachers' (2009) 21 *Bond L Rev* 26.

S Yeazell, 'The Misunderstood Consequences of Modern Civil Process' (1994) 22 *Wisconsin LR* 631.

W Zeidler, 'Evaluation of the Adversary System: As Comparison, Some Remarks on the Investigatory System of Procedure' (1981) 55 *ALJ* 390.

A Zuckerman, 'Reform of Civil Procedure — Rationing Procedure Rather than Access to Justice' (1995) 22 *J of Law and Society* 155.

1.10.2 Reports

Australian Government Attorney-General's Department, Access to Justice Taskforce, *A Strategic Framework for Access to Justice in the Federal Civil Justice System*, 2009.

Department for Constitutional Affairs, *Access to Justice: Interim Report to the Lord Chancellor on the Civil Justice System in England and Wales*, 1995.

Department for Constitutional Affairs, *Access to Justice: Final Report to the Lord Chancellor on the Civil Justice System in England and Wales*, 1996.

National Alternative Dispute Resolution Advisory Council (NADRAC), *The Resolve to Resolve: Embracing ADR to Improve Access to Justice in the Federal Jurisdiction*, 2009.

Victorian Law Reform Commission, *Civil Justice Review*, Report 14, 2008.

Case Management and the Overriding Purpose

## CHAPTER 2

OVERVIEW

2.1.1 The last two decades have seen a move away from adversarialism and party control of litigation as the dominant paradigm of civil procedure to a system where courts control the progress of individual matters in their lists by the use of case management practices. Case management has been facilitated by the development of overarching purpose provisions, that is, legislation and court rules that allow the courts to interpret procedural rules and individual orders to promote an overriding purpose. The enforcement of case management sanctions and the interpretation of the overriding purpose provisions have led to an approach where a court will take into account interests beyond those of the immediate parties to a proceeding when exercising its powers.

This chapter will examine the development of so-called managerial judging which shifted focus away from the judge as referee under a party-controlled system to the judge as a manager of litigation. It will then examine the introduction of case management by Australian courts. There is significant diversity in the detail of case management systems that have been implemented in the various Australian jurisdictions. This chapter attempts to show the distinctive features of different types of case management, exemplified in individual courts. Thereafter, the significant body of case law that considers challenges to case management decisions will be considered, as recently supplemented by the interpretation of overriding objectives which facilitate compliance with case management systems and the interpretation of civil procedural rules generally.

THE ROLE OF THE JUDGE

2.2.1 The adversarial model of litigation is premised upon party control. The parties are left to conduct proceedings as they see fit and according to their own timetable. Judges assume a passive role, intervening, like an umpire, only if the non-delinquent party seeks the imposition of sanctions. The judge does not intervene in the preparation or the presentation of a case; rather the parties plan the preparatory steps which lead to a climactic and self-contained trial: G L Davies and J S Leiboff, 'Reforming the Civil Litigation System: Streamlining the Adversarial Framework' (1994) 14 *Proctor* 18.

Denning LJ asserted in *Jones v National Coal Board* [1957] 2 QB 55 at 65 (*Jones*) that:

> …the judge sits to hear and determine the issues raised by the parties, not to conduct an investigation or examination on behalf of society at large … . If he goes beyond this, he drops the mantle of a judge and assumes the role of an advocate; and the change does not become him well.

However, during the 1990s there was significant criticism in Australia of the model of civil justice which characterises the judge as 'umpire'. For example, in 'Reforms to the Adversarial Process in Civil Litigation — Part 1' (1995) *ALJ* 705 at 713–14, Ipp criticised Lord Denning's comments in *Jones* (above) as follows:

> Lord Denning asserts that the object 'above all, is to find the truth'. On the other hand, the judge, according to his Lordship's view, is to remain a passive spectator until giving judgment, dependent upon the parties to call relevant witnesses and ask appropriate questions. Thus the power of the judge to find the truth is limited by the parties' ability and desire to lay all the relevant facts before her or him. That may result in the judge administering the law as distinct from justice.

Managerial judging

2.2.2   Most judges have shifted from the traditional view to adopt a more active managerial stance. J Resnik, 'Managerial Judges' (1982) 96 *Harvard LR* 376 at 376–7 commented that in growing numbers:

> …judges are not only adjudicating the merits of the issues presented to them by litigants, but also are meeting with parties … to encourage settlement of disputes and to supervise case preparation. Before and after the trial, judges are playing a critical role in shaping litigation and influencing results.

In the following extract, the Australian Law Reform Commission explores some of the wider ramifications of managerial judging for the litigation system.

2.2.3E   **Review of the Adversarial System of Litigation: Rethinking the Federal Civil Litigation System**
ALRC
Issues Paper 20, paras 5.09–5.11

5.09 … [M]anagerial judging has broader implications for civil litigation because the kinds of procedural intervention that typify managerial judging involve nonadversarial decision-making. The judge is not simply responding as a passive umpire to processes initiated by litigants and their lawyers but is active in investigating the best way to define the dispute and to present the case.

5.10 If judges require litigants to present their dispute in a certain manner and with an emphasis on what the judge has decided is the central issue, then the roles of litigants, lawyers and the court are altered. One view is that this approach is an incremental step towards the non-adversarial practice of 'discontinuous trials'. That is, the focus of dispute resolution is no longer solely directed towards the final hearing. Rather, legal proceedings are viewed as a continuous series of meetings, hearings and written communications during which evidence is introduced, witnesses heard and motions made.

2.2.4 Further reading

M Black, 'The Role of the Judge in Attacking Endemic Delays: Some Lessons from Fast Track' (2009) 19 *JJA* 88.

A Rogers, 'The Managerial or Interventionist Judge' (1993) 3 *JJA* 96

R Sackville, 'From Access to Justice to Managing Justice: The Transformation of the Judicial Role' (2002) 12 *JJA* 5.

P Sallmann, 'Impact of Caseflow Management on the Judicial System' (1995) 18 *UNSWLJ* 193.

P Sallmann, 'Musings on the Judicial Role in Court and Caseflow Management' (1989) 63 *ALJ* 98.

CASE MANAGEMENT — CONCEPTS

2.3.1 In Australia, discussion about managerial judging has predominantly taken place within the context of debate about case management. Case management is an approach to the control of litigation in which the court supervises or controls the progress of the case through its interlocutory phase. The term 'case management' encompasses 'caseflow' and 'caseload' management. In particular, the terms 'caseflow management' and 'case management' are used interchangeably in the literature.

2.3.2E   Review of the Adversarial System of Litigation: Judicial and Case Management
ALRC
Background Paper 3, December 1996, pp 5–7
(footnotes omitted)

What is caseflow management?
The progress of cases before the courts has always been 'managed' in one sense, but traditional adversarial case management left the pace of litigation primarily in the hands of legal practitioners. The court's role was simply to respond to processes initiated by practitioners.

Over the last ten years case management by judges and quasi-judicial officers such as registrars has rapidly evolved in many Australian courts. These forms of case management (or, more correctly, caseflow management) … involve the court managing the time and events involved in the movement of cases from commencement to disposition.

The objectives of case management (caseflow and caseload) include:

- early resolution of disputes
- reduction of trial time
- more effective use of judicial resources
- the establishment of trial standards
- monitoring of caseloads
- development of information technology support
- increasing accessibility to the courts

- facilitating planning for the future
- enhanced public accountability
- the reduction of criticism of the justice system by reason of perceived inefficiency. ...

... The fundamental elements of a successful caseflow management system have been said to include:

- judicial commitment and leadership
- court consultation with the legal profession
- court supervision of case progress
- the use of standards and goals
- a monitoring information system
- listing for credible dates
- strict control of adjournments.

Based on these principles, Federal and State courts have implemented a variety of programs adapting case management to suit their own jurisdictions ... Caseflow management has helped bring about substantial procedural, operational and cultural changes in the judicial systems of Australia. ....

Models of caseflow management

Justice David Ipp of the Supreme Court of Western Australia identifies two basic models of pre-trial case management:

- management involving continuous control by a judge, who personally monitors each case on an ad hoc basis; and
- management where control is exercised by requiring the parties to report to the court (often in the form of a master or registrar) at fixed milestones and where the court exercises routine and structured control.

These two models can be referred to as involving 'individual lists' or a 'master list' respectively.

The master list is the method most used in Australian courts. All cases are controlled by the court registry and are assigned to different judges or judicial officers at different times for different purposes. When an event relating to a case has been dealt with it is returned to the pool of cases to await the next event and to be assigned again, not usually to the same judge or judicial officer.

Under an individual list each case is assigned to an individual judge at filing and that judge manages his or her defined group of cases from commencement to conclusion. The judge ensures that the case moves at an appropriate pace. This model is sometimes referred to as 'individual case management' or ... 'individual docket' caseflow management. Although the judge remains responsible for each case on his or her list, the case can be managed by a case team.

Caseflow management regimes may encompass elements of both basic models described above. For example, 'differential case management' ... systems allow for complex cases to be closely managed by the trial judge and others to be managed by judges and judicial officers at different stages. Individual case management may take place within an overall framework of fixed milestone events to which judges are expected to adhere.

2.3.3 The Productivity Commission publishes an annual Report on Government Services that provides data on the case flow of courts, including the Federal Court of Australia and the state and territory Supreme, District/County and Magistrates' (including Children's) Courts. See, for example, Productivity Commission, *Report on Government Services 2012*, Ch 7, Court Administration, (in particular the attachment tables in this chapter), viewed 13 May 2012, <http://www.pc.gov.au>.

2.3.4 Further reading

B Cairns, 'Managing Civil Litigation: An Australian Adoption of American Experience' (1994) 13 *CJQ* 50.

CASE MANAGEMENT — EXAMPLES

An overview of case management practices

2.4.1 The form of case management adopted by courts varies considerably across Australian jurisdictions. It is significant that no Australian jurisdiction maintains a purely 'party initiated' system. The closest equivalent occurs in smaller jurisdictions where a master list is maintained for the majority of matters but particular cases (eg, complex cases) are individually or differentially managed. Where a master list system has been implemented, jurisdictions often create specialist lists for particular types of disputes, such as commercial causes. Within the general lists, differential case management may also be implemented which allows the court to differentiate between cases which have divergent case management requirements. The concept of case management also encompasses encouragement of settlement and so the diversion of cases through alternative dispute resolution processes will also be examined below.

The following discussion will highlight examples of case management techniques that are used in various Australian jurisdictions. The case management system used in each jurisdiction will not be comprehensively described; rather, interesting or unique aspects of each system will be emphasised.

2.4.2 Further reading

B Cairns, *Australian Civil Procedure*, 9th ed, Law Book Co, Sydney, 2011, Ch 2.

C Cameron, 'New Directions for Case Management in Australia' (2010) *CJQ* 337.

Hybrid — Master list with management of certain cases: Australian Capital Territory and Tasmania

2.4.3 Both the Australian Capital Territory and Tasmania rely on a master list for the greater volume of their work. In the Australian Capital Territory, matters involving a claim for debt or death or bodily injury fall within the master list system (the plaintiff must nominate the cause of action on the originating claim — r 1302) and in Tasmania, the master list operates with respect to claims for damages for personal injuries. For these matters, in both jurisdictions, a Certificate of Readiness is filed by one or both parties to set down a matter for trial. A Certificate of Readiness generally certifies that interlocutory procedures are complete and provides details of the anticipated trial, such as witnesses. The Tasmanian procedure is discussed below.

2.4.4   In the Australian Capital Territory, for master list matters ie, those matters involving a claim for debt, death or bodily injury other than medical negligence (Categories A and B — r 1302), the Certificate of Readiness is usually prepared by the plaintiff but may be prepared by either party: r 1306(1). It must be signed by both parties: r 1306(3). Following the filing of the Certificate of Readiness, a listing hearing is held with both parties in attendance. If the matter does not settle at the listing hearing, the court allocates a hearing date for trial: r 1309. Complex claims that need case management directions such as defamation, building and commercial claims (Category C — r 1302) are subject to a Directions Hearing after an appearance (notice of intention to respond) has been filed (Notice to Practitioners 22 August 1997; r 1303).

The Australian Capital Territory Supreme Court undertook a 'blitz' of its listings in 2012, and has foreshadowed the introduction of an individual docket system covering both civil and criminal matters: Practice Direction No 2 of 2011.

2.4.5   As stated above, in the Supreme Court of Tasmania proceedings (other than claims for damages for personal injuries) are subject to case management: r 414 and Practice Direction No 11 of 2005. The principal tool of case management is a directions hearing before a judge. Rule 415(2) states:

> (2) The purpose of a directions hearing is to eliminate any lapse of time from the commencement of a proceeding to its final determination beyond that reasonably required for pleadings, affidavits, discovery and other interlocutory matters essential to the fair and just determination of the issues in contention between the parties and the preparation of the case for trial.

At the directions hearing, the judge may make an order with respect to the future conduct of the matter; for example, an order with respect to the simplification or more adequate definition of issues or the amendment of pleadings.

For personal injury matters, when the matter is ready for trial the parties may file a Certificate of Readiness (r 544) or a joint letter of readiness: r 545. However, the parties to an action must confer together beforehand to reach agreement on as many matters as possible and discuss the possibility of settlement of the action: r 541. After the certificate or letter has been filed, the Registrar gives notice of a pre-trial conference: r 547. At the pre-trial conference, the parties discuss whether the matter is ready for trial: r 549.

At the conclusion of the pre-trial conference, a judge may order that the matter be listed for trial or adjourn the conference: r 550. Either way, the court will manage the conduct of the proceedings until their conclusion.

Court initiated directions hearings: New South Wales — Supreme Court Common Law Division, South Australia and Western Australia

2.4.6   In New South Wales (Common Law Division of the Supreme Court), South Australia and Western Australia upon a triggering event (for example, the filing of a defence, (NSW — Practice Note No SC CL 1, 17/08/2005 at [12]); the notification of an address for service

(SA r 125); or an appearance (WA O 4A r 18(2)), the court requires the parties to attend court for a Directions Hearing (also known as a status conference or status hearing). The obligation applies to all cases commenced, with minor exceptions.

2.4.7   Question

1. Has the implementation of case management brought down the cost of litigation? The Law Reform Commission of Western Australia in its *Final Report of its Review of the Criminal and Civil Justice System*, September 1999, (viewed 12 June 2012, <http://www.lrc.justice.wa.gov.au>) states at Ch 12, para 12.4:

> There seems little doubt that the current trend towards increased judicial involvement has the potential to absorb more court resources and to increase the costs of the parties by subjecting the pre-trial stage of litigation to constant intervention. It also appears that the most expensive case management schemes are those which involve multiple conferences. The regime recommended by us seeks, so far as possible, to minimise the number of interlocutory conferences. In our view those conferences largely should follow the form of the current case management structure — with an initial case management conference (to assess ADR options), a status conference and a listing conference.

2.4.8   Further reading

T Matruglilo and J Baker, *An Implementation and Evaluation of Differential Case Management*, Law Foundation, New South Wales, 1995.

Timelines: Queensland

2.4.9   In the Supreme Court of Queensland, case management of proceedings in the civil jurisdiction of the court in Brisbane is effected by the setting of timelines by which proceedings should progress to specific stages, for example from service to filing a defence, and monitors the progress of proceedings against those timelines. The system is described in Practice Direction No 4 of 2002.

Differential case management: the Northern Territory

2.4.10   As stated in the ALRC Background Paper 3 at **2.3.2E** above, 'differential case management' (DCM) systems are based on the idea that different types of cases need different types of management. DCM systems assign cases on the basis of their individual characteristics to designated procedural 'tracks', which may include prescribed time limits for case progress and different levels of judicial management. Cases are assigned on the basis of case characteristics such as the nature of the dispute and the number of parties. Elements of DCM are used in the Northern Territory. In the Northern Territory Supreme Court, the Master decides the category of case in a directions hearing which is initiated by the court within three weeks to two months of the originating process being filed: rr 48.04, 48.06.

48.06 (2) At the initial directions hearing, the Master must designate the proceeding to be in one of the following categories:

    (a)   if the hearing time is likely to be 1 to 2 days — Category A;

    (b)   if the proceeding is an ordinary matter requiring the supervision of the Master — Category B;

    (c)   if the proceeding is a complex matter requiring the supervision of a Judge — Category C;

    (d)   if the proceeding is an urgent matter requiring the supervision of a Judge — Category D;

    (e)   if the proceeding involves local witnesses only or no witnesses and, when ready for trial, is likely to be capable of being brought on for trial on less than 2 days' notice — Category E.

  (3)   The category to which a proceeding belongs may be altered by a Judge or the Master if there is a good reason for doing so.

2.4.12   Currently the Northern Territory is using a system in which the parties submit a litigation plan (Practice Directions No 4 of 2004, No 7 of 2007 and No 3 of 2011). One month after pleadings have closed, each party files and serves on each other party to a proceeding a litigation plan which must state, among other things, what the party contends are the primary legal and factual issues in the case, necessary evidence, outstanding and required interlocutory steps, a possible timetable for the completion of all outstanding steps and what attempts have been made to settle the proceeding. The Master arranges a directions hearing to take place six weeks after pleadings have closed. At the directions hearing the Master questions the parties' legal representatives about their litigation plans and the progress of the proceeding, makes whatever directions are necessary, and lists the proceeding for trial.

Specialist divisions and lists: Victoria

2.4.13   The Supreme Court of Victoria has introduced a number of judge-controlled specialist lists operating in its civil jurisdiction. For example, matters involving intellectual property, technology, engineering and construction, admiralty, commercial issues, taxation and major torts must be brought before specialist lists. The Judge-in-Charge of each list gives directions to the parties from the early stages of each proceeding in their list.

These lists form part of the Trial Division of the Supreme Court of Victoria. This division is itself divided into three divisions: Commercial and Equity; Common Law; and Criminal. Each division has a principal judge who has the overall supervision of the progress of cases within that division. These judges are responsible for the management of the listing of cases in the division, the review of their progress and the development of procedures appropriate to the particular division. See Practice Note No 4 of 1999.

However, the web page of the Supreme Court of Victoria (viewed 7 January 2012, <http://www.supremecourt.vic.gov.au>) states that the majority of proceedings are not in Specialist Lists. Where a proceeding commenced by writ is not in a Specialist List, it receives directions from a Master who manages the Civil Management List. When these proceedings are ready for trial directions, they are referred to the Listing Master. See generally Practice Note No 1 of 1996.

2.4.14 Note

1. It is reasonably common for the Supreme Courts to arrange their workload to establish lists or divisions which specialise in a particular subject matter such as building disputes or admiralty, or in particular causes of action such as major torts or family provision. The divisions and speciality lists may be ascertained for each court by visiting its web page.

Individual docket: Federal Court

2.4.15 The individual docket system has been adopted in all Federal Court registries. The individual docket system involves each case being allocated to a particular judge who will ordinarily be responsible for that case from commencement to disposition. The rationale of this system is that it is preferable for one judge only to make decisions about the issues in the case and to establish continuity from the pre-trial to trial phases of a proceeding. The extract from the Federal Court home page (**2.4.16E** below) describes the operation of the individual docket system.

The Federal Court has been in the forefront of innovation in case management among Australian courts. For example, in February 2001, it launched eCourt, making it the first court in Australia to hold directions online. eCourt is a virtual courtroom that will assist in the management of interlocutory matters and will allow for directions and other orders to be made online. Via eCourt, the court may receive submissions and affidavit evidence and make orders as if the parties were in a normal courtroom. eCourt may also be used for mediations: viewed 7 January 2012, <https://ecourt.fedcourt.gov.au>.

From 1 May 2007, the court has also introduced a 'fast track' list, also known as the 'rocket docket'. In this list an initial directions hearing (the 'Scheduling Conference') is set down within 45 days of the date of the filing of the application and a trial can expect to be held within two to five months of the Scheduling Conference. The court will endeavour to deliver judgment within six weeks of the trial. The general procedures in these matters are also adapted; for example, there are no pleadings unless the court otherwise orders. See Practice Note CM 8 — Fast Track, 1 August 2011.

2.4.16E   **Individual Docket System**
Federal Court Home Page
<http://www.fedcourt.gov.au/how/ids.html>

Individual Docket System

...

The general principle underlying the individual docket system is that each case commenced in the Court is to be randomly allocated to a judge of the Court, who is then responsible for managing the case until final disposition. The individual docket system aims to encourage the just, orderly and expeditious resolution of disputes. It also seeks to enhance the transparency of the processes of the Court.

Key Elements

Cases are randomly allocated to judges. A case ordinarily stays with the same judge from commencement until disposition. ...

The Docket judge makes orders about the way in which the case should be managed or prepared for hearing. The Court may direct that special procedures be used, including case management conferences and referrals to mediation.

The Docket judge monitors compliance with directions, deals with interlocutory issues and ensures that hearing dates are maintained.

Objectives of the Individual Docket System

Savings in time and cost resulting from the Docket judge's familiarity with the case. In particular, the system seeks to eliminate the necessity to explain the case afresh each time it comes before a judge.

Consistency of approach throughout the case's history.

Fewer management events with greater results. In particular, the system aims at reducing the number of directions hearings and other events requiring appearances before the Court.

Discouragement of interlocutory disputes or, alternatively, swift resolution of those disputes.

Better identification of cases suitable for assisted dispute resolution (mediation). Earlier settlement of disputes or, failing that, a narrowing of the issues and a consequent saving of Court time.

Early fixing of trial dates and maintenance of those dates.

Hearing Dates

Judges allocate hearing dates for matters in their own dockets.

2.4.17 Questions

1. In Issues Paper 20 (extracted above at **2.2.3E**), the ALRC states that under the adversarial system 'the trial is the distinct and separate climax to the litigation process'. Moreover the discussion about the role of the judge above (at **2.2.1–2.2.4**) recognises that, traditionally, trial judges have not dealt with interlocutory applications in civil practice. Does the individual docket system break this tradition? What are the advantages and disadvantages of the individual docket system?

2.4.18 Further reading

Federal Court of Australia and the Law Council of Australia, *Federal Court of Australia Case Management Handbook*, 13 October 2011.

Special leave applications — High Court

2.4.19 The High Court controls its case load in its appellate jurisdiction by requiring appellants to qualify for special leave before an appeal will be heard. To obtain special leave to appeal, the appellant must show 'some special feature of the case which warrants the attention of [the] court': *Morris v R* (1987) 163 CLR 454 at 475 per Dawson J. Section 35A of the

Judiciary Act 1903 (Cth) states inclusive criteria for the grant of special leave. The procedure for applying for special leave is set out in HCR Pt 41. The current rules contemplate that applications for special leave may be decided on the basis of written summaries of argument, without an oral hearing: r 41.15.

2.4.20 Further reading

M Kirby, 'Maximising Special Leave Performance in the High Court of Australia' (2007) 30 *UNSWLJ* 753.

A Mason, 'The High Court as Gatekeeper' (2000) 24 *MULR* 784.

D O'Brien, *Special Leave to Appeal*, Supreme Court of Queensland Library, 2007.

J West et al, *Practice and Procedure — High Court and Federal Court*, LexisNexis Butterworths, Sydney, looseleaf, [15,100.5]ff.

Integration of alternative dispute resolution processes

2.4.21   In most jurisdictions, the court will consider whether the case should be referred to mediation or another form of alternative dispute resolution (ADR) and make orders accordingly: ACT r 1179; FCR r 28.01, NSW Civil Procedure Act 2005 (NSW) ss 26, 28; NT r 48.13; Qld rr 319, 320; SA rr 220, 221; Tas r 518; Vic Civil Procedure Act 2010 (Vic) s 66; Vic rr 50.07, 50.08; WA Practice Direction 4.2 — Mediation and Compromise, O 4A, s 167(1)(q). Pursuant to Pt 4 of the Uniform Civil Procedure Rules 1999 (Qld), ADR is part of the pre-trial management process. See also Pt 6 of the Civil Proceedings Act 2011 (Qld), once this Part enters into force.

2.4.22   The Victorian provisions illustrate a more expansive approach that is now taken by many legislatures and courts to the use of dispute resolution processes in case management. In s 66 of the Civil Procedure Act 2010 (Vic), the court has power to make an order referring all or part of a civil proceeding to appropriate dispute resolution. Such an order may be made without the consent of the parties unless the proposed dispute resolution process is arbitration, reference to a special referee, expert determination or, more generally, one which results, directly or indirectly, in a binding outcome. 'Appropriate dispute resolution' is defined in s 3 of the Civil Procedure Act 2010 (Vic) to mean a process attended, or participated in, by a party for the purposes of negotiating a settlement of the civil proceeding or resolving or narrowing the issues in dispute. This includes, but is not limited to:

• mediation;

• early neutral evaluation;

• judicial resolution conference;

• settlement conference;

• reference of a question, a civil proceeding or part of a civil proceeding to a special referee;

• expert determination;

• conciliation; or

• arbitration.

The concept of a *judicial resolution conference* has recently been developed in the Victorian justice system and is defined in s 3 of the Civil Procedure Act 2010 (Vic). For example, in the Victorian Supreme Court it is 'a resolution process presided over by a Judge of the Court, an Associate Judge or ... a judicial registrar for the purposes of negotiating a settlement of a dispute including, but not limited to, mediation ... early neutral evaluation; settlement conference [or] conciliation ...'.

2.4.23E   **Mediation as Case Management**

H Gamble and L Curtis

Litigation Reform Commission Conference Brisbane, 6–8 March 1996

---

[1] [E]arly settlement assists in managing the workload of the courts and reduces costs for the parties.

There is still much work to be done in identifying the points in the process at which cases settle and the reasons why they settle. If cases likely to settle can be identified early they may be put on a track which does not involve all of the preparation required to bring a case to trial, with consequent savings to the parties and to the court.

More attention is being paid to methods of dispute resolution which produce the best outcome for the parties, not simply achieving a result. Recognition is also being given to the role of the courts in consensual non-adjudication, non-arbitration methods of resolving matters in dispute. Courts are encouraging parties to resort to mediation and, in some cases, providing facilities within the court structure for mediation to occur ...

Mediation as case management

[3] Referral to mediation as part of a case management process must facilitate the progress of litigation and not be another cause of delay:

- the consequences of failed mediation for delay and attitudes of parties need to be understood;
- when their staff act as mediators courts have an extra investment of resources in the process.

If outside mediators are used, the cost of the mediation will be an additional cost to the parties when agreement is not reached. There is an issue whether these should be costs in the proceedings if the court has been involved in referral and the question will arise of who should bear these costs, especially if the breakdown of the mediation is not the fault of the eventual losing party.

Using mediation as case management

To use mediation responsibly, as an effective part of their case management procedures, courts need to address these issues and to find solutions. There are no certain answers to the question — which cases are suitable for early resolution through mediation? However, if the courts are to continue to take part in the referral of cases to mediation attempts have to be made to provide guidelines for those making referral decisions ...

The guidelines must give assistance on:

Characteristics of the parties

- relationship between the parties
  - gauged in part from the nature of the litigation, but also perhaps a matter for advice from instructing solicitors.

- parties' understanding of the process and likely outcomes
  - the increasing use by courts of pre-litigation information sessions seems an appropriate response to this need.
- assessment of the bargaining power of each party
  - specialist mediation services commonly employ intake assessment techniques to prevent gross inequality between the parties.
- parties' willingness to settle
  - in part this may be a matter of balancing the amount at stake against the likely cost of recovery using another process and may have as much to do with the parties' understanding of the costs and likely outcomes as with the merit of the case or with 'doing justice'.

Characteristics of the case
- amount at stake
  - although the complexity of legal issues involved does not necessarily relate to the amounts of money at risk, the willingness of parties to pursue expensive litigation must influence the decision to proceed in court. ...
- complexity of legal issues.

2.4.24 Note and questions

1. Refer to Chapter 3 for a detailed discussion of ADR processes, including court annexed mediations.

2. What 'characteristics' of a party might make him or her less amenable to mediation? Consider one particular characteristic: whether a party is a 'repeat player' or is involved in litigation for the first time. What bearing would this quality have upon a party's amenability to mediation?

2.4.25 Further reading

H Astor, *Quality in Court Connected Mediation Programs: An Issues Paper*, Australian Institute of Judicial Administration, Carlton, 2001.

D Hensler, 'Court-Ordered Arbitration: An Alternative View' in *The Legal Forum*, University of Chicago Law School, 1990, pp 399–420.

R Ingleby, 'Court-Sponsored Mediation: The Case against Mandatory Participation' (1993) 56 *MLR* 441.

K Mack, *Court Referral to ADR: Criteria and Research*, NADRAC, 2003.

J Martin, 'Friendly Persuasion — How Mediation Benefits Case Management' (1996) 6 *JJA* 65.

M Tyler and J Bornstein 'Court Referral to ADR: Lessons from an Intervention Order Mediation Pilot'(2006) 16(1) *JJA* 48.

THE DEVELOPMENT OF THE OVERRIDING PURPOSE

2.5.1   As discussed above, case management shifts the control of the process of litigation from the parties to the court. As Sorabji states, 'it transfers the steering wheel to a new driver'. However, case management does not of itself 'alter in any way the *purpose* for which the litigation process is carried out' (emphasis added): J Sorabji, 'The Road to New Street Station: Fact, Fiction and the Overriding Objective' (2012) 23 *Eur Bus L Rev* 77 at 78.

Therefore as case management became increasingly interventionist, it was necessary for the courts to articulate this purpose through the overriding objective or overriding purpose. The importance of the development of the overriding objective cannot be underestimated. It 'represents ... civil procedure's first explicit guiding principle, its first explicit "all controlling policy objective"'. (Sorabji above, quoting D Greenslade, 'A Fresh Approach: Uniform Rules of Court' in A Zuckerman and R Cranston (eds), *Reform of Civil Procedure: Essays on 'Access to Justice'*, Clarendon Press, 1995, p 127). This objective introduced 'a new concept of justice into ... civil procedure; [which was] committed to proportionality rather than ... an unalloyed commitment to the achievement of ... justice on the merits'. Sorabji, above, at 77–8. See further discussion on the 'justice on the merits approach' at 1.9.1.

The overriding objective was originally developed by Lord Woolf in his recommendations about reform of the civil justice system in England: Department for Constitutional Affairs, *Access to Justice: Interim Report to the Lord Chancellor on the Civil Justice System in England and Wales*, 1995 and *Access to Justice: Final Report to the Lord Chancellor on the Civil Justice System in England and Wales*, 1996.

It may be defined as a statement of an overriding philosophy expressed in legislation or court rules that 'the court must manage litigation to bring cases to an early and economical disposition consistently with the needs of justice': B Cairns, *Australian Civil Procedure*, 9th ed, 2011, p 48.

The Woolf recommendations were implemented in the Civil Procedure Rules (UK) as follows:

2.5.2E   **Civil Procedure Rules (UK)**
Part 1

The Overriding Objective

1.1 (1) These Rules are a new procedural code with the overriding objective of enabling the court to deal with cases justly.

   (2)   Dealing with a case justly includes, so far as is practicable —

      (a)   ensuring that the parties are on an equal footing;

      (b)   saving expense;

      (c)   dealing with the case in ways which are proportionate —

          (i)   to the amount of money involved;

          (ii)   to the importance of the case;

          (iii)   to the complexity of the issues; and

          (iv)   to the financial position of each party;

      (d)   ensuring that it is dealt with expeditiously and fairly; and

      (e)   allotting to it an appropriate share of the court's resources, while taking into account the need to allot resources to other cases.

Application by the court of the overriding objective
1.2 The court must seek to give effect to the overriding objective when it —
  (a) exercises any power given to it by the Rules; or
  (b) interprets any rule subject to rule 76.2 and 79.2.

Duty of the parties
1.3 The parties are required to help the court to further the overriding objective.

2.5.3 The overriding objective clause in r 1.1 of the Civil Procedure Rules (UK) was considered by Einstein J of the NSW Supreme Court in *Idoport Pty Ltd v National Australia Bank Ltd* (2000) 49 NSWLR 51; *Idoport Pty Ltd v National Australia Bank Ltd* [2001] NSWSC 838 and in *National Australia Bank Ltd v John Edward Roberts* [2002] NSWSC 1048 and by the Queensland Court of Appeal in *Gray v Morris* [2004] QCA 5 and *Deputy Commissioner of Taxation v Salcedo* [2005] 2 Qd R 232.

2.5.4 Australian jurisdictions reshaped their rules following the Woolf reforms, engaging in a 'fundamental rethink of rules of court, commencing with first principles and providing a statement of "overriding purpose" to inform all applications of court rules': G Lindsay, *Dynamics of the Civil Procedure Regime in NSW*, University of New South Wales CLE Program, 2005, para 45.

Overriding purpose clauses

2.5.5 Every jurisdiction in Australia has adopted an overriding purpose clause, as follows:

Federal Court

Section 37M of the Federal Court of Australia Act 1976 (Cth):

  (1) The overarching purpose of the civil practice and procedure provisions is to facilitate the just resolution of disputes:
      (a) according to law; and
      (b) as quickly, inexpensively and efficiently as possible
  (2) Without limiting the generality of subsection (1), the overarching purpose includes the following objectives:
      (a) the just determination of all proceedings before the Court;
      (b) the efficient use of the judicial and administrative resources available for the purposes of the Court;
      (c) the efficient disposal of the Court's overall caseload;
      (d) the disposal of all proceedings in a timely manner;
      (e) the resolution of disputes at a cost that is proportionate to the importance and complexity of the matters in dispute.

Australian Capital Territory

Rule 21:

  ...to facilitate the just resolution of the real issues in civil proceedings with minimum delay and expense

New South Wales

Section 56 of the Civil Procedure Act 2005 (NSW):

...to facilitate the just, quick and cheap resolution of the real issues in the dispute or proceedings.

Northern Territory

Rule 1.10:

...shall endeavour to ensure that all questions in the proceeding are effectively, completely, promptly and economically determined.

Queensland

Rule 5:

...to facilitate the just and expeditious resolution of the real issues in civil proceedings at a minimum of expense.

South Australia

Rule 3:

(a)   to establish orderly procedures for the just resolution of civil disputes; and
(b)   to facilitate and encourage the resolution of civil disputes by agreement between the parties; and
(c)   to avoid all unnecessary delay in the resolution of civil disputes; and
(d)   to promote efficiency in dispute resolution so far as that object is consistent with the paramount claims of justice; and
(e)   to minimise the cost of civil litigation to the litigants and to the State.

See also r 116 which states that the court has:

...the power to manage litigation to the extent necessary to ensure that it is conducted (a) fairly; and (b) as expeditiously and economically as is consistent with the proper administration of justice.

Tasmania

Rule 414A:

to ensure that proceedings are conducted and resolved justly and effectively.

Victoria

Section 7 of the Civil Procedure Act 2010 (Vic):

...to facilitate the just, efficient, timely and cost-effective resolution of the real issues in dispute.

See also s 47 of the same Act and r 1.14 that articulate the nexus between the court's case management powers and the overarching purpose.

Western Australia

Order 1 r 4B:

(a) promoting the just determination of litigation; and

(b) disposing efficiently of the business of the court; and

(c) maximising the efficient use of available judicial and administrative resources; and

(d) facilitating the timely disposal of business; and

(e) ensuring the procedure applicable, and the costs of the procedure to the parties and the State, are proportionate to the value, importance and complexity of the subject matter in dispute; and

(f) that the procedure applicable, and the costs of the procedure to the parties, are proportionate to the financial position of each party.

2.5.6 Several jurisdictions also impose an obligation or duty on the parties to further the overriding purpose which is modelled on the Civil Procedure Rules (UK) r 1.3 extracted at **2.5.2E** above: Federal Court of Australia Act 1976 (Cth) s 37N; ACT r 21(3); NSW Civil Procedure Act 2005 (NSW) s 56(3); Vic Civil Procedure Act 2010 (Vic) ss 16–26.

2.5.7 A survey by Cairns and Williams published in 2005 was designed to determine whether the overriding purpose in the Queensland rules was being achieved in practice. The results indicate a reduction in the time from initiation of a proceeding to termination as compared to a sample of similar cases determined under the previous regime: B C Cairns and S C Williams, 'Pace of Civil Litigation in the Queensland Supreme Court' (2005) 24 *CJQ* 337.

2.5.8 Further reading

R Cranston, *How Law Works: The Machinery and Impact of Civil Justice*, Oxford University Press, Oxford, 2006, Ch 5.

D Piggott, 'Relief from Sanctions and the Overriding Objective' (2005) 24 *CJQ* 103.

N Thomson, 'Life After Woolf: Impact of the Civil Procedure Reforms' (2001) 11 *JJA* 81.

The Hon Marilyn Warren, 'Act Paves the Way for Best Practice' (2011) 85(3) *LIJ* 44.

CHALLENGING CASE MANAGEMENT DECISIONS AND THE INTERPRETATION OF THE OVERRIDING PURPOSE

2.6.1 Each jurisdiction imposes sanctions for non-compliance with the Rules of Court. These sanctions are dealt with generally in **Chapter 5**. However, in some jurisdictions additional sanctions have been created in the rules or by legislation to support the overriding purpose and by corollary, case management. A New South Wales example is set out below.

> | 2.6.2E | **Civil Procedure Act 2005 (NSW)** |
>
> **61 Directions as to practice and procedure generally**
> (1)   The court may, by order, give such directions as it thinks fit (whether or not inconsistent with rules of court) for the speedy determination of the real issues between the parties to the proceedings. ...
> (3)   If a party to whom such a direction has been given fails to comply with the direction, the court may, by order, do any one or more of the following:
>   (a)   it may dismiss the proceedings, whether generally, in relation to a particular cause of action or in relation to the whole or part of a particular claim,
>   (b)   it may strike out or limit any claim made by a plaintiff,
>   (c)   it may strike out any defence filed by a defendant, and give judgment accordingly,
>   (d)   it may strike out or amend any document filed by the party, either in whole or in part,
>   (e)   it may strike out, disallow or reject any evidence that the party has adduced or seeks to adduce,
>   (f)   it may direct the party to pay the whole or part of the costs of another party,
>   (g)   it may make such other order or give such other direction as it considers appropriate.
> (4)   Subsection (3) does not limit any other power the court may have to take action of the kind referred to in that subsection or to take any other action that the court is empowered to take in relation to a failure to comply with a direction given by the court.

Judicial interpretation

2.6.3   Where a judicial case management decision is challenged, conflicting views are often expressed as to the relative weight to be given to court efficiency and the interests of the parties to the individual case. These conflicting views are illustrated by the two High Court decisions in *Sali v SPC Ltd* and *Queensland v JL Holdings Pty Ltd*. Short excerpts of these cases are extracted below. However, the High Court settled the uncertainty created by *JL Holdings* in *AON Risk Services v Australian National University*, extracted at **2.6.8C**.

> | 2.6.4C | **Sali v SPC Ltd** |
>
> (1993) 116 ALR 625
> High Court of Australia
>
> [The appellant had sued the first respondent for an allowance he alleged was due to him upon his retirement from the first respondent's board of directors. In the alternative, he sued the second respondents, a firm of solicitors, for damages for negligent advice in relation to the retirement allowance. Both claims were dismissed by Ormiston J of the Victorian Supreme Court on 1 November 1991. The appellant lodged a notice of appeal, within time, against the decision. The appeal was to be listed in a callover on 9 December 1992 and a hearing date fixed no earlier than February 1993. The appellant's solicitor secured the services of a senior counsel, anticipating a February hearing of the appeal.

In February 1992, the appellant was ordered to pay the respondent's costs of the proceeding at first instance, and when he failed to pay these a bankruptcy notice was issued. Subsequently, the respondents gave an undertaking that they would not seek a sequestration order and the appellant similarly undertook to prosecute the appeal with the utmost expedition.

In late 1992 the Supreme Court of Victoria launched a 'Spring Offensive', with the aim of accelerating the disposition of cases pending in that court. Around 13 November 1992, the Listing Master's office asked the appellant's solicitor if he was prepared to have the matter listed, but was advised that counsel was not available until February. The matter was listed for 30 November 1992. The appellant's solicitors immediately caused extensive enquiries to be made for an 'appropriate' Queen's Counsel, but alleged that they were unable to secure the services of such counsel. This contention was disputed by the second respondent, who filed an affidavit by an employee who deposed that on that day she had spoken to four barristers' clerks regarding the availability of Queen's Counsel for the appeal and had been told that approximately 29 such counsel were available.

On 30 November junior counsel appeared for the appellant before the Full Court, but was only instructed to appear for the purpose of seeking an adjournment of the appeal for two weeks. The Full Court refused this application. Junior counsel then referred to the alleged availability of the 29 senior counsel, and asked for an adjournment until 2.15 pm to enable the instructing solicitor to advise that counsel had been obtained and for the matter to proceed the next day. The court refused.

The appellant appealed to the High Court arguing that the refusal to grant an adjournment resulted in a miscarriage of justice.]

Brennan, Deane and McHugh JJ (at 626): In our opinion, the refusal did not amount to a miscarriage of justice. Nor did the Full Court fall into error in refusing to adjourn the hearing of the appeal ...

[After discussing the factual background, their Honours continued (at 629):]

[629] In determining whether to grant an adjournment, the judge of a busy court is entitled to consider the effect of an adjournment on court resources and the competing claims by litigants in other cases awaiting hearing in the court as well as the interests of the parties. ... What might be perceived as an injustice to a party when considered only in the context of an action between parties may not be so when considered in a context which includes the claims of other litigants and the public interest in achieving the most efficient use of court resources. ...

[630] Tadgell J said that he sympathised with counsel for the applicant 'who has been obliged to fashion submissions based upon instructions which to me smack of humbug'. His Honour also said that he was quite unable to accept the submission that it had been impossible to obtain the services of counsel for the purposes of arguing the appeal that morning. His Honour [631] was of the view that the appeal was of a kind that 'could be worked up by counsel in two or three days'. For the reasons we have already given, it was open to Tadgell J to conclude that counsel's instructions smacked 'of humbug' ...

Although there is force in the argument that no injustice would have been done to the respondents by adjourning the matter until 2.15 pm, that application had to be considered in the light of the findings of the Full Court in the first application. If the Full Court was entitled, as we think it clearly was, to regard the appellant's application as mere delaying tactics, there was no warrant for granting any adjournment. ...

[632] The appellant has failed to show error on the part of the Full Court in refusing the successive applications for an adjournment of the hearing of the appeal. The appeal must be dismissed with costs.

Toohey and Gaudron JJ (dissenting) (at 635): Subject to what follows, the reasons expressed by their Honours in refusing an adjournment for two weeks cannot legitimately be the subject of attack. However, underlying the refusal is a rejection of the explanation offered in Mr McLindin's affidavit. While the account of his efforts to obtain senior counsel seems at odds with the picture presented by Ms Hibberd, the two are not irreconcilable. In any event, there was no application to cross-examine Mr McLindin on his affidavit. It is one thing to treat the contents of that affidavit as inadequate justification for an adjournment. It is another thing, and unwarranted in the circumstances, to reject the explanation which it contains (See *Smith v NSW Bar Association* (1992) 176 CLR 256, at pp 267–269). And to describe the contents as 'humbug' can only, given the general and judicial understanding of the term be taken to mean an attempt to deceive the Full Court. "'Humbug" is an imposition, imposture, deception; and as a verb, signifies to impose upon, to cozen, to swindle; all implying intention to misrepresent, by the assertion of what is not the actual condition or the suppression or concealment of what is': *Nolte v Herter* (1895) 65 Ill App 430, at pp 432–433, adopted in *McDonald v Sun Printing and Publishing Ass'n* (1906) 98 NYS 116, at p 117. That was not a conclusion open on the evidence.

This aspect assumes particular importance because of what followed. On refusal of his original application, Mr Jones made a further application in these terms:

> I am instructed that my instructor will endeavour this morning to obtain the services of senior counsel, if the matter could be adjourned until 2.15 to enable him to advise the Court that such counsel has been obtained and then for the matter to proceed tomorrow.

Counsel for each respondent opposed that application and Marks J said: 'The application is refused.' The appeal was called on. As Mr Jones had no instructions to proceed further, there was no appearance for the appellant and the appeal was dismissed with costs. The appellant thereby lost his right of appeal. ...

[636] The contemporary approach to court administration has introduced another element into the equation or, more accurately, has put another consideration onto the scales (see *GSA Industries Pty Ltd v NT Gas Ltd* (1990) 24 NSWLR 710). The view that the conduct of litigation is not merely a matter for the parties but is also one for the court and the need to avoid disruptions in the court's lists with consequent inconvenience to the court and prejudice to the interests of other litigants waiting to be heard are pressing concerns to which a court may have regard. ...

Having regard to these matters, it is clear that the Full Court's decision to refuse an adjournment for two weeks was correct. Nevertheless, in our respectful view, the Full Court was in error in refusing the application to stand the matter down until 2.15 pm. ...

The refusal to stand the appeal down until 2.15 pm was only warranted on the basis that the application to do so was no more than a ploy. There was insufficient material before the Full Court to support that conclusion.

2.6.5 Notes and questions

1. Consider the comments of the majority judges in *Sali* in the light of the comments made by Zuckerman at 1.9.4E and Leubsdorf at 1.9.7E.

2. Can efficiency be divorced from justice? How might Toohey and Gaudron JJ respond to the issues raised by Zuckerman?

3. Traditionally, the award of costs against a dilatory party was regarded as an effective discouragement of delay. The majority and dissenting judges in *Sali* disagreed about the efficacy of costs in that case. What other factors should the courts take into account when allowing or disallowing an application for adjournment?

2.6.6 In *Sali v SPC Ltd* (1993) 116 ALR 625 at 629, the majority in the High Court considered that a judge is entitled to consider the effect of an adjournment upon court resources and the competing claims of litigants in other cases awaiting hearing. More recently in the following case, the High Court placed greater emphasis upon justice between the immediate parties to litigation when considering the efficacy of case management sanctions. The facts are stated in the majority judgment, but note that the reasoning was *overruled* by the plurality in *Aon Risk Services v Australian National University*, extracted below at 2.6.8C.

2.6.7C   **Queensland v JL Holdings Pty Ltd**
                                       (1997) 189 CLR 146
                                      High Court of Australia
                                        (footnotes omitted)

Dawson, Gaudron and McHugh JJ (at 150): At Kangaroo Point on the south side of the Brisbane River is Crown land, part of which ('the land') is held by the Brisbane City Council ('the Council') as trustee under s 334 of the Land Act 1962 (Qld). The Council called for tenders to develop the land and JL Holdings Pty Ltd ('JLH') became the preferred developer. The Council proposed to grant JLH a 30 year lease to develop the land into an amusement park. By virtue of s 343(1) of the Land Act the Council could not lease the land without the written approval of the Minister of Lands. Sub-section (2) of s 343 provides that such approval is to be sought by way of application to the Minister and, pursuant to sub-section (3), an application must be accompanied by a draft of the proposed lease. JLH claims that on 23 October 1989 it obtained the Minister's written consent to a lease agreed upon between it and the Council, but that when the duly executed lease was submitted for endorsement by the [151] Minister pursuant to s 345 of the Land Act, the Minister wrongly refused to endorse his approval on it. That section relevantly provides:

> When a lease under this Division has been duly executed in accordance with the terms and conditions approved by the Minister the original and all other executed copies of such lease shall be forwarded to the Minister for endorsement thereon of his approval of the lease …
>
> A lease to which this Division applies which is not endorsed with the Minister's approval shall have no validity or effect in law and in the case of a lease with respect to land granted in trust shall not be capable of registration under 'The Real Property Acts, 1861 to 1960'.

JLH sued the present applicants, the State of Queensland and South Bank Corporation, in the Federal Court, seeking damages in the vicinity of $60 million. A number of causes of action were pleaded including breach of copyright, breach of agreement for lease, breach of lease, inducement to breach a lease, civil conspiracy, defamation, negligence, breach of statutory duty, estoppel, contravention of s 45D of the Trade Practices Act 1974 (Cth) and fraud. JLH claims that once the Minister had given written approval to the proposed lease under s 343 of the Land Act, the Minister or (as in this case) the Minister's successor in office is obliged to endorse his consent on the executed lease under s 345. In their defence, the applicants deny this claim.

Pursuant to O 13 r 2 of the Federal Court Rules, the applicants by motion sought to amend their defence in a number of respects, including the addition of grounds why the Minister was not required to endorse his approval. ...

[152] In short, the proposed additions allege that the draft lease submitted for endorsement pursuant to s 345 was different from the executed lease which had been approved pursuant to s 343 because it had been altered by a deed of variation entered into between JLH and the Council.

The applicants explained their delay in making application for leave to amend, saying that it was only recently discovered that there was a material discrepancy between the lease originally submitted and the lease submitted for the endorsement of the Minister's approval. That explanation was accepted by the primary judge, Kiefel J, who nevertheless questioned why it had taken so long to uncover the matter and refused leave to amend. However, the principal reason why her Honour refused the application appears from the following passage in her judgment which refers to other amendments which were sought, as well as that in question:

> I have, in the context of this case, where there is only a period of about six months from the time that leave was sought to the commencement of the hearing, taken the view that the most relevant consideration is whether the amendments would jeopardise those hearing dates. If that were the case, I would be inclined to disallow the amendments. Such an approach takes account that the loss of the hearing at that time could be said to amount to severe prejudice to the applicant, particularly since the matter, I would think, would be unlikely to be relisted until the following year. It also takes account of a shift in attitude and that in these times a party's 'right' to present their case or their defence is viewed as subject to some limitation.

... [153] The majority also referred to the decision of this Court in *Clough and Rogers v Frog* (1974) 48 ALJR 481; 4 ALR 615 where applications for leave to amend the defences in two actions by adding a new defence had been refused. The actions had been commenced more than five years previously and the applications were made two days before the actions were listed for hearing. The Court in allowing the appeals before it adopted the words above of Bowen LJ *in Cropper v Smith* and said (1974) 48 ALJR 481 at 482; 4 ALR 615 at 618:

> As the defence, if established, would be a complete answer in either action, the amendments sought should have been allowed unless it appeared that injustice would thereby have been occasioned to the respondent, there being nothing to suggest fraud or improper concealment of the defence on the part of the appellants....

The majority in the Full Court dismissed these remarks saying that 'times have changed since 1884, and even since 1974'. They referred to a passage from the judgment of Toohey and Gaudron JJ in *Sali v SPC Ltd* (1993) 67 ALJR 841 at 849; 116 ALR 625 at 636 [which is quoted above at [636] of the judgment]. ...

[154] It may be said at once that in the passage which we have cited from *Sali v SPC Ltd* Toohey and Gaudron JJ are not to be taken as sanctioning any departure from the principles established in *Cropper v Smith* and accepted in *Clough and Rogers v Frog*. *Sali v SPC Ltd* was a case concerning the refusal of an adjournment in relation to which the proper principles of case management may have a particular relevance. However, nothing in that case suggests that those principles might be employed, except perhaps in extreme circumstances, to shut a party out from litigating an issue which is fairly arguable. Case management is not an end in itself. It is an important and useful aid for ensuring the prompt and efficient disposal of litigation. But it ought always to be borne in mind, even in changing times, that the ultimate aim of a court is the attainment of justice and no principle of case management can be allowed to supplant that aim.

The majority emphasised that the primary judge, Kiefel J, was the trial judge, had been responsible for the management of the present case since 1994 and was in the best position to judge the effect of the proposed amendment. Even so, the application for leave to amend was made before a date was fixed for hearing. The date when fixed was six or so months ahead. It is not apparent that any complex issues of fact are raised by the amendment sought, but even if they are, in a hearing that is estimated to last some four months, they must surely be able to be accommodated. ...

[155] In our view, the matters referred to by the primary judge were insufficient to justify her Honour's refusal of the application by the applicants to amend their defence and nothing has been made to appear before us which would otherwise support that refusal. Justice is the paramount consideration in determining an application such as the one in question. Save in so far as costs may be awarded against the party seeking the amendment, such an application is not the occasion for the punishment of a party for its mistake or for its delay in making the application. Case management, involving as it does the efficiency of the procedures of the court, was in this case a relevant consideration. But it should not have been allowed to prevail over the injustice of shutting the applicants out from raising an arguable defence, thus precluding the determination of an issue between the parties. In taking an opposite view, the primary judge was, in our view, in error in the exercise of her discretion.

For these reasons we took the view that we should grant special leave to appeal, allow the appeal and order that the applicants have leave to amend.

[**Kirby J** delivered a separate concurring judgment.]

2.6.8C   **Aon Risk Services v Australian National University**
(2009) 239 CLR 175
High Court of Australia (footnotes omitted)

[In December 2004, the Australian National University (ANU) commenced proceedings in the Australian Capital Territory Supreme Court against three insurers for an indemnity for loss suffered due to damage caused to its Mount Stromlo Observatory during the 2003 Canberra bushfires. In their defences filed in April 2005, two insurers alleged, first, that certain property was not covered by ANU's insurance policies and, second, that they were entitled to reduce their liability to indemnify as the property had been substantially undervalued by ANU. In response, in June 2005, ANU joined as a defendant its insurance broker, Aon Risk Services

Australia Ltd (Aon). ANU claimed, as an alternative to its claim against the insurers, that if the property was not covered by its insurance policies, then Aon had breached its contract with, and duty of care to, ANU by failing to arrange insurance for it.

On 13 November 2006, the first day appointed for a four-week trial, ANU commenced mediation with those two insurers, having already settled its claim against the third. On 15 November, ANU settled with the insurers and consent judgments were entered. ANU then applied for an adjournment and leave to amend its statement of claim to add a substantial new claim against Aon: essentially, that Aon had breached a different contract for services and its duty of care in failing to declare the correct value of the property to the insurers. ANU stated that the decision to amend was made based on information received during mediation, asserted the mediation was confidential, and refused to explain further. (Summary of facts is drawn from A Lyons, 'Recasting the Landscape of Interlocutory Applications: *Aon Risk Services Australia Ltd v Australian National University*' (2010) *Syd L Rev* 549 at 552–3.)

At first instance before Gray J and on appeal to the Australian Capital Territory Court of Appeal, ANU's application for an adjournment and amendment were granted because in both cases their Honours considered that they were bound to follow *JL Holdings* and therefore allow the amendment.

The rules that were under consideration in the judgments are ACT rr 501 and 502 which concern the court's power to amend documents and ACT r 21, the overriding purpose, which is quoted at **2.5.5**. The High Court's consideration of the power to amend documents under ACT rr 501 and 502 is extracted at **5.2.12C**. The excerpt below focusses primarily upon the High Court's discussion of the overriding purpose in ACT r 21.]

French CJ (at 181): 4. Save for the dissenting judgment of Lander J in the Court of Appeal, the history of these proceedings reveals an unduly permissive approach at both trial and appellate level to an application which was made late in the day, was inadequately explained, necessitated the vacation or [182] adjournment of the dates set down for trial, and raised new claims not previously agitated apparently because of a deliberate tactical decision not to do so. In such circumstances, the party making the application bears a heavy burden to show why, under a proper reading of the applicable Rules of Court, leave should be granted.

5. In the proper exercise of the primary judge's discretion, the applications for adjournment and amendment were not to be considered solely by reference to whether any prejudice to Aon could be compensated by costs. Both the primary judge and the Court of Appeal should have taken into account that, whatever costs are ordered, there is an irreparable element of unfair prejudice in unnecessarily delaying proceedings. Moreover, the time of the court is a publicly funded resource. Inefficiencies in the use of that resource, arising from the vacation or adjournment of trials, are to be taken into account. So too is the need to maintain public confidence in the judicial system. Given its nature, the circumstances in which it was sought, and the lack of a satisfactory explanation for seeking it, the amendment to ANU's statement of claim should not have been allowed. The discretion of the primary judge miscarried.

6. It appears that a factor in the decision of the primary judge and of the Court of Appeal was the decision of this Court in *JL Holdings*. That case arose out of an entirely different factual setting. However, to the extent that statements about the exercise of the discretion to amend pleadings in that case suggest that case management considerations and questions of proper use of court resources are to be discounted or given little weight, it should not be regarded as authoritative. For the reasons set out more fully below, I would allow the appeal. I agree with the orders proposed in the joint judgment (44). ...

[192] 30. It might be thought a truism that "case management principles" should not supplant the objective of doing justice between the parties according to law. Accepting that proposition, *JL Holdings* cannot be taken as authority for the view that waste of public resources and undue delay, with the concomitant strain and uncertainty imposed on litigants, should not be taken into account in the exercise of interlocutory discretions of the kind conferred by r 502. Also to be considered is the potential for loss of public confidence in the legal system which arises where a court is seen to accede to applications made without adequate explanation or justification, whether they be for adjournment, for amendments giving rise to adjournment, or for vacation of fixed trial dates resulting in the resetting of interlocutory processes. ...

[195] 36. The above conclusion is able to be reached on the facts of this case without having regard to r 21. But r 21 strengthens the conclusion. It mandates consideration of the effect of the proposed amendment on the just resolution of the real issues in the proceeding "with minimum delay and expense". It informs both the requirements set out and the discretions conferred in rr 501 and 502.

Gummow, Hayne, Crennan, Kiefel and Bell JJ (at 212):
94. It will be recalled that in *JL Holdings* the plurality said that nothing in *Sali v SPC* suggested that principles of case management might be employed "except perhaps in extreme circumstances, to shut a party out from litigating an issue which is fairly arguable".. Their Honours said that case management was not to be seen as an end to itself and that the ultimate aim of the court remained the attainment of justice, even in changing times. ...

95. The statement of Waller LJ [that the courts are concerned to do justice to all litigants] identifies a fundamental premise of case management. What may be just, when amendment is sought, requires account to be taken of other litigants, not just the parties to the proceedings in question. The statement is consistent with what was said in *Sali v SPC*, which reflected a proper understanding of case management. The statements in *JL Holdings* do not reflect such an understanding and are not consistent with what was said in *Sali v SPC*. To say that case management principles should only be applied "in extreme circumstances" to refuse an amendment implies that considerations such as delay and costs can never be as important as the raising of an arguable case; and it denies the wider effects of delay upon others.

96. An important aspect of the approach taken by the plurality in *JL Holdings* was that it proceeded upon an assumption that a party should be permitted to amend to raise an arguable issue subject to the payment of costs occasioned by the amendment. So stated it suggests that a party has something approaching a right to an amendment. That is not the case. ... It is more accurate to say that parties have the right to invoke the jurisdiction and the powers of the court in order to seek a [213] resolution of their dispute (193). Subject to any rights to amend without leave given to the parties by the rules of court, the question of further amendment of a party's claim is dependent upon the exercise of the court's discretionary power.

97. The objectives of case management are now expressly stated in r 21 of the *Court Procedures Rules*. It cannot be overlooked that later rules, such as r 21, are likely to have been written with the decision in *JL Holdings* in mind. The purposes stated in r 21 cannot be ignored. The *Court Procedures Rules* make plain that the Rules are to be applied having regard to the stated objectives of the timely disposal of the proceedings at an affordable cost. There can be no doubt about the importance of those matters in litigation in the courts of the Australian Capital Territory.

98. Of course, a just resolution of proceedings remains the paramount purpose of r 21; but what is a "just resolution" is to be understood in light of the purposes and objectives stated. Speed and efficiency, in the sense of minimum delay and expense, are seen as essential to a just resolution of proceedings. This should not detract from a proper opportunity being given to the parties to plead their case, but it suggests that limits may be placed upon re-pleading, when delay and cost are taken into account. The Rule's reference to the need to minimise costs implies that an order for costs may not always provide sufficient compensation and therefore achieve a just resolution. It cannot therefore be said that a just resolution requires that a party be permitted to raise any arguable case at any point in the proceedings, on payment of costs. ...

[214] 102. The objectives stated in r 21 do not require that every application for amendment should be refused because it involves the waste of some costs and some degree of delay, as it inevitably will. Factors such as the nature and importance of the amendment to the party applying cannot be overlooked. Much may depend upon the point the litigation has [215] reached relative to a trial when the application to amend is made. There may be cases where it may properly be concluded that a party has had sufficient opportunity to plead their case and that it is too late for a further amendment, having regard to the other party and other litigants awaiting trial dates. Rule 21 makes it plain that the extent and the effect of delay and costs are to be regarded as important considerations in the exercise of the court's discretion. Invariably the exercise of that discretion will require an explanation to be given where there is delay in applying for amendment.

103. The fact that an explanation had been offered for the delay in raising the defence was regarded as a relevant consideration in *JL Holdings* (202). Generally speaking, where a discretion is sought to be exercised in favour of one party, and to the disadvantage of another, an explanation will be called for. The importance attached by r 21 to the factor of delay will require that, in most cases where it is present, a party should explain it. Not only will they need to show that their application is brought in good faith, but they will also need to bring the circumstances giving rise to the amendment to the court's attention, so that they may be weighed against the effects of any delay and the objectives of the Rules. There can be no doubt that an explanation was required in this case.

[Their Honours discussed the application of the amendment powers in r 502 and continued.]

105. ... Rule 502(1) read with r 21 did not provide an unfettered discretion to grant leave to amend. The objectives of r 21 were to be pursued in the exercise of the power conferred by r 502(1). The fact that ANU's new claims were arguable was not itself sufficient to permit amendment and could not prevail over the objectives of r 21. A "just" resolution of the proceedings between ANU and Aon required those objectives to be taken into account.

[216] 106. Given the requirements of the Rule and the effects associated with delay, it was incumbent upon ANU to tender an explanation as to why the matter had been allowed to proceed to trial in its existing form. It needed to explain why it was seeking leave to amend at the time of the trial, when the two insurer's defences had identified the issue central to the claim it sought to bring against Aon more than twelve months earlier. None was given. His Honour was in error in accepting that ANU had provided a satisfactory explanation. ...

[217] **Conclusion and orders**
111. An application for leave to amend a pleading should not be approached on the basis that a party is entitled to raise an arguable claim, subject to payment of costs by way of compensation. There is no such entitlement. All matters relevant to the exercise of the power

to permit amendment should be weighed. The fact of substantial delay and wasted costs, the concerns of case management, will assume importance on an application for leave to amend. Statements in *JL Holdings* which suggest only a limited application for case management do not rest upon a principle which has been carefully worked out in a significant succession of cases. On the contrary, the statements are not consonant with this Court's earlier recognition of the effects of delay, not only upon the parties to the proceedings in question, but upon the court and other litigants. Such statements should not be applied in the future.

112. A party has the right to bring proceedings. Parties have choices as to what claims are to be made and how they are to be framed. But limits will be placed upon their ability to effect changes to their pleadings, particularly if litigation is advanced. That is why, in seeking the just resolution of the dispute, reference is made to parties having a sufficient *opportunity* to identify the issues they seek to agitate.

113. In the past it has been left largely to the parties to prepare for trial and to seek the court's assistance as required. Those times are long gone. The allocation of power, between litigants and the courts arises from tradition and from principle and policy. It is recognised by the courts that the resolution of disputes serves the public as a whole, not merely the parties to the proceedings.

114. Rule 21 of the *Court Procedures Rules* recognises the purposes of case management by the courts. It recognises that delay and costs are undesirable and that delay has deleterious effects, not only upon the party to the proceedings in question, but to other litigants. The Rule's objectives, as to the timely disposal of cases and the limitation of cost, were to be applied in considering ANU's application for amendment. It was significant that the effect of its delay in applying would be that a trial was lost and litigation substantially recommenced. It would impact upon other litigants seeking a resolution of their cases. What was a "just resolution" of ANU's claim required serious consideration of these matters, and not merely whether it had an arguable claim to [218] put forward. A just resolution of its claim necessarily had to have regard to the position of Aon in defending it. An assumption that costs will always be a sufficient compensation for the prejudice caused by amendment is not reflected in r 21. Critically, the matters relevant to a just resolution of ANU's claim required ANU to provide some explanation for its delay in seeking the amendment if the discretion under r 502(1) was to be exercised in its favour and to the disadvantage of Aon. None was provided. ...

116. Since the drafting of these reasons we have had the opportunity to read the reasons, in draft, of the Chief Justice. There may be some point of distinction in our views as to what *JL Holdings* holds. We do not understand there to be any difference between us as to the principles which should now be applied in relation to applications for amendment.

117. The appeal should be allowed with costs ...

Heydon J (concurring) (at 222):
133. In relation to *Queensland v JL Holdings Pty Ltd* (217), it is sufficient to hold that, at least in jurisdictions having rules similar to rr 21 and 502, that case has ceased to be of authority. It is necessary to apply the Rules without any preconceptions derived from what was said in that case. There is a common opinion — it is far from universal, but it is common — within the judiciary and the legal profession that *Queensland v JL Holdings Pty Ltd*, whether it has been correctly understood or not, has had a damaging influence on the conduct of litigation.

[The decision of the Australian Capital Territory Court of Appeal was reversed.]

2.6.9   Cameron in 'New Directions for Case Management in Australia' (2010) *CJQ* 337 at 349 argues that the overruling of *JL Holdings* was justified:

> If it was good law in 1997, 12 years later it had become inconsistent with prevailing views about litigation and case management. *Aon v ANU* improves Australian jurisprudence by bringing the principles of case management into step with state and Commonwealth legislatures and rule-making bodies, law reform commissions, and other common law jurisdictions.
>
> Finally, the scant attention given by the High Court in *JL Holdings* to the earlier precedent of *Sali v SPC Ltd* is a factor justifying interference with *JL Holdings*. In *Sali,* the High Court had endorsed a concept of justice that transcended individual interests. *Sali* was therefore more consistent with modern views about case management than *JL Holdings*, even though it predated *JL Holdings* by four years. At the very least, the High Court in *JL Holdings* should have tackled the clash between the "costs as panacea" approach and the emerging (if not already emerged) views about modern case management.
>
> ... The end result of *Aon v ANU* is that *JL Holdings* and the restricted approach to judicial case-management that it has engendered have been discredited. We now have a clear statement that the case and the principles for which it stands should not be followed. Post-*Aon v ANU* jurisprudence shows that this message has been heard and is being acted on by Commonwealth and state courts.

2.6.10   *Aon* has been applied with great vigour by the courts and it has been discussed many hundreds of times in case law in the relatively short time that has elapsed since it was handed down. The following list demonstrates its adoption in the case law of jurisdictions covered by this book, predominately at the appellate level:

- **Federal Court:** *Cement Australia Pty Ltd v Australian Competition and Consumer Commission (ACCC)* (2010) 273 ALR 147; [2010] FCAFC; *Dye v Commonwealth Securities Ltd (No 2)* [2010] FCAFC 118; *Grimaldi v Chameleon Mining NL (No 2)* [2012] FCAFC 6;

- **ACT:** *Davey v Herbst* [2011] ACTCA 27; *Davey v Herbst, Herbst and Bray (No 2)* [2012] ACTCA 19, *Tran t/as Canberra Direct v Calvista Australia Pty Ltd* [2010] ACTCA 5;

- **NSW:** *Bellingen Shire Council v Colavon Ltd* [2012] NSWCA 34; *Halpin v Lumley General Insurance Ltd* (2009) 78 NSWLR 265; (2009) 261 ALR 741; [2009] NSWCA 372; *Palavi v Radio 2UE Sydney Pty Ltd* [2011] NSWCA 264; *Richards v Cornford (No 3)* [2010] NSWCA 134; *Hamod v State of New South Wales* [2011] NSWCA 375;

- **NT:** *RTA Pty Ltd v Brinko Pty Ltd* [2012] NTSC 3;

- **Qld:** *Barton v Atlantic 3-Financial (Aus) Pty Ltd* [2010] QCA 223; *Crompton, now aka Boettcher v Buchanan* [2010] QCA 250; *Hartnett v Hynes* [2010] QCA 065; *Johnson v Public Trustee of Queensland as Executor of Will of Brady (decd)* [2010] QCA 260; *Multi-Service Group Pty Ltd (in liq) v Osborne* [2011] 1 Qd R 245; [2010] QCA 72;

- **SA:** *Channel Seven Adelaide Pty Ltd v Manock* [2010] SASCFC 59; *Jury v McCue* [2010] SASC 222;

- **Tas:** *Dodge v Snell* [2010] TASSC 12;

- **Vic:** *MWH Australia Pty Ltd v Wynton Stone Australia Pty Ltd (in liq)* [2010] VSCA 245; *Spotlight Pty Ltd v NCON Australia* [2011] VSCA 267; *Trevor Roller Shutter Service Pty Ltd v Crowe* [2011] VSCA 16;

- **WA:** *Brocx v Hughes* (2010) 41 WAR 84; [2010] WASCA 57; *Swansdale Pty Ltd v Whitcrest Pty Ltd* [2010] WASCA 129; *Ibrahim v Wadworth* [2012] WASCA 47.

An extract of one of these cases is set out below:

2.6.11C   Cement Australia Pty Ltd v Australian Competition and Consumer Commission (ACCC)
(2010) 273 ALR 147; [2010] FCAFC 101
Full Court — Federal Court of Australia

[The Australian Competition and Consumer Commission (the ACCC) commenced proceedings against the appellants and others alleging contravention of ss 45, 46 and 47 of the Trade Practices Act 1974 (Cth). The ACCC alleged a market for the supply and acquisition of unprocessed fly ash in the South-East Queensland (SEQ) region and a market for the supply of concrete-grade fly ash in the SEQ region. The second market was denied by the Cement Australia parties, although they admitted a demand from time to time for concrete-grade fly ash including by persons resident in the geographic region identified by the ACCC.

At the beginning of trial set down for six weeks, counsel for the Cement Australia parties opened on the basis that there was only demand for fine-grade fly ash in the SEQ region. Counsel for the ACCC indicated they were taken by surprise, and sought leave to amend so as to plead an alternative market, being a market for the supply of fine-grade fly ash in the SEQ region. Leave was opposed by the Cement Australia parties but granted by the trial judge, notwithstanding that the trial judge was of the view that the necessity for amendment was occasioned primarily by the fault of the ACCC. The trial was adjourned. The Cement Australia parties sought leave to appeal. (Summary of facts is drawn from the headnote of the ALR report.)]

Keane CJ, Gilmour and Logan JJ: [51] *Aon Risk* is not a one size fits all case. While various factors are identified in the judgment as relevant to the exercise of discretion, the weight to be given to these factors, individually and in combination, and the outcome of that balancing process, may vary depending on the facts in the individual case. As the plurality in *Aon Risk* observed at [75], statements made in cases concerning amendment of pleadings are best understood by reference to the circumstances of those cases, even if they are stated in terms of general application.

[52] The responsibility as to how the respondent's case was pleaded, having regard to the available evidence and the applicable law, ultimately belonged to counsel for the respondent. In our opinion, the explanation from them, accepted albeit in the limited sense as it was by senior counsel for the appellants, was in this circumstance a sufficient explanation capable of acceptance by the primary judge. There was no need for an enquiry beyond that given by the counsel whose responsibility it was to plead the ACCC's case. This is a very different position to that in *Aon Risk*. There the reason the claim introduced by amendment had not been raised before was the result of a deliberate tactical decision on the part of the ANU: *Aon Risk* at [4] and [24]. The delay in proposing the amendment in *Aon Risk* was such as to demand an explanation. As the plurality noted at [106] none was given.

[53] Counsel for the Cement Australia parties made much of the absence of an affidavit from an officer of the ACCC or its solicitors to explain that the problem with too broad a definition of the product dimension of the markets had not previously been identified. In this court, counsel for the Cement Australia parties contend that the reasons of the High Court in *Aon Risk* require such evidence. We do not agree. ...

[55] It is apparent from these passages [in the judgment of the plurality in *Aon Risk* at [103] and [106], (extracted above)] that their Honours were more concerned that there be an explanation as to how the late application comes to be made, than the form in which the explanation was proffered. It is apparent from [34] of the reasons of the trial judge … that his Honour was alive to the absence of a sworn affidavit by an officer of the ACCC as to the reason for the late application for an amendment to ACCC's statement of claim. It is also apparent that his Honour was disposed to accept the explanation proffered by the ACCC's counsel (to which no objection was taken) as an explanation of how the need for the amendment arose. His Honour was content to regard the reason for the late application as an error of judgment by counsel. That view of the facts of this case distinguishes this case from *Aon Risk* where the view which prevailed was that the origin of the problem was a deliberate decision on behalf of the plaintiff.

[56] In summary on this point, the gravamen of the submission put by the Cement Australia parties under this heading is that those instructing counsel for the ACCC may actually have appreciated that the Cement Australia parties' case was that only fly ash of a fineness of 75% or better was in demand by manufacturers of concrete and deliberately refrained from drawing that appreciation to the attention of counsel for the ACCC. The trial judge was entitled to regard that hypothesis as so far-fetched — especially in the absence of any apparent tactical reason for deliberately taking such a decision — that he could reject it, even in the absence of a sworn denial by an officer of the ACCC.

[The application for leave to appeal was refused.]

2.6.12   Question

1. In *Cement*, the Full Federal Court emphasises the importance of determining why a late application to amend has come to be made, and discusses the form in which the explanation must be proffered. *Aon* is distinguished on its facts. Do you agree with the reason relied upon by their Honours in distinguishing *Aon*?

Case management — the future?

2.6.13   Smith has described the movement from the party control of litigation to case management as a movement from due process to due progress: R Smith, 'The Context' in R Smith (ed), *Achieving Civil Justice*, Legal Action Group, London, 1995, p 24. Others argue that case management has become 'the prevailing theory with respect to the proper performance of the judicial function in modern society': *Cockerill v Collins* [1999] 2 Qd R 26 at 28 per Fitzgerald P. Although, as Sackville reminds us, fairness in individual cases has an irreducible quality due, in part, to constitutional imperatives, case management has redefined the concept of fairness to meet the demands pressing on the civil justice system in the 21st century: R Sackville, 'The Future of Case Management in Litigation' (2009) 18 *JJA* 211 at 217–18.

However, Bell responds that the enthusiasm for case management is not universal, and it may be proper to regard its most radical or intrusive forms as still experimental. Therefore, the evolution of the judicial role has not concluded: E Bell, 'Judicial Case Management' (2009) 2 *JSIJ* 76 at 121.

Further reading

2.7.1   Books, articles and papers

L Arthur, 'Does Case Management Undermine the Rule of Law in the Pursuit of Access to Justice?' (2011) 20 *JJA* 240.

E Bell, 'Judicial Case Management' (2009) 2 *JSIJ* 76.

B C Cairns, 'A Review of Some Innovations in Queensland Civil Procedure' (2005) 26 *ABR* 158.

D Hensler, 'Court-ordered Arbitration: An Alternative View' (1990) *U Chi Legal F* 399.

R Ingleby, 'Court Sponsored Mediation: The Case Against Mandatory Participation' (1993) 56 *MLR* 441.

M Legg, *Case Management and Complex Civil Litigation*, Federation Press, 2011.

R McGarvie, 'Judicial Responsibility for the Operation of the Court System' (1989) 68 *ALJ* 79.

C Pincus, 'Court Involvement in Pre-trial Procedures' (1987) 61 *ALJ* 471.

S Rares, 'What is a Quality Judiciary?' (2011) 20 *JJA* 133.

P Sallmann, *Change in the Adversarial System of Civil Dispute Resolution and Some Implications for the Role of the Judiciary*, Civil Justice Project, 1997.

P Sallmann, 'Towards a More Consumer-oriented Court System' (1993) 3 *JJA* 47.

P Sallmann, 'Where are We Heading with Court Governance?' (1994) 4 *JJA* 5.

J Sher, 'Aon Risk Services Australia Ltd v Australian National University: The Triumph of Case Management' (2010) *CJQ* 13.

M von Dadelszen, 'Caseflow Management — In Search of the "Meaningful Event"' (1997) 6 *JJA* 171.

J Wood, 'The Changing Face of Case Management: The New South Wales Experience' (1995) 4 *JJA* 121.

2.7.2   Reports

Australian Government Attorney-General's Department, Access to Justice Taskforce, *A Strategic Framework for Access to Justice in the Federal Civil Justice System*, 2009.

Department for Constitutional Affairs, *Access to Justice: Final Report to the Lord Chancellor on the Civil Justice System in England and Wales*, 1996.

Department for Constitutional Affairs, *Access to Justice: Interim Report to the Lord Chancellor on the Civil Justice System in England and Wales*, 1995.

National Alternative Dispute Resolution Advisory Council (NADRAC), *The Resolve to Resolve: Embracing ADR to Improve Access to Justice in the Federal Jurisdiction*, 2009.

Victorian Law Reform Commission, *Civil Justice Review*, Report 14, 2008.

## CHAPTER 3

Alternative Dispute Resolution

OVERVIEW

This chapter provides an overview of the theory and practice of Alternative Dispute Resolution (ADR). It outlines the demand for methods other than litigation to resolve disputes, and focuses upon the growth of mediation, arbitration, and court-annexed procedures in Australia. Other methods of dispute resolution are also discussed.

In the context of mediation, the structure of the mediation process is outlined, and the nature of consensual dispute resolution is explained. Four of the key features of mediation, namely accessibility, voluntariness, confidentiality and facilitation are analysed. Other issues such as power imbalance, enforceability of agreements to mediate and evaluation of mediation are also discussed.

The process of arbitration is then introduced, and the requirements of the Commercial Arbitration Acts are outlined. The process of international arbitration, the most popular form of cross-border dispute resolution, is briefly discussed. Finally, court-annexed mediation and arbitration, mediator certification and practice standards, and the role of the legal profession in ADR practice are discussed.

Underlying the discussion in this chapter are four broader goals:

1. to encourage readers to recognise some of the limitations of litigation and competitive negotiation;
2. to provide an evaluative introduction to mediation;
3. to help readers understand that the practice of law is broader than the practice of litigation; and
4. that the litigation rules themselves and professional responsibility statutes require that a case has a reasonable prospect of success and that reasonable efforts have been made to resolve the dispute without recourse to litigation.

INTRODUCTION

3.1.1 In human society, conflict is inevitable. Throughout history, people have used a variety of ways to resolve their conflicts — from walking away from it, to employing gentle persuasion, negotiation, litigation, coercion, force, and even warfare. The vast majority of disputes are resolved through informal means, sometimes with the help of families, community processes, or counsellors. Often this can result in a win–win solution, where each party achieves some or all of what they expected. When informal means of resolution fail, litigation may seem the next logical step. But this mostly results in a win–lose outcome. In the preface to this book, litigation was compared to a sanctioned form of warfare. It was described as the method of dispute resolution where parties fight to regain lost territory and rights, with lawyers as generals, the Rules of Court the terrain, and judges as all-powerful nature. In the warfare model of litigation, strategy and tactics dominate over rational solutions, and the parties' and societies' resources are consumed at an astonishing rate.

This description of the adversarial system of litigation reveals why litigation does not work for everyone. First, the financial costs of litigation are often so high that only the wealthy and powerful can make effective use of it. Second, litigation is rarely easy. Its adversarial, defensive and hostile methods, combined with the time delays often involved in cases, can leave parties feeling alienated, and emotionally, physically and psychologically exhausted. Third, litigation only deals with the legal issues in dispute between the parties. Yet few conflicts are confined to legal issues. Just as wars have been fought over issues as broad as 'national security', allocation of resources, or even conflicting values and issues of power, so also the disputes underlying litigation involve a wide range of rights, interests, values and aspirations. Often the basic issue underlying a dispute has to do with the nature of the parties' relationship rather than with the overt topic of dispute. A court judgment may not provide an effective solution to the real conflict. Effective solutions to disagreements may require more than the legal determination of rights and remedies. Business and other relationships may need to be maintained.

On the other hand, while litigation does not satisfactorily resolve many kinds of disputes, neither does informal or extra-legal dispute resolution. Left to themselves, parties in conflict may be unable to reach any resolution. If conflict festers unresolved, parties may find themselves stressed or depressed, and may even resort to violence.

Alternative Dispute Resolution (ADR, sometimes also called Additional, Assisted or Appropriate Dispute Resolution) developed to fill the gap between informal, unregulated forms of extra-legal dispute resolution and formal adversarial litigation. ADR is an umbrella term for a variety of private and court-annexed dispute resolution process options — such as mediation, conciliation, expert referral and arbitration. These processes are designed to provide disputants with procedural options that are appropriate to the dispute. The procedures may be faster, cheaper, less adversarial and more flexible than litigation, but more structured and regulated than the disputants' own efforts to resolve the conflict by themselves. ADR aspires to provide a broad framework for resolving disputes in ways that are accessible, effective, psychologically satisfactory and procedurally fair to the disputants.

To assist parties in resolving disputes, the National Alternative Dispute Resolution Advisory Council (NADRAC) defined seven National Principles for Resolving Disputes, viewed 25 April 2012, <http://www.nadrac.gov.au>.

3.1.2E   **National Principles for Resolving Disputes**

Greater understanding of difference and communication about those differences at an early stage will help to prevent or minimise many disputes. Where disputes cannot be prevented, there are many ways to resolve them.

Methods of resolution range from informal discussion and negotiation to formal determination by a court and include dispute resolution processes like mediation, conciliation and arbitration.

These principles set out a fundamental approach to dispute resolution that is consistent with better access to justice.

The principles address people involved in dispute and government and service providers. For specific information on the principles, please consult the *Interim Report to the Attorney-General on the Key National Principles for the Resolution of Disputes* available at www.nadrac.gov.au.

1. People have a responsibility to take genuine steps to resolve or clarify disputes and should be supported to meet that responsibility.

2. Disputes should be resolved in the simplest and most cost effective way. Steps to resolve disputes including using ADR processes, wherever appropriate, should be made as early as possible and both before and throughout any court or tribunal proceedings.

3. People who attend a dispute resolution process should show their commitment to that process by listening to other views and by putting forward and considering options for resolution.

4. People in dispute should have access to, and seek out, information that enables them to choose suitable dispute resolution processes and informs them about what to expect from different processes and service providers.

5. People in dispute should aim to reach an agreement through dispute resolution processes. They should not be required or pressured to do so if they believe it would be unfair or unjust. If unable to resolve the dispute people should have access to courts and tribunals.

6. Effective, affordable and professional ADR services which meet acceptable standards should be readily available to people as a means of resolving their disputes.

7. Terms describing dispute resolution processes should be used consistently to enhance community understanding of, and confidence in, them.

[See also NADRAC, *National Principles for Resolving Disputes and supporting Guide*, April 2011, viewed 25 April 2012, <http://www.nadrac.gov.au>.]

3.1.3 The term 'Alternative Dispute Resolution' may be somewhat misleading. Although processes like mediation can be seen as alternatives to adversarial litigation or traditional informal resolution processes, they are not alternatives in the sense of being independent of each other. ADR and litigation should be conceived of as intertwined processes for legal dispute resolution. Over the past two decades, ADR processes have been thoroughly incorporated into the formal justice system. The relationship between ADR and litigation can be described as 'complex, interactive, even enmeshed': H Astor and C Chinkin, *Dispute Resolution in Australia*, 2nd ed, LexisNexis Butterworths, Sydney, 2002, p 43.

Research has shown that even where litigation is initiated, most disputes are resolved through negotiation or mediation rather than trial: M Galanter, 'The Vanishing Trial: An Examination of Trials and Related Matters in Federal and State Courts' (2004) 1 *Journal of Empirical Legal Studies* 459; J Fitzgerald, 'Grievances, Disputes and Outcomes: A Comparison of Australia and the United States' (1983) 1 *Law in Context* 15. Conversely, although trials resolve relatively few disputes, participants in negotiations, mediations and other non-binding processes know that the litigation option is available if settlement is not reached. When mapping out their negotiating positions, disputants often take into account the likelihood that their claim or defence would succeed at trial and the cost and time delay of going to trial. Therefore, negotiations take place in the 'shadow of the law' and with the underlying threat of costly litigation: R Mnookin and L Kornhauser, 'Bargaining in the Shadow of the Law: The Case of Divorce' (1979) 88 *Yale Law Journal* 950.

Over the past 20 years the perception that litigation is at the heart of dispute resolution in Australia has gradually eroded in the 'mind-set' of many lawyers. Earlier publications on ADR suggest that when people think about disputes, they think about rights; when they think about rights, they think of the law; when they think of the law, they think of litigation: see C Sampford, S Blencowe and S Condlin, *Educating Lawyers for a Less Adversarial System*, The Federation Press, Sydney, 1999, p 176; H Genn, *Paths to Justice: What People Do and Think About Going to Law*, Oxford University Press, Oxford, 1999. However, these perceptions are no longer current. The growth in and acceptance of ADR, the desire of clients to avoid costly litigation, and the education of lawyers in ADR, have achieved this change in practice. In relation to ADR education, K Douglas, 'The Teaching of ADR in Australian Law Schools: Promoting Non-adversarial Practice in Law' (2011) 22 *ADJR* 49 discusses the inclusion of ADR electives in Australian Law School curriculum and how this is improving student mental health and countering any perception of the law as being purely adversarial. See also J Howieson, 'ADR Education: Creating Engagement and Increasing Mental Well-being through an Interactive and Constructive Approach' (2011) 22(1) *ADRJ* 58.

3.1.4   Questions

1. Is it in lawyers' interests to facilitate early and inexpensive resolution of disputes? Some have suggested that ADR stands for 'alarming drop in revenue'. Does ADR threaten the livelihood of lawyers? Or does it make their services more relevant and accessible? See J Macfarlane, *The New Lawyer: How Settlement is Transforming the Practice of Law*, UBC Press, Vancouver, 2008.

2. In *Aboriginal Dispute Resolution*, Federation Press, Sydney, 1995, p 6, L Behrendt writes:

> Alternative dispute resolution mechanisms offer many advantages over court litigation. But the Aboriginal community needs more than to have programs of mediation, arbitration and negotiation which exist within the dominant legal structures merely transferred into the Aboriginal community with mediators who have had cultural training so that they are sensitive to Aboriginal concerns.
>
> Aboriginal and Torres Strait Islander communities should be able to implement models in their own communities, which recognise traditional cultural values and traditional structures of decision making.

Alternative methods of dispute resolution should be developed that embody the cultural values of indigenous people and are perceived as acceptable by Aboriginal and Torres Strait Islander people. Ideally and necessarily these processes would be developed by the Aboriginal communities themselves.

How far has dispute resolution in Australia come in incorporating this viewpoint? Does ADR offer real possibilities for developing models of dispute resolution that work for indigenous communities? See also L Kelly, 'Elements of a "Good Practice" Aboriginal Mediation Model: Part II' (2008) 19(4) *ADRJ* 223; L Kelly, 'Elements of a "Good Practice" Aboriginal Mediation Model: Part I (2008) 19(3) *ADRJ* 198; Committee of Inquiry into Aboriginal Customary Law, *Legal Recognition of Aboriginal Customary Law*, Northern Territory Law Reform Committee, 2003.

3. Australia is a multicultural society. To what extent does the adversarial nature of litigation meet the needs of cultural groups within the community? See T Trenczek and S Loode, 'Mediation "Made in Germany" — A Quality Product' (2012) 23(1) *ADRJ* 61; S Armstrong, 'Developing Culturally Reflexive Practice in Family Dispute Resolution' (2011) 22(1) *ADRJ* 30; J Crockett, 'Cross-Cultural Mediation and the Multicultural/Natural Model' (2003) 14 *ADRJ* 257.

4. Does the growth in globalisation also suggest we should be learning about the way other cultures in our region resolve disputes? See S Law, 'The Construct of Neutrality and Impartiality in Chinese Mediation' (2011) 22(2) *ADRJ* 118; A Ali and F Lee, 'Resolving Financial Disputes in the Context of Australian and Canadian Civil Justice Reform' (2011) 22(2) *ADRJ* 126; G Lipert, 'A New Playing Field: Hong Kong's Civil Procedure Practice Directions and Mediation' (2010) 21(4) *ADRJ* 234; S Hilmer, 'Mediation in the People's Republic of China: History and Recent Developments' (2010) 21(2) *ADRJ* 104.

5. The Australian Law Reform Commission in *Review of the Adversarial System of Justice: Rethinking the Federal Civil Litigation System*, Issues Paper 20, ALRC, Sydney, 1997, p 98, stated:

    ... [m]ost lawyers are not litigators. There is nevertheless a pervading consciousness in legal practice that litigation is the possible conclusion of any contract, trust or deed of conveyance drawn up or any legal advice tendered. The attitude of the lawyer is one of precaution and anticipation of litigation.

    Do you believe that this is still an accurate reflection of legal practice?

3.1.5 Further reading

H Astor and C Chinkin, *Dispute Resolution in Australia*, 2nd ed, LexisNexis Butterworths, Sydney, 2002, pp 43–73.

J Balstad, 'What Do Litigants Really Want? Comparing and Evaluating Adversarial Negotiation and ADR' (2005) 16 *ADRJ* 244.

H Brown and A Marriott, *ADR Principles and Practice*, 3rd ed, Sweet & Maxwell, 2011, London.

B French, 'Dispute Resolution in Australia — The Movement from Litigation to Mediation' (2007) 18 *ADRJ* 213.

M Galanter and M Cahill, 'Most Cases Settle: Judicial Promotion and the Regulation of Settlements' (1994) 46 *Stanford LR* 1339.

M King, A Freiberg, B Batagol and R Hyams, *Non-adversarial Justice*, The Federation Press, Sydney, 2009, Ch 1.

T Sourdin, *Alternative Dispute Resolution*, 4th ed, Thomson Reuters, Sydney, 2012.

D Spencer, *Principles of Dispute Resolution*, Thomson Reuters, Sydney, 2011.

THE GROWTH IN ADR

3.2.1 Although mediation, arbitration and other forms of dispute resolution have ancient origins, western industrialised countries 'rediscovered' ADR in the 1970s: H Astor and C Chinkin, *Dispute Resolution in Australia*, 2nd ed, LexisNexis Butterworths, Sydney, 2002, p 5. The momentum for the diversification of resolution processes was established by neighbourhood justice centres and other community groups in the 1970s and 1980s. Taking their inspiration from the blossoming civil rights movements in Australia and around the world, these groups argued that the traditional legal system of adversarial litigation was not an accessible or effective means of resolving the types of disputes faced by many ordinary Australians. The concerns raised by these groups were soon echoed by the business community and other critics of the justice system, who pointed out that litigation is frequently too expensive or protracted to be financially viable or effective for business needs. Others voiced concern about the effect of adversarial litigation on parties' ongoing relationships: L Boulle, *Mediation — Principles, Process and Practice*, 3rd ed, LexisNexis Butterworths, Sydney, 2011, pp 427–9. Litigation, unlike many ADR outcomes, is often corrosive of parties' ongoing relationships. Where the parties need to continue a relationship after litigation, the adversarial process was in many cases unsuitable. Taken as a whole, these critiques of the adversarial system of litigation presented a compelling case for reform.

3.2.2 Since the 1970s, there has been rapid expansion, development and consolidation of ADR processes. Professor Tania Sourdin writes:

> Mediation is now used within Australia almost everywhere there is conflict. For example, it can be used to deal with conflict that arises in communities, families, workplaces, hospitals, and in respect of consumer issues. It can be used to resolve conflict in the corporate sector as well as large scale environmental conflict. It has been used to resolve conflicts over construction and over refugee rights. In short, mediation is now used wherever there is conflict and conflict is ubiquitous.

T Sourdin, 'Australian National Mediator Accreditation System: Report on Project' (2007) *Australian Centre for Peace and Conflict Studies* 1, 4, viewed 22 April 2012, <http://www.wadra. law.ecu.edu.au>.

3.2.3 ADR mechanisms have now been incorporated into the formal justice system throughout Australia. Every state and the federal government now have statutory provisions for judicial referral of matters to ADR processes. Most of these statutes provide for a judge to use discretion in determining which cases are appropriate for referral to ADR processes. Significantly, however, there are now several legislative provisions requiring people with certain types of claims to attend some form of ADR as a pre-condition to litigation. For example, the Native Title Act 1993 (Cth) requires mandatory pre-litigation attendance at mediation for certain native title claims. Pre-litigation mediation is also required under the Retail Leases Act 1994 (NSW) and the Farm Debt Mediation Act 1994 (NSW). The Civil Procedure Resolution Act 2011 (Cth) requires genuine steps to resolve a dispute prior to litigation in the Federal Court and Federal Magistrates Court: see 3.9.2. The largest and most significant scheme for mandatory pre-litigation ADR was implemented in July 2007 under amendments to the Family Law Act 1975 (Cth). With certain exceptions — such as in cases where there is a threat of family violence or child abuse — a would-be litigant may not file an application in a child-related proceeding without first obtaining a certificate from a family dispute practitioner saying that they attended family dispute resolution 'and made a genuine attempt to resolve the issues': Family Law Act 1975 (Cth) s 60I(8)–(10). Family dispute resolution, a statutorily defined species of mediation, is no longer an 'alternative' method for resolving parenting disputes. It is the primary method. See R Field, 'FDR and Victims of Family Violence: Ensuring a Safe Process and Outcomes' (2010) 21(3) *ADRJ* 185.

3.2.4 Just as the use and availability of ADR within the legal system has grown, so too has the application of ADR processes outside the legal system. For example, the use of ADR techniques has now become well established in the design of dispute management processes aimed at the prevention or early resolution of disputes in government, organisations, schools and communities: see generally R Charlton, *Dispute Resolution Guidebook*, LBC Information Services, Sydney, 2000, Chs 13, 15 and 24; P Condliffe, *Conflict Management: A Practical Guide*, LexisNexis Butterworths, Sydney, 2002, Ch 7; T Sourdin, *Alternative Dispute Resolution*, 4th ed, Thomson Reuters, Sydney, 2012, Ch 9. ADR has also become well established in various dispute resolution contexts including community justice, neighbourhood, banking and finance, construction, farm debt, indigenous and native title, industrial, family, franchising, insurance, local government, personal injury, securities, superannuation and trade practices disputes: see T Sourdin, *Australasian Dispute Resolution: Duncombe & Heap*, Law Book Co, looseleaf, 2012, Vol 1, [2.200]–[2.340].

ADR has affected business dispute resolution on multiple levels. Management theory is now adopting a consultative approach as distinct from the former command and control models. ADR has become a primary dispute resolution process for many businesses, not only for dealing with traditional commercial disputes, but also for addressing consumer complaints. See M Redfern, 'Mediation is Good Business Practice' (2010) 21(1) *ADRJ* 53 who suggests mediation should be adopted as a process of first choice in dealing with business disputes. Many consumer service corporations have developed dispute resolution schemes to deal with consumer issues. These schemes are generally funded by a cooperative of businesses within a particular industry and include the Financial Services Ombudsman, the Telecommunications Industry Ombudsman, the Financial Industry Complaints Service, the Financial Co-operatives Dispute Resolution Service, Insurance Enquiries and Complaints Ltd, Insurance Brokers Disputes Ltd and the Credit Union Dispute Reference Centre. Although developments such as these have provided consumers with more accessible ways for raising complaints, there is little research or evaluation available on the overall accessibility, efficacy or fairness of these schemes for consumers: T Sourdin and L Thorpe, 'How Do Financial Services Consumers Access Complaints and Dispute Resolution Processes', (2008) 19 *ADRJ* 25; P O'Shea, 'Underneath the Radar: The Largely Unnoticed Phenomenon of Industry Based Consumer Dispute Resolution Schemes in Australia' (2004) 15 *ADRJ* 156, 163. The need for monitoring was also highlighted by the NADRAC which suggested that there is wide variation in consumer satisfaction with the independence of industry-based schemes and a general level of dissatisfaction with the outcome of disputes: NADRAC, *Maintaining and Enhancing the Integrity of ADR Processes: From Principles to Practice through People*, viewed 18 May 2012, <http://www.nadrac.gov.au>. The complaints process is addressed in NADRAC, *National Principles for Resolving Disputes and Supporting Guide*, 2011, s 6.3, viewed 26 April 2012, <http://www.nadrac.gov.au> — Practitioner conduct (Chs 2 and 3) and Liability (Ch 5).

3.2.5   The development and diversification of ADR processes has recently been accelerated by changes in information technologies. With videoconferencing, teleconferencing, and online exchange of documents becoming cheaper, faster and more accessible, more disputants are turning to online ADR (also called ODR, or Online Dispute Resolution) to assist with the resolution of their disputes: see T Sourdin, *Alternative Dispute Resolution*, 4th ed, Thomson Reuters, Sydney, 2012, pp 327–54, and A Tidwell, 'Handling Disputes in Cyberspace' (1996) 7 *ADRJ* 245. There are now online mediation services, virtual courtrooms, and online ombudsman programs: see, e.g. Technology Dispute Centre, viewed 26 April 2012, <http://tdc.org.au/facilities/odr> (Aust site); The Mediation Room, viewed 26 April 2012, <http://www.themediationroom. com> (UK site); Cybersettle, viewed 26 April 2012, <http://www.Cybersettle.com> (USA site); The National Center for Technology and Dispute Resolution, viewed 26 April 2012, <http://www.odr.info/index.php> (USA site); Online Ombud: Justice Without Tears, viewed 26 April 2012, <http://www.onlineombud.com/index.html>,(South Africa); ICourthouse, viewed 26 April 2012, <http://www.icourthouse.com> (USA site).

Technology has the capacity to globalise dispute resolution, bridging the barrier of distance by allowing for instant communication of information, documents, offers, etc, around the world. Online dispute resolution may also have other effects flowing from the increased speed and reduced emotional intensity of online communication: S Hardy, 'Online Mediation: Internet Dispute Resolution' (1998) 9 *ADRJ* 216; J Goodman, 'The Pros and Cons of Online Dispute Resolution: An Assessment of Cyber-Mediation Websites' (2003) *Duke L & Tech Rev* 4.

More importantly, the ability to exchange information with multiple parties in multiple locations has the potential to provide greater equality to traditionally disempowered disputants. The individual or one-time player in a commercial dispute may be empowered by greater access to information. Rabinovich-Einy argues:

> The new possibilities for information gathering and publication are unprecedented in the power they offer private individuals who previously had to rely on others for information gathering and/ or for publication. Those who have traditionally been in possession of information — seldom private individuals — have been in a position to control the release of such data, distributing it selectively or keeping it completely confidential. This reality, at times, made it futile for individuals to dispute with larger, better-organized corporations with deep pockets who had long-term stakes in obtaining favorable results.

O Rabinovich-Einy, 'Balancing the Scales: The Ford-Firestone Case, the Internet, and the Future Dispute Resolution Landscape' (2003–2004) 6 *Yale Journal of Law and Technology* 1.

It is clear that developments in information technology are already significantly transforming dispute resolution processes both within and outside the legal system. As Clark and Hoyle explain:

> ... [D]igital communication media and internet-based systems have ... added new dimensions and tools to the dispute resolution process. There may now be little or no need for face-to-face meetings in a confidential setting. This new medium has given birth to virtual meetings for dispute resolution and created in cyberspace a virtual courtroom with mediators or magistrates performing roles equivalent to those they perform in the real world (footnotes omitted).

E Clark and A Hoyle, 'Online Dispute Resolution: Present Realities and Future Prospects' (2002) *17th Bileta Conference* 2, viewed 14 April 2012, <http://www.bileta.ac.uk>.

3.2.6 The development of ADR mechanisms has not been the only way the adversarial system has sought to answer its critics. Particularly in the context of concern about the long delays and high costs of litigation, case management has now been widely introduced in Australian jurisdictions to deal with such issues: see **2.4.21–2.4.25**. The report of the Australian Law Reform Commission on the federal justice system highlights the continuing importance placed on reform to litigation: ALRC, *Managing Justice: A Review of the Federal Civil Justice System*, Report No 89, ALRC, Canberra, 2000. There is also a growing relationship between case management strategies and the use of ADR, with diversion of cases to mediation and arbitration now an important part of the mechanisms employed by Australian courts to facilitate the early resolution of disputes: see **3.9.1** below and **2.4.21–2.4.25**.

It is important that reform to the litigation system continues to be balanced with the promotion, monitoring and evaluation of ADR processes. The integration of ADR practice has accelerated with the release of major government reports and policy documents, increased ethical conduct standards, the implementation of the National Mediator Accreditation System (NMAS) and associated development of a national system of uniform standards and accreditation, changes in the approach of courts to ADR — including pre-action protocols, the emergence of judicial mediation, and the emergence of family dispute resolution practitioners and associated regulation.

3.2.7 Notes and questions

1. It is often presumed that the nature of litigation is well suited to the resolution of commercial disputes. In what contexts could the need to preserve relationships affect commercial disputants? See M Redfern, 'Mediation is Good Business Practice' (2010) 21(1) *ADRJ* 53; NADRAC, *ADR: A Better Way to Do Business, Summary of Proceedings*, 4–5 Sept 2003, Sydney; S C Sable, 'Changing Assumptions About Mediation in Commercial Matters: Resolving Disputes and (Re)Building Relationships' (2001) 12 *ADRJ* 275.

2. At present there is no comprehensive system for reviewing finance industry based ADR schemes. Do you think there is a danger that these processes will perpetuate inequalities between consumers and businesses? See P O'Shea, 'Underneath the Radar: The Largely Unnoticed Phenomenon of Industry Based Consumer Dispute Resolution Schemes in Australia' (2004) 15 *ADRJ* 156; T Sourdin

and L Thorpe, 'How do Financial Services Consumers Access Complaints and Dispute Resolution Processes' (2008) 19 *ADRJ* 25; S Varnham and M Evers, 'The Challenges and Opportunities of the Role of Student Ombudsmen in an Australian University' (2011) 22 *ADRJ* 228; P Kell, 'Consumer Concerns' (2008) 16 *TPLJ* 66; D Sams, 'Judicial Review of Decisions Made by Industry Ombudsman Schemes' (2007) 18 *ADRJ* 222; B French, 'Dispute Resolution in Australia — The Movement from Litigation to Mediation' (2007) 18 *ADRJ* 213.

3. In E Clark and A Hoyle, 'On-Line Dispute Resolution: Present Realities and Future Prospects' (2002) *17th Bileta Conference* 6, viewed 18 May 2012, <http://www.bileta.ac.uk>:

> Negotiation and dispute resolution is fundamentally a 'people' oriented task. The use of e-DR may miss out on non-verbal clues: body language, touch, smell. It is not as holistic and interactive as face-to-face. The nuances of expression, timing, communication, framing and persuasion often make the difference between success and failure in bargaining and mediation.

How do you think the development of online dispute resolution could change the way litigation and dispute resolution processes are conducted? Have improvements in teleconferencing partially allayed the concerns raised by Clark and Hoyle? In what ways do you think these developments would be positive? See also D King, 'Internet Mediation' (2000) 11 *ADRJ* 174.

3.2.8   Further reading

T Altobelli, 'A Generational Change in Family Dispute Resolution in Australia' (2006) 17(3) *ADRJ* 140.

F Gibson, 'Alternative Dispute Resolution in Residential Tenancy Cases', (2007) 18(2) *ADRJ* 101.

P O'Shea, 'The Lion's Question Applied to Industry Based Consumer Dispute Resolution' (2006) 25 *Arbitrator and Mediator* 63.

TYPES OF ADR PROCESSES

3.3.1   Numerous dispute resolution methods have developed over the last 20 years to operate in addition to, or as alternatives to, adjudication. Of these, the most commonly used in Australia are arbitration, mediation, conciliation, facilitation and early neutral evaluation. There is also a range of hybrid processes that have developed, including expert appraisal or determination, private judging and fact-finding, less adversarial trial, multidisciplinary collaborative approach in family law, collaborative law/practice, criminal facilitation/practice, circle sentencing, convening clauses and partnering. As a result, depending upon the nature of the dispute and the circumstances of the parties, one or more of these methods may be used to form part of a dispute resolution process.

Defining ADR processes is no easy task. ADR methods are evolutionary and applied flexibly to suit the nature of the dispute concerned. ADR terms may have different meanings in different contexts or cultures. Further, because many ADR processes are privately arranged, the parties have a significant level of freedom to define and design the process to suit the dispute and their own needs. Decisions about the nature and timing of the process, the qualifications of the facilitator or decision-maker, and the enforceability of the outcome of the process are frequently determined by contract between the disputing parties. Nevertheless, it is helpful for ADR users, practitioners and policy-makers to have a degree of common understanding and consistency in the use of terms. With this in mind, the National Alternative Dispute Resolution Council (NADRAC) put forward a paper to 'describe' rather than define dispute resolution terms: see NADRAC, *Dispute Resolution Terms*, 2003, viewed 26 April 2012, <http://www.nadrac.gov.au>. The following descriptions of the main dispute resolution processes in Australia are drawn primarily from this glossary. The Association of Dispute Resolvers (LEADR) also has a useful list of definitions: viewed 26 April, <http://www.leadr.com.au/adr.htm>.

In evaluating these processes it is useful to bear in mind the following issues:

- Who resolves the dispute?
- Is the process determinative, facilitative or advisory?
- In what way do procedural issues regulate the conduct of the process?

Determinative processes

3.3.2 Determinative processes involve a third party making a decision or determination on the dispute, usually after hearing arguments and evidence. The outcome of most determinative processes — particularly adjudication and arbitration — is enforceable through the courts. In some determinative processes, however, the determinations are made primarily for the benefit of the parties and may be enforceable only to the extent provided for by contract between the parties.

Adjudication

3.3.3 NADRAC defines adjudication in the following terms:

Parties present arguments and evidence to a dispute resolution practitioner (the adjudicator) who makes a determination which is enforceable by the authority of the adjudicator. The most common form of internally enforceable adjudication is determination by state authorities empowered to enforce decisions by law (courts) within the traditional judicial system. However, there are also other in ternally enforceable adjudication processes (for example, internal disciplinary or grievance processes implemented by employers): Source: viewed 18 May 2012, <http://www.nadrac.gov.au/>.

Arbitration

3.3.4 Parties submit the dispute to a third party (the arbitrator) who renders a determination (an award) after hearing arguments and reviewing evidence. The determination is usually binding, and is only reviewable on limited grounds. It has no precedential effect.

Arbitration is most commonly used in commercial, construction, labour and international trade disputes. Arbitration is also the most common form of transnational commercial dispute resolution. Often the parties agree at the outset of their dealings that any disputes that arise are to be referred to arbitration. Alternatively, the parties may agree to arbitration once a dispute has arisen. The arbitrator can also be chosen before or after the dispute, and is usually selected for his or her expertise in the subject matter of the dispute.

The agreement that defines the arbitrator's powers is generally the source of the standard for the resolution of the dispute, although the industry practice and provisions of Commercial Arbitration Acts may come into play: Commercial Arbitration Act 2011 (Cth), International Arbitration Act 1974 (Cth); Commercial Arbitration Act 1986 (ACT); Commercial Arbitration Act 2010 (NSW); Commercial Arbitration Act 1990 (Qld); Commercial Arbitration Act 2011 (SA); Commercial Arbitration Act 2011 (Tas); Commercial Arbitration Act 2011 (Vic); Commercial Arbitration Act 1985 (WA). Parties to an arbitration are usually represented by lawyers, who are responsible for researching and presenting the evidence and arguments at the arbitration. The proceedings are less formal than in court. The parties often determine the venue of the hearing.

Fast-track arbitration is the process in which the parties present arguments and evidence to an arbitrator at an early stage in the dispute. The arbitrator makes a determination on the most important and most immediate issues to be resolved.

Expert determination

3.3.5   The parties appoint an independent expert to make a binding determination on some disputed facts or issues after hearing arguments and evidence from the parties. The expert is chosen on the basis of their specialist qualification or experience in the subject matter of the dispute. The expert's role often includes investigation and inquiry to ascertain necessary information.

Expert appraisal is a very similar process to expert determination, except that the expert provides an advisory opinion rather than a determinative one. The appraiser provides advice on the facts and possible and desirable outcomes and the means whereby these may be achieved. Source: viewed 25 April 2012, <http://www.nadrac.gov.au/>. The point of both processes is to avoid having two or more partisan experts presenting conflicting opinions on important issues or facts by submitting them to a single expert agreed to by the parties. The determination or appraisal may resolve the issue between the parties, it may be used as the basis for further negotiations, or it may reduce the matters in dispute at trial.

Private judging

3.3.6   Parties present arguments and evidence to a private (usually retired) judge who makes a determination based on what, in their opinion, the likely decision would be if the matter went to court. This rare process is often formal and adversarial, and the judge makes the decision according to substantive legal rules.

Fact-finding

3.3.7   NADRAC defines fact-finding in the following terms:

> Parties to a dispute present arguments and evidence to a dispute resolution practitioner (the investigator), who makes a determination as to the facts of the dispute, but who does not make

any finding or recommendations as to outcomes for resolution: Source: viewed 25 April 2012, <http://www.nadrac.gov.au/>. This is not a common approach.

Early neutral evaluation

3.3.8   Parties (or more often their lawyers) present arguments and evidence at an early stage in a dispute to an evaluator (usually a Queen's Counsel or Senior Counsel). The evaluator assesses the merits of the case, identifies and clarifies issues and encourages the parties to settle the matter by consensus. The evaluator may take on the role of chair to assist in a settlement discussions process.

If settlement does not occur, the neutral assessment may be used to focus the issues, identify areas for further discovery, plan litigation, or identify further ADR processes that may be employed. There is no determination on the facts in dispute, and the process can often appear like a mini trial with the goal being to encourage the parties to reach a negotiated settlement.

Case appraisal

3.3.9   Case appraisal is a process in which a dispute resolution practitioner (the case appraiser) investigates the dispute and provides advice on possible and desirable outcomes and the means whereby these may be achieved. Source: viewed 25 April 2012, <http://www. nadrac.gov.au/>.

Mini-trial

3.3.10   Mini-trial is a process in which the participants present arguments and evidence to a dispute resolution practitioner who provides advice as to the facts of the dispute, and advice regarding possible, probable and desirable outcomes and the means whereby these may be achieved. Source: viewed 25 April 2012, <http://www.nadrac.gov.au/>.

Facilitative processes

3.3.11   Facilitative processes involve a third party providing assistance in the management of the process of dispute resolution. This is mostly used for community or public disputes, e.g., where a government agency wants to build a prison near a town resulting in objections. A community meeting will be arranged, concerns are documented and information provided. The facilitator does not make a decision. Rather, the process facilitates the parties' efforts to resolve the dispute for themselves. To the extent that any of the facilitative processes culminate in an agreement or settlement of the dispute by the parties, that agreement or settlement is enforceable at law to the same extent as any other settlement.

Facilitation

3.3.12   NADRAC defines facilitation in the following terms:

> In this collaborative process the parties (often a group), with the assistance of a neutral third party (the facilitator), identify problems to be solved, tasks to be accomplished or disputed issues to be resolved. Facilitation may end at this point, or the facilitator may continue to assist

the parties to develop options, consider alternatives and endeavour to reach agreement. The facilitator has no advisory or determinative role on the content of the matters discussed or the outcome of the process: Source: viewed 25 April 2012, <http://www.nadrac.gov.au/>.

Conciliation

3.3.13   Parties, with the assistance of a neutral third party (the conciliator), identify the disputed issues, develop options, consider alternatives and endeavour to reach an agreement. This is a similar process to mediation. The conciliator can have an advisory, but not a determinative role. Conciliation is one of the oldest and most successful forms of alternative dispute resolution in Australia dating from 1902 with the advent of Industrial Commissions. It is particularly important for resolving industrial disputes both on an individual employee basis and in respect of collective awards.

Conciliation is often used by public agencies that administer rights granted under legislation (for example, the NSW Health Conciliation Registry, the Financial Services Complaints Resolution Scheme, the Family Court, the Equal Opportunity Commission, and the Aged Care Dispute Resolution Scheme). In many cases, one party initiates the matter and the other party is drawn into the process once a complaint has been made. Usually, if no outcome is reached, the dispute will go to a tribunal or other body for a binding decision.

The conciliator is obliged to advocate the rules and standards promoted by the agency. They are usually empowered to make suggestions as to the terms of settlement and will be mindful to ensure there is conformity to any requirements of the legislation under which the conciliation is attempted.

Mediation

3.3.14   Mediation is a process of facilitated negotiation where the parties to a dispute, with the assistance of a neutral third party (the mediator), identify the issues in dispute, develop options, consider alternatives and endeavour to reach an agreement. The issues raised and resolved are not limited to legal issues and may include any range of interests and needs that are important to the parties.

A mediator has no advisory or determinative role and cannot impose a decision or result upon the parties. Instead, the mediator facilitates or assists the parties' effort to reach their own agreement. The mediator does, however, often determine how the process will be conducted, and uses a structured or systematic process as the basis for the mediation.

Mediation can be connected to court proceedings (such as family mediation) or conducted in its own right as a dispute resolution process (as in commercial, neighbourhood and community mediations). When mediation is connected to a court, the mediator is often assigned to the dispute rather than chosen by the parties.

Since mediation ultimately seeks agreement between the parties, the mediator does not evaluate the strengths or weaknesses of evidence or arguments. Instead, they seek to identify common ground between the parties concerning facts, standards and needs. Lawyers may or may not be present, and any settlement reached usually results in a signed agreement, which may be enforceable as a contract.

Mediation addresses the parties' interests in an attempt to achieve a win–win solution, whereas litigation addresses the parties' legal rights, which often results in a win–lose outcome.

Ombudsman

3.3.15   An ombudsman is an impartial third party who investigates complaints against an institution by its constituents, clients or employees. An ombudsman may take action such as bringing an apparent injustice to the attention of higher level officials, advising the complainant of available options and resources, proposing a settlement of the dispute or proposing systematic change to the institution. In Australia, all jurisdictions have the position of ombudsman to investigate complaints against state agencies and officials. There is also an increasing number of industry-based ombudsmen, such as the Private Health Insurance Ombudsman, Australian Banking Industry Ombudsman and the Telecommunications Industry Ombudsman.

3.3.16   Further reading

H Astor and C Chinkin, *Dispute Resolution in Australia*, 2nd ed, LexisNexis Butterworths, Sydney, 2002, pp 82–95.

L Boulle, *Mediation — Principles, Process and Practice*, 3rd ed, LexisNexis Butterworths, Australia, 2011.

L Boulle and N Alexander, *Mediation — Skills and Techniques*, LexisNexis Butterworths, Australia, 2011.

S L Burns, *Making Settlement Work: An Examination of the Work of Judicial Mediators*, Ashgate Publishing Co, England, 2000.

D Spencer, *Principles of Dispute Resolution*, Thomson Reuters, Sydney, 2011, pp 1–21.

Sir L Street, 'The Language of Alternative Dispute Resolution' (1992) 99 *ALJ* 194.

G Tillet, 'Terminology in Dispute Resolution: A Review of Issues and Literature' (2004) 15 *ADRJ* 178.

MEDIATION

3.4.1   Mediation deserves particular attention in discussing ADR mechanisms as it has become the most widely used alternative to litigation, adjunct to negotiated settlement and dispute management process in Australia. NADRAC states:

> Mediation is usually considered to be a process in which the participants, with the assistance of the dispute resolution practitioner (the mediator), identify the disputed issues, develop options, consider alternatives and endeavour to reach an agreement. The mediator is usually regarded as having a facilitative role and will not provide advice on the matters in dispute. The mediator may have no particular experience or expertise in the subject area of the dispute but should be expected to be experienced and have expertise in the mediation process itself: See viewed 30 April 2012, <http://www.nadrac.gov.au>.

D Spencer, *Principles of Dispute Resolution*, Thomson Reuters, Sydney, 2011, p 49 argues that the key elements of mediation, which may change depending on the type of mediation and the desire of the parties, include:

- that the parties to the dispute are assisted by a mediator;
- issues are identified;
- options are developed;
- there is an effort to reach agreement;
- the mediator is not an advisor;
- the mediator does not make a determination;
- the mediator may advise on the process that will lead the parties to resolution; and
- mediation may or may not be voluntary.

3.4.2E   **Alternative Dispute Resolution**
T Sourdin, 4th ed, Thomson Reuters, Sydney, 2012, p 69

Mediation — is there a common definition?

[3.10] The description that has been accepted by the National Alternative Dispute Resolution Advisory Council (NADRAC) assumes that a "facilitative" model will operate (see description below). However, NADRAC has noted that:

> NADRAC prefers to see the term mediation used for processes where "… The mediator has no advisory or determinative role in regard to the content of the dispute or the outcome of its resolution, but may advise on or determine the process of mediation whereby resolution is attempted". In practice, however, the term "mediation" is often used in instances where the dispute resolution practitioner gives advice on the substance of the dispute.
>
> These issues of practice may be better addressed through regulation or codes of practice in specific areas, rather than by a stand-alone definition. Regulations or codes would clearly spell out practitioner roles and responsibilities, and the consequences associated with non-compliance.

Many practitioners consider that two main forms of mediation exist: facilitative and evaluative. Despite more widespread acceptance of the facilitative NADRAC description and the increasing use of mediation standards (see below), in some jurisdictions the mediator is perceived to be active in making recommendations, evaluating the dispute and furnishing advice to the parties about the range of likely outcomes should a matter be litigated. Under the *National Mediation Accreditation System and Standards* (which commenced on 1 January 2008), these processes that involve an evaluative or advisory component are regarded as "blended" — that is, they are not defined as mediation but as an amalgam of processes — and the consent of disputants is required for this amalgam to be used (see Appendix E *NMAS Standards*, s 2(4)).

In most jurisdictions within Australia, the mediator's role is perceived to be purely facilitative (rather than evaluative), and it has been recommended that "the mediator's hand not be seen in the outcome". In the Federal Court of Australia, it has been said that the process follows "Most closely the 'purist' [p 70] (model)". However, this does not mean that the primary focus is not on compromise (rather than more creative options as in interest-based negotiation). In other areas of practice, the processes used may not follow a pure mediation mode (where the mediator may not proffer any opinion or advice) but may more closely resemble an evaluative model.

Many mediation practitioners consider there to be a distinction between asking questions that "reality test" the options that may be put forward by parties to a dispute and suggesting what the likely outcome could be if the matter proceeded to litigation or did not resolve at the mediation. The timing of any reality testing may also vary and in most facilitative models option exploration and testing is discouraged until there has been a full conversation about interests.

Where lawyers expect and promote evaluative mediation models, the mediator chosen is more likely to have a background in law and will be more likely to adopt a more evaluative or directive approach. Once the mediation commences, lawyers may seek to focus on the legal rights of the parties involved rather than the broader interests and issues. This approach can also mean that a more evaluative approach is adopted and the questioning approach is not "elicitative" but directive ...

An empowering process

[3.15] The different approaches to mediation have also been categorized as process-oriented (facilitative) or substance-oriented (evaluative) mediation. In a process-oriented approach the parties, rather than the mediator, are said to provide the solution to their dispute and the mediator is the facilitator of the process rather than an authority figure providing substantive advice or pressure to settle. In the process model, a mediator does not require knowledge of the subject matter of the dispute. Process oriented mediation can be facilitative, settlement focused, transformative, narrative or therapeutic (or a mix of these approaches).

Substance-oriented mediation?

[3.20] Substance-oriented "mediation" is at the opposite end of the scale to the process oriented model and the participants in this model are focused on persuading the ADR practitioner (rather than each other) and the decision making is dependent on the advice of the ADR practitioner. The mediator in this model is often an authority figure who evaluates the case based on experience and offers recommendations on how the case should be resolved. Some practitioners consider that the basic philosophy of mediation requires recognition that the process is to be empowering and that therefore substance-oriented mediation cannot be defined as mediation. This view is also supported in the NADRAC descriptions and the NMAS Standards.

Aside from the definitional differences, there are also liability issues for mediator practitioners who provide a view as to outcome. In these situations, practitioners are more likely to be sued if a party has settled a dispute following "advice" (which may be incorrect) that has been provided to a party or parties. Clearly an "adviceless" mediator cannot be sued regarding incorrect or uninformed advice (as they have not given any). Providing advice is of particular concern in any advisory models that are blended with mediation as any "advice" given by the third party is unlikely to have been tested and will be based on information that may be gathered in the private meetings held in a mediation ...

Substance-oriented mediation, in which a practitioner provides a view as to the outcome, is also known in the United States as "muscle", "rhino" or "rambo" mediation. This process does not appear to offer the same empowerment opportunities and the mediator will often adopt a directive rather than an "elicitative" approach, which essentially locates the mediator as the controller of both process and outcome. The participants in such a mediation may not feel that they have solved their own problem and may have their issues more narrowly defined by a reference to legal rights rather than interests. [E]mpowerment is often viewed as an essential characteristic of mediation ... derived from the recognition that participants are quite capable of negotiating for themselves in reaching their own decision. The parties' ability in this regard was acknowledged and respected. As any solution was not imposed, but arose out of the empowerment of the parties, it was more likely to be acceptable to both sides in adhered to.

Transformative mediation

[3.25] Another form of mediation is known as "transformative" mediation, in which the emphasis is not on problem-solving but on the nature of the process itself. Transformative models are increasingly used in community conflict, victim–offender conferencing and complex family conflict. In the transformative model, the mediator's role is to foster empowerment and recognition in the parties; this is done by encouraging parties to communicate and make decisions more effectively, subject to their own choices and limits. Some mediators consider that the transformative model of mediation existed as part of the New South Wales Community Justice Centre mediation model however in recent years the model has become more structured and facilitative with a greater focus on agenda setting. The transformative form of mediation does not focus on resolution but changes in the individual and group dynamics that can lead to social change as well. A model that is often seen as related is "therapeutic mediation" where professional therapeutic techniques are used to encourage communication and behavioural concerns.

The transformative mediation model has been explored in a series of research projects that have focused on the United States Postal Service (USPS) REDRESS program. The USPS originally employed over 800,000 employees (the number of employees has declined in recent years as e-mail communication has increased) and receives over 25,000 informal equal opportunity (EEO) complaints each year. In 1997 it implemented the REDRESS program, which offered transformative mediations to EEO complainants. Exit surveys conducted following the implementation of the project conducted by the USPS demonstrated high levels of participant satisfaction with the program. Ninety six per cent of complainants and 97 per cent of supervisors reported that they were "very satisfied" or "somewhat satisfied" with the practitioners conducting the transformative mediations. Recent evaluations of this program have achieved similarly high levels of satisfaction.

Other surveys also suggest that the transformative model can cause behavioural shifts in participants. Antes, Folger and Della Noce interviewed mediators about behaviours the mediators had observed during at least two transformative mediations they had either conducted or observed. This research was regarded as somewhat questionable given the focus on mediator perceptions of behaviour. However, the research did suggest that participants tend to become more open and confident as mediations progress and productive engagement can occur following difficult discussions. In addition, participants were said to be more likely to establish personal connections and understand more about themselves and others after engaging in the process.

However, transformative mediation has also been the subject of criticism. This is particularly because some transformative mediation practitioners consider that the process can lead to substantive changes in the way that individuals deal with conflict and each other — in short, that the process can assist with the "moral development" of an individual. In a review of Bush and Folger's book *The Promise of Mediation*, Menkel-Meadow argues that the objective of transformative mediation is not clearly articulated and that it is almost impossible to determine whether individuals become more skilled at dealing with conflict. To some extent, the criticism also relates to what is perceived to be a lack of theoretical underpinning.

3.4.3   Mediation is based on empowering the parties to identify the issues in dispute and then find solutions that meet their interests and needs. There is a distinctive structure to mediation, which, by and large, is complied with in all mediations. This forms the procedural aspect of mediation. In contrast to litigation, it is highly flexible, essentially non-evidentiary and focuses on the mediator directing the process and the parties deciding the issues and the outcome.

Various models have been put forward to explain the mediation process: see R Charlton and M Dewdney, *The Mediator's Handbook: Skills and Strategies for Practitioners*, 2nd ed, Lawbook Co, Sydney, 2004, pp 3–9; T Sourdin, *Alternative Dispute Resolution*, 4th ed, Thomson Reuters, Sydney, 2012, p 551; L Boulle, *Mediation — Principles, Process, Practice*, 3rd ed, LexisNexis Butterworths, 2011, pp 261–3; D Spencer, *Principles of Dispute Resolution*, Thomson Reuters, Sydney, 2011, pp 50–68. Two of the most well known in Australia are set out in **Figures 3.1** and **3.2**.

Figure 3.1:   Mediation process model. (The opening perhaps more accurately should be labelled the mediator's opening. Reproduced with permission of LEADR.)

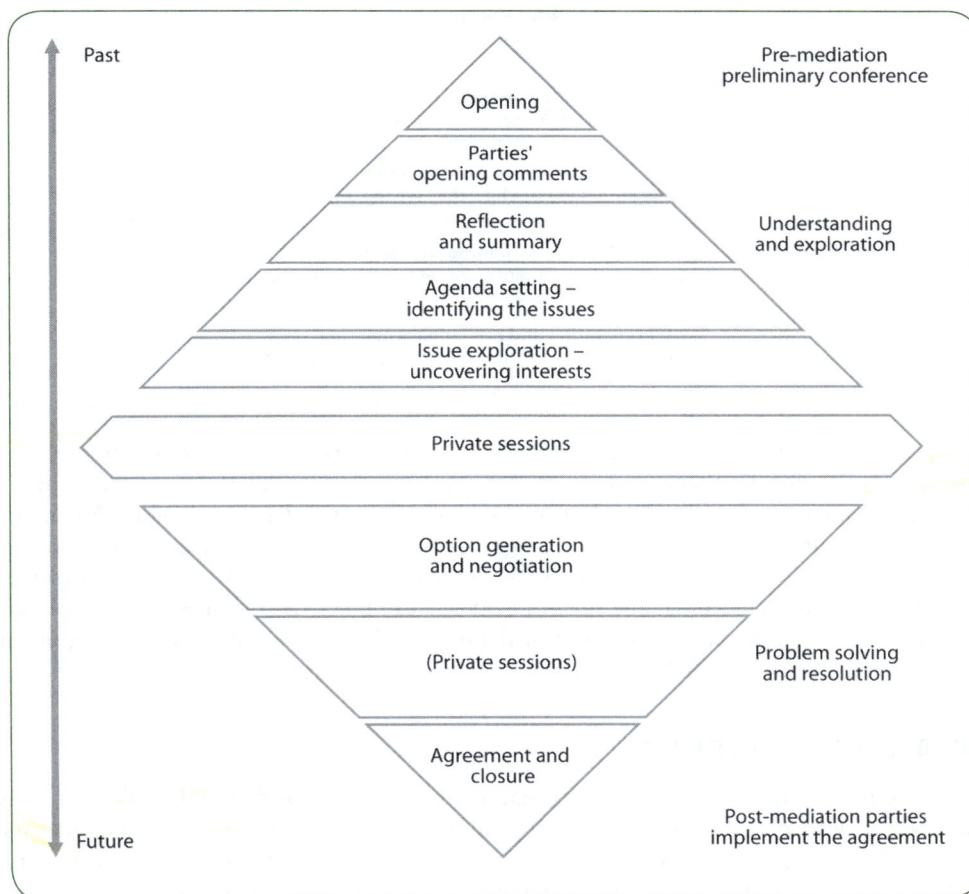

Figure 3.2:   Classical mediation model. (Adapted from D Spencer, *Principles of Dispute Resolution*, Thomson Reuters, Sydney, 2011, p 68.)

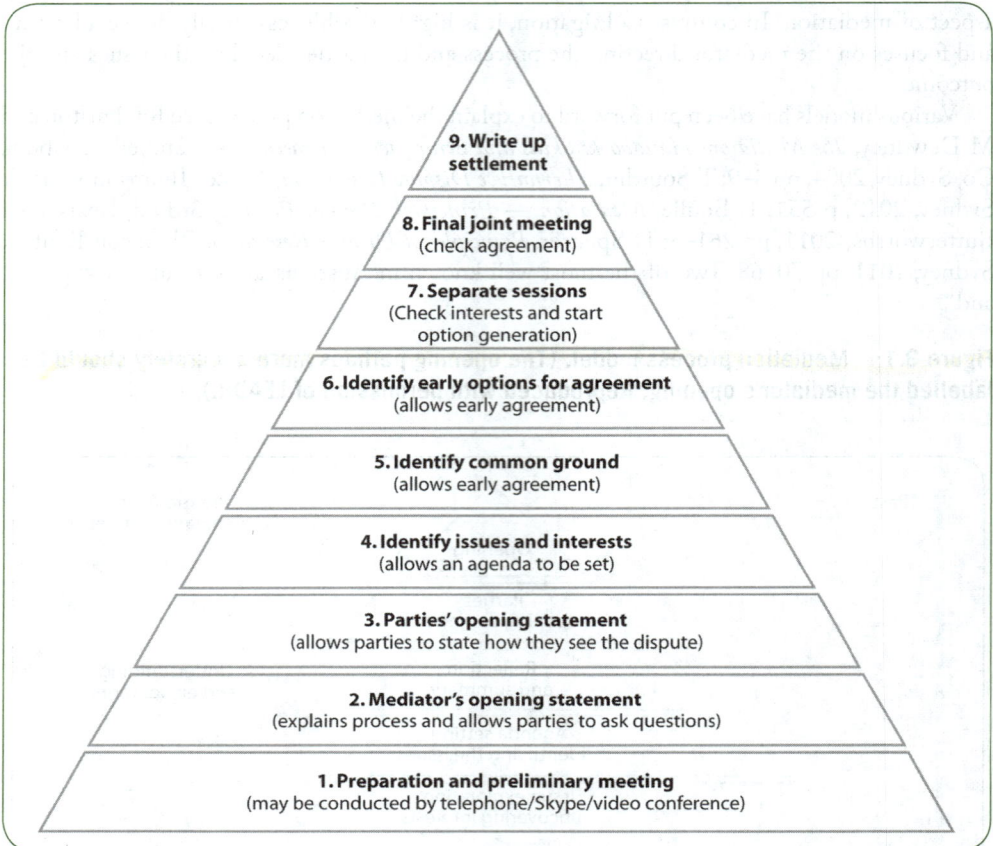

In the opening statement it should be noted that the parties are not bound by the rules of evidence. This enables them to say what they think is relevant. This is part of the cathartic process. The mediator listens. Brett Walker QC calls this the 'Haka step'. Most Australian mediators encourage parties — not their legal representatives — to deliver the narrative. Catharsis, 'getting it off your chest' makes parties more receptive to compromise. ADR preserves dignity as someone is listening. The rules of evidence can preclude this. It is an essential part of the process to be listened to. Australian mediators usually formalise the mediator agreement and review all documentation before commencing the first meeting.

Approaches to negotiation

3.4.4   A mediation is a facilitated negotiation. Therefore, to understand mediation, it is important to understand negotiation and the differences in negotiating styles and theories. A model for principled (also known as problem-solving or cooperative) negotiation was first developed at the Law School at Harvard University in the late 1970s, and later set out in the book by R Fisher and W Ury, *Getting To Yes: Negotiating Agreements Without Giving In*.

3.4.5E   **The Problem**
R Fisher and W Ury (with B Patton)
Getting to Yes: Negotiating an Agreement Without Giving In,
2nd ed, Arrow Books Ltd, London, 1997, pp 10–11.

The game of negotiation takes place at two levels. At one level, negotiation addresses the substance; at another it focuses — usually implicitly — on the procedure for dealing with the substance. The first negotiation may concern your salary, the terms of a lease, or a price to be paid. The second negotiation concerns how you will negotiate the substantive question: by soft positional bargaining, by hard positional bargaining, or by some other method. This second negotiation is a game about a game — a 'meta-game'. Each move you make within a negotiation is not only a move that deals with rent, salary or other substantive questions; it also helps structure the rules of the game you are playing. Your move may serve to keep the negotiations within an ongoing mode, or it may constitute a game-changing move.

This second negotiation by and large escapes notice because it seems to occur without conscious decision. Only when dealing with someone from another country, particularly someone with a markedly different cultural background, are you likely to see the necessity of establishing some accepted process for the substantive negotiations. But whether consciously or not, you are negotiating procedural rules with every move you make, even if those moves appear exclusively concerned with substance.

The answer to the question of whether to use soft positional bargaining or hard is 'neither'. Change the game. At the Harvard Negotiation Project we have been developing an alternative to positional bargaining: a method of negotiation explicitly designed to produce wise outcomes efficiently and amicably. This method, called *principled negotiation or negotiation on the merits*, can be boiled down to four basic points.

These four points define a straightforward method of negotiation that can be used under almost any circumstances. Each point deals with a basic element of negotiation, and suggests what you should do about it.

People: Separate the people from the problem.
Interests: Focus on interests, not positions.
Options: Generate a variety of possibilities before deciding what to do.
Criteria: Insist that the result be based on some objective standard.

3.4.6 Competitive negotiation is usually based upon positional bargaining, and is the style of negotiation traditionally adopted by lawyers. It typically involves each party (or their lawyer) making a high opening claim, and then attempting to persuade, coerce or manipulate the other party into making concessions. Depending upon the extent to which the parties want an outcome, the matter may become deadlocked, or the parties may move closer to each other through incremental concessions. The point of compromise will usually be in a predictable range around the middle of the parties' opening claims, although the party with the least bargaining power or most in need of an outcome will usually make greater concessions to get an agreement. It is a form of negotiation, which assumes that resources are limited and that a gain for one party entails a loss for the other: L Boulle, *Mediation: Principles, Process and Practice*, 3rd ed, LexisNexis Butterworths, Sydney, 2011, pp 46–8. See also discussion at 17.4.1–17.4.14.

In contrast, principled negotiation starts by focusing on the interests and needs that underlie the parties' positions. Positions are often described as the particular outcome a party wants, whereas interests and needs are the reason why the party seeks that outcome. In a principled negotiation, the process is directed towards generating options, identifying objective standards against which to test the results, and separating the people from the problem.

Competitive and cooperative negotiation are further discussed by Menkel-Meadow in the following extract:

3.4.7E   **Toward Another View of Legal Negotiation:**
The Structure of Problem Solving
C Menkel-Meadow, *Alternative Dispute Resolution*,
(ed M Freeman), Vol 26,
The International Library of Essays in Law & Legal Theory,
Dartmouth Publishing Co, England, 1995, pp 203–5, 279–80

Much of the legal negotiation literature emphasizes an adversarial model, implying an orientation or approach that focuses on 'maximizing victory'. This approach is based on the assumption that the parties desire the same goals, items or values. It is assumed that the parties must be in conflict and since they are presumed to be bargaining for the same 'scarce' items, negotiators assume that any solution is predicated upon division of the goods. In the language of game theorists, economists and psychologists, such negotiations become 'zero-sum' or 'constant-sum' games and the bargaining engaged in is 'distributive' bargaining. Simply put, in the adversarial case, each party wants as much as he can get of the thing bargained for, and the more one party receives, the less the other party receives. There is a 'winner' in the negotiation, determined by which party got more.

Legal negotiations, at least in dispute resolution cases, are marked by another adversarial assumption. Because litigation negotiations are conducted in the 'shadow of the law', that is in the shadow of the courts, the negotiators assume that what is bargained for are the identical, but limited, items a court would award in deciding the case. Typically, it is assumed that all that is bargained for is who will get the most money and who can be compelled to do or not to do something. Indeed, it may be because litigation negotiations are so often conducted in the shadow of the court that they are assumed to be zero-sum games.

The creative problem-solving approach ... depends on two structural components: (1) identifying the parties' underlying needs and objectives, and (2) crafting solutions, first by attempting to meet those needs directly, and second, by attempting to meet more of those needs through expanding the resources available. By utilizing such a framework for negotiations, the parties should recognise the synergistic advantage of an approach over the adversarial and manipulative strategies of zero-sum negotiations. Parties should be able to achieve solutions to disputes that would not have been possible in court-ordered resolutions. ...

3.4.8 Questions

1. G Tillett writes 'stress increases the risk of destructive conflict, which, in turn, increases the level of stress; therefore effective stress management is an integral part of conflict resolution': *Resolving Conflict: A Practical Approach*, 2nd ed, Oxford University Press, Melbourne, 1999, p 2. Do some procedural rules lead to 'destructive conflict'? Are these rules necessarily problematic or is it the way they are implemented that is 'destructive'? Is the discussion of stress management and conflict resolution one example of where ADR becomes difficult for the legal system because of its multidisciplinary foundations, or is it a point at which the law needs to grow? See R Fisher and D Shapiro, *Beyond Reason: Using Emotions as You Negotiate*, Viking, New York, 2005.

2. In discussing an approach to conflict, Tillett also writes:

> A collaborative cooperative approach should usually be attempted initially. By assuming cooperation, one can often promote cooperation. The type of approach can be changed (and quickly) if cooperation fails. Direct confrontation (including threat) usually provokes an aggressive response and should be avoided where possible.

How does this fit with the principles of competitive negotiation discussed above? Do you think lawyers and the adversarial setting accommodate an approach such as this? See A Schneider, 'Shattering Negotiation Myths: Empirical Evidence on the Effectiveness of Negotiation Style' (2002) 7 *Harvard Negotiation Law Review* 143.

3.4.9 Further reading

N Alexander and J Howieson, *Negotiation Strategy Style Skills*, 2nd ed, LexisNexis Butterworths, Sydney, 2010.

H Astor and C Chinkin, *Dispute Resolution in Australia*, 2nd ed, LexisNexis Butterworths, Sydney, 2002, pp 105–33, 135–45.

H J Brown and A L Marriott, 'Negotiation' in *ADR: Principles and Practice*, 3rd ed, Sweet & Maxwell, London, 2011.

R Charlton, *Dispute Resolution Guidebook*, LBC Information Services, Sydney, 2000, pp 13–33.

R Fells, 'Of Models and Journeys: Keeping Negotiation and Mediation on Track' (2000) 11 *ADRJ* 209.

T Sourdin, *Alternative Dispute Resolution*, 4th ed, Thomson Reuters, Sydney, 2012, pp 39–66.

FEATURES OF MEDIATION

3.5.1   While there is a general process to mediation, it is important to realise that, in practice, mediators and mediation schemes often demonstrate marked variations in how that process is implemented. For example, different opinions have been expressed on whether a mediator should meet privately with the parties, how best to generate options, and the extent to which a mediator should intervene to move a mediation forward if it reaches an impasse: see L Boulle, *Mediation — Principles, Process, Practice*, 3rd ed, LexisNexis Butterworths, Sydney, 2011, pp 254–63; R Field, 'Rethinking Mediation Ethics: A Contextual Method to Support Party Self-Determination' (2011) 22 *ADRJ* 8, 11–12; R Thirgood, 'Mediator Intervention to Ensure Fair and Just Outcomes' (1999) 10 *ADRJ* 142; B Wolski, 'Mediator Strategies: Winning Friends and Influencing People' (2001) 12 *ADRJ* 248. It is also suggested that different processes are appropriate for conducting single and co-mediation, and for 'evaluative', 'active', 'therapeutic' and 'transformative' mediation: see D Spencer, *Principles of Dispute Resolution*, Thomson Reuters, Sydney, 2011, pp 50–1; L Boulle and M Nesic, *Mediator Skills and Techniques: Triangle of Influence*, Bloomsbury Professional, Haywards Heath, England, 2010; M Noone, *Mediation, Essential Legal Skills Series*, Cavendish Publishing Ltd, London, 1996, pp 5–6; M Brenner, 'What is "Transformative" Mediation?' (2000) 11 *ADRJ* 155.

   Ultimately, because of the flexible and private nature of mediation, the differences in training and characteristics of mediators, and the range of disputes in which mediation is used, it is not surprising that these variations exist. However, it is still important that the mediation process incorporates certain fundamental qualities, and that practitioners understand these characteristics in more than a superficial way.

3.5.2   Noone identifies four principal characteristics of mediation. These are that the process is accessible, voluntary, confidential and facilitative: pp 7–8. While the importance of these characteristics is not disputed, they may not always be present in each and every mediation.

Accessibility

3.5.3   Mediation is accessible in a number of ways. First, it is available to resolve any kind of dispute at any stage. Mediation can and often must be conducted before any litigation has been initiated, but it is still available after trial and verdict if there is a need to settle issues that might give rise to appeal. Parties may use mediation to settle issues relating to legal rights or to deal with problems that do not give rise to legal rights. Second, mediation may be structured in a variety of ways to suit the needs of the parties and may take place in a variety of settings and even become a court-annexed process.

   Traditionally, direct participation in mediation has been an important part of the process of mediation: see C D Schneider, 'What it Means to Be Sorry: The Power of Apology in Mediation' (2000) 17 *Mediation Quarterly* 265. Compared to litigation, arbitration and other formal means of dispute resolution:

> ... [m]ediation is also promoted as being an accessible system in terms of prospective clients' abilities to understand the process and to represent themselves in the procedure. It is relatively devoid of formality, technicality and jargon and parties can participate in it with relative ease.

It has an undemanding familiarity and need not be an alienating experience. Developments in online mediation further enhance its accessibility for some parties: L Boulle, *Mediation: Principles, Process, Practice,* 3rd ed, LexisNexis Butterworths, Sydney, 2011, p 92.

Although the parties to mediation are almost always directly involved in deciding how their dispute will be resolved, direct involvement does not necessarily mean face-to-face negotiations. For example, face-to-face mediation is generally not available as part of industry-based ADR processes: see P O'Shea, 'Underneath the Radar: The Largely Unnoticed Phenomenon of Industry Based Consumer Dispute Resolution Schemes in Australia' (2004) 15 *ADRJ* 156 at 160. Instead, almost all complaints are resolved on the basis of written material passed between the parties on a 'shuttle mediation' basis. In reality, the extent of party participation is also affected by the approach and style of the mediator, the confidence and ability of the parties, the existence of power imbalances, time limitations and the presence of professional advisers, such as lawyers at the mediation: L Boulle, *Mediation: Principles, Process, Practice,* 3rd ed, LexisNexis Butterworths, Sydney, 2011, p 41.

It is also not the case that every dispute is appropriate for mediation, and it is generally accepted that some disputes are better suited to litigation: L Boulle, *Mediation: Principles, Process, Practice*, 3rd ed, LexisNexis Butterworths, Sydney, 2011, p 196; H Astor and C Chinkin *Dispute Resolution in Australia*, 2nd ed, LexisNexis Butterworths, Australia, 2002, pp 276–82; Access to Justice Advisory Committee, *Access to Justice: An Action Plan*, AGPS, Canberra, 1994, pp 292–3. The Australian Law Reform Commission has suggested factors that may indicate whether ADR processes are suitable or not: ALRC, *Managing Justice: A Review of the Federal Civil Justice System*, ALRC Report 89, 25 February 2000, para 6.62, pp 427–9. These include:

- when a definitive or authoritative resolution of the matter is required for precedential value;

- when the matter significantly affects persons or organisations who are not parties to the ADR processes;

- when there is a need for public sanctioning of conduct or where repetitive violations of statutes and regulations need to be dealt with collectively and uniformly;

- when a party is, or parties are, not able to negotiate effectively themselves or with the assistance of a lawyer; and

- in family law matters, where there is a history of family violence.

Even where mediation is appropriate, it is important to ensure that access to a service is available in practice. For example, there can be significant cost differences between schemes (such as community justice mediations) being offered at very low cost, and others (such as private mediations and private judging) that can be very expensive. It is therefore obvious that not all parties have access to the same mediation services: L Boulle, *Mediation: Principles, Process, Practice,* 3rd ed, LexisNexis Butterworths, Sydney, 2011, pp 92, 325. See also R Tomasic, 'Mediation as an Alternative to Adjudication — Rhetoric to Reality in the Neighbourhood Justice Movement' in Tomasic and Feeley (eds), *Common Neighborhood Justice: Assessment of an Emerging Idea*, Longman, New York, 1982.

Some government agencies interpret their duty to be a model litigant as fostering mediation. Some also adopt a policy of paying the mediator's fees, no matter what the outcome: See 3.10.1.

> **3.5.4   Further reading**
>
> L Boulle, *Mediation: Principles, Process and Practice*, 3rd ed, LexisNexis Butterworths, Sydney, 2011, pp 30–4, 357.
>
> C Menkel-Meadow, 'The Transformation of Disputes by Lawyers: What the Dispute Paradigm Does and Does Not Tell Us' (1985) *Journal of Dispute Resolution* 31.

Voluntary

3.5.5   M Noone, *Mediation, Essential Legal Skills Series*, Cavendish Publishing Ltd, London, 1996, p 7 describes the characteristic of voluntariness as follows:

> Mediation expects the parties to take responsibility for resolving their own dispute. Each party to the mediation must freely agree in their choice of mediator, freely choose to participate in the process and freely reach or not reach agreement. Both the mediator and the parties are free to withdraw from the process at any time without giving any reasons. The parties can never be forced to either continue a mediation or reach a settlement. The fact that mediation is voluntary may largely account for the success and finality of most agreements reached through the process, as psychologically, persons are much more likely to feel committed to an agreement which they have personally negotiated and agreed to accept than to one which is imposed upon them by an external judge or arbitrator.

On one view, parties become more likely to compromise because they have taken ownership of the matter. Another factor is that the mediator treats the parties with dignity by listening to them. Finally, making the opening statement results in a catharsis that leads to a susceptibility to compromise.

In the best-case scenario, it is true that the voluntary nature of mediation is an advantage of the process. Consensual participation has always been a fundamental assumption of mediation, and it is often stated as the basis for its effectiveness and legitimacy: H Astor, 'Rethinking Neutrality: A Theory to Inform Practice — Part 1' (2000) 11 *ADRJ* 73. Even when courts require parties to attend mediation, parties are not required to reach agreement or settlement. Instead, they are required, for example, to make a 'genuine effort to resolve the dispute by participating in dispute resolution' or to participate in the mediation 'in good faith': Family Law Rules 2004 r 1.05, Sch 1; Civil Procedure Act 2005 (NSW) s 27. In theory, any agreement or resolution of the dispute is entered into entirely voluntarily.

In reality, however, the idea of a truly voluntary process of mediation may be unrealistic. Parties may experience pressure to enter into mediation as a result of court referral, or 'because of inability to afford litigation or to withstand its accompanying pressures': B Wolski, 'Voluntariness and Consensuality: Defining Characteristics of Mediation?' (1997) 15(3) *Australian Bar Review* 213 at 219. Most parties engage in dispute resolution processes based upon a range of considerations including financial issues, legal advice, available information, desired outcome and availability of services. Their willingness to leave the process, just as to participate, is also determined by the other options available to them. As L Boulle, *Mediation: Principles, Process and Practice*, 3rd ed, LexisNexis Butterworths, Sydney, 2011 writes at p 69 [footnotes omitted]:

[3.22] The reality of widespread mandatory mediation in Australia raises several unresolved issues. The first concerns safeguards, standards and quality control in those situations in which parties are required to use the system against their wishes, partly addressed by the advent of the NMAS in 2008. Another concerns the question of whether it should be publicly funded or paid for by users. There is also a range of structural issues which arise where mandatory mediation is attached to courts or tribunals. In most of these situations compulsion to attend mediation has potential sanctions attached for non-attendance or failure to participate authentically, and this raises issues as to when and how they should be imposed. However, whatever the unresolved policy and practice issues mandatory mediation has come to stay in Australian dispute resolution culture, as it has in many overseas jurisdictions. While it eliminates voluntariness as a mediation value it leaves intact consensuality ...

Where participation in mediation is compelled or directed by a court, it has been suggested that governments have a 'special responsibility for the quality, integrity and accountability of the ADR processes provided': Access to Justice Advisory Committee, *Access to Justice: An Action Plan*, AGPS, Canberra, 1994, p 294. This suggestion has been included in the NADRAC charter. See also NADRAC, *The Resolve to Resolve: Embracing ADR to Improve Access to Justice in the Federal Jurisdiction*, September 2009. It is important that appropriate information be provided to the participants about the nature of the proceedings, and that care be taken to identify cases where mediation may not be appropriate: see discussion at 3.5.3 and 3.6.2.

3.5.6   Further reading

L Boulle, *Mediation: Principles, Process and Practice*, 3rd ed, LexisNexis Butterworths, Sydney, 2011, pp 63–9.

R Field, 'Using the Feminist Critique of Mediation to Explore "the Good, the Bad and the Ugly" Implications for Women of the Introduction of Mandatory Family Dispute Resolution in Australia' (2006) 40 *AJFL* 45.

R Ingleby, 'Compulsion is not the Answer' (1992) 27 *Australian Law News* 17.

M McIntosh, 'A Step Forward — Mandatory Mediations' (2003) 14(4) *ADRJ* 280.

A Robertson, 'Compulsion, Delegation and Disclosure: Changing Forces in Commercial Mediation' (2006) 9(3) *ADR Bulletin* 50.

P Venus, 'Court Directed Compulsory Mediation: Attendance or Participation?' (2004) 15(1) *ADRJ* 29.

P Wulf, 'Court-Ordered Mediation in the Planning and Environment Court: Does it Assist Self-represented Litigants?' (2007) *ADRJ* 49.

Confidential

3.5.7   M Noone, *Mediation, Essential Legal Skills Series*, Cavendish Publishing Ltd, London, 1996, pp 7–8 describes this characteristic as follows:

The parties to a mediation must be free to speak openly about their needs, interests and feelings. They must also be certain that what they say at all stages of the mediation will be treated as confidential and will be without prejudice, and will not be used as evidence in any later arbitral or judicial proceedings. The parties normally expressly agree that the mediator cannot later be called to give evidence about what occurred in the mediation and that all documents will be returned to the parties or destroyed at the conclusion of the mediation.

The issue of confidentiality is of central importance to an effective mediation as the parties must be 'able to reveal all relevant matters without an apprehension that the disclosure may subsequently be used against them': *AWA Ltd v Daniels* (1992) 7 ASCR 463 at 468 per Rogers CJ. The positive aspects of confidentiality are its potential to encourage frank and open discussions, to create an atmosphere conducive to cooperative decision-making, and to encourage trust between the parties and the mediator. Indeed, confidentiality is often one of the main features that draw parties to use mediation, particularly where the matters to be discussed are private or relate to confidential commercial issues.

In *Lukies v Ripley (No 2)* (1994) 35 NSWLR 283, Young J reviewed the *AWA* decisions and concluded that Rogers CJ had given 'some force to the view that it was public policy that statements made in mediation should not be admitted in evidence'. Young J said at 287:

> If parties have attempted to settle the whole or part of litigation and if they have agreed between themselves expressly or impliedly that they will not give in evidence any communication made during those discussions, then public policy makes those discussions privileged from disclosure in a court of law or equity.

There are a number of sources of protection of confidentiality in mediations. These include:

- procedural rules and statutes that relate only to mediations;
- evidentiary privilege that may have broader application;
- contractual terms between the parties entering into mediation;
- court orders;
- the mediator's adherence to voluntary standards of practice that require confidentiality; and
- public policy reinforced by common law.

The confidentiality provisions create overlapping, often redundant, realms of secrecy to encourage an atmosphere of trust during mediation. As discussed below, however, confidentiality in mediation is not absolute — and information learned during a mediation session may not necessarily be protected from subsequent disclosure in discovery or use at trial.

Statutory provisions that relate only to mediations

3.5.8   Where a particular matter is referred to mediation by a court or other relevant organisation, the extent of confidentiality may be provided for by legislation. This legislation takes two forms. The first creates a statutory privilege that applies in later proceedings if the mediation fails to reach a settlement. The second imposes a duty on the mediator to maintain the secrecy or confidentiality of information disclosed during a mediation.

An example of a statutory privilege for mediation sessions is found in s 28 of the Community Justice Centres Act 1983 (NSW). Section 28 provides that admissions made in the course of community mediation, and documents prepared for a mediation session are not later admissible in proceedings before a court or tribunal. The statutory privilege extends to the entire session, including the steps taken to arrange for mediation or the follow-up of a mediation session. See also Supreme Court of Queensland Act 1991 (Qld) s 114; Civil Procedure Act 2005 (NSW) s 30; General Rules of Procedure in Civil Proceedings 1996 (Vic) r 50.07(6); Supreme Court Act 1935 (SA) s 65; Alternative Dispute Resolution Act 2001 (Tas) s 10.

A number of statutes impose a duty of confidentiality on mediators. For example, the Community Justice Centres Act 1983 (NSW) s 29 precludes community justice centre mediators from commencing to exercise the functions of a mediator without first taking an oath of secrecy before a justice of the peace. Other statutes require mediators to maintain confidentiality, and describe a limited set of circumstances where a mediator may disclose information learned in connection with a mediation. For example, s 112 of the Supreme Court of Queensland Act 1991 (Qld) makes it an offence for a mediator to disclose information learned in a mediation session without a reasonable excuse. A 'reasonable excuse' is defined to include:

- if the disclosure is made with the parties' agreement;

- for statistical purposes where the identity of a person is not revealed, or likely to be revealed;

- for an inquiry or proceeding relating to an offence occurring in the course of the ADR process;

- for a proceeding based on a fraud alleged to relate to or to have occurred in the course of the ADR process; or

- to fulfil a statutory requirement.

Under the Civil Procedure Act 2005 (NSW) s 31, Mediation Act 1997 (ACT) s 10, and the Alternative Dispute Resolution Act 2001 (Tas) s 11, similar rules relating to mediator confidentiality apply. However, under these provisions there are additional exceptions that allow mediators to disclose information, if the mediator believes that disclosure is necessary to prevent or minimise danger to life or property.

Privilege

3.5.9 Certain categories of evidentiary privilege that apply in other contexts may also apply in mediations. These categories include the legal professional privilege, the privilege for evidence of settlement negotiations, also known as the 'without prejudice privilege', and the marital privilege.

Legal professional privilege applies to confidential communications between a party and his or her legal adviser made during the mediation process for the purpose of providing legal advice in relation to pending or contemplated litigation. As discussed at **13.5.1–13.5.15**, this privilege can be waived in certain circumstances, including where the legal advice is disclosed to the other party. As a result, for communications made during mediation to remain confidential, they must be covered by terms in the mediation agreement or be disclosed on a 'without prejudice' basis.

The privilege for evidence of settlement negotiations and the 'without prejudice' privilege apply to communications between parties to a dispute made for the purpose of negotiating a settlement, including the process of mediation: Evidence Act 1995 (Cth) s 131; *AWA Ltd v Daniels* (1992) 7 ACSR 463. Generally, settlement discussions and documents created for the purpose of settlement negotiations are excluded as a matter of public policy from being used as evidence if the matter goes to trial: *Lukies v Ripley (No 2)* (1994) 35 NSWLR 283; *Rush & Tompkins v Greater London Council* [1989] 1 AC 1280; see **13.5.25**. The privilege can, however, be overridden where it is being used to protect documents that should have been discovered in the ordinary course of litigation (*AWA Ltd v Daniels*); or where it is in the public interest to do so based on considerations of the welfare of a child (*Hutchings v Clarke* (1993) 113 ALR 709); or where there has been misleading and deceptive conduct in the mediation: *Quad Consulting Pty Ltd v David R Bleakley & Associates Pty Ltd* (1990) 98 ALR 659.

Marital privilege is a form of public policy privilege and arises in the context of marital conciliation or mediation. It only applies to the parties to the mediation, and applies regardless of whether other legal privileges apply. It can, however, be overridden where another public interest, such as the protection of a child, outweighs the interest in confidentiality: L Harman, 'Confidentiality in Mediation', in *Cases for Mediation*, ed G Raftesath and S Thaler, LBC Information Services in association with LEADR, 1999, pp 31–2.

Contractual terms

3.5.10   Where there are provisions in the mediation agreement or in a separate confidentiality agreement that information revealed during the process is confidential, these have effect as contractual terms to bind the parties. They will not usually bind a third party such as a mediator.

Court orders

3.5.11   Where a matter is referred to mediation by a court, the scope of confidentiality attaching to the mediation may be dependent upon the court order: Harman, p 32. In other cases, the outcome of the mediation may require the approval of a court or tribunal, in which case it is only the mediated settlement that is disclosed. See 3.9.1–3.9.21 for specific state provisions relating to court-annexed mediation.

Mediator standards and ethical codes

3.5.12   The mediator's duty of maintaining confidentiality is also found in various codes of practice that apply to mediators. Some of these are found in individual state statutes like the Mediation Act 1997 (ACT). Others are found in industry-based codes of practice. The most important of these is the National Mediator Accreditation Standards (NMAS). The Practice Standards for accredited mediators require mediators to respect the confidentiality of the participants: Australian National Mediation Practice Standards, *Confidentiality*, September 2007, s 6, viewed 24 April 2012, <http://www.leadr.com.au>. These standards, which began operating in January 2008, require a mediator not only to refrain from disclosing information obtained in a mediation, but also to take further steps to safeguard the confidentiality of the mediation. These steps include, among other things, clarifying the parties' expectations about confidentiality, and to ensuring that the mediator's office and administrative staff maintain confidentiality.

Confidentiality in Court-Sponsored Mediation: Disclose at Your Own Risk?
V Vann
(1999) 10 *ADRJ* 195

[While it would appear from the above discussion that the confidentiality of matters discussed in mediation is protected via various legal mechanisms, the extent of this protection is not absolute. In the following extract, V J Vann discusses the case of *Williamson v Schmidt* [1998] 2 Qd R 317, and demonstrates that the information disclosed during a mediation session is not completely shielded from being used in a later proceeding.]

Williamson v Schmidt: The Factual Background

The plaintiffs were all directors of a construction and earthmoving company which was wound up for insolvency in February 1992. Nine separate actions had previously been commenced against the directors claiming damages for insolvent trading pursuant to s 592 of the Corporations Law. Dowsett J ordered that all nine actions be heard together in April 1993, on the basis that the plaintiffs in each suit were effectively relying on the same facts. (These actions will be referred to as the *ANI v Williamson* matter.) Mediation followed, attended by the parties and their legal advisors. The respective merits of the claims and the defences of the company directors were discussed fully and frankly at that mediation. The financial positions of the individual directors were also discussed, and a statement of their positions was circulated. *ANI v Williamson* settled on 7 June 1996.

The defendant was a senior associate in the firm of Brisbane solicitors, and had acted on behalf of one of the plaintiffs in *ANI v Williamson*, including the mediation. Some months after the settlement, another firm employed him. That firm has also taken action against the company directors for insolvent trading on behalf of a client called Quarry Products Pty Ltd. The instructions dated back some four years, and it is unclear why that matter was not heard together with *ANI v Williamson*. It was alleged that through his attendance at the mediation of the *ANI v Williamson* matter, the defendant had 'acquired an array of knowledge going to issues ... identical to the issues' in the *Quarry Products Pty Ltd* action.

Confidentiality had been discussed at the commencement of *ANI v Williamson*. The mediator stated that nothing said during the mediation was to leave the room. A mediation agreement between the parties was signed. However, the former directors feared that the defendant had learned much about their positions during the mediation. They were disturbed that he was now acting as solicitor against them, in an action based on largely similar facts.

A Contractual Liability to Maintain Confidentiality?

Counsel for the directors argued that the defendant had signed the mediation agreement, and was therefore bound by its terms. These included an obligation to keep confidential all information and documents concerning the dispute which had been disclosed during mediation. Lee J had no difficulty in rejecting this proposition. The mediation agreement was drafted as one between the parties to the original litigation. The defendant was not one of those parties and signed only as solicitor for one of the parties. ...

What Use Can be Made of Information Obtained in Mediations? Policy Concerns and Case Law

There are opposing schools of thought as to what use should be made of information obtained during mediation. On the one hand, it is argued that no evidence as to what occurred should be used in subsequent proceedings by anyone, without consent. In short, mediation discussion should remain truly confidential. This is to encourage parties to approach mediation in the best possible settlement spirit. ...

The opposing view rejects the idea of a blanket cover for mediation discussions. It argues that although a subsequent tribunal should not consider any matter arising from a mediation, it should be open to a person to prove that information by other means. This is in the interests of the truth of the matter appearing and a just result being reached. It is argued that 'subsequent litigation should not be stifled by an over-rigid approach to mediation confidentiality' [L Boulle, 'Confidentiality and the Mediation Process' (1992) 3 *ADRJ* 272 at 274]. The policy interest in seeing such a result is said to outweigh the policy interests in protecting confidentiality at mediation as a means of promoting settlements. ...

Lee J began his discussion of these matters by considering the statutory scheme established under the Supreme Court of Queensland Act 1991 (Qld). He noted that the Act places an absolute prohibition on disclosures without consent being made by the ADR convenor, and applies a penalty for breach. The legislation places no such prohibition on other participants. Some restriction on information released by other than the convenor appears to have been provided by s 114(1). This provides that evidence of anything done or said, or an admission made during an ADR process, is only admissible in that dispute or other proceedings if all the parties to the dispute agree. Lee J thought this provision appeared to 'inhibit' a new party (or rather his solicitor who took part in the earlier mediation) from seeking to use such information in a later action. The section appeared to be sufficiently wide in its terms to cover 'all statements about the dispute oral or in writing, any discussions oral or in writing, or any documents made in the course of the mediation proceedings providing they are about the dispute' [p 331]. This protection, though, 'would not ... enable a party to hide documents which should be disclosed ... nor does it protect evidence of fraud during the ADR process.' [pp 331–2].

Certainly the non-admissibility provision provides some protection to the mediating parties. However, it appears as something of a toothless tiger. No penalty attaches to breach of the section, because it only deals with whether a matter is admissible or inadmissible. The provision does not deal with use by a participant or anyone else for purposes other than admissibility, nor does it address the question of whether matters disclosed can be proved by other means. It may be that the legislature had not considered the possibility of the need to restrict the use of confidential information disclosed in ADR processes in any other ways.

The absence of statutory guidance on the use of information led Lee J to a discussion of the *AWA v Daniels* debate. That case concerned an attempted mediation. At mediation, the plaintiff's solicitors had prefaced his comments with the statement, 'Upon the basis that what I am about to say is without prejudice and confidential to this mediation I state ...' [(1992) 7 ACSR 463 at 466] and then referred to the existence of certain documents. After the mediation failed, the defendant's solicitors issued a notice to produce those documents. Rolfe J of the Supreme Court of New South Wales then had to consider whether the notice to produce was an abuse of process as the existence of the documents had been disclosed in confidence and without prejudice. Rolfe J approached the matter by considering the similarities and differences between mediation and more traditional without prejudice discussions. Perhaps the greatest difference was that mediation required a greater degree of frankness and disclosure than other settlement discussions. On the other hand both mediation and traditional settlement discussions were similar in their goal of settlement. Rolfe J rejected what he called the 'sterilizing' argument, saying:

an absurd position could arise. A party could make admissions about all manner of things going directly to the issues in the proceedings and then object to any attempt by the other party to prove them at the hearing by legitimate means. That consequence would more completely stifle mediation and settlement negotiations than allowing matters to be proved by admissible evidence.

[200] Rolfe J applied *Field v Commissioner for Railways for New South Wales* [(1957) 99 CLR 285] and held that objective facts ascertained during the course of negotiations could be proved by direct evidence. The defendants could not prove any admission or statement made at mediation, but they could follow a line of inquiry learned about at mediation and later seek to prove that matter. They could not be excluded from leading the evidence merely because it had first come to their attention at mediation.

Later in the epic *AWA v Daniels* [(1992) 7 ACSR 463] proceedings, the trial judge Rogers CJ also considered how much evidence should be excluded following upon a mediation. He showed some discomfort with Rolfe J's view that discovering evidence in the course of mediation would not cause its immediate exclusion. ...

[201] [L]ee J preferred to adopt Rolfe J's approach to the problem. For the purposes of the Queensland mandated mediation scheme, it would appear that a participant cannot lead evidence of anything said or done at mediation in later proceedings. The participant is, though, entitled to prove by admissible evidence the existence of any fact or matter disclosed at mediation. ...

Statements made to the parties at the commencement of mediation that the mediation will be confidential, or that nothing said or done will leave the room, appear to be misleading at best. The parties to mediation disclose their information at their own risk. The danger is present both from the other party to the mediation and from any other participants. Even assuming the case that an obligation of confidentiality arose out of attendance at the mediation, and the confidential information was imparted, Quarry Products Pty Ltd were not prevented from proving any fact relevant to their suit by admissible means. This was so even if the fact was learned at the former mediation for the first time by the defendant who was not their solicitor. (footnotes omitted)

3.5.14 As this extract shows, although the communications, admissions and documents created for or during a mediation will be inadmissible in a later proceeding, the underlying facts or information is not put 'off limits' by being discussed in a mediation. If a party can prove facts by independent means, the disclosure of those facts during mediation will not insulate the information from production in discovery or from being adduced at trial. See also *789ten v Westpac* [2004] NSWSC 594.

Finally, the broader social policy aspects of confidential mediation must be recognised. Although there have always been private and confidential ways of resolving disputes, many cases that are now mediated might formerly have gone to trial. To that extent, the increased use of mediation represents a shift away from a public system of dispute resolution to a private one. There are potential costs to the increased use of private justice. In particular, it has been argued that confidentiality of mediations can result in whole areas of law being diverted away from the legal system with the result that legal doctrine is not developed and there is no opportunity for public awareness and comment on the issues involved: O Fiss, 'Against Settlement' (1984) 93 *Yale LJ* 1073; J Auerbach, *Justice Without Law*, OUP, New York, 1983, pp 112–13. It has been suggested that this is of particular concern with anti-discrimination complaints, medical malpractice cases and consumer complaints where there is a legitimate public interest in the facts or outcomes of cases: M Thornton, 'Equivocations of Conciliation: the Resolution of Discrimination Complaints in Australia' (1989) 52 *Mod L R* 733 at 737. Concern has also been raised that confidentiality can protect improperly conducted mediations and mediator misconduct. This has led to calls for reporting requirements of matters such as the outcome, if any, in mediations, and the process used: M Dewdney, 'The Partial Loss of Voluntariness and Confidentiality in Mediation' (2009) 20 *ADJR* 17 at 20; Access to Justice Advisory Committee, *Access to Justice: An Action Plan*, AGPS, Canberra, 1994, pp 298–9. However, no recommendations were made in this regard by the Australian Law Reform Commission in its review of the federal litigation system: *ALRC, Review of the Adversarial System of Litigation: Rethinking the Federal Litigation System*, Issues Paper 20, ALRC, Canberra, 1997.

3.5.15   Further reading

L Boulle, *Mediation: Principles, Process and Practice*, 3rd ed, LexisNexis Butterworths, Sydney, 2011, Ch 16.

H Gabrielle, 'Mediation Where a Party Represents the Australian Government: Are There Limits to Confidentiality?' (2006) 17 *ADRJ* 29.

B Meyerson, 'The Dispute Resolution Profession Should Not Celebrate the Vanishing Trial' (2005) 7 *Cardozo Journal of Conflict Resolution* 77.

T Sourdin, *Alternative Dispute Resolution*, 4th ed, Thomson Reuters, Sydney, 2012, [12.10], [12.20], [12.45].

Facilitative

3.5.16   M Noone, *Mediation, Essential Legal Skills Series*, Cavendish Publishing Ltd, London, 1996, p 8 describes the facilitative nature of mediation as follows:

Mediation is interest-based and problem-solving. It avoids position-based bargaining. The mediator's job is to assist the disputants in retaining control of their dispute whilst working out their own solution. In a neutral and impartial way, the mediator assists the parties by helping them:
(a)   identify each other's needs and underlying interests, whether these be substantive, procedural or psychological;
(b)   develop as many options as possible for settlement; and
(c)   reach an agreement which satisfies them and accommodates all their needs.

Most practitioners and writers agree that this feature of mediation is desirable, although it is not always present in practice. For example, it has been suggested that mediators vary in the extent to which they allow the parties to retain control of their dispute, and that there are good arguments to support both an interventionalist and a minimalist role by mediators: L Boulle, *Mediation: Principles, Process and Practice*, 3rd ed, LexisNexis Butterworths, Sydney, 2011, pp 37–43; S Roberts, 'Toward a Minimal Form of Alternative Intervention' (1986) 11 *Mediation*

Quarterly 25, 37; R Thirgood, 'Mediator Intervention to Ensure Fair and Just Outcomes' (1999) 10 *ADRJ* 142; B Wolski, 'Mediator Strategies: Winning Friends and Influencing People' (2001) 12 *ADRJ* 248.

Sir Laurence Street, one of Australia's leading mediators, expressed his view on how a mediation contributes to the resolution of a dispute as follows:

3.5.17E **Mediation — A Practical Outline**
Sir Laurence Street, 5th ed, 2003,
viewed 26 April 2012, <http://www.laurencestreet.com.au/pub02.htm>

5. How does a mediator contribute to the resolution of a dispute?

The mediator is an independent neutral who serves both parties jointly and each party separately. The object of the mediator is to inter-act with the parties (jointly and separately) and to move them through three stages:

- **the first stage** focuses on opening up **channels of communication** between the parties; see Channels of Communication on page 13;
- **the second stage** focuses on using the channels of communication to develop **bridges of understanding** between the parties of each other's perceptions of the dispute and their respective strengths and weaknesses;
- **the third stage** focuses on the **emergence of a negotiated resolution** of the dispute.

The first two stages — communication and understanding — overlap to a greater or lesser extent. Both are directed towards enabling the parties to discuss their dispute, to exchange views and thus more fully to understand their own and, very importantly, the other party's points of view. The mediator's task is to guide and facilitate the flow of communication and to assist the parties to gain a sufficient understanding of the total dispute and of each other's respective points of view that will enable each party to make a **dispassionate, objective appraisal** of the total dispute situation. This can be described as taking a 'helicopter overview' of the black–grey–white continuum that constitutes the dispute. See Annexure: The Symbolism of the Logo. From that point, **assisted by the guidance of the mediator,** the parties move towards a negotiated resolution of their dispute.

THE SYMBOLISM OF THE LOGO

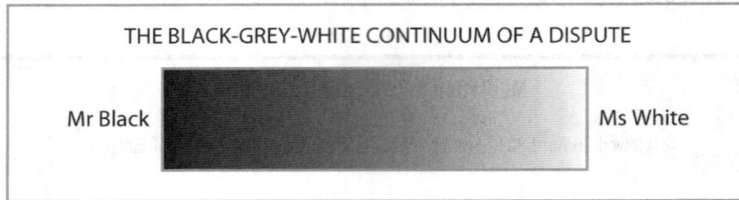

THE BLACK-GREY-WHITE CONTINUUM OF A DISPUTE

Mr Black　　　　　　　　　　　　　　　　　　　　Ms White

ONLY TWO OUTCOMES ARE POSSIBLE ON EACH ISSUE THROUGH AN EXTERNALLY **IMPOSED DECISION** AFTER ADVERSARIAL LITIGATION OR ARBITRATION

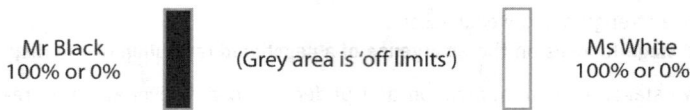

Mr Black
100% or 0%　　　　(Grey area is 'off limits')　　　　Ms White
100% or 0%

"At the end of a trial, at the end of an appeal, the judge will be compelled to reduce a complex slice of human experience, with all its subtlety, to what is, in essence, a one line answer. 'A wins; B loses'."

(The Hon Justice K M Hayne, High Court of Australia, 74 ALJ 377)

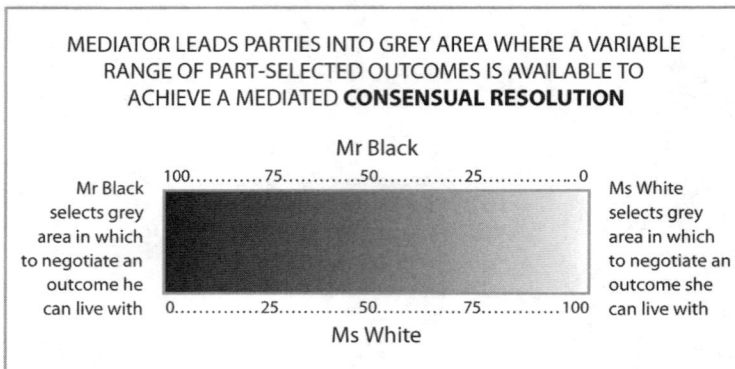

MEDIATOR LEADS PARTIES INTO GREY AREA WHERE A VARIABLE RANGE OF PART-SELECTED OUTCOMES IS AVAILABLE TO ACHIEVE A MEDIATED **CONSENSUAL RESOLUTION**

Mr Black

Mr Black
selects grey
area in which
to negotiate an
outcome he
can live with

100.............75.............50.............25.................0

0.............25.............50.............75.............100

Ms White
selects grey
area in which
to negotiate an
outcome she
can live with

Ms White

3.5.18   Although the distinction between the mediator controlling the process and the parties controlling the outcome is a useful starting point for understanding and explaining the mediation system, it is unclear and misleading in a number of respects. As L Boulle, and M Nesic, *Mediation: Principles, Process and Practice*, 2nd ed, Butterworths, London, 2001, pp 20–1 explain:

(a)   Process can never be completely separate from substance. Many conventional 'procedural' interventions by mediators can affect matters of substance, for example, when they assist the parties to develop an agenda, reinterpret the parties' dialogue or obstruct (or fail to obstruct) a particular negotiating behaviour.

(b)   Sometimes the practice of mediation involves significant interventions on matters of content. Thus parties might select a certain mediator in the expectation that, without imposing a decision, he or she will guide them to an outcome which is reasonable and within the normal range of outcomes for a particular problem, based on his or her expertise in the area of the dispute.

(c)   The style of some mediators may involve direct and indirect interventions into the content of the dispute. Thus through a recurrent style of questioning, or merely through expressive body language, the mediator may be having a significant influence on the substance of the dispute, again without directly recommending a particular course of action or imposing a final decision.

(d)   In some cases, mediators share control of the process with the parties, by inviting their opinion or accepting their decisions on matters of organisation, changes in procedure, adjournments, and the like. Mediators do not, in all respects, control the process alone.

L Boulle, *Mediation: Principles, Process and Practice*, 3rd ed, LexisNexis Butterworths, Sydney, 2011, pp 35–6 [footnotes omitted] further explains:

> Some approaches to mediation define the system in terms of a distinction between its process and its content. It is claimed that mediators do, or should, control a process of decision-making while the parties are, and should be, responsible for the content of what is discussed and the substantive outcomes which emerge from the process. In a commercial leasing dispute, in this view, the mediator assists lessor and lessee to prepare for the meeting, to communicate with each other, to negotiate productively and to record outcomes, but decisions on the valuations, rentals and outgoings are made by the parties themselves. To express it metaphorically, the mediator provides a framework within which parties construct and build according to their own design. This conception is found in early Australian literature on mediation, in mediator codes of conduct and occasionally in court references. It is also reflected in the 2008 NMAS as follows:
>
> > Mediation processes are primarily facilitative processes. The mediator provides assistance in managing a process which supports the participants to make decisions about future actions and outcomes.

> The 'process' focus emanates in part from philosophical assumptions about mediation. A mediator function restricted to process is compatible with the principle of party self-determination, referred to in the following chapter, and the presumed entitlement of parties to make choices about their own personal and business issues rather than have professionals telling them, in however disguised a form, what to do. This contrasts with other dispute resolution systems in which professionals can engage in the substantive content of disputes, such as case appraisal, arbitration and expert determination. The mediation emphasis on process control by the mediator and party control of the content underlies other claimed values such as the neutrality of mediators and the system's potential for party empowerment.

There has also been considerable discussion on the issues of mediator neutrality, impartiality, independence and the extent to which they are possible in practice: H Astor, 'Rethinking Neutrality: A Theory to Inform Practice — Part 1' (2000) 11 *ADRJ* 73 at 74–81; L Boulle, *Mediation: Principles, Process and Practice*, 3rd ed, LexisNexis Butterworths, Sydney, 2011, pp 71–80. Ideally, a neutral and impartial mediator does not have a direct personal or professional association with the parties and acts even-handedly, fairly and without bias towards the parties. The term 'neutrality' is sometimes interpreted as requiring mediators not to favour one party over another or one solution over another. It is particularly in relation to this vision of strict neutrality that there has been uncertainty and debate: Is it possible or desirable for a mediator to maintain strict neutrality?

Conduct that might be regarded as partial includes focusing on one party more than the other and expressing a personal opinion on the merits, even when asked to do so by the parties. Research findings do not address the specific issue of how a mediator remains neutral, particularly where the merits of a dispute heavily favour one side over another or where substantial power imbalance exists between the parties.

Astor argues that much of the debate that has taken place on neutrality is misguided and unhelpful: 'Rethinking Neutrality: A Theory to Inform Practice — Part 1' (2000) 11 *ADRJ* 73. She suggests that it will always be difficult to define what it means in practice to be neutral, as neutrality itself is a problematic concept. Mediators have natural biases, likes and dislikes. It may be easier for the mediator to empathise with one party than the other. It may not be humanly possible to maintain strict neutrality. Instead, she argues, mediators should abandon the task of defining strict neutrality and concentrate on maximising the parties' control over the resolution of the dispute. She explains at 145:

> … [F]ocusing on maximising party control has many advantages. It does not demand scrutiny of a personal quality of a mediator. Instead, it asks questions about what the mediator is doing to achieve a goal. The focus is on a task, the performance of which can be improved. … Maximising party control seems also to describe more accurately what good mediators do in practice. [It] also better explains the diversity of mediation practice, deals better with the challenge of power relations in mediation and is responsive to the dynamic, fluid and changing nature of the interactions in mediation.

3.5.19   Further reading

H Astor, 'Mediator Neutrality: Making Sense of Theory and Practice' (2007) 16 *Social Legal Studies* 221.

L Boulle, *Mediation: Principles, Process and Practice*, 3rd ed, LexisNexis Butterworths, Sydney, 2011, [3.25]ff, [9.21].

R Field, 'The Theory and Practice of Neutrality in Mediation' (2003) 22(1) *The Arbitrator and Mediator* 79.

T Sourdin, *Alternative Dispute Resolution*, 4th ed, Thomson Reuters, Sydney, 2012, [3.05], [3.10], [3.15], [3.50], [3.60], [3.115], [7.25].

A Taylor, 'Concepts of Neutrality in Family Mediation: Contexts, Ethics, Influence and Transformative Process' (1997) 14 *Mediation Quarterly* 215.

OTHER ISSUES WITH MEDIATION
National Mediator Accreditation System

3.6.1   Mediators come from diverse educational and cultural backgrounds and may take different approaches to the mediation process. They may be lawyers, preachers, social workers, teachers, doctors, scholars, homemakers, counsellors, or none of the above. Traditionally, there has been no barrier to entry into practice. Mediators gained clients based on their skill, connections, and reputation for integrity and results. However, as courts have begun requiring parties to attend mediation as a condition precedent to litigation, a need for standards of practice has been recognised.

To ensure the suitable quality of practitioners involved in family dispute resolution under the Family Law Act 1975, regulations were enacted for the registration of family dispute practitioners. These require a minimum standard for education, training and experience and ongoing professional development activity: see Family Law Regulations 1984 (Cth) reg 83. The regulations were fully implemented on 1 July 2009.

Mediators outside the family dispute resolution realm are governed by the National Mediator Accreditation System (NMAS), which came into effect in January 2008. As Sourdin observes at p 471, the NMAS scheme:

> ... has established a framework that is directed at enabling the largely self-regulated mediation area to manage issues relating to credentialing and quality improvement into the future in a coherent manner.
>
> The NMAS scheme has three tiers:
> (1)   a system of accreditation which involves approval and practice requirements for mediators (the NMAS *Australian National Mediator Standards: Approval Standards* and *Practice Standards* ...); and
> (2)   a self-recognition framework for recognized mediation accreditation bodies (RMABs) ... these include professional bodies, mediation agencies, courts, tribunals and other entities;
> (3)   an implementation body ... the Mediators Standards Board (MSB) that was officially launched in 2010.
> The MSB has been established to fully implement the NMAS. It is also involved in developing complaints handling processes, the improvement of standards, the governance and funding of the MSB ...

The NMAS program also monitors and reviews mediation practice and deals with complaints. See further information, viewed 30 April 2012, <http://www.msb.org.au/mediator-standards>. It is expected that a national, uniform program of mediator accreditation will lead to higher standards of practice and increased public confidence in mediation as a process for resolving disputes. See also T Sourdin, *Alternative Dispute Resolution*, 4th ed, Thomson Reuters, Sydney, 2012, [3.35], [3.55], [3.65], [3.70].

Power imbalances

3.6.2   One of the most written about issues in mediation has been the effect of serious power imbalances between the parties upon the appropriateness and effectiveness of mediation. As mediation is essentially a consensual process, it has been suggested that there is a real danger that the outcome of the process will simply reflect the power relationship between the parties themselves: see H Astor and C Chinkin, *Dispute Resolution in Australia*, 2nd ed, LexisNexis Butterworths, Sydney, 2002, pp 160–163; O Fiss, 'Against Settlement' (1984) 93 *Yale LJ* 1073 at 1073–90. In particular, there may be a risk that the less powerful party in mediation will accept a less satisfactory outcome than would have been decided by a neutral third party, or may have such an outcome forced upon them by a stronger party. See L Boulle, *Mediation: Principles, Process and Practice*, 3rd ed, LexisNexis Butterworths, Sydney, 2011, [6.24]–[6.33].

The mediator's role does not include guaranteeing a 'fair' outcome for both parties. The mediator facilitates the parties' self-determination. Therefore, where there are power imbalances, or where one party is willing (for whatever reason) to accept an 'unfair' outcome, mediation may produce 'unfair' results. It has been said, however, that 'the fairness of an outcome, like beauty, is in the eye of the beholder': T Sourdin, *Alternative Dispute Resolution*, 4th ed, Thomson Reuters, Sydney, 2012, [3.75], p 90. When parties feel that the process is fair and feel that they have been allowed to speak and be heard (especially in their opening statement), they may be satisfied with both the process and the outcome — even if the parties do not reach agreement: Sourdin [3.75], p 91.

On the other hand, if mediation were to consistently assist some parties in bullying others, it could hardly merit a place in the justice system. Commentators have suggested that some kinds of power imbalance make mediation inappropriate. For example, mediation has been described as 'problematic' in situations involving domestic abuse or violence, and in cases such as anti-discrimination cases and environmental rights disputes where an individual complainant may face the arrayed forces of developers, big business and government: L Boulle, pp 198–202. Especially in cases where parties are unable to communicate, or where they may be subject to retaliation or abuse outside the mediation room, mediation may be inappropriate.

It is important, however, to keep the issue of power imbalance in perspective. Some degree of power imbalance will exist in most mediations. It cannot be avoided and does not mean mediation is necessarily inappropriate. This is especially true because the weaker party in the mediation may also be the one with fewer resources (both personal and financial) to spend on litigation. Moreover, the traditional justice system is not free of bias in favour of the rich and powerful. The outcome of litigation often favours the party with greater ability to litigate over the party with the more righteous cause. Because it may be faster, cheaper and less complex than traditional litigation, mediation provides an avenue for assisted dispute resolution to people who might otherwise have none. The goal of empowering people to resolve their own disputes has been a major impetus behind the growth of mediation and other alternatives to traditional litigation.

Further, it is not always immediately apparent where the power in a particular relationship lies. The reality of power imbalance is often elusive. When parties sit down around a table and enter into a problem-solving negotiation, multiple types of power may come into play. The interaction may be complex and dynamic. B Mayer, 'The Dynamics of Power in Mediation and Negotiation' (1987) 16 *Mediation Quarterly* 75 at 78 summarises some of the most important types of power to include:

(1) **Formal authority** — The power that derives from a formal position within a structure that confers certain decision-making prerogatives. This is the power of a judge, an elected official, a CEO, a parent, or a school principal.

(2) **Expert/information power** — The power that is derived from having expertise in a particular area or information about a particular matter.

(3) **Associational power** (or referent power) — The power that is derived from association with other people with power.

(4) **Resource power** — The control over valued resources (money, materials, labour or other goods and services). The negative version of this power is the power to deny needed resources or to force others to expend them.

(5) **Procedural power** — The control over the procedures by which decisions are made, separate from the control over the decisions themselves (for instance, the power of a judge in a jury trial).

(6) **Sanction power** — The ability (or perceived ability) to inflict harm or to interfere with a party's ability to realise his or her interests.

(7) **Nuisance power** — The ability to cause discomfort to a party, falling short of the ability to apply direct sanctions.

(8) **Habitual power** — The power of the status quo that rests on the premise that it is normally easier to maintain a particular arrangement or course of action than to change it.

(9) **Moral power** — The power that comes from an appeal to widely held values. Related to this is the power that results from the conviction that one is right.

(10) **Personal power** — The power that derives from a variety of personal attributes that magnify other sources of power, including self-assurance, the ability to articulate one's thoughts and to understand one's situation, one's determination, endurance and so forth.

See also B Mayer, *Staying with Conflict: A Strategic Approach to Ongoing Disputes*, Jossey-Bass, 2009; C Baylis and R Carroll, 'Power Issues in Mediation' (2005) 7(8) *ADR Bulletin* 1.

3.6.3 It is generally accepted that mediators and other ADR practitioners need to be aware of the different forms of power and the ways in which they can manifest and be used by the parties. The Australian National Mediator Standards: Practice Standards, 4 — Power Issues, for example, requires:

> Mediators shall have completed training that assists them to recognise power imbalance and issues relating to control and intimidation and take appropriate steps to manage the mediation process accordingly.

> For the most recent standards, see <http://www.msb.org.au>.

Mediation cannot, and does not, rearrange the reality of the power relationship between parties. What it may be able to do is provide mediators who are sensitive to such imbalances, procedures and strategies, which help to reduce these imbalances in the communications and negotiations between the parties, and allow the parties to move to terms mutually acceptable for the resolution of their differences. Appropriate strategies might include ensuring proper information is brought to the proceedings; allowing all parties a proper opportunity to express their views; preventing abusive, threatening or harassing behaviour; agreeing upon rules of behaviour that are based upon respect; and suggesting each party have access to independent legal advice: H J Brown and A L Marriott, *ADR Principles and Practice*, 3rd ed, Sweet & Maxwell, 2011. Ultimately, however, a mediator must make a judgment call if the power imbalance is substantial. If, for example, a mediator believes one party is unwilling or unable to fully participate in the process, the mediation should be terminated: L Boulle, *Mediation: Principles, Process and Practice*, 3rd ed, LexisNexis Butterworths, Sydney, 2011, p 196.

In some cases, parties redress the balance of power by retaining counsel. There are instances where the less powerful party retains senior counsel, but the more powerful party does not. This practice can often redress the power balance.

3.6.4 Further reading

J Agustí-Panareda, 'Power Imbalances in Mediation: Questioning Some Common Assumptions' (2004) 59 *Dis Res J* 24.

D Bagshaw, 'Language, Power and Mediation' (2003) 14 *ADRJ* 130.

M Greenberg, 'Mediating Massacres: When "Neutral, Low-Power" Models Of Mediation Cannot and Should Not Work' (2003) 19 *Ohio Journal of Dispute Resolution* 185.

Enforcement of agreements to mediate

3.6.5   Agreements to mediate can either be written into a contract between the parties or entered into after a dispute has arisen. An important issue is whether these agreements can be enforced, because the law has been reluctant to uphold agreements to agree and agreements to negotiate. This issue of enforceability was directly considered in several decisions, summarised below by I Nosworthy.

3.6.6E   **Improving Arbitration and Mediation: Creative Approaches in the 21st Century**
Ian Nosworthy
(2005) 21 *BCL* 166 at 170–1

Drive for certainty

Probably the most prominent early decision in this area was *Hooper Bailie Associated Ltd v Natcon Group Pty Ltd* (1992) 28 NSWLR 194.

Hooper Bailie was the contractor for certain portions of the work on the new Parliament House building. It subcontracted some of the work to Natcon. Disputes arose and they were submitted to arbitration. By letter dated 16 February 1990, Hooper Bailie wrote to Natcon suggesting that the parties undergo conciliation prior to commencing arbitration with a view to narrowing the issues in dispute and consequently shortening the arbitration time. The letter called for, inter alia, attendance before a conciliator, the giving of evidence and the making of submissions and rulings or determinations. Following an exchange of information between the parties relating to the conciliation, attempts at conciliation occurred. Before there was any resolution, Natcon sought to proceed with the arbitration. Hooper Bailie sought to stay the arbitration proceedings for as long as Natcon refused to participate in the conciliation.

Hooper Bailie submitted that there came into existence a legally binding agreement — either as a variation of the arbitration agreement or standing independently or pursuant to an estoppel — that the matters identified in the letter would be conciliated, and that the arbitration would not resume until the conciliation had concluded. Hooper Bailie further submitted that it was an implied term of the agreement that the parties 'would take all reasonable steps to endeavour to resolve the conciliation issues by discussion, consideration and agreement'.

Giles J (at 203, 205, 210) held that the agreement was enforceable in that the parties agreed to conciliate the issues identified in the letter, and that the arbitration would not resume until the conciliation had concluded. He held that an agreement to conciliate is not to be likened to an agreement to agree. Such an agreement is enforceable in principle if the conduct required of parties for participation in the process is sufficiently certain.

At 206 Giles J said:

> What is enforced is not co-operation and consent but participation in a process from which co-operation and consent might come.

He concluded that the procedure outlined in the letter was sufficiently certain to be given legal effect.

The court found it unnecessary to decide, or to express any view on, whether there was an implied term that Hooper Bailie and Natcon should participate in the conciliation in good faith, simply because Natcon had declined to participate in the process at all.

The second significant authority is *Elizabeth Bay Developments Pty Ltd v Boral Building Services Pty Ltd* (1995) 36 NSWLR 709.

In 1993, Elizabeth Bay entered into two written contracts: a construction management contract and a building contract with Boral involving the construction of a residential subdivision on the central coast of New South Wales.

The relevant mediation clauses of both contracts stated:

> The parties agree to first endeavour to settle the dispute or difference by mediation administered by the Australian Commercial Disputes Centre (ACDC).

In mid-1994, Boral ceased its involvement in the project. Elizabeth Bay treated the cessation as a repudiation and terminated the contracts. It claimed damages for breach. Boral invoked the mediation clauses in the contracts and sought a stay of the proceedings pending mediation. Elizabeth Bay declined to participate and asserted that the agreement was not sufficiently certain to be given effect. Giles J declined to stay the proceedings, saying at 715:

> At first sight the guidelines did not take up ACDC's form of mediation agreement, since although para 6 of the guidelines spoke of terms which "are" consistent with the guidelines it did not otherwise identify that form and the form was not wholly consistent with the guidelines. In para 6 and elsewhere the guidelines contemplated some kind of agreement, but its terms were left to be settled. If this be so, then by the incorporation of the guidelines the parties had agreed (inter alia) to sign mediation agreements the terms of which were not settled beyond the necessity that they be consistent with the guidelines. The agreements to mediate were open-ended, indeed unworkable because the process to which the parties had committed themselves would come to an early stop when, prior to the mediation, it was asked what the parties had to sign and the question could not be answered.
>
> No doubt it would be possible to prepare an agreement consistent with the guidelines, but there would be an infinite combination of provisions which would not be inconsistent with the guidelines, and for this reason alone the agreement of the parties fell down for lack of certainty in the process which they should follow in their mediation.

This decision was followed by *Aiton Australia Pty Ltd v Transfield Pty Ltd* (1999) 153 FLR 236. Aiton and Transfield contracted for Aiton to conduct certain works on a construction project. Disputes arose and Aiton commenced proceedings against Transfield for damages. Transfield sought a stay of proceedings on the basis that the dispute resolution procedures provided for by the contract had not been carried out prior to the commencement of proceedings. In support of its motion, Transfield argued, inter alia, that the relevant mediation clause lacked sufficient certainty to be given legal effect because (a) there were no provisions dealing with the remuneration to be paid to the mediator if agreed or appointed; (b) what was to happen if one or both of the parties did not agree with the fees proposed by any such mediator; and (c) what was to happen if the nominated or agreed mediator declined appointment for any reason.

Einstein J held (at 246) that:

> The Court will not adjourn or stay proceedings pending alternative dispute resolution procedures being followed, if the procedures are not sufficiently detailed to be meaningfully enforced.

He added (at 252) that, in his opinion, the minimum requirements applying to a dispute resolution clause, not just to mediation, included the following:

> It must be in the form described in *Scott v Avery* [(1856) 5 HL Cas 811]. That is, it should operate to make completion of the mediation a condition precedent to commencement of court proceedings.
>
> The process established by the clause must be certain. There cannot be stages in the process where agreement is needed on some course of action before the process can proceed because if the parties cannot agree, the clause will amount to an agreement to agree and will not be enforceable due to this inherent uncertainty. The administrative processes for selecting a mediator and in determining the mediator's remuneration should be included in the clause and, in the event that the parties do not reach agreement, a mechanism for a third party to make the selection will be necessary.
>
> The clause should also set out in detail the process of mediation to be followed — or incorporate these rules by reference. These rules will also need to state with particularity the mediation model that will be used.

As a result of these decisions it is clear that the two main issues that affect enforceability of ADR agreements are whether the clause is drafted with sufficient certainty and whether it includes in it an obligation to use 'good faith'. These issues have subsequently been discussed in both cases and commentary.

Following *Hooper Bailie* and *Elizabeth Bay*, Angyal stated the following guidelines on enforceability of agreements to mediate and certainty.

3.6.7E **The Enforceability of Agreements to Mediate**
R S Angyal, *Cases for Mediation,*
ed G Raftesath and S Thaler, LBC Information Services
in association with LEADR, 1999, pp 7–9

- *Hooper Bailie* makes it clear that equity is unlikely to order specific performance of an agreement to mediate, because supervision of performance would be impossible. Hence an agreement that merely imposes a positive obligation to mediate is unlikely to be enforceable.
- It follows that, to be enforceable, agreements to mediate should make concluding the mediation a condition precedent to commencing an arbitration or litigation. In other words, the agreement to mediate, to be enforceable, must be in *Scott v Avery* form (see (1856) 5 HL Cas 811; 10 ER 1211). The Court can then enforce the agreement (as in *Hooper Bailie*) by staying an arbitration or litigation commenced in breach of an agreement to mediate.
- Above all, *Hooper Bailie* and *Elizabeth Bay* demonstrate the need to specify what it is the parties are to do, and to specify it with certainty, in order to minimise the risk of the agreement being unenforceable. While of course the agreement cannot require the parties in a substantive sense to agree on how to resolve a dispute that arises between them, it should in a procedural sense define the steps they are to take to attempt to resolve it by mediation.
- There should not be stages in the process where the parties need to agree on a course of action before the process can proceed further. If there are, the agreement risks being characterised as an unenforceable agreement to agree. Alternatively, if the parties reach that stage and cannot agree on what to do next, the agreement then is spent: *TA Mellen Ltd v Allgas Energy Ltd* (unreported, Supreme Court of Queensland, Mackenzie J, 16 July 1992).
- An agreement to mediate thus should set out the steps to be followed in the conduct of the mediation, or it should clearly incorporate reference rules or guidelines that themselves do this. The rules or guidelines should state with particularity the process the parties are to follow.

Either the agreement or the rules/guidelines should state that, if the parties do not agree on a mediator, a nominated third party is to select the mediator and determine the mediator's remuneration. ...

3.6.8 The courts require that dispute resolution clauses include detail on all matters important to conducting the ADR process. In *State of New South Wales v Banabelle Electrical Pty Ltd* (2002) 54 NSWLR 503, three construction contracts specified that should a dispute arise, an expert was to be appointed that was agreed to 'between the parties or if they fail to agree, a person nominated by the person prescribed in the Annexure'. There was no person prescribed in the annexure and Einstein J found the term void for uncertainty because, among other reasons, the nomination mechanism in the second part of the clause was considered an essential machinery provision giving the entirety of the clause its character and certainty.

In *The Heart Research Institute Ltd v Psiron Ltd* [2002] NSWSC 646, Einstein J again found a dispute resolution clause void for uncertainty. In this case, a research contract specified that, in the event that a dispute could not be resolved through other specified means, the dispute was to be submitted to expert determination conducted in accordance with the Australian Commercial Disputes Centre, *Expert Determination Guidelines*. In fact, the guidelines required the execution of an expert determination agreement the terms of which were to be consistent with the guidelines. Einstein J found the clause in the contract void for uncertainty as the terms of the guidelines and the appointment agreement were not consistent with each other and the guidelines did not precisely identify which terms were to be included in the appointment agreement. Similarly, in the recent case of *Dualcorp Pty Ltd v Remo Constructions Pty Ltd* [2008] NSWSC 749, the New South Wales Supreme Court confirmed that it will not enforce alternative dispute resolution clauses unless it is satisfied that the proposed process is complete and appropriate.

Spencer has noted that the requirement that all matters important to the operation of the dispute resolution be specified at the time of drafting the contract is potentially inconsistent with the nature of ADR: D Spencer, 'To What Degree of Certainty Must a Dispute Resolution Clause be Drafted?' (2003) 14 *ADRJ* 153. Spencer states:

> ... [D]rafters are caught between 'the devil and the deep blue sea' when it comes to drafting dispute resolution clauses in contracts. They quite rightly seek to give the parties the freedom to determine the procedures to be [162] followed should a dispute arise under the contract. However, they must take account of the courts' views on enforcing the uncertainty rule of contract law. If courts did not enforce such a rule then parties would be breaching contracts regularly because they would not be sure of the procedures they should be following under a poorly drafted contract that leaves performance open to wide interpretation. ...
>
> [163] [However] Einstein J's warning about certainty in drafting dispute resolution clauses becoming something akin to litigation is a cogent warning that needs to be taken seriously. A complex set of procedures that wrests control from the disputants themselves is an anathema to the very concept of dispute resolution. The benefits of dispute resolution, particularly from the courts' perspectives, are its simplicity, cost efficiency and speed that together are said to relieve the pressure on an overburdened court system. If because of the uncertainty rule in contract law, such processes become bogged down in complex and lengthy procedures, its benefit to the court system and the community at large will begin to disappear.

Good faith

3.6.9   Generally courts have been reluctant to enforce agreements to mediate in good faith. As stated in *Walford v Miles* [1992] 2 AC 128 at 138:

> ... [T]he concept of a duty to carry on negotiations in good faith is inherently repugnant to the adversarial position of the parties when involved in negotiations. Each party to the negotiations is entitled to pursue his (or her) own interest, so long as he avoids making misrepresentations. To advance that interest he must be entitled, if he thinks it is appropriate, to threaten to withdraw from further negotiations or to withdraw in fact, in the hope that the opposite party may seek to reopen the negotiations by offering him improved terms.

See also Giles J in *Elizabeth Bay Developments Pty Ltd v Boral Building Services Ltd* (1995) 36 NSWLR 709. However, in *Aiton Australia Pty Ltd v Transfield Pty Ltd* (1999) 153 FLR 236, Einstein J thought there was not necessarily a tension between the maintenance of good faith and acting with regard to one's own self interest. He considered that good faith did not mean having to forfeit one's own position in deference to the other party's and that an obligation to negotiate or mediate in good faith could include undertaking to take part in the process of negotiation or mediation, and undertaking to have an open mind in terms of a willingness to consider options raised by the other party or the mediator.

However, most commentators agree that drafters of dispute resolution clauses should omit a requirement to act in good faith: Spencer, p 153; G Raftesath and S Thaler (eds), *Cases for Mediation*, LBC Information Services in association with LEADR, 1999, pp 7–8.

Finally, while contractual agreements to mediate in good faith may be too uncertain to be enforceable, the courts have been willing to uphold the requirement to mediate in good faith when imposed under statute: see Farm Debt Mediation Act 1994 (NSW) s 11(1)(c) and (2)(a); Native Title Act 1993 (Cth) s 31(1)(b); *Western Australia v Taylor* (1996) 134 FLR 211.

There is a distinction in the approach to good faith between NSW and Victoria. NSW observes the concept; Victoria does not in situations where the parties are balanced and not at a disadvantage. In relation to 'good faith' in contracts generally see: Sir Anthony Mason, 'Contract, Good Faith and Equitable Standards in Fair Dealing' (2000) 116 *LQR* 66; *Burger King Corporation v Hungry Jacks Pty Ltd* (2001) 69 NSWLR 558; *Esso Australia Resources Pty Ltd v Southern Pacific Petroleum NL* [2005] VSCA 228.

3.6.10   Further reading

D Jones, *Commercial Arbitration in Australia*, Lawbook Co, Australia, 2011.

P Mead, 'ADR Agreements: Good Faith and Enforceability' (1999) *ADRJ* 41.

M Pryles, 'Alternative Dispute Resolution Clauses in Contracts' (1990) 1 *ADRJ* 116.

D Spencer, 'Case Notes: Complying with a Requirement to Negotiate in Good Faith — Further Developments' (2000) *ADRJ* 5.

D Spencer, 'Remedies: A Bar to Enforceability of Dispute Resolution Clauses' (2002) 13 *ADRJ* 85.

D Spencer, 'Case Notes: Drafting Dispute Resolution Clauses with Certainty' (2003) 14 *ADRJ* 85.

Evaluating mediation

3.6.11   In recent years there have been an increasing number of empirical studies aimed at evaluating ADR processes. From this work, it is apparent that when litigants are made aware of ADR processes, many tend to prefer ADR over litigation and experience a high degree of satisfaction with its results: T Sourdin, *Alternative Dispute Resolution*, 4th ed, Thomson Reuters, Sydney, 2012, p 515. It remains difficult, however, to assess the quality of justice afforded by mediation processes. L Boulle, *Mediation — Principles, Process, Practice*, 3rd ed, LexisNexis Butterworths, Sydney, 2011, p 114 writes:

> The mediation movement has emphasized the need to define success in dispute resolution processes in terms broader than only whether there was a short term settlement. ... Settlement has a one-dimensional quantitative focus which does not take account of the fairness of outcomes or whether they endure overtime; it also fails to recognize the qualitative features of dispute resolution processed in terms of user satisfaction, practitioner competence, and the

like. Surveys of mediation participants reveal high levels of satisfaction in both quantitative and qualitative dimensions of effectiveness.

The Australian Law Reform Commission has suggested five key objectives for the civil litigation system, including that the process should be just, accessible, efficient, timely and effective: ALRC, *Review of the Adversarial System of Litigation: Rethinking the Federal Litigation System*, Issues Paper 20, ALRC, Sydney, 1997, pp 27–8. Sourdin suggests that other considerations may also be appropriate when seeking to evaluate the impact of mediation. She points out (at pp 517–18):

> … [S]ome of the benefits of ADR are difficult to measure. The increased use of ADR may lead to a decrease in litigious or adversarial behaviour, foster better relationships between parties to disputes or result in higher levels of compliance with outcomes.

It may also be appropriate to evaluate whether mediation threatens to create a type of 'second-class' justice for the poor, whether the public loses when justice is privatised, and whether mediation can be fair when there are power imbalances: L Boulle, *Mediation: Principles, Process and Practice*, 3rd ed, LexisNexis Butterworths, Sydney, 2011, p 196. A large body of research has considered the wide variety of potential costs and benefits of mediation, but no large-scale research has been done to evaluate the overall impact of mediation on the civil justice system. See bibliography of research collected in Sourdin, App G.

3.6.12   Further reading

N Alexander, 'Mediation on Trial: Ten Verdicts on Court-Related ADR' (2004) 22 *Law in Context* 8.

B Niemeijer and M Pel 'Court-Based Mediation in the Netherlands: Research, Evaluation and Future Expectations' (2005) 110 *Pennsylvania State Law Review* 345.

J D Rosenberg and H J Folberg, 'Alternative Dispute Resolution: An Empirical Analysis' (1994) 46 *Stanford L R* 1487.

T Sourdin, *Alternative Dispute Resolution* 4th ed, Thomson Reuters, Sydney, 2012, pp 515–31.

ARBITRATION

3.7.1   The process of arbitration has been used for centuries for the settlement of disputes between states, state entities, companies and private parties. In the context of private disputes, arbitration has traditionally developed to provide an alternative process for the resolution of commercial disputes. As J Auerbach, *Justice Without Law*, OUP, New York, 1983, p 5 writes:

> For centuries merchants and businessmen have been among the most outspoken proponents of non-legal dispute resolution. At each crucial stage in the development of commercial arbitration, it represented the effort of businessmen to elude lawyers and courts to retain control over their

disagreements. The familiar patterns of commercial custom were (and remain) vastly preferable to the alien procedures, frustrating delays, and high costs of litigation.

Australian arbitration law is shared between the International Arbitration Act 1974 (Cth) and a set of state laws governing non-international arbitration. In 2009, the Standing Committee of Attorneys-General announced the overhaul of the then existing state arbitration acts, based on the Arbitration Act 1979 (UK), by a new domestic version of the UNCITRAL Model Law on International Commercial Arbitration. An example of the implementation of the new state model is the Commercial Arbitration Act 2010 (NSW), which adopted the UNCITRAL Model Law with additions.

H Astor and C Chinkin, *Dispute Resolution in Australia,* 2nd ed, LexisNexis Butterworths, 2002, p 12 wrote:

> Arbitration is an ADR process that has been used in Australia since white settlement, arbitration provisions having been inherited from English law. The English Arbitration Act 1697 provided a procedure whereby parties to a civil action could refer their matter to arbitration and have the ensuing award enforced as a judgment of the court.

In more recent times, arbitration has increasingly developed in the context of the legal system. In particular, arbitration has become a 'quasi-judicial' process in which the arbitrator hears arguments and evidence, and renders a determination (an award) that is binding upon the parties. The process is adversarial in nature, and the arbitrator is required to act in a judicial manner and to apply legal principles in determining the dispute. As Astor and Chinkin write at p 297:

> ... [A]rbitration is essentially a bilateral adversarial process with an impartial third party providing a decision based on law. The decision maker is required to observe the rules of natural justice, a requirement that is traditionally associated with judicial or quasi-judicial decision making. In these ways arbitration appears aligned with adjudication, including its formalism and formality. On the other hand, with the exception of court-associated arbitration, arbitration requires the consent of the parties. ... [It] takes place outside the public court structures, before an arbitrator (or arbitral panel) chosen directly or indirectly by the parties and arbitral awards are binding only on the parties to the case. The distinguishing features of arbitration are that it is private, the parties select the arbitrator(s) ... there are no third party procedural rights and there is no supporting hierarchical structure to arbitration allowing for appeal from or review of the arbitral decision, except through the national courts in limited, statutorily defined circumstances.

Arbitration is, in some ways, so similar to traditional adjudication that some commentators have argued that it is not really an alternative dispute resolution process at all. As M Fulton, *Commercial Dispute Resolution*, Law Book Co, Sydney, 1989, p 67 writes:

> Arbitration is an attempt to achieve a judicial outcome to a dispute without the delay and expense which characterise the litigation process proper. It is *not* an attempt to create an alternative model, rather it is an attempt to simulate the litigation process and achieve the same outcome without the detail and complexity (and hence expense) of that process. In colloquial terms arbitration attempts to be a 'Clayton's process', that is to say, it is the litigation you have when you are not having litigation. However, it does not always achieve its goal as a speedy, inexpensive, quasi-judicial dispute resolution process.

Domestically, arbitration is most common in the construction industry, in business disputes generally and in shipping and commodities disputes. In some other areas such as consumer disputes, domestic building contracts and farm debt dispute resolution, arbitration is considered inappropriate or excluded: see Domestic Building Contracts and Tribunal Act 1995 (Vic) s 14 and Farm Debt Mediation Act 1994 (NSW). See also D Dugdale, 'Arbitration as Oppression' (1992) *NZLJ* 135.

Internationally, arbitration is the most common and most popular method of resolving transnational commercial disputes. According to research conducted by Pricewaterhouse Coopers and the University of London's Queen Mary School of International Arbitration, international arbitration is preferred over international litigation and other methods of dispute resolution, particularly because of the enforceability of arbitral awards, the flexibility of the procedure and the ability to select experienced arbitrators: PricewaterhouseCoopers, *International Arbitration: Corporate Attitudes and Practices 2008*, viewed 1 May 2012, <http://www.pwc.co.uk>.

Enforcement of foreign arbitral awards is accomplished pursuant to an international agreement, the 1958 New York Convention on Recognition and Enforcement of Arbitration Awards. Under this convention, an arbitral award issued in any of the 142 signatory countries is enforceable in any of the other signatory countries. In Australia, the International Arbitration Act 1974 (Cth) (IAA) implements the international agreement. The IAA restricts the range of defences to enforcement 'to ensure that awards circulate freely throughout the world with minimal obstruction by national courts or laws': R Garnett, 'International Commercial Arbitration in Australia: Legal Framework and Problems' (2008) 19 *ADRJ* 249 at 525. By contrast, there is no comparable international treaty that provides a swift and regularised process for the international recognition and enforcement of judgments of foreign domestic courts.

FEATURES OF ARBITRATION

3.8.1   Arbitration can be conducted under a court-annexed scheme, under specific legislation, or pursuant to a private agreement between the parties. Court-connected arbitration has been primarily developed in Australia to facilitate the early resolution of disputes: see **3.9.1**. For example, since 1983 the New South Wales District and Local Courts have been referring cases to arbitration. Indeed, thousands of cases have been determined by court-mandated arbitration within these two jurisdictions: F Herron, 'Arbitrate or Litigate' (1987) 25 *LSJ* 52 at 53.

Even when arbitration is not ordered by a court, it can still take place pursuant to an arbitration agreement between the parties. This agreement may be entered into before or after a dispute has arisen, and is covered by the Commercial Arbitration Acts. The uniform legislation was introduced in Australia to promote a non-interventionalist environment in which business and commercial disputes could be resolved using the expertise of individual specialist arbitrators. It now exists in all federal and state jurisdictions in Australia, and allows parties to determine numerous matters related to the process of arbitration or, in the absence of express agreement, for the provisions of the Act to apply.

Arbitration can also be required by statute for the settlement of certain disputes. For example, the Aboriginal Land Rights (Northern Territory) Act 1976 (Cth) s 12B; Postal and Telecommunications Commission (Transitional Provisions) Act 1975 (Cth) s 36; Property Law Act 1974 (Qld) s 159 all provide for arbitration.

Court-connected schemes vary in the extent to which they follow the procedures and rules that apply to private arbitrations, and the operation of the Commercial Arbitration Acts is generally excluded from these schemes. The following discussion therefore focuses upon circumstances where there is an arbitration agreement between the parties, and the uniform legislation applies.

3.8.2 Under the Uniform Commercial Arbitration Acts, there must be an agreement to submit a dispute to arbitration. 'Agreement' is defined as an agreement in writing to submit a present or future difference to arbitration: Commercial Arbitration Acts, s 4(1). 'Agreement in writing' does not imply signature by or on behalf of both parties: *Re Davis and Browns' Arbitration (No 2)* (1957) VR 127 at 137. If a person has accepted a written agreement and acted upon it, that person is bound by the agreement regardless of whether it is unsigned or partly oral. In these circumstances, it is for the party asserting the existence of an arbitration agreement to prove on the balance of probabilities that an arbitration agreement exists: *Halsbury's Laws of Australia*, Arbitration, [25-70]. An arbitration agreement may still exist even though a clause states that only one party may elect to refer disputes to arbitration, or that some event must occur or some condition must be satisfied before disputes can be referred to arbitration: *PMT Partners Pty Ltd (in liq) v Australian National Parks and Wildlife Service* (1995) 184 CLR 301 at 307–10.

It has been suggested that an agreement to refer future disputes to arbitration takes effect as a standing offer or mutual option agreement, which is activated once a dispute comes into existence and the procedure is invoked by a party: *Halsbury's Laws of Australia*, Arbitration, [25-75]. It is clear, however, that an agreement to refer disputes to arbitration, whether present or future, is a binding contract at common law, and breach of an agreement gives right to an action for damages. Further, in *Comandate Marine Corp v Pan Australia Shipping Pty Ltd* (2006) 157 FCR 45 at 87, the Full Federal Court confirmed that its approach to construing agreements to refer disputes to commercial arbitration is 'benevolent and encouraging'. '[W]ords capable of broad and flexible meaning will be given liberal construction and content' by the court: *Comandate* at 87. Like any contract, however, an arbitration agreement can be terminated or cancelled by agreement between the parties.

The dispute or difference, which the parties agree to refer to arbitration, must consist of a justiciable issue triable civilly: *Halsbury's Laws of Australia*, Arbitration, [25-20]. While arbitration proceedings are usually private in the sense that only the parties to the dispute and their representatives are present during the process, they are not necessarily confidential. In particular, the proceedings are not regarded as implicitly confidential, and an express confidentiality agreement is required to ensure the content of the arbitration is protected: *Esso Australia Resources Ltd v Plowman (Minister for Energy and Minerals)* (1995) 183 CLR 391.

3.8.3 The judicial system plays an important role in arbitrations. The Commercial Arbitration Acts confer on the courts extensive powers, which are supportive of the arbitration process. They are also given supervisory power to ensure that the arbitral procedure is properly exercised by the arbitrator. In addition, the Supreme Courts of each jurisdiction are given the power to determine preliminary questions of law, and an appellate jurisdiction on questions of law arising out of an award: *Halsbury's Laws of Australia*, Arbitration, [25-20], [25-490], [25-530]. However, the court's role in reviewing arbitral awards is intended to be limited:

> Ultimately, it can be said that 'the scope of judicial review of arbitration awards necessarily determines the utility of the arbitration process'. If judicial review is too broad, arbitration merely

becomes an entrée to litigation. If judicial review is too restricted, the efficacy of arbitration will be eroded, as disputants are unlikely to submit to a system without any legal protections against rampant bias or total incompetence (footnotes omitted).

V Donnenberg, 'Judicial Review of Arbitral Awards under the Commercial Arbitration Acts' (2008) 30 *ABR* 177.

The state court's role under the domesticated UNCITRAL Model Law, International Arbitration Act 1974 (Cth); Commercial Arbitration Act 2010 (NSW); Commercial Arbitration Act 2011 (SA); Commercial Arbitration Act 2011 (Tas); Commercial Arbitration Act 2011 (Vic) includes:

- appointing an arbitrator where a person who has power to appoint an arbitrator fails to do so, and no other method for appointment is provided for — s 11 (Model Law Art 11);

- requiring interim measures, e.g. evidence by affidavit, injunction, preserving assets and evidence, or the production of documents — s 17 (Model Law Art 17);

- enforcing an arbitral award in the same manner as a judgment or order of the court — s 33 (Model Law Art 33);

- power of an arbitrator to act as a mediator, conciliator or other non-arbitral intermediary — s 27D (no equivalent in the Model Law);

- setting aside an award with leave — s 34A (no equivalent in the Model Law); and

- recognition and enforcement of awards — s 35 (Model Law Art 35).

The Australian Capital Territory, Queensland and Western Australia are yet to enact the model scheme and are still operating under older legislation: Commercial Arbitration Act 1986 (ACT); Commercial Arbitration Act 1990 (Qld); Commercial Arbitration Act 1985 (WA).

Section 36 of the Commercial Arbitration Act 2010 (NSW) specifies grounds for refusing recognition or enforcement.

3.8.4E   Commercial Arbitration Act 2010 (NSW)

36 Grounds for refusing recognition or enforcement
   (cf Model Law Art 36)
   (1)   Recognition or enforcement of an arbitral award, irrespective of the State or Territory in which it was made, may be refused only:
      (a)   at the request of the party against whom it is invoked, if that party furnishes to the Court proof that:
         (i)   a party to the arbitration agreement was under some incapacity, or the arbitration agreement is not valid under the law to which the parties have subjected it or, failing any indication in it, under the law of the State or Territory where the award was made, or
         (ii)   the party against whom the award is invoked was not given proper notice of the appointment of an arbitrator or of the arbitral proceedings or was otherwise unable to present the party's case, or
         (iii) the award deals with a dispute not contemplated by or not falling within the terms of the submission to arbitration, or it contains decisions on matters beyond the scope of the submission to arbitration, provided that,

if the decisions on matters submitted to arbitration can be separated from those not so submitted, that part of the award which contains decisions on matters submitted to arbitration may be recognised and enforced, or

(iv) the composition of the arbitral tribunal or the arbitral procedure was not in accordance with the agreement of the parties or, failing such agreement, was not in accordance with the law of the State or Territory where the arbitration took place, or

(v) the award has not yet become binding on the parties or has been set aside or suspended by a court of the State or Territory in which, or under the law of which, that award was made, or

(b) if the Court finds that:

(i) the subject-matter of the dispute is not capable of settlement by arbitration under the law of this State, or

(ii) the recognition or enforcement of the award would be contrary to the public policy of this State.

(2) If an application for setting aside or suspension of an award has been made to a court referred to in subsection (1) (a) (v), the Court may, if it considers it proper, adjourn its decision and may also, on the application of the party claiming recognition or enforcement of the award, order the party to provide appropriate security.

3.8.5 The arbitration process normally consists of six steps: commencement; preliminary conference; information exchange; hearing; formulating a decision; and an award: M Fulton, *Commercial Alternative Dispute Resolution*, Law Book Co, Sydney, 1989, p 63. At the preliminary meeting, procedural and other matters will be discussed including:

- challenges to the nomination of the arbitrator;

- the arbitrator's formal acceptance of nomination;

- choice of law matters;

- jurisdiction of the arbitrator to determine the dispute;

- appropriate procedure;

- financial arrangements including the arbitrator's remuneration and security for its payment;

- interlocutory matters including pleadings and discovery if appropriate; and

- arrangements for the hearing including legal representation, venue and dates.

Unlike mediation, where the mediator may hold a caucus with each party separately, in arbitration it is considered a fundamental principle of natural justice that the arbitrator may not hear one party in the absence of the others: *Oxford Clothing Co Pty Ltd v GIO (Tas)* (1994) 4 Tas R 1. However, where the time and place of a meeting appointed by the arbitrator are reasonable, and due notice has been given to the parties, if one party fails, without good cause, to attend, the arbitrator may proceed regardless: *E Kontek v Daveyduke Industries Mimivic Nominees Pty Ltd* (1987) 6 *Aust Const LR* 34.

Under s 20A of the Commercial Arbitration Act 2010 (NSW) (no equivalent in the Model Law), parties may appear or act in person, or may be represented by another person of their choice in oral hearings. A person representing another does not have to be a lawyer.

Under s 27D of the Commercial Arbitration Act 2010 (NSW) (no equivalent in the Model Law), the parties may, at any point, seek to have their dispute mediated or conciliated by the arbitrator.

Unless the parties have agreed otherwise, arbitration is an adversarial process: *Halsbury's Laws of Australia*, Arbitration, [25-465]. Some of the procedures that apply to the arbitration, unless otherwise agreed by the parties in the arbitration agreement or in writing, include:

- the parties are free to determine the number of arbitrators, otherwise one is appointed (s 10);

- arbitrators are under an obligation of disclosure of any circumstances likely to give rise to justifiable doubts as to the person's impartiality or independence and may be challenged (ss 12, 13);

- an arbitral tribunal may rule on its own jurisdiction (s 16);

- an arbitral tribunal, may at the request of a party, grant interim measures, e.g. preserve evidence and assets, maintain the status quo etc. (s 17);

- an arbitral tribunal may require the provision of security (s 17E), disclosure of material changes (s 17F);

- the parties must be treated with equality and be given a reasonable opportunity of presenting their case (s 18);

- the parties are free to agree on the procedure to be followed by the arbitral tribunal, including admissibility, relevance, materiality and weight of evidence, orders in relation to examination of a party or witness (s 19);

- the parties are free to agree on the place of arbitration (s 20) and language used (s 22);

- parties produce statements of claim and defence (s 23) and conduct a hearing (s 24) unless otherwise agree;

- parties may appear or act in person or be represented by another person (not necessarily a lawyer) (s 24A);

- default of a party may result in termination of the arbitration, an award etc. (s 25);

- the arbitral tribunal may appoint experts (s 26);

- various provisions deal with confidential information (ss 27E–27I);

- there is provision for the making of an award and termination of proceedings (Pt 6: ss 28–33F);

- provision is made for recourse against awards (Pt 7: ss 34–34A); and

- there is provision for the recognition and enforcement of awards: Pt 8: ss 35–36.

The arbitrator's fundamental duty, to which all else is subordinate, is to conduct the arbitration fairly: *Varley v Spatt* [1956] ALR 71. This means the arbitrator must give each of the parties the opportunity to know the case of the opponent and to present their own case, and apply to the material a fair and unbiased mind: *Halsbury's Laws of Australia*, Arbitration, [25-450]. A failure to comply with this duty will expose the arbitrator to removal for misconduct.

3.8.6 Further reading

H Astor and C Chinkin, *Dispute Resolution in Australia*, 2nd ed, Butterworths, Sydney, 2001, pp 297–309.

H J Brown and A L Marriott, *ADR Principles and Practice*, 3rd ed, Sweet & Maxwell, London, 2011.

V Donnenberg, 'Judicial Review of Arbitral Awards under the Commercial Arbitration Acts' (2008) 30 *ABR* 177.

R Garnett, 'International Commercial Arbitration in Australia: Legal Framework and Problems' (2008) 19 *ADRJ* 249.

D Jones, *Commercial Arbitration in Australia*, Thomson Reuters, Sydney, 2011.

J Laurie, 'New Directions in Arbitration' (2006) 25(2) *Arbitrator and Mediator* 13.

R Rana and M Sanson, *International Commercial Arbitration*, Thomson Reuters, Sydney, Australia, 2011.

COURT-ANNEXED ADR

3.9.1 Two important reasons for the growth in ADR in Australia has been the increased incorporation, referral and use by Australian courts of mediation and arbitration processes, and the procedural requirement to take genuine or reasonable steps to resolve a dispute before litigation.

In most jurisdictions, courts have the express power to refer all or part of a civil dispute to an ADR process. Court rules and practice directions have also incorporated ADR into the case management system of most courts: see **2.4.21–2.4.25**. ADR may also be provided by the courts, with registrars acting as mediators, conciliators, evaluators or arbitrators, or they may be provided by external ADR professionals.

Court-referral makes ADR processes accessible to the many litigants, who may not be aware of ADR process options before they come to court. It also promotes appropriate use of ADR 'in situations where the parties or their lawyers are so accustomed to the litigation process that they are unlikely to use ADR voluntarily': Commonwealth Attorney-General's Department, Civil Jurisdiction and Federal Courts Branch, *Federal Civil Justice Strategy Paper*, December 2003, p 148, viewed 1 May 2012, <http://www.ag.gov.au>. Other advantages of court-annexed ADR may include a lower cost than private ADR and court-monitoring for quality control of the professionals and the processes: D Spencer, 'Mandatory Mediation and Neutral Evaluation: A Reality in New South Wales' (2000) 11 *ADRJ* 237 at 245–6.

One of the most commonly claimed disadvantages of court-annexed ADR is that the parties do not perceive the process as voluntary. Parties who expect courts to decide the issues for them may misunderstand the process and misconstrue the power and role of the mediator: see Spencer, pp 242–4. Of more concern, however, is the suggestion that, as part of management strategies, particular kinds of cases can be streamlined into ADR. See M Redfern, 'Should Pre-litigation Mediation be Mandated?' (2012) 23 *ADRJ* 6. This approach can result in 'privatising' certain types of disputes based on assumptions about which matters are more appropriate to mediation and which to adjudication. More worryingly, the availability of ADR processes might take the pressure for reform off the court system. The problem of the high cost of access to justice cannot be resolved by simply diverting cases into ADR. ADR should not be allowed to facilitate the creation of a second-class justice for the poor or ethnic: M Thornton, 'Equivocations of Conciliation: the Resolution of Discrimination Complaints in Australia' (1989) 52 *Mod L R* 733 at 737.

Federal Court

Civil Dispute Resolution Act 2011 (Cth)

3.9.2   The Civil Dispute Resolution Act 2011 (Cth) as it applies to the Federal Court and Federal Magistrates Court has as its object 'to ensure that, as far as possible, people take genuine steps to resolve disputes before certain civil proceedings are instituted': s 3. The legislation is modeled on the National Alternative Dispute Resolution Advisory Council (NADRAC) report, *The Resolve to Resolve — Embracing ADR to Improve Access to Justice in the Federal Jurisdiction*, prepared for the Attorney-General of the Commonwealth of Australia, September 2009.

3.9.3E   **Civil Dispute Resolution Act 2011 (Cth)**

Genuine steps to resolve a dispute

4 (1A) For the purposes of this Act, a person takes *genuine steps to resolve a dispute* if the steps taken by the person in relation to the dispute constitute a sincere and genuine attempt to resolve the dispute, having regard to the person's circumstances and the nature and circumstances of the dispute.

  (1)   Examples of steps that could be taken by a person as part of taking genuine steps to resolve a dispute with another person, include the following:
    (a)   notifying the other person of the issues that are, or may be, in dispute, and offering to discuss them, with a view to resolving the dispute;
    (b)   responding appropriately to any such notification;
    (c)   providing relevant information and documents to the other person to enable the other person to understand the issues involved and how the dispute might be resolved;
    (d)   considering whether the dispute could be resolved by a process facilitated by another person, including an alternative dispute resolution process;
    (e)   if such a process is agreed to:
      (i)   agreeing on a particular person to facilitate the process; and
      (ii)   attending the process;
    (f)   if such a process is conducted but does not result in resolution of the dispute — considering a different process;
    (g)   attempting to negotiate with the other person, with a view to resolving some or all the issues in dispute, or authorising a representative to do so.
  (2)   Subsection (1) does not limit the steps that may constitute taking genuine steps to resolve a dispute.

Definitions

5 In this Act:

"applicant in proceedings" means a person who institutes the proceedings.

"application" means an application (however described) by which civil proceedings are instituted.

"civil penalty provision" means a civil penalty provision however described.

"Commonwealth authority" means a body corporate established for a public purpose by or under a law of the Commonwealth.

"eligible court" means the following:

(a)   the Federal Court of Australia;

(b)   the Federal Magistrates Court.

"excluded proceedings" means proceedings that are excluded proceedings under Part 4.

"genuine steps statement":

(a)   for an applicant — see section 6;

(b)   for a respondent — see section 7.

"lawyer" has the same meaning as in the Federal Court of Australia Act 1976.

"respondent" in proceedings means a person against whom the proceedings are instituted.

Genuine steps statement to be filed by applicant

6 (1) An applicant who institutes civil proceedings in an eligible court must file a genuine steps statement at the time of filing the application.

(2)   A genuine steps statement filed under subsection (1) must specify:
   (a)   the steps that have been taken to try to resolve the issues in dispute between the applicant and the respondent in the proceedings; or
   (b)   the reasons why no such steps were taken, which may relate to, but are not limited to the following:
      (i)   the urgency of the proceedings;
      (ii)   whether, and the extent to which, the safety or security of any person or property would have been compromised by taking such steps.

(3)   A genuine steps statement need not be filed under subsection (1) in relation to proceedings that are wholly excluded proceedings.

(4)   A genuine steps statement must be filed under subsection (1) in relation to proceedings that are in part excluded proceedings, but the statement need not relate to the parts of the proceedings that are excluded proceedings.

Genuine steps statement to be filed by respondent

7 (1) A respondent in proceedings who is given a copy of a genuine steps statement filed by an applicant in the proceedings must file a genuine steps statement before the hearing date specified in the application.

(2)   A genuine steps statement filed under subsection (1) must:
   (a)   state that the respondent agrees with the genuine steps statement filed by the applicant; or
   (b)   if the respondent disagrees in whole or part with the genuine steps statement filed by the applicant — specify the respect in which, and reasons why, the respondent disagrees.

Genuine steps statements must comply with Rules of Court

8 A genuine steps statement must comply with any additional requirements specified in the Rules of Court of the eligible court (see section 18) in which the statement is filed.

Duty of lawyers to advise people of the requirements of this Act

9 A lawyer acting for a person who is required to file a genuine steps statement must:

    (a)   advise the person of the requirement; and

    (b)   assist the person to comply with the requirement.

Effect of requirements of this Part

10 (1) The requirements of this Part are in addition to, and not instead of, requirements imposed by any other Act.

    (2)   A failure to file a genuine steps statement in proceedings does not invalidate the application instituting the proceedings, a response to such an application or the proceedings.

3.9.4 The court may have regard to genuine steps requirements in exercising powers and performing functions (s 11) and in exercising a discretion to award costs (s 12). These powers are in addition to powers under other this and other Acts (s 13). Certain proceedings are excluded (s 15), most notably an order imposing a pecuniary penalty, criminal offences, and appellate proceedings.

3.9.5   Further reading

The Right Hon R Jackson LJ, *Review of Civil Litigation Costs: Final Report*, Ministry of Justice, TSO, 2009.

M Legg and D Boniface, *Pre-action Protocols*, Non-adversarial Justice: Implications for the Legal System and Society Conference 4–7 May 2010, viewed 1 May 2012, <http://aija.org.au/NAJ%202010/Papers/Legg&Boniface.pdf>.

T Sourdin, 'Making an Attempt to Resolve Disputes Before Using Courts: We All Have Obligations' (2010) 21(4) *ADRJ* 225.

D Spencer, 'Should Pre-litigation Mediation be Mandated?' (2012) 23(1) *ADRJ* 1.

A Wahab and B Van Gramberg, 'Court-annexed and Judge-led Mediation in Civil Cases: The Malaysian Experience' (2010) 21(4) *ADRJ* 251.

Court-annexed alternative dispute resolution

3.9.6 Court-annexed alternative dispute resolution processes are dealt with in Pt 28 of the Federal Court Rules. Parties must, and the court will consider options for ADR, including mediation, as early as possible: r 28.01. A party may apply for an order that the proceeding, or part of a proceeding be referred to an arbitrator, mediator, or some suitable person for ADR: r 28.02. The proceeding may be adjourned or stayed and the person conducting the ADR process may be ordered to report to the court: r 28.02. A party may apply to the court to terminate mediation or an ADR process: r 28.04. Part 28 does not preclude parties from engaging in an ADR process outside the court-annexed processes: r 28.05.

In the event that an order referring a proceeding to an ADR process does not nominate a suitable person, the Registrar will nominate a Registrar or other person to conduct the ADR process: r 28.31.

Part 28 is divided into specific rules for:

- arbitration — Div 28.2;

- mediation — Div 28.3;

- international arbitration — Div 28.5; and

- referral by a court to a referee — Div 28.6.

The Family Court of Australia

3.9.7 The federal Family Court system is now structured to assist families to reach agreement while minimising conflict and avoiding litigation wherever possible. Following extensive amendments to the Family Law Act 1975 (Cth), the process for resolving child-related disputes can be described as the most comprehensive statutory mediation scheme in Australia. Under the amendments parties must, with certain exceptions, undertake some form of family dispute resolution before filing an application in child-related proceedings. Mediation is offered through community-based programs that use mediators who have a minimum level of training and experience and are registered by the court. See Family Law Regulations 1984 (Cth) regs 60–61C. Arbitration is also available for financial disputes in family law: see Family Law Regulations 1984 (Cth) regs 67A–67T. More recently the Family Court is trialing the less adversarial trial.

3.9.8E **Finding a Better Way**
Margaret Harrison, Family Court of Australia, April 2007.

In an approach pioneered by the Family Court of Australia, family law has recently undergone the most significant change to the way in which litigation is conducted in this country in modern history. The change, from a traditional common law approach to a less adversarial trial, has significant implications, not only for the conduct of family law litigation but also for the conduct of litigation as a whole. It represents a bold step towards bridging the gap between common law systems of litigation and the European civil law system. So far as family law is concerned, the change received legislative force with the passage of Division 12A of Part VII of the *Family Law Act 1975* (Cth) …

In children's cases, Division 12A swept away the restrictive rules of evidence and the control of the proceedings was placed in the hands of the judge, rather than the parties or their legal representatives. The focus is a future looking one, geared to the needs of the child. As a consequence of the new procedures, parties are no longer free to conduct litigation as a forensic war between each other at the expense of the interests of the child. At the same time the best features of the Court's highly developed system for mediation and resolution of disputes has not only been preserved but also enhanced, and the role of what is now called the family consultant has become even more significant. The unique approach retains and relies on the special assistance provided by family consultants, whilst providing a clear child focus underpinned by active judicial leadership and direction … It became mandatory for parents filing a child-related application after 1 July 2006.

Other federal legislation

3.9.9   ADR processes are also available under the following federal legislation:

- Federal Magistrates Act 1999 (Cth);
- Administrative Appeals Tribunal Act 1975 (Cth); and
- Native Title Act 1993 (Cth).

Australian Capital Territory

3.9.10   Under the Court Procedures Rules 2006 (ACT), the court may — on application or on its own initiative — refer a proceeding to mediation or neutral evaluation: r 1179. Parties have a duty to take part in the process 'genuinely and constructively': r 1180. Mediation referral programs are also available under the Domestic Relationships Act 1994 (ACT) s 8(1). Mediation practice in the Australian Capital Territory is governed by the Mediation Act 1997 (ACT), which provides for mediator registration, confidentiality and protection against defamation. The Australian Capital Territory has also adopted uniform legislation for commercial arbitration: See Commercial Arbitration Act 1986 (ACT).

New South Wales

3.9.11   The Civil Procedure Act 2005 (NSW) permits the court to refer any proceeding to mediation, with or without the consent of the parties: see Pt 4 Mediation of Proceedings. Parties participating in mandatory mediation are required to participate 'in good faith': s 27. Alternatively, the court may refer claims for money damages (and ancillary claims) to arbitration, after dealing with the matters that can be resolved before a hearing: s 38. Rules for the conduct of mediations (Div 1) and arbitrations (Div 2) are found in the Uniform Civil Procedure Rules 2005 (NSW), Pt 20. Supreme Court Practice Note No SC Gen 6 (Supreme Court — Mediation) dated 10 March 2010 details the considerations for referral to mediation in civil matters. See also J Spigelman, 'Mediation and the Court' (2001) 39 *LSJ* 63.

Court-ordered mediations have been successfully conducted in New South Wales over the past two decades and judges have shown increasing willingness to order parties to try it. For example, in *Remuneration Planning Corp Ltd v Fitton* [2001] NSWSC 1208 at 1212, Hamilton J made these comments:

> This is an area in which the received wisdom has in my experience changed radically in a period of a few months. A short time ago there was general acceptance of the view adopted by Barrett J in the decision to which I have referred [*Morrow v Chinadotcom Corp* [2001] NSWSC 209], that there may be situations where the Court will, in the exercise of its discretion, take the view that mediation is pointless in a particular case because of the attitudes of the parties or other circumstances and decline to order a mediation. However, since the power was conferred upon the Court, there have been a number of instances in which mediations have succeeded, which have been ordered under opposition, or consented to by the parties only when it is plain that the Court will order the mediation in the absence of consent. It has become plain that there are circumstances in which parties insist on taking the stance that they will not go to mediation, perhaps from a fear that to show willingness to do so may appear to be a sign of weakness, yet engage in successful mediation when mediation is ordered.

The mediator appointed in court-mandated mediation may be one agreed by the parties (a private or external mediator) or one nominated by the court: s 26. According to Sourdin, the internal mediation process in the Supreme Court of NSW is free, but involves a one to six week waiting time: T Sourdin, *Alternative Dispute Resolution*, 4th ed, Thomson Reuters, Sydney, 2012, p 256. ADR referrals in NSW have been quite successful. See *Unconventional Conventions Pty Ltd v Accent OZ Pty Ltd (in liq)* [2004] NSWSC 1050; The Hon T Bathurst, Chief Justice of New South Wales, 'Opening Address', *2011 Advanced Dispute Resolution Workshop*, Westin Hotel, Sydney, 13 August 2011.

Various forms of ADR are also available in New South Wales under the following legislation:

- Commercial Arbitration Act 2010 (NSW) (arbitration);

- Community Justice Centres Act 1983 (NSW) (mediation);

- Community Services (Complaints, Reviews and Monitoring) Act 1993 (NSW) (ombudsman);

- Farm Debt Mediation Act 1994 (NSW) (mediation);

- Industrial Relations Act 1996 (NSW) (conciliation and arbitration); and

- Retail Leases Act 1994 (mediation).

3.9.12 The New South Wales Government established the Alternative Dispute Resolution Directorate in 2009 to coordinate, manage and drive ADR government policy, strategy and growth in New South Wales. See viewed 25 April 2012, <http://www.courts.lawlink.nsw.gov.au/cats/catscorporate_adrdirectorate.html>. In 2010, New South Wales amended the Civil Procedure Act 2005 (NSW) adding Pt 2A which was in similar terms to the Civil Procedure Resolution Act 2011 (Cth). In 2011, the amendments were postponed 18 months due to adverse comment and controversy.

3.9.13E **NSW Government to Postpone Pre-Litigation Reforms**
Media Release, The Hon Greg Smith (NSW Attorney General), 23 August 2011

Part 2A of the Civil Procedure Act 2005 requires parties to take reasonable steps to resolve their dispute by mutual agreement or to more narrowly define the contentious issues before commencing court action. The provisions were passed in late 2010, but would only have applied to matters filed from 1 October 2011.

... the reasonable steps provisions would be postponed by 18 months to enable NSW to monitor the success of similar provisions that commenced in federal Courts on August 1.

The NSW Government will ultimately make informed decisions about the future of Part 2A, using all of the available evidence ...

Compliance with pre-trial obligations should reduce, not add to, the cost of resolving disputes. The purpose of this postponement is to ensure this is the case.

3.9.14   Further reading

New South Wales Justice and Attorney General, *ADR Blueprint — Draft Recommendations Report 1: Pre-action Protocols & Standards*, NSW Justice and Attorney General, Sydney, 2009, viewed 1 May 2012.

<http://www.courts.lawlink.nsw.gov.au/agdbasev7wr/_assets/cats/m40265213/adr_blueprint.pdf>.

Northern Territory

3.9.15   Under the Northern Territory rules (r 48.13(1)), a judge or Master can refer a matter to mediation without the parties' consent where they are of the opinion that the proceeding is capable of settlement or ought to be settled. If a party fails to attend a mediation, or refuses to participate, or applies to adjourn without the other party's consent, they must pay the costs of the mediation and the costs of the other party: r 48.13(13). Otherwise, the costs of the mediation are to be borne equally. Within seven days of the conclusion of the mediation, the mediator must file a signed report indicating whether the proceedings have been resolved, some issues have been resolved and others remain unresolved, or whether no issues at all have been resolved: r 48.13(16).

Under s 16 of the Local Court Act 1989 (NT), the Local Court may, either on its own motion or on a party's application, order a pre-hearing conference, a mediation conference or an arbitration conference. The conference must be conducted in accordance with the Local Court Rules, and if the matter is not settled, may be referred back to court by the presiding person. When a matter is settled at a conference, the presiding person may make a final order, which has the effect as an order of court.

Queensland

3.9.16   The Supreme Court of Queensland Act 1991 (Qld), the Uniform Civil Procedure Rules 1999 (Qld), and the District Court of Queensland Act 1967 (Qld) establish mediation and case appraisal as part of the pre-trial management process: see 2.4.21. Even before a trial date is allocated, the court considers whether a case should be referred to mediation or case appraisal. An action goes to trial only if these processes fail to reach an agreement.

Mediation is also available in Queensland through dispute resolution centres established pursuant to the Dispute Resolution Centres Act 1990 (Qld). Arbitration is also available under the Commercial Arbitration Act 1990 (Qld).

South Australia

3.9.17   In South Australia, there are provisions for referral to mediation or arbitration in the Supreme Court Act 1935 (SA) ss 65–66, the District Court Act 1991 (SA) ss 32–33, and the Magistrates Court Act 1991 (SA) ss 27–28. In the Supreme Court, a judge may, with or without the consent of the parties, and a Registrar or Master may, with the consent of the parties, refer a civil proceeding or any related issue to a mediator: Supreme Court Act 1935

(SA) s 65(1): see *Barry Hopcroft and Barameda Fishing Co v A M Olsen* [1998] SASC 7009; *Addstead Pty Ltd (in liq) v Simmons (No 2)* [2005] SASC 25.

Supreme Court Practice Directions 2006 (SA) Ch 9 Mediations provide for the parties to be jointly and severally liable for mediator's fees, which cannot exceed established guidelines. Further practice directions describe, among other things, the referral process, the preliminary conference, and implementation of a settlement agreement: see Directions 9.5–9.16.

Mediation and conciliation are also available for dealing with environmental and development matters under the Environment, Resources and Development Court Act 1993 (SA) s 28B. Commercial arbitration is provided for in the Commercial Arbitration Act 2011 (SA).

Tasmania

3.9.18 Under the Supreme Court Rules 2000 (Tas), a judge may, at any stage in the proceedings, order that the proceedings or any part of it be referred to mediation: r 518. If a matter is referred to mediation, the mediator is to be the Principal Registrar or a suitable person appointed by the Principal Registrar. Unless otherwise ordered, a referral to mediation does not stay proceedings.

A mediator may, and if ordered to do so, must report to the court, when a mediation is finished: r 520(1). Where a mediation does not result in an agreement on all the issues in dispute between the parties, the plaintiff or applicant must immediately notify the court in writing that the mediation has taken place and state the issues left to be determined by the court or a judge: r 521.

The Alternative Dispute Resolution Act 2001 (Tas) makes provisions for mediator secrecy, privilege from defamation, evidentiary privilege and costs.

Victoria

3.9.19 In Victoria, the Supreme Court (General Civil Procedure) Rules 2005 (Vic) provides for the referral of civil matters to arbitration or mediation. The Supreme Court may, with or without the consent of the parties, refer the whole or part of a civil proceeding to mediation or arbitration. Under r 50.07(4), (5) a mediator may report, or be ordered to report, to the court as to whether the mediation is finished, but no other report shall be submitted to court. The mediator's remuneration is to be determined by the court: r 50.07(8).

Practice Note 2 of 2012 provides a set of Judicial Mediation Guidelines whose purpose is to encourage, and where appropriate direct, parties to engage in private mediation in the majority of civil proceedings coming before the Supreme Court. Civil Procedure Act 2010 (Vic) s 66 enables the court to order a judicial resolution conference, which includes judicial mediation. A judicial mediation is conducted according to the guidelines of PN 2 of 2012. See M Warren, 'Should Judges be Mediators?' (2010) 21 *ADRJ* 77; I Field, 'Judicial Mediation, the Judicial Process and Ch III of the Constitution' (2011) 22(2) *ADRJ* 72.

Arbitration may, with the consent of the parties, be ordered in relation to a proceeding or part of a proceeding: r 50.08. The reference to arbitration may be made at any stage, and the arbitration is conducted in accordance with the Commercial Arbitration Act 2011 (Vic).

In Victoria, like New South Wales, reasonable steps obligations were introduced into the Civil Procedure Act 2010 (Vic), but the section dealing with pre-litigation requirements was repealed in 2011.

Western Australia

3.9.20   Under the Supreme Court Act 1935 (WA) s 167(1)(q), and the Supreme Court Rules 1971 (WA) O 4A r 2(2)(l)(i), mediation is made part of case management. Supreme Court Act 1935 (WA) Pt VI — Mediation s 69 defines a mediator as a Registrar or other person approved by the Chief Justice under the rules of court, or a person agreed by the parties. Mediators when carrying out a mediation have the same privileges and immunities as a judge (s 70) with evidence of anything said or done in the mediation privileged (s 71) and confidential: s 72.

Order 4A r 8 r 11 sets out the procedural requirements for the conference of the parties with a mediator. These include in the absence of an order:

- that the parties must take steps to ensure that the mediation takes place as soon as possible;
- that the fees and expenses of a private mediator are to be paid by the parties equally unless otherwise ordered;
- that the plaintiff must lodge with the court a report signed by or on behalf of each party confirming that the conference took place and the substance of any resolution or the narrowing of points of differences; and
- that, unless the parties agree, the mediator shall not report to the court on the mediation conference, except that the mediator can report on a party's failure to cooperate in a mediation conference which may be used by the court for the purposes of determining costs.

The increasing importance of mediation is reflected in Practice Direction No 2 of 2008, Supreme Court Mediation Program, which states:

> Mediation is an integral part of the case management process and, in general, no case will be listed for trial without the mediation process having first been exhausted.

3.9.21   Further reading

ALRC, *Review of the Adversarial System of Litigation: ADR — Its Role in Federal Dispute Resolution*, Issues Paper 25, ALRC, Sydney, 1997, pp 38–57, 91–8.

M Black, 'The Courts, Tribunals and ADR — Assisted Dispute Resolution in the Federal Court of Australia' (1996) 7 *ADRJ* 138.

M McIntosh, 'A Step Forward — Mandatory Mediations' (2003) 14 *ADRJ* 280.

T Sourdin, *Alternative Dispute Resolution*, 4th ed, Thomson Reuters, Sydney, 2012, pp 251–99.

ADR AND THE LEGAL PROFESSION

3.10.1   Statutory obligations, regulatory schemes, guidelines, and court requirements to negotiate in good faith and promote exchange of information all support the uptake of ADR by the legal profession. L Boulle, *Mediation: Principles, Process and Practice*, 3rd ed, LexisNexis Butterworths, Sydney, 2011, pp 143–144 observes:

Various strands of litigation management enable courts to impose obligations and time-frames on litigants and to require them to participate in settlement conferences, case appraisal or mediation proceedings, drawing ADR closely into court proceedings. Moreover, costs sanctions can be imposed to deter parties from conducting their cases in an excessively adversarial manner. These innovations have been influenced by mediation thinking and ADR-inspired innovations. As a result modern litigation is not as formalized, adversarial and outcome-restricted as traditionally depicted and litigation, on one hand, and negotiation and mediation, on the other, can be viewed as systems on a continuum rather than distinct processes.

There are a range of matters related to ADR that lawyers may be involved in. These include:

- obligations to use ADR as a precondition to litigation;
- ethical obligations to swear that their client's case has reasonable grounds for success;
- understanding and advising on appropriate dispute resolution methods;
- structuring a dispute resolution process for a particular client or dispute;
- drafting ADR provisions for agreements and understanding which clauses are likely to be enforceable;
- preparing information to be used in a dispute resolution process;
- identifying and arranging parties to be included in a dispute resolution process;
- preparing or advising upon agreements to participate, such as mediation agreements;
- attending dispute resolution processes, and if appropriate participating in the process;
- providing advice to clients on their legal rights, obligations and duties with the aim of assisting in the generation and evaluation of options and solutions in ADR processes;
- preparing or advising upon the legality, workability or enforceability of ADR agreements;
- explaining rules and limitations of confidentiality in ADR processes; and
- providing advice and assistance where appropriate to address any power imbalance faced by a client.

See further: H Astor and C Chinkin, *Dispute Resolution in Australia*, 2nd ed, LexisNexis Butterworths, Sydney, 2002, pp 85–212.

Some commentators suggest that parties or their lawyers who do not take court-annexed ADR seriously, or fail to advise their parties on ADR, are susceptible to sanctions: G Dearlove, 'Court-ordered ADR: Sanctions for the Recalcitrant Lawyer and Party' (2000) 11 *ADRJ* 12. Dearlove argues that the court may penalise a party or their lawyer for failure to attend ADR processes; using ADR as a 'fishing expedition'; blatant unwillingness to take part in the ADR processes; and using the ADR for an ulterior purpose such as a delaying tactic or additional financial pressure imposed on a less financially strong party: Dearlove, 19–22. Penalties could include penalising a party with costs, penalising a lawyer with costs, or charging a party with abuse of process or contempt. See also, D Spencer, 'Case Notes: Costs Sanctions against Recalcitrant Parties Who Frustrate Mediation' (2003) 14 *ADRJ* 5.

The draft version of the Legal Profession National Law s 5.4.4, viewed 1 May 2012, <http://www.ag.gov.au/legalprofession> provides for mediation of complaints between clients and their lawyers.

The Legal Services Directions 2005 (Cth) App B, made under the Judiciary Act 1903 (Cth) s 55ZF, requires Commonwealth Government agencies to act as 'model litigants'. Appendix B includes the following provisions with respect to ADR:

Alternative dispute resolution

5.1   The Commonwealth or an agency is only to start court proceedings if it has considered other methods of dispute resolution (eg alternative dispute resolution or settlement negotiations).

5.2   When participating in alternative dispute resolution, the Commonwealth and its agencies are to ensure that their representatives:

     (a)   participate fully and effectively, and

     (b)   subject to paragraph 2 (e) (iv), have authority to settle the matter so as to facilitate appropriate and timely resolution of a dispute.

See generally, viewed 1 May 2012, <http://www.comlaw.gov.au>. These model litigant provisions are also found in the states and territories. For example, in Victoria they are found in the standard legal services to contract panel contract, viewed 1 May 2012, <http://www.justice. vic.gov.au>. In New South Wales see, viewed 1 May 2012, <http://www.lsc.lawlink.nsw.gov. au>. In Queensland see, viewed 1 May 2012, <http://www.justice.qld.gov.au>.

3.10.2   Further reading

A Ardagh, 'The Legal Profession Post-ADR: From Mediation To Collaborative Law' (2007) 18(4) *ADRJ* 205.

L Boulle, *Mediation: Principles, Process and Practice*, 3rd ed, LexisNexis Butterworths, Sydney, 2011, para 8.33–8.65, pp 289–312.

N Cukier, 'Lawyers Acting as Mediators: Ethical Dilemmas in the Shift from Advocacy to Impartiality' (2010) 21 *ADRJ* 59.

M Dewdney, 'Party, Mediator and Lawyer-driven Problems and Ways of Avoiding Them' (2007) 17(4) *ADRJ* 200.

G Gibson, 'Horses for Courses: Warlords as Peacemakers: Are Trial Lawyers Bad for ADR?' (2002) 122 Spring *Victorian Bar News* 30.

O Rundle, 'A Spectrum of Contributions that Lawyers Can Make to Mediations' (2009) 20 *ADRJ* 220.

T Sourdin, *Alternative Dispute Resolution*, 4th ed, Thomson Reuters, Sydney, 2012, [11.10], [11.30].

CONCLUSION

3.11.1   In the past 20 years, ADR has become definitively mainstream in Australia. ADR processes are now widely available through private sources and in court-annexed contexts. In many jurisdictions and for many types of cases, mediation, conciliation or settlement conferences are now prerequisites to litigation. The conduct and practice of mediation, arbitration and conciliation have become regularised through legislation that spells out the duties of third party neutrals in these processes. Private providers of mediation have also stepped up their own efforts to ensure high-quality dispute resolution and have developed national standards for accreditation of mediators and national standards of practice.

The growth of ADR has opened opportunities for lawyers to develop and practise a broader range of skills. It has also fostered the realisation that litigation is not suited to all contexts, and that other dispute resolution processes serve an important function in providing options for dealing with conflict. Restraint, on the other hand, has reminded us that it is important not to throw out the old in embracing the new. It is now understood that reform to the legal system is just as important as developing and expanding new dispute resolution processes.

The growth in ADR has gone a long way to creating a broader framework for dispute resolution in Australia. As Jeremy Gormly SC, Chair of NADRAC (Foreword to T Sourdin, *Alternative Dispute Resolution*, 4th ed, Thomson Reuters, Sydney, 2012) writes:

> … Dispute has always been with us; but this book deals with a relatively recent, worldwide quite revolution in the field of dispute resolution.
>
> There is nothing wrong with dispute. It is normal. Indeed it is an expression of the basic right to differ. In this sense dispute is closely related to freedom of speech. The right to express contrary views is part of the fabric of a free society and of healthy relationships. When a dispute is connected with an interest whether in money, domestic peace, a decision to acquire or sell or in the use of a right of way, both disputants ad society need the dispute to resolve.
>
> Just as the dispute is healthy, we know that unresolved disputes are costly, damaging and debilitating. They interfere with ordinary discourse. They bring productive activity to a halt. They generate animosity. They fracture otherwise good human relationships and they can interfere with any field of activity in which resolution does not occur.
>
> We recognize not only a right to dispute but also a need and even an obligation to resolve our disputes. Usually that is what we do. Only a tiny sliver of daily disputes find their way to the courts. Indeed only a tiny sliver of the disputes of daily life are amenable to judicial determination. Of those that are, only a small proportion have to be determined by a judge because the rest are settled by agreement between the parties. Courts are the first to recognize that and encourage parties to resolve their own disputes. Courts and judges have been one of the great supports of ADR.
>
> Dispute in daily life is usually resolved by disputants at what amounts to lightening speed. Parties to a dispute do not usually refer to lawyers, to legislation or decided cases to resolve their dispute. They look to the value and preservation of the relationship, to their immediate and long term interests and to the harm of not resolving the dispute. Compromise is made. Risks are covered. Both parties come away with something. Courts cannot do that. They do not resolve disputes. They determine them by application of the law to the facts found after an historical examination of behavior and events. It is fair, clean and resected. It is also labour intensive, disruptive and very stressful. The outcome is not one of mutuality or compromise. It is one of win or loss. It is inevitably expensive and it takes time. Judicial determination is a different process from the dispute-solving we engage in ourselves on a day-to-day basis. In daily life we do not look at the legal detail to settle an argument but courts are obliged to do that.

Jurisdiction

## CHAPTER 4

OVERVIEW

Before a court proceeding can be instituted or an appeal brought, it is necessary to consider whether the court in which it is proposed to commence the proceeding or launch the appeal has the necessary jurisdiction to determine it. In general terms this chapter will deal with two types of jurisdiction:

- subject matter jurisdiction, which refers to the nature of the disputes which may be adjudicated upon by the particular court; and
- territorial jurisdiction, which refers to the person or bodies over whom the court may exercise jurisdiction.

This chapter considers the nature of the subject matter which may be determined by each of the High Court, the Federal Court, the Federal Magistrates' Court and the state and territory Supreme Courts, and of the parties over whom that jurisdiction may be exercised. It also explains the operation of the Cross-vesting of Jurisdiction Scheme which was established in 1987 and involves the Federal Court, the Family Court and each of the state and territory Supreme Courts. The scheme has been declared by the High Court to be partially invalid, but it nevertheless alleviates some of the jurisdictional disputes and difficulties which had arisen from the strict jurisdictional limitations which otherwise applied to those courts.

SUBJECT MATTER JURISDICTION

4.1.1 It is not possible for a work of this nature to provide a comprehensive commentary covering all aspects of jurisdiction of the High Court, the Federal Court, and each of the state and territory Supreme Courts. This section will, however, provide an overview of the principal legislation which defines the jurisdiction of the various courts.

> **4.1.2E**   **Commonwealth Constitution**
>
> **Judicial Power and Courts**
> **71** The judicial power of the Commonwealth shall be vested in a Federal Supreme Court, to be called the High Court of Australia, and in such other federal courts as the Parliament creates, and in such other courts as it invests with federal jurisdiction. The High Court shall consist of a Chief Justice, and so many other Justices, not less than two, as the Parliament prescribes.

4.1.3   Chapter III of the Commonwealth of Australia Constitution Act (ss 71–80) sets out the constitutional framework through which courts are or may be invested with the judicial power of the Commonwealth to enforce its laws. Commonwealth judicial power may only be exercised by one of the three classes of courts listed in s 71, namely the High Court, a Federal Court created by the Commonwealth Parliament, and state and territory courts which are vested with jurisdiction pursuant to Ch III. Jurisdiction which any federal or state or territory court has by virtue of a provision of Ch III is federal jurisdiction.

The High Court

Original jurisdiction

> **4.1.4E**   **Commonwealth Constitution**
>
> **Original jurisdiction of High Court**
> **75** In all matters —
>   (i)   arising under any treaty;
>   (ii)   affecting consuls or other representatives of other countries;
>   (iii) in which the Commonwealth, or a person suing or being sued on behalf of the Commonwealth, is a party;
>   (iv)   between States, or between residents of different States, or between a State and a resident of another State;
>   (v)   in which a writ of mandamus or prohibition or an injunction is sought against an officer of the Commonwealth;
>   the High Court shall have original jurisdiction.
>
> **Additional original jurisdiction**
> **76** The Parliament may make laws conferring original jurisdiction on the High Court in any matter —
>   (i)   arising under this Constitution or involving its interpretation;
>   (ii)   arising under any laws made by the Parliament;
>   (iii) of Admiralty and maritime jurisdiction;
>   (iv)   relating to the same subject matter claimed under the laws of different States.

Power to define jurisdiction

77 With respect to any of the matters mentioned in the last two sections the Parliament may make laws —

   (i)   defining the jurisdiction of any federal court other than the High Court;

   (ii) defining the extent to which the jurisdiction of any federal court shall be exclusive to that which belongs to or is invested in the courts of the States;

   (iii) investing any court of a State with federal jurisdiction.

4.1.5 Parliament exercised the power in s 76(i) through the Judiciary Act 1903 (Cth) s 30(a), through which it conferred original jurisdiction on the High Court 'in all matters arising under the Constitution or involving its interpretation'. Section 40 of the Judiciary Act 1903 (Cth) allows a party to such a cause which is pending in a federal court (other than the High Court) or in a state or territory court, to apply to the High Court for an order removing the matter to the High Court. It directs that the order must be made if the application is made by the Commonwealth Attorney-General or by the Attorney-General of a state or territory.

4.1.6E   **Judiciary Act 1903 (Cth)**

Matters in which jurisdiction of High Court exclusive

38 Subject to sections 39B and 44, the jurisdiction of the High Court shall be exclusive of the jurisdiction of the several courts of the states in the following matters:

   (a) matters arising directly under any treaty;

   (b) suits between states or between persons suing or being sued on behalf of different states, or between a state and a person suing or being sued on behalf of another state;

   (c) suits by the Commonwealth, or any person suing on behalf of the Commonwealth, against a state, or any person being sued on behalf of a state;

   (d) suits by a state, or any person suing on behalf of a state, against the Commonwealth or any person being sued on behalf of the Commonwealth;

   (e) matters in which a writ of mandamus or prohibition is sought against an officer of the Commonwealth or a federal court.

Note: Under the Jurisdiction of Courts (Cross-resting) Act 1987, State Supreme Courts are, with some exceptions and limitations, invested with the same civil jurisdiction as the Federal Court has, including jurisdiction under section 39B of this Act.

4.1.7 Section 38 of the Judiciary Act 1903 (Cth) is an exercise of the power given in s 77 of the Commonwealth Constitution. In effect, it vests within the exclusive jurisdiction of the High Court those matters which are within the original jurisdiction of the High Court and which may be regarded as having the greater national or federal significance. (Other matters are left to concurrent jurisdiction: see **4.1.26E–4.1.27**.) Section 38 is expressed to be subject to ss 39B and 44. Section 39B stipulates a range of matters as falling within the original jurisdiction of the Federal Court: see **4.1.12E**. In very broad terms, s 44 enables the High Court, either of its own motion or on the application of a party, to remit a matter or any part of a matter pending in the High Court to the Federal Court, or to a court of a state or territory. Further proceedings are to be as directed by the court to which the proceedings are remitted but subject to any directions of the High Court.

Appellate jurisdiction

4.1.8E   **Commonwealth Constitution**

Appellate jurisdiction of High Court
73 The High Court shall have jurisdiction, with such exceptions and subject to such regulations as the Parliament prescribes, to hear and determine appeals from all judgments, decrees, orders, and sentences —

  (i)   of any Justice or Justices exercising the original jurisdiction of the High Court;
  (ii) of any other federal court, or court exercising federal jurisdiction; or of the Supreme Court of any State, or of any other court of any State from which at the establishment of the Commonwealth an appeal lies to the Queen in Council;
  (iii) of the Inter-State Commission, but as to questions of law only;
    and the judgment of the High Court in all such cases shall be final and conclusive.
But no exception or regulation prescribed by the parliament shall prevent the High Court from hearing and determining any appeal from the Supreme Court of a state in any matter in which at the establishment of the Commonwealth an appeal lies from such Supreme Court to the Queen in Council.

    Until the Parliament otherwise provides, the conditions of and restrictions on appeals to the Queen in Council from the Supreme Courts of the several states shall be applicable to appeals from them to the High Court.

4.1.9 The High Court's jurisdiction under s 73 to hear and determine appeals from justices exercising the original jurisdiction of the High Court is limited by s 34 of the Judiciary Act 1903 (Cth) so as to require the leave of the High Court to bring an appeal from any interlocutory judgment.

Parliament has also created a number of exceptions to, and restrictions on, the jurisdiction granted under s 73(ii). In relation to the Federal Court of Australia these include the Federal Court of Australia Act 1976 (Cth) s 33, which provides that there shall be no appeal from a decision of a single judge exercising the original jurisdiction of the court, except as otherwise provided by another Act: s 33(2). Special leave of the High Court is required for an appeal from a decision of a single judge exercising the appellate jurisdiction of the court: s 33(4). Except as otherwise provided by another Act, special leave of the High Court is also required for any appeal from a judgment of the Full Court of the Federal Court: s 33(3). There are further limitations contained in s 33(4A), which prohibits any appeal to the High Court from judgments of a Full Court of the Federal Court exercising the original jurisdiction of the Federal Court in relation to decisions of the specific types set out in the subsection. Section 33(4B) also contains prohibitions on the bringing of an appeal to the High Court from judgments of the Federal Court (whether constituted by a Full Court or a single judge) in the exercise of its appellate jurisdiction if the judgments are of the nature of any of the decisions as described in that subsection. The restriction relating to appeals to the High Court from an interlocutory judgment does not prevent a party from founding an appeal from a final judgment in the proceeding on the interlocutory judgment, or prevent the High Court from taking account of the interlocutory judgment in determining an appeal from a final judgment in the proceeding or an application for special leave to appeal from a final judgment in the proceeding: s 33(6).

Appeals from state Supreme Courts (whether the judgments were given or pronounced in the exercise of federal jurisdiction or otherwise) are limited by the Judiciary Act 1903 (Cth) s 35, so as to also require the special leave of the High Court.

The Supreme Court of a federal territory is not a federal court or a court exercising federal jurisdiction within s 73 of the Constitution: *Capital TV and Appliances Pty Ltd v Falconer* (1971) 125 CLR 591. However, under the general legislative power in s 122 of the Constitution to make laws for the government of a territory, the Commonwealth Parliament has created a statutory right of appeal from the Supreme Court of a territory (Judiciary Act 1903 (Cth) s 35AA), but it is essential to obtain the special leave of the High Court to bring the appeal.

The Federal Court

Original jurisdiction

4.1.10E   **Federal Court of Australia Act 1976 (Cth)**

Original jurisdiction

19 (1) The court has such original jurisdiction as is invested in it by laws made by the Parliament.

(2) The original jurisdiction of the court includes any jurisdiction vested in it to hear and determine appeals from decisions of persons, authorities or tribunals other than courts.

4.1.11 The Federal Court of Australia was created by the Federal Court of Australia Act 1976 (Cth) in the exercise by the Commonwealth Parliament of the power conferred on it by s 71 of the Commonwealth Constitution.

The original jurisdiction of the court under s 77(i) of the Commonwealth Constitution and s 19 of the Federal Court of Australia Act 1976 (Cth) is limited to those matters in respect of which parliament has specifically invested the court with jurisdiction. Further, it follows from the wording of ss 75–77 of the Constitution that jurisdiction can only be conferred on the court in relation to the 'matters' mentioned in ss 75 and 76: see 4.1.4E.

A key provision investing the court with jurisdiction in respect of a significant proportion of those matters is s 39B of the Judiciary Act 1903 (Cth).

Original jurisdiction of Federal Court of Australia
Scope of original jurisdiction
39B(1) Subject to subsections (1B) and (1C) and (1EA), the original jurisdiction of the Federal Court of Australia includes jurisdiction with respect to any matter in which a writ of mandamus or prohibition or an injunction is sought against an officer or officers of the Commonwealth.

  (1A) The original jurisdiction of the Federal Court of Australia also includes jurisdiction in any matter:
  (a) in which the Commonwealth is seeking an injunction or a declaration; or
  (b) arising under the Constitution, or involving its interpretation; or
  (c) arising under any laws made by the Parliament, other than a matter in respect of which a criminal prosecution is instituted or any other criminal matter.

4.1.13   The jurisdiction conferred by s 39B(1) corresponds with the jurisdiction conferred on the High Court by s 75(v) of the Constitution, while that conferred by s 39B(1A)(a) is equivalent to part of the jurisdiction conferred on the High Court by s 75(iii). The matters mentioned in s 39B(1A)(b) and (c) correspond with those contained in s 76(i) and part of that contained in s 76(ii) of the Constitution respectively.

Subsection 39B(1A) was inserted into the Judiciary Act 1903 (Cth) on 17 April 1997 by the Law and Justice Legislation Amendment Act 1997 (Cth) and it clearly effected a significant extension of the Federal Court's original jurisdiction. Before the introduction of this section, Act by Act conferral of jurisdiction had given the Federal Court jurisdiction over a broad range of matters, including admiralty, bankruptcy, intellectual property, native title, trade practices, taxation and social security, but in all cases the jurisdiction was limited to those matters where there was a specific federal statute explicitly giving the court jurisdiction. The Explanatory Memorandum to the Law and Justice Legislation Amendment Act 1997 states:

> The additional jurisdiction of the Federal Court is concurrent with the federal jurisdiction of State and Territory Courts in civil matters. The jurisdiction gives the Federal Court a greater role in the administration of federal laws, by ensuring that the Court is able to deal with all matters that are essentially of a federal nature.

Section 39B(1A) has been expansively interpreted as a general conferral of jurisdiction: *Transport Workers Union v Lee* (1998) 84 FCR 60 at 67. In respect of s 39(1A)(c) a matter may be said to arise under a federal law if a claim is made for, or in respect of, a right that owes its existence to federal law, even if the only relief claimed is relief at common law or equity rather than a right to relief under a specific provision of a federal law. It is essential, however, that the relief sought can only be granted if some right exists by force of a federal law: *Elders v Swinbank* (2000) 96 FCR 303. See also *Federal Airports Corporation v Aerolineas Argentinas* (1997) 147 ALR 649; *Fejo v Northern Territory of Australia* (1998) 152 ALR 477.

Appellate jurisdiction

4.1.14   The appellate jurisdiction of the Federal Court and its exercise are prescribed in Div 2 Pt III of the Federal Court of Australia Act 1976 (Cth). The key provision is s 24(1), which provides that subject to that section and to any other Act, the Federal Court has jurisdiction to hear and determine:

(a)   appeals from a single judge of the Federal Court;

(b)   appeals from the Supreme Court of a territory (other than the Australian Capital Territory or Northern Territory);

(c)   appeals from judgments of a court (but excluding Full Courts) of a state, the Australian Capital Territory or the Northern Territory, exercising federal jurisdiction;

(d)   appeals from judgments of the Federal Magistrates Court exercising original jurisdiction under a Federal Law other than the Family Law Act 1975, the Child Support (Assessment Act) 1989, or the Child Support (Registration and Collection) Act 1988, or regulations under any of these Acts; and

(e)   appeals from judgments of the Federal Magistrates' Court exercising jurisdiction under s 72Q of the Child Support (Registration and Collection) Act 1988.

There is, however, no jurisdiction in respect of appeals from a decision of a single judge of the court exercising the original jurisdiction of the court in respect of judgments of the nature as set out in s 24(1AA).

In the case of an interlocutory judgment, s 24(1A) requires that court or judge must give leave to appeal. This requirement is qualified by s 24(1C), which removes any requirement for leave to appeal an interlocutory judgment which affects the liberty of an individual or which is made in proceedings relating to contempt of the Federal Court or any other court. Judgments by consent, and decisions granting or refusing applications for summary judgment, are taken to be interlocutory judgments for the purpose of these provisions: s 24(1D). A party may nevertheless found an appeal from a final judgment on an interlocutory judgment in the proceeding, and the court may take account of the interlocutory judgment in determining an appeal from a final judgment: s 24(1E).

Section 25 governs the exercise of the appellant jurisdiction of the Federal Court. Although this jurisdiction is generally to be exercised by a Full Court, there are a range of circumstances set out in the section where the jurisdiction may, or in some instances must, be exercised by a single judge. The manner in which a court may deal with an appeal is set out in s 28.

Reference jurisdiction

4.1.15   Section 25(6) of the Federal Court of Australia Act 1976 (Cth) provides that a single judge of the Federal Court may state any case or reserve any question concerning a matter (whether or not an appeal would lie from a judgment of the judge to the Full Federal Court on the matter) for the consideration of the Full Federal Court, and gives the Full Federal Court jurisdiction to hear and determine the case or question.

Section 26(1) of the same Act provides that a court from which an appeal lies to the Federal Court may state any case or reserve any question for the consideration of the Federal Court, and that the Federal Court has jurisdiction to determine that case or question. Subject to any other Act, the jurisdiction is to be exercised by a Full Court, except if the referring court is one of summary jurisdiction, in which case it may be exercised by a single judge or by a Full Court: s 26(2).

Associated jurisdiction; accrued jurisdiction

4.1.16E   **Federal Court of Australia Act 1976 (Cth)**

32 Jurisdiction in associated matters
Associated matters — civil proceedings

  (1) To the extent that the Constitution permits, jurisdiction is conferred on the Court in respect of matters not otherwise within its jurisdiction that are associated with matters (the *core matters*) in which the jurisdiction of the Court is invoked.

  (2) The jurisdiction conferred by subsection (1) extends to jurisdiction to hear and determine an appeal from a judgment of a court so far as it relates to a matter that is associated with a matter (the *core matter*) in respect of which an appeal from that judgment, or another judgment of that Court, is brought.

    ...

4.1.17   As previously noted, it follows from the wording of ss 75–77 of the Commonwealth Constitution (see **4.1.4E**) that jurisdiction can be conferred on a Federal Court, only with respect to 'matters' mentioned in ss 75 and 76 of the Constitution, and that 'the Constitution gives no power to confer jurisdiction on a federal court with respect to a matter simply because it is associated with any of the matters mentioned in ss 75 and 76, however close that association may be': *Philip Morris Inc v Adam P Brown Male Fashions Pty Ltd* (1981) 148 CLR 457 at 493; 33 ALR 465 at 489 per Gibbs J; *Fencott v Muller* (1983) 152 CLR 570 at 581; 41 ALR 41 at 46 per Gibbs CJ. Accordingly, the associated jurisdiction conferred by the Federal Court of Australia Act 1976 (Cth) s 32 enables the Federal Court to determine only *federal* claims otherwise outside the Federal Court's jurisdiction but which are associated with the claim within the court's primary jurisdiction. Both claims must arise out of facts substantially the same or closely connected.

    Although at one time an important source of additional jurisdiction for the Federal Court, the enactment of s 39B(1A) of the Judiciary Act 1903 (Cth) (see **4.1.12E**) has greatly diminished the significance of the associated jurisdiction.

4.1.18   The Federal Court also has an 'accrued jurisdiction' based upon ss 76(ii) and 77(i) of the Commonwealth Constitution and ss 19 and 22 of the Federal Court of Australia Act 1976 (Cth) (rather than s 32). (Section 22 directs that the court shall grant all remedies to which any of the parties before it appear to be entitled so that, so far as possible, all matters in controversy between the parties may be completely and finally determined and all multiplicity of proceedings concerning any of those matters avoided.) This is a discretionary jurisdiction enabling determination of claims which arise under the common law or state legislation if they are part of the same 'matter' as the claim within the Federal Court's primary jurisdiction. Thus in *Philip Morris Inc v Adam P Brown Male Fashions Pty Ltd* (1981) 148 CLR 457 (HC); (1980) 31 ALR 232 (FC), the High Court held that the Federal Court of Australia had jurisdiction to decide a passing off claim in an action which also involved an alleged contravention of the Trade Practices Act 1974 (Cth) (now Competition and Consumer Act 2010 (Cth)), although there were significant variations in the reasons given in the judgments. The decision in *Philip Morris* was considered by the High Court in *Fencott v Muller* (1983) 152 CLR

570; 46 ALR 41, and subsequently in *Re Wakim; Ex parte McNally* (1999) 198 CLR 511; 163 ALR 270. In general terms those cases make it clear that the federal and non-federal claims joined in a proceeding must both fall within the scope of one controversy, and hence within the ambit of the one 'matter'.

4.1.19C   **Fencott v Muller**
                                        (1983) 152 CLR 570
                                        High Court of Australia

[In complex proceedings before the Federal Court, claims were made for damages for breach of the Trade Practices Act 1974 (Cth) s 52 (see now Australian Consumer Law s 18), along with alternative claims at common law for fraud, negligence or breach of contract. These claims related to allegedly false representations made by the respondents as to the profits and turnover of a business subsequently purchased by one of the applicants. Additional parties were also involved in related claims which included breach of fiduciary duty and a claim for an indemnity. An objection was taken in the Federal Court to the jurisdiction of the court, which was allowed in part but otherwise dismissed. The appellants, who were three of the respondents to the proceedings in the Federal Court, appealed to the Full Court of the Federal Court, contending that the proceedings were entirely outside the jurisdiction of the Federal Court, so that the objection to the jurisdiction should have been allowed in full. There was no cross-appeal against that part of the judgment which held that certain parts of the proceedings were beyond jurisdiction. The appeal was removed into the High Court. The High Court, by majority, affirmed the decision of the Federal Court. The brief extract here is from that part of the majority judgment which relates to the 'accrued' jurisdiction of the Federal Court.]

Mason, Murphy, Brennan and Deane JJ (at CLR 603–608): Though the concept of 'matter' may be narrower than that of a 'legal proceeding', it is a term of wide import. 'The word "matters"', Griffith CJ said in *South Australia v Victoria* [(1911) 12 CLR 667 at 675], 'was in 1900 in common use as the widest term to denote controversies which might come before a Court of Justice'. The concept of 'matter' as a justiciable controversy, identifiable independently of the proceedings which are brought for its determination and encompassing all claims made within the scope of the controversy, was accepted by a majority of the Court in *Philip Morris*. Barwick CJ said [(1981) 148 CLR at 475]:

> It is settled doctrine in Australia that when a court which can exercise federal jurisdiction has its jurisdiction attracted in relation to a matter, that jurisdiction extends to the resolution of the whole matter. This accrued federal jurisdiction is not limited to matters incidental to that aspect of the matter which has, in the first place, attracted federal jurisdiction. In [sic] extends, in my opinion, to the resolution of the whole matter between the parties. This accrued jurisdiction carries with it the authority to make such remedial orders as are necessary or convenient for or in consequence of that resolution. For this [604] purpose, the court exercising federal jurisdiction may enforce rights which derive from a non-federal source. This exercise of this jurisdiction, which for want of a better term I shall call 'accrued' jurisdiction, is discretionary and not mandatory, though it will be obligatory to exercise the federal jurisdiction which has been attracted in relation to the matter.

And thus his Honour, in defining the matter in the proceedings between Philip Morris and Adam P Brown did not identify it as a cause of action but said [(1981) 148 CLR at 479–80]:

> The substantial matter between the parties was their difference as to the assertion of and attempt to protect the rights claimed to belong to the plaintiffs by reason of the trade marks or the acquired business reputation. The claim to relief under Ch V of the Act was one endeavour to protect these rights. The claim to equitable relief for passing off was another. The former attracted federal jurisdiction: the latter, not being disparate and independent of the former, was part of the whole matter between the parties and thus within the accrued federal jurisdiction. Thus, it seems to me that the federal jurisdiction attracted by the claim for misleading and deceptive conduct extends to the resolution of the entire matter between the parties, which includes the claim for passing off, not merely as an associated claim but as part of the entirety of the matter between the parties in relation to which federal jurisdiction has been attracted. ...

Subject to any contrary provision made by federal law and subject to the limitation upon the capacity of non-federal laws to affect federal courts, non-federal law is part of the single, composite body of law applicable alike to cases determined in the exercise of federal jurisdiction and to cases determined in the exercise of non-federal jurisdiction (cf *Felton v Mulligan* [(1971) 124 CLR at 392, 399]).

It follows also that, though the facts upon which a non-federal claim arises do not wholly coincide with the facts upon which a federal claim arises, it is nevertheless possible that both may be aspects of a single matter arising under a federal law. Mason J in *Philip Morris* [(1981) 148 CLR at 512], following what was said in *Moorgate Tobacco* [(1980) 145 CLR 457], gave an indication of a non-federal claim which would not be severable:

> Likewise, it may appear that the attached claim and the federal claim so depend on common transactions and facts that they arise out of a common substratum of facts. In instances of this kind a court which exercises federal jurisdiction will have jurisdiction to determine the attached claim as an element in the exercise of its federal jurisdiction.

His Honour's reference to a dependence of federal and non-federal claims upon common transactions and facts approximates the test in *United Mine Workers of America v Gibbs* [(1966) 383 US at p 725 [16 Law Ed (2nd) at p 228]] that the claims 'must derive from a common nucleus of operative fact'. Barwick CJ thought [(1981) 148 CLR at p 476] that that test, if applied to Ch III of the Constitution, may be too wide because it 'would seem to warrant an accretion of non-federal jurisdiction which is not necessary or convenient for the resolution of the case or controversy which has been the source of the federal jurisdiction in the first place, but extends to what is described as "an associated matter". As I remark in relation to s 32 of the Federal Court Act, the word "associated" embraces matter which may be disparate from each other.'

Perhaps it is not possible to devise so precise a formula that its application to the facts of any controversy would determine accurately what claims are disparate and what claims are not. Whatever formula be adopted as a guide and the formula of 'common transactions and facts' is a sound guide for the purpose it must result in leaving outside the ambit of a matter a 'completely disparate claim constituting in substance a separate proceeding' (per

Barwick CJ in *Felton v Mulligan* [(1971) 124 CLR at p 373]), a non-federal matter which is 'completely separate and distinct from the matter which attracted [608] federal jurisdiction' (per Murphy J in *Philip Morris* [(1981) 148 CLR at p 521]) or 'some distinct and unrelated non-federal claim' (per Stephen, Mason, Aickin and Wilson JJ in *Moorgate Tobacco* [(1980) 145 CLR at p 482]).

Claims which are described by these or similar phrases cannot be determined by exercise of the judicial power referred to in s 71 of the Constitution, for that power can be exercised only to determine those matters in which federal jurisdiction is or can be conferred under Ch III of the Constitution. For precisely this reason, however, it is necessary to attribute to 'matter' in ss 75 and 76 of the Constitution a connotation which does not deny to federal judicial power its primary character: that is, the power of a sovereign authority 'to decide controversies between its subjects, or between itself and its subjects, whether the rights relate to life, liberty or property' (per Griffith CJ in *Huddart, Parker & Co Pty Ltd v Moorehead* [(1909) 8 CLR 330 at p 357]). The unique and essential function of the judicial power is the quelling of such controversies by ascertainment of the facts, by application of the law and by exercise, where appropriate, of judicial discretion. In identifying a s 76(ii) matter, it would be erroneous to exclude a substantial part of what is in truth a single justiciable controversy and thereby to preclude the exercise of judicial power to determine the whole of that controversy. What is and what is not part of the one controversy depends on what the parties have done, the relationships between or among them and the laws which attach rights or liabilities to their conduct and relationships. The scope of a controversy which constitutes a matter is not ascertained merely by reference to the proceedings which a party may institute, but may be illuminated by the conduct of those proceedings and especially by the pleadings in which the issues in controversy are defined and the claims for relief are set out. But in the end, it is a matter of impression and of practical judgment whether a non-federal claim and a federal claim joined in a proceeding are within the scope of one controversy and thus within the ambit of a matter.

4.1.20C   **Re Wakim; Ex parte McNally**
(1999) 198 CLR 511; 163 ALR 270
High Court of Australia

[In July 1985, Mr Wakim was awarded damages in the Supreme Court of New South Wales for personal injuries sustained in an accident in the course of his employment by Tedros Nader and Nawal Nader. His action was brought against Tedros Nader only. In October 1985, Tedros Nader was declared bankrupt and the Official Trustee in Bankruptcy (the Trustee) was appointed trustee of his estate. In June 1987, the Trustee brought proceedings in the Supreme Court of New South Wales against Nawal Nader, seeking orders that her partnership with Tedros Nader was or had been dissolved. A firm of solicitors in which Messrs McNally were partners was retained by the Trustee, and the firm in turn retained Mr Darvall QC.

In March 1990, the parties settled. It was agreed that Mr Wakim be paid $10,000. In July 1993, Mr Wakim brought proceedings in the Federal Court against the trustee. One of his claims was made pursuant to s 176 of the Bankruptcy Act 1966 (Cth), on the basis that the trustee had been guilty of a breach of duty as trustee of the bankrupt estate. Following the commencement of those proceedings, Mr Wakim brought two further actions against Mr Darvall and the firm of solicitors in negligence.

Mr Darvall and the solicitors contended that the Federal Court had no jurisdiction to hear the action in negligence and sought a writ of prohibition. The decision involved a successful challenge to the constitutional validity of those provisions of the scheme for cross-vesting of jurisdiction through which state jurisdiction was conferred on federal courts. The case is considered in that context at 4.3.2. However, in view of the court's finding in that regard it became necessary for the court to consider whether the Federal Court would determine the negligence claims in the exercise of its accrued jurisdiction.]

Gummow and Hayne JJ (at CLR 585–588): In *Fencott* it was said that [(1983) 152 CLR 570 at 608 per Mason, Murphy, Brennan and Deane JJ]: 'in the end, it is a matter of impression and of practical judgment whether a non-federal claim and a federal claim joined in a proceeding are within the scope of one controversy and thus within the ambit of a matter.' The references to 'impression' and 'practical judgment' cannot be understood, however, as stating a test that is to be applied. Considerations of impression and practical judgment are relevant because the question of jurisdiction usually arises before evidence is adduced and often before the pleadings are complete. Necessarily, then, the question will have to be decided on limited information. But the question is not at large. What is a single controversy 'depends on what the parties have done, the relationships between or among them and the laws which attach rights or liabilities to their conduct and relationships' [*Fencott* (1983) 152 CLR 570 at 608 per Mason, Murphy, Brennan and Deane JJ]. There is but a single matter if different claims arise out of 'common transactions and facts' or 'a common substratum of facts' [*Philip Morris* (1981) 148 CLR 457 at 512 Mason J], notwithstanding that the facts upon which the claims depend 'do not wholly coincide' [*Fencott* (1983) 152 CLR 570 at 607 per Mason, Murphy, Brennan and Deane JJ]. So, too, there is but one matter where different claims are so related that the determination of one is essential to the determination of the other [*Philip Morris* (1981) 148 CLR 457 at 512 Mason J], as, for example, in the case of third party proceedings or where there are alternative claims for the same [586] damage and the determination of one will either render the other otiose or necessitate its determination. Conversely, claims which are 'completely disparate' [*Felton v Mulligan* (1971) 124 CLR 367 at 373 per Barwick CJ], 'completely separate and distinct' [*Philip Morris* (1981) 148 CLR 457 at 521 Mason J], or 'distinct and unrelated' [*Moorgate Tobacco Co Ltd v Philip Morris Ltd* (1980) 145 CLR 457 at 482 per Stephen, Mason, Aickin and Wilson JJ] are not part of the same matter.

Often, the conclusion that, if proceedings were tried in different courts, there could be conflicting findings made on one or more issues common to the two proceedings will indicate that there is a single matter. By contrast, if the several proceedings could not have been joined in one proceeding, it is difficult to see that they could be said to constitute a single matter.

Here, the three proceedings could have been joined in one. The fact that those advising Mr Wakim chose to issue separate proceedings at different times does not mean that the scope of the controversy is limited to the matters raised in the first proceeding. Had the Official Trustee brought a cross-claim against both the solicitors and Mr Darvall immediately after Mr Wakim commenced his proceeding against it and if Mr Wakim had then joined the cross-respondents as respondents to his principal claim, the existence of a single controversy involving several parties would be more apparent than it may be in the present circumstances. But neither the differences in the present procedural history nor the absence of any claim by the Official Trustee against the solicitors and Mr Darvall determines the question whether there is a single controversy.

The applicants submitted that the test should be qualified by restricting cases of accrued jurisdiction to those in which no party was added in reliance upon accrued jurisdiction. That is, the applicants contended that there must be some federal claim against every respondent in the proceedings ...

[587] As we have said, the bringing of separate proceedings and the joining of different parties will often be important facts in deciding whether there is a single justiciable controversy for the purposes of Ch III of the Australian Constitution. But there is no basis in principle for concluding that there can never be accrued jurisdiction where a new party is joined. To adopt such a rule would mean that third party proceedings could never be brought in a federal court unless those third party proceedings were founded in some federal claim. And that points to the underlying difficulty in principle. If the 'matter' is to be identified from what the parties allege and how they conduct the proceeding (as *Fencott* and *Stack* hold) and if the 'justiciable controversy' refers (in part, at least) to the factual dispute between them, there is no warrant for holding that federal jurisdiction ends as soon as a new party (against whom no federal claim is made) is added. Each of these proceedings brought by Mr Wakim centres upon the making of claims and bringing of action against Mrs Nader and the prosecution and settlement of those claims and that action. Mr Wakim alleges against the Official Trustee that it was negligent and guilty of breach of duty in not continuing the action against Mrs Nader; he alleges against the solicitors that they negligently failed to advise the Official Trustee of its rights against her; he alleges against Mr Darvall that he negligently failed to advise the Official Trustee of its rights against her. It may be noted that nowhere in the Official Trustee's defence to Mr Wakim's claim does it allege that it acted in reliance on the advice of the solicitors or counsel and it makes no cross-claims against them. Indeed, the pleadings in the proceeding between Mr Wakim and the Official Trustee say nothing whatever about the role of the solicitors or counsel in the matter.

The cases arise out of one set of events. Of most significance is the fact that the damage which Mr Wakim alleges he has suffered as a result of what he says are the various breaches of duty by the Official Trustee, the solicitors and Mr Darvall is, in each case, the loss of what he might have recovered in the bankruptcy had the claims against [588] Mrs Nader been prosecuted differently. There is, then, but a single claim for damages that he seeks to pursue against each of the parties he has sued. And judgment and recovery against one will diminish the amount that may be recovered from the others. There is, in these circumstances, that common substratum of facts in each proceeding of which Mason J spoke in *Philip Morris* [(1981) 148 CLR 457 at 512. See also *Fencott* (1983) 152 CLR 570 at 604–5 per Mason, Murphy, Brennan and Deane JJ].

In *Philip Morris* [(1981) 148 CLR 457 at 475], Barwick CJ said that the exercise of the 'accrued' jurisdiction 'is discretionary and not mandatory, though it will be obligatory to exercise the federal jurisdiction which has been attracted in relation to the matter'. In *Stack* [(1983) 154 CLR 261 at 294–5], Mason Brennan and Deane JJ refer to this proposition with approval [(1983) 154 CLR 261 at 294–5] but say that the idea is similar to the process of identification of a related matter mentioned in *Fencott* as being 'a matter of impression and of practical judgment' [(1983) 152 CLR 570 at 608 per Mason, Murphy, Brennan and Deane JJ]. There may be some difficulty in analysing the question as one of 'discretion'. It is not clear what principles or criteria would inform the exercise of a discretion of this kind. It may be that the better view is that the references to 'discretion' are not intended to convey more than that difficult questions of fact and degree will arise in such issues — questions about which reasonable minds may well differ. It is, however, not necessary to decide what is meant by the references to discretion in this context.

[**Gleeson CJ** and **Gaudron J** agreed with the reasons of **Gummow** and **Hayne JJ**. **McHugh J** expressed doubt as to whether there was a single controversy in the matter but regarded the applications for prohibition as premature. **Callinan J** dissented on this issue. His Honour concluded that there was not one justiciable controversy. **Kirby P** would have upheld the validity of the relevant provisions of the cross-vesting scheme and did not therefore consider whether the Federal Court would also have accrued jurisdiction.

The applications for prohibition in these matters were dismissed.

See also: *Stack v Coast Securities (No 9) Pty Ltd* (1983) 154 CLR 261; 49 ALR 193; *New South Wales Aboriginal Land Council v Aboriginal and Torres Strait Islander Commission* (1995) 131 ALR 559 at 574–5; *Johnson Tiles Pty Ltd v Esso Australia Pty Ltd* (2000) ATPR 41-743; *Elders v Swinbank* (2000) 96 FCR 303.]

4.1.21 The Federal Court will not have any accrued jurisdiction if the primary claim is untenable or not genuinely pursued, or is clearly so untenable that it could not possibly succeed: *New South Wales Land Council v Aboriginal and Torres Strait Islander Commission* (1995) 131 ALR 559 at 572. But if that primary claim is genuine, the court will retain the accrued jurisdiction to determine the attached non-federal claims, even if the primary federal claim fails: *Burgundy Royale Investments Pty Ltd v Westpac Banking Corp* (1988) 76 ALR 173. See also *Johnson Tiles Pty Ltd v Esso Australia Ltd* (2000) 104 FCR 564 at [88] and see **10.9.10**.

Incidental jurisdiction

4.1.22 The Federal Court is declared to be a superior court of record (Federal Court of Australia Act 1976 (Cth) s 5), but it is a court of statutory jurisdiction and accordingly does not have inherent jurisdiction in the same way as the Supreme Courts: see *Jackson v Sterling Industries Ltd* (1987) 162 CLR 612; *Papazoglou v Republic of the Philippines* (1997) 144 ALR 42 at 69.

However, in the exercise of its jurisdiction and in addition to powers which are expressly or impliedly conferred upon it by statute, the Federal Court's powers extend to 'whatever is incidental and necessary to the exercise of that jurisdiction and to the exercise of any powers conferred by legislation': *Wardley Australia Ltd v Western Australia* (1992) 175 CLR 514 at 561; 99 ALR 193. See also *Parsons v Martin* (1984) 5 FCR 235 at 241; *Harris v Caladine* (1991) 172 CLR 84 at 136; 99 ALR 193. This will include powers to control and supervise its own proceedings and to prevent abuse of its process.

The Federal Magistrates' Court

4.1.23 The Federal Magistrates' Court was established as a federal court under Ch III of the Constitution by the Federal Magistrates Act 1999 (Cth). The court was established to deal with a range of matters of a less complex nature that were being dealt with by the Federal Court and the Family Court. It was intended to give litigants a quicker, cheaper option and to ease the workload of the Federal Court and the Family Court. The court derives its jurisdiction from the Federal Magistrates (Consequential Amendments) Act 1999 (Cth). Its jurisdiction is concurrent with the Federal Court or the Family Court, whichever has jurisdiction, and there are provisions for the transfer of matters from the Federal Magistrates' Court to the Federal Court or the Family Court, as well as provisions for the transfer of matters of a less complex nature from the Federal Court or the Family Court to the Federal Magistrates' Court. The procedures applying in the Federal Magistrates' Court will not be examined in this text.

Supreme Courts

Original and appellate jurisdiction

4.1.24E   **Constitution of Queensland Act 1991 (Qld)**

Supreme Court's superior jurisdiction
58 (1) The Supreme Court has all jurisdiction that is necessary for the administration of justice in Queensland.
  (2) Without limiting subsection (1), the court —
      (a) is the superior court of record in Queensland and the supreme court of general jurisdiction in and for the State; and
      (b) has, subject to the Commonwealth Constitution, unlimited jurisdiction at law, in equity and otherwise.

4.1.25   As in Queensland, legislation in the Australian Capital Territory (Australian Capital Territory (Self-Government) Act 1988 (Cth) s 48A; Supreme Court Act 1933 (ACT) s 20), New South Wales (Supreme Court Act 1970, s 23) and Victoria (Constitution Act 1975 s 85) defines the jurisdiction of their respective Supreme Courts as extending to anything which may be necessary to do justice. In the other jurisdictions, Supreme Court jurisdiction is still defined by reference to superior courts in England as they existed before the Judicature Acts 1873–1875 (UK): Supreme Court Act 1979 (NT) s 14 (defined as the jurisdiction of the Supreme Court of South Australia immediately before 1 January 1911; this in turn was defined by reference to the English courts); Supreme Court Act 1935 s 17 (SA); Australian Courts Act 1828 (Imp) ss 3, 11 (Tas); Supreme Court Act 1935 (WA) s 16.

In respect of both categories, the provisions have been widely construed with the result that the Supreme Courts have a wide general jurisdiction. However, as the Victorian Court of Appeal made clear in *City of Collingwood v Victoria (No 2)* [1994] 1 VR 652 (see, in particular, p 663 per Brooking J) the judicial power of the Supreme Courts is not sacrosanct; it may be enlarged, reduced, modified or excluded by legislation. In determining whether a Supreme Court has any particular jurisdiction, it is therefore necessary not only to refer to the general jurisdiction of the court as stated in the legislation governing in general terms jurisdiction of the court, but also to consider the limits imposed upon state courts as being part of the Australian federal structure, and to look at the impact upon the court's jurisdiction of any statutes dealing with specific heads of subject matter: see also *Kable v Director of Public Prosecutions (NSW)* (1996) 138 ALR 577.

Federal jurisdiction

4.1.26E	**Judiciary Act 1903 (Cth)**

Federal jurisdiction of State courts in other matters

39 (1) The jurisdiction of the High Court, so far as it is not exclusive of the jurisdiction of any Court of a State by virtue of section 38, shall be exclusive of the jurisdiction of the several Courts of the States, except as provided in this section.

(2) The several Courts of the States shall within the limits of their several jurisdictions, whether such limits are as to locality, subject-matter or otherwise, be invested with federal jurisdiction in all matters in which the High Court has original jurisdiction or in which original jurisdiction can be conferred upon it, except as provided in section 38, and subject to the following conditions and restrictions —

(a) A decision of a Court of a State, whether in original or in appellate jurisdiction shall not be subject to appeal to Her Majesty in Council, whether by special leave or otherwise.

Special leave to appeal from decisions of State Courts though State law prohibits appeal.

(c) The High Court may grant special leave to appeal to the High Court from any decision of any Court or Judge of a State notwithstanding that the law of the State may prohibit any appeal from such Court or Judge.

Federal jurisdiction invested in State courts by other provisions

39A (1) The federal jurisdiction with which a Court of a State is invested by or under any Act, whether the investing occurred or occurs before or after the commencement of this section, including federal jurisdiction invested by a provision of this Act other than the last preceding section:

(a) shall be taken to be invested subject to the provisions of paragraph (a) of subsection (2) of the last preceding section; and

(b) shall be taken to be invested subject to paragraph 39(2)(c) (whether or not the jurisdiction is expressed to be invested subject to that paragraph), so far as it can apply and is not inconsistent with a provision made by or under the Act by or under which the jurisdiction is invested;

in addition to any other conditions or restrictions subject to which the jurisdiction is expressed to be invested.

...

4.1.27 Section 39(2) of the Judiciary Act is the principal provision conferring jurisdiction on state courts. It seeks to achieve its purpose through a circuitous two-step process. Section 39(1) makes the jurisdiction of the High Court exclusive of the jurisdiction of state courts. This was an exercise of the power in s 77(ii) of the Constitution to 'define the extent to which the jurisdiction of any federal court shall be exclusive of that which belongs to or is invested in the courts of the States'. The subsection therefore divests the state courts of jurisdiction they would otherwise have in all matters referred to in s 75 of the Constitution.

Section 39(2), in exercise of the constitutional power in s 77(iii) of the Constitution, then invests state courts with federal jurisdiction in all matters in which the High Court has original jurisdiction or in which original jurisdiction can be conferred upon it. Excepted are constitutional and other matters which are exclusively the jurisdiction of the High Court pursuant to s 38 of the Judiciary Act 1903 (Cth): see 4.1.6E. Section 39(2) presumably picks up all other matters listed in ss 75 and 76 of the Constitution. There was for many years some confusion as to the scheme of s 39, as it was arguable that what was taken away by s 39(1) and what was vested by s 39(2) were not co-extensive, and that in matters listed in s 76 of the Constitution state courts possessed both federal jurisdiction (which was subject to the conditions listed in s 39(2)) and their own state jurisdiction as courts of general jurisdiction, which was not subject to conditions. The High Court ended this confusion with its decision in *Fenton v Mulligan* (1971) 124 CLR 367, in which it held that federal jurisdiction excluded the operation of concurrent state jurisdiction because of s 109 of the Constitution, which renders a state law inoperative to the extent that it is inconsistent with a Commonwealth law. The result is that there is no state jurisdiction concurrent with federal jurisdiction invested in a state court.

Despite the broad terms of s 39 of the Judiciary Act 1903 (Cth), other federal Acts may impose conditions or restrictions on the exercise of federal jurisdiction by state courts. Examples include: Competition and Consumer Act 2010 ss 138 and 138B (making exclusive the jurisdiction of the Federal Court in relation to matters arising under Div 3 of Pt 3-1, or under Pt 3-5, of the Australian Consumer Law); Patents Act 1990 (Cth) s 154(2) (making exclusive the jurisdiction of the Federal Court to hear and determine appeals against decisions of the Commissioner of Patents); Trade Marks Act 1995 (Cth) s 191 (making exclusive the jurisdiction of the Federal Court to hear and determine appeals against decisions, directions or orders of the Registrar of Trade Marks); and Designs Act 2003 s 83 (making exclusive the jurisdiction of the Federal Court to hear and determine appeals from decisions of the Registrar of Designs).

Inherent jurisdiction

4.1.28 The jurisdiction of a Supreme Court includes all those powers which are necessary to enable it to act effectively and to control its own proceedings and to prevent obstruction or abuse of its process. Examples of the exercise of inherent jurisdiction include: making practice directions (*Langley v North West Water Authority* [1991] 3 All ER 610); awarding costs and making orders for security for costs (*Rajski v Computer Manufacture and Design Pty Ltd* [1982] 2 NSWLR 443); and staying or striking out actions or pleadings which are frivolous, vexatious or an abuse of process: *General Steel Industries Inc v Commissioner for Railways (NSW)* (1964) 112 CLR 125.

The inherent jurisdiction of the court extends to making its own internal arrangements in relation to the exercise of its jurisdiction, subject to any relevant statutory requirements: *Rajski v Wood* (1989) 18 NSWLR 512. See further 1.4.4–1.4.6 and 4.1.29.

4.1.29 Notes and questions

1. Artificial persons or corporations are not encompassed by s 75(iv) of the Commonwealth Constitution; the words 'residents' or 'resident' in that section being interpreted to refer only to natural persons: *Australian Temperance and General Mutual Life Assurance Society Ltd v Howe* (1922) 31 CLR 290.

2. Could federal jurisdiction extend to the provision of an advisory opinion in relation to some subject matter referred to in ss 75 or 76 of the Commonwealth Constitution such as, for example, the meaning of a provision of the Constitution? In *Re Judiciary and Navigation Acts* (1921) 29 CLR 257 at 265–6, the High Court held that a 'matter' within ss 75 or 76 referred to the subject matter for determination and required that there be some immediate right, duty or liability to be established by the determination of the court. The mere provision of an advisory opinion or the making of a declaration at large is not sufficient.

3. The decision in *Momcilovic v The Queen* [2011] HCA 34; 280 ALR 221 provides an interesting illustration of the exercise by a state court of federal jurisdiction as a result of the interaction of s 75(iv) of the Commonwealth Constitution and s 39(2) of the Judiciary Act: see 4.1.4E, 4.1.27). In that case Ms Momcilovic was convicted after a jury trial in the Victorian County Court of trafficking in a drug of dependency, contrary to s 71AC of the Drugs, Poisons and Controlled Substances Act 1981 (Vic). The Victorian Court of Appeal dismissed her application for leave to appeal against conviction. Both the trial in the Victorian County Count and the appeal to the Court of Appeal involved the exercise of federal jurisdiction as a matter between a state (Victoria) and a resident of another state (since by the time of the trial the appellant had become a resident of Queensland) (French CJ at [6], [9] and [99]; Gummow J at [134]–[139]; and Crennan and Kiefel J at [594]). French CJ explained at [99]:

> [99] State Courts may be invested with federal jurisdiction pursuant to s 77(iii) of the Constitution in matters in which the High Court has original jurisdiction conferred on it by s 75 of the Constitution or can have original l jurisdiction conferred on it by the Parliament pursuant to s 76 of the Constitution. The classes of matter in which the High Court has original jurisdiction conferred on it by s 75(iv) include matters "between a State and a resident of another State." By operation of s 39(2) of the Judiciary Act the Supreme Court is "invested with federal jurisdiction in such matters … A 'matter' between a State and a resident of another State is a matter of federal jurisdiction notwithstanding that it arises under a State law or the common law or both.

In this case it was not until submissions made in the High Court presented by Western Australia as intervener that significance of the nature of the jurisdiction as Federal jurisdiction became apparent. For consideration of this aspect of the High Court decision, see: Australian Government Solicitor, 'Inconsistency of Commonwealth and State Laws; Validity and Operation of Victorian Charter of Human Rights', 21 *Australian Government Solicitor Litigation Notes*, 2 November 2011, at <http://www.ags.gov.au/publications/agspubs/legalpubs/litigationnotes/LN21.pdf>.

4. The introduction of s 39B(1A) into the Judicature Act 1903 (Cth) (see 4.1.12E–4.1.13) was intended to avoid consequences which had resulted from the previous position of limited Act by Act conferral of jurisdiction, such as that demonstrated in *Kodak (Australasia) Pty Ltd v Commonwealth* (1988) 22 FCR 197: *Transport Workers Union v Lee* (1998) 84 FCR 60 at 67. In *Kodak*,

the applicant had brought proceedings in the Federal Court seeking recovery of sales tax paid by it under protest, pursuant to s 12A(2) of the Sales Tax Procedure Act 1934 (Cth). That section authorised the bringing of such an action 'in any Commonwealth or State Court of competent jurisdiction'. In dismissing the proceeding, Lockhart J held that s 12A(2) did not confer express or implied jurisdiction on the Federal Court.

5. The authority in s 77(iii) of the Commonwealth Constitution to 'invest' state courts with federal jurisdiction does not enable the Commonwealth Parliament to make laws which affect or alter the structure of state courts or the organisation through which their powers and jurisdiction are exercised: see *Russell v Russell* (1976) 134 CLR 495; *Le Mesurier v Connor* (1929) 42 CLR 481.

6. A 'court of a state' which may be invested with federal jurisdiction in the exercise of the power conferred by s 77(iii) of the Constitution, extends not only to judges but also to other judicial officers such as masters and registrars who, through the structure and organisation of the particular state court, exercise limited judicial functions. The jurisdiction to be exercised by such officers may therefore encompass federal jurisdiction: *Commonwealth v Hospital Contribution Fund of Australia* (1982) 150 CLR 49 (the High Court, by majority, declined to follow earlier authorities on this issue).

7. The Australian Law Reform Commission was asked to examine the application, operation and possible reform of the Judiciary Act 1903 (Cth). The review began in January 2000. One of the key matters for investigation related to the distribution of federal judicial power among federal and state courts: see Australian Law Reform Commission Discussion Paper 64: *The Judicial Power of the Commonwealth: A Review of the Judiciary Act 1903 and Related Legislation*, Canberra, December 2000. The final report of the same name (ALRC 92) sets out 125 recommendations for amendments to the Judiciary Act 1903 and related legislation such as the High Court of Australia Act 1979 (Cth), the Federal Court of Australia Act 1976 (Cth), the Family Law Act 1975 (Cth), and the Federal Magistrates Act 1999 (Cth). The report was tabled in Federal Parliament on 2 October 2001. There has been no formal response to the recommendations in ALRC 92. Some recommendations have been implemented, but there has been no significant change to the distribution of federal judicial power among federal and state courts.

8. In November 2008, the Government released the report *Future Governance Options for Federal Family Law Courts in Australia*, which found that the arrangements for the Federal Magistrates' Court were financially unsustainable, lead to confusion among litigants, conflict over resources and inefficiencies in administration, and impeded access to justice and the delivery of family law services. In line with one of the key recommendations of that report, the Commonwealth Attorney-General announced on 5 May 2009 that the Federal Courts would be restructured, by merging the Federal Magistrates' Court into the Family Court and the Federal Court. All family law matters were to be consolidated under the Family Court, and all general federal law matters were to be consolidated under the Federal Court. However, the Federal Government subsequently shifted its policy to propose a

restructure of the Federal Magistrates Court through the Access to Justice (Family Court Restructure and Other Measures) Bill 2010. Under that proposed new structure, the Federal Magistrates' Court will continue to hear general federal law matters but the court's family law component will operate as a general division of the Family Court.

4.1.30   Further reading

L Aickin, 'The Meaning of "Matter": A Matter of Meaning — Some Problems of Accrued Jurisdiction' (1988) 14 *Mon LR* 158.

The Hon Justice J Allsop, 'Federal Jurisdiction and the Jurisdiction of the Federal Court of Australia in 2002' (2002) 23 *Aust Bar Rev* 29.

M E J Black, 'The Federal Court of Australia: The First 30 Years — A Survey on the Occasion of Two Anniversaries' (2007) 31 *Melb Univ Law Rev* 1017.

N H Bowen, 'The Federal Court of Australia' (1977) 8 *Syd Law Rev* 285.

D Burnett, 'The Commonwealth: A Multitude of Manifestations — Federal Jurisdiction under s 75(iii) of the Constitution' (2007) 81 *ALJ* 195.

C Button, 'The Federal Court's "Arising Under" Jurisdiction and the Development of a "Contingent Jurisdiction"' (2006) 27 *Aust Bar Rev* 327.

E Campbell, 'The Accrued Jurisdiction of the Federal Court in Administrative Law Matters' (1998) 17 *Aust Bar Rev* 127.

Z Cowen and L Zines, *Federal Jurisdiction in Australia*, 3rd ed, Federation Press, Annandale, NSW, 2002.

The Hon Justice P de Jersey, 'The Inherent Jurisdiction of the Supreme Court' (1985) 15 *QLSJ* 325.

P Durack, 'The Special Role of the Federal Court of Australia' (1981) 55 *ALJ* 778.

I H Jacob, 'The Inherent Jurisdiction of the Court' (1970) 23 *Current Legal Problems* 23.

G Kalimnios, 'The Federal Magistrates Court: A Snapshot of its Jurisdiction' (2007) *Qld Lawyer* 138.

P Keyzer, 'Preserving Due Process or Warehousing the Undesirables: To What End the Separation of Judicial Power of the Commonwealth' (2008) 30 *Syd Law Rev* 101.

The Hon Justice S Kiefel, 'The Federal Court of Australia and its Contribution to the Federal Civil Justice System' (2006) 9 *FJLR* 1.

W Lacey, 'Inherent Jurisdiction, Judicial Power and Implied Guarantees under Chapter III of the Constitution' (2003) 31 *Fed LR* 57.

Cases

Orchard v South Eastern Electricity Board
[1987] 20.2.10C
Ormond v Gunnersen [1920] 13.3.8C
O'Reilly's Case (1983) 13.5.4C
Orr v Ford (1989) 6.1.6
— v Holmes (1948) 19.11.1, **19.11.2C**,
19.11.3C, 19.11.4C
Orr Ewing, Re (1882) 9.8.1
Osborne & Co v Anderson [1905] 19.6.7
**Oshlack v Richmond River Council (1998)
.... 20.6.2C**
Otis Elevators Pty Ltd v Zitis (1986) 18.6.2,
18.6.3C
Ottway v Jones [1955] 20.6.7C
Oulton v Radcliffe (1874) 9.7.6, 9.10.2C
Owen v Daly [1955] 21.7.29C, 21.7.30,
21.7.31
— v Sykes [1936] 19.8.13C
Ox Operations Pty Ltd v Landmark Property
Developments (Vic) Pty Ltd 5.1.8C
Oxford Clothing Co Pty Ltd v GIO (Tas) (1994)
.... 3.8.5
Oxley v Link (1914) 5.2.28C

P
P & O Nedlloyd BV v Arab Metals Co [2007]
.... 6.1.9
P S Chellaram and Co Ltd v China Ocean
Shipping Co (1991) 20.8.3
**Packer v Deputy Commissioner of Taxation
[1985]** 13.5.8C
— v Meagher [1984] 17.5.2, **17.5.7C**, 20.3.1,
20.3.2C
Paddock v Forrester (1842) 13.5.26C
Page v Incorporated Nominal Defendant [1981]
.... 17.3.20
Pakuza, Re [1975] 15.6.9, 15.7.4
Palavi v Radio 2UE Sydney Pty Ltd [2011]
.... 2.6.10
Palmco Holding Bhd v Sakapp Commodities
(M) Sdn Bhd (1988) 10.9.4C
Palmos v Georgeson [1961] 11.7.16
Palsgraf v Long Island Railroad Company (1928)
.... 1.5.2E
Pambula District Hospital v Harriman (1988)
.... 18.3.8, 18.3.17C
Panel v Moor (1553) 18.6.3C
Papazoglou v Republic of the Philippines (1997)
.... 4.1.22
Paquin Ltd v Beauclerk [1906] 19.8.11
Paragon Group Ltd v Burnell [1991] 8.8.3

Paramananthan v Minister for Immigration and
Multicultural Affairs (1998) 1.6.5
Paramasivam v Flynn (1998) 6.1.6, 6.5.5,
12.6.6
**Park Rail Developments Pty Ltd v R J Pearce
Associates Pty Ltd** (1987) 18.3.23,
18.3.25C, 18.3.26
Parkin v James (1905) 1.7.9, 7.4.1
Parsons v Martin (1984) 4.1.22
Partington v Booth (1817) 16.5.4C
Partridge v Partridge [1894] 6.1.6
Pasini v Vanstone [1999] **14.5.16C**
Paterson v Paterson (1953) 19.8.8C,
19.8.10C, **19.8.13C**, 19.8.15C
Patrick Stevedores Operations No 2 Pty Ltd
v Maritime Union of Australia [No 3]
(1998) 16.3.5, 16.5.6C
Payabi v Armstel Shipping Corp [1992]
.... 5.2.26, 7.7.4
Payne v Young (1980) 10.4.7, 10.4.9,
10.4.11C, 10.9.4C
PCW (Underwriting Agencies) Ltd v Dixon
[1983] 16.5.5
Peace v Sheriff of Queensland (1890) 21.7.18
Peck v Email Ltd (1987) 18.3.17C
Pedersen v Young (1964) 6.1.3, 6.4.7C
Pegang Mining Co Ltd v Choong Sam [1969]
.... 10.6.4
Pegasus Leasing v Cadoroll Pty Ltd (1996)
.... 4.3.33
Pelechowski v Registrar, Court of Appeal (1999)
.... 16.5.7
Pendal Nominees Pty Ltd v M & A Investments
Pty Ltd (1989) 8.9.37C
Penn-Texas Corporation v Murat Anstalt (No 1)
[1964] 14.5.5C
— v — (No 2) [1964] 14.5.5C
Penrith Whitewater Stadium Ltd v Lesvos
Enterprises Pty Ltd [2007] 19.6.15
Perdrian v Moore (1888) 19.11.1
Perkins v Williams (1900) 4.2.4, 9.7.1
Perpetual Executors & Trustees Association of
Australia Ltd v Wright (1917) 19.8.13C
Perrett v Robinson [1985] 8.1.1, 8.2.1
Perry v Meddowcroft (1846) 18.7.18C
Peruvian Guano Co v Bockwoldt (1883)
.... 11.8.8
Petreski v Cargill (1987) 19.8.17
Pettitt v Dunkley [1971] 19.8.3
Pezzimenti v Seamer [1995] 18.3.6, 18.7.9
Pheeney v Doolan (No 2) (1977) 11.4.18

A Mason, 'The Evolving Role and Function of the High Court of Australia' in B Opeskin and F Wheeler (eds), *The Australian Federal Judicial System*, Melbourne University Press, Melbourne, 2000.

K Mason, 'The Inherent Jurisdiction of the Supreme Court' (1983) 57 *ALJ* 449.

D Mossop, 'The Judicial Power of the Australian Capital Territory' (1999) 27(1) *Fed LR* 19.

R McCallum and M Crock, 'Australia's Federal Courts: Their Origins, Structure and Jurisdiction' (1995) 46 *SC L Rev* 719.

The Hon Justice R Sackville, 'The Re-emergence of Federal Jurisdiction in Australia' (2001) 21 *Aust Bar Rev* 133.

L Zines, 'Federal, Associated and Accrued Jurisdiction' in B Opeskin and F Wheeler (eds), *The Australian Federal Judicial System*, Melbourne University Press, Melbourne, 2000.

L Zines, *The High Court and the Constitution*, 4th ed, Butterworths, Sydney, 1997, Ch 10.

TERRITORIAL JURISDICTION

4.2.1 It is not necessarily sufficient to give a court jurisdiction that the subject matter of a proceeding is a matter which may ordinarily be determined by the court. It is also necessary that the court have jurisdiction over the defendant. This is generally referred to as 'territorial' or '*in personam*' jurisdiction. For instance, a resident and citizen of Uganda cannot choose to sue another Ugandan resident in the Supreme Court of Queensland for a debt arising in Uganda, because ordinarily such an action would clearly fall outside the territorial jurisdiction of the Supreme Court of Queensland. On the other hand, if the potential Ugandan defendant is in Queensland, has submitted to the Queensland court's jurisdiction, or for some other reason can validly be served with the initiating proceeding, then the Queensland court will have territorial jurisdiction.

Presence in the jurisdiction

4.2.2 The principal basis for jurisdiction over an action *in personam* is the presence of a defendant in the jurisdiction. In *Laurie v Carroll* (1958) 98 CLR 310, extracted below, the High Court considered the rationale for this jurisdiction and expounded a number of principles about it.

4.2.3C	**Laurie v Carroll**
	(1958) 98 CLR 310
	High Court of Australia

[The plaintiff had issued a writ of summons out of the Supreme Court of Victoria the day after the defendant, Laurie, had left Victoria, having no intention of returning. The plaintiff obtained orders which included an order giving leave to serve the writ of summons within the jurisdiction by substituted service, being by service upon a nominated firm of solicitors who had acted for Laurie. Laurie applied, without entering an appearance or a conditional appearance, to discharge the *ex parte* order for substituted service, and service pursuant to it, and also to discharge other orders which had been made. The application was dismissed at first instance and the defendant, by special leave, appealed to the High Court.]

Dixon CJ, Williams and Webb JJ (at 322–34): For a point has been reached at which it is better to turn to the question whether it was competent and proper to make the order for substituted service of the writ of summons. Primarily the question is one of jurisdiction. The action is *in personam* and it is transitory; and in such an action the jurisdiction of the Supreme Court of Victoria depends not in the least on subject matter but upon the amenability of the defendant to the writ expressing the Sovereign's command in right of the State of Victoria. The common law doctrine is that the writ does not run beyond the limits of the State. By the federal Service and Execution of Process Act 1901–1953, however, it may, if endorsed under that statute, be served elsewhere within the Commonwealth and its Territories, the conditions in which this may be done and the consequences being defined by the provisions of the Act. Further, by rules made under s 139 of the Supreme Court Act 1928 replacing, but based upon, the fifth schedule of that Act and now contained in O XI, rr 1–5 of the Rules of the Supreme Court 1957, it is provided that in cases answering any of the descriptions in r 1, service of the writ or of notice of the writ in any place outside Victoria may be allowed by the court or a judge. It may be that the cause of action which the plaintiffs seek to set up will fall neither within any of the paragraphs of r 1 of O XI nor within any of those of s 11 of the Service and Execution of Process Act 1901–1953. If so that may explain the importance apparently attached by the parties to this appeal. For except for these extensions of the principle of the common law, it remains true that a writ issued out of the Supreme Court of Victoria does not run outside that State. And in actions *in personam* this must determine the jurisdiction of the [323] court over the defendant ...

The defendant must be amenable or answerable to the command of the writ. His amenability depended and still primarily depends upon nothing but presence within the jurisdiction. 'The service of the writ, or something equivalent thereto, is absolutely essential as the foundation of the court's jurisdiction. Where a writ cannot legally be served upon a defendant the court can exercise no jurisdiction over him. In an action *in personam* the converse of this statement holds good, and wherever a defendant can be legally served with a writ, there the court, on service being effected has jurisdiction to entertain an action against him. Hence, in an action *in personam*, the rules as to the legal service of a writ define the limits of the court's jurisdiction. Now, a defendant who is in England can always, on the plaintiff's taking proper steps, be legally served with a writ. The service should be personal, but if personal service cannot be effected, the court may allow [324] substituted or other service. In other words, the court has jurisdiction to entertain an action *in personam* against any defendant who is in England at the time for the service of the writ': *Dicey — Conflict of Laws*, 6th ed (1949), p 172. It will be noticed that in this passage presence within the jurisdiction at the time of service is regarded as essential. The statutory qualification or exception as to service out of the jurisdiction was of course not under the author's consideration in the foregoing passage. But what is of great importance for the purposes of the case in hand is that to insist on the presence of the defendant within the jurisdiction at the time of service is to exclude the possibility of substituted service when he is no longer within the jurisdiction ...

[328] But the rival theory that the critical time is the issue of the writ means that the issue of the writ is the exercise of jurisdiction over the defendant and accordingly it is enough that he is then present within the jurisdiction. At that moment he may be regarded as falling under the command of the writ as an exercise of jurisdiction. The obligation of its command falls upon him in virtue of his presence within the jurisdiction and his consequent amenability to the writ. Service remains necessary as a condition of his incurring the consequences of default and in that way as a condition perfecting the duty of obedience to the command of the writ. If a defendant knowing of the issue of the writ goes abroad before personal service or, although he does not positively know of the fact of the issue of the writ, goes abroad to evade service, doubtless he may be treated as under notice of the obligation of its command. But without deserting the traditional principle which has governed the jurisdiction of our courts in actions *in personam* and finding a new basis of jurisdiction it is impossible to go back to a point when no writ had been issued, no exercise of jurisdiction had taken place, and to say that because there had been a time when the defendant was amenable to the jurisdiction so that it might then have been exercised over him and because he had quitted the jurisdiction in order that he might cease to be amenable to it, he none the less remained subject to the jurisdiction. For it means that, jurisdiction being based on personal presence it must have ceased when he left, yet none the less he is subject to the jurisdiction still. It must mean this if he is to be served with the writ, not as an extraterritorial exercise of jurisdiction by means of a writ for service out of the jurisdiction, but by substituted service within the jurisdiction of an eight-day writ ...

[331] In the case of personal service within the jurisdiction of a writ of summons in an action *in personam* the view seems to be accepted that it is enough that the defendant is present in England at the time of service. It does not matter why, so long as he has not been enticed there fraudulently for the purpose. It does not matter whether he is a foreigner or a subject of the Crown. It does not matter how temporary may be his presence, how fleeting may be his visit. See *Dicey — Conflict of Laws*, 6th ed (1949), pp 172, 173; *Schmitthoff — The English Conflict of Laws*, 3rd ed (1954), p 428 ...

If the local allegiance (the *ligeantia localis*) of Laurie to the State [332] of Victoria rendering him liable to comply with the mandate of a writ issued from the Supreme Court of Victoria began no earlier and continued no longer than his presence in Victoria, it is surely incongruous that he should be held liable to comply with the mandate of a writ issued after his departure. It is no less incongruous if the ground is that he hastened his departure lest his presence should be used to invoke the exercise over him of the jurisdiction which arose from his presence ...

[333] Laurie neither by reason of past history nor by reason of present domicile, residence or course of business stood in any general relation to the State of Victoria which would make him naturally or prima facie subject to the jurisdiction of the courts of the State. He was about to leave the State within a short time and all that can be meant by the inference that he left to evade service is that he accelerated his departure because of the threat of suit. In all these circumstances the substance of the matter was that, unless [334] the case could be brought within O XI or the Service and Execution of Process Act, a contingency that must have appeared very dubious, the Supreme Court by ordering substituted service was really asserting a jurisdiction over the defendant Laurie which otherwise it could not possess, save in so far as it arose from the accidental circumstances of his brief visit to Melbourne. These are considerations which show that O IX, r 2, ought not to have been used. It was invoked by the plaintiffs only for the purpose of giving the Supreme Court of Victoria jurisdiction where

otherwise it did not exist. Accordingly the order for substituted service of the writ of summons ought not to have been made.

[The court rejected an argument raised on behalf of the plaintiff that, by seeking the other relief as claimed by Laurie in his application, he had waived his right to object or had voluntarily submitted to the jurisdiction. It ordered that the order for substituted service and the purported service of the writ in pursuance of the order be set aside.]

Submission to the jurisdiction

4.2.4   A court will also gain jurisdiction where a defendant, though not present in the jurisdiction, *voluntarily submits* to the jurisdiction.

A party will be taken to have submitted to the jurisdiction of the court if the party's conduct is inconsistent with the maintenance of an objection to the court's jurisdiction. A defendant will, for example, be held to have submitted to the jurisdiction if he or she enters an unconditional appearance (see **9.7.1**), at least where it is possible to test the jurisdiction of the court without entering such an appearance: *Perkins v Williams* (1900) 17 WN (NSW) 135. There will be no submission, however, if a defendant files a conditional appearance and applies to the court to set aside orders on the basis that the court did not have jurisdiction to make them because of significant defects in the service of the originating process: *Robinson v Kuwait Liaison Office* (1997) 145 ALR 68 at 75. See also *United Group Resources Pty Ltd v Calabro (No 4)* [2010] FCA 791.

In respect of an action on a contract, the parties may submit to the jurisdiction by an express agreement in the contract that disputes be referred to a particular court: *Vogel v Kohnstamm Ltd* [1973] QB 133 (a case dealing with enforcement of foreign judgments). A mere choice of law clause, however, does not amount to a submission: *Dunbee Ltd v Gilman & Co (Australia) Pty Ltd* (1968) 70 SR (NSW) 219 at 225.

Statutory extension of territorial jurisdiction

4.2.5   As well as having jurisdiction over a defendant present in the jurisdiction or who submits to the jurisdiction, the court may have *in personam* jurisdiction over a defendant *outside* the jurisdiction who is validly served with the proceeding. This was recognised in the joint judgment of Dixon CJ, Williams and Webb JJ in *Laurie v Carroll* (1958) 98 CLR 310 at 323.

Significant changes came into effect in 1993, in relation to the rules which extend the *in personam* jurisdiction of the Supreme Courts of the states and territories, and which provide for service of a defendant outside the territorial limits of the court. It is necessary to draw a distinction between service outside a state or territory, but within Australia on the one hand and service outside Australia on the other. For state and territory Supreme Courts, service outside the state or territory but within Australia is now governed primarily by the Service and Execution of Process Act 1992 (Cth), which in effect gives the courts of the states and territories Australia-wide *in personam* jurisdiction: *Kontis v Barlin* (1993) 115 ACTR 11 at 18–19 per Master Hogan; *McEntee v Connor* (1994) 4 Tas R 18. The rules in New South Wales also provide for service of originating process in Australia: r 10.13. Service outside Australia is governed exclusively by the Rules of Court. The Federal Court, the High Court, and all state and territory Supreme Courts have rules which allow an initiating process to be served on a defendant outside Australia: HCR r 9.07; FCR Ch 2 Pt 10 Div 10.4; ACT Pt 6.8.9; NSW Pt 11; NT O 7; Qld Ch 4, Pt 7; SA rr 40, 41; Tas Pt 7 Div 10; Vic O 7; WA O 10; see **8.9.9–8.9.35**. As will be seen, these rules require some *nexus* between the case or the defendant and the forum before the court will have jurisdiction.

The Service and Execution of Process Act 1992 (Cth) and the Rules of Court relating to service out of the jurisdiction are generally concerned with *in personam* jurisdiction, not *subject matter* jurisdiction of the courts. For individual recognition of the distinction between the two, see *Flaherty v Girgis* (1987) 162 CLR 574 at 598 in the joint judgment of Mason ACJ, Wilson and Dawson JJ. See also *David Syme & Co Pty Ltd v Grey* (1992) 38 FCR 303: **4.3.11**.

4.2.6   Further reading

A Beech, 'Discretion in the Exercise of Jurisdiction: Recent Developments' (1989) 19 *UWALR* 8.

P Nygh, 'Choice of Law Rules and Forum Shopping in Australia' (1995) 6 *PLR* 237 (see, in particular, 238–41, 244–55).

CROSS-VESTING OF JURISDICTION

The purpose of the cross-vesting scheme

4.3.1   It was the desire to overcome some of the difficulties of overlapping and competing jurisdictions inherent in a federal system, and to ensure that one superior court could give complete relief, that in 1987 caused state and federal legislatures to pass a number of Acts, which collectively are referred to as the cross-vesting scheme. As it was not intended to make any general change in the distribution of business among the courts, it was necessary to also provide a mechanism to ensure that people continued to bring their actions in the most appropriate courts (and so not make any change in the distribution of business among the courts). Accordingly, the scheme has two basic components:

1. The investment or conferral, as the case requires, of the original and appellate jurisdiction of each of the participating courts in or on each of the other participating courts (although with some exclusions). The participating courts are the Federal Court, the Family Court, the Supreme Courts of each of the states and territories, and the Family Court of Western Australia. The scheme does not apply to the High Court: Jurisdiction of Courts (Cross-vesting) Act 1987 (Cth) s 3(1). The scheme does not include magistrates' courts and district and county courts, although certain matters can be remitted to those courts: see **4.3.21E**, **4.3.22**.

2. A mechanism for the transfer of proceedings to the best suited court.

Through these two components it was intended to ensure that, within the ambit of the scheme, a proceeding could not fail because of a lack of jurisdiction, but that jurisdictional balance would be maintained between courts through the appropriate exercise by the courts of the power to transfer proceedings.

The cross-vesting scheme took effect from 1 July 1988. It comprises corresponding state and territorial legislation comprising: Jurisdiction of Courts (Cross-vesting) Act 1987 for each of the states (the State Acts): Jurisdiction of Courts (Cross-vesting) Act 1987 (Cth); Jurisdiction of Courts (Miscellaneous Amendments) Act 1987 (Cth); Jurisdiction of Courts (Cross-vesting) Act 1987 (NT) (and now includes the Jurisdiction of Courts (Cross-vesting) Act 1993 (ACT)) (the Territory Acts). The state and territory Acts are in very similar terms, but they differ in some respects from the Commonwealth Act.

Constitutional invalidity

4.3.2 An aspect of the cross-vesting scheme has been held to be constitutionally invalid. In *Re Wakim; Ex parte McNally* (1999) 198 CLR 511; (1999) 163 ALR 270 (and see 4.1.20C above), the High Court held that those provisions of the cross-vesting scheme which purported to confer state jurisdiction on federal courts were invalid. In its earlier decision in *Gould v Brown* (1998) 193 CLR 346; 151 ALR 395, the High Court had been evenly divided on the issue and had therefore affirmed the decision of the Full Court of the Federal Court in *BP Australia Ltd v Amann Aviation Pty Ltd* (1996) 137 ALR 447, which had upheld the validity of the cross-vesting scheme.

The High Court's finding of invalidity in *Re Wakim* was held to flow from Ch III of the Constitution. Under s 77(i) of the Constitution, the Commonwealth Parliament may make laws defining the jurisdiction of a federal court, but only with respect to those (federal) matters which are set out in ss 75 and 76 of the Constitution: see 4.1.4E. The High Court held that s 77(i) was an exhaustive statement of the jurisdiction which the Commonwealth Parliament could confer on a federal court, and further that no entity other than the Commonwealth Parliament had power to confer jurisdiction on a federal court. Accordingly, state parliaments could not confer any jurisdiction on a federal court. The High Court further held that there was no power in the Commonwealth Parliament to authorise a federal court to exercise jurisdiction which the Commonwealth Parliament could not itself confer.

The decision in *Re Wakim* did not invalidate the entire cross-vesting scheme, but only those provisions which purported to confer state jurisdiction on federal courts. As will be seen, the provisions of the Jurisdiction of Courts (Cross-Vesting) Act 1987 of each of the states which were affected were s 4(1) and (2). In each state these provisions have since been omitted by amending legislation. In respect of the Jurisdiction of Courts (Cross-Vesting) Act 1987 (Cth), the affected provision was s 9(2). Those provisions of the scheme which confer federal jurisdiction on state courts or which confer state jurisdiction on the courts of other states and territories remain operative. Similarly the provisions which facilitate the transfer of proceedings between courts are valid, but it will now only be possible to transfer proceedings between courts if both the transferring court and the court to which it is sought to transfer the proceedings have jurisdiction. Amendments have been made to the transfer provisions in each state to accurately reflect that circumstance.

The Australian Capital Territory and the Northern Territory have legislation corresponding with that of the states, and both the Commonwealth and the state and territory Acts treat them as states: s 3. The decision in *Re Wakim*, however, concerns cross-vesting of state, not territorial, jurisdiction on a federal court. As the conferring of territorial jurisdiction on a federal court was not in issue, the decision does not invalidate s 4 of the Jurisdiction of Courts (Cross-vesting) Act 1993 (ACT) or the Jurisdiction of Courts (Cross-vesting) Act (NT).

Investment and conferral of jurisdiction

4.3.3E   **Jurisdiction of Courts (Cross-vesting) Act 1987 (Qld)**
                                    (as originally enacted)

Vesting of additional jurisdiction in certain courts

4 (1) The Federal Court has and may exercise original and appellate jurisdiction with respect to State matters.

   (2)   The Family Court has and may exercise original and appellate jurisdiction with respect to State matters.

   (3)   The Supreme Court of another State or of a Territory has and may exercise original jurisdiction with respect to State matters.

   (4)   The State Family Court of another State or of a Territory has and may exercise original and appellate jurisdiction with respect to State matters.

   (5)   Subsection (1), (2), (3) or (4) does not:

      (a)   invest the Federal Court, the Family Court or a Supreme Court with; or

      (b)   confer on any such court;

  jurisdiction with respect to criminal proceedings.

4.3.4E   **Jurisdiction of Courts (Cross-vesting) Act 1987 (Qld)**
                (as amended by the Federal Courts (Consequential Amendments) Act 2001)

Vesting of additional jurisdiction in certain courts

4 (1) The Supreme Court of another State or of a Territory has and may exercise original and appellate jurisdiction with respect to State matters.

   (2)   The State Family Court of another State has and may exercise original and appellate jurisdiction with respect to State matters.

   (3)   Subsection (1) or (2) does not —

      (a)   invest a Supreme Court or a State Family Court with; or

      (b)   confer on any such court;

  jurisdiction with respect to criminal matters.

4.3.5 There were only immaterial variations between the various state and territory versions of this section as originally enacted. In its original form the provision purported to confer jurisdiction with respect to 'state matters' on the Federal Court, the Family Court and the Supreme Court of the other states or territories. In *Re Wakim; Ex parte McNally* (1999) 198 CLR 511; 163 ALR 270, the High Court held, however, that state parliaments have no power to confer any jurisdiction on a Federal Court. Accordingly, in their original form s 4(1) and (2) of each of the state Acts were invalid: see **4.3.2**. In Queensland, s 4 of the Jurisdiction of Courts (Cross-vesting) Act 1987 (Qld) was amended by s 39 of the Federal Courts (Consequential Amendments) Act 2001, to delete the invalid provisions and appropriately reflect the position resulting from the decision in *Re Wakim*. The other states have passed similar amendments: Federal Courts (Consequential Provisions) Act 2000 (NSW) s 3; Statutes Amendment (Federal Courts — State Jurisdiction) Act 2000 (SA) s 35; Federal Courts (Consequential

Amendments) Act 2001 (Tas) s 34; Federal Courts Consequential Amendments) Act 2000 (Vic) s 24; Acts Amendment (Federal Courts and Tribunals) Act 2001 (WA). As it was the vesting of state, not territorial, jurisdiction that was in issue in *Re Wakim*, s 4 of each of the territory Acts has not been amended.

Section 3(1) of each state Act defines 'state matter' as extending to any matter in which the Supreme Court has jurisdiction other than by reason of a law of the Commonwealth or of another state, or any matter which is removed to the Supreme Court from an inferior court for the purpose of transfer under the scheme. This means that a state matter is any matter that would fall within the ordinary jurisdiction of a state court regardless of the cross-vesting scheme.

Section 3A of each state Act provides that the Act does not apply to the jurisdiction of courts to which Div 1 of Pt 9.6A of the Corporations Act 2001 (Cth) applies. That division deals with the jurisdiction of the Federal Court, and the state and territory courts with respect to civil matters arising under the corporate legislation.

The jurisdiction which is vested by s 4 is both original and appellate. Only civil jurisdiction is covered; jurisdiction with respect to criminal matters is expressly excluded.

4.3.6E   **Jurisdiction of Courts (Cross-vesting) Act 1987 (Cth)**

Additional jurisdiction of certain Courts

4 (1) Where:

    (a)   the Federal Court or the Family Court has jurisdiction with respect to a civil matter, whether that jurisdiction was or is conferred before or after the commencement of this Act; and

    (b)   the Supreme Court of a State or Territory would not, apart from this section, have jurisdiction with respect to that matter;

then:

    (c)   in the case of the Supreme Court of a State (other than the Supreme Court of the Australian Capital Territory and the Supreme Court of the Northern Territory) that court is invested with federal jurisdiction with respect to that matter; or

    (d)   in the case of the Supreme Court of a Territory (including the Australian Capital Territory and the Northern Territory) jurisdiction is conferred on that court with respect to that matter.

  (2) Where:

    (a)   the Supreme Court of a Territory has jurisdiction with respect to a civil matter, whether that jurisdiction was or is conferred before or after the commencement of this Act; and

    (b)   the Federal Court, the Family Court or the Supreme Court of a State or of another Territory would not, apart from this section, have jurisdiction with respect to that matter;

jurisdiction is conferred on the court referred to in paragraph (b) with respect to that matter.

  (3) Where a proceeding is transferred to the Federal Court, the Family Court or a State Family Court of a State, that court has, by virtue of this subsection, jurisdiction with respect to so many of the matters for determination in the proceeding as that court would not have apart from this subsection.

  (4) This section does not apply to a matter arising under:

(a)   the Conciliation and Arbitration Act 1904; or

(aa) the Building and Construction Industry Improvement Act 2005; or

(ab) the Fair Work Act 2009; or

(ac) the Fair Work (Registered Organisations) Act 2009; or

(ad) the Fair Work (Transitional Provisions and Consequential Amendments) Act 2009; or

(b)   the Workplace Relations Act 1996; or

(ba) the Native Title Act 1993; or

(c)   section 45D, 45DA, 45DB, 45E, 45EA, 46A, 155A or 155B of the Competition and Consumer Act 2010; or

(d)   a provision of Part VI or XII of the Competition and Consumer Act 2010 so far as the provision relates to section 46A, 155A or 155B of that Act.

4.3.7   Section 4 of the Commonwealth Act varies from the state and territory Acts as necessitated by the different constitutional position of the Commonwealth, the fact that federal courts are not courts of general civil jurisdiction, and in order to make provision for territory courts and courts established under Ch III of the Commonwealth Constitution.

Section 3 of the Commonwealth Act defines 'state' as including the Australian Capital Territory and the Northern Territory, and it excludes both territories from the definition of 'territory'. Section 4 of the Commonwealth Act therefore vests in, or confers on, state and territory Supreme Courts, federal jurisdiction where the state or territory courts would not otherwise have jurisdiction and also confers the jurisdiction of the external territory Supreme Courts on the Federal Court, the Family Court and the state Supreme Courts and the Supreme Courts of the Australian Capital Territory and the Northern Territory (where these courts would not otherwise have jurisdiction). The constitutional validity of the conferral of territory jurisdiction on the Federal Court was upheld in *Northern Territory of Australia v GPAO* (1999) 196 CLR 553; 161 ALR 318, and *Spinks v Prentice* (1999) 198 CLR 511.

As is the position under the state and territory Acts, the jurisdiction is both original and appellate, but criminal jurisdiction is excluded: Jurisdiction of Courts (Cross-vesting) Act 1987 (Cth) s 4(1), (2). Unlike the provisions of the state and territory Acts, however, the civil jurisdiction which is conferred by the Commonwealth Act is not unqualified. Section 4(4) expressly excludes matters arising under several stipulated Commonwealth statutes. The Federal Court retains exclusive jurisdiction in respect of those matters.

4.3.8E   **Jurisdiction of Courts (Cross-vesting) Act 1987 (NSW)**

Exercise of jurisdiction pursuant to cross-vesting laws

9 The Supreme Court —

(a)   may exercise jurisdiction (whether original or appellate) conferred on that court by a provision of this Act or of a law of the Commonwealth or a State relating to cross-vesting of jurisdiction; and

(b)   may hear and determine a proceeding transferred to that court under such a provision.

4.3.9E   **Jurisdiction of Courts (Cross-vesting) Act 1987 (Cth)**

Exercise of jurisdiction pursuant to cross-vesting laws

9 (1) Nothing in this or any other Act is intended to override or limit the operation of a provision of a law of a State relating to cross-vesting of jurisdiction.

   (2) The Supreme Court of a Territory may:

      (a) exercise jurisdiction (whether original or appellate) conferred on that court by a provision of this Act or of a law of a State relating to cross-vesting of jurisdiction; and

      (b) hear and determine a proceeding transferred to that court under such a provision.

   (3) The Federal Court or the Family Court may:

      (a) exercise jurisdiction (whether original or appellate) conferred on that court by a provision of this Act or of a law at the Australian Capital Territory or the Northern Territory relating to cross-vesting of jurisdiction; and

      (b) hear and determine a proceeding transferred to that court under such a provision.

4.3.10 Sections 4 of the state, territory and Commonwealth legislation, while granting jurisdiction, are not sufficient in themselves to allow the court to which jurisdiction is granted to exercise that jurisdiction. Section 9 of the cross-vesting legislation applicable for the court to which the jurisdiction is conferred resolves that problem by authorising the exercise of the additional jurisdiction so conferred.

(In its original form s 9 of the Commonwealth Act purported to authorise Federal and Family Courts to exercise jurisdiction as then thought to be conferred by the state Acts. The section was amended consequent on the finding of the High Court in *Re Wakim Ex parte McNally* (1999) 198 CLR 511; 163 ALR 270 that the provision was, to that extent, invalid: Jurisdiction of Courts Legislation Amendment Act 2000, Sch 1): see **4.3.2**.

Nature of jurisdiction cross-vested

4.3.11 Except to the extent of the constitutional invalidity of an aspect of the cross-vesting scheme as has been seen (see **4.3.2**), there is no doubt that the cross-vesting scheme has the effect of vesting the 'subject matter jurisdiction' of a particular court in the scheme in any of the other courts (with significant exceptions to be discussed), but there is some doubt as to whether it extends, in effect, to the 'territorial' jurisdiction: see **4.2.1–4.2.6**.

The issue is illustrated by *David Syme & Co Ltd v Grey* (1992) 38 FCR 303. In that case the respondent issued a writ against the appellant out of the Supreme Court of the Australian Capital Territory. The writ claimed in respect of defamatory material concerning the plaintiff 'published in the Australian Capital Territory and throughout Australia'. The writ was indorsed to be served out of the Australian Capital Territory and in Victoria. The appellant was never present, nor did it carry on any business, in the Australian Capital Territory. The appellant entered no appearance, but gave notice of motion to stay the proceedings as being inappropriate for the granting of liberty to proceed under the Service and Execution of Process Act 1901 (Cth) s 11(1). Section 11(1) of that Act authorised service out of the jurisdiction if there was sufficient nexus with the jurisdiction (as set out in the section), but it was necessary to obtain liberty to proceed if no appearance was entered. The respondent obtained an order of the Supreme Court of the Australian Capital Territory giving it liberty to proceed, and the appellant appealed, by leave, to the Full Court. The Full Court allowed the appeal. It held that in relation to the claims for damages based upon publication outside the Australian Capital Territory, there clearly was not a sufficient nexus with the Australian Capital Territory for the granting of leave under s 11(1). It was argued, however, that the Supreme Court of the Australian Capital Territory had cross-vested jurisdiction which could be exercised without regard to nexus requirements as to service contained in the Service and Execution of Process Act 1901 (Cth), or the relevant Rules of Court relating to service out of the territory. The Full Court of the Federal Court rejected the contention. It held that the cross-vesting legislation should be construed as affecting only the subject matter jurisdiction. It did not vest the 'personal' jurisdiction of the participating courts, leaving service of process to be dealt with under the otherwise applicable rules: see at 310 per Neaves J; at 331–2 per Gummow J.

As noted in the judgments in *David Syme & Co Ltd v Grey* (1992) 38 FCR 303 (see at 332 per Gummow J), K Mason and J Crawford ('The Cross-Vesting Scheme' (1988) 62 *ALJ* 328 at 335–6) had earlier argued for the position accepted in *David Syme & Co Ltd v Grey*, namely that the scheme for cross-vesting of jurisdiction did not extend to vest the personal jurisdiction of the participating courts, leaving personal jurisdiction (including service of process) to be dealt with under the otherwise applicable rules. That view also has some academic support: P Nygh, 'Choice of Law Rules and Forum Shopping in Australia' (1995) 6 *PLR* 237 at 241–2. It should be noted, however, that a number of authors have expressed a contrary view, that there is no need to read down the legislation, and that it should in principle cover the jurisdiction which the Supreme Court of a state can exercise in actions *in personam* merely by reason of the presence of the defendant within the territorial jurisdiction of that state court: see Professor J Davies, *Annual Survey of Law*, 1987, pp 58–9; G Griffith, D Rose and S Gageler, 'Further Aspects of the Cross-Vesting Scheme' (1988) 62 *ALJ* 1016 at 1022–3; The Hon Justice C Pincus, 'Cross-vesting of Jurisdiction' (1989) 19 *QLSJ* 259 at 261; G Lindell, 'The Cross-Vesting Scheme and Federal Jurisdiction Conferred upon State Courts by the Judiciary Act 1903 (Cth) (1991), 17 *Mon LR* 64 at 73–4. This view also finds judicial support in *Seymour-Smith v Electricity Trust of South Australia* (1989) 17 NSWLR 648 at 657–60 per Rogers J (not followed in *David Syme & Co Ltd v Grey*).

The jurisdictional point discussed in *David Syme & Co Ltd v Grey*, and in the other case and articles noted, is no longer important for interstate service under the Service and Execution of Process Act 1992 (Cth) because of the effect of that Act in giving Supreme Courts of the state and territories Australia-wide *in personam* jurisdiction: see 8.9.3.

Transfer of proceedings

4.3.12 If the cross-vesting scheme merely conferred jurisdiction and contained no mechanisms to ensure that proceedings were brought in the most appropriate courts, it could have resulted in a significant change in the distribution of business among the courts and allowed parties to conduct proceedings in courts which were clearly inappropriate forums for the particular disputes. Obviously that would not be a desirable result. To ensure that the scheme does not foster forum shopping and that, so far as possible the jurisdictional balance between the various courts is maintained, the scheme contains provision for the transfer of proceedings in certain cases to a more appropriate court. The key provision for the transfer of proceedings is s 5 of each of the Jurisdiction of Court (Cross-vesting) Acts, which requires transfer of a pending proceeding (where specified conditions are met) between the various superior courts.

4.3.13E   Jurisdiction of Courts (Cross-vesting) Act 1987 (WA)

Transfer of proceedings

5 (1) Where —

    (a) a proceeding (in this subsection referred to as the *relevant proceeding*) is pending in the Supreme Court; and

    (b) it appears to the Supreme Court that, having regard to —

        (i)   whether, in the opinion of the Supreme Court, apart from any law of the Commonwealth or another State relating to cross-vesting of jurisdiction and apart from any accrued jurisdiction of the Federal Court or the Family Court, the relevant proceeding or a substantial part of the relevant proceeding would have been incapable of being instituted in the Supreme Court and capable of being instituted in the Federal Court or the Family Court; and

        (ii) the extent to which, in the opinion of the Supreme Court, the matters for determination in the relevant proceeding are matters arising under or involving questions as to the application, interpretation or validity of a law of the Commonwealth and not within the jurisdiction of the Supreme Court apart from this Act and any law of the Commonwealth or another State relating to cross-vesting of jurisdiction; and

        (iii) the interests of justice,

it is more appropriate that the relevant proceeding be determined by the Federal Court or the Family Court, as the case may be, the Supreme Court shall transfer the relevant proceeding to the Federal Court or the Family Court, as the case may be.

  (2) Where —

    (a) a proceeding (in this subsection referred to as the *relevant proceeding*) is pending in the Supreme Court (in this subsection referred to as the *first court*); and

    (b) it appears to the first court that —

        (i)   the relevant proceeding arises out of, or is related to, another proceeding pending in the Supreme Court of another State or of a Territory and it is more appropriate that the relevant proceeding be determined by that other Supreme Court

        (ii) having regard to —

             (A) whether, in the opinion of the first Supreme Court, apart from this Act and any law of the Commonwealth or another State relating to cross-vesting of jurisdiction, the relevant proceeding or a substantial part of the relevant proceeding would have been incapable of being instituted in the first Court and capable of being instituted in the Supreme Court of another State or Territory;

             (B) the extent to which, in the opinion of the first court, the matters for determination in the relevant proceeding are matters arising under or involving questions as to the application, interpretation or validity of a law of the State or Territory referred to in sub-subparagraph (A) and not within the jurisdiction of the first court apart from this Act and any law of the Commonwealth or another State relating to cross-vesting of jurisdiction; and

        (C)   the interests of justice, it is more appropriate that the relevant proceeding be determined by that other Supreme Court or

    (iii) it is otherwise in the interests of justice that the relevant proceeding be determined by the Supreme Court of another State or of a Territory,

the first court shall transfer the relevant proceeding to that other Supreme Court.

(3)   Where —

    (a)   a proceeding (in this subsection referred to as the *relevant proceeding*) is pending in the Supreme Court of another State or of a Territory (in this subsection referred to as the *first court*); and

    (b)   it appears to the first court that —

      (i)   the relevant proceeding arises out of, or is related to, another proceeding pending in the Supreme Court of Western Australia and it is more appropriate that the relevant proceeding be determined by the Supreme Court of Western Australia;

      (ii) having regard to —

         (A) whether, in the opinion of the first court, apart from this Act and any law of the Commonwealth or another State relating to cross-vesting of jurisdiction, the relevant proceeding or a substantial part of the relevant proceeding would have been incapable of being instituted in the first court and capable of being instituted in the Supreme Court of Western Australia; and

         (B) the extent to which, in the opinion of the first court, the matters for determination in the relevant proceeding are matters arising under or involving questions as to the application, interpretation or validity of a law of the State and not within the jurisdiction of the first court apart from this Act and any law of the Commonwealth or another State relating to cross-vesting of jurisdiction; and

         (C) the interests of justice;

        it is more appropriate that the relevant proceeding be determined by the Supreme Court of Western Australia; or

      (iii) it is otherwise in the interests of justice that the relevant proceeding be determined by the Supreme Court of Western Australia,

the first court shall transfer the relevant proceeding to the Supreme Court of Western Australia.

[Section 5(4) provides for the transfer of proceedings between the Supreme Court of Western Australia and the state Family Court of Western Australia. Section 5(5) is in corresponding terms to s 5(3), except that it provides for the transfer of proceedings by the Federal Court or the Family Court, rather than by the Supreme Court of another state or territory.]

(6)   [Repealed]

(7)   Where —

    (a)   a court (in this subsection referred to as the *first court*) transfers a proceeding to another court under a law or laws relating to cross-vesting of jurisdiction; and

    (b)   it appears to the first court that —

      (i)   there is another proceeding pending in the first court that arises out of, or is related to, the first-mentioned proceeding; and

(ii)   it is in the interests of justice that the other proceeding be determined by
       the other court;

the first court shall transfer the other proceeding to the other court.

(8)   A court may transfer a proceeding under this section on the application of a party to
      the proceeding, of its own motion, or on the application of the Attorney-General of the
      Commonwealth or of a State or Territory.

...

(10) Nothing in this section confers on a court jurisdiction that the court would not
     otherwise have.

4.3.14   In its original form, s 5(1) of each of the state Acts included a purported jurisdiction
for a state Supreme Court to transfer to the Federal Court or Family Court a proceeding
arising out of, or related to, a proceeding in the Federal Court or Family Court. Following
the decision of the High Court in *Re Wakim Ex parte McNally* (1999) 198 CLR 511;
163 ALR 270 (see 4.3.3), s 5 of each of the state Acts, as originally enacted, was amended to its
current form to reflect the position that proceedings can only be transferred between courts if
both the transferring court and the court to which it is sought to transfer the proceedings have
jurisdiction: Federal Courts (Consequential Provisions) Act 2000 (NSW) s 3; Federal Courts
(Consequential Amendments) Act 2001 (Qld) s 40; Statutes Amendment (Federal Courts
— State Jurisdiction) Act 2000 (SA) s 36; Federal Courts (Consequential Amendments)
Act 2001 (Tas) s 35; Federal Courts (Consequential Amendments) Act 2000 (Vic) s 24; Acts
Amendment (Federal Courts and Tribunals) Act 2001 (WA) s 24.

Section 5 of the Jurisdiction of Courts (Cross-vesting) Act 1987 (Cth) is in broadly
similar terms to the state Acts. That provision was amended by the Jurisdiction of Courts
(Miscellaneous Amendments) Act 2000 (Cth) to more accurately reflect the position resulting
from the decision in *Re Wakim*.

It has been held on numerous occasions that despite the decision in *Re Wakim*, the venue
transfer provisions in s 5(4) of the Commonwealth Act remain operable so that proceedings
pending in the Federal Court falling within that court's jurisdiction may be transferred to the
Supreme Court of a state: see eg, *Johnson Tiles Pty Ltd v Esso Australia Ltd* (2001) 113 FLR 42;
[2001] ATPR 41-818: see 10.9.10.

In all cases, the court in which a proceeding (referred to in the legislation as 'the relevant
proceeding') is pending is required to transfer the proceeding to another court in stipulated
circumstances. The legislation provides for two quite distinct circumstances.

The first is where 'related' proceedings have been commenced in different courts participating
in the cross-vesting scheme. It is not essential that the 'related' proceeding be between the
same parties; there need only be some degree of causality between them (*Re Hamilton-Irvine*
(1990) 94 ALR 428 at 432–3 per Beaumont J), or a substantial common question arising in
both proceedings: *Skaventzon v Tirimon* (1993) 61 SASR 103. Provided the other court has
jurisdiction, in general terms the effect of the legislation is that the court should transfer the
proceeding brought before it to the other court if it is 'more appropriate' for that other court to
hear the case or if it is 'otherwise in the interests of justice' that the proceeding be transferred to
that other court.

The second case specifically provided for does not require any 'related proceeding', and clearly
reflects an intention of the cross-vesting legislation (as reflected in the preamble) that courts
should in most situations continue to hear and determine only those proceedings which would

otherwise fall within their ordinary fields of jurisdiction: see s 5(1)(b)(ii) at 4.3.13E. It is important to note, though, that there is no requirement that the transferring court must be exercising cross-vested jurisdiction; the provisions apply to *any* proceeding pending in a relevant court. Again the proceeding must be transferred to another participating court if it is 'more appropriate' that the other court deal with the case, but here the court is specifically directed when making that determination to have regard to three criteria (to be considered cumulatively), namely:

(1) whether, apart from the cross-vesting scheme and any accrued jurisdiction, 'the relevant proceeding or a substantial part of the relevant proceeding' would have been incapable of being instituted in the court in question; and

(2) the extent to which the case involved an issue of 'the application, interpretation or validity of a law' of the receiving court, and the court would not, apart from the cross-vesting legislation, have had jurisdiction over that issue; and

(3) the interests of justice.

As is apparent, the first two of these criteria will require a consideration as to the 'traditional forum' for the subject matter of the litigation. It is necessary to inquire as to whether the court to which the application for transfer is made has jurisdiction independent of the cross-vesting scheme; whether the proposed transferee court has jurisdiction independent of the cross-vesting scheme; and whether it is clearly improper for either of such courts to exercise jurisdiction. In some circumstances (eg, if a matter which would, apart from the cross-vesting scheme, be within the exclusive jurisdiction of the Federal Court is commenced in a state Supreme Court), the first two criteria may well be decisive.

The 'interests of justice' is also a factor to which regard is to be had in considering whether it is 'more appropriate' that a matter be heard in another court. In addition, it forms a third category which may permit transfer to another court within the cross-vesting scheme with jurisdiction to hear the matter, regardless of whether there is a related proceeding pending or any issue involving cross-vested jurisdiction: see, eg, s 5(3)(b)(iii) of the Jurisdiction of Courts (Cross-vesting) Act 1987 (WA) at 4.3.13E.

4.3.15 Questions arise as to what are the criteria for transfer in the 'interests of justice' and what is the role of the court in exercising the discretion under s 5. In particular, do the principles of private international law, such as *forum non conveniens*, have a role to play when the court is considering an application for transfer? This issue will rarely be considered by an appellate court because there is no appeal from the decision of a court upon an application for transfer. It was first considered by the New South Wales Court of Appeal in *Bankinvest AG v Seabrook* (1988) 14 NSWLR 711. In that case Rogers AJA (with whom Street CJ agreed) said that the principles of private international law such as *forum non conveniens* have no place when judges consider the making of a transfer order, that the only lodestar is what the interests of justice dictate and that the question should not be encumbered by judge-made pronouncements of principle, although the considerations were essentially the same as those specified in *Spiliada Maritime Corp v Cansulex Ltd* [1987] 1 AC 460. (*Spiliada* is the leading English authority for the proposition that in that jurisdiction a stay of a proceeding will only be granted on the grounds of *forum non conveniens* if there is some other available forum having competent jurisdiction which is a clearly more appropriate forum for the action.)

Although this approach was not universally accepted it became over time the law applied in all jurisdictions except Western Australia. In that jurisdiction the narrower view was taken that, in determining the interests of justice under para (iii), the courts should start from the premise that the plaintiff's choice of forum should be respected and that a transfer should only be ordered if the defendant can satisfy the court on the test established in *Voth v Manildra Flour Mills* (1990) 171 CLR 538 that the forum is clearly inappropriate: *Mullins Investments Ltd v Elliott Exploration Co Pty Ltd* [1990] WAR 531; *Whyalla Refiners Pty Ltd v Grant Thornton (a firm)* (2001) 182 ALR 274.

The High Court confirmed the approach in *Bankinvest* in *BHP Billiton Ltd v Schultz* (2004) 221 CLR 400; 211 ALR 523. That case also provides an illustration of the factors which might be weighed by the court, in considering which is the more appropriate court having regard to the interests of justice. The decision in *Amor v Macpac Pty Ltd* (1989) 95 FLR 10 (4.3.17C) provides an earlier illustration of the factors which may be weighed on a transfer application in considering which is the more appropriate court in the interests of justice.

4.3.16C   **BHP Billiton Ltd v Schultz**
(2004) 221 CLR 400; 211 ALR 523
High Court of Australia

[The first respondent suffered from asbestosis and asbestos-related pleural disease, which he claimed was the result of exposure to asbestos over various periods while he worked for the appellant in Whyalla in South Australia. He brought proceedings against the appellant in the Dust Diseases Tribunal of New South Wales (the Tribunal), alleging negligence, breach of contract and breach of statutory duty. He included four other corporations in the proceedings, also respondents to the appeal, alleging they were negligent in the manufacture and supply of materials that found their way to Whyalla. The appellant applied to have the action removed from the Tribunal to the Supreme Court of New South Wales, and then transferred to the Supreme Court of South Australia. The appellant brought this appeal, by special leave, from the decision of Sully J in the Supreme Court who had dismissed the application.

A number of significant issues arose for determination on the appeal. The extract below relates to the questions whether error had been shown in the exercise by the Supreme Court of New South Wales of the jurisdiction and power conferred on that court by the Jurisdiction of Courts (Cross-vesting) Act 1987 (NSW).]

Gleeson CJ, McHugh and Heydon JJ (at [418–24]):
At the time of the commencement of the proceedings, the first respondent was a resident of South Australia. The appellant is incorporated in Victoria, and carries on business both in South Australia and in New South Wales. The second respondent is incorporated in the United Kingdom, and is registered as a foreign corporation in New South Wales. The third and fourth respondents are incorporated in the Australian Capital Territory. The fifth respondent is incorporated in New South Wales. According to the first respondent, products containing the asbestos were manufactured, sold and supplied to the appellant and the second respondent in New South Wales by the fifth respondent. According to the appellant, the products were supplied to the appellant in South Australia. There are cross-claims between the appellant and the respondents other than the first respondent ...

... In this Court, the first respondent did not challenge the view that the law of South Australia would be the substantive law that would govern his claim against the appellant, but asserted that the law of New South Wales could govern some of the claims against the other respondents and the cross-claims.

Subject to proof of exposure and diagnosis, liability will not be in issue between the first respondent on the one hand and the appellant and the other respondents on the other hand. Subject to the qualification mentioned, the only issues affecting the first respondent will relate to damages and a claim that a limitation period has expired. The lay witnesses, and most (but not all) of the medical witnesses, reside in South Australia.

Sully J pointed out that s 11A of the Dust Diseases Tribunal Act 1989 (NSW) ('the Tribunal Act'), a provision unique to the Tribunal, empowered the Tribunal to make an award of damages in stages ...

The first respondent sought from the Tribunal an order preserving his right to make a future and additional claim for damages should he develop any of the conditions of asbestosis-induced lung cancer, asbestos-induced carcinoma of any other organ, pleural mesothelioma, or peritoneal mesothelioma.

The Cross-vesting Act

The purpose of the proposed removal of the proceedings from the Tribunal to the Supreme Court of New South Wales under s 8 of the Cross-vesting Act was so that it could then be transferred to the Supreme Court of South Australia under s 5 of the same Act. The criterion for transfer established by s 5 is that it is in the interests of justice that the proceedings be determined in the Supreme Court of South Australia.

From the outset, it has been recognised by courts applying the Cross-vesting Act that, although an application for transfer under s 5 will often involve evidence and debate about matters of the same kind as arise when a court is asked to grant a stay of proceedings on the ground of forum *non conveniens*, there are differences between the two kinds of application. Because of one controversial aspect of the reasoning of Sully J, it is useful to refer to some matters of history in order to explain those differences.

The current English common law on the subject of *forum non conveniens* was established by the decision of the House of Lords in *Spiliada Maritime Corp v Cansulex Ltd* [1987] AC 460.

The current Australian common law is to be found in the decision of this Court in *Voth v Manildra Flour Mills Pty Ltd* (1990) 171 CLR 538. To the extent to which they differ, the difference can be traced to a view about the nature of the power to stay proceedings.

[10] The earlier English view, overturned later by the House of Lords, was expressed by Scott LJ in *St Pierre v South American Stores (Gath & Chaves) Ltd* [1936] 1 KB 382 at 398: 'A mere balance of convenience is not a sufficient ground for depriving a plaintiff of the advantages of prosecuting his action in an English Court if it is otherwise properly brought. The right of access to the King's Court must not be lightly refused.' That approach, which stressed the duty of a court to exercise a jurisdiction that had been regularly invoked, was abandoned in [420] England. In *Spiliada* [1987] AC 460 at 476, Lord Goff of Chieveley said that a stay would be granted on the ground of *forum non conveniens* 'where the court is satisfied that there is some other available forum, having competent jurisdiction, which is the appropriate forum for the trial of the action, i.e. in which the case may be tried more suitably for the interests of all the parties and the ends of justice.'

When *Spiliada* was first considered by this Court, in *Oceanic Sun Line Special Shipping Company Inc v Fay* (1988) 165 CLR 197 some members of the Court expressed concern about the 'duty of an Australian court to exercise its jurisdiction' (1988) 165 CLR 197 at 238 per Brennan J. Deane J said: 'It is a basic tenet of our jurisprudence that, where jurisdiction exists, access to the courts is a right. It is not a privilege which can be withdrawn otherwise than in clearly defined circumstances' (1988) 165 CLR 197 at 252. Later, in *Voth* (1990) 171 CLR 538 this Court settled upon the 'clearly inappropriate forum' test as the basis of granting a stay of proceedings. The reason for adopting a test somewhat stricter than the English test emerges from the joint judgment of Mason CJ, Deane, Dawson and Gaudron JJ in *Voth*, which referred back to what Deane J had said in *Oceanic*, and stated that '[t]he selected forum's conclusion that it is a clearly inappropriate forum is a persuasive justification for the court refraining from exercising its jurisdiction' (1990) 171 CLR 538 at 559. This emphasis upon the need for justification of a judicial refusal to exercise a jurisdiction that has been regularly invoked underlay the selection of the 'clearly inappropriate forum' test, in contrast to the modern English test. It has overtones of what Scott LJ said in *St Pierre* about the right of access to a court being something that is not lightly refused.

The national scheme of legislation, of which the Cross-vesting Act is a part, was intended to operate, and to be applied, in a different juridical context. This was clearly stated in the first case to come before the Court of Appeal of New South Wales under the Cross-vesting Act: *Bankinvest AG v Seabrook* (1988) 14 NSWLR 711. It has been recognised by the Court of Appeal in later cases in which jurisdiction of one kind or the other has been invoked. (Compare, e.g., *Goliath Portland Cement v Bengtell* (1994) 33 NSWLR 414 with *James Hardie & Coy Pty Ltd v Barry* (2000) 50 NSWLR 357.)

In *Bankinvest* (1988) 14 NSWLR 711 at 713–714, Street CJ said:

> The cross-vesting legislation passed by the Commonwealth, the States and the Territories both conferred on each of the ten courts Australia-wide jurisdiction and set up the mechanism regulating the [421] transferring of proceedings from one of these ten courts to another. In relation to transfer, the common policy reflected in each of the individual enactments is that there must be a judicial determination by the court in which proceedings are commenced either to transfer or not to transfer the proceedings to one of the other nine based, broadly speaking, upon consideration of the interests of justice ... It calls for what I might describe as a 'nuts and bolts' management decision as to which court, in the pursuit of the interests of justice, is the more appropriate to hear and determine the substantive dispute.

In the context of the Cross-vesting Act, one is not concerned with the problem of a court, with a prima facie duty to exercise a jurisdiction that has been regularly invoked, asking whether it is justified in refusing to perform that duty. Rather, the court is required by statute to ensure that cases are heard in the forum dictated by the interests of justice. An application for transfer under s 5 of the Cross-vesting Act is brought upon the hypothesis that the jurisdiction of the court to which the application is made has been regularly invoked. If it appears to that court that it is in the interests of justice that the proceedings be determined by another designated court, then the first court 'shall transfer' the proceedings to that other court. There is a statutory requirement to exercise the power of transfer whenever it appears that it is in the interests of justice that it should be exercised. It is not necessary that it should appear that the first court is a 'clearly inappropriate' forum. It is both necessary and sufficient that, in the interests of justice, the second court is more appropriate.

The reason why a plaintiff has commenced proceedings in a particular court might, or might not, concern a matter related to the interests of justice. It might simply be that the plaintiff's lawyers have their offices in a particular locality. It is almost invariably the case that a decision as to the court in which an action is commenced is made by the plaintiff's lawyers, and their reasons for making that choice may be various. To take an example at the other extreme, it might be because a plaintiff is near death, and has a much stronger prospect of an early hearing in one court than in another. The interests of justice are not the same as the interests of one party, and there may be interests wider than those of either party to be considered. Even so, the interests of the respective parties, which might in some respects be common (as, for example, cost and efficiency), and in other respects conflicting, will arise for consideration. The justice referred to in s 5 is not disembodied, or divorced from practical reality. If a plaintiff in the Tribunal were near to death, and, in an application such as the present, it appeared that the Supreme Court to which transfer was sought could not deal with the case expeditiously, that would be a consideration relevant to the interests of justice. Justice would ordinarily dictate that the interest of the plaintiff in having a hearing would prevail over the interest of the defendant in such benefit as it might obtain from the [422] plaintiff's early death. The capacity of the Tribunal to deal expeditiously with cases has always, and rightly, been regarded as relevant to the interests of justice, bearing in mind the condition of many sufferers from dust diseases.

On the other hand, there may be conflicting interests of such a kind that justice would not attribute greater weight to one rather than the other. The advantage which a plaintiff might obtain from proceeding in one court might be matched by a corresponding and commensurate disadvantage to a defendant. The reason why a plaintiff commenced proceedings in one court might be the same as the reason why the defendant seeks to have them transferred to another court. In such a case, justice may not dictate a preference for the interests of either party.

As was pointed out in *John Pfeiffer Pty Ltd v Rogerson* (2000) 203 CLR 503 at 517[13], referring to *Gosper v Sawyer* (1985) 160 CLR 548 at 564–565 the ordinary basis of jurisdiction of common law courts in personal actions is the presence of the defendant within the court's territory, and the defendant's resulting amenability to the court's process. In most cases, the jurisdiction of an Australian court, in the sense of authority to decide, depends upon the location of the defendant, rather than that of the plaintiff. Suing a large corporation in the place where it has its headquarters would not ordinarily be regarded as 'forum-shopping', although the location of the headquarters would not necessarily be decisive as to which was the most appropriate forum. *John Pfeiffer Pty Ltd v Rogerson* involved an action brought in the Supreme Court of the Australian Capital Territory, against a company which had its principal place of business in the Territory, for damages for personal injury arising out of a work-related accident in New South Wales. No one suggested that the Australian Capital Territory was an inappropriate forum. The decision of this Court established that the law governing the quantum of damages, which was treated as a matter of substance, was the *lex loci delicti*, the law of New South Wales.

There is nothing unusual, either in the State or the federal judicature, about actions between residents of different Australian law areas. Federal diversity jurisdiction is an obvious example. Actions in New South Wales courts are commonly brought by residents of other States, especially when the residence or principal place of business of the defendant is New South Wales. Reference is sometimes made to one forum or another being the 'natural forum'. Such a description is usually based upon a consideration of 'connecting factors', described by Lord Goff in *Spiliada* [1987] AC 460 at 478 as including matters of convenience and expense, such as availability of witnesses, the places where the parties respectively reside or carry on business, and the law governing the relevant transaction. Lord Templeman described such factors as [423] 'legion', and said that it was difficult to find clear guidance as to how they are to be weighed in a particular case [1987] AC 460 at 465. Thus, New South Wales might well be the 'natural forum' for an action for damages brought by a passenger in a motor vehicle against the driver if they were both residents of New South Wales, even though the injury resulted from a collision that occurred on the other side of the Queensland or Victorian border.

In many cases, there will be such a preponderance of connecting factors with one forum that it can readily be identified as the most appropriate, or natural, forum. In other cases, there might be significant connecting factors with each of two different forums. Some of the factors might cancel each other out. If the action is between two individuals, and the plaintiff resides in one law area and the defendant in another, there may be no reason to treat the residence of either party as determinative, although, as already noted, it will ordinarily be the residence of the defendant that is important to establish jurisdiction. Weighing considerations of cost, expense, and convenience, even when they conflict, is a familiar aspect of the kind of case management involved in many cross-vesting applications ...

There will often be overlapping, but there is no necessary coincidence, between factors which connect litigation to a forum, and factors which motivate one party to prefer, and another party to resist, litigating in that forum. In the context of the Cross-vesting Act, the treatment by the Court of Appeal of New South Wales, in *James Hardie & Coy Pty Ltd v Barry* (2000) 50 NSWLR 357, of the special procedural powers of the Tribunal is illuminating. The Court of Appeal pointed out that these were not merely forensic advantages to one party that represented a corresponding disadvantage to the other party, but were factors relevant to a decision under s 5 because they have the capacity to assist both plaintiffs and defendants in the efficient and economical resolution of disputes, and therefore serve the public interest.

[Their Honours then examined the reasoning of **Sully J** at first instance and in an earlier case of *BHP Co Ltd v Zunic* (2001) 22 NSWCCR 92 which he imported by reference. They concluded that, although correctly referring to *Bankinvest AG v Seabrook* (1988) 14 NSWLR 711 as the principal authority to follow, his reasoning revealed he had proceeded on the basis that the plaintiff's choice of forum was 'not lightly to be overridden' and also that the 'unusual advantages' conferred on a plaintiff under the New South Wales legislation were to be kept open. They concluded that in the result his decision was affected by a material error. As to the appropriate course to be taken, in the light of this finding, these judges determined that the proceeding should be remitted to the Supreme Court of New South Wales for further consideration.

Kirby, Hayne, Callinan and **Heydon JJ** delivered separate judgments. All expressed similar views as to the proper approach to be taken on an application to transfer proceedings under the cross-vesting legislation. They each concluded, however, that 'the interests of justice dictated that the Supreme Court of South Australia was the more appropriate' court in the circumstances and that the proceedings should be removed into the Supreme Court of New South Wales and then be transferred to the Supreme Court of South Australia.]

Amor v Macpac Pty Ltd
(1989) 95 FLR 10
Supreme Court of New South Wales

[The plaintiff was the owner–driver of a semi-trailer engaged in long distance haulage. His home was in Coffs Harbour. In the course of his business he had hauled a load from Sydney to Brisbane. He was injured while unloading in Brisbane when an employee of the defendant who was operating a forklift pushed the forklift into the load and caused some of it to roll off and crush him. He was severely injured. He was treated at the Princess Alexandra Hospital in Brisbane and subsequently at a hospital in Coffs Harbour, and was subsequently treated by specialists at various places in New South Wales. He commenced the action out of the Supreme Court of New South Wales and the defendant applied for an order under to the Jurisdiction of Courts (Cross-vesting) Act 1987 (NSW) that the proceedings be transferred to the Supreme Court of Queensland. There was no 'related proceeding' pending in Queensland or elsewhere.]

Allen J (at 12–16): Practical guidance as to the considerations which are relevant to determining which is the most appropriate court having regard to the interests of justice is given by the adoption by Rogers AJA [in *Bankinvest AG v Seabrook* (1988) 14 NSWLR 711] of what was said by Lord Goff in *Spiliada Maritime Corp v Cansulex Ltd; The Spiliada* [1987] 1 AC 460. His Lordship in *Spiliada* accepted that the appropriate court is that with which the action had the most real and substantial connection. He continued (at 478):

> So it is for connecting factors in this sense that the court must first look; and these factors will include not only factors affecting convenience or expense (such as availability of witnesses), but also other factors such as the law governing the relevant transaction ..., and the places where the parties respectively reside or carry on business.

In the present case it is a matter of great importance that the accident occurred wholly in the State of Queensland. No negligent act or omission outside that State is relied upon to establish the cause of action. The plaintiff of his own free will chose to accept a contract to haul goods into Queensland. As Mason CJ said in *Breavington v Godleman* (1988) 62 ALJR 447 at 453:

> Australia is one country and one nation. When an Australian resident travels from one state or territory to another state or territory he does not enter a foreign jurisdiction. He is conscious that he is moving from one legal regime to another in the same country and that there may be differences between the two which will impinge in some way on his rights, duties and liabilities so that his rights, duties and liabilities will vary from place to place within Australia. It may come as no surprise to him to find that the local law governed his rights and liabilities in respect of wrong he did or any wrong he suffered in a state or territory. He might be surprised if it were otherwise.

Indeed in respect of any tort committed within a state or territory a claim for damages in respect of it would have to be determined in accordance with any legislation of that state or territory which dealt with substantive law as distinct from procedural matters, no matter in what state or territory it is that the action is brought: *Breavington* (supra). Where the wrongful acts charged are all alleged to have been committed in a particular state or territory the 'connection between the proceedings' in that state or territory is, in the words of Rogers, AJA, 'exceedingly close'.

It has not been argued, in the present case, that there is any relevant difference between the law of New South Wales and the statute law of Queensland as to any matter of the substantive law. There is, however, Queensland legislation which, if applied, well may markedly affect the quantum of any damages which the plaintiff recovers. The prescribed discount rate in Queensland is 5 per cent: Common Law Practice Act 1867 (Qld), s 5. This is procedural rather than a substantive matter. If the proceedings remain in this Court this provision of Queensland legislation will not be applied: *Guidera v Government Insurance Office of New South Wales* (unreported, Supreme Court of New South Wales, Studdert J, 16 January 1989). This Court would apply a discount of 3 per cent: *Todorovic v Waller* (1981) 150 CLR 402. The distinction between substantive law and procedural law is an important one for the purpose of private international law. But it is a distinction which owes more to convention than to reason. The classification of individual matters as being substantive or procedural frequently seems artificial. For present purposes this Court should have regard to the reality — namely that if the proceedings are tried in Queensland the discount rate will be 5 per cent whereas if they remain to be tried in New South Wales it will be 3 per cent. It is not to be expected that the plaintiff would have known that when he hauled the load of steel over the border into Queensland. But he would have expected, or should have expected, that there would be differences between the law of Queensland and the law of New South Wales and that these might affect the damages he could recover if he were injured.

The fact that the accident occurred in Queensland and that all the allegations of negligence relate to conduct in Queensland is not conclusive. It may be appropriate nevertheless that the proceedings remain in this Court. All the relevant facts must be weighed before the decision is reached, on balance, as to whether this Court or the Supreme Court of Queensland is the more appropriate court.

In weighing those other considerations it is material that if the proceedings remain in this Court the place of trial is likely to be in Coffs Harbour — not in Sydney. The plaintiff has given an undertaking to the court that if the proceedings do remain in this Court he will apply for an order that the place for trial be at Coffs Harbour and, if such an order is made, he will not seek another venue without the leave of the court.

A relevant matter is the prospective place of residence of the parties. The defendant was and still is a company incorporated in Queensland and [14] carrying on business solely in that State. The plaintiff was a resident of New South Wales at the time of the accident. He has been living in Fingal Heads for the past 14 months and it is anticipated that he will continue to do so unless suitable work for him becomes unavailable in that area. It is not unimportant that at the time of the accident the plaintiff's home was in New South Wales and that he was across the border, in Queensland, only for the purpose of delivering a load of steel. But this is far from being a case in which in fact that the accident occurred in Queensland was adventitious — for example as would be the case where a passenger in his car sued his driver both of them being New South Welshmen passing through. In such a case the connection with Queensland would carry substantially less weight than in a case such as the present where the defendant was and remains a Queensland resident and the proceedings concern an accident which occurred at its factory in Queensland.

The availability of witnesses (including the plaintiff), considerations of their convenience and considerations of the relative costs of litigation must be assessed and weighed. In those respects the question is not one of a comparison between the State of New South Wales and the State of Queensland. It is a question of a comparison between a trial at Coffs Harbour in New South Wales and a trial at Brisbane in Queensland. Those are the likely venues in New South Wales or Queensland respectively.

The date for trial, whether it be in Coffs Harbour or in Brisbane, is so far away that it is not to be expected that any firm decision has been made by either party as to the witnesses to be called (save, of course, the calling of the plaintiff himself). The court must be guided by its experience as to the ordinary course of events in litigation of this character. Although no formal defence has as yet been filed it may be anticipated that, in the ordinary course of events, the defendant's insurer, who has the conduct of the litigation, will deny liability and allege contributory negligence. On these issues I accept that there are three persons, apart from the plaintiff, whom the solicitor for the defendant describes as 'major witnesses'. The first is the man who operated the forklift. He lives near Brisbane. The second is the receivables clerk of the defendant. He lives at Aspley, a Brisbane suburb. The third is the driver of another semi-trailer which was being unloaded at the time of the accident. He lives near Brisbane. It is not to be anticipated that if the trial were held at Coffs Harbour the distance which any of these witnesses would have to travel to court would result in them not being available to give evidence. The first two of them are still in the employment of the defendant. The third, the driver of the other semi-trailer, has indicated to the plaintiff's solicitors that he is willing to attend court in New South Wales. Nevertheless, their convenience has to be considered — as well as the cost involved in their travelling and accommodation. Consulting a standard set of road maps it appears the Coffs Harbour is some 401 kilometres by road from Brisbane. There is an air service, of sorts, between the cities. It is by a small seven-seater aircraft crewed by one pilot. The witnesses might or might not be happy to fly in it. The evidence to the frequency of flights is vague. It is: 'It may have been a daily flight'.

Although, as I have already indicated, the plaintiff's claim appears to be based primarily on the negligence of the driver of the forklift the claim is not restricted to that head of negligence. It extends to failure to provide a safe system for the unloading of the steel pipes. It is likely that this alternative [15] particular of negligence will be pressed at the hearing so that the plaintiff will not necessarily fail should he not succeed in establishing the personal negligence of the driver of the forklift. The negligence claim insofar as it is based upon failure to provide a safe system of work may well involve the calling of an expert in unloading procedures and it well may be that the expert would wish to have an inspection of the premises to assist him in forming his views. Clearly it would be more convenient and less expensive to qualify a Brisbane expert and to have the trial in Brisbane than it would be to have the trial in Coffs Harbour — whether a Brisbane expert or a Sydney expert is qualified.

On behalf of the defendant it was urged that the treating surgeon at the Princess Alexandra Hospital probably would be a witness. I doubt it. Comprehensive reports have been obtained from the hospital and its records could be subpoenaed. Medical issues are likely to turn on his progress since he has been discharged from that hospital rather than upon the treatment which he received during his hospitalisation. Nevertheless there is a significant possibility that the surgeon would be called.

It is probable that it will be more convenient and less expensive to the plaintiff personally for the hearing to be in Brisbane rather than in Coffs Harbour. Fingal Heads, where he is living, is only some 10 kilometres south of Tweed Heads. The map shows that Tweed Heads is 109 kilometres from Brisbane. This gives a road distance of 119 kilometres between Fingal Heads and Brisbane as compared with 282 kilometres between Fingal Heads and Coffs Harbour. There is the possibility that the plaintiff will return to Coffs Harbour before the trial.

But this is only a possibility. It may be anticipated that the plaintiff's wife will give evidence but there being no evidence to the contrary I shall assume that she is living with and will go with her husband.

It may be anticipated that the plaintiff's witnesses would include the orthopaedic surgeon who currently is treating him, namely Dr Oliver. Dr Oliver practises in Coffs Harbour. Clearly it would be inconvenient for him to have the trial in Brisbane. It may be anticipated, also, that evidence will be called by at least one of the psychiatrists whom he has already seen. These are Dr McCombie who practises in Coffs Harbour and Dr Cole who practises in Murwillumbah. It would be inconvenient to Dr McCombie to have the trial in Brisbane. But it probably would be more convenient for Dr Cole. The road maps show that Murwillumbah is 140 kilometres from Brisbane. It is 261 kilometres from Coffs Harbour.

Having regard to the ordinary course of the conduct of litigation of this type it may be considered quite unlikely that all the other doctors who have treated the plaintiff will be called. In large measure their evidence would be only of the history of his progress up to the time that he became fit for resumption of some work. It may be anticipated that as to some of them at least the defendant would be given consent to the tendering of his reports and that the tendering of the reports would suffice. This I would consider particularly likely to be the case in respect of the two doctors who treated the plaintiff after his discharge from the Princess Alexanrda Hospital and before he moved to Iluka. These were Dr Brand, a consultant surgeon practising at Lismore and Dr Ruthnam, a general practitioner practising at Coffs Harbour. I note that the road map shows that Lismore is 255 kilometres from Brisbane. But it is not close to Coffs Harbour. The distance by road between Lismore and Coffs Harbour is 186 kilometres. In the unlikely event that Dr Brand was called as a witness it would not be much more inconvenient for him to drive to Brisbane than it would be for him to drive to Coffs Harbour.

I consider it unlikely that the plaintiff would call as a witness the general practitioner, Dr Taylor, who treated him at Iluka. It is more likely that he would call Dr Delaney, the orthopaedic surgeon, who treated him in that township. The road map shows that Iluka is 250 kilometres from Brisbane and 151 kilometres from Coffs Harbour. The statement in the affidavit of the plaintiff's solicitor that Iluka is about 250 kilometres from Coffs Harbour is inaccurate.

If the trial is had in Brisbane it may be expected that the plaintiff's solicitor would have him examined by one or more Brisbane specialists to supplement the evidence of the specialists who have treated him so far. That would have the benefit, also, of reducing the number of the treating doctors who would need to be called. Bearing in mind that he is living in Fingal Heads it would not impose a substantial hardship upon the plaintiff to attend for examination by Brisbane specialists.

I accept that it may become necessary for the plaintiff to call his accountant in respect of economic loss. His accountant is in Newcastle. The most convenient way for him to travel to the place of trial, whether it be Coffs Harbour or Brisbane, probably would be to come to Sydney and to fly. It will make little difference to him whether the trial is in Coffs Harbour or in Brisbane.

I accept also that the plaintiff may find it necessary to call someone from the Melbourne firm which, prior to his accident, was seeking to have him enter its employment as a removalist. Again any witness from that firm would fly to the place of trial. It makes little difference whether the place of trial is in Coffs Harbour or Brisbane so far as such a witness is concerned.

In my judgment it does not appear clearly whether in respect of the convenience of witnesses and the availability of witnesses it would be more convenient to have the trial in Coffs Harbour or in Brisbane.

A further consideration is the expense of the trial. Having regard to such matters as country loadings of counsel and accommodation expenses, where required, for members of the legal profession as well as for witnesses I am satisfied that a trial in Coffs Harbour would be significantly more costly than a trial in Brisbane.

Weighing all the considerations to which I have referred I consider that the appropriate place of trial is Brisbane. Pursuant to s 5(2) of the Jurisdiction of Courts (Cross-vesting) Act I transfer these proceedings to the Supreme Court of Queensland.

As to costs I consider that the plaintiff acted quite reasonably in commencing the proceedings in this Court and in not consenting to an order for transfer to the Supreme Court of Queensland rather than putting evidence to this Court and argument on that matter. This is not a case in which it was obvious that the transfer would be ordered. The costs of the proceedings in this Court up to and including the making of the transfer order are to be costs in the cause.

4.3.18   Each of the cross-vesting Acts provides that where a proceeding is transferred the legal practitioners involved have the same right to practise in the court to which the proceeding is transferred as if that court were a federal court exercising federal jurisdiction: s 5(8) (WA s 5(9)). The court to which the proceeding is transferred may determine costs in relation to steps taken prior to transfer, unless those costs have already been dealt with by the court which transferred the proceeding: s 12. Judgments which are given by any court in the exercise of any cross-vested jurisdiction are as enforceable as if given in the exercise of that court's own jurisdiction, apart from the cross-vesting scheme: s 14.

Applicable law

4.3.19   Section 11 of the Commonwealth Act and of the state Acts provides for the appropriate law to be applied in the conduct of proceedings where the court is or is likely to be exercising cross-vested jurisdiction. The basic rule is that the law in force in the state or territory in which the court is sitting (including choice of law rules) is to be applied: s 11(1)(a). The specification in relation to choice of law rules is important, as it may well be that the effect of those rules means that the substantive law of some other place applies. In the case of any proceeding arising from an intranational tort, e.g., the applicable choice of law rule, as settled by the High Court in *John Pfeiffer Pty Ltd v Rogerson* (2000) 203 CLR 403; 172 ALR 625, will mean that the law of the place of commission of the tort (the *lex loci delicti*) should be applied as the law governing questions of substance. The High Court in that case also determined that laws that bear on the existence, extent or enforceability of remedies, rights and obligations should be characterised as substantive and not as procedural laws. This is a matter which is considered fully in standard works on conflict of laws in Australia: see generally M Davies, A Bell and P Brereton, *Nygh's Conflict of Laws in Australia*, 8th ed, LexisNexis Butterworths, Australia, 2010.

There are two qualifications to the basic rule. The first applies where the right of action arises under the written law of another state or territory. In that case the written and unwritten law of that state is to be applied: s 11(1)(b). The second qualification relates to the rules of evidence and procedure to be applied. Section 11(1)(c) specifies the applicable rules to be those that the hearing court 'considers appropriate in the circumstances', being rules that are applied in a superior court in Australia or in an external territory.

Section 11(3) provides that if a proceeding is transferred or removed from a court, the procedural steps taken prior to transfer are to be regarded as if they had been taken in the court to which the proceeding is transferred.

Special federal matters

4.3.20   Special provisions govern the transfer of proceedings which involve 'special federal matters'. 'Special federal matters' are defined in s 3(1) of the Jurisdiction of Courts Act 1987 (Cth) to mean any of the following matters in respect of which the Supreme Court of a state or territory would not, apart from under the Jurisdiction of Courts (Cross-vesting) Act 1987 (Cth), have jurisdiction: matters arising under Pt IV of the Competition and Consumer Act 2010 (Cth) (other than under ss 45D, 45DA, 45DB, 45E or 45EA); matters arising under the Competition Code (as defined in the Competition and Consumer Act 2010 (Cth) s 150A) of the Australian Capital Territory or the Northern Territory; appeals on questions of law from Commonwealth tribunals; matters arising under the Administrative Decisions (Judicial Review) Act 1977 (Cth); matters arising under the Family Law Act 1975 (Cth) s 60G (in a court other than the Family Court of Western Australia or the Supreme Court of the Northern Territory); and matters within the original jurisdiction of the Federal Court by virtue of the Judiciary Act 1903 (Cth) s 39B; The definition is incorporated into the state Acts by reference: s 3.

Where any of these matters arise in a proceeding pending in a state or territory Supreme Court, the effect of s 6(1), (2) and (3) of each of the Commonwealth and state Acts is that the proceeding must be transferred to the Federal Court (or in the case of a matter arising under the Family Law Act 1975 (Cth) s 62AA to the Family Court, the Family Court of Western Australia or the Supreme Court of the Northern Territory, as appropriate in the circumstances), unless the state or territory Supreme Court orders that the proceeding be determined by that Supreme Court. The Supreme Court may only make such an order if it is satisfied that there are 'special reasons for doing so in the particular circumstances of the proceeding, other than reasons relevant to the convenience of the parties'.

Following amendments made in recognition of the effect of the decision of the High Court in *Re Wakim; Ex parte McNally* (see 4.3.2), s 6(1A) of the Commonwealth Act and of each of the state Acts make it clear that it is only permissible to transfer so much of the proceeding as is, in the opinion of the transferring court, within the jurisdiction, including the accrued jurisdiction (see 4.1.18–4.1.21) of the Federal Court (or the jurisdiction of the Family Court, Family Court of Western Australia, or Supreme Court of the Northern Territory, as the case may be). It is likely that any state matters which are properly joined in the proceeding would fall within the Federal Court's accrued jurisdiction. In the event that a special federal matter is included with a state matter not within the accrued jurisdiction, the Supreme Court may be expected to regard the joinder as providing 'special reason' for it to determine the federal matter, so that the whole controversy may be determined in one court: *Computershare Ltd v Perpetual Registrars Ltd (No 3)* [2000] 2 VR 666 at 679 per Warren J.

Section 6(4) of the Commonwealth and state Acts requires that before a Supreme Court may make an order that the matter should be determined by that court, it must be satisfied that the Commonwealth Attorney-General and the Attorney-General of the state or territory where the proceeding is pending have been notified of the nature of the special federal matter, and allowed a reasonable time to consider whether submissions should be made to the court about the proceeding. In considering whether there are 'special reasons' for not transferring a special federal matter, s 6(6) directs that the state or territory Supreme Court must have regard to 'the general rule that special federal matters should be heard by the Federal Court' (or in the case of a matter arising under the Family Law Act 1975 (Cth) s 62AA by the Family Court, the Family Court of Western Australia or the Northern Territory Supreme Court, as the case may be) and must take into account any submission made by the Commonwealth Attorney-General or the Attorney-General of the state or territory where the proceeding is pending.

Despite the provisions of s 6, the Supreme Court is not prevented from granting urgent relief of an interlocutory nature if it is in the interests of justice to do so: s 6(7).

Inferior courts

4.3.21E   **Jurisdiction of Courts (Cross-vesting) Act 1987 (Vic)**
Orders by Supreme Court

8 (1) Where —
    (a) a proceeding (in this subsection referred to as the 'relevant proceeding') is pending in —
        (i) a court, other than the Supreme Court; or
        (ii) a tribunal established by or under an Act; and
    (b) it appears to the Supreme Court that —
        (i) the relevant proceeding arises out of, or is related to, another proceeding pending in the Federal Court, the Family Court or the Supreme Court of another State or of a Territory and, if an order is made under this subsection in relation to the relevant proceeding, there would be grounds on which that other proceeding could be transferred to the Supreme Court; or
        (ii) an order should be made under this sub-section in relation to the relevant proceeding so that consideration can be given to whether the relevant proceeding should be transferred to another court —
the Supreme Court may, on the application of a party to the relevant proceeding or of its own motion, make an order removing the relevant proceeding to the Supreme Court.
    (2) Where an order is made under subsection (1) in relation to a proceeding, this Act applies in relation to the proceeding as if it were a proceeding pending in the Supreme Court.
    (3) Where a proceeding is removed to the Supreme Court in accordance with an order made under subsection (1), the Supreme Court may, if the Supreme Court considers it appropriate to do so, remit the proceeding to the court or tribunal from which the proceeding was removed.

4.3.22 Inferior courts do not have any cross-vested jurisdiction, but they are included in the scheme in a limited way. First, s 8 of each of the state and territory Acts provides for the Supreme Court, on the application of a party to the proceeding or of its own motion, to remove proceedings pending in a court (other than the Supreme Court of the state or territory) or a tribunal (established by or under an Act) up into the Supreme Court for the purpose of considering transferring them to another court in accordance with the cross-vesting scheme.

Section 8 of the Commonwealth Act provides for removal of proceedings from a lower court or tribunal in an external territory into the Supreme Court of the territory for the purpose of considering whether the proceeding should be transferred.

Second, s 10 of the Jurisdiction of Courts (Cross-vesting) Act 1987 (Cth) permits the Federal Court, the Family Court or the Supreme Court of a state or territory, on the application of a party to the proceeding or of its own motion to transfer to an *inferior* state court a proceeding otherwise within that inferior court's jurisdictional limits, if the proceeding involves a matter arising under Pts 2-2, 3-1, 3-3 or 3-4 of Sch 2 to the Competition and Consumer Act 2010 (Cth) (consumer protection matters), as that Part applies as a law of the Commonwealth and is not an appeal or a special federal matter. Section 10 of the state Acts is in similar terms, although it applies to matters pending in state or territory Supreme Courts, and extends only to matters arising under Ch 3, Pt 3-1, Divs 1, 2, 4 or 5; Ch 3, Pt 3-3; and Ch 3 Pt 3-4 of Sch 2 of the Competition and Consumer Act 2010 (Cth), applying as a law of the Commonwealth.

Limitation on appeals

4.3.23 The jurisdiction and transfer provisions of the cross-vesting legislation apply to matters within both original and appellate jurisdiction. If it was not then qualified this would mean, for example, that an appeal could be brought from a single judge of the Federal Court to a Full Court or Court of Appeal of a state. Section 7 of each of the Cross-vesting Acts therefore imposes limitations which generally require that appeals be brought within the appellate system of the court by which the primary decision was made.

Most appeals from decisions of Supreme Courts of a state (whether the court in which the proceeding was commenced, or that to which it has been transferred) are to be brought before that state Full Court. An exception is contained in the Jurisdiction of Courts (Cross-vesting) Act 1987 (Cth) s 7(5), which has the effect that certain appeals (primarily those relating to bankruptcy and intellectual property matters) must be brought to the Full Court of the Federal Court, and that appeals in family law matters must go to the Full Court of the Family Court. With the special leave of the High Court, appeals in respect of these matters may also go to the High Court. Appeals cannot be taken from the Federal Court or the Family Court to the other of those courts, or to the Full Court of a state.

4.3.24 Section 13 of each of the Cross-vesting Acts provides that no appeal lies from a decision of a court in relation to the transfer or removal of a proceeding pursuant to the cross-vesting legislation, and further that there is no right of appeal in relation to the rules of evidence and procedure which are to be applied pursuant to s 11(1).

Procedure

4.3.25 Each of the courts in the cross-vesting scheme has their own rules providing for the procedural and mechanical means of implementing the scheme. These rules vary significantly.

Federal Court

4.3.26 The Federal Court Rules provide that a party may apply to the court for an order that the proceeding be transferred to another court: r 27.21. If a transfer application is made by the Attorney-General, or by the Attorney-General of a state or territory, the Attorney-General does not, because of the application, become a party to the proceeding: r 27.22.

Rule 27.23 provides some appropriate mechanisms for the transfer of proceedings under a cross-vesting law. These include a requirement that the party who applied for the order must file a copy of the order in the District Registry named in the order, or if no District Registry is so named the District Registry of the state or territory where the order was made. The Registrar will attach a notice to the order in the prescribed form. The party filing the order must serve a copy of the order, and the notice that has been attached by the Registrar, on each party to the proceeding in the court which made the transfer order. The service is to be effected at the party's address for service, but personal service is required if the party does not have an address for service. After an order is filed and the notice is attached, the Federal Court rules apply to the proceeding as if it had been started in the Federal Court. The party who files the order must, as soon as practicable after service of the order and attached notice, and before taking any further step in the proceeding, apply to the court for directions in relation to the further conduct of the proceeding.

Australian Capital Territory

4.3.27 Applications under a cross-vesting law for the transfer of a proceeding are made by an application to the court under Pt 6.2 of the rules. Applications under s 8 for an order removing a proceeding from an ACT court (other than the Supreme Court) or a tribunal to the Supreme Court must be made by originating application: r 3303. The Attorney-General (whether of the Commonwealth or of a state or territory) may make a transfer application without becoming a party to the proceeding: r 3304.

If a proceeding is removed from a lower court or tribunal under s 8, the Supreme Court may give any directions it considers appropriate: r 3305. If a party to a proceeding relies on cross-vesting legislation, the party must include particulars of the cross-vested claim in the process, pleading or affidavit by which the cross-vested law is relied on. If a matter to be decided in the proceeding is a special federal matter, the statement must also identify the special federal matter and explain why it is a special federal matter: r 3306.

Rule 3307 states that a proceeding in which cross-vested jurisdiction is invoked may be served outside the territory, but if the defendant fails to serve a defence the plaintiff cannot take any further step unless the court gives leave. The leave is only to be given if the court is satisfied that it is a convenient court in which to decide the matter. If the court gives leave, it is not prevented from later transferring the matter to another court.

The first party to rely on a cross-vesting law must apply to the court for directions: r 3308.

A party who wants the court to apply the written law of another state or territory or the rules of evidence and procedure of another court under s 11(1)(b) or s 11(1 (c) of the Jurisdiction of Courts (Cross-vesting) Act 1987 (ACT) (see **4.3.19**) must include in their pleading a statement identifying the right of action and the written law under which it arises, or the rules they seek to have applied, as the case may be: rr 3311, 3312.

New South Wales

4.3.28 Applications for an order under any provision of the cross-vesting legislation (except s 8) are to be made by motion: r 44.3.

Applications for transfer made by the Attorney-General do not, by reason of the application, make the Attorney-General a party to the proceeding: r 44.4.

A party who intends to contend either that the court should exercise cross-vested jurisdiction, or that the court should make an order for transfer pursuant to the cross-vesting scheme should make an application to the court as soon as practicable after the commencement of the proceeding for determination of the question whether or not the proceedings should be transferred to another court: r 44.5.

A party who wishes to contend that the court should apply the written law of another state or territory or the rules of evidence and procedure of another court under s 11(1)(b) or s 11(1)(c) of the Jurisdiction of Courts (Cross-vesting) Act 1987 (NSW) (see 4.3.19) shall, as soon as practicable, file and serve on each other party notice of the contention specifying the law or rule and stating the grounds relied on in support of the contention. The court may give directions in relation to the application of such a law or rule either on the application of a party or of its own motion: r 44.6.

The Northern Territory and Victoria

4.3.29   There are common rules in the Northern Territory and Victoria. Any originating summons or motion under cross-vesting law must be headed 'In the matter of the Jurisdiction of Courts (Cross-vesting) Act 1987': NT r 89.03; Supreme Court (Miscellaneous Civil Proceedings) Rules 2008 (Vic) r 13.03 (references for Victoria in this section are to these rules).

As in the other jurisdictions, the Commonwealth or a state or territory Attorney-General may apply for transfer of a proceeding without becoming party to the proceeding: NT 89.04; Vic r 13.04. If a proceeding is removed from a lower court or tribunal to the Supreme Court, the Supreme Court can give any direction which could have been given in the tribunal or lower court: NT r 89.05; Vic r 13.05.

A party to a proceeding who proposes to invoke a jurisdiction arising under a provision of a cross-vesting law, or otherwise to rely on a provision of a cross-vesting law, is required to file and serve a notice which identifies the provision and the claim in relation to which reliance is placed on the provision, and state the grounds upon which reliance is placed on the provision. That party must also seek directions as soon as practicable as to whether the proceeding should be transferred. If there is a special federal matter involved in the proceeding, the notice must identify the special federal matter and the grounds which make it a special federal matter: NT r 89.06; Vic r 13.06.

If a proceeding is transferred to the court, the party who commenced the proceeding is to apply for directions as soon as practicable. There are also requirements in relation to the transfer of documents filed and orders made when a proceeding is transferred by the court, and as to the numbering and titling of a proceeding transferred to the court: NT r 89.08; Vic r 13.07.

A party seeking to have the court apply the written law of another state or territory, in determining a right of action arising under that written law or the rules and procedure of another court under s 11(1)(b) or 11(1)(c) respectively of the Jurisdiction of Courts (Cross-vesting) Act 1987, is required to file and serve a notice identifying the right of action and written law or the relevant rules of evidence and procedure, as the case may be. That party must then seek directions on the subject matter of the notice before the proceeding is set down for trial: NT r 89.09; Vic r 13.08. The court has an express power to give, set aside, or vary any directions in relation to a proceeding to which a cross-vesting law applies: NT r 89.10; Vic r 13.09.

Queensland and Western Australia

4.3.30   In Queensland (r 53) and Western Australia (O 81E r 3), a party who relies on cross-vesting laws is required to indorse the process by which those laws are invoked with a statement identifying each claim or ground of defence, as the case may be, about which the cross-vesting laws are invoked. These rules assist in ensuring that reliance upon the cross-vesting laws is identified as early as possible in the proceeding. However, a failure to include the indorsement does not invalidate the process.

If a matter for determination is a special federal matter, the indorsement is to include particulars of that special federal matter, and the court is not permitted to determine a proceeding which raises such a matter for determination, unless it is satisfied that the notice required by s 6(4)(a) of the cross-vesting laws sufficiently specifies the nature of the special federal matter: Qld r 54; WA O 81E r 4. These rules assist to ensure that the Supreme Court is in a position to adequately assess whether it should proceed to hear the matter or whether it should transfer it to the Federal Court. It is further provided that in the case of doubt or difficulty as to the manner of commencement of a proceeding, the court may give directions: Qld r 53; WA O 83E r 3. This may be necessary if the legislation or rules under which the proceeding may be commenced do not have a counterpart in the rules in Queensland or Western Australian (as the case may be). The rules specify that the first party to invoke the cross-vesting laws must make an application for directions (Qld) or take out a summons for directions (WA) and serve it on all other parties: Qld r 56; WA O 83E r 6. If it is the plaintiff who first invokes the cross-vesting laws, he or she must make and serve the application within seven days after being served with the first notice of intention to defend (Qld) or notice of appearance (WA). If a defendant is required to make the application, he or she must make and serve the application within seven days of the delivery or service of the process which invokes the cross-vesting laws.

In the situation where a proceeding is transferred to the Queensland or the Western Australian Supreme Court from another court, the party who started the proceeding is required to file and serve an application for directions (Qld) or summons for directions (WA) within 14 days of the date of the order transferring the proceeding. In default, any other party may file and serve the application or summons, or the court may call the parties before it on its own initiative. On the hearing of the application or summons, the court is to give any direction or make any decision as to the conduct of the proceeding that it thinks proper. Any order or decision made may subsequently be varied by the court at the trial or hearing of the proceeding. The rules provide some appropriate mechanisms to facilitate the transfer of proceedings pursuant to the cross-vesting scheme: Qld rr 56, 57; WA O 81E rr 6, 7.

The requirement of making the application (Qld) or taking out a summons (WA) for directions at an early stage enables the court to consider whether special directions are required. Such directions may well be needed when pleading or other procedural rules of the court where the proceeding would ordinarily be brought are different from the procedural rules which normally apply in the Queensland or Western Australian Supreme Court, for example, where a family law proceeding is commenced in the Supreme Court (proceedings in the Family Court are conducted on affidavit rather than pleadings).

It is further provided that if a proceeding is removed to the Supreme Court under s 8 of the cross-vesting laws, the court may immediately, on that removal, give any direction or make any decision or direct the parties to take any step that the court sees fit: Qld r 59; WA O 81E r 10. These powers are in addition to the powers exercisable under Qld r 56 and WA O 81E r 6, and include powers to give any directions that could have been given by the court or tribunal from which the proceeding was removed.

It is specifically provided that an application by an Attorney-General under s 5 or s 6 of the cross-vesting laws for the transfer of a proceeding may be made by application (Qld) or summons (WA) without the Attorney-General becoming a party to the proceeding: Qld r 58; WA O 81E r 9.

The Western Australian rules contain an additional provision regulating the conduct of proceedings. If the law of another state or territory must be applied under s 11(1)(b) of the Jurisdiction of Courts (Cross-vesting) Act 1987 (WA) in determining a right of action arising under a written law of that state or territory, or if a party seeks to have the rules of evidence or procedure of another court applied under s 11(1)(c) (see **4.3.19**) the pleadings must identify the right of action and the written law under which it arises, or state the particular rules of evidence sought to be applied, as the case may be: WA O 81E r 11. In either case, the party concerned is to apply for directions on the matter before the proceeding is set down for trial. There is no equivalent rule in Queensland.

In Western Australia (O 81E r 8), any application for the transfer or removal of a proceeding under cross-vesting laws must be determined by a judge. In Queensland (r 451), any application about cross-vesting under Ch 2 Pt 7 is to be determined by a judge.

South Australia

4.3.31   Orders for the transfer of actions under the Jurisdiction of Courts (Cross-vesting) Act 1987 (SA) can only be made by a judge or the Full Court: r 313(2). An application for an order for the transfer of an action under the Act must clearly identify any special federal matter as defined in the Act, and also identify any action that the applicant has begun, or intends to begin in another court, involving the same or similar issues to those involved in the action for which the order for transfer is sought: r 313(3). If a party asserts that a matter is to be, or may be, determined by the court in accordance with the law of another place under s 11 of the Act, the party's pleadings must state which law must, or should, according to the party's assertion, be applied: r 313(4). If a party seeks an order under s 11(1)(c) of the Act for the application to an action of laws of evidence or procedure differing from those normally applied in the court, an interlocutory application may be made for such an order: r 313(5).

Tasmania

4.3.32   In Tasmania, as in the other jurisdictions, the Attorney-General of the Commonwealth, a state or a territory may apply for the transfer of a proceeding without becoming a party: r 779.

If a matter is removed into the court from a lower court or tribunal under the Jurisdiction of Courts (Cross-vesting) Act 1987 (Tas), the court may give any directions which could have been given by that court or tribunal: r 780.

Rule 781 regulates procedures whereby jurisdiction under cross-vesting laws is or may be invoked. A party who proposes to invoke a jurisdiction arising under a cross-vesting law or otherwise relies on a cross-vesting law is required to identify the provision relied on, the claim to which it relates, and the grounds upon which reliance is placed on that provision. This is to be done in the originating process or the pleadings or by notice filed and served on the other parties. The first party to invoke a cross-vesting law must also take out an application for directions within seven days of the service of the pleading which invoked the cross-vesting law. In the case of a proceeding transferred to the court, the plaintiff is to make the application for directions within 14 days of the transfer order. In default the application may be made by any party or the court may call the parties before it of its own motion. Directions given or orders made may be varied at the trial. If any special federal matter is involved, it must be identified as such in the pleading and directions must be sought by the party pleading it as to whether the proceeding should be transferred to the Federal Court. Rule 782 provides some appropriate mechanical matters which apply when proceedings are transferred pursuant to the cross-vesting scheme.

If the court may apply the law of another state or territory under s 11(1)(b) of the Jurisdiction of Courts (Cross-vesting) Act 1987 (Tas) in determining a right of action arising under a written law of that state or territory, the pleadings must identify the right of action and the written law under which it arises. A party must also identify in his or her pleadings any rules of evidence and procedure other than those of the court which that party seeks to have applied under s 11(1)(c) of that Act. Whenever a party seeks to have such laws or rules of evidence applied, he or she must seek directions on the matter before the proceeding is set down for trial, and the court may, at any time, of its own motion, given directions and revoke any such directions in relation to the matter: r 783.

4.3.33   Notes and questions

1. In response to the decision in *Re Wakim* (1999) 198 CLR 511, legislation was enacted by each of the states in an attempt to palliate the potentially devastating blow dealt to litigants in Federal Courts: Federal Courts (State Jurisdiction) Act 1999 (NSW), (Qld), (SA), (Tas), (Vic), (WA). The legislation in each jurisdiction follows the same template, although there are some minor differences. One of the key provisions of these Acts is s 11 which, in essence, provides that existing ineffective judgments of the Federal Court in the purported exercise of state jurisdiction are taken to be judgments of the Supreme Court. It also provided a mechanism for the transfer of proceedings then pending before the Federal Court in relation to state matters to the Supreme Court. The High Court upheld the constitutional validity of that provision in *Residual Assco Group Ltd v Spalvins* (2000) 202 CLR 629; 172 ALR 366.

2. A scheme that was separate from but similar to the cross-vesting scheme was enacted for corporations. Mirror state Acts applied the Corporations Act 1989 (Cth) and the Corporations Law promulgated by the Commonwealth for the Australian Capital Territory. Section 42 of the state Acts conferred jurisdiction on the Federal Court with respect to civil matters arising under the Corporations Law. The Federal Court's jurisdiction was restored following the decision in *Re Wakim* (1999) 198 CLR 511 by the commencement of the Corporations Act 2001 (Cth) on 15 July 2000.

3. It has been seen that lower courts do not have any cross-vested jurisdiction. Is there any logical justification for this? In *Cross-Vesting of Jurisdiction: A Review of the Operation of the National Scheme*, Australian Institute of Judicial Administration Incorporated, 1992, Moloney and McMaster recommended that the cross-vesting scheme should be expanded to include at least the major trial courts in each jurisdiction (for example, the Queensland District Court, the New South Wales District Court and the Victorian County Court) with suitable appellate or review procedures to ensure the proper operation of the scheme in those lower courts.

4. The decision of the Court of Appeal of the Northern Territory of Australia in *Scott v NTA* [2005] NTCA 1; (2005) 147 NTR 6; (2005) 226 FLR 1 provides an interesting illustration of circumstances (which are not common) in which the Supreme Court of a state or territory might obtain jurisdiction over a matter within the jurisdiction of a Supreme Court of another state or territory, only by virtue of the cross-vesting scheme. In that case, the Supreme Court of the Northern Territory

did not in its own right have jurisdiction to make the order sought, namely an order for the exhumation of the remains of a deceased person who had been buried in Queensland. The application was not assisted in this instance by the Service and Execution of Process Act 1992 (Cth). As Mildren J noted (at [29]), that legislation enables lawful service or process interstate, but 'it does not confer jurisdiction over a subject matter such as the power to order the exhumation of a body in another state ... '. It was held the Supreme Court of the Northern Territory obtained the jurisdiction 'with respect to State matters' by virtue of the Jurisdiction of Courts (Cross-vesting) Act 1987 (Qld), and could exercise that jurisdiction under s 9 of the Jurisdiction of Courts (Cross-Vesting) Act 1987 (NT).

5. In their review of the cross-vesting scheme, Moloney and McMaster (*Cross-Vesting of Jurisdiction: A Review of the Operation of the National Scheme*, Australian Institute of Judicial Administration Incorporated, 1992) indicated that there is scope for greater communication between judges of participating courts in relation to cross-vesting matters generally, and in relation to particular cases under the scheme. One of the suggestions mentioned as warranting detailed consideration on the question of better communication between the courts in particular cases was a suggestion that, in relation to proceedings sought to be transferred, 'teleconferencing' should be available in appropriate cases, to bring together the judges of the two courts involved in the 'presence' of the legal representatives of the parties. What are the advantages and disadvantages of this suggested procedure?

6. It has been noted that there is some uncertainty as to whether the cross-vesting scheme vests only the subject matter jurisdiction of the participating courts, or whether it also extends to territorial jurisdiction. It has also been noted that the issue is no longer relevant in respect of proceedings served interstate under the Service and Execution of Process Act 1992 (Cth), which gives state Supreme Courts Australia-wide *in personam* jurisdiction. Could the issue be relevant to service out of Australia? Could a plaintiff argue, for example, that if personal jurisdiction is cross-vested, the Supreme Court of Victoria could assume jurisdiction in respect of a proceeding to be served on a defendant in another country where there is sufficient connection with another state so that, under its Rules of Court, that other state could have *in personam* jurisdiction?

7. It is possible for there to be separate proceedings in two different courts which are part of the cross-vesting scheme involving the same parties and raising essentially the same issues, which each court refuses to transfer to the other. How should such a situation be resolved? The position arose in *Pegasus Leasing v Cadoroll Pty Ltd* (1996) 59 FCR 152, regarding parallel proceedings in the Federal Court and the Supreme Court of South Australia. Both courts had declined to transfer the proceeding before it to the other court and each had also refused an application to stay the proceeding in that court. The Full Federal Court, by majority, upheld the decision of Neaves J to restrain the parties from taking any further steps in the South Australian proceeding until the hearing and determination of the application was brought in the Federal Court. The decision includes consideration of the circumstances in which such a restraining order might be appropriately granted: Lee and Tamberlin JJ at 156–8.

Further reading

4.4.1 Articles

V Anetta and K Fraser, 'Transfer Provisions of the Cross-vesting Legislation — The Need for Clarification' (1996) 24 *ABLR* 208.

C Baker, 'Cross-Vesting of Jurisdiction between State and Federal Courts' (1987) 14 *UQLJ* 118.

E Campbell, 'Cross-vesting of Jurisdiction in Administrative Law Matters' (1990) 16 *Monash LR* 1.

G Griffith, D Rose and S Gageler, 'Choice of Law in Cross-vested Jurisdiction: A Reply to Kelly and Crawford' (1988) 62 *ALJ* 698.

G Griffith, D Rose and S Gageler, 'Further Aspects of the Cross-vesting Scheme' (1988) 62 *ALJ* 1016.

D Kelly and J Crawford, 'Choice of Law Under the Cross-vesting Legislation' (1988) 62 *ALJ* 589.

D Kovacs, 'After the Fall: Recovering Property Jurisdiction in the Family Court in the Post Cross-vesting Era' (2001) 25 *MULR* 58.

D Kovacs, 'Cross-Vesting of Jurisdiction — New Solutions or New Problems?' (1988) 16 *MULR* 669.

K Mason and J Crawford, 'The Cross-vesting Scheme' (1988) 62 *ALJ* 328.

S Miller and O Nicholls, 'Cross-vesting of Civil Proceedings — A Practical Analysis of some of the Interests of Justice in the Determination of Cross-vesting Applications' (2004) 30 *Monash LR* 95.

P Nygh, 'Choice of Law Rules and Forum Shopping in Australia' (1995) 6 *PLR* 237.

B O'Brien, 'Arid Jurisdictional Disputes: The Federal Court Versus the State Supreme Courts' (1985) 13 *ABLR* 77.

C Pincus, The Hon Justice, 'Cross-vesting of Jurisdiction' (1989) 19 *QLSJ* 259.

D Rose, 'The Bizarre Destruction of Crossing-vesting' in A Stone and G Williams, *The High Court at the Crossroads*, Federation Press, Sydney, 2000, Ch 6.

G E Santow, The Hon Justice and M Leeming, 'Refining Australia's Appellate System and Enhancing its Significance in Our Region' (1995) 69 *ALJ* 348.

C Saunders, 'In the Shadow of *Re Wakim*' (1999) 17 *C & SLJ* 507.

L W Street, 'Consequences of a Dual System of State and Federal Courts' (1978) 52 *ALJ* 424.

L W Street, 'Towards an Australian Judicial System' (1982) 56 *ALJ* 515.

M Whincop, 'Trading Places: Thoughts on Federal and State Jurisdiction in Corporate Law after *Re Wakim*' (1999) 17 *C & SLJ* 489.

P Young, The Hon Justice, 'Cross-vesting Legislation' (1995) 69 *ALJ* 473.

4.4.2   Looseleaf

W P M Zeeman, The Hon Justice, 'Courts and the Judicial System', *Halsbury's Laws of Australia*, LexisNexis Butterworths, Sydney, vol 8.

4.4.3   Reports

G Moloney and S McMaster, *Cross-vesting Jurisdiction: A Review of the Operation of the National Scheme*, The Australian Institute of Judicial Administration Incorporated, 1992; 'National Scheme for Cross-vesting of Jurisdiction' (1993) 19 *Cth LB* 1005 (summary of the Review by Maloney and McMaster).

4.4.4   Tex ts

M Davies, A Bell and P Brereton, *Nygh's Conflict of Laws in Australia*, 8th ed, LexisNexis Butterworths, Australia, 2010, Chs 4–8.

M Davies, S Ricketson and G Lindell, *Conflict of Laws Commentary and Materials*, Butterworths, Australia, 1997, Chs 3 and 4.

R Mortensen, R Garnett and M Keyes, *Private International Law in Australia*, 2nd ed, LexisNexis Butterworths, Australia, 2011.

## CHAPTER 5

Non-compliance, Amendment and Time

OVERVIEW

Litigation is costly and corrosive. The courts are anxious to ensure that litigation proceeds expeditiously. However, courts must balance the need for expedition with the object of ensuring that justice is done between the parties. Non-compliance with a party's process obligations and applications to amend court documents are perennial issues for courts and litigants. There has been a perceptible change in emphasis in the courts' approach to these issues in recent times.

In the previous edition of this book, reference was made to *Queensland v J L Holdings Pty Ltd* (1997) 189 CLR 146. In that case, the plurality found in the context of an amendment application that principles of case management should not be employed 'except in extreme circumstances, to shut a party out from litigating an issue which is fairly arguable' (Dawson, Gaudron and McHugh JJ at 154). Within 12 years that statement was disapproved by the High Court in *Aon Risk Services Australia Ltd v Australian National University* (2009) 239 CLR 175: see 5.2.7–5.2.12C. In *Aon*, the court considered the extent to which an application to amend a pleading should be determined by reference to principles of case management. For a detailed examination of case management, see **Chapter 2**.

It must be said that 12 years is a relatively short period in the life of the law. In *Aon*, the High Court held that applications to amend will be determined in light of all matters relevant to the exercise of the power to allow amendment: Gummow, Hayne, Crennan, Kiefel and Bell JJ at 217. Principles of case management are important considerations in the court's determination: Gummow, Hayne, Crennan, Kiefel and Bell JJ at 215; see also French CJ at 182 and Heydon J at 222–5. Litigants do not have an entitlement to amend pleadings in order to raise an arguable claim or defence subject to the payment of costs in order to compensate other parties for prejudice occasioned by the amendment. The break with the past was decisive. Gummow, Hayne, Crennan, Kiefel and Bell JJ said at 212 that '[w]here a party had had a sufficient opportunity to plead his or her case, it may be necessary for the court to make a decision [to refuse an amendment] which may produce a sense of injustice in that party, for the sake of doing justice to the opponent and to other litigants'. These statements have application beyond the issue of pleading amendment. If a party fails to use reasonable diligence in preparing and presenting their case, they can be shut out from arguing a triable issue.

The object of this chapter is to discuss the consequences of a party's failure to comply with the rules of procedure or orders made by the court in respect of procedural matters. This chapter will also deal with amendment of documents and the dismissal of proceedings for want of prosecution in cases in which a plaintiff fails to comply with procedural steps requiring the diligent prosecution of proceedings. It also considers the effect of non-compliance with self-executing orders. Finally, there will be a discussion of the question of time in litigation which otherwise relates to the matters dealt with in this chapter.

NON-COMPLIANCE

5.1.1 Two questions arise where a party does not comply with court orders or rules of court. The first concerns the proper characterisation of the non-compliance. Non-compliance in some cases can result in a step taken in the proceeding or the proceeding itself being a nullity. The second question is whether the non-compliance may be validated by the court. The tendency under the rules of most jurisdictions is to provide the court with a wide discretion to deal with non-compliance. Again, case management considerations will inform the court's approach. In that regard, reference can again be made to the decision of the High Court in *Aon Risk Services Australia Ltd v Australian National University* (2009) 239 CLR 175: see **5.2.11–5.2.12C**.

The following extract from the Rules of the Supreme Court 1971 (WA) provides an example of the rules governing non-compliance.

[*NOTE:* in this chapter a reference, such as WA O 9 r 2, is a reference to the relevant Rules of Court. All other legislation will be specified.]

5.1.2E   **Rules of the Supreme Court 1971 (WA)**
Order 2 — Non-compliance with Rules

Non-compliance with rules

1 (1) Where in beginning or purporting to begin any proceedings or at any stage in the course of or in connection with any proceedings, there has, by reason of anything done or left undone, been a failure to comply with the requirements of these Rules, whether in respect of time, place, manner, form or content or in any other respect, the failure shall be treated as an irregularity and shall not nullify the proceedings, any step taken in the proceedings, or any document, judgment or order therein.

(2) Subject to subrule (3) the Court may, on the ground that there has been such a failure as is mentioned in paragraph subrule (1), and on such terms as to costs or otherwise as it thinks just, set aside either wholly or in part the proceedings in which the failure occurred, any step taken in those proceedings, or any document judgment or order therein or exercise its powers under these Rules to allow such amendments (if any) dealing with the proceedings generally as it thinks fit.

(3) The Court shall not wholly set aside any proceedings or the writ or other originating process by which they were begun on the ground that the proceedings were required by any of these Rules to be begun by an originating process other than the one employed.

Application to set aside for an irregularity

2 (1) An application to set aside for irregularity any proceedings, any step taken in any proceedings or any document, judgment or order therein shall not be allowed unless it is made within a reasonable time and before the party applying has taken any fresh step after becoming aware of the irregularity.

(2) An application under this Rule shall be made by summons or motion, as the case may require, and the grounds of objection must be stated in the summons or notice of motion.

5.1.3   Order 2 WA has counterparts in other jurisdictions: HCR r 2.04; Judiciary Act 1903 (Cth) s 77K; Court Procedures Rules (ACT) r 1450; Civil Procedure Act 2005 (NSW) s 63; Uniform Civil Procedure Rules (NSW) rr 6.5–6.6; Supreme Court Rules (NT) rr 2.01–2.03; Uniform Civil Procedure Rules 1999 (Qld) rr 371, 373–374; Supreme Court Civil Rules (SA) rr 12–13; Rules of the Supreme Court 2000 (Tas) rr 13–15; Supreme Court (General Civil Procedure) Rules 2005 (Vic) rr 2.01–2.03. Section 51 of the Federal Court of Australia Act (Cth) 1976 provides that proceedings are not invalidated by a formal defect or irregularity unless the court determines that it has caused a substantial injustice which cannot be remedied by a court order. Rule 1.42 of the Federal Court Rules 2011 provides that the court may specify within an order the consequences of non-compliance with the order.

5.1.4   A general power which permits the court to dispense with the rules is set out in the following: HCR r 2.03; FCR 2011 r 1.34; Court Procedures Rules (ACT) r 6; Civil Procedure Act 2005 (NSW) s 14; Supreme Court Rules (NT) r 2.04; Supreme Court Civil Rules 2006 (SA) r 10; Supreme Court (General Civil Procedure) Rules 2005 (Vic) r 2.04.

Section 14 of the Civil Procedure Act 2005 (NSW) provides that: '[i]n relation to particular civil proceedings, the court may, by order, dispense with any requirement of rules of court if satisfied that it is appropriate to do so in the circumstances of the case.' This section replaces Pt 1 r 12 of the Supreme Court Rules 1970, which was described in the following terms by Kirby P in *Bay Marine Pty Ltd v Clayton Country Properties Pty Ltd* (1986) 8 NSWLR 104 at 108–9:

> … [It was] designed to bring into the general practice of the Court the approach of courts of equity to their rules. It was long ago said that 'the rules must be the servant not the master of the Court' … It is all too easy for those whose lives are daily engaged in the administration of rules to overlook the fact that they exist and are designed, not as an end in themselves but as a means to the attainment of justice. There is no necessary justice in the inflexible and unthinking application of rules for neatness' sake, especially when the rules themselves contain ample powers of dispensation which may be utilised in appropriate cases … It would be undesirable for that beneficial rule [Pt 1 r 12] for dispensation to be given a narrow construction. Its language, the history which preceded it in courts of equity, its position in the first part of the rules and the utility of such a provision to promote the interest in justice all suggest that a meaning should be given to the rule which permits the Court to dispense with the [requirement of the rules that a corporation carry on proceedings by a solicitor].

5.1.5   The general thrust of the rules is to avoid the distinction previously made between a failure to comply with rules which might render the proceeding a nullity incapable of remediation and a failure which might simply constitute an irregularity: *Pontin v Wood* [1962] 1 QB 594 at 608–10 per Holroyd Pearce LJ. An irregularity may be validated by the court.

5.1.6   Notwithstanding the width of the rules and the obvious intention to provide as much scope as possible to correct errors and irregularites, there are cases in which courts are unable to deal with a party's non-compliance. For example, the failure of a party to comply with a statute which prescribes conditions to be satisfied before proceedings are commenced, will render the proceeding void: *Beugelaar v City of Springvale* [1969] VR 3, where there was failure to serve notices prescribed by the Local Government Act 1958 (Vic) prior to issue of proceedings; *Zentahope Pty Ltd v Bellotti* (unreported, SC (Vic), Appeal Division, Fullagar, Brooking and Tadgell JJ, 2 March 1992, BC9203164), where there was a failure to secure a consent to representation in proper form on behalf of represented plaintiffs as required by statute. The court will simply have no jurisdiction.

Similarly, where a party does not exist and proceedings are brought in his, her or its name, the proceeding will be regarded as a nullity; e.g., where a plaintiff is dead and proceedings are brought in his or her name (*Re Pritchard (dec'd)* [1963] Ch 502) and *Deveigne v Askar* (2007) 239 ALR 370; [2007] NSWCA 45 where the distinction between a deceased plaintiff and a deceased defendant is discussed, or where proceedings are brought by or against a company which has ceased to exist: *Re Kilkenny Engineering Pty Ltd (in liq)* (1976) 13 SASR 258.

In the cases mentioned, the error is so fundamental as to be incapable of rectification. They are not cases in which the error is a failure to comply with the rules and, therefore, the rules will not operate to correct such error.

Where an order is made by a superior court in circumstances where it had no jurisdiction to make that order, either on the basis that the proceeding is a nullity or otherwise, the party to whom the order is directed is nonetheless bound to comply with it until such time as it is set aside: *Isaacs v Robertson* [1985] AC 97.

5.1.7 Where a representative proceeding is issued by solicitors without the authority of the named representative plaintiff, the question arises as to whether the proceeding is a nullity or whether the commencement of the proceeding is an irregularity capable of remediation. This question is explored in the following case with respect to representative proceedings under Pt 4A of the Supreme Court Act 1986 (Vic).

5.1.8C **Matthews v SPI Electricity Pty Ltd**
[2011] VSC 167
Supreme Court of Victoria

Forrest J

Introduction

[1] Within 10 days of the Black Saturday bushfires which devastated so much of Victoria on 7 February 2009, Slidders Lawyers (now Oldham Naidoo) issued this proceeding for damages against two power companies in relation to the Kilmore East and Beechworth fires.

[2] Mr Leo Keane was the named representative plaintiff in what is colloquially known as a class action — a group proceeding under Part 4A of the *Supreme Court Act* 1986 (Vic).

[3] Oldham Naidoo did not have instructions or authority from Mr Keane to issue the writ. Indeed, it was the Kilmore East fire that burnt out Mr Keane's property; his claim was unrelated to the Beechworth fire. Within days, he asked the solicitors to remove his name from the writ.

[4] Oldham Naidoo made no attempt to remove Mr Keane as plaintiff for over a year, notwithstanding that the proceeding had been brought without his authority and involved a risk that Mr Keane would be liable for any order for costs obtained by the defendants against him. The solicitors' conduct was a patent and egregious abuse of process, particularly given that the representative claim was brought on behalf of many injured and grieving persons who could not have known what was going on behind the scenes in the solicitors' office.

[5] In July last year Mrs Carol Matthews replaced Mr Keane as the representative plaintiff in this proceeding. Subsequently, another four defendants were added to Mrs Matthews' claim ... Maurice Blackburn & Co (which had the joint conduct of the proceedings) ... played no part in the abuse of the Court's processes and acted promptly and diligently in bringing Oldham Naidoo's conduct to the attention of the Court and the other parties.

[6] Mrs Matthews now applies to the Court to regularise the proceeding to overcome the deficiencies caused by the conduct of Oldham Naidoo.

...

[8] Essentially, I am required to determine three interwoven issues:

(a)   whether the lack of authority of the solicitors in issuing the proceeding is fatal to the claim now brought on behalf of the group members by Mrs Matthews under Part 4A of the *Supreme Court Act*;

(b)   whether the purported ratification by Mr Keane or Mrs Matthews of the institution of the proceeding, in effect, regularises the claim notwithstanding the lack of authority of Oldham Naidoo at the outset; and

(c)   whether, regardless of any conclusion as to ratification, the proceeding should, in the interests of justice, be allowed to continue and Mrs Matthews' application granted, or as the Defendants maintain should it be dismissed as an abuse of process. Alternatively, as I will explain, whether the interests of justice dictate any other course.

...

Non-controversial matters

[38] A number of matters are not in issue:

(a)   at the time that the proceeding was instituted, it was not authorised by Mr Keane nor was there any principal/agent relationship between Mr Keane and Oldham Naidoo;

(b)   Mrs Matthews authorised Maurice Blackburn and Oldham Naidoo (joint solicitors at that time) in May 2010 to apply for her to be substituted as the representative plaintiff;

(c)   Mrs Matthews has, since the time of her substitution (July 2010), authorised the solicitors to maintain the action on her behalf;

(d)   Mr Keane, on 23 March 2011, ratified the institution of the proceeding by Oldham Naidoo;

(e)   Oldham Naidoo consented to being substituted for Mr Keane for the purpose of any costs order against Mr Keane prior to 23 July 2010.

The first issue — Does the lack of authority on the part of the solicitor in issuing a proceeding under Part 4A render it a nullity?

[39] This was the primary submission of SPI which was, somewhat begrudgingly, adopted by the State defendants, but enthusiastically by USC.

[40] The State defendants' reluctance to adopt this proposition, I think, was understandable. In effect, the submission means that any proceeding brought irregularly (in this case without the authority of the named plaintiff), under Part 4A of the *Supreme Court Act* is incapable of cure by either subsequent action (such as ratification) or order of the Court.

[41] If correct, this proposition results in the representative plaintiff and the group members suffering real detriment. All would necessarily be affected by an order dismissing the claim, even if that prejudice was limited to the delay caused by the institution of a fresh proceeding. That of course would be the minimal amount of prejudice — in a case involving the expiry of a limitation period, the prejudice would be far more substantial. Here such an order would deprive the plaintiff and the group members of any entitlement to interest until a fresh

proceeding is issued. That is notwithstanding that since Mrs Matthews was substituted as representative plaintiff the proceeding has been regularly maintained.

[42] I have concluded that SPI's argument is inconsistent with statements of principle of the High Court as to irregularities relating to the commencement of proceedings. It runs contrary to a long line of authority enabling a court to regularise proceedings irregularly commenced. It is also not supported by an analysis of the provisions of Part 4A. Finally, to accept this proposition would be to act inconsistently with the legislative intent and underlying purpose of Part 4A.

[43] I will now explain my reasoning on each of these matters.

[44] Section 33C of the Supreme Court Act reads as follows:

33C Commencement of proceeding
(1) Subject to this Part, if —
    (a) seven or more persons have claims against the same person; and
    (b) the claims of all those persons are in respect of, or arise out of, the same, similar or related circumstances; and
    (c) the claims of all those persons give rise to a substantial common question of law or fact —
a proceeding may be commenced by one or more of those persons as representing some or all of them.

[45] The current version of Mrs Matthews' statement of claim describes the group as follows:

Group members
4. The group members to whom this proceeding relates are:
(a) all those persons who suffered personal injury (whether physical injury, mental injury, psychiatric injury or nervous shock) as a result of:
    (i) the Kilmore bushfire (including, without limitation, an injury suffered as a result of attempts to escape the Kilmore bushfire or other emergency action taken by any person in response to the Kilmore bushfire); and/or
    (ii) the death or injury to another person as a result of the Kilmore bushfire.
(b) the estates or dependants of any person who died in or as a result of the Kilmore bushfire (including, without limitation, a death resulting from attempts to escape the Kilmore bushfire or other emergency action in response to the Kilmore bushfire); or
(c) all those persons who suffered loss or damage to property as a result of the Kilmore bushfire (including, without limitation, loss or damage resulting from emergency action taken by any person in response to the Kilmore bushfire); or
(d) all those persons who at the time of the Kilmore bushfire resided in, or had real or personal property in, the Kilmore bushfire area and who suffered economic loss, which loss was not consequent upon injury to that person or loss or damage to their property.

[46] The number of group members represented by Mrs Matthews will be measured in the thousands. It is common knowledge that over a hundred people died as a result of this bushfire and many more, it can be readily surmised, suffered physical and psychological injury. Thousands more have property damage claims and, presumably, many others sustained "pure economic loss".

[47] This group proceeding is "open" in the sense that its size will not be finally determined until a judgment or settlement — assuming, of course, success on the question of liability. There is no suggestion here that the group is not properly defined in the pleadings or that in some way the definition of the group is amenable to attack for failure to comply with s 33C or the pleading requirements of s 33H.

[48] The role of the plaintiff as the representative of the group is emphasised by other provisions of Part 4A. For instance, s 33D permits a person who has commenced a representative proceeding to maintain that proceeding even though he or she ceases to have a claim against the defendant. A group member does not need to give consent to be part of the group (s 33E), but may opt out of the proceeding if he or she so wishes (s 33J). However, the conduct of the proceeding is, at least nominally, undertaken by the representative plaintiff. It is the representative plaintiff, not a group member, who carries the potential costs liability (s 33ZD).

[His Honour considered the role of the representative plaintiff and group members under the provisions of Pt 4A of the Supreme Court Act 1986 (Vic) and continued.]

[54] It follows from the above that the claims of the group members are, in a practical sense, carried forward by the representative plaintiff. Once the proceeding has been issued, the Court is seized not merely of a claim by the representative plaintiff, but of the group's claims as well. Absent an order of the Court (which necessarily must take into account the interests of the group members), the claim will proceed to trial (or settlement) where orders will be made which bind all members of the group who have not elected to opt out.

[55] There can be no doubt that Part 4A of the Supreme Court Act radically enlargened the scope by which representative proceedings could be brought in this State. What emerges, starkly, from this analysis of the legislation in the context of these applications is that once a group proceeding is on foot, then the interests of all group members must be considered in any application which may, in some way, affect their rights.

[56] It is in this statutory context that I turn to the primary assertion of SPI which is to this effect: once it was accepted that the writ had been issued without the authority of Mr Keane, then the proceeding is a nullity and, therefore, must be dismissed. In its written submissions on this point, SPI said as follows:

  (b) the firm having commenced the proceeding in the absence of any agency relationship with Mr Keane, without any instructions or authority and contrary to Mr Keane's wishes:
    (i) no proceeding was "commenced" within the meaning of s 33C of the *Supreme Court Act* or at all;
    (ii) if any proceeding was "commenced" it was not commenced by Mr Keane;
    (iii) if any proceeding was commenced by Mr Keane, it was not commenced by Mr Keane "as representing some or all" of the persons referred to in section 33C; and
    (iv) the proceeding was accordingly, a nullity.
  (d) The proceeding being commenced without authority and not ratified by Mr Keane before the purported substitution of Mrs Matthews on 23 July 2010, that substitution was ineffective such that she is not and never has been a plaintiff.
  (f) It is not possible to ratify or adopt a Part 4A proceeding commenced without authority so as to regularise it and cure the original lack of authority. The provisions of

Part 4A should be construed as precluding the operation of any curative common law principles that might apply in the individual proceeding context.

[57] Unsurprisingly in oral argument, counsel for SPI sought to shy away from expressions such as "nullity" or "voidable". This was understandable, as the statements of principle of the High Court in *Berowra Holdings Pty Ltd v Gordon* stand squarely in the path of this proposition advanced by SPI.

[58] Before turning to the reasoning of the Court, the history and relevant legislation in *Berowra Holdings* is of some significance to this application. The proceeding had, on its face, been instituted irregularly. Mr Gordon had been injured on 2 October 2001 in the course of his employment. He gave notice of injury to his employer, Berowra Holdings, under the Workers' Compensation Act 1987 (NSW) on 12 October 2001. He then issued his common law proceeding for damages on 23 November 2001. However, there was a problem in the form of s 151C of the Workers' Compensation Act which provided:

A person to whom compensation is payable under this Act is not entitled to commence court proceedings for damages in respect of the injury concerned against the employer liable to pay that compensation until six months have elapsed since notice of the injury was given to the employer.

[59] On the day prior to the trial of Mr Gordon's common law damages claim, the employer gave notice that it proposed to rely upon the non-compliance with s 151C and to argue that the proceeding was invalid or a nullity.

[60] In *Berowra Holdings*, the High Court described concepts such as "nullity" and "invalidity" as misleading because they "tend to obscure the discretion between superior courts of record of general jurisdiction and courts of limited jurisdiction".

[61] The Court rejected the characterisation of the proceeding as being either a nullity or invalid, saying as follows:

There also is a very real difficulty in characterising proceedings as "invalid". The institution of an action or other proceeding is the exercise by the litigant of the freedom to invoke the jurisdiction of the judicial arm of government to determine a dispute. That step engages the procedural law appurtenant to the relevant court, which in modern times is found primarily in the Rules.

Professor Jolowicz describes procedural law as creating choices or a sequence of choices in the sense that each procedural step taken by a litigant requires the other party or the court to take some action, so affecting the path which the proceedings take towards ultimate disposition. *This is the case even where a procedural rule is expressed in mandatory form; if the party to whom it is addressed chooses to disregard it, the normal outcome is that a choice accrues to the other party either to do nothing or to seek an appropriate order from the court.* Once the procedural law has been engaged, all parties to the litigation are subject to it.

In the adversarial system of justice, choice rests primarily with the parties and it is generally the case that the court's power of decision or order is exercised upon the application of a party. *Generally there is in law no restriction upon a person's right to start an action and to carry it to the point at which a choice is cast upon the defendant to make some response in order to avoid judgment in default.* Once the procedural law has been engaged, all parties to the litigation are subject to it.

None of the above denies the possibility of a defendant denying the plaintiff's right to invoke the jurisdiction of the court, for example where the plaintiff's right is conditional upon there being an action cognisable within that jurisdiction ... However, the invocation of jurisdiction ordinarily enlivens the authority of the court in question at least in the first instance to decide whether it has jurisdiction. (emphasis added and citations omitted)

[62] *Berowra Holdings* demonstrates that where a proceeding has been issued in contradiction of a specific statutory provision, it is nonetheless capable of being litigated and is neither *void ab initio* nor a nullity. On a more general level it establishes that an irregularity in the institution of a proceeding does not render the proceeding invalid. Rather, its future prosecution may be attacked by engaging the appropriate procedural measures.

[63] The result in *Berowra Holdings* is also illustrative in the context of this case. The employer had raised s 151C of the Workers' Compensation Act point at the last moment — just prior to the trial commencing. The trial Judge permitted the employer to raise the point notwithstanding its timing. The High Court held that it was unfair to Mr Gordon to have the point raised at that time (particularly as it was still open to Mr Gordon to accept the offer of compromise made by the employer — which he had endeavoured to do). Leave should not have been granted permitting the employer to amend its defence. Notwithstanding his failure to comply with what might have been thought to be a precondition to jurisdiction, the High Court held that Mr Gordon was entitled to accept the offer of compromise and have judgment entered for that amount.

[64] Cases decided under Part IVA of the Federal Court Act are also consistent with the reasoning of the High Court. Proceedings "not properly commenced" by reason of non-compliance with the "threshold requirements of s 33C(1)" are neither a nullity nor invalid. They are, as Sackville J said in *Philip Morris (Australia) Ltd v Nixon* "liable to be dismissed or the applicants' pleading struck out".

[65] The decision in *Berowra Holdings* also sits comfortably with the established line of authority to the effect that a proceeding issued by a solicitor without the authority of a plaintiff be regarded, to use the terminology eschewed by the High Court, as neither "void" nor a "nullity".

[66] The point is demonstrated by the decision of the Court of Appeal in *Danish Mercantile Co Ltd & ors v Beaumont*. In that case, the argument put by the defendant was that:

... where an action is brought without the authority of the purported plaintiff, the action is an utter and complete nullity, so that no amount of subsequent ratification can cure the defect.

The Court of Appeal rejected the proposition that the action was *void ab initio* and concluded that notwithstanding this defect in the proceeding as originally constituted, it could be cured if ratified by the "purported plaintiff". It was a nullity only in the sense that it could be stayed on application by the defendant.

[67] In *Presentaciones Musicales S.A. v Secunda & anor*, the Court of Appeal summarised the position in England:

It is well recognised law that where a solicitor starts proceedings in the name of a plaintiff — be it a company or an individual — without authority, the plaintiff may ratify the act of the solicitor and adopt the proceedings. In that event, in accordance with the ordinary law of principal and agent and the ordinary doctrine of ratification the defect in the proceedings as originally constituted is cured.

[68] Recently in this country, the principle was affirmed by Finkelstein J in *Ox Operations Pty Ltd v Landmark Property Developments (Vic) Pty Ltd in liquidation*:

> The usual course when a company is improperly made a plaintiff is to stay or dismiss the action and require the solicitor who purported to act for the company to pay the cost. *The cases also show that the action though brought without authority is not a nullity in the sense that it is void ab initio without the possibility of subsequent ratification. To the contrary, it is well established that it is possible for the company to ratify the unauthorised act of the solicitor in bringing an action in its name without its actual or implied authority.* And, because ratification is possible, a practice has developed that when an action is brought without authority it will not be stayed or dismissed forthwith, but the company will be permitted to convene a general meeting or a meeting of its directors to consider whether to adopt the action. (emphasis added)

[69] It follows, I suggest, that the proposition that the proceeding once issued was either *void ab initio* or a nullity could not be sustained unless it was demonstrated that Part 4A, in some way, quarantines a representative proceeding from the application of these general principles. This, it seems to me, requires an extraordinary leap of faith. The Workers' Compensation Act 1987 (NSW) provided, specifically, that a person was not entitled to commence proceedings unless there was compliance with its provisions. The High Court ruled that Mr Gordon's claim was not a nullity. Here Part 4A is silent about both invalidity and ratification — not a word is said to displace the general proposition that a representative proceeding, irregularly commenced, cannot either by way of ratification or order of the Court be maintained subsequently.

[70] As I followed the argument of SPI, it was said that by reason of the special role taken on by the plaintiff in representing the group members (as demonstrated by a number of the provisions I have referred to), then a claim issued without authority could not be cured. This it argued flows from the Part 4A regime. Also, so the argument went, absent a specific provision permitting ratification then a representative plaintiff cannot ratify an irregularly commenced group proceeding.

[71] Counsel for Mrs Matthews rightly, I think, characterised SPI's argument as treating a representative proceeding as an island, immune to authority governing every other form of proceeding. Counsel for SPI was unable to direct me to any other decision to the effect that statements of principle in *Berowra Holdings* or, for that matter, in relation to ratification, are not of general application. Nor was he able to direct me to any authority that other forms of representative proceeding (such as that involving a litigation guardian acting for a person under a disability or a trustee acting on behalf of a beneficiary) are in some way isolated from the application of the principles I have referred to.

[72] In *Wong v Silkfield*, the High Court said of Part IVA of the *Federal Court Act*:

> Like other provisions conferring jurisdiction upon or granting powers to a court, Part IVA is not to be read by making implications or imposing limitations not found in the words used; this is so even if the evident purpose of the statute is to displace generally understood procedures.

[73] There is, in my view, no warrant to draw an implication that a Part 4A proceeding irregularly commenced is therefore invalid or void from commencement; nor to conclude that the general principles relating to irregularly commenced proceedings (including that of ratification) do not apply to such a proceeding.

...

[77] Then, there was the contention that absent the existence of a principal/agent relationship between Mr Keane and Oldham Naidoo, the proceeding should be treated as a nullity. The first hurdle, as I have repeatedly said, is the decision in *Berowra Holdings*: the absence of the relationship rendered the proceeding open to attack by SPI as an abuse of process but it was not a "nullity".

[78] In any event, the existence of such a relationship is not essential to a subsequent act of ratification. In *Bowstead and Reynolds On Agency*, the following is said of ratification:

> Where an act is done purportedly in the name or on behalf of another by a person who has no actual authority to do that act, the person in whose name or whose behalf the act is done may, if the third party has believed the act to be authorised, by ratifying the act, make it as valid and effectual ... as if it had been originally done by his authority, whether the person the act was an agent exceeding its authority, *or as a person having no authority to act for him at all.* (emphasis added)

[79] Returning to Part 4A, it seems to me that the result pressed by SPI flies in the face of the clear purpose of this Act particularly in the context of this case - which enables many persons, either injured or who have suffered the loss of a loved one, or those who have sustained damage to property, or have suffered economic loss, to be represented by one person in a group proceeding and to have their rights determined (as far as possible) in a single proceeding. To suggest that Part 4A would render nugatory a group proceeding because of a solicitor's failure to obtain the authority of the representative plaintiff would, I think, go against the very objective of the legislation. It cannot be thought that the legislature would have intended that the rights of group members be so adversely affected, particularly say in a situation where a limitation provision could be invoked by a defendant if the proceeding was held to be a nullity from its commencement.

[80] So to summarise; the proceeding, although commenced without the authority of Mr Keane, remains alive. The claim now brought on behalf of group members, with instructions from Mrs Matthews, is not a nullity nor is it void.

[After rejecting submissions to the effect that the proceeding was a nullity, Forrest J considered the effect of the document signed by Mr Keane purporting to ratify the institution and maintenance of the proceeding in his name until Mrs Matthews was substituted as representative plaintiff.]

The second issue — Was it possible for Mr Keane and/or Mrs Matthews to ratify the institution of the proceeding?

...

[86] I have already rejected the proposition that the proceeding was a nullity. On the second point Mr Keane, has, by the document signed by him on 23 March 2011 ratified the institution and maintenance of the proceeding in his name until replaced by Mrs Matthews. But SPI (supported by the other Defendants) says that this ratification counts for nothing — as Mr Keane is no longer the representative plaintiff.

[87] I do not accept this contention. No authority was cited to suggest that a person ratifying the issue of a proceeding needed to be the plaintiff at the time of ratification. Nor can I see any justification for the proposition emerging impliedly out of Part 4A.

[88] The proceeding was issued in Mr Keane's name. He was subsequently capable of authorising the issue of the proceeding notwithstanding he was no longer the plaintiff. I shall set out my reasoning briefly on this point and commence with article 15 of *Bowstead and Reynolds on Agency* which reads:

> The only person who has power to ratify an act is the person *in whose name or on whose behalf the act* was purported to be done. (emphasis added)

[89] In *PMSA*, the English Court of Appeal concluded that the "nominal plaintiff" could ratify a proceeding issued without its authority (in that case after the limitation period had expired) provided it was lawful to do so:

> Where a writ is issued without authority, the cases show that the writ is not a nullity. For the nominal plaintiff to adopt the writ, or ratify its issue, does not require any application to the court. Accordingly, on the same general principle that justifies *Pontin v Wocd*, the plaintiff, in the simple example of an action raising a single cause of action which has been begun by solicitors without authority, must be entitled to adopt the action notwithstanding the expiration of the limitation period applicable to that cause of action.[1] (citations omitted)

[90] It follows that the nominal plaintiff at the time of issue, Mr Keane, may adopt the proceeding and ratify its initiation and maintenance up until the time of the substitution of Mrs Matthews.

[91] It was argued by SPI that by implication drawn from the terms of s 33C, which provides that "a proceeding may be commenced by one or more persons as representing some or all of them", then only if that person remains as the representative plaintiff was he or she capable of ratifying the proceeding. I disagree.

[92] Section 33C enables the representative plaintiff to institute the proceeding and operates in tandem with s 33H to ensure that the group is sufficiently identified to satisfy the criteria for the maintenance of the claim under Part 4A. It says nothing either expressly or by implication about ratification, and, more importantly, about the principle of ratification being excluded in Part 4A proceedings.

[93] It was also contended that because of the structure of a representative proceeding and the role of the representative plaintiff, a member of the group (which Mr Keane now is) could not subsequently ratify the institution of the representative proceeding. It was said to be a "special creature".

[94] In my view the provisions of Part 4A have no bearing, either expressly or impliedly, on questions of ratification or lack of authority. The Part 4A regime does not prohibit the application of the general principles of ratification to a group proceeding. There is no reason to treat a group proceeding differently to any other proceeding and the matters I set out at [57]–[79] are applicable here.

[95] There is nothing in the principles of agency which suggest that the person ratifying the unauthorised act needs to be a party to the proceeding at time of the subsequent authorisation.

Rather, the enquiry is whether at that time it was lawful for the person in whose name the proceeding was issued to do so. For the reasons I have set out I think that it was.

[96] It is sufficient (and consistent with the principles I have adverted to), that Mr Keane now says that he ratifies the institution of the proceeding notwithstanding that it was issued without his authority.

[97] Given this conclusion, it is not necessary to determine whether Mrs Matthews had the capacity to ratify the proceeding issued in Mr Keane's name.

[Forrest J rejected the contention that the proceeding should be dismissed as an abuse of process and ordered, among other things, that the proceeding commenced without authority in the name of Leo Keane stand as a proceeding regularly commenced and continued by Carol Ann Matthews pursuant to Pt 4A of the Supreme Court Act 1986 (Vic).]

5.1.9   Notes and questions

1. How important is the fact that a willing representative plaintiff could be found?
2. What consequences would be likely to flow from an inability to substitute a representative plaintiff? See *Cohen v State of Victoria* [2011] VSC 165.
3. Can a failure to comply with the rules of procedure constitute a nullity?
4. In what circumstances may a court refuse to ratify an irregularly issued proceeding? See Williams, *Civil Procedure Victoria*, LexisNexis Butterworths, Sydney, looseleaf, [2.01.20].
5. For further examples of irregularly issued proceedings, see Williams, *Civil Procedure Victoria*, LexisNexis Butterworths, Sydney, looseleaf, [2.01.35].

AMENDMENT

5.2.1   Amendment is governed by the applicable rules in the relevant jurisdiction. There are provisions in all Australian jurisdictions for the amendment of documents. Some rules of court provide specifically for the amendment of pleadings: FCR Div 16.5, especially r 16.51; ACT r 5.05; NSW r 19.1; NT r 36.03; Qld r 377; SA r 55; Tas r 428; Vic r 36.04; WA O 21 r 3.

Amendment rules

5.2.2   There are two main categories of amendment rules. Rules which fall within the first category direct themselves to the determination of the real issues in dispute, the correction of an error or defect and the avoidance of multiplicity of proceedings. The following extract is an example.

5.2.3E   **Supreme Court Rules (Northern Territory)**

36.01(1) For the purpose of determining the real question in controversy between the parties to a proceeding or of correcting a defect or error in a proceeding or of avoiding multiplicity of proceedings, the Court may at any stage order that a document in the proceeding be amended or that a party have leave to amend a document in the proceeding.

[See Supreme Court Act (NT) s 80; See also: HCR r 3.01.2; FCR r 16.53; Judiciary Act 1903 (Cth) s 77J; ACT r 501; Civil Procedure Act 2005 (NSW) s 64(2); Qld r 375; SA rr 54 and 57; Tas r 427; Vic r 36.01; WA O 21 rr 5(1), 7(1).]

5.2.4 In *Aon Risk Services Australia Ltd v Australian National University* (2009) 239 CLR 175 (see **5.2.7–5.2.12C**), the court found that the real issues in the proceeding may extend beyond the pleadings but are confined to issues which exist in the proceeding at the time of the application for amendment. See the judgments of Gummow, Hayne, Crennan, Kiefel and Bell JJ at 205 and Heydon J at 218–19. This case provides an authoritative example of a new issue which falls outside the scope of the 'real' issues in the proceeding within the meaning of r 501(a) of the Court Procedures Rules 2006 (ACT). The new issues raised were allegations that Aon Risk Services had breached a services contract pursuant to which it was required to ascertain and declare correct values of specified property and provide certain advice. The original claim against Aon Risk Services, which had been on foot for 17 months, alleged that Aon had breached a different contract by failing to arrange for renewal of insurance over certain property. The amendment in question was found to raise entirely new issues and therefore r 501(a) did not apply. Such amendments fell to be considered under the court's general discretion to amend considered at **5.2.6** and **5.2.7E** below (see French CJ at 192–3; Gummow, Hayne, Crennan, Kiefel and Bell JJ at 205 and Heydon J at 218–19).

5.2.5 In determining whether an amendment was necessary to avoid a multiplicity of proceedings under r 501(c), the plurality in *Aon* considered whether an exercise of reasonable diligence on the part of ANU would have led to the bringing of the claim in question in the existing proceedings so that subsequent proceedings might be met with an application for a stay based upon *Port of Melbourne Authority v Anshun Pty Ltd* (1981) 147 CLR 589 (Gummow, Hayne, Crennan, Kiefel and Bell JJ at 209–10: see **5.2.12C** below). French CJ said as follows at 192:

> The requirement under r 501(c) to avoid a multiplicity of proceedings is to be understood as operating within the framework of an ordered progression to a fixed trial date. It does not oblige the court to accept the addition of new claims at the last moment before trial, on the basis that if they are not allowed there might be subsequent proceedings in which those claims are raised. The steps which r 501(c) requires to be taken to avoid multiple proceedings are "all necessary amendments". The Court had no basis for inferring that, absent the amendments, there would be further proceedings.

5.2.6 Where an amendment is found to be necessary to determine the real issues in dispute, to correct an error or defect or avoid multiplicity of proceedings, the court must grant the amendment. These rules offer little scope for discretion beyond that entailed in the determination of what is necessary. In contrast, the second category of amendment rule falls within the courts' general discretion. The following is an example.

5.2.7E   **High Court Rules 2004**

3.01.1 The Court or a Justice may, at any stage of a proceeding, allow a party to amend any document in the proceeding.

[See also FCR rr 8.21, 15.15; ACT r 502; Civil Procedure Act 2005 (NSW) s 64(1); NT r 36.03; Tas r 427; Vic r 36.03; WA O 21 rr 1, 3].

Factors affecting amendment

5.2.8 The party seeking amendment must satisfy the court that its opponent will not suffer prejudice by reason of the amendment which cannot be remedied by an adjournment, an award of costs or in some other way. In *Queensland v JL Holdings* (1997) 189 CLR 146, the High Court held that a party should be permitted to raise an arguable defence subject to the payment of costs by way of compensation: see **2.6.5C**. This approach was disapproved in *Aon Risk Services Australia Ltd v Australian National University* (2009) 239 CLR 175 (see **5.2.11–5.2.12C**), where the court found that a party seeking to amend a pleading does not have an entitlement to amend subject to payment of costs by way of compensation. The adequacy of costs in compensating an opposing party's prejudice is considered by Gummow, Hayne, Crennan, Kiefel and Bell JJ at 99–100. Their Honours considered that indemnity costs are not always sufficient to address prejudice suffered by other litigants in the form of duplication and lost time, inconvenience and stress.

5.2.9 In *Aon Risk Services Australia Ltd v Australian National University* (2009) 239 CLR 175, French CJ stated at 194 that:

> ... [a] court faced with a late amendment seeking to raise new claims and the *in terrorem* prediction that a multiplicity of proceedings may follow if the amendment is not allowed, is entitled to have regard to the barriers to the implementation of suggestions of that kind.

Such barriers include the danger that subsequent proceedings may be considered an abuse of process and the form of estoppel considered by the High Court in *Port of Melbourne Authority v Anshun Pty Ltd* (1981) 147 CLR 589: see **5.2.5** above.

5.2.10 In *Queensland v J L Holdings Pty Ltd* (1997) 189 CLR 146 at 169–70, Kirby J enumerates the considerations which guide the exercise of judicial discretion in determining an amendment application.

Considerations which favour the grant of leave to amend include:

- that the amendment sought is the only way in which the true issues and the real merits, factual and legal, can be litigated and artificiality avoided;

- that the relevant oversight is adequately explained;

- that the proposed amendment is of considerable importance to the rights of a party, particularly where it provides a complete answer to a claim;

- that any fault is attributable to the party's legal representatives;
- that there has been the perception of an important new point by new legal representatives; and
- that the hearing date is not jeopardised.

Considerations which militate against the grant of leave to amend include:

- the absence of explanation for a late application;
- the blamelessness of the resisting party and the extent to which the applicant is at fault in its breach of clear directions;
- the strain which litigation may place upon those involved and the natural desire of most litigants to be freed, as quickly as possible, from the anxiety, distraction and disruption which litigation causes;
- the proximity to the hearing date;
- the length of time that the proceedings have been pending; the longer the time, the more reasonable it is to expect that the matter should have been raised earlier;
- the extent to which a new issue would give rise to a substantial and new case in reply; and
- 'litigation abuse' manifest in repeated default on the part of a litigant whose conduct has the effect of frustrating a proper timetable fixed for the trial.

The relevance of case management

5.2.11 The adversarial model of litigation has evolved: see 2.1.1–2.3.3 on case management. Party control over the progress of proceedings has been qualified by case management schemes. In jurisdictions where courts have adopted case management, the power of the court to allow an amendment must be considered in the context of the objects sought to be achieved through the judicial control of litigation: Federal Court of Australia Act 1976 Pt VB; ACT r 21, r 1402; Civil Procedure Act 2005 (NSW) ss 56–60; NT r 1.10; Qld r 5; SA r 3; Tas rr 414, 414A, 427(3); Civil Procedure Act 2010 (Vic) ss 7–9; WA O 1 r 4A, O 1 r 4B.

The extent to which case management is relevant in determining applications for amendment has been considered by the High Court in *Sali v SPC Ltd* (1993) 67 ALJR 841, *Queensland v J L Holdings Pty Ltd* (1997) 189 CLR 146 and *Aon Risk Services Australia Ltd v Australian National University* (2009) 239 CLR 175.

In *Sali v SPC*, case management was characterised by Toohey and Gaudron JJ at 636 as another element in the equation of determining an adjournment application or another consideration put onto the scales. Thus case management reflects the position that 'the conduct of litigation is not merely a matter for the parties but is also one for the court and the need to avoid disruptions in the court's lists with consequent inconvenience to the court and prejudice to the interests of other litigants waiting to be heard' (at 636). Brennan, Deane and McHugh JJ explained at 629 that:

> ... [i]n determining whether to grant an adjournment, the judge of a busy court is entitled to consider the effect of an adjournment on court resources and the competing claims by litigants in other cases awaiting hearing in the court as well as the interests of the parties ... What might be perceived as an injustice to a party when considered only in the context of an action between

parties may not be so when considered in a context which includes the claims of other litigants and the public interest in achieving the most efficient use of court resources.

In *Queensland v J L Holdings Pty Ltd*, Dawson Gaudron and McHugh JJ at 154 considered that *Sali v SPC* did not suggest that case management principles 'might be employed, except perhaps in extreme circumstances, to shut a party out from litigating an issue which is fairly arguable'. Their Honours said at 154 that:

> ... [c]ase management is not an end in itself. It is an important and useful aid for ensuring the prompt and efficient disposal of litigation. But it ought always be borne in mind, even in changing times, that the ultimate aim of a court is the attainment of justice and no principle of case management can be allowed to supplant that aim.

They concluded (at 155) that while case management was a relevant consideration, 'it should not have been allowed to prevail over the injustice of shutting the applicants out from raising an arguable defence, thus precluding the determination of an issue between the parties'.

The High Court in *Aon Risk Services Australia Ltd v Australian National University* accorded greater weight to case management concerns. The court unanimously allowed an appeal against an order granting leave to amend the respondent's statement of claim to add a substantial new claim. The facts of the case are set out at **2.6.6C**. After noting that the case in *Queensland v J L Holdings Pty Ltd* arose out of a completely different factual setting, French CJ considered in *Aon Risk Services Australia Ltd v Australian National University* (at 182) that:

> ... to the extent that statements about the exercise of the discretion to amend pleadings in that case suggest that case management considerations and questions of proper use of court resources are to be discounted or given little weight, it should not be regarded as authoritative.

French CJ considered that concerns of case management extend beyond those of the immediate parties and other litigants awaiting trial (at 182):

> ... the time of the court is a publicly funded resource. Inefficiencies in the use of that resource, arising from the vacation or adjournment of trials, are to be taken into account. So too is the need to maintain public confidence in the judicial system.

The plurality (Gummow, Hayne, Crennan, Kiefel and Bell JJ) similarly observed (at 217) that 'it is recognised by the courts that the resolution of disputes serves the public as a whole, not merely the parties to the proceedings'. Their Honours considered (at 212 and 217) that the statements in *Queensland v JL Holdings* which suggest only a limited application for case management should not be applied in the future. These statements were not consonant with the court's earlier recognition of the effects of delay on parties to a proceeding, the court and other litigants. The judgment of the plurality is extracted in part at **5.2.12C** below.

Heydon J said in *Aon Risk Services Australia Ltd v Australian National University* at 222 that there is a common opinion that *Queensland v JL Holdings Pty Ltd*, whether correctly understood or not, has had a 'damaging influence on the conduct of litigation'. His Honour described the conduct of the litigation by the Australian National University as reflecting 'a certain culture and mentality' which common opinion attributed to the decision in *Queensland v JL Holdings*.

The delays in the conduct of the proceeding were considered by Heydon J in the context of the importance of expedition in commercial litigation. His Honour stated (at 224):

> Commercial life depends on the timely and just payment of money. Prosperity depends on the velocity of its circulation. Those who claim to be entitled to money should know, as soon as possible, whether they will be paid. Those against whom the entitlement is asserted should know, as soon as possible, whether they will have to pay. In each case that is because it is important that both the claimants and those resisting claims are able to order their affairs. How they order their affairs affects how their creditors, their debtors, their suppliers, their customers, their employees, and, in the case of companies, their actual and potential shareholders, order their affairs. The courts are thus an important aspect of the institutional framework of commerce. The efficiency or inefficiency of the courts has a bearing on the health or sickness of commerce.

5.2.12C   Aon Risk Services Australia Ltd v Australian National University
(2009) 239 CLR 175; 258 ALR 14
High Court of Australia

[The facts of the case are set out in 2.6.8C and referred to at 5.2.4 above. Leave to amend the statement of claim was granted to the Australian National University (ANU) by Gray J in the Australian Capital Territory Supreme Court. An appeal to the Court of Appeal was dismissed and Aon Risk Services Australia Ltd (Aon) appealed to the High Court. The High Court unanimously allowed the appeal. The following three rules were considered by the court:

- r 501 of the Court Procedures Rules 2006 (ACT) which concerns amendments which are necessary for determining the real issues in the proceeding. This rule falls within the first category of amendment rule considered above at 5.2.3–5.2.4;
- r 502 of the Court Procedures Rules which concerns the court's discretionary power to permit amendments 'in the way it considers appropriate': see 5.2.5 above; and
- r 21 of the Court Procedures Rules which sets out the overriding purpose of facilitating the just resolution of the real issues in civil proceedings with minimum delay and expense. The court's discretion to grant an amendment under r 502 is guided by the case management purposes set out in r 21.]

Gummow Hayne, Crennan, Kiefel and Bell JJ (at 196):

The background to the amendments

…

The original claim brought by ANU against Aon was based upon a contract dated 28 June 1999, the term of which was said to have been extended until 30 June 2004. ANU alleged that the agreement required Aon to arrange for the renewal of insurance cover for the period in question for all buildings and their contents which were then the subject of insurance which was due to expire. It was alleged to be an implied term of that agreement that Aon would exercise reasonable care, skill and diligence in arranging for the renewal of the expiring cover.

The claim against Aon was expressed to be in the alternative to the claims brought against the insurers and to arise in the event that the buildings and contents referred to in the two Schedules were not the subject of a contract of insurance. Understood in light of the insurers' defences, the claim was limited to the property in the PNI Schedule, which was alleged not to have been insured. ANU alleged that if insurance had not been effected, Aon had breached its retainer and breached its duty of care to it by failing to arrange insurance or to advise ANU that it had not been arranged.

On the first day appointed for trial ANU, Chubb and CGU commenced a mediation and a settlement was reached two days later. ... It was later alleged that the amounts paid left a substantial shortfall remaining in the claim with respect to the Sch C property in consequence of the insurers' claim to reduction of liability and no payment at all for the claim with respect to the property in the PNI Schedule.

After dealing with orders which were made by consent with respect to the insurers, counsel for ANU advised the court that ANU would apply for leave to amend its claim against Aon and sought an adjournment of the trial. In the events which followed the adjournment was effectively granted. The trial did not proceed. The applications were not heard until 27 November 2006. The decision to grant leave was not made until 12 October 2007. This delay is regrettable given the nature of the applications, the time at which they were brought and their importance for the future of the litigation.

The amendments

The amendments permitted to be made to ANU's claim as a result of the grant of leave were substantial. The contract between ANU and Aon was now said to be one for insurance broking and advisory services and to have come into effect from 1 July 1999. It is not apparent from the documents particularised whether it was referable, in part, to the agreement earlier pleaded. Pursuant to this agreement Aon was to review ANU's policies of insurance; meet with ANU on a regular basis in the process of review; prepare submissions to insurers which would ensure all material facts were disclosed and enable the insurers to determine their criteria for indemnity; and place insurance upon instructions from ANU. It was to provide an annual stewardship report.

Central to the new claim was the allegation that Aon knew or ought to have known that the true replacement value of both building and contents were material to the insurers' consideration of indemnity, including the decision to reinsure. ANU alleged breaches of the services agreement, and of Aon's duty of care to it, by its failure to arrange insurance on declared values which were the true replacement values of the property; that it failed altogether to obtain valuations of the contents of the property; and that it was negligent in failing to obtain accurate valuations.

The claims with respect to Aon's failure to effect insurance of the PNI Schedule property were maintained, but in the context of the new agreement for services. It was now alleged that Aon knew that ANU required renewal of insurance cover in 2003 over all the property which had been listed in three Schedules, which included the PNI and Sch C lists, and which had been the subject of its express instruction to insure in the preceding year. It was alleged that Aon failed to obtain ANU's instructions before placing the insurance in question and that it had failed to advise of the effect of the provision for a 'deductible', which is to say an 'excess', on the amount ANU was not entitled to recover. The contract of insurance was alleged to have applied a deductible of $1 million to 'each and every loss' with the effect that ANU might not be able to recover where buildings had a value less than the deductible.

It was further alleged that Aon had breached provisions of the Australian Securities and Investments Commission Act 2001 (Cth) in the provision of its services; it had made representations as to future matters without reasonable grounds for doing so (120); and had been guilty of misleading and deceptive conduct (121).

211

The 'explanation'

The proposed amended pleading had not been drawn when ANU sought an adjournment of the trial. Senior counsel for ANU outlined three matters as necessitating the foreshadowed application for amendment: the settlements which had just taken place with the insurers; the recent receipt by ANU of affidavits of evidence from Chubb and CGU and of discovery from Chubb of documents relating to its underwriting processes; and conversations with the insurers during mediation. It was said that it was now apparent that the declared value of the property had critical significance to the insurers, beyond the calculation of premium, and that Aon was directly responsible for the valuations ...

Statements in *JL Holdings*

The starting point in this appeal is the provisions of the Court Procedures Rules which govern the application to amend ... However, it is convenient to refer at this point to statements made in *JL Holdings* which pre-date those Rules. Those statements were considered by the primary judge and members of the Court of Appeal as authoritative in limiting the application of the case management principles to which those Rules give expression.

It is not necessary to recite the facts of *JL Holdings*. It is sufficient to observe that the defendant, the State of Queensland, sought leave to amend its defence to raise a clearly arguable matter, which depended upon the terms of a statute but which had been overlooked in the course of the litigation towards a trial. The primary judge refused leave to amend, on the basis that it would jeopardise the dates allocated for hearing. The plurality (Dawson, Gaudron and McHugh JJ) did not accept that JL Holdings would necessarily be prejudiced by the amendments, given the nature of the issue raised, the fact that the hearing was some months ahead and the likelihood that the length of the trial would be such as to accommodate it.

More important, for present purposes, is what their Honours said concerning the requirements of case management, which had been referred to by the Full Court of the Federal Court in dismissing the appeal from the primary judge's orders. Referring to the previous decision of this Court in *Sali v SPC Ltd*, the plurality said of case management principles:

> ... nothing in that case suggests that those principles might be employed, except perhaps in extreme circumstances, to shut a party out from litigating an issue which is fairly arguable. Case management is not an end in itself. It is an important and useful aid for ensuring the prompt and efficient disposal of litigation. But it ought always to be borne in mind, even in changing times, that the ultimate aim of a court is the attainment of justice and no principle of case management can be allowed to supplant that aim.

In their conclusion, their Honours said:

> In our view, the matters referred to by the primary judge were insufficient to justify her Honour's refusal of the application by the applicants to amend their defence and nothing has been made to appear before us which would otherwise support that refusal. Justice is the paramount consideration in determining an application such as the one in question. Save in so far as costs may be awarded against the party seeking the amendment, such an application is not the occasion for the punishment of a party for its mistake or for its delay in making the application. Case management, involving as it does the efficiency of the procedures of the court, was in this case a relevant consideration. But it should not have been allowed to prevail over the injustice of shutting the applicants out from raising

an arguable defence, thus precluding the determination of an issue between the parties. In taking an opposite view, the primary judge was, in our view, in error in the exercise of her discretion.

The Court Procedures Rules

As earlier stated, the starting point for any application to amend must be the rules governing such applications in the relevant jurisdiction. In this case rr 501 and 502 appear in Ch 2 of the Court Procedures Rules, which is concerned with civil proceedings in courts in the Territory. Rule 501 provides:

> All necessary amendments of a document (126) must be made for the purpose of —
> (a) deciding the real issues in the proceeding; or
> (b) correcting any defect or error in the proceeding; or
> (c) avoiding multiple proceedings.

Rule 502 provides:

> (1) At any stage of a proceeding, the court may give leave for a party to amend, or direct a party to amend, an originating process, anything written on an originating process, a pleading, an application or any other document filed in the court in a proceeding in the way it considers appropriate.
> (2) The court may give leave, or give a direction, on application by the party or on its own initiative.
> ...
> (3) The court may give leave to make an amendment even if the effect of the amendment would be to include a cause of action arising after the proceeding was started.
> (4) If there is a mistake in the name or identity of a party, the court must give leave for, or direct the making of, amendments necessary to correct the mistake, even if the effect of the amendments is to substitute another person as a party.
> (5) This rule does not apply in relation to an amendment of an order.
> ...

Rule 21 states the purposes of the Rules in Ch 2 and requires that they be applied to those ends. The Rule is in these terms:

> (1) The purpose of this chapter, and the other provisions of these rules in their application to civil proceedings, is to facilitate the just resolution of the real issues in civil proceedings with minimum delay and expense.
> (2) Accordingly, these rules are to be applied by the courts in civil proceedings with the objective of achieving —
> (a) the just resolution of the real issues in the proceedings; and
> (b) the timely disposal of the proceedings, and all other proceedings in the court, at a cost affordable by the respective parties.
> (3) The parties to a civil proceeding must help the court to achieve the objectives.
> (4) The court may impose appropriate sanctions if a party does not comply with these rules or an order of the court.

[Their Honours considered the decision of the primary judge and Court of Appeal and continued (at 204):]

Rule 501(a)

The judgments below dealt with the question of amendment by reference to discretionary considerations, despite their reference to r 501. The general discretion is given by r 502(1). On this appeal ANU relied upon the importance placed by the Court Procedures Rules on the need for the courts to decide the 'real issues in the proceedings', and more particularly upon the terms of r 501(a), which obliges amendments that are necessary for deciding the real issues in the proceeding. ANU did not dispute that the substance of its contention was that the 'real issues in the proceeding' extended to any issues which a party sought in good faith to advance and which were arguable. For the reasons which follow, that contention cannot be accepted.

Rules 501 and 502 are more recent adaptations of Rules of the Supreme Court 1883 (Eng), which dealt with amendment of pleadings after the passage of the Judicature Acts. Those earlier Rules provided the pattern for rules adopted by many courts in this country. They included power to correct errors, occasioned by way of 'slip' or omission and mistakes in the identities of parties.

The Rule which gave power to amend defects or errors in any proceedings contained the statement, in imperative terms: 'and all necessary amendments shall be made for the purpose of determining the real question or issue raised by or depending on the proceedings.' The Rule containing the general discretionary power to amend pleadings or indorsements contained a similar command, except that the purpose of the amendments considered to be necessary was the determination of 'the real questions in controversy between the parties'. There is no relevant distinction between questions or issues raised and controversies.

The purpose of these earlier Rules, to permit a determination of the real issue or controversy in the proceedings, which informed those r 501(a). The question which arises from the terms of r 501(a) is whether it is necessary to make an amendment for the purpose of deciding the real issues in the proceeding. Some general observations concerning rr 501(a), 502(1) and 21 are necessary at this point.

The words 'the real issues in the proceeding' in r 501(a) obviously refer to issues raised, perhaps unclearly, in the pleadings at the time of the application for leave to amend. The 'real' issues may also extend beyond the pleadings, as cases concerned with the purpose stated in the original Rules show. But, as is explained in these reasons, to be regarded as a real issue, and for amendment therefore to be necessary, the relevant dispute or controversy must exist at the time of the application. Amendments raising entirely new issues fall to be considered under the general discretion given by r 502(1), read with the objectives of r 21.

The purposes of r 21, to minimise the delay and expense of proceedings, are plainly intended to guide the exercise of discretion in r 502. There may be questions as to the extent to which the objectives there stated apply where a matter is identified as a 'real issue' in the proceedings and one therefore within the terms of r 501(a). The Rule would appear to oblige amendment without more. The amendments necessary for the purpose of r 501 may be less likely to be productive of delay and cost and therefore not cut across the objectives to a substantial degree. And it may be that the 'real' issues in civil proceedings, referred to in r 21 and read with that Rule's objectives, are intended to refer to issues which are not peripheral. In referring to the 'just resolution of the real issues' in the proceedings, r 21 may be intending to refer to those issues which are determinative of the matter in dispute. It is not necessary to further consider these questions. Even if r 21 and the objectives there stated have no real significance for the application of r 501(a), r 501(a) did not apply to the amendments proposed by ANU.

[Their Honours then considered statements made in a number of seminal English cases with respect to the amendment of pleadings and continued (at 208):]

The need for amendment will often arise because of some error or mistake having been made in the drafting of the existing pleading or in a judgment about what is to be pleaded in it. But it is not the existence of such a mistake that founds the grant of leave under rules such as r 501(a), although it may be relevant to show that the application is bona fide. What needs to be shown for leave to amend to be given, as the cases referred to above illustrate, is that the controversy or issue was in existence prior to the application for amendment being made. It is only then that it is necessary for the court to allow it properly to be raised to enable a determination upon it.

The existence of a controversy may be seen in the way in which the matter had already been pleaded, albeit inferentially, in *Tildesley v Harper* and *Dwyer v O'Mullen*; or where the issue is raised by another party in the same proceedings but in respect of which the party applying was inextricably involved, as in *Cropper v Smith*. It may be present in the nature of the bargain struck, as in *O'Keefe v Williams*. A consideration of these cases does not suggest that an unduly narrow approach should be taken to what are the real issues in controversy, although they are not, or are not sufficiently, expressed in the pleading.

These observations do not avail ANU. True it was that the insurers had pleaded that the values declared for the purposes of insurance had been substantially understated, but this had no relevance to Aon, having regard to the extent of the contractual obligations ANU had identified as in issue. The insurers' defences should have alerted ANU to the need to reconsider its claim against Aon, if its contractual relationship was other than it had alleged. Prior to the application to amend there was no issue about Aon's involvement with respect to the declared values. Indeed there was no issue concerning any aspect of the insurance effected with respect to the Sch C property. There was no dispute about deductibles and none about Aon having made misrepresentations or engaging in misleading conduct. The dispute was only as to whether Aon had been obliged to effect cover over the PNI Schedule property but had not done so.

Rule 501(a) did not require the allowance of the amendment sought by ANU.

A multiplicity of proceedings: r 501(c)

In the course of argument ANU submitted that the order for amendment could be seen as supported by r 501(c) because it overcame the need for ANU to bring further proceedings. ANU submitted that, at the time the application for leave to amend was heard, the time for the bringing of the claims which were the subject of the amendment had not expired. Nonetheless, in the event that leave to amend was refused, the possibility of ANU bringing further proceedings depended upon a number of matters. It required that ANU be able to abandon its case against Aon in such a way as would not preclude a later claim. Discontinuance of the existing proceeding required leave. The case having been fixed for trial and leave to amend having been refused, Aon might have led evidence to answer the claim originally framed against it and moved for judgment. It cannot be assumed that ANU could have avoided a judgment being entered. That raises the question of whether further proceedings would be met by an application for a stay based upon *Port of Melbourne Authority v Anshun Pty Ltd*. The issue would then be whether an exercise of reasonable diligence on the part of ANU would have led to the bringing of the claim in these, the earlier proceedings.

It is not immediately obvious how ANU could have dealt with an Anshun point in the further proceedings to which it refers. Further consideration of these matters is not required.

It is sufficient for present purposes that ANU did not seek to show this Court how it might have done so. It is therefore not demonstrated that the amendment proposed was necessary to avoid multiple proceedings.

Rule 501(c) did not apply. The application fell to be determined solely by exercise of the power conferred by r 502(1), read in conjunction with the purposes in r 21.

Rules 502(1) and 21(1) — the power to allow amendment and the objectives

A power is given to the court by r 502(1) to permit the amendment of pleadings 'in the way it considers appropriate'. Rule 21(2) specifies, in paras (a) and (b), the objectives to be sought by the exercise of the power conferred by r 502(1). In this setting, some care is called for in describing the grant or refusal of an application to amend in such a way as to suggest a very wide discretion in the decision whether to permit amendment. The observations by Gleeson CJ, Gaudron and Hayne JJ in *Coal and Allied Operations Pty Ltd v Australian Industrial Relations Commission* are apposite:

> "Discretion" is a notion that "signifies a number of different legal concepts". In general terms, it refers to a decision-making process in which "no one [consideration] and no combination of [considerations] is necessarily determinative of the result" (179). Rather, the decision-maker is allowed some latitude as to the choice of the decision to be made.

Their Honours went on to point out that the latitude as to choice may be considerable or it may be narrow. Given the terms of r 21, it could not be said that the latitude as to the choice of decision, as to whether to grant or refuse leave to amend, was at large. The objectives in r 21(2) are to be sought in the exercise of the power given by r 502(1).

The overriding purpose of r 21, to facilitate the just resolution of the real issues in civil proceedings with minimum delay and expense, is stated in the rules of other courts in Australia, although those purposes and the obligations cast upon the court and the parties may be stated in somewhat different terms.

In submissions before Gray J, Aon relied upon a decision of the New South Wales Court of Appeal which distinguished *JL Holdings* on the basis of later provisions of the Civil Procedure Act 2005 (NSW).

His Honour did not consider those provisions to be comparable with the Court Procedures Rules and the Act under which they were made, the Court Procedures Act 2004 (ACT). No issue is taken concerning that aspect of his Honour's decision. The importance of r 21 to an application for leave to amend is to be determined by reference to its own terms.

The purposes stated in r 21 reflect principles of case management by the courts. Such management is now an accepted aspect of the system of civil justice administered by courts in Australia. It was recognised some time ago, by courts here and elsewhere in the common law world, that a different approach was required to tackle the problems of delay and cost in the litigation process. In its report in 2000, *Managing Justice: A review of the federal civil justice system*, the Australian Law Reform Commission noted that: 'Over the last ten years Australian courts have become more active in monitoring and managing the conduct and progress of cases before them, from the time a matter is lodged to finalisation'.

Rule 21(2)(b) indicates that the rules concerning civil litigation no longer are to be considered as directed only to the resolution of the dispute between the parties to a proceeding. The achievement of a just but timely and cost-effective resolution of a dispute has an effect upon the court and upon other litigants. In *Sali v SPC Ltd*, Toohey and Gaudron JJ explained that case management reflected:

> ... [t]he view that the conduct of litigation is not merely a matter for the parties but is also one for the court and the need to avoid disruptions in the court's lists with consequent inconvenience to the court and prejudice to the interests of other litigants waiting to be heard ...

In the past it has more readily been assumed that an order for the costs occasioned by the amendment would overcome injustice to the amending party's opponent. In *Cropper v Smith* Bowen LJ described an order for costs as a panacea that heals all. Such a view may largely explain the decision of this Court in *Shannon v Lee Chun*, which upheld a decision allowing the plaintiff to raise a new case at the second trial, but which imposed a condition as to costs. The modern view is that even an order for indemnity costs may not always undo the prejudice a party suffers by late amendment. In the present case it is difficult to see that such an order could be sufficient compensation, given that Aon would be required to again defend litigation which was, effectively, to be commenced afresh.

The views expressed by Lord Griffiths in *Ketteman v Hansel Properties Ltd*, that justice cannot always be measured in money and that a judge is entitled to weigh in the balance the strain the litigation imposes upon litigants, are also now generally accepted. In *Bomanite Pty Ltd v Slatex Corporation Aust Pty Ltd* (200), French J said of Bowen LJ's statements in *Cropper v Smith*:

> ... That may well have been so at one time, but it is no longer true today ... Non-compensable inconvenience and stress on individuals are significant elements of modern litigation. Costs recoverable even on an indemnity basis will not compensate for time lost and duplication incurred where litigation is delayed or corrective orders necessary.

In *Ketteman* Lord Griffiths recognised, as did the plurality in *JL Holdings*, that personal litigants are likely to feel the strain more than business corporations or commercial persons. So much may be accepted. But it should not be thought that corporations are not subject to pressures imposed by litigation. A corporation in the position of a defendant may be required to carry a contingent liability in its books of account for some years, with consequent effects upon its ability to plan financially, depending upon the magnitude of the claim. Its resources may be diverted to deal with the litigation. And, whilst corporations have no feelings, their employees and officers who may be crucial witnesses, have to bear the strain of impending litigation and the disappointment when it is not brought to an end. The stated object in the *Court Procedures Rules*, of minimising delay, may be taken to recognise the ill-effects of delay upon the parties to proceedings and that such effects will extend to other litigants who are also seeking a resolution in their proceedings. ...

Application of rr 502(1) and 21 to this case

The salient features of the application for leave to amend in this case were, as Lander J pointed out in his dissent, that the amendments sought to introduce new and substantial claims; they were so substantial as to require Aon, in effect, to defend again, as from the beginning; the application was brought during the time set for the trial of the action and would result in the abandonment of the trial if granted; and there was a question whether costs, even indemnity costs, would overcome the prejudicial effects on Aon if the litigation to this point was not productive of an outcome.

The primary judge was in error in failing to recognise the extent of the new claims and the effect that amendment would have upon Aon. His Honour was in error in failing to recognise the extent to which the objectives of r 21 would not be met if the amendments were allowed. The known ill-effects of a delayed determination, which informed the purposes and objectives of the Rule, were present. Rule 502(1) read with r 21 did not provide an unfettered discretion to grant leave to amend. The objectives of r 21 were to be pursued in the exercise of the power conferred by r 502(1). The fact that ANU's new claims were arguable was not itself sufficient to permit amendment and could not prevail over the objectives of r 21. A 'just' resolution of the proceedings between ANU and Aon required those objectives to be taken into account.

Given the requirements of the Rule and the effects associated with delay, it was incumbent upon ANU to tender an explanation as to why the matter had been allowed to proceed to trial in its existing form. It needed to explain why it was seeking leave to amend at the time of the trial, when the two insurers' defences had identified the issue central to the claim it sought to bring against Aon more than twelve months earlier. None was given. His Honour was in error in accepting that ANU had provided a satisfactory explanation. The statements made by counsel foreshadowing leave to amend were not evidence. The ANU's solicitor's later affidavit did not support them. In addition to the defences, the letters written by Chubb in 2003 showed that ANU was told of the importance of the valuation of the property to the insurers long before the receipt of more recent documentation. ANU's solicitor did not suggest that the defences, raising the same matter in connection with the misrepresentations, were misunderstood in their potential relevance to Aon. He did not say that ANU was *first* alerted to Aon's possible involvement as a result of what was said in mediation.

The possibility that ANU was not in a position to explain itself was adverted to in argument on the appeal but that possibility could not be taken very far. ANU's solicitor could have said that ANU only realised the potential for claim as a result of confidential communications, but he made no such claim. In a carefully worded affidavit he merely said (i) that the discussions were agreed to be kept confidential; and (ii) at the conclusion of mediation senior counsel advised of the need to amend. In cross-examination he agreed that the decision to amend was made on the basis of information received during mediation. At no point did he suggest that this was the first time that ANU appreciated that it had a claim against Aon of the kind it sought to raise by amendment.

This evidence was no basis for a finding that there had been an oversight and that ANU's lawyers had not appreciated Aon's possible involvement until the mediation talks. It invited speculation as to whether ANU first realised the potential for a claim against Aon during mediation, assuming there to be a basis for such a claim. One possibility is that ANU only decided to proceed against Aon when it realised the insurers would not settle for a higher sum. If so, that was the basis upon which it had determined to proceed to trial. The absence of explanation suggests the possibility that none which favoured ANU could be offered.

Whatever was the reason for the delay in applying for the amendment, none was provided. There was no mistake of judgment, such as that to which Bowen LJ referred, which might be weighed against the effects of the delay, effects which r 21 required to be taken seriously into account.

The primary judge was mistaken as to the extent of the new claims and what would be required of Aon if they were permitted and the matter effectively re-litigated. His Honour incorrectly elevated the fact that the claim was arguable to a level of importance it did not have. His Honour failed to recognise the importance of the objective stated in r 21, of the timely disposal of the proceedings. The exercise of the power conferred by r 502(1) miscarried. The application should have been refused.

5.2.13   Notes and questions

1. *Aon Risk Services Australia Ltd v Australian National University* is widely seen to have overruled the High Court's earlier decision in *Queensland v JL Holdings*. Is this view accurately borne out from a reading of the joint judgment in *Aon Risk Services Australia Ltd v Australian National University*? If a trial judge were considering similar facts to *Queensland v JL Holdings* today with the benefit of the decision in *Aon Risk Services Australia Ltd v Australian National University*, would the same decision be reached?

2. *Queensland v JL Holdings* was considered by the High Court to be a clear case. The court was able to deliver its judgment after a short period of deliberation, with its reasons published afterwards.

3. Are perceived swings in judicial authority a chimera? Is *Aon Risk Services Australia Ltd v Australian National University* an unusual case? The conduct of the proceedings was such that Aon alleged an abuse of process. Footnote 221 in Heydon J's judgment (at 225) states the following:

    > On 15 November 2006 counsel for Aon contended that ANU had not complied with the court's orders to prepare and file an agreed bundle of documents, a chronology and an opening. He continued: "Now, that leads, critically, to the assessment that this plaintiff was never intending to run this case against us if it couldn't settle with us, and we made it clear at the mediation what our position was. Now, your Honour, it's transparent, in our submission, that the plaintiff is now seeking to avoid starting the case against us, seeking to avoid having to run a case on the basis that it pleaded, and on the basis that it was prepared to go to trial." The primary judge did not deal with this question in his reasons for his decision to allow the amendment.

4. Heydon J identified a certain culture and mentality in the running of the litigation by the Australian National University and the approach taken by the Supreme Court to its resolution. Can you find other examples of this culture and mentality? If so, is it attributable to *Queensland v JL Holdings*? See, eg, Bryson J in *Maronis Holdings Ltd v Nippon Credit Australia Ltd* [2000] NSWSC 753 at [15] as cited by Heydon J in *Aon Risk Services Australia Ltd v Australian National University* at 222; *Black & Decker (Australasia) Pty Ltd v GMCA Pty Ltd* [2007] FCA 1623 at [3]–[4] per Finkelstein J (26 October 2007).

5. Is the High Court's decision in *Aon Risk Services Australia Ltd v Australian National University* a bar to all successful applications for late amendment?

Amendment to add statute-barred claims

5.2.14　What is the position where the plaintiff seeks to add a cause of action which has become statute-barred since the date of commencement of the proceeding? In accordance with the old rule of practice in *Weldon v Neal* (1887) 19 QBD 394, a court would not permit a plaintiff to amend its statement of claim to plead a cause of action which had become statute-barred since the date of commencement of the proceeding. The rule has been abrogated in the Federal Court, New South Wales, the Northern Territory, Queensland and Victoria: Civil Procedure Act 2005 (NSW) s 65; Limitation Act 1981 (NT) s 48A; Civil Proceedings Act 2011(Qld) s 16 (previously Supreme Court of Queensland Act 1991 (Qld) s 81); Federal Court of Australia Act (Cth) s 59(2B). Section 34 of the Limitation of Actions Act 1958 (Vic) is set out below at **5.2.15E**.

5.2.15E	**Limitation of Actions Act 1958 (Vic)**
	Abrogation of rule in *Weldon v Neal* (1887) 19 QBD 394

34 (1) If a court would, but for the expiry of any relevant period of limitation after the day a proceeding in the court has commenced, allow a party to amend a document in the proceeding, the court must allow the amendment to be made if it is satisfied that no other party to the proceeding would by reason of the amendment be prejudiced in the conduct of that party's claim or defence that could not be met by an adjournment, an award of costs or otherwise.

　　(2) This section does not apply to an amendment in a proceeding commenced before 1 January 1987.

[Section 48A of the Limitation Act 1981 (NT) is set out in the same terms.]

5.2.16　Section 59(2B) of the Federal Court of Australia Act 1976 provides that the Rules of Court may make provision for the amendment of (or leave to amend) a document in a proceeding even if the effect of the amendment would be to allow a person to seek a remedy that would have been barred because of the expiry of a limitation period if the remedy had originally been sought at the time of the amendment. Rules 8.21 and 15.15 were made pursuant to s 59(2B) and allow amendment of an originating application or cross-claim even if the application is made after the expiry of any relevant limitation period which applied when the proceeding was started. An amendment to an originating application under r 8.21 or a cross-claim under r 15.15 may be made to:

- correct a mistake in the name of a party to the proceeding;
- correct the identity of a party to the proceeding;
- change the capacity in which the party is suing in the proceeding; or
- add or substitute a new claim for relief, or a new foundation in law for a claim for relief, that arises out of the same facts or substantially the same facts as those already pleaded to support an existing claim for relief by the applicant.

　　Section 16 of the Civil Proceedings Act 2011 (Qld) confers a broad power on the court to order or grant leave to a party to make an amendment even though the amendment will include or substitute a cause of action or add a new party; the cause of action included or substituted arose after the proceeding was started; or a relevant limitation period which was current at the commencement of the proceeding has ended. This section replaces s 81 of the Supreme Court of Queensland Act 1991(Qld), which was set out in the same terms. Rule 376 of the Uniform Civil Procedure Rules 1999 (Qld) allows an amendment notwithstanding the expiry of a limitation period applicable upon commencement of the proceeding in order to:

- correct the name of a party (even if the effect of the amendment is to substitute a new party) (r 376(2)); or

- change the capacity in which a party sues (r 376(3)); or

- add a new cause of action in circumstances where the court considers it appropriate (r 376(4)(a)) and the new cause of action arises out of the same (or substantially the same) facts as a cause of action for which relief has already been claimed by the party applying for leave to amend: r 376(4)(b).

The requirements set out in r 376(4)(b) are narrower than the terms of s 16 of the Civil Proceedings Act 2011. The Queensland Court of Appeal considered the operation of r 376 in the context of s 81 of the Supreme Court of Queensland Act 1991, now reflected in s 16 of the Civil Proceedings Act 2011. The court held that despite this restrictive criterion, the court has a general discretion under s 81 to add a cause of action out of time when the interests of justice demand it: *Draney v Barry* [2002] 1 Qd R 145; [1999] QCA 491 per Pincus JA at [22] to [23], McMurdo P concurring at [2]. Thomas JA (at [56]) agreed with Pincus JA's reasoning that s 81 created a source of power over and above that stated in r 376 but took the view that r 376 sets out the principles upon which the judicial power recognised by s 81 is to be exercised. His Honour observed that he could not envisage any situation where a court would act upon any different principles under s 81 than those set out in r 376.

The amendment rules applicable in Victoria and the Northern Territory are set out in the same terms. Rule 36.01(1) of the Supreme Court (General Civil Procedure) Rules (Vic) and r 36.01(1) of the Supreme Court Rules (NT) allow the court to order that a document in the proceeding be amended or that a party have leave to amend a document in the proceeding. Rule 36.01(1) (NT) is extracted at **5.2.3E** above. An order may be made in both jurisdictions notwithstanding the expiry of any relevant limitation period after the day a proceeding is commenced where the court is satisfied that any other party to the proceeding would not by reason of the order be prejudiced in the conduct of that party's claim or defence in a way that could not fairly be met by an adjournment, an award of costs or otherwise: NT r 36.01(6); Vic r 36.01(6).

In New South Wales, ss 64 and 65 of the Civil Procedure Act 2005 operate to abrogate the rule in *Weldon v Neal*. Sections 64 and 65 are extracted at **5.2.17E** below. These sections replaced Pt 20 rr 1 and 4 of the Supreme Court Rules 1970 which were expressed to the same effect. In *McGee v Yeomans* [1977] 1 NSWLR 273 (per Moffit P, Glass and Mahoney JJA) and *Proctor v Jetway Aviation Pty Ltd* [1984] 1 NSWLR 166 (per Moffit P and Glass JA), the Court of Appeal accepted that Pt 20 r 4 had the effect of a statute enacted subsequent to the applicable statute of limitations, thus conferring a power to amend notwithstanding the terms of the statute. With reference to the Court of Appeal's decisions, Brereton J observed in *Street v Luna Park Sydney Pty Ltd* [2006] NSWSC 230 at [50] that:

> … [t]hat is no less the case now that the authority for amendments is contained, not in Rules of Court, but in the Civil Procedure Act ss 64 and 65. In other words, because the statutory authority to permit amendments notwithstanding the Limitation Act is sourced in an Act later in time than the Limitation Act, it prevails.

5.2.17E   **Civil Procedure Act 2005 (NSW)**

64 (1) At any stage of proceedings, the court may order:

    (a)   that any document in the proceedings be amended, or

    (b)   that leave be granted to a party to amend any document in the proceedings.

  (2)   Subject to section 58, all necessary amendments are to be made for the purpose of determining the real questions raised by or otherwise depending on the proceedings, correcting any defect or error in the proceedings and avoiding multiplicity of proceedings.

  (3)   An order under this section may be made even if the amendment would have the effect of adding or substituting a cause of action that has arisen after the commencement of the proceedings but, in that case, the date of commencement of the proceedings, in relation to that cause of action, is, subject to section 65 taken to be the date on which the amendment is made.

65 (1) This section applies to any proceedings commenced before the expiration of any relevant limitation period for the commencement of the proceedings.

  (2)   At any time after the expiration of the relevant limitation period, the plaintiff in any such proceedings may, with the leave of the court under section 64(1)(b), amend the originating process so as:

    (a)   to enable the plaintiff to maintain the proceedings in a capacity in which he or she has, since the proceedings were commenced, become entitled to bring and maintain the proceedings, or

    (b)   to correct a mistake in the name of a party to the proceedings, whether or not the effect of the amendment is to substitute a new party, being a mistake that, in the court's opinion, is neither misleading nor such as to cause reasonable doubt as to the identity of the person intended to be made a party, or

    (c)   to add or substitute a new cause of action, together with a claim for relief on the new cause of action, being a new cause of action that, in the court's opinion, arises from the same (or substantially the same) facts as those giving rise to an existing cause of action and claim for relief set out in the originating process.

5.2.18   The rule in *Weldon v Neal* is not abolished by statute in the Australian Capital Territory, South Australia, Tasmania and Western Australia. Nevertheless, these jurisdictions have rules which effectively limit its application: ACT r 503; SA r 54(7); Tas r 427(2A); WA O 21 r 5. Rule 427(2A) of the Supreme Court Rules (Tasmania) allows the court to grant leave to a party to amend if it is satisfied that any other party to the proceedings would not be prejudiced by the amendment in the conduct of their claim or defence in a way that could not be fairly met by an adjournment, an award of costs or otherwise. The remaining rules provide that the court can allow an amendment which adds or substitutes a statute-barred cause of action if it arises out of substantially the same facts as the original cause of action.

In *Dye v Griffin Coal Mining Co Pty Ltd* (1998) 19 WAR 431, the Full Court of the Supreme Court of Western Australia rejected the argument that O 21 r 5 permits amendment in circumstances where the conditions set out in the rule are not met. Owen J (with Malcolm CJ and Kennedy J concurring) considered (at 439) that 'the rule in *Weldon v Neal* continues in force in truncated form, being qualified only to the extent that O 21 r 5 allows some amendments out of time for certain limited purposes' by giving the court a discretion to add a cause of action that is otherwise statute-barred in circumstances where the conditions set out in the rule are met.

5.2.19 The rules examined at 5.2.14–5.2.18 above operate subject to the principle of relation back. An amended pleading generally takes effect from (i.e. relates back to) the date of the original pleading: *Sneade v Wotherton Barytes & Lead Mining Company Ltd* [1904] 1 KB 295 at 297–8; *Air Link Pty Ltd v Paterson (No 2)* (2003) 58 NSWLR 388. If an amendment substitutes or adds a cause of action, that new cause of action operates as if it had been included in the original document. If an amendment adds a new cause of action which has become statute-barred since the date of commencement of proceedings, the date on which the amendment takes effect is significant. If the amendment were to take effect from the date on which it is made, the new cause of action would be statute-barred. The relation back of the amendment to the date of the original document will defeat the limitations defence.

In the Supreme Court of Tasmania, Crawford J considered that in the absence of any special order, an amendment to a pleading will date back to the time when the pleading was originally delivered: *Webster Ltd v Roberts* [1989] Tas R 37. His Honour later observed in *Tassal Ltd v Russfal Pty Ltd* [2006] TASSC 33; BC200603276 at [11] that it was generally accepted as a rule that unless it is otherwise ordered, an amendment to a pleading takes effect from the date of the original pleading.

In *Agtrack (NT) Pty Ltd (t/as Spring Air) v Hatfield* (2003) 174 FLR 395, Ormiston J (at 416–17) considered that the relation back of amendments is a matter of practice 'hardly to be called a principle or rule, for it is merely the commonsense characterisation of what is in fact sought and done' and is (at 434) 'the accepted construction of the effect of rules of superior courts' (see also *Proctor v Jetway Aviation Pty Ltd* [1984] 1 NSWLR 166 at 182 per Priestley JA). Ormiston J observed (at 419) that the courts may nevertheless specify within the terms of an order the date upon which the amendment takes effect.

Section 64 of the Civil Procedure Act 2005 (NSW) (extracted at 5.2.17E) above provides that amendments to add or substitute a new cause of action take effect as from the date of amendment but s 65 provides that an amendment to add or substitute a cause of action which would otherwise be statute-barred takes effect from the date of commencement of proceedings.

Rule 387 of the Uniform Civil Procedure Rules 1999 (Qld) and r 514 of the Court Procedures Rules 2006 (ACT) provide that an amendment takes effect on and from the date of the amendment but an amendment including or substituting a cause of action arising after the commencement of the proceeding takes effect on and from the date of the order giving leave unless the court orders otherwise. Nevertheless, where a limitation period is being considered, such amendment is taken to have commenced when the original proceeding commenced unless the court otherwise orders.

In *Wilkinson v Rockdril Contractors Pty Ltd* [1997] 1 Qd R 560, Pincus and Davies JJA in the Queensland Court of Appeal rejected the argument (at 565) that *any* amendment to a statement of claim, whether made with or without the court's leave, relates back to the original statement of claim. While an amendment made with the court's leave takes effect from the date of the original statement of claim, an amendment made without leave does not take effect from the date of the writ or the original statement of claim so as to defeat the limitations defence (at 566). The same approach has been adopted in the Federal Court Rules 2011 and is outlined below.

The Federal Court Rules 2011 qualify the practice of relation back in specified circumstances. An amendment to a pleading which pursuant to r 16.51 does not require the court's leave takes effect on the date the amendment is made. Rule 8.22 provides that an amendment to an originating application which has the effect of substituting another person as a party will take effect for that person on the day that the originating application is amended. An amendment to a notice of cross-claim with the same effect is to be taken to have started for a person substituted as a party on the date on which the notice of cross-claim is amended: r 15.16.

Amendment of parties

5.2.20   Where a party to a proceeding has been misjoined, the rules allow for their removal as a party to the proceeding: FCR r 9.08; ACT r 230; NSW r 6.29; NT r 9.06; Qld r 69(1)(a); SA r 74; Tas r 184; Vic r 9.06; WA O 18 r 6. Where the correct party has not been joined in the proceeding, they may be added as a party to the proceeding: FCR r 9.05; ACT rr 220–221; NSW r 6.24; NT r 9.06; Qld r 69(1)(b); SA r 74; Tas r 184; Vic r 9.06; WA O 18 r 6.

5.2.21   In each jurisdiction where application is made to add a defendant as a party to the proceeding, the addition of such party operates prospectively. For example, in Victoria r 9.11(3) provides that where an order is made for the addition or substitution of a person as a defendant, the proceeding against the new defendant commences upon the amendment of the filed originating process in the court. See also *Philip Morris Ltd v Bridge Shipping Ltd* [1994] 2 VR 1. The rules in other jurisdictions reflect the prospective nature of addition or substitution of defendants: FCR r 9.05; ACT r 242; NSW r 19.2.4; NT r 9.11(3); SA r 74(1); Tas r 184(6); WA O 18 r 8(4) (the High Court rule is not explicit: see r 3.01(3)). If the time prescribed by any relevant statute of limitations has expired, the court should refuse an application to add a defendant. The question is referred to in the judgment of Dawson J in *Bridge Shipping Pty Ltd v Grand Shipping SA* (1991) 173 CLR 231 at 236:

> At one time it was thought that the substitution or addition of a defendant by amendment related back to the commencement of the proceedings so that, if the proceedings were commenced before the expiry of the limitation period, the amendment would defeat the limitation period even though the amendment was made after the expiry of that period. Upon that view, the reason for not allowing the amendment was that it would deprive the defendant substituted or added of the benefit of the limitation period: see *Mabro v Eagle, Star and British Dominions Insurance Co Ltd* [1932] 1 KB 485, cf *Davies v Elsby Brothers Ltd* [1961] 1 WLR 170; [1960] 3 All ER 672. The accepted view now is: particularly having regard to the present form of the relevant rule (r 9.11(3)): that the substitution or addition of a defendant by amendment does not relate back to the commencement of proceedings but takes effect from the time of the amendment. That means that the amendment cannot prejudice any existing rights under a statute of limitations (or any other limitation period). Accordingly, leave to amend to substitute or add a defendant who has a good defence under a period of limitation will generally be refused as serving no useful purpose: *Liff v Peasley* [1980] 1 WLR 781; [1980] 1 All ER 623; *Ketteman v Hansel Properties Ltd* [1987] AC 189.

In *Agtrack (NT) Pty Ltd (t/as Spring Air) v Hatfield* (2003) 174 FLR 395, Ormiston J observed (at 419) that an amendment adding a party does not relate back to the commencement of a proceeding 'for the very good reason that there has been in existence no document, writ or statement of claim between the plaintiff and the added defendant, unless and until the order adding the defendant is made'.

In Queensland, the abrogation of the rule in *Weldon v Neal* had led to amendments to the Uniform Civil Procedure Rules 1999 which allow the relation back of orders adding or substituting a party. Section 16 of the Civil Proceedings Act 2011(Qld) (see **5.2.16**) confers a broad power of amendment which extends to the addition of a new party after the expiry of a relevant limitation period. Rule 69(2) of the Uniform Civil Procedure Rules 1999 provides that the court must not include or substitute a party after the end of a limitation period unless specified conditions are met. Rule 74(4) provides that if an order is made including or substituting a person as a defendant or respondent, the proceeding against the new defendant or respondent starts on the filing of the amended copy of the originating process. An exception is made under r 74(5) for limitation purposes; with the addition or substitution operating retrospectively to the date upon which the proceeding was commenced against the original defendant, unless the court otherwise orders.

5.2.22 Where it can be said that a mistake has been made in the name of a party, the amendment rules in most jurisdictions can be used to correct that mistake. Where the amendment rules apply, the amendment will operate retrospectively by relating back to the date of the commencement of the proceeding, so as to overcome any difficulties created by any limitation provision: see **5.2.19**. The Victorian rule is extracted in part below:

5.2.23E   **Supreme Court (General Civil Proceedure) Rules 2005 (Vic)**
                            Order 36 — Amendment

36.01 ... (1) For the purpose of —

   (a)   determining the real question in controversy between the parties to any proceeding; or
   (b)   correcting any defect or error in any proceeding; or
   (c)   avoiding multiplicity of proceedings —

the Court may, at any stage [stage,] order that any document in the proceeding be amended or that any party have leave to amend any document in the proceeding.

   ...

(4) A mistake in the name of a party may be corrected under paragraph (1), whether or not the effect is to substitute another person as a party.

5.2.24 There are equivalent provisions in most other jurisdictions: FCR rr 8.21 and 15.15; ACT r 503(2); Civil Procedure Act 2005 (NSW) s 64(4); NT r 36.01; Qld r 376; SA r 54(7)(b); Tas r 184; WA O 21 r 5. The Victorian and Northern Territory provisions are broader, adding that where 'an order to correct a mistake in the name of a party has the effect of substituting another person as a party, the proceeding shall be taken to have commenced with respect to that person on the day the proceeding commenced': r 36.01(5).

What is a mistake in the name of a party?

5.2.25C	**Bridge Shipping Pty Ltd v Grand Shipping SA**
	(1991) 173 CLR 231
	High Court of Australia

[Bridge Shipping was engaged by Philip Morris Ltd to arrange for the shipment of 32 containers of tobacco from Rio Grande in Brazil to Melbourne. The bills of lading issued by the master of the ship the 'Green Sand' made no reference to the identity of the carrier. A number of containers were found to be missing and the contents of others were damaged. Philip Morris sued Bridge Shipping. Bridge Shipping's solicitors searched the Lloyd's Register and found that Grand Shipping was the owner of the 'Green Sand'. It issued third party proceedings against Grand Shipping assuming that the owner was also the carrier.

The carrier was, in fact, Rainbow Line SA. The 'Green Sand' had been chartered by Grand Shipping to Rainbow Line. Bridge Shipping sought to substitute Rainbow Line as third party in place of Grand Shipping. Any claim against Rainbow Line had become time-barred. The principal judgment (in which **Brennan** and **Deane JJ** concurred) was delivered by **McHugh J**.]

McHugh J (at 252): The question in this appeal is whether O 36.01 of the Supreme Court Rules (Vic) authorises the substitution of another person for the person named as defendant in the action after the expiration of the relevant limitation period for bringing an action against the first person ...

[His Honour then referred to the facts and to O 36 of the Supreme Court Rules and continued (at 253):]

The competing interpretations of O 36.01

Bridge contends that the case is within O 36.01(4) because the mistake which it made was a mistake as to which person or corporation fell within the description of the carrier of the tobacco. Bridge says that the mistake which it made was not a mistake as to the category of persons who were subject to the legal liability. If, for example, Bridge had mistakenly sued the wharfinger, thinking it was liable, and now wished to sue the carrier, it concedes that there would not be a mistake 'in the name of a party'. But Bridge contends that, since it has made a mistake as to the name of the carrier, it has made a 'mistake in the name of a party' within the meaning of O 36.01(4). In the Full Court, Crockett J, with whose judgment Kaye and Southwell JJ agreed, held that the class of mistake with which the sub-rule deals is more limited. His Honour said:

> [254] I should have thought that the better view is that the rule as to correction of a mistake in the name of a party was intended to (and, in fact, must) be confined to mere cases of misnomer, misdescription, typographical or clerical error and the like. That is to say, cases in which there was no merit in the joined defendant's being able to claim immunity from action nor hardship to him by his inability to rely on a time bar. Accordingly, despite O 36 in general being remedial in its operation, sub-r (5) (sic) (sub-r (4)) should, I consider, be strictly construed.

His Honour went on to say:

> It (Bridge) never intended to sue Rainbow. That was because it made an error as to who was the carrier. That mistake was not one as to the name of the person it intended to sue. It was a mistake as to the identity of the person sued. That is not a mistake of the kind that should allow Rainbow to be deprived of its time-bar defence. Nor should the rule be construed so as to permit such a deprivation.

If the reasoning of the Full Court in the present case is correct, the enactment of O 36.01 has made little, if any, difference to the pre-1986 position.

History of Order 36.01

Order 36 was introduced into the Supreme Court Rules in 1986. Before that time, the practice in Victoria was that, where a person was entitled to rely on a defence of the statute of limitations, an amendment to substitute him or her as a party would be permitted only in cases of misnomer, misdescription or clerical error: *Attorney-General (Enq) v Sorati* [1969] VR 88, at pp 94–95; *Hubbard Assoc v The Attorney-General for Victoria* [1976] VR 119, at pp 126–128. The decisions in *Sorati* and *Hubbard Assoc* were based on the practice concerning amendment which applied in England for much of this century. In *Davies v Elsby Brothers Ltd* [1961] 1 WLR 170; [1960] 3 All ER 672 the Court of Appeal held that a plaintiff could not be permitted to amend 'if that would deprive the defendant of the benefit to which he had become entitled as of right under the Statute of Limitations' and 'the amendment involves the addition of a party and not the mere correction of a misnomer' at (173; 674). Devlin LJ said (at 176; 676):

> I think that the test must be: how would a reasonable person receiving the document take it? If, in all the circumstances of the case and looking at the document as a whole, he would say to himself: "Of course it must mean me, but they have got my [255] name wrong," then there is a case of mere misnomer. If, on the other hand, he would say: "I cannot tell from the document itself whether they mean me or not and I shall have to make inquiries," then it seems to me that one is getting beyond the realm of misnomer.

In *Davies*, the plaintiff had issued a writ against 'Elsby Brothers — a firm' for damages for negligence in respect of injuries sustained during the course of his employment. The date of injury was not specified in the writ. Originally, the plaintiff had been employed by the firm of Elsby Brothers, but in 1955 that firm's business was taken over by Elsby Brothers Ltd. The plaintiff's injury occurred in 1956. The Court of Appeal dismissed an appeal against a decision of Elwes J who had held that the writ could not be amended by striking out the words 'a firm' and adding the word 'Limited' to 'Elsby Brothers' because the plaintiff's claim against the company was barred by a statute of limitations.

The principle in *Davies* was applied in *Whittam v W J Daniel and Co Ltd* [1962] 1 QB 271 where, however, the decision went the other way. There the plaintiff had issued a writ against 'W J Daniels and Co (a firm)'. Later the Master allowed the amendment of the writ by substituting as defendant 'W J Daniel and Co Ltd'. The Court of Appeal upheld the Master's order. Danckwerts LJ said that the case was distinguishable from *Davies* 'because in the present case there is no other entity to which the description in the writ could be taken to refer' ibid, at 282.

In *J Robertson and Co Ltd (in liq) v Ferguson Transformers Pty Ltd* (1970) 44 ALJR 441 in this Court, Walsh J applied the test stated by Devlin LJ in *Davies* but allowed a plaintiff to amend its writ from 'Philips Electrical Pty Ltd' to 'Philips Industries Pty Ltd.' His Honour said ibid, at 443:

> It has been held, in my opinion correctly, that a misdescription of a corporate body is capable of being regarded as a mere misnomer and of being corrected by amendment in the same way as the misnomer of a natural person ... It must be acknowledged however, that when, as in the present case, there were two companies in existence to which the writ could refer, it is more difficult to regard the name of one of them, set out in the writ, as being a misnomer, than it would be if there were no other entity in existence than the one to which the writ was intended to refer. The importance of this has been recognized in the cases but in my opinion it has not been laid down that it is decisive.

[256] However, this Court had no rule equivalent to O 36.01.

Nevertheless, the principle in *Davies* was capable of working injustice as the decision in that case demonstrated. Consequently, the power to make amendments was changed in England by the promulgation of O 20 r 5 of the Supreme Court Rules which empowers the Court to allow a plaintiff to amend the writ or a party to amend his or her pleading on such terms as may be just. Sub-rule (2) enables an application for leave to make an amendment to be made 'after any relevant period of limitation current at the date of issue of the writ has expired' if the court thinks it is just to do so. Sub-rule (3) provides:

> An amendment to correct the name of a party may be allowed under paragraph (2) notwithstanding that it is alleged that the effect of the amendment will be to substitute a new party if the Court is satisfied that the mistake sought to be corrected was a genuine mistake and was not misleading or such as to cause any reasonable doubt as to the identity of the person intending to sue or, as the case may be, intended to be sued.

In *Mitchell v Harris Engineering Company Ltd* [1967] 2 QB 703, at 718 Lord Denning MR said:

> Sub-rule (3) has removed the injustice caused by the decision in *Davies v Elsby Brothers*.

In *Evans Constructions Co Ltd v Charrington and Co Ltd* [1983] QB 810 the Court of Appeal, by majority, gave O 20 r 5 a wide meaning. In August 1970, Evans Constructions Co Ltd ('Evans') had taken a lease of various buildings from Charrington and Co Ltd ('Charringtons') for use in connection with its business. Charringtons assigned the reversion to Bass Ltd ('Bass'), another company in the same commercial group, but continued to act as managing agent for Bass. In 1981, Charringtons, as agent for Bass, wrote to Evans enclosing a notice terminating the tenancy in April 1982. Under the Landlord and Tenant Act 1954 (UK), Evans was entitled to apply to the County Court for a new tenancy. The application had to be made not less than two months nor more than four months after the serving of the landlord's notice. The application which Evans made to the County Court contained the error that Charringtons was the other party to the lease and the respondent to the application. Subsequently, Evans sought to join Bass as an additional respondent. The County Court allowed the application under the provisions contained in O 20 r 5. The Court [257] of Appeal dismissed the appeal but decided that Bass should be substituted for Charringtons.

On appeal, Donaldson LJ accepted that it was the intention of the solicitor for Evans to sue the relevant landlord. Accordingly, his Lordship found that there was a genuine mistake of a character to which O 20 r 5(3) could apply. Donaldson LJ said ibid, at p 821:

> In applying O 20 r 5(3) it is, in my judgment, important to bear in mind that there is a real distinction between suing A in the mistaken belief that A is the party who is responsible for the matters complained of and seeking to sue B, but mistakenly describing or naming him as A, and thereby ending up suing A instead of B. The rule is designed to correct the latter and not the former category of mistake. Which category is involved in any particular case depends upon the intentions of the person making the mistake and they have to be determined on the evidence in the light of all the surrounding circumstances.

Waller LJ who dissented said ibid, at 816:

> In the present case there was no mistake as to name. Mr Greenwood, Evans' solicitor, in his affidavit frankly stated he thought Charringtons was the landlord. The mistake here was not a mistake as to name; it was a mistake as to identity.

In *Central Insurance Co Ltd v Seacalf Shipping Corporation (The 'Aiolos')* [1983] 2 Lloyd's Rep 25 the Court of Appeal refused to extend *Evans v Charrington* to a case where the applicants were mistaken as to the nature of the rights which they had as plaintiffs. The Court upheld the refusal of an application to add the names of the buyers of goods to the names of the plaintiffs who were the insurers of the buyers. The insurers had sued the defendants in reliance on their rights of subrogation under their contracts of insurance with the buyers. Oliver LJ said ibid, at 30–31:

> The analogy which Mr Gruder seeks to draw with the *Charrington* case is not, in my judgment, a permissible one. No doubt if the fact were that the actual insurer was not the plaintiff, but, say, a subsidiary company there could or might be a true analogy with that case. But the instant case was not a case, as was the *Charrington* case, of a mistaken belief that the person made party to the proceedings fulfilled a particular description, videlicet that of landlord or insurer, but a case of an erroneous belief that the plaintiff, because he was in fact what he was thought to be, that is, the insurer, had as a result of that certain legal rights which he did not in fact have. There was therefore no error either as to the name or as to the identity of the party which fell to be corrected, but simply an error of law as to the rights possessed by the correctly identified party. Order 20, r 5(3) simply does not extend to this sort of error and the application under this rule must, therefore, fail.

Evans v Charrington was followed by Clarke J in *Lloyd Steel (Aust) Pty Ltd v Jade Shipping SA* [(1985) 1 NSWLR 212]. His Honour had to consider an application under Pt 20 r 4 of the Supreme Court Rules (NSW) in circumstances which were not materially different from the circumstances of the present case. Part 20 r 4 relevantly provided:

> (1) Where any relevant period of limitation expires after the date of filing of a statement of claim and after that expiry an application is made under rule 1 for leave to amend the statement of claim by making the amendment mentioned in any of subrules (2), (3), (4) and (5), the Court may in the circumstances mentioned in that subrule make an order giving leave accordingly, notwithstanding that that period has expired.

> ... Where there has been a mistake in the name of a party and the Court is satisfied that the mistake was not misleading nor such as to cause reasonable doubt as to the identity of the person intended to be made a party, the Court may make an order for leave to make an amendment to correct the mistake, whether or not the effect of the amendment is to substitute a new party.

Clarke J said that he found the statement of Donaldson LJ in *Evans v Charrington* 'utterly persuasive' ibid, at 218.

Despite the similarity between O 36.01 and O 20 of the English Rules and Pt 20 of the New South Wales Rules, however, the Full Court of the Supreme Court of Victoria in the present case refused to follow *Evans v Charrington* and *Lloyd Steel* and the reasoning which is the basis of those decisions. In *Teys Bros Pty Ltd v ANL Cargo Operations Pty Ltd* [1990] 2 Qd R 288, Cooper J also distinguished *Evans v Charrington* and *Lloyd Steel* and gave O 32 of the Rules of the Supreme Court of Queensland a narrow construction despite its similarity to O 20. Cooper J said ibid, at 292:

> The test as to misnomer to be applied in this Court is that formulated by Devlin LJ in *Davies v Elsby Brothers Limited* [1961] 1 WLR 170, 176.

Later his Honour said ibid, at 294:

> The test as to misnomer adopted by the majority of the Court [259] of Appeal in *Evans Limited v Charrington and Co Limited* is not consistent with the test to be applied in Queensland as laid down in the decisions of the Full Court to which I have earlier referred. Importantly, Donaldson LJ (as he then was) construed O 20 r 5(3) as "reflecting and overruling the objection which prevailed in *Beardmore Motors Limited v Birch Bros (Properties) Limited* [1959] Ch 298 and in *Davies v Elsby Bros Ltd* [1961] 1 WLR 170". Such a view cannot stand with the decisions of this Court subsequent to 1965, when O 32 r 1(3) was introduced into the Rules, continuing to apply *Davies v Elsby Brothers Limited* as the authoritative statement of the test relevant to the application of the Rules. The dissenting judgment of Waller LJ is, in my view, closer to the position which is applied in this State.

His Honour's reference to the decisions of the Full Court was a reference to *Harstoff v Allen* (1967) Qd R 211, *Lynch v Keddell* [1985] 2 Qd R 103 and *Lynch v Keddell (No 2)* [1990] 1 Qd R 10. In *Harstoff*, both parties to the appeal accepted that, in a case where a limitation period had expired, the test to be applied in determining whether an amendment should be applied was that formulated by Devlin LJ in *Davies*. In *Lynch v Keddell*, the Full Court held that, when an application to join a defendant was made after the expiration of a limitation period, the discretion to order the joinder was to be exercised only in peculiar or special circumstances. However, *Lynch v Keddell* was not a case where the plaintiff claimed that she had made 'a mistake in the name of a party'.

The construction of r 36.01

Having regard to the history of O 20 r 5(3) of the English Rules, it is obvious, as the English Court of Appeal pointed out in *Mitchell v Harris Engineering*, that the sub-rule was intended to overcome the decision in cases such as *Davies*. There is no reason why its Australian counterparts should be given a more restricted meaning. Consequently, in so far as cases in Queensland and the judgment of the Full Court of the Supreme Court of Victoria in the present

[Toohey ⌐ delivered a judgment in which he broadly agreed with the approach taken by McHugh J. Dawson J delivered a judgment which tends to require an objective determination of the question, who was it that the party intended to sue? There appears to be no radical difference in approach by Dawson J to the question whether a mistake in name has been made.]

5.2.26   Note and question

1. Can the decision in *Davies v Elsby Brothers Ltd* [1961] 1 WLR 170; [1960] 3 All ER 672 be sustained on any, and if so what, basis?

2. The decision in *Bridge Shipping Pty Ltd v Grand Shipping SA* (1991) 173 CLR 231 has been applied in the Northern Territory in *Smart v Stuart* (1992) 83 NTR 1. Compare *Payabi v Armstel Shipping Corp* [1992] 2 WLR 898. See also *Stiles v Permanent Trustee Australia Ltd* [2005] VSC 86, Mandie J.

Slip rule

5.2.27   In each jurisdiction there is provision for the court to correct a mistake or error in a judgment or order. Rule 3.01.2 of the High Court Rules 2004 provides that '[t]he Court or a Justice may, at any time, correct a clerical mistake in a judgment or order, or an error arising in a judgment or order from any accidental slip or omission'.

There are similar rules in other jurisdictions: FCR r 39.05; ACT r 1452(8); NSW r 36.17; NT r 36.07; Qld r 388; SA r 242; Tas r 435; Vic r 36.07; WA O 21 r 10. The court also has an inherent jurisdiction to amend or vary an order for error. The slip rule and the court's inherent jurisdiction were discussed by Gillard J of the Victorian Supreme Court in *Abacus Australia Ltd v Bradstock GIS Pty Ltd* [2001] VSC 19, where the plaintiff had obtained a judgment in default of defence: see **10.2.1–10.2.17C**. There was an error in the judgment as authenticated by the court, in that the judgment, while providing for assessment of damages, did not give judgment for damages. See **5.2.28C** below. His Honour referred to the slip rule and said:

5.2.28C   **Abacus Australia Ltd v Bradstock GIS Pty Ltd**
[2001] VSC 19
Supreme Court of Victoria

Gillard J [His Honour referred to the slip rule and said]:

[33] In addition to the powers in the Rules, the court has an inherent jurisdiction to amend or vary a judgment or order which has been authenticated where there is some error and the court takes steps to ensure that the authenticated order states correctly what the court decided and intended. See *Lawrie v Lees* (1881) 7 App Cas 19 at 34–5. The inherent power also enables the court to clear up any ambiguity or uncertainty and also to correct any mistake or error made by an officer of the court in drawing up the judgment. See *Oxley v Link* (1914) 2 KB 734 at 738 and 746.

[34] But the general rule is that once a judgment or order has been authenticated in a form which correctly expresses the intention with which it was made by the court, the court has no jurisdiction to review, vary or set it aside and the only avenue open to any party to attack the judgment is to appeal.

[35] In *Bailey v Marinoff* (1971) 125 CLR at p 530 Barwick CJ said —

Once an order disposing of a proceeding has been perfected by being drawn up as the requisite record of a court, that proceeding apart from any specific and relevant statutory provision is at an end in that court and is in its substance, in my opinion, beyond recall by that court.

[36] In the same case at p 539 Gibbs J said —

It is a well settled rule that once an order of a court has been passed and entered or otherwise perfected in a form which correctly expresses the intention with which it was made the court has no jurisdiction to alter it. ... The rule rests on the obvious principle that it is desirable that there be an end to litigation on the view that it would be mischievous if there were jurisdiction to re-hear a matter decided after full hearing. *However, the rule is not inflexible and there are a number of exceptions to it in addition to those that depend on statutory provisions such as the slip rule found in most rules of court.* Indeed, as the way in which I have already stated the rule implies, the court has the power to vary an order so as to carry out its own meaning or to make plain language which is doubtful, and that power does not depend on rules of court but is inherent in the court. (Emphasis added.)

[37] This present application is unusual in that it is the plaintiff who obtained the judgment who seeks to have it varied to give effect to what it sought in the summons seeking judgment in default of defence. In my opinion the rules referred to and the inherent power of the court permit a plaintiff to make application to vary the judgment in its favour.

The slip rule

[38] There is no evidence as to what occurred before Beach J on the application which led to the judgment being pronounced. Further, the judgment as authenticated followed precisely the court record prepared by the Associate.

[39] In my opinion there is no evidence that there was a clerical mistake made in the judgment. Further, I am not persuaded that there was an error in the judgment arising from some accidental slip or omission. The Court Record of Hearing completed by the Associate records the judgment of the Court. The summons sought a number of orders including interlocutory judgment for damages to be assessed. The application was unopposed and it would be expected that the court would pronounce judgment in accordance with the terms of the summons.

[40] But it is not possible to say what the learned Judge said at the time. What his Associate recorded became the authenticated judgment of the Court.

[41] It follows that the Court could not find that the circumstances which attract the operation of the slip rule have been established. What was recorded could have been what the Judge pronounced.

[Nevertheless, Gillard J was satisfied that there was power in the default judgment rules (Vic r 21.07) and the court's inherent jurisdiction to allow correction of the order in circumstances where it could be shown that it did not reflect the intention of the court in making the order.]

WANT OF PROSECUTION

5.3.1   A proceeding may be brought to an untimely end where the plaintiff or the plaintiff's legal advisers fail to prosecute the proceeding with due diligence. The jurisdiction to dismiss a proceeding for want of prosecution derives from the superior courts' inherent jurisdiction and the court rules. Whether the court is exercising its inherent jurisdiction or determining an application brought under the court rules, the same principles will apply: *Allen v Sir Alfred McAlpine & Sons Ltd* [1968] 2 QB 229; [1968] 1 All ER 543; *Birkett v James* [1978] AC 297; [1977] 2 All ER 801; *Schiffbau und Maschinenfabrik v South India Shipping Corp Ltd* [1981] AC 909; *Weston v Publishing and Broadcasting Ltd* (2011) 83 ACSR 206; [2011] NSWSC 433; BC201103172.

Dismissal under the courts' inherent jurisdiction

5.3.2   Each superior court in Australia has an inherent power to dismiss a proceeding for want of prosecution. Dismissal for want of prosecution under the courts' inherent jurisdiction is discretionary. In exercising its discretion, the court must determine each case on the merits: *McKenna v McKenna* [1984] VR 665; *Ulowski v Miller* [1968] SASR 227; *Witten v Lombard Australia Ltd* (1968) 88 WN (Pt 1) (NSW) 405. The court will consider all the circumstances, including the length of and reasons for the delay, the conduct of the parties and their lawyers, the impact of the delay on the availability of evidence and the risk that a fair trial of the issues in dispute would not be possible: see *Birkett v James* [1978] AC 297, [1977] 2 All ER 801; *Allen v Sir Alfred McAlpine & Sons Ltd* [1968] 2 QB 229 at 259; *Ulowski v Miller* [1968] SASR 227; *Cooper v Hopgood and Ganim* [1999] 2 Qd R 113. The court will also consider the hardship on the plaintiff which would result from an order for dismissal and the prejudice which would flow to the defendant from the continuation of the action.

In *Birkett v James* [1978] AC 297, [1977] 2 All ER 801 at 805, Lord Diplock said:

> The power should be exercised only where the court is satisfied either· (1) that the default has been intentional and contumelious, eg disobedience to a peremptory order of the court or conduct amounting to an abuse of the process of the court; or (2)(a) that there has been inordinate and inexcusable delay on the part of the plaintiff or his lawyers, and (b) that such delay will give rise to a substantial risk that it is not possible to have a fair trial of the issues in the action or is such as is likely to cause or have caused serious prejudice to the defendant either as between themselves and the plaintiff or between each other or between them and a third party.

In *Department of Transport v Chris Smaller (Transport) Ltd* [1989] 1 AC 1197, the House of Lords considered that prejudice occasioned to the defendant by the plaintiff's delay in commencing proceedings (at 1206) or by the mere fact of the anxiety that accompanies any litigation (at 1209) were insufficient grounds for dismissal. Lord Griffiths said (at 1209) that:

> … [i]t would be foolish to attempt to define or categorise the type of prejudice justifying striking out an action, but there can be no doubt that if the defendants had been able to establish significant damage to their business interests, flowing directly from the culpable delay of 13 months after the issue of a writ, a judge would have been entitled to regard it as prejudice justifying striking out the action.

5.3.3   An order for dismissal for want of prosecution brings a plaintiff's proceeding to an end. If the limitation period has not expired, the plaintiff may issue fresh proceedings. Because there is no judgment for the defendant or determination on the merits, fresh proceedings will not be subject to the defence of *res judicata*: *Pople v Evans* [1969] 2 Ch 255; [1968] 2 All ER 743; *Hart v Hall & Pickles Ltd* [1969] 1 QB 405 at 411. Fresh proceedings may be determined to be an abuse of process: *Arbuthnot Latham Bank Ltd v Trafalgar Holdings Ltd* [1998] 2 All ER 181; [1998] 1 WLR 1426; *Lenijamar Pty Ltd v AGC (Advances) Ltd* (1990) 96 ALR 197 at 204.

The issue of a fresh writ after dismissal for want of prosecution would increase delay. Courts are therefore reluctant to order dismissal if the limitation period has not expired. In *Birkett v James*, Lord Diplock said (at 808) that:

> ... the fact that the limitation period has not yet expired must always be a matter of great weight in determining whether to exercise the discretion to dismiss an action for want of prosecution where no question of contumelious default on the part of the plaintiff is involved; and in cases where it is likely that if the action were dismissed the plaintiff would avail himself of his legal right to issue a fresh writ, the non-expiry of the limitation period is generally a conclusive reason for not dismissing the action that is already pending.

Applications for dismissal for want of prosecution are usually brought after the expiry of the limitation period. The defendant will not be disadvantaged by the mere fact that they have waited for the limitations period to expire prior to bringing such an application unless their conduct is misleading or amounts to a breach of an undertaking: *McKanna v Aspect Homes Pty Ltd* (1983) 51 ALR 603; 72 FLR 476; *Vidler v Merit Engineering Pty Ltd* (1986) 86 FLR 213.

Dismissal under the rules of court

5.3.4   The plaintiff is required by the rules of court to take certain steps within a specified time. The rules in most jurisdictions provide for dismissal in defined circumstances. For example, a proceeding may be dismissed for want of prosecution when the plaintiff fails to provide a Statement of Claim as required by the rules or fails to take steps to set a proceeding down for trial: HCR r 27.09.7; ACT r 1110(1); NT r 24.01; Qld r 280; Tas rr 265 and 371; Vic r 24.01 and r 48.04; WA O 20 r 1 and O 33 r 33.

Further criteria for dismissal include the following:

- the failure to prosecute the proceeding with due dispatch: NSW r 12.7;

- the failure of any party to take a step for more than five months in circumstances where the matter has not been listed for hearing and no interlocutory application is pending: NSW r 12.8;

- the failure to do an act within a specified time or take a step required by the rules within a prescribed period: Qld r 280; and

- an action remaining on the list of inactive cases two months after being entered on the list: SA r 123(4). An action becomes liable for entry in the inactive cases list if three months after the expiry of the time allowed for serving the originating process, no application for extending the time for serving originating process has been made (or such an application has been made and refused), the defendant has not filed an address for service and the plaintiff has not applied for judgment in default of a defence: SA r 123(1).

Section 22 of the Civil Proceedings Act 2011 (Qld) allows the District and Magistrates Courts to dismiss a proceeding if two years have passed since the last step was taken in the proceeding.

Rule 1110 of the ACT Court Procedures Rules 2006 permits dismissal for want of prosecution where the plaintiff does not take a step as required by the rules or fails to comply with an order of the court. The Federal Court Rules 2011 permit dismissal under r 5.23 where a party is in default on the grounds enumerated in r 5.22, namely that the party has failed to:

(a)   do an act required to be done, or to do an act in the time required by the Rules; or

(b)   comply with an order of the Court; or

(c)   attend a hearing in the proceeding; or

(d)   prosecute or defend the proceeding with due diligence.

Dismissal and case management

5.3.5   With the advent of case management and timetables for the completion of interlocutory proceedings, the kind of delay which would give rise to dismissal for want of prosecution is less likely to occur: *Spitfire Nominees Pty Ltd v Hall & Thompson (a firm)* [2001] VSCA 245; BC200108136 at [32]–[34]. In jurisdictions which have adopted case management schemes, courts will take a less forgiving approach to plaintiffs' defaults: see **5.2.11–5.2.12C** above.

The approach to dismissal since the advent of case management in England is described thus by Lord Woolf in *Arbuthnot Latham Bank Ltd v Trafalgar Holdings Ltd* [1998] 2 All ER 181 at 191:

> In *Birkett v James*, the consequence to other litigants and to the courts of inordinate delay was not a consideration which was in issue. From now on it is going to be a consideration of increasing significance. Litigants and their legal advisers must recognise that any delay which occurs from now on will be assessed not only from the point of view of the prejudice caused to the particular litigants whose case it is, but also in relation to the effect it can have on other litigants who are wishing to have their cases heard and the prejudice which is caused to the due administration of justice. The existing rules do contain the limits which are designed to achieve the disposal of litigation within a reasonable time scale. Those rules should be observed.

In *Re Lenijamar Pty Ltd v AGC (Advances) Ltd* [1990] FCA 520; 27 FCR 388 (20 December 1990), Wilcox and Gummow JJ held (at 395) that the case management system adopted by the Federal Court '[renders] inapplicable most, if not all, of the principles evolved by the English courts in relation to their own procedures' and 'the existence of a case management system within this Court is the backdrop against which the relevant rules must be considered and applied'. Their Honours considered whether an order dismissing the proceeding for want of prosecution should have be granted under O 10 r 7 of the Federal Court Rules 1976. The rule allowed for dismissal where a party failed to comply with a court order directing the party to take a step in the proceeding. This is now reflected in part in r 5.23 of the Federal Court Rules 2011.

The court set aside the order of the primary judge dismissing the proceeding for want of prosecution. In considering whether the proceeding should have been dismissed for want of prosecution, Wilcox and Gummow JJ said at 395–7:

> It is to be noted that the power given by this rule is conditioned on one circumstance only: the failure of a party to comply with an order of the Court directing that party to take a step in the

proceeding. There is no requirement of intentional default or contumelious conduct, although the attitude of the applicant to the default and the Court's judgment as to whether or not the applicant genuinely wishes the matter to go to trial within a reasonable period will usually be important factors in weighing the proper exercise of the discretion conferred by the rule. There is no requirement of 'inordinate and inexcusable delay' on the part of the applicant or the applicant's lawyers, although any such delay is likely to be a significant matter. There is no requirement of prejudice to the respondent, although the existence of prejudice is also likely to be significant. And it must be remembered that, in almost every case, delay adversely affects the quality of the trial and is an additional burden upon the parties ...

The observations which we have just made about the scope of O 10, r 7 are not intended to convey the impression that any failure to comply with a procedural direction will appropriately result in the dismissal of the proceeding. On the contrary, the rules must be administered sensibly and with an appreciation both of the fact that some delays are unavoidable, and unpredictable, by even the most conscientious parties and their lawyers, and of the likely serious consequences to an applicant of staying or dismissing a claim ... We would not wish our observations to cause respondents to apply for dismissal of proceedings simply because there has been a non-compliance with a direction by the applicant, even though it does not cause or indicate a continuing problem in preparing the matter for an early trial.

The discretion conferred by O 10, r 7 is unconfined, except for the condition of non-compliance with a direction. As it is impossible to foresee all of the circumstances under which the rule might be sought to be used, it is undesirable to make any exhaustive statement of the circumstances under which the power granted by the rule will appropriately be exercised. We will not attempt to do so. But two situations are obvious candidates for the exercise of the power: cases in which the history of non-compliance by an applicant is such as to indicate an inability or unwillingness to co-operate with the Court and the other party or parties in having the matter ready for trial within an acceptable period and cases — whatever the applicant's state of mind or resources — in which the non-compliance is continuing and occasioning unnecessary delay, expense or other prejudice to the respondent. Although the history of the matter will always be relevant, it is more likely to be decisive in the first of these two situations. Even though the most recent non-compliance may be minor, the cumulative effect of an applicant's defaults may be such as to satisfy the judge that the applicant is either subjectively unwilling to co-operate or, for some reason, is unable to do so. Such a conclusion would not readily be reached; but, where it was, fairness to the respondent would normally require the summary dismissal of the proceeding.

In the second of the two situations we postulate, a significant continuing default, it does not really matter whether there have been earlier omissions to comply with the Court's directions. *Ex hypothesi* the default is continuing and is imposing an unacceptable burden on the respondent. But the continuance of the non-compliance is of the essence of this situation. If, when the Court looks at the matter, the direction has already been complied with, the defaulting applicant may be ordered to pay any wasted costs; but it would be difficult to justify the dismissal of the proceeding solely because of that default.

In *Luck v University of Southern Queensland (No 4)* [2011] FCA 433; BC201102698, Bromberg J cited the above judgment of Wilcox and Gummow JJ and considered that the court is reposed with a wide discretion and that dismissal does not follow inevitably from default (at [25]). Bromberg J nevertheless determined that the applicant had failed to prosecute two proceedings with due diligence. In deciding to exercise his discretion in favour of dismissal of the proceedings, his Honour took account of the following matters (at [26]–[31]):

* the nature and substance of the proceedings;

* the applicant's failure to progress the proceedings;

* the applicant's inability or unwillingness to cooperate with the court (manifested most notably in a tone of correspondence which "may be regarded as high-handed, disrespectful and defiant");

* the applicant's refusal to deal with an asserted need for more time through a proper application to the court;

* the applicant's failure to apprise the court of her future capacity to prosecute the proceedings;

* the advantage gained by the applicant from delaying the payment of costs orders through failing to prosecute the proceedings; and

* the real prospect that the pursuance of the proceedings would not be of benefit to the applicant.

His Honour also took into account (at [32]) the case management objectives in ss 37M and 37N of the Federal Court of Australia Act 1976, namely the need to bring finality to the litigation and the court's obligation to facilitate the just resolution of disputes according to law as quickly, inexpensively and efficiently as possible.

5.3.6   An order dismissing a proceeding for want of prosecution may be set aside in Victoria (r 24.06) and the Northern Territory: r 24.06. Under the Court Procedures Rules (ACT), an order dismissing the proceeding for want of prosecution may ordinarily be set aside only on appeal or with the agreement of the parties (r 1110(3)), but the court may amend or set aside an order dismissing the proceeding for want of prosecution made in the absence of the plaintiff without the need for an appeal: r 1110(4). In all other jurisdictions, an order dismissing a proceeding for want of prosecution can only be set aside on appeal.

SELF-EXECUTING ORDERS

5.4.1   A self-executing order sets out consequences which take effect upon non-compliance with the terms of the order. The party to whom the order is directed is required to take a procedural step by a fixed date, failing which specified consequences will ensue. For example, an order may require a defendant to provide answers to interrogatories within a specified time, failing which their defence will be struck out.

Self-executing orders are also known as springing, guillotine or peremptory orders and in the United Kingdom are often referred to as unless orders. They may be made against a plaintiff or defendant and may be distinguished from dismissal for want of prosecution which addresses itself to the plaintiff's failure to prosecute the proceeding with diligence.

5.4.2E **Federal Court Rules 2011**
Division 5.2 — Orders on Default

5.21 Self-executing orders
A party may apply to the Court for an order that, unless another party does an act or thing within a certain time:

(a)   the proceeding be dismissed; or
(b)   the applicant's statement of claim be struck out; or
(c)   the respondent's defence be struck out; or
(d)   the party have judgment against the other party.

[See also FCR r 1.42; ACT r 671; Civil Procedure Act (NSW) s 86(1) CPA; NT rr 24.02, 48.27; Qld r 374; SA rr 116(2), 117; Tas r 372; Vic rr 24.02, 24.05; WA O 4A, r 23]

5.4.3   The consequences of the order may be avoided by compliance with its terms. The party to whom the order is directed may apply for an extension of time under the rules: see **5.5.9–5.5.10E**. In *FAI General Insurance Company Ltd v Southern Cross Exploration NL* (1988) 165 CLR 268, the High Court considered the power to grant an extension of time now reflected in NSW r 1.12 (Pt 2, r 3 of the Supreme Court Rules 1970). The court found that the rule conferred a power on the court to extend the time for compliance with a self-executing order even after the period for compliance had elapsed. On the exercise of the power, Wilson J said at 283:

> It is a remedial provision which confers on a court a broad power to relieve against injustice. The discretion so conferred is not readily to be limited by judicial fiat. The fact that it manifestly is a power to be exercised with caution and, in the case of conditional orders, with due regard to the public policy centred in the finality of litigation does not warrant an arbitrary limitation of the power itself, not expressed in the words of the rule, so as to deny its capacity to apply to circumstances such as those which are to be found in the present case. It would be wrong to so read the rule as to deny to a court power to prevent injustice in circumstances where the party subject to a conditional order ought to be excused from non-compliance.

5.4.4   A party may seek to set aside or vary a self-executing order if it is affected by error or if an injustice in the result flowed from the operation of the order. In *Freeman v Rabinov* [1981] VR 539, an order was made to the effect that the plaintiff must make, file and deliver a supplementary affidavit of documents failing which his action will be dismissed and his defence to the defendant's counterclaim struck out. The plaintiff provided a supplementary affidavit of documents within the stipulated time. The affidavit was insufficient because it was not sworn in proper form. It did not include a statement as required by the rules to the effect that the documents listed in the original and supplementary affidavits constituted all of the documents which were or had been in the deponent's possession. The affidavit also failed to provide a sufficient description of some cheque butts.

The plaintiff applied for an extension of time for compliance with the court's order or alternatively, for leave to appeal against the order while the defendants sought judgment on the counterclaim and an assessment of damages. The judge refused to grant the plaintiff an extension of time and granted the defendants interlocutory judgment on the counterclaim. The plaintiff appealed to the Full Court of the Supreme Court (as it then was). Lush J (with

Murray and King JJ concurring) found that although the affidavit was not in proper form and was provided around a month after it should have been delivered, the defendants had obtained the information that they required. The plaintiff was at risk of suffering an injustice by the operation of the self-executing order in the form of a significant judgment in damages without a trial. The Full Court allowed the appeal and varied the self-executing order to extend the time for delivery of a supplementary affidavit of documents.

5.4.5 Some court rules enable a party to make an application to set aside judgment entered upon non-compliance with a self-executing order: ACT r 1128; NT r 24.06; NSW r 36.16(2); Qld r 290; SA r 230; Tas r 255; Vic r 24.06(b).

TIME

5.5.1 All jurisdictions have provisions relating to time. These provisions deal with reckoning, extension and abridgment, fixing times, provisions dealing with proceedings taken after a year, and vacation and registry hours provisions. Most jurisdictions also have a provision explicitly stating that 'month' refers to a calendar month, rather than to a lunar month (as month was defined under common law principles of interpretation).

Reckoning

5.5.2 Some jurisdictions reckon time exclusively of the first and last day, as in WA O 3 r 2 (extracted below).

5.5.3E **Rules of the Supreme Court 1971 (WA)**
Order 3 rule 2

(1) Where clear days are prescribed by these Rules or fixed by any judgment, order or direction, the time shall be reckoned exclusively of the first and last day. Where any number of days not expressed to be clear days is prescribed or fixed the time shall be reckoned exclusively of the first and inclusively of the last day.

(2) Where less than 7 days is prescribed by these Rules or limited by any judgment, order or direction for doing any act any day on which the Central Office is closed for business shall not be reckoned.

5.5.4 See also: FCR r 1.61; NSW r 1.11; and see and compare SA r 5(1) which provides:

(1) When a rule or judgment fixes prospectively the time within which something is required or permitted to be done, the period runs from the end of the day from which the calculation is to be made.

5.5.5 Others reckon time exclusively of the first day and inclusively of the last, such as Tas r 47 and HCR r 4.01 (extracted below).

5.5.6E   **Rules of the Supreme Court 2000 (Tas)**
Part 4 — Time

Computation of number of days
47 A period of a particular number of days, not expressed to be clear days, excludes the first day and includes the last day.

[See also: Legislation Act 2001 (ACT) s 151.]

5.5.7E   **High Court Rules 2004**

Time
4.01.1 Any period of time fixed by or under these Rules shall be calculated in accordance with this Part.

4.01.2 Where a time of 1 day or longer is to begin on or to be calculated from a day or event, the day or the day of the event shall be excluded.

4.01.3 Where a time of 1 day or longer is to end on or to be calculated to a day or event the day or the day of the event shall be included.

4.01.4 Where a period of 5 days or less would include a day on which the office of the Registry is not open in the State or Territory where the act is to be done or may be done that day shall be excluded.

4.01.5 Where the last day for doing any act is a day on which the office of the Registry is not open in the State or Territory where the act is to be done or may be done the act may be done on the next day the Registry is open.

4.01.6 In calculating any period of time fixed by or under these Rules an act done after 4.00 pm on a day shall be taken to have been done on the next day on which the Registry in the State or Territory where that act was done is open.

[See also NT r 3.01(1); Vic r 3.01.]

5.5.8 In general, the rules provide that the court's Christmas vacation time is not to be taken into account: FCR r 1.61; ACT r 6350; NT r 3.04; Acts Interpretation Act 1954 (Qld) s 38; SA r 5(6); Tas r 48; Vic r 3.04; WA O 3 r 3. Where there is a limited time within which a step must be taken, Sundays and days in which the court's offices are not open are not included in that time limit. Where the last day in which a given act is to be done falls upon a Sunday or a day in which the court's offices are closed, then that act may be done on the next day in which the registry is open: HCR r 4.01.5; FCR r 1.61; ACT r 6350; NSW r 1.11; NT r 3.01; Acts Interpretation Act 1954 (Qld) s 38; SA r 5; Tas r 51; Vic r 3.01; WA O 3 r 4.

Extension and abridgment

5.5.9   Each of the jurisdictions has rules which allow the court to extend or abridge time. The Tasmanian rule is set out below:

5.5.10E   **Supreme Court Rules 2000 (Tas)**

Extension or abridgment of period

52 (1) The Court or a judge may extend or abridge the period for doing any act or taking any proceedings allowed or limited by these rules or by any order of the Court or a judge on any terms the Court or judge considers just.

(2) An extension of any period may be ordered although the application is made after the expiration of the period originally allowed or limited.

[See also: HCR r 4.02; FCR r1.39; ACT r 6351, Legislation Act 2001 (ACT) s 151C; NSW r 1.12; NT r 3.02; Qld r 7; SA r 117; Vic r 3.02; WA O 3 r 5.]

5.5.11   The courts may make an order effective from the date upon which a particular step in the litigation ought to have been taken. Where they do so, the order is said to have effect *nunc pro tunc*: see, eg, **8.7.10**.

Further reading

5.6.1   Looseleaf

B C Cairns, 'Practice and Procedure', *Halsbury's Laws of Australia*, LexisNexis Butterworths, Sydney, looseleaf, vol 20.

N J Williams, *Civil Procedure Victoria*, LexisNexis Butterworths, Sydney, looseleaf.

5.6.2   Texts

B C Cairns, *Australian Civil Procedure*, 9th ed, Thomson Reuters, Sydney, 2011, Chs 2, 8 and 9.

J Hunter, C Cameron and T Henning, *Litigation I: Civil Procedure*, LexisNexis Butterworths, Sydney, 2005, Ch 5, [5.34]–[5.49].

Limitation of Actions

OVERVIEW

This chapter examines statutory limitation periods which dictate the time within which plaintiffs must commence their actions. The chapter begins by exploring the purpose of limitation periods; that is, the discouragement of stale claims which may cause evidentiary difficulties and injustice to defendants. The running of time is then outlined; that is, how a cause of action accrues, qualities which suspend the running of time, the expiry of time and the judicial discretion to extend the limitation period. This will be followed by an analysis of the operation of the limitation acts in personal injury actions. Not only is personal injury the most commonly litigated cause of action, it gives rise to particular issues involving limitation periods such as latent injury or disease, as well as complicated questions about achieving justice between plaintiffs and defendants. The chapter will conclude with a brief discussion of limitation periods and choice of law.

INTRODUCTION

State and territory jurisdictions

6.1.1   For most types of legal action there are time periods known as 'limitation periods' within which proceedings must be commenced. Statutes of Limitation are in force in every Australian jurisdiction: Limitation Act 1985 (ACT), Limitation Act 1969 (NSW), Limitation Act 1981 (NT), Limitation of Actions Act 1974 (Qld), Limitation of Actions Act 1936 (SA), Limitation Act 1974 (Tas), Limitation of Actions Act 1958 (Vic), Limitation Act 2005 (WA) (referred to collectively hereafter as the 'Limitation Acts'). They prescribe the general period within which an action to enforce a right must be commenced. Failure to commence proceedings within this limitation period will bar the action, subject to possible suspension or extension of the limitation period, or the other side failing to take the issue. The existence of the Limitation Acts is based on the policy that stale claims should not be brought. This policy is justified in two major respects:

(1)   *Injustice*: it would be an injustice to defendants to have proceedings hanging over their heads for too long since people should be able to arrange their affairs on the basis that

claims cannot be made against them after a certain time. Further, the attainment of justice is precarious where witnesses' memories have faded or documentary material is no longer available.

(2)   *Efficiency*: litigants should be encouraged to bring their actions within a reasonable period since there is a public interest in having claims settled as quickly as possible.

6.1.2   The origins of the Australian Limitation Acts are found in English legislation dating from 1623–1888. The Limitation Acts apply to all actions of any class for which a limitation period is prescribed by the Acts. Most actions stipulated in the Acts are common law actions as equity developed its own limitation principles, which are discussed at **6.1.6ff**. The Limitation Acts do not generally apply where a specific period of limitation is provided for in another enactment, although SA s 47 extends some limitation periods under other enactments and SA s 48 gives the court power to extend a time limitation contained in another Act, regulation, rule or by-law.

Federal jurisdiction

6.1.3   Although limitation periods may be nominated in particular Commonwealth statutes, such as the Corporations Act 2001 (Cth) and the Competition and Consumer Act 2010 (Cth) (see **6.1.5**), there is no general federal statute governing limitation periods. Importantly, the Limitation Acts of the Australian states and territories are not ordinarily applicable to courts exercising federal jurisdiction, for example, the High Court or Federal Court, or where a state court exercises federal jurisdiction. eg, where it exercises jurisdiction under a federal statute.

Section 79 of the Judiciary Act 1903 (Cth) provides that the laws of each state, including the laws relating to procedure, are binding on all courts exercising federal jurisdiction in that state or territory, except as otherwise provided by the Commonwealth Constitution or the laws of the Commonwealth. This provision may 'pick up' a state or territory limitation provision if a High Court or Federal Court action is commenced and heard in a state or territory: *Pedersen v Young* (1964) 110 CLR 162, *Montgomery v Pickard* [2007] QCA 203. As stated by the High Court in *Commissioner of Stamp Duties v Owens (No 2)* (1953) 88 CLR 168 at 170:

> The purpose of [s 79] is to adopt the law of the State where federal jurisdiction is exercised as the law by which, except as the Constitution or federal law may otherwise provide, the rights of the parties ... are to be ascertained and matters of procedure are to be regulated.

Some commentators have expressed hesitation about the characterisation of limitation periods as procedural for the purpose of s 79 of the Judiciary Act following the High Court judgment in *John Pfeiffer Pty Ltd v Rogerson* (2000) 203 CLR 503, which classified them as part of the substantive law for choice of law purposes: P Handford, *The Laws of Australia*, [5.10.340]. Another approach is to regard s 79 as operating on legislation that regulates the exercise of jurisdiction, which Hill and Beech refer to as 'incidental' legislation. Hill and Beech consider that incidental legislation would include, but is not limited to, 'procedural' legislation; that is, legislation that regulates the mode or conduct of court proceedings. However, incidental legislation also includes measures that are sometimes characterised as 'substantive', such as limitation periods that bar the remedy: G Hill and A Beech, "'Picking

Up" State and Territory Laws under s 79 of the Judiciary Act — Three Questions' (2005) 27 *Aust Bar Rev* 25 at 30. For a discussion of the relationship between substantive and procedural law, see **1.2.1–1.3.3**.

It has been said that s 79 in 'picking up' state law, transforms it into 'surrogate Commonwealth laws': *Commonwealth of Australia v Mewett* (1997) 191 CLR 471 at [554] per Gummow and Kirby JJ, extracted at **6.4.7C**.

The Queensland Court of Appeal considered the operation of s 79 of the Judiciary Act in *Du Boulay v Worrell* [2009] QCA 63. In that case, the previous director of a deregistered company commenced proceedings in the Queensland Supreme Court against the administrators of the company seeking damages and alleging various breaches of the Corporations Act 2001 (Cth). One of the allegations against the administrators was 'fraud', which was said to be in breach of s 590 of the Corporations Act 2001 (Cth). It was held by the Court of Appeal (at [22] per Keane JA) that s 79 of the Judiciary Act 1903 (Cth) had the consequence of applying the Limitation of Actions Act 1974 (Qld) to the appellant's putative claims under the Corporations Act. Consequently, the claim would be defeated by the expiration of the limitation period applicable to the claim.

Where the Commonwealth or a state is a party in federal proceedings, s 64 of the Judiciary Act 1903 (Cth) may also make a state limitation law applicable: *Maguire v Simpson* (1977) 139 CLR 362; *Commonwealth v Dixon* (1988) 13 NSWLR 601.

6.1.4 Further reading

Australian Law Reform Commission, *The Judicial Power of the Commonwealth: Review of the Judiciary Act 1903 and Related Legislation*, Discussion Paper 64, December 2000.

J Kirk, 'Conflicts and Choice of Law within the Australian Constitutional Context' (2003) 31(2) *Fed LR* 247.

S Kneebone, 'Claims against the Commonwealth and States and their Instrumentalities in Federal Jurisdiction: Section 64 of the Judiciary Act' (1996) 24 *Fed LR* 93.

P Nygh, 'Choice of Law in Federal and Cross-vested Jurisdiction', B Opeskin and F Wheeler (eds), *The Australian Federal Judicial System*, Melbourne University Press, 2000, p 335.

R Sackville, 'The Re-emergence of Federal Jurisdiction in Australia' (2001) 21 *Aust Bar Rev* 133.

6.1.5   As discussed above at **6.1.3**, federal statutes may nominate limitation periods within the particular statute. For example, the Competition and Consumer Act 2010 (Cth) provides for:

* three years for civil actions seeking damages for personal injury or death (ss 87F–87K);
* six years for civil actions alleging various contraventions of the Act: for damages (s 82(2)) or other orders (s 87(1CA); and
* six years for actions to enforce a pecuniary penalty: s 77(2).

Note that the remedies available under the Competition and Consumer Act 2010 (Cth) must be distinguished from those obtainable under the Australian Consumer Law (ACL), which is set out in Sch 2 to the Competition and Consumer Act 2010 (Cth). The ACL (constituted by Sch 2 to the Competition and Consumer Act 2010 (Cth)) operates as a law of the Commonwealth, but the ACL was also picked up as an 'applied law' by the states and territories. The latter operates as state or territory law, depending on the jurisdiction.

Section 236(2) of the ACL stipulates that an action in damages for contravention of a consumer protection provision found in Chs 2 and 3 of the ACL (eg, misleading and deceptive conduct under s 18 of the ACL) is six years from the date of accrual. See generally: A Bruce, *Consumer Protection Law*, LexisNexis Butterworths, 2011, Chs 1 and 2.

[*Note:* in this chapter a reference such as NSW s 9(2) is a reference to the relevant Limitations Act. All other legislation will be specified.]

Equitable remedies

6.1.6   With the exception of the Australian Capital Territory and Western Australia, the limitation statutes do not generally apply to claims for equitable relief. There are some individual equitable causes of action that are expressly dealt with in the limitation legislation, for example, a beneficiary's action for breach of trust: see 6.3.2. Some Limitation Acts exclude the equitable remedies of specific performance and injunction from the provisions dealing with contract and tort actions (s 10(6)(b) (Qld); s 9 (Tas); s 5(8) (Vic)) and the legislation in New South Wales and the Northern Territory provides that various provisions of the Act do not apply to causes of action for equitable relief: s 23 (NSW); s 21 (NT). Moreover, express provisions of the Limitation Acts provide that the Acts do not apply to the exercise of the equitable jurisdiction to refuse relief on the ground of acquiescence or otherwise: s 6 (ACT); s 9 (NSW); s 7 (NT); s 43 (Qld); s 26 (SA); s 36 (Tas); s 31 (Vic); s 80 (WA).

In the Australian Capital Territory, s 11 states that 'an action on any cause of action is not maintainable if brought after the end of a limitation period of 6 years'. The phrase 'cause of action' is defined in the Dictionary as 'the fact or combination of facts that gives rise to a right to bring a civil proceeding'. It was held by the Full Federal Court in *Paramasivam v Flynn* (1998) 90 FCR 489 at 501; 160 ALR 203 at 215, that these provisions clearly encompass equitable claims, in particular, breach of fiduciary duty.

Similarly, in Western Australia s 13 states that 'an action on any cause of action cannot be commenced if 6 years have elapsed since the cause of action accrued'. 'Action' is defined, among other things, to mean 'any civil proceeding in a court, whether the claim that is the subject of the proceeding or relief sought is under a written law, at common law, in equity or otherwise': s 3(1)(a) (WA). Section 27 (WA) nominates the relevant limitation periods and the running of time for equitable actions: see *Neilson v City of Swan (No 2)* [2007] WASC 278 at [12].

In jurisdictions other than the Australian Capital Territory and Western Australia, the time for commencement of an equitable cause of action is determined by the doctrine of laches. Laches was described in *Partridge v Partridge* [1894] 1 Ch 351 at [360] as 'an Old French word for slackness or negligence or not doing'. The court may, in its discretion, refuse to grant equitable relief where the plaintiff's delay makes it unjust for the court to award equitable relief: see *Orr v Ford* (1989) 84 ALR 146 at 151ff per Wilson, Toohey and Gaudron JJ and at 159ff per Deane J.

The following case explains the operation of laches:

6.1.7C   **Crawley v Short**
(2009) 262 ALR 654; (2009) 76 ACSR 286
Supreme Court of New South Wales — Court of Appeal

Young JA (at [163]): The elements of the defence of laches are: (i) knowledge of the wrong; (ii) delay; and (iii) unconscionable prejudice caused to the opponent by the delay.

[164] The key element is whether, in all the circumstances, "it would be practically unjust to give a remedy": per Lord Selborne LC in *Lindsay Petroleum Co v Hurd* (1874) LR 5 PC 221 at 239–40. Normally, that means that the defendant must show both delay and detriment suffered by the delay, *Fisher v Brooker* [2009] 4 All ER 789; [2009] 1 WLR 1764; [2009] UKHL 41 at [64] (*Fisher*) per Lord Neuberger with whom Lord Hope, Lord Walker, Baroness Hale and Lord Mance agreed. ...

[168] The authorities give little guidance on the extent of the knowledge required. One of the leading statements is in Lord Blackburn's speech in *Erlanger v New Sombrero Phosphate Co* (1878) 3 App Cas 1218 at 1279 that the plaintiff must be shown to have "such notice or knowledge as to make it inequitable to lie by". That statement was approved by this court in *Savage v Lunn* (unreported, NSWCA, Handley, Sheller JJA and Sheppard AJA, 9 March 1998, BC9800548) ... . Lord Blackburn acknowledged that his statement was very general, but said that he had "looked in vain" for any more distinct rule.

[169] That general statement does not, of itself, assist in fixing the degree of knowledge required, but points to it being a question of fact and degree in each case to be taken together with all the other facts of the particular case.

6.1.8   For a further overview of the principles of laches and their application, see *Cubillo v Commonwealth of Australia* (1999) 89 FCR 528; 163 ALR at [1426]–[1434] per O'Loughlin J; *Trevorrow v State of South Australia (No 5)* (2007) 98 SASR 136; *The Salvation Army (South Australia Property Trust) v Rundle* [2008] NSWCA 347; *Streeter v Western Areas Exploration Pty Ltd (No 2)* (2011) 278 ALR 291; (2011) 82 ACSR 1 at [632]–[682] per Murphy JA and *Bell Group Ltd v Westpac Banking Corp (No 9)* (2008) 39 WAR 1 per Owen J at [9303]–[9308].

Application of Statutory Limitation Periods to Equitable Claims by Analogy

6.1.9   Pursuant to the maxim that 'equity follows the law', a court exercising equitable jurisdiction may apply a statutory limitation period by analogy to the grant of an equitable remedy. Lord Westbury LC in *Knox v Gye* (1872) LR 5 HL 656 at 674–5 has been treated as authoritative. He said:

> For where the remedy in Equity is correspondent to the remedy at Law, and the latter is subject to a limit in point of time by the Statute of Limitations, a Court of Equity acts by analogy to the statute, and imposes on the remedy it affords the same limitation ...

For example, the court in *Duke Group Ltd (in liq) v Alamain Investments Ltd* [2003] SASC 415 needed to decide whether claims for equitable compensation for breach of directors' fiduciary duty were analogous to claims in tort for negligence. Doyle CJ found that authority supported the contention that:

> ... there are causes of action in tort against the directors sufficiently similar to the claim against the directors for breach of fiduciary duty, and which are subject to a six year time limit, to warrant in principle the application of that time limit to a claim against the directors for breach of fiduciary duty: at [133].

However, it is necessary to consider whether, despite the similarity, it would be unjust to rely on the analogy (at [114]) and on an application for summary disposition in *Duke*, Doyle CJ was not prepared to find that the claim should be struck out because it was barred by the application by analogy of the statutory time limit: at [134].

This issue was tested in the New South Wales Supreme Court in the Joy Williams litigation: *Williams v Minister, Aboriginal Land Rights Act 1983* (1994) 35 NSWLR 497. In 1942, Joy Williams was removed from her mother, an Aboriginal woman, by the Aborigines Welfare Board. In 1993, Williams sought to commence proceedings for damages for negligence, wrongful imprisonment and breach of fiduciary duty. She brought preliminary proceedings for an order extending time under the Limitation Act 1969 (NSW). At first instance, Studdert J found that it was not 'just and reasonable' to extend the limitation period (pursuant to NSW s 60G) because of the prejudice suffered by the defendant. The evidence of the defendant was that it was unable to find written records pertaining to the plaintiff and possible witnesses for the defendant were either very elderly or deceased.

Studdert J's decision was reversed by a majority of the Court of Appeal in *Williams v Minister, Aboriginal Land Rights Act 1983* (1994) 35 NSWLR 497. Kirby P, with whom Priestley JA agreed, found that Williams' claim for breach of fiduciary duty did not fall within s 60G of the Limitation Act 1969 (NSW). His Honour stated at 509:

> It is therefore clear that the scheme of the Limitation Act does not apply, in its own terms, to a cause of action for equitable relief. It only applies by analogy. ... [I]t is a mistake of law to assume that an equitable claim, based on an equitable cause of action, not for damages but for equitable compensation, is to be dealt with under s 60G of the Limitation Act. It is not. It raises separate and different questions. Nor can the application of the Act "by analogy" lead to the automatic application of s 60G to such a claim. Analogous application of the statute does not necessarily mean exact application of its terms. The considerations that may be relevant to a defence of laches will be different from (or not exactly the same as) the considerations relevant to the application of the Act.

For further analysis of the application of the limitation legislation by analogy, see *Bell Group Ltd (in liq) v Westpac Banking Corp (No 9)* (2008) 39 WAR 1 at [9246]–[9302] per Owen J; *P&O Nedlloyd BV v Arab Metals Co* [2007] 1 WLR 2288; [2007] 2 All ER (Comm) 401, *Hewitt v Henderson* [2006] WASCA 233 and *Barker v Duke Group Ltd (in liq)* (2005) 91 SASR 167; [2005] SASC 81.

6.1.10 Further reading

P Batley, 'The State's Fiduciary Duty to the Stolen Children' (1996) 2 *Australian Journal of Human Rights* 177.

G Dal Pont, *Equity and Trusts: Commentary and Materials*, Lawbook Co, 2011, 5th ed, pp 985–97.

A Marfording, 'Access to Justice for Survivors of Child Sexual Abuse' (1997) 5 *Torts Law Journal* 221.

N Mullany, 'Civil Actions for Childhood Abuse in Australia' (1999) 115 *LQR* 565.

N Skead, 'Limitation Act 2005 (WA) and Equitable Actions: A Fatal Blow to Judicial Discretion and Flexibility — How Other Australian Jurisdictions Might Learn from Western Australia's Mistakes' (2009) 11 *The University of Notre Dame Australia Law Review* 1.

THE PURPOSE OF LIMITATION PERIODS

6.2.1E	**Limitation of Actions for Latent Personal Injuries** Law Reform Commissioner of Tasmania (Report No 69, 1992)

POLICY UNDERLYING THE LEGISLATION

The purpose of Statutes of Limitations

The purpose and effect of Statutes of Limitation is to protect defendants. The Courts have expressed frequently three reasons for supporting the existence of Statutes of Limitation, namely:

(a) that plaintiffs with good causes of actions should pursue them with reasonable diligence;

(b) that a defendant might have lost evidence to disprove a stale claim; and

(c) that long dormant claims have more of cruelty than justice in them (*Halsbury's Laws of England* (4th edition) Volume 28, at page 266).

Statutes of Limitation are intended to bring *certainty* to legal proceedings by preventing old and stale claims from being resurrected. After the expiry of the prescribed limitation period, defendants can with reasonable certainty assume that if legal proceedings have not been commenced they are free from the threat of future legal proceedings. This aspect of certainty has been expressed by Lord Atkinson in *Board of Trade v Cayzer Irving and Co* [1927] AC 610:

> ... the whole purpose of this Limitation Act is to apply to persons who have good causes of action which they could, if so disposed, enforce and to deprive them of the power of enforcing them after they have lain by for the number of years respectively and omitted to enforce them. They are thus deprived of the remedy which they have omitted to use ... (at 628)

The need for certainty can be justified in many cases. For example, manufacturers need to be able to 'close their books' and calculate the potential liability of their business enterprise with some degree of certainty before embarking on future development. Under modern circumstances, an award of damages compensation may be so large as to jeopardise the financial viability of a business. The threat of open-ended liability from unforeseen claims may be an unreasonable burden on a business. Limitation periods may allow for more accurate and certain assessment of potential liability.

Statutes of Limitation have also been defended on the ground that there may be *difficulties with evidence* if actions are not pursued within reasonable time periods. So, for instance, the Tucker Committee in the United Kingdom noted that actions in contract or tort ought to be brought within the prescribed period ... 'having regard to the desirability of such actions being brought to trial quickly, whilst evidence is fresh in the minds of the parties and witnesses' (*Report of the Committee on the Limitation of Actions* Cmnd. 7740 (1949) at paragraph 22). ...

Perhaps most persuasive is the argument that periods of limitation are intended to achieve *justice* between the parties. In the early nineteenth century, Best CJ in *A Court v Cross* (1825) 130 ER 540; 3 Bing 329 stated that the legislation is 'an act of peace. Long dormant claims have often more of cruelty than justice in them'. A plaintiff ought to take legal proceedings promptly whilst a defendant should know after the expiry of the prescribed period of time that no legal threat continues. The need for finality in litigation was stressed by Streatfield J in *R B Policies v Butler* [1949] All ER 226:

> ... one of the principles of the [Limitation] *Act* is that those who go to sleep on their claims should not be assisted by the courts in recovering their property. But another equally important principle is that there shall be an end of these matters, and that there shall be protection against stale demands. (at 229)

Limitations, however, bar plaintiffs — not defendants. These justifications aside, the interests of defendants ought not to outweigh completely the interests of plaintiffs, especially when the claim is based on a personal injury rather than damage to property. A balance must be struck in order to ensure that justice is done between the parties.

THE RUNNING OF TIME

6.3.1   Generally speaking, the limitation period commences to run upon accrual of a cause of action and the obligation to bring a claim within time will be satisfied by the plaintiff commencing proceedings within the statutory time frame. Commencement occurs when the relevant originating process is issued by the plaintiff; that is, when it is accepted in the court registry: see 7.4.7.

However, even if proceedings are commenced within the original limitation period, the plaintiff may still be in jeopardy, because the limitation period continues to run and if the plaintiff's proceeding is dismissed prior to judgment or settlement, an attempt to bring new proceedings may be statute-barred, see, for example, *Van Leer Australia Pty Ltd v Palace Shipping KK* (1981) 180 CLR 337, extracted at 7.7.11C.

There must be proper compliance with the requirements for the issue of originating process in order for the plaintiff to resist the defendant's claim that the limitation period has expired: *Turagadamudamu v PMP Ltd* (2009) 75 NSWLR 397; [2009] NSWCA 120; *Windsurf Holdings Pty Ltd v Leonard; Carson v Leonard; Wyvill v Leonard* [2009] NSWCA 6 at [9]–[24] per Bell JA (with whom Beazley JA agreed) where the plaintiffs purported to commence proceedings using a notice of motion rather than originating process (a statement of claim in New South Wales).

If proceedings are not commenced within the limitation period, the time for bringing an action will expire, rendering the cause of action unenforceable. However, in certain circumstances the plaintiff may seek an extension of time within which to bring the action. Certain occurrences also have the effect of suspending the operation of the limitation period, such as disability (see **6.3.25ff**) or delaying the running of time until the cause of action is discoverable by the plaintiff: see **6.3.10ff** and **6.6.7ff**.

Examples of limitation periods — General

6.3.2   The following table gives examples of the limitation period in years applying to certain causes of action and the relevant state or territory provision of the Limitation Acts pertaining to the nominated causes of action. The stipulated periods for personal injury actions are set out at **6.6.2**.

	ACT	NSW	NT	Qld	SA	Tas	Vic	WA
Contract	6 s 11(1)	6 s 14(1)(a)	3 s 12(1)(a)	6 s 10(1)(a)	6 s 35(a)	6 s 4(1)(a)	6 s 5(1)(a)	6 s 13(1)
Tort general	6 s 11(1)	6 s 14(1)(b)	3 s 12(1)(b)	6 s 10(1)(a)	6 s 35(c)	6 s 4(1)(a)	6 s 5(1)(a)	6 s 13(1)
Actions by a beneficiary against a trustee to recover trust property, or for breach of trust	6 s 11	6 s 48	3 s 33	6 s 27(2)	N/A	6 s 24(2)	6 s 21(2)	6 s 13(1)
Deed or Specialty	12 s 13	12 s 16	12 s 14(1)	12 s 10(3)	15 s 34	12 s 4(3)	15 s 5(3)	12 s 18
Recovery of Land	N/A *	12 s 27(2)	N/A *	12 s 13	15 s 4	12 s 10(2)	15 s 8	12 s 19(1)
Judgment	12 s 14(1)	12 s 17(1)	12 s 15(1)	12 s 10(4)	15 s 34	12 s 4(4)	15 s 5(4)	6 s 13(1)

	ACT	NSW	NT	Qld	SA	Tas	Vic	WA
Defamation/	1	1	1	1	1	1	1	1
Slander	s 21B(1)	s 14B	s 12(2)(b)	10AA	s 37(1)	**	s 5(1AAA)	s 15

*   In the Australian Capital Territory and the Northern Territory, the title of the registered proprietor of land is not extinguished by the operation of a Limitation Act: Land Titles Act 1925 (ACT) s 69; Land Title Act 2004 (NT) s 198.

** In Tasmania, the relevant limitation period is found in s 20A of the Defamation Act 2005 (Tas).

6.3.3   For a comprehensive table of Australian limitation periods, see P Handford, 'Table of Limitation of Actions', *The Laws of Australia*, [5.10.10].

Accrual of cause of action

6.3.4   The general rule is that the limitation period commences to run when the plaintiff's cause of action accrues or is complete. The Limitation Acts generally stipulate that an action must be brought within a stated number of years from the date on which the plaintiff's right or cause of action accrues, as illustrated in the extract below:

6.3.5E   **Limitation Act 1969 (NSW)**

14(1) An action on any of the following causes of action is not maintainable if brought after the expiration of a limitation period of six years running from the date on which the cause of action first accrues to the plaintiff or to a person through whom the plaintiff claims:

(a) a cause of action founded on contract (including quasi contract) not being a cause of action founded on a deed,

(b) a cause of action founded on tort, including a cause of action for damages for breach of statutory duty,

(c) a cause of action to enforce a recognizance,

(d) a cause of action to recover money recoverable by virtue of an enactment, other than a penalty or forfeiture or sum by way of penalty or forfeiture.

6.3.6   A cause of action accrues when the necessary facts have occurred, and there is in existence a competent plaintiff who can sue and a competent defendant who can be sued: *Thomson v Lord Clanmorris* [1900] 1 Ch 718 at 728–9 per Vaughan Williams LJ. The requirements of a cause of action vary according to the type of case and are determined by the substantive law. For specific applications, in contract, the cause of action is said to arise from the breach, whereas in the tort of negligence, damage is necessary to perfect the cause of action. Therefore, generally speaking, in contract the limitation period will run from the breach whereas in negligence, damage must be suffered before the limitation period commences: see *Price, Higgins & Fidge v Drysdale* [1996] 1 VR 346, *Guthrie v Spence* [2009] NSWCA 369 at [120] per Campbell JA and *Commonwealth of Australia v Cornwell* (2007) 229 CLR 519, as discussed hereafter.

6.3.7 In *Commonwealth of Australia v Cornwell* (2007) 229 CLR 519; (2007) 234 ALR 148; (2007) 61 ACSR 118, the respondent, Cornwell, was employed by the appellant, the Commonwealth, from 1962 until his retirement in 1994. In 1965, another employee of the Commonwealth negligently advised Cornwell that he could not join the Commonwealth Superannuation Fund because his employment status was 'temporary' rather than 'permanent'. In fact, Cornwell could have joined the fund despite his employment status being temporary. Cornwell ultimately joined the fund when the status of his position was reclassified as permanent in 1987.

In 1999, Cornwell instituted proceedings in the Supreme Court of the Australian Capital Territory against the Commonwealth for damages for negligent misstatement. The amount of damages claimed was the difference between the retirement benefit he would have received if he had joined the fund in or about 1965 and the retirement benefit which he in fact received. The question for the court was when Cornwell's causes of action 'first accrue[d]' under s 11 of the Limitation Act (ACT). The Commonwealth argued that the claim was statute-barred because, among other things, his loss had ceased to be contingent and had accrued in 1987 when he joined the fund. It was held by the High Court that his cause of action in contract accrued upon breach, ie, upon the giving of negligent advice in 1965, therefore was statute-barred: (2007) 61 ACSR 118 at 120. However, Cornwell had suffered economic loss in tort because his retirement benefit was worth less than it would otherwise have been and this loss could only be determined by how he ceased to be employed by the Commonwealth. Therefore his cause of action accrued upon his retirement in 1994 and was not statute-barred: summary of facts provided by Australian Corporation and Securities Reports (2007) 61 ACSR 118 at 120.

6.3.8 For a further example of the running of the limitation periods in tort and contract within the one factual matrix, see *Sullavan v Teare* [2011] 1 Qd R 292.

6.3.9   Questions

1. In 1970, a testator made a will in New South Wales appointing an executor and leaving him the residue of her estate. The will was retained by the solicitors by whom it was drawn. The testator died in January 1975, but the solicitors made no attempt to locate the executor and inform him of the will until March 1981. In October 1982, the executor obtained a grant of probate. Between the testator's death and March 1981, the main asset of her estate, the house, was permitted to fall into disrepair and to lie vacant for a substantial time. Who might bring an action against the solicitors? What causes of action might be pleaded by which parties? When did the limitation period relevant to each cause of action accrue? See *Hawkins v Clayton* (1988) 164 CLR 539.

2. In June 1943, FD deposited gold bars and gems in a safe with TB Ltd for TB Ltd to hold in safe custody at the company's premises until such time as FD required them. The gold and gems disappeared sometime between 1950–53. Around April–May 1953, an employee of TB Ltd noticed that the safe previously containing the gold and gems was empty.

In 1959, FD demanded the return of the articles deposited. In January 1960, FD issued a writ against the company, claiming the return of the chattels or their value and damages for their detention and conversion. He alternatively claimed damages for breach of contract of bailment and conversion. When did the limitation period commence to run for each of the causes of action pleaded by FD? Were any of the claims statute-barred? See *Thomas Brown & Sons Ltd v Fazal Deen* (1962) 108 CLR 391.

Discoverability

6.3.10   Accrual of a cause of action may occur without reference to the knowledge of the plaintiff, for example, where the plaintiff has suffered latent injury due to the negligence of the defendant. In such cases, the Limitation Acts now generally substitute the date of discoverability as the relevant date from which the limitation period runs. McGee discusses this issue in the following extract:

6.3.11E   **A Critical Analysis of the English Law of Limitation Periods**
Andrew McGee
(1990) 9 *Civil Justice Quarterly* 366

[369] If it were possible to design a system of limitation periods from scratch, good sense would surely dictate that time should run at the earliest from the date when there is a plaintiff who can sue, a defendant who can be sued and a legally recognised wrong, all of whose constituent elements are present. The same system would conclude that the latest date at which time could legitimately start to run is when the plaintiff is actually aware of these facts. It might be said that the choice between date of accrual, date of discoverability and date of actual awareness was then one of the difficult matters of judgment which would have to be resolved in designing the system. A question arising out of this would be whether it is legitimate to have different starting dates for different types of action, and if so, on what basis such distinctions should be drawn. As a general point it is suggested that date of actual knowledge is too late a starting date from the point of view of the general principle of English law that parties are expected to be mindful of their own interest and cannot rely on ignorance which is caused by their own negligence or indolence. ... A simple rule of [370] date of accrual causes fewer uncertainties but is of course more likely to cause injustice in individual cases, and the choice between this and a discoverability rule seems to depend largely on whether justice or certainty is valued more highly.

6.3.12   The concept of discoverability is now commonly adopted by legislatures in formulating limitation periods for personal injury actions: see generally **6.6.1ff.** The reasons for this development are discussed in the following extract from the Ipp Report:

6.3.13E	**Review of the Law of Negligence: Final Report**
	Commonwealth of Australia, 2002

The date of discoverability

[6.18] The date of discoverability is the Panel's preferred option.

[6.19] The date of discoverability means the date on which the plaintiff knew, or ought to have known, that personal injury or death:

    (a)   Had occurred; and

    (b)   Was attributable to negligent conduct of the defendant; and

    (c)   In the case of personal injury, was sufficiently significant to warrant bringing proceedings. ...

[6.28] The fact that the test proposed for determining the date of discoverability is objective will make it easier to prove when the date for commencement of the limitation period occurs. The date of discoverability is not when the claimant in fact discovered the damage and that the damage was caused by the negligence of another, but rather when a reasonable person in the claimant's position should have made the discovery. Accordingly, the evidence about what individual plaintiffs knew will carry less weight, as the date of discoverability will depend on what a reasonable person in the plaintiff's position would have known, and not what the plaintiff personally knew.

6.3.14 The test for discoverability recommended by the Ipp Committee has been adopted in the following jurisdictions: NSW s 50D; Tas s 2(1); Vic s 27F. For applications, see *Baker-Morrison v State of New South Wales* (2009) 74 NSWLR 454; *Bostik Australia Pty Ltd v Liddiard* [2009] NSWCA 167; *Foster v QBE Insurance (Australia) Ltd* [2008] NSWSC 1004; *Kaye v Hoffman (No 2)* [2008] TASSC 2 (and on appeal [2009] TASSC 5); *Spandideas v Vellar* [2008] VSC 198; and *Delai v Western District Health Service* [2009] VSC 151.

6.3.15 As stated above, the test of discoverability commonly applies to latent injuries (where the plaintiff has suffered an injury but does not know that the injury has occurred, eg, asbestosis). Where the claim involves a latent injury, the date of discoverability is frequently relied upon by legislatures as a trigger for the limitation period to run. This issue is discussed in more detail in relation to personal injuries below at **6.6.7 ff**.

The operation of the discoverability test and its interaction with the extension provisions (see **6.5.1ff** and **6.7.1ff**) are discussed in the following case.

6.3.16C	**Caven v Women's and Children's Health**
	(2007) 15 VR 447; [2007] VSC 7; BC200700246
	Supreme Court of Victoria

[In December 2004, the parents of a child born in September 1997 and soon thereafter diagnosed as suffering from a congenital heart defect, Down's Syndrome and other disabilities, commenced an action claiming damages for personal injury and economic loss alleging that the hospital authority responsible for the antenatal care of the child's mother had negligently failed to advise her of foetal defects disclosed during an ultrasound conducted when she was approximately 18-weeks pregnant. In January 1998, the parents had been told by a cardiologist that the defect should have been picked up in the ultrasound, and by March 2000 (during antenatal testing in a subsequent pregnancy) they had become aware that the foetal heart defect could be an indicator of Down's Syndrome. The plaintiffs claimed that the mother had lost the opportunity for further antenatal investigation and the opportunity to terminate her pregnancy. When the defendant pleaded that the claims were barred by s 5(1)(a) and/ or s 27D of the Act, the plaintiffs applied under s 27K(1) to extend the time within which to commence the proceeding, in so far as their claim was otherwise barred. (Facts extracted from The Victorian Reports Headnote (2007) 15 VR 447).

This excerpt of the case deals with the question of when the limitation period began to run ie, when it was discoverable under s 27F of the Limitation of Actions Act 1958 (Vic). Kaye J's reasoning in relation to the application to extend the limitation period under s 27K of the Limitation of Actions Act 1958 (Vic) is extracted below at **6.7.6C.**]

Kaye J (at 453): [24] Section 27D prescribes the relevant period of limitation for a cause of action to which Pt 2A applies. Section 27D(1)(a) provides:

> (1) An action in respect of a cause of action to which this Part applies shall not be brought after the expiration of whichever of the following periods is first to expire —
> (a) the period of 3 years from the date on which the cause of action is discoverable by the plaintiff; ...

[25] Section 27F defines when a cause of action is 'discoverable'. It provides:

> (1) For the purposes of this Part, a cause of action is discoverable by a person on the first date that the person knows or ought to have known of all of the following facts —
> (a) the fact that the death or personal injury concerned has occurred;
> (b) the fact that the death or personal injury was caused by the fault of the defendant;
> (c) in the case of personal injury, the fact that the personal injury was sufficiently serious to justify the bringing of an action on the cause of action.
> (2) A person ought to know of a fact at a particular date if the fact would have been ascertained by the person had the person taken all reasonable steps before that date to ascertain the fact.

[26] Sections 27K and 27L entitle a person, claiming to have a cause of action to which Pt 2A of the Act applies, to apply to the court for an extension of the period within which the action might be brought.

[His Honour found that the claim brought by the plaintiffs might properly be described as 'a personal injury' within the meaning of s 27B(1) of the Limitation of Actions Act. The following arguments were made by the parties on the issue of discoverability and possible extension of the limitation period.]

[27] The ... propositions advanced by the plaintiffs in this application may be summarized as follows:

> ...
> (2) Those claims were not 'discoverable' by the plaintiffs, pursuant to s 27D, until they received the report of Dr Ramsey in November 2005. Accordingly the claims are not barred under s 27D(1).

...

(4)   If those claims are barred under s 27D(1)(a), the court should extend the time within which the action might be commenced pursuant to ss 27K and 27L.

[28] The ... propositions argued by the defendant may be summarised as follows:

(2)   [t]he plaintiffs' cause of action was discoverable by January 1998 (when the plaintiffs consulted the cardiologist and were told that the heart defect should have been detected on the ultrasound) or alternatively in March 2000 (when the plaintiffs consulted Dr De Crespny and understood that the detection of a heart defect on ultrasound might be a pointer to the existence of Down's Syndrome). Accordingly the claims are barred under s 27D(1).

...

(5)   The court should not extend the time within which the plaintiffs might commence their proceedings pursuant to ss 27K and 27L.

...

[464] Section 27F: When was the plaintiffs' cause of action discoverable?

[55] The next question is whether the claims of the plaintiffs in these proceedings are barred by s 27D of the Act. That question depends on whether the cause of action on which the plaintiffs rely was 'discoverable', within the meaning of that term as defined in s 27F, more than three years before the writ was issued in these proceedings in December 2004. Thus the question is whether the plaintiff knew or ought to have known each of the three prescribed facts under s 27F(1) before December 2001. It is common ground that the critical question is whether the plaintiffs, on or about that date, knew or ought to have known of the facts prescribed in s 27F(1)(b), namely that 'personal injury was caused by the fault of the defendant'. [His Honour construed the word 'fault' n s 27D to mean 'act or omission'.]

[57] Mr Noonan submitted that the plaintiffs each knew, or ought to have known, that the personal injury was caused by the 'fault' of the defendant in January 1998 or, alternatively, in March 2000. In support of that submission Mr Noonan referred to evidence which he submitted establishes that by those dates the plaintiffs knew each of the following facts:

1.   Jared was born with Down's Syndrome.
2.   Jared was born with a heart defect.
3.   In May 1997 Ms Caven had undergone an ultrasound conducted by the defendant.
4.   Ms Caven had not been told that the ultrasound demonstrated that the baby carried by her had a heart defect.
5.   [465] The heart defect which was suffered by Jared should have been disclosed by the ultrasound.
6.   There was a strong connection between a baby having a heart defect and the possibility of the baby being affected by Down's Syndrome.

[58] Based on those six facts, Mr Noonan submitted that the plaintiffs either knew or ought to have known, by January 1998, or alternatively March 2000, that, following the performance of the ultrasound in May 1997, the defendant hospital had failed to inform the plaintiffs that the baby carried by Ms Caven had a heart defect which might indicate that the baby was affected by Down's Syndrome.

[59] It is not in dispute that the first four facts, relied upon by Mr Noonan, were clearly known to the plaintiffs shortly after the birth of Jared in September 1997. The fifth fact, to which I have referred above, is based on the evidence of the plaintiffs. ...

[61] ... I accept that the plaintiffs were informed by a cardiologist, in January 1998, that Jared's heart defect which had then been diagnosed should have been disclosed on the ultrasound of May 1997.

[62] Mr Noonan submitted that the plaintiffs' knowledge of the sixth fact, which I set out above, was based on two pieces of evidence given by each plaintiff.
[The two pieces of evidence presented by the defendant were firstly, a book on Down's Syndrome that Ms Caven and Mr Huysing agreed they had read and secondly, evidence that Ms Caven and Mr Huysing agreed that they understood that if an ultrasound identified a defect in the baby's heart there was a possibility that the child may be affected by Down's Syndrome.]

[64] Mr Noonan submitted that, based on those six facts, it was 'inevitable', and I should find, that the plaintiffs realised, by at least March 2000 that the defendant had failed to advise them that the ultrasound of March 1997 demonstrated the evidence of a heart defect in the foetus which was an indicator that the baby might be affected by Down's Syndrome. He submitted that both plaintiffs are intelligent people who were well alert to the nature of Jared's problems after he was born. He therefore submitted that I should conclude that both plaintiffs had become aware, at least by 2000, of the fact that after the ultrasound the defendant had failed to disclose to the plaintiffs that Jared had a heart defect which, if disclosed to the plaintiffs in May 1997, would have indicated the possibility that the baby might suffer from Down's Syndrome.

[65] In their evidence, both plaintiffs swore that until their solicitor, Mr Henderson, told them of the report of Dr Phillipa Ramsey, they did not know whether the cardiac views of Jared on the ultrasound conducted in May 1997 should have alerted the radiographer to the potential that the baby suffered from Down's Syndrome. In other words both plaintiffs swore that they did not draw the inference which Mr Noonan has submitted inevitably must have been drawn by them, based on all the facts with which they were seized. Both plaintiffs were skilfully and thoroughly cross-examined by Mr Noonan. I closely observed both of them under cross-examination. ... I consider that both plaintiffs were candid and reliable witnesses. I do not accept that they have untruthfully denied knowing that the cardiac views of the ultrasound should have alerted the radiographer, in May 1997, to the potential that the baby had Down's Syndrome. Indeed, it would seem to me that if that circumstance had dawned on the plaintiffs during those years, it is most unlikely that they would have done nothing about it. Neither plaintiff struck me as being an entirely passive person. Ms Caven, despite her heavy load at home, has returned to the work force, involved herself in part-time study, and continued her duties as a Sergeant in the Army Reserve. I consider it most unlikely that she, or her husband, would have simply remained inactive had either of them realised that the defendant had failed to advise them of a critical fact which might have alerted them to the fact that the baby carried by Ms Caven in May 1997 might be affected by Down's Syndrome.

[66] There is of course a fundamental difference between facts which the plaintiff might have known, and facts which they might have simply suspected. Furthermore, there is an important and substantial difference between, on the one hand, knowing a fact in question, and, on the other hand, being seized of certain other facts which are capable of leading to an inference

or suspicion as to the existence of the fact in question. In other words it is one thing for the plaintiffs to have had in their possession and known of the six facts relied upon by Mr Noonan. It is another matter for them to have subjectively drawn the inference on which Mr Noonan relies, namely, that the ultrasound in May 1997 should have disclosed to the plaintiffs a heart defect which was commonly associated with Down's Syndrome. In hindsight the drawing of such an inference might be logical and even obvious. However that does not mean that the plaintiffs themselves did, in the circumstances in which they found themselves, subjectively draw that inference or, to adopt the phrase used in the course of argument, 'join the dots'.

[67] Accordingly I reject the proposition advanced on behalf of the defendant that by January 1998 or March 2000 the plaintiffs knew that the continued pregnancy of Ms Caven, which resulted in the birth of Jared, was 'caused by the fault of the defendant'.

[68] The question which then arises is whether, before December 2001, the plaintiffs ought to have known that the personal injury of which they complain was caused by the 'fault' of the defendant. As I have stated, the personal injury relied on by the plaintiffs is the continued pregnancy of Ms Caven, which she lost the opportunity to terminate after the ultra-sound in 1997. The question is whether, before December 2001, the plaintiffs ought to have known that the cardiac views of the ultrasound should have alerted the radiographer to the possibility that the baby might suffer from Down's Syndrome. In turn, s 27F(2) raises the question whether that fact would have been ascertained by the plaintiffs had they taken all reasonable steps before December 2001 to ascertain it.

[69] The answer to this question is not easy. It involves an exercise obscured by the wisdom of hindsight. It requires me, as a judge, to postulate what reasonable steps ought to have been taken by the plaintiffs in the circumstances in which they found themselves, and what they might have learnt, had they taken such reasonable steps.

... [71] The question is, then, given the information in the possession of the plaintiffs in January 1998 or alternatively March 2000, should they have then consulted a solicitor, as a consequence of which they would have, ultimately, gained the knowledge which is contained in the report of Dr Ramsey. In my view it would be setting too high a standard of reasonableness to have expected the plaintiffs to have made inquiries of the solicitor when the cardiologist first spoke to them in January 1998. At that time they were under considerable pressure. Jared was gravely ill. They were adjusting to their lives with a seriously ill young baby with Down's Syndrome. In my view they did not, at that time, fail to take the reasonable steps postulated by Mr Noonan, namely, to instruct a solicitor to inquire whether the hospital had failed to inform them that the ultrasound disclosed a cardiac defect which might have alerted them to the potential for the baby to have Down's Syndrome.

[72] However, the position did change somewhat by March 2000. By then, although Jared's health was still poor, they were not confronted with the immediate and pressing health crises of Jared's earlier days. Further, in March 2000, their knowledge as to the link between heart defects and Down's Syndrome, which they had gained from a book, was reinforced by what they learnt when consulting Dr De Crespny. By then they knew that if the ultrasound of the next baby indicated a heart defect, that was a potential indication that that baby was affected with Down's Syndrome. By then they knew each of the six facts on which Mr Noonan has relied. In particular they knew that Jared had a heart defect, that he had Down's Syndrome, and that they had not been informed that the ultrasound performed in 1997 had disclosed either such

matter. They also knew, from what they were told by the radiologist in January 1998, that the heart defect should have been disclosed by the ultrasound. Finally, their knowledge as to the potential link between the detection of a heart defect, and the detection of Down's Syndrome, had been reinforced. In those circumstances, and even allowing for judicial wisdom of hindsight, it would seem to me that ordinary reasonable parents would have been particularly curious as to why, after the ultrasound, they had not been informed that Jared might have a heart defect, which might be a pointer to the existence of the Down's Syndrome. In my view it would not be unreasonable to have expected persons in the position of the plaintiffs to have consulted a solicitor, at least with a view to making inquiries as to whether the ultrasound did in fact disclose a heart defect, and if so whether that heart defect might have been a pointer to the baby then carried by Ms Caven being affected with Down's Syndrome. If the plaintiffs had made such inquiries, then it is probable that a prudent solicitor would have done just what Mr Henderson did, namely, consult an appropriately qualified obstetric radiologist.

[73] Dr Ramsey, when consulted, advised that the cardiac view should have alerted the radiographer to the potential for Down's Syndrome because 50% of Down's Syndrome foetuses have some sort of heart defect. Dr Ramsey does not state that that knowledge only lay within the expertise of any particular narrow specialty. In those circumstances I consider it appropriate to infer that, if the plaintiffs had consulted a solicitor in 2000, then the solicitor would have received the type of advice obtained by Mr Henderson, which would have informed the plaintiffs of the fact that the defendant had failed to inform the plaintiffs that the ultrasound conducted in May 1997 showed a heart defect which was commonly associated with Down's Syndrome. Thus I conclude that at some time after March 2000 the plaintiffs ought to have known that the personal injury which is the basis of their action (the continued pregnancy of Ms Caven) was caused by the fault of the defendant under s 27F(1)(b) of the Act.

[74] It thus becomes necessary to determine, for the purposes of s 27D, when it was that those facts ought to have been ascertained by the plaintiffs. The answer to that question lies in determining when information of the type contained in Dr Ramsey's report would have been available to the plaintiffs, had they consulted a solicitor shortly after March 2000.

[75] The affidavits of Ms Caven and of the plaintiffs' solicitor, Mr Henderson, set out the events which occurred after the plaintiffs first consulted the solicitors in April 2004. In the upshot it was not until 29 November 2005 that the solicitors received Dr Ramsey's report. ... In the absence of any other evidence, on the balance of probabilities I would infer that such a delay [between consultation with solicitors and the receipt of an appropriate expert's report] would have been in the order of some 12 months or so. It therefore follows that if, shortly after March 2000, the plaintiffs had consulted solicitors, then they would have ascertained the relevant facts set out in s 27F by approximately April 2001. In the terms of s 27D, it was then that the cause of action relied on by the plaintiffs was 'discoverable'. The writ in this proceeding was not issued until December 2004. I therefore conclude that the proceedings have commenced more than three years after the expiration from the date on which the cause of action of the plaintiffs was discoverable by them.

[Kaye J then proceeded to determine whether he should grant the plaintiffs' application to extend the limitation period pursuant to ss 27K and 27L of the Act. His Honour found that in all the circumstances it was just and reasonable to extend the time under ss 27K and 27L within which the proceeding might be commenced. This aspect of the judgment is extracted at **6.7.6C**].

6.3.17   For an analysis of the operation of discoverability in s 50D (NSW) (ie, the New South Wales equivalent to s 27F(Vic) discussed in *Caven* above), see *Baker-Morrison v State of New South Wales* (2009) 74 NSWLR 454 and *Bostik Australia Pty Ltd v Liddiard* [2009] NSWCA 167.

6.3.18   The Western Australian Limitation Act 2005 (extracted below) has created an accrual provision for personal injuries which has elements of discoverability.

6.3.19E   **Limitation Act 2005 (WA)**

Personal injury — general
55 (1) A cause of action for damages relating to a personal injury to a person accrues when the only or earlier of such of the following events as are applicable occurs —
  (a) the person becomes aware that he or she has sustained a not insignificant personal injury;
  (b) the first symptom, clinical sign or other manifestation of personal injury consistent with the person having sustained a not insignificant personal injury.
  (2) This section does not apply to a personal injury that is attributable to the inhalation of asbestos.

6.3.20   In relation to the proviso in WA s 55(2) above, note that s 56 of the same Act applies to asbestos-related diseases.

6.3.21   Further reading

P Handford, 'A New Limitation Act for the 21st Century' (2007) 33 *UWAL Rev* 387.

Postponement

6.3.22   The limitation periods stipulated by the Limitation Acts may be suspended or postponed in particular circumstances. Postponement or suspension of the limitation period may arise where there has been:

• fraud, deceit, concealment or mistake: ACT ss 33–34; NSW ss 55–56; NT ss 42–43; Qld s 38; SA s 25; Tas s 32; Vic s 27;

• an acknowledgment or part-payment by the defendant: ACT s 32; NSW s 54; NT s 41; Qld ss 35–37; Tas ss 29–31; Vic ss 24–26; WA ss 47–51; or

• where the plaintiff is under a disability: ACT s 30; NSW s 52–53; NT s 36-40; WA ss 35–36 (mental disability).

  For a discussion of disability, see **6.3.25** below. Note also that the limitation period may be extended, rather than suspended, in Western Australia where there has been a fraud or mistake: s 38.

6.3.23 The High Court in *Hawkins v Clayton* (1988) 164 CLR 539 held that where the wrongful conduct of the defendant has the effect of preventing the institution of proceedings against the defendant, the commencement of the limitation period is suspended for as long as that prevention continues. Deane J noted that equity could intervene to grant relief due to unconscionable reliance upon the provisions of a Statute of Limitation where the cause of action had been concealed until after the limitation period had expired. See also *Hutchinson v Equititour Pty Ltd* [2011] 2 Qd R 99.

6.3.24 For a discussion of acknowledgment by the defendant, see *Alcock v Casey* [2007] ACTSC 87 and, on appeal, *Casey v Alcock* [2009] ACTCA 1.

Disability

6.3.25 In some cases, plaintiffs will be under a disability which prevents them from taking prompt action. Generally speaking, the plaintiff is under a disability if he or she is under 18 years of age or suffering from a mental disability. In some jurisdictions the term 'unsound mind' is used to describe mental disability. See generally: ACT s 2, Dictionary; NSW s 11(3); NT s 4(1); Qld s 5(2); SA s 45(2); Tas s 2(2); Vic s 3(2); WA ss 3(1), 30–33.

However, each jurisdiction defines disability in a slightly different way. Some jurisdictions include physical disability (ACT s 2, Dictionary; NSW s 11(3)(b); NT s 4(1)), detention in custody (NSW s 11(3)(b)), undergoing a term of imprisonment (Qld s 5(2)) and involvement in war or war-like activities: ACT s 2, Dictionary; NSW s 11(3)(b).

A plaintiff is under a mental disability or of unsound mind when they are incapable of managing their affairs, as explained in the following extract.

6.3.26C   **Kirby v Leather**
                               [1965] 2 QB 367
                 High Court of England, Queens Bench Division

[On 15 May 1959, the plaintiff was involved in a motor vehicle accident when his motor scooter collided with a van. He suffered serious injuries, including brain damage. He was unconscious for several weeks after the accident, but eventually regained consciousness. He had no recollection of the accident and needed constant care, which was rendered by his mother. On 2 October 1963, a writ was issued claiming damages against the driver of the van.]

Lord Denning MR (at 382): Under the Statutes of Limitation an action for personal injuries 'shall not be brought after the expiration of three years from the date on which the *cause* of action accrued': see section 2(1) of the Limitation Act, 1939 ... In calculating the three years, you exclude the day of the accident itself: see *Marren v Dawson, Bentley & Co Ltd* [1961] 2 QB 135. The accident here took place on May 15, 1959. The cause of action accrued on that date. The three years started at midnight on May 15–16, 1959, and ran up to midnight on May 15–16, 1962, and then expired.

There is an extension of time when a person is under a disability: 'If on the date when any right of action accrued ... the person to whom it accrued was under a disability, the action may be brought at any time before the expiration of three years from the date when the person *ceased* to be under a disability': see section 22 ... A person is deemed to be under a disability 'while he is an infant or of unsound mind': see section 31(2) of the Act ... In this particular case, the right of action accrued at 8.50 pm on May 15, 1959. If on that date David Kirby was under [333] a disability, the period of three years would not begin to run until he had ceased to be under a disability. 'On the date' means, I think, at any time before the end of the day, because the law takes no account of fractions of a day. So if David Kirby was rendered of unsound mind at 8.50 pm on May 15, 1959, owing to the accident, the three years would not begin to run against him until he recovered his soundness of mind ...

So the question comes down to this. Was David Kirby, at and after 8.50 pm on May 15, 1959, of unsound mind? ... [I]t seems to me in this statute a person is 'of unsound mind' when he is, by reason of mental illness, ... So here it seems to me that David Kirby was of unsound mind if he was, by reason of mental illness, incapable of managing his affairs in relation to this accident ...

[The medical evidence established that] after David Kirby recovered consciousness, he was badly affected mentally, his behaviour being extremely abnormal. After a time he was to some extent able to appreciate (from being told by others) something of what had happened to him .... But he could not concentrate on it for any length of time: not long enough to be able to appreciate the nature and extent of any claim that he might have. In particular he had no insight at all into his own mental state. He was not capable of instructing a solicitor properly. He certainly was not capable of exercising any reasonable judgment upon a possible settlement. [The trial judge at first instance] came to the conclusion, following [the medical] evidence, that David Kirby had been of unsound mind and under a disability from the moment of this accident onwards. I think that there was ample evidence on which the judge was entitled so to hold. Accordingly the action is not statute-barred.

6.3.27 The interpretation of 'unsound mind' pursuant to Qld ss 5(2) and 29 was considered by Macrossan J in *King v Coupland* [1981] Qd R 121 at 123. His Honour commented that Lord Denning's judgment in the extract above was referring to 'relevant aspects of unsoundness' such as the capacity to instruct a solicitor properly, capacity to exercise reasonable judgment upon a possible settlement and capacity to appreciate the nature and extent of any available claim. Macrossan J found that these matters were 'aspects of a broader concept of a mental illness causing an incapacity to manage affairs in relation to the accident that is to manage them in the manner that a reasonable man would achieve'. His Honour stated that medical witnesses should provide an opinion about the plaintiff's disability and base this opinion upon the abovementioned guidelines.

6.3.28 In *State of New South Wales v Harlum* [2007] NSWCA 120 the New South Wales Court of Appeal identified the court's task as the determination of whether the person claiming to be under the relevant disability was able to reason normally about the matters relevant to a potential cause of action, to understand and consider advice, and to give instructions about any action. The judgment in *Harlum* was discussed by Master Harper in *Brown v Haureliuk* [2011] ACTSC 9 at [36] as follows:

It was a fundamental aspect of bringing a claim that it required the exercise of willpower to initiate the claim and continue with it. The trial judge had accepted psychiatric evidence that the ordeal the plaintiff had been through constituting his cause of action, had caused a severe adjustment disorder with depression and chronic post-traumatic stress disorder. The trial judge accepted that the plaintiff was disabled as defined by the legislation, that the impairment arose from his mental condition, and that it substantially impeded him in the management of his affairs in relation to his cause of action. He accepted as a matter of probability that the plaintiff was unable, during the period in question, to make a rational judgment or exercise the will to seek advice to address the wrong that had been done to him. The trial judge accordingly declared that the plaintiff had been disabled for the purposes of the legislation and that the proceedings he had instituted some nine years after the event had been brought within time. Beazley JA found no error in the approach of the trial judge. A disability for the purposes of the section could arise during the course of the limitation period and did not need to exist at its commencement. It was not necessary that the applicant be under a disability for the whole of the limitation period.

6.3.29   In some cases there may be several grounds of disability. For example, in *State of Queensland v RAF* [2010] QCA 332 the respondent, a 48-year-old woman, commenced proceedings in 2007 for damages against the State of Queensland for personal injury consequent upon the sexual abuse that she had suffered at the hands of her stepfather. The abuse commenced when she was aged 10 years. She alleged that the abuse had come to the notice of the relevant government department but no proper action was taken to protect her and the abuse continued for many years thereafter. The appellant relied on the expiry of the limitation period to preclude her pursuing her action and the respondent sought a declaration pursuant to Qld s 29 that she was under a relevant disability, ie, that she was a minor and suffered from an unsound mind due to post-traumatic stress disorder and hence the limitation period did not run against her. The declaration was granted at first instance and was upheld by the Queensland Court of Appeal, applying Macrossan J's test in *King v Coupland* [1981] Qd R 121 at 123, which is set out at **6.3.27** above.

6.3.30   Notes

1. In *State of Queensland v RAF* [2010] QCA 332, the respondent also made an application to extend the limitation period under s 31 (Qld). See the discussion of this provision at **6.7.8ff**.

2. For a discussion of the questions raised by limitation defences in cases involving allegations of sexual abuse of children, see **6.5.5, n 4**.

6.3.31   The effect of the plaintiff's disability is to either prevent the running of the limitation period — thereby effecting an extension of the limitation period from the date that a person ceases to be under a disability — (Qld s 29; SA s 45(1); Tas s 26(1); Vic s 23(1); WA s 42) or to suspend the running of the limitation period (ACT s 30; NSW s 52; NT s 36; WA ss 35–36) for the duration of the disability. For example, where the plaintiff is a minor, the limitation period will only begin to run upon him or her attaining majority, which is now 18 years of age.

6.3.32E   **Limitation Act 1981 (NT)**

4 Interpretation

In this Act, unless the contrary intention appears — ...

disabled person means a person who by reason of age, disease, illness or mental or physical infirmity, is incapable of managing his affairs in respect of legal proceedings;

...

36 Time not to run where person under disability

(1) Subject to this Division, where —
   (a) a person has a cause of action;
   (b) the limitation period fixed by this Act for the cause of action has commenced to run; and
   (c) the person is under a disability, in that case —
   (d) the running of the limitation period is suspended for the duration of the disability; and
   (e) if, but for this paragraph, the limitation period would expire before the lapse of 3 years after —
      (i) the date on which he has, before the expiration of the limitation period, ceased to be under a disability; or
      (ii) the date of his death, whichever is the earlier, the limitation period is extended so as to expire 3 years after the earlier of those dates.
   ...
(4) This section does not operate so as to extend a limitation period to more than 30 years from the date when the cause of action arose.

6.3.33   Where the disability prevents the limitation period from starting to run, its effect is to give the plaintiff the full limitation period after the disability ceases in which to bring an action. In each Australian jurisdiction where a suspension occurs, there is procedure which extends the time period for the duration of the disability. Legislation in the Australian Capital Territory (s 31), New South Wales (s 53), the Northern Territory (s 38) and Tasmania (s 27) provides a procedure under which a putative defendant may give notice to proceed to the plaintiff's guardian.

6.3.34   For an analysis of disability under the New South Wales Act and the effect of disability on the running of the limitation period in New South Wales, see *Guthrie v Spence* [2009] NSWCA 369 at [109]–[182] per Campbell JA and *State Rail Authority of New South Wales v Hammond* (1988) 15 NSWLR 395.

6.3.35   For personal injury actions in New South Wales and Victoria, the legislation provides that a minor is only under a disability for the purposes of suspending or preventing the running of time if they do not have a capable parent or guardian: NSW s 50F(2); Vic s 27J(1). In Tasmania, where the victim was a minor not in the custody of a parent at the time of accrual, the limitation period is suspended until the end of the period of legal incapacity: Tas s 26(6). See generally 6.6.1 and 6.6.4.

6.3.36 Notes and questions

1. In jurisdictions where a disability prevents the limitation period from starting to run, what happens when the plaintiff suffers from a mental disability caused by the defendant's negligence, but never recovers sufficiently for the disability to cease? Is it possible in this circumstance that there is no limitation period? Can the court impose one? See *Williams v Zupps Motors Pty Ltd* [1990] 2 Qd R 493 and *Batistatos v Roads and Traffic Authority of NSW* (2006) 226 CLR 256; (2006) 227 ALR 425; extracted at 12.7.9C.

2. For a general discussion of the running of time involving multiple causes of action and disability, see the judgment of McLure J of the Supreme Court of Western Australia in *Australia and New Zealand Banking Group Ltd v Dzienciol* [2001] WASCA 305.

6.3.37 Further reading

M A Jones, 'Limitation Periods and Plaintiffs under a Disability — A Zealous Protection?' (1995) 14 *Civil Justice Quarterly* 258.

B Mathews, 'Limitation Periods and Child Sexual Abuse Cases: Law, Psychology, Time and Justice' (2003) 11 *Torts Law Journal* 218.

THE EFFECT OF EXPIRY OF THE LIMITATION PERIOD

6.4.1   Where the limitation period has expired the general rule is that the right remains in existence, but may no longer be enforced. In other words, the remedy is barred, but not the right. So the underlying right may be enforced by means other than court procedures, for example, where the defendant voluntarily repays a statute-barred debt.

Despite the general rule, the right may still be enforced in court where the defendant waives his or her right to plead the relevant Limitation Act, for example where they take a step in the action.

In certain instances however, the running of the limitation period extinguishes the right in question and not just the remedy. For example, the running of the limitation period for an action to recover land extinguishes the title of the landowner in all jurisdictions except the Australian Capital Territory and the Northern Territory: NSW s 65; Qld s 24; SA s 28; Tas s 21; Vic s 18; WA s 75. The Western Australian Act, however, contemplates that the limitation period may be extended and the extinguishment operates after expiry of an extended period: WA s 74. Some jurisdictions also extinguish the title of a chattel owner by expiration of the period within which an action must be brought to recover goods: ACT s 43(1); NSW s 65(1); NT s 19(2); Qld s 12(2); Tas s 6(2); Vic s 6(2).

However, the Limitation Act 1969 (NSW) is exceptional in that the right and title of a person having an action for debt, damages or account is extinguished by the running of the period: ss 63, 64.

Where the plaintiff is suing on a statutory cause of action, it is a matter of statutory construction whether a limitation provision extinguishes the cause of action or merely bars the remedy. It was held by French J, as he then was, in *Carey-Hazell v Getz Bros & Co (Aust) Pty Ltd* (2001) 112 FCR 336; BC200103004 that the limitation provisions under the Trade Practices Act 1974 (Cth) barred the plaintiff's remedy rather than her cause of action under ss 74J, 75AO of the Trade Practices Act 1974 (Cth) for an allegedly defective heart valve device. Therefore proceedings commenced by her out of time were not an abuse of process on that ground alone. The Trade Practices Act 1974 (Cth) has now been superceded by the Competition and Consumer Act 2010 (Cth) and the Australian Consumer Law. See 6.1.5.

In the following extract, McGee explores the distinction between extinguishment of the right and barring of the remedy.

Barring the remedy or right?

6.4.2E   **A Critical Analysis of the English Law of Limitations Periods**
Andrew McGee
(1990) 9 *Civil Justice Quarterly* 366
(footnotes omitted)

[373] ... The effect of the expiry of time is by no means uniform. This is so for two reasons. The first is that there is a distinction between those cases where the expiry of time extinguishes the plaintiff's right and those where it merely bars his remedy. The second is that in a few cases there is the possibility of an extension of time being granted by the Court. The distinction between the extinguishing of the right and the barring of the remedy is a difficult one. It is first necessary to explain what the distinction means. In cases where the plaintiff's right is extinguished the effect is that he loses title to any property to which he may wish to assert a claim; thus, any extra-legal action taken by him to reclaim the property is likely to be unlawful, and any judicial process instituted by him to secure the return of the property is doomed to failure, since he has no title to the property and therefore cannot possibly have better title than the person in possession of it. By contrast, where the remedy is merely barred, there is no general prohibition on taking extra-legal action to secure the plaintiff's rights (provided of course that such action is not in its self unlawful) and judicial process is not doomed to failure. This follows from the principle that in cases where the remedy is barred the court will not of its own motion raise the question of the Limitation Act, and it is for the defendant to plead the Act specifically.

6.4.3   As stated by McGee and discussed in more detail at 6.5.1ff, a person with a statute-barred right to bring an action may apply in certain circumstances to the court to seek an extension of time to bring the action. The question therefore arises as to the nature of the right held by the potential plaintiff after the expiration of the limitation period, but before the limitation period is extended by the courts. A further question arises as to the status of the right or remedy where the defendant does not plead the Statute of Limitations, or waives the right to do so: *Verwayen v Commonwealth of Australia* (1990) 170 CLR 394.

6.4.4   Handford argues that in Australia the effect of the limitation period having run is to bar the remedy rather than the right (see for example *WorkCover Queensland v Amaca Pty Ltd*

(2010) 241 CLR 420; (2010) 271 ALR 203 at [31]), except in New South Wales where, as stated above, the operation of ss 63 and 64 result in the cause of action being extinguished on expiration of the period: P Handford, *Limitation of Actions — The Laws of Australia*, 3rd ed, Thomson Reuters, 2011, [5.10.510].

6.4.5   The question of what interest is held by the plaintiff in a stature-barred cause of action is explored in the following cases: *Georgiadis v Australian and Overseas Telecommunications Corp* (1994) 179 CLR 297; 119 ALR 629; *Commonwealth of Australia v Mewett* (1995) 59 FCR 391; *Commonwealth of Australia v Mewett* (1997) 191 CLR 471; 146 ALR 299. For most causes of action where the remedy is barred but not the right, the claim is capable of being regarded as sufficiently proprietary in character to be counted among the 'innominate and anomalous interests' that may be protected under s 51(xxxi) of the Constitution: see *Bank of NSW v The Commonwealth* (1948) 76 CLR 1 at 349 per Dixon J.

6.4.6   In *Commonwealth of Australia v Mewett* (1997) 191 CLR 471, two different approaches to the analysis of whether a statute-barred cause of action can constitute 'property' for the purposes of s 51(xxxi) of the Commonwealth Constitution were adopted. Dawson, Toohey and Gaudron JJ relied upon the construction of the relevant Limitation Acts. In a joint judgment, Gummow and Kirby JJ decided the question in more global terms: see the extract below.

6.4.7C   **Commonwealth of Australia v Mewett**
                              (1997) 191 CLR 471; 146 ALR 299
                              High Court of Australia

Gummow and Kirby JJ (at 337): [I]n our view, a cause of action of this nature upon which there has operated a bar of the kind imposed by a statute of limitations in the traditional form still has sufficient substance to answer the constitutional description of 'property' in s 51(xxxi) of the Constitution.

This follows from a consideration of the rights and liabilities of the parties in that situation. First, a statutory bar, at least in the case of a statute of limitations in the traditional form, does not go to the jurisdiction of the court to entertain the claim but to the remedy available and hence to the defences which may be pleaded. The cause of action has not been extinguished. Absent an appropriate plea, the matter of the statutory bar does not arise for the consideration of the court (*The Commonwealth v Verwayen* (1990) 170 CLR 394 at 473–474). This is so at least where the limitation period is not annexed by statute to a right which it creates so as to be of the essence of that right (*Australian Iron & Steel Ltd v Hoogland* (1962) 108 CLR 471 at 488–489; *Pedersen v Young* (1964) 110 CLR 162 at 169; *The Commonwealth v Verwayen* (1990) 170 CLR 394 at 497–498; *McKain v R W Miller & Co (SA) Pty Ltd* (1991) 174 CLR 1 at 43). Secondly, in the circumstances the defendant may be estopped from pleading the statutory bar or otherwise be deemed to have waived the right to do so (see *The Commonwealth v Verwayen* (1990) 170 CLR 394 at 482–486; *Roebuck v Mungovin* [1994] 2 AC 224 at 234–236).

The constitutional guarantee operates in respect of a 'species of valuable right and interest' (*Minister of State for the Army v Dalziel* (1944) 68 CLR 261 at 290). Despite the existence of the statutory bar, the subsistence of the cause of action, particularly one for a liquidated sum, means that it still may be turned by the plaintiff to valuable account. A creditor may exercise rights in relation to a time-barred debt in a number of ways which do not require recourse to the courts. Where a debtor makes a payment to the creditor without directing that it be paid in reduction of a particular debt, the right of appropriation which thereby devolves upon the creditor may be exercised by application to payment of the time-barred debt rather than to another debt which is still enforceable (*Mills v Fowkes* (1839) 5 Bing (NC) 455). A possessory lien may be exercised in respect of a statute-barred debt (*Higgins v Scott* (1831) 2 B & Ad 413). Further, where the debtor approaches the court for equitable relief in aid of other rights against the creditor, the debtor will be required to do equity. Thus, a mortgagor seeking equitable relief in a redemption action is obliged to do equity by paying [338] to the mortgagee all arrears of interest from the date of the mortgage, not merely that interest due and owing for less than six years (*Dingle v Coppen; Coppen v Dingle* [1899] 1 Ch 726 at 746; *In re Lloyd; Lloyd v Lloyd* [1903] 1 Ch 385 at 402).

These latter considerations may not bear upon the facts of the particular case, being but illustrations of the proposition that the existence of direct curial remedy is not coextensive with the juridical existence of the right. However, as we have indicated, it is the subsistence of the latter which suffices to engage the constitutional guarantee.

6.4.8   In relation to the broader issues raised in *Mewett* about the juridical nature of a claim or a cause of action, the High Court has recently held that a company's claim for restitution was capable of assignment to a third party: see *Equuscorp Pty Ltd v Haxton* [2012] HCA 7.

EXTENSION OF THE LIMITATION PERIOD

6.5.1   The limitation statutes of all Australian jurisdictions contain provisions that allow the potential plaintiff to seek an extension of time to bring proceedings where the limitation period has expired. Generally speaking, extensions may be sought for the following claims: personal injury; wrongful death; property damage and economic loss; admiralty actions; and arbitrations. The majority of applications for extension made under the Limitation Acts are actions for damages for personal injury. These applications are discussed separately at **6.7.1ff**.

In the Northern Territory and South Australia, the court's discretion to extend limitation periods applies to all kinds of civil proceedings: NT s 44; SA s 48. The court must be satisfied that the plaintiff's failure to institute proceedings was because facts material to the plaintiff's case had not been ascertained or was due to representations or conduct of the defendant. The South Australian Act was amended in 2004 to provide guidance on the question of materiality of facts and criteria for the judicial discretion to extend. Section 48(3a) states that a fact is material if it forms an essential element of the plaintiff's cause of action or it would have major significance on an assessment of the plaintiff's loss. Section 48(3b) states that the court should have regard to the following criteria in deciding whether to grant the extension:

(a)   the period of extension sought and, in particular, whether the passage of time has prejudiced a fair trial; and

(b)   the desirability of bringing litigation to an end within a reasonable period and thus promoting a more certain basis for the calculation of insurance premiums; and

(c)   the nature and extent of the plaintiff's loss and the conduct of the parties generally; and

(d)   any other relevant factor.

See *Salvation Army (South Australia Property Trust) v Rundle* [2008] NSWCA 347; BC200810947; *Trevorrow v South Australia (No 5)* (2007) 98 SASR 136; *Pomeroy v Thwaites Witham Pty Ltd* (2001) 79 SASR 489.

In the Australian Capital Territory, the court has the discretion under s 40 to extend the limitation period where the plaintiff alleges loss through latent damage to property or economic loss. However, the discretion is subject to a 15-year ultimate limitation period: s 40(1).

The extension provisions in the limitation statutes apply where no proceedings have been commenced within the limitation period so that a person's claim is statute-barred. Where proceedings have been commenced, several applications may be made under the relevant rules:

(a)   The plaintiff may seek to amend the originating process to insert a fresh cause of action against the defendant which is now statute-barred: see **5.2.14–5.2.19**.

(b)   Where the plaintiff has proceeded against a defendant (D1) he or she may seek to add or substitute another defendant (D2), where the claims against D2 are statute-barred: see **5.2.20–5.2.21**.

(c)   Where the plaintiff has issued an originating process which he or she has failed to serve during its currency and the claim against the defendant is now statute-barred, the court may exercise its discretion for or against renewal of the originating process: see **7.7.8ff**.

6.5.2   The following extracts examine the nature of the competing interests of the parties where the plaintiff seeks to extend the time limit after it has expired. Morgan in his article entitled 'Limitation and Discretion' (extracted below), and McHugh J in *Brisbane v Taylor* (1996) 186 CLR 541; 139 ALR 1 (see below at **6.5.4C**) discuss the policy issues that underpin the discretion to extend the limitation period. McHugh J also considers how the burden of proof operates when an extension is sought.

6.5.3E   Limitation and Discretion Procedural Reform and Substantive Effect
Derek Morgan
(1982) 1 *Civil Justice Quarterly* 109

---

[120] The effect of the court acceding to the plaintiff's request to override the time limit, and its only effect, is to deprive the defendant of what would otherwise be a complete defence to the action, viz that the writ was issued too late. A [finding for the plaintiff] must therefore always be highly prejudicial to the defendant. A defendant is put to the expense of time and money in establishing a defence on the merits of the case ... When the Court upholds the time bar, the defendant gains, at worst, freedom from establishing a good defence, at best a windfall (if there is no substantive defence to liability).

As to the effects on the plaintiff, the matter is somewhat more complicated:

The degree to which the plaintiff would be prejudiced by being prevented from proceeding with his action will be affected by how good or bad would have been his prospects of success; so too it will be affected by the extent to which the plaintiff will be able to recover in an action for negligence against his own solicitor the value of his lost prospects of success [*Thompson v Brown* [1981] 2 All ER 296 at 301] ...

In addition two other considerations have much wider implications for striking the equitable difference between the plaintiff's and the defendant's interests.

Firstly, if the plaintiff's application for extension of time is refused, suing solicitors may not be easy. Not only is the plaintiff put to proof of the particulars of negligence, but insofar as the plaintiff wishes to recover in damages from the solicitor the quantum of a successful claim against the defendant, the plaintiff must surely prove that had the original case gone to judgement, liability on the defendant would have been established. ...

Secondly, when suing solicitors for negligence, the question inevitably arises, 'what would the reasonable solicitor have done?'

6.5.4C	**Brisbane South Regional Health Authority v Taylor** (1996) 186 CLR 541; 139 ALR 1 High Court of Australia (footnotes omitted)

McHugh J (at 7): The issue in the case is a simple one. It is whether the Court of Appeal erred in setting aside the exercise of the discretion which s 31 of the Limitation of Actions Act 1974 (Qld) ('the Act') invested in the District Court judge. But lurking behind this question is another, a question that made this case one for the grant of special leave to appeal. It is whether an applicant who has adduced evidence to establish that she had a right of action against the defendant and that a material fact of a decisive character relating to that right was not within her means of knowledge during the period specified in s 31 of the Act is entitled 'to an extension of time unless there is some matter justifying the exercise of a discretion against the granting of an extension.' In the Court of Appeal, Davies JA and Ambrose J held that the scheme of s 31 indicated that it did. Fitzgerald P agreed with this judgment although he added some observations of his own.

With great respect to their Honours, s 31 should not be read as giving an applicant a presumptive right to an order once he or she satisfies the two conditions laid down in s 31(2) of the Act. An applicant for an extension of time who satisfies those conditions is entitled to ask the court to exercise its discretion in his or her favour. But the applicant still bears the onus of showing that the justice of the case requires the exercise of the discretion in his or her favour.

[8] The discretion to extend time must be exercised in the context of the rationales for the existence of limitation periods. For nearly 400 years, the policy of the law has been to fix definite time limits (usually six but often three years) for prosecuting civil claims. The enactment of time limitations has been driven by the general perception that '[w]here there is delay the whole quality of justice deteriorates'.

Sometimes the deterioration in quality is palpable, as in the case where a crucial witness is dead or an important document has been destroyed. But sometimes, perhaps more often than we realise, the deterioration in quality is not recognisable even by the parties. Prejudice may exist without the parties or anybody else realising that it exists. As the United States Supreme Court pointed out in *Barker v Wingo* (1972) 407 US 514 at 532, 'what has been forgotten can rarely be shown.' So, it must often happen that important, perhaps decisive, evidence has disappeared without anybody now 'knowing' that it ever existed. Similarly, it must often happen that time will diminish the significance of a known fact or circumstance because its relationship to the cause of action is no longer as apparent as it was when the cause of action arose. A verdict may appear well based on the evidence given in the proceedings, but, if the tribunal of fact had all the evidence concerning the matter, an opposite result may have ensued. The longer the delay in commencing proceedings, the more likely it is that the case will be decided on less evidence than was available to the parties at the time that the cause of action arose.

Even before the passing of the Limitation Act 1623 (Imp), many civil actions were the subject of time limitations. Moreover, the right of the citizen to a speedy hearing of an action that had been commenced was acknowledged by Magna Carta itself. Thus for many centuries the law has recognised the need to commence actions promptly and to prosecute them promptly once commenced. As a result, courts exercising supervisory jurisdiction over other courts and tribunals in their jurisdictions have power to stay proceedings as abuses of process if they are satisfied that, by reason of delay or other matter, the commencement or continuation of the proceedings would involve injustice or unfairness to one of the parties.

The effect of delay on the quality of justice is no doubt one of the most important influences motivating a legislature to enact limitation periods for commencing actions. But it is not the only one. Courts and commentators have perceived four broad rationales for the enactment of limitation periods. First, as time goes by, relevant evidence is likely to be lost. Second, it is oppressive, [9] even 'cruel', to a defendant to allow an action to be brought long after the circumstances which gave rise to it have passed. Third, people should be able to arrange their affairs and utilise their resources on the basis that claims can no longer be made against them. Insurers, public institutions and businesses, particularly limited liability companies, have a significant interest in knowing that they have no liabilities beyond a definite period. As the New South Wales Law Reform Commission has pointed out:

> The potential defendant is thus able to make the most productive use of his or her resources and the disruptive effect of unsettled claims on commercial intercourse is thereby avoided. To that extent the public interest is also served.

Even where the cause of action relates to personal injuries it will be often just as unfair to make the shareholders, ratepayers or taxpayers of today ultimately liable for a wrong of the distant past, as it is to refuse a plaintiff the right to reinstate a spent action arising from that wrong. The final rationale for limitation periods is that the public interest requires that disputes be settled as quickly as possible.

In enacting limitation periods, legislatures have regard to all these rationales.

A limitation period should not be seen therefore as an arbitrary cut off point unrelated to the demands of justice or the general welfare of society. It represents the legislature's judgment that the welfare of society is best served by causes of action being litigated within the limitation period, notwithstanding that the enactment of that period may often result in a good cause of action being defeated. Against this background, I do not see any warrant for treating provisions that provide for an extension of time for commencing an action as having a standing equal to or greater than those provisions that enact limitation [10] periods. A limitation provision is the general rule; an extension provision is the exception to it. The extension provision is a legislative recognition that general conceptions of what justice requires in particular categories of cases may sometimes be overridden by the facts of an individual case. The purpose of a provision such as s 31 is 'to eliminate the injustice a prospective plaintiff might suffer by reason of the imposition of a rigid time limit within which an action was to be commenced.' But whether injustice has occurred must be evaluated by reference to the rationales of the limitation period that has barred the action. The discretion to extend should therefore be seen as requiring the applicant to show that his or her case is a justifiable exception to the rule that the welfare of the State is best served by the limitation period in question. Accordingly, when an applicant seeks an extension of time to commence an action after a limitation period has expired, he or she has the positive burden of demonstrating that the justice of the case requires that extension.

The scheme of the Act is that s 11 forbids the bringing of an action for damages for negligence after the expiration of three years from the date on which the cause of action arose unless leave is given under s 31. It follows that an applicant for extension must show that justice will be best served by excepting the particular proceedings from the general prohibition which s 11 imposes. In this context, justice includes all the relevant circumstances relating to the application including the various rationales for the enactment of the limitation period involved. That the applicant had a good cause of action and was unaware of a 'material fact of a decisive character relating to the right of action' does not alter the burden on the applicant to show that the justice of the case favours the grant of an extension of time. Those facts enliven the exercise of the discretion, but they do not compel its exercise in favour of the applicant. Without them, the applicant has no right to call for the discretion to be exercised in his or her favour. Proof of them does not give the applicant a presumptive right to the exercise of the discretion, as Davies JA and Ambrose J held. As Wells J has pointed out, 'to qualify is not to succeed.' The object of the discretion, to use the words of Dixon CJ in a similar context, 'is to leave scope for the judicial or other officer who is investigating the facts and considering the general purpose of the enactment to give effect to his view of the justice of the case.' In determining what the justice of the case requires, the judge is entitled to look at every relevant fact and circumstance that does not travel beyond the scope and purpose of the enactment authorising an extension of the limitation period.

6.5.5 Notes and questions

1. The two extracts above represent a dichotomy of views about applications to extend the limitation period. Morgan refers to the 'defendant's windfall', which occurs when the court upholds a statutory time bar. McHugh J urges that the policy of the law is to fix definite time limits, which should generally be adhered to in order to preserve the quality of justice. Consider the competing interests of plaintiff and defendant in this context. What general factors should be taken into account by the court when exercising its discretion to extend a limitation period?

2. As stated above, extensions of the limitation period are most commonly sought for personal injuries actions. These applications are dealt with separately under 6.7.1ff.

3. Some jurisdictions place an overriding or ultimate time bar within which actions must be brought regardless of extensions of the limitation period granted by the court: ACT s 40 (in relation to claims for latent property damage); NSW s 51.

4. When limitation defences are raised in cases involving child sexual abuse, the court must carefully weigh up the rights of the parties and adopt a procedure that fairly and sensitively deals with the contentions. An important question is whether the court should decide the limitation issues at an early stage using summary procedures

(for example, upon an application by the defendant for summary judgment or a preliminary application by the plaintiff to extend the limitation period) or after a full hearing of the evidence.

Des Rosiers argues (N Des Rosiers, 'Childhood Sexual Abuse and the Civil Courts' (1999) 7 *Tort Law Review* 201) that the 'awkward procedure for summary motion' should be avoided and that the request for an extension of time should come after a full trial of the issues. She argues that this approach may improve judicial understanding of the problems and the reasons for the delay in proceeding. This in turn may lead to a better application of the limitation legislation, particularly in relation to cases of alleged sexual abuse.

Compare, for example the procedures adopted in *State of Queensland v RAF* [2010] QCA 332 and *Paramasivam v Flynn* [1998] FCA 1711. See also *GGG v YYY* [2011] VSC 429. The summary procedures are discussed in **Chapter 12**.

5. For a further discussion of the policy underpinning of the extension of limitation periods and the *Brisbane South Regional Health Authority v Taylor* case, see *Pomeroy v Thwaites Witham Pty Ltd* (2000) 79 SASR 489; *Clark v McGuinness* [2005] VSCA 108; *Queensland v Stephenson* (2006) 226 CLR 197; (2006) 227 ALR 17 (particularly Kirby J at 212–15 who emphasises the remedial nature of the extension provisions of the Limitation Acts) and *Conray v Scotts Refrigerated Freightways Pty Ltd* [2008] NSWCA 60, (2008) Aust Torts Reports ¶81-944.

PERSONAL INJURY ACTIONS

6.6.1   'Personal injury' is defined in the Limitation Acts of all jurisdictions to include any disease and any impairment of a person's physical or mental condition: ACT s 2, Dictionary; NSW s 11(1); NT s 4(1); Qld s 5(1); SA s 36(2); Tas ss 5(5), 5A; Vic s 3(1); WA s 3(1). A personal injury victim who can establish a cause of action at law is entitled to claim damages except to the extent that that right has been modified or abolished by statute. In Australia, these rights have been significantly modified by statute particularly to exclude certain causes of action such as claims arising out of motor vehicle accidents eg, NSW s 50A, Vic s 27B. See generally, **6.8.1ff** and the references at **6.8.5**.

Common law actions for damages for personal injury are among the most commonly litigated matters in the state and territory Supreme Courts. Although the cause of action pleaded is generally common law negligence, many jurisdictions apply special limitation periods for personal injuries, rather than relying upon the general limitation period applicable to tort actions. In the Northern Territory (s 12(1)(b)), the limitation period for personal injury actions is the same as for other tort actions. In other jurisdictions the limitation period for personal injury actions is shorter than that applicable to tort actions generally.

6.6.2   Examples of limitation periods — personal injury actions:

Jurisdiction	Limitation period		Cause of action	Dates of operation
ACT	3 ****	S 16A	Actions for personal injury where a claim could be made under the Workers Compensation Act 1951 (ACT)	Actions arising on or after 01/07/03
	3 **	s 16B(2)(a)	Actions for damages for personal injury consisting of disease or disorder	
	3 ****	s 16B(2)(b)	Actions for damages for other personal injury	
Cth (Competition and Consumer Act 2010)	3 ** OR 12 *** whichever ends first	s 87F(1)(a); s 87G s 87F(1)(b); s 87H	Actions for damages for personal injury or death taken under the Australian Consumer Law that relate to Pt 2-2 (unconscionable conduct), 3-3 (safety of consumer goods and product related services, 3-4 (information standards) or 3-5 (liability of manufacturers for goods with safety defects), or Div 2 of Pt 5-4 (action for damages against manufacturers of goods) (s 87E)	—
NSW	3 *	s 18A(2)	Actions for damages for personal injury founded on negligence, nuisance, breach of duty	Action relates to an act/ omission occurring from 01/09/90 to 05/12/02
	3 ** OR 12 *** whichever ends first	s 50C(1)(a) s 50C(1)(b)	Actions for damages for personal injury or death regardless of the nature of the cause of action	Action relates to an act/ omission occurring on or after 06/12/02
NT	3 *	s 12(1)	Actions for personal injury in contract, tort or founded on a breach of statutory duty	—

Jurisdiction	Limitation period		Cause of action	Dates of operation
Qld	3 *	s 11	Actions in negligence, trespass, nuisance or for breach of duty (whether in contract, under statute or otherwise) where damages claimed consist of or include damages for personal injury	—
SA	3 * **	s 36(1) s 36(1a)	All actions which consist of or include damages in respect of personal injuries	—
Tas	3 *	s 5(1)	Actions in negligence, nuisance or for breach of duty (whether in contract, under statute or otherwise) where damages consist of or include damages for personal injuries	Action accrued before 01/01/05
	3 ** OR 12 *** whichever ends first	s 5A(3)(a) s 5A(3)(b)	Actions in negligence, nuisance or for breach of duty (whether in contract, under statute or otherwise) where damages consist of or include damages for personal injuries	Action accrued on or after 01/01/05
Vic	3 ** OR 12 *** whichever ends first	s 27D(1)(a) s 27D(1)(b)	Actions for damages for personal injury or death regardless of the nature of the cause of action	Action is commenced on or after 01/10/03 regardless of when act/omission occurred
WA	3 *****	s 14	Any action for damages relating to personal injury or death under the Fatal Accidents Act 1959	On or after 15 November 2005

* From the date of accrual.

** From the date of discoverability.

*** From the date of the act or omission alleged to have resulted in the personal injury/death.

**** From the date the injury occurred.

***** WA has a hybrid test for the running of the limitation period, extracted at 6.3.19E.

Date of accrual v date of discoverability in personal injuries actions

6.6.3 The table above reveals the two alternative methods of commencing the running of time. For the date of accrual, the limitation period will begin to run when the injury first occurs. An alternative formula is the date of discoverability where the statute begins to run when the plaintiff discovers the injury and the cause of action. This issue is discussed at **6.3.10ff**.

Special limitation periods for personal injuries to minors

Minors injured by close relatives or associates

6.6.4 Recommendations made by the *Ipp Review of the Law of Negligence* for a special limitation period for cases where a child is injured by a parent or a person in a close relationship with the child's parent, have been implemented in New South Wales, Tasmania, Victoria and Western Australia. In New South Wales and Victoria, the legislation now stipulates a limitation period of three years from the date when the victim turns 25 or three years from the date of discoverability, whichever is the later: NSW s 50E; Vic s 27I. See *AM v KB* [2007] VSC 429 for a discussion of the Victorian provision. In Tasmania, the limitation period is three years from the date the victim turns 25 with a discretion to extend this period to three years from the date of discoverability: Tas s 26(7), (9). A Western Australian provision provides that a cause of action can be commenced up until, but not after, the relevant person has turned 25 if the cause of action accrued before the person turned 18 and the defendant is in a close relationship with the relevant person: s 33. Similar provisions now exist in relation to certain actions for personal injury or death under the Competition and Consumer Act 2010: s 87K.

6.6.5 Further reading

B Matthews, 'Post-Ipp Special Limitation Periods for Cases of Injury to a Child by a Parent or Close Associate: New Jurisdictional Gulfs' (2004) 12 *Torts Law Journal* 239.

Injuries to children arising from the provision of health services

6.6.6 In the Australian Capital Territory (s 30B), special limitations provisions apply to children who suffer personal injuries arising from the provision of a health service where the cause of action arose on or after 1 July 2003. Such a claim must be brought within six years of the date the accident giving rise to the injury occurred. If the injury includes a disease or disorder, then the applicable period is six years from the date of discoverability (either by the plaintiff or the plaintiff's parent or guardian) or 12 years after the day the accident giving rise to the injury occurred, whichever period ends sooner.

Latent injuries

6.6.7 Significant difficulties arise where the plaintiff suffers an injury and the limitation period begins to run, but the plaintiff has no means of discovering the damage until the expiry of the relevant period. This is the issue of latent injury. Michael Green ('The Paradox of Statutes of Limitations in Toxic Substances Litigation' (1988) 76 *California LR* 965 at 972) argues that personal injury claims came within the purview of the Limitation Acts at a relatively late stage and tended to involve cases where the plaintiff's injury occurred within a short time period, that is, 'snapshot' cases. He states (at 972):

> The primary form of proof in those cases — witness recollection of previous perceptions unaided by documentary evidence — was consistent with the major functions of the statute of limitations; ensuring early notice to defendants and resolving factual disputes before witnesses disappeared and memories faded irreparably.

However, tortious actions causing latent injury are fundamentally different to the snapshot torts described above. An example is provided by the case of *Cartledge v Jopling and Sons Ltd* [1963] AC 758. In that case, the defendant was sued for negligence and breach of statutory duty by a number of its former employees and the personal representatives of two others who had since died. It was established that all the employees had contracted the disease pneumoconiosis before October 1950 as a result of inhaling invisible and infinitesimal particles of fragmented silica while working in the defendant's steel factory, and that the defendant had been in breach of duty in not taking proper steps to guard against this. However, the employees did not discover that they had contracted the disease until after 1950 and it was not until 1955 that all of them were certified to be suffering from it. Although it was not suggested that they had been dilatory or unreasonable in failing to do so, the employees did not commence proceedings against the defendant within six years of October 1950. As a result, it was held that their causes of action were barred by the Act.

However, their Lordships called for reform to reverse the effect of their decision. As stated by Lord Evershed (at 774):

> In another generation science may ... if the present statute for limiting causes of action remains unamended, render justice unattainable for ordinary men in cases of this kind.

6.6.8   Question

1. How does the law respond to the difficulties caused by the interaction between latent injuries and limitation periods?

6.6.9E   Limitation of Actions for Latent Personal Injuries
Law Reform Commissioner of Tasmania
Report No 69
(footnotes omitted)

The Case for Reform: The Problem of Latent Injuries

In recent decades, the problems created by certain latent injuries have become more pronounced. Cases of injustice have been identified where a plaintiff's action for compensation arising from a once latent injury is statute-barred. A latent injury describes the circumstances in which an illness is contracted and the symptoms lie dormant before manifesting themselves at a time later than the period prescribed in the Limitation Act for commencement of legal proceedings. Some latent injuries are the so-called 'toxic torts' based in negligence, nuisance or breach of duty. In these cases, the plaintiff sustains injury or contracts a disease as a result of contact with substances which, by their nature, are toxic unless handled with caution. The characteristics of latent injuries are frequently the same; the injury is sustained as a result of repeated exposure to a toxic substance, the exposure is over many years and the exposure occurred many years before and the symptoms appear outside the limitation period. Common amongst this class of Plaintiffs are people suffering from diseases caused by inhalation of toxic types of dust, eg, asbestosis, silicosis, pneumoconiosis, and mesothelioma. These insidious diseases have a long latency period, sometimes more than thirty years from the date of the inhalation. Other toxic substances such as radioactive minerals and dangerous chemicals have also given rise to instances of statute-barred claims.

Apart from latent injury there may be cases of undiagnosed injury. In some cases, a person may be medically examined and according to the prevailing standard and level of medical knowledge no adverse symptoms may be indicated. However, a disease may be discovered later with new or improved diagnostic techniques.

The potential class of plaintiffs with latent injury type claims may not be confined to those suffering from diseases and may expand. This class of case could extend to an adult Plaintiff claiming compensation for psychological injuries sustained as a result of repeated sexual abuse as a child. ...

6.6.10 The Limitation Acts of most Australian jurisdictions deal with latent injuries either by ensuring that the limitation period does not run until after the injury is discovered (the date of discoverability) or under the general discretion to extend the limitation period: NT s 44. As discussed above at 6.3.14, the test for discoverability recommended by the Ipp Committee has been adopted in three jurisdictions: NSW s 50D; Tas s 2(1); Vic s 27F. However, the test for discoverability differs in jurisdictions that did not adopt the Ipp recommendations: ACT s 16B; SA s 36(1a); WA s 55 (for non-asbestos-related diseases — extracted at 6.3.19E) and s 56 (for asbestos-related diseases).

For example, the South Australian Act states that the limitation period begins to run 'when injury first comes to a person's knowledge' (s 36(1a)) and the ACT s 16B(2)(a) states that when 'the injury is or includes a disease or disorder' the limitation period runs after the injured person first knows that the injury includes a disease or disorder and that the injury is related to someone else's act or omission. There is no express provision stating that the limitation period may run from the date that the person 'ought to have known' these elements.

The New South Wales Act makes specific provision for latent injury (see NSW ss 60F–60J) and applies to latent injuries arising prior to December 2002, apart from proceedings for dust diseases which may be brought under the Dust Diseases Tribunal Act 1989 (NSW): see below at 6.6.12ff.

6.6.11 In *Stingel v Clarke* (2006) 226 CLR 442; 228 ALR 229, Stingel commenced a proceeding against Clarke in August 2002 in the County Court of Victoria. She alleged that she had been assaulted and raped by Clarke in 1971 and that in consequence she suffered injury in the form of post-traumatic stress disorder. At first instance, it was held that s 5(1A) of the Limitation of Actions Act 1958 (Vic) applied and that the proceeding was not statute-barred. Section 5(1A) provided:

An action for damages for negligence nuisance or breach of duty ... where the damages claimed by the plaintiff consist of or include damages in respect of personal injuries consisting of a disease or disorder contracted by any person may be brought not more than six years from, and the cause of action shall be taken to have accrued on, the date on which the person first knows:

(a)   that he has suffered those personal injuries; and

(b)   that those personal injuries were caused by the act or omission of some person.

The judge accepted Stingel's evidence that she suffered from post-traumatic stress disorder of delayed onset, that the onset was in 2000, and that she first knew of that condition and of its causal connection with the alleged acts of Clarke at a time after then. The cause of action was taken to have accrued when she first had that knowledge and the proceeding was commenced within six years of that time.

An appeal to the Victorian Court of Appeal was allowed on the ground that the facts alleged did not bring the case within the concept of a 'disease or disorder contracted' within s 5(1A). On further appeal to the High Court, it was held by the majority (Gleeson CJ, Hayne, Callinan, Heydon and Crennan JJ) that s 5(1A) was not limited in its operation to insidious diseases, such as mesothelioma or lung cancer, which were contracted many years before any symptoms were apparent to the plaintiff. It could apply where the plaintiff's knowledge of a disorder, and of its cause, occurred at or about the same time as the occurrence of the disorder. Further, the damages claimed by Stingel included damages in respect of personal injuries of a psychiatric nature consisting of a disorder contracted by her. The disorder alleged by Stingel was of a delayed type and did not exist until there were symptoms in 2000. Section 5(1A) applied in relation to the disorder and, accordingly, her claim was not barred by s 5(1)(a). (Summary is based on the Commonwealth Law Reports headnote (2006) 226 CLR 442 at 442–3.)

For further discussion, see L Sarmas, 'Mixed Messages on Sexual Assault and the Statute of Limitations: *Stingel v Clark*, the Ipp "Reforms" and an Argument for Change' (2008) *32 MULR* 609.

Dust-related conditions

6.6.12   In New South Wales, proceedings in relation to 'dust-related conditions' are to be determined exclusively by the Dust Diseases Tribunal, established by the Dust Diseases Tribunal Act 1989 (NSW). This tribunal has no limitation period: Dust Diseases Tribunal Act 1989 (NSW) s 12A. 'Dust-related conditions' is defined in s 3 by reference to specific diseases nominated in Sch 1 (for example, asbestosis, coal dust pneumoconiosis, farmers' lung, mesothelioma and silicosis) or by any other pathological condition of the lungs, pleura or peritoneum that is attributable to dust. Similarly, Queensland has no limitation period applying to 'dust-related condition', which is defined in the Dictionary in Sch 2 of the Civil Liability Act 2003 (Qld) in similar terms to the New South Wales legislation. Victoria has no limitation period for dust-related or tobacco smoke-related conditions: s 27B(2). As stated above, Western Australia uses a test of discoverability for asbestos-related diseases: WA s 56.

For definitions of asbestos, asbestosis, dust disease, mesothelioma, pneumoconiosis, and silicosis, consult the *Encyclopaedic Australian Legal Dictionary*, LexisNexis.

6.6.13   The High Court considered the operation of the general New South Wales latent injury provisions (ss 60F–60J) in *Harris v Commercial Minerals Ltd* (1996) 186 CLR 1; 135 ALR 353. The plaintiff in that case suffered from silicosis. The plaintiff sought an extension of time to bring an action against three former employers alleging their negligence had caused him to contract the disease. Proceedings had been commenced in 1991, although the Dust Diseases Board had informed the plaintiff periodically between 1971 and 1986 of his disease's progression. After the expiration of the limitation period but before the application for extension, the plaintiff developed depression and impotence as consequences of the silicosis. The question for the High Court was whether it is the actual awareness of the plaintiff which must be considered when determining the matters in s 60I(1)(a)(ii) and (iii), or whether awareness may be constructive or based on reasonable foreseeability. The High Court (Dawson, Toohey, Gaudron, McHugh and Gummow JJ) held that the plaintiff's actual awareness alone is relevant and that the extent of the injury is to be determined at the time of the application for extension and not at the expiration of the limitation period. Since the plaintiff was not aware of the consequences of the silicosis at the time of the expiration of the limitation period he was entitled to an extension of the limitation period. See also *Commonwealth of Australia v McLean* (1996–97) 41 NSWLR 389 and *Commonwealth of Australia v Smith* [2005] NSWCA 478.

6.6.14   Further reading

P Handford, 'Damages and Limitation Issues in Asbestos Cases' (1991) 21 *UWALR* 63.

D Jackson, *Report of the Special Commission of Inquiry into Medical Research and Compensation Foundation*, September 2004.

M Joseph, 'Asbestos Related Diseases' (1995) 27 *Australian Journal of Forensic Sciences* 13.

J McCulloch, *Asbestos — Its Human Cost*, University of Queensland Press, 1986.

EXTENSIONS OF TIME FOR PERSONAL INJURIES ACTIONS

6.7.1   The limitation period stipulated for each cause of action may be extended in appropriate circumstances; however, these circumstances vary remarkably from jurisdiction to jurisdiction. The main grounds for extending limitation periods in this context are:

- just and reasonable ground (NSW, Tas, Vic) **(6.7.2ff)**;

- the plaintiff's awareness of material facts of a decisive nature (Qld) or of facts establishing the cause of action (WA) **(6.7.8ff)**; and

- a general power to extend a time stipulation in a statute (NT and SA): **6.5.1**.

In the Australian Capital Territory, the judicial discretion to extend the limitation period for many personal injury claims (ie, those not arising out of employment claims) has been removed by the operation of ss 16B and 36(5) of the Limitation Act 1985 (ACT) — *DJ v RHS* [2004] ACTSC 12, but note the reasoning in *Doyle v Gillespie* (2010) 173 ACTR 66 per Refshauge J. Where a claim concerns a cause of action for personal injury that could have been made under the Workers Compensation Act 1951 (ACT), s 16A of the Limitation Act 1985 (ACT) may apply. In the Australian Capital Territory, extensions for causes of action under s 16A are permitted under s 36.

The concept of a fair trial has been influential in the reasoning of courts when exercising the power to extend the limitation period. This concept is explicit in some of the legislative provisions eg, Vic s 27L(2)(a) extracted below, but in other contexts it appears to be developing in the appellate case law, particularly in New South Wales and Queensland. Note for example, the comments of Santow JA (with whom Handley JA agreed) in *Commonwealth of Australia v Smith* [2005] NSWCA 478 at [128] who considered that significant prejudice means 'such prejudice as would make the chances of a fair trial unlikely'. For further examples, see *The Salvation Army (South Australian Property Trust) v Rundle* [2008] NSWCA 341 at [96] per McColl JA; *HWC v The Corporation of the Synod of the Diocese of Brisbane* [2009] QCA 168 at [41] per Keane JA (with whom Fraser and Chesterman JJA agreed) at [41], [55]–[58] and [68]–[76], *Spain v WorkCover Queensland* [2009] QCA 323, per McMurdo JA at [33] and [54]; contra *Windsurf Holdings Pty Ltd v Leonard* [2009] NSWCA 6 at [83] per Sackville JA.

Just and reasonable

6.7.2 In New South Wales (s 60G(2) applying to latent injuries arising before 6 December 2002; ss 60C, 60E applying to ordinary actions arising between 1 September 1990–5 December 2002; and ss 62A, 62B applying after 6 December 2002), Tasmania (ss 5(3), 5A(5)) and Victoria (ss 27K, 27L), the court may extend the limitation period if it is just and reasonable to do so.

6.7.3E   **Limitation of Actions Act 1958 (Vic)**

27K Extension of limitation periods
  (1) A person claiming to have a cause of action to which this Part applies may apply to a court for an extension of a period of limitation applicable to the cause of action under Division 2.
  (2) Subject to section 27L, the court —
     (a) may hear any of the persons likely to be affected by the application as it sees fit; and
     (b) may, if it decides that it is just and reasonable to do so, order the extension of the period of limitation applicable to the cause of action for such period as the court determines.
  (3) If a court orders the extension of a period of limitation applicable to a cause of action under this section, that period of limitation is accordingly extended for the purposes of an action brought by the applicant in that court on the cause of action that the applicant claims to have.

27L Matters to be considered in determining applications for extension of limitation period
  (1) In exercising the powers conferred on it by section 27K, a court shall have regard to all the circumstances of the case, including (but not limited to) the following —
     (a) the length of and reasons for the delay on the part of the plaintiff;
     (b) the extent to which, having regard to the delay, there is or is likely to be prejudice to the defendant;
     (c) the extent, if any, to which the defendant had taken steps to make available to the plaintiff means of ascertaining facts which were or might be relevant to the cause of action of the plaintiff against the defendant;
     (d) the duration of any disability or legal incapacity of the plaintiff arising on or after the date of discoverability;
     (e) the time within which the cause of action was discoverable;
     (f) the extent to which the plaintiff acted promptly and reasonably once the plaintiff knew that the act or omission of the defendant, to which the injury of the plaintiff was attributable, might be capable at that time of giving rise to an action for damages;

> (g)   the steps, if any, taken by the plaintiff to obtain medical, legal or other expert advice and the nature of the advice he or she may have received.
>
> (2)   To avoid doubt, the circumstances referred to in sub-section (1) include the following —
>
>   (a)   whether the passage of time has prejudiced a fair trial of the claim; and
>
>   (b)   the nature and extent of the plaintiff's loss; and
>
>   (c)   the nature of the defendant's conduct.

6.7.4   The jurisdictions that have adopted the just and reasonable test as the basis for extending the limitation period impose different criteria to guide and, in some cases, to limit the exercise of judicial discretion. In Victoria, the court must consider the circumstances set out in s 27L (extracted above) but may extend the limitation period for such time as it determines. Although the circumstances to be considered by the court are similar, in New South Wales (s 62A(2)) the court may only extend the 12-year long-stop limitation period for up to three years from the date of discoverability for cases arising after 2002. For older cases, before the discretion to extend under s 60G may be exercised, the plaintiff must establish the elements of latent injury under s 60I (*Commonwealth of Australia v Shaw* (2006) 66 NSWLR 325; 91 ALD 401) and the court may only extend the limitation period under s 60C for up to five years. In Tasmania, the court's discretion to extend is also limited, in that the limitation period may only be extended having regard to the justice of the case and to the circumstances set out in s 5A(5)(a)–(c), for such period which does not exceed three years from the date of discoverability.

Exercise of judicial discretion upon the just and reasonable ground

6.7.5   The following case provides an example of the operation of the judicial discretion to extend time under ss 27K and 27L (extracted at 6.7.3) and their counterparts. The facts of the case and the reasons why Kaye J found that that the limitation period had expired are set out at 6.3.16C.

6.7.6C	**Caven v Women's and Children's Health** (2007) 15 VR 447; [2007] VSC 7 Supreme Court of Victoria

Section 27K(2): Application to extend period of limitation

[77] Section 27K(1) provides that a person claiming to have a cause of action to which Pt 2A applies may apply to a court for an extension of a period of time applicable to that cause of action. Section 27K(2)(b) provides that the court may 'if it decides that it is just and reasonable to do so' order the extension of the period of limitation applicable to the cause of action for such period as the court determines. Section 27L provides that in exercising the powers provided by s 27K the court shall have regard to all the circumstances including (but not limited to) the set of factors numerated in s 27L(1). It is convenient if I consider the application by the plaintiff by reference to those factors.

(a) Length of and reasons for delay

The first factor is the length of and the reasons for the delay on the part of the plaintiff. In the context of s 23A(3)(a) [the predecessor to s 27L], which is in identical terms, the courts have construed the 'delay' to be the period from the accrual of the cause of action to the making of the application for extension of time or the issue of the writ. [*Repco Corporation Ltd v Scardamaglia* [1996] 1 VR 7 at 11; *Lord v Australian Safeway Stores Pty Ltd* [1996] 1 VR 614 at 616.]

I have already held that the plaintiffs ought to have known all of the facts necessary to constitute the cause of action by approximately April 2001. If they had learnt of those facts by then, proceedings would have been issued shortly thereafter. Accordingly the relevant period of delay is approximately three and a half years.

The explanation for that delay is contained in the affidavit of Ms Caven. There she states that she contacted her solicitors in March 2004 because at that time Jared's heart condition had deteriorated. Furthermore, it was becoming apparent to Ms Caven that Jared's development 'when considered against the development of my other children was significantly delayed'. She states that she was also informed that he may require further surgery as his heart enlarged with age.

In cross-examination by Mr Noonan, Ms Caven stated that in 1999 it was evident to her that Jared's development was significantly delayed compared with the development of her eldest child, Maddison, at a similar age. By that time Jared was already attending EPIC, the early intervention centre. Accordingly Mr Noonan contended that the explanation of the delay given by Ms Caven in her affidavit was substantially discredited.

In re-examination Ms Caven stated that until Jared commenced school her main concerns with him related to matters of health rather than his development. However when he commenced school she stated 'I see it as my eyes were opened, in that school isn't going to provide him with everything he needs in terms of speech, because ... he seemed to understand the routine and what was happening, but he was not able to verbalise it'. She stated that she became concerned as to Jared's ability to cope in a mainstream school.

It seems clear that, from an early stage, Ms Caven, and indeed Mr Huysing, were each aware that Jared's development was and would be substantially delayed behind that of other children. None the less, I accept that it was not until Jared commenced school that the full impact of that developmental delay was brought home to the plaintiffs, when they had the opportunity to compare his development with that of other children who were in mainstream education. It is understandable that a parent might not fully appreciate, subjectively, the full extent and effect of the child's disability until the child can be compared in a situation such as the commencement of school. That explanation does, in some measure, provide some palliation of the delay of the plaintiffs in commencing with litigation. However, it does not entirely excuse that delay. After all, as pointed out by Mr Noonan, the plaintiffs were well aware that Jared did have significant developmental problems from as early as 1999. Those developmental problems were sufficient to require him to attend EPIC. There is little evidence before me as to the nature and extent to which Jared suffers from Down's Syndrome. However, in re-examination Ms Caven did tell me that in his early years he lagged significantly behind her elder child in achieving the usual milestones such as sitting up, crawling and walking.

(b) The extent to which, having regard to the delay, there is or is likely to be prejudice to the defendant

The defendant has not sought to establish, or contend, that it has suffered, or will suffer, any prejudice to it in the conduct of the litigation, or otherwise, as a consequence of the delay in the commencement of proceedings. In some cases, it is appropriate that to infer that, none the less, some prejudice may be occasioned, even if the defendant is unable to establish such prejudice [*Brisbane South Regional Health Authority v Taylor* (1996) 186 CLR 541 at 551–3]. Certainly in some cases of professional liability, it is clear that delay in the commencement of proceedings redounds to the disadvantage of a defendant, particularly where there is a dispute as to what advice was or was not given to a patient or client. However, that is not the case here. It was accepted by Mr Noonan that the issue of liability in this case will depend, significantly, on expert evidence as to what may be observed on the video of the ultrasound performed on Ms Caven on 12 May 1997, and what advice ought to have been given to Ms Caven as a result of that procedure. There is no suggestion that Ms Caven was informed, at all, that the ultrasound disclosed a heart defect, or gave any indication of Down's Syndrome or indeed any other abnormality in the foetus. In those circumstances the question of the potential for prejudice to exist is of little significance in this application.

(c) The extent if any to which the defendant had taken steps to make available to the plaintiff means of ascertaining facts which were or might be relevant to the cause of action of the plaintiff against the defendants

Mr O'Dwyer submitted that the defendant had the means available to it to inform the plaintiff of the **facts** which are relevant to the present cause of action. To some extent that proposition is correct. The ultrasound was taken by the defendant, and it was the defendant's expert radiologist who viewed and interpreted the film. None the less the plaintiffs did know that the first plaintiff had undergone the ultrasound in May 1997. As I have found, by March 2000, they knew of sufficient facts to put them on inquiry as to what the ultrasound should have disclosed to them. Accordingly I do not consider this circumstance to be particularly significant in the determination of this application.

(d) The duration of any disability or legal incapacity of the plaintiff arising on or after the date of discoverability

This consideration is not relevant.

(e) The time within which the cause of action was discoverable

I have already found that the cause of action was discoverable by approximately April 2001.

(f) The extent to which the plaintiff acted promptly and reasonably once the plaintiff knew that the act or omission of the defendant to which the injury of the plaintiff was attributable might be capable at that time of giving rise to an action for damages

This subparagraph relates to a different consideration to that set out in subpara (e). This consideration focuses on the time when the plaintiff actually knew that the defendant's act or omission, to which the plaintiffs' injury was attributable, might be capable of giving rise to an action of damages. The plaintiffs did not know that fact until they received the report of Dr Ramsey.

(g) The steps if any taken by the plaintiff to obtain medical, legal or other expert advice and the nature of the advice he or she may have received

This consideration is allied to the previous consideration, namely, the plaintiffs obtained the report of Dr Ramsey in November 2005.

[78] Section 25L(2) provides that to avoid doubt the circumstances referred to in subs (1) include (inter alia) the nature and extent of the plaintiffs' loss. The plaintiffs did not adduce any medical or other evidence as to the nature and extent of the Down's Syndrome condition suffered by Jared. None the less the evidence of the nature of his developmental delays, both

in Ms Caven's affidavit and in her evidence, make it clear that the claim by the plaintiffs, particularly for the cost of care of Jared, is not insubstantial. In addition Jared has had significant health problems, particularly relating to his cardiac condition. On any view, it is reasonable to assess the plaintiffs' claims, if they are successful, as being of some substance.

[79] In light of the considerations that I have set out above, the question is whether it is just and reasonable in the circumstances to order that the period of limitation applicable to the plaintiffs' cause of action be extended to the date upon which proceedings are issued in this case, 21 December 2004. Essentially that question involves a proper assessment and balancing of all of the relevant factors to which I have already adverted. There has been reasonably significant delay. On the other hand, the reasons for that delay advanced by Ms Caven are to some extent at least 'understandable'. The defendant has not demonstrated that it will suffer any prejudice, whether in the litigation or otherwise, as a result of the delay. The claim by the plaintiffs, if it succeeds, is not insubstantial. If they are deprived of the ability to pursue that claim, they would lose the opportunity to vindicate a substantial right. Having regard to all those circumstances it is my conclusion that it is just and reasonable to extend the time within which the proceeding might be commenced to 24 December 2004. Therefore I order that the period of limitation applicable to the cause of action on which the plaintiffs have brought these proceedings be extended to that date.

6.7.7 Notes and questions

1. Does the nature of the case affect the exercise of the judicial discretion? Is there any difference in the application of the criteria in Victoria s 27L and its equivalents, where the plaintiff is seeking damages for sexual assault compared to damages for injuries sustained in a motor vehicle accident? See *A v D* (1995) 127 FLR 372; *McIntosh v Southern Meats Pty Ltd* (1997) *Aust Torts Reports* 81–424.

2. For a commentary on actions for wrongful birth and the operation of limitation periods in that context, see C Lake, 'The Kid and the Cash: Categorising Damage in Wrongful Birth and Wrongful Pregnancy' (2009) 17 *TLJ* 55.

3. For further cases that apply the just and reasonable criterion, see *Tsiadis v Patterson* (2001) 4 VR 114; *Hill v Iluka Corp Ltd* [2002] TASSC 113; *Berriman v Cricket Australia* (2007) 17 VR 528; *Certain Lloyds Underwriters v Giannopoulos* [2009] NSWCA 56; *Doyle v Gillespie* (2010) 173 ACTR 66; and *Norris v McGeachy* [2010] TASFC 4.

Material facts of a decisive nature

6.7.8 In Queensland and in New South Wales for causes of action accruing before 1 September 1990, the limitation period may be extended if material facts of a decisive nature are not within the plaintiff's means of knowledge at the relevant time: NSW ss 57B, 58; Qld ss 30, 31.

30 Interpretation

(1) For the purposes of this section and sections 31, 32, 33 and 34 —

   (a) the material facts relating to a right of action include the following —

      (i)   the fact of the occurrence of negligence, trespass, nuisance or breach of duty on which the right of action is founded;

      (ii) the identity of the person against whom the right of action lies;

      (iii) the fact that the negligence, trespass, nuisance or breach of duty causes personal injury;

      (iv) the nature and extent of the personal injury so caused;

      (v)   the extent to which the personal injury is caused by the negligence, trespass, nuisance or breach of duty;

   (b) material facts relating to a right of action are of a decisive character if but only if a reasonable person knowing those facts and having taken the appropriate advice on those facts, would regard those facts as showing —

      (i)   that an action on the right of action would (apart from the effect of the expiration of a period of limitation) have a reasonable prospect of success and of resulting in an award of damages sufficient to justify the bringing of an action on the right of action; and

      (ii) that the person whose means of knowledge is in question ought in the person's own interests and taking the person's circumstances into account to bring an action on the right of action;

   (c) a fact is not within the means of knowledge of a person at a particular time if, but only if —

      (i)   the person does not know the fact at that time; and

      (ii) as far as the fact is able to be found out by the person — the person has taken all reasonable steps to find out the fact before that time.

(2) In this section —

   appropriate advice, in relation to facts, means the advice of competent persons qualified in their respective fields to advise on the medical, legal and other aspects of the facts.

31 Ordinary actions

(1) This section applies to actions for damages for negligence, trespass, nuisance or breach of duty (whether the duty exists by virtue of a contract or a provision made by or under a statute or independently of a contract or such provision) where the damages claimed by the plaintiff for the negligence, trespass, nuisance or breach of duty consist of or include damages in respect of personal injury to any person or damages in respect of injury resulting from the death of any person.

(2) Where on application to a court by a person claiming to have a right of action to which this section applies, it appears to the court —

   (a) that a material fact of a decisive character relating to the right of action was not within the means of knowledge of the applicant until a date after the commencement of the year last preceding the expiration of the period of limitation for the action; and

(b)   that there is evidence to establish the right of action apart from a defence founded on the expiration of a period of limitation; the court may order that the period of limitation for the action be extended so that it expires at the end of 1 year after that date and thereupon, for the purposes of the action brought by the applicant in that court, the period of limitation is extended accordingly.

(3)   This section applies to an action whether or not the period of limitation for the action has expired —

     (a)   before the commencement of this Act; or

     (b)   before an application is made under this section in respect of the right of action.

6.7.10   The operation of ss 30 and 31 were discussed by the Queensland Court of Appeal in *HWC v The Corporation of the Synod of the Diocese of Brisbane* [2009] QCA 168. In that case, the Court of Appeal upheld a decision dismissing an application for an extension of the limitation period because, among other things, certain witnesses had died, leading to prejudice to the defendants and the unlikelihood of a fair trial. See also *Spain v WorkCover Queensland* [2009] QCA 323.

6.7.11   Note that the Northern Territory, South Australia and Western Australia provide similar tests to these provisions, though there are important differences in the drafting of the statutory provisions. The Limitation Acts in Northern Territory (s 44) and South Australia (s 48) provide a general power to the court to extend the limitation period, discussed at **6.5.1**. A precondition for the exercise of the general power is that material facts were not ascertained by the plaintiff within the requisite time frame.

Pursuant to s 39(3) of the Limitation Act 2005 (WA), the court may extend time for personal injuries where a person:

(a)   was not aware of the physical cause of the … injury;

(b)   was aware of the physical cause of the … injury but was not aware that the … injury was attributable to the conduct of a person; or

(c)   was aware of the physical cause of the … injury and that the … injury was attributable to the conduct of a person but after reasonable enquiry, had been unable to establish that person's identity.

6.7.12   The High Court held in *Queensland v Stephenson* (2006) 226 CLR 197; (2006) 227 ALR 17 (Gummow, Kirby, Hayne and Crennan JJ, Heydon J dissenting) that the phrase 'material fact of a decisive character relating to a right of action' in s 31(2)(a) (above) is a composite expression and therefore each element of the phrase must be within the means of knowledge of an applicant at any particular time. In that case it was held that although the material facts relating to a right of action were known to the plaintiffs at the relevant date, the decisive character of those facts was not within the plaintiffs' means of knowledge.

Similarly in the leading decision of *Sola Optical Australia Pty Ltd v Mills* (1987) 163 CLR 628; 75 ALR 513, the High Court held that facts, in order to be material, need not be decisive. A fact is material to the plaintiff's case if it is both relevant to the issue to be proved and is of sufficient importance to be likely to have a bearing on the case. The requirements are satisfied by objective inquiry, without subjective assessment of the plaintiff's decisions or intentions.

In New South Wales (s 57B(1)(b)) and Queensland (s 30(1)(a)), there is a list of factors to be taken into account in deciding materiality.

These factors were considered by the High Court in the following case:

Do Carmo v Ford Excavations Pty Ltd
                          (1984) 154 CLR 234; 52 ALR 231
                               High Court of Australia

[The appellant, while working for the respondent between 1971 and 1975, was exposed to silica dust which eventually caused silicosis-tuberculosis, rendering him totally disabled for work. He sought legal advice in 1976 but was given the impression that there was no reasonable basis for bringing an action. In 1979 he changed solicitors and learned that certain precautions could have been adopted by his employer which would have minimised the risk of contracting the disease. These procedures had been generally available to the industry in 1971. He then sought an extension of the limitation period pursuant to the Limitation Act 1969 (NSW) s 58. It was necessary for the High Court to construe s 57B(1)(b) that 'material facts' included 'the fact of the occurrence of negligence ... on which the cause of action is founded'.]

Dawson J (at 256): The form of the legislation requires, I think, a step-by-step approach. The first step is to inquire whether the facts of which the appellant was unaware were material facts: s 57(1)(b). If they were, the next step is to ascertain whether they were of a decisive character: s 57(1)(c). If so, then it must be ascertained whether those facts were within the means of knowledge of the appellant before the specified date: s 58(2).

Having formed the conclusion, as I have, that the reference in s 57(1)(b)(i) to the fact of the occurrence of negligence — by definition a material fact — is an elliptical reference to those facts which must be proved in order to establish the negligent conduct upon which the cause of action in negligence is founded, it is necessary to identify those facts in this case. In most cases, proof of negligent conduct requires no more than proof of the act or omission which is relied upon as constituting the negligent conduct. This, however, is a case in which it is alleged that the respondent was negligent by failing to provide a safe system of work for the appellant. That is no more than an allegation that the respondent failed to take reasonable steps for the safety of the appellant but in such a case it may not be enough merely to establish the actual omission constituted by the employer's conduct in order to establish the negligent character of the conduct. It may be necessary to establish as a fact that the system of work was defective by calling evidence of the steps which might have been taken to minimise or eliminate the risk of injury in the performance of the work: [257] *Neil v NSW Fresh Food and Ice Pty Ltd* (1963) 108 CLR 362. As Windeyer J pointed out in *Vozza v Tooth & Co Ltd* (1964) 112 CLR 316, at pp 318–319:

> The statement that the common law requires that an employer have a safe system of work for his employees means only that he must take reasonable care for their safety. It does not mean that he must safeguard them completely from all perils. The ruling principle is that an employer is bound to take reasonable care for the safety of his workmen, and all other rules or formulas must be taken subject to this principle. That statement, made by Lord Keith of Avonholm in *Cavanagh v Ulster Weaving Co Ltd* [1960] AC 145, at p 165 was repeated and approved in the House of Lords in *Brown v Rolls Royce Ltd* [1960] 1 WLR 210; [1960] 1 All ER 577. The latter case and *Neill v NSW Fresh Food and Ice Pty Ltd* establish that the legal burden of proving an absence of reasonable care on the part of a defendant employer remains on the plaintiff workman throughout. For a plaintiff to succeed it must appear, by direct evidence or by reasonable inference from the evidence, that the defendant unreasonably failed to take measures or adopt means, reasonably open to him in all the circumstances, which would have protected the plaintiff from the dangers

of his task without unduly impeding its accomplishment. To quote a sentence from one of the cases to which counsel referred, 'What is "a proper system of work" is a matter for evidence, not for law books': per Lord Denning in *Qualcast (Wolverhampton) Ltd v Haynes* [1959] AC 743, at p 760.

In other words, where a safe system of work cannot otherwise be inferred, evidence will be necessary to identify it: *Da Costa v Australian Iron & Steel Pty. Ltd* (1978) 20 ALR 257 at p 266, per Mason J. One way of providing that evidence may be by calling an expert witness. Another may be by calling evidence of the practice in the industry. But what is clear is that in such a case the safe system of work is a fact to be proved in order to establish the negligent character of the conduct of the employer before reliance can be placed upon that conduct. It is one of the ingredients which go to make up 'the fact of the occurrence of negligence' and for that reason is, in my view, and [sic] material fact within the meaning of s 57(1)(b) of the Act on which the cause of action in negligence is founded. ...

[258] Was the lack of knowledge of an alternative safe system of work a material fact of a decisive character? The test laid down by s 57(1)(c) is an objective one to be applied by reference to the reaction of a reasonable man who has taken appropriate advice. I think that it must be assumed that the reference to appropriate advice contemplates not only the taking, but also the receiving, of such advice upon the facts which are relied on as being of a decisive character. Whatever else may be said of this paragraph of the section, it is clear to my mind that it characterises as decisive at least each of those facts which must be proved in order to establish a cause of action. The question is whether a reasonable man, having received appropriate advice, would regard at least that concatenation of facts as showing 'a reasonable prospect of success'. In this case the appellant would not have been advised that that prospect of success was shown if the fact of an alternative safe system of work was omitted from the facts upon which advice was sought. The existence of an alternative safe system of work was, in this case, a material fact of a decisive character.

The next question is whether the existence of an alternative safe system of work was, for the purposes of s 58(2), 'within the means of knowledge' of the appellant during the relevant period. It is not enough that the appellant did not know. It is not really in dispute that he did not. It is a question of his means of knowledge. Moreover, it is to be noted that unlike s 57(1)(c), s 58(2) posits a subjective rather than an objective test. It is the means of knowledge [259] which were available to the appellant which are relevant and not the means of knowledge of a hypothetical reasonable man. And s 57(1)(e) provides that a fact is outside his means of knowledge if he does not know it and he has taken reasonable steps to ascertain it. The remarks of Lord Reid in *Smith v Central Asbestos Co* [1973] AC, at p 530, made in reference to a similarly worded provision, are to the point:

> In order to avoid constructive knowledge the plaintiff must have taken all such action as it was reasonable for him to take to find out. I agree with the view expressed in the Court of Appeal that this test is subjective. We are not concerned with 'the reasonable man'. Less is expected of a stupid or uneducated man than of a man of intelligence and wide experience.

It is also to be noted that it does not matter what advice the appellant received. In fact he sought advice and, it would appear, did not receive the advice which he ought to have been given. However, s 58(2), unlike s 57(1)(c), makes no assumption that appropriate advice was received when it was sought. What is important is the means of knowledge which were reasonably available to the appellant. And that must mean available in a practical and not a theoretical sense.

The master found, as I have said, that the appellant had not failed to take, before the specified time, reasonable steps to ascertain those facts which would have provided him with knowledge of an alternative safe system of work. There is no reason to doubt this finding of the master. The appellant is, as he found, 'a non-English speaking, poorly educated, ... immigrant in this country'. Within some four or five months after experiencing the symptoms of his lung disease he saw his union representative and inquired about his rights. He was referred by the union to the union solicitors. He was medically examined at the instance of the union solicitors but was given no indication during the relevant period that he had the basis of an action against the respondent and certainly no indication that an alternative system of work was available during the appellant's period of employment with the respondent. It was not until the appellant sought advice from solicitors other than the union solicitors that he or those solicitors learnt from a medical report that the risk of injury from dust could be minimised by hosing the area of operations with water and the wearing of face masks and that this information would have been generally available at the relevant time. Within a month those solicitors commenced an action on behalf of the appellant. Having consulted his union, the solicitors to whom the union referred him and the medical advisers [260] to whom those solicitors in turn referred him and having received no advice of an alternative safe system of work, it could not have been said that during the relevant time the appellant had within his means of knowledge at least one material fact of a decisive character within the meaning of the Limitation Act.

6.7.14   Notes and questions

1. The result of the appeal in the *Do Carmo* case was that the High Court allowed the appeal. Murphy ACJ, Brennan and Dawson JJ allowed the appeal, with Wilson and Deane JJ dissenting. However, there is no ratio in the case because the reason given by Murphy ACJ for allowing the appeal (that ignorance of a right of action was a material fact) was disagreed with by each of the other four judges. Brennan J agreed with Dawson J's judgment (above). Wilson and Deane JJ considered that the availability of precautions was a material fact, but that it was not of a decisive nature. Wilson J considered that the fact of an alternative safe system of work was a secondary fact and that its relevance and importance lay in determining whether primary facts (the inhalation of dust in a working environment where no provision had been made to reduce the hazard) were wrongful. Deane J agreed with this analysis of primary and secondary facts, while Dawson J found it to be unhelpful.

2. The *Do Carmo* case was discussed by the Queensland Court of Appeal in *Dick v University of Queensland* [2000] 2 Qd R 476. The *Do Carmo* and *Dick* cases are discussed and applied in *Castensen v Frankipile Australia* [2004] QSC 145 and *Hodgson v Dimbola Pty Ltd t/as Towers Removals* [2010] ACTCA 22.

3. The Queensland tests for the extension of the limitation period, contained in ss 30–31, have been repealed in New South Wales and Victoria and replaced by a just and reasonable test for extension, discussed at 6.7.2. In 1998 the Queensland Law Reform Commission issued a report, which recommended that a modified just and reasonable test be adopted in that jurisdiction: *Review of the Limitations of*

Actions Act 1974 (Qld), Report No 53, September 1998. What are the advantages and disadvantages of the just and reasonable model as opposed to the material facts model for the granting of an extension of time? For a discussion of the application of Qld ss 30–31 to cases involving psychiatric conditions, see *NF v State of Queensland* [2005] QCA 110 and *Stephenson v State of Queensland* [2004] QCA 483.

4. In 1970, S, a 22-year-old woman, underwent an operation to remove her gall bladder. During the surgery, her bile duct was severed, although this was not realised at the time. As a result she suffered extreme ill health and complications. During her subsequent treatment, S became aware that doctors were critical of the doctor who performed the first operation, but she did not know that her bile duct had been severed. When asked why she had not asked what had gone wrong in the 1970 operation, S stated that she did not know who to ask or how to go about it. S alleged that she became aware that her bile duct had been severed in 1992–93, when her solicitors obtained a report from the hospital where the operation had been performed. In May 1993, S sought an extension of time under the Victorian equivalent of Qld ss 30, 31. Would she be entitled to an extension of time? See *Koehne v Stanbury* [1996] 1 VR 203.

5. Section 30(1)(c)(ii) (Qld) requires the applicant to take reasonable steps in the circumstances of the case to ascertain the material facts. In *McManamny v Hadley* [1975] VR 705, the Full Supreme Court of Victoria held that the test to be applied in these circumstances is not a subjective one, rather it is an objective test to be applied to a person of the applicant's background and understanding. In *Koehne,* discussed at note 4 above, the applicant had left school at year eight, had married early in life and had three children with congenital heart defects, causing the death of two children. She had also had considerable ill-health since the operation, necessitating over 40 admissions to hospital. Did the court in *Koehne* consider that the applicant had acted reasonably in not ascertaining the material facts before 1992?

6. Where a newly-discovered fact goes to enlargement of the damages that may be recouped by the plaintiff, is this a 'material fact' within the terms of Qld s 30? What if the amount which the plaintiff had thought was previously recoverable was too small to bother about? See *Taggart v Workers' Compensation Board of Queensland* [1983] 2 Qd R.

NOTICE OF CLAIMS FOR PERSONAL INJURY ACTIONS INVOLVING MOTOR VEHICLES AND WORKERS' COMPENSATION

6.8.1 When a personal injury claim arises out of the use of a motor vehicle or in the context of employment, it is common for additional steps and notices to be mandated by legislation. These additional requirements are beyond the scope of this book, however the following commentary provides a general overview of this issue.

6.8.2 Some Australian jurisdictions have placed restrictions upon the recovery of common law damages for personal injury or death arising out of the use of a motor vehicle. These provisions mandate time frames within which steps must be taken. See, for example, the Motor Accidents Compensation Act 1999 (NSW); Motor Accidents (Compensation) Act 1979 (NT); and Transport Accidents Act 1986 (Vic). *Builders and Contractors v Rawlings* [2010]

VSCA 306 which examines the operation of the Limitation of Actions Act 1958 (Vic) in conjunction with s 135AC of the Accident Compensation Act 1985 (Vic).

6.8.3 Similarly, in every Australian jurisdiction there is in force a no-fault workers' compensation scheme which provides compensation in respect of injury or death attributable to employment. Each jurisdiction places limitations upon the time within which notice of the injury must be submitted. See generally Safety, Rehabilitation and Compensation Act 1988 (Cth); Seafarers Rehabilitation and Compensation Act 1992 (Cth); Workers Compensation Act 1951 (ACT); Workers Compensation Act 1987 (NSW); Workplace Injury Management and Workers Compensation Act 1998 (NSW); Workers Rehabilitation and Compensation Act 2008 (NT); Workers' Compensation and Rehabilitation Act 2003 (Qld); Workers Rehabilitation and Compensation Act 1986 (SA); WorkCover Corporation Act 1994 (SA); Workers Rehabilitation and Compensation Act 1988 (Tas); Accident Compensation Act 1985 (Vic); Accident Compensation (WorkCover Insurance) Act 1993 (Vic); Workers' Compensation and Injury Management Act 1981 (WA)

For an example of the relationship between this legislation and the Limitation Acts, see *Morris & Joan Rawlings Builders and Contractors v Rawlings* [2010] VSCA 306 which examines the operation of the Limitation of Actions Act 1958 (Vic) in conjunction with s 135AC of the Accident Compensation Act 1985 (Vic).

6.8.4 Additional time periods may also be mandated in legislation. For example, legislation may require that the plaintiff serve a notice of claim upon a respondent as a prerequisite to commencing personal injury proceedings. The time frames for such notices are stipulated in the legislation and such time stipulations are in addition to the requirements in the Limitation Acts, see s 51 of the Civil Law (Wrongs) Act 2002 (ACT), s 8 of the Personal Injuries (Civil Claims) Act 2002 (NT) and ss 9–9A of the Personal Injuries Proceedings Act 2002 (Qld). See *Davison v State of Queensland* (2006) 226 CLR 234; (2006) 227 ALR 1 for a discussion of the relationship between the Personal Injuries Proceedings Act 2002 (Qld) and the Limitation of Actions Act 1974 (Qld).

6.8.5 Further reading

CCH IntelliConnect, *Torts and Personal Injury Law,* 2012.

CCH IntelliConnect, *Workers Compensation,* 2012.

J Glissan, et al, *Personal Injury Litigation NSW,* LexisNexis, looseleaf.

P Mullins et al, *Personal Injury Litigation Qld,* LexisNexis, looseleaf.

Halsbury's Laws of Australia, 'Accident Compensation Schemes', [425–1500]ff, LexisNexis, looseleaf.

LIMITATIONS PERIODS AND CHOICE OF LAW

6.9.1 Some states and territories have longer limitation periods than others for certain causes of action. Plaintiffs may seek to commence their actions in jurisdictions where their claims are not statute-barred. This raises the question of whether a court has jurisdiction to hear a case brought by a particular plaintiff, which is decided by reference to the principles of choice of law. Due to factors such as the increasing globalisation of transactions, plaintiffs have become increasingly adventurous in commencing actions in a wider range of jurisdictions. Plaintiffs or defendants may also argue that a matter should be transferred to a more appropriate jurisdiction under the cross-vesting legislation: eg, the Jurisdiction of Courts (Cross-vesting) Act 1987 (Cth). The choice of law rules require the court to decide which limitation period applies to the action which has been commenced in that jurisdiction. This involves deciding whether limitation periods are substantive or procedural.

Substantive or procedural?

6.9.2 Traditionally, under the general law, limitation provisions were regarded as procedural and therefore the forum court would apply its own limitation provisions, for example, the limitation provisions of the state or territory where the court was physically located. In a series of tort cases (*Koop v Bebb* (1951) 84 CLR 629; *McKain v R W Miller & Co (SA) Pty Ltd* (1991) 174 CLR 1; *Stevens v Head* (1993) 176 CLR 433), the High Court held that the law of the forum was to apply where the tort occurred in another jurisdiction.

6.9.3 The Australian Law Reform Commission in its Report No 58, *Choice of Law*, p 8, made the following statement about the *McKain* case:

> The inability of the High Court to reform rules which preserve a special position for forum law, both in regard to substance and procedure ... make it necessary for these areas of law to be reviewed.

That review has now taken place in most Australian jurisdictions and the decision of the majority in *McKain* was reversed by the following state and territory legislation: Limitation Act 1985 (ACT) ss 55–57; Choice of Law (Limitation Periods) Act 1993 (NSW); Choice of Law (Limitation Periods) Act 1994 (NT); Choice of Law (Limitation Periods) Act 1996 (Qld); Limitations of Actions Act 1936 (SA) s 38A; Limitation Act 1974 (Tas) ss 32A–32D; Choice of Law (Limitation Periods) Act 1993 (Vic); Choice of Law (Limitation Periods) Act 1994 (WA).

6.9.4E **Limitation Act 1974 (Tas)**
Limitation periods for choice of law purposes

Characterization of limitation laws
32C If the substantive law of another place, being another State, a Territory or New Zealand, is to govern a cause of action before a court of this State, a limitation law of that place is to be regarded as part of that substantive law and applied accordingly by the court.

Exercise of discretion under limitation law
32D Where a court of this State exercises a discretion conferred under a limitation law of a place, being another State, a Territory or New Zealand, that discretion, as far as practicable, is to be exercised in a manner in which it is exercised in comparable cases by the courts of that place.

6.9.5 These provisions and their equivalents require courts to regard a 'limitation law' (defined as one which prescribes a time limit for the commencement of proceedings) of another state or territory or of New Zealand, as part of the substantive law of that place 'if the substantive law of [that place] is to govern a claim before a court of [the State or Territory concerned]'. For an interesting application of ss 36, 45 and 48 of the South Australian Limitation Act by a Victorian Court, see *Berriman v Cricket Australia* (2007) 17 VR 528.

A similar result was reached by the High Court in *Pfeiffer v Rogerson* (extracted below) as least as regards actions in tort. The High Court held in *Pfeiffer* that the substantive law of the place where the tort occurred is the law that must be applied in the forum.

6.9.6C   **John Pfeiffer Pty Ltd v Rogerson**
                                   (2000) 203 CLR 503; 172 ALR 625
                                        High Court of Australia
                                         (footnotes omitted)

Gleeson CJ, Gaudron, McHugh, Gummow and Hayne JJ (at 650):
Substance and procedure
[97] As already indicated, the choice of law rules traditionally distinguish between questions of substance and questions of procedure. There is much history that lies behind the distinction, but search as one may, it is very hard, if not impossible, to identify some unifying principle which would assist in making the distinction in a particular case. But, as the majority said in McKain:

> Though the dividing line is sometimes doubtful or even artificial, the need to distinguish between substantive law and procedural law is clearly recognized for a number of forensic purposes.

[98] Some statutes of limitation have traditionally been held to be procedural on the basis that they bar the remedy not the right; other limitation provisions have been held to be substantive. But all limitation provisions can affect whether a plaintiff recovers. Questions of what heads of damage are allowable have been held to be substantive; but questions of quantification of damages have been held to be procedural. But all questions about damages can affect how much a plaintiff recovers and, thus, statutes such as the NSW Compensation Act, which is in issue in this case, alter the rights of plaintiffs and, also, the obligations of defendants.

[99] Two guiding principles should be seen as lying behind the need to distinguish between substantive and procedural issues. First, litigants who resort to a court to obtain relief must take the court as they find it. A plaintiff cannot ask that a tribunal which does not exist in the forum (but does in the place where a wrong was committed) should be established to deal, in the forum, with the claim that the plaintiff makes. Similarly, the plaintiff cannot ask that the courts of the forum adopt procedures or give remedies of a kind which their constituting statutes do not contemplate any more than the plaintiff can ask that the court apply any adjectival law other than the laws of the forum. Secondly, matters that affect the existence, extent or enforceability of the rights or duties of the parties to an action are matters that, on their face, appear to be concerned with issues of substance, not with issues of procedure. Or to adopt the formulation put forward by Mason CJ in McKain, 'rules which are directed to governing or regulating the mode or conduct of court proceedings' are procedural and all other provisions or rules are to be classified as substantive.

[100] These principles may require further elucidation in subsequent decisions but it should be noted that giving effect to them has significant consequences for the kinds of case in which the distinction between substance and procedure has previously been applied. First, the application of any limitation period, whether barring the remedy or extinguishing the right, would be taken to be a question of substance not procedure (which is the result arrived at by the statutes previously referred to). The application of any limitation period would, therefore, continue to be governed (as that legislation requires) by the lex loci delicti. Secondly, all questions about the kinds of damage, or amount of damages that may be recovered, would likewise be treated as substantive issues governed by the lex loci delicti.

Conclusion

[101] Development of the common law in the manner we propose is consistent with the assumption that underlies the State legislation with respect to limitation periods to which we have earlier referred and, also, with the terms of that legislation. That being so, there is no reason why the Court should leave the common law to operate in a manner that does not properly take account either of the fact of federal jurisdiction or the nature of the Australian federation.

[102] Development of the common law to reflect the fact of federal jurisdiction and, also, the nature of the Australian federation requires that the double actionability rule now be discarded. The lex loci delicti should be applied by courts in Australia as the law governing all questions of substance to be determined in a proceeding arising from an intranational tort. And laws that bear upon the existence, extent or enforceability of remedies, rights and obligations should be characterised as substantive and not as procedural laws.

6.9.7   Notes and questions

1. Do you agree with the comment in para 102 above that 'laws that bear upon the existence, extent or enforceability of remedies, rights and obligations *should* be characterised as substantive and not as procedural laws'? See P Spender, *Oxford Companion to the High Court*, M Coper, T Blackshield and G Williams (eds), Oxford University Press, Melbourne, 2001, p 105.

2. The High Court provided further guidance on the *Pfeiffer* substantive/ procedural analysis in *BHP Billiton Ltd v Schultz* (2004) 211 ALR 523 and *Blunden v Commonwealth of Australia* (2003) 203 ALR 189.

Further reading

6.10.1   Articles

L Bunney, 'Limitation of Actions: Effect on Child Sexual Abuse Survivors in Queensland' (1998) 18 *Qd L* 128.

T Buti, 'Removal of Indigenous Children from their Families: The Litigation Path' (1998) 27 *Univ WAL Rev* 203.

P J Davies, 'Limitations of the Law of Limitation' (1982) 82 *LQR* 249.

S Gray, 'Holding the Government to Account: The "Stolen Wages" Issue, Fiduciary Duty and Trust Law' (2008) 32 *MULR* 115.

M Green, 'The Paradox of Statutes of Limitations in Toxic Substances Litigation' (1988) 76 *Calif L Rev* 965.

P Handford, 'Limitation of Actions and Tort Reform' (2002) 25 *UNSWLJ* 871.

D Jackson, 'The Legal Effect of the Passing of Time' (1969–70) 7 *MULR* 407.

R James, 'New Claims and Limitations Periods' [1995] *CJQ* 42.

M Jones, 'Limitation Periods and Plaintiffs under a Disability — A Zealous Protection?' [1995] *CJQ* 258.

R Kune, 'The Stolen Generations in Court: Explaining the Lack of Widespread Successful Litigation by Members of the Stolen Generations' (2011) 30 *UTLR* 32.

B Mathews, 'Judicial Considerations of Reasonable Conduct by Survivors of Child Sexual Abuse' (2004) 27(3) *UNSWLJ* 631.

B Matthews, 'Limitation Periods in Child Sex Abuse Cases in Queensland: Recent Cases Provide Both Hope and Caution' (2003) 57 *Plaintiff* 12.

B Mathews, 'Queensland Government Actions to Compensate Survivors of Institutional Abuse: A Critical and Comparative Evaluation' (2004) 4 *QUTLJJ* 23.

A McGee, 'A Critical Analysis of the English Law of Limitations Periods' (1990) 9 *CJQ* 366.

A McGee and G Scanlan, 'Constructive Knowledge within the Limitation Act' (2003) *CJQ* 248.

A McGee and G Scanlan, 'Fraud, Concealment and Mistake in the Limitation Act 1980' (2001) 20 *CJQ* 171.

A McGee and G Scanlan, 'Judicial Attitudes to Limitation' (2005) 24 *CJQ* 460.

D Morgan, 'Limitation and Discretion: Procedural Reform and Substantive Effect' (1982) 1 *CJQ* 109.

K Patten, 'Limitation Periods in Personal Injury Claims — Justice Obstructed' (2006) 25 *CJQ* 349.

6.10.2 Books

'Civil Procedure — Limitation of Actions', *Laws of Australia*, Thomson Reuters, Ch 5.10, viewed 13 June 2012.

P Handford, *Limitations of Actions: The Australian Law*, Lawbook Co, 2nd ed, 2007.

A McGee, *Limitation Periods*, Sweet & Maxwell, United Kingdom, 6th ed, 2010.

Commencing Proceedings

## CHAPTER 7

OVERVIEW

This chapter will outline the law and practice which governs the commencement of proceedings in the Supreme Courts, Federal Court and High Court. The chapter canvasses issues that must be heeded by the plaintiff's lawyer prior to drafting court documents. For example, certain jurisdictions require pre-action protocols to be observed. The forms and history of originating process are then discussed. The term 'action' applies to disputes predominantly involving factual issues. This category is the major type of dispute dealt with by the Supreme Courts and is commonly commenced by writ. Conversely, the term 'matter' referred to disputes which were predominantly about legal issues. The various forms of originating process for both types of dispute will be reviewed. Finally, the duration of originating process and criteria for renewal will be considered.

CLIENT CARE

7.1.1   In a lawyer–client relationship, 'client care' means ensuring that all contacts made between the lawyer and the client promote a positive and fruitful relationship. Critical to the development of such a relationship is effective communication. A common complaint to professional associations is the failure of lawyers to communicate adequately with their clients. When litigation is commenced it is necessary to keep the client informed of all steps in the process and of the consequences of each step. Initiating proceedings may lead to prolonged involvement in a court action with significant costs.

7.1.2   Client care practices are promoted by effective interviewing. The legal interview is a vital aspect of lawyer-client communication and represents the primary means of access to the law for many people. For an example of good legal interviewing practice when considering litigation, see K Lauchland and M Le Brun, *Legal Interviewing: Theory, Tactics and Techniques*, Sydney, Butterworths, 1996, pp 79–80, 86–7.

Costs disclosures

7.1.3   Provisions requiring legal practitioners to make disclosures about legal costs to prospective clients were included in the National Legal Profession Model Bill, 2nd ed

(Pt 3.4, Div 3), a joint initiative of Commonwealth, state and territory attorneys-general to comprehensively reform the legal profession in Australia. These provisions are being gradually enacted across state and territory jurisdictions: Legal Profession Act 2006 (ACT) Pt 3.2; Legal Profession Act 2004 (NSW) Pt 3.2; Legal Profession Act (NT) Pt 3.3 Div 3; Legal Profession Act 2007 (Qld) Pt 3.4 Div 3; Legal Profession Act 2007 (Tas) Pt 3.3; Legal Profession Act 2004 (Vic) Pt 3.4; Legal Profession Act 2008 (WA) Pt 10. The provisions specify what information must be disclosed to clients regarding legal costs and provide that disclosure is to be made in writing before, or as soon as practicable after, a practitioner or firm is retained.

7.1.4   Further reading

A J Chay and J Smith, *Legal Interviewing in Practice*, LBC Information Services, Sydney, 1996.

G D Lewis, E J Kyrou and A Dinelli, *Handy Hints on Legal Practice*, 3rd ed, Sydney, Law Book Co, 2004.

PRE-ACTION PROTOCOLS

7.2.1 The term 'pre-action protocols' refers to steps that must be taken by parties prior to commencing litigation. These protocols were originally introduced in England as part of the reforms to civil procedure that followed Lord Woolf's *Access to Justice* Report discussed at **2.5.1**. The protocols are designed to encourage the early disclosure of relevant documents and information to better enable parties to assess their cases and settle: A Marriott, 'Breaking the Dispute Resolution Deadlock: Civil Litigation and ADR in the United Kingdom and beyond' (2006) 17 *ADRJ* 157 at 157. In the UK, practice directions set out the requirements for pre-action protocols both generally (Civil Procedure Rules, Practice Direction: Pre-action Conduct (UK)) and for specific claims. There are currently 11 pre-action protocols in the UK covering claims such as construction and engineering disputes, defamation, personal injury claims, judicial review, professional negligence, and disease and illness claims: see generally, viewed at 25 April 2012, <http://www.justice.gov.uk/courts/procedure-rules/civil/protocol>.

7.2.2 The Civil Dispute Resolution Act 2011 (Cth) seeks to ensure that parties take 'genuine steps' to resolve a civil dispute before proceedings are commenced in the Federal Court or the Federal Magistrates' Court. When commencing proceedings in those jurisdictions, parties are required to file a statement saying what steps they have taken to resolve their dispute or, if they have not taken any steps, the reasons why not (eg, urgency or personal safety): ss 6 and 7.

Lawyers are under an obligation to advise their clients of the requirement and assist them to comply with it: s 9. The court can take into account the failure to take steps when exercising its existing case management directions and costs powers: ss 11 and 12.

7.2.3E **Civil Dispute Resolution Act 2011 (Cth)**
Part 1 — Preliminary

4 Genuine steps to resolve a dispute

(1A) For the purposes of this Act, a person takes **genuine steps to resolve a dispute** if the steps taken by the person in relation to the dispute constitute a sincere and genuine attempt to resolve the dispute, having regard to the person's circumstances and the nature and circumstances of the dispute.

(1) Examples of steps that could be taken by a person as part of taking genuine steps to resolve a dispute with another person, include the following:

    (a) notifying the other person of the issues that are, or may be, in dispute, and offering to discuss them, with a view to resolving the dispute;

    (b) responding appropriately to any such notification;

    (c) providing relevant information and documents to the other person to enable the other person to understand the issues involved and how the dispute might be resolved;

    (d) considering whether the dispute could be resolved by a process facilitated by another person, including an alternative dispute resolution process;

    (e) if such a process is agreed to:

        (i) agreeing on a particular person to facilitate the process; and

        (ii) attending the process;

    (f) if such a process is conducted but does not result in resolution of the dispute— considering a different process;

    (g) attempting to negotiate with the other person, with a view to resolving some or all the issues in dispute, or authorising a representative to do so.

(2) Subsection (1) does not limit the steps that may constitute taking genuine steps to resolve a dispute.

7.2.4 For a discussion of the obligations of the applicant, respondent and their respective lawyers to comply with the Civil Dispute Resolution Act 2011 (Cth), see *Superior IP International Pty Ltd v Ahearn Fox Patent and Trade Mark Attorneys* [2012] FCA 282. See also rr 5.03 and 8.02 of the Federal Court Rules 2011 (Cth) regarding compliance with ss 6 and 7 of the same Act.

7.2.5 Although pre-action protocols were introduced in New South Wales and Victoria in Pt 2A of the Civil Procedure Act 2005 (NSW) and Ch 3 of the Civil Procedure Act (Vic) respectively, commencement of the New South Wales provisions has been deferred until March 2013 (by the Courts and Other Legislation Further Amendment Act 2011 (NSW)) and repealed in Victoria (by the Civil Procedure and Legal Profession Amendment Act 2011 (Vic)). The *uncommenced* New South Wales provisions at s 18E require persons who are involved in a civil dispute to take reasonable steps, having regard to the person's situation, the nature of the dispute, (including the value of any claim and the complexity of the issues) to resolve the dispute by agreement or to clarify and narrow the issues in dispute.

7.2.6   Further reading

C Bush and K Evans, 'Who's Afraid of the Civil Dispute Resolution Act and its Requirement to Take "Genuine Steps"?' (2011) 8(1) *Australian Civil Liability* 150.

O Dinkha, 'The Introduction of Pre-litigation Dispute Resolution Requirements to the NSW Civil Procedure Act 2005' (2011) 7(9) *Australian Civil Liability* 114.

M Legg and D Boniface, 'Pre-action Protocols in Australia' (2010) 20 *JJA* 39.

LETTERS OF DEMAND

7.3.1   A letter of demand is often used by solicitors prior to instituting proceedings. These letters may be useful to bring about a speedy resolution of matters in dispute between the parties. If a negotiated settlement is desired, the letter may be accompanied by a 'without prejudice' offer to settle the dispute, so that if settlement is not reached, admissions may not be put into evidence. Alternatively, the letter may disclose deficiencies in the instructions provided by the client; for example, where the defendant is dead, is not incorporated or has been placed into liquidation, has a different name to that advised by the client or cannot be located. A letter of demand might also seek information about insurers or other potential parties to the litigation.

7.3.2   While letters of demand might be inappropriate in the context of particular disputes, for example, where there are concerns about evidence being destroyed or violent behaviour, generally speaking, putting the defendant on notice might increase the costs and statutory interest which may be recouped by the client: *R v Inland Revenue; Ex parte Opman* [1986] 1 WLR 568. Further, a successful application for costs may be jeopardised if proceedings are commenced before making a demand, see *In the Estate of Lucas* (1895) 1 ALR 61. This approach may apply where interlocutory proceedings are brought without first asking the other party to consent: *Moore v Gannon* (1915) 32 WN (NSW) 60.

7.3.3   Lawyers' professional associations have made rulings about the content of letters of demand. For example, it is unethical to threaten criminal proceedings as an alternative to available civil redress. It is also improper to demand payment of a debt from someone with no legal liability to pay an alleged debt (Law Society of New South Wales, 'Letters of Demand Threatening Criminal Proceedings' (1992) 30 *L Soc J* 37) or to claim costs that are unreasonable or excessive in the circumstances (Law Institute of Victoria, 'Letters of Demand' (1993) 67 *L Inst J* 146). See generally V Shirvington, 'Letters of Demand — Just How Demanding Can You Be?' (1996) 34 *L Soc J* 28.

7.3.4   When lawyers are acting for defendants, they will have to make tactical decisions about whether or not to reply to a letter of demand. Clearly, sometimes such letters are written without the intention of instituting proceedings. However, a failure to answer a letter of demand may amount to an admission of its correctness in certain circumstances: *Thomas v Hollier* (1984) 156 CLR 152 at 157 per Gibbs CJ. Misuse of letters of demand by a solicitor may amount to professional misconduct: *In Re X (a Solicitor)* [1935] ALR 263.

COMMENCING PROCEEDINGS

Terminology

7.4.1 The different forms of modern originating process are derived from the historical distinction between a cause and a matter. A *cause* had two or more parties and a *matter* had only one. The most common kind of civil cause is an action. An *action* is a cause which was traditionally commenced by a *writ of summons*: *Herbert Berry Associates Ltd v Inland Revenue Commissioners* [1978] 1 All ER 161 at 170; *Parkin v James* (1905) 2 CLR 315 at 342. The substantive legal issue upon which the plaintiff relies may also be referred to as a *cause of action*, for example, breach of contract, negligence etc. An action will generally involve a factual dispute, although there may also be legal arguments.

Even though some jurisdictions no longer employ the term 'action' (and other jurisdictions have defined the term so that proceedings other than those commenced by writ fall within it), most of the proceedings which are dealt with in the Supreme Courts and regulated by the rules of the Supreme Courts fall within the description of 'action' discussed above.

By comparison, a *matter* was a proceeding where there was no dispute with another party; for example, a trustee applying for directions as to how to administer a trust or a law graduate applying to the court for admission as a solicitor. However, the word 'matter' has now acquired a vernacular meaning which is synonymous with 'court proceeding' and lawyers frequently say that they are dealing with a matter even though they are not referring to the technical sense of the word.

7.4.2 The forms of originating process emanated from England with the enactment of the Judicature Acts from 1873–75. These Acts allowed for four types of originating process: the writ of summons, originating summons, petition and originating motion. Those forms of process were adopted in the High Court of Australia and in the Supreme Courts of the states by rules which largely followed the Rules of the Supreme Court 1883 (UK). Those rules drew a distinction between the various forms of originating process on the basis that an action was commenced by a writ of summons, a written application was made to the court by petition, an oral application was made to the court on motion and an application to a judge in chambers was made by summons. The rules in force in Tasmania follow the 1883 English rules, though they provide for different forms of originating process.

7.4.3E   **Supreme Court Rules 2000 (Tas)**
Part 7 — Proceedings
Division 3 — Commencement of proceedings

Actions
88. The following classes of proceedings are to be commenced by a writ, unless these rules provide that they are to be commenced by application:
   (a)   for the recovery of a debt;
   (b)   for the recovery of wages or other remuneration;
   (c)   for the restitution or return of money paid;
   (d)   for the assessment of a sum as the value of goods or services, including claims on a quantum meruit or quantum valebat;

(e)   proceedings based on a common count;

(f)   for the recovery of a sum due on a negotiable instrument;

(g)   for the return of goods or their value;

(h)   for the recovery of money due in respect of necessaries supplied;

(i)   for the enforcement of a bond;

(j)   for the enforcement of a contract, an indemnity or a guarantee;

(k)   for the specific performance of a contract;

(l)   for the recovery of rent or mesne profits;

(m)   for the recovery of land;

(n)   for the recovery of damages, however arising;

(o)   for the declaration of a private right, including a right to ownership of personal property, except one to which rule 89(a) or rule 90(1)(a) applies;

(p)   for the declaration of a public right, except one to which rule 89(a) or rule 90(1)(a) applies;

(q)   for the rectification of a deed or other instrument;

(r)   for the setting aside of a contract or a gift;

(s)   for the setting aside of a deed, conveyance, transfer or other instrument;

(t)   in the nature of an action of replevin;

(u)   for an injunction, except if it is sought as ancillary to relief claimed in an application;

(v)   for the enforcement of a statutory right if the statute creating the right specifies that the proceeding to enforce the right is to be by way of an action;

(w)   for other relief which, before the commencement of the Act, was sought by action commenced by —

     (i)   writ or plaint and summons; or

     (ii)   bill or information in the equity jurisdiction of the Court; or

     (iii)   citation or otherwise in the ecclesiastical jurisdiction of the Court;

(x)   for the repeal, revocation, cancellation or vacation of any grant or charter granted or issued by the Crown or of any record;

(y)   against the Crown.

7.4.4   The method adopted by Tasmania of nominating most of the forms of relief which might be sought by the plaintiff in an action, is unique among Australian jurisdictions. The other jurisdictions create overarching forms of originating process. Some jurisdictions have one form of originating process, that is, the Federal Court (originating application — r 8.01); and South Australia: summons — r 34. Other jurisdictions have two principal forms of originating process which broadly maintain the historical dichotomy between the action and the matter. Therefore:

•   procedures which are based on the *action* contemplate that the dispute primarily concerns factual issues, thus anticipates pleadings and an eventual trial in open court. Examples are the statement of claim in New South Wales, the claim in Queensland, the originating claim in the Australian Capital Territory and the writ in Northern Territory, Tasmania, Victoria and Western Australia;

•   procedures which are based on the *matter* contemplate that the dispute predominantly involves the resolution of legal issues, and the plaintiff wishes to proceed by way of affidavit rather than pleadings. These processes are derived from the chamber jurisdiction of the court;

that is, where the plaintiff applies to a judicial officer in chambers. They are commonly used for equity and probate matters. See, eg, the originating application (ACT); the summons (NSW); the application (Qld); the originating motion (NT) and (Vic); and the originating summons: WA.

This chapter will primarily use the *writ* to exemplify originating procedures which are based on the action at 7.5.1. Thereafter, at 7.5.9, it will examine other types of originating process for disputes involving factual issues. At 7.6.1 it will examine disputes predominantly based on legal issues, ie, procedures which evolved from the matter.

7.4.5 A third form of initiating process is the motion. A motion is used where a party applies in open court for a favourable outcome. In other words, the party moves for an outcome, as they would in a debate. Motions are commonly sought where a dispute arises between the parties at the interlocutory stage. Where there is an unresolved interlocutory dispute between the parties, for example a dispute about discovery, one party will generally file a motion to seek orders from the court. Where the other party is involved, the process is called a notice of motion. However, motions are commonly made *ex parte*, so that a party merely obtains a time from the court and puts the motion to the relevant court officer. The motion is now commonly referred to as an 'application' or 'summons' and is discussed in more detail at 16.2.3.

7.4.6 The High Court Rules recognise several forms of initiating process where proceedings are commenced in the High Court's original jurisdiction, such as applications and petitions, but the main form is the writ of summons: HCR r 20.01.

7.4.7 Originating process commences as of right upon its presentation in proper form to the court's registry with the appropriate filing fee. The Court Rules generally refer to proceedings being 'issued' by the plaintiff or the court (HCR r 20.01.4; Qld r 8; Tas r 105; WA O 5 r 6) or describe this process as 'filing' or 'commencing': FCR r 8.01; ACT r 32(1); NSW r 6.2(1); NT r 5.11; SA r 34(1); Vic r 5.11. The issue, filing or commencing of an originating process is not regarded as a judicial act by the court. The time of issue or commencement is when the originating process is sealed by the relevant court registrar or otherwise accepted by the court registry: Vic r 5.11(1A)(a); WA O 5 r 6. In practical terms, the originating process and the number of copies of it that are required for service are stamped at the court registry and the stamped copies for service are returned to the filing party: HCR r 20.02; NSW rr 4.10, 4.12; NT r 5.11(3); Vic r 5.11(3); at common law, see *The Espanoleto* [1920] 125 LT 121 and *Cheney v Spooner* (1929) 41 CLR 532 at 536–7.

Proceedings may sometimes be commenced orally, for example when urgent relief is sought: ACT r 37, NT r 4.08, Qld r 12. Increasingly, the court rules provide for electronic lodgment of originating process and for the sealed copies for service to bear a computer-generated image of the court's seal: NSW r 3.4; SA r 51(2); Vic rr 5.11, 28.10, 28.11.

[*Note:* In this chapter a reference, such as WA O 9 r 2, is a reference to the relevant Rules of Court, set out in full at 1.4.2. All other legislation will be specified.]

Ethical considerations

7.4.8 When a lawyer decides to institute proceedings on behalf of a client, the lawyer should be satisfied that the case has merit. However, sometimes plaintiffs make claims that are not well-supported by the law in the hope that an early negotiated settlement will obviate the need to commence proceedings. If the client has a hopeless case, is the plaintiff's lawyer under any ethical obligation to refuse to commence proceedings?

If a lawyer commences proceedings which have no legal foundation, the proceedings may constitute an abuse of process. Such proceedings could be struck out or permanently stayed by the court: *Williams v Spautz* (1992) 174 CLR 509: see **12.7.5Cff**. The major disciplining factor is that a costs award may be made against the client and potentially against the lawyer personally. Courts have express power to order a party's lawyer to pay or forgo costs where the lawyer has incurred costs improperly or without reasonable cause: FCR r 40.07; ACT rr 1753, 1754; Civil Procedure Act 2005 (NSW) s 99; NT r 63.21; Qld r 690; SA r 13; Tas r 61; Vic r 63.23; WA O 66 r 5. This power was discussed by Goldberg J in *White Industries (Qld) Pty Ltd v Flower & Hart (a firm)* (1998) 156 ALR 169 at 231:

> I consider there are limitations on the proposition that commencing or maintaining proceedings which have no or substantially no prospects of success may result in a costs order being made against a practitioner. Something more must be added to the equation such as, for example, an ulterior purpose, abuse of process or a serious dereliction of duty.

The summary procedure is also available to the other party where the proceedings do not disclose a reasonable cause of action: see generally **Chapter 12**.

However, it may be a dereliction of the lawyer's duty to expose the client to liability for unnecessary costs. The classic statement of a lawyer's professional responsibility when requested to take on a hopeless case was made by Lord Esher in *Re Cooke* (1889) 5 TLR 407. His Lordship opined that if the lawyer is unable to form the certain and absolute opinion that the case is hopeless and the client insists upon commencing proceedings even though he or she is fully informed of the risks of taking that course, the lawyer will not be behaving dishonourably by taking instructions: at 408.

However, his Lordship's views have been superseded in some jurisdictions by statutory provisions which provide that lawyers must not provide legal services for certain claims, unless they reasonably believe that the claim or defence has reasonable prospects of success. Failing to comply with this requirement may amount to professional misconduct or lead to adverse costs orders against the lawyer personally. In Australian Capital Territory and New South Wales, this requirement applies to claims or defences for actions seeking for damages. In these jurisdictions, lawyers must provide a certificate that the claim or defence has reasonable prospects of success when lodging a pleading in a damages action: Civil Law (Wrongs) Act 2002 (ACT) ss 188–190; Legal Profession Act 2004 (NSW) Pt 3.2 Div 10 ss 344–349. A similar process applies in the Federal Court where lawyers representing an applicant who is commencing migration litigation must certify that they have reasonable grounds for believing that the migration litigation has a reasonable prospect of success: Migration Act 1958 (Cth) s 486I; FCR r 8.04.

7.4.9 The New South Wales Court of Appeal discussed Pt 3.2 Div 10 of the Legal Profession Act 2004 (NSW) in *Lemoto v Able Technical Pty Ltd* [2005] NSWCA 153; *Firth v Latham* [2007] NSWCA 40; and *Fowler v Toro Constructions Pty Ltd* [2008] NSWCA 178 and the Full Federal Court dealt with arguments about s 486I of the Migration Act 1958 (Cth) in *Nguyen v Minister for Immigration and Citizenship* [2007] FCAFC 38.

7.4.10 Victoria goes further than other jurisdictions in requiring that parties certify adherence to the overarching obligations (see **2.5.6ff**) as well as requiring legal representatives to certify that allegations of fact, denials and non-admissions have a proper basis, as follows:

7.4.11E | **Civil Procedure 2010 (Vic)**

41 Overarching obligations certification by parties on commencement of civil proceeding

(1) Each party must personally certify that the party has read and understood the overarching obligations and the paramount duty.

(2) The overarching obligations certification must be—

    (a) filed with the first substantive document in the civil proceeding filed by the party; and

    (b) otherwise in accordance with the rules of court. ...

42 Proper basis certification

(1) On the filing of a party's first substantive document in a civil proceeding and any document that contains significant amendments to the first substantive document, a legal practitioner acting for or on behalf of a party to the proceeding must certify that, on the factual and legal material available —

    (a) each allegation of fact in the document has a proper basis;

    (b) each denial in the document has a proper basis;

    (c) there is a proper basis for each nonadmission in the document.

7.4.12 Note and questions

1. Should the Australian Capital Territory, the Commonwealth and New South Wales follow the example set by Victoria and require certification for all types of proceedings, not just claims for damages or migration claims?

2. Alternatively, does the Victorian standard stifle the development of the law by discouraging doubtful cases?

3. For a further discussion of *White Industries (Qld) Pty Ltd v Flower & Hart*, see *Steindl Nominees Pty Ltd v Laghaifar* [2003] 2 Qd R 683. Compare the approach of Weinberg J in *Tran v Minister for Immigration and Multicultural and Indigenous Affairs (No 2)* (2006) 228 ALR 727.

7.4.13 Further reading

G Dal Pont, *Lawyers' Professional Responsibility*, 4th ed, Lawbook Co, Sydney, 2009.

Y Ross, *Ethics in Law: Lawyers' Responsibility and Accountability in Australia*, 5th ed, LexisNexis Butterworths, 2009.

DISPUTES PREDOMINANTLY INVOLVING FACTUAL ISSUES

The writ of summons

7.5.1 The main type of originating process used in Australian state and territory Supreme Courts is the writ. Where a dispute involves factual issues, proceedings must be commenced by writ in the High Court (r 20.01.4), the Northern Territory (rr 4.01, 4.04), Tasmania (r 88), Victoria (rr 4.01, 4.04) and Western Australia: O 4 r 1. Originally, the writ was a written command of the sovereign which summoned the defendant to enter an appearance in the court.

Indorsements

7.5.2 A writ must contain an indorsement, also known as an 'endorsement'. There are two types of indorsement, general and special, although the terminology for these categories varies between jurisdictions.

7.5.3 A general indorsement is not a pleading; rather, it is a general statement which puts the defendant on notice of the claim and foreshadows a statement of claim. Barwick CJ and McTiernan J described the indorsement in *Renowden v McMullin* (1970) 123 CLR 584 at 595:

> The indorsement on the writ not being a statement of claim is not in the nature of a pleading. In our opinion, it should not be construed as such but read for what it is, namely, a notice of the nature of the plaintiff's claim, of the cause thereof and of the relief sought in the action. ... On the other hand, the indorsement marks out the perimeter or range of the area within which the plaintiff may express his claim in a formal fashion in his statement of claim whether as originally filed or as sought to be amended.

For a general discussion of the relationship between writs and statements of claim, see 7.5.6.

The rules of each jurisdiction mandate the content of the general indorsement, but generally require a statement of the nature of the claim made and the relief or remedy sought in the action: HCR r 27.01; NT r 5.04; Tas r 108; Vic r 5.04; WA O 6 r 1.

Ruzeu v Massey-Ferguson [1983] 1 VR 733 concerned what was then O 3 r 1 of the Victorian Supreme Court Rules, which required a statement of the nature of the claim, the cause relied upon and the relief or remedy sought. The general indorsement on the writ stated as follows:

> The Plaintiff's claim is for damages for injuries he received to his back in an accident which occurred in [sic] or about 2 December 1975 whilst he was in the course of his employment with the Defendant. The accident occurred as a result of the negligence of the Defendant its servants or agents and the Plaintiff claims damages.

The Full Court held that the question of whether the indorsement complies with the rules is to be determined by examining the indorsement and evidence is not generally admissible to assist in that task. The court also held that 'cause' means the legal category, rather than the physical acts which caused the injury or damage. Their Honours' reasoning was based on what is stated in the Limitation Acts. See also *Dowling v Watson* [2000] TASSC 165 and *Watch Tower Bible Society v Sahas* (2008) 36 WAR 234.

7.5.4 Notes and questions

1. Some jurisdictions require indorsements to be made on the originating process where it is to be served outside the jurisdiction, particularly outside Australia. For example, where the plaintiff wishes to serve outside Australia, the writ must generally state the facts and particular rule upon which the plaintiff relies in order to support service. This requirement is in addition to the requirements for the general or special indorsement: NT r 7.02; Vic r 7.02; WA O 5 r 2.

2. What are the consequences of an inadequate general indorsement on a writ? Does it mean that the writ is a nullity? See *Ruzeu v Massey-Ferguson*, discussed above.

7.5.5 A special indorsement is a statement of claim that is contained within the writ which pleads the cause of action. Western Australia appears to be the only state in Australia that expressly retains the device: O 6 r 3.

A special indorsement should show that the plaintiff has a right to relief and plead all the material facts: *Geelong Retreads Pty Ltd v Allstates Transport Pty Ltd* (1973) 22 FLR 255. In Western Australia, the rules exclude certain claims from this type of originating process, for example, a claim containing allegations of fraud and slander: O 6 r 3.

Since a specially indorsed writ contains a statement of claim, its service will generally trigger commencement of the time within which the defendant must deliver a defence as well as an appearance. See *Clayton v Thomas Denton & Co Pty Ltd* [1972] VR 46.

Relationship between the writ and the pleadings

7.5.6 Where the writ is generally indorsed and a statement of claim does not accompany the writ, the rules require that a statement of claim be served within a stipulated period of time. Where a statement of claim is served in a proceeding commenced by writ, the plaintiff may alter, modify or extend the claim as indorsed on the writ without amending the indorsement: NT r 14.03; Tas r 117; Vic r 14.03; WA O 20 r 2(3). However, the causes of action upon which the plaintiff relies are to be ascertained exclusively by the statement of claim.

How does the court treat causes of action raised in the indorsement but not included in the statement of claim? This issue was discussed by the High Court in *Renowden v McMullin* (1970) 123 CLR 584. In that case the plaintiff, who was a solicitor, brought an action for damages against the defendants, who were members of a firm of accountants, for loss arising from alleged breaches of duty by them in auditing his books of account. The writ contained a general indorsement alleging breach of contract and breach of duty of care imposed on the defendants by the provisions of the Legal Profession Practice Act 1958 (Vic). A statement of claim was subsequently delivered which made no claim based on breach of contract. More than six years after the events alleged to have given rise to the claims in question, the plaintiff sought leave to amend the statement of claim to introduce the claim based on alleged breaches of contract. By this time the contract claims were statute-barred. The High Court held (Kitto, Menzies and Owen JJ, Barwick CJ and McTiernan J dissenting), that the causes of action on which a plaintiff relies are to be ascertained exclusively by reference to the statement of claim without regard to the indorsement on the writ. The amendments proposed by the plaintiff sought to raise a cause of action which was statute-barred and had not been mentioned in the statement of claim, and therefore was not allowed.

7.5.7   Notes

1. Central to the High Court's reasoning in *Renowden v McMullin* was the 'rule in *Weldon v Neal*'. This rule prohibits amendment to introduce statute-barred causes of action. The current status of the rule in *Weldon v Neal* is discussed at 5.2.14. In jurisdictions where the rule operates, the question of whether the statement of claim introduces a new cause of action has become quite complex. See, for example, *Bateman Project Engineering Pty Ltd v Pegasus Gold Australia Pty Ltd* (1998) 8 NTLR 132; *Ritchie & Parker Alfred Green & Co v Gornalle* [2000] TasSC 8; *Summit Chemicals Pty Ltd v Vetrotex Espana SA* [2004] WASCA 109; and *Jeffrey v Witherow* (2006) 31 WAR 236.

2. On the general issue of variance between the plaintiff's indorsement on the writ and pleadings, see *Turner v Bulletin Newspaper Co Pty Ltd* (1974) 131 CLR 69; *Elsum v Jameson* [1974] VR 529; and *Shell Co of Australia Ltd v Esso Aust Ltd* [1987] VR 317.

Concurrent writs

7.5.8   Some jurisdictions authorise the plaintiff at the time of issuing the writ or during the currency of the writ (see below) to issue one or more concurrent writs: Tas r 102; WA O 7 r 3. A concurrent writ bears the same date as the original writ and is in force for the same period of time as the original writ, although it is generally marked 'concurrent'. Traditionally the procedure was used because although the defendant was served with a copy of the writ, he or she was entitled to have the original writ produced. For the purpose of service, a concurrent writ is the equivalent of the original writ. The plaintiff usually issues a concurrent writ where there are multiple defendants, some of whom are within the jurisdiction and some of whom need to be served outside. It might also be prudent to issue a concurrent writ where there is a single defendant to be served, but it is unclear whether service will be effected within the jurisdiction or outside.

As an alternative to the concurrent writ procedure, a court officer may seal as many copies of the originating process as there are defendants and those copies are duly authorised for the purpose of service: HCR r 20.02; FCR r 2.21(4); ACT rr 70, 71; NSW r 4.12; NT r 5.11; Qld rr 978, 980; SA r 51; Vic r 5.11.

Other types of originating process for disputes involving factual issues

7.5.9   In New South Wales actions are commenced by a statement of claim, thus the functions of originating process and pleadings are merged in the one document. Rule 6.3 states which claims must be commenced by a statement of claim.

The Federal Court uses an originating application as the originating process. The jurisdiction of the Federal Court differs from the Supreme Courts of the states and territories because it is conferred by federal statute. In the Federal Court Act 1976 (Cth) and Federal Court Rules 2011 (Cth), there is no differentiation between actions, causes and matters; there is only a proceeding. A proceeding is defined in the Federal Court Act as a proceeding in the court: s 4. The term, therefore, contemplates proceedings based on both causes and matters.

Proceedings in the Federal Court's original jurisdiction are commenced by filing an originating application in the prescribed form: r 8.01. Pursuant to r 8.03, the application must state the relief claimed by the applicant and, if the relief depends on a provision of an Act, the Act and the provision.

The grounds of the application are usually set out in a statement of claim or an affidavit which is filed and served with the application: r 8.05.

In the Australian Capital Territory, actions in the Supreme Court are generally commenced by an originating claim: r 33. The originating claim must set out briefly and specifically the nature of the claim and the relief sought: r 50(1). For all actions commenced by originating claim, a statement of claim must be attached to the originating claim: r 50(2). For certain types of claim, such as motor vehicle personal injury claims or personal injury claims arising from the negligence of an employer, the rules provide that the statement of claim must satisfy certain requirements: see rr 52, 53. The information that is required to satisfy rr 52 or 53 is set out in the court-approved Forms 2.3 and 2.4. Similarly, if the action includes a claim for debt or liquidated demand, the rules require certain information to be included in the statement of claim, such as the period for which interest is claimed: r 51.

In Queensland where a dispute involves factual issues, proceedings must be commenced by a claim unless there is insufficient time to prepare a claim because of the urgent nature of the relief sought: rr 9, 11. In the latter situation, a party may commence proceedings by way of application: r 11. The Queensland rules state that the claim must state briefly the nature of the claim made, or the relief sought in the proceeding (r 22). This requirement is analogous to the general indorsement requirement for a writ (see 7.5.3ff), but r 22 also requires that a statement of claim be attached to the claim.

In South Australia, the summons is used for factual and legal disputes: r 34. The summons must be in the approved form and bear the following endorsements (r 38):

- those required by statute or the Supreme Court Rules;

- the time allowed for service;

- where the full name of the party is not known, an indorsement to that effect; and

- where the action is brought in a representative capacity, an endorsement of the capacity in which the plaintiff brings the action.

DISPUTES PREDOMINANTLY INVOLVING LEGAL ISSUES

7.6.1 In this category, the process is used primarily for resolving legal disputes and utilises affidavits rather than pleadings. For a discussion of affidavits, see **Chapter 15**. Most equity and probate matters begin this way. It is called the following in various jurisdictions: in the Australian Capital Territory (rr 31, 34–36) and Tasmania (r 89) an originating application; in the Northern Territory and Victoria an originating motion (r 4.05); in New South Wales a summons (rr 6.2, 6.4); in Queensland an application (r 11); and in Western Australia an originating summons: O 4 r 1. Like Tas r 88, extracted above at **7.4.3E**, Tasmania follows the same model of nominating the types of matters which might be instituted by an originating application. Rule 89 nominates many different types of proceedings which must be commenced by application, although the rule also contains a catch-all provision which refers to proceedings which are directed to be begun by motion or petition and cases in which an application is authorised to be made.

As stated above, at **7.5.9**, the Federal Court and South Australia use the same originating process for both types of dispute ie, those predominantly involving factual issues and those primarily involving legal issues. Further, as noted at **7.4.6**, proceedings in the original jurisdiction of the High Court are usually commenced by a writ of summons but the High Court Rules nominate particular forms of initiating process for particular forms of relief, eg, an application where writs of mandamus (r 20.01.1(a)) or habeus corpus (r 20.01.1(b)) are sought or a petition where the validity of an election is disputed: r 20.01.3.

DURATION OF ORIGINATING PROCESS

7.7.1   In most jurisdictions, the writ or other originating process is valid for a threshold period of three to 12 months. Most jurisdictions also allow the originating process to be extended by order of the court: HCR r 27.01; ACT r 74; NT r 5.12; Qld r 24; SA r 39; Tas r 107; Vic r 5.12; WA O 7 r 1. The situation regarding New South Wales and the Federal Court is discussed at **7.7.3**.

7.7.2E   **Court Procedures Rules (ACT)**

Originating process — duration and renewal
74 (1) An originating process is valid for service for 1 year starting on the day it is filed in the court.
  (2)   The plaintiff may apply to the court to renew the originating process if the process has not been served on the defendant.
  (3)   If the court is satisfied that reasonable efforts have been made to serve the defendant or that there is another good reason to renew the originating process, the court may renew the process for a further period, of not longer than 6 months at a time, starting on the day after the day the process would otherwise end.
  (4)   The originating process may be renewed whether or not it is valid for service.
  (5)   Before an originating process renewed under this rule is served, it must be stamped and show the period for which the process is renewed.
  (6)   Despite subrule (1), for any time limit (including a limitation period), an originating process that is renewed is taken to have started on the day the process was filed in the court.
  (7)   Failing to serve an originating process within the time limited by these rules does not prevent the plaintiff from starting a fresh proceeding by filing another originating process.

7.7.3   In New South Wales (r 6.2) the two forms of originating process — the statement of claim and the summons — are in force for six months and neither is renewable. However, in New South Wales, courts may use the general power to enlarge time, discussed at **5.5.9ff** below to exercise a discretion to extend the time for service of originating process. This strategy was discussed by the New South Wales Court of Appeal in *Arthur Andersen Corporate Finance Pty Ltd v Buzzle Operations Pty Ltd (in liq)* [2009] NSWCA 104 and *Agricultural & Rural Finance Pty Ltd v Kirk* (2011) 82 ACSR 390.

In the Federal Court, the period that an originating application is valid is determined by court order due to the court's individual docket case management system.

Although writs are used in the following commentary to exemplify the law and practice concerning duration, the principles apply with any necessary changes to other forms of originating process where renewal is permitted.

7.7.4 A writ that is not served within the relevant period (usually 12 months) is said to be 'stale'. A stale writ is not a nullity, therefore it may be effective to commence the proceedings even if it is stale at the time of service: *Re Kerly, Son and Verden* [1901] 1 Ch 467; *Simpson v Brereton* [1964] VR 332; *Payabi v Armstel Shipping Corp* [1992] 1 QB 907; *Jadwan Pty Ltd v Porter* (2004) 13 Tas R 162. If the defendant enters an unconditional appearance to a writ that has been served upon him or her out of time, the appearance is a step in the action and amounts to a waiver by the defendant of the irregularity in the service of the writ: *Sheldon v Brown Bayley Steel Works Ltd* [1953] 2 QB 393.

7.7.5 The following case — *Brealey v Board of Management Royal Perth Hospital* — demonstrates the complex relationship between the duration of the writ, service and appearance. Appearance is discussed in more detail in **Chapter 9**.

7.7.6C   **Brealey v Board of Management Royal Perth Hospital**
(1999) 21 WAR 79
Supreme Court of Western Australia — Full Court

Anderson J: ... [69]. The issues relating to service are complicated because wrong procedures were followed at the outset due to what, I think, were two misconceptions. The first misconception was that a defendant can refuse to accept service of a 'stale' writ. The second was that the court can exercise the power under O 7 r 1(2) to extend the validity of a stale writ when the writ has already been served on the defendant.

[70] This writ was issued on 21 February 1997 against the surgeon Mr Hardcastle as first defendant and the Board of Management of Royal Perth Hospital (that is the respondent) as second defendant. The writ was not served on either defendant within the 12 months prescribed by O 7 r 1(1). The 12 months expired on 20 February 1998. Without making any application for a renewal of the writ, the plaintiff's solicitors caused the writ to be served on the respondent on 27 February 1998, that is, seven days after it had become stale.

[71] The respondent sent the writ to its solicitors, who wrote to the appellant's solicitors informing them to the effect that, because the writ was stale when served, the respondent had not 'accepted service' of it. In other words, because the writ was more than a year old, the respondent intended to simply ignore it.

[72] Implicit in this approach must be the proposition that service of a stale writ (and perhaps also the writ itself) is a nullity. That this idea underlay the respondent's approach appears from par 5 of the affidavit of the respondent's solicitor, Ms Williams, sworn on 9 September 1998 in which she deposes:

> On 3 March 1998 I wrote to the plaintiff's solicitors advising that the writ purportedly served on the Board at Royal Perth Hospital on 27 February 1998 was dated 21 February 1997 and, therefore, was out of time for service prescribed by the Rules of the Supreme Court. I advised that the writ was stale and that the Board had not accepted service of the stale writ.

[73] It is, however, well settled that neither a stale writ, nor service of it, is a 'nullity'. The only quality lacking in the stale writ is that of not being in force for the purpose of service. It is still a writ. *Sheldon v Brown Bayley's Steel Works Ltd and Dawnay's Ltd* [1953] 2 QB 393, per Singleton LJ at 400 and Denning LJ at 402; *Van Leer Australia Pty Ltd v Palace Shipping KK* (1981) 180 CLR 337, at 341. And it can still be served. Service of a stale writ s not a nullity. As Lord Denning said in *Sheldon v Brown Bayley's Steel Works Ltd and Dawnay's Ltd* (loc cit):

... The service of the writ after the 12 months was not a nullity but an irregularity ...

[74] Therefore, it was not open to the respondent in this case to refuse to accept service. The respondent should have entered a conditional appearance as provided for in O 12 r 6 and should have applied to the court under O 2 r 1(2) to set aside the service of the writ on the ground of the irregularity. The court would then exercise the discretion conferred by O 2 r 1(2) to either set the service aside or not.

[75] Personal service had not been effected on Mr Hardcastle, although I think his solicitors had been sent a copy of the writ at about the same time as it was served on the respondent. It was, therefore, appropriate for the appellant's solicitors to apply for an order extending the validity of the writ for the purpose of service upon Mr Hardcastle. An *ex parte* application was made to that effect [on 6 March 1998]. ...

[76] Order 7 lays down the procedure to be followed only when a writ has not yet been served. It enables the plaintiff to renew the writ so that, when it is served, it will not be open to the objection that it is stale. This is made very clear by the opening words of O 7 r 1(2), which are:

(2) **Where a writ has not been served on a defendant** (my emphasis), the Court may by order extend the validity of the writ ...

It is also made clear by other provisions of O 7 as to how an extended writ is to be specially endorsed for service.

[77] It is my experience of practice in this Court and the District Court, that applications for renewal under O 7 r 1(2) are made *ex parte* and are invariably supported by an affidavit giving reasons why service has not been effected. That this is the practice here and elsewhere is confirmed by Seaman, 'Civil Procedure', par 7.1.2 and by the case cited in that work, *Ramsay v Madgwicks* [1989] VR 1, especially at 6.

[78] This time-honoured procedure, especially the *ex parte* aspect of it, would seem quite inappropriate to a case in which service (albeit irregular service) has already been effected on the defendant. Anyway, as I have said, I am of the opinion that the introductory words in O 7 r 1(2) preclude its operation where service of the writ has already been effected. In my opinion, where a stale writ has been served and the irregularity is not waived by, for instance, the entry of an unconditional appearance, the procedure to be followed is that which is laid down in O 2 r 1(2) and O 12 r 6. ...

[81] On this *ex parte* application [to extend the writ for service upon the defendant Hardcastle] ... Deputy Registrar Wallace made an order on 12 March 1998 extending the writ for a further three months. At that stage, as I have mentioned, the writ had not been personally served on the first defendant, Mr Hardcastle. Personal service of the extended writ was effected on Mr Hardcastle on 8 April 1998, and he filed a conditional appearance and an application to set aside the order of 12 March 1998 whereby the writ had been extended as against him.

[82] Finally, on 20 July 1998, the respondent's solicitors did what I think should have been done in the first place. They filed a conditional appearance under O 12 r 6(2) and an application under O 2 r 1(2) seeking an order that the service of the writ on the respondent be set aside 'on the grounds of irregularity which renders the service invalid'. Curiously, they also sought to set aside the order of the Deputy Registrar extending the validity of the writ.

[83] These applications came before Deputy Registrar Hewitt, who granted Mr Hardcastle's application to set aside the order extending the validity of the writ. He did so on discretionary grounds. Deputy Registrar Hewitt then considered the respondent's application to set aside the extension order. He came to the conclusion it was not necessary to set aside the extension as against the respondent because the writ had been served on the respondent before the order was made for its extension. He put it as follows:

The writ was served before the extension of time was granted and as a consequence I take the view that the extension of time was quite irrelevant to the second defendant.

[84] In my opinion, the Deputy Registrar was quite correct. The case stood or fell on the Deputy Registrar's determination not as to whether the writ ought to have been renewed as against the respondent but whether the irregular service, that is, the service on 27 February of the stale writ, ought to be set aside. And this is the issue which the Deputy Registrar proceeded to consider. As I understand his reasons, he took the view that the irregularity had been waived. ... He therefore dismissed the application and the result was that the action could proceed against the respondent but not against the first defendant, Mr Hardcastle.

7.7.7 On the issue of waiver, the Full Court disagreed with the Registrar that the first defendant had waived the irregularity in service. In the final result, the plaintiff was unsuccessful in her application to extend the validity of the writ as against both defendants. The case fell into the third category of *Kleinwort Benson v Barbrak Ltd*: see the discussion below at **7.7.8**. On that application, Ipp J made the following comments in *Brealey*:

[68] In the present case the delay on the part of the appellant involved a very considerable period. The appellant has failed to give a satisfactory explanation for that delay. It was quite deliberate, there being no question of mishap or oversight. The prejudice suffered by the appellant were the validity of the writ not to be extended would be self-inflicted. Were the validity of the writ to be extended the prejudice the respondent would suffer would not be insignificant. In my opinion, good reason to exercise the discretion under O 7 r 1 has not been shown and I am not persuaded that the interests of justice require the exercise of a remedial discretion under O 2 r 1. I would dismiss the appeal.

Renewal of originating process

7.7.8 As demonstrated by *Brealey*'s case (above at **7.7.6C**), if service is not effected within the duration of the originating process, renewal of the writ may be sought by application to the court. The application is usually made *ex parte* and supported by an affidavit. The court has discretion to extend the writ if good cause is shown: HCR r 27.01(f); ACT r 74(3); NT r 5.12(2); Qld r 24(2); SA r 39(2); Tas r 107(2); Vic r 5.12(2); WA O 7 r 1(2).

The rules grant the court a wide discretion to consider the individual circumstances of the application, taking into account the efforts that have been made to serve the defendant and the potential prejudice to the defendant. Because of the width of the discretion conferred by the rules, previous examples of the exercise of the discretion cannot create a formula: *McKenna v McKenna* [1984] VR 665 at 674 per McGarvie J. Nevertheless there are certain recurring themes which guide the exercise of the discretion. One critical theme is the potential prejudice suffered by the defendant if the plaintiff applies to renew the writ after the expiration of the limitation period. This is a common occurrence, because before expiry of the limitation period it will generally be more cost-effective for the plaintiff to simply file another originating process than to apply to the court for a renewal.

Lord Brandon discussed the categories of case in which limitation issues arise in this area in the case of *Kleinwort Benson Ltd v Barbrak Ltd* [1987] 2 All ER 289 at 294:

> My Lords, there are three main categories of cases in which, on an application for extension of the validity of a writ, questions of limitation of action may arise, all being cases in which the writ has been issued before the relevant period of limitation, that is to say the period applicable to the cause of action on which the claim made by the writ is founded, has expired. Category (1) cases are where the application for extension is made at a time when the writ is still valid and before the relevant period of limitation has expired. Category (2) cases are where the application for extension is made at a time when the writ is still valid but the relevant period of limitation has expired. Category (3) cases are where the application for extension is made at a time when the writ has ceased to be valid and the relevant period of limitation has expired. In both category (1) cases and category (2) cases, it is still possible for the plaintiff (subject to any difficulties of service there may be) to serve the writ before its validity expires, and, if he does so, the defendant will not be able to rely on a defence of limitation. In category (1) cases, but not category (2) cases, it is also possible for the plaintiff, before the original writ ceases to be valid, to issue a fresh writ which will remain valid for a further 12 months. In the time when the application for extension is made, a defendant who has not been served has an accrued right of limitation. In category (3) cases, however, it is not possible for the plaintiff to serve the writ effectively unless its validity is first retrospectively extended. In category (3) cases, therefore, it can properly be said that, at the time when the application for extension is made, a defendant on whom the writ has not been served has an accrued right of limitation.

7.7.9   Notes

1. The Western Australian Court of Appeal has dealt with two of Lord Brandon's categories: *Bell Group NV (in liq) v Aspinall* (1998) 19 WAR 561 (category 2 case); and *Brealey v Board of Management Royal Perth Hospital* (1999) 21 WAR 79 (category 3 case): extracted above at **7.7.6C**.

2. In relation to Lord Brandon's discussion of the category 3 cases, the rules in the Australian Capital Territory (r 74(4)), Northern Territory (r 5.12(3)), Victoria (r 5.12(3)), South Australia (r 39(3)) and Western Australia (O 7 r 1(2)) expressly state that the renewal may be granted upon application made after the writ has become stale. But the courts of other jurisdictions may achieve the same result by first extending the time for making such an application, then granting it: *Victa*

Ltd v Johnson (1975) 10 SASR 496; *Travis v CML Assurance Society Ltd* [1977] VR 249; *Verdich v McKechnie*[1981] Tas R 91.

3. The rules of each jurisdiction give the court the power to enlarge and abridge time, generally even after the time appointed for an act has expired: HCR r 4.02; FCR r 1.39; ACT r 6351, Legislation Act 2001 (ACT) s 151C; NSW r 1.12; NT r 3.02; Qld r 7; SA r 117(2), (3); Tas r 52; Vic r 3.02; WA O 3 r 5. See generally **5.5.9ff** and *Arthur Andersen Corporate Finance Pty Ltd v Buzzle Operations Pty Ltd (in liq)* [2009] NSWCA 104 for an example of the exercise of this power where renewal of originating process was sought.

7.7.10   There is some debate in the cases about the defendant's 'accrued right of limitation' referred to by Lord Brandon in *Kleinwort Benson v Barbrak,* extracted at **7.7.8**. The operation of the Limitation Acts is discussed in **Chapter 6**. Is it accurate to say generally that the defendant attains 'an accrued right of limitation' under the Australian law? If the defendant does acquire an accrued right of limitation, what is the nature of such a right? When the limitation period expires under the relevant limitation statute, the defendant does not acquire immunity from proceedings. In most limitation statutes, the court has the power to extend the limitation period and the defendant has the right to ask the court not to grant the application: *Finlay v Littler* [1992] 2 VR 181 at 186–7. No immunity is conferred by the expiry of the limitation period, but it is a factor that the court would take into account when exercising the discretion under the court rules to renew originating process.

     An important consideration in these cases is that the proceedings have been commenced before the expiry of the limitation period and an exercise of power to extend the duration of the writ after the limitation period has expired raises interesting questions about the relationship between the operation of the limitation statutes and the rules. This is discussed by Stephen J in the following case.

7.7.11C   **Van Leer Australia Pty Ltd v Palace Shipping KK**
(1994) 180 CLR 337
High Court of Australia

Stephen J (at 338): The disposal of these applications, made respectively by the plaintiff and by the first-named defendant, Palace Shipping, requires some description of the nature of the plaintiff's action and of its initiation and prosecution to date.

     The plaintiff imported from Japan two consignments of steel, which arrived in Australia in November and December 1977. The plaintiff alleges that much of the steel, shipped in good condition, was rusty on arrival. It accordingly sued Simsmetal, a New South Wales company, alleged to have been the charterer of the ship which carried the steel to Australia, and Palace Shipping, alleged to be the Japanese owner of the ship. The steel was carried under bills of lading issued by Hong Kong and Eastern (Japan) Ltd, alleged to be the agent either of Simsmetal or of Palace Shipping.

The plaintiff did not issue its writ until November 1978, almost a year after the arrival of the consignments of steel. The writ was served on Simsmetal in September 1979 but notice of the writ was not served on Palace Shipping in Japan until much later. Therein lies the occasion for these applications.

The plaintiff's writ was 'stale' when notice of it was served on Palace Shipping because, being issued on 24 November 1978 and renewed for a further six months on the plaintiff's *ex parte* motion [339] on 23 November 1979, service was not effected on Palace Shipping within those eighteen months nor was the writ further renewed. Only on 2 October 1980, almost twenty-three months after issue, was notice of the writ served on Palace Shipping.

The plaintiff seeks an order that will have the effect of renewing its writ of summons, while Palace Shipping seeks to have the writ and the service upon it of notice of the writ set aside. Palace Shipping, in attacking the writ and service of notice of it, has also sought to have set aside the order for renewal of the writ which the plaintiff obtained *ex parte* in November 1979.

Pursuant to O 8, r 1(1) of the Rules of this Court, a writ issued out of this Court remains in force for only twelve months unless renewed for a further six months upon application made before the expiration of the initial twelve months. The Court may order renewal if it is satisfied that 'reasonable efforts have been made to serve the defendant, or for other good reason' — r 1(2). Under that rule further applications for renewal may also be made 'from time to time during the currency of the renewed writ'.

Since the plaintiff's present application is made well after the end of the six months' period of first renewal, the 'currency of the renewed writ' referred to in O 8, r 1(2) having expired, the plaintiff must also rely on O 60, r 6. That rule both confers power to enlarge 'the time appointed by these Rules ... for doing an act ...' — sub-r (1), and permits of such an enlargement 'although the application for it is not made until after the expiration of the time appointed ...' — sub-r (2). It is well established that, whatever infelicities of language this may appear to involve, the power conferred by this rule applies to such an application as the plaintiff now makes.

Each of these applications raises the general question of how the Court should exercise its power to order renewal of a writ and also the specific question of how that power should be exercised in the particular facts of this case. Central to this question is how the expiration of a limitation period should affect the exercise of the discretionary power to renew the plaintiff's writ. The Hague Rules, which are scheduled to the Sea-Carriage of Goods Act 1924 (Cth), are applicable to the present bills of lading. By r 6 of Art III of those Rules a carrier is discharged from all liability in respect of loss or damage unless suit is brought within a year after delivery of the goods.

That period of a year has, of course, long since expired. It had long expired when the *ex parte* order for the first renewal of the writ was made. Accordingly, Art III, r 6 would bar the plaintiff were it to institute fresh proceedings against Palace Shipping. Dr Griffith, [340] appearing for that defendant, relies upon the proposition that to accede to the plaintiff's application, and, indeed, to have acceded to its earlier application for renewal, has the effect of depriving his client of the absolute defence to the plaintiff's claim available to it were the plaintiff forced to issue a new writ. Mr Searby, on the other hand, says that the time bar is of little relevance. He contends that had application for a second renewal of the writ been made, as was the first application, while the writ was still current, the existence of the time bar should have proved no obstacle so long as good grounds were shown for its renewal. Since, as he contends, there have all along been such good grounds, both for extending the time within which to make the application and for granting it, the existence of the time bar should be no more an obstacle than it would be had application been made during the currency of the writ.

The plaintiff did in fact 'bring suit' within the twelve months specified in Art III, r 6 of the Hague Rules. Article III, r 6 is, like most conventional limitation of action statutes of common law jurisdictions, concerned with the institution of proceedings within limited times after an event and not with the subsequent service of process: the judgments of the several members of the Court of Appeal in *The Merak* ((1965) P 223, esp at pp 252, 257, 258, 260–261) make it clear that in Art III, r 6 'unless suit is brought' refers to the issue of proceedings and not to service upon the defendant. The Hague Rules thus rely, in effect, upon the procedural requirements of the particular *lex fori* to ensure that defendants will not for an inordinate time be left in ignorance of claims against them.

Accordingly it is non-compliance with the procedural rules of this Court, rather than with the limitation provisions of the Hague Rules, that the plaintiff must overcome in its present application. Only if it fails to attract in its favour the exercise of this Court's discretionary power will Art III, r 6 affect it. It therefore rather overstates the matter to speak of the plaintiff's application as seeking to deprive the defendant of a limitation defence. ...

All this is not to deny the considerable relevance to the plaintiff's application of the fact that the period of twelve months prescribed by the Hague Rules has long since passed. That period, prescribed in an international code which has found its place in the domestic law of most trading nations, no doubt reflects the need for relatively prompt initiation of claims which arise in the international shipping trade. On any view this is a matter to which regard must be had in considering these applications: the question is what weight is to be accorded to it. The modern English authorities, and they are numerous, place considerable weight upon the expiration of periods of limitation, partly under the influence of older cases such as *Doyle v Kaufman* (1877) 3 QBD 7; 3 QBD 340 and of what was said by Lord Goddard in *Battersby*. They treat renewal after a time bar has arisen as only to be permitted in quite exceptional circumstances.

[His Honour discusses the English authorities.]

The two South Australian cases already referred to, *Krawszyk v Graham* and *Victa Ltd v Johnson*, supra, are among the most fully reasoned of these decisions. I will cite at length from the judgment of Bray CJ in the second of these cases since in his discussion of the authorities and his reasoning generally his Honour expresses, [343] with respect, much of what I would wish to say on the subject. ...:

> ... [T]here is discernible in this [area], as in cognate branches of the procedural law, a tendency to relax rigid time [344] limits where that is legal, possible and where it can be done without prejudice or injustice to other parties.

His Honour went on to say [in *Victa Ltd v Johnson*] at pp 503–504:

> It follows then that it is incorrect to talk about allowing a cause of action or a new cause of action to be set up after the expiry of the period of limitation. Once the writ is issued within the period, the Statute of Limitations is ousted or rather never comes into operation. It is not the statute, which the court must obey on what it thinks is its proper interpretation, but the rule of court which takes over then. That rule has the discretion built into it and that discretion is to be exercised judicially, indeed, but not fettered by inflexible prescriptions ...

It is not correct to say that the defendant has acquired an absolute right to immunity when a writ issued within the limitation period is not served within twelve months of its issue and the limitation period has in the meantime expired. What has expired is in reality not the limitation period but the period which would have been the limitation period if no writ had ever been issued. What the failure to serve a writ within twelve months gives the defendant is no more than a right to contend that the Court in the exercise of its discretion should not renew the writ. The efficacy of the writ does not expire absolutely at the end of the twelve months, it only expires if and in so far as the Court sees fit not to renew it.

The rule first directs the Court to inquire whether reasonable efforts have been made to serve the defendant. If they have, it seems to me that the Court should renew the writ. If not, the Court has to consider whether other good reasons exist for the renewal. I will not attempt an exhaustive category of such reasons. That would probably be impossible and would certainly be undesirable. Prominent, however, amongst the matters for the consideration of the Court, apart from whatever attempts have been made at service, will be the length of the delay, the reasons for the delay, the conduct of the parties and the hardship or prejudice caused to the plaintiff by refusing the renewal or to the defendant by granting it.

[345] ... [T]he Canadian cases have approached the matter very much as has the South Australian Supreme Court. The Saskatchewan Court of Appeal considered the matter in detail in *Simpson v Saskatchewan Government Insurance Office* (1967) 65 DLR (2d) 324. ... Culliton CJ, speaking for the Court, said at p 332:

... when the action is one that is subject to a limitation either by statute or rule, once the writ is issued within the time limitation, any defence based upon the limitation is gone forever in respect to that writ. If the writ is not served within the period limited therefore, it is not a nullity and there is no revival of the limitation defence in respect of that writ. Such defence becomes available to the defendant only if a new writ is required to be issued. Thus, in my opinion, it is not strictly accurate to say that the renewal of a writ to which the limitation does not apply is a denial of a defence open to the defendant. In my view the real significance of the intervention of a limitation, created by statute or rule, is to alert the Court that the case is likely to be one in which the delay occurred by [346] non-service may have resulted in substantial injury or prejudice to the defendant. As long as the Rules give to the Court the discretionary right of renewal, it cannot be said that the exercise of that discretionary right defeats or contravenes either a rule or a statute which provides for limitation. ...

For the reasons which appear in the passages which I have cited from the judgments of Bray CJ and of Culliton CJ I have concluded that in the exercise of discretion in renewal of a writ I should, with the support of this substantial body of Commonwealth authority, adopt the approach favoured by the South Australian Supreme Court and by the Canadian courts.

I turn now to the circumstances which have led to this application. It seems that a number of factors led to the plaintiff initially making no endeavour to serve Palace Shipping. Leave to serve notice of a concurrent writ upon Palace Shipping in Japan was granted by me [347] on 15 December 1978, less than a month after issue of the writ. Palace Shipping was a Japanese company which had no presence within Australia which would have allowed it to be served here. On the other hand, the defendant Simsmetal was thought to be the demise charterer of the vessel which had carried the steel to Australia and could be served readily enough in Sydney. The plaintiff's solicitors accordingly sought an admission that it was the demise charterer, believing that if such admission were obtained it would be unnecessary to pursue the claim against Palace Shipping. As early as February 1979 there were discussions between the solicitors for the plaintiff and for Simsmetal, in which the latter suggested that pending investigations the writ should not be served upon their client or upon Palace Shipping. Thenceforth all question of service upon Palace Shipping seems to have been deferred for some seven months until, in September 1979, it became clear to the plaintiff that the desired admission was not forthcoming. The plaintiff then effected service upon Simsmetal but still took no step towards effecting service upon Palace Shipping.

Then, in October 1979, Simsmetal delivered its defence. According to the solicitor for the plaintiff, it was only then that it became clear that the plaintiff 'would have to pursue proceedings against the first named Defendant and that led to the first application for extension of the Writ', by which time almost twelve months had elapsed since its issue and almost two years since the consignments of steel had arrived in Australia. The plaintiff had taken no steps in those two years to inform Palace Shipping of its complaint about the condition of the steel. This was not, however, to be the full extent of delay in notifying that defendant of the claim made against it.

While, so far as appears, Palace Shipping continued to remain in ignorance of the claim against it, the plaintiff began for the first time to attend to service in Japan of notice of the writ.

Once leave to serve out is obtained there is a variety of ways in which writs issued out of this Court may be served on defendants out of the jurisdiction. ....

Instead the plaintiff sought to effect service by means of a letter of request, pursuant to O 10, r 7 of the High Court Rules and this it only accomplished some twelve months later. Service by letters of request may commend itself in terms of international comity, but is not always expeditious. In the present case it of course proved to be extraordinarily slow.

While the plaintiff is not to be criticised merely because of the mode of service which it chose, it might have been expected that, once it became clear that this method was leading to long delays, the availability of other speedier means of service would have been investigated. Especially is this so in view of the already substantial delays and obvious need, since September 1979, to serve Palace Shipping.

[His Honour provides a narrative of events whereby the plaintiff sought to effect service by a letter of request. This involved various steps such as contacting the Australian Attorney-General's Department, the Department of Foreign Affairs and the Japanese authorities as well as translating the writ and orders.]

In mid-July 1980, the plaintiff's solicitors were told that the Japanese Ministry of Foreign Affairs required a further document to accompany the notice of writ. This led them to reexamine their files and to note that the six-months' period of extension of the writ had by then long since expired. This the principal responsible for the matter had not previously appreciated: he had mistakenly believed that the period of renewal had been for twelve months (although the Rules only permit of six months' extension at a time). His clerk had known all along that the renewal was only for six months but had both assumed that his principal knew likewise and that the latter's lack of concern was because it was enough that within the six month period the plaintiff had taken the initiating steps necessary to effect service overseas. Moreover he apparently thought it likely that service had in fact been effected soon after dispatch of the notice of writ to the Attorney-General's Department, the delay being only in receiving confirmation of service rather than in the effecting of service.

I have recounted the events leading ultimately to the service [350] of notice of the writ on the defendant in Japan in October 1980. However in determining how I should exercise my discretion I will initially confine myself to what has now emerged concerning the position in November 1979, when the order was obtained *ex parte* to extend the writ for six months.

Some two years had then passed since delivery of the steel and almost a year since both issue of the writ and also expiration of the twelve months' limitation period. During that time the plaintiff had done nothing directly to inform Palace Shipping of the damaged condition of the steel; it had informed other parties, including Simsmetal, and may have assumed that Palace Shipping would have heard of the matter. However there is no evidence from which I can infer that Palace Shipping had in fact become aware of the claim against it before it was served with notice of the writ in October 1980.

Moreover, until October 1979 the plaintiff had done nothing in preparation for effecting service on Palace Shipping in Japan. For example, what proved to be the very time-consuming preliminary of having prepared in acceptable form a Japanese translation of the notice of writ had not been set in train. The reason for this inaction was neither mishap nor oversight. It seems, rather, to have been due to a calculated decision to incur no costs in prosecuting the case against Palace Shipping so long as there were thought to be prospects of a successful outcome against Simsmetal. It follows from what I have already said that Palace Shipping, who, for all that appears, knew nothing of the proceedings, can have played no part in encouraging the plaintiff to adopt this course.

In the light of the circumstances as they now appear, it is clear that in November 1979, when the *ex parte* application to renew the writ was made, it could not be said, as the terms of O 8, r 1(2) require, that 'reasonable efforts have been made to serve the defendant'. It follows that, unless 'other good reason' existed, the writ should not then have been renewed.

In considering whether there did exist such 'other good reason', I do not, for the reasons already stated, regard the expiration of the limitation period of twelve months as of itself casting upon the plaintiff that heavy onus which the English decisions would impose. However I do take account of the long delay in serving Palace Shipping. It bears at least three aspects: first, it involved a very considerable period, secondly, it was quite deliberate, there being no question of mishap or oversight; thirdly, no notice was given to the defendant in this case, although the giving of such notice may sometimes mitigate the prejudice which a defendant may otherwise suffer through delay in actual service of process.

[351] These are all substantial considerations. To be weighed against them is the plaintiff's effective loss of its rights against Palace Shipping if the renewal of the writ in November 1979 is to be set aside. But this seriously prejudicial consequence will be present whenever renewal of a writ is in question after a limitation period has run its course; and in the present case the prejudice is self-inflicted in the sense that Palace Shipping did nothing to induce delay in service or to encourage a belief that the claim against it might be settled without recourse to litigation.

In these circumstances I conclude that, on a proper exercise of discretion and in the light of the facts as now known to me, the writ should not have been renewed as a result of the *ex parte* application made to me in November 1979. ...

[352] On the first-named defendant's application, it is enough that I order that the service upon Palace Shipping of notice of the writ be set aside on the ground that the *ex parte* order for its renewal, made in November 1979, should not have been made. The plaintiff's application, which seeks a further renewal of the writ, will be dismissed.

7.7.12 Notes and questions

1. See also *Woodcock v State of Tasmania* [2003] TasSC 81, *Gillies v Dibbetts* [2001] 1 Qd R 596, and *Muirhead v Uniting Church in Australia Property Trust (Q)* [1999] QCA 513.

2. When exercising the discretion to renew originating process, the courts will take into account case management principles (*Irvine Haulage Pty Ltd (in liq) v Irvine* [1993] SASC 4122) and the overriding purpose, see generally **Chapter 2**. In *IMB Group Pty Ltd (in liq) v ACCC* [2007] 1 Qd R 148, the Queensland Court of Appeal applied the overriding purpose to deny a plaintiff's application to renew a claim for the ninth time. The defendant had not been served despite eight previous renewals.

3. An application to renew a writ is made *ex parte*; therefore the applicant has an obligation to the court of utmost good faith to disclose all facts material to the court's determination: see *Savcor Pty Ltd v Cathodic Protection International Aps* (2005) 12 VR 639.

4. Is potential prejudice to a third party motor vehicle insurer relevant to the decision whether or not to renew a writ? See *Foxe v Brown* (1984) 59 ALJR 186; 58 ALR 542.

5. If plaintiffs have a potential claim in negligence against the solicitor acting for them, should this affect the exercise of the judicial discretion to renew the writ? Is it an appropriate matter for a judge to take into account on an application to renew a writ? See *Ramsay v Madgwicks* [1989] VR 1.

Further reading

7.8.1 Articles

P Alexander, 'Reasonable Prospects of Success and Costs Orders against Solicitors' (2006) 75 *Precedent* 44.

M I Aronson, 'Amendments and Limitations Acts — The Effects of Some Recent English Decisions in New South Wales' (1975) 13 *Law Society Journal* 185.

R Buth, 'Responding to Resolve: Considering Pre-action Requirements in Relation to ADR' (2010) 21 *ADRJ* 179.

R French CJ, 'Litigating in a Statutory Universe', *Victorian Bar Association 2nd Annual CPD Conference — The New Litigation Landscape — Challenges and Opportunities*, 18 February 2012, Melbourne.

R Kambar and G Walsh, 'A Critical Evaluation of the Pre-litigation Protocols' (2011) 106 *Precedent* 42.

T Sourdin, 'Making an Attempt to Resolve Disputes before Using Courts: We All Have Obligations' (2010) 21 *ADRJ* 225.

J G Starke, 'Grounds for Renewal of Writ' (1989) 63 *ALJ* 567.

7.8.2   Reports

Australian Government Attorney-General's Department, Access to Justice Taskforce, *A Strategic Framework for Access to Justice in the Federal Civil Justice System*, 2009.

National Alternative Dispute Resolution Advisory Council (NADRAC), *The Resolve to Resolve: Embracing ADR to Improve Access to Justice in the Federal Jurisdiction*, 2009.

Victorian Law Reform Commission, *Civil Justice Review*, Report 14, 2008

Service

CHAPTER **8**

OVERVIEW

Service is the procedure by which a plaintiff informs a defendant of the claim being made against them. Personal service is the foundation of jurisdiction and is required for originating proceedings. It is also an essential requirement of natural justice.

Ordinary service has less stringent requirements than personal service and is sufficient for interlocutory proceedings. Special service rules have developed for certain types of parties, such as corporations and those parties under a disability. Special rules exist in relation to certain types of actions, for example, motor vehicle personal injury actions. Technical service rules have also developed for service out of the jurisdiction, both within and outside the Commonwealth of Australia.

Where a plaintiff experiences difficulties in serving a defendant, the plaintiff may seek an order for substituted service, provided the method proposed is likely to bring the proceeding to the attention of the defendant.

INTRODUCTION

8.1.1 At common law an action based on the *in personam* jurisdiction of the court could not proceed unless the person against whom a relief or remedy is sought had been served with an originating process: *Laurie v Carroll* (1958) 98 CLR 310 at 323–4. For a full explanation of *in personam* or territorial jurisdiction, see **3.2.1**. *In personam* jurisdiction broadly extends to all civil cases, except claims in relation to ships (known as actions *in rem*), property or status. Service was only possible upon persons who were actually present within the jurisdiction at the time of filing the originating process; there was no power to serve outside the jurisdiction: *Re Sherlock* (1991) 102 ALR 156. The basis for the common law rule was that natural justice prevented courts making orders affecting parties in their absence and without notice. The rationale of service was stated by Lord Cranworth LC in *Hope v Hope* (1854) 4 De GM & G 328 at 342; 43 ER 534, in the following terms:

> The object of all service is of course only to give notice to the party on whom it is made, so that he may be made aware of and may be able to resist that which is sought against him; and when that has been substantially done, so that the Court may feel perfectly confident that service has reached him, everything has been done that is required.

The common law limitations imposed upon service have been modified by statute. The Service and Execution of Process Act 1992 (Cth) enables service of state and territory proceedings throughout Australia: see **8.9.3**. The Rules of Court enable service outside the jurisdiction: see **8.9.10**.

All applications and procedures required to be made to a court must be served in accordance with the Rules of Court. *Ex parte* applications are an exception to this general rule, and then, only in cases of emergency. *Ex parte* applications are made in the absence of the other party. Examples of *ex parte* applications include interim injunctions and Anton Piller orders.

Having been served, a defendant has four choices:

1. do nothing, in which case a default judgment may follow: see **Chapter 12**;

2. enter an appearance indicating that the action is to be defended and providing an address for all future documents to be sent to: see **Chapter 9**;

3. enter a conditional appearance, objecting to the court's jurisdiction, except in the Australian Capital Territory and New South Wales, where conditional appearances no longer exist: see **9.8.1**. Possible bases of objection include:

   (a) the plaintiff's cause of action has no nexus with the jurisdiction and that service was invalid (see **8.9.10**); or

   (b) the plaintiff tricked the defendant into coming into the jurisdiction so as to serve the originating process; or

4. if in the High Court (r 23.02), enter a Submitting Appearance, submitting to any order the court may make in a matter save as to costs.

A defendant may, however, submit to the jurisdiction and waive irregularities and lack of service by:

• entering into a contract for consensual service: see **8.2.7**;

• taking a step in the action: see **9.9.1**;

• entering the jurisdiction to accept service: *Perrett v Robinson* [1985] 1 Qd R 83;

• instructing his or her solicitor to accept service and enter an appearance. Once an appearance is entered, proof of service is no longer required; or

• creating an estoppel by conduct which amounts to waiver: *Ditfort v Temby* (1990) 26 FCR 72 at 80.

Once service of an initiating process is effected, it may be necessary to prepare an affidavit of service within a prescribed period. Service is usually required for all documents filed in a proceeding, eg, NSW r 10.1; SA r 60. Service is also required in relation to other documents related to an action after the primary action has been commenced, eg, documents relating to interlocutory proceedings, pleadings etc. Exceptions to this general rule include:

• documents relating to *ex parte* applications (ie, applications made without notice to other parties);

• requests for the issue of a subpoena; and

• documents excluded by practice direction or specific direction of the court.

[*Note:* in this chapter a reference, such as WA O 9 r 2, is a reference to the relevant Rules of Court. All other legislation will be specified.]

PERSONAL SERVICE

Foundation of jurisdiction

8.2.1   Service is the foundation of jurisdiction (*Laurie v Carroll* (1958) 98 CLR 310 at 323–4), hence a superior court will not exercise its jurisdiction unless the person against whom the relief or remedy is sought has been served with notice of the proceedings: High Court Rules 2004 rr 9.01.1, 22.01.2; Federal Court Rules 1979 r 13.01; Court Procedures Rules 2006 (ACT) rr 54 (originating claim), 61 (originating application); Uniform Civil Procedure Rules 2005 (NSW) r 10.20; Supreme Court Rules 1987 (NT) r 6.02; Uniform Civil Procedure Rules 1999 (Qld) r 105; Supreme Court Rules 2006 (SA) r 39; Rules of the Supreme Court 2000 (Tas) r 133; Supreme Court (General Civil Procedure) Rules 2005 (Vic) r 6.02; Rules of the Supreme Court 1971 (WA) O 9 rr 1, 5; O 72 r 1.

Originating process must be served personally on a party against whom a remedy or relief is sought, unless otherwise provided. Where personal service is not required ordinary service will suffice. Such is the case with interlocutory procedures, for example, an application to grant interim relief to prevent injury to a party: see 'Ordinary service' at **8.3.1**.

In the absence of fraud inducing a defendant to enter the jurisdiction, where at the time of service of the writ a defendant is within the jurisdiction, courts have *in personam* jurisdiction with respect to any action. It is immaterial whether the cause of action arose outside the jurisdiction or the defendant is only within the jurisdiction for a short time: *Colt Industries Inc v Sarlie* [1966] 1 WLR 440. It is not fraud where a defendant is brought within the jurisdiction by force of law, for example, for examination under the corporate legislation (*John Sanderson & Co (NSW) Pty Ltd (in liq) v Giddings* [1976] VR 421) or where the defendant willingly travels to the jurisdiction to accept service: *Perrett v Robinson* [1985] 1 Qd R 83.

Manner of service

8.2.2   At common law the process server had to physically touch the defendant with the document, describe its nature and offer the defendant the opportunity to compare the service copy with the original. While there is some unnecessary diversity among the rules, personal service is now generally effected by leaving a copy of the originating process with the defendant: HCR r 9.02.1; FCR r 10.01; ACT r 6405; NSW r 10.21; NT r 6.03; Qld r 106; Tas rr 132, 135; Vic r 6.03; WA O 72 r 2.

The High Court Rules (r 9.02.3) provide it is not necessary to show the original document. The Western Australian rules require the leaving of a copy of the document with the person to be served. However, the duplicate original need be produced only if the person served demands it: WA O 72 r 2.

In the High Court (rr 9.02.1, 9.02.2 (sealed copy)), Federal Court (rr 10.01, 10.12), the Australian Capital Territory (r 6405), New South Wales (r 10.21), the Northern Territory (r 6.03), Queensland (r 106) and Victoria (r 6.03), the rules once again provide two methods of service: (a) leaving a copy of the document with the person to be served, or (b) if the person to be served does not accept the copy, by putting the copy down in their presence and telling them the nature of the document. The Federal Court Rule gives the court a discretion to direct how personal service will be effected: see *Amalgamated Wireless (Australia) Ltd v McDonnell Douglas Corp* (1987) 16 FCR 238.

In Tasmania, r 135 provides that the person serving the document must both deliver and leave the document with the person to be served, or offer to do so. The Australian Capital Territory rule (r 6405) is similar to Tasmania's, except in so far as the Australian Capital Territory rule requires that a sealed copy be served.

In New South Wales, if the person attempting service is prevented by violence or the threat of violence from approaching the person to be served, personal service is effected by leaving the document as near as practicable to the person to be served: r 10.20.

In South Australia, r 67 provides that personal service of a document is effected if:

(a)   the document is given to, and accepted by, the person to be served;

(b)   the person to be served is offered the document and, if he or she appears unwilling to accept it, is informed orally of the nature of the document;

(c)   a solicitor accepts service of the document on behalf of the person to be served (whether the solicitor is served personally with the document or not) and issues an acknowledgment to that effect; or

(d)   the document is served in accordance with an agreement between the parties as to the manner of service.

8.2.3C   **Ainsworth v Redd**
(1990) 19 NSWLR 78
Court of Appeal (NSW)

[This case is relevant to the Federal Court, New South Wales, the Northern Territory, South Australia, Queensland and Victoria. The appellant sued the respondent claiming damages for defamation and injurious falsehood. The respondent resided in the United States of America and had visited New South Wales for the purpose of obtaining a poker machine licence. The process server held out the statement of claim to the respondent at arm's length and said: 'These documents are for you.' The nature of the documents was not identified. The respondent appeared to look at the documents but did not take them. The respondent's American attorney took the documents, thinking that they had something to do with the poker machine licence.

The respondent was overheard to say to his attorney: 'We had better take a look at these.' The attorney did not take the documents intending to do so for the defendant either personally or on his behalf.

The issue was whether personal service of a document was effected by leaving a copy of the document with the person to be served within the meaning of NSW Pt 9 r 3(1). Hunt J at first instance held that service had not been effected. The issue was then tested in the Court of Appeal.]

Kirby ACJ (at 85–6): The relevant object is to ensure that originating process in the form of a document will come to the notice of the person named as a party so that any later default in defending his or her position (for example, by entering an appearance and being represented before the Court) is fairly to be attributed to a decision of that person. The obligation of personal service thereby removes the risk that the jurisdiction of the Court over the person named will be asserted, conclusions reached and orders made, without a proper initial opportunity being given to the person named to appear and defend the proceedings: cf *Hope v Hope* (1854) 4 De G M & G 328; 43 ER 534.

It is in that context that the obligation to ensure that the document is 'left with the person served' is to be construed. In the light of this consideration of the purpose of the Rule, there can be no gainsaying the fact that the statement of claim was sufficiently 'left ... with' the respondent in the present case. The fact that the respondent did not know the nature of the document until the day following the service relied upon is a matter which seemed relevant to Hunt J. However it is, with respect, irrelevant to that part of the Rule upon which the appellants relied. This was what has been [86] described as the first or primary mode of service provided for in the opening words of the Rule. Under those words, it is sufficient that the document should be left with the person to be served. It is not necessary that its nature and purpose should be identified, described or brought to the attention of the person to be served. Such an obligation is indeed required under the secondary mode of service. But that only applies where the person to be served 'does not accept the copy'. As I have said, there is no suggestion that that is the case here. This juxtaposition between the requirements of the primary and of the secondary modes of service provided for in the rule helps to throw light upon the requirement of the former. In the case of the latter, the person may walk away refusing to pick up the document which is set down in that person's presence. In those circumstances, to fix the person with all of the consequences that may follow, the law understandably requires that the 'nature of the document' should be described. But that is not required where the actual document itself is left with the person. Then, it may be inferred, the law presumes that the person will become aware of the document. Self–interest may then be relied upon to ensure that an appearance is entered and a defence mounted, if that is desired.

Clarke JA (at 88–9): Counsel for the plaintiffs contends that Mr Slone did leave the statement of claim, or more accurately a copy of the statement of claim, with Mr Redd [89] and that therefore, contrary to his Honour's ruling, personal service had been effected. In my opinion this contention should be upheld. I am satisfied that Mr Slone did, in the circumstances described above, leave the statement of claim with Mr Redd and thereby personally served him with it.

My reasons for this conclusion can be shortly stated. There is a dichotomy in the rule between a case in which the person proposed to be served accepts the document and the case in which he does not do so. If the proposed recipient does not accept the document, then the server who wishes to effect personal service is obliged to put the copy document down in his presence and describe its nature to him. If, however, the proposed recipient does not decline to accept the document then effective service is achieved by 'leaving a copy of the document' with him.

Accordingly, when an issue is raised as to whether personal service has been effected in accordance with r 3 the first question which needs to be answered is whether or not the proposed recipient declined to accept the document. If he did then it is incumbent upon the person seeking to establish that service was effected to show that there had been compliance with the second mode of service described in r 3. If, on the other hand, it is not shown that the recipient declined or failed to accept the document, then it is necessary merely to leave the document with him. In this instance there is no obligation, either express or implied, imposed on the server to inform the proposed recipient of the nature of the document or to read it to him. Nor is there any obligation on the server to take any steps to bring to the notice of the recipient the nature of the document which he is endeavouring to serve. All that he has to do is to leave a copy of the document with the recipient.

[**Samuels AP** agreed with **Clarke JA.**]

8.2.4   Service may be carried out by the plaintiff or the plaintiff's agent. The document should be left as near to the possession or control of the person to be served as circumstances will allow: *Thomson v Pheney* (1832) 1 Dowl 441 at 443 per Patteson J who said:

> I do not mean to say, that it is necessary to leave the process in the actual corporal possession of the defendant; for, whether the party touches him or puts it into his hand, is immaterial for the purpose of personal service. Personal service may be, where you see a person and bring the process to his notice ... I am quite of opinion, that in this case there are not sufficient facts to warrant any man in making an affidavit of personal service. If the deponent had informed the defendant of the nature of the process, and thrown it down, that would do.

The mode of service is required to bring the nature of the document to the defendant's attention for service to be valid: see *Taylor v Marmaras* [1954] VLR 476.

8.2.5   Provided the correct method of service is adopted, service will be valid even in the event a defendant refuses to accept it.

Exceptions to personal service

8.2.6   Personal service is usually required in respect of:

- preliminary originating process;
- secondary originating process, eg, introducing a new party or an existing party in a different capacity;
- documents initiating contempt or attachment proceedings;
- injunctions; and
- where required by statute, rules, or court order.

However, ordinary service is sufficient in respect of interlocutory applications. There are a number of situations where personal service is not required, even though the process to be served may initiate the proceedings. In those situations, service is either dispensed with, or may be effected in a different way. The main categories are as follows:

- *ex parte* interim applications: FCR r 7.01; ACT rr 728, 729; NSW r 25.9; NT r 38.02; Qld r 27; SA r 131; Tas rr 185, 530; Vic r 38.02; WA O 52 r 1;
- where a solicitor accepts service: see **8.2.9**;
- where an appearance or an unconditional notice of intention to defend (Qld r 105(2)) is entered before service: see **Chapter 9**;
- selected Queensland Magistrates' Court documents: Qld r 111;
- where substituted service is ordered: see **8.8.1**;
- where service is by means of a mode specified in an agreement: see **8.2.2, 8.2.7**;
- where there is an action for the recovery of land within the jurisdiction: see **8.5.2**;
- where there is an action *in rem* against a ship;
- where the rules or a statute expressly permit other means of service, for example, Corporations Act 2001 (Cth) (see **8.4.2**); Service and Execution of Process Act 1992 (Cth) ss 10, 11 (see **8.9.3**) and in special types of actions: see **8.5.1**; and

- in the Australian Capital Territory (ACT r 6438), where the plaintiff acts in person and no-one can be found at the plaintiff's address for service. This rule does not apply to documents that are required to be personally served on a party by a territory law including the Court Procedures Rules 2006.

In most other cases ordinary service is sufficient. For a discussion of ordinary service, see 8.3.1.

Consensual service

8.2.7 Some jurisdictions permit the parties to agree upon a mode for valid service: FCR r 10.28; NSW r 10.6; NT r 6.13; Qld r 119 (service under contract); SA r 67(1)(d); Vic r 6.14; WA O 9 r 3. For example, in *Samarni v Williams* [1980] 2 NSWLR 389, service of a statement of claim on the defendant's third party insurer was held to be valid service where the insurer was willing to accept service, and was conducting the defence pursuant to an insurance policy. The rule covers both contractual and informal agreements about service (see also Informal service 8.3.6). There are no equivalent rules in the other jurisdictions. See also *Ditfort v Temby* (1990) 26 FCR 72.

8.2.8C	**Kenneth Allison Ltd v A E Limehouse & Co (a firm)**
	[1992] 2 AC 105
	House of Lords

[The plaintiff sued the defendant accountants claiming damages for a negligent audit. The day prior to the expiry of the limitation period, a process server attended the defendant's offices and told the senior partner's personal assistant he wished to serve a writ. The personal assistant was authorised by a partner to accept the writ. The personal assistant told the process server she had been authorised to accept service, received a sealed copy of the writ and a form of acknowledgment of service. The defendant sought to set aside service as it had not been served on a partner personally: Supreme Court Rules 1965 (UK) O 10 r 1(1); O 81 r 3. A district registrar dismissed the summons, but a judge allowed an appeal which was in turn upheld by the Court of Appeal. The decisions of the judge at first instance and of the Court of Appeal were overturned by the House of Lords.]

Lord Bridge of Harwich (at 113, 119–20): [113] The important question which lies at the heart of the appeal is whether the provisions of the Rules of the Supreme Court which relate to the process of service of originating process constitute an exclusive code by which alone such service may be effected, as McCullough J and the majority of the Court of Appeal held, or whether, if the parties agree between themselves on a mode of service outside the ambit of the rules, service in that mode ('consensual service', as Lord Donaldson M.R. aptly called it) will, as he held, be effective. ...

[119] It is said that it is necessary to require strict adherence to the rules in order to achieve certainty with respect to the date of service. I see no reason why it should be more difficult to establish the date when consensual service was effected by whatever method the parties may have chosen for their own convenience than to establish the date when the defendant was served personally. There is certainly no difficulty in this case. Consensual service was effected on the last date possible before the plaintiff's claim became statute-barred. That explains the defendants' motivation in challenging the validity of service, but it has no other relevance.

> Lord Donaldson of Lymington M.R. summed the matter up in words with which I entirely agree and on which I could not hope to improve when he said [1990] 2 Q.B. 527 at 533–4:
>
> > The rules are the servants of the courts and of their customers, not their masters, unless expressed in a wholly mandatory and exclusive [220] fashion which these rules are not. It would be wholly contrary to the spirit of the times that the rules should be construed in a manner which would forbid parties to litigation to act reasonably with a view to eliminating or reducing the acerbities inevitable in litigation, when to do so creates no problems whatsoever for the defendant in terms of deciding precisely when service was effected for the purposes of the Limitation Acts or otherwise.
>
> I would allow the appeal, set aside the order of the Court of Appeal and of McCullough J and dismiss the defendants' summons with costs here and below.

Solicitor's undertaking to accept service

8.2.9   An alternative to personal service is for the defendant's solicitor to undertake in writing to accept service of the originating process or indorse acceptance of service on the service copy: FCR r 10.22; ACT r 6464; NSW rr 10.6, 10.13; NT r 6.08; Qld r 115; SA r 67(1)(c) (the solicitor issues an acknowledgment to that effect); Tas rr 134, 144; Vic r 6.09; WA O 9 r 1; or undertake in writing to enter an appearance: HCR r 9.01.1 (or Submitting Appearance). The Northern Territory, Queensland and Victorian rules apply to service of all documents, not just originating process.

Where a party is legally represented, the address of the solicitor or agent is the address for service.

A solicitor should have specific instructions to accept service. General instructions to conduct the litigation are not sufficient. The undertaking is normally expressed as 'I accept the service of this writ and undertake to enter an appearance': see **9.3.8**. The solicitor is bound by the undertaking even if the client's instructions change: *Re Crimdon* [1900] P 171. Service is deemed to have been effected on the date of such indorsement (FCR r 10.22; ACT r 6464; NSW r 10.13; NT r 6.08; Qld r 115; Tas r 134; Vic r 6.09; WA O 9 r 1) unless, in some jurisdictions, it is shown that the solicitor did not have authority to accept service: FCR r 10.22; NT r 6.09; Qld r 115; Vic r 6.09. These rules appear to state what would be the position even in their absence.

Where, with the authority of the defendant in an action, a solicitor accepts service of a writ on the defendant's behalf and gives a written undertaking to 'enter an appearance in due course', that undertaking is unconditional and must be performed forthwith. It can be enforced by attachment of the solicitor: *Re Kerly, Son & Verden* [1901] 1 Ch 467.

In Tasmania (r 127), a practitioner, on demand in writing by any person served or appearing, must declare in writing whether the process has been issued by, or with the authority of that practitioner.

8.2.10 Notes and questions

1. Service within the precincts of the court is valid (*R v Jones; Ex parte McVittie* [1931] 1 KB 664; *Baldry v Jackson* [1976] 1 NSWLR 19).

2. In *Taylor v Marmaras* [1954] VLR 476 personal service was effected even though the application was enclosed in an envelope in circumstances where the defendant was aware of the application, but rejected it without opening the envelope.

3. Do the following situations give rise to valid service?

   • Attaching the document to the defendant's closed door while explaining the nature of the document, the defendant at the same time refusing to open the door. (In *Re Hudson; Ex parte G E Crane & Sons Ltd* (1990) 25 FCR 318 such service was held to be valid under r 15 of the Bankruptcy Rules 1968 (Cth) — would this be acceptable under the Rules of Court?; see also *Re Ditfort; Ex parte Deputy Commissioner of Taxation* (1988) 19 FCR 347; 83 ALR 265 which held that in cases where a defendant refuses to accept service, it is sufficient for a process server to state the nature of the process and leave it before or near the defendant, who has unimpeded and immediate access to it; *Graczyk v Graczyk* [1955] ALR (CN) 1077 (pushing the document under the door with the defendant on the other side was valid service).)

   • Poking the document into the passenger side window of a fleeing defendant's car while describing the nature of the document: see *Re Rosenberg; Ex parte Westpac Banking Corp* (unreported, FCA, Sweeney J, No VP 851 of 1992) where service of this nature was considered valid.

4. If the copy served is not a true copy, will service be ineffective? See *McArthur v Herald & Weekly Times Ltd* [1957] QWN 16 where O'Hagan J held that service of a writ without a time limited for appearance was a nullity (ie, of no legal effect).

5. A court may release a solicitor from an undertaking to accept service and enter an appearance where good cause is shown: *Simpson v Brereton* [1964] VR 332. While a court has a discretionary jurisdiction to release a solicitor's undertaking to enter an appearance, this is unlikely where a solicitor accepts service of a writ more than 12 months after its issue, undertakes to enter an appearance, then seeks to be relieved from the undertaking in circumstances where the solicitor is attempting to defeat the plaintiff's action through expiry of a limitation period: *Simpson v Brereton* [1964] VR 332.

Time requirements

8.2.11 In most jurisdictions the originating process must be served within 12 months of issue unless extended by court order, otherwise it becomes 'stale' or no longer in force: HCR r 27.01(f); NT r 5.12; Qld r 24; Vic r 5.12; WA O 7 r 1. In South Australia (r 39) the period is six months (with a possible extension of a further six months, even if the time limited for service or continuing an action has expired); and in the Federal Court (r 1.39) there is no set period as time may be extended by order. In Tasmania (r 107), the period is six months with further extension possible, provided the application is made while the original writ is in force. After the time period has expired the originating process is said to be stale, if it is not renewed before the time expired. Service of stale process is not a nullity (of no legal effect), but an irregularity.

Failure to serve originating process within these time limits does not prevent a plaintiff from commencing fresh proceedings by filing another originating process, provided a limitation period has not expired.

The rules specify how time is calculated: HCR Pt 4; FCR r 1.61; ACT r 6350; NSW rr 1.11–1.13; NT r 3.01; SA r 5; Tas rr 46–56; Vic r 3.01; WA O 3; except in Queensland where time is governed by the Acts Interpretation Act 1954 (Qld) s 38. For example:

- time does not run during court vacations;

- month means calendar month;

- a period of days is calculated by excluding the first day, but including the last day. The phrase 'clear days' excludes both the first and last day;

- short service periods exclude the days on which the registry is closed: HCR r 4.01.4 (five days); FCR r 161(3) (five days); ACT r 6350; (five days); NSW r 1.11(3) (five days); NT r 3.01(4) (five days); Acts Interpretation Act 1954 (Qld) s 38; SA r 5(3) (seven days); Tas r 50 (six days); Vic r 3.01(4) (five days); WA O 3 r 2(2) (seven days); and

- when a time period expires, if the registry is closed, the period is extended until the day on which the registry is next open: HCR r 4.01.5; FCR r 161(4); NSW r 1.11(4); NT r 3.01(5); Acts Interpretation Act 1954 (Qld) s 38; SA r 5(4); Tas r 51; Vic rr 3.01(5), 3.05; WA O 3 r 4. Courts have a power to enlarge or abridge time for service: HCR r 4.02; FCR r 1.61; ACT r 6351; NSW r 1.12; NT r 3.02; Qld r 7; SA r 10; Tas r 52; Vic r 3.02; WA O 3 r 5.

At common law, service could not be effected on a Sunday. The prohibition is still retained to varying degrees. In Tasmania, service on a Sunday is prohibited with limited exceptions: Tas r 49. See also the Sunday (Service of Process) Act 1984 (NSW) and the Hon Justice D Byrne, 'Practice and Procedure', *Halsbury's Laws of Australia*, LexisNexis, Sydney, looseleaf, vol 20, [325–2025]. Elsewhere service is permitted on a Sunday. For example, it is permissible in South Australia to serve legal process on any day: Supreme Court Act 1935 (SA) s 118.

Some jurisdictions also specifically exclude service on other days such as Good Friday and Christmas Day: Qld r 101 (unless court otherwise orders); Tas r 49. In New South Wales, the Sunday (Service of Process) Act 1984 prohibits service on a Sunday on which Christmas Day falls. In South Australia, see SA r 5(6) in relation to the Christmas vacation.

In some jurisdictions the rules regulate the time within which service is required and impose deeming provisions. In the High Court, r 4.01.6 provides that an act done after 4 pm is taken to have been done on the next day the Registry is open. Similar provisions exist in other jurisdictions: Qld r 103; SA r 5(1); Tas r 51; Vic r 3.05(2); WA O 72 r 5A. There are no equivalent deeming provisions in the Australian Capital Territory, the Federal Court, or New South Wales.

The rules prescribe time delay between service and hearing of an originating application. For example, Tas r 123 requires nine clear days, where an appearance is required, otherwise two clear days.

Cross-vesting schemes

8.2.12 It appears that the cross-vesting schemes have not altered the procedural requirements for service (*David Syme & Co Ltd (rec and mgr apptd) v Grey* (1992) 38 FCR 303; 115 ALR 247), although the issue is not beyond doubt: see **4.3.10E**.

Concurrent summons

8.2.13   A concurrent summons is a duplicate of the original summons indorsed with the word 'concurrent'. Concurrent summons are available in Western Australia (O 7 r 3). Elsewhere, copies of the originating process are used. Concurrent summons enable service to be effected in several jurisdictions simultaneously or on several defendants. The summons will vary to reflect the altered time periods for entry of appearance (see **9.6.1**) together with any other necessary indorsements for service outside Australia: see **8.9.35**.

Affidavit of service

8.2.14   A plaintiff or applicant is required to file an affidavit of service deposing to the time and manner of service of an initiating process within a set time frame: HCR r 22.02 (seven days).

8.2.15E	Uniform Civil Procedure Rules 2005 (NSW)
	Form 41 (version 1)
	UCPR 35.8

AFFIDAVIT OF SERVICE [NAME] [DATE]

COURT DETAILS
Court
Division
List
Registry
Case number

TITLE OF PROCEEDINGS

[First] plaintiff	**[name]**
# Second plaintiff # Number of plaintiffs	
(if more than two)	
[First] defendant	**[name]**
# Second defendant # Number of defendants	
(if more than two)	

FILING DETAILS

Filed for	**[name]** [role of party eg, plaintiff]
# Filed in relation to	[eg, plaintiff's claim, (number) cross-claim]
	[include only if form to be eFiled]
# Legal representative	[solicitor on record] [firm]
# Legal representative reference	[reference number]
Contact name and telephone	[name] [telephone]
[on separate page]	

AFFIDAVIT
Name
Address
Occupation
Date
1.   I [# say on oath affirm]:
2.   I am [role of deponent].
3.   I am over the age of 16 years.
4.   On [date] at [place], I served [name of person served] with the following documents [describe documents served. If the document served is a filed document, include the date the document was filed in the description eg, statement of claim filed (date). Do not attach a copy of any document already filed.]
5.   I served the documents by [method of service].
At the time of service [name of person served] stated [record what, if anything, the person served said].
SWORN # AFFIRMED at
Signature of deponent
Signature of witness
Name of witness
Address of witness
Capacity of witness

[#Justice of the peace # Solicitor # Barrister # Commissioner for affidavits # Notary public]
Note: The deponent and witness must sign each page of the affidavit. See UCPR 35.7B.

8.2.16   Question

1.   How is personal service of an originating process achieved on a person who evades service by travelling between Australia and New Zealand? In Western Australia, a concurrent writ together with the original writ will need to be prepared. Each document will have different time periods for entry of appearance. In the remaining jurisdictions copies of the originating writ need only be prepared. Service may then be effected at each of the locations. If service still proves difficult, an order for substituted service may be sought: see **8.8.1**.

ORDINARY SERVICE

8.3.1   More relaxed rules apply in respect of the service of interlocutory processes as distinct from originating processes. Generally, only initiating proceedings are required to be personally served: for example, writs, originating summonses, orders to show cause, and third party notices.

Most documents do not require personal service. While such documents may be served personally (see **8.2.1**), ordinary service by sending or delivering the document to a party's proper address for service is sufficient and more convenient: HCR rr 9.01.5, 9.04.1; FCR O 7 rr 3, 4; ACT r 6420; NSW r 10.5; NT r 6.06; Qld r 112; SA r 68; Tas r 144; Vic r 6.07; WA O 72 r 5. The address for service is stated in the originating process or appearance. In South Australia, a document filed in the court by or on behalf of a party must be endorsed with the party's address for service: r 59. If the person is legally represented, the address for service will be that of the solicitor or their agent. In some jurisdictions, the rules specifically provide that one means of ordinary service is the making by a solicitor of an indorsement or note on a copy of the service document, that service has been accepted: FCR r 10.22; ACT r 6464; NSW r 10.13; NT r 6.08; Qld r 115; Vic r 6.09. The other jurisdictions have no equivalent rule, but rely on the personal service rule equivalent.

The rules also provide for ordinary service by other means including:

- service by filing: see **8.3.4**;
- service by the court: see **8.3.5**;
- informal service: see **8.3.6**;
- service by facsimile: see **8.3.7**;
- service by post: see **8.3.9**;
- service by document exchange (DX): see **8.3.13**; and
- service by electronic means: see **8.3.14**.

There are also special service rules in relation to special types of parties including corporations, partnerships, business names, unincorporated associations, agents, spouses, infants, mentally ill persons, the Crown, third parties and prisoners (see **8.4.1**) or special types of action, including actions for the recovery of land (see **8.5.2**) and motor vehicle personal injury claims: see **8.5.3**.

8.3.2E   **Supreme Court (General Civil Procedure) Rules 1996 (Vic) r 6.07**
Order 6 — Service

How ordinary service effected

6.07 (1) Where personal service of a document is not required, the document may be served —

(a) by leaving the document at the proper address of the person to be served on any day on which the Prothonotary's [registrar's in the other jurisdictions] office is open;

(b) by posting the document to the person to be served at his proper address;

(c) where provision is made by or under any Act for service of a document on a corporation, by serving the document in accordance with that provision;

(d) where the solicitor of a party has facilities for the reception of documents in an exchange box in a document exchange, by leaving the document in that exchange box or in another exchange box for transmission to that exchange box; or

(e) where the solicitor for a party has facilities for the reception by telephone transmission of a facsimile of a document, by telephone transmission of the document in accordance with paragraph (2.1) …

Address for service

8.3.3   Where a person has nominated an address for service, that is their proper address for service: HCR rr 9.05.1, 9.05.2; FCR O 7 rr 4, 6; ACT r 6420; NSW r 4.5; NT r 6.06; Qld r 112(3) (relevant address), Form 8; Tas r 128; Vic r 6.07; WA O 72 r 5. The originating process or appearance sets out an address for service within a prescribed distance from the registry: HCR r 9.05.1 (plaintiff), r 9.05.2 (defendant); FCR rr 8.01, 11.01; ACT r 50; NT r 6.05; Qld r 17 (plaintiff), r 140 (defendant); SA r 58; Tas rr 128, 144; Vic r 6.06; WA O 6 r 7, O 12 r 2 (defendant), O 71A.

In New South Wales r 4.5 states that a person's address for service is an address in NSW (other than a DX address):

(a)   at which documents in the proceedings may be left for the person during ordinary business hours; and

(b)   to which documents in the proceedings may be posted for the person.

An address for service continues to be relevant when a new proceeding commences in a higher court, which is related to the proceedings in a lower court: NSW r 10.18.

If at the time of service a person has no address for service, the proper address is usually:

• for individuals, their usual or last known residential or business address;

• for firms, the principal or last known place of business; or

• for corporations, the registered or principal office.

See NT r 6.06; Qld r 112(3); Vic r 6.07; WA O 72 r 5. The Australian Capital Territory (r 6421) and New South Wales (rr 4.5, 10.16) provide for filing in the registry in these circumstances. Failure to give an address for service or giving a false address may also result in an order for security for costs: *Knight v Ponsonby* [1925] 1 KB 545. For a defendant, the court may decide to strike out an appearance: *A v B* [1883] WN 174.

In South Australia, an address for service of a party is an address recorded (or to be recorded) in the court records as an address at which documents may be served on the party: r 58(1). A party must submit a physical address for service which is defined as an address of premises at which service may be effected by leaving the document for the party or in the absence of a separate postal address by sending the document by prepaid post in an envelope addressed to the party: r 58(3). The premises must be in separate occupation and be either where the party's lawyer practices in South Australia or be within 50 km of the Adelaide GPO: r 58(4). The party may submit in addition to the physical address for service, a postal, DX, facsimile, email address or combinations of these addresses for service: r 58(5). Rule 59 has detailed requirements concerning the obligation to give an address for service. It should also be noted that in South Australia, notice of an address for service has replaced the concept of an appearance.

In Tasmania, r 128A provides for an illusory, fictitious, or in some other way not genuine or appropriate address for service. The judge may make any order including setting aside a notice of appearance, providing for or dispensing with service.

All the Rules of Court provide for changing an address for service: see for example HCR rr 9.05, 9.06; FCR r 11.09; NSW r 4.6; SA r 59(4).

In the Federal Court (r 10.11), the respondent, in the absence of a r 13.01 application, will by filing an address for service, defence or affidavit, or appearing in response to the originating application, be deemed to have been personally served.

Service by filing

8.3.4   It is sufficient for ordinary service to be effective to file or post a notice on a public notice board in the court registry in circumstances where the person to be served is in default of appearance, or has no address for service: FCR r 10.25; ACT r 6421; NT rr 6.06(3), (3.1),

6.11; Tas r 145; Vic r 6.12(1). In South Australia (r 68(2)(d)) and Western Australia (O 72 r 8) a direction of the court is required. There is no equivalent provision in Queensland, though it may be dealt with by substituted service: r 116. In Tasmania, the document filed in the registry must be endorsed with the name of the person served and that the document is filed as service: Tas r 146A. In New South Wales, service by filing is permitted in relation to a person in default of appearance or a person who has entered an appearance, but is not an active party in the proceedings: r 10.16. The New South Wales rule does not apply to any document required to be served personally.

Service by the court

8.3.5   The rules in several jurisdictions provide that where under the rules an order, notice or other document is to be served by the court or officer of the court, it is sufficient if done by ordinary service: ACT r 6420; FCR r 10.26; NSW r 10.7; NT r 6.15; SA r 68 (post, fax, DX or other order); Tas r 145 (post); Vic r 6.16; WA O 72 r 6. There is no equivalent provision in Queensland.

Informal service

8.3.6   In some jurisdictions, courts may dispense with compliance with the rules, typically where the document has come to the attention of the party to be served, or in Queensland, came into their possession, and no prejudice arises: FCR r 10.23; NSW r 10.14(3) (taken to constitute personal service); NT r 6.10; Qld r 117 (possession); SA r 67(2) (presumption of personal service), r 69 (ordinary presumptive service). It may also be necessary to establish that proper service was impracticable. Service occurs when it comes to the attention of the party to be served. In South Australia, personal service will be presumed if an answering document is filed or served on the party required to serve a document or it is established in some other way that the document and its contents have come to the attention of the person to be served: SA r 67(2). See also Vic r 6.11. Elsewhere there are no equivalent provisions. In Tasmania, r 146B deems a document to be served on the day on which it came to the person's notice despite not being served in the manner required by the rules.

Service by facsimile

8.3.7   In the High Court, Federal Court, South Australia, Tasmania and Victoria, documents not required to be served personally may be served by facsimile: HCR rr 9.04.1, 9.04.2; FCR rr 10.31, 10.32; Qld rr 112, 122; SA r 68(3)(c) (assuming the party has an address for service); Tas r 144(5), (6); Vic rr 6.07(1)(e), 6.07(2.1). The Victorian rule is slightly narrower than in the Federal Court and Queensland as the facsimile must be directed to a solicitor representing a party.

The Australian Capital Territory and New South Wales rules enable service by facsimile where a solicitor's office is the address for service: ACT r 6450 (after 4 pm deemed next day — r 6450); NSW r 10.5(2), (3) (taken to be served at the end of the first day following the day of the facsimile). Elsewhere, in the absence of a rule, service by facsimile is not necessarily valid. If, however, a legible and complete copy of the document is received by the person to be served, courts have held the requirements of ordinary service have been fulfilled: see *Hastie & Jenkerson v McMahon* [1990] 1 WLR 1575; *NM Superannuation Pty Ltd v Baker* (1992) 7 ACSR 105;

and *Ralux NV/SA v Spencer Mason, The Times,* 18 May 1989 as discussed by J G Starke QC in practice note, 'Service by Fax — Conditions for a Valid Service' (1989) 63 *ALJ* 500.

South Australian r 68(4) provides for re-transmission on request of illegible facsimiles. A facsimile sent before 5 pm on a business day is taken to be served on that day, otherwise it is taken to be served on the next business day after transmission: SA r 71(3).

8.3.8   Question

1.   Tom faxed a copy of a summons to Peter. Peter received the complete legible copy. Has ordinary service been effected? Would your answer depend on whether the fax is that of an originating process? Do you need to confirm whether your fax has been received? See *N M Superannuation Pty Ltd v Hughes* (1992) 27 NSWLR 26.

Service by post

8.3.9   Ordinary service may be effected by prepaid post, addressed to the person to be served at their proper address for service: HCR r 9.04.1; FCR r 10.31; ACT r 6420, Legislation Act 2001 (ACT) s 247; NSW r 10.5(1)(b); NT r 6.06; Qld r 112(1)(d); SA r 68(2)(b); Tas r 144(1) (posted to the person's address for service); Vic r 6.07 (sent by post); WA O 72 r 5 (sent by pre-paid post). For proper address for service, see **8.3.3**. In New South Wales, documents relating to inactive parties may be posted to the person's business or residential address: r 10.5(1)(b). The foregoing rules state that a person's address for service is the address nominated for the purpose of the proceedings. Service will be deemed to be effected when the process would be delivered in the ordinary course of the postal service unless proved to the contrary or the relevant rule specifies a set time period: FCR r 10.32 (four business days); Acts Interpretation Act 1901 (Cth) s 29; ACT r 6450 (four days); Evidence Act 1995 (NSW) s 160 (four working days after posted); Interpretation Act 1987 (NSW) s 76; Acts Interpretation Act 1954 (Qld) s 39A; SA r 71(1); Tas r 144(2); Acts Interpretation Act 1931 (Tas) ss 5, 30; Vic r 6.07(5); Interpretation of Legislation Act 1984 (Vic) s 49; Interpretation Act 1984 (WA) s 75. There is no equivalent provision in the Northern Territory.

8.3.10   At common law there is a rebuttable presumption that a prepaid, stamped and addressed envelope which has been posted and has not been returned, has, in the ordinary course, reached its destination: *Re Gasbourne Pty Ltd* [1984] VR 801. A return address is required, since if the letter is returned, service is invalid. The above Rules of Court and common law presumptions may be rebutted if non-service can be proved: *Fancourt v Mercantile Credits Ltd* (1983) 154 CLR 87 at 96.

8.3.11   Sections 9 and 10 of the Service and Execution of Process Act 1992 (Cth) also permit service of originating process by post with respect to companies and body corporates. Section 27 provides that service upon an individual must be effected in the same way as service of such a process in the place of issue, including those rules governing service by post.

8.3.12   Questions

1. Is postal service valid when a letter is returned marked 'return to sender'?
2. Is postal service valid when a letter is returned marked 'undelivered' or 'no response'? See *Hewitt v Leicester City Council* [1969] 2 All ER 802 at 804.
3. Is it preferable to send a document to be served by registered post or by certified mail? This procedure is required by the High Court and Tasmanian rules respectively. Elsewhere prepaid post is sufficient.

Service by document exchange (DX)

8.3.13   Ordinary service is permissible through the document exchange system where the address for service is the office of a solicitor who has a document exchange box: HCR r 9.04.1; FCR O 7 rr 4(1)(d), (3)(b) (two days), 4A(1)(c), (2)(b), 7; ACT r 6450 (two days); NSW r 10.5(2), (3) (taken to be served at the end of the second day after delivery); NT rr 6.06(1)(d), (4), (5); Qld rr 112(1)(f), 102; SA rr 68(3)(b) (addressed to the party's DX address), 71(2); Tas r 144(4); Vic rr 6.07(1)(d), (5)(b), (6); WA O 72 r 5A. The same rules also contain deeming provisions concerning the time of service. There is no equivalent High Court rule.

Service by electronic means

8.3.14   In Queensland, a document may be served if the person to be served has a solicitor with an email address, by emailing the document to the solicitor (Qld r 112(1)(f)(iii)) or by using an electronic means prescribed by practice direction: r 112(1)(g). The New South Wales provision is similar: rr 3.8, 10.5(2)(c). The Electronic Transactions Act 2000 (NSW) and other state equivalents specify when an electronic copy of a document is taken to be delivered. WA O 72 r 5A allows service by fax (cover page O 72 r 5(4)) and email. See also WA O 72 r 6A. Federal Court r 10.31 enables a person to file a notice authorising documents to be served by electronic communication to the email address specified in the notice. This is a valid form of ordinary service one day after the copy is sent: r 10.32. In Tasmania, when an address for service and email address is endorsed, stated or advised, a document may be served by sending it to the email address: r 144(7). Service occurs on the first day, not being a court holiday, following the sending of the email. For the detailed requirements for the Australian Capital Territory, see r 6466.

In South Australia, provided the person to be served has an email address for service, they may be served by email: r 68(3)(a). Incomplete or unintelligible emails may be resent or sent by post or personally served: r 68(4)(b). For the time of service in South Australia, see r 71.

Interlocutory injunctions

8.3.15   In the Federal Court (r 10.27) and New South Wales (r 10.17) there are unique rules which permit notice of an interlocutory injunction to be served by telegram or letter signed by or on behalf of the registrar.

Statutory modification

8.3.16   The various Acts Interpretation Acts provide general rules for service of documents under any Act: Acts Interpretation Act 1901 (Cth) s 28A; Service and Execution of Process Act 1992 (Cth) (see **8.9.3**); Legislation Act 2001 (ACT) Pt 19.5; Interpretation Act 1987 (NSW) s 76; Acts Interpretation Act 1954 (Qld) ss 39, 39A; Acts Interpretation Act 1915 (SA) s 33; Interpretation of Legislation Act 1984 (Vic) s 49. These provisions do not affect specific provisions as to service in Acts, nor the power of the court to authorise or require service in another way.

The Federal Court also has special rules for service in relation to patents (r 10.07) and trade marks (r 10.08).

8.3.17E	**Acts Interpretation Act 1901 (Cth)**

Service of documents

28A (1) For the purposes of any Act that requires or permits a document to be served on a person, whether the expression 'serve', 'give' or 'send' or any other expression is used, then, unless the contrary intention appears, the document may be served:

  (a)   on a natural person:
     (i)   by delivering it to the person personally; or
     (ii)   by leaving it at, or by sending it by pre-paid post to, the address of the place of residence or business of the person last known to the person serving the document; or
  (b)   on a body corporate: by leaving it at, or sending it by pre-paid post to, the head office, a registered office or a principal office of the body corporate. Note: The Electronic Transactions Act 1999 deals with giving information in writing by means of an electronic communication.

(2) Nothing in subsection (1):

  (a)   affects the operation of any other law of the Commonwealth, or any law of a State or territory, that authorizes the service of a document otherwise than as provided in that subsection; or
  (b)   affects the power of a court to authorize service of a document otherwise than as provided in that subsection.

SPECIAL PARTIES

8.4.1   The Rules of Court contain special service rules applicable to certain types of parties. The main categories are as follows:

- corporations: see **8.4.2**;

- partnerships, business names, and unincorporated associations: see **8.4.9**;

- agents: see **8.4.10**;

- spouses: see **8.4.13**;

- infants: see **8.4.14**;

- mentally ill persons: see **8.4.15**;

- Crown and judicial officers: see **8.4.16**;

- third parties: see **8.4.17**;

- prisoners or detainees: see **8.4.18**; and

- parties keeping house: see **8.4.19**.

Corporations

8.4.2 Most jurisdictions have Rules of Court enabling personal service on corporations, in addition to those of the Corporations Act 2001 (Cth): HCR r 9.03(2) (service on the secretary or other proper officer of the body corporate); ACT r 6432 (extracted below); NSW r 10.22 (personal service on the principal officer); NT r 6.04(a); SA r 62 (director, secretary or public officer of the company); Tas r 137; Vic r 6.04(a); WA O 72 r 3 (mayor, president or other head officer of the body, chief executive officer, clerk, treasurer, manager, secretary or similar officer). Personal service may be effected under the Rules of Court or the Corporations Act. The Federal Court (r 10.02) and Queensland (r 107) have adopted service as provided for by the Corporations Act or other applicable law.

Domestic corporations

8.4.3 Under the Corporations Act 2001 (Cth) domestic companies are served in accordance with s 109X (extracted below).

8.4.4E   **Corporations Act 2001 (Cth)**

Service of documents

109X(1) For the purpose of any law, a document may be served on a company by:

  (a)   leaving it at, or posting it to, the company's registered office; or
  (b)   delivering a copy of the document personally to a director of the company who resides in Australia or in an external Territory; or
  (c)   if a liquidator of the company has been appointed — leaving it at, or posting it to, the address of the liquidator's office in the most recent notice of that address lodged with ASIC; or
  (d)   if an administrator of the company has been appointed — leaving it at, or posting it to, the address of the administrator in the most recent notice of that address lodged with ASIC.

109X(2) For the purposes of any law, a document may be served on a director or company secretary by leaving it at, or posting it to, the alternative address notified to ASIC under subsection 5 H(2), 117(2), 205B(1) or (4) or 601BC(2). However, this only applies to service on the director or company secretary:

  (a)   in their capacity as a director or company secretary; or
  (b)   for the purposes of a proceeding in respect of conduct they engaged in as a director or company secretary.

109X(3) Subsections (1) and (2) do not apply to a process, order or document that may be served under section 9 of the Service and Execution of Process Act 1992.

109X(6) This section does not affect:

(a)   any other provision of this Act, or any provision of another law, that permits; or

(b)   the power of a court to authorise;

a document to be served in a different way.

109X(7) This section applies to provisions of a law dealing with service whether it uses the expression "serve" or uses any other similar expression such as "give" or "send".

8.4.5   The Corporations Act 2001 (Cth) permits ordinary service of originating process: s 109X. Throughout Australia, service may be effected by posting the process to the company's registered office. This procedure is an alternative to using the Service and Execution of Process Act 1992 (Cth). Section 28(A) of the Acts Interpretation Act 1901 (Cth) only requires a properly addressed envelope and prepaid postage. Registered or certified mail is not required. If certified mail is returned, the Acts Interpretation Act 1901 (Cth) s 38(2) deems that service has not been effected.

It is not valid service under s 109X if:

(a)   a document is mailed by registered post, the postal delivery worker is not able to obtain a signature, and instead leaves a card requesting the addressee to contact the post office: *Giustginiano Nominees Pty Ltd v Redan Pty Ltd* [1999] WASC 95;

(b)   a document posted to the registered company office is returned unclaimed: *Re Rustic Homes Pty Ltd* (1988) 49 SASR 41 at 45.

An inference that directors are neglecting their duty to collect documents from their company's registered office postbox, may be sufficient to sustain effective service: *Liberty Funding Pty Ltd v Drakeswood Pty Ltd* [2002] SASR 54.

8.4.6   If the corporation is a public authority, in the absence of a statutory provision, the service rules apply. Service should be effected on the head officer of the body (for example, the mayor, head officer or general manager): ACT r 6431; NSW r 10.22 (principal officer); NT r 6.04(a); SA r 62 (director, secretary or public officer); Tas r 137; Vic r 6.04(a) (officer apparently 16 years old); WA O 72 r 3. In the case of municipalities, New South Wales and Victorian legislation specifically provide for service on the clerk: Local Government Act 1993 (NSW) s 727; Local Government Act 1989 (Vic) s 233. There are no equivalent provisions elsewhere.

Foreign corporations

8.4.7   Foreign corporations may be registered or unregistered. Registered foreign corporations are served by leaving the document at, or by sending it by post to, the address of the local agent: Corporations Act 2001 (Cth) s 601CX.

Unregistered foreign corporations may be resident or non-resident in Australia. Resident foreign corporations are served under the Rules of Court by serving the process at the principal office or place of business on a senior officer of the body corporate: HCR r 9.03.2 (service on the secretary or other proper officer of the body corporate); FCR r 10.02; ACT r 6432; NSW r 10.22 (service upon a principal officer or service in accordance with any applicable Act: Local Government Act 1993 (NSW) s 727; Strata Schemes Management Act 1996 (NSW) s 235); NT r 6.04(a); Qld r 112(3)(c); SA r 62 (director, secretary or public officer of the company); Tas r 137 (served on a head officer, general manager, treasurer, manager or secretary); Vic r 6.04(a); WA O 72 r 3. As to service on a foreign corporation, see *BHP Petroleum Pty Ltd v Oil Basins Ltd* [1985] VR 725. As to residence, see *Okura & Co Ltd v Forsbacka Jernverks Aktiebolag* [1914] 1 KB 715.

Service on a non-resident unregistered foreign corporation is governed by the Rules of Court mentioned in **8.4.2**, together with the Rules of Court dealing with international service: see **8.9.10**.

Any difficulties associated with service of foreign corporations may be avoided where there is an express agreement to submit to the jurisdiction: see **8.2.7**, *Emanuel v Symon* [1908] 1 KB 302.

Government owned corporations

8.4.8 In Queensland, the Government Owned Corporations Act 1993 provides for (i) statutory government owned corporations and (ii) company government owned corporations. The former are body corporates established under an Act and are not bound by the Corporations Act (see Government Owned Corporations Act 1993 (Qld) ss 65, 67). Statutory government owned corporations are served according to their creating Act, or if there is no specific provision, in accordance with the Acts Interpretation Act 1954 (Qld) s 39(1)(b). Company government owned corporations are public companies limited by shares. They are bound by and served under s 109X of the Corporations Act (Government Owned Corporations Act 1993 ss 66, 69).

Partnerships, business names, and unincorporated associations

8.4.9 In all jurisdictions except the High Court and New South Wales, partners may sue or be sued in the firm name: FCR r 9.41; ACT r 286; NT r 17.01; Qld r 83; SA r 85; Tas r 308; Vic r 17.01; WA O 71 r 1; *Kenneth Allison Ltd (in liq) v A E Limehouse & Co (a firm)* [1990] 2 All ER 723. In New South Wales (r 7.20), partners are sued individually or under an unregistered business name.

Originating process may be personally served on any one or more partners, or at the principal place of business on anyone having the control or management of the business at the time of service: FCR r 10.05; ACT r 6433; NT r 17.03; Qld r 114; SA r 64; Tas r 310; Vic r 17.03; WA O 71 r 3. There is no equivalent High Court rule. The same rules also provide that in the event a partnership has been dissolved prior to the commencement of the proceeding, originating documents must be served on all parties sought to be made liable. Queensland r 114(1)(c) also permits service at the registered office of a partnership under the Partnership Act 1891 (Qld).

Notice in writing needs to be given to the person served, indicating the capacity in which they are served (for example, as a partner or person having apparent control of the business). Where there is a failure to give notice, the person so served is deemed to be served as a partner: NT r 17.03; Tas r 310; Vic r 17.03(4); WA O 71 r 4. There are no equivalent provisions in the remaining jurisdictions.

Persons carrying on a business in a name or style, other than his or her name or style, may be served in that name or style as if the name or style were a firm name, and the partnership service rules apply. In all jurisdictions except the Federal Court, New South Wales, Queensland and Tasmania, such persons may be served in the same way as partnerships: ACT r 291 (unregistered name); NT r 17.10; SA r 85; Vic r 17.10; WA O 71 r 12. It is implicit that these rules permit suing in the business name. In the Federal Court, r 10.06 permits personal service on any individual trading under a business name, by leaving a copy of the document at the place where the business is carried on with the person, or another person apparently an adult, and appears to be engaged in the service of the business.

In New South Wales, rr 10.9, 10.10 apply to unregistered and registered business names respectively. Service may be effected on an unregistered business name by leaving a copy of the process where the business is carried on with a person apparently engaged in the business apparently of or over 16 years of age, or by sending a copy by post to the business address: r 10.9. Registered businesses are dealt with by the Commonwealth under the Business Names (Commonwealth Powers) Act 2011 (NSW) and r 10.10 (a similar process to that described for unregistered business names). With respect to limited partnerships, documents may be served on a defendant, whether sued in his or her name or under the firm name of the partnership. The process is similar to that for unregistered business names: r 10.11.

In Queensland (r 113), if a proceeding is brought against a person in relation to a business carried on by the person under a name or style other than the person's name, the name is not registered under the Business Names Act 1962 (Qld), and the proceeding is started in that name or style, then the originating process may be served by leaving a copy at the person's place of business with a person who appears to have control or management of the business at the place.

Unincorporated associations do not have a distinct legal personality. Such associations cannot sue or be sued in a group name, save in the absence of legislation. In all jurisdictions except the Federal Court, New South Wales, South Australia and Tasmania, the ordinary Rules of Court applicable to representative proceedings apply (HCR r 21.09; ACT r 266; NT r 18.02; Qld r 75; Vic r 18.02; WA O 18 r 12) or, alternatively, every member of the association can be served. See *Healey v Ballarat East Bowling Club* [1961] VR 206; *M & M Civil Engineering Pty Ltd v Sunshine Coast Turf Club* [1987] 2 Qd R 401 (members of the Management Committee).

In the Federal Court (r 10.03), unincorporated associations can be served personally by leaving a copy of the document at the principal place of business or office of the association with a person who is apparently an adult and appears to be engaged in the service of the association. There are also similar provisions in relation to organisations: FCR r 10.04.

In South Australia (SA r 64), an unincorporated association sued in the name of the association is served by service on any member of the committee of management, a person who holds property on trust for the purposes of the association, or a person who has management or control of the business of the association.

In Tasmania (r 138), originating process may be served on persons who constitute an unincorporated body, by serving the president, chairperson, other presiding officer, secretary or treasurer of the body or on any other officer holding a similar office.

Agents

8.4.10   In some jurisdictions an agent may be served on behalf of a principal who is outside the jurisdiction: NT r 6.12; Qld r 118; SA r 65; Tas r 139; Vic r 6.13; WA O 9 r 2. A copy of the order and the originating process is sent by post to the principal. There is no equivalent rule in the other jurisdictions. The South Australian rule applies to principals whether in or outside the jurisdiction.

8.4.11 On the *ex parte* application it will be necessary to establish that the agent's authority is still current before leave is granted: *Russell Wilkins & Co Ltd v Peck & Co* [1908] St R Qd 134. The procedure is an alternative to procedures allowing service outside the jurisdiction (see **8.9.10**) and is permitted in exceptional circumstances and may have special conditions attached.

8.4.12   Notes and questions

1. Is there valid service on a foreign company by serving an agent:
   (a) who has authority to receive and dispatch cargo?; or
   (b) who has no authority to accept service?

   See *The Lalandia* [1933] P 56 (In this case, service on general shipping agents inside the jurisdiction with respect to a foreign defendant was held to be bad. The defendant had no financial interest in the foreign defendant; the shipping agency transactions were on a commission-only basis. The agents had no authority to make or vary contracts all of which were fixed by a foreign corporation abroad.); *The 'Holstein'* [1936] 2 All ER 1660 (where service on local shipping agents with respect to a foreign defendant was held to be bad; the agents 'sold' but did not 'make' contracts on behalf of the foreign defendant); *Glanville v J B Lippincott* (1900) 17 WN (NSW) 74 (where the limited extent of the local agency prevented valid service on the agent with respect to a foreign defendant); *Rudd v John Griffiths Cycle Co Ltd* (1897) 23 VLR 350 (which held that where an agent has a power of attorney to defend actions brought against their foreign corporate principal, service on the agent will be valid).

2. Is service of originating process by post to a corporation's branch office or place of business valid? See **8.4.5**.

Spouses

8.4.13 In all jurisdictions, the standard rules as to personal service apply: see **8.2.1**. Whether service of the spouse of a defendant is valid personal service of the defendant depends on the facts: see *Pino v Prosser* [1967] VR 835.

Infants

8.4.14 An infant is a natural person under 18 years old (under 16 years old in New South Wales). Infants are served via their guardian, or, if no guardian is appointed, via their parents or the person with whom the infant resides (or who takes care of him or her): HCR r 9.03.3(a); FCR rr 10.09, 10.10; ACT r 6435 (litigation guardian); NSW r 10.12 (tutor); NT r 6.04; Qld r 108 (litigation guardian); SA r 63 (guardian, administrator or other person with responsibility for administering the affairs of the person under a disability); Tas r 136 (or authorised person under the Guardianship and Administration Act 1995 (Tas));

Vic r 6.04(b); WA O 70 r 13 (guardian or next friend); *Re Williams; Ex parte Official Assignee v Williams* (1907) 7 SR (NSW) 422. In Tasmania (r 136), the court or a judge may order that service made, or to be made, personally on a person under a disability is good service.

In New South Wales, judgments, orders, notices of motion and subpoenas (but not orders for interrogatories, discovery or inspection of documents) must be personally served on a person under a legal incapacity.

In South Australia, r 63(2) provides that service is to be regarded as valid service on a person under a disability if:

(a)   service is effected in the usual way;

(b)   the party effecting service is, at the time of service, unaware that the party is a person under a disability; and

(c)   the court is satisfied that the document came to the attention of someone who could deal with the document in an appropriate way for the person under a disability.

Mentally ill persons

8.4.15   Mentally ill persons are served via a guardian *ad litem*, or via a person who may occupy this position: HCR r 9.03.3 (guardian or other person having responsibility for the conduct of the person's affairs, or if there is none, on the person with whom the person with a disability resides or who has the care of the person with a disability); FCR rr 10.09, 10.10 (guardian, or a person responsible for their care); ACT r 6436 (litigation guardian or if none, a person who cares for the person or with whom he or she lives); NSW r 10.12 (tutor, or if a protected person within the meaning of the New South Wales Trustee and Guardian Act 2009 (NSW), the manager of his or her estate or, if no manager, the person with whom the protected person resides or in whose care he or she is); NT r 6.04(c) (litigation guardian); Qld r 109 (impaired person's litigation guardian); SA r 63, see **8.4.14**; Tas r 136 (authorised person under the Guardianship and Administration Act 1995 (Tas)); Vic r 6.04(c) (litigation guardian); WA O 70 r 13.

Crown and judicial officers

8.4.16   The Crown in the right of a state or the Commonwealth is served by serving the Attorney-General or Crown Solicitor: Judiciary Act 1903 (Cth) s 63; Court Procedures Act 2004 (ACT) s 33 (Chief Solicitor); NSW r 10.23; Crown Proceedings Act 1988 (NSW) s 6; NT r 6.04; Crown Proceedings Act 1980 (Qld) s 19 (Chief Solicitor); Crown Proceedings Act 1976 (SA) s 5; Vic r 6.04(d) (secretary to the Attorney-General's Department (Cth); Victorian Government Solicitor (Vic)), (e); Crown Proceedings Act 1958 (Vic) Pt 2; WA O 72 r 3A, Crown Suits Act 1947 (WA) s 5. In Tasmania, the appropriate officer is the Director of Public Prosecutions: Crown Proceedings Act 1993 (Tas) s 13. The High Court r 9.03.1 provides that personal service of a document may be effected on a body politic by serving the document on the government solicitor for that polity. In Queensland, bodies politic are served in the same manner as corporations: r 107 — Acts Interpretation Act 1954 (Qld) s 36.

In New South Wales (r 10.24), personal service on a judicial officer is effected by leaving a copy of the document at the office of the Principal Registrar addressed to the judicial officer.

Third parties

8.4.17   A defendant using a third party notice may claim against a person not already a party to the action (known as the third party), a contribution or indemnity, or a relief or remedy related to or connected with the original subject matter of the action. Personal service is required on the third party: HCR rr 9.01.1, 21.05.1; FCR rr 15.01, 15.08, 8.01; ACT r 308; NSW r 9.7; NT r 11.04; Qld r 195; SA r 39; Tas r 203; Vic r 11.04; WA O 19 rr 1, 3.

Prisoners or detainees

8.4.18   Queensland r 110 provides for personal service of prisoners via the Public Trustee, if he or she manages the prisoner's estate and the proceeding is of a property nature or relates to the recovery of debt or damage. Otherwise, the prisoner's litigation guardian, or the person in charge of the prison in which the prisoner is imprisoned may be served. In New South Wales, personal service may be effected on an inmate of a correctional centre by leaving a copy of the document with the governor of the correctional centre or centre manager of a child detention centre: r 10.25. See also ACT r 6437, which is of similar effect. High Court r 9.03.3 deals with personal service of a person under a disability. There are no equivalent Rules of Court in other jurisdictions.

Keeping house

8.4.19   New South Wales has a special rule to deal with a person who remains in premises to which a person attempting service cannot lawfully or practicably obtain access: r 10.26. This rule originates from the bankruptcy jurisdiction.

SPECIAL ACTIONS

8.5.1   Special rules exist in relation to certain types of action. These relate mainly to actions for the recovery of land and to motor vehicle personal injury claims.

Action for recovery of land

8.5.2   In proceedings for recovery of land, service may be effected in the case of vacant possession by leaving the process on a conspicuous part of the property: ACT r 6439; NSW r 10.15; NT r 6.14; SA r 69; Tas r 140; Vic r 6.15; WA O 9 r 4. There is no equivalent provision in the Federal Court or Queensland rules. In Victoria (r 6.15) and Western Australia (O 9 r 4), an *ex parte* application is required. The court is required to be satisfied that no person appears to be in possession of the land and that the originating process cannot otherwise be served without undue expense or delay. In South Australia, r 204 provides for service in respect of an action for possession of land.

Motor vehicle personal injuries claims

8.5.3   In Victoria, r 6.05 requires a plaintiff who claims damages in respect of death or bodily injury caused by or arising out of the use of a motor vehicle to serve a copy of the originating process on the Transport Accident Commission. While there is no equivalent Rule of Court in the other jurisdictions, there are provisions contained in legislation. See, for example, Motor Accident Insurance Act 1994 (Qld) s 37 (notice requirements); Motor Vehicles Act 1959 (SA) s 125a.

INDORSEMENTS

8.6.1   Indorsements of service on originating process have been superseded in the Rules of Court.

However, indorsements are required for service pursuant to the Service and Execution of Process Act 1992 (Cth) (see s 16 and see Service and Execution of Process Regulations (Cth) Sch 1 Form 1.

PROOF OF SERVICE

8.7.1   Proof of service is not required when a defendant enters an unconditional appearance (see ACT r 73 (Notice of Intention to Respond)), a defence, or the defendant's solicitor indorses acceptance of service on the originating process (see 8.2.9), otherwise an affidavit proving service is required: ACT r 6467; NT r 6.16; Qld r 120; SA r 72; Tas r 143; Vic r 6.17; WA O 72 r 7; *Warringah Shire Council v Magnusson* (1932) 49 WN (Pt 1) (NSW) 187. The Service and Execution of Process Act 1992 (Cth) has its own special rules: s 11. The rules in several jurisdictions assist in proving service by providing that evidence of a statement by a person as to his or her identity or the holding of an office is evidence of identity or the holding of the office: Service and Execution of Process Act 1992 (Cth) s 11(7); FCR r 10.21; ACT r 6468; NSW r 10.27; NT r 6.07; Qld r 121; Vic r 6.08. There is no such assistance in the other jurisdictions.

8.7.2E   **Uniform Civil Procedure Rules (Qld)**
                            Rule 120 — Affidavit of service

120. (1) If an affidavit of service of a document is required under these rules or an Act or law, the affidavit —

    (a)   for an affidavit of personal service — must be made by the person who served the document and include the following —

        (i)   the person's full name;

        (ii)   the time, day and date the document was served;

        (iii)   the place of service;

        (iv)   the name of the person served and how the person was identified; or

    (b)   otherwise —

        (i)   must state the relevant dates and the facts showing service; and

        (ii)   may be made on information given to, or the belief of, the person causing the service; and

        (iii)   if made on information given to the person — must state the source of the information.

(2) An affidavit of service must —
- (a) have the document filed with it as an exhibit or be written on the document; or
- (b) if the document has been filed — mention the document in a way sufficient to enable the document to be identified.

SUBSTITUTED SERVICE

8.8.1   All jurisdictions permit substituted service (or presumptive service, as it is known in South Australia) as an alternative to personal service, if certain preconditions are satisfied. In Tasmania (r 141), an order for substituted service may be obtained where prompt personal service cannot be effected on a defendant.

In the other jurisdictions there are two requirements:
- (a) personal service must be too difficult or impracticable; and
- (b) the substituted method proposed must be likely to bring the proceedings to the defendant's attention: ACT r 6460; FCR r 10.24; NSW r 10.13; NT r 6.09; Qld r 116; Vic r 6.10; WA O 72 r 4. The South Australian rules dispense with the second requirement (SA r 69(3)) but retain the first requirement: SA r 69(2). See SA r 69(4) in relation to insurers.

The case law and grounds for both approaches are identical: *O'Neil v Acott* (1988) 59 NTR 1. In Queensland, r 116(3) provides that the court may, in the order, specify that the document is to be taken to have been served on the happening of a specified event or at the end of a specified time.

8.8.2C	**Porter v Freudenberg**
	[1915] 1 KB 857
	High Court of England, Court of Appeal

[An action was brought against an alien enemy resident in an enemy country, who by means of an agent, carried on a branch business within the jurisdiction. Leave was given to the plaintiff to issue a concurrent writ and to make substituted service of a notice of the writ by service of the notice upon the defendant's agent within the jurisdiction.]

Lord Reading CJ (at 888–9): In order that substituted service may be permitted, it must be clearly shown that the plaintiff is in fact unable to effect personal service and that the writ is likely to reach the defendant or to come to his knowledge if the method of substituted service which is asked for by the plaintiff is adopted. The Court may then make such order as may seem just: Order IX r 2. The terms of this rule are of very wide application, and give a very wide discretion which we are not inclined to limit. In the case of *a writ* properly issued under one of the heads of Order XI r 1, for service out of the jurisdiction, substituted service either within or without the jurisdiction may be permitted in special circumstances, as, eg, that the defendant is evading personal service of such writ, and that the proposed form of substituted service will be effectual in bringing the writ to the defendant's knowledge: *Ford v Shephard* (1895) 34 WR 63; *Western, &c, Building Society v Rucklidge* [1905] 2 Ch 472. In the case of *a notice in lieu of writ* to be served on a foreigner out of the jurisdiction on order properly so obtained under Order XI r 1, there is no reason why substituted service of that notice should not be permitted in similar circumstances to those in which it is permitted in the case of a writ for service [889] out of the jurisdiction. As to substituted service of such a notice, Order XI r 7, and Order IX r 2 give power to order it. Certainly under Order XI rr 8(4) and 8(5), it is contemplated that this may be done, for it prescribes the method of doing it, and *Ditton v Bornemann* (1886) 3 Times LR 3 (a decision on the practice before the introduction of rr 8 and 8(a)) favours the view that the substituted service of a notice of a writ may be allowed. Lord Coleridge CJ and Bowen LJ, sitting as a Divisional Court, made the order, which has been refused by the judge in chambers, that service of the notice of the writ should be made by registered letter to Germany to the trustee of the estate of the defendant, whose affairs were in compulsory liquidation in Germany, and also to the defendant's wife, and that the defendant should have a month to appear after letter would arrive. The judge in chambers before whom the application is made for substituted service of a writ for service out of the jurisdiction or of a notice of such a writ ought to be careful before acceding to the application —

(a) To satisfy himself that there exists a practical impossibility of actual service, as otherwise, inasmuch as there is always a certain amount of difficulty and delay in effecting service out of the jurisdiction under Order XI a plaintiff will always seek to obtain an order for substituted service, with the serious risk that the defendant may never have notice of the proceedings and judgment in default of appearance may be given against him unjustly;

(b) To satisfy himself for the same reason that the method of substituted service asked for by the plaintiff is one which will in all reasonable probability, if not certainty, be effective to bring knowledge of the writ or the notice of the writ (as the case may be) to the defendant.

8.8.3   An order for substituted service should not be made unless it appears:

(a)   that there exists a practical impossibility of actual service: *Re Conan Doyle's Will Trusts; Harwood v Fides Union Fiduciaire* [1971] Ch 982; *Paragon Group Ltd v Burnell* [1991] 2 All ER 388; *Kendell v Sweeney* [2002] QSC 404;

(b)   that the method of substituted service asked for is one which will in all reasonable *probability*, if not certainty, be effective to bring knowledge of the writ to the defendant: *Porter v Freudenberg* [1915] 1 KB 857; *Miscamble v Phillips (No 2)* [1936] St R Qd 272; and

(c)   but for practical difficulties, that personal service is legally permissible: see **8.8.12**.

An order for substituted service cannot be based on a stale writ (*Bernstein v Jackson* [1982] 2 All ER 806; see **8.2.11**), nor made against a foreign sovereign: *Mighell v Sultan of Jahore* [1894] 1 QB 149.

In Western Australia (O 72 r 4), substituted service is limited to documents for which personal service is required. The other jurisdictions allow substituted service of any documents: FCR r 10.24; ACT r 6460; NSW r 10.14; NT r 6.09; Qld r 116; SA r 69(1); Tas r 141; Vic r 6.10. It is unusual to use substituted service for processes other than originating process as ordinary service is a simpler process.

8.8.4E **Uniform Civil Procedure Rules 2005 (NSW)**

10.14 Substituted and informal service generally
(cf SCR Part 9, rules 10 and 11; DCR Part 8, rules 5 and 16; LCR Part 7, rules 5 and 16)

(1) If a document that is required or permitted to be served on a person in connection with any proceedings:
  (a) cannot practicably be served on the person, or
  (b) cannot practicably be served on the person in the manner provided by law,
the court may, by order, direct that, instead of service, such steps be taken as are specified in the order for the purpose of bringing the document to the notice of the person concerned.
(2) An order under this rule may direct that the document be taken to have been served or the person concerned on the happening of a specified event or on the expiry of a specified time.
(3) If steps have been taken, otherwise than under an order under this rule, for the purpose of bringing the document to the notice of the person concerned, the court may, by order, direct that the document be taken to have been served on that person on a date specified in the order.
(4) Service in accordance with this rule is taken to constitute personal service.

Practical impossibility of actual service

8.8.5 The issue is whether, at the date of the application for substituted service, the plaintiff, despite reasonable efforts, was unable to serve the document in accordance with the rules: *Foxe v Brown* (1984) 58 ALR 542 at 546–7; *Zinc Corp Ltd v Hirsch* [1916] VLR 550; *Syndicate Mortgage Solutions Pty Ltd v Khaled El-Sayed* [2009] NSWLR 207. The plaintiff must also show that extensive efforts were made to effect personal service: *Munkarra v Fischer* (1980) 5 NTR 3.

8.8.6C **Amos Removals & Storage Pty Ltd v Small**
[1981] 2 NSWLR 525
Supreme Court of New South Wales

[An action arose in tort alleging conspiracy to interfere with contractual relations. The plaintiffs sought a representative order and interlocutory injunctions against 19 defendants, who were committee members of a union. Leave was granted to effect substituted service on the defendants by serving a solicitor acting in other litigation on behalf of some of the defendants, but who was paid by all of them.]

Hunt J (at 528): The first matter to be decided, then, is whether it was impractical to effect prompt personal service upon the defendants named in the summons. The plaintiffs point to a number of factors which they say rendered such service impractical. Firstly, there was the cost of service upon nineteen different defendants. That factor does not impress me by itself. Secondly, there was the geographical spread of the defendants as shown by their personal addresses. That factor is not of any weight by itself. Thirdly, there was the short period within which service had to be effected. The summons was issued on a Thursday and, because of the apparent urgency of the matter, it was made returnable for the following Wednesday. The time for service was abridged by Fisher J to 5 pm on the Friday. In these circumstances, the geographical spread of the defendant's personal addresses — at which personal service would (as a matter of practical reality in the industrial scene) have to be effected — assumes considerable importance. I am satisfied that, in the circumstances of leave having been granted to serve short notice, prompt personal service on the defendants named in the summons was impractical.

8.8.7 Notes and questions

1. While the underlying principle is that a person to be served receives notice of proceedings, the method of notice must be in accordance with the Rules of Court. However, where a substituted service order is effected, the person is deemed to be served whether they actually receive notice or not. See *Grice v Grice* [1930] St R Qd 261, where it was held that in the absence of evidence of a failure of the originating process to reach the person to be served, substituted service is valid and service is deemed to have happened. Substantial compliance with an order for substituted service combined with personal service is sufficient service — see *Bulldogs Rugby League Club v Williams* [2008] NSWSC 822.

2. Will substituted service be ordered where:

   (a) it is sought to prevent foreign trustees disposing of the estate of a testator in circumstances where personal service could not be effected until after the likely sale? See *Re Conan Doyle's Will Trusts; Harwood v Fides Union Fiduciaire* [1971] 1 Ch 982 where substituted service was ordered; or

   (b) the defendant has not been heard of for many years (*Union Trustee Co of Australia Ltd v Carr* [1942] QWN 18 where an order for substituted service was refused) or there is good reason to believe that the defendant is dead? See *Simpson v Young* (1922) 39 WN (NSW) 126 — apply for leave to presume a person is dead, not for substituted service; or

   (c) the order sought is in respect of personal service of a subpoena to give evidence? See *Nash v Stewart* [2010] NSWSC 513 where Barrett J refused to make the order. Personal service was required.

3. Will substituted service be permitted where a defendant cannot be located and it is proposed to deliver the statement of claim to an authorised insurer, where the latter is not a party to the proceedings? See *O'Neil v Acott* (1988) 59 NTR 1; *Chappell v Coyle* (1985) 2 NSWLR 73 (where such an approach was rejected); *Lawford v Hosth* (1974) 5 ALR 57 and *Foxe v Brown* (1984) 58 ALR 542 (where such an approach was accepted). See also SA r 69(4) (there being no equivalent rule in the other jurisdictions) which states:

   > If it appears that a party not served is insured against liability in respect of the claim sought to be made against that party, substituted service may be ordered to be made upon the insurer where reasonable efforts to serve or locate the party personally have failed.

4. Can service be effected by Facebook? Perhaps only as a last resort — see P Young, 'Service by Facebook' (2010) 84(10) *ALJ* 669 referring to a consultation paper by the Singapore Supreme Court.

8.8.8C   **Munkarra v Fischer**
(1980) 5 NTR 3
Supreme Court of the Northern Territory

[The plaintiff suffered personal injuries when struck by the defendant's motorcycle. The motorcycle was insured and registered in Western Australia. The defendant was unable to be located. An application was made for substituted service.]

Gallop J (at 5–6): The solicitors caused a field officer of the North Australian Legal Aid Service to make certain inquiries regarding the whereabouts of the defendant. They also requested the Aboriginal Legal Aid Office in Perth to make inquiries and placed advertisements in newspapers circulating in the Northern Territory. In particular, searches of the Northern Territory electoral roll for all electors in the Northern Territory of Australia and the telephone directory were made without success and no information as to the defendant's whereabouts could be obtained from the Motor Vehicle Registry in Darwin. Searches were made in the electoral roll in both Houses of Parliament in Western Australia and all Commonwealth electoral rolls for each seat of the House of Representatives in Western Australia and the Senate. No elector by the name of the defendant could be found. On 8 December 1979 an advertisement appeared in the public notices section of *The West Australian* newspaper seeking information concerning the whereabouts of the defendant, but without success. Similar advertisements were placed in *The Northern Territory News* on 8 February 1980 and in the *Central Advocate* on 7 February 1980, both being newspapers circulating in the Northern Territory. There was no response to either advertisement. Inquiries were also made from the Clerk of Courts, Darwin, concerning any prosecution of the defendant, but no useful information was received. Finally on 2 April 1980 the police officer who investigated the subject accident was interviewed on behalf of the plaintiff. It was ascertained that at the time of the accident the defendant was travelling on an international driver's licence and also on a Northern Territory licence. It was confirmed that the defendant had no fixed place of abode except the Beatrice Caravan Park, Bagot Road, Darwin. By letter dated 1 May 1980 the Department of Immigration and Ethnic Affairs confirmed that the defendant was a German national and arrived at Perth Airport on 15 May 1977. There was no record of the defendant having departed from Australia. It was argued that if the defendant had left Australia the Department of Immigration and Ethnic Affairs would probably have had a record to this effect and that therefore the defendant is on the probabilities still in Australia.

[6] No inquiries have been made in other States and Territories of Australia to ascertain the whereabouts of the defendant. No inquiries have been made to ascertain whether the defendant holds a driver's licence in those parts nor have inquiries been made of the German Embassy or any German clubs. On ordinary principles, therefore, I would refuse the order for substituted service.

Method of substituted service

8.8.9   Substituted service (or presumptive service as it is known in South Australia) is effected by the method prescribed by order of the court. The various methods include:

* post: *Bradvica v Radulovic* [1975] VR 434 per Gillard J at 439–40; *Wray v Wray* [1901] P 132;

* advertising (newspaper, registry): *Hilaire v Harvie* (1950) 68 WN (NSW) 61;

* serving someone closely connected with the defendant on the basis they will bring the process to the notice of the defendant. For example, the defendant's:

  (i)   spouse;

  (ii)   solicitor (acting or formerly acting for the defendant);

  (iii)   agent (acting or formerly acting for the defendant);

  (iv)   attorneys under a power of attorney: *Rosenbaum v Rosenbaum* [1926] VLR 280;

  (v)   compulsory insurer (this is not permissible where there is no likelihood of the process coming to the defendant's attention): *Chappell v Coyle* (1985) 2 NSWLR 73 (see **8.8.11C**); compare *Hunt v Molk* (1976) 11 ALR 288.

8.8.10C   **Miscamble v Phillips (No 2)**
[1936] St R Qd 272
High Court of Australia

[The plaintiff filed a notice of appeal to the High Court then sought leave to serve the notice by substituted service. In the Supreme Court the writ of summons had been served by substituted service in circumstances where the defendant's whereabouts had been unknown for 45 years.]

Starke J (at 274): The question is whether we should allow substituted service of the notice of appeal in the same manner as it was allowed by the Supreme Court. In my opinion, we should not. The object of substituted service, the primary object, is to bring to the knowledge of the person in respect of whom substituted service is sought the whole proceedings, so that he can take such steps as he thinks proper to protect his interests and rights. It is not proper to substitute service of process in a Court of law when there is no belief that the service will bring the proceedings to the knowledge of the person in question or of any person representing his interests. It is on these grounds that I think the motion must be rejected.

[**Dixon** and **McTiernan JJ** agreed with **Starke J**.]

8.8.11C   **Chappell v Coyle**
(1985) 2 NSWLR 73
Supreme Court of New South Wales

[Chappell was injured by a motor vehicle driven by Coyle. Coyle was insured by the Government Insurance Office of New South Wales. The plaintiff issued a statement of claim claiming damages for negligence. Attempts at service of the statement of claim were unsuccessful as Coyle had disappeared and could not be located. In New South Wales a statement of claim is an originating process, which is required to be served personally.

An application for substituted service on the insurer was successful before the master. The insurer appealed, arguing that it was unlikely that any order for substituted service would bring the statement of claim to the notice of the defendant and that service should be set aside.]

Yeldham J (at 86): I have come to the conclusion that, although an order that a statement of claim may be served upon the authorized insurer in the type of case with which we are dealing could be said, in most circumstances, to accord with the justice of the situation, that fact cannot serve to bring within the relevant rule [Pt 9 r 10] that which is outside it. The court is only empowered to order steps to be taken by way of substituted service for the purpose of bringing the statement of claim to the notice of the named defendant. In the present case that, admittedly, was not the object of the application, nor will it be the result of the order, which, for that reason, must be set aside. I do not consider that provisions such as the Supreme Court Act [1970], s 81, or Pt 1, r 12, of the rules made thereunder may be called in aid if the order for substituted service is not in accordance with the requirements of the relevant rule.

[Service of the statement of claim was set aside.]

Jurisdictional limitations

8.8.12   A person who is not amenable to personal service within the jurisdiction, cannot be served by substituted service of a writ for service inside the jurisdiction. It is possible to serve such a person by substituted service of a writ for service outside the jurisdiction, provided the court has jurisdiction: see **4.2.5**. If a person was within the jurisdiction at the time of issue of the writ, but then deliberately goes outside the jurisdiction to evade service of process, there may be grounds for an order for substituted service.

The rules in some jurisdictions, consistent with *Laurie v Carroll* (1958) 98 CLR 310, permit an order for substituted service notwithstanding the defendant was outside the jurisdiction when the proceedings commenced: ACT r 6460; NT r 6.09(3); Qld r 116(4); and Vic r 6.10(3). The rules do not give the court jurisdiction to order substituted service where the court does not have jurisdiction to order personal service. For a detailed discussion of *Laurie v Carroll*, see **4.2.3C**.

8.8.13C	**Myerson v Martin**
	[1979] 1 WLR 1390
	High Court of England, Court of Appeal

[The plaintiff was a solicitor who practised in London. The defendant was a solicitor who lived and practised in Jersey, but who frequently visited England to attend corporate board meetings. The plaintiff issued a writ claiming damages for conspiracy to defraud which was indorsed for service within the jurisdiction. The defendant was not in England at the time of the issue of the writ. Several unsuccessful attempts were made to serve the defendant while he was in the jurisdiction. The plaintiff sought an order for substituted service by serving the English company of which the defendant was a board member. The defendant was not in England at the time of the application.]

Lord Denning MR (at 1394–5): The weight of authority is overwhelming that one should look at the time when the writ was issued. If the defendant was in fact outside the jurisdiction at the time the writ was issued — and the plaintiff in ignorance of it issued a writ for service *within* the jurisdiction — then the plaintiff must wait until the defendant comes back *within* the jurisdiction and serve him personally on his return. There cannot be substituted service on the defendant. If the defendant was in fact *within* the jurisdiction at the time the writ was issued — and the plaintiff issues a writ for service *within* the jurisdiction — the plaintiff can get an order for substituted service on him, even if he has gone overseas since the issue of the writ.

If the defendant was in fact *outside* the jurisdiction at the time the writ was issued— and the plaintiff knows it — the plaintiff can take his choice and issue a writ for service *within* the jurisdiction: but in that case he has to wait his opportunity and hope that the defendant will return to England and be served personally. There cannot be substituted service.

Otherwise if the defendant was in fact outside the jurisdiction when the writ was issued — and is likely to remain outside — the proper course for the plaintiff is to apply for leave to serve out of the jurisdiction: in which case he can only get it if the case comes within R.S.C Ord. 11.

In the present case Mr Martin was *outside* the jurisdiction at the time the writ was issued. There cannot therefore be substituted service. The only course for the plaintiff is to try to serve him personally when he comes here. Or, alternatively, apply for leave to issue a writ for [1395] service out of the jurisdiction — and get leave if he brings the case within R.S.C., Ord. 11.

I would therefore dismiss the appeal.

[The order sought was denied.]

The application

8.8.14 The *ex parte* application for an order permitting substituted service should be supported by an affidavit, setting out the circumstances justifying the application, attempts made at service (time and place), and the alternative methods of service which are likely to bring the matter to the defendant's attention: ACT r 6460; SA r 69(1); WA O 72 r 4. In the other jurisdictions, it is nevertheless necessary to accompany your application with a supporting affidavit. Proof is on the balance of probabilities.

The order

8.8.15 The usual practice is to order that at the expiration of a specified period after compliance with the order, the writ shall be deemed to have been personally served. Service effected in accordance with an order for substituted service is as effectual as personal service: *Grice v Grice* [1930] St R Qd 261. A copy of the order itself will usually be required to be served in addition to the copy of the originating process. Time for entry of appearance runs from the time that service pursuant to the order is effected: *Cook v Dey* [1876] 2 Ch D 218. Costs of the application are usually in the cause: see Chapter 20.

SERVICE OUT OF THE JURISDICTION

8.9.1 Service out of the jurisdiction from state and territory courts can be broadly classified into two categories: service out of the jurisdiction but within Australia, and service outside

Australia. The former category is governed by the Service and Execution of Process Act 1992 (Cth). The latter category is governed by the Rules of Court (including diplomatic channels) and international conventions, such as the Hague Convention. Federal courts have Australia-wide jurisdiction, but like state and territory courts, their international service requirements are also governed by the Rules of Court and international conventions.

Service out of the jurisdiction but within Australia

8.9.2 Before the Service and Execution of Process Act 1992, each Australian jurisdiction was regarded as a foreign territory with respect to service of process. Originating process at common law did not extend beyond the limit of the jurisdiction: *Flaherty v Girgis* (1987) 162 CLR 574 at 598. Rules existed for service outside the jurisdiction and a federal scheme for service was developed under the service and Execution of Process Act 1901 (Cth). In both cases it was necessary to have a territorial nexus with the jurisdiction of issue, among other procedural requirements. The nexus requirements for international service (see **8.9.10**) do not appear in the Service and Execution of Process Act 1992 (Cth).

In New South Wales, r 10.3 recognises that originating process may be served anywhere in Australia, but if served outside New South Wales, must bear a statement either that the plaintiff is proceeding under the Service and Execution of Process Act 1992 (Cth) or intends to proceed under the Uniform Civil Procedure Rules 2005 (NSW). This election may be varied with leave. Part 10 Service of documents is not expressed to limit the operation of any law of the Commonwealth: r 10.4. In Western Australia, O10 r 1A requires service inside Australia, but outside WA, to be served according to the Service and Execution of Process Act 1992 (Cth).

Service and Execution of Process Act 1992 (Cth)

8.9.3 The Service and Execution of Process Act 1992 (Cth) enables service of process in civil proceedings in any state or territory anywhere in Australia without leave. In effect it gives state and territory courts Australia-wide *in personam* jurisdiction.

The Act applies to the exclusion of state law except with respect to:

- substituted service: s 8(1);

- certain legislation relating to prisoners and the Family Law Act 1975 (Cth):

- s 8(2); and

- subpoenas: s 8(3).

Section 3 contains several important definitions for understanding this Act. 'Initiating process' means a process by which a proceeding is commenced, or by reference to which a person becomes a party to a proceeding. A 'proceeding' (other than a proceeding before a tribunal) means a proceeding in a court including an interlocutory or similar proceeding and a proceeding heard in chambers. A 'civil proceeding' means a proceeding other than a criminal proceeding.

Section 8(4) details the matters to which the Act applies to the exclusion of a law of a state.

8.9.4 Territories are regarded as states for the purposes of the Act: s 5. The operation of the Act extends to each external Australian territory, eg, Christmas Island Territory: s 7. The

Act has its own code with respect to service on companies and other registered bodies to the exclusion of the Corporations Act 2001 (Cth): ss 9, 10.

8.9.5 The Act provides a strict method of proof of service in s 11. Requirements are specified in relation to:

- service by post on individuals: s 11(3); and
- service by post on a company, a registered body or other body corporate: s 11(4); and any other case: s 11(1).

The evidence in satisfaction of these requirements is generally deposed to in an affidavit (s 11(5)) or by oral testimony if the court so requires: s 11(6).

Service under the Act has the same effect and gives rise to the same proceedings as if the process had been served in the place of issue: s 12. The Act applies to both service of initiating process and non-initiating process: ss 15, 27 respectively.

Initiating process issued in a state may be served in another state:

- in the case of an individual or body politic, in the same way as in the state of issue: s 15(3), (5); or
- in the case of a company or body corporate, in accordance with s 10: s 15(3), (4).

In each case, service is only valid if certain prescribed notices are attached: s 16.

The Act enables any process which is not an initiating process or subpoena issued in a state to be served in another state:

- in the case of an individual or body politic in the same way as in the state of issue: s 27(2), (5); or
- in the case of a company or body corporate, in accordance with s 10: s 27(3), (4).

The following procedures protect a defendant against proceedings being brought in the wrong court:

- stay of proceedings (s 20) or under the court's rules or inherent jurisdiction;
- transfer of proceedings: jurisdiction of courts (cross-vesting) legislation s 5; and
- security for costs (s 19) or under the court's rules or inherent jurisdiction.

The issuing court may stay the proceedings if the court of another state is the appropriate court to determine the matter; the factors are specified in s 20(4).

The jurisdiction based on the Act is not affected by limitations concerning the locality in which the process may be served, apparent in state laws in the place where service is effected: s 130.

8.9.6 Service is governed by the place of issue. The affidavit of service will include: the identity of the process server; time and day of service; place of service; manner of service; and how a person was identified if necessary. Prescribed notice must be attached: see Service and Execution of Process Regulations (Cth) Sch 1, Form 1.

8.9.7 Further reading

W Harris, 'Life after Voth: The Application of Forum Non Conveniens by Australian Courts in Transnational Proceedings' (1992) 22 *QLSJ* 21.

J Martin, 'Service and Execution of Process Act 1992 (Cth)' (1993) 23 *UWALRev* 156.

B Nicholas, 'New Act Tidies Up Interstate Service' (1993) 15 *Law Society of South Australia Bulletin* 33.

M Pryles, 'Forum Non Conveniens — The Next Chapter' (1991) 65 *ALJ* 442.

A Wallace and M Shirley, 'Are You Being Served? The New Service and Execution of Process Act 1992' (1993) 23 *QLSJ* 211.

Service and Execution of Process Regulations (Cth)

8.9.8   The Service and Execution of Process Regulations (Cth) specify prescribed notices which must be attached to service documents. Failure to attach a prescribed notice is an irregularity which may be waived by a party appearing in the court of issue and arguing the substance of an application: *C & P Trading Pty Ltd v Roladuct Spiral Tubing Pty Ltd* [1994] 2 Qd R 247.

Service outside Australia

8.9.9   International service is relevant to federal, state and territory courts and may be permitted under the Rules of Court (see **8.9.10**), including by diplomatic channels (see **8.9.31**), and under the Hague Convention: see **8.9.33**. The common law prohibiting service beyond the jurisdiction has been altered by the Rules of Court, extending jurisdiction by allowing service or granting leave to serve limited types of claim (originating and subsequent process) in the appropriate form outside Australia: HCR r 9.07.1; FCR Div 10.4; ACT r 6501; NSW Pt 11; NT O 7; Qld Ch 4 Pt 7; SA r 40; Tas Div 10, r 147A; Vic O 7; WA O 10. Leave is not required to serve process in specified cases in some jurisdictions (HCR r 9.07.1; ACT r 6501; NSW r 11.2; NT r 7.02(1)(b), (c); Vic r 7.01), otherwise, leave to proceed is required before taking another step in the process where there is no appearance: ACT r 6505; NSW r 11.4; NT r 7.02; Vic r 7.04; c.f. SA r 40(2). In Queensland, leave is not required for the extensive list of matters under r 124. Leave is possible for a proceeding under an Act if service is not authorised under r 124, or with respect to an application, order, notice or document in a pending proceeding: r 127. Leave is required to serve process in the remaining jurisdictions: FCR r 10.43; WA O 10 r 1(1). The Rules of Court govern service of process outside Australia: Service and Execution of Process Act 1992 (Cth) s 8(4). Any application for leave will need to be supported by an affidavit. The High Court Rules provide for service outside Australia, without order of the court, in situations where under the Federal Court Rules originating process may be served out of Australia: r 9.07.1.

Service outside Australia under the Rules of Court — Nexus

8.9.10   For service outside Australia according to the Rules of Court, there must be a sufficient nexus with the jurisdiction as specified by the Rules of Court. The main categories of nexus are:

- possession of or title to land within the jurisdiction: see **8.9.15**;
- contract or breach of contract connected to the jurisdiction: see **8.9.16**;
- submission to the jurisdiction: see **8.9.17**;
- acts, deeds, wills and other instruments affecting land within the jurisdiction: see **8.9.18**;
- persons domiciled or ordinarily resident in the jurisdiction: see **8.9.19**;
- administration of deceased estates and execution of trusts: see **8.9.20**;
- agent for a foreign principal: see **8.9.21**;
- injunction with respect to an act within the jurisdiction: see **8.9.22**;
- necessary or proper party: see **8.9.23**;
- damages occurred within the jurisdiction: see **8.9.24**;
- tort committed within the jurisdiction: see **8.9.25**;
- perpetuation of testimony as to land within the jurisdiction: see **8.9.26**;
- membership of a corporation incorporated with the jurisdiction: see **8.9.27**;
- claims relating to shares of a corporation within the jurisdiction: see **8.9.28**; and
- statute: see **8.9.29**.

All jurisdictions permit service of foreigners who submit to the jurisdiction: HCR r 9.07.1; FCR r 10.42 (Item 19); ACT r 6501; NSW r 11.2, Sch 6(h); NT r 6.13, 7.02(1)(c) (contract); Qld r 124(1)(r); SA r 40(1)(j); Tas r 147A(1)(f); Vic rr 6.14, 7.01(1)(h) (contract); WA O 10 r 2 (contract). The rules also apply to service of interlocutory process.

Service out of the jurisdiction for interlocutory and other processes is allowed with leave of the court: HCR r 9.07.1; FCR r 10.44; ACT r 6504; NSW r 11.5 (or if confirmed by the Supreme Court); NT r 7.03; Qld r 127 (if not covered by r 124); SA r 40(1)(l); Vic r 7.06; WA O 10 r 7. An application for leave accompanied by a supporting affidavit may be required: NT r 7.03; Vic r 7.08. In Tasmania, r 147A is limited to originating process.

8.9.11C	**Agar v Hyde**
	(2000) 201 CLR 552; 173 ALR 665
	High Court of Australia

Gaudron, McHugh, Gummow and Hayne JJ: [25] These two appeals raise questions about the assumption and exercise of jurisdiction by the Supreme Court of New South Wales over defendants who have been served with originating process outside Australia. Both appeals are brought by defendants who were served outside Australia with a Statement of Claim by which (in each case) the plaintiff claimed damages for personal injuries he sustained when playing rugby union football in a match conducted in New South Wales. ...

[47] The applicable Rules [UCPR Pt 11], however, mark the departure from the models based on the Chancery practice and do not require leave to serve out of the jurisdiction and do not require that the party seeking to serve out demonstrate a prima facie entitlement to the relief sought in the originating process. All that the applicable Rules say is that "the plaintiff shall

not proceed against [a defendant served outside Australia who has not entered appearance] except with the leave of the Court" [Pt 10 r 2(1)]. The applicable Rules are silent about what matters can or should be taken into account in granting or refusing that leave.

[48] Part 10 r 1A [UCPR r 11.2, Sch 6] of the applicable Rules permits the service of originating process outside Australia only in certain specified cases. If a defendant served outside Australia has not entered an appearance, an applicant for leave to proceed must demonstrate that one or more of the cases set out in r 1A [Sch 6] applies. Those cases are described either as "where the proceedings are founded on" a particular kind of claim, or as "where the subject matter of the proceedings" is of a particular kind.

[49] To take the particular paragraphs which the respondents relied on in these matters, it was said that the originating process in each action might be served outside Australia because:

(a)   … the proceedings are founded on a cause of action arising in the State;
…
(d)   … the proceedings are founded on a tort committed in the State;
(e)   … the proceedings, wholly or partly, are founded on, or are for the recovery of damages in respect of, damage suffered in the State caused by a tortious act or omission wherever occurring;
…
(i)   … the proceedings are properly brought against a person served or to be served in the State and the person to be served outside the State is properly joined as a party to the proceedings.

[50] In deciding whether Pt 10 r 1A [UCPR r 11.2, Sch 6] applied, and thus permitted service outside Australia of the originating process in these two actions, attention must be directed to the way in which the claims made by the respondents are framed. The paragraphs speak of "proceedings [which] are founded on" a specified matter such as a cause of action arising in the State or a tort committed in the State. That focuses attention upon the nature of the claim which is made. That is, is the claim a claim in which the plaintiff alleges that he has a cause of action which, according to those allegations, is a cause of action arising in the State?

[51] The inquiry just described neither requires nor permits an assessment of the strength (in the sense of the likelihood of success) of the plaintiff's claim. The Court of Appeal was wrong to make such an assessment in deciding whether the Rules permitted service out. In so far as the contrary was held in *Bank of America v Bank of New York* [(1995) ATPR 41-390] it should be overruled. The application of these paragraphs of r 1A depends on the nature of the allegations which the plaintiff makes, not on whether those allegations will be made good at trial. Once a claim is seen to be of the requisite kind, the proceeding falls within the relevant paragraph or paragraphs of Pt 10 r 1A, service outside Australia is permitted, and prima facie the plaintiff should have leave to proceed.

[52] Often enough, the statement of claim will reveal all that it is necessary to know to assess whether a plaintiff's claim is of the requisite kind. But that may not always be so. For example, the place of making of a contract, or the place of breach of a contract, may not appear from the pleading and some evidence may be required to establish that a relevant paragraph of Pt 10 r 1A [In the examples given, paras (c)(i) and (iii).] is engaged. And where, as here, a plaintiff relies on Pt 10 r 1A(1)(i), which provides for service outside the State on a person who is properly joined as a party to proceedings "properly brought against a person served or to be served in the State", other considerations may arise in deciding both whether the

joinder is proper and whether the action is "properly brought". Those questions may, however, be left to one side in the present cases because (subject to one consideration to which it will be necessary to return) it is clear that each of the proceedings is "wholly or partly ... founded on, or [is] for the recovery of damages in respect of, damage suffered in the State caused by a tortious act or omission wherever occurring"[Pt 10 r 1A(1)(e)]. The claim in each of the present matters is framed in negligence and alleges that tortious acts or omissions caused the damage which the respondent suffered when injured in New South Wales.

The intersection of applications for leave to proceed and applications to set aside service

[53] In some cases, an application for leave to proceed will not be opposed. It is an application which may be made without serving notice of the motion on the defendant [Pt 10 r 2(2)]. Where the application is made without notice to a defendant, there will be no occasion to consider any question about the strength of the plaintiff's claim. If, however, as was the case in each of these matters, the application for leave to proceed is opposed, and is joined with an application by parties served outside Australia to set aside service or to have the Court decline to exercise its jurisdiction [Under Pt 10 r 6A], other considerations arise. It is necessary, in such a case, to recall that there are different issues raised on the hearing of an application for leave to proceed from those that arise on the hearing of applications to set aside service or to decline to exercise jurisdiction.

[54] Central to the inquiry on an application for leave to proceed is whether the originating process makes claims of a kind which one or more of the paragraphs in Pt 10 r 1A mention. If the originating process makes such a claim, r 1A provides that the process may be served outside Australia and, on proof of service of the process, the Court's jurisdiction is, prima facie, properly invoked over the party who has been served. In the absence of some countervailing consideration, leave to proceed should then be given.

[55] On an application to set aside service, or to have the Court decline to exercise jurisdiction, attention might be directed to any of a number of features of the proceeding, the claims made in it, or the parties to it, in aid of the proposition that the Court should not exercise jurisdiction. Part 10 r 6A is cast in general terms and it would be wrong to attempt some exhaustive description of the grounds upon which the rule might be invoked. Nevertheless, it may be expected that three common bases for doing so are first, that the claims made are not claims of a kind which are described in Pt 10 r 1A [Pt 10 r 6A(2)(a)], secondly, that the Court is an inappropriate forum for the trial of the proceeding [Pt 10 r 6A(2)(b)] and thirdly, that the claims made have insufficient prospects of success to warrant putting an overseas defendant to the time, expense and trouble of defending the claims. Whether the Rules prescribe a different test for determining questions of inappropriate forum from that developed at common law [*Voth v Manildra Flour Mills Pty Ltd* [1990] HCA 55; (1990) 171 CLR 538] is a question which we need not stay to consider. In these cases, it is necessary to deal only with the last of the bases we have mentioned. It was on this that the appellants chiefly relied.

Insufficient prospects

[56] If service was authorised by the Rules, and has been properly effected, the Court's authority to determine the issues that are raised by the proceeding has been regularly invoked. If the Court is *not* persuaded that it is an inappropriate forum for trial of the proceedings, it will have reached that conclusion having given due weight to the considerations of comity and

restraint which we mentioned earlier. Only then do the prospects of success of a claim made in originating process served outside Australia fall for consideration.

[57] It is, of course, well accepted that a court whose jurisdiction is regularly invoked in respect of a local defendant (most often by service of process on that defendant within the geographic limitations of the court's jurisdiction) should not decide the issues raised in those proceedings in a summary way except in the clearest of cases. Ordinarily, a party is not to be denied the opportunity to place his or her case before the court in the ordinary way, and after taking advantage of the usual interlocutory processes. The test to be applied has been expressed in various ways [Dey v Victorian Railways Commissioners [1949] HCA 1; (1949) 78 CLR 62 at 91 per Dixon J; General Steel Industries Inc v Commissioner for Railways (NSW) [1964] HCA 69; (1964) 112 CLR 125 at 130 per Barwick CJ], but all of the verbal formulae which have been used are intended to describe a high degree of certainty about the ultimate outcome of the proceeding if it were allowed to go to trial in the ordinary way.

[58] It was suggested, in the present matters, that some less demanding test should be adopted in cases where a defendant served overseas seeks to have that service set aside. There are at least two reasons why that should not be done. First, and most fundamentally, what is the criterion which is to be applied? Are proceedings to be terminated upon a prediction (on what almost invariably will be less evidence and argument than would be available at trial) of the "likely" or "probable" outcome of the proceeding? That cannot be so. It would be wrong to deny a plaintiff resort to the ordinary processes of a court on the basis of a prediction made at the outset of a proceeding if that prediction is to be made simply on a preponderance of probabilities. And if it is not to be enough to persuade the court that it is more probable than not that the case against a defendant will fail, and some higher test (less than that now applied in applications for summary judgment) is to be applied, how is that test to be described? The attachment of intensifying epithets, such as "very" or "highly", offers little useful guidance for those judicial officers who would have to apply the test and who would have to do so, often enough, in a busy practice list. Such a test would be unworkable.

[59] Secondly, as the present proceedings show, the application of some different, and lower, test in favour of overseas defendants would lead to unacceptable results. It would mean that proceedings must continue to trial against those defendants who happen to have been served with the originating process within the jurisdiction, but can be brought to a summary end by those who are served overseas even where the claims against the local and overseas defendants are identical.

[60] For these reasons, the same test should be applied in deciding whether originating process served outside Australia makes claims which have such poor prospects of success that the proceeding should not go to trial as is applied in an application for summary judgment by a defendant served locally.

[61] The appellants submitted that the respondents' claims against them were doomed to fail: first, because the claims made were statute barred and secondly, because the appellants owed no duty of care to the respondents. We deal first with the appellants' alleged duty of care. ...

The appeals to this Court should each be allowed with costs.

8.9.12 The Rules of Court require a nexus to be established between the action and the jurisdiction. The nexus requirements vary widely as do the associated procedural rules. Often the connection with the forum is tenuous, at best, leading to claims of an 'exorbitant jurisdiction' over foreigners. The cases in this area may be divided into:

- those dealing with the discretionary criteria for refusing service overseas; and

- the discretionary criteria for staying a case where service overseas has occurred.

The test for both categories is whether the local court is a 'clearly inappropriate forum' (*Voth v Manildra Flour Mills Pty Ltd* (1990) 171 CLR 538; 97 ALR 124), having regard to the circumstances of the particular case and the availability of a foreign tribunal to whose jurisdiction the defendant is amenable. The issue is the inappropriateness of the local court, not the appropriateness or comparative appropriateness of the suggested foreign forum. It is not necessary to compare the pros and cons of having the case determined in Australia or overseas (*Leigh-Mardon Pty Ltd v PRC Inc* (1993) 44 FCR 88); rather, the focus is on the plaintiff's choice of forum. The *forum non conveniens* issue arises where a party outside the jurisdiction objects to the court hearing and determining the matter.

For jurisdiction to exist it must be found within the four corners of the rules. The absence of jurisdiction will render all consequential proceedings invalid: *Deputy Commissioner of Taxation v Ahern* [1986] 2 Qd R 342.

Where there are multiple causes of action joined in the proceedings, some of which do not come within the rules for service outside the jurisdiction, the actions within the rule may proceed after striking out those which are not within the rule: *Gosman v Ockerby* [1908] VLR 298.

8.9.13 Further reading

A Beech, 'Discretion in the Exercise of Jurisdiction' (1989) 19 *WALR* 8.

A Briggs, 'Forum Non Conveniens in Australia' (1989) 105 *LQR* 200.

D Charles, 'Serving Process on Foreign Defendants: Getting it Right Not Always Easy' (1994) 32 *LSJ* 27.

L Collins, 'The High Court of Australia and the Doctrine of Forum Non Conveniens: A Further Comment' (1989) 105 *LQR* 364.

A Ehrenzweig, 'The Transient Rule of Personal Jurisdiction: The "Power" Myth and Forum Conveniens' (1956) 65 *Yale LJ* 289.

M Garner, 'Towards an Australian Doctrine of Forum Non Conveniens' (1989) 38 *ICLQ* 361.

M Pryles, 'Judicial Darkness on the Oceanic Sun' (1988) 62 *ALJ* 774.

F Reynolds, 'Forum Non Conveniens in Australia' (1989) 105 *LQR* 410.

Categories of nexus

8.9.14 The categories of nexus between the proceeding and the jurisdiction vary. The categories are listed below, together with citation of the rules of each jurisdiction to which they relate. Each is a separate ground for deciding whether an originating process can be served outside Australia, but do not extend nor limit the jurisdiction of the court. It is possible for a proceeding to encompass several categories, eg, NSW r 11.2, Sch 6(w).

8.9.15   Possession of or title to land within the jurisdiction A claimant may serve a party outside the jurisdiction if the claim relates directly to the possession of or title to land or other property within the jurisdiction: HCR r 9.07.1; FCR r 10.42 (Item 21); ACT r 6501(1)(b), (s); NSW r 11.2, Sch 6(j); NT r 7.01(1)(a); Qld r 124(1)(b); SA r 40(1)(a)(i); Vic r 7.01(1)(a); WA O 10 r 1(1)(a)(i).

8.9.16   Contract or breach of contract connected to the jurisdiction A claimant may serve a party outside the jurisdiction if the action is based on a contract connected to the jurisdiction: HCR r 9.07.1; FCR r 10.42 (Items 2, 3); ACT r 6501(1)(g), (h), (i); NSW r 11.2, Sch 6 (b), (c); NT r 7.01(1)(f)–(h); Qld r 124(1)(g), (h), (i); SA r 40(1)(d), (e); Tas r 147A(1)(h), (n) (affecting property in the state); Vic r 7.01(1)(f)–(h); WA O 10 r 1(1)(e), 1(1)(f), O 10 r 2; *W A Dewhurst & Co Pty Ltd v Cawrse* [1960] VR 278; *Entores Ltd v Miles Far East Corp* [1955] 2 QB 327. If the action is founded on breach of contract committed within the state, it is irrelevant where the contract was made.

8.9.17   Submission to the jurisdiction Service may be effected upon a foreign party who agrees to submit to the jurisdiction: HCR r 9.01; FCR r 10.42 (Item 19); ACT r 6501(1)(i), (r); NSW r 11.2, Sch 6(h); NT rr 6.13, 7.02(1)(c) (but only in contract actions); Qld r 124(1)(r); SA r 40(1)(j); Tas r 147A(1)(f); Vic rr 6.14, 7.01(1)(h) (but only in contract actions).

8.9.18   Acts, deeds, wills and other instruments affecting land within the jurisdiction Service may be effected on a party outside the jurisdiction in respect of acts, deeds, wills and other instruments affecting land within the jurisdiction: HCR r 9.07.1; FCR r 10.42 (Item 6); ACT r 6501(1)(c); NSW r 11.2, Sch 6(m) (affecting property in NSW); NT r 7.01(1)(b); Qld r 124(1)(c) (affecting property); SA r 40(1) (a)(ii); Tas r 147A(1)(n) (affecting property in the state); Vic r 7.01(1)(b); WA O 10 r 1(1)(b). See *Official Solicitor v Stype Investments (Jersey) Ltd* [1983] 1 All ER 629; [1983] 1 WLR 214.

South Australian r 40(1)(i) extends this category to probate actions relating to the will or testamentary intentions of a person who died domiciled in the state or who made a will or expressed testamentary intentions in circumstances governed by the law of the state.

8.9.19   Persons domiciled or ordinarily resident in the jurisdiction Relief may be claimed against a person ordinarily resident or domiciled within the jurisdiction, regardless of where the cause of action arose. The person can be served overseas if they are only temporarily resident outside the Commonwealth of Australia: HCR r 9.07.1; FCR r 10.42 (Item 18); ACT r 6501(1)(d)(i); NSW r 11.2, Sch 6(g); NT r 7.01(1)(c); Qld r 124(1)(d); SA r 40(1)(b); Tas r 147A(1)(a); Vic r 7.01(1)(c); WA O 10 r 1(1)(c).

8.9.20   Administration of deceased estates and execution of trusts Actions in respect of the administration of deceased estates and execution of trusts may be served overseas if the deceased was domiciled in the jurisdiction at the date of death, or trust property is within the jurisdiction: HCR r 9.07.1; FCR r 10.42 (Item 7) (trust); ACT r 6501(1)(e) (administration of an estate), (1)(f) (trust and administration); NSW r 11.2 Sch 6(o) (administration), Sch 6(p) (trust); NT r 7.01(1)(d) (administration), (1)(e) (trust); Qld r 124(1)(e) (administration), (1)(f) (trust); SA r 40(1)(g) (trust); Tas r 147A(1)(p) (administration), (1)(q) (trust); Vic r 7.01(1)(d) (administration), (1)(e) (trust); WA O 10 r 1(1)(d) (trust and administration).

As to trust property, see *Winter v Winter* [1894] 1 Ch 421.

8.9.21   **Agent for a foreign principal** Originating process may be served outside the jurisdiction where it is sought to sue on a contract made by an agent who trades or resides in the jurisdiction, on behalf of a principal trading or residing out of the jurisdiction: HCR r 9.07.1; FCR r 10.42 (Item 3); ACT r 6501(1)(g)(iii); NSW r 11.2, Sch 6(c)(ii); NT r 7.01(1) (f)(ii); Qld r 124(1)(g)(iii); SA r 40(1)(d)(ii); Vic r 7.01(1)(f)(ii); WA O 10 r 1(1)(e)(ii). There is no equivalent rule in Tasmania.

8.9.22   **Injunction with respect to an act within the jurisdiction** Service may be effected out of the jurisdiction in proceedings for injunction with respect to an act within the jurisdiction: HCR r 9.07.1; FCR r 10.42 (Item 23); NSW r 11.2, Sch 6(n) (whether damages are also sought or not); NT r 7.01(1)(k); Qld r 124(1)(o) (whether or not damages are also claimed); SA r 40(1)(k); Tas r 147A(1)(b); Vic r 7.01(1)(k); WA O 10 r 1(1)(g); *BHP Petroleum Pty Ltd v Oil Basins Ltd* [1985] VR 725 at 753. There is no equivalent rule in the Australian Capital Territory or South Australia.

8.9.23   **Necessary or proper party** Service may be effected out of the jurisdiction if the party to be served out of the jurisdiction is a necessary or proper party to an action which has been properly brought against another party within or beyond the jurisdiction: HCR r 9.07.1; FCR r 10.42 (Item 20); ACT r 6501(1)(p); NT r 7.01(1)(l); Qld r 124(1)(p); SA r 40(1)(c); Tas r 147A(1)(g); Vic r 7.01(1)(l); WA O 10 r 1(1)(h); *Richardson v Tiver* [1960] VR 578. There is no equivalent rule in New South Wales.

8.9.24   **Damages occurred within the jurisdiction** Originating process may be served out of the jurisdiction if damages arising from a tortious act or omission occurred within the state or territory, regardless of where the act or omission occurred: FCR r 10.42 (Items 3(f), 5); (breach of an Act which causes damage in the Commonwealth); ACT r 6501(1)(l); NSW r 11.2, Sch 6(e); NT r 7.01(1)(j); Qld r 124(1)(l); SA r 40(1)(f)(ii); Tas r 147A(1)(d); Vic r 7.01(1)(j); WA O 10 r 1(1)(j); see also *Darrell Lea Chocolate Shops Pty Ltd v Spanish Polish Shipping Co Inc ('The Katowice II')* (1990) 25 NSWLR 568; *MacGregor v Application Des Gaz* [1976] Qd R 175; *Challeno v Douglas* [1983] 2 NSWLR 405; *Russell Wilkins & Co Ltd v Peck & Co* [1908] St R Qd 134. For an example of a tort committed outside the jurisdiction resulting in damage inside the jurisdiction, and the application of the clearly inappropriate forum test, see *Voth v Manildra Flour Mills Proprietary Ltd* (1990) 171 CLR 538. There are no equivalent rules in the other jurisdictions.

8.9.25   **Tort committed within the jurisdiction** Service may be effected out of the jurisdiction for any tort committed within the jurisdiction: HCR r 9.07.1; FCR r 10.42 (Items 4, 5); ACT r 6501(1)(k); NSW r 11.2, Sch 6(d); NT r 7.01(1)(i); Qld r 124(1) (k); SA r 40(1)(f); Tas r 147A(1)(c); Vic r 7.01(1)(i); WA O 10 r 1(1)(k). There must be some real substance in the wrong complained of as having been committed within the state: *Kroch v Rossell et Compagnie Société des Personnes à Responsibilité Limitée* [1937] 1 All ER 725. In the Northern Territory (r 7.01(1)(k)), New South Wales (Pt 10 r 1A(e)), South Australia (r 40(1)(f)(ii)) and Victoria (r 7.01(1)(j)) the rule extends to a tort causing damage within the forum, wherever occurring.

8.9.26   Perpetuation of testimony as to land within the jurisdiction Service may be effected out of the jurisdiction in proceedings for the perpetuation of testimony as to land that is within the jurisdiction: HCR r 9.07.1; FCR r 10.42 (Item 22); (property in the Commonwealth); NSW r 11.2, Sch 6(k) (all property); NT r 7.01(1)(a); Qld r 124(1)(b)(ii); Tas r 147A(1)(j) (relating to property in the state); Vic r 7.01(1)(a); WA O 10 r 1(1)(a)(i). There is no equivalent rule in South Australia.

8.9.27   Membership of a corporation incorporated within the jurisdiction Service may be effected out of the jurisdiction for claims relating to a person's membership of a corporation carrying on business or incorporated in the jurisdiction: HCR r 9.07.1; FCR r 10.42 (Items 8, 24); ACT r 6501(1)(m)(i); NSW r 11.2, Sch 6(q); Qld r 124(1)(m) (also extends to partnerships and other associations or entities); Tas r 147A(1)(r) (also extends to associations). There are no equivalent rules in the other jurisdictions.

8.9.28   Claims relating to shares of a corporation within the jurisdiction Service may be effected out of the jurisdiction for claims relating to shares or stock of a corporation having its principal place of business within the jurisdiction: WA O 10 r 1(1)(a)(ii). See also FCR r 10.42 (Item 18). There are no equivalent rules in the other jurisdictions.

8.9.29   Statute Service may be effected out of the jurisdiction to enforce an Act, statutory instrument or administrative act pursuant to an Act: HCR r 9.07.1; FCR r 10.42 (Items 12–16); ACT r 6501(1)(t); NSW r 11.2, Sch 6(r),(s) (NSW Acts), r 11.2, Sch 6(l) (Imperial or Commonwealth Acts); Qld r 124(1)(t), (u) (or an amount payable under an Act: r 124(1)(j)); SA r 40(1)(i) (Commonwealth and State); Tas r 147A(1)(k)–(m). There are no equivalent provisions in the remaining jurisdictions.

8.9.30   Other There are other categories appearing in the rules (but not in all jurisdictions), including:

- a proceeding based on a cause of action arising in the state: NSW r 11.2, Sch 6(a), Qld r 124(1)(a), Tas r 147A(1)(b), Vic r 7.06 (Originating motion, Summons, Order or Notice), or in Australia FCR r 10.42 (Item 1);

- if the proceedings are properly commenced against a person served or to be served in New South Wales and the person to be served outside New South Wales is properly joined as a party to the proceedings: NSW r 11.2, Sch 6(i);

- a proceeding for a contribution or indemnity for a liability enforceable in the court: FCR r 10.42 (Item 17); NSW r 11.2, Sch 6(f); Qld r 124(1)(n); Tas r 147A(1)(i);

- a proceeding brought under the Civil Aviation (Carrier's Liability) Act 1959 (Cth) by a resident of the jurisdiction or in relation to damage that happened in the jurisdiction: ACT r 6501(1)(q); Qld r 124(1)(q); WA O 10 r 1(1)(l);

- a proceeding in which the subject matter, so far as it concerns the person, is property in the state: ACT r 6501(1)(s); Qld r 124(1)(s); SA r 40(1)(a)(i); Tas r 147A(1)(e);

- a proceeding relating to an arbitration held in the state: ACT r 6501(1)(v); NSW r 11.2, Sch 6(t): Qld r 124(1)(v), FCR r 10.42 (Items 9, 10); or governed by the law of the state: SA r 40(1)(a)–(h); Tas r 147A(1)(s);

- a proceeding about a person under a legal incapacity who is domiciled or present, or a resident of the jurisdiction: ACT r 6501(1)(x); Qld r 124(1)(w);

- proceedings for the construction, rectification, setting aside or enforcement of an obligation or liability affecting property in the state: SA r 40(1)(a); Tas r 147A(1)(n), (v), (vi);

- proceedings to enforce a judgment in the state, regardless of where the judgment was made: ACT r 6501(1)(w); NSW r 11.2, Sch 6(u); SA r 40(1)(a)(h); Tas r 147A(1)(t);

- proceedings for relief relating to custody, guardianship, protection or welfare of a minor, whether or not the minor is in the state and that the court has jurisdiction to grant: FCR r 10.42 (Item 11); NSW r 11.2, Sch 6(v); Tas r 147A(1)(u), Vic 7.06;

- proceedings in relation to the effect or enforcement of an executive, ministerial or administrative act: ACT r 6501(1)(u); FCR r 10.42 (Item 16);

- proceedings in relation to the recovery of taxes or duty (WA O10 r 1(1)(j));

- proceedings by a mortgagee or mortgagor in relation to a mortgage of personal property situate within the jurisdiction (O10 r 1(1)(j)); and

- proceedings affecting the person to be served in relation to their membership of or office in a corporation or an association, or organisation formed, or carrying on business, in Australia (FCR r 10.42 (Item 24)).

In South Australia, r 41(2) specifies that for service in non-Hague Convention countries, subject to the law of the country in which service is to be effected, originating process is to be served outside Australia in the same way as if it were served in Australia. The court may give directions that may be appropriate to avoid conflict of laws or for any other reason. Rule 41 is not limited to service pursuant to a convention.

Service outside Australia under the Rules of Court (diplomatic channels)

8.9.31   Various jurisdictions allow for service by diplomatic channels within their rules: HCR r 9.07; FCR Div 10.5; ACT r 6511; NSW rr 11.8A–11.12; NT rr 7.08–7.09; Qld Ch 4 Pt 7 Div 2; SA rr 41, 41C; Tas Pt 38; Vic rr 7.09–7.15; WA O 10 rr 9–11.

8.9.32E   **Australian Government Attorney-General's Department Service Overseas — Diplomatic Channels**
viewed at 27 February 2012, <http://www.ag.gov.au>

Diplomatic channels are used for the communication of information between diplomats and foreign States. In Australia, the sending and receiving of these communications is carried out by the Department of Foreign Affairs and Trade.

Introduction
Diplomatic channels can be used, in some circumstances, to serve court documents abroad. Using diplomatic channels is only possible if the country in which service is to be effected accepts this method of service.

Advantages and disadvantages of this method include:
- Service via diplomatic channels may be the only method permitted in the absence of multilateral or bilateral service agreements
- Service by this method is the most formal and official method
- Service by this method is the most complex method and can be very time-consuming.

These and other considerations, in particular the individual circumstances of each case, should be used to guide each litigant when deciding whether service by diplomatic channels should be used.

Important note: Countries may object to service via diplomatic channels for reasons of sovereignty. Countries may also object to service via diplomatic channels on their own citizens or limit the scope of service to Australian citizens only. ...

The steps in Australia
Australian law governs the initial steps for service using diplomatic channels. Litigants will generally be required to apply to the court for a request for overseas judicial assistance. This includes requests for the transmission of documents via diplomatic channels.

The matter is litigated in a State or Territory court
If the matter is before a State or Territory court, the local court rules will outline how to make a request for judicial assistance for the service of documents via diplomatic channels. Please refer to the Relevant Australian Legislation page for links to the relevant court rules. The request for judicial assistance, together with the documents to be served abroad, is then transmitted to the Department of Foreign Affairs and Trade.

The matter is litigated in the Federal Court of Australia
If the matter is before the Federal Court of Australia, the Federal Court's court rules will govern how to make the request for judicial assistance for the service of documents via diplomatic channels. Please refer to the Relevant Australian Legislation page for links to the relevant court rules. The request for judicial assistance, together with the documents to be served abroad, is then transmitted the Commonwealth Attorney-General's Department and from there to the Department of Foreign Affairs and Trade.

The transmission
The Department of Foreign Affairs and Trade facilitates the transmission of the documents to the foreign country using its established diplomatic channels. Where service is to occur in a non-convention country, the documents will be transmitted to the Australian Embassy in that country first.

Processing the request for service overseas
The request will be processed according to the laws and particular institutional arrangements of the foreign country. However, a typical process is as follows:

- The Australian Embassy transmits the request for judicial assistance, together with the documents, to the foreign country's Foreign Affairs Ministry (or other relevant agency)
- The Foreign Affairs Ministry (or other relevant agency) then transmits the request for judicia assistance, together with the documents, to the authority competent to deal with the execution of requests for judicial assistance
- The competent authority executes the request and arranges for service.

The formal confirmation that service was successful or unsuccessful

The formal confirmation that service was successfully or unsuccessfully executed will be returned to the foreign litigant using the same path by which service was effected.

Costs

It is possible that costs may be associated with the execution of diplomatic channel request. If so, the relevant Australian court registrar will receive an invoice with the formal confirmation of service or non-service. The registrar will pass on the invoice to the legal practitioner, or if none, the litigant who must pay the registrar the amount specified in the notice. ...

Service outside Australia under the Hague Convention

8.9.33 Service may be effected in a foreign country pursuant to a convention (convention country or any other country the Attorney-General, by instrument filed in the proceeding, specifies): HCR r 9.07.1; FCR r 10.51; ACT r 6510; NSW Pt 11A; NT O 7A Pt 1; Qld Ch 4, Pt 7, Div 2; SA Ch 3 Div 3; Tas Pt 38A; Vic O 80; WA O 11, r 3, O 11A. For example, service in the United Kingdom would proceed via the Rules of Court, whereas service in France would proceed via convention procedures. The laws of most non-common law countries effectively preclude the service of foreign originating process except pursuant to a convention or following a government-to-government request.

Translations and notices may be required: see *Williams v Lips-Heerlen BV* (unreported, SC(NSW), Common Law Div, Giles J, 17209/1990). As to the operation of the Hague Convention, see *Channar Mining Pty Ltd v CMIEC (Channar) Pty Ltd* [2003] WASC 253. The term 'convention' is generally defined widely. For example in Qld r 100, 'convention' means an agreement, arrangement, treaty or convention, relating to legal proceedings in civil matters, made between Australia and another country.

The party seeking service in a foreign jurisdiction files a request accompanied by the original document, and a translation in the language of the country in which service is to be effected, certified by the person making the request. The documents and further copies are sealed and forwarded by the registrar to the Attorney-General of the Commonwealth for transmission through diplomatic channels to the foreign country. Service is effected by the person appointed by the foreign judge, by delivering to and leaving with the person to be served the relevant documents. The conventions Australia has entered into can be found on the Department of Foreign Affairs, Registry of Treaties' website: <http://www.dfat.gov.au>. See also G Elliot and D Hughes, 'Australia Joins the Hague Service Convention' (2010) 84(8) *ALJ* 532.

Service is also possible under bilateral treaties that Australia has entered with other countries, eg, South Korea and Thailand: viewed at 27 February 2012, <http://www.ag.gov.au>.

Australian Government Attorney-General's Department Service Overseas — Hague Service Convention.
Viewed at 27 February 2012 <http://www.ag.gov.au>

Australia is a party to the *Convention on the Service Abroad of Judicial and Extrajudicial Documents in Civil or Commercial Matters 1965* (the Hague Service Convention). Please visit the Hague Service Convention website for the full text of the Convention and a full list of participating countries.

Introduction

The Hague Service Convention provides one of the most effective methods to serve overseas legal documents in Australia.
Advantages of this method include:

- it is quick and efficient, as it utilises a network of designated central and additional authorities
- it is cost efficient as only certain costs incurred by the country requested to effect service can be passed on to the requesting party
- the transmission of documents has been harmonised between countries, therefore reducing the risk that service will be challenged
- harmonisation also facilitates proof of service through the use of standardised certificates of service, and
- the above factors reduce transactional and litigations risks for parties.

Disadvantages of this method include:

- involuntary service requests (made under article 5(a) of the Hague Service Convention) to foreign jurisdictions may need to meet the following minimum requirements:
  ○ two copies of the request, certificate of service, summary of documents and *all* documents to be served including any requested translations.
  ○ **all** documents may need to be translated from English into the official language of the foreign jurisdiction.
  ○ certification of the translation and/or the translator may be necessary.
- Failure to comply with these minimum requirements may result in non-service or delayed service. …

The steps in Australia

Australian law governs the initial steps for service using the method established under the Hague Service Convention. Please refer to the relevant Federal Court or State and Territory court rules for the steps prospective litigants need to take to effect service abroad using this method. A non exhaustive list of these rules can be found on the Relevant Australian Legislation page [<http://www.ag.gov.au>].

General y, the litigant has to apply to the Registrar for service under the Hague Service Convention. This request is subject to certain mandatory form requirements. In particular the litigant must include the following:

- model letter of request
- Summary of Documents to be Served
- Certificate of Service for the foreign court to complete
- documents to be served

- certified translations where necessary, and
- an undertaking as to costs.

Please refer to the relevant court rules and forms which are based on the model letter of request, Summary of Documents to be Served and Certificate of Service annexed to the Hague Service Convention [<http://www.hcch.net>]. Links to the relevant court rules can be found on the Relevant Australian Legislation page. ...

The transmission

If the Registrar is satisfied that the form requirements are complied with, the documents can be transmitted to the designated Foreign Competent Authority by mail. A current list of Foreign Central and Additional authorities is maintained on the Hague Service Convention Authorities Index [<http://www.hcch.net>]. The documents should **not** be forwarded to the Commonwealth Attorney-General's Department.

Important note: Whilst the additional authority in Queensland is the Department of Justice and Attorney General, litigants will need to apply to the Supreme Court Registrar for service under the Hague Service Convention.

Processing the request for service overseas

The Foreign Competent Authority will process the request in accordance with the laws in that country and will arrange for the request to be executed.

The formal confirmation that service was successful or unsuccessful

The Foreign Competent Authority will formally advise the Registrar that the Request was executed by transmitting back a Certificate of Service. This certificate is evidence of service in the proceedings to which it relates. Where service was unsuccessful, the certificate records the reasons why. The certificate can then serve as evidence for non-service and may provide the basis for an application for substituted service.

Costs

It is possible that costs may be associated with the execution of a bilateral treaty request. If so, the Registrar will receive a Statement of Costs with the Certificate of Service. The Registrar will pass on the Statement of Costs to the legal practitioner, or if none, the litigant who must pay the Registrar the amount specified in the notice. ...

Effecting service outside Australia: notices and indorsements

8.9.35   In some jurisdictions notice of the originating process, not the process itself, is served in a foreign country in the manner in which writs are served in the relevant Australian jurisdiction: WA O 10 r 3. The Australian Capital Territory Rules allow an alternative, rarely used procedure enabling service by letters of request (r 6540). In Tasmania, r 147C requires a notice to be served with the originating process. If a defendant so served does not enter an appearance, the plaintiff requires leave of the court to proceed: Tas r 147B.

In other jurisdictions, the originating process must contain a special indorsement, statement or notice and is served in accordance with the law of the foreign country in which service occurs: NSW r 11.3; NT rr 7.02(3); Vic rr 7.02, 7.03. In the Federal Court (r 10.45) the normal rules of service apply, subject to any convention.

Personal service of originating process may not be required, provided it is served in accordance with the law of the foreign country in which service is effected: HCR r 9.07.2; FCR r 10.46; NSW r 11.6; NT rr 7.02(3), 7.05; Vic r 7.03; WA O 10 r 10(3). There are no equivalent rules in the other jurisdictions. See *Richard Crookes Constructions (Qld) Pty Ltd v Wendell* [1990] 1 Qd R 392. Substituted service may also be available, eg, NT r 7.06.

High Court r 9.07.3 provides that a plaintiff may proceed against a party duly served with originating process, having appropriate nexus outside Australia, who does not file an appearance.

Setting aside service outside Australia

8.9.36   A court may, on application by a defendant or respondent, set aside service of the originating process for failure to comply with the Rules of Court: see 8.11.1.

Stay of proceedings served outside Australia

8.9.37C	**Garsec v His Majesty The Sultan of Brunei**
	(2008) 250 ALR 682
	New South Wales Court of Appeal

Campbell JA (Spigelman CJ and Hodgson JA agreeing):

Nature of the Case

[33] The Claimant brought proceedings in the Equity Division of this Court relating to an alleged agreement for the sale of an old, rare and beautiful manuscript copy of the Holy Koran ("the Manuscript"). As the Claimant's claim was ultimately put, three causes of action were relied on, against two defendants.

[34] The first defendant was His Majesty the Sultan and Yang Di-Pertuan of Brunei Darussalam ("the Sultan"). The second defendant, Pehin Nawawi, at all relevant times was the Private and Confidential Secretary of the Sultan. The Sultan was served out of the jurisdiction. Pehin Nawawi has not been served, but the proceedings have come to his attention and he has engaged the same Australian solicitors as has the Sultan to deal with the matter on his behalf.

[35] The first cause of action sued upon alleged that a contract was made in April 2005 between the Claimant and the Sultan for the sale of the Manuscript to the Sultan for a price of US$8m, that the Sultan has failed to perform that contract, and that by virtue of the unique character of the Manuscript it was appropriate to order that the contract be specifically performed. The second and third causes of action were brought against Pehin Nawawi in the alternative to the claim against the Sultan. The contractual claim against the Sultan had alleged that Pehin Nawawi was part of a chain of communication through which the Claimant had communicated to the Sultan an offer to sell the Manuscript to the Sultan, and the Sultan had communicated acceptance of that offer to the Claimant. The alternative claims against Pehin Nawawi alleges that he had represented that he had authority from the Sultan to receive

the offer, and to communicate acceptance of the offer, and (in the event that Pehin Nawawi did not have that authority) that he is liable both for breach of warranty of authority, and also for the tort of negligent misstatement.

[36] McDougall J has ordered that the proceedings be stayed permanently: *Garsec v His Majesty The Sultan of Brunei* [2007] NSWSC 882; (2007) 213 FLR 331. This is an application for leave to appeal from that decision of McDougall J. It was argued on the basis that in the course of the application for leave to appeal each party put all arguments on which he or it would wish to place reliance if leave were to be granted.

Common Law Principles Concerning Stay of Proceedings Against Foreign Defendants

[37] Both Opponents filed a Notice of Appearance in the proceedings ...

[38] When both Opponents have appeared, the Supreme Court clearly has jurisdiction to deal with the case alleged against them. The effect of the stay granted by McDougall J is that, notwithstanding that it has jurisdiction over the dispute, the Court declines to exercise that jurisdiction.

[39] Quite independently of any particular rules of court, courts have on occasions declined to exercise jurisdiction vested in them. A circumstance in which a question has commonly arisen of whether a court should decline to exercise jurisdiction is when proceedings are brought in the court against a foreign defendant, and the foreign defendant alleges that the dispute should be tried in some foreign court, rather than in the local court. It has been in that context that principles have developed about the circumstances in which the local court should, or should not, decline to exercise jurisdiction.

[40] Principles governing that topic that were developed in 19th-century England were encapsulated by Scott LJ in *St Pierre v South American Stores (Gath & Chaves) Ltd* [1936] 1 KB 382, at 398:

> The true rule about a stay ... may I think be stated thus: (1.) A mere balance of convenience is not a sufficient ground for depriving a plaintiff of the advantages of prosecuting his action in an English Court if it is otherwise properly brought. The right of access to the King's Court must not be lightly refused. (2.) In order to justify a stay two conditions must be satisfied, one positive and the other negative: *(a)* the defendant must satisfy the court that the continuance of the action would work an injustice because it would be oppressive or vexatious to him or would be an abuse of the process of the Court in some other way; and *(b)* the stay must not cause an injustice to the plaintiff. On both the burden of proof is on the defendant.

[41] The principle in *St Pierre* came to be questioned in the House of Lords in *The "Atlantic Star"* [1974] AC 436; *MacShannon v Rockware Glass Ltd* [1978] AC 795; *Amin Rasheed Shipping Corporation v Kuwait Insurance Co* [1984] AC 50 and *Spiliada Maritime Corporation v Cansulex Ltd* [1987] AC 460. In summary, the English position came to be that a court should stay litigation against a foreign defendant if the English court was not the appropriate forum for the resolution of the dispute.

[42] In *Oceanic Sun Line Special Shipping Company Inc v Fay* [1988] HCA 32; (1988) 165 CLR 197 a majority of the High Court (Brennan, Deane and Gaudron JJ, Wilson and Toohey JJ dissenting)

adhered to the principle stated in St Pierre, but differed in their explanation of what that principle meant. Given its adoption by later authority, [it] is appropriate to set out the explanation given by Deane J. At [6]–[7]; 247–248 his Honour said that the words "oppressive" and "vexatious" as used by Scott LJ in St Pierre:

> ... were not used as directly descriptive of the conduct of the plaintiff but as descriptive of the objective effect which continuance of the action would have on the defendant: *"the defendant must satisfy the Court that the continuance of the action would work an injustice because it would be oppressive or vexatious to him ... "*. On that approach which, in my view, should be accepted as correct, I do not think that one should read into the words a requirement that the continuance of the action would involve moral delinquency on the part of the plaintiff: note the contrary view expressed by Lord Kilbrandon in *The "Atlantic Star"*, at p 477, and by Lord Salmon in *MacShannon*, at pp 818–819. Rather, it seems to me that those words should be read, in the *St. Pierre* formulation, as describing and characterizing the objective effect, on balance, of a continuation of the particular forum as the venue of the proceedings rather than as describing the conduct of the plaintiff in selecting or persisting with that forum (cf. per Gibbs J, *Cope Allman*, at p 494: *"the exercise ... of ... jurisdiction would be vexatious to the defendants or would result in any real injustice to them"*). That reading of the words is consistent with the approach adopted by this Court in *Maritime Insurance Co*, at pp 200–201, where the Court engaged in an assessment of what the effect of continuation of the proceedings in the Victorian Supreme Court would, on balance, be as a matter of objective fact. If the plaintiff is not acting bona fide or in pursuit of a legitimate advantage in pursuing the proceedings in the legal system of this country, that will, of course, make it much easier for a continuation of the proceedings to be characterized as vexatious or oppressive, since there will be little if anything to put into the balance against the inconvenience which would be sustained by the defendant. On that approach, *"oppressive"* should, in this context, be understood as meaning seriously and unfairly burdensome, prejudicial or damaging while *"vexatious"* should be understood as meaning productive of serious and unjustified trouble and harassment.

In the light of the foregoing and at the cost of some repetition, it is possible to identify in summary form what I see as the modern content of the traditional principles governing the power of a court in this country to order that proceedings which have been regularly instituted within jurisdiction should be dismissed or stayed on inappropriate forum grounds. That power is a discretionary one in the sense that its exercise involves a subjective balancing process in which the relevant factors will vary and in which both the question of the comparative weight to be given to particular factors in the circumstances of a particular case and the decision whether the power should be exercised are matters for individual judgment and, to a significant extent, matters of impression. The power should only be exercised in a clear case and the onus lies upon the defendant to satisfy the local court in which the particular proceedings have been instituted that it is so inappropriate a forum for their determination that their continuation would be oppressive and vexatious to him. Ordinarily, a defendant will be unable to discharge that onus unless he can identify some appropriate foreign tribunal to whose jurisdiction the defendant is amenable and which would entertain the particular proceedings at the suit of the plaintiff. Otherwise, that onus will ordinarily be discharged by a defendant who applies promptly for a stay or dismissal if he persuades the local court that, having regard to the circumstances of the particular case and the availability of the foreign tribunal, it is a clearly inappropriate forum for the determination of the dispute between the parties. The reason why that is so is that, once it is accepted that the adjectives "*oppressive*" and "*vexatious*" are not to be narrowly or rigidly construed and are to be applied in relation to the effect of the continuation of the proceedings rather than the conduct of the plaintiff in continuing them, the continuation of proceedings in a tribunal which is a clearly inappropriate forum would, in the absence of exceptional circumstances being established by the plaintiff (cf *Spiliada Maritime Corp v Cansulex Ltd* (1987) 1 AC 460, at p 478), be oppressive or vexatious to such a defendant if there is some available and appropriate tribunal in another country. Admittedly, that approach to the "*vexatious*" and "*oppressive*" test is less stringent and less rigid than would have been accepted in the nineteenth century. Under it, the applicable test pursuant to traditional principles can, in the ordinary case, properly be seen as an "*inappropriate forum*" test. It cannot, however, properly be seen as a "*more appropriate forum*" test since the mere fact that a tribunal in some other country would be a more appropriate forum for the particular proceeding does not necessarily mean that the local court is a clearly inappropriate one.

[43] *Voth v Manildra Flour Mills Proprietary Ltd* [1990] HCA 55; (1990) 171 CLR 538 established that the test in Australian law by reference to which a court should decide whether to stay proceedings that had been commenced in it was whether the court was a "*clearly inappropriate forum*"; the test was not whether there was a more appropriate forum somewhere else. The joint judgment of Mason CJ, Deane, Dawson and Gaudron JJ at [30]; 554 identified four principles that were common ground to the majority in *Oceanic Sun*:

> First, a plaintiff who has regularly invoked the jurisdiction of a court has a prima facie right to insist upon its exercise. Secondly, the traditional power to stay proceedings which have been regularly commenced, on inappropriate forum grounds, is to be exercised in accordance with the general principle empowering a court to dismiss or stay proceedings which are oppressive, vexatious or an abuse of process and the rationale for the exercise of the power to stay is the avoidance of injustice between parties in the particular case. Thirdly, the mere fact that the balance of convenience favours another jurisdiction or that some other jurisdiction would provide a more appropriate forum does not justify the dismissal of the action or the grant of a stay. Finally, the jurisdiction to grant a stay or dismiss the action is to be exercised "*with great care*" or "*extreme caution*".

[44] Concerning the first of those principles, the majority also recognised at [54]; 566 that in some cases too much weight may have been given to "*the notion that a proceeding regularly invoked provides a prima facie right to have the proceeding continue in that forum*". (The majority in *Henry v Henry* [1996] HCA 51 at [28]; (1996) 185 CLR 571 at 589 also drew attention to that passage.) Further, the majority in *Voth* stated, at [40]; 559, the circumstances in which that prima facie right did not arise:

> Granted that there is an obligation on the domestic courts of this country to exercise jurisdiction which is conferred upon them — a matter on which the majority in *Oceanic Sun* was united — it does not extend to cases where it is established that the forum is clearly inappropriate.

[45] Concerning the second of those principles, the joint judgment in *Voth* identified the substantial differences of approach between Brennan J on the one hand, and Deane and

Gaudron JJ on the other in *Oceanic Sun* as either being, or arising from, differences of view about the shade of meaning to be attributed to *"oppressive"* and *"vexatious"*. They said, at [31]; 555, that Deane J in *Oceanic Sun* said that:

> …*'oppressive'* should, in this context, be understood as meaning seriously and unfairly burdensome, prejudicial or damaging while *'vexatious'* should be understood as meaning productive of serious and unjustified trouble and harassment" (1988) 165 CLR, at p 247. His Honour also took the view that the words should be read as describing and characterizing the objective effect, on balance, of a continuation of the proceedings and a particular forum as the venue of proceedings rather than as describing the conduct of the plaintiff in selecting or persisting with that forum. Gaudron J (1988) 165 CLR, at p 266, stated her agreement with the test stated by Deane J, subject to a qualification to which we shall refer later in these reasons.

[46] The joint judgment reached the conclusion, at [51]; 564–5, that, subject to a question of onus which is not of present relevance:

> … the principles to be applied in applications to set aside service and in applications for a stay on inappropriate forum grounds are those stated by Deane J in *Oceanic Sun* (1988) 165 CLR, at pp 247–248. In the application of those principles the discussion by Lord Goff in *Spiliada* [1987] AC, at pp 477–478, 482–484 of relevant *"connecting factors"* and *"a legitimate personal or juridical advantage"* provides valuable assistance.

[47] The discussion of Lord Goff that has thus been recognised by the High Court as providing *"valuable assistance"* for the purpose of identifying connecting factors is, at 477–478:

> Since the question is whether there exists some other forum which is clearly more appropriate for the trial of the action, the court will look first to see what factors there are which point in the direction of another forum. These are the factors which Lord Diplock described, in *MacShannon's* case [1978] AC 795, 812 as indicating that justice can be done in the other forum at *"substantially less inconvenience or expense"*. Having regard to the anxiety expressed in your Lordships' House in the *Société du Gaz* case, 1926 SC (HL) 13 concerning the use of the word *"convenience"* in this context, I respectfully consider that it may be more desirable, now that the English and Scottish principles are regarded as being the same, to adopt the expression used by my noble and learned friend, Lord Keith of Kinkel, in *The Abdin Daver* [1984] AC 398, 415 when he referred to the *"natural forum"* as being *"that with which the action had the most real and substantial connection."* So it is for connecting factors in this sense that the court must first look; and these will include not only factors affecting convenience or expense (such as availability of witnesses), but also other factors such as the law governing the relevant transaction (as to which see *Crédit Chimique v James Scott Engineering Group Ltd*, 1982 SLT 131), and the places where the risk parties respectively reside or carry on business.

[48] The discussion of Lord Goff that has been recognised by the High Court as providing *"valuable assistance"* for the purpose of identifying the type of matters that count as a *"legitimate personal or juridical advantage"* for the application of the principle concerning grant of a stay is, at 482–484:

"(8) Treatment of "a legitimate personal or juridical advantage"
Clearly, the mere fact that the plaintiff has such an advantage in proceedings in England cannot be decisive. As Lord Sumner said of the parties in the *Société du Gaz* case, 1926 S.C.(H.L.) 13, 22:

> I do not see how one can guide oneself profitably by endeavouring to conciliate and promote the interests of both these antagonists, except in that ironical sense, in which one says that it is in the interests of both that the case should be tried in the best way and in the best tribunal, and that the best man should win.

Indeed, as Oliver LJ [1985] 2 Lloyd's Rep 116, 135, pointed out in his judgment in the present case, an advantage to the plaintiff will ordinarily give rise to a comparable disadvantage to the defendant; and simply to give the plaintiff his advantage at the expense of the defendant is not consistent with the objective approach inherent in Lord Kinnear's statement of principle in *Sim v Robinow*, 19 R. 665, 668.

The key to the solution of this problem lies, in my judgment, in the underlying fundamental principle. We have to consider where the case may be tried "suitably for the interests of all the parties and for the ends of justice." Let me consider the application of that principle in relation to advantages which the plaintiff may derive from invoking the English jurisdiction. Typical examples are: damages awarded on a higher scale; a more complete procedure of discovery; a power to award interest; a more generous limitation period. Now, as a general rule, I do not think that the court should be deterred from granting a stay of proceedings, or from exercising its discretion against granting leave under R.S.C. Ord. 11, simply because the plaintiff will be deprived of such an advantage, provided that the court is satisfied that substantial justice will be done in the available appropriate forum. Take, for example, discovery. We know that there is a spectrum of systems of discovery applicable in various jurisdictions, ranging from the limited discovery available in civil law countries on the continent of Europe to the very generous pre-trial oral discovery procedure applicable in the United States of America. Our procedure lies somewhere in the middle of this spectrum. No doubt each of these systems has its virtues and vices; but, generally speaking, I cannot see that, objectively, injustice can be said to have been done if a party is, in effect, compelled to accept one of these well-recognised systems applicable in the appropriate forum overseas. ... Then take the scale on which damages are awarded. Suppose that two parties have been involved in a road accident in a foreign country, where both were resident, and where damages are awarded on a scale substantially lower than those awarded in this country. I do not think that an English court would, in ordinary circumstances, hesitate to stay proceedings brought by one of them against the other in this country merely because he would be deprived of a higher award of damages here.

But the underlying principle requires that regard must be had to the interests of all the parties and the ends of justice; and these considerations may lead to a different conclusion in other cases ...

[49] The power to stay proceedings on grounds of clearly inappropriate forum has been held to be an aspect of the inherent or implied power which, in the absence of some statutory provision to the same effect, every court must have to prevent its own processes being used to bring about injustice: *CSR Limited v Cigna Insurance Australia Ltd* [1997] HCA 33; (1997) 189 CLR 345 at 391.

[50] A further source of the power of the Court to stay proceedings is section 67 *Civil Procedure Act* 2005:

> Subject to rules of court, the court may at any time and from time to time, by order, stay any proceedings before it, either permanently or until a specified day.

The Relevant Rules

[51] The following provisions of the Uniform Civil Procedure Rules are relevant to an application for stay of proceedings served outside Australia: [UCPR rr 11.7, 12.11(1)(h) reproduced].

[52] Apart from insertion of the express reference to the Supreme Court in UCPR 11.7, and some purely stylistic changes, those rules are identical to Part 10 r 6A and Part 11 r 8 Supreme Court Rules 1970, introduced in 1988.

[53] UCPR 12.11(1)(h) appears in a Part of UCPR entitled "Discontinuance, Withdrawal, Dismissal and Setting Aside of Originating Process", that deals in a perfectly general way with the topics identified in the title of the Part. In terms, UCPR 12.11(1)(h) applies to all proceedings whatever, regardless of whether they have been served in Australia, or served outside Australia or never served. When UCPR 11.7 makes specific provision that the Supreme Court may make an order of a kind referred to in rule 12.11 on application by a defendant on whom originating process is served outside Australia, it is not, it seems to me, making any provision that extends the scope of the types of actions to which UCPR 12.11 would have applied in its own terms. That is of some significance in the present case, as Pehin Nawawi has not been served outside Australia (or indeed at all), and so does not come within the literal terms of the UCPR 11.7.

[54] UCPR 11.7(2)(b) identifies one of the grounds on which the Court can stay proceedings as being that "the court is an inappropriate forum for the trial of the proceedings". Purely as a matter of construction of the rule, it does not seem to me that that statement of the grounds operates as a limitation on the generality of the power of the Court under UCPR 12.11(1)(h) to decline to exercise jurisdiction in the proceedings. That is because, while UCPR 11.7(2) sets out some of the grounds on which an order can be made under UCPR 11.7, it explicitly states that it is not limiting the power of the court to make such an order.

[55] In Pendal Nominees Pty Ltd v M & A Investments Pty Ltd (1989) 18 NSWLR 383 Rogers CJ Comm D pointed out at 395 that the 1988 amendments to the New South Wales rules concerning "long arm" jurisdiction were made prior to the decision of the High Court in Oceanic Sun. (The rules were gazetted on 17 June 1988, and the decision in *Oceanic Sun* was delivered on 30 June 1988.) Rogers CJ Comm D expressed the view at 396–7 that it was *"the philosophy which informs Lord Goff's Speech in Spiliada that the new r 6A attempted to capture"*. He foreshadowed that:

> ... the subrule may require reconsideration of the applicability, in New South Wales, in applications of this kind, of the decision in *Oceanic Sun*.

[56] That view was rejected in the joint judgment of Spigelman CJ, Mason P and Stein JA in *Hyde v Agar* (1998) 45 NSWLR 487 at 510:

> ... r 6A picks up the principles of forum non conveniens as they are enunciated from time to time in Australian law. This requires fidelity to *Voth* not *Spiliada* where there is inconsistency. We do not agree with the suggestion to the contrary of Rogers CJ Comm D in *Pendal Nominees Pty Ltd v M & A Investments Pty Ltd* (1989) 18 NSWLR 383 at 396–397.

[57] In *James Hardie Industries Pty Ltd v Grigor* (1998) 45 NSWLR 20 the Court of Appeal applied the *"clearly inappropriate forum"* tests to an application for stay of proceedings, but (as Spigelman CJ recorded at 28) no argument was put that the introduction of Part 10 rule 6A(2)(b) of the Supreme Court Rules made any difference to the common law principles that the High Court had laid down in *Voth*.

[58] The decision of the Court of Appeal in *Hyde v Agar* was reversed on appeal (*Agar v Hyde* [2000] HCA 41; (2000) 201 CLR 552), principally on the ground that a duty of care that the Court of Appeal had thought arguable was held by the High Court not to be arguable. The majority judgment of Gaudron, McHugh, Gummow and Hayne JJ at [55], expressly declined to enter into the question of whether the Rules prescribed a different test for determining questions of inappropriate forum from that developed at common law (which, by the time the decision in Agar v Hyde was given, meant the principles adopted in Voth).

[59] Any uncertainty that that might have left about the status as a precedent of the Court of Appeal decision in Hyde v Agar in so far as it related to the construction of Part 10 rule 6A was removed in the majority judgment of the High Court in Regie Nationale des Usines Renault v Zhang [2002] HCA 10; (2002) 210 CLR 491 at [25]:

> Because a court's power to stay proceedings is an aspect of its inherent or implied power to prevent its own process is being used to bring about injustice, the same concept and considerations necessarily inform the tests of "inappropriate forum" in par (b) of Part 10 r 6A (2) as inform the "clearly inappropriate forum" test adopted in *Voth*.

[60] Thus it is clear that the power that is given by the rules is exercised on the same principles as the common law concerning stay of proceedings brought against a foreign defendant, notwithstanding that it uses the expression *"inappropriate forum"* instead of *"clearly inappropriate forum"*: ...

Legitimacy of Bringing the Substantive Proceedings in NSW

[161] In *CSR Limited v Cigna Insurance Australia Limited* [1997] HCA 33; (1997) 189 CLR 345 the High Court granted a stay of New South Wales proceedings that had been brought by certain insurers against their insured, seeking a declaration that the insurers were not liable under certain policies of insurance. Those New South Wales proceedings were begun when some United States proceedings were already on foot, brought by the insured against the insurers. The United States proceedings alleged that a document that the insured had given the insurers, and that on its face appeared to bear upon the scope of cover, had been procured by conduct in breach of the *Sherman Act* and its New Jersey counterpart. The United States proceedings included a claim for treble damages under those Acts. Those antitrust claims could not have been brought by the insured in Australian proceedings. A significant part of the reasons of the majority in the High Court for granting the stay was that the central purpose of the insurers in bringing the New South Wales proceedings was to stifle the US proceedings. For that reason the New South Wales proceedings were oppressive in the *Voth* sense.

[162] In the present case, the primary judge took the view that the purpose of the Claimant in bringing proceedings in New South Wales was to prevent the Opponents from enjoying defences available to them in the Brunei courts. In his view, just as it was oppressive in *CSR v Cigna* for a plaintiff to bring New South Wales proceedings to prevent the defendant in

those proceedings from pursuing a remedy available in the foreign court, but not available in Australia, so it could be oppressive in the *Voth* sense for a plaintiff in New South Wales proceedings to bring those proceedings to prevent the defendant from enjoying a defence available to him in the courts of another country.

[163] Mr Hutley submitted that reasoning in this way involved error on the primary judge's part. He submitted that it is quite common in proceedings involving foreign elements that the plaintiff is seeking to pursue a juridical advantage in bringing proceedings in the local forum rather than the foreign forum, and that there is no general principle to the effect that a plaintiff who brings proceedings in the only available forum is to be criticised for pursuing an illegitimate juridical advantage. He points out that in Voth one of the legitimate juridical advantages relied upon by the plaintiff in bringing proceedings in New South Wales was the avoidance of an effective limitation bar, which would have been available to the defendant in Missouri. He submits that while the defendant in Voth gave an undertaking that it would not rely on the limitation defence if the proceedings were brought in Missouri, there is nothing in the High Court's reasoning that suggests that, absent the undertaking, the avoidance of that juridical d sadvantage was in any way illegitimate or decisive against the plaintiff.

[164] In my view there is no error of the type Mr Hutley submits that requires this court to reconsider the stay for itself.

[165] A sufficient reason arises from the use that the primary judge made of his view that it would be oppressive in the Voth sense to bring proceedings in New South Wales to prevent the other party from enjoying defences available in the courts of another country and not available in this country. He quite explicitly called that consideration into aid only if he was wrong in his view that the immunities available under Article 84B of the Constitution of Brunei are matters of substance and not procedure. I have already held that the primary judge was right in regarding those immunities as substantive. Thus, even if the primary judge had been wrong in taking the view that bringing proceedings in New South Wales to prevent an opposing party from pursuing remedies available in Brunei but not available in Australia was in itself oppressive, it would not have a material effect on the conclusion reached.

[166] Indeed, in light of the account of substantive law given in John Pfeiffer, it is hard to see how a situation could ever arise where a defence was available in the courts of another country, but was not available in this country. The situation that arose in *Voth*, where the High Court granted the stay on terms of the limitation defence not being relied on in Missouri, will never arise under the choice of law rules laid down in *John Pfeiffer*.

Conclusion and Orders

[167] In my view none of the errors alleged by the Claimant are made out.

[168] The Claimant's submissions raised some important matters of principle. I would grant leave to appeal, but dismiss the appeal.

Service of foreign legal process inside the jurisdiction

8.9.38   The Supreme Court Rules provide for service in Australian jurisdictions of documents associated with civil or commercial proceedings pending before a court or tribunal in a foreign country: ACT r 6540; NSW rr 11.13–11.17; NT rr 80.01–80.05; Qld Ch 4 Pt 8; SA r 70;

Tas rr 966–70; Vic rr 80.13–80.16; WA O 11 rr 1–5. There are no equivalent rules in the remaining jurisdictions.

JUDGMENTS AND ORDERS

8.10.1　Generally a judgment or order requiring the doing of an act by a person should be served before enforcement: HCR r 8.05; FCR r 30.02; ACT r 1610; NT rr 59.03, 59.05; Qld r 906; SA r 260(1) (with exceptions); Tas r 142(2) (personal service or showing the original is not necessary unless demanded by the party served); Vic r 68.04(4) (service of accompanying affidavit). Personal service is required to enforce an order or judgment by attachment (sequestration) or committal: FCR r 41.07; NSW r 40.7; NT r 66.10; Qld r 926; SA r 260(2); Tas r 142; Vic r 66.10(1)(a). There is no equivalent High Court, ACT, or WA provision. In the Federal Court a judgment or order takes effect on the date on which it is made or pronounced (r 39.01). A person ordered to do an act or thing or to pay money must comply with times specified in the order, or if no time is specified, after 14 days of service of the order: r 30.02.

8.10.2　Question

1.　Under what circumstances would a litigant use the Service and Execution of Process Act 1992 (Cth) procedure to serve a judgment or order?

SETTING ASIDE SERVICE IRREGULARITIES

8.11.1　Any person may apply to set aside service of any originating process on the basis that the process or its service is irregular: HCR r 2.03; FCR r 13.01; ACT r 111 Conditional Notice of Intention to Respond; NSW rr 11.7, 12.11; NT r 8.09; Qld r 126; SA r 12; Tas rr 14, 168; Vic rr 7.05, 8.09; WA O 2 r 1, Federal Court of Australia Act 1976 (Cth) s 51. In South Australia (r 100) a dispute as to a preliminary issue such as the validity of service must be pleaded.

Typical challenges relate to:

(a)　whether the court is a 'clearly inappropriate forum': *Voth v Manildra Flour Mills Pty Ltd* (1990) 171 CLR 538; 97 ALR 124, see Chapter 4;

(b)　orders for substituted service: *Bradvica v Radulovic* [1975] VR 434, see 8.8.1;

(c)　deemed service: *Towers v Morley* [1992] 2 All ER 762, see 8.3.9 in relation to post; or

(d)　agreements to litigate elsewhere: *Lewis Construction Co Pty Ltd v Tichauer Societé Anonyme* [1966] VR 341.

Success on any of these grounds is most likely going to result in a stay of proceedings.

Further reading

8.12.1 Articles

J Castelan, 'Service of Proceedings Overseas' (2004) 78(4) *LIJ* 54.

M Elliott, 'Service Out of Jurisdiction Reviewed' (2001) 39(11) *LSJ* 64.

D Jackson QC, 'Practice in the High Court of Australia' (1997) 15 *Aust Bar Rev* 187.

8.12.2 Looseleaf

R Steinwall, D Cremean, P Fary, P Hanks, J West, N Moshinsky, L Armstrong, J Clarke, A Black, D William and P Nichols, *Practice and Procedure of the High Court and the Federal Court of Australia*, LexisNexis, Sydney.

K Tronc and B Gribbin, *Civil Procedure in the Queensland Magistrates Courts*, Law Book Co, Sydney.

I Wylie, *District Courts Practice Queensland*, LexisNexis, Sydney.

8.12.3 Texts

D Boniface, M Kumar and M Legg, *Principles of Civil Procedure*, 2nd ed, Thomson Reuters, 2012, Ch 10.

B Cairns, *Australian Civil Procedure*, 9th ed, Law Book Co, Sydney, 2011, Ch 4.

M Davies, S Ricketson and G Lindell, *Conflict of Laws — Commentary and Materials*, Butterworths, Sydney, 1997, Ch 3.

J Hunter, C Cameron and T Henning, *Litigation 1 Civil Procedure*, 7th ed, LexisNexis Butterworths, Sydney, 2005, Ch 3.

P Nygh, *Conflict of Laws in Australia*, 7th ed, Butterworths, Sydney, 2002, Ch 4.

M Smith, *ABC Guide to the Federal Court of Australia*, Law Book Co, Sydney, 1986.

Appearance

## CHAPTER 9

OVERVIEW

An appearance is the procedure used by the defendant to inform the plaintiff that he or she intends to defend the proceedings. The procedure prevents the plaintiff entering a default judgment or taking further steps without notice to the defendant. In Queensland, an appearance is known as a Notice of Intention to Defend. In the Australian Capital Territory, it is called a Notice of Intention to Respond. Appearances are of two types, though both types are not available in all jurisdictions. The most common type is an unconditional appearance, which acknowledges the court's jurisdiction and waives any irregularity in service or commencement of proceedings. The other form of appearance is a conditional appearance. Conditional appearances do not waive procedural irregularities, but preserve arguments based on lack of jurisdiction and other irregularities. In the event that an appearance is not entered, the defendant is at risk of a default judgment being entered. Appearances have been abolished in South Australia and in the Federal Court in favour of filing a Notice of Address for Service or alternatively in South Australia, a defence. In New South Wales a Submitting Appearance (r 6.11) and in the Australian Capital Territory, Notice of Intention to Respond (r 106), may be used by a defendant to submit to the orders of the court save as to costs, and take no part in the proceedings.

INTRODUCTION

9.1.1 The general rule is that a defendant files or enters an appearance in person or through their solicitor (High Court Rules 2004 r 23.01.2; Federal Court Rules 2011 r 4.01; Court Procedure Rules 2006 (ACT) — Notice of Intention to Respond; Uniform Civil Procedure Rules 2005 (NSW) rr 6.9, 7.1; Rules of the Supreme Court of the Northern Territory of Australia (NT) r 8.03; Uniform Civil Procedure Rules 1999 (Qld) r 136; Supreme Court Rules 2000 (Tas) rr 154, 159; Supreme Court (General Civil Procedure) Rules 2005 (Vic) r 8.03; Rules of the Supreme Court 1971 (WA) O 12 r 1; *Tucker v Walker* [1920] VLR 385 at 386; *Flatau v Best* (1897) 13 WN (NSW) 147). Some rules provide that an appearance must be entered before taking a step in a proceeding (HCR r 23.01.1; ACT r 100 (c.f. where a defence is filed); NSW r 6.1; NT r 8.02; Qld r 135; Vic r 8.02) or filing any document: FCR r 11.06. There are a number of exceptions whereby a party may proceed without entering an appearance, including:

- applying to set aside the originating process or its service: FCR r 13.01; NSW rr 6.1(2), 12.11(2); NT r 8.09; Tas r 167; Vic r 8.09; WA O 12 r 7; *Australian Insurance Brokers Ltd v Hudig Langeveldt Pty Ltd* [1988] WAR 44 at 46; *TPC v The Gillette Company (No 1)* (1993) ATPR 41-267;

- objecting to the court's jurisdiction — appearance under protest: see **9.9.1**;

- with leave of the court or a judge: HCR r 23.01.1; ACT r 100; NSW r 6.1; NT r 8.02; Qld r 135; Vic r 8.02; there are no equivalent provisions in the other jurisdictions;

- seeking to stay execution: FCR r 41.11; ACT r 2013; NT r 66.16; Qld r 800; Enforcement of Judgments Act 1991 (SA) s 17; Tas r 887; Vic r 66.16; Civil Judgments Enforcement Act 2004 (WA) s 15;

- applying to set aside a judgment in default of appearance: see **Chapter 12**;

- High Court r 23.01.1 gives a defendant wishing to object to the jurisdiction, to the originating process, or to the service of the originating process, a discretion as to whether to file a conditional appearance. High Court r 2.02 enables the court or a justice to dispense with compliance with the rules, before or after the occasion for compliance arises;

- a party has filed a statement of claim or summons in the proceedings: NSW r 6.1;

- where a defendant files a defence: ACT r 100(1)(b), Form 2.9; NSW r 6.9; SA r 59;

- applications for preliminary discovery and inspection (NSW Pt 5) or orders in urgent cases before the commencement of proceedings (NSW r 25.2): NSW r 6.1(2).

Further exceptions are listed by Cairns in 'Practice and Procedure', *Halsbury's Laws of Australia*, LexisNexis, Sydney, looseleaf, vol 20, [325]–[2505].

In South Australia, the concept of an appearance has been abandoned in favour of simply filing an address for service.

[*NOTE:* in this chapter a reference, such as WA O 12 r 7, is a reference to the relevant Rules of Court. All other legislation will be specified.]

WHY ENTER AN APPEARANCE?

9.2.1   Appearances are filed and served for five reasons:

    (1)   failure to enter an appearance will enable the plaintiff to obtain judgment in default of appearance: see also **Chapter 12**;

    (2)   to inform the plaintiff the action is to be defended, the name of the defendant's solicitors, and an address where service can be effected;

    (3)   in the case of an unconditional appearance, to acknowledge the court's jurisdiction;

    (4)   as a precondition before a defendant can take a step in proceedings otherwise than with leave of the court (see 'Introduction' above); and

    (5)   in the case of conditional appearances, to prevent waiver of procedural irregularities and of the right to object to the court's jurisdiction.

WHO MAY ENTER AN APPEARANCE?

9.3.1 Only a defendant may enter an appearance, either in person or through a solicitor: see **9.1.1**; *Caltex Oil (Aust) Pty Ltd v The Dredge 'Willemstad'* (1976) 136 CLR 529 at 539. Where a solicitor enters an appearance on behalf of a client, the solicitor's details need to be entered on the appearance (name, address, telephone number and so on). In South Australia, a party may only be represented in proceedings by a lawyer: rr 22, 23.

Special rules apply in relation to appearances by infants or others under a disability under which a guardian or similar person needs to be appointed: HCR r 21.08; FCR r 9.61; ACT rr 275, 279; NSW r 7.17; NT rr 15.02, 15.04; Qld rr 93, 96, 136; Tas rr 292, 345; Vic r 15.02, 15.04; WA O 70 rr 2, 3, 5. In some jurisdictions special rules apply in relation to recovery of land by which a person in possession of the land, either directly or by a tenant, may enter an appearance: ACT rr 150–153; NT r 53.06; Qld r 143 (possession of land); Tas r 166; Vic r 53.06; WA O 12 rr 8–10. In New South Wales the occupier may become a defendant: r 6.8.

Corporations

9.3.2 In the absence of leave of the court, or in WA as expressly provided by an Act, a corporation enters an appearance through its solicitor: HCR r 23.01.2; FCR r 11.02, O 45 r 1; ACT r 30; Qld rr 135, 136; Tas r 11; WA O 4 r 3(2), O 12 r 1(2). See also *Bay Marine Pty Ltd v Clayton Country Properties Pty Ltd* (1986) 8 NSWLR 104; *Simto Resources Ltd v Normandy Capital Ltd* (1993) 43 FCR 78. In New South Wales a company, within the meaning of the Corporations Act 2001 (Cth), may commence and carry on proceedings by a solicitor or by a director who is a plaintiff in the proceedings: r 7.1. There are variations to this procedure in lower New South Wales courts.

In Victoria and the Northern Territory, a corporation may file an appearance by any person duly authorised by it to so act: NT r 8.03(2); Vic r 8.03(2). However, as a general rule it cannot take any other step in the proceeding, or attend before the court, except by a solicitor or by counsel instructed by a solicitor: see *Hubbard Association of Scientologists International v Anderson* [1971] VR 788.

In South Australia, r 27 enables the court to give leave for a company to act through a director.

Partnerships

9.3.3 When a partnership is sued in the firm name, a partner must appear individually in his or her own name: FCR r 11.04; ACT r 108; NSW r 7.19; NT rr 17.04–17.06; Qld r 85; Tas r 311; Vic rr 17.04–17.06; WA O 71 r 5. There is no equivalent provision in the High Court or South Australia. The time for appearance runs from when the partner, or last partner is served.

Business name

9.3.4 Appearances must not be filed in a business name, even if a registered business name: ACT r 110, Qld r 91.

Multiple defendants

9.3.5 Where two or more defendants appear by the same solicitor at the same time, only one appearance needs to be entered: FCR r 11.07 (Form 10); ACT r 107; Tas r 162; WA O 12 r 2(3). There is no equivalent provision in the High Court, New South Wales, Northern Territory, Queensland and Victoria.

Third parties

9.3.6 Third parties are required to enter appearances or risk default judgment: HCR r 23.01.1 (if a defendant); ACT r 311 (Notice of Intention to Respond); NSW r 6.27; NT r 11.08; Qld r 197 and subsequent parties r 207; Tas r 205; Vic r 11.08; WA O 19 r 3. See *O'Neill v Cowan's Scaffolding Hire Service* [1983] 2 Qd R 40. Persons added or substituted as defendants must also enter an appearance: HCR rr 21.05.1, 23.01.1; FCR r 9.11; ACT r 243; NSW r 6.32; NT r 9.11; Qld r 135, Sch 4 (definition of 'defendant'); Tas r 184; Vic r 9.11; WA O 18 rr 6, 8. As to non-parties served with a defence and counterclaim, see: HCR r 21.05.1; FCR r 15.10; ACT r 462; NSW r 6.1; NT r 10.04; Qld r 178; Tas r 197; Vic rr 10.04, 10.04(4); WA O 18 r 3(4).

Undertakings

9.3.7 Where a solicitor undertaking in writing to enter an appearance fails to do so, the plaintiff has three options:

(1)   ignore the undertaking and seek default judgment;

(2)   compel the solicitor to enter an appearance: *Re Kerly, Son & Verden* [1901] 1 Ch 467; *Squires v Weeks* (1893) 9 WN (NSW) 122; or

(3)   bring the breach of undertaking to the court's attention (in such cases, personal liability for attachment or for contempt may result): HCR r 11.02.1; Qld r 900; Tas r 163; there are no specific rules in the other jurisdictions. See *Darley v Hyman* (1893) 10 WN (NSW) 212.

A solicitor who enters an appearance without the authority of the defendant may be liable to pay the costs of the defendant and plaintiff: *Yonge v Toynbee* [1910] 1 KB 215; *Porter v Fraser* (1912) 29 TLR 91. A defendant whose solicitor enters a appearance without authority may have the appearance vacated: *Re Gray; Gray v Coles* (1891) 65 LT 743; *Porter v Fraser* (1912) 29 TLR 91. Notice should be given to the party in whose name the appearance was filed: *Place v Williams* [1969] VR 703.

An appearance entered on behalf of a non-existent person is a nullity, not an irregularity. A nullity is a process that is legally void or inoperable, whereas an irregularity is a failure to comply with a procedural formality. Courts cannot cure a nullity, whereas an irregular proceeding may be set aside in whole or in part, or an order may be made to cure the irregularity. See **Chapter 5**.

9.3.8   Notes and questions

1.   Can corporations enter an appearance otherwise than through their solicitors? See *Bay Marine Pty Ltd v Clayton Country Properties Pty Ltd* (1986) 8 NSWLR 104, where it was held that the New South Wales Supreme Court has an inherent power to permit a corporation to carry on proceedings otherwise than by a solicitor (but exceptional circumstances are required). Cf NSW r 7.1.

2. What is the role and responsibility of a solicitor entering an appearance? What reliance can courts and other members of the profession put upon such a solicitor's assumption of authority? See *Simmons v Liberal Opinion Ltd; In Re Dunn* [1911] 1 KB 966 at 972–3; *Yonge v Toynbee* [1910] 1 KB 215 at 233.

TYPES OF APPEARANCES

9.4.1 Appearances may be either conditional or unconditional, except in New South Wales where there is only one type of appearance: an appearance (in effect an unconditional appearance). In Queensland (r 144(6)), and Western Australia (O 12) unconditional appearances at common law have the effect of waiving procedural irregularities and objections to jurisdiction. Conditional appearances preserve such rights in these jurisdictions. While conditional appearances also remain in the High Court (r 23.03), the Northern Territory (O 8) and Tasmania (rr 168, 326), objections can be made before the requirement for any appearance. In New South Wales (r 6.11(1)) a defendant who intends not to contest or take no active part in the proceedings may enter an appearance, including a statement to the effect that the defendant submits to the making of all orders sought and the giving or entry of judgment in respect of all claims made save as to costs. Such a defendant may not file a defence or affidavit or take any other step in the proceedings without leave (r 6.11(2)): see *Trust Co of Australia Ltd v Perpetual Trustees WA Ltd* (1995) 36 NSWLR 654. In Queensland, with respect to minor debt claims, a notice of intention to defend and a defence are combined into one form: Form 4.

High Court r 23.02 creates an 'Appearance' (Form 8), where a defendant/respondent submits to any order the court may make in the matter save as to costs. FCR r 12.02 and ACT r 106 are of similar effect

PROCEDURE FOR ENTRY OF APPEARANCE

9.5.1 A defendant in person or by a solicitor may enter an appearance by filing a notice of appearance (HCR r 23.01.3; FCR r 11.07 — notice of address for service (Form 10); NSW r 6.9; NT r 8.05; Tas rr 154, 159, Forms 14–16), notice of intention to respond (ACT rr 100, 101, 152, Form 2.8), notice of intention to defend (Qld r 136, Form 006), mode of filing appearance (Vic r 8.02), or memorandum of appearance (WA O 12 r 2, Form No 6) in the registry out of which the originating process issued.

The requirements as to contents and procedure for entry of the appearance include:

(a) for stating the name and address or contact details of the person entering the appearance: HCR r 23.01.4 (address for service); ACT r 101; NSW Form 6; NT r 8.06; Qld r 140; Tas rr 128, 159; Vic r 8.06; WA O 12 r 2;

(b) use of the appropriate form: HCR r 23.01.3, Forms 7–9; FCR rr 8.01(1), 8.04(1), 11.09(a), Forms 15, 28; ACT r 102, Form 2.8; NSW r 6.9, Form 6; NT r 8.05, Form 8A; Qld r 139, Forms 006, 007; Tas r 154(3), Forms 14–16; Vic r 8.05, Forms 8A, B; WA Form 6;

(c) filing or entering the appropriate form: HCR r 23.01.3; FCR r 11.09(a); ACT r 102; NSW r 6.9; NT r 8.05; Qld r 141 (in the registry from which the claim was issued); Tas r 154(3); Vic r 8.05; WA O 12 r 2;

(d) ordinary service of the appearance (HCR rr 9.01.5, 23.04; FCR r 11.08; ACT r 102; NSW r 10.1; NT r 8.05; Qld r 142, Ch 4 Pt 4; Vic rr 6.07(1), 8.05(4); WA O 12 r 4), or by prepaid post (HCR r 9.04; Tas r 157(5)(a), (b); Vic rr 6.07(1), 8.05(4); WA O 12 r 4);

(e) that an address for service be given: defendant's address for service, address of defendant's solicitor, detail of principal and town agent arrangements if relevant: HCR r 23.01.4; FCR r 11.01; ACT r 101; NT r 8.06; NSW Form 6; Qld r 140; Tas rr 128, 159; Vic r 8.06; WA O 12 r 2(2) — geographical address; Service and Execution of Process Act 1992 (Cth) s 18 and NSW r 4.5(3)(d); and

(f) in Queensland (r 139), a notice of intention to defend must be signed, dated, and have the defendant's defence attached. Practitioners are required to complete an appearance slip in the application's jurisdiction: see Practice Direction No 6 of 2004.

9.5.2E | **Rules of the Supreme Court 1971 (WA)**
Form 6 — Memorandum of Appearance Order 12 rule 2(2)

Supreme Court of Western Australia General Division		No:
		Memorandum of appearance
Parties	Plaintiff Defendant	
Appearance [*select one]	Enter an appearance for the defendant [*name of party*]. The defendant *is/is not represented by a solicitor.	
Defendant's details		
Defendant's geographical address 1		
Defendant's service details 1		
Signature and date		
Signature of Defendant or solicitor	Defendant/Defendant's solicitor	Date:
Notes to Form No 6 —		
1. Must be in accordance with Order 71A.		

9.5.3 Notes and questions

1. The address for service so stated in the appearance becomes the address for service or delivery of pleadings and other documents in the action: see **8.3.3**.

2. Assuming an appearance has been entered, does failure to give notice of appearance to the plaintiff render the appearance a nullity or entitle a plaintiff to enter judgment in default of appearance? See *North Melbourne Building Society & C v Vrendenberg* (1885) 7 ALT 38; *Lyman v Franklin* (1889) 15 VLR 2; *Alliance Acceptance Co Ltd v Makas* (1976) 26 FLR 451.

3. Can a defendant apply for leave to appear in their proper and real name to prevent continuation of proceedings as if the appearance had not been entered? See *Allied Mills*

Ltd v Robinson (1981) 2 BPR 9,353; *Alexander Korda Film Productions Ltd v Columbia Pictures Corp Ltd* [1946] 2 All ER 424, where there was a trivial misdescription in the name of the defendant and they, on that basis, entered a conditional appearance. The correct procedure is for the defendant to enter an appearance in their own name, stating in the appearance that the company was sued in the wrong name.

TIME LIMITED FOR APPEARANCE

9.6.1 The initiating proceeding specifies the time within which the appearance is to be entered: HCR r 27.01; FCR r 11.06 (before the return date and before filing any other document); ACT rr 60, 102 (Return date); NSW r 6.10; NT r 8.04; Qld r 137; Tas rr 98, 99; Vic r 8.04; WA O 5 r 11. The actual time periods vary across jurisdictions and within the jurisdiction depending upon the distance from the registry.

The time at which an appearance is actually entered is of critical importance for entry of a default judgment and also for determining the date for delivery of the statement of claim. However, the time limited for appearance, not the time of the actual appearance, determines the time within which a defence must be delivered: see *Anlaby v Praetorius* (1888) 20 QBD 764.

Time periods for entry of an appearance for process to be served inside the jurisdiction are governed by that jurisdiction's Rules of Court. Time periods for entry of an appearance relevant in another state or territory of Australia are governed by s 17 of the Service and Execution of Process Act 1992 (Cth) (21 days). Time periods for an appearance outside Australia are governed by the Rules of Court mentioned above.

9.6.2E **Service and Execution of Process Act 1992 (Cth)**

17 Time for appearance

(1) If the person served is required or permitted to enter an appearance under a law of the place of issue, the period after service within which the person may enter an appearance is:

(a) which ever is the longer of the following periods:

(i) 21 days;

(ii) the period in which the appearance would have been required or permitted to be entered if the process had been served in the place of issue; or

(b) such shorter period as the court of issue, on application, allows.

(1A) If, under a provision (the *State provision*) of the law of the place of issue, the period in which an appearance is required or permitted to be entered in respect of process served in the place of issue varies according to the distance of the place of service from another place, the period referred to in subparagraph (1)(a)(ii) is to be calculated by reference to the longest distance mentioned in the State provision.

(2) The matters that the court must take into account in determining an application to allow a shorter period include:

(a) urgency; and

(b) the places of residence or business of the parties; and

(c) whether a related or similar proceeding has been commenced against the person or another person.

9.6.3   A defendant may enter a late appearance at any time before judgment: ACT r 103; NT r 8.07; Qld r 138; Tas r 164(1); Vic r 8.07; WA O 12 r 5; *Re Thomas, Davies v Thomas* [1940] 4 All ER 145. In jurisdictions where this is permissible, leave is required to enter an appearance after final judgment: NT r 8.07; Vic r 8.07; WA O 12 r 5. The application for leave should be made on notice to the plaintiff by summons: *Stern v Friedmann* [1953] 2 All ER 565. See also *Reid Murray Development Queensland Pty Ltd v Lynwood Holdings (Pty) Ltd* [1964] QWN 1. In the Federal Court, FCR r 11.06 enables a respondent to file a notice of address for service at any time before the return date and the filing of any other document. In New South Wales (r 6.9), there is no restriction as to when a defendant may enter an appearance.

Where an appearance is filed after the time limited in the writ, the time available to deliver a defence or for other purposes is calculated from the last day for appearance specified in the writ or originating application: NT r 8.07(2); Tas r 164(2); Vic r 8.07; WA O 12 r 5; see also *Lloyd v Dixon* [1952] VLR 434. There is no equivalent provision in the High Court, Federal Court, New South Wales or South Australia. In Queensland (r 139(1)(b)) the defence accompanies the notice of intention to defend.

The time for entry of an appearance runs during court vacations.

Finally, a judgment entered before the time for appearance has elapsed is irregular: *Daly v Silley* [1960] VR 353.

UNCONDITIONAL APPEARANCE

9.7.1   In all jurisdictions an appearance may be unconditional or conditional, except in New South Wales where conditional appearances have been abolished, or in South Australia and the Federal Court where appearances have been abolished. Entry of an unconditional appearance waives:

(a) objections to the jurisdiction of the court (*Moore v Gamgee* (1890) 25 QBD 244; *Clutha Developments Pty Ltd v Marion Power Shovel Co Inc* [1973] 2 NSWLR 173; *Henry v Geoprosco International Ltd* [1976] QB 726);

(b) irregularities in the originating process known to the defendant or obvious on the face of the process: *Mulckern v Doerks* (1884) 53 LJQB 526; *Healey v Ballarat East Bowling Club* [1961] VR 206;

(c) irregularities as to commencement: *Edwards v Warden* (1874) LR 9 Ch 495; and

(d) irregularities in service (*Western National Bank of the City of New York v Perez, Triana & Co* [1891] 1 QB 304; *Perkins v Williams* (1900) 17 WN (NSW) 135) or the absence of service: *Green v Braddyll* [1856] 1 H & N 69. Hence there is no need to prove service.

If a defence is not entered after filing an unconditional appearance, then non-service or service irregularities will not prevent entry of a default judgment.

The following extracted forms are examples of unconditional appearances.

Form 6 (version 2)   **Form 6**

UCPR 6.9

                                       APPEARANCE

COURT DETAILS
Court
Division
List
Registry
Case number

TITLE OF PROCEEDINGS

[First] plaintiff   **[name]**

Second plaintiff

Number of plaintiffs

(if more than two)

[First] defendant   **[name]**

Second defendant

Number of defendants

(if more than two)

FILING DETAILS

Filed for   **[name]** [role of party eg, defendant]

Filed in relation to   [eg, plaintiff's claim, (number) cross-claim]

                                       [include only if form to be eFiled]

Legal representative   [solicitor on record] [firm]

Legal representative   [reference number]

Contact name and telephone   [name] [telephone]

APPEARANCE
[name] [role of party eg, defendant] appears.

#STATEMENT OF SUBMISSION
[name] [role of party eg, defendant] submits to the making of all orders sought, and the giving or entry of judgment in respect of all claims made, save as to costs.

SIGNATURE

#Signature of legal Representative

#Signature of or on behalf of party
if not legally represented

Capacity   [eg solicitor, authorised officer, role of party]

Date of signature

                                       [on separate page]

397

DETAILS ABOUT FILING PARTY
Filing party

Name

Address   # Unit/level number]   #[building name]

     [The filing party must   [Street number]   [street name]   [street type]
     give the party's address.]   [suburb/city]   [state/territory]   [postcode]

                           #[country (if not Australia)]

#Frequent user identifier   [include if the filing party is a registered frequent user]

[repeat the above information as required if appearing for more than one party]

#Legal representative for filing party

Name   [name of solicitor on record]

Practicing
certificate number

Firm   [name of firm]

#Contact solicitor   [include name of contact solicitor if different to solicitor
                         on record]

Address   # Unit/level number]   #[building name]

                   [Street number]   [street name]   [street type]
                   [suburb/city]   [state/territory]   [postcode]

DX address

Telephone

Fax

Email

Electronic services address   **[#email address for electronic service eg, service@
emailaddress.com.au #N Not applicable]**

#Contact details for filing party acting in person or by authorised officer

#Name of authorised officer

#Capacity to act for filing   #as above

party

Address for service # Unit/level number] #[building name]

[The filing party must give
an address for service.
This must be an address in
NSW unless the exceptions
listed in UCPR 4.5(3)
apply. State "as above" if
the filing party's address for
service is the same as the
filing party's address stated
above.]

[Street number] [street name] [street type]
[suburb/city] [state/territory] [postcode]

#Telephone

#Fax

#Email

9.7.3E	**Supreme Court (General Civil Procedure) Rules 2005 (Vic)**

IN THE SUPREME COURT OF VICTORIA 20 No.
AT

BETWEEN:

A.B. Plaintiff

And

C.D. Defendant

Date of document:

Filed on behalf of: Plaintiff

Prepared by:

FORM 8A

r 8.05(1)

NOTICE OF APPEARANCE
[heading as in originating process]

FILE an appearance for [full name of defendant] the above named defendant.

Dated [eg, 15 June 20].

[Signed]

The address of the defendant is

[*where the defendant appears in person and the address of the defendant is outside Victoria* The address of the defendant within Victoria for service is].

[*where the defendant appears by a solicitor* The name or firm and the business address within Victoria of the solicitor for the defendant is].

[where the solicitor is agent of another as agent for [name or firm and business address of principal]].

Submission to the jurisdiction

9.7.4 An unconditional appearance is a submission to the jurisdiction of the court but cannot confer jurisdiction which otherwise does not exist: *Colbert v Tocumwal Trading Co Pty Ltd* [1964] VR 820 at 826 per Sholl J obiter. At best the court has jurisdiction to declare the extent of its power: *Wilkinson v Barking Corp* [1948] 1 KB 721. In that latter case, Asquith LJ said (at 725):

> The Supreme Court may by statute lack jurisdiction to deal with a particular matter ... but it has jurisdiction to decide whether or not it has jurisdiction to deal with such matters. By entering an unconditional appearance, a litigant submits to the second of these jurisdictions (which exists) but not to the first (which does not).

The parties cannot confer jurisdiction by consent: *Thomson Australian Holdings Pty Ltd v Trade Practices Commission* (1981) 148 CLR 150 at 163. In *Caltex Oil (Aust) Pty Ltd v The Dredge 'Willemstad'* (1976) 136 CLR 529, Gibbs J said (at 539):

> As a general rule an unconditional appearance amounts to a submission to the jurisdiction of the court and to a waiver of irregularity, eg, in the manner of service. However, only a defendant can enter an appearance. That is the general rule in all proceedings ...

9.7.5 Questions

1. Does an unconditional appearance amount to a submission to the jurisdiction for all purposes? Can an unconditional appearance be limited to issues then in dispute, not necessarily extending to further claims raised by the plaintiff by amendment or be limited to certain capacities? See *Marlborough Harbour Board v Charter Travel Co Ltd* (1989) 18 NSWLR 223 at 229–30 where Hope JA said:

   > It is not in issue between the parties that the mere circumstance that a foreign party has submitted to the jurisdiction of The Court in one proceeding does not mean it has submitted to that jurisdiction for all purposes. Thus a foreign plaintiff who brings proceedings in The Court is not taken to submit to any cross-claim which the defendant may bring against it: *National Commercial Bank v Wimbourne* (1979) 11 NSWLR 156. In the same way a foreign defendant who has submitted to the jurisdiction of The Court to try one case against it will not be taken to have submitted to the jurisdiction of The Court to try all other cases which may be brought against it by the same party, including cases tried by amendment.

2. Does an unconditional appearance cover every capacity of a defendant? Do you think it advisable to enter a limited appearance if appearing and defending in a limited capacity?

Waiver

9.7.6   An unconditional appearance can waive irregularities but not nullities: see **Chapter 5**. For examples of appearances waiving procedural irregularities see: *Oulton v Radcliffe* (1874) 9 CP 189 (service outside the jurisdiction of the court); *Healey v Ballarat East Bowling Club* [1961] VR 206 (defendants not properly named nor address given in the writ). Typical irregularities concern stale or expired writs and the failure to serve the originating process. See also **9.9.1**.

Stale writ

9.7.7   An unconditional appearance makes good the service of an expired or stale writ which has not been renewed.

9.7.8C	**Sheldon v Brown Bayley's Steel Works Ltd**
	[1953] 2 QB 393
	High Court of England and Wales, Court of Appeal

[In an action under the Fatal Accidents Act 1846, the plaintiff failed to serve the writ on the defendants within 12 months of filing it. The writ had become stale. The first defendants entered a conditional appearance and had service against them set aside. The second defendants entered an unconditional appearance, but upon discovering what the first defendants had done, applied to have service of the writ set aside. The question was whether they were prevented from doing so by reason of their unconditional appearance.]

Denning LJ (at 401–2): This writ was not served within the 12 months permitted by the rule. It was served three or four days out of time. The first defendants thereupon entered a conditional appearance and got the service on them set aside. That meant that they obtained the benefit of the statutory limitation; because all that the plaintiff could then do, as against them, was to issue a new writ which would be statute barred. The second defendants, however, did not notice that the writ was served out of time. On October 13, 1952, they entered an unconditional appearance, but they soon afterwards came to know what the first defendants had done, and then they also applied to have the service of the writ set aside. The question is whether they are prevented from so doing by reason of their unconditional appearance. This depends on whether the service of a writ, after the 12 months permitted by the rule has expired, is a nullity or an irregularity. If it was an irregularity, then the irregularity was waived by the unconditional appearance; but if it was a nullity, then it could not be waived at all. It was not only bad, but incurably bad. ...

[402] In my opinion, the service of the writ after the 12 months was not a nullity but an irregularity which was waived by the unconditional appearance.

CONDITIONAL APPEARANCE

9.8.1   A conditional appearance, or conditional notice of intention to defend as it is known in Queensland (Form 007), or Conditional Notice of Intention to Respond as it is known in the ACT (r 111, Form 2.8), provides a method of approaching the court while preserving rights to object to procedural irregularities or jurisdiction. Conditional appearances may be entered in all jurisdictions except New South Wales where they no longer exist. A conditional appearance has the same effect as an unconditional appearance, unless upon application by the defendant within 14 days the court otherwise orders: HCR rr 23.03.3, 23.03.4, Form 9; ACT r 111; NT r 8.08, Form 8B; Qld r 144 (a defence must be filed within a further seven days); Tas r 168; Vic r 8.08(3), (4), Form 8B; WA O 12 r 6.

If a defendant files a conditional appearance, it seems the defendant will be bound by the court's decision if it determines it has jurisdiction: *Forbes v Smith* (1855) 10 Exch 717; *Re Orr Ewing* (1882) 22 Ch D 456; *Moore v Gamgee* (1890) 25 QBD 244; *Moss v Moss* [1937] St R Qd 1. If having entered a conditional appearance the defendant establishes a lack of jurisdiction, defect or irregularity in the process or its service, the court has inherent jurisdiction to stay the proceedings or set them aside.

Leave is not required to enter a conditional appearance. The extract at **9.8.4E** provides an example of a conditional appearance.

9.8.2C   **Glassford, Cook and Co Pty Ltd v William Higson & Co**
                                        (1899) 25 VLR 177
                                     Supreme Court of Victoria

[An unconditional appearance had been mistakenly filed by an articled clerk. Later the same day leave was granted *ex parte* to enter a conditional appearance in its stead. An application was made to set aside the conditional appearance.]

Hodges J (at 179–80): The first is an application to set aside an appearance, or rather an amendment of an appearance, as it really is. It appears that a clerk of the defendants' attorneys entered an appearance without any qualification. An application ex parte was made before [in fact after] the appearance was entered, and [before] notice thereof given to the plaintiffs' attorney for an order to transform that unconditional appearance into a conditional one. I made the order on that ex parte application. It is now contended that such an order was altogether irregular, that there is no authority for allowing a conditional appearance, and that if there were authority the order should not have been made ex parte. In my [180] opinion the order was rightly made, and the materials upon which it was made are sufficient. After having heard counsel for the plaintiffs, I think that if I had heard him similarly then upon the materials now before me I should have done exactly, what I then did. I do not think it can be too clearly remembered what Brett, LJ, said — viz, that parties should succeed, not by the slips of attorneys or their clerks, but by the merits of their cases. This appearance was entirely the mistake of the attorney's clerk, who did not know all that had taken place, and who thought the matter one for immediate action, and therefore entered an appearance without consulting the managing clerk. I therefore have no hesitation in dismissing that application ...

9.8.3C
Firth v John Mowlem and Co Ltd
[1978] 1 WLR 1184
High Court of England and Wales, Court of Appeal

[The plaintiff lorry driver was injured on 1 June 1973 while unloading steel bridging. In March 1976, the plaintiff sued the builders for negligence. The builders delivered their defence on 8 June 1976, one week after the three-year limitation period had expired which indicated that M and J Ltd were in control of the unloading. The plaintiff sought, and was granted, leave by the Master to amend both the writ and the statement of claim to join M and J Ltd as defendants, who on 8 November entered an unconditional appearance. Ten days later, M and J Ltd applied for leave to withdraw their appearance and enter a conditional appearance instead, the limitation period having expired before leave was given. The judge on appeal from the Master allowed the amendment. The plaintiff appealed against this order on the basis that the judge had misdirected himself in holding that accident or mistake justified substitution of a conditional appearance. The appeal was dismissed with costs.]

Megaw LJ (at 1189): Each case has to be looked at on its own particular facts. There was here what can properly be called a 'mistake', and, subject to the question of the proper exercise of the court's discretion, the judge had jurisdiction to make the order which he did and to set aside the unconditional appearance.

Waller LJ (at 1189): Mr Deby, on behalf of the plaintiff, sought to distinguish two kinds of circumstances in which the court might, or might not, exercise the discretion, one of which was when there was an absence of authority which caused the mistake and the other was simply a mistake. He submitted that in the former there was a discretion but in the latter there was no discretion. This was a case where the second defendants had given authority to their solicitors; the solicitors through their clerk, Mr Hardman, had erred: and he submitted, therefore, that there was no discretion. I agree with Megaw LJ that it is not possible to divide up the cases in that way. In my view the court had a complete discretion. No [1190] doubt in relation to questions of entry of appearance such discretion will be exercised sparingly. But it is a matter for the judge, acting judicially. This being a matter of discretion, this court only interferes if the judge was plainly wrong or was acting on a wrong principle or taking wrong matters into account. In this case Mr Hardman erred in entering an unconditional appearance. But he realized that we had done so in a very short space of time, namely, within 10 days, and in particular, before he or the second defendants had taken any further step in the action. I am quite unable to say that there was anything wrong in the way in which the judge exercised his discretion, and I also would dismiss this appeal.

9.8.4E
Supreme Court Forms Rules 2000 (Tas)
Form 15 — Notice of Conditional Appearance Rule 168(2)

Take notice that this conditional appearance has been filed by or on behalf of [*name of party or person filing appearance*], the defendant [*or respondent or third party*] who denies the jurisdiction of the Court (or disputes the validity of the originating process or its service) and reserves the right to apply to the Court or a judge to set aside that process or its alleged service on the following grounds [*specify grounds*].

The defendant's [*or respondent's or third party's*] address for service of documents is [*specify address with particularity*].

Dated

[*Signature of party or practitioner for party*]

Sealed [*date*]

To [*plaintiff or applicant or the practitioner for such party and address*]

9.8.5   Notes and questions

1. Does the 14-day period for bringing an application for a conditional appearance run from the date the conditional appearance is filed, or from the date the summons or application was filed? See NT r 8.08; Qld r 144(3); Tas r 168; Vic rr 8.08(4), 46.02(2); WA O 12 r 6. This question is not relevant to the other jurisdictions.

2. What is the relationship between a conditional appearance and the Service and Execution of Process Act 1992 (Cth)? See *Reid Murray Development Queensland Pty Ltd v Lynwood Holdings (Pty) Ltd* [1964] QWN 1; *Tallerman & Co Pty Ltd v Nathan's Merchandise (Vic) Pty Ltd* (1957) 98 CLR 93 at 107, but note the removal of the nexus requirements. A person served with a state Supreme Court originating process pursuant to the Service and Execution of Process Act 1992 (Cth) cannot sustain a conditional appearance based on the argument that the state that issued the process was not the appropriate forum. Territories are regarded as states under the Act. This question is not relevant to federal courts (the High Court and the Federal Court) as they have Australia-wide jurisdiction.

Examples of appropriate circumstances for a conditional appearance

Objection to jurisdiction

9.8.6   An objection to jurisdiction may occur where it is alleged that a person or corporation outside the jurisdiction is not amenable to the jurisdiction. For example, in *Express Airways v Port Augusta Air Services* [1980] Qd R 543 the plaintiffs (resident in Queensland) sued the defendants (resident in South Australia) in respect of an alleged breach of contract. The defendant entered a conditional appearance and had set aside the writ of summons on the basis that the Queensland Supreme Court had no jurisdiction as the requirements of the Service and Execution of Process Act 1901 (Cth) had not been satisfied. This is no longer a problem for interstate service as the Service and Execution of Process Act 1992 (Cth) no longer retains the nexus requirements contained in the Service and Execution of Process Act 1901 (Cth). The issue remains a problem for service outside Australia, as the nexus requirements in that respect remain: see 6.9.10.

Generally, the action will be stayed and not set aside, particularly if service was pursuant to the Service and Execution of Process Act 1992 (Cth).

Forum non conveniens

9.8.7 Forum non conveniens is a private international law doctrine which states that courts have a discretionary power to refuse jurisdiction when the convenience of the parties and justice would be better achieved by resolving the dispute in another forum. Proceedings should be stayed on the basis that the court is a clearly inappropriate forum for the determination of the application: *Oceanic Sun Line Special Shipping Co Inc v Fay* (1988) 79 ALR 9 at 44–6; *Voth v Manildra Flour Mills Pty Ltd* (1990) 97 ALR 124; see also, M Davies, S Ricketson and G Lindell, *Conflict of Laws Commentary and Materials*, Butterworths, Sydney, 1997, Ch 4; P Nygh, *Conflict of Laws in Australia*, 8th ed, LexisNexis Butterworths, Sydney, 2010, Ch 7; M Pryles, 'Forum Non Conveniens — The Next Chapter' (1991) 65 *ALJ* 442. See also Chapter 4.

Immunity

9.8.8 A foreign sovereign cannot generally be sued without consent: *The Christina* [1938] AC 485. In *Van Heyningen v Netherlands-Indies Government* [1949] St R Qd 54 at 61, the Full Court of the Supreme Court of Queensland had to consider whether the Netherlands-Indies Government was capable of being sued. It was held that the entry of a conditional appearance in which jurisdiction was denied did not mean waiver of objections concerning defective service based on foreign sovereign immunity not raised in the conditional appearance. A conditional appearance may be entered as of right, and the defendant can rely on any circumstances to show that the court has no jurisdiction, including alleged insufficiencies in service. See also *Capewell v Seltino Pty Ltd (Practice Note)* [1986] 2 Qd R 2 at 15.

Service irregularities

9.8.9 Irregularities as to service offer a common basis for entry of a conditional appearance (see *Capewell v Seltino Pty Ltd* [1986] 2 Qd R 2 at 15; *Monteleone v Owners of the Old Soap Factory* [2007] WASCA 79). For example, purported service on a solicitor without instructions to accept service. As to the requirements of personal service, see 8.2.1.

Examples of inappropriate circumstances for entry of a conditional appearance

A different venue within the jurisdiction is required by contract

---

9.8.10C **Roy v Dahl**
[1959] Qd R 332
Supreme Court of Queensland, Full Court

[Two defendants entered separate 'conditional appearances', the first of which stated:

> Enter a conditional appearance in this action for the defendant Australian Guarantee Corporation Limited which defendnt denies the right of the plaintiff to institute or proceed with this action in this court or any court other than a court in Brisbane.]

> **Wanstall J (at 338):** Properly construed, this 'conditional appearance' is not of the kind contemplated by O XII r 22, in that it does not deny the jurisdiction, but merely reserves [the] appellant's contractual right as to venue.
>
> We think that the proper way of dealing with it was to direct that it be treated as an unconditional appearance, once it had achieved its purpose of bringing before the learned judge the questions raised by the appellant's summons.
>
> [**Townley** and **Stable JJ** concurred with **Wanstall J**.]

A compromised cause of action

9.8.11 A compromised cause of action has settled. Typically, as part of the settlement agreement, the original cause of action will be extinguished. It will be inappropriate to enter an appearance as the action no longer exists.

Alternatives to a conditional appearance

9.8.12 There are several alternatives to entering a conditional appearance. It is possible to apply to have the originating process, or its service, set aside (usually before default judgment is entered), without entering an appearance: HCR r 23.03.1 (defendant's discretion); FCR r 13.01; NSW r 12.11; NT r 8.09; Qld r 135 (with leave); Tas r 167; Vic r 8.09; WA O 12 r 7.

The Rules of Court also contain a general rule enabling applications for orders dealing with a failure to comply with the rules: ACT r 1450; NSW r 12.11; NT r 2.03; Qld r 371; SA r 12; Tas rr 13, 14; Vic r 2.03; WA O 2 r 2. There are no such rules in the High Court and the Federal Court. An application to set aside an irregularity should be made within a reasonable time, and before the party applying has taken any fresh steps subsequent to knowledge of the irregularity: see **Chapter 5**.

APPEARANCE UNDER PROTEST

9.9.1 An appearance under protest is a common law equivalent to a conditional appearance. A conditional appearance under the rules is not filed. Queensland r 144 requires that a conditional notice of intention to defend be filed, instead of an appearance under protest. Tasmanian r 125 specifically requires entry of an appearance before a party may be heard, unless the court or a judge otherwise orders. Elsewhere, appearances under protest remain possible though they have been superseded by the following rules which offer an alternative procedure to a conditional appearance: HCR r 23.03.1; FCR r 13.01; NSW rr 10.19, 12.11; NT r 8.09; Tas r 167; Vic r 8.09; WA O 12 r 7.

New South Wales r 10.19 states:

10.19 Waiver of objection to service (cf DCR Pt 8, r 5(3))
A party who files a document in reply to a document alleged to have been served on that party is taken to have waived any objection to the fact or manner of service unless he or she files and serves notice of the objection together with the document so filed.

9.9.2C   **Larsen v The Ship 'Nieuw Holland'**
[1957] St R Qd 605
Supreme Court of Queensland, Full Court

Philp J (at 609–13): On 10th July, 1957, the defendant ship and the owner thereof entered an appearance in the following form:

[610] 'Enter an appearance to this action under protest for the defendant the ship 'Nieuw Holland' and the owner thereof.' ...

A preliminary point was raised for the appellant. It was argued that as the defendant had entered an appearance 'under protest' and not a conditional appearance denying the jurisdiction under O XII r 22, in the form prescribed by the Rules, it had waived its right to contest the jurisdiction of the court and to have the writ set aside. The point was taken before us for the first time. ...

[612] There is no difference between an appearance under protest and a conditional appearance ...

[613] The rules are permissive and neither requires a defendant desiring to appear in order to contest the jurisdiction to use any particular form of words in his entry of appearance. Neither of these rules (nor EO XII r 30) refer to setting aside the writ — they have in view only an application to set aside service. In the instant case the motion is to set aside the writ. It is impossible to hold that a defendant entering an appearance marked 'under protest' is entering an unqualified appearance whereby he evinces an intention to abandon his right to contest the substantive matter of jurisdiction.

9.9.3   Question

1. Would *Larsen v The Ship 'Nieuw Holland'* [1957] St R Qd 605, have the same result under the Queensland UCPR?

APPEARANCE GRATIS

9.10.1   A defendant does not have to wait until service before entering an appearance. He or she may enter an 'appearance gratis' upon issue of the originating process. An appearance gratis can take the form of either a conditional or an unconditional appearance, depending on the jurisdiction. The rules in all jurisdictions, except South Australia and the Australian Capital Territory, permit unconditional appearances, and in the case of the High Court, a Submitting Appearance, before service of originating process: HCR r 9.01.1 (solicitors only); FCR r 12.01; NSW rr 6.11, 10.20(5); NT r 6.02; Qld r 105(2); Vic r 6.02; WA O 9 r 1(3). In relation to submitting appearances, see *Trust Co of Australia Ltd v Perpetual Trustees WA Ltd* (1995) 36 NSWLR 654. The following jurisdictions also permit conditional appearances before service of the originating process: HCR r 9.01.1; Tas r 168.

The practice in the Australian Capital Territory is consistent with the remaining jurisdictions.

407

The plaintiff cannot set aside an appearance where it has been entered by a defendant before service of the originating process: *The Gniezno* [1968] P 618; [1967] 2 All ER 738.

9.10.2C   **Farley & Lewers (Qld) Pty Ltd v Fitzgerald**
[1983] 1 Qd R 231
Supreme Court of Queensland

[A plaintiff was allowed to enter judgment in default of defence against a defendant who entered an unconditional appearance, despite not having previously been served with a writ of summons. The registrar pursuant to O 31 had regard to the date of entry of appearance as the date of service of the writ for the purposes of calculating the time limited for defence.]

Master Lee (as he then was, at 233): [When referring to *Pioneer Concrete (North Coast) Pty Ltd v Bennett* [1972] Qd R 544, the Master observed:] As indicated by His Honour in that case, it is clear that an unconditional appearance could be entered before service. This was known as appearance *gratis* under which a person could at any time after the issue of a writ or an originating summons, waive service and enter an unconditional appearance: *Oulton v Radcliffe* (1874) LRCP 189; *Pike v Nairn & Co Ltd* [1960] Ch 553.

9.10.3   Notes and questions

1. Will a writ be deemed to be served if an appearance gratis is entered? See *Pioneer Concrete (North Coast) Pty Ltd v Bennett* [1972] Qd R 544 at 550–2, 555 (where it was held that a defendant may, although not served with process, waive the necessity for service and enter an appearance by solicitors); *Farley & Lewers (Qld) Pty Ltd v Fitzgerald* [1983] 1 Qd R 231 (see **9.10.2C**); *Tucker v Walker* [1920] VLR 385; *Collins v Hudson* [1953] VLR 396.

2. Does it make any difference if the writ is no longer valid for service? See *The Gniezno* [1968] P 618; [1967] 2 All ER 738 (where an entry of appearance was entered without previous service even after the validity of the writ for service had expired); and see **9.7.7** in relation to a stale writ.

FAILURE TO ENTER AN APPEARANCE

9.11.1   Failure to enter an appearance enlivens the issues of waiver and default judgment.

Waiver

9.11.2   Waiver is constituted by words or conduct of such a nature, that an inference can properly be drawn that the party does not intend to rely on the objection upon which he or she may otherwise be entitled to rely: *Lindgran v Lindgran* [1956] VLR 215 at 220; *Colbert* *v Tocumwal Trading Co Pty Ltd* [1964] VR 820 at 826 (obiter). Waiver can arise in the context of an appearance under protest: see **9.9.1**.

In *Boyle v Sacker* (1888) 39 Ch D 249, an order had been made for substituted service in England, of a writ and notice of motion for injunction, on a person resident abroad. The defendant declined to enter an appearance, but appeared by counsel on the motion, filed affidavits and argued the case opposing the injunction on the merits. The conduct amounted to a waiver of any objection to an order for substituted service, since it went beyond merely challenging jurisdiction.

9.11.3   The following conduct would appear to give rise to waiver in this context:

- an application for security for costs and an extension of time for appearance: see *White v Hardwick* (1922) 23 SR (NSW) 6; and

- an application for an adjournment and to serve and answer interrogatories: see *Kingstone Tyre Agency Pty Ltd v Blackmore* [1970] VR 625.

However, the following conduct does not appear to give rise to waiver in this context:

- seeking particulars of a statement of claim on a summons to have service of the writ set aside: see *Williams v Society of Lloyd's* [1994] 1 VR 274; and

- attempting to discharge an interim injunction on an application to set aside service prior to an appearance: see *Laurie v Carroll* (1958) 98 CLR 310.

For further examples of waiver or otherwise, see Williams, *Civil Procedure Victoria*, LexisNexis, Sydney, looseleaf, [18.02.45].

Default judgment

9.11.4   Failure to enter an appearance is a common ground for applying for a default judgment: see **Chapter 12**.

AMENDMENT, WITHDRAWAL AND REMOVAL

9.12.1   Appearances may be withdrawn only with leave of the court: HCR r 27.10.1; NSW r 12.5; NT r 25.01; Qld r 306 (also with the consent of the other parties), Form 028; Tas r 375; Vic r 25.01; WA O 23 r 1. Either the plaintiff consents or the court believes the appearance was entered accidentally or by mistake. It is unlikely leave will be given where the appearance was entered intentionally with proper legal advice. See *Sambroke v Hayes* (1835) 4 LJ Ch 175; *Somportex Ltd v Philadelphia Chewing Gum Corp* [1968] 3 All ER 26; *Firth v John Mowlem & Co Ltd* [1978] 3 All ER 331. After withdrawal of an appearance, the proceeding continues as if there had never been an appearance. The defendant will then be at risk of default judgment.

Once notice of an appearance has been given to the plaintiff, an application to amend the appearance will need to be made on notice (*Glassford, Cook & Co Pty Ltd v William Higson & Co* (1889) 25 VLR 177: see **9.8.2C**) otherwise the application may be *ex parte*. Leave may be granted to amend an irregularity or mistakenly entered appearance.

> **9.12.2C** **Camm v Linder**
> Unreported, SC(Qld), Master Lee, W918/1982
>
> [The defendant applied for leave to amend an unconditional entry of appearance to make it conditional. The defendants sought to deny the jurisdiction of the court and for an order setting aside service upon them of the writ of summons. The application was refused because of delay, prejudice to the plaintiff, and because it was a result of mere oversight and not due to any accident or mistake.]
>
> **Master Lee:**
> (1) An unconditional appearance without the words 'under protest' or some other indication that there was in reality no intention to submit to the jurisdiction, will usually bind a defendant except in the rarest cases: *Larsen v The Ship 'Nieuw Holland'* [1957] St R Qd 605 at 611–12. In other words, any objection to jurisdiction is ordinarily waived by the unconditional appearance.
> (2) For the discretion to amend the appearance to arise, it must have been entered by accident or mistake, eg, a solicitor acting without proper authority or instructions, but not when it is entered deliberately and on proper advice. There must be some evidence of a mistake, eg, failure of communication or misunderstanding: *Somportex Ltd v Philadelphia Chewing Gum Corp* [1968] 3 All ER 26 at 28.
> (3) The mistake may be of a specific kind: *Somportex Ltd v Philadelphia Chewing Gum Corp, supra*; *Glassford Cook & Co Ltd v William Higson & Co* (1899) 25 VLR 177; or it may be perfectly general in nature: *Firth v John Mowlem & Co Ltd* [1978] 1 WLR 1184 ...
> (4) If there is evidence of mistake, which appears to be essential, then there is a complete discretion in the court to allow an amendment subject to established rules: see *Firth v John Mowlem & Co Ltd, supra,* particularly at 1189 ...
> (5) The discretion will rarely be exercised if the application to amend is not made promptly or if there *is* any prejudice to the plaintiff: *Glassford Cook & Co Ltd v William Higson & Co, supra* (application made same afternoon). See also *Somportex Ltd v Philadelphia Chewing Gum Corp, supra* at 32 where Salmon LJ said:
>
> > I think that if a party, who has had the best professional advice, elects to take a course of this kind, acts on it and that action has the effect of postponing the proceedings for three months, he should not subsequently be able to say that he resiles from what he has done and would now rather elect one of the other courses which had been open to him ...

9.12.3 A defendant sued in the wrong name should enter an appearance in the correct name, also stating that the defendant has been sued in the wrong name: *Alexander Korda Film Production Ltd v Columbia Pictures Corp Ltd* [1946] 2 All ER 424. The plaintiffs should amend their proceedings accordingly.

9.12.4 An appearance may be removed or set aside by the court where it contains no address for service, or if the address so provided is fictitious or illusory: Tas r 128A (an order providing for or dispensing with service may also be made). In the remaining jurisdictions, if the address for service is false, the plaintiff or applicant may, with leave of the court, continue to litigate as if an appearance had not been made: NT r 8.06; Vic r 8.06. In the High Court (r 2.03), New South Wales Civil Procedure Act 2005 s 63 and Queensland (r 371), the issue is dealt with as a failure to comply with the rules. In Tasmania (r 160), a Notice of Appearance not containing an address for service required by rr 128, 159 cannot be filed.

Further reading

9.13.1 Looseleaf

N Williams, *Civil Procedure Victoria*, LexisNexis, Sydney.

9.13.2 Reports

Evershed *Report*, 1953, Cmnd 8878, [112]–[115].

9.13.3 Texts

H Astor and C Chinkin, *Dispute Resolution in Australia*, 2nd ed, LexisNexis Butterworths, Sydney, 2002.

D Boniface, M Kumar and M Legg, *Principles of Civil Procedure in NSW*, 2nd ed, Thomson Reuters, Sydney, 2012, Ch 8.

B Cairns, *Australian Civil Procedure*, 9th ed, Thomson Reuters, Sydney, 2011, Ch 5.

J Hunter, C Cameron and T Henning, *Litigation 1: Civil Procedure*, 7th ed, LexisNexis Butterworths, Australia, 2005, [3.27].

Joinder of Parties and Actions, and Particular Parties

## CHAPTER 10

OVERVIEW

This chapter is concerned with, to what extent, and how, parties and causes of action can be joined in the one proceeding. Joinder of claims and parties raises many issues which need to be addressed, such as: To what extent do the judges attempt to give effect to the legislative direction in the interpretation and application of the joinder rules? What factors influence the litigant's decision to join a party or a claim in a proceeding? To what extent do the Rules of Court reflect this legislative direction? In the context of mediation, the structure of the mediation process is outlined, and the nature of consensual dispute resolution is explained. Four of the key features of mediation, namely accessibility, voluntariness, confidentiality and facilitation are analysed. Other issues such as power imbalance, enforceability of agreements to mediate and evaluation of mediation are also discussed.

INTRODUCTION

10.1.1   Each Australian jurisdiction has provisions derived from the English Judicature Act 1873 (UK) s 24(7) designed to avoid multiplicity of proceedings and inconsistency of result, and to promote finality in litigation. The following extract from the Supreme Court Act 1986 (Vic) is an example. The provision should be liberally construed: *Roberts v Gippsland Agricultural and Earth Moving Contracting Pty Ltd* [1956] VLR 555 at 564.

10.1.2E   **Supreme Court Act 1986 (Vic)**

Law and equity to be concurrently administered
29 ... (2) Every court referred to in sub-section (1) must give the same effect as before the commencement of this Act —
    (a)   to all equitable estates, titles, rights, reliefs, defences, and counterclaims, and to all equitable duties and liabilities; and
    (b)   subject thereto, to all legal claims and demands and all estates, titles, rights, duties, obligations and liabilities existing by the common law or created by any Act

---

and, subject to the provisions of this or any other Act, must so exercise its jurisdiction in every proceeding before it as to secure that, as far as possible, all matters in dispute between the parties are completely and finally determined, and all multiplicity of proceedings concerning any of those matters is avoided.

[See also: Federal Court of Australia Act 1976 (Cth) s 22; Supreme Court Act 1933 (ACT) s 25; Supreme Court Act 1970 (NSW) s 63; Supreme Court Act 1979 (NT) s 19; Supreme Court Act 1995 (Qld) s 244(9); Supreme Court Act 1935 (SA) s 27; Supreme Court Civil Procedure Act 1932 (Tas) s 10(7); Supreme Court Act 1935 (WA) s 24(7).]

10.1.3   Note

1. For the rules regarding joinder of parties and causes of action, cross-claims, counterclaims and third party proceedings, see: High Court Rules 2004 Pt 21; Federal Court Rules Pt 9; Court Procedures Rules 2006 (ACT) Pt 2.4; Uniform Civil Procedure Rules 2005 (NSW) Pt 6 Divs 5 and 6 and Pt 9; Supreme Court Rules (NT) Orders 9–11; Civil Proceedings Act 2011 s 7(1); Uniform Civil Procedure Rules 1999 (Qld) Ch 3 Pt 1 r 173, Ch 6 Pts 5, 6; Supreme Court Civil Rules 2006 (SA) rr 28–31, 35–37, 73–77; Supreme Court Rules 2000 (Tas) rr 169–212; Supreme Court (General Civil Procedure) Rules 2005 (Vic) Orders 9–11; Rules of the Supreme Court 1971 (WA) Orders 18, 19.

   [*Note*: in this chapter a reference, such as WA O 9 r 2, is a reference to the relevant Rules of Court. All other legislation will be specified.]

RES JUDICATA AND ISSUE ESTOPPEL

Introduction

10.2.1   The plea of *res judicata* applies where a court has given judgment in relation to matters that are the subject of litigation. It precludes the relitigation of claims made in earlier proceedings between the same parties (or their privies; ie, persons closely connected with the parties and their claims), in respect of the same subject matter. It is sometimes described as cause of action estoppel. Issue estoppel is concerned with the redetermination of a finding made in earlier litigation. Issue estoppel is explained more fully below at **10.2.6–10.2.12**.

Since the decision of the High Court in *Port of Melbourne Authority v Anshun Pty Ltd (No 2)* (1981) 147 CLR 589 (see **10.2.4C**), it has become common to refer to a further form of estoppel, namely, litigation estoppel or *Anshun* estoppel. Litigation estoppel applies to those claims which could have been made in an earlier proceeding and which are subsequently sought to be litigated. It would appear that this form of estoppel is an instance of *res judicata*: see *Port of Melbourne Authority v Anshun Pty Ltd (No 2)* (1989) 147 CLR 589 at 598 where reference is made to the speech of Lord Wilberforce in the *Carl Zeiss* case [1967] 1 AC 853 at 966.

Res judicata and issue estoppel are important considerations in relation to the joinder of claims and parties. The failure to join a claim in a proceeding may preclude the pursuit of such a claim in a later proceeding. The failure to join a person as a party will normally mean that a decision made in the proceeding will not be binding upon that person.

Res judicata

10.2.2 As noted in 10.2.1, *res judicata* extends to claims which could have been made in an earlier proceeding.

The objectives underlying the Judicature Act 1873 (UK) s 24(7) (and its Australian equivalents) referred to above at 10.1.2E and, in particular, the desire for complete and final determination of all matters between the parties, are given full force through the doctrine of *res judicata*. The risk that non-joinder of a claim may result in the later estoppel of that claim, will be a powerful factor in a litigant's decision to join that claim in the proceeding. The classic formulation of the relevant principle is found in *Henderson v Henderson* (1843) 3 Hare 100; 67 ER 313, a case on cause of action estoppel. Sir James Wigram VC formulated the principle as follows (at 3 Hare 114–15; 67 ER 319):

> … [W]here a given matter becomes the subject matter of litigation in and of adjudication by a Court of competent jurisdiction, the Court requires the parties to that litigation to bring forward their whole case, and will not (except under special circumstances) permit the same parties to open the same subject of litigation in respect of matter which might have been brought forward as part of the subject in contest, but which was not brought forward, only because they have, from negligence, inadvertence, or even accident, omitted part of their case. The plea of *res judicata* applies, except in special cases, not only to points upon which the Court was actually required by the parties to form an opinion and pronounce a judgment, but to every point which properly belonged to the subject of litigation, and which the parties, exercising reasonable diligence, might have brought forward at the time.

10.2.3 This passage was referred to with apparent approval in *Port of Melbourne Authority v Anshun Pty Ltd (No 2)* (1981) 147 CLR 589 at 598 by Gibbs CJ, Mason and Aickin JJ.

10.2.4C   **Port of Melbourne Authority v Anshun Pty Ltd (No 2)**
(1981) 147 CLR 589
High Court of Australia

[A worker had been injured by a load of girders handled by a crane hired by Anshun Pty Ltd (Anshun) from the Port of Melbourne Authority (the Authority). In an earlier action brought by the injured worker against Anshun and the Authority, the defendants sought contribution from each other pursuant to the Wrongs Act 1958 (Vic) (Lord Campbell's Act). It was ordered in the contribution proceedings that Anshun should recover 90 per cent of the damages awarded to the plaintiff from the Authority and that the Authority should recover 10 per cent of the damages from Anshun. The Authority then brought proceedings against Anshun, claiming an entitlement to an indemnity from Anshun pursuant to the crane hire agreement.

It was held at first instance that the case was governed by the principle in *Henderson v Henderson*: see 10.2.2. A stay of the proceeding was granted. It was held that the claim for indemnity ought to have been pursued in the original proceeding. That decision was upheld on appeal by the Full Court of the Supreme Court of Victoria.

It was noted in the High Court by Gibbs CJ, Mason and Aickin JJ (at 595), and by Brennan J (at 607) that a claim to an indemnity may be litigated as between a defendant and a third party (or between defendants) even though the right to indemnity arises only on payment of the liability to which it relates, that is, payment to the plaintiff who seeks damages. The fact that liability to the plaintiff has not been established (or discharged) is no bar to the third party claim: see third party proceedings below.]

Gibbs CJ, Mason and Aickin JJ (at 598): [Their Honours referred to the passage from *Henderson v Henderson* (see 10.2.2), and continued:] Although it has been said that the principle operates so as to extend the doctrines of issue estoppel as well as res judicata, its application to cases of issue estoppel is to be treated with [599] caution. Lord Wilberforce in *Carl Zeiss* [1967] 1 AC 853, at p 966 observed that *Henderson v Henderson* was an instance of res judicata. Lord Reid in the same case [1967] 1 AC, at p 916 noted that confusion had been introduced by applying to issue estoppel without modification rules designed to deal with res judicata.

Indeed, for a long time Wigram VC's statement did not express the principle that was applied to a case in which it was contended that a party, whether plaintiff or defendant, was estopped from asserting a matter in a new action by reason of his failure to plead that matter as a defence in an earlier action. As applied to such a case Wigram VC's statement of principle suggests that there will be an estoppel except in special circumstances. The English and United States authorities establish that this was certainly not the law and that it was only an omission to deny by way of a defence a traversable allegation that gave rise to an estoppel. In *Howlett v Tarte* (1861) 10 CB (NS) 813 at p 827 (142 ER 673 at p 679), Willes J went so far as to say: 'nobody ever heard of a defendant being precluded from setting up a defence in a second action because he did not avail himself of the opportunity of setting it up in the first action.'

However, it seems that Williams J in the same case expressed the proposition with greater accuracy when he said (1861) 10 CB (NS), at p 826 (142 ER, at p 678): 'if the defendant attempted to put upon the record a plea which was inconsistent with any traversable allegation in the former declaration, there would be an estoppel.'

In considering whether failure to plead a defence available in an earlier action gives rise to an estoppel in subsequent litigation, early authorities distinguished between failure to traverse an allegation made by the other side and failure to plead affirmative matters which would not have conflicted with any traversable allegation, eg, a plea by way of confession and avoidance. The general rule was that a general adverse decision imported also a particular adverse decision on any traversable allegation made by the successful party which the unsuccessful party omitted to traverse but did not import an adverse decision as to affirmative matters which, if pleaded, would not have conflicted with any traversable allegation. This appears to have been the basis of the judgment of Williams J in *Howlett v Tarte*. See also Field J in *Cromwell v County of Sac* (1876) 94 US 351, at pp 356–357 (24 Law Ed 195, at p 199); Spencer-Bower and Turner, *Res Judicata*, 2nd ed (1969), pp 165–167 and [600] *Halsbury's Laws of England*, 4th ed, vol 16, par 1533. Thus in *Davis v Hedges* (1871) LR 6 QB 687 a plaintiff was not precluded from claiming damages for non-performance and improper performance of work by reason of his failure to raise this claim when earlier sued by the defendant for the price of the work alleged to have been improperly done. A similar distinction seems to have been drawn in the United States. 46 *American Jurisprudence* 2d, Judgements, par 433 states:

... the general rule is that a judgment in a prior action in which a claim might have been but was not asserted as a setoff counterclaim, or cross action does not conclude the defendant ... and is no bar to a subsequent independent action based on the claim ...

An Annotation, ALR vol 8 (1920) 694, at p 695 says:

The general rule is that a defendant, having a claim available by way of setoff, counterclaim, or cross petition, has an election so to plead it, or to reserve it for a future independent action, and a prior action in which a claim might have been asserted as a set-off, counterclaim, or cross petition is no bar to a subsequent independent action thereon.

If a defendant did elect in the first action to raise a plea which did not traverse the allegation of the other party and which could have been pleaded as a counterclaim or setoff he would be bound by a general adverse decision (*Davis v Hedges* (1871) LR 6 QB, at p 692; in the United States, *Brown v First National Bank of Newton, Kansas* (1940) 132 F 450).

There were several reasons why a distinction was drawn between the effect of failure to plead to traversable allegations and failure to raise matters which could be pleaded as a counterclaim or setoff. Some, but not all, are still applicable. The right to plead by way of cross claim or setoff is a relatively modern development for the benefit of defendants. (See *Davis v Hedges* (1871) LR 6 QB, at p 690, per Hannen J speaking for Blackburn J and himself and *Merchants Heat and Light Co v Clow & Sons* (1907) 204 US 286, at pp 289–290 (51 LawEd 488, at pp 489–490), per Holmes J delivering the opinion of the Court.) To require that the defendant always raise his crossclaim or setoff at the first available time could cause great inconvenience. Hannen J in *Davis v Hedges* (1871) LR 6 QB, at p 640 noted that an action for the price of goods delivered or work performed may be maintainable before it is possible for a defendant to ascertain the [601] extent to which breach of warranty or breach of contract may afford a defence.

Other justifications suggested for the distinction such as that consequential damages could not be recovered (*Davis v Hedges* (1871) LR 6 QB, at p 691) or the old rule against double pleading (*Howlett v Tarte* (1861) 10 CB (NS), at p 828 (142 ER, at p 679)) are no longer relevant to the post Judicature Acts system (see Hoysted (1925) 37 CLR, at p 302; Hoystead [1926] AC, at pp 168–169).

This may explain why the old distinction between allegations which are traversable and those which are not is not always rigorously applied. Spencer-Bower and Turner (p 165) notes that 'according to the more recent authorities, an allegation may be "traversable", for the purposes of the rule, not only when it is express and direct, but also when it is reasonably implied.' Thus in *Humphries v Humphries* [1910] 2 KB 531 in an action upon an agreement for a lease the Court of Appeal held that there is an implied allegation that the agreement is valid so that a defendant could not in subsequent litigation with the plaintiff allege for the first time that it did not conform with s 4 of the Statute of Frauds. Even so, in the judgment of the Court delivered by Farwell LJ the decision is expressed to be based on the statement of principle by Williams J in *Howlett v Tarte*.

That statement of principle became less instructive as the old rules of pleading became obsolete. The remarks of Wigram VC did not suffer from this disadvantage: they were not tied to the elements of common law pleading. It is significant that in *Hoysted* both statements were approved. Subsequently, Viscount Radcliffe in *Kok Hoong* [1964] AC, at pp 1011–12 noted that the effect of the judgments in *Howlett v Tarte* is that a defendant 'is estopped only from asserting something which, if pleaded in the earlier action, would have amounted to a direct traverse of what was there asserted' and that 'if what he wishes to set up in the second action would have been matter only for a plea by way of confession and avoidance or, it seems, a special plea in the first action, there is no estoppel.' He went on to observe, rightly in our opinion, that this formula based on an obsolete and complicated system of pleading, was of limited utility in resolving questions of estoppel. For this reason, it was jettisoned in favour of the formulation by Wigram VC.

However in *Yat Tung* [1975] AC 581 the adoption of the principle in *Henderson v Henderson* (1843) 3 Hare 100 (67 ER 313) was taken too far. Lord Kilbrandon [602] spoke of it becoming 'an abuse of process to raise in subsequent proceedings matters which could and therefore should have been litigated in earlier proceedings' [1975] AC, at p 590. As we have seen, this statement is not supported by authority. And if we are to discard the traditional statement of principle because it was linked to the rules of common law pleading, there is no reason for rejecting the powerful arguments based on considerations of convenience and justice which were associated with it.

Lord Kilbrandon's remarks go further than the statement of Somervell LJ in *Greenhalgh v Mallard* [1947] 2 All ER 255, at p 257 which was recently approved by Lord Wilberforce in *Brisbane City Council* [1979] AC, at p 425. Somervell LJ had said: 'res judicata for this purpose is not confined to the issues which the court is actually asked to decide, but ... it covers issues or facts which are so clearly part of the subject matter of the litigation and so clearly could have been raised that it would be an abuse of the process of the court to allow a new proceeding to be started in respect of them.' Yet, *Greenhalgh v Mallard* and *Brisbane City Council*, unlike *Yat Tung*, were not cases in which the alleged estoppel arose from a defendant's failure to plead a defence. They were cases in which it was argued that a plaintiff was estopped from bringing a new proceeding by reason of dismissal of an earlier action.

In these cases in applying the *Henderson v Henderson* principle to a plaintiff said to be estopped from bringing a new action by reason of the dismissal of an earlier action, Somervell LJ and Lord Wilberforce insisted that the issue in question was so clearly part of the subject matter of the initial litigation and so clearly could have been raised that it would be an abuse of process to allow a new proceeding. Even then the abuse of process test is not one of great utility. And its utility is no more evident when it is applied to a plaintiff's new proceeding which is said to be estopped because the plaintiff omitted to plead a defence in an earlier action.

In this situation we would prefer to say that there will be no estoppel unless it appears that the matter relied upon as a defence in the second action was so relevant to the subject matter of the first action that it would have been unreasonable not to rely on it. Generally speaking, it would be unreasonable not to plead a defence if, having regard to the nature of the plaintiff's claim, and its subject matter it would be expected that the defendant would raise the defence and thereby enable the relevant issues to be determined in the one proceeding. In this respect, we need to [603] recall that there are a variety of circumstances, some referred to in the earlier cases, why a party may justifiably refrain from litigating an issue in one proceeding yet wish to litigate the issue in other proceedings eg, expense, importance of the particular issue, motives extraneous to the actual litigation, to mention but a few. See the illustrations given in *Cromwell v County of Sac* (1876) 94 US (24 Law Ed, at p 199).

It has generally been accepted that a party will be estopped from bringing an action which, if it succeeds, will result in a judgment which conflicts with an earlier judgment. In this respect the discussion in *Brewer v Brewer* (1953) 88 CLR 1 is illuminating. There it was held that the wife's omission to plead matters which would have constituted a discretionary bar to her husband's suit for dissolution of marriage on the ground of adultery did not estop her from raising those matters in subsequent proceedings for maintenance. Fullagar J with whom Dixon CJ agreed, said (1953) 88 CLR, at p 15:

> In *Hoysted's Case* (1925) 37 CLR 290; [1926] AC 155 the Commissioner was not merely seeking to raise on the second appeal a point which he might have raised but had omitted to raise on the first appeal. He was seeking to raise a point which could not be decided in his favour consistently with the decision on the first appeal. The point had not been argued on the first appeal, and there was therefore no express decision on the point. But the Commissioner had allowed it to be assumed against him, and the assumption was fundamental to the decision in the sense that, if the assumption had not been made, the decision must have been different. As Somervell LJ said: 'He was therefore seeking to obtain an order which was on the face of it and in form in direct conflict with the order which had been made previously' (1949) Ch, at p 360. The point in question had been 'the groundwork of the decision itself, though not then directly the point at issue' (per Coleridge J in *Reg v Township of Hartington* (1855) 4 El & Bl 780, at p 794 (119 ER 288, at p 293)).

This was also the conclusion reached by Williams, Webb and Taylor JJ (1953) 88 CLR, at p 10.

The likelihood that the omission to plead a defence will contribute to the existence of conflicting judgments is obviously an important factor to be taken into account in deciding whether the omission to plead can found an estoppel against the assertion of the same matter as a foundation for a cause of action in a second proceeding. By 'conflicting' judgments we include [604] judgments which are contradictory, though they may not be pronounced on the same cause of action. It is enough that they appear to declare rights which are inconsistent in respect of the same transaction.

It is for this reason that we regard the judgment that the Authority seeks to obtain as one which would conflict with the existing judgment, though the new judgment would be based on a different cause of action, a contractual indemnity.

Taking into consideration the relevant factors we conclude that the Full Court was right in holding that there was an estoppel. The matter now sought to be raised by the Authority was a defenece to Anshun's claim in the first action. It was so closely connected with the subject matter of that action that it was to be expected that it would be relied upon as a defence to that claim and as a basis for recovery by the Authority from Anshun. The third party procedures were introduced to enable this to be done. If successful, the indemnity case would have obviated an inquiry into contribution. If reserved for assertion in a later action, it would increase costs and give rise to a conflicting judgment.

The Authority did not adduce evidence at the trial to show why it failed to raise the indemnity issue in the first action. Apart from considerations such as the ability to overcome any prejudice to Anshun by orders for costs and the fact that O'Bryan J refused to strike out the action summarily — matters mainly associated with the conduct of this action — the Authority's case is that the principle in *Henderson v Henderson* (1843) 3 Hare 100 (67 ER 313) does not apply.

There is, however, one other factor which should be mentioned. It is that the defence of an indemnity required to be specially pleaded at common law. It was not covered by a general or particular traverse. Consequently the failure to plead it would not have founded an estoppel under the old law in its strictest formulation. But the evolutionary development of that rule evidenced by the decision in *Humphries v Humphries* [1910] 2 KB 531 may well have resulted in releases and indemnities being equated to traversable allegations for the purposes of estoppel. In any event the fact that the defence required to be specially pleaded at common law is not now a material consideration. It does not derogate from the conclusion that it was unreasonable for the Authority to refrain from raising its case of indemnity for disposition in the first action.

We would dismiss the appeal.

Murphy J (at 605): [His Honour delivered a short concurring judgment, in which he stated:] These notions of res judicata and issue estoppel are founded on the necessity, if there is to be an orderly administration of justice, of avoiding reagitation of issues, and of preventing the raising of issues which could have been and should have been decided in earlier litigation. ... The judgment in [the earlier] case is inconsistent with the judgment now sought by the plaintiff.

Brennan J (at 609–10): The recovery of a judgment which declares or enforces rights or liabilities between parties inconsistent with an earlier judgment binding upon them is precluded by the operation of the rules of estoppel and res judicata.

[His Honour continued (at 611):]

If cause of action is taken to mean a right, the rule is stated in terms of the passing of the right into judgment, and the rule precludes a party bound by the judgment from maintaining against another party bound by it any subsequent proceeding to recover a judgment giving a remedy to enforce or to compensate for an infringement of that right.

10.2.5   Note and questions

1. In *Triantafillidis v National Australia Bank Ltd* [1995] VConvR 54–536, the Victorian Court of Appeal expressed the view that the precise parameters of the High Court's decision were not known. Brooking JA said that there had to be a determination of the question, whether the plaintiff in the second action *had acted* unreasonably in not relying on its claims in the first proceeding. Phillips and Ormiston JJA rested their decision on the risk of inconsistency of judgment. Judgment for possession of land had been entered in default of defence against one of two mortgagors by the respondent bank. The land had been sold. The appellant sought to litigate claims for damages based on unconscionability against the respondent. The Victorian Court of Appeal held that she could do so, provided that she did not seek to challenge the validity of the mortgage itself upon which the respondent's judgment for possession rested.

2. Is it possible to discern any overriding test from the judgments in *Port of Melbourne Authority v Anshun Pty Ltd* as to when litigation estoppel will arise?

3. For an interesting decision in which *Anshun* estoppel was held not to apply, see *Running Pigmy Productions Pty Ltd v AMP General Insurance Co Ltd* [2001] NSWSC 431, a decision of Palmer J of the Supreme Court of New South Wales.

The plaintiff had commenced proceedings as one of two co-plaintiffs against the defendants, although arising out of the same events and under the same insurance policy. It had discontinued those proceedings, with leave of the court, and the proceedings by the co-plaintiff were settled. It was held that it was not unreasonable to discontinue the earlier proceeding so as to prosecute the fresh proceeding.

His Honour said:

> [33] It is not an abuse of process for a plaintiff to discontinue a proceeding merely in order to be able to bring the same proceeding later in circumstances in which the plaintiff believes there will be a greater prospect of success or a more substantial recovery: see eg, *Castanho v Brown & Root (UK) Ltd* [1981] AC 557, at 576. These circumstances may legitimately include the possibility of a subsequent increase in the limit of recoverable damages due to legislative amendment (see *Brown v Parker* [1961] WAR 194) and the enhanced prospect of enforcing a verdict by commencing proceedings in another jurisdiction (eg, *Castanho v Brown & Root (UK) Ltd* (supra)). I would include amongst such circumstances the prospect of the plaintiff being able to conduct the second proceedings more effectively than the first by reason of an improvement in the plaintiff's financial position enabling the plaintiff to procure expert evidence which would have been prohibitively expensive at the time of the first proceedings. A fortiori is this so when the plaintiff's financial inability to conduct the first proceedings effectively is the result of the defendant's own act or omission, whether or not that act or omission ultimately proves to be legitimate.
>
> [34] I am of the view that if RP had commenced its own separate proceedings against the Insurers and had sought leave to discontinue for the reasons which Mr Preston gave, it would have been granted leave subject only to the appropriate conditions as to payment of the Insurers' costs. The fact that RP was a co-plaintiff seeking leave to discontinue in the Earlier Proceedings rather than the plaintiff in its own separate action would have made no difference to the granting of leave. The possibility of a conflict of interest arising if APC and RP were retained as co-plaintiffs in the Earlier Proceedings with the same legal representation would have been a further ground justifying the grant of leave to RP to discontinue.
>
> [35] If, as I hold, the discontinuance by RP as co-plaintiff in the Earlier Proceedings was not an abuse of process, then no question of 'Anshun estoppel' arises in the present case. As noted by Handley JA in *'Anshun Today'* (1997) 71 ALJ 934, the decision in *Port of Melbourne Authority v Anshun Pty Ltd* (supra) is part of an extended doctrine of abuse of process which has been developed from *Henderson v Henderson* (1843) 3 Hare 100; (1843) 67 ER 313. As his Honour says:
>
>> The extended doctrine, of which Anshun is only part, supplements the doctrines of merger, cause of action estoppel and issue estoppel. It can apply where the parties or the causes of action are different. It has never been suggested, however, that it extends an issue estoppel to decisions on questions of fact or law which were not fundamental to the earlier decision. The extended doctrine also applies to later proceedings which are vexatious and hopeless in the light of an earlier decision, and to proceedings which are a collateral attack on an earlier decision ...

[36] It is clear, in my opinion, that the category of abuse of process represented by 'Anshun estoppel', in so far as it is applicable to a plaintiff, is concerned with the situation which arises when that plaintiff prosecutes a cause of action to its conclusion by judgment or settlement and later that plaintiff, or that plaintiff's privy, seeks to prosecute against the same defendant another cause of action which should reasonably have been prosecuted in the first proceedings. The rationale for the doctrine in *Henderson v Henderson*, as developed by *Anshun*, has no application to the case where the plaintiff, or the plaintiff's privy, has commenced earlier litigation against the defendant, but has, with the Court's leave, discontinued that litigation rather than prosecuting it to a conclusion by judgment or settlement.

[37] I am of the view that the Insurers' defence based upon abuse of process or 'Anshun estoppel' fails.

4. In most jurisdictions, an employer (or more particularly, its insurer) is given a statutory right to seek indemnity from a third party tortfeasor for compensation which the employer has been bound to pay to its employee under workers' compensation legislation: see for example, Workers Compensation Act 1987 (NSW) s 151Z(1)(d). The employee may have a common law right to sue the tortfeasor in negligence. Suppose the employee sues the tortfeasor and recovers a judgment in respect of his or her injuries *less* any monies received by way of workers' compensation. Can the workers' compensation insurer (or employer) take proceedings against the tortfeasor for the compensation paid to the employee or is there an estoppel (*res judicata*) created by the judgment? Is the insurer 'privy in interest' to the claim brought by the employee? See *QBE Workers Compensation (NSW) Pty Ltd v Dolan* (2004) 62 NSWLR 42. It was held by the New South Wales Court of Appeal that the statutory right existed independently of the employee's right to bring a claim for damages; there was no privity of interest and no *res judicata*.

Issue estoppel

Definition

10.2.6   Issue estoppel occurs where there is an essential element common to two or more sets of proceedings involving the parties. For example, this might occur when a common issue of liability arises in two actions involving a motor vehicle collision, where, if each proceeding were tried separately, mutually inconsistent decisions might be reached, with the result that a party in one proceeding might be bound by a decision in the other. In such a case the proceedings might be consolidated: *Todd v Jones* [1969] VR 169; *Hinchcliffe v Carroll* [1969] VR 164. The earlier decision might be reopened in light of subsequent evidence becoming available: *Mills v Cooper* [1967] 2 QB 459. Issue estoppel will only apply where the previous determination was made by a court of competent jurisdiction; that is, a court able to hear and determine the earlier proceeding. Otherwise the status of the court is immaterial: *Kosanovic v Sarapuu* [1962] VR 321 (referred to with approval in *Azzopardi v Bois* [1968] VR 183 at 185).

A case which illustrates the distinction between cause of action estoppel and issue estoppel, and which deals with the operation of issue estoppel and exceptions to it, is the decision of the House of Lords in *Arnold v National Westminster Bank Plc* [1991] 2 AC 93, which is extracted below: 10.2.7C.

Arnold v National Westminster Bank Plc
                                         [1991] 2 AC 93
                                         House of Lords

[A judgment adverse to tenants of premises in a rent review case had been given by a High Court judge. The judgment was shown to be erroneous by two Court of Appeal decisions in later cases. The tenant brought proceedings seeking, in effect, the reopening of the findings made in the earlier High Court action.]

Lord Keith of Kinkel (at 104): It is appropriate to commence by noticing the distinction between cause of action estoppel and issue estoppel. Cause of action estoppel arises where the cause of action in the later proceedings is identical to that in the earlier proceedings, the latter having been between the same parties or their privies and having involved the same subject matter. In such a case the bar is absolute in relation to all points decided unless fraud or collusion is alleged, such as to justify setting aside the earlier judgment. The discovery of new factual matter which could not have been found out by reasonable diligence for use in the earlier proceedings does not, according to the law of England, permit the latter to be reopened ... The principles upon which cause of action estoppel is based are expressed in the maxims *nemo debet bis vexari pro una et eadem cause* and *interest rei publicae ut finis sit litium.* Cause of action estoppel extends also to points which might have been but were not raised and decided in the earlier proceedings for the purpose of establishing or negativing the existence of a cause of action.

[His Lordship then referred to the passage from *Henderson v Henderson* set out above at **10.2.2** and continued (at 105):]

It will be seen that this passage appears to have opened the door towards the possibility that cause of action estoppel may not apply in its full rigour where the earlier decision did not in terms decide, because they were not raised, points which might have been vital to the existence or non-existence of a cause of action. The passage has since frequently been treated as settled law, in particular by Lord Shaw, giving the advice of the Judicial Committee of the Privy Council, in *Hoystead v Commissioner of Taxation* [1926] AC 155, 170. That particular part of it which admits the possible existence of exceptional cases was approved by Lord Kilbrandon in *Yat Tung Investment Co Ltd v Dao Heng Bank Ltd* [1975] AC 581, 590:

> The shutting out of a 'subject of litigation' — a power which no court should exercise but after a scrupulous examination of all the circumstances — is limited to cases where reasonable diligence would have caused a matter to be earlier raised; moreover, although negligence, inadvertence or even accident will not suffice to excuse, nevertheless 'special circumstances' are reserved in case justice should be found to require the nonapplication of the rule.

Issue estoppel may arise where a particular issue forming a necessary ingredient in a cause of action has been litigated and decided and in subsequent proceedings between the same parties involving a different cause of action to which the same issue is relevant one of the parties seeks to reopen that issue. This form of estoppel seems first to have appeared in *Duchess of Kingston's* case (1776) 20 St Tr 355. A later instance is *Reg v Inhabitants of the Township of Hartington Middle Quarter* (1855) 4 E & B 780. The name 'issue estoppel' was first attributed to it by Higgins J in the High Court of Australia in *Hoysted v Federal*

Commissioner of Taxation (1921) 29 CLR 537, 561. It was adopted by Diplock LJ in *Thoday v Thoday* [1964] P 181. Having described cause of action estoppel as one form of estoppel *per rem judicatam*, he said, at p 198:

> The second species, which I will call 'issue estoppel,' is an extension of the same rule of public policy. There are many causes of action which can only be established by proving that two or more different conditions are fulfilled. Such causes of action involve as many separate issues between the parties as there are conditions to be fulfilled by the plaintiff in order to establish his cause of action; and there may be cases where the fulfillment of an identical condition is a requirement common to two or more different causes of action. If in litigation upon one such cause of action any of such separate issues as to whether a particular condition has been fulfilled is determined by a court of competent jurisdiction, either upon evidence or upon admission by a party to the litigation, neither party can, in subsequent litigation between one another upon any cause of action which depends upon the fulfillment of the identical condition, assert that the condition was [106] fulfilled if the court has in the first litigation determined that it was not, or deny that it was fulfilled if the court in the first litigation determined that it was.

Issue estoppel, too, has been extended to cover not only the case where a particular point has been raised and specifically determined in the earlier proceedings, but also that where in the subsequent proceedings it is sought to raise a point which might have been but was not raised in the earlier. In *Fidelitas Shipping Co Ltd v VLO Exportchleb* [1966] 1 QB 630, 642, Diplock LJ said:

> In the case of litigation the fact that a suit may involve a number of different issues is recognized by the Rules of the Supreme Court which contain provision enabling one or more questions (whether of fact or law) in an action to be tried before others. Where the issue separately determined is not decisive of the suit, the judgment upon that issue is an interlocutory judgment and the suit continues. Yet I take it to be too clear to need citation of authority that the parties to the suit are bound by the determination of the issue. They cannot subsequently in the same suit advance argument or adduce further evidence directed to showing that the issue was wrongly determined. Their only remedy is by way of appeal from the interlocutory judgment and, where appropriate, an application to the appellate court to adduce further evidence: but such application will only be granted if the appellate court is satisfied that the fresh evidence sought to be adduced could not have been available at the original hearing of the issue even if the party seeking to adduce it had exercised due diligence.
>
> This is but an example of specific application of the general rule of public policy, *nemo debet bis vexari pro una et eadem cause*. The determination of the issue between the parties gives rise to what I ventured to call in *Thoday v Thoday* [1964] P 181, 198 an 'issue estoppel.' It operates in subsequent suits between the same parties in which the same issue arises. A fortiori it operates in any subsequent proceedings in the same suit in which the issue has been determined. The principle was expressed as long ago as 1843 in the words of Wigram VC in *Henderson v Henderson*, 3 Hare 100, 114 which were expressly approved by the Judicial Committee of the Privy Council in *Hoystead v Commissioner of Taxation* [1926] AC 155, 170. I would not seek to better them: ...

Then in *Brisbane City Council v Attorney-General for Queensland* [1979] AC 411, 425, Lord Wilberforce, giving the advice of the Judicial Committee of the Privy Council, said:

> The second defence is one of 'res judicata.' There has, of course, been no actual decision in litigation between these parties as to the issue involved in the present case, but the appellants invoke this defence in its wider sense, according to which a party may be shut out from raising in a subsequent action an issue which he could, and should, have raised in earlier proceedings. The classic statement of this doctrine is contained in the judgment of Wigram VC in *Henderson v Henderson* (1843) 3 Hare 100 and its existence has been [107] reaffirmed by this Board in *Hoystead v Commissioner of Taxation* [1926] AC 155. A recent application of it is to be found in the decision of the Board in *Yat Tung Investment Co Ltd v Dao Heng Bank Ltd* [1975] AC 581. It was, in the judgment of the Board, there described in these words: 'there is a wider sense in which the doctrine may be appealed to, so that it becomes an abuse of process to raise in subsequent proceedings matters which could and therefore should have been litigated in earlier proceedings:' p 590. This reference to 'abuse of process' had previously been made in *Greenhalgh v Mallard* [1947] 2 All ER 255 per Somervell LJ and their Lordships endorse it. This is the true basis of the doctrine and it ought only to be applied when the facts are such as to amount to an abuse: otherwise there is a danger of a party being shut out from bringing forward a genuine subject of litigation.

It thus appears that, although *Henderson v Henderson*, 3 Hare 100, was a case of cause of action estoppel, the statement there by Wigram VC has been held to be applicable also to issue estoppel. That statement includes the observation that there may be special circumstances where estoppel does not operate. The instant case is concerned with the nature of such special circumstances.

[His Lordship then considered cases in which the special circumstances exception had been considered and continued (at 108):]

> It was argued that there was no logical distinction between cause of action estoppel and issue estoppel and that, if the rule was absolute in the one case as regards points actually decided, so it should be in the other case. But there is room for the view that the underlying principles upon which estoppel is based, public policy and justice, have greater force in cause of action estoppel, the subject matter of the two proceedings being identical, than they do in issue estoppel, where the subject matter is different. Once it is accepted that different considerations apply to issue estoppel, it is hard to perceive any logical distinction between a point which was previously raised and decided and one which might have been but was not. Given that the further material which would have put an entirely different complexion on the point was at the earlier stage unknown to the party and could not by reasonable diligence have been discovered by him, it is hard to see why [109] there should be a different result according to whether he decided not to take the point, thinking it hopeless, or argue it faintly without any real hope of success. In my opinion your Lordships should affirm it to be the law that there may be an exception to issue estoppel in the special circumstances that there has become available to a party further material relevant to the correct determination of a point involved in the earlier proceedings, whether or not that point was specifically raised and decided, being material which could not by reasonable diligence have been adduced in those proceedings. One of

the purposes of estoppel being to work justice between the parties, it is open to courts to recognise that in special circumstances inflexible application of it may have the opposite result, as was observed by Lord Upjohn in the passage which I have quoted above from his speech in the *Carl Zeiss* case [1967] 1 AC 853, 947.

[His Lordship then found that there were special circumstances, namely, the fact that the law had changed since the original decision in the High Court. The action was not barred by issue estoppel. Lords Griffiths, Oliver of Aylmerton and Jauncey of Tullichettle concurred. Lord Lowry delivered a speech in which he adopted Lord Keith's conclusions.]

10.2.8   Note and questions

1. See also *Chamberlain v Deputy Commissioner of Taxation* (1988) 164 CLR 502 at 504–550 per Brennan J; at 512 per Dawson J on the special circumstances exception to issue estoppel. See also *Murphy v Abi-Saab* (1995) 37 NSWLR 280 (only a decision on a matter which it is necessary to decide can create an issue estoppel).

2. Is there any reason in principle why the courts should permit an exception to issue estoppel, but not to cause of action estoppel? Should there be any exception to *Port of Melbourne Authority v Anshun Pty Ltd (No 2)* (1981) 147 CLR 589? Is it necessary?

10.2.9 The general view has been that issue estoppel does not apply in cases where separate proceedings are brought for property damage on the one hand, and personal injuries on the other arising out of a tortious act by the defendant. So much was established by a majority of the English Court of Appeal in *Brunsden v Humphrey* (1884) 14 QBD 141 where the plaintiff brought proceedings in the County Court for damages to his cab caused by the defendant's employee. The plaintiff recovered damages. He then brought proceedings in the High Court seeking damages for personal injury arising from the same incident. It was held that the second action was not barred by the previous action.

10.2.10 The New South Wales Court of Appeal in *Marlborough Harbour Board v Charter Travel Co Ltd* (1989) 18 NSWLR 223, a case concerning the founder of the ship the 'Mikhail Lermontov' off the coast of New Zealand, described the majority's view in *Brunsden v Humphrey* as 'curious' (at 230) and noted that its effect ought to be confined to the distinction between personal injury and property damage cases. Hope JA, speaking for the Court of Appeal, said (at 231):

The better view would seem to be that, although for pragmatic and possibly historical reasons separate actions can be brought for damages in respect of personal injuries and damage to property, if an action has been brought for damage to property, or for both personal injury and damage to property, other actions cannot be brought for damage to other property as the result of the same 'causality'. There would not be, as has been submitted in the present case, a separate cause of action in respect of each knife and fork lost when the 'Mikhail Lermontov' sank.

The appellant objected to an application by the respondents to amend their cross-claim (third party notice) against it. It argued that it had submitted to the jurisdiction of the New South Wales courts, as a foreign litigant, on the basis of the claims made in the original cross-claim and that the amendments raised separate causes of action not within the ambit of its original submission. On the assumption that the proposed amendments did in fact raise separate causes of action, it would be appropriate that they be made in the one proceeding. Such causes of action clearly arose out of the essential subject matter of the original cross-claim: at 232.

10.2.11 See also *Azzopardi v Bois* [1968] VR 183 where, in proceedings before a court of petty sessions dealing with a claim and counterclaim for the cost of repairs to their respective motor vehicles, it had been found that both parties were negligent and their claims were reduced accordingly. It was held by Adam J that the plaintiff was estopped from alleging, in Supreme Court proceedings for damages for personal injury, that the accident was wholly due to the defendant's negligence, and from denying that he had been contributorily negligent. The court could, however, vary the apportionment made in the court of petty sessions.

See further, the decision of the Victorian Court of Appeal in *Linsley v Petrie* [1998] 1 VR 427 in which the court followed *Brunsden v Humphrey* (1884) 14 QBD 141. The plaintiff's insurer had brought proceedings in the name of the plaintiff against the defendant seeking damages for damage to her vehicle. A magistrate found that the accident had been the result of circumstances beyond the defendant's control, and that the defendant had not therefore been negligent. There had been judgment for the defendant. The plaintiff sought to sue the defendant for damages for personal injury.

Hayne JA expressed the view that while there was one duty of care owed by the alleged tortfeasor, there might be a different standard of care owed depending upon whether the claim was one for personal injuries or property damage: at 433–5. Smith AJA was of a similar view: at 450. Issue estoppel did not apply. The court did not consider it necessary to decide whether exceptional circumstances should be recognised. In particular, the court refused to decide whether the fact that the first proceeding had been brought by the insurer in the name of the plaintiff made a difference.

10.2.12 Questions

1. Should courts engage in such subtle distinctions?
2. Consider the following situations:
    (a) P, a passenger in a motor vehicle, seeks damages for personal injuries against T, the driver of the vehicle. T's insurers commence third party proceedings against a local government authority (B) seeking contribution in respect of P's claim (but not in respect of T's own claim for damages for personal injuries). B is subsequently joined as a defendant. At trial, liability for P's damages is apportioned two-thirds against T and one-third against B. T sues B for damages for personal injuries. Should T's action be allowed to proceed? See *Talbot v Berkshire County Council* [1994] QB 290 (English Court of Appeal).
    (b) Bank (B) sues T for possession of land mortgaged by T to B. A default judgment for possession is obtained by B against T. T issues proceedings seeking,

among other things, damages for misrepresentation by B to T in respect of the mortgage. Should T's action be allowed to proceed? See *Triantafillidis v National Australia Bank Ltd* [1995] VConvR 54–536: 10.2.5 n 1.

(c) T and J are involved in a two-car collision. T is killed. T's widow commenced an action for damages against J in respect of the death of her husband in a motor vehicle accident. J brought proceedings against T's estate claiming damages for personal injuries. Is J likely to succeed? See *Todd v Jones* [1969] VR 169.

(d) B commences proceedings against C for damages for negligence. A defence is filed in which the defendant relies upon the statute of limitations. S is appointed as the new solicitor for B. S is of the view that, if the defence is made out, B's former solicitors are liable for professional negligence. If the existing action proceeds to judgment, will the solicitors in an independent action be bound by any findings of fact or law in the action against C? See *Birtles v Commonwealth* [1960] VR 247 at 249 per Adam J (10.4.5C), referring to *Green v Berliner* [1936] 2 KB 477.

3. What is the effect of an order at trial that the plaintiff's claim and the defendant's claim/cross-claim be dismissed? Is there any way in which *Port of Melbourne Authority v Anshun Pty Ltd (No 2)* (1981) 147 CLR 589 may be avoided where orders are sought disposing of a proceeding? See *Melbourne Money Pty Ltd v Bryant* [1994] ASC 58,899 (Victorian Appeal Division). It really depends upon whether the proceeding or claims in the proceeding are dismissed. If so, estoppel will operate. Does the discontinuance or withdrawal of a proceeding give rise to the litigation estoppel? See *Running Pigmy Productions Pty Ltd v AMP General Insurance Co Ltd* [2001] NSWSC 431: 10.2.5 n 3.

4. What might constitute special circumstances sufficient to take a matter outside the litigation estoppel principle? See *Arnold v National Westminster Bank Plc* [1991] 2 AC 93: 10.2.7C (change in law between earlier determination and second action); *New Brunswick Railway Co v British and Trust Corp Ltd* [1939] AC 1 (where the earlier judgment is a default judgment).

5. What is the position with a test case or, as it is sometimes called, a lead case? Will the defendant in a test case, in the absence of agreement to that effect, be estopped upon an adverse finding of liability in respect of claims by other claimants arising out of the same circumstances? Will prospective plaintiffs be bound by a finding of liability in favour of the defendant? See *Bishop v Bridgelands Securities* (1990) 25 FCR 311 at 313 per Wilcox J. Is the position different where the prospective plaintiff actively encourages or acquiesces in the test case? See *Ashmore v British Coal Corp* [1990] 2 QB 338 in which the court thought that the prospective plaintiff might be estopped.

6. Does issue estoppel apply to interlocutory applications, such as applications to bring a proceeding out of time? For example, if an injured applicant makes an application to commence proceedings outside a relevant limitation period and fails, can they make a further application based upon fresh evidence? See *D A Christie Pty Ltd v Baker* [1996] 2 VR 582.

RULES GOVERNING JOINDER

The rules and their interpretation

10.3.1 The courts seek to promote and control joinder in a number of ways:

- The courts have created flexible rules regarding joinder of parties and causes of action, and seek to give a liberal construction to those rules.

- The rules regarding consolidation seek to prevent a multiplicity of proceedings.

- The courts will use the amendment rules to ensure that the real issue or issues between the parties are determined. Indeed, the court will allow amendment even during the trial to ensure that the real issue or issues are determined: *Queensland v J L Holdings Pty Ltd* (1997) 71 ALJR 294 (**1.11.7C, 11.2.4**); *Howarth v Adey* [1996] 2 VR 535 (**11.2.4**): compare *Ketteman v Hansel Properties Ltd* [1987] AC 189 where the amendment was sought during the final address of counsel for the plaintiffs. It was held, by majority, that the amendment ought to have been refused. See also *Spiteri v Visyboard Pty Ltd* [2005] VSCA 132. A defendant may conduct a trial in a particular way, having regard to the plaintiff's statement of claim, namely through cross-examination of the plaintiff, on the basis that the plaintiff does not rely upon a particular claim. If the plaintiff applies to amend its pleading to rely upon such claim (in which case, an adjournment would almost be inevitable), the defendant may suffer prejudice by reason of having to conduct a new trial after conducting the first trial in the way that it did. This may occur, for example, through implied admissions made in cross-examination designed to discredit the claim made, but which supports the existence of the claim sought to be made by amendment.

Other matters affecting joinder

10.3.2 The following considerations will be relevant to the question as to who to join and whether to join:

- A litigant's decision to join a party or parties will be dictated by the need to effect a joinder prior to the expiry of any relevant limitation period, in the absence of an agreement of such party or parties that they will not rely on the limitation provision.

- In some jurisdictions, interest on damages is available only from the date upon which a proceeding commenced. This is the position in Victoria (Supreme Court Act 1986 s 60(1)), and Tasmania: Supreme Court Civil Procedure Act 1932 s 34. This will almost certainly require a litigant to effect an immediate joinder in the absence of an agreement to pay interest from an earlier date. In other jurisdictions, statutory interest will run from the date of the accrual of the cause of action: Federal Court of Australia Act 1976 s 51A; ACT r 1616; Civil Procedure Act 2005 (NSW) s 100; Supreme Court Act 1979 (NT) s 84; Supreme Court Act 1995 (Qld) s 47; Supreme Court Act 1935 (SA) s 30C; Supreme Court Act 1935 (WA) s 32.

- With claims in tort, the fact that the doctrine of joint and several liability enables a plaintiff to effect a full recovery against a defendant, even if only liable to a small degree for the plaintiff's loss, will encourage a plaintiff to join as many defendants as possible looking for the defendant with the 'deep pocket': see, in this respect, the *Reports of the Inquiry into the Law of Joint and Several Liability*, July 1994 and January 1995, Commonwealth

Government, in which it was recommended that there be proportionate liability as between joint tortfeasors. In line with the recommendations made by the Ipp Report (*Review of the Law of Negligence*) in relation to civil liability reform, all jurisdictions have moved towards proportionate liability for economic loss in non-personal injuries cases. See, for example, Proportionate Liability Act (NT) and Wrongs Act 1958 (Vic) Pt IVAA. Unfortunately, there has been no real uniformity achieved in relation to these provisions. And see the article, D Byrne J, 'Proportionate Liability in Construction Claims' (2007) 23 *BCL* 10.

- In Victoria, South Australia and the Northern Territory, legislation had previously been enacted to create proportionate liability in building disputes: Building Act 1993 (NT) s 155; Development Act 1993 (SA) s 72; Building Act 1993 (Vic) s 131. What if a plaintiff in a proceeding to which this legislation applies sues one defendant to avoid proportionality? The defendant may apply to join others as defendants (**10.6.3**) or as third parties or cross-defendants (**10.10.1**) who may in turn apply to be added as defendants in the proceeding: see *Boral Resources (Vic) Pty Ltd v Robak Engineering and Construction Pty Ltd* [1999] 2 VR 507. This will then ensure proportionality.

- A party effecting a joinder must consider the consequences for costs in doing so. It does not follow automatically that a plaintiff will be entitled to a Bullock or Sanderson order; that is, an order that an unsuccessful defendant pay directly, or indirectly, the costs of a defendant who successfully defends the plaintiff's action: see **20.5.3–20.5.6**.

- The availability of representative proceedings or class action provisions in a particular jurisdiction will be relevant to the question whether a party opts for traditional joinder: see **10.9.1–10.9.16**.

JOINDER OF PARTIES

10.4.1   In all jurisdictions, other than the Federal Court, a party bringing a proceeding is known as the plaintiff, and the party against whom the proceeding is brought is known as the defendant. In the Federal Court, the names of the parties are applicant and respondent respectively: FCR Sch 1, Dictionary.

Any natural person may be a party. Corporations incorporated under the Corporations Act, bodies given incorporated status under associations incorporation legislation and entities recognised as having status to sue or be sued under the law of a foreign company may also be parties. (See also **10.7.1–10.7.13**). A government may also be a party to a proceeding, whether the government of the Commonwealth, a state or territory or a foreign state. Where a government is party to a proceeding, legislation may require it to act as a model litigant: see, for example, Judiciary Act 1903 (Cth) s 55ZF.

The party bringing the proceeding will normally have the carriage of it and is often referred to as *dominus litus* (see **10.6.2** for an example of this). The party against whom the proceeding is brought may also have their own claim, either against the plaintiff/applicant, or the plaintiff/applicant and some other person (**10.5.4**), or a claim against a non-party: **10.10.1**.

10.4.2   In theory, joinder is concerned with the decision taken by the plaintiff prior to the drawing and issue of proceedings as to who should be party to the proceedings: *Walker v Commonwealth Trading Bank of Australia* (1985) 3 NSWLR 496 at 503 per Needham J. In the post-proceeding period, it is appropriate to speak of addition of parties. In most cases, however, the distinction is blurred because the addition rules often lead back to the joinder rules: see *Birtles v Commonwealth* [1960] VR 247 at 249 per Adam J (**10.4.5C**) where the plaintiff sought to, and was successful in, adding his former solicitors as defendants in circumstances where it was alleged by the initial defendants to an action for personal injuries, among other things, that the claim against them had become statute-barred.

10.4.3E   **Supreme Court (General Civil Procedure) Rules 2005 (Vic)**
                Order 9 — Joinder of Parties and Claims

Permissive joinder of parties
9.02 Two or more persons may join as plaintiffs or defendants in any proceeding —
  (a) where —
     (i) if separate proceedings were brought by or against each of them, some common question of law or fact would arise in all the proceedings; and
     (ii) all rights to relief claimed in the proceeding (whether joint, several or alternative) are in respect of or arise out of the same transaction or series of transactions; or
  (b) where the Court, before or after joinder, gives leave to do so.

10.4.4   There are rules in each of the other jurisdictions which reflect the two arms of Vic r 9.02(a): HCR r 21.01; FCR r 9.02; ACT r 211; NSW r 6.19; NT r 9.02(a); Qld r 65(1); Tas rr 176, 179; WA O 18 r 4(1). In South Australia, it should be noted that the relevant rule (r 73) is broader in that it requires the fulfillment of only one condition. The Australian Capital Territory rule does not refer to the joinder of defendants in the same terms as joinder of plaintiffs. Rule 9.02(a) and its equivalents have been construed liberally: see *Birtles v Commonwealth* [1960] VR 247.

10.4.5C   **Birtles v Commonwealth**
                [1960] VR 247
                Supreme Court of Victoria

[The plaintiff brought proceedings for damages for personal injury arising out of an industrial accident. Each of the defendants maintained that the plaintiff's cause of action was statute-barred. One of the defendants, the State Electricity Commission, alleged that the plaintiff had failed to serve a notice upon it, as required by statute, within six months of the accident. The plaintiff sought to add his original solicitors as defendants to the action alleging negligence in failing to serve the notice. Adam J proceeded to deal with the application on the basis that it fell within the then equivalent of Vic r 9.02(a) (O XVI rr 1, 4, 7).]

Adam J (at 249): [His Honour considered the meaning of the word 'transaction', saying:] [It is] of vague import, but I see no reason why in the circumstances of this case it should not be treated as comprehending, in addition to the accident and the injury sustained by the plaintiff, the further matters of relevance in the action against the original defendants; that is the payments subsequently received by the plaintiff alleged to have been received as weekly payments of compensation, and the fact of the [250] commencement of the action more than two years after the accident. It is in relation to this transaction viewed as a whole that the plaintiff is or is not entitled to relief against the original defendants, and in respect of this transaction as a whole a question of law or fact common to the causes of action alleged against the original defendants and the applicants (the solicitors) arises.

[Of the possibility of the plaintiff commencing an independent action against the former solicitors, his Honour said:]

A grave objection, however, to his adopting this course would have been the risk that he might fail in the action against the original defendants because of the defences taken ... and then fail also in the new action against the solicitors, heard before another tribunal, because he failed to satisfy that tribunal that these defences were soundly based — a prerequisite to his success in the later action. ...

In other words, by litigating their claims against the solicitors in a separate action the plaintiff might possibly, to use a homely phrase, 'fall between two stools'.

10.4.6   This, indeed, might be advanced as a reason why a plaintiff with an alternative claim against a second defendant dependent upon the outcome of an earlier claim against the original defendant, ought always to be permitted to join the first and second defendants as defendants to the one proceeding. In such circumstances, the plaintiff ought to be entitled to a Bullock order in respect of the successful defendant's costs: compare *Norwest Refrigeration Services Pty Ltd v Bain Dawes (WA) Pty Ltd* (1984) 157 CLR 149, and *Reid v Campbell Wallis Moule & Co Pty Ltd* [1990] VR 859. See also **20.5.3–20.5.6**.

10.4.7   In *Payne v Young* (1980) 145 CLR 609, Mason J said regarding HCR O 16 r 1(1) (at 618):

The consequence is that under para (a) of the rule joinder of separate causes of action accruing to different plaintiffs is authorised when the relief claimed is in respect of, or arises out of, the same or a particular series of transactions. Joinder is not authorized when the relief claimed is in respect of, or arises out of, two or more different series of transactions, when the participation of each individual plaintiff is limited to participation in one series of transactions, the other plaintiffs not participating in that series.

In that case, in each plaintiff's claim, a declaration was sought as to the invalidity of regulations affecting abattoirs in Western Australia. Each plaintiff operated a different abattoir. It was said that the claim for a declaration did not arise out of any transaction or series of transactions: at 614 per Barwick CJ. Mason J (at 618) said that there was no common participation by the plaintiffs in the inspection services the subject of the impugned regulations; 'each series of transactions was peculiar to each individual plaintiff'. Murphy J (at 623) dissented, regarding the rule as remedial, to be construed liberally.

See also the High Court's decision in *Richardson v Trautwein* (1942) 65 CLR 585, where the official receiver and trustee of the estate of a bankrupt sought relief against several respondents in respect of different properties said to belong to the bankrupt estate.

10.4.8   In Victoria, there is a series of unreported decisions which support the proposition that if only one arm of r 9.02(a) can be satisfied, this may provide a basis upon which the court can grant leave to join (see further **10.4.10**): *Glenwood Management Pty Ltd v Mayo* (unreported, SC(Vic), Young CJ, No 8421 of 1990, 14 August 1990, BC9000705); *Zentahope Pty Ltd v Bellotti* (unreported, SC(Vic), Fullagar, Brooking and Tadgell JJ, No 3474 of 1989,

2 March 1992, BC9203164); *A & J Partitions Pty Ltd v Jolly* (unreported SC(Vic), Beach J, 16 February 1993, BC9300648); *Meadow Gem Pty Ltd v ANZ Executors and Trustee Co Ltd* (unreported, SC(Vic), Hedigan J, F3968, 25 August 1993, BC9300768).

10.4.9 Questions

1. Does the decision in *Payne v Young* mean that, where several plaintiff's make claims in respect of the validity of legislation or regulations, the 'same transaction or series of transactions' condition will never be satisfied? What is the position with regard to several plaintiffs each of whom is party to a separate contract with the defendant, albeit in identical terms where it is alleged that each plaintiff was induced to enter into the contract as the result of similar, though not identical, representations made by the defendant? See *Hagan v Bank of Melbourne Ltd* [1994] 2 Qd R 507.

2. D purchased a cello from F, an antique dealer. The cello was stolen from M. The cello was returned to M, its true owner. D brought proceedings against F for damages. He joined M as a defendant so that he might obtain an order for inspection of the cello to establish his damages. He had no other claim against M. Should the joinder be allowed? See *Douibech v Findlay* [1990] 1 WLR 269.

10.4.10 In most jurisdictions there is a rule equivalent to Vic r 9.02(b) which enables the court to give leave to join: HCR r 21.01; ACT r 211(1)(b); NSW r 6.19(1); NT r 9.02(b); SA r 73(1)(c) and (2)(c). There is no equivalent provision in the Federal Court, but the court has an express general power to dispense with compliance with its rules: FCR r 1.34. In Queensland and Tasmania there is no equivalent to the Victorian r 9.02(b), but in each of those states there are rules which permit joinder of defendants and respondents where there is doubt as to the person from whom the plaintiffs are entitled to relief or as to the defendants' respective liability: Qld r 65(2); Tas r 178. *Bishop v Bridgelands Securities* (1990) 25 FCR 311 (10.4.11C) examines the scope of Vic r 9.02(b) and its equivalents in other jurisdictions.

10.4.11C	**Bishop v Bridgelands Securities**
	(1990) 25 FCR 311
	Federal Court of Australia

[The applicant to proceedings in the Federal Court sought both declarations that the respondents had engaged in conduct in contravention of the Trade Practices Act 1974 (Cth) s 52 and Securities Industry Act 1980 (Cth) s 68E(1) and also damages. The proceedings concerned representations made in letters sent by the respondent to the applicant and some 114 other persons who, as the result of the representations, had invested monies on an unsecured basis with a company which failed. Reference was made to the High Court's decision in *Payne v Young* (1980) 145 CLR 609. It was accepted that the investors' claims could not be said to arise out of the same transaction or series of transactions.]

Wilcox J (at 314): However, counsel for the applicant pressed a claim for the grant of leave under subr (b). This subrule, which has no counterpart in the High Court Rules, confers a general discretion on the Court to permit joinder in any appropriate case, without any of the limitations which are contained in subr (a). Subrule (b) has not often been used. The only case of which I am aware is *Trade Practices Commission v Westco Motors (Distributors) Pty Ltd* (1981) 58 FLR 384, a case whose facts were so different from those of the present case as to afford no guidance to me.

As the discretion conferred by subr (b) is, in terms, unconfined, it would be inappropriate to specify circumstances in which it might be applied. Everything must depend upon the facts of the particular case. But it is appropriate to consider what principles ought to guide the exercise of such a discretion. The basic principle, as it seems to me, is that the Court should take whatever course seems to be most conducive to a just resolution of the disputes between the parties, but having regard to the desirability of limiting, so far as practicable, the costs and delay of the litigation. Considerations of costs and delay may often support the grant of leave under subr (b); but, in my opinion, leave ought not to be granted unless the Court is affirmatively satisfied that joinder is unlikely to result in unfairness to any party. Secondly, regard must be had to practical matters. For example, it would normally be inappropriate to grant leave for the joinder of applicants who were represented by different solicitors. There must be a single solicitor, or firm of solicitors, who is accountable for the conduct of the proceeding on the applicants' side of the case. Similarly, although all applicants might propose to rely upon some common, or similar facts, there may be such differences between the evidence intended to be relied upon in support of the claims of particular applicants as to make it inexpedient to join the claims. The discrete material may overbear that which is common to all the claims. Again, there may be cases in which the sheer number of the claims, if joinder [315] is permitted, will impose an undue burden on the respondent; although it seems to me unlikely that this will be so except in cases where separate evidence is proposed to be adduced in support of individual claims.

When the present matter was argued, a point which troubled me was Mr Clay's reference to some oral representations. Depending, perhaps, upon the number of such conversations, it seemed to me that these conversations might result in joinder proving unduly burdensome to the respondents. It might be one thing to require respondents to meet 114 claims which all depend upon the contents of three particular letters; it might be another thing altogether to require them to deal with a host of separate conversations involving individual applicants.

However, when this question was raised, counsel for the applicant informed me that, if joinder was permitted, each of the applicants would be prepared to forgo any reliance upon the oral communications. Each of them would be prepared to limit their case, in relation to misrepresentations, to the letters which they had received. Most of the applicants claimed to have received all three letters. Nineteen conceded that they had not received the letter of 24 October 1989, two conceded that they had not received the letter of 3 July 1990. Counsel submitted that, if the cases were so confined, the only task of the court, in connection with misrepresentation, would be to determine the meaning of the letters; a task which would have to be undertaken even if Ms Bishop's claim stood alone. In relation to loss, it would be necessary to trace the funds managed by Bridgelands and deal with recoverability of the loan; but, once again, this would be necessary in any event. Of course, it would also be necessary to adduce evidence, in respect of each applicant, of the amount of that person's deposit, the receipt of the relevant letters and of reliance upon the representations which they contained. Counsel for the applicants conceded that the issue of reliance might involve cross-examination of each of the applicants, with the possibility of differing findings on that issue as between different applicants. But they submitted that, otherwise, the case was substantially a documentary case. They said that, although joinder would make the proceeding more complex and expensive than a proceeding in which Ms Bishop was the sole applicant, a joint proceeding would be markedly more satisfactory than the alternative, 114 separate proceedings.

The application ... for leave under O 6, r 2(b) was opposed by counsel for the respondents. They emphasised the matters already noted by me, as concessions of the applicant. They made the point that, traditionally, the common law courts have required that separate causes of action be separately litigated. They suggested that r 2(a) was carefully framed so as to indicate the types of cases suitable for joinder and that the Court ought not to exercise its discretion in other cases in such a manner as to force joinder upon an unwilling respondent.

At the conclusion of the argument on 28 August, I reached a tentative conclusion that this was a case in which leave ought to be granted under O 6 r 2(b). Although I think that this power ought to be cautiously exercised, it seemed to me that there were a number of unusual features of this case which enabled me to reach the affirmative conclusion that joinder would be unlikely to result in unfairness to any party.

In relation to unfairness, I thought that it was important that the case was substantially dependent upon documents. The terms of the letters were likely [316] to be of critical importance, but there would be no extra burden imposed on the respondents in arguing the proper construction of those letters in the context of a claim by 114 persons rather than one. The financial records would also be important, but the respondents already have possession of records relating to all claimants. Little additional work would be involved in tracing the deposits claimed to have been made by the extra applicants. The fate of the money placed by the respondents with Estate Mortgage Financial Services would need to be investigated, but this would be so even if there was but a single claim. The major complication of the joinder of the additional applicants would be in connection with the reliance evidence. However, it seemed to me that, whilst it would be burdensome to challenge evidence of reliance from 114 separate applicants in one proceeding, the burden was not so great that this factor ought to be determinative. I had in mind that affidavits could be directed and that the respondents could determine which if any, of the applicants would be required for cross-examination. Even if all applicants were cross-examined on this point, the length and cost of the proceeding would be much less than if 114 separate claims were litigated.

Moreover, it seemed to me that there were advantages in all the claims being litigated at one time. I was told that the total value of all the claims lay between $5 million and $6 million. I do not know the extent of the respondents' resources but it is possible that they would not extend to payment of all claims, if all were successful. It seemed to me to be inherently undesirable to take a course which would allow one claimant to advance her claim to judgment, and so be in a position to recover in full against the respondents, while the claims of other persons, in a like situation, were, in a practical sense, stayed. [I say this because it would be quite unreasonable to expect the respondents simultaneously to work on 114 separate claims, with separate, perhaps different pleadings, directions etc. Nor could the court accommodate the hearing of a multitude of separate cases within an acceptable period of time.]

10.4.12 Questions

1. Is the discretion given by Vic r 9.02(b) in fact unconfined as suggested by Wilcox J?

2. In *Hagan v Bank of Melbourne Ltd* [1994] 2 Qd R 507, there were claims by several plaintiffs in respect of separate contracts with the defendant. In respect of two of those contracts, it was alleged that similar, though not identical, representations

had been made by the defendant. That factor did not exist in respect of the third contract. Should joinder be allowed in respect of all plaintiffs? If not, why not?

3. Can a party be joined solely for the purpose of obtaining discovery from that party? A good example is an application to join a defendant's liability insurer to gain access to documents held by the insurer, including the policy of insurance and the insurer's file relating to the question of indemnity. The question whether the defendant has insurance and whether it will grant indemnity, and for what sum, are matters of great interest to the plaintiff. Recent decisions hold that joinder should not be permitted, at least where the insurer has not denied indemnity: *C E Heath Casualty and General Insurance Ltd v Pyramid Building Society (in liq)* [1997] 2 VR 256 (Victorian Court of Appeal); *Beneficial Finance Corp Ltd v Price Waterhouse* (1996) 68 SASR 19 (South Australian Full Court) (special leave to appeal to the High Court refused). In that case, the court rejected the view taken at first instance that it was in the interest of case management for the plaintiff to know what the position might be in relation to the liability insurance held by the defendant; the defendant's insurer had refused to either admit or deny indemnity. See and compare *J N Taylor Holdings Ltd (in liq) v Bond* (1993) 59 SASR 432 (where indemnity had been denied).

4. How are discovery (disclosure in Queensland) and interrogation to be handled in cases involving multiple plaintiffs (or defendants)?

Mandatory or compulsory joinder

10.4.13E	Uniform Civil Procedure Rules 2005 (NSW)

6.20 Proceedings affecting persons having joint entitlement

(1) Unless the court orders otherwise, all persons jointly entitled to the same relief must be joined as parties in any claim for that relief that is made by any one or more of them.

(2) Unless the court orders otherwise, any other such person is to be joined:

  (a) as a plaintiff, if he or she consents to being a plaintiff, or

  (b) as a defendant, if he or she does not consent to being a plaintiff.

(3) Despite subrule (1), a person may not be joined as a party to proceedings in contravention of any other Act or law.

6.21 Proceedings affecting persons having joint or several liability

(1) A person who is jointly and severally liable with some other person in relation to any act, matter or thing need not be a defendant in proceedings with respect to that act, matter or thing merely because the other person is a defendant in those proceedings.

(2) In any proceedings in which a defendant is one of a number of persons who are jointly, but not severally, liable in contract or tort, or under an Act or statutory instrument, the court may order that the other persons be joined as defendants and that the proceedings be stayed until those other persons have been so joined.

...

> **6.23 Effect of misjoinder or non-joinder of parties**
> Proceedings are not defeated merely because of the misjoinder or non-joinder of any person as a party to the proceedings.
>
> [See also: FCR rr 9.03, 9.04, 9.07; ACT rr 213–214, 218 and see also r 215; NT rr 9.03, 9.05; Qld rr 62, 63, 64, 67; SA rr 73(3), 74(1), 77; Vic rr 9.03, 9.05; WA O 18 rr 4(2), 4(3), 6. In the High Court and Tasmania, there are no rules for mandatory joinder. There is, however, provision in relation to misjoinder (HCR r 21.04 and Tas r 181) and misjoinder where there is a counterclaim: Tas r 175. Cf Civil Proceedings Act 2011 (Qld) s 17(2): a person given notice of an order that it be a party to litigation will be bound by the outcome if it elects not to be included.]

10.4.14   Rule 6.23 and its counterparts are designed to eliminate the plea in abatement, which was available in common law actions prior to the Judicature Acts; that is, where two or more persons were jointly liable upon a contract, the failure to join one of them as defendant released those persons joined as defendants, and gave rise to a substantive defence in the defendant or defendants joined: *Van Gelder v Sowerby Bridge Society* (1890) 44 Ch D 374 at 391, 394. The rule is consistent with the objectives underlying the Judicature Act provision to be found, for example, in the Supreme Court Act 1986 (Vic) s 29(2): see **10.1.2E**. Speaking of the English equivalent, Lord Esher MR in *Byrne v Brown* (1889) 22 QBD 657 at 666–766 said that the rule should be construed so as to give effect to the objectives of the Judicature Act.

JOINDER OF CLAIMS

By the plaintiff

> **10.5.1E**   **Supreme Court (General Civil Procedure)**
> Rules 2005 (Vic)
> Order 9 — Joinder of Claims and Parties
>
> **Joinder of claims**
> **9.01** A plaintiff may join any number of claims against a defendant whether the plaintiff makes the claims in the same or in different capacities and whether the claims are made against the defendant in the same or in different capacities.
> ...
>
> **Joinder inconvenient**
> **9.04** Notwithstanding Rules 9.01 and 9.02, where any joinder of claims or of parties may embarrass or delay the trial of the proceeding or cause prejudice to any party or is otherwise inconvenient, the Court may order that —
> (a) there be separate trials;
> (b) any claim be excluded;
> (c) any party be compensated by an award of costs or otherwise for being required to attend, or be relieved from attending, any part of a trial in which he has no interest;
> (d) any party made a party cease to be a party on condition that he be bound by the determination of the questions in the proceeding or without any such condition.
>
> [See also: HCR r 21.03 ; FCR r 9.06; ACT rr 200–202; NSW rr 6.18, 6.22; NT rr 9.01, 9.04; Qld rr 60, 68; SA r 30 ; Tas rr 169, 179(3); WA O 18 rr 1(1), 5(1)].

10.5.2   It will be noted that Vic r 9.04 and its counterparts apply to both joinder of claims and parties. The power given to the court by the rule is discretionary: *Thomas v Moore* [1918] 1 KB 555. However, in determining whether joinder should be permitted or whether one of the courses referred to in r 9.04 should be adopted, the court will naturally be concerned to consider matters of *res judicata* and issue estoppel: see **10.2.1–10.2.12**.

10.5.3   Question

1.   Two plaintiffs claim damages for slander against two defendants. Some slanders are alleged to have been published by defendant 1, others by defendant 2. Should both claims proceed in the one action? See *Sandes v Wildsmith* [1893] 1 QB 771. Are they separate claims by different plaintiffs in respect of different slanders? There might be evidence admissible in an action against defendant 1 which would be inadmissible in an action against defendant 2, but which might be damaging to defendant 2. Is this a factor which might require separate trials, assuming the plaintiff's elect for trial by jury? See *Sandes v Wildsmith* [1893] 1 QB at 774 per Wills J.

By the defendant — counterclaims and set-off

10.5.4   See further **10.6.1E–10.6.5**.

Counterclaim

10.5.5   Prior to the Judicature Act there was no provision for counterclaim. By counterclaim, the defendant may not only make a claim against the plaintiff, but seek to join a third person or persons to the counterclaim. Claims other than monetary claims can be made the subject of a counterclaim, unlike a defendant's claim to set-off. In the absence of any rule or statutory provision to the contrary, a claim and counterclaim would result in two judgments, although for the purpose of execution, they would be set off against each other. It follows that the plaintiff would normally be entitled to its costs of the claim and the defendant to its costs of the counterclaim: *McDonnell & East Pty Ltd v McGregor* (1936) 56 CLR 50 at 62 per Dixon J (McTiernan J concurring).

All jurisdictions, other than the High Court, have rules regarding counterclaims or their equivalents: FCR Pt 15; ACT rr 460–474; NSW Pt 9 and see Civil Procedure Act 2005 (NSW) s 22; NT O 10; Qld rr 175–85; SA r 35; Tas rr 192–200; Vic O 10; WA O 18 rr 2, 3. In the Federal Court and in New South Wales, counterclaims are a form of 'cross-claim', as are third party proceedings (and see r 35 of the SA rules which refers to cross-action). In the Federal Court and in New South Wales, a cross-claim against a person not party to the original proceeding will be permitted only where the relief claimed against that person is related to, or connected with the subject of the proceeding: FCR r 15.01(b); Civil Procedure Act (NSW) s 22. This may also be said of Western Australia: see O 18 r 3(1).

10.5.6   Question

1. S sues for the price of goods sold to B by way of a contract where the risk of damage would pass to B upon delivery to the railway (an FOB contract). B counterclaims for damages, alleging, against S, that the goods were not delivered in good condition and, against the railway, a new defendant by counterclaim, that if the goods had been delivered to them in good condition, any damage was due to their negligence as carriers. Should the counterclaim be struck out? Can claims be made against the plaintiff and the additional party in the alternative? See *Smith v Buskell* [1919] 2 KB 362. See also *Re Richardson* [1933] WN 90 and *D G Madin Ltd v Gordon* [1964] SASR 64.

10.5.7   In the Northern Territory and Victoria, r 10.03 provides:

A defendant may join with the plaintiff as defendant to the counterclaim any other person, whether a party to the proceeding or not, who, if the defendant were to bring a separate proceeding, could properly be joined with the plaintiff as a party in accordance with Rule 9.02.

The defendant must satisfy the ordinary joinder rules.

In other jurisdictions there is no express restriction in the rules on the joinder of non-parties to a counterclaim, although it is implicit that there should be some common question in the proceedings. Consider *Smith v Buskell* [1919] 2 KB 362 in respect of jurisdictions other than the Federal Court and New South Wales.

An example of a notice of counterclaim where a defendant is a new party is extracted below.

10.5.8E   **Supreme Court (General Civil Procedure) Rules 2005 (Vic)**
                 Form 10A — Heading and Notice on Counterclaim Where Defendant New
                                  [Supreme Court only]

IN THE SUPREME COURT
OF VICTORIA
AT 20 *No.*
BETWEEN
AB Plaintiff
and
CD Defendant

                              (by original proceeding)

AND BETWEEN
CD Plaintiff
and
AB and *EF* Defendants
(by counterclaim)

To *EF*
of [*address*]

TAKE NOTICE that this proceeding has been brought against you by the defendant for the claim set out in this counterclaim.

IF YOU INTEND TO DEFEND the claim YOU MUST GIVE NOTICE of your intention by filing an appearance within the proper time for appearance stated below.

YOU OR YOUR SOLICITOR may file the appearance. An appearance is filed by:

- (a) filing a 'Notice of Appearance' in the Prothonotary's office in the Law Courts, William Street, Melbourne, or, where the counterclaim has been filed in the office of a Deputy Prothonotary, in the office of that Deputy Prothonotary; and
- (b) on the day you file the Notice, serving a copy, sealed by the Court, at the defendant's address for service, which is set out at the end of the counterclaim.

IF YOU FAIL to file an appearance within the proper time, the defendant may OBTAIN JUDGMENT AGAINST YOU on the counterclaim without further notice.

*THE PROPER TIME TO FILE AN APPEARANCE is as follows —

- (a) where you are served with the counterclaim in Victoria, within 10 days after service;
- (b) where you are served with the counterclaim out of Victoria and in another part of Australia, within 21 days after service;
- (c) where you are served with the counterclaim in New Zealand or in Papua New Guinea, within 28 days after service;
- (d) where you are served with the counterclaim in any other place, within 42 days after service.

COUNTERCLAIM

[Set out in separate, consecutively numbered paragraphs all the material facts relied upon for the counterclaim and state precisely the relief claimed.]

The address of the defendant is —

The address for service of the defendant is —

*[Strike out this paragraph where order made fixing time for appearance and substitute

'THE PROPER TIME TO FILE AN APPEARANCE is within … days after service on you of this counterclaim.']

What is the nature of a counterclaim?

10.5.9C   Aurel Forras Pty Ltd v Graham Karp Developments Pty Ltd
[1975] VR 202
Supreme Court of Victoria

[The plaintiff was a builder and the defendant an owner. The plaintiff sued for monies said to be due under building contracts. The defendant counterclaimed. The plaintiff, in a counterclaim, served with its reply and defence to the defendant's counterclaim, made claims under a further contract which had largely arisen after the filing of the writ in the proceeding, alternatively, before the filing of the writ. Menhennitt J was asked to determine whether the plaintiff's counterclaim should be struck out. He decided that a plaintiff was able to counterclaim against a defendant, at least in respect of claims which had arisen after the commencement of the action. In so doing, his Honour examined the nature of a counterclaim.]

Menhennitt J (at 218): Thus in *Winterfield v Bradnum* (1873) 3 QBD 324 Brett, LJ said at p 326:

> [219] I think the true mode of considering the claim and counterclaim is, that they are wholly independent suits which, for convenience of procedure, are combined in one action.

Cotton, LJ said at p 326:

> The counterclaim is in the nature of a new action.

In *Stooke v Taylor* (1880) 5 QBD 569, Cockburn, CJ said at pp 573–4:

> Let us see, then, how the matter stands under the new system introduced by the Judicature Acts. A defendant, who, having a claim for unliquidated damages against the plaintiff suing him, must before have brought a crossaction, is now enabled to meet the plaintiff's claim by counterclaim, in other words, by a proceeding which, without being in form a crossaction, is so in substance — for that is what a counterclaim in effect amounts to.

He further said at p 574:

> In effect each party establishing his claim recovers to that amount in his own action.

At p 576 he said:

> This reasoning does not apply to a counterclaim, the effect of which, as distinguished from a mere setoff, is altogether different. It is, as I have already pointed out, to all intents and purposes an action by the defendant against the plaintiff ... But the most striking difference is that the counterclaim operates not merely as a defence, as does the setoff, but in all respects as an independent action by the defendant against the plaintiff.

Manisty, J said at p 587:

> A counterclaim, properly so called, is the creature of the Judicature Act 1873. It is an independent suit, which, for the sake of convenience of procedure may be tried at the same time as the claim (see per Brett, LJ, in *Winterfield v Bradnum* 3 QB 324).

However, the decision most directly in point is that of the Court of Queens Bench Division (Field J and Huddleston B) in *Toke v Andrews* (1882) 8 QBD 428, where it was held that a plaintiff was entitled to counterclaim against the defendant's counterclaim for an amount which became due after the issue of the writ. The Court held that the right in the plaintiff to counterclaim against the defendant's counterclaim was within the words and spirit of the provisions of s 24(3) and s 24(7) of the Judicature Act 1873, equivalent to what are now s 61(3) and s 61(7) of the Victorian Supreme Court Act 1958 [since repealed]. Further, although the Court did not expressly so decide, it was very strongly disposed to think that the plaintiff's right to counterclaim fell within O 19 r 3 of the English rules the terms of which were identical with the present O 19 r 3 of the Victorian Supreme Court Rules.

In my opinion there is no later decision of which I am aware which is to the contrary of this basic approach to the matter. Accordingly I conclude that a plaintiff's right to counterclaim against a defendant's counterclaim is to be found in s 61(3) and s 61(7) of the Supreme Court Act 1958 [since repealed] and O 19 r 3 [now O 10 r 3] of the Supreme Court Rules ...

[220] This leaves two further matters. One is as to the position where the plaintiff seeks to rely on a claim which he puts in the alternative, primarily as arising after the issue in the writ but, in the alternative, as arising before the issue of the writ. In so far as it is claimed as arising after the issue of the writ, the only way in which he can raise it, except with the consent of the defendant, is in the plaintiff's counterclaim. The only thing which might stand in the way of him raising it in the alternative, on the basis that it arose before the issue of the writ, is O 19 r 16. However, overriding all the rules is [221] the provision of s 61(7) of the Supreme Court Act that the Court in every cause or matter pending before it shall grant all such remedies whatsoever as any of the parties appear to be entitled to in respect of any legal or equitable claim properly brought forward, so that as far as possible all matters in controversy between the parties may be completely and finally determined and all multiplicity of legal proceedings concerning any of such matters avoided. Further, in *Renton Gibbs and Coy, Ltd v Neville and Co* [1900] QB 181, the Court of Appeal, whilst recognizing that as a rule a plaintiff who seeks to raise an additional claim should seek an amendment to his statement of claim and not raise it in a plaintiff's counterclaim, none the less held that there are exceptions to that rule and in that case refused to strike out the plaintiff's counterclaim, which raised a claim that clearly arose before the issue of the writ. The Court of Appeal so decided because the plaintiffs were primarily denying that the contract relied upon by the defendant in its counterclaim bound the plaintiff but were contending that, if it did, then the plaintiff made a counterclaim under it. Accordingly, it appears to me that where, as here, the prime basis upon a claim is made by a plaintiff is that it arose after the issue of the writ, it is permissible to include in a plaintiff's counterclaim claims in the alternative on the basis that they arose before the issue of the writ, including, in the alternative, claims on a quantum meruit or quantum valebant basis which arose partly before and partly after the issue of the writ.

The second point is whether on the plaintiff's counterclaim the plaintiff is entitled to claim and recover any amount in excess of the amount claimed or for which the defendant is entitled to recover on the defendant's counterclaim. If the rules apply in their entirety to the plaintiff's counterclaim, the plaintiff is, because r 16 and r 17 of O 21 expressly so provide. However it is contended for the defendant that the plaintiff can use his counterclaim only as a shield and not as a sword. One question is what this expression means. If something is raised as an answer to a claim, it is in one sense always a shield and it does not cease to be a shield because it is larger than the claim. A shield is commonly larger than the offensive weapon against which protection is sought. If the contention that a plaintiff's counterclaim can be used only as a shield and not a sword means that the plaintiff cannot recover on it an amount in excess of the amount to which the defendant may be entitled under the defendant's counterclaim, it would be clearly contrary to the provisions of O 21 r 17. Even more clearly, if the defendant's counterclaim were dismissed altogether, it would be quite contrary to the provisions of not only O 21 r 16 but also s 61(7) of the Supreme Court Act to hold that at that stage of the proceedings, after the whole issues had been litigated, judgment could not be given for the plaintiff on its counterclaim. The contention that the plaintiff may use a counterclaim only as a shield not as a sword might refer to the principle that, as a general rule, a plaintiff should not raise in a plaintiff's counterclaim a claim which unequivocally arose before the issue of the writ. The contention might also be claimed to cover a situation where a plaintiff seeks in a counterclaim to raise a matter which is so unrelated to the plaintiff's original claim or to the defendant's counterclaim that it could properly be said not to be a counterclaim at all, but this would run contrary to the principle that a counterclaim may raise claims quite unrelated to the opposing claim (see *Williams Supreme Court Practice* (2nd ed) p 1301). [222] Further in the present case no such issue arises. In the defendant's counterclaim the defendant itself brought into the litigation claims in respect of the third contract and I dismissed the plaintiff's application for those claims to be struck out, and the main claims by the plaintiff in its counterclaim relate to this third contract and are clearly raised as counter to the defendant's claims in its counterclaim and the only other claim raised by the plaintiff in its counterclaim is one under the first contract which is claimed as arising after the issue of the writ.

It is important, I think to examine the context in which the expression 'not as a shield but as a sword' was used. In *Renton Gibbs and Co Ltd v Neville and Co* [1900] 2 QB 181, the Court of Appeal permitted a plaintiff to rely in a plaintiff's counterclaim on a claim which clearly arose before the issue of the writ. It did so on the basis that the plaintiff denied that it was a party to the contract on which the defendant was relying in the defendant's counterclaim but said that, if the defendant could rely on that contract, it, the plaintiff, then wanted to make a counterclaim thereunder. To distinguish *James v Page* (1888) 85 LT (Jo) 157, Collins, LJ said that there 'a counterclaim was used not as a shield but as a sword'. This was, I think, a reference to the fact that the plaintiff in *James v Page* wanted to rely in a counterclaim on a new claim which stood on its own feet and which clearly arose before the issue of the writ. Collins, LJ did not say a plaintiff on his counterclaim cannot be given the full relief to which he is entitled on the claims there put forward and the Court of Appeal did not decide that a plaintiff on his counterclaim cannot recover any amount in excess of the amount for which the defendant is counterclaiming or in excess of any amount the defendant may recover on his counterclaim. In *Herbert v Vaughan* [1972] 1 WLR 1128, the plaintiffs sought to rely in a counterclaim on what was held to be a new claim and one inconsistent with their statement of claim, and it was held, in accordance with the general rule stated in *Renton Gibbs and Co Ltd v Neville and Co*, that the plaintiff's counterclaim should be struck out and that the plaintiffs should apply to amend their statement of claim. In *The Normar* [1968] P 362; [1968] 1 All ER 753, Cairns J said at p 370 that the statement by Collins LJ in *Renton Gibbs and Co Ltd v Neville and Co* that a plaintiff's counterclaim was permissible as a shield rather than as a sword meant 'that it could be used only to such extent as might be necessary to defeat the counterclaim of the defendant, but not by way of claiming something against the defendant over and above the amount for which he was counterclaiming.' In my respectful opinion, this statement, which was not essential to the decision, gives an unjustifiable meaning to the expression 'not as a shield but as a sword'. In my view, there is nothing in the Supreme Court Act 1958 or the Supreme Court Rules and no principle or judicial decision which leads to the conclusion that there is any limit on the amount a plaintiff may recover on a plaintiff's counterclaim. In my view, all that is involved in Collins LJ's statement that in *James v Page* the counterclaim was sought to be used not as a shield but as a sword is that, where a plaintiff seeks to rely upon a claim which stands on its own feet and could have been included in his statement of claim, he should, in general, apply to amend his statement of claim. Where, however, as in *Renton Gibbs and Co Ltd v Neville and Co* the plaintiff is advancing a counterclaim only if, contrary to its prime contention, the basis of the defendant's counterclaim is upheld, [223] or where, as in the present case, the prime claims made by the plaintiff in its counterclaim are ones which the plaintiff is precluded from having included in its statement of claim, except by the consent of the defendant, because they are claimed to arise after the issue of the writ, and those claims are put forward in the alternative only if it should be held that they arose before the issue of the writ, then I think that, not only is the plaintiff entitled to raise its claims in its counterclaim, but there is no limit to the amount which the plaintiff can recover on its counterclaim.

For all the reasons I have given, my conclusion is that the plaintiff's counterclaim should not be struck out.

10.5.10   Note and questions

1. Menhennitt J referred to *Toke v Andrews* (1882) 8 QBD 428 as authority for the view that the plaintiff might counterclaim for an amount which became due after the issue of the writ. At that time, Victoria did not have a rule in terms of the present r 36.01(3), which permits a plaintiff to amend a proceeding to add a cause of action arising after the date of issue of proceedings. Was his Honour correct? See *Baldry v Jackson* [1976] 2 NSWLR 415, where the plaintiff had issued his own proceeding for contribution and indemnity in respect of any damages which he might be liable to pay as defendant in an action that had already been commenced, but had not been finalised. It was held that the plaintiff's statement of claim should be struck out as being in respect of an inchoate cause of action, although the New South Wales Court of Appeal stated that had the proceeding been brought by cross-claim in the other proceeding, the cross-claim might have been sustained: at 419–20.

2. Can a defendant against whom judgment has been entered in default of defence and who subsequently files a defence and counterclaim obtain judgment against the plaintiff in default of defence to counterclaim? See *Shanks & Co Pty Ltd v Hohne* [1963] VR 1 98, and also Qld R 183.

10.5.11   A court has power to exclude a counterclaim from a proceeding or to order that it be separately determined: FCR r 15.3 (through directions); ACT r 471; NSW r 9.8(a); NT r 10.06; Qld r 182; Tas r 198; Vic r 10.06; WA O 18 r 5(2). There is no equivalent rule in South Australia, but the same result could be achieved under the more general rules relating to consolidation and separation of actions: r 31.

Set-off

10.5.12E   **Supreme Court Rules 1987 (NT)**
Order 13 — Pleadings

Money claim as a defence

13.14 Where a defendant has a claim against a plaintiff for the recovery of a debt or damages, the claim may be relied upon as a defence to the whole or part of the claim made by the plaintiff for the recovery of a debt or damages and may be included in the defence and set off against the plaintiff's claim, whether or not the defendant also claims for that debt or damages.

10.5.13 This rule relates to pleading. The rule would appear to abolish the distinction between set-off and counterclaim in most cases, but recognises that, particularly with regard to claims other than monetary claims, the distinction will continue: *M E K Nominees Pty Ltd v Billboard Entertainments Pty Ltd* (1993) VConvR 544-68; see G McEwan, 'An Update on Equitable Estoppel' [1993] *LIJ* 264.

Historically, set-off was used by a defendant as a shield rather than a sword. A single judgment only would be obtained. The defendant relying upon a set-off was not entitled to judgment for any sum which might be shown to be due in excess of the plaintiff's claim: *Bow v McLachlan & Co v The Ship Camosun* [1909] AC 597. In that situation, there would simply be judgment for the defendant on the plaintiff's claim. Unlike a counterclaim, a set-off has no life once the plaintiff's action is determined through discontinuance or otherwise: *Gathercole v Smith* (1881) 7 QBD 626. Moreover, set-off was available only in limited circumstances originally derived from the Statutes of Set-off of 1728 and 1734. In *Stehar Knitting Mills Pty Ltd v Southern Textile Converters Pty Ltd* [1980] NSWLR 514, it was stated that the effect of the Judicature Act was to take over the work previously performed by the Statutes of Set-Off: at 517 per Hutley JA; at 523 per Glass JA. The right to set-off liquidated debts in New South Wales is established by the Civil Procedure Act 2005 s 21. Unliquidated debts may be set-off under a judgment: Civil Procedure Act 2005 (Qld) s 90(2)(a).

In *Re Interesting Developments Pty Ltd v Pital Business Pty Ltd* [2009] VSC 12, J Pital Business Pty Ltd (Pital) sought to enter judgment pursuant to terms of settlement entered into between it and the respondents, Giuseppe De Simone Nominees and others. The respondents sought to resist judgment asserting a cross-claim by way of equitable set-off based upon the alleged breach by Pital of certain warranties said to have been given by Pital regarding its entitlement to certain assets under a joint venture agreement.

For the purpose of the argument, Robson J assumed the correctness of the respondents' contention. His Honour then said:

> A set-off is said to exist where a defendant, in answer to a plaintiff's claim, is able to plead successfully that a countervailing claim, which he has against the plaintiff, absolves him, wholly or partially, from liability to the plaintiff. At common law, the right of set-off was unknown and was established by statute. At law, a claim can not ground a plea for set-off unless it is liquidated Equity, however, allows a setoff in certain circumstances as a defence to a legal or equitable claim. The authors of Meagher, Gummow and Lehane's *Equity Doctrines and Remedies* assert that it is tolerably clear that in equity a claim for an unliquidated amount is sufficient to establish an equitable set-off. They say that in equity the set-off must go to the root of, be essentially bound up with and 'impeach' the title of the plaintiff. In *Indrisie v General Credits Ltd*, the Full Court of the Supreme Court of Victoria comprising Young CJ, Crockett and Nicholson JJ held that:
>
> > In order to rely upon a cross-claim as an equitable set-off, there must be such a nexus between the claim and cross-claim that the cross-claim can be said to impeach the plaintiff's claim.

In Meagher, Gummow and Lehane's *Equity Doctrines and Remedies*, the authors say:

> The defendant, in order to make out an equitable set-off, had to establish that he possessed some equitable right to be protected from the plaintiff's claim.

The authors assert that the most famous exposition of this doctrine is that of Lord Cottenham LC in *Rawson v Samuel*. This case is relied upon by the respondents in support of their equitable set-off defence. In that case, the defendant to a suit of law sought to restrain the plaintiff at law from executing on an action for damages until an account of complicated dealings between the parties had been taken. It was uncertain whether, on the taking of that account, the plaintiff at law would end up owing any money to the defendant at law or rather the defendant at law would end up owing money to the plaintiff. The Lord Chancellor said:

> It was said that the subjects of the suit in this Court, and of the action at law, arise out of the same contract; but the one is for an account of transactions under the contract, and the other for damages for the breach of it. The object and subject-matters are, therefore, totally distinct; and the fact that the agreement was the origin of both does not form any bond of union for the purpose of supporting an injunction.

> The question then comes to this: Is the Defendant, in a suit in this Court for an account, the balance of which I will suppose to be uncertain, to be restrained from taking out execution in an action for damages against the other party to the account until after the account shall have been taken, and it shall thereby have been ascertained that he does not owe to the Defendant at law, upon the balance of the account, a sum equal to the amount of the damages? If so, it cannot be open upon the ground of set-off, because there is not at present any balance against which the damages can be set off; nor can it be because the damages are involved in the account, for certainly they can form no part of it.

> We speak familiarly of equitable set-off, as distinguished from the set-off at law; but it will be found that this equitable set-off exists in cases where the party seeking the benefit of it can shew some equitable ground for being protected against his adversary's demand. The mere existence of cross-demands is not sufficient; *Whyte v O'Brien* [(1824) 1 Sim & St 551; 57 ER 218]; although it is difficult to find any other ground for the order in *William v Davies* [(1829) 2 Sim 461; 57 ER 860], as reported. In the present case, there are not even cross-demands, as it cannot be assumed that the balance of the account will be found to be in favour of the Defendants at law. Is there, then, any equity in preventing a party who has recovered damages at law from receiving them, because he may be found to be indebted, upon the balance of an unsettled account, to the party against whom the damages have been recovered? Suppose the balance should be found to be due to the plaintiff at law, what compensation can be made to him for the injury he must have sustained by the delay? The jury assess the damages as the compensation due at the time of their verdict. Their verdict may be no compensation for the additional injury which the delay in payment may occasion. What equity have the Plaintiffs in the suit for an account to be protected against the damages awarded against them? If they have no such equity, there can be no good ground for the injunction.

The applicability of this test was affirmed by Gummow J in *Re Just Juice Corp Pty Ltd*. See also the observations of Tadgell J in *Eagle Star Nominees Ltd v Merril*. In *Galambos v McIntyre* Woodward J, sitting as a judge of the Supreme Court of the Australian Capital Territory, examined this principle of equitable set-off and in particular the decision in *Rawson v Samuel*. Woodward J concluded the prerequisites of an equitable set-off to be:

(i)   Clear crossclaims for debts or damages, which
(ii) were so closely related as to the subject-matter that the claim sought to be set-off impeached the other in the sense that it made it positively unjust that there should be recovery without deduction. [30]–[33] [*Endnotes omitted*]

It could not be said that the warranties given by Pital, the breach of which was disputed by the respondents in proceedings before the New South Wales Supreme Court, could give rise to an equitable set-off sufficient to deny Pital judgment. The claims for breach of warranty were contingent. Pital was entitled to judgment.

The Statutes of Set-off applied to set-off of debts at common law. In equity, a claim by the defendant for unliquidated damages might be set off against the plaintiff's claim where there was 'such a nexus between the claim and cross-claim [as] to … impeach the plaintiff's claim': *Indrisie v General Credits Ltd* [1985] VR 251 at 254 *per curiam*.

10.5.14 The relevant rule in the Australian Capital Territory (r 473) provides:

> If a defendant establishes a counterclaim against the plaintiff and there is a balance in favour of 1 of the parties, the court may give judgment for the balance.

There are similar rules to ACT r 473 in Victoria and the Northern Territory, in relation specifically to counterclaims (NT r 10.09; Vic r 10.09) and in most of the other jurisdictions: Qld r 184; SA r 224; Tas r 200; WA O 18 r 2. See also Civil Procedure Act 2005 (NSW) s 90(2)(a).

10.5.15 The effect of the rules is to enable the court to give a single judgment in respect of the competing claims of plaintiff and defendant in circumstances where money claims are made and the competing claim can be properly categorised as a set-off, cross-claim or counterclaim. In Victoria (r 13.14) and the Northern Territory (r 13.14), the claim may arise by way of defence.

In order to do justice to the parties, however, it may be necessary to make separate orders for costs in favour of the plaintiff and the defendant where the defendant's claim (or in Victoria and the Northern Territory, its defence) is truly in the nature of a counterclaim. See *Chell Engineering Ltd v Unit Tool and Engineering Co Ltd* [1950] 1 All ER 378 where the English Court of Appeal held that, despite the English rule similar to ACT r 473, the more convenient course might not be to enter judgment for the balance found due, but rather, to enter separate judgments with costs and, where necessary, to make an adjustment for legal costs not readily severable from the claim and counterclaim. In this case an offer of compromise had been made by the defendant which exceeded the balance found due but did not exceed the sum found due on the plaintiff's claim. The plaintiff also sought its costs on the High Court scale rather than the County Court scale. In order that there be a just result, the Court of Appeal held that there should be separate judgments.

10.5.16 Questions

1. Is there any real basis for favouring the plaintiff as happened in *Chell Engineering Ltd*?

2. In what other circumstances might it matter that judgment is given for the balance rather than separately in relation to the claim and counterclaim?

Addition, substitution and removal of parties

> **10.6.1E**   **High Court Rules 2004**
>
> **Addition, removal and substitution of party**
>
> **21.05.1** At any stage of a proceeding the Court or a Justice may order that:
>
> (a) a person who is not then a proper or necessary party cease to be a party;
>
> (b) any person who ought to have been joined as a party or whose presence in the proceedings is necessary to ensure that all questions in the matter are effectually and completely determined be joined as a party; or
>
> (c) any person between whom and any party to the proceeding there may exist a question arising out of or relating to or connected with any claim in the proceeding which it is just and convenient to determine as between that person and the party as well as between the parties to the proceeding be joined as a party.
>
> **21.05.2** A person shall not be added as plaintiff without that person's written consent.
>
> [See also: FCR r 9.05; ACT r 220; NSW r 6.25; NT r 9.07(1); Qld r 69; Tas r 184(4); Vic r 9.07(1); WA O 18 rr 6(2), 9. The South Australian provisions regarding addition are, however, broader: SA r 74]

10.6.2   The courts have tended to read rules such as HCR r 21.05.1 quite liberally, where the plaintiff seeks to add a party to the proceeding: *Birtles v Commonwealth* [1960] VR 247 (**10.4.5C**); *J N Taylor Holdings Ltd (in liq) v Bond* (1993) 59 SASR 432, where a plaintiff company in liquidation in proceedings against its former directors was able to join the directors' liability insurers as defendants. The insurers had denied indemnity. The plaintiff, as *dominus litus*, should be entitled to add parties subject to being penalised by way of order for costs should the plaintiff's claim against the added party fail.

10.6.3   Courts are generally reluctant to permit a defendant to add another defendant or to accede to an application by a non-party to be added as a defendant. To permit addition is to force a defendant on an often unwilling plaintiff. In *Walker v Commonwealth Trading Bank of Australia* (1985) 3 NSWLR 496, Needham J refused leave to a defendant who was sued for recovery of preferential payments by a company liquidator to add persons against whom they might have a right to indemnity under mortgages and guarantees taken as security for the company's debt. It was not for the conduct of the action that they be added.

In *National Australia Bank Ltd v Bond Brewing Holdings Ltd* [1991] 1 VR 386, the Appeal Division of the Victorian Supreme Court refused an application by a member of the Bond Brewing Group of companies to be added as a defendant to an action brought by the plaintiff bank upon an agreement with other companies in the group. The applicant was not party to the agreement, so it was not necessary that it be added: at 579–80 per Kaye J.

Both cases illustrate a narrow approach to the addition rules, an approach given authority by the decision of the House of Lords in *Vandervell Trustees Ltd v White* [1971] AC 912, where Viscount Dilhorne said (at 936) the addition rule gave power to add a party 'only if he ought to have been joined as a party or if his presence is necessary for the effectual and complete determination and adjudication upon all matters in dispute in the cause or matter'.

10.6.4 In Vic r 9.06(b)(ii), NT r 9.06(b)(ii), and Qld r 69(1)(b)(ii) the following provision is found:

> A person between whom and any party to the proceeding there may exist a question arising out of or relating to or connected with any claim in the proceeding which it is just and convenient to determine as between that person and that party as well as between the parties to the proceeding.

This provision is a direct response to the narrowness of the interpretation of the addition rules in *Vandervell Trustees*. The Malaysian equivalent of Vic r 9.06(b)(ii) was given a broad interpretation by the Privy Council in *Pegang Mining Co Ltd v Choong Sam* [1969] 2 MLJ 52. It does not appear that the Victorian Appeal Division was referred to Vic r 9.06(b)(ii) in the *Bond Brewing* case. For a recent decision on Vic r 9.06(b)(ii), see *Boral Resources (Vic) Pty Ltd v Robak Engineering and Construction Pty Ltd* [1999] 2 VR 507: **10.3.2**.

10.6.5 Question

1. If a person cannot be added under the addition rules, how should one proceed? Does the answer lie in the issue of separate proceedings and an application for consolidation? See **10.8.1–10.8.3**. Of course, a defendant may have a claim which can be made the subject of third-party proceedings: See **10.10.1–10.10.3**.

DEALING WITH PARTICULAR PARTIES

10.7.1 There are statutory provisions and rules designed to facilitate or regulate proceedings involving particular parties. The most important of these are discussed in this section.

Persons under a disability

10.7.2 Each jurisdiction has rules or provisions which require persons under a disability, namely, minors and handicapped persons unable to themselves conduct litigation, to sue or be sued through a litigation guardian or next friend: HCR r 21.08; FCR Div 9.6; ACT rr 275–282; NSW Pt 7 Div 4; NT O 15; Qld rr 93–98, Public Trustee Act 1978 (Qld) s 59; SA rr 78, 79; Tas rr 292–301; Vic O 15; WA O 70.

The following extract from the South Australia rules is an example of the provisions covering persons with a disability.

10.7.3E   **Supreme Court Civil Rules 2006 (SA)**
Parties under Disability

78 (1) As a general rule, a person under a disability (a protected person) may only take or defend proceedings through a guardian who has authority to represent the interests of the protected person (a litigation guardian).

Exception —

The Court may, however, permit a protected person to act personally in bringing, or taking any step in, proceedings.

(2)   The litigation guardian is responsible for the conduct of the proceedings on behalf of the protected person and may take any step in the proceedings and do anything else that the protected person might have done if of full age and capacity.

(3)   A party who becomes aware that another party is a protected person and is not represented by a litigation guardian as required by this rule must inform the Court of that fact.

(4)   A judgment or proceeding of the Court is not invalid because a party was not represented by a litigation guardian as required by this rule, but the Court may set aside the judgment or proceeding if satisfied that the party has been substantially prejudiced through the lack of such representation.

[See also r 79.]

10.7.4   The litigation guardian or next friend will be a person who has no interest in the proceeding adverse to the interests of the litigant, normally a close relative of the litigant. The rules applicable to persons under a disability contain provisions dealing with offers of compromise and approval of settlements by the court.

Partners

10.7.5   Each jurisdiction, other than the High Court and New South Wales, has rules which facilitate proceedings by or against partners in the name of the firm of which they are partners: FCR r 9.41; ACT rr 285–292; NT O 17; Qld rr 82–88; SA rr 86–88; Tas rr 307–314 (see **10.7.6E**); Vic O 17; WA O 71 rr 1, 2. There is nothing which precludes proceedings by or against the individuals comprising the firm. In New South Wales proceedings are taken by or against the individual partners of the firm: see r 7.19. There are rules dealing with service upon partners, appearance and execution of judgments against the firm and the partners of the firm, following the abovementioned rules.

The following extract from the Tasmanian rules is an example.

10.7.6E	**Supreme Court Rules 2000 (Tas)**

308 (1) Any 2 or more persons claiming, or being liable, as partners and carrying on business in Tasmania may sue or be sued in any firm name under which those persons carried on business in partnership at the time of the accrual of the cause of action.

Executors, administrators and trustees

10.7.7   There is provision in each jurisdiction for proceedings relating to any estate or trust to be taken against the executor, administrator or trustee of the estate. It is not necessary to join those beneficially entitled: HCR r 21.06; FCR r 9.23; ACT rr 255–261; NSW Pt 7 Div 3; NT O 16; Qld r 71, Supreme Court of Queensland Act 1991 (Qld) ss 93I, 93J; SA rr 83–84; Tas rr 302–306; Vic O 16; WA O 18 rr 13–15.

Corporations

10.7.8   Each company has an Australian Company Number (ACN), and, in the case of foreign and certain other companies, an Australian Registered Body Number (ARBN). Section 153(1) of the Corporations Act 2001 provides:

> A company must set out its name on all its public documents and negotiable instruments.

In s 9 it is provided that 'public document', in relation to a body corporate, has the meaning given by s 88A. This provides that public document includes an 'official notice' which, according to the Australian Securities and Investments Commission (ASIC), includes any document which is part of legal proceedings.

Accordingly, a company plaintiff should include its ACN as part of the description of its name in any legal proceeding. A defendant company should include its ACN as part of its name in any document involved in any legal proceeding.

10.7.9 Question

1.   Does the omission of the ACN invalidate the proceeding?

Corporations under administration, dissolved or otherwise defunct

10.7.10   Where a company is being wound up by the court or is in provisional liquidation, s 471B of the Corporations Act requires any person wishing to commence or continue proceedings against the company to seek leave of the court (Supreme Court) to do so. Where proceedings are taken against a company without the requisite leave, an order can be made by the court which has the effect of deeming that the proceeding was commenced with leave (leave is granted *nunc pro tunc*: *Re Testro Consolidated Pty Ltd* [1965] VR 18 at 34 per Sholl J, that is, the order is effective retrospectively to a time immediately prior to the taking of proceedings). Normally, leave to proceed under s 471B will be given where the company in liquidation is insured and the 'real' defendant is the insurer. See *Re Gordon and Grant Pty Ltd* (1982) 1 ACLC 196 generally as to the circumstances in which leave to proceed will be granted.

It might be noted here, in relation to matters where insurance is involved, that where an insured has died, or cannot with reasonable diligence be found, a third party claimant may recover directly against the insurer: Insurance Contracts Act 1984 (Cth) s 51. Reference can also be made to the Law Reform (Miscellaneous Provisions) Act 1946 (NSW) s 6 which enables a plaintiff to proceed directly against the defendant's liability insurer. There is similar legislation in the Australian Capital Territory: Law Reform (Miscellaneous Provisions Act 1955 (ACT) ss 206–208.

10.7.11   Section 440D of the Corporations Act should be noted where the company is under administration pursuant to Pt 5.3A of the Corporations Act. Administration operates as a stay on proceedings. It is necessary to obtain the consent of the administrator or leave of the court to proceed against the company under administration.

Note the effect of deregistration: s 601AD of the Corporations Act. A company may be reregistered: s 601AH.

10.7.12   A proceeding brought by or against a dissolved (or deregistered) company is a nullity: *Re Kilkenny Engineering Pty Ltd (in liq)* (1976) 13 SASR 258. Therefore, it is imperative that a search be conducted at ASIC, of any company to be involved to ascertain the status of any corporate litigant before joinder or addition in any proceeding.

Bankrupt persons

10.7.13   It is provided in s 58(3)(b) of the Bankruptcy Act 1966 (Cth) that it is not competent for a creditor to commence or continue any proceeding against a person who has become a bankrupt, without the leave of the court in respect of a debt which is provable in bankruptcy. Importantly, this does not include claims for unliquidated damages in tort: s 82(2). In relation to proceedings brought by a person who becomes bankrupt, see the Bankruptcy Act 1966 (Cth) s 60(2)–(4).

CONSOLIDATION

10.8.1   In most jurisdictions there is provision for the consolidation of proceedings: FCR r 30.11; ACT r 270; NSW r 28.5; NT r 9.12; Qld rr 78–81; SA r 31, Tas r 188; Vic r 9.12; WA O 83. Typically, consolidation permits two or more proceedings to be tried jointly or certain issues in them, although there is no uniformity in approach in the rules in the various Australian jurisdictions. The following extract from the Western Australia rules is an example.

10.8.2E   **Rules of the Supreme Court 1971 (WA)**
                              Order 83 — General Rules

Causes may be consolidated

1   Whenever any issues between the same parties can be conveniently tried together, or wherever it appears desirable notwithstanding that the parties are not identical and that the evidence necessary to prove the issues is not identical, the Court may consolidate any number of causes or matters in order to quiet all claims relating to one subject matter, transaction or event, or to substantially similar subject matters, transactions or events.

Consolidation with action removed from another court

2   In the exercise of jurisdiction under this Order the Court may order the consolidation with any action pending in the Supreme Court of any action remitted or removed to the Supreme Court from any other court.

Directions

3   The Court shall make all necessary directions for the pretrial procedure, and for the trial or determination of such consolidated causes or matters.

10.8.3 The court will not normally permit consolidation, unless it would have been proper to join the claim between the plaintiff in the one proceeding with the claim between the parties in the second proceeding: *Bolwell Fibreglass Pty Ltd v Foley* [1984] VR 97.

REPRESENTATIVE PROCEEDINGS

10.9.1 The following item appeared in the Melbourne *Age* on 2 January 1992:

> Fourteen United States prisoners on California's death row have sued for the right to impregnate their wives or girlfriends through conjugal visits or artificial insemination.
>
> The suit was filed in the Federal Court in San Francisco on Monday on behalf of the condemned inmates at San Quentin prison, their spouses and other women who might want to bear the prisoners' children and potential grandparents.

We do not know what became of this action, but it perhaps illustrates the perceived excesses of class actions in the United States of America.

The Australian position

The traditional representative proceeding

10.9.2 Each of the Australian jurisdictions, other than New South Wales, has rules derived from equitable practice, which permit a person to represent a group of plaintiffs or defendants having the same interest in the litigation: HCR r 21.09; FCR r 9.21; ACT rr 265–267; NT O 18; Qld rr 75–77; SA rr 80–82; Tas rr 335–336; Vic O 18; WA O 18 r 12.

The ACT r 266(1) provides:

> If numerous people have the same interest or liability in a proceeding, the proceeding may be started and, unless the court otherwise orders, continued by or against any 1 or more of them as representing all of them.

In the High Court and Tasmania, there is a requirement that there be at least seven persons having the same interest. In Tasmania there is also reference to 'common rights' and 'common interests' in a 'subject matter or controversy'. In South Australia, r 80(1) refers to 'common interest in the subject matter of an action or proposed action'. It requires authority in writing by members of the group to bring or defend the action.

10.9.3 The words 'same interest' have, until recently, been narrowly construed as the result of the decision of the English Court of Appeal in *Markt & Co Ltd v Knight Steamship Co Ltd* [1910] 2 KB 1021. In that case it was held that where proceedings are brought on behalf of a group of plaintiffs under separate but otherwise identical contracts, the same interest requirement was not satisfied. It was also held that where damages were in issue and had to be separately assessed, that the representative proceeding rule could not be used. This decision must now be read in the light of the High Court's decision in *Carnie v Esanda Corp Ltd* (1995) 182 CLR 398, extracted below.

Carnie v Esanda Finance Corp Ltd
                                     (1995) 182 CLR 398
                                     High Court of Australia

[The plaintiff appellants were farmers who had obtained credit from the defendant respondent to purchase farm equipment and had sought relief by way of declaration that certain agreements (variation agreements) were in breach of the Credit Act 1984 (NSW) and therefore were void. They sought to represent all other persons, party to similar agreements with the defendant under NSW Pt 8 r 13(1) (the equivalent of ACT r 266(1)). The defendant challenged the plaintiffs' pleading in so far as it sought to plead a representative action.]

Mason CJ, Deane and Dawson JJ (at 403): Subject to the comments which follow, we agree with the reasons given by Toohey and Gaudron JJ for allowing the appeal. We would, however, remit the matter to the Court of Appeal for the purpose of considering whether an order should be made that the action not continue as a representative action.

We do not agree with the statement of Kirby P in the Court of Appeal that the majority in that Court (Gleeson CJ and Meagher JA) failed to answer the correct question because their Honours assumed that the appellants were bringing a class action. Properly understood, the majority concluded that the particular procedure adopted by the appellants in this case — which their Honours happened to characterize as a 'class action' — was not within the Supreme Court Rules 1970 (NSW), Pt 8 r 13(1). This conclusion is contained in the following passage of Gleeson CJ [(1992) 29 NSWLR 382 at 389]. [Meagher JA agreed with the Chief Justice in a short concurring judgment.]:

> To say that each borrower has the same interest in the proceedings as [the appellants], for the purpose of the rule relating to representative actions, goes well beyond received notions of the scope and purpose of the rule.

Whether the present case was or was not a class action is not the critical question. More than that, it is not a question which is susceptible of a precise or an instructive answer. The term 'class action' is used in various senses. Sometimes it is employed as a generic term to comprehend any procedure which allows the claims of many individuals against the same defendant to be brought or conducted by a single representative [Australian Law Reform Commission, Report No 46, Grouped Proceedings in the Federal Court, (1988) at 1]. At other times, when the 'same interest' stipulation was thought to preclude the application of the representative action procedure to actions for damages on the ground that each individual's entitlement to damages would have to be independently assessed [at page 3], the term 'class action' was employed to refer to an extension of the representative action to cover such actions.

The remaining sense in which the term 'class action' is used is by way of reference to the class action procedures prescribed and applied in the United States, such as the procedures prescribed by [404] the Federal Rules of Civil Procedure, r 23 [See Appendix C, 'Other models for class actions', at 191]. This is the sense in which the majority in the Court of Appeal used the term. It would be unprofitable and difficult to make a precise comparison between a representative action under r 13 and a class action under r 23 but we see no reason to doubt that the two rules could cover much common ground. The elaborate set of provisions contained in r 23 would create some differences. But this does not seem to be of much moment for present purposes. What the majority in the Court of Appeal thought to be important was that, in the absence of legislation or a rule of court prescribing an elaborate set of rules regulating representative actions, a representative action could not be constituted in the manner contended for by the appellants.

But we do not think that this approach of the majority of the Court of Appeal can prevail in the face of the language of r 13(1). All that this subrule requires is numerous parties who have the same interest. The subrule is expressed in broad terms and it is to be interpreted in the light of the obvious purpose of the rule, namely, to facilitate the administration of justice by enabling parties having the same interest to secure a determination in one action rather than in separate actions. It has been suggested that the expression 'same interest' is to be equated with a common ingredient in the cause of action by each member of the class [*Prudential Assurance v Newman Industries* [1981] Ch 229 at 255]. In our view, this interpretation might not adequately reflect the content of the statutory expression. It may be it extends to a significant common interest in the resolution of any question of law or fact arising in the relevant proceedings. Be that as it may, it has now been recognized that persons having separate causes of action in contract or tort may have 'the same interest' in proceedings to enforce those causes of action.

Much as one might prefer to have a detailed legislative prescription by statute or rule of court regulating the incidents of representative action, r 13 makes provision for an action to proceed as a representative action in a context in which there is no such legislative prescription. The absence of such a prescription does not enable a court to refuse to give effect to the provisions of the rule. Nor, more importantly, does the absence of such prescription provide a sufficient reason for narrowing the scope of the operation of the rule, as the Court of Appeal did, without giving effect to the purpose of the rule in facilitating the administration of justice.

[405] Once the existence of numerous parties and the requisite commonality of interest are ascertained, the rule is brought into operation subject only to the exercise of the court's power to order otherwise. And that leaves for consideration the question whether the case is one in which the court should, in the exercise of that power, make an order that the action should not continue as a representative action. Relevant to that question are some of the comments of Gleeson CJ in the course of explaining his concern about the absence of a detailed legislative prescription. In that context, Gleeson CJ mentioned the need to deal with such important matters as [(1992) 29 NSWLR at 388]: (1) whether or not consent is required from group members; (2) the right of such members to opt out of the proceedings; (3) the position of persons under a disability; (4) alterations to the description of the group; (5) settlement and discontinuance of the proceedings; and (6) the giving of various notices to group members.

The question of the importance of those matters, in the context of the particular case, in determining whether an order should be made that the action not continue as a representative action is by no means free from difficulty. However, the Court is not in a position to deal with them or with the consequences of the absence of a legislative prescription with respect to them. Indeed, argument has not been directed to that issue in this Court. The Court should not embark upon an examination of the question whether such an order should be made in the absence of such argument and without having the benefit of the views of the Court of Appeal.

In the result, we would allow the appeal, set aside the orders made by the Court of Appeal striking out the further amended statement of claim in so far as it purports to plead a representative action and remit the matter to the Court of Appeal for consideration of the question whether it should 'otherwise order' within the meaning of r 13(1).

Brennan J (at 407): [After referring to the facts, his Honour continued:] The defendant submits that the scope and purpose of the procedure under Pt 8 r 13(1) is to overcome or to provide an exception to the practice of the courts of equity that all persons having an interest in the subject matter of the suit ought to be made parties [*Templeton v Leviathan Proprietary Ltd* (1921) 30 CLR 34 at 43, 75–6]. And, as [408] each member of the putative class would have a distinct cause of action arising out of distinct transactions, there is no common interest in the proceedings. For that reason the class sought to be represented could not be joined as plaintiffs, nor could their respective causes of action be joined, in the same proceeding [*Payne v Young* (1980) 145 CLR 609 at 611, 614, 615, 617].

For the reasons stated by Toohey and Gaudron JJ, I would reject the proposition that the scope and purpose of Pt 8 r 13(1) is limited in the manner submitted. Rule 13(1) requires 'the same interest' in the proceeding, not necessarily the same cause of action nor an entitlement to have or to share in the same relief. I respectfully agree with McHugh J that the test for determining whether an action is within the scope of Pt 8 r 13(1) is whether the plaintiff and the members of the represented class have a community of interest in the determination of some substantial issue of law or fact.

Here, the further amended statement of claim raised an issue in which there is a community of interest, namely, whether s 70(1)(a) permits the inclusion of unpaid credit charges under an original loan or credit sale contract in the calculation of 'the outstanding balance of the amount financed' for the purposes of that provision.

However, it is precisely because of the flexible utility of the representative action that judicial control of its conduct is important, to ensure not only that the litigation as between the plaintiff and defendant is efficiently disposed of but also that the interests of those who are absent but represented are not prejudiced by the conduct of the litigation on their behalf. The self-proclaimed carrier of a litigious banner may prove to be an indolent or incompetent champion of the common cause in the courtroom. As Vinelott J said in the course of his judgment in *Prudential Assurance v Newman Industries* [1981] Ch 229 at 255, the court must be satisfied that — 'the issues common to every member of the class will be decided after full discovery and in the light of all the evidence capable of being adduced in favour of the claim.' I would add that if, for any reason, the court is not satisfied that the interests of the absent but represented class are being properly advanced, the court should exclude the represented persons from the action [It was the attempt to allow any one shipper to conduct litigation on behalf of another without his leave and yet so as to bind him that was branded as a 'fundamental error' by Fletcher Moulton LJ in *Markt & Co, Limited v Knight Steamship Company, Limited; Sale & Frazar v Knight Steamship Company, Limited* [1910] 2 KB 1021 at 1040]. That power can be exercised at any time before the judgment is perfected.

In the present case at the time when the plaintiffs delivered their [409] statement of claim, there appeared to be a live issue as to whether, in the case of a variation agreement, 'the amount financed' as that term is used in s 70(1)(a) of the Act must exclude credit charges under the original loan contract. In the course of argument, counsel for the defendant conceded that if the plaintiffs brought themselves within subpars (a), (b)(i) and (c) of par 6 of the further amended statement of claim, they would be entitled to relief under s 42. If it be conceded that the issue relating to the interpretation of s 70(1)(a) is to be determined in favour of the plaintiffs and of all members of the represented class coming within subpar (b)(i) of par 6, there can be no doubt that the action is prima facie one appropriate to be conducted as a representative action subject to the court's supervision. The concession eliminates any risk that the issue can be determined adversely to the members of the represented class coming within subpar (b)(i). If it continues as a representative action and that concession is not withdrawn, there will be a binding declaration in favour of the plaintiffs and all members of the represented class.

Counsel for the defendant submits, however, that the pleading which identifies the persons represented is unsatisfactory and really denies any issue of common interest for determination. He draws attention to par 6 of the further amended statement of claim which does not plead the facts which bring the contracts referred to in that subparagraph within the definition of regulated loan or credit sale contracts, nor the facts establishing noncompliance with the requirements of ss 35 and 36. The facts are unique to each contract but the criterion of the represented class is pleaded as a conclusion that the contracts of all members of the class answer the description therein alleged. Counsel further submits that a 'variation agreement' falling under subpar (b)(ii) of par 6 might not be supported by consideration, though consideration is needed to constitute a 'loan contract' under s 3 of the Act. And, finally, it is said that the credit charges in respect of which Mr and Mrs Carnie seek relief under s 42 are pleaded as the credit charges under the variation agreement, but par 7(2) may be seeking (it is said to be ambiguous) relief under s 42 not only in respect of the credit charges under the variation agreements but in respect of credit charges under the original loan agreements. However, the plaintiffs [410] accept, and intend, that the declaration sought in par 7(2) relates only to credit charges under the variation agreements.

The defendant's objections are without substance so far as they challenge the availability of the representative procedure. Subparagraphs (a) and (c) of par 6 simply ensure that the issue of common interest and the declaration as to that issue are confined to the issue arising under s 70(1)(a). And subpar (b)(ii) clearly relates to a variation agreement enforceable subject to the Act. The questions whether the arrangement with the defendant into which any particular person has entered is a regulated loan or credit sale contract and whether a particular variation agreement is supported by consideration will be answered according to the circumstances of each case. They do not arise and need not be addressed in the present action except in respect of Mr and Mrs Carnie.

However, the defendant's objections are relevant to the second aspect of Pt 8 r 13(1): should the action be permitted to continue as a representative action? If it be conceded, or held, that s 42(1)(b) applies to all variation agreements falling within par 6, s 85 entitles the defendant to apply to the Commercial Tribunal 'for an order increasing the liability of the debtor to the credit provider'. In other words, the application of s 42(1)(b) could prove to be a pyrrhic victory for a debtor. The discretionary powers of the Tribunal are to be exercised according to the individual circumstances of the case. Is it appropriate, then, to permit the action to continue as a representative action when, in any given case, it will be necessary to determine whether the person seeking relief against the defendant has entered into a loan or credit sale contract [Issues arising under subpar (a) and arguably under subpar (b)(ii) of par 6] and whether there has been a noncompliance with s 35 or s 36 [Issues arising under subpar (c) of par 6], and the ultimate benefit of the litigation to that person will depend on the prospect of the defendant's obtaining an order under s 85 increasing the liability of the particular debtor. These are matters which it is appropriate for the Supreme Court to consider in supervising the conduct of the litigation.

As these matters were not material to the decision of the majority of the Court of Appeal once their Honours decided that the plaintiffs and the represented debtors did not have the 'same interest in [the] proceedings', I would agree with the order proposed by Mason CJ, Deane and Dawson JJ. It will be for the Court of Appeal, appreciating the nature of the interest common to the plaintiffs and the represented class and evaluating the factors [411] relevant to the obtaining of substantive relief by each of the represented persons, to determine (or to direct the determination of) the question whether the action should continue as a representative action.

Toohey and Gaudron JJ (at 415):

The approach to a claim for a representative action
It is necessary to go back to Pt 8 r 13(1) itself and not merely assume that it is a class action that the appellants wish to bring and for which the Rules do not adequately provide. The starting point is whether the procedure which the appellants wish to adopt is within the Rules. If it is, a subsidiary question arises, whether the Supreme Court should exercise its discretion to 'otherwise order' and so prevent the continuance of the proceedings in that form. With respect to their Honours in the majority in the Court of Appeal, those two necessary steps appear to have been taken as one.

In ascertaining whether the procedure which the appellants wish to adopt is within the Rules it is helpful to consider the history and interpretation of r 13(1), the ancestor of which is to be found in the English Rules of the Supreme Court and which appears in various forms in other common law countries. Rule 13(1) is almost identical in language with O 15 r 12(1) of the English Rules of the Supreme Court, from which it was clearly taken. The English rule was in turn derived from an earlier rule which itself was derived from the practice of the Court of Chancery [*The Supreme Court Practice*, (1993), vol 1, 15/12/1; and see *Duke of Bedford v Ellis* [1901] AC 1].

Historically the common law courts had no power to hear an action by a representative plaintiff. However, in the Court of Chancery representative actions were permitted in certain cases. With the merger of common law and equity, the new rules of procedure scheduled to the Supreme Court of Judicature Act 1873 (UK) incorporated the chancery practice [Rule 10 of the Rules of Procedure. Rule 10 was subsequently replaced in 1883 by O 16 r 9 and then in 1962 by the current O 15 r 12(1)]. That practice was described by Lord Macnaghten in *Bedford v Ellis* [1901] AC at 8 as follows:

> The old rule in the Court of Chancery was very simple and perfectly well understood. Under the old practice the Court required the presence of all parties interested in the matter in suit, in order that a final end might be made of the controversy. But when the parties were so numerous that you never could 'come at justice', to use an expression in one of the older cases, if everybody interested was made a party, the rule was not allowed to stand in the way. It was originally a rule of convenience; for the sake of convenience it was relaxed.

Initially the courts construed the rule narrowly. In *Temperton v Russell* [1893] 1 QB 435 the requirement for those represented to have the [416] 'same interest' was interpreted as applying only to individuals who had a 'beneficial proprietary right' in the matter [at 438]. However, in *Bedford v Ellis* that narrow approach was rejected by the House of Lords and, apart from one significant exception [*Markt & Co Ltd v Knight Steamship Co Ltd* [1910] 2 KB

1021], in the cases that followed the general approach to interpretation and application of the English rule became increasingly liberal.

In *Bedford v Ellis* a number of plaintiffs were permitted to sue on behalf of themselves and all other growers of fruit, flowers, vegetables, roots and herbs within the meaning of the Covent Garden Market Act 1828 (UK) to enforce statutory preferential rights to stands in the market. The plaintiffs sought a declaration as to the true construction of the Act, an injunction to restrain the infringement of their statutory rights and an account of the sums which they had allegedly been overcharged. Lord Macnaghten, with whom the majority concurred, identified three criteria which must be satisfied before the representative rule can apply [[1901]) AC at 8]:

> Given a common interest and a common grievance, a representative suit was in order if the relief sought was in its nature beneficial to all whom the plaintiff proposed to represent.

The majority held there was a common interest and it did not matter that the group was a fluctuating body which would be difficult to catalogue. It was enough that there was a clear description of the growers sought to be represented in the Act. The fact that the plaintiffs were claiming separate and different rights under the Act did not detract from the practicality of using the representative procedure.

This broad and liberal approach suffered a setback with the decision of the Court of Appeal in *Markt & Co Ltd v Knight Steamship Co Ltd* which had the effect for some time afterwards of limiting the scope of the representative action to exclude those cases where the relief claimed was damages and where separate and individual contracts were involved. In that case the plaintiff shippers had various goods aboard the defendant's vessel which was sunk by Russians who suspected it of carrying contraband during the Russo–Japanese war. The plaintiffs sued the defendant on behalf of themselves and the 44 other owners of cargo for 'damages for breach of contract and duty in and about the carriage of goods [417] by sea' [(1910) 2 KB at 1025]. The majority in the Court of Appeal held that the shippers did not have the same interest because each contract was manifestly different. Different defences such as estoppel and set off may have existed so that no representative action could settle the rights of the individual members of the class.

But the subsequent history of representative actions evidences a greater readiness to sanction them. In *John v Rees* [1970] Ch 345 Megarry J referred to the broad approach of Lord Macnaghten in *Bedford v Ellis* with approval, saying [at 369–370]:

> This seems to me to make it plain that the rule is to be treated as being not a rigid matter of principle but a flexible tool of convenience in the administration of justice.

His Honour said this approach was consistent with the language of the rule which was wide and permissive in its scope while providing adequate safeguards for the substance and that he 'would therefore be slow to apply the rule in any strict or rigorous sense' [at 370].

In *Prudential Assurance v Newman Industries* [1981] Ch 229 Vinelott J traced the history of the rule and its application in the United Kingdom. He distinguished *Markt* on its particular facts, saying [at 254]:

> It is clear on authority and principle that a representative action can be brought by a plaintiff, suing on behalf of himself and all other members of a class, each member of which, including the plaintiff, is alleged to have a separate cause of action in tort, provided three conditions are satisfied.

The first condition was that no order could be made if the effect might be to confer a right of action on a member of the class represented who would not otherwise have been able to assert such a right in separate proceedings, or to bar a defence which might otherwise have been available to the defendant in a separate action. The second was that the common interest requirement, where there are separate causes of action in tort, is a requirement for a common ingredient in the cause of action of each member of the class. In this case the representative action resulted in a declaration that was common in terms of relief to all the members of the class: whether a circular sent to shareholders was misleading and contained statements that were untrue. The third condition was that it must be [418] for the benefit of the class that the plaintiff be permitted to sue in a representative capacity.

Likewise, in *R J Flowers Ltd v Burns* [1987] 1 NZLR 260, McGechan J of the New Zealand High Court held that the fact that claims arose under separate contracts was not an objection to the use of a representative action. The defendant pleaded defences which, if established, would remove any common interest. But at an early interlocutory stage of the proceedings the Court was not prepared to elevate the mere expression of contest by a defendant into an automatic barrier to a representative action, saying [at 271]:

> The traditional concern to ensure that representative actions are not to be allowed to work injustice must be kept in mind. Subject to those restraints however the rule should be applied and developed to meet modern requirements.

In *Irish Shipping Ltd v Commercial Union* [1991] 2 QB 206 the defendant sought to rely on *Markt* for the proposition that there can be no common interest where there are separate contracts and the claim of the plaintiff is damages. Staughton LJ reviewed the English authorities and came to the conclusion that the law had been reformed by decisions since *Markt* [at 227]. The case involved insurance contracts containing a leading underwriter's clause which made it possible to regard the 77 individual contracts as one contract. However, while this was an important factor in finding a common interest in this particular case, further authority has held that this was not the decisive factor [*Bank of America v Taylor* (1992) 1 Lloyd's Rep 484 at 494].

In *Naken v General Motors of Canada Ltd* (1983) 144 DLR (3d) 385 at 410 the Supreme Court of Canada found the O 8 r 13(1) equivalent in Canada to be 'totally inadequate for employment as the base from which to launch an action of the complexity and uncertainty' as the one before it. In the Court of Appeal Gleeson CJ referred to that decision and appeared to treat the present case as one which fell within the parameters of that conclusion. In *Naken* the applicants sued General Motors on behalf of persons who purchased new 1971 and 1972 Firenza motor vehicles in Ontario and who had not at the date of the writ sold the cars. Due to a defect the value of the cars was allegedly diminished by $1,000. The claim was based on a [419] breach of implied and express warranty. The express warranty was contained in newspaper advertisements. In order to prove their membership of the class individuals would have had to prove they had responded to the advertisement. Estey J gave the decision of the Court that the case was inappropriate for a representative action. A catalogue of problems against such a course was listed, including the complexity of determining the class which would entail the Master trying up to 4,932 claims; the lack of authority to award costs against unsuccessful claimants for membership of the class; and the possibility of future tort actions for personal injury arising out of reliance on the defect being estopped.

However, *Naken* was carefully distinguished by the Alberta Court of Appeal in *Swift Canadian Co v Alberta Pork Producers' Marketing Board* (1984) 9 DLR (4th) 71. In that case the plaintiffs claimed a declaration of entitlement to an orderly market and free competition, together with a claim for damages suffered by the class by reason of the tortious conspiracy of the defendants to purchase hogs from the class for prices lower than those which would otherwise have prevailed. The damages claimed were restricted to the difference on each transaction made during the period between the price actually paid and the price which would have been paid under the marketing system but for the tortious conduct of the defendants. The Court held that a representative action was appropriate because there was a common interest in securing a declaration that the activities of the defendants were unlawful and in recovering the losses sustained by virtue of those activities. The damages of the class could be determined by mathematical computation. The defendants would not be prejudiced by inability to have discovery of all the members claiming as plaintiffs.

In *Shaw v Real Estate Board of Greater Vancouver* (1973) 36 DLR (3d) 250 at 254 Bull JA observed:

> It appears to me that the many passages uttered by Judges of high authority over the years really boil down to a simple proposition that a class action is appropriate where if the plaintiff wins the other persons he purports to represent win too, and if he, because of that success, becomes entitled to relief whether or not in a fund or property, the others also become likewise entitled to that relief, having regard, always, for different quantitative participations.

In our view that observation is apposite to r 13(1), notwithstanding the use of 'representative action' rather than 'class action'.

[420] The operation of r 13(1)

It is against this background that the operation of r 13(1) falls to be considered though in the end it is the language of the rule which must determine its meaning. The critical words are: 'Where numerous persons have the same interest in any proceedings.' In the course of his judgment Kirby P referred to the requirements identified by Lord Macnaghten in *Bedford v Ellis*, namely, that all persons to be represented have a common interest, that they have a common grievance and that they stand to receive relief which, in its nature, would be beneficial to all. This, of course, is not the precise language of r 13(1) but Kirby P said [(1992) 29 NSWLR at 394] that the present appellants accepted the need to bring themselves within these criteria and he was content to adopt the same approach. In this Court the appellants placed greater emphasis on the actual terms of r 13, arguing that a representative action should be available whenever the two prescribed criteria are established, namely, numerous persons having bona fide claims against another party and having the same interest in the proceedings.

Although the judgments below and the argument in this Court focused on r 13(1), reference should be made to other aspects of the rule. Subrule (4) provides:

> A judgment entered or order made in proceedings pursuant to this rule shall be binding on all the persons as representing whom the plaintiffs sue or, as the case may be, the defendants are sued but shall not be enforced against any person not a party to the proceedings except with the leave of the Court.

Though any judgment or order will be binding on those for whom a plaintiff sues, the represented parties are not liable for costs [*Marks & Co Ltd v Knight Steamship Co Ltd* [1910] 2 KB at 1039]. Subrule (6) allows any person against whom a judgment or order is sought to be enforced to dispute liability 'on the ground that by reason of facts and matters particular to his case he is entitled to be exempted from the liability'.

Objections to a representative order: 'same interest'

As Gleeson CJ observed [(1992) 29 NSWLR at 389]: 'It is the meaning of the expression "the same interest" ... that lies at the heart of the problems'.

The authorities are clear that the fact that claims arise under separate contracts does not mean that the requirement for the same [421] interest is defeated [*R J Flowers Ltd v Burns* [1987] 1 NZLR 260; *Irish Shipping Ltd v Commercial Union* [1991] 2 QB 206; *Bank of America v Taylor* [1992] 1 Lloyd's Rep 484; *Palmco Holding Bhd v Sakapp Commodities (M) Sdn Bhd* (1988) 2 MLJ 624 and *Voon Keng v Syarikat Muzwina Development Sdn Bhd* (1990) 3 MLJ 61]. A refusal to allow a representative action on this ground is open to the criticism that it looks to the question of the Court's discretion to allow a representative action to proceed rather than to the basic question of whether the rule is applicable. That question, stated in terms of the rule, is this: Do numerous persons have the same interest in the action which the appellants have commenced? If they do not then that is the end of the matter. If they do, then the action is properly begun and, unless the Court otherwise orders, it may be continued.

Then it was argued that the same interest was lacking because the relief might not be beneficial to all members of the class, that some parties might not want to contend that their variation agreements were null and void because they had the benefit of the extended time for repayment provided by the variation agreements and that they might be content with their arrangements. However, in the Court of Appeal the appellants, without objection, abandoned the pursuit of a declaration that the variation agreements were null and void. Kirby P would have given leave to amend the statement of claim so that that claim could be deleted, substituting declaratory relief that went no further than determining the meaning of the Act so far as it affects those concerned on matters in which they have a common interest. In that event those debtors who do not wish to take advantage of a favourable judgment would be under no obligation to do so. That is the basis on which the matter was argued in this Court.

There are many persons who have entered into variation agreements with the respondent. They have the 'same interest' in testing those agreements against the Act to see if the method of calculating the amount owed was correct. If that method was not in accordance with the Act, then those persons have a common interest in obtaining the relief of being released from liability for the credit charges. That is, they have the same interest in these proceedings in the sense that there is a significant question common to all members of the class and they stand to be equally affected by the declaratory relief which the appellants seek.

Although each contract will be different in the details of the amounts involved, this will not eliminate the convenience of finding [422] a right to a release which is common to all of them. As Lord Macnaghten said [*Bedford v Ellis* [1901] AC at 7]:

In considering whether a representative action is maintainable, you have to consider what is common to the class, not what differentiates the cases of individual members.

Identification of class

The respondent contended that there were particular difficulties in identifying the class which the appellants wished to represent. But the onus on the appellants is not to identify every member of the class; rather it is to identify the class with sufficient particularity [at 11]. They have done this in par 6 of the statement of claim. The class is not open ended; it is limited to those persons who have credit sale or loan contracts with the respondent which have been varied in circumstances where the variation has been executed in such a way as to be inconsistent with the Act. Furthermore the situation here, unlike cases such as *Naken v General Motors Canada* 144 DLR (3d) 384, is one in which the respondent knows or has the means of knowing better than anyone else the members of the class.

Adequacy of r 13

As noted earlier, Gleeson CJ regarded the present case as an attempt to make r 13(1) the foundation of a class action. Questions of nomenclature aside, it is true that r 13 lacks the detail of some other rules of court. But there is no reason to think that the Supreme Court of New South Wales lacks the authority to give directions as to such matters as service, notice and the conduct of proceedings which would enable it to monitor and finally to determine the action with justice to all concerned. The simplicity of the rule is also one of its strengths, allowing it to be treated as a flexible rule of convenience in the administration of justice and applied 'to the exigencies of modern life as occasion requires' [*Taff Vale Railway Co v Amalgamated Society of Railway Servants* [1901] AC 426 at 443]. The Court retains the power to reshape proceedings at a later stage if they become impossibly complex or the defendant is prejudiced.

[423] Res judicata

In the course of argument a question arose as to the effect of a judgment in these proceedings, if constituted as a representative action. Strictly speaking, the question does not arise at the stage where the issue is whether 'numerous persons have the same interest in any proceedings'. Rather, it goes to the issue whether the Court 'otherwise orders' the continuance of the proceedings in that form. Nevertheless, it is appropriate to say something about the effect of a judgment on the represented persons; it has a bearing on the outcome of this appeal.

If the action, constituted as a representative action, succeeds those represented will have the benefit of declaratory relief as to the meaning of the Act. Whether they choose to take advantage of such a declaration will be a matter for them. But what if the action fails? Counsel for the appellant conceded that each of the members of the class would be 'estopped'. Later, in response to a question from the Court, counsel agreed that 'in theory' if the action failed borrowers within the class would lose the right to take advantage of s 42 of the Act. Section 42 provides that where there has been a failure to comply with certain requirements of the Act, particularly relating to disclosure, the debtor is not liable to pay to the credit provider the credit charges under the contract. But it may be said that in the light of such a decision there was no such right in any event.

The relevant principle is stated in the following way by Spencer-Bower and Turner [The *Doctrine of Res Judicata,* 2nd ed (1969) at par 231]:

> A judicial decision inter partes operates as an estoppel in favour of, or (as the case may be) so as to bind, ... in the case of a 'representative' or 'test' action, all members of the class, whom a party purports to represent therein, ... but not those who, though alleged to be so represented, insist and establish that they are not.

In *Naken v General Motors of Canada Ltd* Estey J in delivering the judgment of the Court, was clearly concerned as to the consequences of res judicata for those sought to be represented, particularly as a fixed sum was claimed for the purchaser of each motor vehicle though each might 'still have rights flowing from the formal contract of purchase and the warranties and covenants contained therein' [(1983) 144 DLR (3d) at 407]. In *Zhang De Yong v Minister for Immigration, Local Government and Ethnic Affairs* (1993) 118 ALR 165 French J ordered that proceedings in the Federal Court should not continue as a [424] representative proceeding under Pt IVA of the Federal Court of Australia Act 1976 (Cth) because of the implications of res judicata for other applicants for refugee status.

In the argument before this Court nothing emerged to show that members of the class in question would be prejudiced by the outcome of this action other than in the obvious sense that they would be bound by a judgment acceding to or rejecting the claim for relief. It would not affect other rights they might have against the respondent, for instance a claim that a member of the class had entered into a contract as a result of misrepresentation or false or misleading conduct. If it did appear that other rights would be affected, it would be a matter for consideration in determining whether the Court should otherwise order. But it is not a consideration in deciding whether the action is properly constituted in terms of r 13(1). And, as mentioned earlier, the members of the class are not liable to the respondent in costs.

The appellants have brought themselves within r 13(1)

The appellants have brought themselves within r 13(1). There are numerous other persons capable of being clearly defined who have the same interest in these proceedings in that they will be equally affected by the declaratory relief which the appellants seek. Whether, in the end, they take advantage of that relief if granted is another matter. But that consideration cannot disqualify the appellants from invoking r 13(1). ...

[Toohey and Gaudron JJ then considered the provisions of the Credit Act. They concluded (at 426):]

On this footing, those whom the appellants seek to represent have the same interest as the appellants. They have entered into loan contracts with the respondent in circumstances where, if the appellants can make good their claim, the variation of those contracts was not in accordance with Pt 3 of the Act. Accordingly, they are not obliged to pay any amount on account of credit charges. In terms of r 13(1) all have the same interest in the proceedings. While it is not known how many other borrowers might wish to take advantage of the declaratory relief the appellants seek, all potentially stand to benefit from a successful action.

In view of the conclusion that the decision of the Court of Appeal was in error in holding that the appellants' action did not fall within r 13, the appeal should be allowed.

It might be said that there is no point in allowing the appeal if, in all the circumstances, the Supreme Court should 'otherwise order' in respect of the continuance of the proceedings. If the appellants had persisted with their claims for declarations that the variation agreements were null and void and of no effect, we would be disposed to remit the matter to the Court of Appeal on the basis that the appellants' action fell within r 13(1) and that it was for that Court to decide whether the action should continue.

However, since the appellants do not persist with this particular aspect of their claim, there appears to be no answer to what Kirby P said at the end of his judgment [(1992) 29 NSWLR at 403]:

Once these are excised, what remains is a proper case for a representative order. The class of person affected is clear, defined and now closed. The primary relief sought is a declaration as to the meaning of an Act of Parliament as it affects the members of that claim in respect of which all of them will have a common interest and a common legal grievance. So far as the orders are concerned, as so amended, they seek relief which is wholly beneficial to all the persons represented.

The trial judge has it within his or her power to 'otherwise order' if, as the action proceeds, circumstances make that course appropriate.

We would therefore allow the appeal and set aside the orders of [427] the Court of Appeal striking out the further amended statement of claim in so far as it purports to plead a representative action.

[McHugh J delivered a judgment in which he concurred with Toohey and Gaudron JJ. The case was remitted to the New South Wales Court of Appeal which sent the matter to Young J for consideration: see *Carnie v Esanda Finance Corp Ltd* (1996) 38 NSWLR 465.]

10.9.5 Notes and questions

1. To what extent has the decision in *Carnie* overridden the decision of the English Court of Appeal in *Markt*? See also *Jameson v Professional Investment Services Pty Ltd* [2009] NSWCA 28, where the New South Wales Court of Appeal held that a representative proceeding may be brought for alleged misleading and deceptive conduct provided that a substantial common issue can be identified.

2. If damages are in issue, can the representative proceeding rule be used? In what circumstances can it be used? What practice has been adopted in England? See the joint judgment of Toohey and Gaudron JJ in *Carnie* where their Honours refer to the English cases. It is not uncommon in England to sue for a declaration on liability so that damages can be resolved at a later date.

3. The rule requires that there be actual persons represented in the proceeding when it is commenced; it is not sufficient that there is provision for persons to opt in to the proceeding subsequently: *Campbells Cash and Carry Pty Ltd v Fostif Pty Ltd* (2006) 80 ALJR 1441. What then is the nature of the representation under the rule? Is it an example of 'opt in', 'opt out' or a hybrid of these?

4. The rule permits representative proceedings to be brought against one or more defendants representing numerous defendants. Historically, the rule would facilitate proceedings against the members of an unincorporated association (most of these will now be incorporated under legislation which permits the incorporation of non-profit making organisations, such as sporting and social clubs: see, for example, the Associations Incorporation Act 1981 (Vic)). The rule may be used where an injunction is sought against a group of people: see 16.2.11.

'Opt in' provisions

10.9.6 In Victoria, prior to Pt 4A of the Supreme Court Act 1986 (Vic), which applies to causes of action in existence on or after 1 January 2000, there were provisions which permitted a representative proceeding where persons seeking the same, or substantially the same, relief consented in writing to be represented by others in the proceeding. This was an example of an 'opt in' class action. The provisions were contained in the Supreme Court Act 1986 (Vic) ss 34 and 35. They have now been repealed and are of historic interest only.

'Opt out' provisions

10.9.7   Part IVA of the Federal Court of Australia Act 1976 came into effect on 2 March 1992. It applies to causes of action arising after 3 March 1992. It is an example of an 'opt out' representative proceeding. The legislation is the result of the ALRC Report No 46, *Grouped Proceedings in the Federal Court*, AGPS, Canberra, 1988.

10.9.8E	**Federal Court of Australia Act 1976 (Cth)**
	Part IVA — Representative Proceedings

DIVISION 1 — PRELIMINARY

Interpretation

33A In this Part, unless the contrary intention appears:

'group member' means a member of a group of persons on whose behalf representative proceeding has been commenced;

'representative party' means a person who commences a representative proceeding;

'representative proceeding' means a proceeding commenced under section 33C;

'respondent' means a person against whom relief is sought in a representative proceeding;

'subgroup member' means a person included in a subgroup established under section 33Q;

'subgroup representative party' means a person appointed to be a subgroup representative party under section 33Q.

Application

33BA A proceeding may only be brought under this Part in respect of a cause of action arising after the commencement of the Federal Court of Australia Amendment Act 1991.

DIVISION 2 — COMMENCEMENT OF REPRESENTATIVE PROCEEDING

Commencement of proceeding

33C (1) Subject to this Part, where:

    (a)   7 or more persons have claims against the same person; and

    (b)   the claims of all those persons are in respect of, or arise out of, the same, similar or related circumstances; and

    (c)   the claims of all those persons give rise to a substantial common issue of law or fact;

a proceeding may be commenced by one or more of those persons as representing some or all of them.

  (2)   A representative proceeding may be commenced:

    (a)   whether or not the relief sought:

       (i)   is, or includes, equitable relief; or

      (ii)   consists of, or includes, damages; or

     (iii)   includes claims for damages that would require individual assessment; or

     (iv)   is the same for each person represented; and

    (b)   whether or not the proceeding:
        (i)   is concerned with separate contracts or transactions between the respondent in the proceeding and individual group members; or
        (ii) involves separate acts or omissions of the respondent done or omitted to be done in relation to individual group members.

Standing

33D (1) A person referred to in paragraph 33C(1)(a) who has a sufficient interest to commence a proceeding on his or her own behalf against another person has a sufficient interest to commence a representative proceeding against that other person on behalf of other persons referred to in that paragraph.

    (2)   Where a person has commenced a representative proceeding, the person retains a sufficient interest:
        (a)   to continue that proceeding; and
        (b)   to bring an appeal from a judgment in that proceeding; even though the person ceases to have a claim against the respondent.

Is consent required to be a group member?

33E (1) The consent of a person to be a group member in a representative proceeding is not required unless subsection (2) applies to the person.

    (2)   None of the following persons is a group member in a representative proceeding unless the person gives written consent to being so:
        (a)   the Commonwealth, a State or a Territory;
        (b)   a Minister or a Minister of a State or Territory;
        (c)   a body corporate established for a public purpose by a law of the Commonwealth, of a State or of a Territory, other than an incorporated company or association; or
        (d)   an officer of the Commonwealth, of a State or of a Territory, in his or her capacity as such an officer. ...

Representative proceeding not to be commenced in certain circumstances

33G A representative proceeding may not be commenced if the proceeding would be concerned only with claims in respect of which the Court has jurisdiction solely by virtue of the Jurisdiction of Courts (Cross-vesting) Act 1987 or a corresponding law of a State or Territory.

Originating process

33H (1) An application commencing a representative proceeding, or a document filed in support of such an application, must, in addition to any other matters required to be included:
        (a)   describe or otherwise identify the group members to whom the proceeding relates; and
        (b)   specify the nature of the claims made on behalf of the group members and the relief claimed; and
        (c)   specify the questions of law or fact common to the claims of the group members.
    (2)   In describing or otherwise identifying group members for the purposes of subsection (1), it is not necessary to name, or specify the number of, the group members. ...

Right of group member to opt out

33J (1) The Court must fix a date before which a group member may opt out of a representative proceeding.

(2) A group member may opt out of the representative proceeding by written notice given under the Rules of Court before the date so fixed.

(3) The Court, on the application of a group member, the representative party or the respondent in the proceeding, may fix another date so as to extend the period during which a group member may opt out of the representative proceeding.

(4) Except with the leave of the Court, the hearing of a representative proceeding must not commence earlier than the date before which a group member may opt out of the proceeding.

Causes of action accruing after the commencement of representative proceedings

33K (1) The Court may at any stage of a representative proceeding, on application made by the representative party, give leave to amend the application commencing the representative proceeding so as to alter the description of the group.

(2) The description of the group may be altered so as to include a person:

(a) whose cause of action accrued after the commencement of the representative proceeding but before such date as the Court fixes when giving leave; and

(b) who would have been included in the group, or, with the consent of the person would have been included in the group, if the cause of action had accrued before the commencement of the proceeding.

(3) The date mentioned in paragraph (2)(a) may be the date on which leave is given or another date before or after that date.

(4) Where the Court gives leave under subsection (1), it may also make any other orders it thinks just, including an order relating to the giving of notice to persons who, as a result of the amendment, will be included in the group and the date before which such persons may opt out of the proceeding. ...

Order that proceeding not continue as representative proceeding where cost excessive

33N (1) The Court may, on application by the respondent or of its own motion, order that a proceeding no longer continue under this Part where it is satisfied that it is in the interests of justice to do so because:

(a) the costs that would be incurred if the proceeding were to continue as a representative proceeding are likely to exceed the costs that would be incurred if each group member conducted a separate proceeding; or

(b) all the relief sought can be obtained by means of a proceeding other than a representative proceeding under this Part; or

(c) the representative proceeding will not provide an efficient and effective means of dealing with the claims of group members; or

(d) it is otherwise inappropriate that the claims be pursued by means of a representative proceeding.

(2) If the Court dismisses an application under this section, the Court may order that no further application under this section be made by the respondent except with the leave of the Court.

(3) Leave for the purposes of subsection (2) may be granted subject to such conditions as to costs as the Court considers just. ...

Settlement and discontinuance — representative proceeding

33V (1) A representative proceeding may not be settled or discontinued without the approval of the Court.

(2) If the Court gives such an approval, it may make such orders as are just with respect to the distribution of any money paid under a settlement or paid into the Court.

Settlement of individual claim of representative party

33W (1) A representative party may, with leave of the Court, settle his or her individual claim in whole or in part at any stage of the representative proceeding.

(2) A representative party who is seeking leave to settle, or who has settled, his or her individual claim may, with leave of the Court, withdraw as representative party.

DIVISION 3 — NOTICES

Notice to be given of certain matters

33X (1) Notice must be given to group members of the following matters in relation to a representative proceeding:

(a) the commencement of the proceeding and the right of the group members to opt out of the proceeding before a specified date, being the date fixed under subsection 33J (1);

(b) an application by the respondent in the proceeding for the dismissal of the proceeding on the ground of want of prosecution;

(c) an application by a representative party seeking leave to withdraw under section 33W as representative party.

(2) The Court may dispense with compliance with any or all of the requirements of subsection (1) where the relief sought in a proceeding does not include any claim for damages.

(3) If the Court so orders, notice must be given to group members of the bringing into Court of money in answer to a cause of action on which a claim in the representative proceeding is founded.

(4) Unless the Court is satisfied that it is just to do so, an application for approval of a settlement under section 33V must not be determined unless notice has been given to group members.

(5) The Court may, at any stage, order that notice of any matter be given to a group member or group members.

(6) Notice under this section must be given as soon as practicable after the happening of the event to which the notice relates. ...

DIVISION 4 — JUDGMENT ETC

Judgment — powers of court

33Z (1) The Court may, in determining a matter in a representative proceeding, do any one or more of the following:

(a) determine an issue of law;

(b) determine an issue of fact;

(c) make a declaration of liability;

(d) grant any equitable relief;

(e) make an award of damages for group members, subgroup members or individual group members, being damages consisting of specified amounts or amounts worked out in such manner as the Court specifies;

(f) award damages in an aggregate amount without specifying amounts awarded in respect of individual group members;

(g) make such other order as the Court thinks just.

(2) In making an order for an award of damages, the Court must make provision for the payment or distribution of the money to the group members entitled.

(3) Subject to section 33V, the Court is not to make an award of damages under paragraph (1)(f) unless a reasonably accurate assessment can be made of the total amount to which group members will be entitled under the judgment.

(4) Where the Court has made an order for the award of damages, the Court may give such directions (if any) as it thinks just in relation to:

(a) the manner in which a group member is to establish his or her entitlement to share in the damages; and

(b) the manner in which any dispute regarding the entitlement of a group member to share in the damages is to be determined.

Constitution of fund

33ZA (1) Without limiting the operation of subsection 33Z(2), in making provision for the distribution of money to group members, the Court may provide for:

(a) the constitution and administration of a fund consisting of the money to be distributed; and

(b) either:

(i) the payment by the respondent of a fixed sum of money into the fund; or

(ii) the payment by the respondent into the fund of such instalments, such terms, as the Court directs to meet the claims of group members; and

(c) entitlements to interest earned on the money in the fund.

(2) The costs of administering a fund are to be borne by the fund, or by the respondent in the representative proceeding, as the Court directs.

(3) Where the Court orders the constitution of a fund mentioned in subsection (1), the order must:

(a) require notice to be given to group members in such manner as is specified in the order; and

(b) specify the manner in which a group member is to make a claim for payment out of the fund and establish his or her entitlement to the payment; and

(c) specify a day (which is 6 months or more after the day on which the order is made) on or before which the group members are to make a claim for payment out of the fund; and

(d) make provision in relation to the day before which the fund is to be distributed to group members who have established an entitlement to be paid out of the fund.

(4) The Court may allow a group member to make a claim after the day fixed under paragraph (3)(c) if:

(a) the fund has not already been fully distributed; and

(b) it is just to do so.

(5) On application by the respondent in the representative proceeding after the day fixed under paragraph (3)(d), the Court may make such orders as are just for the payment from the fund to the respondent of the money remaining in the fund. ...

DIVISION 6 — MISCELLANEOUS

Suspension of limitation periods

33ZE (1) Upon the commencement of a representative proceeding, the running of any limitation period that applies to the claim of a group member to which the proceeding relates is suspended.

(2)   The limitation period does not begin to run again unless either the member opts out of the proceeding under section 33J or the proceeding, and any appeals arising from the proceeding, are determined without finally disposing of the group member's claim.

General power of court to make order

33ZF (1) In any proceeding (including an appeal) conducted under this Part, the Court may, of its own motion or on application by a party or a group member, make any order the Court thinks appropriate or necessary to ensure that justice is done in the proceeding.

(2)   Subsection (1) does not limit the operation of section 22.

10.9.9   Victoria has enacted Pt 4A of the Supreme Court Act 1986 which replaces O 18A of the Victorian rules. Part 4A applies to causes of action which arose before or after 1 January 2000. New South Wales has followed suit (and in so doing has also repealed the old representative proceedings rules): Civil Procedure Act 2005 (NSW) Pt 10. While there are some differences between the Victorian and New South Wales provisions and the provisions of Pt IVA of the Federal Court of Australia Act 1976, the differences are not significant and it is convenient to deal simply with the Federal Court provisions. The Federal Court provisions can only be used where there is a federal claim: see **4.1.10E–4.1.12E**. Where there is a federal claim, then the Federal Court may exercise an accrued jurisdiction: see **4.1.16E–4.1.19C**. Since the decision in *Re Wakim; Ex parte McNally* (1999) 198 CLR 511, the Federal Court has been unable to exercise cross-vested jurisdiction. The court had not been able to adopt the Pt IVA provisions to a wholly cross-vested claim in any event: see s 33G.

10.9.10   What is the position where an applicant seeks to use Pt IVA of the Federal Court of Australia Act by putting forward a federal claim which is subsequently struck out? In *Johnson Tiles Pty Ltd v Esso Australia Ltd* (the *Longford Gas Explosion* case, in Gippsland, Victoria) (2000) 104 FCR 564 at [88], the Full Federal Court said:

In the ordinary course the contention that a claim is not tenable will not go to jurisdiction unless dependent upon a submission that the claim is outside jurisdiction. And indeed, within that class a claim may be untenable because its very nature denies its character as an element of any matter or controversy in respect of which the Court can exercise jurisdiction. So a proceeding based upon the proposition that the Commonwealth Constitution is invalid does not disclose a matter arising under the Constitution or involving its interpretation — *Nikolic v MGICA Ltd* [1999] FCA 849. A claim may also be a sham reflecting no genuine controversy and therefore establishing no matter in respect of which the Court may exercise its jurisdiction. There has been discussion of so called 'colourable' claims made under the Trade Practices Act for the improper purpose of fabricating jurisdiction. The mere fact that a claim is struck out as untenable does not mean it is colourable in that sense. The pleading of the s 52 claim in this case advanced the legitimate forensic purpose of endeavouring to establish a cause of action which would not require proof of a duty of care. Notwithstanding its precipitate initiation and chequered history, I am not satisfied that it was colourable in the sense that would deprive this Court of jurisdiction to deal with the matter including any non-federal claims that may form part of it.

The court was of the view that the proceeding could continue as a representative proceeding under Pt IVA.

Merkel J transferred the proceeding to the Supreme Court of Victoria on 12 April 2001 to be litigated as a representative proceeding under Pt 4A of the Supreme Court Act: (2001) 113 FCR 42.

10.9.11   The validity of Pt IVA of the Federal Court of Australia Act 1976 was challenged unsuccessfully in *Femcare Ltd v Bright* (2000) 100 FCR 331, as was the validity of the Victorian provisions in *Mobil Oil Australia Ltd v Victoria* (2002) 211 CLR 1. Central to those challenges was the opt-out nature of the provisions, the way in which damages are to be assessed and the effect that this has on the rights of persons within the class.

10.9.12C	**Wong v Silkfield Pty Ltd** (1999) 199 CLR 215; [1999] HCA 48; (1999) 73 ALJR 1427 High Court of Australia

[The appellants brought proceedings under Pt IVA of the Federal Court of Australia Act 1976 seeking relief. This included a declaration that the respondent had engaged in misleading and deceptive conduct, in respect of the sale or proposed sale of lots in a residential building known as 'the Phoenician North Tower', Broadbeach, Queensland, and damages. The proceeding was brought by the appellants as a 'representative party' and the group members were identified in the statement of claim, namely persons who entered into contracts to purchase lots in the building from Silkfield. The appellants complained of certain representations allegedly made by the respondent's agent.

At issue were the requirements in ss 33C(1)(c) and 33H(1)(c) and, in particular, the meaning of the phrase in para (c) of s 33C(1) — 'give rise to a substantial common issue of law or fact'.

The court said at ALJR 1427 [11]:]

In *Carnie v Esanda Finance Corporation Ltd* this Court construed Pt 8 r 13(1) of the Supreme Court Rules 1970 (NSW). That sub-rule provided:

> Where numerous persons have the same interest in any proceedings the proceedings may be commenced, and, unless the Court otherwise orders, continued, by or against any one or more of them as representing all or as representing all except one or more of them.

The Court determined that persons having separate causes of action in those causes of action within the meaning of this Rule. Order 6 r 13(1) of the Federal Court Rules is in the same terms as the New South Wales Supreme Court Rule. Part IVA provides its own more detailed regime. Like other provisions conferring jurisdiction upon or granting powers to a court, Pt IVA is not to be read by making implications or imposing limitations not found in the words used; this is so even if the evident purpose of the statute is to displace generally understood procedures.

In particular, the scope of s 33C is not confined by matters not required by its terms or context; however, the terms must be construed and the context considered. Section 33C attempts to resolve issues which bedevilled representative procedures as they had been developed, particularly by courts of equity. This is apparent from the terms of s 33C(2). Thus, the relief may consist only of damages and may not include equitable relief and the proceeding may be concerned with separate contracts or transactions and involve separate acts or omissions. What is required is that the claims give rise to a common issue of law or fact which is 'substantial'. ...

[At ALJR 1433 [27]:]

The term 'substantial' may have various shades of meaning. Having regard to the context, it may mean 'large or weighty' or 'real or of substance as distinct from ephemeral or nominal'. Some assistance for the present case may be derived from authorities construing provisions in the form of that rule considered in *Carnie*. This rule provided for the commencement of proceedings by numerous persons having 'the same interest in any proceeding'. In *Carnie*, Mason CJ, Deane and Dawson JJ expressed the view that to equate the meaning of the phrase 'same interest' with a common ingredient in the cause of action by each member of the class might not adequately reflect the content of the statutory expression. Their Honours said that the expression may extend 'to a significant common interest in the resolution of any question of law or fact arising in the relevant proceedings'. Brennan J and McHugh J were of opinion that a plaintiff and the represented persons had 'the same interest' when they had a community of interest 'in the determination of any substantial question of law or fact that arises in the proceedings'. Toohey and Gaudron JJ treated as sufficient 'a significant question common to all members of the class', to be determined by the grant of declaratory relief.

Clearly, the purpose of the enactment of Pt IVA was not to narrow access to the new form of representative proceedings beyond that which applied under regimes considered in cases such as *Carnie*. This suggests that, when used to identify the threshold requirements of s 33C(1), 'substantial' does not indicate that which is 'large' or 'of special significance' or would 'have a major impact on the litigation' but, rather, is directed to issues which are 'real or of substance'.

The circumstance that proceedings which pass the threshold requirement of s 33C may later be terminated as representative proceedings, by order made under s 33N, confirms rather than denies such a construction of s 33C(1). Further, as Foster J pointed out, the broadening provisions in sub-s (2) of s 33C emphasise the width of the entitlement conferred by s 33C(1) to commence a representative proceeding.

Foster J noted that the only issue of fact which could be common to all members of the postulated group, identified and unidentified, would be that raised in the statement of claim respecting the representation as to the accuracy of the s 49 statements. His Honour, like Spender J at first instance, regarded the identified common issue as 'substantial' in the necessary sense. This was because the allegations involved were serious and significant and detrimental misrepresentations were claimed. It was not to the point that, in the final resolution of the litigation, this might not prove to be the 'major' or 'core' issue. It was not necessary to show that litigation of this common issue would be likely to resolve wholly, or to any significant degree, the claims of all group members.

The Statement of Claim alleged various misrepresentations made by Skye for the purposes of promoting sales of lots in the building, and consequent contraventions of s 52 of the Trade Practices Act. The issue respecting the s 49 certificates was but one of these matters. However, on the face of the Application and the Statement of Claim, the issue was one of substance.

Spender J correctly refused the declaration sought on the motion by Silkfield, and the Full Court erred in upholding the appeal and granting relief to Silkfield.

10.9.13   The following case considers other threshold requirements prescribed in s 33C.

10.9.14C   **Philip Morris (Australia) Pty Ltd v Nixon**
                      (2000) 199 CLR 215; 170 ALR 487; [2000] FCA 229
                                  Full Federal Court

[The proceedings were brought by six named applicants, for themselves, and as representing the class of persons defined in an amended statement of claim. The three sets of respondents to the representative proceedings comprised manufacturers or distributors of cigarettes in Australia. The applicants claimed that they, and each group member, had contracted a smoking-related disease in consequence of being influenced by the respondents' conduct to begin or continue smoking the respondents' cigarettes.

The relief sought by the applicants in the proceedings included damages under the general law and under the Trade Practices Act 1974 (Cth) and exemplary damages.

Sackville J's principal judgment, which is reproduced below, relates to an application for leave to appeal an earlier determination of a pleading application by Wilcox J.]

Sackville J (at [107]):
The Common Ground

There was some common ground among the parties on important issues. *First*, it seems to have been accepted on all sides that the applicants were obliged to plead adequately the case alleged by the applicants on their own behalf and on behalf of all members of the represented class. Reference was made to the observation of Beaumont J in *Cameron v Qantas Airways Ltd* (1993) ATPR 41–251, at 41,370, that it is axiomatic that a respondent in a representative proceeding, like the respondent in any proceedings, is entitled to the benefit of a properly pleaded case, so that a proper defence can be filed. According to his Honour, it is no answer to an inadequate pleading to say that the position might be clarified at a subsequent directions hearing. Reference was also made to the holding by Hely J in *Harrison v Lidoform Pty Ltd* (Hely J, 24 November 1998, unreported), that the statement of claim in a representative proceeding 'needs to identify what the rights of those represented are claimed to be, and how they are said to arise' (at 14).

Secondly, Senior Counsel for the applicants expressly accepted that in order to satisfy par (a) of what the High Court has described as the 'threshold requirements' imposed by s 33C(1) of the Federal Court Act (*Wong v Silkfield*, at 381, *per curiam*), it was necessary that the applicants' pleading allege facts that establish that they and every member of the represented class have a claim against every respondent. For their part, the respondents accepted that the expression 'the same person' in s 33C(1)(a) is to be read as including more than one person (see Acts Interpretation Act 1901 (Cth), s 23(b)), provided that all applicants and members of the represented class make claims against all respondents to the proceedings.

Perhaps because there was no dispute on these questions, the parties did not explore further the relationship between the procedural requirements of Part IVA of the *Federal Court Act* and the general principles governing pleadings in the Federal Court. It is nonetheless important to address these questions, as they have a bearing on the outcome of the present appeals. A useful starting point is the report of the Law Reform Commission ('LRC'), *Grouped Proceedings in the Federal Court* (Report No 46, 1988) ('*Grouped Proceedings*').

The LRC's Report on Grouped Proceedings

Part IVA of the Federal Court Act does not follow precisely the recommendations of the LRC in *Grouped Proceedings.* Nevertheless, Part IVA follows reasonably closely the substance of the LRC's proposals concerning procedural requirements for representative proceedings. (*Grouped Proceedings* included in Appendix A a draft Federal Court (Grouped Proceedings) Bill ('Draft Bill') that has similarities with the legislation ultimately enacted.) For this reason, the LRC's analysis sheds light on the objectives underlying key provisions now contained in Part IVA.

As has been noted, s 33C(1) of the Federal Court Act sets out threshold requirements for representative proceedings. Section 33C(1)(a) of the Federal Court Act does two things. First, it stipulates that seven is the minimum number of persons who may make claims in a representative proceeding. (In this respect it broadly corresponds to the LRC's proposal: see par 140). Secondly, and more importantly for present purposes, it requires that the seven or more persons 'have claims against the same person'.

The second requirement in s 33C(1)(a) implements the LRC's clearly expressed view that group proceedings should be available only where the applicant and all group members seek relief against the **same respondent.** The LRC saw its task as considering whether there was a need for procedural changes to make it easier and less costly for people to obtain remedies in cases of 'multiple wrong[doing]' (par 13). It used the term 'multiple wrong' to describe situations:

> ... where a **single respondent** has caused or threatened to cause loss, damage or injury to a number of people in circumstances where there is a legal liability to pay compensation ... or where injunctive or declaratory relief is available (par 13). (Emphasis added.)

The LRC's recommendations were specifically designed to provide an effective procedure to enable people suffering loss or damage in common with others as a result of a wrongful act or omission **by the same respondent** (par 69, 95, 133). It therefore plainly did not envisage that the grouped procedure could be employed to bring a proceeding against more than one respondent, in circumstances where some members of the group make a claim against one respondent only and others make a claim against another respondent.

Section 33C(2) of the Federal Court Act closely mirrors the LRC's recommendations that the grouped procedure should be available where group members:

- claim damages as a result of a wrongful act or series of wrongful acts by another even though damages might need to be assessed separately (par 64); and
- have different claims for relief against the respondent or rely on different transactions or events to establish their claims (par 134–135).

The LRC saw these recommendations as justifiable extensions of the scope of existing procedures under Rules of Court, such as FCR, O 6 r 13, which permit representative proceedings where numerous people have 'the same interest' in the proceedings. (*Grouped Proceedings* was published before the decision in *Carnie v Esanda Finance Corporation Ltd* (1995) 182 CLR 398, which gave a liberal construction to an equivalent rule).

In view of its recommendations extending the scope of existing representative procedures, the LRC considered that provision should be made to ensure that grouped proceedings involve common issues. Accordingly, it proposed that the various claims brought by the applicant and group members should be based on similar or related facts:

> ... [t]he material facts on which a claim is based [footnote: that is, those that must be pleaded: FCR O 4 r 6(2)] — every fact upon which a party must rely to make out their

claim — should therefore have to be the same, similar or related in order to ensure a community of interest between the principal applicant and group members and to prevent disparate matters from being brought together. (par 134.)

This recommendation is reflected in the terms of s 33C(1)(b) of the Federal Court Act, which requires that the claims of all applicants and group members be 'in respect of, or arise out of, the same, similar or related circumstances'.

The LRC recognised that a requirement of 'common or related circumstances' would not of itself ensure that there is a single issue or question which arises in all proceedings. Unless such a requirement were imposed, the LRC took the view that the advantages of grouping could be outweighed by diversity and unmanageability of issues (par 136). Therefore it recommended that each group member's proceeding should have to raise at least one question of law or fact that is common to the proceedings of each other group member and the principal applicant (par 138). This recommendation is reflected in the terms of s 33C(1)(c), although the word 'substantial' (the significance of which was considered by the High Court in *Wong v Silkfield*) does not appear in the LRC's *Draft Bill* (see App A, cl 12(1)(a)).

The LRC specifically addressed the question of pleadings in grouped proceedings. It noted that the originating process for proceedings in the Federal Court is an application and either a statement of claim or an affidavit in support (FCR, O 4, rr 1–6). The LRC observed that the application in grouped proceedings would need to include:

- the relief claimed by the principal applicant
- the relief claimed by the group members
- a sufficient description or identification of the group members (par 141).

The LRC reiterated that the group members would not have to be named in the application, but would usually be described as persons suffering a particular kind of loss or injury.

The LRC proposed that, in order to give the respondent 'the appropriate information', the statement of claim or affidavit should set out:

- the nature of the principal applicant's claim or claims and the material facts on which they are based
- the nature of the group members' claims and the material facts on which they are based
- a question or questions common to the principal proceeding (so far as that proceeding is in respect of a federal or Territory matter) and each group member's proceeding (par 142).

The LRC also recommended that the statement of claim or affidavit should declare that the material facts in the applicant's proceedings are the same, similar or related to the material facts giving rise to such claim in each group member's proceeding.

It is clear from these recommendations that the Commission envisaged that in a grouped proceeding commenced by application and statement of claim, the pleading would specify the material facts on which the claims of the principal applicant and group members were based. However, it seems that the Commission also envisaged that pleadings in grouped proceedings would not necessarily plead in detail the individual case of each group member.

This is demonstrated by the sample statement of claim included in an Appendix to *Grouped Proceedings* report (App B). The sample statement of claim pleads a hypothetical case founded on misleading advertising by a vendor of fax machines. The representative group is identified as comprising all persons who purchased a particular brand of fax machine from the respondent. The sample statement of claim pleads precise dates of purchase and installation of a fax machine by the principal applicant. But so far as group members are concerned, the sample pleading simply alleges that each group member purchased a relevant fax machine after a particular date and prior to the institution of proceedings. Similarly, the sample statement of claim does not identify when each group member saw the misleading advertisement or purchased the fax, but alleges only that each member relied on the advertisement when purchasing the machine.

Section 33H of the Federal Court Act also has its origins in the LRC's recommendations, although the section does not exactly follow the LRC's proposals. For example, s 33H(1) (c) requires the common questions of law and fact to be specified in the application, rather than in the statement of claim or supporting affidavit, while s 33H(1)(b) requires the application to specify the nature of the claims made on behalf of group members, as well as the relief claimed.

Finally, the LRC considered that adequate provision had to be made to ensure that the grouped procedure is not abused or used inappropriately or inefficiently. For this reason, the LRC proposed that the Court's existing powers under FCR O 11 r 16 and O 20 r 2(1) should be available in grouped proceedings. To stress this point, the LRC recommended (par 149) that the legislation should specifically refer to the Court's power to stay, dismiss or strike out proceedings. Section 33ZG(b) of the Federal Court Act implements this recommendation.

Procedural Requirements for Representative Proceedings

It follows from Part IVA of the Federal Court Act, when construed in context (including the LRC's report on *Grouped Proceedings*), that representative proceedings must satisfy a number of procedural requirements.

First, in order for representative proceedings to be properly constituted, the application (or a supporting document) must include the three categories of information specified in s 33H(1). If, for example, the application does not describe or otherwise identify the group members, as required by s 33H(1)(a), the application is liable to be struck out or the proceedings dismissed, pursuant to the Court's powers under the FCR specifically preserved by s 33ZG(b).

Secondly, a proceeding is not properly commenced unless it satisfies each of the three threshold requirements specified in s 33C(1). If the proceeding does not comply with these requirements, for example because seven or more persons do not have claims against the same person as required by s 33C(1)(a), the proceeding is liable to be dismissed or the applicants' pleading struck out. (An alternative procedure was adopted in *Silkfield v Wong*, where the Full Federal Court made a declaration that the proceedings continue as proceedings brought by the respondents on their own behalf, to give effect to the majority holding that s 33C(1)(c) had not been complied with. The High Court, although allowing the appeal, did not comment adversely on this form of relief.)

Thirdly, as the parties accepted, s 33C(1)(a) requires every applicant and represented party to have a claim against the one respondent or, if there is more than one, against all respondents. This conclusion follows from the language of s 33C(1)(a) itself and is consistent with the approach taken by the LRC in *Grouped Proceedings*. It is also consistent with the structure of the legislation. For example, s 33D(1)(a) (which provides that a person who has a sufficient interest to commence a proceeding on his or her own behalf against another person has a sufficient interest to commence a representative proceeding **against that person** on behalf of other persons referred to in s 33C(1)(a)) is clearly drafted on the assumption that all applicants and represented persons will have claims against the same person.

It follows that s 33C(1)(a) is not satisfied if some applicants and group members have claims against one respondent (or group of respondents) while other applicants and group members have claims against another respondent (or group of respondents). The requirement in s 33C(1)(b), that the claims of all group members are in respect of or arise out of the same, similar or related circumstances, is a necessary but not sufficient condition for the commencement of representative proceedings. Of course, if there are two sets of claims against two sets of respondents, it may well be that each can be the subject of representative proceedings. It may even be that directions can be made for them to be heard together: *Ryan v Great Lakes Council* (1997) 149 ALR 45, at 48, per Wilcox J. But they cannot both be the subject of the same representative proceedings.

Fourthly, in a representative proceeding commenced by application and statement of claim, the pleading must demonstrate that each of the conditions laid down in s 33C(1) has been satisfied. Since s 33C(1) is concerned with the commencement of proceedings, compliance with its terms can be assessed only by reference to the case pleaded by the applicants (or set out in affidavit form if pleadings are not used). This is consistent with the approach taken by the High Court in *Wong v Silkfield*. Thus, for example, the pleading must make claims on behalf of the applicant and each member of the represented class against the same respondent or, if more than one, against all respondents. It is not permissible in a representative proceeding to plead a claim on behalf of some group members against one respondent and a separate claim on behalf of other group members against another respondent.

Fifthly, Part IVA of the Federal Court Act does not abrogate the general pleading requirements applicable to proceedings in the Federal Court by virtue of FCR, O 11. An inadequately pleaded representative proceeding is liable to be struck out or dismissed in the exercise of the Court's powers under FCR, O 11 r 16 or O 20 r 2(1). So much follows from s 33ZG(b) of the Federal Court Act which, as has been seen, gives effect to recommendations of the LRC in *Grouped Proceedings*.

Unlike the threshold requirements for a representative proceeding specified in s 33C(1) of the Federal Court Act, inadequacies in the pleadings do not necessarily mean that the proceeding cannot continue as a representative action. Whether that is the consequence of pleaded deficiencies will depend on the nature of the deficiencies and whether they are curable by amendment. The Court has powers to manage representative proceedings which are no less extensive than its powers to manage other proceedings: FCR, O 10 r 1; Federal Court Act s 33ZF(1) (empowering the Court to make any order in a representative proceeding that the Court thinks appropriate or necessary to ensure that justice is done).

The fact that Part IVA of the Federal Court Act preserves the ordinary rules of pleading in representative proceedings does not, however, necessarily mean that the applicant in such proceedings is bound to plead material facts specific to each individual member of the represented class. The principal functions of pleadings are to furnish a statement of the case sufficient to allow the opposing party a fair opportunity to meet it:

- to define the issues for decision in the litigation and thereby enable the relevance and admissibility of evidence to be determined at the trial; and
- to enable the opposing party to understand and assess the pleaded case for the purposes of settling the litigation.

See *Dare v Pulham* (1982) 148 CLR 658, at 664, *per curiam*.

The requirement imposed by FCR O 11 r 2, that a pleading contain a statement in summary form of the material facts on which the party relies, is to be understood by reference to the functions of pleadings. Thus it is a well established rule that the permitted level of generality of a pleading must depend on the general subject matter and on what is required to convey to the opposite party the case that is to be met: *Ratcliffe v Evans* [1892] 2 QB 524 (CA). For example, in some circumstances, it may be permissible to plead a conclusion rather than the material facts underlying the conclusion: *Kernel Holdings Pty Ltd v Rothmans of Pall Mall Australia Pty Ltd* (French J, 3 September 1991, unreported); *Queensland v Pioneer Concrete (Qld) Pty Ltd* (1999) ATPR 41–691 (Drummond J), at 42,829.

In the context of representative proceedings, it may be sufficient for the applicant to plead the case of each member of the represented class at a reasonably high level of generality. (I use 'sufficient' in the sense of adequate to enable the applicant to resist an application to strike out the pleading or dismiss the proceedings.) This is illustrated by the sample statement of claim appended to the LRC's report on *Grouped Proceedings*. As has been explained, the sample statement of claim alleges material facts, such as the purchase of a defective product by group members and their reliance on misleading representations, only in the most general terms. ...

[At [165]–[166]:]

The representative procedure provided for by Part IVA of the Federal Court Act is plainly designed to accommodate a case where the applicants and group members rely on a series of related but not identical transactions, such as similar representations being made separately to different individuals: *Grouped Proceedings,* par 134. But this case involves vastly different forms of advertising, promotions and other public statements by the three respondents over four decades. It is true that the applicants allege that the various public statements — ranging from a single brand name on a billboard at a sporting match to a submission to a Senate Committee — all make substantially the same representations. Yet to test that allegation it would be necessary to examine each of the public statements made over the four decades in its own context, having regard to the characteristics of the likely audience. This is a far cry from the kind of case envisaged by the LRC as falling within the purview of the representative procedure.

In the end, as the primary Judge acknowledged, a judgment must be made as to whether the circumstances giving rise to each claim are so disparate as to merit their grouping as a representative proceeding. His Honour's judgment that the circumstances of this case are not too disparate for this purpose rested heavily on his view, with which I respectfully disagree, that the applicants' pleaded case included a claim that the respondents engaged in a collective course of conduct designed to mislead or deceive consumers. Once it is accepted that the case is founded on the separate conduct of each set of respondents, the difficulty in concluding that s 33C(1)(b) is satisfied becomes apparent. The circumstances of each of the thousands of claims pleaded in the statement of claim are so disparate and involve such varied conduct on the part of the several respondents that they cannot be said to arise out of related circumstances.

The Court ordered that the proceedings not continue under Part IVA.

10.9.15　Notes and questions

1. Section 43(1A) of the Federal Court of Australia Act 1976 (Cth) provides that a represented person will not be liable for any costs payable to a respondent. This is the legislative response to the decision of the Victorian Appeal Division in *Burns Philp & Co Ltd v Bhagat* [1993] 1 VR 203, where in *obiter* the view was expressed that a represented person in proceedings under the Victorian provisions (extracted above) might be liable for a defendant's costs by virtue of s 24 of the Supreme Court Act 1986 (Vic): see 20.2.1. (In Pt 4A proceedings, the Victorian rules are the same as the Federal rules: Supreme Court Act 1986 (Vic) s 33SZB.)

2. Can Pt IVA work in the absence of contingency fees? The adoption of contingency fees was recommended by the ALRC in its report on grouped proceedings. It was not adopted in Pt IVA.

3. It would appear from *Philip Morris (Australia) Pty Ltd v Nixon* (10.9.14C) that unless each applicant has claims against each respondent, the representative procedure in Pt IVA cannot be adopted. But see *Bray v F Hoffman-La Roche Ltd* (2003) 130 FCR 317 where two members of the Full Federal Court, Carr and Finkelstein JJ, expressed doubt about *Philip Morris v Nixon* and declined to follow it. The matter may need to be resolved by the High Court as suggested by Branson J in that case. See further V Morabito, 'Class Actions against Multiple Respondents' (2002) 30 *FLRev* 295.

4. Note that s 486B of the Migration Act 1958 (Cth) is designed to prevent non-citizens exercising rights by way of representative proceeding in migration matters. Quite apart from any other consideration, do you think this assists judicial administration?

5. The court has a discretion as to whether to allow a proceeding to continue as a representative proceeding, notwithstanding the fact that the threshold requirements have been satisfied. On the exercise of the discretion, see *Dagi v Broken Hill Proprietary Co* [2000] VSC 486 per Hedigan J.

6. The Full Federal Court has held that a represented group in proceedings under Pt IVA can be defined by reference to the entry of group members into litigation funding agreements with a litigation funder: see *Multiplex Fund Managers Ltd v P Dawson Nominees Pty Ltd* [2007] FCAFC 200. And see also *Jameson v Professional Investment Services Pty Ltd* [2009] NSWCA 28, where the New South Wales Court of Appeal indicated that it would follow the *Multiplex* case in the context of NSW r 7.4.

7. How should the court manage multiple class actions, that is, different class actions which rest broadly on the same facts and issues? Finkelstein J has suggested the formation of a litigation committee for each of the class actions: see *Kirby v Centro Properties Ltd* [2008] FCA 1505.

8. How is the court to deal with settlements? What factors need to be taken into account, particularly where there are group members who are under a disability? See *Lopez v Star World Enterprises Pty Ltd* (1999) ATPR 41-678; per Finkelstein J. And see also *Verschuur v Vynotas Pty Ltd* [2004] VSC 130.

10.9.16 Further reading

P Cashman, *Class Action Law and Practice*, The Federation Press, Sydney, 2007.

V Morabito, 'Class Actions: The Right to Opt Out under Part IVA of the Federal Court of Australia Act 1976 (Cth)' (1994) 19 *MULR* 615.

The Hon Justice M Wilcox, 'Representative Proceedings in the Federal Court: A Progress Report' (1997) 15 *Aust Bar Rev* 91.

THIRD PARTY PROCEEDINGS

10.10.1 There is provision in most jurisdictions for claims by defendants against third parties: FCR r 15.01(b); ACT rr 301–318; NSW r 9.1; NT r 11.01; Qld rr 191– 207; SA r 36; Tas rr 201–210; Vic r 11.01; WA O 19 r 1. In the Federal Court and in New South Wales, third party proceedings are subsumed within the broader category of 'cross-claims'. The following extract from the Tasmanian rules is an example of third party rules.

10.10.2E   **Rules of the Supreme Court 2000 (Tas)**

202 (1) Subject to sub-rule (2) a defendant who claims as against any person not already a party to the action to be entitled to contribution or indemnity or any relief or remedy relating to, or connected with, the original subject matter of the action, may file and serve on that person a third party notice directed to that person.

    (2)   A defendant may file and serve a third party notice —

        (a)   without leave at any time before delivering the defence; and

        (b)   at any other time with the leave of the Court or a judge.

204 On being served with the third party notice, the third party becomes a party to the action with the same rights in respect of the defence against the claim and otherwise as if sued by the defendant in the ordinary way.

10.10.3 Question

1. Can a defendant commence third party proceedings against X where the liability of X is an alternative liability to that of the defendant rather than a concurrent liability? See *Lauren v Jolly* [1996] 1 VR 189. The answer is no.

One example given by the court in that case is as follows:

> A pedestrian is knocked down by a motor car, but is uncertain whether it was car A or car B. If suit is brought against driver A, then A cannot properly bring a third party claim for contribution against driver B. Only one of the drivers is liable and there is no concurrent liability. The claims are true alternative claims. Of course the

position would be different if it were alleged that the negligence of both drivers had in some way caused the plaintiff's injury, even if only one vehicle actually struck the plaintiff.

On the question of the parties' entitlement to claim contribution, see *James Hardie & Coy Pty Ltd v Seltsam Pty Ltd* (1998) 196 CLR 53; *Burke v LFOT Pty Ltd* (2000) 178 ALR 161.

Contribution

10.10.4 In most jurisdictions, there are rules which enable parties to the proceeding to seek contribution or indemnity from another party or parties: FCR r 15.01(b); ACT r 321; NSW r 9.11; NT r 11.15; Qld rr 206, 208; SA r 35; Tas rr 211, 212; Vic r 11.15; WA O 1 9 r 8. The following extract from the Victorian rules is an example.

10.10.5E **Supreme Court (General Civil Procedure) Rules 2005 (Vic)**
Order 11 — Third Party Procedure

Claim against another party

11.15 (1) Where a third party claims as against another party to the proceeding any relief of the kind described in Rule 11.01, the party may make the claim against the other party by filing and serving a notice in accordance with this rule —

    (a) within 60 days after the service on the party of the document in the proceeding by which the claim in respect of which the notice is served was made; or

    (b) if when the document was served the other party was not a party, then within 60 days after the party became a party.

(2) Paragraph (1) shall not apply where the claim could be made by counterclaim in the proceeding.

10.10.6 It is important that notice of contribution be given if the court is to make an order for contribution. Contribution should be sought in the proceeding rather than in a later proceeding: *Port of Melbourne Authority v Anshun Pty Ltd (No 2)* (1981) 147 CLR 589. See **10.2.4C**.

Further reading

10.11.1 Looseleaf and electronic sources

N R Burns, 'Parties to Proceedings', *Court Forms Precedents and Pleadings New South Wales*, LexisNexis, Sydney looseleaf.

B K Grossman, 'Parties to Proceedings', *Court Forms Precedents and Pleadings Victoria*, LexisNexis, Sydney looseleaf.

Halsbury's Laws of Australia, Practice and Procedure, 'Parties', LexisNexis, [325-1300]–[325-1515].

B Springer et al, 'Parties to Actions', *Court Forms Precedents and Pleadings Queensland*, LexisNexis, Sydney looseleaf.

10.11.2 Texts

B Cairns, *Australian Civil Procedure*, 9th ed, Thomson Reuters, Sydney, 2011, Ch 9.

## CHAPTER 11

Pleading

OVERVIEW

Pleadings are documents exchanged between the parties to litigation, in which they set out the material facts they intend to allege at the hearing of the action. They serve a number of purposes, including:

- informing the court of the matters on which its decision is sought;
- defining the issues, and so limiting the ambit of discovery and the evidence which needs to be prepared for trial; and
- providing a record of all of the matters involved in the action, and in that way preventing further actions between the same parties in relation to them.

 The usual pleadings are:

- the plaintiff's statement of claim;
- the defendant's defence, or defence and counterclaim; and
- the plaintiff's reply (and answer if there is a counterclaim).

 Pleadings are often the first documents read by the judge; therefore, well-drafted pleadings will assist a party to create a favourable impression. The rules include a number of sanctions against a party that does not comply with the rules of pleading. The result in such a case may be that a party is deprived of some right to relief, or of some defence, unless the court gives leave to amend.

PURPOSE OF PLEADINGS

11.1.1   Pleadings define the issues in dispute between the parties, which are to be determined by the court.

 Because the purpose of pleadings is to define the issues, they are usually only required in 'actions', which, in most jurisdictions, are defined as matters commenced either by writ or by statement of claim. In some circumstances, however, the court can order that a matter commenced in another way proceed by exchange of pleadings, or that the parties file points of claim and defence in a similar form to pleadings: see generally Chapter 7.

Proper pleading ensures that both the court and the parties know the matters in issue: *Bruce v Odhams Press Ltd* [1936] 1 KB 697 at 712; *Banque Commerciale* SA (*en liq*) *v Akhil Holdings Ltd* (1990) 169 CLR 279 (extracted below); *Suvaal v Cessnock City Council* [2003] HCA 41; (2003) 200 ALR 1: extracted below at 11.1.4C. This assists the parties to properly prepare for trial. Once they know exactly what is in dispute, the parties are able to determine what evidence has to be led at the trial. For instance, they know they do not need to lead evidence of matters which have been admitted by the other side, and that they must lead evidence of allegations essential to their case which have been put in issue. In the same way, the pleadings will assist pre-trial in determining which documents must be discovered to the other side, and in the scope of any interrogatories.

A case can be decided on a different basis to that set out in the pleadings only if the parties agree to depart from what is alleged, and the court permits such a departure.

11.1.2C   **Banque Commerciale SA (en liq) v Akhil Holdings Ltd**
                          (1990) 169 CLR 279
                          High Court of Australia

[In 1978, the plaintiff sued the defendant bank and two other parties in the Supreme Court of New South Wales. It alleged that one of the other parties had caused the bank to transfer from its ownership certain shares in a mining company which were held by it in trust for the plaintiff. Each defendant filed a defence pleading that the action was statute-barred.

The plaintiff did not reply to the bank's defence, but in its reply to the defences of the other parties it alleged that its action was one in respect of a fraudulent breach of trust by the bank, in which event the usual six-year time bar did not apply. A copy of that reply was served on the bank's solicitors. The bank did not appear at the trial.

The trial judge gave judgment for the defendants on the ground that the plaintiff had not established a beneficial interest in the shares. On appeal by the plaintiff, the Court of Appeal found the bank was a party to the fraudulent breach of trust and gave judgment against all defendants. The bank appealed to the High Court. It was not in issue that the action against the bank was statute-barred after six years unless there was a fraudulent breach of trust to which the trustee was party or privy; nor that the breach complained of occurred more than six years before the action was commenced. The bank argued that the finding of fraud against it was not open on the pleadings and that, but for that finding, its plea that the action was statute-barred must result in judgment in its favour.]

Mason CJ and Gaudron J (at 286–7): The argument that, notwithstanding that fraud was neither pleaded nor particularised against the Bank, the Court of Appeal was entitled to make a finding of fraud on the part of the Bank was made by reference to service on the Bank's solicitors of the Amended Reply to Defence of Third Defendant (Mr Messara). As previously noted, that pleading asserted that the action was for 'fraudulent breach of trust by the [Bank]'. In substance the argument was that, the allegation of fraud having been brought to the notice of the Bank, and the Bank nonetheless having elected not to be present at the hearing, it should not now be allowed to claim the benefit of the rule that, in general, relief should be restricted to that available on the pleadings.

The function of pleadings is to state with sufficient clarity the case that must be met: *Gould and Birbeck and Bacon v Mount Oxide Mines Ltd (in liq)* (1916) 22 CLR 490, at p 517 per Isaacs and Rich JJ. In this way, pleadings serve to ensure the basic requirement of procedural fairness that a party should have the opportunity of meeting the case against him or her and, incidentally, to define the issues for decision. The rule that, in general, relief is confined to that available on the pleadings secures a party's right to this basic requirement of procedural fairness. Accordingly, the circumstances in which a case [287] may be decided on a basis different from that disclosed by the pleadings are limited to those in which the parties have deliberately chosen some different basis for the determination of their respective rights and liabilities. See, eg, *Browne v Dunn* (1893) 6 R, at p 76; *Mount Oxide Mines* (1916) 22 CLR, at pp 517–518.

Ordinarily, the question whether the parties have chosen some issue different from that disclosed in the pleadings as the basis for the determination of their respective rights and liabilities is to be answered by inference from the way in which the trial was conducted. It may be that, in a clear case, mere acquiescence by one party in a course adopted by the other will be sufficient to ground such an inference. In the present case, the Bank not having been present at the hearing, there could be no acquiescence by it in such course, if any, by which Akhil might have attempted to extend the issues at the hearing to encompass a case of fraud as against the Bank. Nor, in our view, can acquiescence be inferred from the Bank's failure to participate in the hearing coupled with its knowledge that an allegation of fraud on its part had been raised in the amended reply to the defence filed against Mr Messara. That was a bare and unparticularised assertion. In that context, a choice by the Bank to have its liability determined on the basis of fraud would be tantamount to a decision to forego the right to be informed of the case to be made against it. The facts will not support such an inference. Accordingly, Akhil was entitled only to such relief as was available on the pleadings. In particular, it was not entitled to relief on the basis that the Bank was party to a fraudulent breach of trust. The Bank is therefore entitled to judgment in the action on the basis that its defence that the action was statute-barred was made out.

The appeal should be allowed. The orders of the Court of Appeal should be set aside in so far as the appeal was allowed and judgment entered against the Bank. In lieu thereof it should be ordered that the appeal as against the Bank be dismissed with costs.

Brennan J (at 289–90): In the present case, the defendant Bank (the appellant) pleaded in its defence that 'the Plaintiff's claim [was] barred by the provisions of the *Limitation Act*, 1969 and the provisions of Section 69 of the *Trustee Act*, 1925.' In the absence of any reply to this pleading the Bank was entitled to succeed as the breaches of trust alleged against the Bank were alleged to have occurred more than six years before the proceedings were commenced. There was no issue of fact which the Bank was required to prove to make good its defence based upon the statutes. As of right it was entitled to judgment at the trial and the order that 'the proceedings be dismissed with costs' was rightly made — albeit for reasons which the Court of Appeal held to be erroneous.

The Court of Appeal found that the Bank had committed breaches of trust the last of which occurred on or before 27 November 1970, a date more than six years before the proceedings commenced. The Court of Appeal held that s 69 of the *Trustee Act* 1925 (NSW) rather than ss 47 and 48 of the *Limitation Act* 1969 (NSW) was the provision governing the time within which proceedings had to be brought against the bank. That view may be correct; at all events it was not challenged by either party in this Court. Holding that s 69(3) of the *Trustee Act* imposed a six-year limitation period on the bringing of a suit for breach of trust, the Court of Appeal considered the application of sub-s (1) to which sub-s (3) is subject:

In any action suit or other proceeding against a trustee or any person claiming through him, the provisions of this section shall have effect:

Provided that this section shall not affect any action suit or other proceeding where the claim is founded upon any fraud or [290] fraudulent breach of trust to which the trustee was party or privy, or is to recover trust property, or the proceeds thereof still retained by the trustee, or previously received by the trustee and converted to his use.

Although no issue of fraud on the part of the Bank had been raised in the pleadings between the plaintiff and the Bank, the Court of Appeal allowed the plaintiff (the appellant in that Court) to raise that issue in order to take advantage of the proviso to sub-s (1). The issue of fraud on the part of the Bank had been raised on the pleadings between the plaintiff and the Bank's co-defendants (though in terms relevant to the Limitation Act, not the Trustee Act). The Bank had notice that that issue was raised by the plaintiff's reply to its co-defendants' defences but it had not been raised in the pleadings against the Bank. The notice was not tantamount to a reply to the Bank's defence. The Court of Appeal, allowing the issue to be raised before it, found the Bank guilty of fraud on the evidence admitted at the trial. But it was too late to raise that issue against the Bank on appeal and to decide it on the evidence at the trial. If recent authority for such a long-established proposition be needed, reference may be made to what was said by Mason CJ, Wilson, Brennan and Dawson JJ in *Water Board v Moustakas* (1988) 62 ALJR 209, at p 211; 77 ALR 193, at p 196.

The judgment of the Court of Appeal must be set aside and the judgment of the trial judge restored.

11.1.3 Toohey J delivered a judgment to similar effect. However, rather than simply allowing the appeal and entering judgment for the bank, as was the order made by the majority, he would have preferred (at 305) that the matter go back to the Court of Appeal (where the plaintiff's answer to the limitations defence was crucial) to enable the parties to make submissions as to whether, and if so on what terms, the plaintiff should be permitted to raise by way of reply to the bank's defence the matters raised in its reply to the defences of the other defendants: (1990) 169 CLR 279 at 305.

Dawson J dissented. He noted (at 293) that fraud had been pleaded against the other parties to the proceeding and that evidence was admissible in support of it. He thought the statutory limitation should not have been imposed in the face of admissible evidence which established its inapplicability, particularly where that evidence was of fraud. Further, the failure to plead fraud against the bank here was not a matter of substance, as the substance of the allegation was contained in the statement of claim. His Honour concluded that if the plaintiff was in breach of the Rules of Court in relation to pleading by failing to serve a reply on the bank identifying its conduct as fraudulent, the breach was technical only, and should not deprive the plaintiff of the relief it claimed against the bank: (1990) 169 CLR 279 at 298. His Honour further indicated that, if his view did not prevail, he favoured the course proposed by Toohey J that the matter should be sent back to the Court of Appeal to determine whether and, if so, on what terms, the plaintiff should then be permitted to raise fraud by way of reply.

Suvaal v Cessnock City Council
                                    (2003) 200 ALR 1; [2003] HCA 41
                                         High Court of Australia

[The plaintiff had been a professional cyclist. On 2 February 1993 he was cycling at 40km per hour on the edge of a public road near Cessnock as part of training with a view to returning to professional racing. He claimed that he was brushed by an unidentified motor vehicle and pushed into potholes on the left shoulder of the road. The handlebars then collapsed, causing him to lose control of the bicycle and to crash into a ditch on the opposite side of the road. As a result of the accident, the plaintiff became a quadriplegic.

The plaintiff sued the Nominal Defendant in relation to the negligent driving of the unidentified driver, and the Cessnock City Council for negligent road construction and maintenance. As damages had been agreed, the hearing in the New South Wales Supreme Court concerned only liability. That court found in favour of the Nominal Defendant, rejecting the plaintiff's claim that a car was involved, but found against the Council. The court found that the plaintiff had briefly lost concentration, struck potholes and rough round edges on the left side, and that the handlebars had then fractured and turned anti-clockwise, causing the bike to career to the other side of the road. There was also a finding of contributory negligence against the plaintiff in the proportion of 20 per cent.

The Council appealed. The New South Wales Court of Appeal allowed the appeal. It found that there was no basis for the finding for the plaintiff, once his evidence that an unidentified car caused the sudden deviation into the potholes had been rejected. The plaintiff appealed, with special leave, to the High Court of Australia.]

Callinan J (at 31–8):

[126] The appellant sued the Nominal Defendant (as the legal alter ego of the driver of an unidentified motor vehicle) and the respondent in negligence and nuisance in the Supreme Court of New South Wales. This was the appellant's case on his pleading:

4. At all material times, the [respondent] was responsible for carrying out maintenance and repairs on the said road and, *in particular, the edges of the road alongside the sealed bitumen surface.*

5. At all material times the said edges of the road contained fragmented and broken bitumen or tar pieces, the surface of which was rough and uneven.

6. On 2 February 1993, the [appellant] was riding his bicycle in a westerly direction along Quorrobolong Road, Kitchener, when an unidentified motor vehicle proceeding in [32] the same direction brushed against the [appellant] on his right side, forcing him off the sealed bitumen surface onto the said edges of the road whereupon the handle bar assembly of his bicycle broke, causing the [appellant] to lose control of his bicycle, leading him to crash into a ditch on the opposite side of the road, in consequence whereof he sustained severe injuries, loss and damage.

7. The identity of the said motor vehicle, after due search and inquiry, cannot be established.

8. The said injuries, loss and damage occasioned by the [appellant] was caused by the said unidentified motor vehicle which was driven negligently.

...

9. Further or in the alternative, the said injuries, loss and damage occasioned to the [appellant] was caused by the negligence of the [respondent].

PARTICULARS OF NEGLIGENCE

(a) Failing to design and construct the bitumen surface so as to prevent the development of fragmented and broken pieces on the edge of the road.

(b) Designing and constructing the bitumen surface in such a way that it was susceptible to the development of fragmented and broken pieces on the said edges.

(c) Failing to design and construct the roadway so as to provide uniformity in the width of the bitumen surface.

(d) Failing to repair the broken pieces on the said edges.

(e) Failing to ensure that the said edges of the road were completely and evenly covered by a sealed bitumen surface.

(f) Allowing or permitting repairing or patching of the road surface on the said edges that was inadequate and unsafe for traffic users.

(g) Permitting or allowing the break-up of the bitumen surface to occur on the edges of the road.

(h) Failing to inspect or check the road in order to properly repair the edges of the bitumen surface.

(i) Failing to maintain the road in a proper condition.

(j) Failing to erect a sign, notice or other warning indicating to users of the roadway that the edge of the road contained fragmented and broken pieces and that the road surface was rough and uneven.

10. Alternatively, the said injuries, loss and damage were caused by the nuisance in the roadway created by the [respondent], by leaving the said edges of the said road in a dangerous condition for persons lawfully using the same. (emphasis added)

...

[33] The appellant was consistently emphatic throughout the trial that the [34] driver of an unidentified motor vehicle caused the accident. This was, despite his allegation in the alternative in paragraph 10 of his statement of claim, his case, and indeed his only case at the trial. He did not offer any other hypothesis for the accident, indeed he expressly rejected that any other explanation was open.

...

[36] In my opinion the Court of Appeal had no option but to allow the appeal. The approach of the Master was an incorrect one. She seemed to think that, rather than decide whether the appellant had proved the case that he sought repeatedly to make at the trial and which she concluded she was bound to reject, she was obliged to find some other explanation for the accident. This was to misunderstand the nature of the task she had to perform.

It was not open to the Master to find that a momentary lapse in concentration caused the appellant to deviate from the bitumen surface and into the potholes. That was something that the appellant had not claimed, and which as between him and the respondent, the latter was not required to answer. Even the appellant's first version of the accident, the one that he gave to the police [37] officer at the scene, made no reference to a momentary or any lapse in attention. It was not pleaded in paragraph 10 of the statement of claim, and was not even submitted to be so by the other defendant, the Nominal Defendant. It was, in short, not an issue in the case, and certainly was not an issue between the appellant and the respondent. As an operative cause, momentary inattention seems to have been entirely the invention of the Master ...

The appellant argued that the submission of the other defendant, that the respondent had negligently allowed potholes in the shoulders of the roadway to develop, put the respondent "in the frame" and argued that the Master's reasoning was within that submission. That is not the position so far as the issues between the appellant and the respondent were concerned. The frame upon which the appellant was, and remained exclusively focussed, always had in it the driver of an unidentified motor vehicle as the cause of the accident. And in any event, there was certainly no clear focus by any party upon a momentary lapse of concentration. Furthermore the appellant was not entitled to succeed on a case not put by him, and indeed one which he dared not put, either in the alternative or otherwise, because it starkly contradicted his true case.

...

[38] The appellant expressly denied the absence of an unidentified motor vehicle at the relevant time. That denial was rejected by the Master. Its rejection had nothing whatsoever to say about any other cause of the accident. It was probative of nothing and certainly not of any other affirmative cause.

I agree with Giles JA that the Master's explanation of the accident was no more than "a rationalisation of what occurred ... from final overload before the [appellant] went into the potholes." [*Cessnock City Council v Suvaal* [2001] NSWCA 428 at [10]]. The principle that findings by judges of first instance are owed much deference because of the judge's advantage over appellate courts by reason of seeing and hearing the witnesses can have little useful application to a case in which the judge has found in favour of a party who was a witness, a version which he has not only not given but which he has also resolutely and repeatedly rejected. The appellant's so-called alternative case in paragraphs 9 and 10 of the statement of claim was not in truth an alternative case at all. For it to have any credibility, or indeed even relevance, required first the essential presence of a carelessly driven motor vehicle.

A further submission that the appellant made was that it was not his fault that the respondent did not explore at the trial the ramifications of a finding of loss of concentration by the appellant. The submission must be rejected. It was precisely because the appellant did not claim, indeed because he asserted the contrary of, a loss of concentration, that these were not explored. There may be multi-party cases in which an issue not initially raised between two of the parties, does become an issue between one or more of them and another party who raises it. This is not such a case however. As between the respondent and the appellant the issue that was critical was the one to which the appellant irrevocably committed himself, negligence by a motorist, and uncontrollable propulsion by that negligence on to a section of the roadway which he well knew was not nearly as even as the bitumen surface upon which he was riding.

The appeal should be dismissed with costs.

[Gleeson CJ and **Heydon J** agreed that the appeal should be dismissed with costs for the reasons given by **Callinan J.** They also added additional reasons. These included further analysis of the plaintiff's pleaded case and the view that in proceedings based in negligence the plaintiff may be confined to the issue chosen through the allegations in the pleadings of particular acts or omissions on the part of the defendant, unless at the trial the plaintiff be allowed to amend. This had not occurred here.

McHugh and **Kirby JJ** dissented. Their Honours declined to accept the argument that the court at first instance was, as a result of the way the trial was pleaded and conducted, forbidden from accepting the pothole hypothesis, with the explanation of loss of concentration, as that court ultimately concluded. Their Honours were satisfied on the basis of Council's written submissions at the trial that the court and the parties were fully aware at the trial of the pothole hypothesis, and that there was no procedural unfairness in the court accepting that hypothesis, as it had.

See also *Cameron v Troy* [2001] WASCA 400, extracted at **11.5.16C**.]

11.1.5   The pleadings also act as a record of the precise issues raised, so that the parties may be met by the plea *res judicata*, or issue estoppel, if they seek to re-litigate them, or any of them: *Blair v Curran* (1939) 62 CLR 464. *Res judicata* is the estoppel that prevents the same cause of action being litigated again in a later action. The cause of action merges in the judgment. It is the pleadings (and the judgment) that reveal the nature of the cause of action and the facts on which it is based. An issue estoppel arises where a particular issue is deemed to have been adjudicated upon in an earlier action. Again the pleadings assist to determine what issues have been resolved in a previous action: see further **Chapter 10**.

11.1.6   The narrowing of issues through pleadings may assist in determining the appropriate manner of trial. It may appear, for example, that the parties are at odds on a pure point of law which should be decided in advance of a full trial: *CB Darvall & Darvall v Maloney* (2006) 236 ALR 796.

11.1.7 Notes and questions

1. In his article, 'The Purpose of Pleadings' (2004) 25 *Aust Bar Rev 116*, J C Campbell J explains that pleadings are referred to by the judge at all stages of the pleading process and, for this reason, they act in some respects as a piece of advocacy. Preparation of a pleading requires the same qualities as are needed for good advocacy, including a clear understanding of legal principle and clarity of expression. His Honour notes that pleadings have traditionally, though not necessarily, been drafted by counsel, and he considers the role of both counsel and solicitors in the pleading process.

2. A plaintiff proceeds in a Magistrates' or Local Court in respect of damage to her motor vehicle involved in a collision with that of the defendant. Liability is apportioned 15 per cent to the plaintiff and 85 per cent to the defendant. The plaintiff subsequently brings separate proceedings in the Supreme Court for personal injuries suffered in the same accident. Is the Supreme Court bound by the previous apportionment of liability? Do you think this is an appropriate result? See *Bollen v Hickson* [1981] Qd R 249; *Hawira v Suncorp Metway Insurance Ltd* [2007] QSC 158.

11.1.8   Further reading

S Dunstone, *A Practical Guide to Drafting Pleadings*, LBC Information Services, 1997, pp 7–17.

I H Jacob, 'The Present Importance of Pleadings' (1960) 13 *Current Legal Problems* 171.

J Jacob and I S Goldrein, *Pleadings: Principles and Practice*, Sweet & Maxwell, London, 1990, pp 1–12.

CONTENTS OF PLEADINGS

Usual pleadings

Pleading generally

11.2.1   Pleadings usually comprise a statement of claim; a defence (and possibly counterclaim); and a reply (and answer, if there is a counterclaim). This may differ in the Federal Court (Federal Court Rules r 8.05) and in South Australia (Supreme Court Civil Rules 2006 (SA) rr 91, 96), where some matters will proceed by way of affidavit. If a matter in the Federal Court is to proceed by pleadings, the Federal Court Rules provide for a statement of claim (or cross-claim), defence, and a reply to the defence.

There are a number of special rules which apply to each of the particular pleadings. These are considered under separate sections below.

There are a number of principal rules of pleading common to all pleadings. It is intended here to consider the general principles, as well as some important and/or unique variations which may apply in some jurisdictions. It must be borne in mind, however, that there are a large and varied number of specific rules and exceptions in each jurisdiction. For close analysis of any particular pleading rules, looseleaf or online annotated rules for the relevant jurisdiction should be consulted. Numerous specialist precedent works on pleadings are also available and provide greater assistance for drafting of particular pleadings.

[*Note:* in this chapter a reference, such as WA O 9 r 2, is a reference to the relevant Rules of Court. All other legislation will be specified.]

11.2.2E   **Supreme Court (General Civil Procedure) Rules 2005 (Vic)**
                                           Order 13 — Pleadings

Content of pleading

13.02 (1) Every pleading shall —
    (a)   contain in a summary form a statement of all the material facts on which the party relies, but not the evidence by which those facts are to be proved.

11.2.3   This rule is sometimes described as the 'fundamental rule' of pleading. See also: HCR 2004 rr 27.04, 27.05; FCR 2011 r 16.02(1)(d); Court Procedures Rules 2006 (ACT) r 406(1); Uniform Civil Procedure Rules 2005 (NSW) r 14.7; Supreme Court Rules (NT) r 13.02(1)(a); Uniform Civil Procedure Rules 1999 (Qld) r 149(1); SA r 98(2)(b); Supreme Court Rules 2000 (Tas) r 227(1); Rules of the Supreme Court 1971 (WA) O 20 r 8(1).

Material facts

11.2.4   In order to plead the material facts, a party must plead all the facts which are necessary to constitute a complete cause of action or defence, so that if the facts pleaded are proved or admitted, the party pleading them will be entitled to the relief sought in the pleading. Material facts also extend to the relief being sought and such other facts as will ensure the other party is not taken by surprise.

Immaterial facts clearly should not be pleaded, but in practice the rule is not so strictly interpreted as to preclude appropriate introductory matters, such as descriptions of the parties, their occupations, locations of their businesses, and so on.

The requirement that a party must plead all material facts does not mean that a party must be committed to one assertion or consistent series of assertions as to what are the facts, but inconsistent allegations of fact or grounds of claim must be clearly pleaded as alternatives: FCR r 16.06; ACT r 414; NSW r 14.18; NT r 13.09; Qld r 154; SA r 98(7); Tas r 230; Vic r 13.09; WA O 20 r 11.

The decision of the Supreme Court of the Northern Territory in *RTA Pty Ltd v Brinko Pty Ltd* [2012] NTSC, extracted below, provides a case illustration where the court was satisfied the plaintiff had not pleaded necessary material facts to comply with the pleading requirements under applicable rule of court.

11.2.5C   **RTA Pty Ltd v Brinko Pty Ltd**
[2012] NTSC 03
Northern Territory Supreme Court

[The plaintiff's cause of action was based partly on misleading and deceptive conduct pursuant to the Trade Practices Act 1974 (Cth) (now the Competition and Consumer Act 2010 (Cth)) and the Consumer Affairs and Fair Trading Act (NT). The second defendant applied to strike out the statement of claim, alleging that it did not adequately set out the case the second defendant was required to meet.]

Master Luppino (at [5]–[6]; [16]–[26]):

[5] The Rules specifically provide that a pleading is to contain a statement of all the material facts on which the party relies. (Order 13.02(1)(a)). In that context the material facts are those necessary to formulate the complete cause of action. They are not to be expressed in terms of great generality but must inform a defendant of the case the defendant must meet and are to be set out with sufficient particularity to enable the trial to be conducted fairly to all parties. (*Northern Territory of Australia v John Holland & Ors Pty Ltd* (2008) 22 NTLR 58).

[6] The cause of action in the subject claim is partly based on misleading and deceptive conduct pursuant to the Trade Practices Act and the Consumer Affairs and Fair Trading Act. Some specific requirements for pleadings in such cases were prescribed in *Miller & Associates*

Insurance Broking Pty Ltd v BMW Australia Finance Limited (2010) 241 CLR 357. In that case French CJ and Kiefel J said:-

> It [Section 52 Trade Practices Act] requires a clear identification of the conduct said to be misleading or deceptive. Where silence or non-disclosure is relied upon, the pleading should identify whether it is alleged of itself to be, in the circumstances of the case, misleading or deceptive conduct or whether it is an element of conduct, including other acts or omissions, said to be misleading or deceptive. (*Miller & Associates Insurance Broking Proprietary Limited v BMW Australia Finance Limited* (2010) 241 CLR 357 at p 364)

...

[16] The parts of the Amended Statement of Claim which are under challenge are paragraphs 16 and 17. It is now acknowledged and accepted by all parties that the particulars provided in respect of paragraphs 7 and 8 of the first Statement of Claim (those paragraphs are now paragraphs 16 and 17 in the Amended Statement of Claim), still apply and are still relied on. For the purposes of the argument, I read the Particulars together with the Amended Statement of Claim.

[17] It is apparent from the Particulars that a number of obvious material facts have been provided as particulars in lieu of pleading them in the Amended Statement of Claim. If that were to be the only issue then there could be some scope for acceptance of Mr Christrup's argument that nonetheless the purposes of pleadings have been satisfied in that all the material facts have been provided in one form or another and therefore that the Defendants are informed of the case they must meet.

[18] However I agree with Mr Roper that there remains an unacceptable flaw in the current pleadings even when read with the Particulars. To properly understand that requires consideration of the allegations and the pleadings as a whole. Paragraphs 4 and 5 of the Amended Statement of Claim plead an industry practice or arrangement whereby publishers have divided the Darwin metropolitan area into areas and have appointed persons to be the exclusive agents in those areas for sales of various publications. Paragraph 9 of the Statement of Claim defines the "Business" sold by the First Defendant to the First Plaintiff by reference to one of those defined exclusive areas, specifically the Nightcliff exclusive area. Paragraphs 16 and 17 of the Amended Statement of Claim allege false representations as to turnover, profitability and the extent of the customer base of the Business. The Particulars elaborate and allege that representations were made based on the provision of sales and trading figures in various accounting documents. The falsity that is alleged in respect of those representations is indirect as apparently the figures provided were correct. The allegation is that the basis of the representations, specifically the extent of the customer base to which those figures related, is misrepresented. That is essentially what the representation defined as "the Customer Base Representation" in the Particulars purports to allege. The Plaintiffs allege that the net result is to render misleading the figures that were provided as the figures include sales outside the Nightcliff exclusive area.

[19] Mr Christrup argues that the pleading in paragraphs 4, 5 and 9 of the Amended Statement of Claim, coupled with the Particulars defining the Customer Base Representation and the definition of "Business" by reference to the Nightcliff exclusive area, set out all of the relevant material facts to notify the Defendants of the claim they have to meet.

[20] I do not agree. The overall effect of the Amended Statement of Claim and the Particulars is merely to allege representations as to turnover, profitability and the customer base of the Business. As to the turnover and profitability, there are no material facts as to the precise nature of the representations made, how they arise or the extent of the overstating. I note that to some extent the provision of further particulars awaits the obtaining of evidence which is currently being pursued by way of subpoenas. That will not necessarily or entirely satisfy the pleading requirements as in my view the Plaintiffs are required to plead all the material facts relevant to the alleged overstating of turnover and profitability. Ideally that should occur as an amendment to the pleadings and not by way of particulars. However given that the falsity alleged in the Particulars is with respect to the customer base, I would not expect this to remain a contentious issue once all the material facts have been pleaded.

[21] The allegation of falsity of the Customer Base Representation however is pivotal to the Plaintiffs' claim of misrepresentation. In my view the material facts pleaded in the Amended Statement of Claim as to how such a representation arises are either insufficient or unclear. On the available material, the Customer Base Representation could arise in a number of ways. It could be a specific representation (including in, or by the provision of, documents), or it could be by implication arising out of industry practice. The Defendants are entitled to know specifically how the Plaintiffs claim that the Customer Base Representation arises and until material facts to demonstrate that are pleaded, it cannot be said that the Defendants know the case they have to meet. The relevance of the industry practice pleaded in paragraphs 4 and 5 of the Amended Statement of Claim is not sufficiently clear at present.

[22] The net result is that the Amended Statement of Claim contains only a bare allegation of a representation as to the customer base. The absence of pleading of material facts to establish how it arises makes that a plea of conclusion and that is insufficient. (*Northern Territory of Australia v John Holland & Ors Pty Ltd* (2008) 22 NTLR 58)

[23] Further, it is clear that the Plaintiffs rely on silence by the Second Defendant and the Third Defendant. Silence can give rise to actionable misrepresentation at common law and can also be the basis of a claim for statutory misleading and deceptive conduct under both Acts relied on when the circumstances of the case give rise to an obligation to disclose the relevant facts (*Henjo Investments Pty Ltd v Collins Marrickville Pty Ltd* (1988) 79 ALR 83, *Winterton Constructions Pty Ltd v Hambros Australia Pty Ltd* (1992) 111 ALR 649.) The pleadings must therefore set out the circumstances or material facts on which the Plaintiffs will rely to establish the duty to disclose.

[24] The pleadings are also insufficient to satisfy the requirements of pleadings in the case of statutory misleading and deceptive conduct based on silence in accordance with *Miller & Associates Insurance Broking Pty Ltd v BMW Australia Finance Limited* (2010) 241 CLR 357. Specifically the pleadings are required to set out whether silence is alleged to be only an element of the misleading or deceptive conduct or whether the silence itself is the conduct complained of.

[25] Although the Defendants have some knowledge of the facts, that is not relevant for the purposes of determining the sufficiency of the pleadings. The test is whether the Defendant knows what the Plaintiffs allege are the material facts. (*Whelan v John Fairfax & Sons Ltd* (1988) 12 NSWLR 148). The Amended Statement of Claim in its current form fails to satisfy that requirement. For those reasons in my view there is no scope for the exercise of

any discretion in favour of the Plaintiff. I am satisfied that in all of the circumstances case management issues do not significantly impact on the making of the orders sought.

[26] For these reasons I order that the Plaintiffs' Amended Statement of Claim filed 9 June 2011 be struck out. I give leave to the Plaintiffs to file a Second Amended Statement of Claim.

Facts, not evidence

11.2.6   A distinction is drawn between the material facts upon which a pleading party relies and evidence by which those facts are to be proved. Facts which merely evidence the facts establishing the cause of action or defence should not be pleaded, although sometimes it may be difficult to distinguish material facts from evidence.

Facts and law

11.2.7   What is not stated in the rule, but may be implied from it, is that the pleader is generally not required to state the legal consequences flowing from the facts on which he or she relies. South Australia is a partial exception because its rules specify that the pleading must state each cause of action (r 99(1)(a)) and any special defence on which the defendant relies (r 100). In the other jurisdictions, the general principle is that it is for the court to declare the law arising upon the facts proved before it. Except in very limited circumstances (see **11.2.10E–11.2.11**, **11.5.11–11.5.13**), a pleading will be sufficient if it pleads the 'essential ingredients' of the cause of action or defence and puts the other party in a position to know the case to be met at trial. The case extracted below illustrates this.

11.2.8C   **Creedon v Measey Investments Pty Ltd**
                              (1988) 91 FLR 318
                        Supreme Court of the Northern Territory

[The plaintiff brought proceedings against several defendants seeking damages for personal injuries, which he suffered in a motor vehicle accident. The only allegation in the statement of claim against the fourth defendant was that it owned the vehicle driven by the third defendant. The fourth defendant applied to strike out the statement of claim as against it.]

Martin J (at 320–1): Plainly what the plaintiff had in mind was that the fourth defendant should be held vicariously liable for the alleged negligence of the third defendant in his driving of the truck. To suggest that there is anything in the statement of claim which might be seen as smacking of any other cause of action against the fourth defendant is fanciful and on the facts such as are pleaded no other possible cause of action presents itself. It is not a case where 'this statement of claim in no way enables the defendants to know what case they have to meet at the trial of this action' per Cotton LJ: *Philipps v Philipps* (1878) 4 QBD 127 at 138.

Order 23, r 4 of the former rules provided that every pleading shall contain, and contain only, a statement in a summary form of the material facts on which the party pleading relies for his claim or defence.

In *Williams v Milotin* (1957) 97 CLR 465 at 474 the High Court said:

> When you speak of a cause of action you mean the essential ingredients in the title to the right which it is proposed to enforce.

That case and others are cited by Williams in '*Civil Procedure in Victoria*' Vol 1 at par 13.02.30, for the proposition that: 'The pleader is not bound to state the legal effect of the facts upon which he relies; he is only bound to state the facts themselves'. The learned author goes on:

> It is sufficient if the pleader states the material facts, and at the trial he is free to present in argument whatever legal consequences are appropriate to the facts as found by the Court.

It is not necessary that the plaintiff plead a conclusion of law, ie, that the facts disclose as a matter of law the fourth defendant is vicariously liable for the alleged negligence of the third defendant. However, the plaintiff must plead the 'essential ingredients'.

One of those ingredients is the relationship between the person alleged to be negligent and the person whom it is sought to hold vicariously liable. Here nothing is pleaded other than the third defendant was driving a truck owned by the fourth defendant. In New South Wales it has long been held that the ownership of a motor vehicle, especially a commercial motor vehicle, is prima facie evidence, fit to be left to a jury, that any person driving it and causing damage to another was driving with the authority and for the purpose of the owner: *Jennings v Hannan* (No 2) (1969) 71 SR (NSW) 226. His Honour Walsh JA said at 233 that the Court of Appeal in New Zealand had adopted the same view. In the decision of the Privy Council in [321] *Rambarran v Gurrucharran* [1970] 1 All ER 749, in which *Jennings v Hannan* was considered, Lord Donovan at 751 said:

> Where no more is known of the facts, therefore, than that at the time of an accident the car was owned but not driven by A it can be said that A's ownership affords some evidence that it was being driven by his servant or agent.

It is to be noted that ownership of a vehicle is only prima facie evidence fit to be left to the jury, or in this jurisdiction, the Court, that the person driving it and causing damage did so with the authority and for the purposes of the owner. It is not conclusive evidence and the evidence at trial may disclose facts which require the application of the law to determine whether or not the owner is vicariously liable. As Lord Donovan went on to say:

> But when the facts bearing on the question of service or agency are known, or sufficiently known, then clearly the problem must be decided on the totality of the evidence.

Milkovits v Federal Capital Press of Australia Pty Ltd (1972) 20 FLR 312 and *Lanchbury v Morgans* [1973] AC 127, to which I was referred by counsel for the fourth defendant, are but examples of the application of the law to the facts in those cases, facts which went beyond what is pleaded here.

I hold that the statement of claim discloses a cause of action by the plaintiff against the fourth defendant, and dismiss the application.

11.2.9 Sometimes a pleading will be more intelligible if it sets out the conclusion for which the pleader contends. A party, though not bound to do so (except in South Australia (see 11.2.7)), may choose to state the conclusion of law, provided that material facts in support of the conclusion are also stated. In Queensland (r 149 (2)), Victoria (r 13.02(2)(b)) and the Northern Territory (r 13.02(2)(b)), the Rules of Court expressly authorise this. A party who alleges the legal result of pleaded facts may nevertheless seek to persuade the court at trial that it should draw different conclusions of law from those pleaded: *Re Vandervell's Trusts (No 2)* [1974] Ch 269; *Hancock Family Memorial Foundation Ltd v Belle Rosa Holdings Pty Ltd* (1992) 8 WAR 435.

Pleading a statutory provision

11.2.10E **Uniform Civil Procedure Rules 1999 (Qld)**

Statements in pleadings

149 (1) Each pleading must —

...

(e) if a claim or defence under an Act is relied on identify the specific provision under the Act.

11.2.11 In the Federal Court (r 16.02(1)(e)), the Australian Capital Territory (r 406(1)(e)), South Australia (r 99(1)(b) (statement of claim), r 100(1)(d) (defence)), Victoria (r 13.02(1)(b)) and the Northern Territory (r 13.02(1)(b)), as in Queensland, parties proposing to rely on a statutory cause of action or defence must identify the specific provision in their pleading. A similar requirement applies in the High Court (r 27.04(c)) for statements of claim. It is suggested that in the other jurisdictions parties should do likewise whenever they are relying on a statutory provision for a claim or defence. To plead the statutory provision complies with the general obligation to inform the other party of the case to be answered and not take them by surprise. It also makes the pleading more meaningful and intelligible.

11.2.12E **C Wood, 'Pleading in Commercial Cases',**
29 November 2007,
<http://www.13wentworthselbornechambers.com.au>

[When a statutory provision is pleaded, it remains important to ensure the material facts supporting the statutory cause of action or defence are pleaded first. In his paper, Christopher Wood provides the following helpful discussion and illustration of the appropriate approach to the pleading of a statutory cause of action:]

Don't plead the section

19. Commercial law is increasingly governed by statutory provisions. The necessary elements of a particular statutory cause of action may be perfectly obvious on a reading of the provision.

However, the individual facts need to be pleaded first, rather than pleading the conclusion which is the formula expressed in the section.

20. For example, under s 79 of the Corporations Act 2001, a person involved in another person's contravention may be liable to remedies including damages. However, it is not acceptable to simply plead the section itself. For example:

The third defendant has [sic]:
(a)   has aided, abetted, counselled or procured the contravention; and/or
(b)   has induced, by threats or promises or alternatively otherwise, the contravention; and/or
(c)   has, by act and/or omission, been directly and/or indirectly, knowingly concerned in, and/or a party to, the contravention; and/or
(d)   has conspired with others to effect the contravention.

21. What is necessary is to break up the individual conduct. For example:

41.   The third defendant was, from 1 January 2004 to 30 October 2006, a director of Dodgy Dealings Pty Limited.
42.   The third defendant controlled the company's share register.
43.   The third defendant was the controlling mind of the company to the extent that the company engaged in the share transfer set out in paragraph 21 above.
44.   The third defendant executed the share transfer set out in paragraph 21 above.
45.   By reason of the facts set out in paragraph 41 to 45 above, the third defendant aided, or alternatively procured the contravention set out in paragraph 36 above.
46.   By reason of the facts set out in paragraph 45, the third defendant was involved in the contravention set out in paragraph 36 above.
47.   Pursuant to s.79 of the Corporations Act 2001, and by reason of her involvement set out in paragraph 46, the third defendant is liable for the breach contravention set out in paragraph 36 above.

Miscellaneous rules of pleading

11.2.13   There are numerous specific pleading rules, many of which are unique to one or more jurisdictions. As previously mentioned, it is not possible to discuss all or even most of those miscellaneous rules in this work, but some of the more common or significant are outlined.

Documents and conversations

11.2.14   Where the effect of documents are material but not the particular words used, the rules in most jurisdictions allow the effect of the document to be pleaded, without setting out the precise terms of the document: FCR r 16.04; ACT r 411; NSW r 14.9; NT r 13.03; Qld r 152; SA r 98(3); Tas r 234; Vic r 13.03; WA O 20 r 8(2). Except in Tasmania, the same rules also apply to the contents of oral conversations. If there is controversy in relation to the construction of a document (or of words spoken), the material words alleged should be set out in the pleading in full.

Conditions precedent

11.2.15 In most instances a plaintiff need not specifically plead the performance of any condition precedent (ie, of any condition which the parties have agreed, or which the law requires, must be fulfilled before the plaintiff is entitled to succeed in the action). Fulfillment of conditions precedent is implied by force of the Rules of Court: FCR r 16.05; ACT r 412; NSW r 14.11; NT r 13.05; Qld r 153; SA r 98(8); Tas r 236; Vic r 13.05; WA O 20 r 8(4). However, the situation is different if performance of any condition precedent is also of the essence to the cause of action, such as the making of a demand in an action in detinue or the giving of a notice of dishonour in an action on a bill of exchange.

In the Federal Court, the Australian Capital Territory, Queensland and Tasmania, the rules referred to above also state that any party who intends to contest the performance or occurrence of any condition precedent should distinctly plead the denial. The position is clearly the same in the other jurisdictions, despite the absence of a separate specification to that effect in the relevant rule.

Presumptions

11.2.16 A party is not required to plead any matter of fact which the law presumes in his or her favour, or in respect of which the other party bears the onus of proof, unless there has been a specific denial of that fact: FCR r 16.03(2); ACT r 409; NSW r 14.10; NT r 13.04; Qld r 151; Tas r 227(4); Vic r 13.04; WA O 20 r 8(3).

An illustration of the application of this principle, which is set out in the relevant rule in several of the jurisdictions, is that a plaintiff need not plead consideration for a bill of exchange where he or she sues only on the bill, and not for the consideration as a substantive ground of claim. Actions for defamation provide another example. In these actions the falsity of defamatory words is presumed, and the burden of proving the truth of the defamatory imputation is placed on the defendant: *Age Company Pty Ltd v Elliott* (2006) 14 VR 375.

Points of law

11.2.17E **Uniform Civil Procedure Rules 2005 (NSW)**
Pt 14 — Pleadings

Pleadings may raise points of law
14.19 A pleading may raise any point of law.

[See also: FCR O r 16.02(3); ACT r 406(2); NT r 13.02(2)(a); Qld r 149(2); SA r 100 (defence), r 101 (reply); Tas r 249; Vic r 13.02(2)(a); WA O 20 r 12.]

11.2.18 This rule and its equivalents permit a party to raise a point of law in a pleading so that if, eg, the defence is that the plaintiff's claim is not maintainable in law, or that the plaintiff's statement of claim does not establish a cause of action, this may be pleaded in the defence. Similarly, in appropriate cases the plaintiff may plead in the reply that the defendant's defence does not in law reveal a defence. In raising an objection in point of law in this way, a party in effect assumes as truth the facts alleged by his or her opponent, and alleges those facts are insufficient in law for the purpose for which they are pleaded.

The Rules of Court also set out procedures by which points of law (ACT r 1521; Tas r 249) or 'any question' in a 'proceeding' (FCR r 30.01; NSW r 28.2; NT r 47.04; Qld r 483; Vic r 47.04; WA O 32 r 4) or an issue of fact or law (or an issue involving mixed questions of fact and law) (SA r 211) may be tried separately. If the determination of that issue substantially disposes of the action, or a distinct cause of action within the action, the court may dismiss the action or make such other order as is just: FCR r 30.02; ACT r 1523; NSW r 28.4; NT r 47.05; Qld r 485; Tas rr 249, 806; Vic r 47.05; WA O 32 r 7; in South Australia judgment is given under the court's inherent jurisdiction: *Landsal Pty Ltd (in liq) v R E I Building Society* (1993) 41 FCR 421; 113 ALR 643.

In the High Court (r 27.08), a special procedure is available to enable the parties to agree in stating the questions of law arising in the proceeding in the form of a special case for the opinion of the Full Court. The special case is to state the facts and identify the documents necessary to enable the court to decide the questions raised.

11.2.19   In the High Court (r 27.07), the parties also have the right to 'demur' to their opponent's pleading, and to obtain a ruling on the demurrer. This is an old procedure which is no longer available elsewhere. The demurrer is a plea which, only for the purpose of obtaining a ruling on some question of law, admits the truth of the opponent's pleading but asserts that it does not lead to the conclusion for which the opponent contends. Although the procedure is less commonly used than it once was, it was retained when the High Court Rules were replaced in 2004 because it remains a useful procedure for determining some questions of constitutional validity and it was regarded as unnecessary to rename it.

Formal requirements

11.2.20E   **Supreme Court (General Civil Procedure) Rules 2005 (Vic)**
Order 13 – Pleadings

Formal requirements

13.01 (1) Every pleading shall bear on its face —

    (a)   a description of the pleading; and

    (b)   the date on which it is served.

  (2)   A pleading shall be divided into paragraphs numbered consecutively, and each allegation so far as practicable shall be contained in a separate paragraph.

  (3)   A pleading which is settled by counsel shall be signed by that counsel, and if it is not so settled, it shall be signed by the solicitor for the party, or if there is none, by the party.

11.2.21   In all jurisdictions, there are some formal requirements applying to all pleadings. Though there are variations in detail, all jurisdictions except South Australia specify that the pleading must be divided into consecutively numbered paragraphs and that, so far as practicable, each allegation is to be contained in a separate paragraph: HCR r 27.02; FCR r 16.02(1)(a);

ACT r 405(2); NSW r 14.6; NT r 13.01 (1); Qld r 146(1)(f); Tas r 227(2); Vic r 13.01(2); WA O 20 r 7(2). Most also require the pleading to be as brief as the nature of the case will allow: FCR r 16.02(1)(b); NSW Pt 14.8; Qld r 149(1)(b); SA r 98(2)(a); Tas r 227(2); WA O 20 r 8(1).

Although these rules may appear rather mechanical, they should be considered in the context of the key purpose of pleadings of defining the issues between the parties: see 11.1.1. If paragraphs are confined to separate allegations, a practitioner is able to respond to each paragraph by stating whether the allegation it contains is admitted, denied, not admitted, or whether some special pleading is to be made about it. Provided the paragraphs are discretely numbered, pleadings in response can be made by reference to the paragraph numbers. In practice, it is common for both parties' representatives and the judge to annotate a pleading to indicate the status of each allegation and so to assist in understanding and clearly identifying what the issues are.

In most jurisdictions there are rules relating to the signing of pleadings: HCR rr 27.02.3, 27.02.4; NT r 13.01(3); Qld r 146(1); SA r 98(1); Tas r 226; Vic r 13.01(3); WA O 20 r 7(5). The rules in the High Court, the Northern Territory, Victoria and Western Australia require counsel's signature if the pleading was settled by counsel; the party's solicitor's signature if not settled by counsel; or the party's signature if he or she sues or defends in person. In Queensland the solicitor is to sign if the party is represented, or otherwise the party personally. In South Australia the pleading is to be endorsed with a certificate signed by the solicitor representing the party as discussed below, but if the party is not represented by a solicitor, the pleading is to be signed by the party. In Tasmania, the pleading may be signed by the party or his or her counsel or solicitor. The rules in the Federal Court (r 16.01) and the Australian Capital Territory (r 405(5)) do not require signing, but do require (in all cases in the Federal Court and in the Australian Capital Territory if the pleading has been settled by counsel) that the pleading state the name of the person who prepared the pleading. The Federal Court rules also requires a statement by the person that the person prepared the pleading.

The signature to a pleading, however, is not an oath or affirmation. As a matter of practice pleadings have usually been drawn as widely as the applicable rules permit. This enables parties to preserve their options in relation to evidence to be presented at the trial. This practice also places the maximum obligation on opposing parties.

In some jurisdictions, however, legislation or rules of court now impose obligations on parties or their solicitors to verify to some degree the accuracy of the content of the pleadings: see 11.2.22–11.2.25. Further, the rules of court are restricting the ability of parties to plead allegations, denials or non-admissions for which they may not have adequate foundation: see 11.2.22–11.2.25 and 11.5.3–11.5.7.

Certificate of Legal Representative: Australian Capital Territory, Federal Court and South Australia

11.2.22   In the Australian Capital Territory, s 188 of the Civil Law (Wrongs) Act 2002 (ACT) imposes an obligation on lawyers who are providing legal services on a claim for damages, or in defence of a claim for damages. The lawyer is prohibited from lodging a pleading in court for filing, or filing a pleading in a court, in relation to the claim, unless a certificate as required by the section has been lodged or filed in court, or accompanies the pleading. The certificate must state that the lawyer believes, on the basis of provable facts and a reasonably arguable view of the law, that the claim or defence has reasonable prospects of success. Contravention of this requirement by a lawyer is not an offence, but can be professional misconduct or unsatisfactory professional conduct under the Legal Profession Act 2006, Ch 4 (Complaints and discipline). See further **7.4.8–7.4.11**.

11.2.23 The Rules in the Federal Court include a requirement for a form of verification of pleadings: r 16.01. Any pleading prepared by a lawyer must include a certificate signed by the lawyer that any factual and legal material available to the lawyer provides a proper basis for each allegation in the pleading, and for each denial and non-admission in the pleading.

In South Australia a pleading must be endorsed with a certificate signed by the solicitor representing the party, certifying that the pleading has been prepared in accordance with the party's instructions and complies with the rules of court: r 98(1)(b)(i).

Pleadings to be verified: New South Wales

11.2.24 In New South Wales, s 347 of the Legal Profession Act 2004 (NSW) imposes obligations on law practices in respect of claims or defences of claims for damages. A law practice cannot file court documentation on a claim or defence of a claim for damages unless a principal of the practice, or a legal practitioner associate responsible for the provision of the legal services concerned, provides a certificate as required by the section. The certificate is to state that there are reasonable grounds for believing, on the basis of provable facts and a reasonably arguable view of the law, that the claim or the defence (as appropriate) has reasonable prospects of success. 'Court documentation' is defined so as to include an originating process (eg, a statement of claim, summons or cross-claim), defence or further pleading or amended pleading. The provision of legal services by a law practice without reasonable prospects of success does not constitute an offence, but is capable of being unsatisfactory professional conduct or professional misconduct by a legal practitioner associate of the law practice who is responsible for the provision of the service, or by a principal of the practice. See further **7.4.8–7.4.11**.

In addition, the Rules of Court require parties to file affidavits to verify their pleadings in certain circumstances. The effect of r 14.23 is that, except in actions for the recovery of damages for defamation, malicious prosecution, false imprisonment, or in respect of death or personal injury (which are exempted from the requirement by r 14.22(1), unless the court orders under r 14.22(2) that the verification requirements apply to a particular matter falling within these categories), both statement of claim and defence must be so verified.

The affidavit is generally to be made by the party pleading. Special provision is made, however, for particular parties. For example, in the case of corporations, the affidavit may be made by a member or officer having knowledge of the facts deposed to in the affidavit: r 35.3.

The affidavit verifying the pleading is to state:

- as to any allegations of fact in the pleading, that the deponent believes the allegations are true;

- as to any allegations of fact denied in the pleading, that the deponent believes those allegations to be untrue; and

- as to any allegations of fact that the pleading does not admit, that, after reasonable inquiry, the deponent does not know whether or not the allegations are true: r 14.22(3).

If there is some reason why the deponent cannot comply with all of these requirements, the affidavit should comply with so much as is practicable, and provide reasons why the party pleading cannot comply with the remainder: r 14.23(4).

The affidavit verifying the pleading must be subscribed to the pleading, unless the court otherwise orders: r 14.23(6).

Pleadings optional: South Australia

11.2.25   The plaintiff may choose that the matter proceed by affidavit rather than by pleadings: rr 91, 96. The court has wide powers, however, to order that any particular matter continue by pleadings or affidavits: r 96. If the matter is conducted by affidavit, the defendant is required to file an affidavit setting out all the facts on which he or she wishes to rely. In respect of any matters not within the direct knowledge of the deponent, he or she must affirm the belief in those facts and provide the source and grounds of the information and his or her belief. The South Australian rules (r 217) expressly provide that if a party using pleadings gives evidence at the trial of an action, he or she may be cross-examined on the pleadings, and the court may draw an adverse inference to the party's credit from a discrepancy between what it finds proved and the allegations of fact as stated in the party's pleadings.

Plain English

11.2.26   There is nothing in the Rules of Court about the writing style that should be adopted in the drafting of a pleading. As with drafters of other legal documents, however, pleaders have developed their own 'legalese' characterising pleadings, and apparent even in very modern works providing precedents of pleadings.

The reassessment over recent years of the writing and drafting skills of lawyers has focused on the writing of letters, wills and commercial documents. It could be argued that until comparatively modern times, complete court documents could not be produced in 'plain English' because the forms prescribed under the Rules of Court were in antiquated styles, and completing them in 'plain English' could go only part of the way. Fortunately the forms approved under the modern rules of court have been drafted in simple English. In this environment, practitioners should make a conscious move towards the production of pleadings in jargon-free, simple English.

For comprehensive guidance about writing in plain language, reference should be made to one of the many specialist works now available. There are, however, some simple ways to avoid most of the 'legalese' commonly found in pleadings:

11.2.27   Avoid 'legal fossils'   As with other forms of legal writing, pleadings commonly incorporate words common hundreds of years ago, but having no place in current legal drafting. Many of these words have preferable modern day substitutes; others add nothing at all and can be completely omitted.

For example, a precedent recently published for a statement of claim relating to personal injury suffered in the course of employment, included the following:

> … the defendant was driving the *said* [defendant's vehicle] in a southerly direction along the *said* highway.

The same facts should be more simply stated: the defendant was driving her vehicle along the highway in a southerly direction. The following is a list of words commonly found in pleadings, and suggested alternatives. It has, in part, been extracted from a broader list set out in

R MacDonald and D Clark-Dickson, *Clear and Precise: Writing Skills for Today's Lawyer*, 2nd ed, Thomson Custom Publishing, Sydney, 2005, pp 38–9, 129–44.

Avoid	Alternatives
abovementioned	omit/recast
aforesaid	omit/recast
herein	omit/recast
hereinafter	recast
hereinbefore	recast
hereof	omit
said (used as an adjective)	omit
save as	except
such	omit/recast
thereof	of that or it/recast
thereunder	under the
whereupon	recast

11.2.28   **Omit surplus words**   Another common but unwelcome feature of some pleadings is the incorporation of groups of words and phrases that add nothing in terms of clarity, but certainly make a pleading longer. These should be omitted or recast as appropriate. Some examples contained in recently published precedents, together with suggested alternatives follow:

Avoid	Preferred alternative
negligence on the part of the said defendant	the defendant's negligence
at that time and on that date	at the same time
for the duration of	during
the agreement referred to in paragraph two hereof	the agreement
the agreement the terms of which have been set out above	the agreement
each and every one of the allegations	the allegations
together with interest thereon pursuant to the provisions of	and interest under

11.2.29 Adopt other principles of plain English drafting Other standard strategies for achieving simplicity and clarity in legal writing should be adopted, unless they would require a departure from a specific Rule of Court regulating the content of pleadings. Examples include using:

- active, not passive, verbs;

- defined terms, if they have a specific and necessary role (In complicated matters, defining all relevant terms in a 'dictionary' section at the beginning of the pleading may make the pleading more readable.);

- non-discriminatory language;

- headings to signpost longer pleadings; and

- vertical lists when appropriate to break up detailed information.

11.2.30 Notes and questions

1. In what circumstances would a court order that a point of law or other question in a proceeding be set down as a preliminary issue? Clearly a question should be set down as a preliminary issue if its determination will settle the question between the parties, but this is not essential. The question is one of discretion, and the court will look for convenience and saving of expense. Examples of points of law which have been determined as preliminary issues include: whether a matter was action-barred by a statute of limitation (*Attorney-General (Vic) v Craig* [1958] VR 34; *Hewson v Burke* [2000] QCA 434); whether, upon the proper construction of a building agreement, the liability of a party was conditional upon an arbitration award in respect of that liability (*Ropux v Langtree* [1985] VR 799); and which of two arguable interpretations of a clause in a building contract was the correct construction: *Re Multiplex Constructions Pty Ltd* [1999] 1 Qd R 287.

   An order was also made allowing the hearing of a separate issue relating to the appropriate standard of proof in *The Chief Executive Officer of Customs v Labrador Liquor Wholesale Pty Ltd* [1999] QSC 384. The trial in this case was expected to last more than three weeks, and if it proceeded on an incorrect assumption as to the standard of proof, a retrial would be necessary.

2. A division of the Queensland Litigation Reform Commission recommended in 1994 (G L Davies J and J S Lieboff, 'Reforming the Civil Litigation System: Streamlining the Adversarial Framework', *Proctor*, November 1994, 10) that the pleading rules should be changed to require that, if a party makes an allegation of fact, he or she is also required to state in the pleading the evidence which proves the fact; if oral, the name and address of each witness; or if in writing, sufficient facts to identify the documents. The party would then be required to state each contention, whether of fact or law, to be made on that fact. This change was not incorporated into the Uniform Civil Procedure Rules 1999 (Qld). Is there a danger in requiring a party to provide names and addresses of witnesses who will prove any allegation of fact in that party's pleading? Would the benefits of this change outweigh the dangers?

3. One particular phrase that has been judicially considered in the context of clarity and precision in pleadings is 'and/or'. The use of that expression was criticised in *Re Moage Ltd* [1998] FCA 296; (1998) 153 ALR 711 at 716–17 and in *Laing v Construction, Forestry, Mining and Energy Union* [2005] FCA 765 at [78]–[79]. In *St Clair v Timtella Pty Ltd (No 2)* [2010] QSC 480 Martin J discussed (at [11]–[13]) a number of authorities in which the use of that expression has been considered. His Honour concluded (at [14]):

> While the conjunction "and/or" is now almost a commonplace in commercial documents and some other forms of legal drafting, it should not be used in a pleading. Pleadings are intended to clarify and concentrate the issues in an action. They will not do that if the language used leaves open to reasonable construction a large number of permutations and combinations such as occurs in this case. Thus, a construction of them ranges from alleging that one defendant of the five is liable to all defendants being liable.

4. In his article, 'Seven Deadly Sins of Pleading' (2008) 32 *Hearsay*, <http://www.hearsay.org.au>, Anthony Morris QC helpfully considers the various ways in which relevant documents may be appropriately pleaded. He also discusses a number of common pleading practices which he argues are poor practice. These include pleading to the effect that 'The Plaintiff will refer to the said [document] at the trial of this action for its full terms, true meaning and effect', (which, as he explains, is 'a meaningless and worthless piece of verbage'), and the expression 'repeats and relies upon' (which he also regards as 'entirely unnecessary'.)

5. It has been noted at 11.2.19 that the High Court has retained a procedure entitling a party to 'demur' to an opponent's pleading and to obtain a ruling on the demurrer. For the purpose of obtaining the ruling, the demurrer admits the truth of the opponent's pleading but asserts that it does not lead to the conclusion for which the opponent contends. An example of the raising of this plea occurred in *Wurridjal v The Commonwealth of Australia* (2009) 237 CLR 309; [2009] HCA 2; (2009) 252 ALR 232. In that case a challenge was brought before the High Court to the constitutional validity of the Federal Government's emergency response to deal with sexual abuse of Aboriginal children in the Northern Territory, along with alcohol and drug abuse, pornography and gambling. Two key Bills concerned were the Northern Territory National Emergency Response Bill 2007 (Cth) and the Families, Community Services and Indigenous Affairs and Other Legislation Amendment Bill 2007. The Commonwealth demurred to the claim on the basis that it did not show any cause of action to which the court could give effect. The High Court, by a 6:1 majority, held that the demurrer should be allowed. The judgments include analysis of the function and purpose of the demurrer procedure, and the extent to which facts expressly or impliedly averred in the statement of claim might be taken as admitted for the purposes of demurrer.

11.2.31 Further reading

M Asprey, *Plain Language for Lawyers*, 4th ed, Federation Press, Australia, 2010.

Australian Law Reform Commission, *Managing Justice: A Review of the Federal Civil Justice System*, Report No 89, 2000, pp 285–9.

Centre for Plain Legal Language, *Words and Phrases*, Faculty of Law, University of Sydney, Sydney, 1992–93.

S Dunstone, *A Practical Guide to Drafting Pleadings*, LBC Information Services, 1997, pp 41–64.

The Hon M Kirby, 'Ten Commandments for Plain Language in Law' (2010) 33 *Aust Bar Rev* 10.

R Macdonald and D Clark-Dickson, *Clear and Precise: Writing Skills for Today's Lawyer*, 3rd ed, Thomson Reuters, Australia, 2010.

P McNamara, 'Cross-Examination of a Party on Pleadings' (1989) 5 *Aust Bar Rev* 176.

K C Oliver, 'Preliminary Determination of Questions' in *Court Forms, Precedents & Pleadings*, Vol 4, LexisNexis, Sydney, looseleaf.

PROCEDURE

11.3.1   In all jurisdictions, pleadings are filed and copies either delivered (Tas r 264) or served: HCR r 27.03 (statements of claim); FCR rr 8.06, 16.31–16.33; ACT r 6401; NSW r 10.1, Pt 14; NT O 14; Qld rr 146(1) (filing), 22(3), 139(1), 142, 164 (service); SA rr 34, 92–97 (filing); rr 39, 60 (service); Vic O 14; WA O 20 r 3.

11.3.2   The pleading process continues with the exchange of pleadings, within the varying time periods permitted for each pleading prescribed by the rules, or fixed by the court at a directions hearing. The rules in most jurisdictions also prescribe the time when pleadings close. A further pleading cannot be delivered after that time without the leave of the court: FCR r 16.12; ACT rr 481, 483; NSW r 14.5; NT r 14.08; Qld r 169; SA r 4; Tas r 228; Vic r 14.08; WA O 20 r 20.

STATEMENT OF CLAIM

Procedural matters

11.4.1E	**Supreme Court (General Civil Procedure) Rules 2005 (Vic)**
	Order 14 — Service of Pleadings

Statement of claim indorsed on writ

14.01 Where the endorsement of claim on a writ constitutes a statement of claim in accordance with Rule 5.04, no statement of claim shall be served.

Statement of claim not indorsed on writ

14.02 Where the endorsement of claim on a writ does not constitute a statement of claim in accordance with Rule 5.04 and a defendant files an appearance, the plaintiff shall serve a statement of claim on that defendant within 30 days after the defendant's appearance, unless the Court otherwise orders.

11.4.2   The opening pleading is the 'statement of claim'. In the High Court (r 27.03), the Northern Territory (r 14.02), Tasmania (r 265(2)) and Western Australia (O 20 r 1), as in Victoria, the statement of claim is often a separate document which follows the writ, although in the High Court and Tasmania the plaintiff may choose to deliver the statement of claim with the writ.

In the High Court, the Northern Territory and Victoria, the plaintiff may indorse the writ with the statement of claim (HCR r 27.01; NT r 5.04; Vic r 5.04), and if that alternative is taken, no further statement of claim is delivered: HCR r 27.03; NT r 14.01; Vic r 14.01. The position in Tasmania (r 265(1)) and Western Australia (O 20 r 1) is similar, with the statement of claim forming part of the writ in the situations where the writ is specially indorsed: see **7.4.3**.

In New South Wales (r 6.3), a statement of claim must be used to commence proceedings for a range of specified claims. In general terms, these claims are those likely to involve a substantial dispute of fact: see also **7.4.1**. In the Australian Capital Territory (r 50(2)), a statement of claim must be attached to the originating claim.

In Queensland (r 22(1)), any claim must have the statement of claim attached to it.

In South Australia (rr 91, 96), the plaintiff may choose to accompany the summons commencing a proceeding with either a statement of claim or an affidavit, but practice directions may require that a case proceed on affidavits rather than pleadings. The court may order that an action begun on pleadings continue on affidavits or that an action begun on affidavits continue on pleadings. There is also provision for a party to seek exemption from the obligation to file formal pleadings.

In the Federal Court (r 8.05), proceedings are commenced by application. If the applicant seeks relief that includes damages, the originating application must be accompanied by a statement of claim. The applicant may otherwise choose to accompany the application with either a statement of claim, or an affidavit. The future course of the matter is determined at the first directions hearing, where pleadings may be ordered: FCR r 5.04.

Content

11.4.3   The statement of claim must disclose a cause of action (see **11.4.9–11.4.10E**) and generally comply with the rules of pleading. In the High Court (r 27.04), the statement of claim must allege that the matter is one within the original jurisdiction of the High Court and set out the facts on which that allegation is based.

Order of statement of claim

11.4.4   In some jurisdictions the Rules of Court contain rules and/or forms which prescribe generally the layout of the statement of claim, although not the substantive content: see, eg, FCR r 8.05, Form 17; ACT Forms 2.2–2.6; NSW Civil Procedure Act 2005 (NSW) s 17,

Forms 3A, 3B; Qld Form 16; SA r 98, Form 3; Vic r 23.03. Provided the statement of claim meets these requirements, its final presentation is a matter for the plaintiff, but the usual (and logical) order involves the following:

Introductory statements

11.4.5 Introductory statements should cover matters such as who the parties are, how they are connected to the dispute, and individual facts that apply to all parties, such as uncontroversial dates and events. If a plaintiff or a defendant is a corporation, the statement of claim should contain an allegation that that party is and was at all material times incorporated, or is otherwise entitled to sue or to be sued, as the case may be, in its own name: *Moldex v Recon Ltd* [1948] VLR 590. The introductory statements should also include the involvement of either party to the action in a representative capacity. Where necessary, this part of the pleading will also include facts establishing the court's jurisdiction.

The body

11.4.6 The body should include, in numbered paragraphs, substantive allegations sufficient to establish each element of each cause of action relied on. In most circumstances, the most appropriate way to plead these allegations will be to follow the natural chronology of events.

Claim for relief

11.4.7 See 11.4.13E–11.4.19.

Prescribed details — ACT

11.4.8 In the Australian Capital Territory, the rules prescribe the details which must be included in statements of claim for certain types of originating claims. These claims include a claim for damages for death or a personal claim for injury caused by, or arising out of, either the negligent use of a motor vehicle (r 52), or negligence or breach of statutory duty by an employer (r 53). Statements of claim are sufficient if the prescribed particulars are included.

Must disclose a cause of action

11.4.9 The most important feature of a statement of claim is that it must set out the material facts relied on to support the claim made. In other words, it must disclose a cause of action. If a party is bringing a proceeding for defamation, eg, the statement of claim must allege material facts sufficient to establish identification of the plaintiff, a statement likely to injure the plaintiff's reputation, publication of the statement and damage. In a similar way, a statement of claim in which a party is seeking to bring the action in negligence must contain material facts sufficient to establish a duty of care owed by the defendant to the plaintiff, a breach of that duty and consequential damage: see *McCauley v Hamilton Island Enterprises Pty Ltd* (1987) 75 ALR 257 at 263.

From a practical perspective this means it is appropriate, before commencing to draft a statement of claim, to consider exactly what causes of action the plaintiff has against each defendant, whether statutory, common law or in equity. It will frequently be necessary for the pleader to undertake research to ensure that all the elements of the causes of action, and the associated remedies, have been correctly identified.

Once the elements of each cause of action and the remedies available have been listed, the pleader can then consider what allegations of fact should be pleaded for each element of each cause of action against each defendant. A common defect in pleadings is a lack of precision in pleading which remedies are sought against which of several defendants. To avoid this problem, it may well be preferable to plead facts comprising the elements of each cause of action against each individual party separately. Of course this will depend upon the complexity of the proceeding.

If a statement of claim or part of a statement of claim fails to plead material facts sufficient to establish the cause of action relied upon, the pleading or the affected part of the pleading may be struck out, and in appropriate cases judgment may be entered for the defendant. For case examples where the plaintiff's claim, or that part of the statement of claim under challenge, were struck out as failing to disclose a cause of action, see **11.8.5C** and **11.8.6C**.

11.4.10E   **An Overview of Pleadings, Statements of Claim, Defences and Reply**
Justice J H Phillips
(1988) 62 *ALJ* 718

[In his article, Justice JH Phillips provides helpful, practical suggestions about the preparation of a statement of claim (or defence) to ensure that it discloses every element in the relevant cause of action (or defence), as follows:]

Preparation

If it is to be held sufficient a pleading must encompass each and every element in the relevant cause of action or defence. Consequently, it is the ascertainment of the legal nature of your client's case which is the essential commencement for all work on pleadings. Failure to make that ascertainment will most probably be accompanied by a failure to take adequate instructions. The first stage of preparation will be completed when you can say to yourself 'I am satisfied my client's cause of action (defence) is...'

Even when dealing with the most frequently pleaded causes of action or defences, it is prudent to write out their constituent elements and then make a cross-check with your instructions. Ask yourself: 'Have I sufficient facts to support this claim (defence)?' But once you are outside the area of causes of action and defences with which you are confident, you should always make a further check. It does not take long to look at the precedents in *Bullen and Leake, Atkin and Jacob*, and then make an additional reference to a textbook. Unless you can confidently answer the question I have posed in the affirmative you must seek further instructions. Finally, unless you are operating under circumstances of emergency try to put your pleading aside for a day or two and then take another look at it. You may find yourself saying: 'Did I really write that?' Ask yourself not only what you think of it, but how it will appear to your opponent and the court.

Should not anticipate the defence

11.4.11   Provided the necessary elements of the cause of action are pleaded, the plaintiff should not try to anticipate the defendant's defence. All the plaintiff should do is to allege the material facts along with such particulars (see 'Particulars' below at **11.7.1Eff**) necessary to prevent surprising the other side. If the plaintiff needs to allege further facts to rebut a defence, that is done in the reply.

The plaintiff should not, eg, raise in the statement of claim that the defendant is estopped from setting up a particular denial, or has waived his or her right to allege or rely upon certain circumstances. As a general rule, these matters should only be raised if and when the defendant has pleaded the particular denial, or the circumstances which the plaintiff asserts have been waived, as the case may be. A possible exception is an allegation that the defendant has waived the performance of a condition precedent or that there is some other reason why the plaintiff was not obliged to perform that condition precedent. In that circumstance, the relevant facts should be pleaded in the statement of claim, as performance of the condition precedent will otherwise be implied from the plaintiff's pleading: *Spicers and Detmold Ltd v Australian Automatic Cigarette Paper Co Pty Ltd* [1942] VLR 97.

Australian Capital Territory and Queensland — nature and amount of damages claimed to be pleaded

11.4.12 The Queensland and the Australian Capital Territory have unique requirements about the pleading of damages. In Queensland, if damages are claimed in a pleading, then r 155(1) makes it mandatory that the pleading state the nature and amount of the damages claimed. If there is a claim for general damages, the pleading must include particulars of the nature of the loss or damage suffered, the exact circumstances in which the loss or damage was suffered, and the basis on which the amount claimed has been calculated or estimated: r 155(2). If practicable, the party must plead each type of general damages and state the nature of the damages claimed for each type: r 155(3). There is also a general requirement in relation to the pleading of damages that a party claiming damages must plead any matter relating to the assessment of damages that, if not pleaded, may take an opposing party by surprise: r 155(4). Rule 155 should be read with r 150(1)(b), which requires a plaintiff to specifically plead every type of damage claimed, including special and exemplary damages.

Rule 155 was considered by the Queensland Court of Appeal in *Meredith v Palmcam Pty Ltd* [2001] 1 Qd R 645. The Court of Appeal made it clear that pleading in terms such as 'full particulars of the plaintiff's special damages will be provided prior to the trial of this action', which were commonly used before the introduction of the Uniform Civil Procedure Rules 1999, does not comply with r 155. The court also indicated that the necessary particulars of the types and amounts of damage should appear in the body of the statement of claim, and not just in the claim for relief at the end of the statement of claim. It is permissible, however, to then refer back to the amounts or matters pleaded in relevant paragraphs of the statement of claim without repeating them in full in the claim for relief at the end.

The Australian Capital Territory has rules modelled on r 155 of the Queensland rules: ACT rr 417, 418. There is a key difference, however, in that the rules in the Australian Capital Territory only require the amount of damages to be claimed for damages that are not general damages, and specify that a pleading must not claim an amount for unliquidated damages.

Claim for relief

11.4.13E   **Rules of the Supreme Court 1971 (WA)**
Order 20 — Pleadings

Statement of claim
2 (1) A statement of claim must state specifically the relief or remedy which the plaintiff claims, but costs need not be specifically claimed.

11.4.14 All jurisdictions have equivalent rules requiring the plaintiff, in the statement of claim, to specify the relief that is claimed in the action: HCR r 27.04; FCR r 16.02(1)(f) Sch 1 Form 7 (a party is not entitled to seek any additional relief to that claimed in the originating application); ACT r 406(1)(d); NSW r 6.12; NT r 13.02(1)(c); Qld r 149(1)(d); SA r 99(1)(d); Tas r 229; Vic r 13.02(1)(c). In the ordinary course it is placed at the end of the statement of claim, and commences 'The plaintiff claims' followed by a statement of the relief sought. If several items of relief are claimed, these should be listed separately and distinctly. If more than one cause of action is relied upon, the pleader should specify clearly the relief sought in respect of each. If the relief claimed is other than an amount of money, the statement of claim should specify the actual order sought. If, eg, injunctive relief or a declaration is claimed, the plaintiff should set out the precise terms proposed.

11.4.15E   **Supreme Court (General Civil Procedure)**
Rules 2005 (Vic)
Order 59 — Judgments and Orders

General relief

59.01 The Court may, at any stage of a proceeding, on the application of any party, give such judgment or make such order as the case requires notwithstanding that the judgment or order had not been sought in the originating process or other document of the party in the proceeding.

[See also: FCR r 1.41; ACT r 419; NSW r 36.1; NT r 59.01; Qld r 156; SA r 223; Tas rr 229, 806; WA O 20 r 2 (this rule is less specific in relation to general relief than those of the other jurisdictions).]

11.4.16 The effect of these rules is that, although the plaintiff will usually state quite specifically the relief sought, the court may also award other general or 'non-specific' relief if the evidence shows that the relief claimed by the plaintiff is inadequate: *Murphy v Murphy* [1963] VR 610; *Belmont Finance Corp Ltd v Williams Furniture Ltd* [1979] Ch 250. In a similar way, the plaintiff will usually list the principal orders sought, but the court may order further or general relief sufficient to make its principal orders effective. For example, if the court makes an order for specific performance of a contract, it will usually supplement that order with a series of mechanical details that make the order for specific performance operational. Non-specific or general relief, however, cannot extend beyond the needs of the case as revealed in the pleadings: *Wicks v Bennett* (1921) 30 CLR 80.

11.4.17 If the plaintiff is suing for damages, the plaintiff should claim damages in the *claim for relief*. If unliquidated damages are claimed, then in most jurisdictions the plaintiff need not claim a specific amount but may ask for damages generally. In the Australian Capital Territory (r 418) and New South Wales (r 14.13), the rules forbid claiming a specific amount for unliquidated damages, and in Tasmania (r 242) the amount of any unliquidated damages claimed is to be stated in a pleading only if it does not exceed $50,000.

A claim for damages will extend only to general damage and will not enable the plaintiff to recover damage which the law regards as special; ie, such damage as is not inferred by law to flow from the defendant's conduct (eg, expenses such as loss of income and medical expenses in personal injury actions). It will also not enable the plaintiff to recover in respect of unusual damage, which the defendant would not have anticipated. In either case, the plaintiff should specifically plead the particular damage suffered.

The position in Queensland is different, as the rules require that the pleading state the nature and amount of the damages claimed: see 11.4.12. The Queensland Court of Appeal has indicated that the details in relation to damages as required by rr 150(1)(b) and 155 should appear as allegations in the body of the statement of claim, and not only in the claim for relief at the end. In appropriate circumstances, however, the claim for relief may simply refer back to the amounts or matters pleaded in the relevant paragraphs of the statement of claim: *Meredith v Palmcam Pty Ltd* [2001] 1 Qd R 645.

In *Dare v Pulham* (1982) 148 CLR 658, evidence admitted at the trial without objection established a claim for damages at a higher amount than that claimed in the particulars in the statement of claim, and the High Court held the plaintiff was not bound by the assessment in the particulars. However, except in Queensland, it is usually advisable to avoid any potential difficulties by leaving at large the amount of any unliquidated damages claimed.

11.4.18 A claim for interest to the date of judgment should be pleaded: *Pheeney v Doolan (No 2)* (1977) 1 NSWLR 601 at 605. In New South Wales (r 6.12), the Rules of Court specifically require this. The Queensland rules go further. They require a party intending to apply for an award of interest to allege particulars of the amount or amounts on which interest is claimed, the interest rate or rates claimed (except if the party is claiming at the rate or rates specified in a practice direction), and the method of calculation: r 159. Proceedings for damages for personal injury or death are expressly excluded (r 159(2)) because in proceedings of that nature it would be difficult, and often impossible, to provide those details.

11.4.19 If the plaintiff has pleaded claims in the alternative, it may be appropriate to also have alternative claims for relief. This is permitted, provided the relief claimed can be justified by pleaded facts: see *Water Wine & Juice Pty Ltd v Steve Konstanopoulos* [2010] NSWSC 312.

11.4.20 Notes

1. In their article, 'Pleadings in Industrial and Employment Cases' (2009) 22 *AJLL*, Stuart Wood and Tim Donaghey provide a number of helpful practical tips to assist a party to appropriately plead the elements of the cause of action, with a particular focus on industrial and employment cases.

2. For a Queensland Court of Appeal decision confirming the striking out of a statement of claim as disclosing no reasonable cause of action, see *Butler v Simmonds Crowley & Galvin* [1999] QCA 475. The case includes consideration of the pleaded causes of action in malicious prosecution and collateral abuse of process. The Court of Appeal confirmed that the statement of claim in question failed to contain the necessary foundation for a successful claim based on either tort and should be struck out.

3. For consideration by the New South Wales Court of Appeal of the principles applicable to pleading material facts necessary to establish a cause of action in defamation, see *Ron Hodgson (Trading) Pty Ltd v Belvedere Motors (Hurstwille) Pty Ltd* [1971] 1 NSWLR 472.

11.4.21   Further reading

D Barnard and M Houghton, *The New Civil Court in Action*, Butterworths, London, 1993, pp 127–31, 143–8 (drafting commentary and simple sample statements of claim for common causes of action).

M Blumberg, 'Pleading Alternative Version of the Facts' (1994) 16(6) *Law Society of South Australia Bulletin* 19.

S Cooper, 'Pleading Vulnerability in Cases of Pure Economic Loss', (2008) 26 *Hearsay*, <http://www.hearsay.org.au>.

S Star and M Pryse, *Pleading and Proving Misleading and Deceptive Conduct*, Leo Cussen Institute, Melbourne, 2008.

DEFENCE

Contents generally

11.5.1E   **Supreme Court (General Civil Procedure) Rules 2005 (Vic)**
                                    Order 13 — Pleadings

Matter which must be pleaded

13.07 (1) A party shall in any pleading subsequent to a statement of claim plead specifically any matter of fact which —

    (a)   the party alleges makes any claim or defence of the opposite party not maintainable; or

    (b)   if not pleaded specifically, might take the opposite party by surprise; or

    (c)   raises questions of fact not arising out of the preceding pleading.

[See also: HCR r 27.05; FCR r 16.08 (this rule also extends to points of law); ACT r 407(3); NSW r 14.14; NT r 13.07; Qld r 150(4); SA r 100; Tas r 251; WA O 20 r 9(1).]

11.5.2 This rule and its equivalents require the defendant to plead in the defence all facts showing that the plaintiff's claim is not maintainable and all grounds of defence which, if not pleaded, may surprise the plaintiff, or which raise matters of fact not arising out of the statement of claim. The provisions of the Australian Capital Territory, New South Wales, South Australia and Western Australian rules also provide instances of matters which will fall within the ambit of the rule and hence require specific pleading. The examples given vary in extent but they include matters such as fraud, statute of limitations, and any fact showing illegality. For the Australian Capital Territory (r 407(1)) and Queensland (r 150(1)), matters such as fraud, illegality, and defences under the Limitations of Actions Act 1974 (Qld) are included in a very extensive list of matters which specifically must be pleaded, regardless of the nature of the particular pleading.

The Rules of Court distinguish between a defendant's:

(a)   pleading negatively (making denials or 'traversing'); and

(b)   pleading affirmatively.

Any combination of these pleas may be used concurrently. As has previously been discussed, the defendant may choose to raise a point of law at the same time: see 11.2.17E–11.2.19. It is also permissible to make inconsistent alternative pleas. A defendant may, for example, deny the making of a contract alleged by the plaintiff, and *also* allege that if there was a contract it is unenforceable because of the absence of writing (in the case of the sale of land), or even proceed to counterclaim for breach of the same contract. However, it must be clear that the inconsistent defences are alternatives. Further, the defendant may not allege a defence known to be false.

As with a statement of claim, the rules in some jurisdictions prescribe a form for the defence, but these forms relate only to basic layout, and not to substantive pleas: see, eg, FCR r 16.02, Form 33; NSW Civil Procedure Act 2005 (NSW) s 17, Forms 7A, 7B; Qld Forms 17 (defence), 18 (defence and counterclaim); SA r 98, Form 9.

Denials

11.5.3   A defence should be formulated so as to identify the issues and give the other party notice of the case to be met at trial. In most jurisdictions, the defendant must plead to each allegation in the statement of claim: FCR r 16.07(1); ACT r 441; NT rr 13.12, 13.13(2); Qld r 165(1); Tas r 243; Vic rr 13.12, 13.13(2); WA O 20 r 14(3). In New South Wales r 14.26 permits general denials, though there is in r 14.20 a prohibition of the pleading of the general issue. It is suggested that in that jurisdiction also the defendant must plead in such a way that it is clear what is admitted and what is denied, and so should endeavour to plead to each specific allegation. The effect of a denial is to put the other party to proof of the allegations denied.

11.5.4   A denial may be express or implied. The rules in most jurisdictions also contemplate that the defendant may plead that certain allegations are 'not admitted': FCR r 16.07(3); ACT r 440; NSW r 14.26; NT r 13.12; Qld r 165(1); Tas rr 243(4), 250(1); Vic r 13.12; WA O 20 r 14(2). This plea is appropriate when the allegation being responded to is outside the knowledge of the defendant. As the rules in some jurisdictions make explicit (FCR r 16.03(7); ACT r 440), a non-admission operates in the same way as a denial: *Ruptic v AW Baulderstone Pty Ltd* (1987) 46 SASR 99 at 102.

11.5.5   There are various specific rules which restrict the making of general denials in respect of particular types of claim, or which give certain denials a limited effect: see 11.5.11–11.5.13. With these specific exceptions it has historically been permissible for defendants to simply deny a plaintiff's allegations, even if the defendant knew those allegations were true, and put the plaintiff to proof. That feature of the pleading rules has been broadly criticised. As long ago as 1968, the Winn Report, *Report of the Committee on Personal Injuries Litigation*, (UK), 1968, Cmnd 3691, pp 76–7, eg, described the defence as 'a blot on our procedure' and recommended that defendants should be required to plead their version of the relevant facts and to indicate the extent of their knowledge of those facts. Davies J, when he was Chair of the Litigation Reform Commission in Queensland, described the pleading rules as 'playing a very expensive game rather than getting to the real issues in dispute': G L Davies J and J S Lieboff, 'Reforming the Civil Litigation System: Streamlining the Adversarial Framework' *Proctor*, November 1994, 10.

To address this concern, the Rules of Court in most jurisdictions now include requirements which, in various ways, force defendants to plead in a way that really does narrow the issues, rather than just put the plaintiff to proof.

11.5.6 The requirements in the Federal Court, the Australian Capital Territory, New South Wales, and South Australia, for the certification or verification of pleadings have already been discussed: see 11.2.22–11.2.25. These requirements apply to defences as well as to statements of claim.

In the Federal Court (r 16.07), Australian Capital Territory (r 441(1), (4)), Tasmania (r 243(1)) and Western Australia (O 20 r 14(3)) the rules expressly state that a general denial is not permitted, and that a party must deal specifically with each allegation of fact the party does not admit.

In the Northern Territory (r 13.12(3)), Tasmania (r 250(3)) and Victoria (r 13.12(3)) a party intending to prove facts different to those pleaded by the opposite party, may not merely deny or 'not admit' the facts pleaded, but must plead the version of events which he or she intends to prove.

In South Australia (rr 100, 101) parties must indicate which allegations of fact in the pleading being responded to are admitted or which the party pleading does not propose to challenge at the trial. They must also raise any special defence or answer to a special defence raised by an opposing party, and in either case state the basis on which they rely. Except with the leave of the court, there is a general prohibition on introducing at the trial evidence of facts that should have been, but were not, alleged in the party's pleadings, or raising at the trial issues of which notice should have been but was not given in the party's pleadings: r 103.

11.5.7 The rules in Queensland contain particularly extensive obligations in relation to denials and non-admissions. Those rules prohibit a party from pleading a non-admission unless the party has made inquiries to find out whether the allegation is true or untrue, and the inquiries for an allegation are reasonable, having regard for the time limited for filing and serving the defence or other pleading in which the denial or non-admission of the allegation is contained, and the party remains uncertain as to the truth or falsity of the allegation: r 166(3). Further, a party's denial or non-admission of an allegation of fact must be accompanied by a direct explanation for the party's belief that the allegation is untrue or cannot be admitted: r 166(4). If a party's denial or non-admission does not do so, the party is taken to have admitted the allegation: r 166(5). A party pleading a non-admission is under a continuing obligation to make further inquiries that become reasonable and, if the results of the inquiries make possible the admission or denial of an allegation, to amend the pleading appropriately: r 166(6). The pleading of a non-admission also now has the serious consequence that the party pleading it may not give or call evidence in relation to a fact not admitted, unless the evidence relates to another part of the party's pleading: r 165(2).

11.5.8 A more subtle encouragement for a party to admit rather than deny an allegation is the court's power, in circumstances where an allegation that should have been admitted is denied or not admitted, to impose a penalty in the form of extra costs occasioned by the denial or failure to admit: *Gordon v Gordon* [1948] VLR 57 at 58. In the Australian Capital Territory (r 448) and Queensland (r 167) this is specifically provided for by the Rules of Court.

11.5.9 In South Australia (rr 100(5), 101(3)) a party is taken to deny any allegation of fact in the pleading being responded to unless the party pleading indicates that the allegation is admitted or that it is not proposed to challenge the allegation at the trial. The rules in most other jurisdictions provide that any allegation in the statement of claim which is not denied or stated to be admitted in the defence will be taken to have been admitted, except in respect of damages (which, if not admitted, are always deemed to be in issue) or where the defendant is under a legal disability: FCR rr 9.67, 16.07 (there is no longer an exception in respect of damages); ACT r 447; NSW r 14.26; NT rr 13.12, 15.06; Qld r 166(1), (2) (there is no longer any exception in respect of damages); Tas rr 250(1), 243(3); Vic rr 13.12, 15.06; WA O 20 r 14(1), 14(4), O 70 r 8. In all jurisdictions which do not permit general denials, this will also apply to allegations not separately addressed in the defence, as illustrated by the classic decision in *Thorp v Holdsworth* (1876) 3 Ch D 637 (extracted below). These rules may also apply if the defendant's plea to an allegation in the statement of claim, when considered with that allegation, is ambiguous, with the result that the allegation may be deemed admitted.

11.5.10C   **Thorp v Holdsworth**
                                      (1876) 3 Ch D 637
                          High Court of England, Chancery Division

[The plaintiffs alleged in their statement of claim that a partnership had been formed, that the terms had been agreed upon and the business of the partnership commenced. The defendant admitted agreeing to enter into partnership as alleged but also pleaded: 'The defendant denies that the terms of the arrangement between himself and the plaintiffs were definitely agreed upon as alleged.' The plaintiffs moved for judgment based upon the defendant's admissions of fact.]

Jessel MR (at 640–2): What amounts to admissions of fact in a pleading ... is defined by the 17th rule of Order XIX: 'Every allegation of fact in any pleading ... if not denied specifically or by necessary implication, or stated to be not admitted in the pleading of the opposite party, shall be taken to be admitted.' Consequently, all you have to find is no specific denial or no definite refusal to admit.

Then the question is what 'if not denied specifically' means, and that is again defined in subsequent rules. The 20th rule says: 'It shall not be sufficient for a Defendant in his defence to deny generally the facts alleged ... in a defence by way of counterclaim, but each party must deal specifically with each allegation of fact of which he does not admit the truth.' There, it will be seen, it is not merely denial which is meant, but the rule covers non-admission, for each party is to deal specifically with every allegation of fact of which he does not admit the truth. Therefore, he must be quite as specific under the 20th rule when he says 'I do not admit' as when he says 'I deny'. In fact, they are both covered by the 20th rule.

Then, in order that there shall be no mistake as to the meaning of the word 'specifically' in the 20th rule, the 22nd rule says this: 'When a party in any pleading denies an allegation of fact in the previous pleading of the opposite party, he must not do so evasively, but answer the point of substance. Thus, if it be alleged that he received a certain sum of money, it shall not be sufficient to deny that he received that particular amount, but he must deny that he received that sum, or any part thereof, or else set out how much he received. And so, when a matter of fact is alleged with divers circumstances, it shall not be sufficient to deny it as alleged along with those circumstances, but a fair and substantial answer must be given.'

Applying that rule to the pleadings in the present case, let us see what comes of it. The Plaintiffs allege an agreement to take a lease and to carry on a partnership. They allege that, in pursuance [641] of the agreement, they took a lease, and that the draft articles were prepared to define the terms of the partnership; that there was an interview on the 17th of September, and that the same were approved by the parties subject to being submitted by the Defendant to his solicitor, and being revised and finally settled; that the draft had not yet been revised, and the articles had not yet been executed, and that, although the draft articles were only settled subject to revision, the terms of the arrangement between the Plaintiffs and Defendant, as therein provided, were definitely agreed upon at the said interview, and the Defendant procured the Plaintiff Stackpoole to sign the draft articles in order to prevent any question being raised by him as to the terms agreed upon. Then they allege that they subsequently carried on the business, and that the Defendant had taken an active part in carrying it on.

The Defendant does not deny a word of these allegations, except that part which alleges that the terms were definitely settled, and as to that he says: 'The Defendant denies that the terms of the arrangement between himself and the Plaintiffs were definitely agreed upon as alleged.' Now that is evasive. 'As alleged' means the whole allegation in the statement of claim, not the allegations of the particular paragraph. I cannot tell from his pleading what part of the allegation of the Plaintiffs the Defendant intends to deny. He may intend to deny that the terms were definitely agreed upon at the interview of the 17th of September, although they were at some other day, or he may have some peculiar view as to the meaning of the word 'definitely.' He may not be able to say that the terms were not arranged as agreed upon, but he may take the word 'definitely,' because he thinks it may give him some mode of escape. I cannot make out what he means. He is bound to deny that any agreements or any terms of arrangement were ever come to, if that is what he means; if he does not mean that, he should say that there were no terms of arrangement come to, except the following terms, and then state what the terms were; otherwise there is no specific denial at all.

Mr Cookson submitted to me that it was a great hardship on a Defendant who was asked to perform a parol agreement, the terms [642] of which were not accurately stated by the Plaintiffs, to be compelled by his own pleadings to state what the terms were. It would be a very extraordinary notion of the administration of justice to treat such a complaint seriously. It is the very object we have always had in view in pleading to know what the Defendant's version of the matter is in order that the parties may come to an issue. If you have an agreement for a lease containing fifty stipulations made by parol, and the Plaintiff and Defendant both agreed that there was such an agreement, and, except as to one of the fifty stipulations, that it had been carried out and acted upon, what would be said of a Court of Justice if it allowed the Defendant simply to deny that there was any such agreement as alleged, so that the Plaintiff should be compelled to come to trial with witnesses to prove every one of the fifty stipulations of the agreement? Of course the Defendant ought to admit that forty-nine were made, and deny the fiftieth, and then the cause would come to a trial upon the question whether the fiftieth stipulation alleged did or did not form part of the agreement. That is not hard upon a Defendant: it is the proper mode of carrying on the administration of justice. That is the meaning of the rules, and I have said as much as I have done in order that solicitors may be aware in future that I shall insist upon the rules of pleading being complied with.

There will be the usual decree for dissolution, and, if desired by the Defendant, an inquiry what were the terms of the partnership.

[See also *Byrd v Nunn* (1877) 7 Ch D 284.]

11.5.11   In addition to the general principles, the rules in the Australian Capital Territory (r 442) and Tasmania (rr 232(2), 243(5)) do not permit a mere denial of a debt in a defence to a claim for debt or a liquidated demand, and require the defence to deny such matters of fact from which the liability of the defendant is alleged to arise as are disputed. In an action on a bill of exchange, promissory note or cheque, any denial must specify the matter of fact which is denied, such as the drawing, making, endorsing, accepting, presenting or dishonouring of the bill, note or cheque: ACT r 444; Tas r 243(6).

11.5.12   In the Australian Capital Territory, the rules detail the matters which must be particularised in the statement of claim when the claim arises out of motor vehicle or workplace accidents: see 11.7.14 and 14.2.7. The rules provide that in such proceedings the defendant must, in the defence, specifically admit or deny every material allegation of fact in the originating claim and statement of claim, including any allegation by way of particulars. The defence must plead every ground of defence to be relied on, together with facts necessary to establish each ground. A defendant wishing to prove a version of facts different from that alleged in the originating claim or statement of claim, must plead that version in the defence: r 443.

11.5.13   A defendant should take special care when denying a negative proposition in the opposing party's pleading. If the plaintiff pleads a negative proposition (eg, that A had no authority) which the defendant denies, the double negative may be construed as an assertion of an affirmative proposition (ie, A had authority). A denial which carries with it an affirmative proposition is known as a 'negative pregnant'. If a positive proposition could arise in this way, the defendant should make the intention clear and provide adequate particulars.

If a negative pregnant is pleaded, the court may strike it out as embarrassing or, more commonly, order the defendant to provide particulars of the case intended to be raised by the plea.

11.5.14C	**Pinson v Lloyds & National Provincial Foreign Bank Ltd**
	[1941] 2 KB 72
	High Court of England, Court of Appeal

[For some years the defendants acted as agents and brokers for the purchase and sale of securities and foreign currencies on behalf of the plaintiff. The plaintiff brought proceedings against the bank claiming damages for breach of contract. By para 7 of her statement of claim the plaintiff had alleged that in respect of certain transactions the bank had not acted in accordance with her instructions and that she had suffered damage as a result. In their defence the defendants denied:

> ... that they effected purchases or sales without having been authorised by the plaintiff to do so either in respect of the matters alleged in the particulars of para 7 of the statement of claim or at all.

The plaintiff brought an application either to strike out the defence or for particulars:

> ... of any authority which the defendants are alleged to have had from the plaintiff to carry out any of the transactions referred to in para 7 of the statement of claim which the defendants were therein alleged to have carried out without such authority.

The application was refused by the Master and by the Chamber Judge on appeal. The plaintiff appealed to the Court of Appeal. The defendants admitted on the appeal that on the pleadings as they stood they intended at the trial to set up an affirmative case of authority.]

Stable J (at 83–5): It remains, therefore, to consider whether or not as it stands the passage in the defence that I have set out is sufficient or not. To determine this question it is necessary to consider the nature of a denial or traverse in a pleading. A traverse in a defence is never an assertion of fact on oath. Often it is not an assertion of fact at all, and may amount to no more than this: 'Prove your allegation if you can. I do not intend to give you any help by admitting it.' Where the traverse is a mere denial or putting in issue of some positive or affirmative allegation in the statement of claim, the rule [84] that a defendant cannot be ordered to give particulars really rests on the commonsense basis that there is nothing which the defendant can particularize, in which case, to say the least of it, there would be no point in ordering him to do something which *ex hypothesis* is impossible. Where the allegation in the statement of claim is a negative allegation, the traverse necessarily involved a double negative. When used in ordinary speech a double negative must involve an affirmative proposition, but where the double negative appears in a defence in the form of a denial of a negative allegation in the statement of claim it does not necessarily follow, by reason of the very nature of a traverse which I have tried to indicate, that a positive or affirmative statement is contained in it. It may or may not be so.

Such a traverse — that is, one involving a double negative — may fall under one of three heads: (i) it may be a mere traverse involving no affirmative allegation; (ii) it may be a negative pregnant which contains within the double negative an affirmative allegation; or (iii) it may leave the matter in doubt what its true nature is. In my judgment, in the first case the defendant at the trial of the action can do no more than put the plaintiff to the proof of the negative alleged. He can seek to shake or destroy by cross-examination any evidence which the plaintiff may bring on the point, but, when once the plaintiff has established a prima facie case, the defendant on such a pleading cannot set up an affirmative case in answer because that, *ex hypothesis*, would be to set up a case which he has not pleaded, and that is what the rules expressly preclude him from doing. If it falls under the second head, the double negative extends beyond a mere traverse and amounts as in the present case to this: 'If you establish a prima facie case that I sold or purchased shares for you and that in so doing I acted without authority, then I intend to call evidence to establish that on each or some of the occasions there was an express authority to act as I did or an implied authority to be derived from certain facts.' That, in my judgment is to set up an affirmative case of which particulars ought to be given and that, none the less, though the affirmative case is [85] concealed, albeit imperfectly, in a negative shell. The third head may be excluded in the present case because Mr Holmes has told us that at the trial of the action, if the pleading rests where it is his intention to contend that he is entitled to set up an affirmative case and to prove the existence of an express authority of which he refuses to give particulars.

In my judgment, in each case where a negative allegation by a plaintiff in a pleading is traversed in the defence, the question whether or not the defendant can be ordered to give particulars depends on whether the traverse is a mere traverse or whether, though negative in form, the negative is pregnant with an affirmative, in which case particulars of that affirmative must be given. This result seems to me to be in accordance with the rules which govern these matters, with common sense, and with the authorities in which the recognition of the importance of this distinction seems to me to be clearly recognized ....

[His Honour concluded (at 88):]

For these reasons, in my judgment, the defendants' counsel having admitted that the double negative in fact contains an affirmative case, he must be ordered to give particulars of what it is … I will only add that, if Mr Holmes had not made the admission he did, he would have been in no better plight, because he would have left the real nature of the traverse in doubt, in which case it would have been embarrassing. That part of the pleading in such circumstances would have been defective in that the limits of the controversy were not properly defined in accordance with the rules of the Supreme Court and should accordingly in default of amendment have been struck out.

[**Goddard LJ** delivered a separate judgment to similar effect. **Scott LJ** dissented. The basis for the dissent, however, was that the plaintiff's statement of claim and particulars were so embarrassing that the exercise of discretion by the judge in chambers should not be interfered with.

See also *Bardenhagen v Neville Smith Group Pty Ltd* [1994] TASSC 175.]

Affirmative pleading

11.5.15 A defendant should make such admissions as are appropriate in the defence. The specific requirement in the rules that a party plead any matter which is likely to take the other party by surprise means there are also certain circumstances where the defendant must plead positively as distinct from a bare or general denial of the allegation in the statement of claim or even a specific denial of any particular fact or circumstance.

The examples given in the rules, which all specify such things as fraud, release, payment, performance and illegality, are not intended to be exhaustive and any unexpected defences must also be pleaded.

One type of allegation which is required to be specifically pleaded in this way is what is known as a 'confession and avoidance'. By this plea a defendant may admit or 'confess' a particular allegation, but couple this admission with further facts which throw new light on the allegation and which thus 'avoid' the effect which those facts would have otherwise. If, for example, the basis of the defence is that the contract upon which the plaintiff sues is illegal, this should be specifically pleaded in the defence.

Frequently, a confession and avoidance will be pleaded with a denial. In that case it should be clear that the pleas are in the alternative. The defendant bears the burden of proof in respect of any matter alleged in avoidance.

11.5.16C **Cameron v Troy**
[2001] WASCA 400
Supreme Court of Western Australia, Full Court

[The respondent sued the appellant in the District Court, alleging that at material times the appellant had carried on business as 'Great Breaks International'. In its statement of claim, the respondent alleged that it had carried out work for the appellant under an oral agreement between them that it would provide accounting services to the appellant in relation to a proposed venture in which the appellant was involved, and that the appellant had agreed to pay its usual professional fees for these services. There was evidence that the appellant's solicitors were instructed that the appellant did not contract with the respondent in his private capacity, but only as agent for Great Brooks International Ltd. However, the appellant's defence consisted of denials of every allegation in the statement of claim, other than non-payment of the respondent's accounts. The appellant admitted he had not paid the respondent any moneys, and stated that he was not obliged to do so. The appellant did not plead that he had not contracted personally or that he had contracted as agent for Great Breaks International Ltd.

During the trial, counsel for the appellant endeavoured to direct cross-examination and to lead evidence directed towards showing that the appellant had contracted with the respondent as agent for Great Breaks International and that he had no dealings in a private capacity with the respondent. The trial judge determined that it was outside the ambit of the pleadings to consider whether the defendant was acting as agent or gave instructions as agent of Great Breaks International or any other company. The judge was satisfied this issue could not be dealt with without injustice to the respondent and made directions that generally confined the trial to the issues that had been raised on the pleadings. The appellant appealed to the Full Court.]

Templeman J (at [9]–[12], [49]–[54]):

[9] At the hearing of the appeal, counsel for the appellant sought to justify his client's position by reference to the text *Pleadings: Principles and Practice*, by Sir Jack Jacob QC and Mr Iain S Goldrein (1990) which contains the following passage:

> The defendant should not confess and avoid where a mere traverse is sufficient. For he will then introduce additional matter which he may have to prove, instead of putting the plaintiff to proof of his allegations. It is not always wise for the defendant to set up an affirmative case, especially if there is a ground for anticipating that the plaintiff may fail to establish a *prima facie* case.

[10] The corollary of that statement is equally true: if it is obvious that the plaintiff will establish a *prima facie* case, it is wise to establish an affirmative case if liability is to be avoided. That should have been obvious to the appellant's solicitor, given the instructions to which I have referred.

[11] That being so, the conduct of the appellant's solicitor in pleading a denial rather than a confession and avoidance, was, in my view, misguided and improper. In so saying, I adopt the following passage from the judgment of Ipp J in *Unioil International Pty Ltd & Ors v Deloitte Touche Tohmatsu & Anor (No 2)* (1997) 18 WAR 190, 193:

> It has long been the practice, for tactical reasons, for lawyers to draft pleadings in such a form as to put the opposing party to proof of allegations, and even to deny allegations, notwithstanding that their factual instructions might not justify such failures to admit or denials. In my view, the circumstances under which litigation is conducted have changed to such a degree that this practice should no longer be tolerated. I do not intend, by saying this, to indicate that there should be any obligation on lawyers to exercise some credibility judgment as to the merits of their factual instructions. But, in my view, where a denial or putting to the proof would be inconsistent with the facts with which the pleader is instructed, the pleader should admit the allegation in question.

[12] In the present case, the denial of the allegation that the respondent had contracted with the appellant, was inconsistent with instructions the appellant had given to his solicitors. On those instructions, the true issue was whether the respondent had contracted with the appellant as agent for Great Breaks International Ltd. But the issue raised by the denial was whether the respondent had contracted with the appellant at all.

...

[49] On the hearing of the appeal, counsel for the appellant submitted that the learned trial Judge attached undue significance to the fact that the appellant had simply denied the respondent's claim without advancing a positive case that the appellant was acting as agent for another party or that the respondent in fact contracted with Great Breaks International Ltd. The essence of the submission was that the Judge was preoccupied with the pleadings.

[50] In my view, that is not so. It may be accepted that pleadings are a means to an end and should not be permitted to govern litigation in which it is necessary to resolve issues which have emerged otherwise than by the pleading process.

[51] In the present case, for example, if counsel for the appellant had informed the Judge that the real issue was whether the appellant had contracted on behalf of Great Breaks International Ltd, the trial could have been conducted on that basis. But, for reasons about which one can only speculate, the appellant chose not to have that issue tried. He must therefore accept the consequences.

[52] Counsel for the appellant provided the Court with the recent recommendations of the Western Australian Law Reform Commission to the effect that pleadings should be abolished and replaced with case statements which set out in a concise narrative and non-legalistic form:

1.   in chronological order, the facts which are material to the claim or defence; and
2.   the legal nature of the claim or defence.

Counsel provided the Court also with a submission made to the Law Reform Commission in which numerous criticisms were made of the present pleading system and recommendations made for its reform. Counsel's object in providing these materials to the Court was to underpin the submission that:

The very situation which occurred here should never be allowed to happen.

[53] The assumption underlying that submission is that the present system of pleadings was responsible for the trial Judge reaching an erroneous conclusion. I do not accept that proposition. The appellant was found liable because he chose not to advance his real case: that he had contracted as agent. He was therefore obliged to conduct his case on a false premise: that he was not the person with whom the respondent contracted.

[54] The result would have been no different under the case statement regime proposed by the Law Reform Commission if the appellant had stated only that his defence arose from the fact that the respondent had not contracted with him.

[Murray J and **Einfield AJ** both agreed with the reasons of **Templeman J.** The appeal was dismissed.]

11.5.17   Notes and questions

1. In addition to the obligations arising under the Rules of Court about the pleading of allegations of fraud, there are also obligations placed upon members of the legal profession who seek to raise them. In particular, legal practitioners must take care to have specific instructions and an appropriate evidentiary foundation, direct or inferred, for alleging and pleading fraud. What is the rationale for such rules of ethical conduct? For discussions of the principles and their justification, see *Saltoon v Lake* [1978] 1 NSWLR 52 at 57–8; *Minister administering the Crown Lands (Consolidation) Act and Western Lands Act v Tweed Byron Aboriginal Land Council* (1990) 71 LGRA 201 at 203–4; *Ghazal v Government Insurance Office of New South Wales* (1992) 29 NSWLR 336 at 348–9 per Mahoney JA; *White Industries (Qld) Pty Ltd v Flower & Hart (a firm)* [1998] FCA 806; on appeal (1999) 87 FCR 134 at 147–50. See further **7.4.8–7.4.11**.

2. A division of the Queensland Litigation Reform Commission recommended in 1994 (Davies and Lieboff, 10: see **11.5.18** below) that the pleading rules should be changed to require that statements made in response to allegations by an opposing party in a pleading must be verified on oath by the party pleading, or if it is a body of persons, by an officer of that body with knowledge of the relevant facts. The proposal also involved that party's solicitor in two ways: the verifying affidavit would require the deponent to say that his or her solicitor has explained the nature and effect of the pleading and the obligations of the party, and the solicitor would also be required to certify that, according to his or her instructions, the pleading was correct. This change was not incorporated into the Uniform Civil Procedure Rules 1999 (Qld). Would you support a proposal to increase the obligations upon solicitors in relation to the preparation of pleadings in the manner outlined?

11.5.18   Further reading

C Beaton-Wells, 'Solving the Problems of Pleadings: Are there Lessons to be Learnt for Civil Justice Reform in General?' (1998) 8 *JJA* 36.

F G Brennan, QC, 'Written Pleadings' (1975) 12 *UWAL Rev* 33.

Justice G L Davies and J S Leiboff, 'Reforming the Civil Litigation System: Streamlining the Adversarial Framework' *Proctor*, November 1994, 10.

J Hamilton, 'Thirty Years of Civil Procedure Reform in Australia: A Personal Reminiscence' (2005) 26 *Aust Bar Rev* 258.

A Jack, 'Radical Surgery for Civil Procedure' [1993] *New LJ* 891 at 893–4.

S Jackson and M Shirley, 'Pleadings' (1999) 20 *Qld Lawyer* 110.

Justice Lander, 'Pleadings: Changes, Risks and Justice' (1996) *Law Society of South Australia Bulletin* 32.

Report of the Committee on Personal Injuries Litigation (UK) Cmnd 3691, Her Majesty's Stationery Office, London, 1968 (the Winn Report).

COUNTERCLAIM AND SET-OFF

Counterclaim

11.6.1   Except in the High Court, the Federal Court and New South Wales, the Rules of Court specifically permit the defendant to bring a counterclaim against the plaintiff. A counterclaim is essentially an action in its own right: ACT r 461; NT r 13.15; Qld r 177; SA r 35 (a counterclaim is encompassed by the procedure referred to as a 'cross-action'); Tas r 192; Vic r 13.15; WA O 18 r 2. The rules permitting counterclaims therefore in effect facilitate the joint trial of two claims. The same position effectively prevails in the Federal Court (Pt 15) and New South Wales (Civil Procedure Act 2005 s 22), where what is termed a 'cross-claim' in effect amalgamates the procedures which, in the other jurisdictions are dealt with separately as counterclaims, notices of contribution and third party notices: see **10.5.5, 10.10.1–10.10.6**.

11.6.2   In pleading the counterclaim, a defendant generally follows the same pleading requirements as for a statement of claim. Accordingly, a counterclaim must reveal a cause of action by the pleading of necessary material facts. It is permissible, however, for the defendant to incorporate matters pleaded in the defence into the counterclaim by reference and usually the affirmative allegations in the defence are so included in the counterclaim, rather than being individually repeated. The counterclaim then proceeds to allege any additional facts necessary to complete the counterclaim.

11.6.3   The plaintiff is an essential party to any counterclaim. As between the plaintiff and the defendant, no limit is imposed upon the nature of the matters that may be the subject of the counterclaim. A counterclaim may also be brought against the plaintiff and other or others, even if these others are not already parties to the action: FCR r 15.01; ACT r 462; Civil Procedure Act 2005 (NSW) s 22; Supreme Court Act 1979 (NT) s 64; Civil Proceedings Act 2011 (Qld) s 7, Qld r 178; SA rr 36, 37 (in South Australia the procedure is a combined cross-action and third party action); Supreme Court Act 1935 (SA) s 23; Supreme Court Civil Procedure Act 1932 (Tas) s 10(3), Tas r 195; Supreme Court Act 1986 (Vic) s 29; WA Supreme Court Act 1935 (WA) s 24(3), WA O 18 r 3. In most jurisdictions, such a counterclaim must relate to or be connected with the subject matter of the original action, although in Victoria (r 10.03) and the Northern Territory (r 10.03) a counterclaim may be brought against defendants additional to the plaintiff in the same circumstances as ordinarily justify the joinder of parties (ie, 'same transaction or series of transactions' and 'common question of law or fact' or by leave of the court: r 9.02.). The criteria for severance in those jurisdictions are also the same, regardless of whether the counterclaim is also brought against parties new to the proceedings: r 10.06.

The principle function of the rules permitting the joinder to a counterclaim of a person not a party to the original is to provide a means of ensuring that such a party may be effectively bound by the result of the proceeding, and so precluded from later asserting that they are not: *Warner v Turning* (1876) 24 WR 536; *Watkins Ltd v Plancorp No 6 Pty Ltd* [1983] 2 Qd R 401; *Williams v Callegari* [1999] QCA 134.

11.6.4   The rules in most jurisdictions permit a plaintiff or a third party joined in the counterclaim to apply to the court for an order either that the counterclaim be disposed of separately from the action, or that it be excluded. The options vary depending upon the particular jurisdiction: ACT r 471; NT r 10.06; Qld r 182, Tas r 198; Vic r 10.06; WA O 18 r 5. In New South Wales the court may give appropriate directions under Pt 6, and the Federal

Court has an appropriate discretion under rr 5.06 and 15.13. The court will usually only exercise its discretion in this way if it is satisfied that the counterclaim cannot conveniently be heard with the main action.

Reply and defence to counterclaim

11.6.5   The plaintiff may reply to the defence but in most jurisdictions this is only necessary (or in the Northern Territory or Victoria, permitted) if the defence has raised a new allegation of fact requiring a response more than a mere denial. If no reply is delivered, the rules in most jurisdictions stipulate that all the allegations in the defence are deemed denied: FCR r 16.11; ACT rr 480, 482, 483; NSW r 14.27; NT r 13.13; Tas r 257; Vic r 13.13; WA O 20 r 15.

In Queensland (r 168(1)), any allegations of fact made in the last pleading filed and served before the time for filing and serving pleadings closes is taken to be the subject of a non-admission and r 165(2) then applies. (Rule 165(2) restricts a party who pleads a non-admission from giving or calling evidence in relation to a fact not admitted, unless the evidence relates to another part of the party's pleading.)

A reply should be delivered if it is appropriate for the plaintiff to plead specifically to any allegation contained in the defence. If, for example, the defendant has raised a defence under any statute of frauds, the plaintiff is obliged to plead any facts alleged to render that defence unmaintainable. The same applies if a defence raises any statute of limitations, although as a matter of practice matters taking a claim outside a statute of limitations are commonly alleged in the plaintiff's statement of claim.

11.6.6   The reply can only be used to *meet* the defence; it is not to raise a new cause of action nor allege any matter which is inconsistent with the statement of claim: FCR r 16.06; ACT r 414; NSW r 14.18; NT r 13.09; Qld r 154; Tas r 233; Vic r 13.09, WA O 20 r 11.

11.6.7   The plaintiff *must* defend any counterclaim, otherwise the defendant may obtain a default judgment on the counterclaim: see **12.2.1–12.2.6**. The defence to the counterclaim is pleaded in the same document as the reply, but it is separate from the reply and must generally follow the same pleading rules as for a defence. It should, accordingly, specifically deal with each matter of fact pleaded in the counterclaim.

Set-off

11.6.8   In limited circumstances, the defendant may make a claim against a plaintiff by way of set-off. Common law set-offs originated with Imperial statutes of set-off, and were allowed only in respect of mutual debts. This meant that only liquidated claims could be set off against claims which were also liquidated (*McDonnell and East Ltd v McGregor* (1936) 56 CLR 50), and that the claims had to be mutual in the sense that the plaintiff and the defendant owed each other a debt: *East Street Properties Pty Ltd v Jamison* [1974] 2 NSWLR 435. The claim sought to be set off must be one which could be sued for in separate proceedings. The set-off does not deny the debt, but rather asserts that despite the existence of the debt the plaintiff is not entitled to payment in respect of it. By contrast, equitable set-offs do not need to be mutual. The defendant can set off against the plaintiff any claim which is recognised in equity, but in equity it is essential that the defendant's claim impeaches the title of the plaintiff to sue, in that it is related to the plaintiff's claim in a way that means it would be inequitable to permit the plaintiff to sue without reduction in respect of the defendant's claim. Although there has been conflicting authority, it now seems that it will be possible, in equity, to set-off an unliquidated demand against a liquidated demand. The dichotomy between the two is of less significance under the judicature system, and either a common law or an equitable set-off may now be raised in the one proceeding.

Set-off and counterclaim contrasted

11.6.9   A set-off must be distinguished from a counterclaim. The main distinction between the two is that a set-off is essentially a defence, whereas a counterclaim is an independent cause of action. This distinction has the following consequences:

- If the set-off equals or exceeds the plaintiff's claim, the plaintiff loses the action. If the set-off exceeds the plaintiff's claim, then strictly there would be no judgment for the defendant for the balance, unless the defendant has also pleaded the set-off as a counterclaim. The rules in the Australian Capital Territory (r 456) and Queensland (r 173(2)) modify this consequence by providing that, if the balance is in favour of the defendant, the court may give judgment for the defendant for the balance, or may otherwise award the defendant such relief as the defendant may be entitled to on the merits of the case. As a counterclaim is regarded as an independent action against the plaintiff (and any third party included in the counterclaim), judgment is pronounced both on the claim and the counterclaim. If there is a balance in favour of the defendant, the court has a discretion as to whether to simply enter judgment for the defendant for the balance (this is the usual course): *Shrapnel v Laing* (1888) 20 QBD 334 at 338. In most jurisdictions this discretion is specifically acknowledged in the Rules of Court: ACT r 473; NT r 10.09; Qld r 184; SA r 224; Tas r 200; Vic r 10.09; WA O 18 r 2.

- If the plaintiff discontinues his or her action, the set-off falls with the discontinuance. This is not so with a counterclaim, which remains on foot and proceeds to trial: *McGowan v Middleton* (1883) 11 QBD 464.

- Limitation periods once had a different effect depending upon whether the defendant raised a set-off or a counterclaim. Lapse of time would not bar a set-off unless the statutory limitation period applying to the set-off had expired before the issue of the plaintiff's writ. The relevant time for a counterclaim, however, was the time when the counterclaim was brought, so that the counterclaim would be barred if not made in the proceeding before the expiration of the statutory limitation period applying to it. In most jurisdictions there are now statutory provisions, which have the effect that both a set-off and a counterclaim are deemed to be a separate action and to have been commenced on the same date as the action in which the set-off or counterclaim is pleaded: Limitation Act 1985 (ACT) s 51; Limitation Act 1969 (NSW) s 74; Limitation Act 1981 (NT) s 8; Limitation of Actions Act 1974 (Qld) s 42; Limitation Act 1974 (Tas) s 35; Limitation of Actions Act 1958 (Vic) s 30.

11.6.10   Notes

1.   A common situation where a counterclaim may be made and will proceed with the claim is where A and B both suffer injuries in a motor vehicle accident. A sues B, alleging B failed to take reasonable care. B denies negligence in his or her defence

and counterclaims against A for personal injury and/or property damage, alleging that the accident was caused by A's negligence. This is a classic situation in which both claim and counterclaim should be disposed of in the same action. On the other hand, A may sue B for assault. The rules would allow B to counterclaim for goods sold and delivered two years earlier. In such a case the court may be expected to strike out the counterclaim, or at least order that it be disposed of separately.

2. If a defendant has a counterclaim available against the plaintiff, but fails to pursue it by way of counterclaim, the defendant may be estopped from pursuing that claim in a subsequent action against the plaintiff if the court finds it was unreasonable for the party bringing the second action to have failed to raise its subject in the first action: *Bryant v Commonwealth Bank of Australia* (1995) 57 FCR 287; see also *Ling v Commonwealth* (1996) 68 FCR 180; 139 ALR 159. These cases apply the principle in *Port of Melbourne Authority v Anshun Pty Ltd (No 2)* (1981) 147 CLR 589 (which related to a claim for indemnity as between the parties to the first proceeding) to cross-claims. They also consider the rationale of the principle and the competing interests to be weighed in determining whether it applies in a given situation.

3. The limitations contained in the rules permitting the joinder in a counterclaim of persons not party to the original action mean there is substantially less freedom to raise issues distinct from those in the original action if the counterclaim is against the plaintiff and a person not already party to the action: see 11.6.3. For an examination of the nature and extent of the power, see *Watkins v Plancorp No 6 Pty Ltd* [1983] 2 Qd R 501. In that case McPherson J concluded the proposed counterclaim related to or was connected with the subject matter of the original action and gave leave to the defendant to deliver an amended defence and counterclaim as requested.

4. For a case illustration where the court struck out part of the plaintiff's reply on the basis that it did more than meet the defence and in fact raised a new cause of action, see *Herbert v Vaughan* [1972] 1 WLR 1128. See also *Harper v Adams* [1976] VR 44; *Duke Group Ltd (in liq) v Arthur Young (Reg)* (1991) 5 SCR 212.

11.6.11   Further reading

B A Barnard and M Houghton, *The New Civil Court in Action*, Butterworths, London, 1993, pp 53–5, 133–4.

G E Dal Pont, *Equity and Trusts in Australia*, 5th ed, Thomson Reuters, Australia, 2011.

R Derham, 'Set-off in Victoria' (1999) 73 *ALJ* 754.

PARTICULARS

Formal requirements

11.7.1E   **Supreme Court (General Civil Procedure) Rules 2005 (Vic)**
Order 13 — Pleadings

Particulars of pleading

13.10 (1) Every pleading shall contain the necessary particulars of any fact or matter pleaded.

   (2) Without limiting paragraph (1), particulars shall be given if they are necessary

      (a)   to enable the opposite party to plead, or

      (b)   to define the questions for trial; or

      (c)   to avoid surprise at trial.

   (3) Without limiting paragraph (1), every pleading shall contain particulars of any —

      (a)   misrepresentation, fraud, breach of trust or undue influence; or

      (b)   disorder or disability of the mind, malice, fraudulent intention or other condition
of the mind, including knowledge or notice

which is alleged.

11.7.2   All jurisdictions have rules which, in general terms, require the giving of appropriate and necessary particulars of the material facts which the parties plead. The rules in most jurisdictions also specify certain allegations in respect of which particulars must be given. These rules vary in detail, but generally include such matters as misrepresentation, fraud, breach of trust, willful default and undue influence: HCR r 27.04; FCR rr 16.41–16.44; ACT rr 407, 430–432 (see also rr 417, 418 in relation to pleading damages); NSW rr 15.2–15.8; NT r 13.10; Qld rr 157, 159 (and see also rr 150, 155). The extensive requirements in Queensland for the pleading of damages and interest are detailed in 11.4.12 and 11.4.18; Tas rr 227, 251, 241 (account stated), Div 18 (building disputes), Div 18A (defamation actions); WA O 20 r 13(1). There is no equivalent rule in South Australia, although there is a broad power in the court to order a party to file further particulars of its case if it is satisfied that the pleadings do not give fair notice of the party's case, and the order is necessary to avoid substantial prejudice to the party in whose favour the order is to be made: r 102. See further 11.7.12.

In the Northern Territory, Queensland, Tasmania, and Victoria the requirements for particulars are incorporated into the rules for pleadings. In the other jurisdictions the relevant rules appear under the heading of 'particulars', rather than 'pleadings'. Although they become incorporated into the pleading for which they are delivered, there is no obligation upon a party to plead separately in response to them; in fact to do so would not be appropriate: *Trade Practices Commission v David Jones (Aust) Pty Ltd* (1985) 7 FCR 109. The notes to the rules in the Federal Court make this explicit: FCR r 16.41.

Purpose of particulars

11.7.3   Consistent with the general function of pleadings, the purpose of particulars is to make sure the other party knows exactly the case to be met and is able to determine what evidence must be prepared for the trial. Particulars limit the generality of the pleadings, and in this way they assist to clarify and narrow the issues and so limit and define the questions to be tried, and the scope of any discovery/disclosure required.

Accordingly, it will be necessary to provide particulars of any allegation so broad that it leaves doubt as to what will be proved under it. For example, if money is owed on a running account for the supply of goods, it is not usually sufficient to plead that the plaintiff sold and delivered certain quantities of goods to the defendant at the defendant's request, and that a specified sum remains owed by the defendant to the plaintiff. Rather, particulars should be provided, specifying the invoice numbers, the quantities delivered on given dates, and the price, as well as the dates and amounts of payments received from the defendant. The provision of these particulars gives the defendant the opportunity to check the facts and figures with his or her own. In a similar way, in an action based in negligence, it will not generally be a sufficient pleading of the breach of the duty of care, simply to allege that the accident resulted from the failure of the defendant to take reasonable care. 'The function of particulars in an action for negligence is not to define the cause of action, which is negligence, but to show what acts or omissions will be put forward as constituting it': *Anchor Products Ltd v Hedges* (1967) 115 CLR 493 at 499 per Windeyer J.

The decision of the High Court in *Bailey v Federal Commissioner of Taxation* (1977) 136 CLR 214, extracted below, provides a discussion of the function of particulars, and an illustration of circumstances in which particulars should be provided.

11.7.4C   **Bailey v Federal Commissioner of Taxation**
                              (1977) 136 CLR 214; 13 ALR 41
                                  High Court of Australia

[The taxpayers appealed against the Commissioner's assessment of their liability to tax. It appeared from correspondence between the parties that the Commissioner relied upon the Income Tax Assessment Act 1936 (Cth) s 260 in making the assessment challenged. The taxpayers requested particulars of the 'arrangement' upon which the Commissioner's application of s 260 was based, but the Commissioner refused to supply them. The taxpayers made an application to the Supreme Court of New South Wales for particulars of the alleged arrangement. That application was dismissed, and the taxpayers appealed to the High Court.]

Aickin J (at 227–9): The purpose of particulars is to assist in the defining of issues and there is in my opinion no reason why in appropriate cases the Commissioner should not give particulars where they are necessary in order that both the appellant and the court may understand the basis upon which the assessment has been made. See *Spedding v Fitzpatrick* (1888) 38 Ch 410, *R v Associated Northern Collieries* (1910) 11 CLR 738, at pp 740–741 and *Astrovlanis Compania Naviera SA v Linard* 1972] 2 QB 611, at pp 619–620. No doubt there are many cases in which the return, the notice of assessment, the alteration sheet and the notice of objection will reveal the issues with sufficient certainty so that no particulars are necessary. This however is seldom the case where an assessment has been issued upon the basis of s 260. To tell a taxpayer and the Court that an assessment is based upon s 260 reveals nothing beyond the fact that the Commissioner contends that there is some contract, agreement or arrangement which falls within the ambit of that section and that either the whole or some part of it, or some step taken pursuant to it, or in the course of carrying it out, is void as against the Commissioner and that a taxable situation stands revealed by such avoidance. If no more is said the taxpayer and the Court are left entirely in the dark as to critical matters and the issues remain undefined except as to the ultimate conclusion contended for by each party.

There is nothing in the policy of the Act nor in general considerations of policy to require that the Commissioner should not inform the appellant prior to the commencement of the hearing of those details so that the case may proceed in an orderly and comprehensible manner. It is not in the interests of the proper administration of justice that, when the matter comes before the court, the appellant should have to speculate about, and adduce evidence to negate, every possible kind of agreement or arrangement and avoidance which the imagination of his advisers can conjure up. Such a process is not merely [228] time-wasting but is likely to obscure the real issues. It is no doubt possible that in the course of the evidence facts may emerge which were not previously known to the Commissioner and which suggest that there was some contract, agreement or arrangement other than that which he had previously supposed existed and which would support the actual assessment, but that is a situation which can readily be cured by amendment and it cannot be doubted that the Commissioner would in those circumstances be permitted to amend his particulars even though he would again have to specify the details of the arrangement which he was then alleging.

An examination of the authorities does not in my opinion suggest that the Supreme Court or this Court has no power to direct the Commissioner to give appropriate particulars of the basis of the assessment. The fact that the Commissioner does not himself have to prove any particular fact and that the onus by proof rests upon the taxpayer by virtue of s 190 cannot determine this question. There are many situations in which the party who gives a general denial to the pleading of the party on whom the onus rests may none the less be required to give particulars if the general denial really involves some positive allegation. This general principle is well established — see, eg, *Pinson v Lloyds and National Provincial Foreign Bank Ltd* [1941] 2 KB 72 and *George v Federal Commissioner of Taxation*, per Kitto J (1952) 86 CLR 183, at p 190. This is exactly the case where s 260 is relied upon to support an assessment.

Gibbs J (at 218–20): I have had the advantage of reading the reasons for judgment prepared by my brother Aickin. I agree with them and would add only a few remarks.

Broadly speaking, the argument advanced on behalf of the Commissioner is put in two ways. The first branch of the argument rests on a sound basis — namely that s 260 of the *Income Tax Assessment Act* 1936 (Cth) is part of the law which the court must apply to the facts whether or not the Commissioner invokes its operation. That being so, it is said that any views that the Commissioner holds as to the application of the section to the circumstances of the case, and any facts on which he bases those views, are irrelevant. It is further suggested that the administration of the revenue laws might be hampered if the Commissioner were required to give particulars, because the Commissioner might commit himself to some view of the operation of the section or of the facts when another view, more favourable to the revenue, might appear and ought to be acted upon. The second branch of the argument is that the facts in a case arising under s 260 are peculiarly within the knowledge of the taxpayer who, for that reason, is not entitled to particulars.

Particulars fulfill an important function in the conduct of litigation. They define the issues to be tried and enable the parties to know what evidence it will be necessary to have available and to avoid taking up time with questions that are not in dispute. On the one hand they prevent the injustice that may occur when a party is taken by surprise; on the other they save expense by keeping the conduct of the case within due bounds. These considerations are no less important in revenue cases than in other cases. A taxpayer who comes to court in a case in which it is suggested that s 260 applies is, as a matter of justice, entitled to know what case it is that the Commissioner intends to raise against him. The circumstance that s 260 must be applied to the facts whether or not the Commissioner holds any opinion on the subject provides no reason why the issues of fact arising in the case should not be defined. The fact that the taxpayer bears the onus of proving that the assessment is excessive makes it all the more necessary that he should be given particulars of the basis of the assessment — cf *R v Associated Northern Collieries* (1910) 11 CLR 738, at p 741. The Commissioner is not likely to be disadvantaged by supplying particulars. In an appropriate case no doubt particulars may be framed in the alternative and if the Commissioner's particulars prove to be too narrow or to be erroneously stated the court may allow him to depart from them if the interests of justice requires such a course — cf *Mummery v Irvings Pty Ltd* (1956) 96 CLR 99, at p 110. The facts in a case arising under s 260 are not necessarily all within the knowledge of the taxpayer. However, it is a misapprehension to think that the only function of particulars is to reveal to a party facts of whose existence he is aware. As I have indicated, particulars have the important function of informing a party of the nature of the case he has to meet and of limiting the issues of fact to be investigated by the court.

The question whether and what particulars should be ordered is one within the discretion of the court. In the present case the learned primary judge indicated that he thought that the taxpayer was morally entitled to particulars but that legally there was no power to order them to be given. In these circumstances this Court may exercise the discretion that the learned primary judge thought was not available to him.

I would allow the appeal and make an order for particulars.

[**Barwick CJ**, **Mason** and **Jacobs JJ** delivered separate judgments to similar effect.]

Pleadings and particulars

11.7.5 'Pleadings define the issues in general terms. Particulars control the generality of pleadings and restrict the evidence to be led by the parties at the trial and give the information enabling the other party to know what case he or she will be met with at the trial and prevent surprise': *Pilato v Metropolitan Water Sewerage & Drainage Board* (1959) 76 WN (NSW) 364 at 365 per McClemmens J. If a pleading has inadequately set out all the material facts, it may be appropriate for that pleading to be supplemented by particulars. Strictly, however, it is not appropriate to endeavour to cure a pleading which does not allege the material facts at all by the delivery of particulars. A pleading of that kind is defective and may be struck out. Increasingly, however, the distinction between 'material facts' and 'particulars' is becoming blurred, and it is not uncommon for parties who have failed to plead all material facts to be permitted to use particulars to supplement their inadequate pleadings. Often this is done without recourse to the court at all.

11.7.6C   Southern Cross Exploration NL v Fire & All Risks Insurance Co Ltd
(1985) 2 NSWLR 340
Supreme Court of New South Wales

[One of the issues before the court was the extent to which one of the defendants was in breach of its obligation to make full discovery of documents relevant to the matters in dispute in the proceedings. The defendants claimed the obligations in this respect had been substantially complied with unless the plaintiff's particulars were taken to have enlarged its statement of claim. The trial judge regarded the particulars as having been intended by the plaintiff to be part of its pleaded case, and took the view that this should have been clear to the defendant.]

Waddell J (at 349–51):

Relationship between pleadings and particulars:
The defendants submit that if the statement of claim is read in the way mentioned the particulars of par 38 have no relationship to that paragraph or to par 51 and so could properly be ignored for the purpose of determining the matters in question in the proceedings for the purpose of giving discovery. The plaintiffs, on the other hand, submit that the particulars given had the effect of enlarging the allegations in the statement of claim and thus incorporating in the matters in question in the proceedings the allegations in the particulars.

Accordingly, there has been a good deal of debate on what are the proper respective roles of pleadings and particulars.

The Supreme Court Rules 1970, Pt 15, r 7(1), requires that a pleading shall contain, and contain only, a statement in a summary form of the material facts relied upon. Part 16, r 1, requires that a party pleading shall give the necessary particulars. The plaintiffs submit that it is sometimes not easy to distinguish between facts which should be given as particulars and those [350] which should be alleged as material facts in a statement of claim. It is said that the distinction is often blurred. It is also said that under the present system of pleading particulars should not be regarded merely as limiting the generality of the statement of material facts contained in a statement of claim but that it is open to the party giving particulars to enlarge the ambit of the statement of claim by adding in the particulars further material facts.

The distinction between the material facts and particulars is described in the well known passage from the judgment of Scott LJ in the decision of the Court of Appeal in *Bruce v Odhams Press Ltd* [1936] 1 KB 697 at 712–713.

[351] In *Bruce v Odhams Press Ltd* the statement of claim alleged a libel but did not state the facts on which the plaintiff, not being actually named in the libel, relied to show that she would have been identified in the minds of some people reasonably reading the libel as the person defamed. On the application of the defendant an order was made that the plaintiff give particulars of these facts. The Court of Appeal held that this order was correct. It was unanimously held that such facts were material facts and should have been included in the statement of claim but that as the defendant was content to have the facts by way of particulars the order was rightly made. But it is also made clear that the defendant might have sought the more drastic remedy of seeking to have the statement of claim struck out. There are some remarks in the decision of the Court of Appeal in *Milbank v Milbank* [1900] 1 Ch 376 at 385 per Vaughan Williams LJ upon which the plaintiffs rely. There it is said that particulars under the Judicature Act are merely supplemental to the pleadings and are 'in fact amendments of the pleadings'. It is said that this is direct authority for the plaintiffs'

proposition that the particulars in the present case might validly have enlarged the allegations made by the statement of claim. These comments are, however, in my opinion, contrary to the whole stream of authority which is binding up [sic] me. The case was one, like *Bruce v Odhams Press Ltd*, in which the applicant for particulars would have been entitled to apply to have the pleading struck out as embarrassing but contented himself with an application for particulars. The case is an instance of the distinction between the particulars and statement of material facts in a pleading being blurred for practical reasons.

In my opinion the authorities cited make it clear that a party is not entitled, in effect, to amend a pleading by giving particulars of further material facts. To permit a party to do so would be to allow amendment contrary to the rules which require, in various circumstances, the filing of an amended pleading, the consent of other parties, or the leave of the court. But it is possible that particulars in effect amending a pleading might be accepted by the opposite party and a proceeding might be conducted on that basis. In *Bruce v Odhams Press Ltd* and *Milbank* the parties seeking the particulars ordered could hardly afterwards complain of a deficiency in the pleading. Similarly, a party to whom particulars have been given which, in effect, amended a pleading, might have so conducted himself as to represent to the party giving the particulars that no objection would be taken to the case being conducted on the basis of them even though, strictly speaking, there should have been an amendment. In such circumstances any objection taken later might be cured by the granting of the necessary amendment.

[See also *Beach Petroleum NL v Johnson* (1992) 7 ACSR 203; (1991) 105 ALR 456 at 466 per von Doussa J.]

Particulars and evidence

11.7.7 It has been seen in the context of the discussion of the purpose of pleadings that the pleadings determine what evidence must be given at the trial. Viewed strictly, this means the court can and should exclude evidence about matters not alleged in the pleadings and particulars. In practice, however, a fairly lenient approach is often taken in this respect. Pleadings and particulars are not strictly enforced, and evidence is admitted if the parties have ignored inadequacies in the pleadings, or if to do so is not likely to cause surprise or injustice to the other party.

11.7.8C	**Katsilis v Broken Hill Pty Co Ltd**
	(1977) 18 ALR 181; (1978) 52 ALJR 189
	High Court of Australia

[The plaintiff, who was employed by the defendant, lost the sight in his left eye after a piece of metal flew into it. The plaintiff had been engaged with other employees in the task of removing old railway lines. Some of the plates which joined one piece of rail to another were difficult to remove because of corrosion and some of the workmen were using a pick and sledgehammer to remove them. It was a fragment from the pick head which flew off when struck by the hammer which was alleged to have hit the plaintiff. The pick should not have been used in the manner in which it was used.

The negligence alleged in the plaintiff's statement of claim was that the defendant failed to provide a safe system of work. The trial judge found that the defendant was not directly negligent, in that the employees had not been instructed to use the pick in the particular manner and that the employees were personally negligent. The trial judge accordingly dismissed the action. The Full Court of the Supreme Court, by majority, dismissed an appeal from the trial judge's decision. The plaintiff appealed to the High Court.]

Stephen, Mason, Jacobs and Murphy JJ (at 201–3): Had the pleading alleged in the alternative the vicarious liability of the defendant for the dangerous method of removal of fish plates no difficulty would have arisen. The defendant would, in accordance with what we have already said, have been liable to the plaintiff. Can it then matter that the pleading does not take that form? We think not, and this for the reason that at least in this instance the case made out by the plaintiff, although framed in terms of a breach of the so-called 'personal' duty resting upon his employer, is in fact no different from that which would establish vicarious liability in the defendant.

The case for the plaintiff, ignoring that concerned with protective glasses, was presented on the footing that it was incumbent on him to prove that Adams gave instructions for, or permitted or suffered, the tools to be used in the manner in which they were used. However, the trial judge was aware that, if the plaintiff succeeded in proving that the piece of metal came from the pick and that the use of the tools in the manner used involved additional risk of splinters over and above unavoidable risks, and the employees had not been instructed otherwise, the plaintiff might well be entitled to succeed. He said:

> In the result, I am not able to find, on the balance of probabilities, that Adams ordered and instructed the men to use the beater pick as they allege, or that he was even aware of its use until after the event. Nevertheless, the very fact that the defendant's employees were using tools in an improper manner, and had not been instructed otherwise, may well be sufficient for the plaintiff's case (even though it was not presented on this footing) if all other relevant issues are decided in the plaintiff's favour.

It is important to draw attention to the recognition by the trial judge that he would, on findings other than those made by him, have needed to consider the matter in this way. If there was a particular risk and the defendant had not instructed the employees using the tools so to use them that the risk was avoided, the defendant's general system of work would be at fault. On the other hand, if the instructions had been given and were disobeyed, and provided, of course, that such a use of the tools did involve an additional risk of flying splinters of metal, the employees would themselves be negligent in the system of work which they chose to adopt and the defendant would be vicariously liable. What happened here is no different, the two fettlers did adopt a method of work regarded by the defendant as improper and it matters not whether they did so at their own instance, as the judge held, or, as they said, against their will and on the specific instruction of their foreman for whom the defendant would be no less vicariously liable.

It is true that the pleadings were not drawn in such a way as to allege a vicarious liability for the negligence either of the foreman Adams or the fettlers actually doing the work. But there is no question of further evidence in the circumstances of this case. In particular the critical questions, so far as concern vicarious liability, of an improper use of tools resulting in enhanced risk, and of that risk maturing into actual injury to the plaintiff, were fully explored and determined. There was, of course, no question of any conduct of the fettlers being otherwise than in the course of their employment. The only question was whether, in the result, the plaintiff proved enough issues to entitle him to a verdict in an action for negligence against his employer. The fact that he undertook, and failed, to prove additional issues, namely that the foreman had ordered or permitted the work to be done in the particular manner and that he knew or ought to have known of the particular risk in so doing the work, cannot affect the result if the plaintiff, within the facts pleaded or particularized, proved sufficient to establish liability for negligence in his employer. The function of particulars is not to circumscribe the cause of action sued on. 'Their function is to limit the issues of fact to be investigated and in doing this they do not modify or alter the cause of action sued upon': *Mummery v Irvings Pty Ltd* (1956) 96 CLR 99 at 110. [202] The abolition of the doctrine of common employment, the history of which against an evolving social and economic background is penetratingly analysed by Friedman and Ladinsky in their article in *Columbia Law Review*, vol 67 (1967) p 50, did not result in the creation of a new cause of action against an employer. The cause of action remained the failure to take reasonable care for the safety of an employee, however the failure might be manifested. The situation is distinguishable from that where the cause of action is based on an occupier's liability. This may be a different cause of action: *Mummery v Irvings Pty Ltd* (1956) 96 CLR 99.

In the present case the issue was whether the method by which work was being undertaken in proximity to the plaintiff was such as to show a lack of reasonable care for the safety of the plaintiff. If so then the defendant was liable in negligence to the plaintiff for injuries sustained in consequence of that lack of care, and this whether it ordered or permitted the method, or its foreman did so, or the actual employees doing the work adopted it contrary to instructions. So far as the plaintiff was concerned that method was what caused his injury and it was irrelevant whether it was approved of by the defendant or was, instead, adopted [203], even against its will, by some person or persons for whose acts or omissions it was vicariously liable.

In our opinion the appellant made out his case of negligence against the respondent. We would allow the appeal, set aside the judgment of the Full Court, and in lieu thereof allow the appeal to that court with costs, set aside the judgment in favour of the respondent, order judgment for the appellant with costs and remit the action to the trial judge for assessment of damages.

[**Barwick CJ**, who took a different view of the evidence, delivered a dissenting judgment. See also *Leotta v Public Transport Commission* (NSW) (1976) 9 ALR 437; 50 ALJR 666.]

11.7.9 The courts have permitted a party to prove his or her case on the basis of the evidence admissible on the pleadings and particulars, even if the court is not satisfied that any specified particular has been proved.

11.7.10C	**Doonan v Beacham** (1953) 87 CLR 346 High Court of Australia

[The plaintiff was injured when struck by a motor vehicle driven by the defendant. The statement of claim set out particulars of the defendant's negligence as:

(a)   driving at an excessive speed under the circumstances;

(b)   failing to keep any or any proper look-out;

(c)   driving on the wrong portion of the roadway;

(d)   failing to observe the plaintiff on the roadway;

(e)   failing to slow down or stop when danger
        arose; and

(f)   failing to apply the brakes at all or in time to avoid the collision.

The trial judge (**Lowe J**) found that it could not be inferred on the evidence that the accident was due to any particular one of the causes particularised and therefore directed the jury to find for the defendant.

The plaintiff appealed to the Full Court on the Supreme Court of Victoria which, by majority, allowed the appeal, but granted leave to appeal from its decision to the High Court of Australia under the Judiciary Act 1903 (Cth) s 35. The defendant's appeal to the High Court was unanimously dismissed.]

Williams ACJ (at 351–2): It was submitted to the learned trial judge that on the evidence which I have shortly stated it was impossible for the jury reasonably to infer that the accident was due to any particular one of the causes itemised in the particulars, and that, unless it could be so attributed, the plaintiff must fail. His Honour gave effect to this submission and for this reason directed the jury to find a verdict for the defendant. On appeal to the Full Supreme Court Martin J took the same view as his Honour, but the other two learned judges of that Court, Smith J and Hudson AJ, whilst agreeing that on the evidence the accident could not be attributed to any definite one or more of the acts and omissions specified in the particulars of negligence, came to the conclusion that on the whole of the evidence there was a case to go to the jury.

It was submitted to us, as it was submitted to the learned trial judge and to the Full Supreme Court, that if the evidence does not disclose any particular act or omission amounting to a failure to take reasonable care then the case cannot be left to the jury. I am quite unable to agree with this submission. In my opinion the jury are entitled to consider the evidence as a whole and if, on the whole of the evidence, the jury can reasonably infer that the accident was due to the negligence of the defendant, then they can find for the plaintiff. When I say the whole of the evidence I mean the whole of the evidence which is admissible within the scope of the particulars. This was the view taken by the majority of the Full Supreme Court and with this view I am in entire agreement. I think that it is succinctly and aptly expressed by Smith J in the following passage:

> A plaintiff in an action for damages for negligence must, it is true, make out his allegation for negligence within the limits of the particulars he has furnished, and any amendments thereto which he may be given leave to make. But if he adduces evidence upon which the jury can properly find, on the balance of probabilities and as a matter of reasonable inference, that the damage was caused by negligence on the part of the defendant which must have taken some form falling within the scope of the particulars, I do not think it is an answer in law to his claim that the evidence does not enable the jury to find more specifically the nature of the defendant's negligence.

His Honour proceeded to discuss a number of cases and then said:

> It follows that in my view the plaintiff in the present case had made out a sufficient case to go to the jury, in that she had adduced evidence upon which it was open to the jury to find,

on the balance of probabilities, and as a matter of reasonable inference, that the collision was caused by negligence consisting either of a failure to keep a [352] proper lookout or else of a failure to slow down or stop when danger arose.

With those remarks of his Honour I find myself in entire agreement and they are sufficient, I think to dispose of the appeal.

In my opinion the appeal should be dismissed with costs.

Kitto J (at 352): I am of the same opinion. I should like to add only this, that in my opinion the argument which has been presented by Mr Revelman rests upon a misconception of the function of particulars of negligence in a case of this description. The function of such particulars is not to divide a single issue of negligence into several distinct issues each requiring a separate finding, and to preclude a verdict from being given for the plaintiff unless he obtains a finding in his favour upon one or more of those issues. It is simply to confine the issue of negligence to the question whether the plaintiff's injury was caused by negligent conduct of the defendant falling within the limited category of acts and omissions which is defined by the particulars considered as a whole.

I agree with the reasons stated by the Acting Chief Justice for dismissing the appeal.

[**Webb, Fullagar** and **Taylor JJ** delivered concurring judgments.

See also: *Mummery v Irvings Pty Ltd* [1965] HCA 45; (1956) 96 CLR 99 at 110; *Crystal Wall Pty Ltd v Pham* [2005] NSWCA 449 at [27]–[40].]

Procedure where particulars are inadequate

11.7.11E   Supreme Court (General Civil Procedure) Rules 2005 (Vic)
Order 13 — Pleadings

Order for particulars

13.11 (1) The Court may order a party to serve on any other party particulars or further and better particulars of any fact or matter stated in the party's pleading or in an affidavit filed on that party's behalf ordered to stand as a pleading.

(2) The Court shall not make an order under paragraph (1) before service of the defence unless the order is necessary or desirable —

(a) to enable the defendant to plead; or

(b) for some other special reason.

(3) The Court may refuse to make an order under paragraph (1) if the party applying for the order did not first apply by letter for the particulars the party requires.

11.7.12 It may be that the other party has not complied with the rules which have been discussed, and that the statement of claim or defence in the action is not sufficiently particularised. The usual procedure for a party who believes the other party has not given particulars; or has given insufficient particulars, is to make a 'request for particulars' or for 'further and better particulars' as the case may be. The Victorian rules and its equivalents in most jurisdictions expressly contemplate the making of such a request: ACT r 6741 (this rule applies the detailed requirements in Pt 6 (Evidence) Div 6.10.3 (exchange of correspondence before making application in a proceeding) to an application under r 434 for particulars); NT r 13.11; Qld r 443 (this rule prescribes that the detailed requirements set out in Ch 11 (evidence) Pt 8 (exchange of correspondence instead of affidavit evidence) must be complied with before an application may be made for an order for particulars); Tas r 253; WA O 20 r 13(6). If satisfactory particulars are not given in response, application may be made to the court for an appropriate order. The rules in most jurisdictions specifically state that the order may be made upon such terms as to costs as may be just, so if the court thinks that the particulars should have been provided, a cost sanction may be imposed upon the defaulting party: FCR r 16.45; ACT r 434; NSW r 15.10; NT r 13.11; Qld r 161; Vic r 13.11; WA O 20 r 13(3).

The South Australian rules (r 102) contemplate that parties should include all material facts in their pleadings as initially filed so that there is no unfairness to another party by any lack of particularity. They do, however, permit an order requiring the pleading of further material facts if insufficient facts have been pleaded to give the other parties fair notice of the case they will have to meet and the party seeking them would be substantially prejudiced in the conduct of the case by not having them. If an order is made requiring the pleading of further material facts, the further particulars are to be provided by substituting for an existing pleading a new pleading incorporating the further particulars required by the court, unless the court directs to the contrary.

Requests and applications for particulars should specify what particulars (or further and better particulars) are to be supplied, and should be made expeditiously once the need for particulars has become apparent. The court will not, however, order particulars a party is simply unable to provide, or in circumstances where to make the order would be harsh or oppressive.

Personal injury

11.7.13E   **Supreme Court (General Civil Procedure) Rules 2005 (Vic)**
                              Order 13 — Pleadings

Particulars of pleading
13.10 (4) The pleading of a party who claims damages for bodily injury shall state —
    (a)   particulars, with dates and amounts, of all earning lost in consequence of the injury complained of;
    (b)   particulars of any loss of earning capacity resulting from the injury;
    (c)   the date of the party's birth;
    (d)   the name and address of each of the party's employers commencing from the day being 12 months before the party sustained the injury, the time of commencement and the duration for each employment and the total net amount, after deduction of tax, that was earned in each employment ...
    (6) Particulars of debt, damages or expenses which exceed three folios shall be set out in a separate document referred to in the pleading and the pleading shall state whether the document has already been served and, if so, when, or is to be served with the pleading.

11.7.14   In most jurisdictions quite detailed particulars are required in cases involving personal injuries, but there are significant variations as to when and how these particulars are to be provided.

As in Victoria, the rule in the Northern Territory (r 13.10) incorporates the requirement as part of the rules relating to pleadings and particulars.

In the Australian Capital Territory, there are special requirements about details to be included in a statement of claim for damages arising out of the negligent use of a motor vehicle (r 52) or the negligence or breach of statutory duty by an employer: r 53. These rules are considered further at 14.2.7.

In South Australia (r 99(3)), the plaintiff is required to plead the general nature of the injury and any resulting disability, the treatment received and of matters relating to economic and non-economic loss, but the detail of these matters is contained in a 'statement of loss' to be delivered subsequently: see 14.2.10.

11.7.15   In New South Wales, Queensland, South Australia, and Tasmania there are rules requiring the provision of detailed statements of particulars in personal injury actions, either with or at nominated times following the delivery of pleadings, but these statements are separate to the pleadings. In some jurisdictions the rules in this respect also require identification and provision of associated documents such as hospital and medical reports and documents relating to the plaintiff's income and taxation position; in others there are separate rules in relation to the production of such documents, either for personal injury actions only, or as part of the broader rules relating to expert evidence. These rules are considered in Chapter 14: see 14.2.

11.7.16   Notes and questions

1. Should a party be entitled to insist upon particulars where he or she is clearly in a position to know the true facts? It seems a party with knowledge of the true facts is still entitled to particulars of the case that his or her opponent will be attempting to make out, which may be something quite different from the true facts of the case: *Palmos v Georgeson* [1961] Qd R 186. The court may, however, refuse to order particulars where the party seeking them already knows the matters on which the other party is relying: *Lawson v Perpetual Trustee Co (Ltd)* (1959) 76 WN (NSW) 367.

2. It has been observed that the rules in most jurisdictions have special requirements for giving particulars in personal injury actions. What do you think is the rationale for these requirements? Is it likely to encourage settlement of such actions if the defendant (usually an insurance company) is placed as early as possible in a position to assess the plaintiff's loss and so to commence settlement negotiations? Is there more justification in the case of personal injury litigation as compared with other types of litigation for a requirement that particulars be supplemented from time to time?

3. In his article, 'Seven Deadly Sins of Pleading' (2008) 32 *Hearsay*, <http://www. hearsay.org.au>, Anthony Morris QC questions whether it is ever necessary or

desirable to adopt the common practice of using the subheading 'particulars' in a pleading. He argues that it is almost invariably preferable to incorporate the relevant factual allegations within numbered paragraphs of the pleading and provides illustrations of the way allegations of the kind commonly pleaded under 'particulars' might be re-cast.

4. For consideration of the decision in *Doonan v Beacham* (1953) 87 CLR 346 (see 11.7.10C) from a perspective of probability theory, see: Sir Richard Eggleston, 'Wignore, Fact-finding and Probability' [1989] *Monash LR* 21. Eggleston argues that the problems of fact-finding, including an understanding of basic rules of probability theory, should be included in the undergraduate law curriculum.

11.7.17 Further reading

H G Fryberg, 'Pleadings — A View from the Bench', speech delivered at the Australian Institute Insurance Law Association Breakfast, 20 April 2003, <http://archive.sclqld.org.au>.

P Heerey QC, 'Talking about Defamation: Pleading Defamatory Meaning' (1987) 61 *LIJ* 442.

W Pengilly, 'Trade Practices and Pleading Particularity' (1992) 8 *Australian & New Zealand Trade Practices Law Bulletin* 7.

A Vassie, 'The Unwise Admission' (1995) 69 *LIJ* 230.

STRIKING OUT PLEADINGS

11.8.1E   Court Procedures Rules 2006 (ACT)
Rule 425 — Pleading — Striking out

(1) The court may, at any stage of a proceeding, order that a pleading or part of a pleading be struck out if the pleading —
   (a) discloses no reasonable cause of action or defence appropriate to the nature of the pleading; or
   (b) may tend to prejudice, embarrass or delay the fair trial of the proceeding; or
   (c) is frivolous, scandalous, unnecessary or vexatious; or
   (d) is otherwise an abuse of the process of the court.
(2) The court may receive evidence on the hearing of an application for an order under this rule.

> (3) If the court makes an order under this rule, it may also make any other order it
>   considers appropriate, including, for example —
>   (a) If the court makes an order under subrule (1) (a) — an order staying or dismissing
>   the proceeding or entering judgment; and
>   (b) An order about the future conduct of the proceeding.

11.8.2   The rules in all jurisdictions give the court a discretionary power to strike out all or part of a pleading which does not disclose a cause of action or is otherwise objectionable. These rules provide a means of redress for a party whose opponent fails to comply with the rules of pleading.

If the court merely strikes out a pleading, this does not end the proceeding, although a judgment might subsequently be obtained by default against a party who fails to serve a rectified pleading: see **12.2.16**. However, depending upon the nature of the objection to the pleading, the relevant rules may authorise the court to make an order staying or dismissing the proceeding or entering judgment: HRC r 27.09; FCR rr 16.21, 26.01; ACT r 425; NSW rr 13.4, 14.28; NT rr 23.01, 23.02; Qld rr 162, 171; SA rr 98(2)(c), 104; Tas rr 258, 259; Vic rr 23.01, 23.02; WA 0 20 r 19(1).

The court also has inherent jurisdiction to stay, strike out or dismiss every action or pleading which is an abuse of its process or is frivolous or vexatious or does not disclose a cause of action: see **12.2.16**. This jurisdiction is part of the court's power to control the conduct of litigation and to ensure that the court's process is not abused or used to inflict injustice or oppression. Commonly a challenge to a pleading on some or all of these grounds will rely upon both the Rules of Court relating to the striking out of pleadings, as well as upon the inherent jurisdiction of the court.

If the court does strike out a pleading and enter judgment, the action is terminated without any hearing on the merits, and the party whose pleading has been successfully challenged in this way is denied the opportunity to fully investigate all the legal and factual circumstances involved in the dispute. The courts will be cautious in exercising that power (whether basing their determination upon the Rules of Court or the inherent jurisdiction of the court) and will do so only in the clearest of cases: *General Steel Industries Inc v Commissioner for Railways (NSW)* [1964] 112 CLR 125, extracted at **11.8.5C**. Certainly if the defect in the pleading is not due to a failure of all of the facts to reveal a cause of action or defence, but rather to a failure by a pleader to plead a material fact, it is to be anticipated the court will permit amendment of the pleading. Even if the whole pleading is so bad that it needs to be totally struck out, the court will usually give leave to the offending party to serve a rectified pleading: see generally *Brimson v Rocla Concrete Pipes* [1982] 2 NSWLR 937 at 943–4.

11.8.3   There are now rules in all jurisdictions which are quite separate from the rules enforcing compliance with the pleading rules and which allow a party to bypass the normal extended procedures in litigation and obtain summary judgment. In general terms, these rules are available only when there is no defence to the claim or the claim is unfounded, though there are significant jurisdictional differences in the formulation of the applicable tests. These rules are considered in detail at **12.3.1Eff**. A party seeking summary judgment under these rules may frequently seek in the alternative an order under the rules relating to the striking out of pleadings or the inherent jurisdiction of the court: see, eg, *Inglis v Commonwealth Trading Bank of Australia* (1972) 20 FLR 30.

No reasonable cause of action

11.8.4   The decisions of the High Court in *General Steel Industries Inc v Commissioner for Railways* (1964) 112 CLR 125 and *Esanda Finance Corporation v Peat Marwick Hungerfords* (1997) 188 CLR 241, extracted below, provide case examples in which the court struck out the whole (*General Steel*) or part (*Esanda Finance*) of the plaintiff's statement of claim as failing to disclose a cause of action. In *General Steel*, the court then dismissed the plaintiff's action, with costs.

> **11.8.5C**   **General Steel Industries Inc v Commissioner for Railways (NSW)**
> (1964) 112 CLR 125
> High Court of Australia

[The plaintiff brought proceedings against the Commissioner for Railways (NSW) and others seeking to restrain the alleged infringement by the defendants of the plaintiff's patent. After delivery of the statement of claim, the defendants sought by summons to set aside the writ and statement of claim, or alternatively to stay further proceedings on the ground that the plaintiff did not have a reasonable, or indeed any, cause of action against them or any of them. The challenge was based both on the High Court Rules, and under the inherent jurisdiction. It was clear the action could not succeed if certain exempting provisions in the Patents Act 1952 (Cth) for the benefit of state authorities and persons authorised in writing by such authorities applied.]

Barwick CJ (at 128–30): At the outset the plaintiff submits that whatever conclusion I might reach upon the legal questions involved, I ought not to deal summarily with the action but should allow it to proceed, leaving the defendants to raise their points in opposition to the plaintiff's claim in proceedings on demurrer or by points of law taken on the pleadings and dealt with under Order 26, r 16, or perhaps by special case under Order 35.

The plaintiff rightly points out that the jurisdiction summarily [129] to terminate an action is to be sparingly employed and is not to be used except in a clear case where the Court is satisfied that it has the requisite material and the necessary assistance from the parties to reach a definite and certain conclusion. I have examined the case law on the subject, to some of which I was referred in argument and to which I append a list of references. There is no need for me to discuss in any detail the various decisions, some of which were given in cases in which the inherent jurisdiction of a court was invoked and others in cases in which counterpart rules to Order 26, r 18, were the suggested source of authority to deal summarily with the claim in question. It is sufficient for me to say that these cases uniformly adhere to the view that the plaintiff ought not to be denied access to the customary tribunal which deals with actions of the kind he brings, unless his lack of a cause of action — if that be the ground on which the court is invited, as in this case, to exercise its powers of summary dismissal — is clearly demonstrated. The test to be applied has been variously expressed; 'so obviously untenable that it cannot possibly succeed'; 'manifestly groundless'; 'so manifestly faulty that it does not admit of argument'; 'discloses a case which the Court is satisfied cannot succeed'; 'under no possibility can there be a good cause of action'; 'be manifest that to allow them' (the pleadings) 'to stand would involve useless expense'.

At times the test has been put as high as saying that the case must be so plain and obvious that the court can say at once that the statement of claim, even if proved, cannot succeed; or 'so manifest on the view of the pleadings, merely reading through them, that it is a case that does not admit of reasonable argument'; 'so to speak apparent at a glance'.

As I have said, some of these expressions occur in cases in which the inherent jurisdiction was invoked and others in cases founded on statutory rules of court but although the material available to the court in either type of case may be different the need for exceptional caution in exercising the power whether it be inherent or under statutory rules is the same. Dixon J (as he then was) sums up a number of authorities in *Dey v Victorian Railways Commissioners* (1949) 78 CLR 62 where he says (1949) 78 CLR, at p 91: 'A case must be very clear indeed to justify the summary intervention of the court to prevent a plaintiff submitting his case for determination in the appointed manner by the court with or without a jury. The fact that a [130] transaction is intricate may not disentitle the court to examine a cause of action alleged to grow out of it for the purpose of seeing whether the proceeding amounts to an abuse of process or is vexatious. But once it appears that there is a real question to be determined whether of fact or law and that the rights of the parties depend upon it, then it is not competent for the court to dismiss the action as frivolous and vexatious and an abuse of process.' Although I can agree with Latham CJ in the same case when he said that the defendant should be saved from the vexation of the continuance of useless and futile proceedings (1949) 78 CLR, at p 84, in my opinion great care must be exercised to ensure that under the guise of achieving expeditious finality a plaintiff is not improperly deprived of his opportunity for the trial of his case by the appointed tribunal. On the other hand, I do not think that the exercise of the jurisdiction should be reserved for those cases where argument is unnecessary to evoke the futility of the plaintiff's claim. Argument, perhaps even of an extensive kind, may be necessary to demonstrate that the case of the plaintiff is so clearly untenable that it cannot possibly succeed.

[**Barwick CJ** proceeded to consider the relevant provisions of the Patents Act 1952 (Cth). His Honour concluded that it was sufficiently clear that the Commissioner was an authority of the state for the purposes of the relevant part of the Act, and that his use of the invention in respect of which the plaintiff complained, was a use for the service of the state. He further concluded that it sufficiently appeared that in respect of the activities of the other defendants of which the plaintiff complained, that the use by those defendants had been duly authorised by the Commissioner in writing. Hence he was satisfied with the requisite certainty that the plaintiff's statement of claim did not disclose a cause of action against any of the defendants. His Honour then considered the appropriate order to be made upon those findings (at 137–8):]

Order 26, r 18 authorises me to strike out a pleading which does not disclose a reasonable cause of action. I am satisfied that the plaintiff's statement of claim does not do so. It seeks to restrain an infringement of the plaintiff's letters patent in stated circumstances which preclude the plaintiff having such a cause of action against any of the defendants. Accordingly, I strike out the whole of the plaintiff's statement of claim.

Rule 18 further authorises me, if I consider it just so to do, to stay or to dismiss the plaintiff's action. This is not a case in which the plaintiff by amendment of the pleading could improve its position. I have been mindful throughout my consideration [138] of this matter of the principles to which I have called attention and which govern the exercise of the power summarily to terminate an action. I have reached the firm conclusion that consistently with those principles I ought to intervene by order under this rule to prevent further proceedings in the action, as, in my opinion, to use one of the expressions which I have quoted, the plaintiff's claim is 'manifestly groundless' and that to allow it to proceed 'would involve useless expense'. In my opinion the proper course is to dismiss the plaintiff's action, which I now do.

My order is that I strike out the whole of the plaintiff's statement of claim and dismiss the plaintiff's action with costs.

11.8.6C   **Esanda Finance Corporation Ltd v Peat Marwick Hungerfords**
(1997) 188 CLR 242
High Court of Australia

[Esanda Finance Corporation (Esanda) sought damages against Peat Marwick Hungerfords (Peat Marwick), an auditor, based on several causes of action, including negligence. In relation to the claim in negligence, Esanda alleged that Peat Marwick failed to comply with accounting standards when auditing the financial accounts of Excel. Esanda also alleged that it was a member of a class of persons, whom the auditors foresaw, or ought reasonably to have foreseen, might reasonably have relied on the audited accounts and report. Esanda relied on the audited accounts and suffered consequential loss. Peat Marwick applied to strike out the claim in negligence on the ground that it failed to disclose a reasonable cause of action, and in particular that the pleaded allegations did not establish that Peat Marwick owed Esanda a duty of care. The application was dismissed at first instance. An appeal to the Full Court of the Supreme Court of South Australia was successful. Esanda appealed, by special leave, to the High Court.]

Toohey and Gaudron JJ (at 258–60): The appellant, Esanda Finance Corporation Limited ("Esanda"), is a finance provider. In that capacity it entered into a number of transactions with Excel Finance Corporation Limited ("Excel") and companies associated with Excel. In short, it lent moneys to associated companies, accepting a guarantee from Excel, and purchased debts from Excel upon terms which included an indemnity by Excel against any shortfall. Excel has since gone into [259] liquidation and Esanda claims to have suffered financial loss as a result of the transactions. It brought proceedings in the Supreme Court of South Australia to recover that loss from the respondent company, Peat Marwick Hungerfords (Reg) ("Peat Marwick"). Peat Marwick were Excel's auditors.

Esanda pleaded several causes of action against Peat Marwick. This appeal is concerned with Esanda's pleaded claim that Peat Marwick were negligent in their conduct of the audit of Excel's accounts for the financial year ending 30 June 1989 and, more particularly, that they failed to take reasonable care in reporting that Excel's true financial position was as represented in those accounts ...

The only question in the appeal is whether the facts pleaded in the contested paragraphs are capable of giving rise to a duty of care between Peat Marwick, as Excel's auditors, and Esanda, as a company providing finance to Excel and its associated companies. In essence, the pleaded facts are:

1.   Peat Marwick were at all material times members of the Institute of Chartered Accountants in Australia and bound by the Australian Accounting Standards (par 84A).
2.   At the relevant time, the Australian Accounting Standards required, in relation to a business entity, the disclosure in its audited accounts of financial information relevant to present and potential providers of equity or loan capital, and creditors (par 84B).

3. Esanda was at all relevant times a member of a class or classes of persons, namely creditors and financiers of Excel, whom Peat Marwick foresaw or ought reasonably to have foreseen might reasonably and relevantly rely on Excel's audited accounts for the year [260] ending 30 June 1989 and the report accompanying those accounts (par 84C).
4. Esanda relied on Excel's audited 1989 accounts and the auditor's report accompanying those accounts in deciding to enter into financial transactions with Excel and its associated companies, those transactions resulting in financial loss (par 87).

The question whether the pleaded facts are capable of giving rise to a duty of care falls to be decided in light of the law's insistence that a plaintiff who sues in negligence to recover pure economic loss must establish more than the foreseeability of loss. In this country, the question whether there is a duty of care to take reasonable steps to avoid another's economic loss depends on whether there is a relationship of proximity, it being said that "the categories of case in which the requisite relationship of proximity with respect to mere economic loss is to be found are properly to be seen as special" (*Bryan v Maloney* (1995) 182 CLR 609 at 619. See also *Hawkins v Clayton* (1988) 164 CLR 539 at 576.)

[Their Honours then examined authorities in relation to the existence of a duty of case in economic loss cases involving negligent misstatement, and proceeded (at 265–6):]

[265] There are, in our view, only two pleaded facts which are relevant to the existence of a special relationship of proximity between Esanda and Peat Marwick. The first is that Peat Marwick were Excel's [266] auditors and, inferentially, were in a situation of particular advantage to know or ascertain its true financial position. The second is that, by virtue of its membership of the Institute of Chartered Accountants in Australia, Peat Marwick accepted a general professional responsibility to ensure that Excel's audited accounts disclosed information relevant to Excel's present and potential creditors.

It was not argued that the facts pleaded are capable of sustaining a suggestion that Peat Marwick intended or encouraged Esanda to rely upon their audit of Excel's accounts. And in our view, they are not. Nor are they capable of giving rise to a relationship of proximity marked either by reliance or the assumption of responsibility for information or advice which is voluntarily provided. It may be accepted that, as Excel's auditors, Peat Marwick were in a particularly advantageous position to know or ascertain Excel's true financial position. However, there is nothing to suggest Esanda was not itself able to have accountants undertake the same task on its behalf as a condition of its entertaining the possibility of entering into financial transactions with Excel. And, which is much the same thing in the circumstances of this case, there is nothing to suggest that it was reasonable for Esanda to act on the audited reports without further inquiry.

The appeal should be dismissed.

[**Brennan CJ, Dawson** and **McHugh** and **Gummow JJ** delivered separate judgments. Though their analyses of the applicable law differed in some respects, all concluded that the appeal should be dismissed because Esanda had not pleaded material facts necessary to establish one of the elements essential to an action in negligence, namely, duty of care. Accordingly the components of the pleading under challenge did not disclose a cause of action.]

Embarrassment

11.8.7E   **The Purpose of Pleadings**
Hon J C Campbell
(2004) 25 *Aust Bar Rev* 116 at 122–3

[In his article, the Hon J C Campbell provides a helpful discussion of the meaning of 'embarrassing' in the context of pleading, along with examples which have been held to meet that description:]

Just as the rule about surprise is concerned with the effect that a pleading has on your opponent, so the rule about a pleading not being embarrassing deals with the effect that the pleading is likely to have on your opponent. One of the purposes of that rule is, like the rule requiring pleading of any matter which might take your opponent by surprise, to let your opponent know what your case really is. But there are other purposes too.

When a lawyer says that an allegation in a statement of claim is embarrassing, the lawyer is not using the most common meaning of 'embarrassing' — he or she does not mean that the pleading alleges something unpleasant or discreditable which the defendant would much rather have not been said. Rather, the meaning of 'embarrassment' which is relevant here is like the use that is involved in saying someone is financially embarrassed when they have a debt which they are obliged to pay but cannot pay. In the sense relevant to pleading, embarrassment is the situation which a defendant is in when it is under an obligation under the court rules to file a defence, but cannot do so because of deficiencies in the statement of claim, or when the pleading does not make clear the case which the opposite party must be ready to meet. In the words of Cotton LJ in *Philipps v Philipps* (1878) 4 QBD 127 at 139:

It is absolutely essential that the pleading, not be embarrassing to the defendants, should state those facts which will put the defendants on their guard and tell them what they will have to meet when the case comes on for trial.

The case law explains what is meant by 'embarrassing' through examples. It would be impossible to give an exhaustive list, but ways in which a statement of claim can be embarrassing include:

- if it leaves the defendant in a situation of not knowing what evidence he ought to file in order to meet it, or if it contains statements which are irrelevant to the relief sought; (*Davy v Garrett* (1877) 7 Ch D 473 at 483, 486, 488; *In re W R Wilcocks & Co Ltd* [1974] 1 Ch 163 at 166–7.)
- if its language is so general that it is not clear what is being alleged; (*Tsatsoulis v Westpac Banking Corp* [1999] NSWSC 193 unreported, Rolfe J, 15 March 1999, BC9901502 at [85], [123].)
- if it 'leaves obscure the facts said to give rise to the duty of care and the content of the duty of care'; (*Agius v New South Wales* (2002) Aust Torts Reps 81-656 at [35].)
- if it makes an allegation which could found a liability in the defendant only if taken in conjunction with some other fact which is not pleaded; (*Re Modular Furniture Pty Ltd* (1981) 5 ACLR 463 at 466.)
- if it uses terminology in a way which is not consistent, and it is not clear which of two or more possible meanings of a word is intended by a particular allegation; (*Garden Mews-St Leonards Pty Ltd v Butler Pollnow Pty Ltd (No 2)* (1984) 9 ACLR 91 at 93.)

- if it 'leaves the accused in a position of material prejudice, derived from the incapacity to know with clarity what case is to be met': (*Chew v R* (1991) 4 WAR 21 at 64; 5 ACSR 473 at 550 (WA FC).)
- if it makes allegations against several defendants, and it is not clear what allegation is made against which defendant; (*South Australia v Peat Marwick Mitchell & Co* (1977) 24 ACSR 231 at 255.)
- if a duty of some particular legal type is alleged to exist without a statement of the facts by virtue of which it exists; (*Charlton v Baber* (2003) 47 ACSR 31 at [19].)
- if it pleads matter in anticipation of a particular defence being raised, when that matter should be reserved for pleading in the reply when, and if, that defence is raised; (*Church of Scientology v Woodward* (1980) 31 ALR 609 at 623.)
- if an allegation 'is a prediction rather than an allegation of fact and is thus not capable of admission or denial by the defendants'; (*East-West Airlines (Operations) Ltd v Commonwealth of Australia* (1983) 49 ALR 323 at 325.)
- if it uses imprecise and inappropriate language; (*McKellar v Container Terminal Management Services Ltd* (1999) 165 ALR 409 at [102], [104].) or
- if it is 'poorly expressed and ... confusing', (*McKellar v Container Terminal Management Services Ltd* (1999) 165 ALR 409 at [255]) or 'susceptible to various meanings' (*Bartlett v Swan Television & Radio Broadcasters Pty Ltd* (1995) ATPR ¶41-43 at 40,889; *Bright v Femcare Ltd* (2000) 175 ALR 50 at [26].)

11.8.8 Notes and question

1. The terms 'frivolous' and 'vexatious' seem to be used interchangeably, and neither has been comprehensively defined. An action, which was obviously unsustainable and an abuse of the process of the court, was regarded as frivolous in *Young v Holloway* [1895] P 87 at 90. A similarly described action was classified as vexatious in *Peruvian Guano Co v Bockwoldt* (1883) 23 Ch D 225 at 230.

   To the extent that a claim has already been made in a pending action, the bringing of a further claim of the same kind would be vexatious: *Butler v Simmonds Crowley & Galvin* [1999] QCA 477. In a similar vein it was said in *Moore v Inglis* (1976) 9 ALR 509 at 514; 50 ALJR 589 at 591 to be prima facie vexatious for the same plaintiff to bring two actions against the same defendant where one lies.

2. The ground that a pleading is unnecessary and/or scandalous may be relied upon, for example, if a pleading contains unnecessary details or material which is indecent or offensive and has no relevance to any issues in the action. An application to the court will not be justified in the case of unnecessary matter, unless that matter is objectionable for some other reason, such as that it makes the pleading difficult to comprehend or is otherwise prejudicial to the applicant's case. See, eg, the comments of McGill DCJ in *Kev Leamon Earthmovers Pty Ltd v Hammond Villages Pty Ltd* (1998) 19 Qld Lawyer Reps 10 at 14.

3. The ground that a pleading is 'otherwise an abuse of process' is an all-embracing ground for cases of abuse not otherwise specifically provided for, *and* it reveals the general principle behind the rules for striking out. The pleading must be so bad

as to amount to an abuse of the process of the court. An illustration is *Yat Tung v Dao Heng Bank* [1975] AC 581. In that case it was held to be an abuse to raise in subsequent proceedings matters which were *res judicata*, or matters which could and should have been raised in earlier proceedings. Abuse of process is examined in detail at 12.7.1ff.

4. If a successful application is made by one of two defendants to have the plaintiff's statement of claim struck out, should that statement of claim be struck out against another defendant who has already pleaded to the statement of claim? See *Madden v Kirkegard Ellwood and Partners* [1975] Qd R 364. In that case Dunn J (at 365) summarised his findings in respect of the plaintiff's statement of claim colourfully:

> Its condition is such that no 'surgery' can save it. It will be an act of mercy to terminate its existence. It should be re-pleaded in such a way as to make it clear to the first defendant, and to the court, what the plaintiff's case really is.

The judge further held that, although the second defendant must be taken to have understood what was alleged against him, it would be confusing to the trial judge to strike out everything alleged in the statement of claim against the first defendant and to require a fresh statement of claim to be delivered to that defendant only. His Honour held that in all the circumstances it was appropriate to strike out the whole of the statement of claim and to order that a fresh statement of claim be delivered to both defendants.

Further reading

11.9.1 Looseleaf and online

M Moynihan and D Skennar (eds), *Court Forms Precedents and Pleadings,* LexisNexis, Sydney.

M Walton, H Keller and P Young (eds), *Court Forms Precedents and Pleadings — NSW*, LexisNexis, Sydney.

N J Williams, D L Bailey and D Davies (eds), *Court Forms Precedents and Pleadings Victoria*, LexisNexis, Sydney.

(These works contain sample pleadings for various causes of action.)

11.9.2 Texts

B Cairns, *Australian Civil Procedure*, 8th ed, Thomson Reuters, Sydney, 2009, Chs 6–7.

J Hunter, C Cameron and T Henning, *Litigation 1: Civil Procedure*, 7th ed, LexisNexis Butterworths, Sydney, 2005, Ch 5.

R Turner, J I Winegarten and M Kershaw (eds), *Atkin's Court Forms*, 2nd ed, LexisNexis, UK, 2011.

P W Young and H Selby, *Pleadings without Tears in Australia*, Federation Press, New South Wales, 1997.

A Zuckerman, *Zuckerman on Civil Procedure: Principles of Practice*, 3rd ed, Sweet & Maxwell, UK, 2011, Chs 6, 8.

11.9.3   Articles

B Cairns, 'A Review of Some Innovations in Queensland Civil Procedure' (2005) *Aust Bar Rev* 158.

Justice RD Giles, 'Pleadings', 2007, <http://www.nswbar.asn.au>.

A Morris QC, 'Seven Deadly Sins of Pleading' (2008) 32 *Hearsay*, <http://www.hearsay.org.au>.

H Selby, 'Pleading for Modern Approach to Civil Pleading', (2010) 33 *Aust Bar Rev* 141.

S Wood and T Donaghey, 'Pleadings in Industrial and Employment Cases' (2009) 22 *Australian Journal of Labour Law* 207.

Summary Disposition

## CHAPTER 12

OVERVIEW

It is a fundamental principle of justice that litigants should have full access to court procedures to prove their claim or defence. However, this principle may become an instrument of tyranny if applied without limitation. The principle is subject to a number of countervailing policies. In particular:

- Litigants should not make spurious or improper claims or defences and the other party should be entitled to deal expeditiously with such claims/defences.

- Litigants should be discouraged from bringing a claim or entering a defence which has no merit. The other party should not be required to compromise or be forced to bear the cost of a full hearing into such claims or defences.

- Some sanctions must be available to force parties to comply with time limits and other procedural requirements mandated by the rules and the courts. If courts are lenient with breaches of time stipulations, parties may be dilatory or engage in tactical behaviour.

Although these policies are to some extent overlapping, they may broadly be described as promoting protection against spurious claims and defences and encouraging accelerated justice.

In this chapter, procedures will be explored which implement these policies and enable litigants to shortcut the usual interlocutory steps and/or a full hearing of a claim. Procedures which emanate from the Rules of Court allow either party to use these shortcuts to obtain default or summary judgment or to have a claim or defence struck out by the court. The court also has powers under the inherent jurisdiction to stay proceedings for abuse of process.

POLICY ISSUES

12.1.1   **Principles of Civil Procedure**
                                              N Andrews
                                Sweet and Maxwell, London, 1994, p 19

Protection against spurious claims and defences

The loudest claims for procedural reform are made by those who clamour for greater access to the courts. The rallying cry is that there should be greater 'access to justice'. But there is another complaint which often gets drowned out by stentorian radicals, but which is no less entitled to close consideration. This complaint is that the legal system is already too accessible and that neither plaintiffs nor defendants are subject to sufficiently exacting control in formulating their case. Bad claims are too easily heard. Bad defences are too often allowed to proceed unextirpated. Both cause delay, expense, anxiety and injustice. The present topic can helpfully be viewed as the obverse of the coin which has access to justice on one face.

What protection does a defendant have against unmeritorious or maliciously inspired actions, or the plaintiff against a bad defence? It will be expensive and time-consuming to nail the bad point at trial or on appeal. Can the victim of such a point snatch himself out of the nightmare and terminate the action or strike out defence on the ground that it is improper? Or might he at least be entitled after the case is concluded to seek compensation from his adversary or his adversary's lawyers?

In abstract form such actions and defences can be placed in the following categories:

(a)   malicious or bad faith claims;
(b)   hopeless or groundless claims brought in good faith;
(c)   'bad' claims which are immediately identifiable as such;
(d)   'weak' claims which are distinctly tenuous but not as obviously bad as the preceding class.

...

The principle of accelerated justice

Most judgments are obtained without trial. A plaintiff might obtain judgment by default ... if the defendant has failed to defend or indicated that he is unwilling to defend. Another possibility is that a plaintiff might win 'summary judgment'. ... In this last situation the plaintiff will go before a [judicial officer] and show that there is no arguable defence disclosed by the defendant's response to the plaintiff's claim. The defendant will then try to argue against that conclusion. ...

Accelerated justice is also achieved through the procedure known as 'striking out' of actions and defences. This enables the court to order that a relevant claim or defence should be erased on the ground that it is technically bad or clearly based on an improper motive, or that it is trivial ('frivolous').

12.1.2   Superior courts use procedures derived from their inherent powers: see 1.4.4 and the court rules to promote the principles discussed by Andrews above. For example, where the defendant does not respond to originating process issued and served by the plaintiff within the time stated in the rules, the plaintiff may obtain judgment in default. If the defendant does respond, the plaintiff may still obtain judgment without a trial by asking for summary determination of the claim. Once the plaintiff makes an application for summary judgment, the burden is cast upon the defendant to show that there should be a trial. If the defendant cannot do this, then the plaintiff may obtain summary judgment. Similar procedures may be used by the defendant, as discussed below.

Comment

12.1.3   When assessing the efficacy of summary disposition procedures, the case management systems used by particular courts must also be considered, see generally **Chapter 2**.

DEFAULT JUDGMENT

12.2.1   Default judgment generally occurs in two instances: (a) where there has been a failure to take a step required by the rules; or (b) where there has been a failure to comply with a peremptory court order, usually called a self-executing or springing order.

The rules prescribe time limits for most steps involved in the interlocutory process. Those limits may be shortened or lengthened, sometimes by agreement, but more commonly by a court order upon application: see generally **Chapter 5**.

Judgment in default of appearance

12.2.2   An appearance is a general term which describes the first formal step taken by the defendant in response to originating process: see generally **Chapter 9**. Where the defendant fails to enter an appearance, the plaintiff may obtain default judgment as of right by filing with the relevant court an affidavit of service and a request for judgment: HCR rr 27.09.1, 27.09.2; FCR Div 5.2 especially rr 5.22, 5.23; ACT Div 2.11.3, especially rr 1117(1), 1118; NSW Pt 16, especially rr 16.2(1), 16.3; NT O 21, especially r 21.01; Qld Ch 9 Pt 1, especially rr 280–281; SA Ch 11, Pt 3, especially r 229; Tas Pt 11, Div 2 especially rr 342, 346, 347; Vic O 21, especially r 21.01; WA O 13.

[*Note:* in this chapter a reference, such as WA O 9 r 2, is a reference to the relevant Rules of Court. All other legislation will be specified. See **1.4.2** which sets out the full titles of all the rules.]

12.2.3E   **Rules of the Supreme Court 1971 (WA)**
Order 13 — Default of appearance to writ

1.   **Prerequisites for judgment in default of appearance etc.**

(1)   Judgment shall not be entered against a defendant under this Order unless —
(a)   an affidavit is filed by or on behalf of the plaintiff proving due service of the writ
...
or
(b)   the plaintiff produces the writ indorsed by the defendant's solicitor with a statement that he accepts service of the writ on the defendant's behalf.

...

---

2. Claim for liquidated demand

(1) Where the writ is indorsed with a claim for a liquidated demand only, then, if a defendant fails to enter an appearance to the writ, the plaintiff may, after the time limited for appearance has expired, enter final judgment against that defendant for a sum not exceeding that claimed by the writ in respect of the demand, and for costs.

...

7. Claims for damages

(1) Where the writ is indorsed with a claim against a defendant for unliquidated damages only, and that defendant fails to enter an appearance within the time limited for appearing, the plaintiff shall be entitled to enter interlocutory judgment against that defendant and obtain an order for directions for the assessment of damages, and proceed with the action against the other defendants, if any.

...

10. Setting aside judgment in default

The Court may, on such terms as it thinks just, set aside or vary any judgment entered in pursuance of this Order.

Default judgment — liquidated claims and damages

12.2.4   As the extract of WA O 13 above exemplifies, the rules of most Australian jurisdictions stipulate that default judgment may be entered if the plaintiff's claim is for damages, a liquidated demand or a debt.

If the claim is for damages, interlocutory judgment is entered for the plaintiff because the court will need to conduct a further hearing to assess the quantum of the judgment; that is, the amount of damages: ACT rr 1118, 1122; NSW r 16.7; NT r 21.03; Qld r 284; SA r 229(1)(b); Tas rr 342, 348; Vic r 21.03; WA O 22 r 7.

If the claim is for debt or a liquidated demand, the plaintiff may enter final judgment: ACT r 1120; NSW r 16.6; NT 21.03; Qld r 283; SA r 229(1)(a); Tas rr 347, 349; Vic r 21.03; WA O 22 r 2.

The entry of default judgment for liquidated claims is an administrative task performed by the registry staff at the offices of the relevant court. The application does not receive judicial consideration. This aspect distinguishes default judgment from summary judgment or a judgment after a hearing. Fisher J made the following comments in *Argento v Cooba Developments Pty Ltd* (1987) 71 ALR 253 at 258, referring to three earlier decisions concerning default judgments:

> However, the circumstances here are significantly different. In each of those three cases the court was concerned with a default judgment where judgment follows administratively and as a matter of course from the default. It involved no consideration by the court of the merits of the case. A summary judgment ... is to be distinguished from a default judgment in that it involves a decision by the court that the defendant has failed to show a triable defence to the plaintiff's claim.
>
> In an application for leave to enter [summary] judgment ... the defendant has the opportunity to point to defects in the plaintiff's [claim] and have it reviewed by the court. A defendant has no such opportunity when default judgment is entered.

Where default judgment is sought for an unliquidated claim, the plaintiff cannot use the administrative procedure and must apply to the court for an assessment of damages.

12.2.5 A debt is a type of liquidated demand: see *Williams' Civil Procedure Victoria*, LexisNexis, at I 21.03.15. What constitutes a liquidated demand or claim? It has been held that whenever the amount to which the plaintiff is entitled can be ascertained by a simple calculation, or fixed by any scale of charges or other positive data, it is liquidated: *Spain v Union Steamship of New Zealand Ltd* (1923) 32 CLR 138, applied by Barrett J in *Rothenberger Australia Pty Ltd v Poulsen* (2003) 58 NSWLR 288, *Environmental Systems Pty Ltd v Peerless Holdings Pty Ltd* (2008) 19 VR 358; (2008) 227 FLR 1 [2008] VSCA 26, per Nettle JA at [79] and *Edwards v Australian Securities and Investments Commission (ASIC)* (2009) 264 ALR 723; (2009) 235 FLR 207; (2009) 76 ACSR 369; [2009] NSWCA 424 at [81]–[88] per Macfarlan JA.

12.2.6 For the application of these criteria to new causes of action, see the following decisions: Full Federal Court of Australia in *Official Trustee in Bankruptcy v C S & G J Handby Pty Ltd* (1989) 87 ALR 734; the NSW Court of Appeal in *Vale v TMH Haulage Pty Ltd* (1993) 12 ACSR 124 and *Taylor v Rudaks* (2007) 245 ALR 91, per Mansfield J.

Setting aside default judgment

12.2.7 Due to the comparative ease with which the plaintiff may obtain default judgment, there are correlative rights vested in the defendant. Where a default judgment has been irregularly obtained (that is, not in accordance with the rules), it will generally be set aside as of right (*ex debito justitiae*): *Anlaby v Praetorious* (1888) 20 QBD 764; *Lam v Gulic* (1979) 25 ACTR 46; and *Deputy Commissioner of Taxation v Abberwood Pty Ltd* (1990) 19 NSWLR 530. So, for instance, judgments signed too soon (*Anlaby v Praetorius* (1888) 20 QBD 764) or for too much (*Hughes v Justin* [1894] 1 QB 667) have been set aside. See also *Westpac Banking Corporation v Garrett* [2004] SASC 265 where the irregularity was the entering of judgment against the defendants in both their personal and representative capacities. However, the court retains a discretion to deal with irregularities; therefore not every irregularity will entitle the defendant to have default judgment set aside as a matter of right: *Commonwealth Bank of Australia v Buffett* (1993) 114 ALR 245 and *Westpac Banking Corporation v Garrett* [2004] SASC 265 at [31], [32]. For a general discussion of the concept of non-compliance and irregularities, see **Chapter 5**.

12.2.8 However, even when properly obtained, the court has discretion to set aside a default judgment upon the application of the defendant: FCR r 10.72; ACT r 1128; NSW 36.16, NT r 21.07; Qld r 290; SA r 230; Tas r 355; Vic 21.07; WA O 13 r 10. The jurisdiction to set aside its orders is inherent in every court, unless displaced by statute and this jurisdiction extends to setting aside a default or *ex parte* judgment: *Taylor v Taylor* (1979) 143 CLR 1; 25 ALR 418; *Allesch v Maunz* (2000) 203 CLR 172; (2000) 173 ALR 648, [2000] HCA 40; *Deputy Commissioner of Taxation v Falzon* (2008) 74 ATR 76; [2008] QCA 327.

12.2.9 In *Cook v DA Manufacturing Co Pty Ltd* (2004) QCA 52, the Queensland Court of Appeal stated that the defendant should address three elements when attempting to set aside default judgment: give a satisfactory explanation for the failure to appear, establish no unreasonable delay in making the application and demonstrate a *prima facie* defence on the merits.

The following two extracts demonstrate the application of two of these criteria. The first — *National Australia Bank Ltd v Singh* — focuses upon delay and the second — *Mearns v Willoughby Community Preschool Inc* — discusses the need for a prima facie defence.

12.2.10C   **National Australia Bank Ltd v Singh**
[1995] 1 Qd R 377
Court of Appeal (Qld)

[The plaintiff issued and served a writ claiming approximately $6 million from the defendant pursuant to a guarantee which the defendant had given to secure a debt owed by a company. The defendant alleged that securities which were available to the plaintiff to recoup part of the debt had been sold by its receiver at undervalue. However, no appearance was entered by the defendant. The plaintiff entered judgment against the defendant for the sum claimed. The defendant did not act until a bankruptcy notice was issued by the plaintiff, but thereafter sought to set aside the judgment and defend the proceedings. The defendant stated that he had become very depressed after the appointment of the receivers, and was unable to attend to his business affairs. The judge at first instance considered that the defendant's condition was not related to the time default judgment was sought and did not accept that the defendant could not attend to his business affairs. His Honour refused to set aside the judgment. The defendant appealed.]

Pincus JA (at 379): Even proceeding on the basis that there was reason to think that the [380] explanation given was dubious, I am, with respect, of the opinion that circumstance did not warrant the course his Honour took. 'It is not often that a defendant who has an apparently good ground of defence would be refused the opportunity of defending, even though a lengthy interval of time had elapsed provided that no irreparable prejudice is thereby done to the plaintiff', per Mr Justice McPherson, *National Mutual Life Association of Australasia Limited v Oasis Developments Pty Ltd,* [1983] 2 Qd R 441 at 449.

It appears that one of the bases on which his Honour declined to set the default judgment aside was that if that is done whenever there is a defence on the merits, defendants might be encouraged to let judgment go by default, in order to produce delay. In my view there is no reason to think that the appellant had any such motive, nor do I think it likely that defendants generally will, having a good defence on the merits, be inclined to let judgment go by default, simply to gain the relatively short time which would be expected to pass before the judgment can be set aside.

The learned primary judge also remarked, 'Where there has been, in effect, no satisfactory explanation of delay, the Court should not, in my view, be overly anxious to accommodate the preferences of the debtor.'

Here it is true that the explanation given was broad and not detailed: further no medical reports were produced. Despite these weaknesses I see no justification for failing completely to act on the explanation, particularly as it derived, as I have mentioned, some support from contemporary correspondence.

In my opinion, the uncontradicted valuation evidence showed a prima facie case of a sale at a quite serious undervalue in circumstances where, as a matter of law, proof of such a sale would provide the appellant with an arguable defence. There is really nothing in the evidence to suggest that the defence is put forward other than bona fide.

I am of the opinion that the learned primary judge erred in failing, as he apparently did, to give any weight to the explanation advanced for the delay, and that his Honour should have approached the matter on the basis that, the appellant's delay not being lengthy and no prejudice being shown, the appellant should have been allowed to litigate a defence which appears to raise a matter of substance.

[**McPherson** and **Davies JJA** agreed with **Pincus JA**. The appeal was allowed and judgment set aside.]

12.2.11C	**Mearns v Willoughby Community Preschool Inc**
	[2003] NSWCA 382
	Supreme Court of New South Wales — Court of Appeal

Hodgson JA:

[1] On 11 September 2003, Acting Judge Bowden dismissed an application by Robyn Haydn Mearns to set aside a default judgment obtained against her by Willoughby Community Preschool. Ms Mearns has applied for leave to appeal to this Court from that decision.

[2] The claim of the preschool was made in a statement of liquidated claim filed on 27 June 2003. It alleged employment of Ms Mearns by the school between 1981 and 28 September 2001. It alleged that Ms Mearns had drawn cheques on school accounts and applied those cheques for her own benefit rather than the benefit of the school.

[3] The Statement of Claim included detailed schedules identifying all the cheques in question, giving in each case a cheque number, amount of cheque, date cheque presented, purported payee noted on the cheque butt, actual payee recorded on the cheque and the purpose of payment as noted on the cheque butt or allocation sheet and, in some cases, purpose of payment as noted in the relevant ledger. In many cases the payee recorded on the cheque was 'cash', with the purported payee recorded on the cheque butt being various suppliers of goods that may have been appropriate for acquisition for the school. The total amount of the cheques was $356,835.50.

[4] As well as alleging that the payments made pursuant to the cheques were used to acquire goods and services not necessary or used in the running of the preschool and that they were used for the personal use of Ms Mearns, the statement of claim specifically alleged that the payments were disguised by falsely recording fictitious payees and by falsely completing cheque butts and other entries to disguise cash cheques as being cheques made out to legitimate payees.

[5] The solicitors acting for Ms Mearns wrote to the solicitor acting for the plaintiff on 28 July 2003, advising that counsel had been briefed to draw a defence and asserting that due to the complex and extensive nature of the allegations, they would require an additional fourteen days to respond; and also stating that they assumed the plaintiff's solicitors would not enter a judgment without reasonable notice to their client. The plaintiff's solicitor responded on 30 July 2003 asserting that the defendant had adequate time to prepare a defence, and advising that the plaintiff's solicitor intended to enter judgment on 13 August 2003 without further notice if a defence was not filed prior to that date.

[6] On 5 August 2003 a letter seeking better particulars of the statement of claim was prepared by the defendant's solicitors, but it appears that it may not have been sent to the plaintiff's solicitor at that time due to a misunderstanding. A copy of it was forwarded on 21 August 2003. However, the plaintiff's solicitors responded by advising that they had attempted to obtain default judgment on 14 August, and although judgment had not been entered at that time because of some procedural difficulty, they were proceeding to obtain default judgment.

[7] An application to set aside that default judgment came before Acting Judge Bowden on 5 September 2003. He was satisfied on that day that an explanation had been given in relation to the delay. However, he noted a requirement that the defendant also show some defence on the merits. He noted that at that stage there was no proposed defence, and only an affidavit from the solicitor asserting instructions that the defendant had not obtained funds for herself from the preschool, and referring to criminal charges that had been brought against the defendant.

[8] His Honour asked the question whether he should dismiss the notice of motion or give the defendant an opportunity to bring forward material to support a defence, and he adjourned the notice of motion to 11 September to give that opportunity to the defendant.

[9] On that day the defendant relied on an affidavit she had sworn on 9 September, which in substance asserted that all expenditure was appropriate and necessary for the running of the preschool. The affidavit dealt with certain particular allegations concerning a life insurance policy in her name, but otherwise did not deal with any specific item in the statement of claim. It made no answer to the allegations concerning the disguising of the payments by falsely recording fictitious payees and falsely completing records to disguise the nature of the payments. No draft defence was submitted.

[10] On that day Acting Judge Bowden delivered a judgment referring to the defendant's affidavit, and indicating that in his view the defence was precisely the sort of defence that the Rules say shall not be pleaded to a matter commenced by way of liquidated statement of claim. He went on to say that what the defendant had to do was a matter of showing the prima facie defence on the merits, but that in doing so:

> the defendant is required to put some factual statements before the Court that would deal with what are very specific allegations and claims that have been made here. That has not been done.

[11] On that basis his Honour dismissed the notice of motion with costs.

[12] The applicant seeks leave to appeal on the following grounds:

1. His Honour erred in determining an application to set aside a default judgment on the basis that

   [']the applicant is required to ... establish that there is a bona fide defence on the merits' and '... it is a matter of showing a prima facie defence on the merits['].

2. His Honour should have held that such application was to be determined on the basis of the fundamental duty of the Court to do justice between the parties. ...

[14] The question for this Court is whether leave should be granted to appeal, on the basis that there is an appeal that has some prospect of success because of an error made by the primary judge, and the interests of justice require that leave should be granted.

[15] I should say at the outset that it seems to me that, right up to the time when the application to set aside the judgment was dismissed, the claimant appeared to be proceeding on the basis that there was no need for a defence to be put on until the request for further particulars had been answered. I have to say that, in my view, the Statement of Claim was pleaded with adequate particularity and that the request that was made for particulars was one to which the defendant was not entitled to have an answer before putting on a defence or, indeed, probably at all.

[16] In those circumstances, it seems to me that the application which the claimant made to have the judgment set aside should have been accompanied by a proposed defence, and the failure to have a proposed defence put to the Judge hearing the application was a significant deficiency in the application that was made.

[17] The deficiency could possibly have been overcome by the Judge setting aside the judgment on condition that a defence be put on within seven days; but it also had the consequence that there were important allegations in the statement of claim that were not addressed at all, even in the affidavit that was put on. There was no addressing in the affidavit of the very significant allegations in the statement of claim of deliberate falsifications in relation to the recording of the transactions so as to disguise the nature of the payments. In any defence, that certainly would have to be addressed.

[18] It may be that, if that question had been squarely addressed and if there had been a verified defence available asserting in relation to some or even all of the transactions that the money was applied for the purposes of the school, that might possibly have been a sufficient indication of a defence on the merits to justify setting aside the judgment. However, in the light of the deficiencies that I have identified, I do not think it can be said that the result to which the District Court Judge came was an incorrect result, even if it may be the case that he placed too high a standard on the defence on the merits that had to be shown.

[19] For those reasons I think this application for leave to appeal should be dismissed.

[**Ipp JA** agreed with **Hodgson JA**. The application for leave to appeal was dismissed with costs].

12.2.12   For further examples of the exercise of discretion to set aside default judgment, see *Troiani v Alfost Properties Pty Ltd* [2002] QCA 281; *GE Personal Finance Pty Ltd v Liddy* [2008] ACTSC 126; *Jiona Investments Pty Ltd v Medihelp General Practice Pty Ltd* [2010] QCA 099; and *Ezekiel–Hart v Law Society of the ACT* [2012] ACTSC 103.

Costs

12.2.13   Where the judgment was regularly obtained, the defendant will usually be ordered to pay the costs thrown away and the costs of the application (*Federal Bank v Bate* (1889) 5 WN (NSW) 67), but costs may be refused if the plaintiff did not give reasonable warning to the defendant of its intention to sign judgment (*Coburn v Brothchie* (1890) 16 VLR 6) or if the plaintiff unreasonably refused to agree to set aside the judgment: *Gorman v Matthews* (1897) 13 (WN) 224.

The operation of the default judgment system

12.2.14E   **Consumer debt-related legal problems**
Louis Schetzer
(2010) 35 *Alt LJ* 107

[107] An analysis of data from the Magistrates' Court of Victoria indicated that civil consumer debt matters make up a significant majority of all civil matters finalised in Victorian Magistrates' Courts. Of the 50,869 civil complaints finalised in the Magistrates' Court in 2005–06, 61 per cent were for civil consumer debt matters. Of these, the overwhelming majority (84 per cent) was for claims of less than $10,000, with almost a quarter for claims of less than $1000. Ninety-eight per cent of matters under $10,000 were finalised by way of default judgment.

The majority of default judgments for civil consumer debt matters of less than $10,000 were for debts, monies due and local government rates/charges. For matters over $10,000, there were significantly proportionally more matters involving breach of contract/agreement (42 per cent of matters over $10,000, compared to only 13 per cent of matters under $10,000).

For civil consumer debt matters under $10,000 finalised by way of default judgment, local councils were one of the most common plaintiff creditors, accounting for 21 per cent of all default judgments for matters under $10,000. Debt collection agents were the second most common type of creditor plaintiffs amongst default judgment creditor plaintiffs for matters under $10,000. Banks and financial institutions also accounted for significant numbers of default judgment civil consumer debt matters under $10,000.

The increasing reliance on debt collection agents for debt recovery raises issues concerning the manner in which debt collection agents pursue outstanding debts. Several of the 90 financial counsellor clients interviewed as part of this project reported intrusive and invasive behaviour on the part of debt collection agents. ...

Over two-thirds of 450 participants in a telephone survey of Magistrates' Court consumer default debtors said that they did not seek any advice/assistance for their debt-related matter. ...

The research found that the most common reasons for not seeking advice/assistance were:

- lack of trust or a belief that they had to deal with it themselves;
- did not think that the debt was owed;
- lack of awareness of how to access advice/ assistance;
- feelings of shame, guilt, embarrassment or stress.

12.2.15   Notes and question

1. In your view, has a balance been achieved between debtor and creditor in the proceedings for default judgment?

2. For further commentary, see D St L Kelly, *Debt Recovery in Australia*, Commission of Inquiry into Poverty, AGPS, Canberra, 1977; Consumer Credit Legal Centre (NSW) Inc, *Report into Debt Collection*, Sydney, April 2004; and L Schetzer, *Courting Debt, The Legal Needs of People Facing Civil Consumer Debt Problems*, Department of Justice, Victoria, Civil Law Policy, July 2008.

Judgment upon striking out or default of pleading

12.2.16 Where there are defects in a party's pleadings, for example, they are vexatious or do not disclose a cause of action, the other party may seek to strike out those pleadings and obtain default judgment: refer to the discussion at **11.8.2ff**.

In some jurisdictions, the plaintiff may apply to the court for judgment where the defendant's defence has been struck out: ACT r 1117(1)(a)(iv); NSW r 16.2(1)(c); NT r 21.02; SA r 229(1); Tas rr 259, 342; Vic r 21.02(3).

Judgment upon failure to comply with a time stipulation

12.2.17 The court has jurisdiction to enlarge or abridge any time period in the rules and this may be done retrospectively; that is, even if the application is made after the relevant time has expired: see generally **Chapter 5**.

Where there is inordinate delay in, or successive extensions in taking a step in proceedings, the court can make orders requiring the step to be taken within a specified time, and then providing that failure to comply with that order will result in a penalty spontaneously arising, without further recourse to the court. The usual penalty in such cases will be judgment for the other party or striking out the pleadings of the defaulting party. This procedure is called a self-executing or 'springing' order and is discussed at **5.4.1ff**.

12.2.18 Further reading

G Munck, 'Adjudicated Debt Resolution (ADR): A Proposal for a Cooperative Approach to Resolving Debt Issues' (2004) 23(1) *The Arbitrator & Mediator* 55.

D St L Kelly, *Debt Recovery in Australia*, Commission of Inquiry into Poverty, AGPS, Canberra, 1977.

J Willis, 'Of Process Servers, Default Summonses and the Judicial Process' (1975) 10 *Melb Univ L Rev* 225.

SUMMARY JUDGMENT

History and purpose of summary judgment

12.3.1E   **The Evolution of the Summary Judgment Procedure**
John A Bauman
(1956) *Ind LJ* 329
(footnotes omitted)

Delay in the disposition of litigation has been one of the enduring problems of the law. In the first English law book ever written for lay persons, an explanation was sought for the 'huge delays' that 'withhold petitioners from their right' and impose 'an intolerable burden of expense'. Not withstanding extensive reforms in judicial administration, the law's delay

---

remains a much mooted question today. As one step toward the solution of this recurrent problem, Parliament, a century ago, enacted Keating's Act providing a summary judgment procedure to facilitate the collection of bills of exchange. The appearance of a summary judgment procedure in England in 1855 was not fortuitous; its enactment was the response to economic and social pressures that could be withstood no longer. These pressures came not from the legal profession, which was notoriously reluctant to make any changes in the existing system, but from lay [people] and in particular the newly ascendant mercantile group that found the delays and technicalities of common law procedure unendurable.

Why the dissatisfaction of the merchants resulted in the enactment of a summary procedure at this particular time may best be understood from a historical perspective. For centuries merchants had little reason to resort to the common law courts for commercial litigation. Commerce was carried on at the borough fairs held pursuant to the King's franchise, and that franchise included the right to hold a fair or piepowder court. Other towns were authorised to conduct the staple trade, and these towns were privileged to hold courts to settle disputes by the law merchant. ... A summary procedure was the noteworthy feature of these courts. 'Justice was administered as speedily as the dust could fall or be removed from the feet of the litigants'. ...

Subsequent developments altered this picture substantially. With increased wealth and the improvement in transport, fairs diminished in importance with a consequent withering of the piepowder courts. .... As a result of these changes in commercial practice and because of the failure of the English to develop the early commercial courts, merchants found it necessary to resort to the common law and chancery courts for the settlement of mercantile disputes. ...

[However, they encountered delays]. Writing in 1740, the winner of a Chancery suit lasting thirteen years found legal expenses so great that he quoted Hannibal [sic] to the effect that a few more such Victories would undo him. ... No doubt some of the delay in the disposition of litigation could be attributed to the increased business of the courts, but there were defects in the prescribed procedure which contributed substantially to this result. In the Chancery Court, the glaring defect was the time consuming procedure for taking testimony by written deposition. In the common law courts, pleading was the chief offender. As that system developed, it became increasingly complex and technical, caus[ing] difficulties. Because the highly technical rules governing pleading were rigidly enforced, a case might be dismissed for some defect in form irrespective of the merits of the case. The more significant defect in the system was its failure to provide a method of determining the factual basis of a pleading prior to trial. It was this weakness that unscrupulous lawyers advised debtors to exploit. ...

To remedy at least some of the evils resulting from sham pleading, Lord Brougham, in 1828, proposed the adoption of the Scottish summary procedure for actions brought on notes, bonds, and bills of exchange. ... Keating's Act, entitled the Summary Procedure on Bills of Exchange Act (1855), became effective on October 24, 1855.

12.3.2   All jurisdictions now empower the court to bypass the normal extended procedures in civil litigation by giving summary judgment to the plaintiff or the defendant who can show (whether on the facts or on the law) that victory is a foregone conclusion. The procedure allows a party to bypass a full trial where there is no defence to the claim or the claim is unfounded. Thus, as demonstrated by Bauman above, the procedure required a reappraisal of pleadings.

Under the traditional common law pleading rules, a party's claim or defence was determined solely on the face of the pleadings. The attacking party could not 'go behind' the pleading to show that it had no basis in fact. It was assumed that pleadings were made in good faith, based on evidence that could be presented at trial. Therefore, any challenge to the truth of a pleading would necessitate a trial. Modern courts have recognised, however, that there are occasions where it appears from the pleadings that a legitimate legal dispute exists when in fact one does not: J H Friedenthal, M K Kane and A R Miller, *Civil Procedure*, West Publishing Co, St Paul, 1993, pp 435–6.

12.3.3E   **Civil Procedure**
                                      F James Jr
                        Little Brown & Co, Boston, 1965

[230] The weakness of [early civil procedures] was that they could not go behind the pleadings. They had to take the adversary's pleading at full face value. They provided no way to test whether the pleader could support his allegations by proof or whether there was anything of substance behind a denial. And since there was no very strong sanction against either pleading or denying groundlessly, it has been traditionally easy for either a plaintiff or defendant to run successfully the gauntlet of ... motions by tendering paper issues in the pleadings which will evaporate when proof is made at trial.

A natural question is why anyone should want to plead groundlessly when he should know that he will not be able to make his pleading good when proof is called for. Unfortunately there are reasons. A defendant from whom payment is sought (eg, for services rendered or goods sold and delivered) often wants delay. Indeed, that may well be the very reason why suit had to be brought. And a defendant can have delay by the simple device of denying the debt, and perhaps gilding the lily by adding pleas of payment and breach of warranty — a trilogy known in the trade as the last refuge of the deadbeat. It is a little less obvious what a plaintiff can gain by pleading falsely, but he, too, may have a reason. Even groundless suits cost money to defend and therefore may have a nuisance value in settlement if they cannot be disposed of by a speedy and inexpensive pretrial device. In addition to the downright dishonest pleader there is the incurable optimist who pleads without presently known grounds in the hope that something may turn up.

12.3.4 The summary procedure allows the plaintiff or defendant to obtain judgment on the whole or part of a claim or defence, even if the other party contests liability. The applicant must show that there is no arguable issue of law or fact disclosed by the other party's pleadings or other documentation.

Lord Halsbury made the following statement in *Jones v Stone* [1894] AC 122 at 124 in relation to summary proceedings by the plaintiff in England:

[It] is ... intended to apply only in cases where there can be no reasonable doubt that a plaintiff is entitled to judgment, and where, therefore, it is inexpedient to allow the defendant to defend for the mere purposes of delay.

12.3.5 The grant of an application for summary judgment effectively denies the other party the chance of testing the applicant's case by discovery and oral evidence and therefore will only be granted where the applicant is able to show an unanswerable case. It is not enough for an applicant to show that it has a strong case or it is likely to succeed. It will only obtain judgment if it can show that it is bound to succeed: D Barnard and M Houghton, *The New Civil Court in Action*, Butterworths, London, 1993, p 149. However, the tests for achieving this outcome differ, see below.

'TRADITIONAL', 'NO REAL PROSPECT' AND 'REASONABLE' APPROACHES TO SUMMARY JURISDICTION

12.4.1   There is a significant diversity in the tests used in different jurisdictions in Australia for summary judgment. An explanation of the differences between some of the tests was given by the High Court in *Spencer v Commonwealth* (2010) 241 CLR 118, which is extracted below at **12.4.5C**. In that case, the High Court distinguished between summary judgment that was given under the inherent jurisdiction (which is referred to below as 'the traditional approach') and where the power to enter summary judgment is articulated by statute or the rules. Therefore, summary judgment must be approached by considering the provisions in which the test is expressed and the expression differs across Australian jurisdictions.

The traditional approach

12.4.2   Traditionally, the summary jurisdiction was exercised when the court found that actions or defences should not be permitted in the ordinary way because it is apparent that they must fail: *Webster v Lampard* (1993) 177 CLR 598. On this traditional view, summary judgment should be approached with 'exceptional caution': *General Steel Industries Inc v Commissioner for Railways* (NSW) (1964) 112 CLR 125 at 129 per Barwick CJ. This approach is used in the following rules: HCR r 27.09; ACT rr 1146, 1147; NSW rr 13.1, 13.4; NT regs 22.02, 23.03; Tas Pt 11, Divs 3 and 4, rr 356–370; WA O 14, O 16.

No real prospect of success

12.4.3   This test is derived from r 24.2 of the Civil Procedure Rules 1998 (UK) and states that the ground for summary judgment is that the claimant or defendant has no real prospect of succeeding in the claim or defence. It is used in Queensland and Victoria.

In relation to Victoria, although the Supreme Court (General Civil Procedure) Rules 2005 (Vic) (O 22, 23) ostensibly adopt a traditional approach to summary disposition, Pt 4.4 of the Civil Procedure Act 2010 (Vic) (ss 60–65) introduced a 'no real prospect' test, i.e. that a plaintiff or a defendant in a proceeding may apply to the court for summary judgment on the ground that the other party's claim/defence or part of it has no real prospect of success. However, the court retains a residual discretion under s 64 of the Civil Procedure Act 2010 (Vic), so it may order that a civil proceeding proceed to trial if the court is satisfied that, despite there being no real prospect of success, the civil proceeding should not be disposed of summarily because it is not in the interests of justice to do so, or the dispute is of such a nature that only a full hearing on the merits is appropriate. This provision is discussed further at **12.6.8**.

Although the Queensland rules (rr 292, 293) are based on the drafting of r 24.2 of the Civil Procedure Rules 1998 (UK) (*DCT v Salcedo* [2005] 2 Qd R 232 at [11]), their wording is also slightly different. For example, under Qld r 292(2), where the plaintiff is applying summary judgment, it will be granted only:

If the court is satisfied that —

(a) the defendant has no real prospect of successfully defending all or a part of the plaintiff's claim; and

(b) there is no need for a trial of the claim or the part of the claim ...

Although the Queensland Court of Appeal in *DCT v Salcedo* [2005] 2 Qd R 232 stated that the traditional approach 'is not compatible with' rr 292 and 293 (at [17] per Williams JA with McMurdo P and Atkinson JA agreeing), a differently constituted Court of Appeal (Holmes and Chesterman JJA and Daubney J) in *Bolton Properties Pty Ltd v JK Investments (Australia) Pty Ltd* [2009] 2 Qd R 202; [2009] QCA 135 questioned this approach. Therefore, at the time of writing, the issue is not settled.

The reasonable approach

12.4.4 The rules which adopt the reasonable approach focus upon the opponent's reasonable prospects of success: Federal Court of Australia Act 1976 (Cth) s 31A; SA rr 232. For example, s 31A of the Federal Court Act states that summary judgment may be given to applicants or respondents if the court is satisfied that the other party has no reasonable prospects of successfully prosecuting/defending the proceeding. A proceeding need not be 'hopeless' or 'bound to fail' for it to have no reasonable prospect of success: s 31A(3). The principles applicable to s 31A were summarised by Foster J in *Wang v Anying Group Pty Ltd* [2009] FCA 1500 at [43], which is extracted below at **12.5.7C**.

12.4.5 The South Australian rule (r 232(2)) states that summary judgment may only be given if the court is satisfied that there is no reasonable basis for the claim or defence. In *Ceneavenue Pty Ltd v Martin* (2008) 67 ACSR 130; [2008] SASC 158, the South Australian Full Court held that the reasoning in *General Steel* is no longer applicable: at [80]–[81] per Debelle J (Duggan and Anderson JJ agreeing). The decision of the plurality of the High Court in *Spencer v Commonwealth* (2010) 241 CLR 118 (extracted below) has been applied to r 232 (SA): see *Davies v Minister For Urban Development and Planning* (2011) 109 SASR 518; [2011] SASC 87 per Bleby J.

12.4.6C   **Spencer v Commonwealth**
                         (2010) 241 CLR 118; (2010) 269 ALR 233; [2010] HCA 28
                                        High Court of Australia
                                         (footnotes omitted)

Hayne, Crennan, Kiefel and Bell JJ:

[50] Consideration of the operation and application of s 31A of the Federal Court Act must begin from consideration of its text. So far as relevant to this matter, s 31A provides: ...

(2) The Court may give judgment for one party against another in relation to the whole or any part of a proceeding if:

(a) the first party is defending the proceeding or that part of the proceeding; and

(b) the Court is satisfied that the other party has no reasonable prospect of successfully prosecuting the proceeding or that part of the proceeding.

(3) For the purposes of this section, a defence or a proceeding or part of a proceeding need not be:

(a) hopeless; or

(b) bound to fail;

for it to have no reasonable prospect of success.

(4) This section does not limit any powers that the Court has apart from this section.

[51] First, the central idea about which the provisions pivot is "no *reasonable* prospect" (emphasis added). The choice of the word "reasonable" is important. If s 31A is to be seen as deriving from r 24.2 of the *Civil Procedure Rules 1998* of England and Wales, its provisions underwent an important change in the course of their translation from that jurisdiction to this. The English rule speaks of "no *real* prospect"; s 31A speaks of "no *reasonable* prospect". The two phrases convey very different meanings.

[52] Second, effect must be given to the negative admonition in subs (3) that a defence, a proceeding, or a part of a proceeding may be found to have no reasonable prospect of successful prosecution even if it cannot be said that it is "hopeless" or "bound to fail". It will be necessary to examine further the notion of "no reasonable prospect". But before undertaking that task, it is important to begin by recognising that the combined effect of subss (2) and (3) is that the enquiry required in this case is whether there is a "reasonable" prospect of prosecuting the proceeding, not an enquiry directed to whether a certain and concluded determination could be made that the proceeding would necessarily fail.

[53] In this respect, s 31A departs radically from the basis upon which earlier forms of provision permitting the entry of summary judgment have been understood and administered. Those earlier provisions were understood as requiring formation of a certain and concluded determination that a proceeding would necessarily fail. That this was the basis of earlier decisions may be illustrated by reference to two decisions of this court often cited in connection with questions of summary judgment: *Dey v Victorian Railways Commissioners* [(1949) 78 CLR 62] and *General Steel Industries Inc v Commissioner for Railways (NSW)* [(1964) 112 CLR 125].

[54] In *Dey*, the defendants moved for summary judgment on the grounds that the action was frivolous, vexatious and an abuse of process. In a passage often later cited, Dixon J said [at 91] that "[a] case must be very clear indeed to justify the summary intervention of the court to prevent a plaintiff submitting his case for determination in the appointed manner by the court with or without a jury". What Dixon J meant by "very clear" was identified by his observation that "once it appears that there is a *real question* to be determined whether of fact or law and that the rights of the parties depend upon it, then it is not competent for the court to dismiss the action as frivolous and vexatious and an abuse of process" (emphasis added). And there would be a "real question" unless the defendant could "show that it was *so certain* that [the question] must be answered in the [defendant's] favour that it would amount to an abuse of the process of the court to allow the action to go forward for determination according to the appointed modes of procedure" (emphasis added). The test identified by Dixon J in *Dey* can thus be seen to be a test requiring certain demonstration of the outcome of the litigation, not an assessment of the prospect of its success.

[55] In *General Steel Industries*, Barwick CJ pointed out that previous decisions about summary termination of actions on the motion of a defendant had been given in cases in which the so-called "inherent" jurisdiction of a court to protect itself and its processes from abuse had been invoked, and in cases where the defendant had relied upon a particular rule of court permitting the court to strike out pleadings or dismiss an action on it being shown that a pleading "does not disclose a reasonable cause of action" or the action "being shown by the pleadings to be frivolous or vexatious". The material available to the court might differ, depending upon which power was invoked, but all the cases emphasised the need for "exceptional caution" in exercising a power to dismiss an action summarily. As Barwick CJ also pointed out in General Steel Industries, the test to be applied was expressed in many different ways, but in the end amounted to different ways of saying "that the case of the plaintiff is so *clearly* untenable that it cannot possibly succeed" (emphasis added). As that formulation shows, the test to be applied was one of demonstrated certainty of outcome.

[56] Because s 31A(3) provides that certainty of failure ("hopeless" or "bound to fail") need not be demonstrated in order to show that a plaintiff has no reasonable prospect of prosecuting an action, it is evident that s 31A is to be understood as requiring a different enquiry from that which had to be made under earlier procedural regimes. It follows, of course, that it is dangerous to seek to elucidate the meaning of the statutory expression "no reasonable prospect of successfully prosecuting the proceeding" by reference to what is said in those earlier cases.

[57] Likewise, it is dangerous to apply directly what has been said in the United Kingdom about the application of a test of "no real prospect" or what has been said in United States decisions about summary judgment. The United Kingdom cases are directed to a different test. The controversies in the United States about what is sufficient to resist a motion for summary judgment, ... turn upon the requirements of the Federal Rules of Civil Procedure applied to a system of "notice" pleading.

[58] How then should the expression "no reasonable prospect" be understood? No paraphrase of the expression can be adopted as a sufficient explanation of its operation, let alone definition of its content. Nor can the expression usefully be understood by the creation of some antinomy intended to capture most or all of the cases in which it cannot be said that there is "no reasonable prospect". The judicial creation of a lexicon of words or phrases intended to capture the operation of a particular statutory phrase like "no reasonable prospect" is to be avoided. Consideration of the difficulties that bedevilled the proviso to common form criminal appeal statutes, as a result of judicial glossing of the relevant statutory expression, provides the clearest example of the dangers that attend any such attempt.

SUMMARY JUDGMENT FOR THE PLAINTIFF

What must the plaintiff establish?

12.5.1   Broadly speaking, the conditions for an application for summary judgment by the plaintiff are:

(a)   in some jurisdictions, a proceeding amenable to summary judgment must be commenced by a writ: HCR r 27.09.1; NT r 22.01; Vic r 22.01;

(b)   except for the Federal Court, New South Wales and South Australia, an appearance (in the Australian Capital Territory a notice of intention to respond or a defence, and in Queensland a notice of intention to defend) must be entered by the defendant;

(c)   verification of the cause of action is usually given by affidavit made by the plaintiff or a person who can swear positively to the facts (although the rules of some jurisdictions allow facts to be verified on information and belief in certain circumstances); and

(d)   that affidavit must contain a statement that the deponent believes that there is either *no defence* to the action ('the traditional approach') or that the defence has '*no real prospect of success*' (Qld and Vic) or there is no *reasonable basis* for defending the plaintiff's claim ('the reasonable approach' — Federal Court and SA).

See generally: HCR r 27.09; FCR Div 26.1; Federal Court of Australia Act s 31A, ACT Div 2.11.5; NSW r 13.1; NT O 22; Qld r 292; SA rr 232, 233; Tas rr 356–366; Vic Civil Procedure Act s 61; O 22; WA O 14.

12.5.2E   **Supreme Court Rules (NT)**

Order 22 — Summary judgment for plaintiff

22.02 Application for judgment

(1) Where the defendant has filed an appearance, the plaintiff may at any time apply to the Court for judgment against the defendant on the ground that the defendant has no defence to the whole or part of a claim included in the writ or statement of claim, or no defence except as to the amount of a claim. ...

22.03 Affidavit in support

(1) An application for judgment shall be made by summons supported by an affidavit verifying the facts on which the claim or the part of the claim to which the application relates is based and stating that, in the belief of the deponent, there is no defence to that claim or part or no defence except as to the amount claimed. ...

(3) An affidavit under subrule (1) may contain a statement of fact based on information and belief if the grounds are set out and, having regard to all the circumstances, the Court considers that the statement ought to be permitted. ...

22.04 Defendant to show cause

(1) The defendant may, by affidavit or otherwise to the satisfaction of the Court, show cause against the application.

(2) An affidavit under subrule (1) may contain a statement of fact based on information and belief if the grounds are set out. ...

Application by the plaintiff for summary judgment — principles and process

12.5.3   As stated by Cameron, '[t]he hearing of an application for summary judgment is not intended to be a type of mini-trial on affidavit evidence': J Hunter, C Cameron and T Henning, *Litigation: Evidence and Procedure*, 7th ed, LexisNexis Butterworths, 2005, vol 1, p 206. The following extract provides a useful example of the procedures adopted by courts when hearing an application for summary judgment in jurisdictions where the traditional approach is used.

Glover v Roche
[2003] ACTSC 19; BC200301405
Supreme Court of the Australian Capital Territory

[The plaintiffs had entered into a deed of agreement with the defendants for the sale of the plaintiffs' legal practice to the defendants. The defendants purchased the plaintiffs' practice on terms requiring the defendants to pay all outstanding amounts equal to the aggregate of fees and disbursements due to the plaintiffs in relation to work in progress by 3 August 2002 and they failed to do so. The plaintiffs commenced proceedings and made an application for summary judgment.]

Crispin J

[1] This is an application for summary judgment. ...

[15] The case of the plaintiffs is a straightforward one. ... Mr Sheils has deposed to the fact that he believes that there is no defence to the claim for the outstanding sum of $423,487.94. He has also deposed to his belief that the defence and counter claim was filed 'purely for the purposes of delay so that they can dispose of or secure assets in order to defeat any judgment obtained in this matter'.

[16] On 4 March 2003, which was the first day of the hearing, I granted leave for the defendants to file an amended defence and counter claim. In response, both defendants filed affidavits and were permitted to give further evidence orally. They contended, in essence, that the agreement was void for illegality, or on the ground of public policy, or that they had been induced to enter into it as a consequence of misrepresentations by the plaintiffs and that they had effectively rescinded it by letter dated 28 February 2002. They also sought to raise other defences based upon allegations that, in some cases, amounts less than that agreed had been received in full satisfaction of their liability and that, in others, the amounts were not payable for various reasons.

[17] The application is brought under O15 r1 of the Supreme Court Rules 1937 (ACT), which permits a plaintiff to make an application for leave to enter judgment when an originating application [now an originating claim] has been accompanied by a statement of claim and the defendant has entered a notice of appearance. Subr(2) provides that the application must be supported by an affidavit or affidavits verifying the cause of action and, in the case of a claim for debt or a liquidated demand, verifying the amount claimed and stating that in the belief of the deponent there is no defence to the action.

[18] Subr(4) provides as follows:

> On an application under this rule, the Court may make such order for the entry of judgment as it considers just having regard to the nature of the remedy or relief claimed, unless the Court is satisfied that —
>
> (a) there is a good defence to the action on the merits; or
> (b) sufficient facts are disclosed to entitle the defendant to defend the action generally; or
> (c) subr(5) applies. ...

[20] In my opinion, once there is prima facie evidence of liability as required by subr(2), the provisions of subr(4) enable the Court to make orders for the entry of judgment if the

defendant does not establish that there is at least an arguable defence or some other reason sufficient to entitle the defendant to defend the action generally. ...

[21] ... [T]he onus that rests upon a defendant by virtue of this sub-rule is not a heavy one. A defendant need only establish a state of facts that displaces the prima facie effect of the sworn statement by the deponent of the affidavit filed in support of the application that he or she believes that there is no defence to the action: *Cloverdell Lumber Co Pty Ltd v Abbott* (1924) 34 CLR 122. It has even been suggested that it may be sufficient for a defendant to show that there is a real case to be investigated: *Australian Can Pty Ltd v Levin & Co Pty Ltd* [1947] VLR 332. A defendant may file an affidavit setting out the material facts upon which a defence might be established without disclosing the evidence by which the defendant hopes to establish those facts: *Country Estates Pty Ltd v Leighton Contractors Pty Ltd* (1975) 49 ALJR 173. A court will not attempt to resolve disputed questions of fact on the basis of competing affidavits: *Evans v Bartlam* [1937] AC 473.

[22] Nonetheless, a defendant cannot rely upon mere denials and must 'condescend to particularity': see *Moscow Narodny Bank Ltd v Mosbert Finance (Aust) Pty Ltd [1976] WAR 109; Wallingford v Mutual Society* (1880) 5 App Cas 685; and *Ritter v North Side Enterprises Pty Ltd* (1975) 132 CLR 301. Furthermore, it has been suggested that if the evidence raising the defence is not credible, there is no reasonable probability of the defence being established and leave to defend should be refused: see *National Westminster Bank plc v Daniel* [1994] 1 All ER 156; *Commonwealth Bank of Australia v Wallace* (1995) ATTR 41-387. ...

[23] In approaching an application of this kind, one must also be conscious of the note of caution sounded by Gaudron, McHugh, Gummow and Hayne JJ in *Agar v Hyde* (2000) 201 CLR 552 at 575–576, albeit in the context of a case decided under the NSW Supreme Court Rules:

> Ordinarily, a party is not to be denied the opportunity to place his or her case before the court in the ordinary way, and after taking advantage of the usual interlocutory processes. The test to be applied has been expressed in various ways, but all of the verbal formulae which have been used are intended to describe a high degree of certainty about the ultimate outcome of the proceeding if it were allowed to go to trial in the ordinary way (footnotes omitted).

[24] The suggested defences must be considered in the context of these principles.

[25] Mr Spinks, who appeared for the defendants, submitted that there was evidence of facts sufficient to establish an arguable case in respect of the defences pleaded.

[His Honour discussed the defences raised by the defendants. The first was that the agreement had been made in contravention of r 59 of the Workers Compensation Rules (ACT) because its effect was to extract from clients fees that were not properly payable and, as a consequence, was illegal and unenforceable against the defendants. He considered at [27] that this argument 'involved several misconceptions' discussed at [28]–[33]].

[34] There was nothing in the terms of the Deed that purported to require the defendants to attempt to extract from clients fees that were not properly payable or to otherwise act illegally or improperly and, even if the language employed in those terms had been sufficient to raise the possibility of such conduct being undertaken in purported performance of the agreement, that would not have invalidated the Deed or rendered it unenforceable. There is no triable issue in respect of this suggested defence.

[35] The other grounds of defence that were strongly pressed on behalf of the defendants relied upon allegations that they were induced to enter into the Deed by various misrepresentations made to them by the plaintiffs and hence had been entitled to rescind the agreement, even if they had not purported to do so until a few days prior to the hearing of the application for summary judgment.

[His Honour discusses the estoppel argument and factual and evidentiary issues raised by it at [36]–[62]].

[63] Dr O'Hair raised a number of other issues in answer to the suggested grounds for rescission, but I have found it unnecessary to examine them. The defences are in my opinion plainly untenable. ...

[His Honour discusses the case law on promissory estoppel.]

[67] In the present case, no particulars of the representation were provided and no evidence was adduced to confirm that it had ever been made. The only evidence as to this issue was given by Mr Sheils who said that the suggestion of such a representation was inconsistent with the discussion he had had with Mr Glover, with the relevant correspondence and with the terms of subsequent demands for payment. He was not challenged in cross-examination as to the truth of this evidence.

[68] The defendants also filed a counter-claim, but it was again based upon allegations of misrepresentation which, in my opinion, they are estopped from raising and which, in any event, the evidence before me does not support. ...

[69] Even on an application of this kind, relief should not be denied to a plaintiff with an apparently valid claim unless the Court is satisfied that there are bona fide defences which, as mentioned earlier, are at least sufficiently credible to warrant further investigation. In the present case, the defences put forward by the defendants do not, in my opinion, satisfy even this test. Having observed each of them give supplementary evidence-in-chief and be cross-examined about the issues raised in the amended defence, I was unable to be satisfied that there was a bona fide dispute as to their liability under the Deed or, at least after Mr Sheils had rechecked the figures and conceded certain amounts, even as to the balance owing to the plaintiffs. On the contrary, I was left with the distinct impression that the defences had been raised only to delay judgment and, perhaps, provide some scope for negotiation.

[70] I am satisfied that the plaintiffs are entitled to summary judgment on their claim for the sum of $423,487.94 plus interest since 3 August 1998 at 9% per annum, which amounts to $25,409.27. There will be judgment in their favour for the sum of $448,897.21. The counter claim will be dismissed.

12.5.5   *Glover v Roche* exemplifies the traditional approach, where the court gives summary judgment only if it is clear that there is no triable issue. On this approach, in order to resist summary judgment, the defendant must show an issue of fact or law which requires resolution by trial: *Jacobs v Booths Distillery Co* (1901) 85 LT 262 (House of Lords). For applications of this test in the jurisdictions that follow the traditional approach, see *ACT v Gaillard & Gaillard* [2009] ACTSC 3; *Kevern v Marshall* [2012] ACTSC 9; *Scott MacRae Investments Pty Ltd v Baylily Pty Ltd* [2011] NSWCA 82; *Australian Co-operative Foods Ltd v SW & JD Reilly & Sons Pty Ltd* (2011) 209 IR 192; [2011] NSWCA 148; *Heller Financial Services Ltd v Roman*

Solczaniuk [1989] NTSC 36; *National Australia Bank v Dixon* [2003] TASSC 57; and *Bosveld v Cardup Industrial Land Holdings Pty Ltd* (2011) 41 WAR 504; [2010] WASC 411.

12.5.6 The following extract sets out the principles that apply in jurisdictions where the reasonable approach has been adopted.

12.5.7C **Wang v Anying Group Pty Ltd**
[2009] FCA 1500

Foster J: [43] The critical words of s 31A(1), when applied to the present case, require me to be satisfied that the respondents have "... no reasonable prospect of successfully defending the proceeding ...". The following principles may be extracted from the authorities:

(a) The moving party does not have to demonstrate that the defence is hopeless or unarguable;

(b) The court must consider the pleadings and the evidence with a "critical eye" in order to see whether the respondent party has evidence of sufficient quality and weight to be able to succeed at trial (*Jefferson Ford Pty Ltd v Ford Motor Co of Australia Ltd* (2008) 167 FCR 372 at [23] (p 382) (per Finkelstein J));

(c) The respondent party is not obliged to present its whole case in order to defeat the summary judgment applicant but must at least present a sufficient outline of the evidence in order to enable the court to come to a preliminary view about the merits for the purpose of considering the statutory test in s 31A(1)(b) (*Jefferson Ford Pty Ltd* 167 FCR 372 at [22] (p 382) (per Finkelstein J)); and

(d) The test may require greater scrutiny of the pleadings and evidence in some cases than in others. In my judgment, the words of s 31A(1) compel a flexible approach. The real question in every case is not so much whether there is any issue that could arguably go to trial but rather whether there is any issue that should be permitted to go to trial. This seems to be the approach of Finkelstein J in *Jefferson Ford Pty Ltd* 167 FCR 372 and of Gordon J in the same case (as to which see [123]–[134] (pp 406–409)), although Rares J in that case at [73]–[74] (p 394) and in *Boston Commercial Services Pty Ltd v GE Capital Finance Australasia Pty Ltd* (2006) 236 ALR 720 esp at [45] (p 731) favoured a test which is much closer to the older test articulated in authorities decided under Rules of Court expressed in terms different from the language of s 31A(1)).

12.5.8 For further applications of the reasonable approach to summary judgment for the plaintiff (adopted in the Federal Court and South Australia), see *Anderson Formrite Pty Ltd v Baulderstone Hornibrook Pty Ltd* [2008] FCA 473; *Ceneavenue Pty Ltd v Martin* (2008) 67 ACSR 130; [2008] SASC 158; *Kleentex (Thailand) Co Ltd v Corporate IM Pty Ltd* [2012] SASC 71.

12.5.9 Applications of the 'no real prospect of success' test (adopted in Queensland and Victoria) where summary judgment is by the plaintiff may be seen in *DCT v Salcedo* [2005] 2 Qd R 232; *Bolton Properties Pty Ltd v JK Investments (Australia) Pty Ltd* [2009] 2 Qd R 202 as discussed above at **12.4.3** and *APN Funds Management Ltd v Australian Property Investments Strategic Pty Ltd* [2011] VSC 555.

12.5.10   Notes and questions

1. On any of traditional, no real prospect or reasonable, approaches, the court may take a robust approach to summary judgment, thus refusing to allow the defendant to go to trial. See, for example, the Queensland Court of Appeal in *Hepburn v McLaughlins Nominee Mortgage Pty Ltd* [1997] QCA 37. This approach has been urged by academics, such as Zuckerman, in order to deal with delays in the court's processing of claims: see the discussion at **1.9.4E**. Importantly, the summary disposition provisions are part of a regime that includes the overriding purpose, overarching obligations, and more rigorous case management provisions, and therefore the powers must be viewed in this context: Clyde Croft J, 'Summary Judgment Part 4.4 of the Civil Procedure Act' (VSC) [2010] *VicJSchool* 25.

2. Traditionally an order for summary judgment was considered an interlocutory order, see *Cox Brothers (Australia) Ltd v Cox* (1934) 50 CLR 314; *RJK Enterprises Pty Ltd v Webb* [2006] 2 Qd R 593; and *Schiffer v Pattison* (2005) 215 ALR 505. However, the Full Federal Court in *Jefferson Ford Pty Ltd v Ford Motor Co of Australia Ltd* (2008) 246 ALR 465 held that whether an order for summary judgment is an interlocutory or final order depends on the rules of the court. See also *Hunt v Knabe (No 2)* (1992) 8 WAR 96 and *King Investment Solutions Pty Ltd v Hussain* [2005] NSWSC 1076.

3. When deciding an application for summary judgment, to what extent must the court undertake a predictive assessment as to the prospects of success of a claim? See *Boston Commercial Services Pty Ltd v GE Capital Finance Australasia Pty Ltd* (2006) 236 ALR 720 at [42] per Rares J.

4. Can the defendant resist summary judgment by arguing that he or she wishes to test the plaintiff's case by cross-examination? See *Rosser v Austral Wine and Spirit Co Pty Ltd* [1980] VR 313.

Issue of law

12.5.11 The defendant should be given leave to defend if he or she raises a difficult and substantial question of law, which cannot be determined without full argument: *Theseus Exploration NL v Foyster* (1972) 126 CLR 507. However, the court may deal with a question of law summarily and it is within its discretion to do so: *Civil and Civic Pty Ltd v Pioneer Concrete (NT) Pty Ltd* (1991) 103 FLR 196.

12.5.12 The Victorian Court of Appeal discussed this issue in *Aquatec-Maxcon Pty Ltd v Minson Nacap Pty Ltd* (2004) 8 VR 16 at [58]–[60], stating that the mere fact that the defendant raised an intricate question of law in answer to an application for summary judgment would not be sufficient to justify refusal of summary judgment. However, their Honours held that it was inappropriate to resolve the legal issue on appeal, stating:

> It may well be that the answer to the question will turn on questions of fact which have not yet been resolved or on policy considerations which have not been ventilated before us and which merit consideration, in the first instance, by a trial judge.

See also *Jefferson Ford Pty Ltd v Ford Motor Co of Australia Ltd* (2008) 246 ALR 465; *Casella v Hewitt* [2008] WASCA 13; and *Hausman v Abigroup Contractors Pty Ltd* (2009) 29 VR 213; [2009] VSCA 288.

Failure by defendant to appear

12.5.13   If the defendant does not appear at the hearing and the plaintiff sufficiently substantiates the grounds of the application and proves service on the defendant, leave will be given to obtain summary judgment: *Traders' Co Ltd v Sutton* (1884) 6 ALT 113. However, a summary judgment given in the defendant's absence may be set aside or varied: FCR r 39.05; ACT r 1613; NSW r 36.16; NT r 22.15; Qld r 302; SA r 242; Tas r 366; Vic r 22.15; WA O 14 r 12. Such a judgment is not a default judgment and generally cannot be set aside by reference to the rules regarding default judgments: *Spira v Spira* [1939] 3 All ER 924.

12.5.14   Question

1. Is the summary procedure available to the plaintiff where the defendant has entered a conditional appearance to originating process? See *Tardiani v Steele* [1943] QWN 48.

SUMMARY JUDGMENT FOR THE DEFENDANT

12.6.1   The defendant may also apply for summary judgment in all jurisdictions: HCR 27.09.6; Federal Court Act (Cth) s 31A; ACT rr 1145, 1147; NSW r 13.4; NT r 23.03; Qld r 293; SA r 232(2)(b); Tas r 367; Civil Procedure Act 2010 (Vic) s 62; Vic r 23.03; WA O 16 r 1. The elements of the plaintiff's application (discussed above) apply with some necessary adaptation. Defendants commonly seek summary judgment where a plaintiff has commenced proceedings which are statute-barred, ie, where the limitation period has expired: see generally Chapter 6. The Tasmanian Supreme Court Rules, extracted below, set out the grounds upon which the defendant may seek summary dismissal:

12.6.2E   **Supreme Court Rules 2000 (Tas)**
Part 11 Division 4 — Summary judgment for defendant

Defendant may apply for summary judgment
367 (1) Within 10 days after appearing, a defendant to an action may apply to a judge for summary judgment.

(2) A judge may do anything set out in subrule (3) if satisfied that —
   (a)   the action is frivolous or vexatious; or
   (b)   the defendant has a good defence on the merits; or
   (c)   the action should be disposed of summarily or without pleadings.

(3) A judge may —
   (a) order that judgment be entered for the defendant, with or without costs; or
   (b) order that the plaintiff proceed to trial without pleadings; or
   (c) if all parties consent, dispose of the action finally and without appeal in a summary manner.

12.6.3 The differentiation between the general approaches to summary judgment and their operation where a plaintiff seeks summary judgment (discussed above at **12.4.1–12.4.6C** and **12.5.1**) is also evident in the case law on defendant applications. For the traditional approach, see *Northern Australian Aboriginal Legal Aid Service Inc v Bradley* (2000) 136 NTR 1; *Leerdam v Noori* [2009] NSWCA 90; *Application under the Status of Children Act* [2002] NTCA 3; *Woodham v Roberts Ltd* [2010] TASSC 31; and *Smec Australia Pty Ltd v Valentine Falls Estate Pty Ltd* [2011] WASCA 138.

12.6.4 For applications of the 'no real prospect of success' test (adopted in Queensland and Victoria) where a defendant seeks summary judgment, see *Bradshaw v Secure Funding Pty Ltd* [2012] QCA 52; *Coldham-Fussell v Commissioner of Taxation* [2011] QCA 45; *Story v Semmens* [2011] VSC; *Tomasevic v State of Victoria* [2012] VSC 148 at [305].

12.6.5 Applications of the reasonable approach to summary judgment for the defendant (adopted in the Federal Court and South Australia) may be seen in *Spencer v Commonwealth* (2010) 241 CLR 118, (2010) 269 ALR 233, [2010] HCA 28, extracted at **12.4.6C**; *Visscher v Teekay Shipping (Australia) Pty Ltd* (2011) 198 FCR 575; (2011) 284 ALR 261; [2011] FCAFC 137; *Wills v Australian Broadcasting Corporation* (2009) 173 FCR 284; (2009) 253 ALR 228; [2009] FCAFC 6; *Kowalski v MMAL Staff Superannuation Fund Pty Ltd* (2009) 178 FCR 401; (2009) 259 ALR 319 and *Davies v Minister For Urban Development and Planning* (2011) 109 SASR 518; [2011] SASC 87.

12.6.6 Where the plaintiff raises novel issues of law in his or her pleadings, an important question arises as to how the court should deal with an application by the defendant for summary judgment and/or to strike out the plaintiff's claim because no reasonable cause of action is disclosed: see **11.8.2ff**. A related question is whether the court should deal with those issues at an interlocutory stage, that is, upon the application by the defendant for summary judgment or only after a full hearing of the evidence.

This issue has arisen in Australia in the context of litigation pursued by the victims of various types of personal and institutional abuse. In some cases, this litigation was seeking to establish a duty owed to child victims of sexual abuse (*Paramasivam v Flynn* (1998) 160 ALR 203), and in other cases it has been argued that a duty is owed to Aboriginal people who are members of the Stolen Generation (*Cubillo v Commonwealth of Australia* (1999) 89 FCR 528; 163 ALR 395) or otherwise institutionalised: see *Williams v Minister Aboriginal Land Rights Act 1983* (1994) 35 NSWLR 497. In each of the cases, the action was brought outside the limitation period, and therefore the defendant sought summary judgment and/or applied to strike out pleadings, arguing that the action could not be sustained due to non-compliance with the limitation legislation: see further **Chapter 6**. In each case the plaintiff sought common law and equitable relief and the defendant argued on a summary judgment application that the claims were barred by lapse of time, either by laches (for equitable doctrines) (see **6.1.6**) or by the relevant Limitation Act. However, in each case, the claim was novel, that is, the plaintiff sought to extend the scope of the relevant duties under the substantive law.

The courts have taken different approaches in determining whether these issues should be dealt with on a motion for summary dismissal. In the *Williams* case, Priestley J (at 516) took a cautious approach:

> To enable a properly satisfactory and fully explored answer to be given to [several of the questions] Mrs Williams wishes to raise, it seems to me desirable that Mrs Williams have the opportunity of putting all relevant evidence before the Court at a trial, rather than that the matters of significance which the case raises should be dealt with on the incomplete state of the evidence at present before the Court.
>
> These considerations have influenced my general agreement with the approach of Kirby P. That approach involves conclusions, favourable to Ms Williams, about the arguability of a number of issues. I have reached some of these conclusions only with hesitation and I recognise they may be vulnerable to a strict approach. However, this case seems to me pre-eminently to be of the kind where a broad approach should be taken to questions of arguability of legal propositions which may be novel but which require careful consideration in the light of changing social circumstances.

However, in *Paramasivam v Flynn* (1998) 90 FCR 489; 160 ALR 203 the Full Federal Court held that novel questions about the operation of fiduciary duty may be dealt with in a summary application. In that case the plaintiff alleged sexual abuse by a guardian and claimed breach of fiduciary duty and assault. The assault claim was barred by the Limitation Acts (both New South Wales and the Australian Capital Territory), although the plaintiff sought to extend the limitation period in both jurisdictions. The equitable claim was potentially subject to the laches doctrine (at least under New South Wales law): see **6.1.6**. The application to extend the limitation period was dismissed due to prejudice to the respondent.

As to whether these issues should be decided at the interlocutory stage, the trial judge (Gallop J) considered that the respondent had not made out a good defence on the merits because he had not gone into evidence. Nevertheless the respondent was entitled to an order for summary judgment because the action was not maintainable, having been instituted out of time and extension of time having been refused: at 210. The Full Court found that it was not necessary for the respondent to go into evidence in order to make out a good defence to the action on the merits. The facts necessary to establish that defence were made out in the appellant's own case, if not on the pleadings, and the respondent had established, on the merits, the defence of expiry of the limitation period: at 225. In *Cubillo v Commonwealth of Australia* (extracted below), O'Loughlin J of the Federal Court held that the request for extension of time should come after a full trial of the issues.

12.6.7C   **Cubillo v Commonwealth of Australia**
                                       (1999) 89 FCR 528; 163 ALR 395
                                          Federal Court of Australia

Application to dismiss actions summarily
Introduction
[1] ... [T]he applicants, Mrs Lorna Cubillo and Mr Peter Gunner, are part-Aboriginal persons who have claimed that, as children, they were removed from their families and thereafter detained in institutions against their will until they attained (in the case of

Mrs Cubillo) the age of 18 years and (in the case of Mr Gunner) the age of 16 years; it has also been alleged that each removal occurred without the consent of the applicant or the applicant's mother.

[2] In the case of Mrs Cubillo, these events are said to have commenced in about 1945, fifty four years ago. In Mr Gunner's case, it is said that he was taken 11 years later, in 1956. Both applicants have claimed that they are members of 'the Stolen Generation', the term that is widely used to refer to the former practice of taking part-Aboriginal children from their families and placing them in dedicated missions or institutions. They have each claimed that it was the Commonwealth who was the party responsible for taking them into custody and thereafter detaining them; they have also alleged that their removal and detention was unlawful. All these claims are denied by the Commonwealth.

[3] The applicants have claimed that their removal and detention constituted 'wrongful imprisonment and deprivation of liberty'. That claim is the first of four alleged causes of action. The remaining causes of action are said to be breaches of statutory duty, of fiduciary duty and of a general duty of care. General damages allegedly arising from mental and emotional distress and a post-traumatic stress syndrome are claimed. There are also claims for aggravated and exemplary damages. ...

[5] Although it is important to recognise that the subject of the removal and detention of part-Aboriginal children has created racial, social and political problems of great complexity, it nevertheless remains the duty of the court, in the determination of the issues that are presently before the court, to limit its observations to the legal issues that have been identified during the course of argument. Historians may wish to adjudicate on the social policies of former governments and it must be left to the political leaders of the day to determine what, if any, action might be taken to arrive at a social or political solution to these problems. It would not be proper for this court to go beyond the boundaries of the legal issues that are to be determined.

The orders sought
[6] These reasons are therefore concerned with and limited to certain of the orders that were sought in a notice of motion dated 5 June 1998 that was filed by the respondent, the Commonwealth of Australia. The orders sought in that notice include orders that the statements of claim in each action be struck out and that each action be dismissed. In taking that action, the Commonwealth is relying upon the provisions of O 20, r 2 of the Rules of Court [now replaced by s 31A of the Federal Court Act]. ...

[His Honour sets out the personal history of Lorna Cubillo and Peter Gunner].

Summary dismissal of proceedings
[52] It is important to note at the outset that the issue before the court on this application for summary dismissal is not whether Mrs Cubillo and Mr Gunner would probably succeed in their action against the Commonwealth. It is whether the material before the court demonstrates that these actions should not be permitted to go to trial in the ordinary way because it is apparent that they must fail: *Webster v Lampard*, above, at CLR 602 per Mason CJ, Deane and Dawson JJ. ...

[His Honour discusses each of the causes of action pleaded by the plaintiffs, that is, guardianship, wrongful imprisonment, breach of statutory duty, breach of duty of care and breach of fiduciary duty and the relief sought. He then discusses the application to extend the relevant limitation periods. His Honour sets out the traditional approach to the summary jurisdiction, set out at 12.4.2 above].

[165] As has been earlier indicated, the Commonwealth sought an order directing that the two applications for extensions of time pursuant to s 44 of the Limitation Act be brought on for hearing and determination. Counsel for the applicants opposed that proposal, arguing that it would be necessary for both applicants to adduce oral evidence in support of their respective claims; submitting that it would not be expedient to conduct 'mini-trials' on this issue, Mr Rush QC argued that the question of the applications for extension should be dealt with as part of the substantive trial. ...

[166] [E]ven though it might ultimately be found that all causes of action accrued many years ago, 'Limitation' legislation can be used to permit extensions of time to persons who have suffered longstanding, but latent, injuries that manifest themselves years after the event: *Williams v Minister, Aboriginal Land Rights Act 1983*, above, at 499 per Kirby P. ...

[167] It has been asserted by both Mrs Cubillo and Mr Gunner that they each now suffer disabilities of that kind and that they have so suffered them from some unspecified date. Whether those injuries exist, whether they have existed for some lengthy period of time, whether they can be traced back in any meaningful way to the Commonwealth, are not matters that can be the subject of findings in these interlocutory proceedings. But their identification is sufficient to establish the need to take evidence on these and related topics. They are all questions of fact that are yet to be determined. ...

[168] Difficulty in fixing the date of the accrual of a cause of action has been the reason, in some cases, it has been held that the 'limitation' defence should be determined at trial after all the relevant evidence has been taken: *Magman International Pty Ltd v Westpac Banking Corp* (1991) 32 FCR 1; 104 ALR 575; *Wardley Australia Ltd v Western Australia* (1992) 175 CLR 514; 109 ALR 247. In *Wardley* the following observations were made by Mason CJ, Dawson, Gaudron and McHugh JJ at CLR 533–4; ALR 259–60:

> We should, however, state in the plainest of terms that we regard it as undesirable that limitation questions of the kind under consideration should be decided in interlocutory proceedings in such proceedings, insufficient is known of the damage sustained by the plaintiff and of the circumstances in which it was sustained to justify a confident answer to the question. ...

[169] A recent example of the application of the decision in *Wardley Australia Ltd v Western Australia* is to be found in *Noble v Victoria* (CA (Qld), 13 April 1999, unreported). The plaintiffs claimed that they were descendants of Jack Noble and Gary Owens, two Aboriginal men who participated in the capture of Ned Kelly and his gang at Glenrowan. It was claimed that they were each granted a reward of £50 but that the rewards were never paid. The plaintiffs' claims had been struck out but, on appeal, the court, by a majority, restored them. McPherson JA (with whom McMurdo P agreed), after referring to the statement in *Wardley's* case that it is undesirable that limitation questions should be decided in interlocutory proceedings said:

> but, for all that, a decision to strike out an action summarily as an abuse of process ought in the end to be based on the inherent weaknesses of the action itself, and not on what appears to be the potential strengths of a defence to which an answer may yet emerge. ...

[172] In *Sola Optical Australia Pty Ltd v Mills* (1987) 163 CLR 628; 75 ALR 513, a decision based on the South Australian Act, the High Court held that a fact does not need to have a bearing on a party's decision to commence proceedings in order to be 'material'; it decided that a fact is material to a party's case 'if it is both relevant to the issues to be proved if the plaintiff is to succeed in obtaining an award of damages sufficient to justify bringing the action and is of sufficient importance to be likely to have a bearing on the case': at CLR 636; ALR 519.

[173] An example of a 'material fact' was the expectation of a political solution to the problems facing the plaintiff: see *South Australia v Johnson* (1982) 42 ALR 161. ...

[177] The Commonwealth flagged its intention to challenge both Mrs Cubillo and Mr Gunner about their first knowledge of their ability to institute these proceedings. There is information on the court file which, says the Commonwealth, would establish that they each would have had much earlier knowledge. It is claimed for example, that Mrs Cubillo participated in the research for a book on the subject of the 'Stolen Generation' and that she attended at a conference dealing with the plight of children who had been removed from their families. Of Mr Gunner, it is said that his work with the Aboriginal Legal Service would have given him considerable knowledge of the legal system. Although these might become important issues, they cannot be assessed at this stage. I have mentioned them only because they were adverted to during the course of submissions on behalf of the Commonwealth. But the time to give them appropriate consideration will be when the applicants seek their extensions of time within which to prosecute their actions.

[178] For the reasons that I have endeavoured to explain, I am not prepared to order that the applications by Mrs Cubillo and Mr Gunner for extensions of time be heard and determined prior to the substantive trial. It follows, in my opinion, that I should reach the same conclusion with respect to the Commonwealth's proposal that there should be a preliminary hearing to determine whether the applicants' claims for equitable damages are barred by analogy to the barring by statute of their claims at common law or by the principle of laches. After all, no matter what cause of action is being considered, they all arise out of the same factual matrix: that is, the removal and detention of the applicants in the institutions, the way in which they were treated while in the institutions and the consequences that have flowed from that removal and detention.

12.6.8 Notes

1. The *Cubillo* case went to a full trial but the plaintiffs were ultimately unsuccessful (*Cubillo v Commonwealth of Australia* (2000) 174 ALR 97), because, among other things, O'Loughlin J declined to exercise the discretion to extend time under s 44 of the Limitation Act (NT). Due to the effluxion of time and the loss of documentary evidence, his Honour found that the Commonwealth's claims of prejudice were 'overwhelming': at 590. See J Clarke, 'Cubillo v Commonwealth' (2001) 25 *Melb Univ L Rev* 218 and R Kune, 'The Stolen Generations in Court: Explaining the Lack of Widespread Successful Litigation by Members of the Stolen Generations' (2011) 30 *U Tas L Rev* 32.

2. See also *Webber v State of New South Wales* (2004) 31 Fam LR 425 and *Brown v NSW* [2008] NSWCA 287.

3. Section 64 of the Civil Procedure Act 2010 (Vic) is designed to provide more flexibility to the court in deciding whether or not to allow a trial to proceed on the merits. That provision states as follows:

> Despite anything to the contrary in this Part or any rules of court, a court may order that a civil proceeding proceed to trial if the court is satisfied that, despite there being no real prospect of success the civil proceeding should not be disposed of summarily because—
>
> (a) it is not in the interests of justice to do so; or
>
> (b) the dispute is of such a nature that only a full hearing on the merits is appropriate.

This provision was based on a recommendation of the Victorian Law Reform Commission that r 24.02(c) of the Civil Procedure Rules (UK) be followed in Victoria. This residual discretion would allow for a full hearing of the matter, for example, in cases of public interest (Victorian Law Reform Commission, *Civil Justice Review Report*, Report No 14, 2008, p 357). Moreover, there are 'powerful public policy considerations in favour of giving litigants their day in court, particularly when the litigant is unrepresented or under-represented': The Hon Justice James Judd, 'Developments in Civil Procedure: Good and Bad', paper presented at the Supreme Court of Victoria Commercial Law Conference, *Current Issues in Commercial Law*, Melbourne, 15 August 2011, [23].

4. For a discussion of the overlap between an application for summary judgment and an application to strike out pleadings for failing to disclose a cause of action, see 11.8.3 and *Imobilari Pty Ltd v Opes Prime Stockbroking Ltd* (2008) 252 ALR 41.

STAYING OR DISMISSING PROCEEDINGS AS AN ABUSE OF PROCESS

12.7.1   If proceedings are an abuse of process, the court may order that they be stayed temporarily or permanently. The power of a superior court to stay proceedings as an abuse of process stems from its inherent power to guard its own processes and to prevent them from being subverted for improper purposes. For further discussion of the inherent jurisdiction, see 1.4.4ff.

There is some overlap between abuse of process and other claims, in particular, contempt of court and the tort of malicious prosecution. The tort of malicious prosecution will give rise to a remedy in damages, however it may only be brought at the completion of the challenged proceedings: *Halsbury's Laws of Australia*, 'Malicious Prosecution', [415-1725], LexisNexis, 2007.

Abuse of process is available to stop an action at any stage of the litigation and applies, though 'with somewhat different emphases attending its exercise', to civil and criminal proceedings: *Moti v R* (2011) 283 ALR 393, [2011] HCA 50 at [11], quoting *Batistatos v Roads and Traffic Authority of New South Wales* (2006) 226 CLR 256; (2006) 227 ALR 425; [2006] HCA 27 at [8]. *Batistatos* is extracted below at **12.7.9C**.

12.7.2   The power of courts to prevent abuse of process is related to their contempt power, in that the court has the power to control proceedings to ensure that its functions and processes are used correctly. These powers are intended to prevent a legal action which has no chance of succeeding or which is being used by one party improperly. In *Rogers v The Queen* (1994) 181 CLR 251; (1994) 123 ALR 417, McHugh J (at 286) observed that abuses of process usually fall into one of three categories:

(1)   the court's procedures are invoked for an illegitimate purpose;
(2)   the use of the court's procedures is unjustifiably oppressive to one of the parties; or
(3)   the use of the court's procedures would bring the administration of justice into disrepute.

McHugh J further commented (at 286) that:

Many, perhaps the majority of, cases of abuse of procedure arise from the institution of proceedings. But any procedural step in the course of proceedings that have been properly instituted is capable of being an abuse of the court's process.

For an application of the wide operation of the doctrine and its interaction with tort and other procedures (eg, summary judgment), see *Bradshaw v Secure Funding Pty Ltd* [2012] QCA 52.

In civil matters, the commencement of proceedings can by itself be an abuse of the process of the court. The rules in each jurisdiction give court officials the power to refuse to accept filed documents or refer a filed document to the court if the document is frivolous or vexatious or is an abuse of process: HCR r 6.07; FCR rr 2.26, 2.27; ACT r 6142; NSW r 4.15; NT r 27.08; Qld r 15; SA r 53; Tas r 82A; Vic r 27.06; WA O 67 r 5.

12.7.3   In all jurisdictions, the court may strike out all or part of the offending party's pleadings (for example, if those pleadings harass, embarrass or intimidate the other party) or the court may stay proceedings permanently. Abuse of process will often be pleaded by the defendant, although the plaintiff may argue that a defence or counterclaim is an abuse of process.

Establishing abuse of process

12.7.4   Abuse of process is a misuse of a court's procedure which would 'be manifestly unfair to a party to litigation before it, or would otherwise bring the administration of justice into disrepute among right-thinking people': *Hunter v Chief Constable of the West Midlands Police* [1982] AC 529 at 536 per Lord Diplock.

In the following extract, the High Court discusses what must be established by the applicant seeking to stay proceedings temporarily or permanently for abuse of process:

12.7.5C   **Williams v Spautz**
(1992) 174 CLR 509
High Court of Australia

Mason CJ, Dawson, Toohey and McHugh JJ (at 513): This appeal is brought by the appellants against orders of the Court of Appeal of New South Wales made 12 December 1990. By those orders, the Court of Appeal set aside orders obtained by the appellants from Smart J in the Supreme Court staying certain prosecutions instituted by the respondent Dr Spautz against the first two appellants and Mr L Gibbs (now deceased) on the ground that the proceedings constituted an abuse of the process of the court.

The facts and the proceedings

From [514] 1973 to 1980, Dr Spautz was a senior lecturer in the Department of Commerce at the University of Newcastle. In 1977, Professor Williams was appointed to the Chair of Commerce at the University. By the end of 1978 and throughout 1979, Dr Spautz was in serious conflict with Professor Williams; he alleged plagiarism in the Professor's doctoral thesis; disputed the Professor's appointment to an administrative post within the Department and threatened litigation. Towards the end of 1979, the dispute reached the University Council and a committee, chaired by Professor Michael Carter, was appointed to report on and attempt to resolve the dispute. Upon the recommendation of the committee, the University Council directed Dr Spautz to stop his one-man campaign against Professor Williams; it also advised Dr Spautz that disobedience of the direction would be regarded as misconduct within the meaning of the relevant University by-law. Subsequently, a further committee, chaired by the Deputy Chancellor, Mr Justice Kirby, was appointed to investigate the conduct of Dr Spautz and, in particular, to report whether he had disobeyed the Council direction. Following the report of this committee, which made no recommendations but found in favour of Professor Williams on a number of issues, the Council resolved on 20 May 1980 to dismiss Dr Spautz, effective as from 23 May, unless he resigned prior to that time. Dr Spautz did not resign and thus his dismissal took effect.

In August 1980 Dr Spautz commenced proceedings in the Equity Division of the Supreme Court of New South Wales seeking a declaration that his dismissal was invalid. ...

Those proceedings were the first of many forays by Dr Spautz into the litigation process. From 11 August 1981 to the present date, Dr Spautz has commenced over thirty proceedings — the majority, criminal prosecutions — against persons who occupy positions of authority at the University or who played a role in the events leading to his dismissal. ...

Each of the appellants [in this case, Professor Williams, Mr Morris and Mr Gibbs] commenced separate proceedings seeking, inter alia, declarations that the prosecutions [for criminal defamation] were an abuse of the process of the court. ... [T]hese proceedings came before Smart J who, in final orders made 17 June 1988, granted the declarations sought and stayed the prosecutions permanently. ...

After examining in detail the conduct of Dr Spautz during his self-proclaimed campaign for justice, Smart J made this finding of fact:

> The predominant purpose of Dr Spautz in instituting and maintaining the criminal proceedings, the subject of the present applications, against Profs Gibbs and Williams and Mr Morris was to exert pressure upon the University of Newcastle to reinstate him and/ or to agree to a favourable settlement of his wrongful dismissal case. ...

On appeal, the Court of Appeal rejected a challenge to the central finding concerning Dr Spautz's predominant purpose.

The trial judge also found that Dr Spautz had other purposes in instituting the various criminal proceedings and that most of those purposes were improper. One such purpose was the collection of material for research which Dr Spautz claimed to be conducting into corrupt practices in Australian institutions. Another purpose was vindication of Dr Spautz's reputation. Although the trial judge referred in one passage in his judgment to vindication of reputation as not being a proper purpose for a person to have in instituting or maintaining proceedings for criminal defamation, later his Honour said that this purpose, though interwoven with the dominant purpose of securing reinstatement, did not detract from the finding that securing reinstatement was the dominant and improper purpose. ...

The jurisdiction to grant a permanent stay for abuse of process

It is well established that Australian [518] superior courts have inherent jurisdiction to stay proceedings which are an abuse of process (*Clyne v NSW Bar Association* (1960) 104 CLR 186, at p 201; *Barton v The Queen* (1980) 147 CLR 75, at pp 96, 107, 116; *Jago v New South Wales District Court* (1989) 168 CLR 23). Although the term 'inherent jurisdiction' has acquired common usage in the present context, the question is strictly one of the power of a court to stay proceedings. That power arises from the need for the court to be able to exercise effectively the jurisdiction which the court has to dispose of the proceedings. ...

Is it essential to the exercise of jurisdiction that the proceedings have been instituted not only for an improper purpose but also without reasonable grounds?

What the appellants assert here is that the court will grant a permanent stay in the exercise of its inherent jurisdiction to prevent abuse of process where the proceedings have been instituted for an improper purpose, notwithstanding that the initial proceedings, if prosecuted to a conclusion, may result in the judgment or conviction sought by the moving party. ...

In our view, the power must extend to the prevention of an abuse of process resulting in oppression, even if the moving party has a prima facie case or must be assumed to have a prima facie case. Take, for example, a situation in which the moving party commences criminal proceedings. He or she can establish a prima facie case against the defendant but has no intention of prosecuting the proceedings to a conclusion because he or she wishes to use them only as a means of extorting a pecuniary benefit from the defendant. It would be extraordinary if the court lacked power to prevent the abuse of process in these circumstances. ...

The boundaries of abuse of process

The observations of the Privy Council in *King v Henderson* [1898] AC, at p 731 and those of Isaacs J in *Dowling* (1915) 20 CLR, at pp 521–522, to which we referred earlier, represent an attempt to achieve a formulation which keeps the concept of abuse of process within reasonable bounds. To say that a purpose of a litigant in bringing proceedings which is not within the scope of the proceedings constitutes, without more, an abuse of process might unduly expand the concept. The purpose of a litigant may be to bring the proceedings to a successful conclusion so as to take advantage of an entitlement or benefit which the law gives the litigant in that event.

Thus, to take an example mentioned in argument, an alderman prosecutes another alderman who is a political opponent for failure to disclose a relevant pecuniary interest when voting to approve a contract, intending to secure the opponent's conviction so that he or she will then be disqualified from office as an alderman by reason of that conviction, pursuant to local government legislation regulating the holding of such offices. The ultimate purpose of bringing about disqualification is not within the scope of the criminal process instituted by the prosecutor. But the immediate purpose of the prosecutor is within that scope. And the existence of the ultimate purpose cannot constitute an abuse of process when that purpose is to bring about a result for which the law provides in the event that the proceedings terminate in the prosecutor's favour.

It is otherwise when the purpose of bringing the proceedings is not to prosecute them to a conclusion but to use them as a means of obtaining some advantage for which they are not designed *(In re Majory* (1955) Ch 600, at pp 623–624) or some collateral advantage beyond what the law offers (*Goldsmith v Sperrings Ltd* (1977) 1 WLR, at pp 498–499; see also *Varawa* (1911) 13 CLR, at p 91). So, in *Dowling,* Isaacs J pointed out that (44) (1915) 20 CLR, at p 524:

> ... if, for instance, it had been shown that the Society had simply threatened Dowling that unless he did what they had no right to demand from him, namely, give up certain names, they would proceed to sequestration, and they had proceeded accordingly, there would have been in law an abuse of the process.

However, because the Society wished to use the process for the very purpose for which it was designed, there was no abuse of process.

Is it essential to the exercise of the jurisdiction that there should be an improper act as well as an improper purpose?

Priestley JA drew heavily on the law relating to the tort of collateral abuse of process, particularly judicial decisions in the United States, to support the proposition that a permanent stay will not be granted in the absence of an improper act, improper purpose alone being insufficient to ground such a stay. His Honour drew a distinction between 'the actual improper use of the process ... [and] the predominant purpose of the party for the misuse' ((1990) 21 NSWLR, at p 278), only the first satisfying the requirement that there be an act. A similar distinction seems to have been drawn by Clarke JA in *Hanrahan v Ainsworth* ((1990) 22 NSWLR 73, at p 118) between the institution or maintenance of an action for an improper purpose and 'an association of process and an overt act which, in combination, demonstrate the improper purpose'.

Neither the authorities in Australia nor those in England insist on the need for an improper act as an essential ingredient in the concept of abuse of process. However, the authorities do speak of the 'use' of process for a purpose which stamps it as an abuse (see, for example, *Varawa* (1911) 13 CLR, at p 55; *Metall and Rohstoff v Donaldson Inc* (1990) 1 QB, at p 469). That is not surprising because an improper act may, in appropriate circumstances, afford evidence of improper purpose and abuse of process. ...

Priestley JA was also concerned to discount the [529] notion that abuse of process calls for an inquiry into the moving party's motivation in instituting the proceedings. Much earlier, Isaacs J was at pains to distinguish between motivation and abuse of process (*Dowling* (1915) 20 CLR, at pp 521–523). Inquiry into motivation alone might prove a fragile foundation on which to base an exercise of the power to grant a permanent stay. For that reason, apart from any other, it is more satisfactory to base an exercise of the jurisdiction in cases of improper purpose upon a use or threatened use of the proceedings for such a purpose. Then the conclusion which the court reaches is more likely to be founded upon objective evidence rather than subjective evidence of intention.

Predominant purpose

It has been suggested that the criterion for abuse of process is whether the improper purpose is the sole purpose of the moving party (see, for example, the use of the word 'merely' by Isaacs J in *Varawa* (1911) 13 CLR, at p 91). ... However, in more recent times it has been said, in our view correctly, that the predominant purpose is the criterion. That was the test applied by Lord Denning in *Goldsmith v Sperrings Ltd* (1977) 1 WLR, at p 496 and by the English Court of Appeal in *Metall and Rohstoff v Donaldson Inc.* In giving the judgment of the Court in the latter case, Slade LJ observed (54) [1990] 1 QB, at p 469:

> [A] person alleging such an abuse must show that the predominant purpose of the other party in using the legal process has been one other than that for which it was designed.

It is, of course, well established that the onus of satisfying the court that there is an abuse of process lies upon the party alleging it. The onus is 'a heavy one', to use the words of Scarman LJ in *Goldsmith v Sperrings Ltd* [1977] 1 WLR, at p 498 and the power to grant a permanent stay is one to be exercised only in the most exceptional circumstances (*Jago* (1989) 168 CLR, at p 34; see also *Sang* [1980] AC, at p 455). ...

Conclusion

Although [530] the primary judge did not express his findings in terms that the use of the proceedings was for an improper purpose, the findings are so expressed as to make it clear that Dr Spautz threatened to use the proceedings for an improper purpose and that his commencement and maintenance of the proceedings were, in pursuance of that purpose, undertaken predominantly to that end. There was therefore a relevant use of the proceedings for an improper purpose.

[The appeal was allowed by **Mason CJ, Brennan, Dawson, Toohey** and **McHugh JJ. Deane** and **Gaudron JJ** dissented.]

12.7.6 *Williams v Spautz* was cited by Mason CJ in *Coe v Commonwealth of Australia (The Wiradjuri Claim)* (1993) 118 ALR 193. In that case, his Honour permanently stayed proceedings by the Wiradjuri people for a declaration that they are the owners of a substantial part of southern and central New South Wales, because the proceedings had been brought for an improper purpose, namely a political purpose. The land claimed extended from the Wambool (Macquarie) River on the northern border, to the Murray River on the southern border, and from the Great Dividing Range and the Murrumbidjeri (Murrimbidgee) River on the eastern border to the flood plains of the Kalar (Lachlan) River on the western border. This comprised approximately 80,000 square kilometres. The owners of the private allotments within the area claimed they had not been joined and his Honour was of the view that without these owners being joined, the court could not make binding declarations adverse to their interests.

In relation to the improper purpose, Mason CJ said (at 207):

> The second defendant contends that the predominant purpose of bringing the proceedings is not to litigate them to a successful conclusion but rather that they should serve as an aid to a political process or campaign foreign to the litigation, namely, to contribute to a political settlement of claims made by the Aboriginal people of Australia or by the Wiradjuri who constitute part of that people. The second defendant submits that the inference that the proceedings have been brought for this ulterior and illegitimate purpose should be drawn from the fact that the core

of the plaintiff's case is the sovereignty claim, notwithstanding that it is an untenable claim. Certainly the sovereignty claim is the central element in the case pleaded in the statement of claim. Furthermore, the genocide claim features prominently in the statement of claim, despite the difficulties associated with it. In addition, there are technical shortcomings: the inadequate description of the lands claimed and the failure to join interested parties. Indeed, the unwieldy nature of the proceedings arising from the joinder of so many grounds for relief in relation to such a large area of land claimed instead of presenting manageable claims to defined parcels of land for resolution points to the purpose of using the proceedings for political purposes.

The affidavit of Mr John McDonnell who deposes to the making of various statements by Mr Paul Coe, the brother of the plaintiff and the Chairman of the Aboriginal Legal Service which acts for the plaintiff in these proceedings, supports the existence of this purpose. These statements indicate that the principal purpose of the proceedings is to pursue the sovereignty claim in order to play a part in creating the impression that the Aboriginal people have rationally based legal claims to much of New South Wales with the consequence that the farming community should start negotiating with the Wiradjuri with respect to the payment of royalties for occupation of traditional Wiradjuri lands. In addition, the statements indicate that the opposition of the States to the Federal *Mabo* legislation left Aboriginal people with no alternative but to bring land claims, such as that involved here, in the eastern States. The plaintiff has not contested the making of these statements.

In the result, his Honour struck out the entire statement of claim, leaving the plaintiff to file an amended statement of claim 'confined to tenable claims pleaded in proper form' (at 207).

12.7.7   Notes and questions

1. See *Roberts v Wayne Roberts Concrete Constructions Pty Ltd* (2004) 208 ALR 532, (particularly at [55]–[56]) Supreme Court of New South Wales per Barrett J for an interesting discussion of improper purpose in the context of abuse of process.

2. To what extent might an arrangement between a party and a non-party (eg, a litigation funder) about the litigation constitute an abuse of process? *Campbells Cash and Carry Pty Ltd v Fostif Pty Ltd* (2006) 229 CLR 386; 229 ALR 58 is authority for the proposition that there is no overarching general rule/public policy that an arrangement with a third party (such as a litigation funder) will constitute an abuse of process. However, the issue remains controversial; see the discussion of the New South Wales Court of Appeal in *Project 28 Pty Ltd v Barr* [2005] NSWCA 240 and Full Federal Court in *Deloitte Touche Tohmatsu v JP Morgan Portfolio Services Ltd* (2007) 240 ALR 540 and the High Court judgments in *Jeffery & Katauskas Pty Ltd v SST Consulting Pty Ltd* (2009) 239 CLR 75; (2009) 83 ALJR 1180; [2009] HCA 43 and *Equuscorp Pty Ltd v Haxton* (2012) 286 ALR 12; [2012] HCA 7. See also A Walters, 'Anonymous Funders and Abuse of Process' (1998) 114 *LQR* 207.

3. For more discussion on the development of litigation funding in Australia and the judicial system's response, see Standing Committee of Attorneys-General, *Litigation Funding in Australia*, Discussion Paper, May 2006; Victorian Law Reform Commission, *Civil Justice Review Report*, May 2008, Ch 6 and P Spender, 'After *Fostif*: Lingering Uncertainties and Controversies about Litigation Funding' (2008) 18 *J Jud Admin* 101.

Delay constituting abuse of process

12.7.8   Pursuant to the inherent jurisdiction and the statutory powers discussed in **Chapter 1**, superior courts may stay proceedings for abuse of process where there has been a considerable delay in the commencement or in the conduct of proceedings. The rationale of this power is that continuation of the proceedings is harsh and oppressive to the defendants: see generally *Walton v Gardiner* (1993) 177 CLR 378; (1993) 112 ALR 289; [1993] HCA 77.

The High Court discussed this power in the following extract:

12.7.9C   **Batistatos v Roads and Traffic Authority of New South Wales**
(2006) 226 CLR 256; 227 ALR 425
High Court of Australia
(footnotes omitted)

[The plaintiff became a quadriplegic after suffering catastrophically disabling injuries in a motor vehicle accident on 21 August 1965. He commenced proceedings in 1994. These proceedings were not statute-barred under the Limitation Act (NSW) due to the plaintiff's disabilities. Between 1996 and 2004, the defendants brought applications for summary disposal, striking out the plaintiff's pleadings as an abuse of process under the Supreme Court Rules and a stay or dismissal based on abuse of process under the inherent jurisdiction. These applications were refused at first instance but allowed on appeal to the New South Wales Court of Appeal: **Mason P, Giles** and **Bryson JJA**.]

Gleeson CJ, Gummow, Hayne and Crennan JJ at 438:

The Court of Appeal

...

[50] The leading judgment in the Court of Appeal was delivered by Bryson JA. His Honour treated as the same in substance the complaints made by the defendants that the proceedings were an abuse of process and that they were irretrievably prejudiced by reason of the delay in the bringing of the proceedings ... .

[53] His Honour ... consider[ed] ... the exercise of the inherent jurisdiction to stay proceedings by reason of the great delay in the commencement of the action. Bryson JA referred to the statement by Dixon J in *Cox v Journeaux (No 2)* (1935) 52 CLR 713 at 720:

> A litigant is entitled to submit for determination according to the due course of procedure a claim which he believes he can establish, although its foundation may in fact be slender. It is only when to permit it to proceed would amount to an abuse of jurisdiction, or would clearly inflict unnecessary injustice upon the opposite party that a suit should be stopped.

[54] His Honour discountenanced any approach which saw the absence of a statutory time bar as in some sense an authorisation to bring proceedings at the particular time within the statutory period when they were instituted. His Honour, correctly, emphasised that statutory time bars speak to the consequence of the passage of time, regardless of other considerations. He said:

> Delay is not what the [Limitation Act] authorises, literally or in substance. It operates in quite another way, by preventing proceedings being brought after prescribed times,

irrespective of whether or not the proceedings can be fairly adjudicated. Some statutory time limits are quite short, for example time limits of 2 years or 3 are sometimes prescribed, and there must be many cases where a fair hearing could be conducted even if those statutory limits have not been observed. The present case is one at the extremes, as almost 3 decades passed before the proceedings were commenced, and 4 decades will have passed before the proceedings ever go to trial. The [Limitation Act] cannot in my view close the court's eyes to the practical inability of reaching a decision based on any real understanding of the facts, and the practical impossibility of giving the defendants any real opportunity to participate in the hearing, to contest them or, if it should be right to do so, to admit liability on an informed basis.

[55] The critical holding by Bryson JA appears in the sentence:

> No more than a formal enactment of the process of hearing and determining the plaintiff's claim could take place; it cannot be expected that the process would be just. ...

[56] In his concurring reasons, Giles JA dealt as follows with the two strands in the defendants' applications for a permanent stay. His Honour dealt with the first strand saying:

> While the defendants did not establish that the plaintiff's case was untenable, nor did the plaintiff demonstrate its strength; on the limited material disclosed, it is not a strong case.

[57] ... [H]is Honour observed that whether the defendants could have a fair trial necessarily required consideration of the negligence alleged against them. The negligence was alleged in broad terms and the more generously the terms of the pleading of the plaintiff's case, the more difficult it was for the defendants to meet the allegations after so long a time. His Honour continued:

> The plaintiff's case was not narrowed by proffering a meaningful account from the plaintiff of how he came to run off the road, or an expert report identifying material deficiencies in the design, construction, maintenance or state of the roadway. It is particularly against that background that it would be unfair and oppressive on the defendants to require them to attempt to meet such a generous case under the difficulties brought about by the lapse of time.

The third member of the Court of Appeal, Mason P, agreed with both judgments.

The appeals to this court

...

[61] Counsel for the plaintiff developed the submission by placing particular emphasis upon the operation of s 52 of the Limitation Act. This had suspended the running of the limitation period for the duration of the disability suffered by the plaintiff. Reference was made to a number of English authorities. These were said to demonstrate that where there is a statutory limitation period any exercise of power to stay proceedings commenced within that period must be exceptional and could not be supported merely by prejudice which might be expected to flow from the effluxion of time within the limitation period. The plaintiff submitted that some element of 'oppressive' conduct on the part of the plaintiff must be discernible before the court would exercise the power to order a permanent stay. The 'oppression' lay in conduct which was burdensome, harsh, wrongful.

Conclusions on the appeals

[62] There is no substance in the negative implication which the plaintiff seeks to draw from an unexpired statutory limitation period. As Bryson JA pointed out, periods of statutory limitation operate indifferently to the existence of what might be classified as delay on the part of a plaintiff. Section 63 of the Limitation Act provides for the extinction of causes of action 'to recover any debt damages or other money'. But s 68A requires a party claiming the benefit of extinction to plead that extinguishment. To say that a limitation period has not run is to say that the potential defendant, if now sued, has no accrued defence to the action.

[63] In that setting it is unsatisfactory to speak of a common law 'right' which may be exercised within the applicable statutory limitation period, and of the enacting legislature as having 'manifested its intention that a plaintiff should have a legal right to commence proceeding with his action'. The words are those of Lord Diplock in *Birkett v James*. The difficulty is in the expression 'a legal right'. The plaintiff certainly has a 'right' to institute a proceeding. But the defendant also has 'rights'. One is to plead in defence an available limitation defence. Another distinct 'right' is to seek the exercise of the power of the court to stay its processes in certain circumstances. On its part, the court has an obligation owed to both sides to quell their controversy according to law.

[64] It is a long, and impermissible, step to deny the existence of what may be the countervailing right of a defendant by imputation to the legislature of an intent, not manifested in the statutory text, to require the court to give absolute priority to the exercise by the plaintiff within the limitation period of the right to initiate proceedings. The truth is that limitation periods operate by reference to temporal limits which are indifferent to the presence or absence of lapses of time which may merit the term 'delay'.

[65] The 'right' of the plaintiff with a common law claim to institute an action is not at large. It is subject to the operation of the whole of the applicable procedural and substantive law administered by the court, whose processes are enlivened in the particular circumstances. This includes the principles respecting abuse of process.

[Their Honours discuss the principles in *Birkett v James* [1978] AC 297 at 320; [1977] 2 All ER 801].

...

[69] The descriptions [of the principles of abuse of process] given in this court ... post-date *Birkett v James* and do not provide any ground for a requirement of oppressive conduct by the plaintiff. Rather, as in the circumstances of the present case, attention must be directed to the burdensome effect upon the defendants of the situation that has arisen by lapse of time. The Court of Appeal held that this was so serious that a fair trial was not possible. The result was that to permit the plaintiff's case to proceed would clearly inflict unnecessary injustice upon the defendants.

[70] What Deane J said in *Oceanic Sun Line Special Shipping Co Inc v Fay*, with respect to the staying of local proceedings, is applicable also to a case such as the present one. His Honour emphasised that there was no 'requirement that the continuance of the action would involve moral delinquency on the part of the plaintiff'; what was decisive was the objective effect of the continuation of the action.

[71] In assessing that effect, there must be taken into account the consideration expressed by Dixon J in *Cox v Journeaux (No 2)* and set out earlier in these reasons. Bryson JA in terms

did so. He went on to remark in that connection that the defendants had not shown that the plaintiff's action was 'clearly without foundation'. But, he concluded that there was 'in practical terms nothing of utility to place in the balance against the defendants' claim for a permanent stay'.

[72] There was no error of principle in the decision of the Court of Appeal.

[**Kirby** and **Callinan JJ** delivered separate dissenting judgments.]

12.7.10 Notes and questions

1. Do you agree with the reasoning of the majority in this case? Compare the comments of Callinan J at [233]:

> I cannot accept that the fact that the holding of a fair trial because of effluxion of time within the limitation period has become very difficult, perhaps even impossible, can justify a stay. There must be many cases in which objectively a fair trial is impossible. A court may not know that this is so in a particular instance but will often be aware that what is taking place in a trial falls far short of the ideal. That cannot justify the stopping of the case by the court.

2. How do the procedures in this case compare to those used in *Cubillo v Commonwealth of Australia*, extracted at **12.6.7C**?

3. The issue of *Birkett v James* [1978] AC 297; [1977] 2 All ER 801 and the timely conduct of claims is discussed at **5.3.1ff**. The law relating to limitation periods is discussed in **Chapter 6**.

4. The power to stay proceedings for delay amounting to abuse of process has been exercised in criminal and civil proceedings. The High Court has opined that the difficulty in dividing litigation into 'criminal' and 'civil' categories is reason enough to reject a principle founded on drawing such a distinction. Moreover, their Honours stated that it is not right to:

> ... see the administration of the civil law as giving rise to judgments worthy of less respect than those reached on the trial of indictable or other offences. No doubt account must be taken of the different standards of proof. Account must also be taken of the fact that there are cases in which issues tried in civil litigation include issues that have been, or could be, the subject of criminal prosecution: *D'Orta–Ekenaike v Victoria Legal Aid* (2005) 223 CLR 1 at 29; 214 ALR 92 at 110.

5. See also J Goudkamp, 'Delay in Commencing Proceedings within the Limitation Period in Australia' (2007) 26 *CJQ* 185; S Henchliffe, 'Abuse of Process and Delay in Criminal Prosecutions — Current Law and Practice' (2002) 22(1) *ABR* 18; J Hunter, 'Abuse of Process Savages Criminal Issue Estoppel' (1995) 18 *UNSWLJ* 151; N Mullany, 'Conduct of Defence and Abuse of Process' (1995) 3 *Tort L Rev* 177.

VEXATIOUS LITIGANTS

12.8.1   Vexatious proceedings are those which are intended to harass or annoy, cause delay or taken for some other ulterior purpose or lack reasonable grounds: B Cairns, *Australian Civil Procedure*, 9th ed, Thomson Reuters, 2011, p 114. In most jurisdictions, the court may restrain specific people from bringing further legal actions without the leave of the court if they have been habitually using the court's processes improperly. Such persons are termed 'vexatious litigants'. Persons declared to be vexatious litigants are prevented from bringing actions without first seeking leave of the court. See *Williams v Spautz* extracted at **12.7.5C** for an example.

12.8.2E	**High Court Rules**
	Rule 6.06 — Vexatious proceedings

6.06.1 Upon the application of a Law Officer, the Australian Government Solicitor, or the Principal Registrar, the Court or a Justice, if satisfied that a person, alone or in concert with any other, frequently and without reasonable ground has instituted or has attempted to institute vexatious legal proceedings may, having given that person an opportunity to be heard, order that he or she shall not, without the leave of the Court or a Justice, commence any proceeding or make any application in the original or the appellate jurisdiction of the Court.

6.06.2 Leave shall not be given under this rule unless the Court or a Justice is satisfied that the proposed proceeding or application is not an abuse of the process of the Court and that there is prima facie ground for the proceeding.

12.8.3   The power to restrain vexatious litigants may be contained in a statute: Supreme Court Act 1933 (ACT) s 67A; Vexatious Proceedings Act 2008 (NSW) s 8; Vexatious Proceedings Act (NT) s 7; Vexatious Proceedings Act 2005 (Qld) s 6; Supreme Court Act 1935 (SA) s 39; Supreme Court Civil Procedure Act 1932 (Tas) s 194G; Supreme Court Act 1986 (Vic) s 21; Vexatious Proceedings Restriction Act 2002 (WA) s 4; and/or the Rules of Court: HCR r 6.06; FCR Div 6.1.

The other statutes and rules dealing with vexatious litigants are in substantially similar terms to HCR r 6.06 (extracted above) and vary mainly in terms of who may apply for an order declaring a person vexatious. Some provide for a person aggrieved to make an application, or for the court to make a decision of its own motion or on an application by a registrar, while others require an application by the relevant Attorney-General.

12.8.4   The legal principles relevant to the declaration of vexatious litigants have been summarised in the following case:

12.8.5C	**Attorney-General for the State of Victoria v Weston**
	[2004] VSC 314
	Supreme Court of Victoria

Whelan J:

Summary of legal principles

[23] It seems to me that the applicable legal principles may be summarised as follows:

(1) The application seeks a remedy of a most serious nature and a clear and compelling case must be shown to warrant it.

(2) The requirements of the section are that the person must have

- instituted proceedings
- which are vexatious
- and to have done so habitually and persistently and without reasonable cause.

If the requirements are met, the Court must then consider whether an order ought to be made.

(3) A proceeding is 'instituted' where originating process is filed, and also where a person counterclaims, appeals against an otherwise final determination of the substantive matter, or applies to have an otherwise final determination set aside. Interlocutory applications and appeals on interlocutory applications do not ordinarily constitute the institution of proceedings.

(4) Vexatious proceedings are proceedings which have either been brought for an improper purpose, or which have been revealed to be hopeless. Hopelessness ought to be apparent from the ultimate disposition. A genuine claim, or element of a claim, may exist within a vexatious proceeding, where it is deeply buried in untenable claims and bizarre allegations.

(5) Vexatious proceedings are instituted 'habitually' where they appear to be commenced as a matter of course. 'Persistence' suggests determination and an element of stubbornness. An absence of reasonable grounds will necessarily be the position where the proceedings have been revealed to be hopeless.

(6) If the requirements of the section are met, the person's conduct as a whole must be then assessed to determine if, in all the circumstances, an order ought to be made.

12.8.6 This statement has been applied in Victorian cases eg, *Attorney-General (Vic) v Moran* [2008] VSC 159 and cited in several South Australian decisions including *Kowalski v Mitsubishi Motors Australia Ltd* [2005] SASC 433.

12.8.7 Guidelines to determine whether a litigant is vexatious were provided by the Full Federal Court in *Freeman v National Australia Bank Ltd* (2006) 230 ALR 213; [2006] FCAFC 67 at [24]. *Freeman* has been applied in *Singh v Secretary, Dept of Families, Housing, Community Services and Indigenous Affairs* (2011) 282 ALR 56; [2011] FCA 833 and note *Singh v Secretary, Dept of Education, Employment and Workplace Relations (No 3)* [2011] FCA 1219 where a person who had been declared to be a vexatious litigant appealed against the decline of permission to proceed in subsequent proceedings.

12.8.8   Further reading

N Kirby, 'When Rights Cause Injustice: A Critique of the Vexatious Proceedings Act 2008 (NSW)' (2009) 31 *Syd L Rev* 163.

C Thompson, 'Vexatious Litigants — Old Phenomenon, Modern Methodology: A Consideration of the Vexatious Proceedings Restriction Act 2002 (WA)' (2004) 14 *J Jud Admin* 64.

Victorian Law Reform Committee, *Inquiry into Vexatious Litigants*, December 2008.

Further reading

12.9.1   Articles

A Beck, 'Onus of Proof in Summary Judgment Proceedings' (1987) *NZLJ* 143.

R Fox, 'Criminal Delay as an Abuse of Process' (1990) 16 *Monash LR* 64.

B Paxton, 'Domestic Violence and Abuse of Process' (2003) 17(1) *AFL* 7.

K Rapael, 'Collection of Commercial Debts — a Case for Summary Judgment' (1984) 22 *LSJ* 156.

S Smith, 'Vexatious Litigants and their Judicial Control' (1989) 15 *Monash LR* 48.

A Zuckerman, 'Quality and Economy in Civil Procedure: The Case for Commuting Correct Judgments for Timely Judgments' (1994) 14 *Oxford J Legal Stud* 353.

Discovery

## CHAPTER 13

OVERVIEW

The term 'discovery' is used to refer to the various procedures by which one party to litigation is able to obtain information and documents held by other parties. The purpose of the rules which facilitate disclosure is to ensure the parties are fully apprised of the case to be met at trial, and have access to relevant information which may support their own cases. It is also important that relevant facts are available to be brought before the court to assist it in its function of determining where the truth lies. By assisting parties to have more detailed knowledge of the evidence available in their case, discovery processes may enable parties to assess their prospects of success earlier and more accurately, and may as a result enhance the prospect of settling disputes.

Discovery encompasses processes by which parties disclose relevant documents to their opponents and make those documents available for inspection. In some jurisdictions this extends to documents in the possession of third parties. It also encompasses processes enabling one party to ask the other a series of questions, known as 'interrogatories', designed to obtain admissions and again to apprise the interrogating party of the case to be met at trial.

There are a number of other procedures available under the rules which, though not strictly encompassed by the term 'discovery', further assist in defining issues and obtaining evidence for trial. These will be considered in Chapter 14.

If limitations were not placed on these procedures, the expenses associated with the discovery processes could be prohibitive, and disproportionate to the relief sought in the litigation. Recent reviews of the court rules have resulted in a range of reforms. In some jurisdictions, for example, discovery of documents is no longer undertaken as of course but requires the leave of the court. Similarly, in several jurisdictions interrogatories may only be delivered with the leave of the court. The reforms are intended to contain costs and prevent abuse, though still endeavouring to ensure the discovery processes are able to achieve their aims.

There are also principles and relationships which are so important that the law must sometimes protect them, even if it means relevant information is not made available to all parties and the courts. The procedures in relation to discovery are therefore also constrained by principles about privilege and other restrictions which attempt to strike a balance between full access and valid protection of important relationships and other interests.

The work undertaken in the High Court in its original jurisdiction is now largely confined to constitutional work. Very often that work proceeds by way of stated case under s 18 of the Judiciary Act 1903 (Cth) or by demurrer (The demurrer is a plea which, only for the purpose of obtaining a ruling on some question of law, admits the truth of the opponent's pleading but asserts that it does not lead to the conclusion for which the opponent contends. See further: **11.2.19**). In recognition of this, the High Court Rules 2004 do not include rules relating to the discovery processes discussed in this chapter. Should circumstances arise where discovery processes are necessary, appropriate orders may be made at a directions hearing.

DISCOVERY AND INSPECTION OF DOCUMENTS

Requirement for discovery and inspection of documents

Australian Capital Territory, Northern Territory, Queensland, South Australia, Tasmania, Victoria, Western Australia

---

13.1.1E   **Civil Procedures Rules 2006 (ACT)**
Division 2.8.2 — Disclosure of documents

605 Discoverable documents

A document that is, or has at any time been, in the possession of a party to a proceeding, is discoverable by the party if it —

    (a)   relates, directly or indirectly, to a matter in issue in the proceeding; or

    (b)   is mentioned, expressly of by necessary implication, in a pleading or notice filed in the proceeding

...

607 Notice to disclose discoverable documents

   (1)   A party to a proceeding may serve on another party a notice requiring the other party to disclose discoverable documents for the proceeding.

       Note For disclosure in relation to third parties, see r 315 (Third parties — disclosure)

   (2)   Unless the court gives leave, the party must not serve a notice —

       (a)   before the close of pleadings; or

       (b)   after the filing of a certificate of readiness

       Note Pt 6.2 (Applications in proceedings) applies to an application for leave

   (3)   The party who is served with the notice must —

       (a)   file the following documents not later than 28 days after the day the party receives the notice:

           (i)   the party's list of documents;

           (ii)   an affidavit verifying the list;

           (iii)   if the party is represented by a solicitor — the solicitor's certificate of advice in relation to the list; and

     Note 1 Rule 608 (List of discoverable and privileged documents etc) sets out requirements for the list, affidavit and certificate.

Note 2 Rule 6351 (Time—extending and shortening by court order) provides for the extending of time by the court.

(b)   serve a copy of each of the documents on each other active party.

608 List of discoverable and privileged documents etc
(1)   A party's list of documents must —
   (a)   set out, in a convenient order —
      (i)   each document discoverable by the party; and
      (ii)   each document discoverable by the party that the party claims to be privileged from production; and
   (b)   describe clearly and briefly —
      (i)   each document set out in the list; and
      (ii)   if the party claims the document is privileged from production — the nature of the claim for privilege; and
   (c)   for each document not in the party's possession, state —
      (i)   when and how it stopped being in the party's possession; and
      (ii)   to the best of the party's knowledge, information and belief, who now has possession of the document or, failing that, what has become of the document.

Note See approved form 2.24 (Affidavit verifying list of documents) AF2006-269

....

13.1.2   In the Australian Capital Territory, the Northern Territory, Queensland, South Australia, Tasmania, Victoria and Western Australia, there is a basic process for discovery of documents similar to that in the Australian Capital Territory: Rules of the Supreme Court of the Northern Territory of Australia (NT) O 29; Uniform Civil Procedure Rules 1999 (Qld) Ch 7; Supreme Court Civil Rules 2006 (SA) Ch 7 Pt 3; Supreme Court Rules 2000 (Tas) Pt 13; Supreme Court (General Civil Procedure) Rules 2005 (Vic) O 29; Rules of the Supreme Court 1971 (WA) O 26. In the Australian Captial Territory, Queensland and South Australia, the process is termed 'disclosure' of documents.

There are substantial differences in the detail of these rules. Illustrations of some of the variations follow, but these are examples only; the rules of the jurisdiction in question should be examined for the detailed procedural requirements of that particular jurisdiction.

- In several of these jurisdictions, as in the Australian Capital Territory, the obligation to make discovery is triggered by the service of a notice requiring discovery. In the Northern Territory (r 29.02), Queensland (r 211) and South Australia (r 136), the obligation arises automatically without any requirement for notice.

- In some jurisdictions, there are particular limitations upon the nature of the matters in which discovery may be required without a court order. In Tasmania (r 383(4)(c)), for example, a plaintiff in any motor vehicle accident litigation who seeks discovery from a defendant requires a court order. It is suggested that the requirement that in certain matters a court order must be obtained reflects a view that, in respect of matters of that nature, the facts are likely to be known to both parties and little is likely to be achieved through the discovery process. If a need for discovery is shown, however, it is to be anticipated the court will grant leave.

- In those jurisdictions where the discovery process is triggered by notice, minor variations apply in relation to the time at which the notice requiring discovery may be served. In Tasmania (r 383(1)) and Victoria (r 29.02), for example, the rules provide that the notice may be served any time after pleadings close, while in Western Australia (O 26 r 1), the notice may be served any time before a matter is entered for trial.

- Where the process is triggered by notice, the time within which the other party is required to comply with the notice varies. For example, it is 42 days in Victoria. Fourteen days is also specified in Tasmania (r 383(2)) (or such greater period but prior to filing the certificate of readiness as may be agreed between the parties or allowed by a judge); while in Western Australia (O 26 r 4) the rules permit 10 days for compliance with the notice; and in the Australian Capital Territory (r 607(3)) the rules permit 28 days for compliance. In the Northern Territory (r 29.03) the parties are obliged to make discovery within 21 days after the close of pleadings, and in Queensland (r 214) in the usual case the initial disclosure is to be made within 28 days after the close of pleadings. In South Australia (r 136(3)) the parties are to make disclosure within 21 days of the close of any first settlement conference or, if there is to be no settlement conference, within 21 days of the close of pleadings.

[*NOTE:* in this chapter a reference, such as WA O 9 r 2, is a reference to the relevant Rules of Court. All other legislation will be specified.]

13.1.3   Except in Queensland, a party required to make discovery must prepare a written list setting out all documents which are or were at any time in that party's possession, custody or power, (in the Australian Capital Territory the rules refer only to 'possession'), to which the duty of discovery otherwise relates (see **13.1.26–13.1.28**) and which either:

(a)   the party making discovery is willing to show to the other party;

(b)   are no longer in the possession or power of the discovering party, in which case the party making discovery must also specify what has become of the documents; or

(c)   the party making discovery declines on a recognised and specified ground of privilege to show to the other party. (Privilege is considered below under 'Privilege' at **13.5.1ff**.)

The list of documents is usually verified on oath and is referred to as an 'affidavit of documents'. In Tasmania (r 383(8)), the party requiring discovery may also serve a notice requiring the party making discovery to make an affidavit verifying the list of discoverable documents. If such a notice is not served, a list of documents in the prescribed form is sufficient. In the Northern Territory (r 29.03), a party entitled to a list of documents by notice may require the list to be verified by affidavit.

In South Australia (rr 136, 137), there is no requirement for a list of documents to be verified on oath, unless the court so directs. The rules in South Australia also provide that the parties to an action may, by agreement (referred to as a 'document disclosure agreement'), dispense with the disclosure of documents, or regulate the extent of disclosure and how it is to be made: r 138. Notice of the agreement must be filed in the court before the time limited for making disclosure. If an agreement is filed, disclosure is taken to have been completed 21 days after close of pleadings, to be verified on oath, unless the court so directs.

13.1.4   In Queensland, the procedure for disclosure is significantly different. Rule 214 provides that, subject to r 216 (which governs disclosure by inspection of documents: see **13.1.6**) and r 223 (which permits the making of special court orders relating to discovery), a party to an action performs the duty of disclosure by delivering to the other parties in accordance with

Ch 7, Pt 1, a list of the documents to which the duty relates, and the documents for which privilege from disclosure is claimed. The list should describe the nature of each document and identify the person who made the document. Under r 211(1), the obligation extends only to documents in the possession or under the control of the first party. Unlike the position in the other jurisdictions, it does not extend to documents which were once in the possession of a party but no longer are. It is possible for a party, by notice, to defer disclosure by the other party in respect of a specified question or class until the party giving the notice requests it: r 220.

13.1.5 A party, upon whom an affidavit or list of documents is served in accordance with the rules, is entitled to inspect any document referred to which is in the possession of the party making discovery, and which the party does not object to producing, and to obtain photocopies of any such documents: ACT r 620; NT r 29.09; SA rr 140, 141 (r 141 includes detailed requirements as to the manner in which production and inspection is to be conducted); Tas r 390; Vic r 29.09; WA O 26 rr 8, 8A (r 8A includes detailed requirements as to the manner in which production and inspection of documents is to be conducted). These rules vary substantially in respect of matters of detail. In short, the procedure commonly adopted is that after the parties have exchanged affidavits or lists of documents, their solicitors arrange for a mutually convenient time for a meeting at which each will bring his or her client's documents for the other party to inspect and photocopy (or request photocopies). In matters which are relatively uncomplicated and where there is no reason to expect it could be important to inspect the original documents themselves, the meeting may be omitted, with the parties' representatives merely requesting by letter copies of certain documents as itemised on the other party's affidavit or list. The South Australian rule (r 140) specifically acknowledges that this may be done either by agreement between the parties or by direction of the court.

13.1.6 In Queensland (r 214(1)), a party who has delivered a list of documents under r 214 must, at another party's request, deliver to the party copies of the documents mentioned in the list, other than the documents for which privilege from disclosure is claimed. Another party can require the production for inspection of the original of any document disclosed: r 215. An alternative means of disclosure is available in circumstances where it is not convenient for a party to deliver documents because of the number, size, quantity or volume of the documents or some of them. In such a case the party effecting disclosure must notify the other party of a convenient time and place at which the documents may be inspected: r 216. Rule 217 includes detailed requirements as to the manner in which disclosure by the production of documents is to be conducted.

13.1.7 The rules also make provision for the inspection of documents referred to in pleadings or particulars: ACT r 620; NT r 29.10; Qld r 222; Tas r 391; Vic r 29.10; WA O 26 r 8. The provisions in the Australian Capital Territory, Queensland, Tasmania and Western Australia specifically extend to any document referred to in another party's affidavits; those in the Northern Territory and Victoria also extend to any document referred to in another party's originating process, interrogatories or answers, affidavit or notice.

13.1.8 There are rules which specifically authorise the making of an order for discovery or for production of documents for inspection where a party fails to make discovery as required by the rules, or objects or refuses to produce any document as required by the rules: ACT r 606 (disclosure), r 621 (production); NT r 29.11; Qld r 223; SA r 145; Tas r 386 (discovery), r 392 (production); Vic r 29.11; WA O 26 r 7 (discovery), O 26 r 9 (production).

There are also rules in more general terms which permit the court to make an order at any stage of a proceeding that a party give discovery, or (subject to any question of privilege) produce documents for inspection, or provide copies of documents: ACT rr 606 (disclosure), 621 (production); NT r 29.07 (discovery); SA r 142 (production); Tas rr 386 (discovery), 392 (production); Vic r 29.07; WA O 26 rr 7 (discovery), 9 (production). As is specifically provided by the rules in most jurisdictions, these orders will usually only be made where the court is satisfied that they are necessary for fairly disposing of the proceeding, or for saving costs.

The Federal Court

13.1.9 There is no longer any general right to discovery and inspection of documents in the Federal Court. The rules in that jurisdiction stipulate that a party must not give discovery unless the court has made an order for discovery: FCR r 20.12. Further, a party is not to apply for such an order unless the making of the order sought will facilitate the just resolution of the proceeding as quickly, inexpensively and efficiently as possible: FCR r 20.11.

An application for an order that another party to the proceeding give discovery may not be made until 14 days after all the respondents have filed a defence, or an affidavit in response to the affidavit accompanying the originating application. The application must state whether the party is seeking 'standard discovery' (see **13.1.17**) or the proposed scope of the discovery: r 20.13.

If an order for discovery is made, the court will, in its order, specify the time for compliance. The party ordered to give discovery gives discovery by serving on all parties to the proceeding a list of documents in accordance with r 20.17. That rule requires that the list of documents must be in accordance with Form 38 and must describe:

(a)   each category of documents in the party's control sufficiently to identify the category but not necessarily the particular document; and

(b)   each document that has been, but is no longer in the party's control; a statement of when the document was last in the party's control and what became of it; and

(c)   each document in the party's control for which privilege from production is claimed and the grounds for the privilege.

Rule 20.32 entitles any party to apply to the court for an order that another party produce for inspection any document that is included in the other party's list of documents and that is in that party's control. The court may order that inspection to be given by electronic means.

Any party also has a right under r 20.31 to inspect any document mentioned in a pleading or affidavit filed by any other party, following the procedure detailed in that rule. If the party from whom the production is sought does not comply with the prescribed procedure, or claims a document sought is privileged, the party seeking inspection may apply to the court for an order for production and inspection of the document.

A party to whom a document is produced for inspection may copy or make an electronic image of the document, subject to any reasonable conditions imposed by the person producing the document: r 20.34.

New South Wales

13.1.10 Part 21 Div 2 of the New South Wales rules substitutes, for the right of general discovery upon service of a notice on another party, a more limited right to require the production of *specific* documents. Any documents referred to in the other party's originating process, pleadings, affidavits or witness statements may be specified. Other documents clearly identified in the notice, and relevant to a fact in issue, may also be specified: r 21.10. Unless the court orders otherwise, the party served with the notice must then produce the required documents in that party's possession, custody or power, and provide any information that he or she may have as to the whereabouts of the specified documents that are not produced: r 21.11. Importantly, a party to proceedings on a claim for damages for personal injuries or death is not required to comply with a notice to produce documents other than those referred to in documents filed by that party unless the court, for special reasons, otherwise orders: r 21.12.

A court order is necessary for any discovery beyond the specific documents which may be sought by notice under r 21.10, but this right is also limited. Rule 21.2 gives the court power to make an order for discovery, but only in relation to a document within a specified class or classes, or to one or more samples of documents within such a class. A class of documents is not to be specified in more general terms than the court considers 'justified' in the circumstances. A class of documents may be specified either by relevance to one or more of the facts in issue, by description of the nature of the documents and the period within which they were brought into existence, or in such other manner as the court considers appropriate in the circumstances. An order for discovery may not be made in respect of a document unless the document is relevant to a fact in issue.

In personal injury and fatal accident proceedings, the court is not to make an order for discovery, unless satisfied there are special reasons: r 21.8.

A party ordered to make discovery must comply with the order within 28 days or within such other period as the court orders. This requires the preparation of a list, verified on oath, which sets out all of the documents within the scope of the order and which are or were at a time later than six months prior to the commencement of proceedings in the 'possession, custody or power' of the party. The list must indicate which of those documents are no longer in the possession of the discovering party and state any belief the party may have as to in whose possession or power those documents may now be. It must also state which documents are claimed to be privileged documents and the basis of that claim: rr 21.3, 21.4.

For discovery made pursuant to a court order under r 21.2, the discovering party must then make the documents available for inspection. Rule 21.5 details the obligations on the discovering party in that respect.

Practice Note SC 11, issued 22 March 2012, imposed additional limitations upon applications for orders for disclosure of documents. The Practice Direction commenced on 26 March 2012, and it applies to all new and existing proceedings in the Equity Division, except in the Commercial Arbitration List. In these matters, the court will not make an order for disclosure of documents until the parties to the proceedings have served their evidence, unless there are exceptional circumstances necessitating disclosure. There is to be no order for disclosure in any proceedings in the Equity Division unless it is necessary for the resolution of the real issues in dispute in the proceedings. Any application for an order for disclosure, consensual or otherwise, must be supported by an affidavit setting out: the reason why disclosure is necessary for the resolution of the real issues in dispute in the proceedings; the classes of documents in respect of which disclosure is sought; and the likely cost of the disclosure. The Practice Direction also specifies that the court may impose a limit on the amount of recoverable costs in respect of disclosure.

Exclusion of privileged documents

13.1.11 The right to inspection of any document is subject to there being no valid claim to privilege in respect of that document. Recognised grounds of privilege are considered below under the heading 'Privilege' at **13.5.1ff**.

Except in the Federal Court, a challenge to any claim for privilege in respect of documents included in an affidavit or list of documents, is appropriately made once the affidavit or list of documents has been served. The rules in Western Australia also make provision for claiming privilege following notice requiring production of documents, in which case the claim may be challenged at that time.

In Queensland (r 212(1)), privileged documents are specifically exempted from the obligation to disclose (see **13.1.25**), although it is necessary to separately list the documents in relation to which privilege from disclosure is claimed: r 214(1)(a). If the claim to privilege is challenged, an affidavit stating the claim to privilege is to be made by an individual knowing the facts giving rise to the claim: r 213.

In New South Wales (r 21.3(2)(d)), when any claim to privilege is made in a list of documents, the rules require that the circumstances under which the privilege is claimed to arise be specified.

In the Federal Court (r 20.32), a party seeking inspection of documents included in another party's list of documents must apply for an order for production, at which time any claim for privilege may be challenged. If a party has served on another party a notice under r 20.31 seeking production of any document mentioned in an affidavit or pleading of the other party and the other party has claimed privilege in respect of the document, it will be necessary for the party seeking production and inspection to challenge the claim to privilege by application to the court for the necessary order.

If any application before the court involves a challenge to a claim for privilege, the court may inspect the document to decide the validity of the claim: FCR r 20.35; ACT r 621; NT r 29.13; Qld r 223(5); SA r 143 (this rule extends to any objection made to production of a document); Tas r 395; Vic r 29.13; WA O 26 r 12. See also Evidence Act 1995 (Cth) s 183; Evidence Act 1995 (NSW) s 183; Evidence Act 2001 (Tas) s 183.

Document

13.1.12 The definitions of 'document' which apply to the discovery procedure are wide enough to encompass audiotapes and videotapes, computer disks and information stored by most other electronic or mechanical means: ACT r 600 and FCR r 1.51 and Sch 1 Dictionary (both rules incorporate the definition of *document* in Pt 1 of the Dictionary to the Evidence Act 1995 (Cth); NSW Interpretation Act 1987 (NSW) s 21(1); NT rr 1.09, 29.12; Qld Acts Interpretation Act 1954 (Qld) s 36 (as to application of that section, see ss 2(1), 7(1)); SA r 4; Tas r 381; Interpretation of Legislation Act 1984 (Vic) s 38, Vic r 29.12; WA O 26 r 1A.

The South Australian rule (r 137(1)) is explicit in requiring that the list of documents must contain a concise description of each document and a means of identifying it so that it is later practicable to identify the document with certainty and precision. Three specific exceptions are provided, when the document is not to be separately listed, namely:

(1)   if a file is listed and the document is part of the file;

(2)   if a document is recorded on a computer disk and the disk is listed; and

(3)   if the document is part of a bundle of documents of the same or similar character

and the bundle is listed with a description of its contents and (if it is not clear from the description) a statement of the number of documents comprised in the bundle (eg, accounting records for a stated financial year). The court may, however, order a party to file a supplementary list identifying documents disclosed under a general description with greater precision than required under subr (1).

One of the areas of increasing importance relates to the breadth of the discovery obligation in relation to emails and other information stored electronically. In *Sony Music Entertainment (Aust) Ltd v University of Tasmania* [2003] FCA 724, Tamberlin J made orders permitting Sony's expert forensic investigator to have access to the university's back-up files and to use specially designed software to recover deleted information, extract information and if necessary convert it into readable form, and to make copies of it. In *Grant v Marshall* [2003] FCA 1161, the applicant wished to trace the source of an email containing false allegations. Emmett J made orders restraining two of the respondents from deleting or erasing material that might assist in identifying the author of the emails and for the production to the court of material that might assist in identifying the author. It was also ordered that a computer forensic expert be given access to the hard drive of the computer upon the giving of appropriate undertakings. See further 13.1.42–13.1.45.

Relevance

13.1.13   In several jurisdictions, discovery is limited to documents which are relevant to a fact in issue in the proceedings as disclosed by the pleadings. A very broad interpretation has been taken as to what is relevant, extending to relevance of an indirect kind. The rules in the Federal Court, New South Wales, the Northern Territory, Queensland, South Australia and Victoria now incorporate more restrictive tests in relation to the nature of documents which must be disclosed.

Australian Capital Territory, Tasmania, and Western Australia

13.1.14   The classic test of 'relevance' is found in the judgment of Brett J in *Compagnie Financière et Commerciale du Pacifique v Peruvian Guano Co* (1882) 11 QBD 55, extracted below.

13.1.15C   **Compagnie Financière et Commerciale du Pacifique v Peruvian Guano Co**
(1882) 11 QBD 55
High Court of England, Court of Appeal

[The plaintiffs brought proceedings against the defendants for breach of contract. The defence included a denial that a contract had been concluded, and alleged that the parties had not proceeded beyond negotiation. The plaintiffs' affidavit of documents included the minute book of proceedings of the plaintiff company. This referred to several documents and letters which were not included in the plaintiffs' affidavit of documents, most of which were dated subsequent to the date of the alleged breach of contract. The defendants brought an application for a further and better affidavit of documents. In respect of all documents dated subsequent to the alleged agreement, the defendants were unsuccessful before the master, the judge in Chambers, and the Queens Bench Division. They appealed to the Court of

Appeal. The defendants claimed that these documents might show that subsequent to the alleged breach, the parties were still negotiating and might tend to disprove the plaintiffs' allegation that a contract had been concluded.]

Brett LJ (at 62–4): The party swearing the affidavit is bound to set out all documents in his possession or under his control relating to any matters in question in the action. Then comes this difficulty: What is the meaning of that definition? What are the documents which are documents relating to any matter in question in the action? In *Jones v Monte Video Gas Co* 5 QBD 556 the Court stated its desire to make the rule as to the affidavit of documents as elastic as was possible. And I think that is the view of the Court both as to the sources from which the information can be derived, and as to the nature of the documents. We desire to make the rule as large as we can with due regard to propriety; and therefore I desire to give as large an interpretation as I can to the words of the rule, 'a document relating to any matter in question in the action'. I think it obvious from the use of these terms that the documents to be produced are not confined to those, which would be evidence either to prove or to disprove any matter in question in the action; and the practice with regard to insurance cases shows, that the Court never thought that the person making the affidavit would satisfy the duty imposed upon him by merely setting out such documents, as would be evidence to support or defeat any issue in the cause.

The doctrine seems to me to go farther than that and to go as [63] far as the principle which I am about to lay down. It seems to me that every document relates to the matters in question in the action, which not only would be evidence upon any issue, but also which, it is reasonable to suppose, contains information which *may* — not which *must* — either directly or indirectly enable the party requiring the affidavit either to advance his own case or to damage the case of his adversary. I have put in the words 'either directly or indirectly', because, as it seems to me, a document can properly be said to contain information which may enable the party requiring the affidavit either to advance his own case or to damage the case of his adversary, if it is a document which may fairly lead him to a train of inquiry, which may have either of these two consequences. ... The question must be, whether from the description either in the first affidavit itself or in the list of documents referred to in the first affidavit or in the pleadings of the action, there are still documents in the possession of the party making the first affidavit which, it is not unreasonable to suppose, do contain information which may, either directly or indirectly, enable the party requiring the further affidavit either to advance his own case or to damage the case of his adversary. In order to determine whether certain documents are within that description [64], it is necessary to consider what are the questions in the action: the Court must look not only at the statement of claim and the plaintiffs' case, but also at the statement of defence and the defendants' case. In the present action it is true to say that the contention of the plaintiffs is that there was a concluded agreement, and that there was a breach of that agreement on a particular day. I quite agree that these documents, which are referred to in the minutes to which our attention has been drawn, cannot affect the plaintiffs' case if it be true; for the documents, of which production is now sought, came into existence after the alleged breach. But the defendants' case is that there never was a concluded agreement, and of course there never was or could be a breach of an agreement which never existed. The defendants' case is that, from beginning to the end of the whole transaction, even up to the time of bringing the action, the whole matter was in negotiation — there was one unbroken series of negotiations. Therefore, if the defendants can show that there are documents in the possession of the plaintiffs which, it is not unreasonable to suppose, do contain information which may support the defendants' case, those documents, as it seems to me, ought to have been set out by the plaintiffs in the original affidavit, and must be set out by them in a further affidavit.

[His Lordship concluded that some of the documents referred to in the minute book could reasonably be supposed to support the defendants' case if the defendants' case was true, and proceeded to order that the plaintiffs were bound to make a further affidavit of documents. **Baggallay LJ** delivered a separate judgment to similar effect.]

13.1.16 The *Peruvian Guano* test has long been adopted in Australia: *Mulley v Manifold* (1959) 103 CLR 341 at 345 per Menzies J; *Commonwealth v Northern Land Council* (1991) 103 ALR 267 (FC); (1993) 176 CLR 604 (HC). Despite the breadth of the test of relevance, the concept does not extend to documents which are relevant only to the credibility of a party, except if the honesty or reliability of that party is actually in issue in the proceeding. It also does not extend to documents which relate to claims which may be regarded as purely speculative: *WA Pines Pty Ltd v Bannerman* (1980) 30 ALR 559.

Federal Court

13.1.17 The Federal Court Rules no longer incorporate a general test of relevance. A party applying for an order that another party to the proceeding give disclosure must state whether the party is seeking 'standard discovery' or the proposed scope of the discovery: r 20.13. Rule 20.14 details the documents which must be discovered if the court orders a party to give standard discovery. This encompasses documents:

(a)   that are directly relevant to the issues raised by the pleadings or in the affidavits; and

(b)   of which, after a reasonable search, the party is aware; and

(c)   that are, or have been, in the party's control.

In order to satisfy the requirement that the documents are directly relevant to matters raised by the pleadings or in the affidavits, the documents must meet at least one of the following criteria:

(a)   the documents are those on which the party intends to rely;

(b)   the documents adversely affect the party's own case;

(c)   the documents support another party's case; or

(d)   the documents adversely affect another party's case.

A number of matters are specified by r 20.14(3) as matters which may be taken into account by a party in making a reasonable search, namely:

(a)   the nature and complexity of the proceeding;

(b)   the number of documents involved;

(c)   the ease and cost of retrieving a document;

(d)   the significance of any document likely to be found; and

(e)   any other relevant matter.

Rule 20.15(1) details the requirements when a party seeks an order for discovery other than standard discovery. The party must identify:

(a)   any of the criteria defining the scope of standard discovery that should not apply;

(b)   any other criteria that should apply;

(c)   whether the party seeks the use of categories of documents in the list of documents;

(d)   whether discovery should be given in electronic format; and

(e)   whether discovery should be given in accordance with a discovery plan.

Rule 20.15(2) stipulates that the application must be accompanied by:

(a)   if categories of documents are sought — a list of the proposed categories; and

(b)   if discovery is sought by an electronic format — the proposed format; and

(c)   if a discovery plan is sought to be used — a draft of the discovery plan.

An application by a party seeking more extensive discovery than is required by standard discovery must be accompanied by an affidavit stating why the order should be made.

Division 20.2 of the Federal Court Rules should be read in conjunction with Practice Note CM 5 (1 August 2011). This Practice Note makes it clear that the court will approach applications for discovery orders with a view to eliminating or reducing the burden of discovery. The court will not order discovery as a matter of course, even where parties consent, unless discovery is necessary for the determination of the issues in the proceeding, and it will fashion any order for discovery to suit the issues in a particular case. The Practice Note specifies a range of questions that should be answered in support of an application for discovery. It also specifies a number of matters to which the court will have regard in determining whether to make any order for discovery, including: the issues in the case and the order in which they are likely to be resolved; the resources and circumstances of the parties; the likely benefit of discovery; and the likely cost of discovery and whether that cost is proportionate to the nature and complexity of the proceeding. Orders will ordinarily be limited to documents required as standard discovery under r 20.14.

New South Wales

13.1.18   In New South Wales, 'relevance' is usually, but not always, one of the applicable tests for determining whether a document must be discovered. It is always necessary if a party is seeking production for inspection of specified documents under r 21.10 that the documents be 'relevant to a fact in issue': see **13.1.10**. If discovery is pursuant to a court order for discovery of a class or classes of documents under r 21.2, it is possible for the classes to be described in the order by description of the nature of the documents and the period when they were made, or in any other manner the court considers appropriate. In that event, clearly the question of which documents are included can only be determined by reference to the terms of the court order. Alternatively, the classes of documents may be described in the order by reference to their 'relevance to one or more facts in issue': see **13.1.10**. For those circumstances in which relevance is a governing test, Pt 21 now incorporates a definition of that term.

13.1.19E   **Uniform Civil Procedure Rules 2005 (NSW)**
Part 21 — Discovery, inspection and notice to produce documents

21.1 Definitions

...

(2) For the purpose of this Division, a document or matter is to be taken to be relevant to a fact in issue if it could, or contains material that could, rationally affect the assessment of the probability of the existence of that fact (otherwise than by relating solely to the credibility of a witness), regardless of whether the document or matter would be admissible in evidence.

13.1.20   This test, which is similar to the test in the Evidence Act 1995 (NSW) s 55, is still fairly wide, and would appear to encompass anything that might throw light on any matter in issue or relevant to an issue between the parties. It does not, however, encompass documents which may only have value under the 'chain of inquiry' test in *Compagnie Financière et Commerciale du Pacifique v Peruvian Guano Co*: *National Australia Bank Ltd v Idoport Pty Ltd* [2000] NSWCA 8: see 13.1.15C.

Northern Territory

13.1.21   In the Northern Territory the rules still require the discovery of documents 'relating' to a question raised by the pleadings (r 29.02(1)), but the scope of the test of relevance became more limited by an amendment made in 2000, which added r 29.02(3). That subrule specifies that a party is not required to discover a document that is relevant only because it may lead to a chain of enquiry, except if a pleading contains allegations of a kind referred to in r 13.10(3). The subrule is also subject to a contrary order by the court. This means that in the ordinary course a more restricted view is to be taken of the test of relevance, except if the pleadings contain allegations of misrepresentation, fraud, breach of trust, wilful default, undue influence, disorder or disability of the mind, malice, fraudulent intention or other condition of the mind, including knowledge or notice.

Queensland and South Australia

> **13.1.22E**   **Uniform Civil Procedure Rules 1999 (Qld)**
> Rule 211
>
> **211** (1) A party to a proceeding has a duty to disclose to each other party each document —
>
>   (a)   in the possession or under the control of the first party; and
>   (b)   directly relevant to an allegation in issue in the pleadings …

13.1.23   In Queensland and South Australia (r 136), the crucial test for determining the scope of disclosure is whether the document is *directly relevant* to an allegation in issue in the proceeding; the *Peruvian Guano* 'chain of inquiry' concept (see 13.1.15C) is gone.

As to the meaning of 'directly relevant', Demack J said in *Robson v Reb Engineering Pty Ltd* [1997] 2 Qd R 102 at 105:

> … the word 'directly' should not be taken to mean that which constitutes direct evidence as distinct from circumstantial evidence. Rather, 'directly relevant' means something which tends to prove or disprove the allegation in issue.

In *Mercantile Mutual Custodians Pty Ltd v Village Nine Network Restaurants and Bars Pty Ltd* [2001] 1 Qd R 276 at 282–3, Pincus JA said that the direct relevance test effected a deliberate narrowing of the obligation to provide disclosure.

The meaning of this test has been considered in a number of decisions in the Supreme Court of South Australia. In *Rehn v Australian Football League* [2003] SASC 159, for example, Doyle CJ said that it was not possible to state precisely the effect of the adverb 'directly'.

He noted a range of matters as relevant to the meaning of the rule including the fact that it assumed that a party is able to decide from the pleading what documents must be discovered, and found this also suggestive of a narrower meaning for 'directly relevant'. The comments in this case were approved in the Full Court in *Channel Seven Adelaide Pty Ltd v Lane & Hurley* [2004] SASC 177.

In South Australia the extent of the disclosure obligation may be cut down by agreement between the parties. Rule 138 provides that the parties to any action may, by agreement (referred to as a 'document disclosure agreement') dispense with the disclosure of documents or regulate the extent of disclosure and how it is to be made. The agreement must be made within seven days after the close of pleadings, and notice of an agreement under the rule must be filed in the court before the time limited for making disclosure. If an agreement is filed under the rule, disclosure is taken to have been completed 21 days after the close of pleadings.

Victoria

13.1.24   In Victoria the broad test of relevance was replaced in 2010, with the insertion of r 29.01.1. The amendments apply to any proceeding commenced on or after 1 January 2011. Rule 29.01.1 restricts the scope of discovery to any of the following documents of which the party giving discovery is, after a reasonable search, aware at the time discovery is given:

(a)   documents on which the party relies;

(b)   documents that adversely affect the party's own case;

(c)   documents that adversely affect another party's case;

(d)   documents that support another party's case.

In making a reasonable search a party may take into account:

(a)   the nature and complexity of the proceeding;

(b)   the number of documents involved;

(c)   the ease and cost of retrieving a document;

(d)   the significance of any document to be found; and

(e)   any other relevant matter.

If a party required to give discovery in accordance with r 29.01.1 does not, in making a reasonable search as required by r 29.01.1, search for a category or class of document, the party must state in the affidavit of documents the category or class of document not searched for, and the reason why: r 29.04(2).

The court may make an order at any stage of a proceeding, expanding a party's obligation to give discovery beyond that required by r 29.01.1. Such an order may specify any document or class of document to which the expanded obligation relates: r 29.05.2.

Documents exempted from discovery

13.1.25   In the Australian Capital Territory, the Federal Court, New South Wales, Queensland, South Australia and Victoria, the rules eliminate certain categories of documents from the requirement to discover or disclose. In respect of most categories of documents excluded, the underlying rationale is that discovery of those documents serves no useful purpose but simply increases the number of documents included.

In the Australian Capital Territory (r 605(2)), a document is not discoverable by a party:

(a)   if it is filed in court in the proceeding;

(b)   if it relates to only one or more items of special damage;

(c)   if it is mentioned in a pleading or notice filed in the proceeding by another party, unless it is discoverable on another ground;

(d)   if it is a written communication in relation to the proceeding between a solicitor for the party requiring disclosure and a solicitor for the disclosing party;

(e)   if it is the party's brief to counsel; or

(f)   if it is an advice to the party from the party's counsel.

Rule 605(3) also excludes from the discovery obligation a range of confidential documents and communications involving legal practitioners.

The Federal Court Rules specify that a party who is required to give discovery need not give discovery of additional copies of documents, which are discoverable purely because the original or any other copy is discoverable: r 20.8.

In New South Wales (r 21.1), Pt 21 excludes certain documents from an order for discovery, unless the court orders to the contrary. The 'excluded documents' are:

• any document filed in the proceedings or served on the party obtaining the order for discovery after the commencement of proceedings;

• any document which wholly came into existence after the commencement of the proceedings;

• extra copies of documents already included in the list of documents and not containing any additional mark, deletion or other matter relevant to a fact in question; and

• any original of a written communication sent by the party obtaining the order for discovery prior to the commencement of proceedings of which a copy is already included in the list of documents.

In Queensland (r 212(1)), the rules specify that the duty of disclosure does not extend to a document in relation to which there is a valid claim to privilege from disclosure (see further under 'Privilege' at **13.5.1ff**): a document relevant only to credit, or an additional copy of a document already disclosed if it is reasonable to suppose the additional copy contains no change, obliteration or other mark or feature likely to affect the outcome of the proceeding. Despite the recognition that the duty does not apply to privileged documents, the privilege which may otherwise apply to a document consisting only of a statement or report of an expert is specifically removed: r 212(2). It is also provided that a document relating only to damages may be disclosed to another party only if the other party requests its disclosure: r 221.

In South Australia (r 136(6)), the documents which need not be disclosed include:

(a)   an investigative film made for the purposes of the action;

(b)   documents filed in the action;

(c)   communications between the parties' lawyers or notes of these communications;

(d)   correspondence between parties and their lawyers or notes of these communications;

(e)   opinions of counsel; and

(f)   copies of documents that have been disclosed or are not required to be disclosed.

Although most of these documents would in any event be privileged from production, this rule means that the existence of the documents need not be disclosed at all.

In Victoria, the obligation to make discovery does not extend to documents that the party giving discovery reasonably believes are already in the possession of the party to which discovery is given, nor to additional copies of documents otherwise discoverable only because the original or any other copy is discoverable: r 29.01.1(4).

Possession, custody or power

13.1.26 A party is only required to discover documents which are or have been in that party's control in the manner contemplated by the rules. In all jurisdictions, except the Australian Capital Territory and Queensland, the test is whether the document has been in the party's 'possession, custody or power': FCR r 20.17, Sch 1 (Dictionary); NSW Pt 21, r 1.2, Dictionary; NT r 29.01; SA r 136, r 4 (interpretation); Tas r 382; Vic r 29.01; WA O 26 r 1.

In the Australian Capital Territory (r 605(1)) the obligation to provide discovery applies only to documents in the discovering party's 'possession', and in Queensland (r 211(1)) the obligation to disclose now applies to documents in a party's 'possession or control'.

For the purpose of the discovery rules, 'possession' means the physical or corporal holding of the document pursuant to the legal right to deal with it, as in the case of an agent or bailee; 'custody' means the mere actual physical or corporal holding of a document, regardless of the right to its possession, as in the case of a servant or employee; and 'power' means an enforceable right to inspect or to obtain possession or control of the document from the person who ordinarily has it in fact: see *Halsbury's Laws of England*, 4th ed, vol 13, para [39]. The case extract below considers authorities relating to the meaning of 'power' in this context, and provides further guidance as to the circumstances in which a document will be in a party's 'power'.

13.1.27C	**Alstom Ltd v Liberty Mutual Insurance Co** [2010] FCA 588 Federal Court of Australia

[The plaintiff, Alstom Ltd, purchased two gas transformers from Crompton Greaves Ltd (CGL). CGL carried on business in Mumbai, India. The transformers were manufactured in Mumbai and were packed by CGL in sealed steel tanks and shipped to Western Australia. During the commissioning, the sealed steel cases housing the transformers were removed. It was then discovered that the transformers were damaged. Alstom made a claim on its marine cargo insurance policy which it had entered into with the defendants, in respect of the damage to the transformers. Under that policy, the defendants agreed to indemnify Alstom in respect of any damage to the transformers during the voyage from India to Australia. However, the defendants contended that the damage to the transformers arose by reason of an inherent vice — an excluded risk under the policy, and refused to indemnify Alstom. The defendants contended that the transformers had been packed in a defective manner which rendered the transformers liable to be damaged by the usual conditions encountered in sea transportation.

In proceedings commenced by Alstom against the defendants seeking an order that the defendants indemnify it under the policy in respect of the damage to the transformers, the court had made orders that Alstom file written statements of evidence from witnesses on which it intended to rely. Alstom had filed statements from several employees of CGL (all residents of India), including Mr Manish and Mr Naik. The evidence showed that CGL was prepared to give only limited cooperation to Alstom, and required that Alstom's solicitors forward to CGL in writing the questions which Alstom wished their relevant employees to answer. The witness statements, therefore, comprised a question and answer format. The witness statements referred to one or more documents and expressed conclusions founded on those documents. However, the witnesses did not attach to their statements all the documents to which they referred. The defendants applied for a range of orders relating to discovery and production of documents, including orders that Alstom produce certain documents which were referred to in the statements of Mr Manish and Mr Naik.]

Siopis J (at [13]–[26]):
Claim for production of documents

[13] The defendants sought orders that Alstom produce for inspection the following categories of documents:

1(b) The following documents identified in the statement of Mr Manish dated 23 July 2009:
   - (i)   Documents for the design, manufacture and preparation for transport of the transformers manufactured by Crompton Greaves Ltd (CGL);
   - (ii) Standard design drawing T63B3781Q;
   - (iii) Quality Control check list.
   ...
1(d) The following documents identified in the statement of Nitik Naik dated 23 July 2009 — CGL documents for the design, manufacture and preparation for transport of the transformers manufactured by CGL.

[14] The defendants say that they are entitled to an order under O 15 r 11(1) of the Federal Court Rules (the Rules). Order 15 r 11(1) reads as follows:

Where –
   - (a)   it appears from a list of documents filed by a party under this Order that any document is in his possession, custody or power;
   - (b)   a pleading or affidavit filed by a party refers to any document; or
   - (c)   it appears to the Court from evidence or from the nature or circumstances of the case or from any document filed in the proceeding that there are grounds for a belief that any document relating to any matter in question in the proceeding is in the possession, custody or power of a party,

   the Court may, subject to any question of privilege which may arise, order the party -
   - (d)   to produce the document for inspection by any other party at a time and place specified in the order; or
   - (e)   to file and serve on any other party a copy of the whole or any part of the document, with or without an affidavit verifying the copy made by a person who has examined the document and the copy.

[15] The defendants contended that by reason of cl 12.3 of the general terms and conditions of the contract between it and CGL, Alstom has a contractual right to have the documents produced to it. The defendants contended, therefore, that the documents are within the power of Alstom and it is on that basis that Alstom should be ordered to produce the documents.

[16] Clause 12.3 provides as follows:

The purchaser or the Owner, as the case may be, will take out a project specific Marine Cargo Insurance (MC) for the benefit of the Supplier (and its Subcontractors) covering the risk of damage and loss of the Work during transportation of the Work from the Supplier's and/or Subcontractor's facility to the named destination and/or the Site.

...

The Supplier shall strictly adhere and cause its Subcontractors to strictly adhere to the terms of the MC ... and shall promptly make all information available required by the Insurer.

[17] The "Supplier" referred to in cl 12.3 is CGL. It is contended by the defendants that cl 12.3 applies because they require inspection of the documents in this proceeding.

[18] In the case *of Lonrho Ltd v Shell Petroleum Co Ltd* [1980] 1 WLR 627 (*Lonrho*), Lord Diplock observed at 635:

[T]he expression "power" must, in my view, mean a presently enforceable legal right to obtain from whoever actually holds the document inspection of it without the need to obtain the consent of anyone else. Provided that the right is presently enforceable, the fact that for physical reasons it may not be possible for the person entitled to it to obtain immediate inspection would not prevent the document from being within his power; but in the absence of a presently enforceable right there is, in my view, nothing in O 24 to compel a party to a cause or matter to take steps that will enable him to acquire one in the future.

[19] In the case of *Taylor v Santos Lt*d (1998) 71 SASR 434 at 438 (*Taylor*), Doyle CJ observed:

But, in my opinion, the obligation to discover hinges upon having a right or actual and immediate ability to examine the document. A person does not have that right or actual immediate ability if the person is able to inspect the document only if a third person, who has control of the document, agrees to permit inspection, or agrees to refrain from so exercising that person's control as to prevent inspection.

[20] The evidence shows that each of Mr Manish and Mr Naik have in the course of answering the questions posed, refused to disclose the documents falling within para 1(b)(i) and para 1(d) of the amended notice of motion (the design documents) (see [13] above), on the basis that the documents were confidential business documents.

[21] It is unnecessary to rule on whether, on its proper construction, cl 12.3 of the terms and conditions applies to documents sought by the insurers in defence of a claim made by Alstom as opposed to a claim made by CGL on an insurance policy taken out for the benefit of CGL. This is because, in my view, even if the clause did apply to that class of documents, it is far from clear that cl 12.3 requires CGL to disclose its confidential documents to the insurer.

[22] Further, by reason of the claim to confidentiality made by CGL, Alstom is not being prevented from inspecting documents, which it would otherwise unquestionably be entitled to inspect, solely because the documents are not in Alstom's physical possession. Rather it is because CGL is claiming a legal entitlement not to disclose the documents. In those circumstances, Alstom does not have, in terms of Lord Diplock's definition in *Lonrho*, a "presently enforceable legal right" to inspect the documents in question. Nor would Alstom have power over the documents under the definition of power adopted by Doyle CJ in *Taylor*.

This is because CGL has not agreed to release its claims to the confidentiality in the documents and to permit Alstom to inspect the documents.

[23] In my view, the defendants have not established that the documents sought are within the power of Alstom such as would permit Alstom to produce the documents if an order was made to that effect.

[24] In those circumstances, the Court will not make an order for the production by Alstom of the documents in question.

[25] However, the Court will make an order for the discovery of the drawing referred to in para 1(b)(ii) of the notice of motion on the basis that there is a real likelihood that the drawing would be produced by CGL to Alstom on Alstom's request (*Sabre Corporation Pty Ltd v Russ Kalvin's Hair Care Company* [1993] FCA 557; (1993) 46 FCR 428). This is because Mr Manish, who referred to this drawing in his witness statement, stated that the drawing may be disclosed in Court.

[26] The position in relation to the "quality control check list", which is referred to in para 1(b)(iii) of the notice of motion, is not as clear. Mr Manish refers in his witness statement to a process occurring as "part of the quality check list". Whilst, it may well be that there is a physical document comprising a "quality control check list", it may be that Mr Manish is speaking metaphorically. I will order that Alstom clarify the position and request that CGL produce the "quality control check list", referred to by Mr Manish, if it, in fact, is a document.

[See also: *Commonwealth Bank of Australia v White (No 5)* [2002] VSC 566; *Reed v Amaca Pty Ltd Formerly James Hardy & Co Pty Ltd* [2010] WASC 14.]

13.1.28 In *Theodore v Australian Postal Commission* [1988] VR 272, a defendant sought discovery of documents to which a plaintiff had possible access under the Freedom of Information Act 1982 (Cth). The court took the view that those documents were not within the plaintiff's 'power' within the meaning of the discovery rules. In *Erskine v McDowall* [2001] QDC 192, Robertson DCJ considered whether applications and other forms which the defendant had submitted to various Commonwealth agencies were in her 'possession or control' and so should be disclosed under r 211 of the Queensland rules. He concluded 'somewhat hesitantly' that 'control', as used in the Queensland rule, was a more stringent requirement than 'power' and it did not extend to documents in respect of which a party had a right to obtain copies under the Freedom of Information Act 1982 (Cth). However, his Honour nevertheless made an order directing the defendant to make the necessary FOI application and upon obtaining copies of the documents (which were critical to a matter in issue) to make disclosure of the relevant parts. His Honour based his order upon either r 367 (directions) or r 223(4)(b) (court orders relating to disclosure) of the Uniform Civil Procedure Rules 1999 (Qld). A similar approach was taken by Reid DCJ in *Bowenbrae Pty Ltd v Flying Fighters Maintenance and Restoration* [2010] QDC 347.

There is now a unique rule in South Australia, which applies if a document is not in a party's immediate possession but is obtainable by the party. In that circumstance, r 140(2) obliges the party to take reasonable steps to obtain the document or a copy of it.

Restricted discovery

13.1.29   Most rules allow the court to restrict discovery to that which is necessary at the particular stage of the proceeding for fairly disposing of an action, or for the saving of costs: ACT r 606; NT r 29.05; Qld r 223; SA r 139 (disclosure); r 140 (production); Tas r 383(6); Vic r 29.05; WA O 26 r 7. In South Australia (r 144), the rules also specifically authorise the court to make orders to protect the confidentiality of documents to be disclosed or produced. In the Federal Court and New South Wales, a separate rule in this respect is not necessary as a right to require discovery by notice is limited to specific documents and a court order will only be in respect of stipulated classes of documents, and only to the extent the court considers justified in the circumstances: see 13.1.9, 13.1.10.

The court may be expected to exercise its power to restrict disclosure in circumstances where compliance with the normal discovery processes would involve disclosure of trade secrets to a competitor, or where there is some other competing interest which weighs against full discovery at the particular time it is sought. Alternatively, the costs associated with full discovery of enormous numbers of documents may not be regarded as justified at the stage which the proceedings have reached.

13.1.30C	**Ammerlaan v Distillers Co (Bio-chemicals) Ltd**
	(1992) 58 SASR 164
	Supreme Court of South Australia, Full Court

[The plaintiff brought an action in negligence against both the manufacturer and the distributor of the drug thalidomide. She claimed damages in respect of deformities alleged to have been caused by her mother's ingestion of the drug when pregnant with the plaintiff in 1961 and 1962. The defendants applied successfully to a master for orders that there be a separate preliminary trial on the questions as to whether or not thalidomide was ingested, whether or not it caused the alleged injuries, and whether or not the plaintiff was entitled to an extension of time under the Limitation of Actions Act 1936 (SA). They also obtained an order restricting discovery to those documents relevant to the preliminary issues. On appeal by the plaintiff, the orders of the master were varied, but only in respect of discovery, ordering that there be discovery on all issues, including the issue of negligence. The defendants appealed against the variation of the order of the master (there was no cross-appeal).]

Millhouse J (at 166–8): Mr F M Douglas QC who led Mr Dean Clayton for the appellants contended that the master's original order should be restored. He had two principal arguments: first that the learned judge was wrong when he said that the respondent had a 'normal right to discovery under the Rules on all issues raised by the pleadings' and secondly because the judge thought the respondent should have an opportunity, through full discovery, to enable her the better to assess her chances of success in the litigation. Mr Douglas submitted first that there is no such general principle and secondly that general discovery would be oppressive to the appellants and this outweighed the benefit to the respondent of being able to assess her case …

[167] With very great respect to him, I think Cox J was in error in assuming the respondent has a 'normal right to discovery'. I have always understood discovery, certainly if challenged,

to be a matter of the discretion of the Court. In *Burmah Oil Co Ltd v Governor and Co of the Bank of England* [1980] AC 1090 at 1141 Lord Scarman said:

> Although in the High Court discovery of documents is automatic in most civil litigation, this is no more than a convenient practice ordered and regulated by rules of court: see RSC O 24, and the recent decision of this House in *Science Research Council v Nasse* [1980] AC 1028. Discovery of documents remains, ultimately, a matter for the discretion of the court.

Mr Martin Frayne, for the respondent, argued that there is a distinction between English O 24, r 8 and our r 58.04 so that Lord Scarman's dictum is not apposite in South Australia. I doubt it. Rule 58.04 gives the Court power, *inter alia*, to:

> order that discovery be limited to certain documents or classes of documents related to the matters specified in the order; and
> if satisfied that discovery is not necessary, or not necessary at that stage, dismiss or adjourn the application.

English O 24, r 8 is:

> On the hearing of an application for an order ... the Court, if satisfied that discovery is not necessary, or not necessary at that stage of the cause or matter, may dismiss or, as the case may be, adjourn the application and shall in any case refuse to make such an order if and so far as it is of opinion that discovery is not necessary either for disposing fairly of the cause or matter or for saving costs.

The wording may be different but the sense of the two rules is the same.
I am fortified in this by what Judge Lunn says in his commentary on r 58.04.6:

> There is always a discretion in the court whether to allow discovery. Usually it will only be allowed if it is necessary for disposing fairly of the action or for the saving of costs.

Mr Douglas succeeds, I suggest, on his first argument.

As for the second we were told that discovery on the issue of negligence would involve many tens of thousands of documents. (Mr Douglas [168] mentioned 30,000 at one stage and 30,000 to 40,000 at another.) It will be extremely expensive in time and money to give discovery on negligence and, if the respondent failed on either of the issues to be tried first — causation and limitation — all that time and money would be wasted. To have to give discovery, at this point in the proceedings, would be oppressive to the appellants and discovery may be refused on that ground. Mr Douglas argued that this consideration outweighed the advantage to the respondent of being able to assess the whole of the case against her and for that reason discovery ought not to be given generally but should be restricted to the issues to be tried first.

My immediate reaction was to wonder whether it would be possible easily to separate documents relevant to the first two issues from those relevant to the third. The respondents acknowledge that there may be some overlap (as there may be of evidence — some witnesses may have to be called at each hearing) but say that it will not be much. When one looks at the issues they really are discrete. The limitation point seems to have nothing to do with negligence: likewise whether the plaintiff's condition is the result of her mother having taken thalidomide seems to have little to do with whether the appellants were negligent in having the drug on the market and selling it. I accept that the risk or rather the inconvenience of the mingling of the issues when giving discovery is small: it is small enough not to be the consideration on which to decide the point.

I have come to the conclusion that Cox J did proceed on a wrong basis and that we are entitled therefore to substitute our own discretion for his. Moreover he was in error in himself thinking that the master's discretion had miscarried.

I suggest that the appeal be allowed and that the order of Cox J varying the order of the master be set aside and the matter be referred back to the master to conclude the directions hearing in accord with these reasons.

[**Legoe J** agreed with the reasons given by **Millhouse J** and the order proposed. **Olsson J** delivered a separate judgment to similar effect.]

13.1.31C   **Magellan Petroleum Aust Ltd v Sagasco Amadeus Pty Ltd**
                              (1993) 25 IPR 455
                          Supreme Court of Queensland

[The plaintiffs were involved in litigation over the defendants' takeover bid for the plaintiffs. The defendants discovered some documents which they claimed were confidential. They applied for orders limiting inspection of the documents to the plaintiffs' counsel and two litigation solicitors upon the provision of undertakings by those persons. It was the detail of the documents, rather than their subject matter in general, which was confidential, in that they contained information as to the assessment by the defendants and their advisers of the plaintiffs' worth and takeover strategies which they might adopt. The plaintiffs resisted the limitations sought, on the basis that such restriction would deprive the plaintiffs' lawyers of the benefit of instructions from the plaintiffs.]

White J (at 459–62): This then leads to what is the real difference between the parties in this application — the difficulties as Magellan sees them in an order that disclosure be limited to counsel and litigation solicitors. This means that Magellan's lawyers may not have the benefit of instructions from their client on, for example, the significance of the documents in themselves and also as leading to a train of enquiry for possible cross-examination and further investigation. The documents might have a meaning for lawyers which would be modified or changed when put against a commercial context which may be known only to the client.

The principles of discovery relating to restricted disclosure have been enunciated by Templeman LJ in *Church of Scientology of California v Department of Health and Social Security* [1979] 1 WLR 723 where his Lordship said at 746:

> The first principle is that the court shall not order discovery which is not necessary for the fair disposal of the action. It follows that the court has power to impose restrictions which ensure that the ambit of discovery is not wider than is necessary to dispose fairly of the action. The second principle is that the court may act to prevent any possibility of conduct which might constitute contempt of court. The third principle is that the court may act to prevent what may be an abuse of the process of the court. Of course a strong case must be made out for the court to impose restrictions, and the court will endeavour to ensure that the litigants are not prejudiced by the restrictions in the reasonable prosecution of their claim, but in the unusual circumstances of this case I am satisfied that the court ought to intervene and that there is jurisdiction for the court so to do.

True, a litigant is entitled to inspect documents disclosed on discovery and to take copies: see *McIvor v Southern Health and Social Services Board* [1978] 1 WLR 757. But if there is a danger that inspection and copying in the manner desired by the litigant may lead to misuse of information, the court in the exercise of its power to prevent a possible contempt of court or in the exercise of its power to prevent an abuse of process and in the exercise of its power to confine discovery to the ambit which alone is necessary for the disposal of the action may dictate the manner in which *inspection* is carried out, whether by an individual litigant or by [460] a corporate litigant, and may regulate the taking and safeguarding of copies, and may impose limitations on the circulation of copies and information ...

It must be able to act similarly to protect the persons or property or even the peace of mind of individuals.

Earlier in the judgment his Lordship held at 746:

> ... the interests of the prudent administration of justice and the interests of the plaintiffs themselves require that reasonable precautions be taken to restrict the circulation of information without hampering or prejudicing the plaintiffs in their pursuit of the remedies they seek in this action.

Warner-Lambert Co v Glaxo Laboratories Ltd [1975] RPC 354 was a patent case in which the court considered restricting disclosure to legal advisers. Buckley LJ at 360 observed:

> If in a particular case it is right that disclosure of any facts should be made by one party to his opponent's advisers before trial, it must normally follow as a matter of course that the opponent should be entitled to know the facts so disclosed. His advisers are his agents in the matter, and strong grounds must be required for excluding the principal from knowledge which his agents properly acquire on his behalf. But this principle must be subject to some modification if trade secrets are to be protected from disclosure to possible competitors ... Where a matter in question in an action, being that matter upon which inspection or disclosure will throw light, is of a technical nature, the parties seeking discovery may well require inspection by, or disclosure to, technical and professional advisers. If the matter be of a kind on which the party will be likely to be able with the aid of those advisers to form some kind of view of his own, it seems to me that he should normally be allowed to know as much about the facts as his advisers. If, however, the case were one of so esoterically technical a character that even with the help of his expert advisers the party himself could really form no view of his own upon the matter in question but would be bound to act merely upon advice on the technical aspects, disclosure to him of the facts underlying the advice might serve little or no useful purpose. In such a case a court might well be justified in directing disclosure of allegedly secret material only to expert or professional agents of the party seeking discovery on terms that they should not, without further order, pass on any information so obtained to the party himself or anyone else, but should merely advise him in the light of the information so obtained. Even so, if the action were to go to trial, it would seem that sooner or later the party would be bound to learn the facts, unintelligible though they might be to him, unless the very exceptional course were taken of excluding him from part of the hearing.

His Lordship went on to note:

> The plaintiff in the present case, being a corporate body, can only acquire knowledge and make decisions by living agents. Its legal and expert advisers are for the relevant purpose

its agents to acquire knowledge but they are not authorised to make any major decisions on the company's behalf such as, for instance, a decision whether to continue or abandon the action. Such a decision should be made by the company, not by its legal advisers, and still less by its scientific advisers. It must be made by a duly authorised officer or agent or body of agents such as a managing director or the board of directors of the company ...

[461] I have concluded that the subject documents are directly relevant to some of the matters in issue between the parties in the litigation and that certain aspects of them can be characterised as commercially sensitive such as to attract the discretion of the court to make an order for restricted disclosure. They are not of a technical nature such that Magellan's officials could form no complete evaluation of them without the assistance of experts such as is often the case with trade secrets. It is highly undesirable that litigation solicitors and counsel should be left without the benefit of instructions from the client, particularly in a situation as here where the issues are much more subtle than a question of, for example, an infringement of a technical process. This does not mean that the balancing process requires general disclosure. The material filed reveals that Mr John Humphreys, a commercial solicitor in Magellan's solicitors' firm has been advising Magellan in relation to the takeover. The danger adverted to by Mr O'Shea for Sagasco that his advice, if the takeover proceeds, to Magellan in the future will be tainted by knowledge acquired from the subject documents can be avoided by undertakings. Russell LJ said of the plaintiff's chairman in *Warner-Lambert Co v Glaxco Laboratories Ltd* at 363:

> I only add this. Mr Giblin, the plaintiff's chairman, must realise that he may find himself in a difficult situation. He will have been told of the employment of this feature in the production of the defendant's material. Suppose some employee of the plaintiff comes to him with a suggestion that the plaintiff might try employing that feature? He will be in a difficulty. This is a difficulty which he must resolve as an honourable man: he must be poker-faced, just as he must if quizzed by members of his board.

The material does not indicate, as far as I am aware, who from Magellan is concerned in giving instructions in relation to this litigation. That individual is the person to whom disclosure may properly be made on that [462] person giving undertakings. I am not persuaded that any other person, at this stage, needs to see the subject documents.

The order of the court should follow this general form — that upon Mr Ray Lindwall, Miss Jayne Steele, Mr John Humphreys, senior and junior counsel retained in the present litigation and [Magellan's official] undertaking in writing to Sagasco and to the court not to divulge the information or any part of it to any other person, firm or company save with the consent of Sagasco or the authority of an order of the court and not to use the information or permit it to be used for any purpose other than a purpose connected with the action, that the documents identified in the plaintiff's summons be disclosed to those persons; that the number of copies made be limited to six; that apart from the copies to counsel, those copies be retained in a safe place in the plaintiff's solicitors' offices and, subject to any earlier or other order, the six copies be returned to the solicitors for the first and second defendants at the conclusion of any appeal period after judgment given in this litigation.

[See also *Davies v Eli Lilley & Co* [1987] 1 WLR 428.]

Deferral of discovery

13.1.32   In several jurisdictions, the court is given a discretion to defer determination as to a party's right to discovery or inspection until after the determination of a particular issue or question in the proceeding: Tas r 387; WA O 26 r 3. In the Australian Capital Territory (r 606) and South Australia (r 139), an order to defer disclosure in this way is within the court's broad power to regulate disclosure of documents under these rules. Such an order may be made if the court is satisfied that the right to discovery or inspection sought depends on the determination of the issue or question, or if for any other reason it is desirable that the issue or question be decided before discovery.

13.1.33   In Queensland (r 220), a party to whom disclosure is to be made may give a notice to the other party stating that documents relating to a specified question or class are not to be disclosed to the first party until requested by that party. A document to which the notice relates may then only be disclosed if the party giving the notice asks for its disclosure. It is also provided that a document only relating to damages may be disclosed only if the other party asks for its disclosure: r 221.

Further discovery and particular discovery

13.1.34   A party to whom discovery of documents has been provided may believe that the discovery is incomplete. It may be thought that a document or class of documents has been overlooked by the discovering party, that privilege has been inappropriately claimed, or even that the discovering party has been deliberately evasive or has intentionally omitted discoverable documents. The historical position in this respect was that a party's affidavit of documents was generally conclusive, and could not be challenged by an affidavit making assertions in reply to it: *Mulley v Manifold* (1959) 103 CLR 341. The reason usually given for this was that discovery takes place quite early in the proceeding and the court is not in a position to determine whether or not adequate discovery has been given simply by considering conflicting affidavits. It has always been possible, however, to challenge an affidavit of documents if it was obvious from the record (pleadings, the list or affidavit of documents, or other discovered documents) that a party had given incomplete discovery.

13.1.35   The Rules of Court now expand, in some circumstances, the bases upon which a party may challenge the sufficiency of discovery made by another. In general terms, this is achieved by giving the court a discretion to make an order for particular discovery.

In Western Australia (O 26 r 6), an application for such an order must be supported by an affidavit which refers to a particular document or class of documents, and deposes to a belief both that the other party has at some time had possession or power of that document (or where applicable, class of documents) and that it is relevant. There is a similar rule in Tasmania (r 392) in relation to orders for production for inspection of particular documents. For a discussion of the then equivalent Victorian rule, see *Beecham Group Ltd v Bristol-Myers Co* [1979] VR 273 at 278.

13.1.36   The practice in relation to further and particular discovery is now much broader in the Northern Territory (r 29.08), Queensland (r 223), Tasmania (r 388) and Victoria (r 29.08). The Victorian rule typifies the procedure in those jurisdictions, although the rules vary in detail.

13.1.37E   **Supreme Court (General Civil Procedure) Rules 2005 (Vic)**
Order 29 — Discovery and Inspection of Documents

Order for particular discovery

29.08 (1) This Rule applies to any proceeding in the Court.

(2) Where, at any stage of a proceeding, it appears to the Court from evidence or from the nature or circumstances of the case or from any document filed in the proceeding that there are grounds for a belief that some document or class of document relating to any question in the proceeding may be or may have been in the possession of a party, the Court may order that party to make and serve on any other party an affidavit stating —

    (a)   whether that document or any, and if so what, document or documents of that class is or has been in that party's possession; and

    (b)   if it has been but is no longer in that party's possession, when the party parted with it and that party's belief as to what has become of it.

(3) An order may be made against a party under paragraph (2) notwithstanding that the party has already made or been required to make an affidavit of documents.

13.1.38   In Queensland (r 223(4)(b)), the order for particular discovery may be made if it appears there is an objective likelihood that the duty to disclose has not been complied with, or that a specified document or class of documents exists or existed and has passed out of the possession or control of a party. The order may also be made if there are special circumstances and the interests of justice require it: r 223(4)(a). In the latter case, it is not necessary that the documents sought to be disclosed be directly relevant to an allegation in issue and hence otherwise encompassed by the general duty of disclosure under r 211(1): *Lampson (Australia) Pty Ltd v Ahden Engineering (Aust) Pty Ltd* (1998) 10 ANZ Ins Cas 61-402.

13.1.39   In the Federal Court (r 20.21), there is a procedure for a party who claims that a document or category of documents may be or have been in another party's control to apply for an order requiring the other party to file an affidavit stating whether the document or any document of that category is or has been in that party's control, and if no longer in the party's control, when it was last in the party's control and what has become of it. The party seeking the order must identify the documents or category of documents as precisely as possible. The procedure is quite separate from the procedure for applying for an order for standard or more extensive discovery: see **13.1.9**.

13.1.40   In South Australia, the basis on which a party may challenge the sufficiency of disclosure or production of documents has also been broadened. Rule 145 provides that if there is reason to doubt whether a party has fully complied with the obligation to disclose and produce documents, the court may make orders it considers appropriate to ensure that the obligations have been fully complied with and, if necessary, to enforce those obligations. Examples of the orders which may be made include: an order requiring the party, or another person who may be in a position to provide relevant information, to appear before the court for examination; and an order requiring the party to answer written questions relevant to ascertaining whether the party has made full disclosure.

13.1.41   It has been seen that in New South Wales, Pt 21 Div 2 enables a party, by notice, to require discovery in respect of specified documents: see **13.1.10**. In respect of discovery made under a court order, there is no rule directed towards challenging the sufficiency of discovery or the contents of a verifying affidavit. There is, however, a general power in the court to determine any question arising under the rules, and for that purpose to inspect any document and if the document is not before the court to order that the document be produced to the court for inspection: r 1.8.

In the Australian Capital Territory (r 606(6)), the rules prohibit the use of an affidavit on an application to the court for an order about disclosure, including an order for a party to make further and better disclosure, unless the court otherwise orders.

Discovery of documents and information technology

13.1.42   One of the challenges for litigation in the electronic age is dealing with the explosion in the number of documents which are discoverable in many civil matters. In *Seven Network Ltd v News Ltd* [2007] 1062 FCA at 15, for example, it is reported there were 85,653 discovered documents, comprising 589,392 pages. In matters involving large volumes of documents which must be gathered, sorted, indexed and classified, it has been common for some time for litigation practitioners to use information technology as an aid in document management. In most jurisdictions, practice notes have been issued to encourage parties to consider, from the start of proceedings, ways to use information technology to manage the discovery and inspection process more efficiently and also to use technology in appropriate cases at trial.

There are such practice notes or directions in the Federal Court (Practice Note CM 6: Electronic Technology in Litigation, issued 1 August 2011; New South Wales (Practice Note SC Gen 7: Supreme Court — Use of Technology, with effect from 1 August 2008); the Northern Territory (Practice Direction No 2 of 2002: Guidelines for the Use of Information Technology in any Civil Matter, issued 13 February 2002); Queensland (Practice Direction No 10 of 2011: Use of Technology for the Efficient Management of Documents in Litigation, issued 22 November 2011); South Australia (Supreme Court Practice Directions 2006, 2.1: Guidelines for the Use of Electronic Technology, substituted Amendment No 2, with effect from 1 May 2007); and Victoria (Practice Note No 1 of 2007: Guidelines for the Use of Technology in any Civil Matter, issued 8 February 2007). In Western Australia, Consolidated Practice Directions 2009, 1.2.5: The Use of Electronic Material in Trials and Appeals, provides guidance to parties who may be required, or who wish, to present material to the court in electronic format, but this practice direction does not cover the use of technology in pre-trial processes. In the Australian Capital Territory, the rule of court providing for orders about disclosure (r 606(1)) permits the court to order that the lists of documents of one or more of the parties be served in a stated electronic form, but there are no relevant practice directions in that jurisdiction, or in Tasmania.

13.1.43E	**Supreme Court Practice Direction No 10 of 2011 (Qld)**
	Use of Technology for the Efficient Management of Documents in Litigation

[Although the practice notes all incorporate a statement about their purpose, the practice notes in the Federal Court and Queensland also helpfully set out a number of propositions about efficient document management that have inspired the development of the practice notes and provide a rationale for most of the requirements they contain. For example, para 2 of Queensland Supreme Court Practice Direction No 10 of 2011, Use of Technology for the Efficient Management of Documents in Litigation, provides:]

2. Purpose

2.1 The purpose of the Practice Direction is to encourage the efficient and cost effective management of documents at all stages of litigation and to facilitate the conduct of electronic trials.

2.2 The Practice Direction is based upon the following propositions: —

(a) documents must be managed efficiently to minimise the cost of litigation to both the Court and litigants;

(b) the earlier the litigants consider the appropriate use of technology in all aspects of litigation, the greater the benefits which will be derived, particularly if the litigation proceeds to a trial;

(c) litigants need to liaise with one another and plan document identification, management and exchange as early as possible, ideally as soon as proceedings have been instituted;

(d) consistent use of an agreed Document Management Protocol from the earliest possible stage should minimize the cost of managing both hard copy and electronic documents in both small and large cases;

(e) printing large volumes of electronic documents for the purpose of disclosure is usually costly and inefficient;

(f) photocopying large volumes of paper documents multiple times for the purpose of litigation is usually costly and inefficient;

(g) litigants must endeavour to exchange documents in a usable, searchable format or in the format in which the documents are ordinarily maintained to allow the party receiving the documents the same ability to access, search, review and display the documents as the party producing them.

13.1.44   Most of the practice notes and directions refer to document 'protocols'. Document protocols may simply set out how documents are to be described. They prescribe what information (known as 'fields') should be included, eg, date, document type, author, author organisation, recipient, recipient organisation. The protocols also explain how the information for each field should be provided. They may, for example, require that the 'author' in the document field should be described with 'last name first then first initial only'. When document management software is used and data and documents are exchanged electronically, protocols may also cover such things as document numbering, imaging standards for documents that have to be scanned and a hard copy stored, virus responsibility, and protocols for updating or adding additional documents or images.

The details of the practice notes or directions vary, but the notes in the Federal Court, New South Wales, the Northern Territory, Queensland, South Australia and Victoria have a number of similarities. They each encourage parties to use electronic data (or databases) to create lists of their discoverable documents, and encourage parties to give discovery by exchanging databases created in accordance with an agreed protocol. They also encourage parties to consider the use of technology, including an electronic court book, at trial.

13.1.45   Until very recently, all the Australian practice notes and directions about the use of information technology were significantly limited, in that they did not cover electronic discovery issues *per se* because they did not cater for the discovery of electronic documents in their native electronic format, such as email and their attachments, and electronic documents found on hard disks. There are a range of issues associated with sourcing documents in native electronic format, particularly those to be found on backup tapes. Rather than deal with these issues, the notes dealt only with the conversion of hard copy documents to an electronic format, ie, the electronic information to which they referred generally related to paper documents that have been scanned and the meta-data used to describe certain details about the document, eg, document type (eg, letter, contract etc), the document date and the document author. Parties were required to print electronic documents onto paper, scan the printed documents into a digitised format, index the scanned documents in a database system, and exchange the scanned documents plus their supporting meta-data with the other litigants and the court.

The latest practice notes in the Federal Court, Queensland, New South Wales and Victoria formally recognise the distinction between paper and electronic documents and attempt to address some of the associated issues. Their requirements include an obligation on the parties to meet and confer for the purpose of reaching agreement about a range of issues relating to efficient document management in a proceeding, including the discovery of electronic documents in their native format.

Parties obliged to make discovery

13.1.46 The rules generally provide that a party to litigation may be obliged to make discovery to any other party: FCR r 20.13; ACT r 607; NSW rr 21.2, 21.10; NT r 29.02; Tas r 383; Vic r 29.02; WA O 26 rr 1, 2. Usually that will mean discovery may be required between parties on different sides of the record as, for example, between plaintiff and defendant or defendant and third party, but the rules are broad enough to extend to any parties between whom there is an issue to be adjusted: *Shaw v Smith* (1886) 18 QBD 193 at 200. See also *Thiess v TCN Channel 9 Pty Ltd (No 2)* [1992] 1 Qd R 237 at 238–9.

The rules in most jurisdictions also make provision in varying degrees for an affidavit of documents by a party to a proceeding to be made available to other parties beyond the party which sought discovery, irrespective of whether there is any issue between the other party and the party making discovery: FCR r 15.14; ACT r 607(3); NT r 29.06; Tas r 385; Vic r 29.06; WA O 26 r 5.

In Queensland (r 211), the obligation on a party to a proceeding is to make disclosure to 'each other party'. The position is similar in South Australia (rr 136, 60) where the list of documents is to be filed and served on all other parties for whom a current address for service is on file in the court.

Solicitor's obligations

13.1.47 In preparing for trial, solicitors bear a heavy burden in relation to discovery, as their clients will not usually know or appreciate the legal requirements relating to discovery. It is a solicitor's professional duty to be personally satisfied that the client is providing complete discovery. In *Myers v Ellman* [1940] AC 282, views were expressed in the House of Lords that if a client will not give information which his or her solicitor is entitled to require, or if the solicitor knows that the affidavit of documents insisted upon by the client is misleading, then the solicitor should withdraw. It was also suggested in that case that the solicitor bears a special burden in this respect when an allegation of fraud is made against his or her client.

The rules in some jurisdictions require a party's solicitor to furnish a certificate about discovery. In the Australian Capital Territory (rr 607(3), 608(4)), a party who is represented by a solicitor must file the solicitor's certificate of advice with the list of documents. The certificate of advice must state that the solicitor has advised the party of their obligations in relation to a notice or order requiring discovery, and the solicitor is not aware of any discoverable documents that are or have been in the party's possession and are not included in the party's list of documents.

In New South Wales (r 21.4), the solicitor must, within the time for compliance with the order for discovery, serve on the party to whom discovery is made a certificate stating that he or she has advised the client as to the obligations arising under an order for discovery, and that he or she is not aware of any documents which are not included in the list of documents but should have been. In Queensland (r 226) and Western Australia (O 26 r 15A), the solicitor having the conduct of the proceeding must, by certificate given at the trial, certify that the duty of disclosure has been explained to the client. If the client is a corporation, the certificate must identify the individual to whom the duty was explained.

Discovery: a continuing obligation?

13.1.48   In the Federal Court (r 20.20), a party who has been ordered to give discovery is under a continuing obligation to discover any document not previously discovered that would otherwise need to be discovered to comply with the order. The position is similar in New South Wales, where a party who has provided discovery under an order made under r 21.2 is under a continuing obligation to give discovery of documents which fall within the ambit of the order and which come into the possession of the discovering party (or which the discovering party becomes aware are in his or her possession, custody or power): r 21.6. It is also specified that if the discovering party becomes aware that a document claimed to be privileged was not, or has ceased to be a privileged document, that party must notify the other party and make the document available for inspection.

In Queensland, r 211(2) states that the duty of disclosure continues until the proceeding is decided. This principle is reinforced by r 214, which specifies several particular times in the course of a proceeding when disclosure of documents must be made. Rule 214(2)(e) stipulates that where, subsequent to a time already covered by earlier sub-paragraphs of the same rule, a document first comes into the possession or control of a party (or is located by a party), the party must make disclosure of the document within seven days.

In the Australian Capital Territory (r 611), the Northern Territory (r 29.16), South Australia (r 136(3) (b)), Victoria (r 29.15) and Western Australia (O 26 r 2), there are also specific rules requiring supplementary discovery of any discoverable documents which have come into a party's possession after the party has given discovery.

These rules abrogate the principle that applied in the absence of a specific rule dealing with the issue that the obligation to give discovery only extended to documents in the possession of the discovering party at the date of the list (and verifying affidavit, if any): *TNT Management Pty Ltd v Trade Practices Commission* (1983) 47 ALR 693.

Permitted use of discovered documents

13.1.49   In relation to documents produced by one party to another in the course of discovery, there is an implied undertaking by each party not to use any document for any purpose, otherwise than in relation to the litigation in which it is disclosed: *Esso Australia Resources Ltd v Plowman* (1995) 183 CLR 10 at 32; 128 ALR 391; *Hearne v Street* (2008) 235 CLR 125 at [96]–[97]. The restriction on the use of documents generated by litigious processes is an obligation of substantive law: *Hearne v Street* (2008) 235 CLR 125 at [106].

The principle applies to parties' solicitors, who may be liable to punishment for contempt of court if they misuse for ulterior purposes documents made available on discovery. It also extends to others who obtain documents they know were produced on discovery: *Hammersley Iron Pty Ltd v Lovell* (1998) 19 WAR 316. In the Australian Capital Territory (r 673) the obligation, in relation to the use of the documents and the exposure to be dealt with for contempt of court if a person contravenes the rule without reasonable excuse, is express.

13.1.50 If special circumstances exist, the court may release or modify the implied undertaking so as to enable the use of discovered documents in another piece of litigation, or for other non-litigious purposes. In *Springfield Nominees Pty Ltd v Bridgelands Securities Ltd* (1991) ATPR 52,162, Wilcox J was satisfied such special circumstances existed. Although not purporting to propound an exhaustive list, his Honour suggested the following factors as relevant to the issue:

(a)   the nature of the document;

(b)   the circumstances under which it came into existence;

(c)   the attitude of the author of the document and any prejudice the author may sustain, whether the document pre-existed litigation or was created for that purpose and therefore expected to enter the public domain;

(d)   the nature of the information in the document (in particular whether it contains personal or commercially sensitive information);

(e)   the circumstances in which it came into the hands of the applicant for leave; and

(f)   the likely contribution of the document to achieving justice in the other proceeding.

It may be argued that once documents that were obtained on discovery have been admitted into evidence and consequently entered the public domain, then unless the court orders to the contrary there is little point in requiring the parties to continue to honour the implied undertaking. However, in *British American Tobacco Australia Services Ltd v Cowell representing the Estate of McCabe (dec'd)* [2003] VSCA 43, the Court of Appeal in Victoria rejected the submission for the respondent that the implied undertaking ceased once the documents were put in evidence. The court accepted the document then became part of the public domain and so could be used by a stranger to the litigation but found it did not mean the document therefore ceased to be subject to the implied undertaking binding the parties themselves.

The authorities considering the nature of the implied undertaking, and the circumstances in which the court may release or modify it, were discussed in the Supreme Court of Queensland in *Northbuild Construction Pty Ltd v Discovery Beach Project Pty Ltd* [2009] QSC 76, extracted below.

13.1.51E   Northbuild Construction Pty Ltd v Discovery Beach Project Pty Ltd
[2009] QSC 76
Supreme Court of Queensland

[The originating proceedings had been commenced in May 2005 for an asset-freezing order over the assets of Discovery Beach Pty Ltd (Discovery Beach) in aid of an arbitration proceeding which was ongoing. It was to be expected that the arbitration proceeding would decide what, if anything, was owing to Northbuild Construction Pty Ltd (Northbuild) by Discovery Beach under complex contractual arrangements between them. The only proceedings in the Supreme Court were ancillary to the arbitration proceedings.

In one of the applications before the Supreme Court, Northbuild sought leave to use documents obtained in the Supreme Court proceeding, including documents obtained by subpoenas, to bring an application to wind up Discovery Beach, the respondent in the Supreme Court proceeding. Northbuild wished to use those documents to demonstrate that Discovery Beach was insolvent and/or that the conduct of the directors vis-à-vis creditors dictated that it was just and equitable that Discovery Beach be wound up. Discovery Beach opposed the grant of leave.]

White J (at [28]–[37]):

[28] It is now accepted that the restriction on the use of documents generated by litigious processes is an obligation of the substantive law. [*Hearne v Street* (2008) 235 CLR 125 at [106]. Justices Hayne, Heydon and Crennan in *Hearne v Street* said: [(2003) 8 VR 571]

> Where one party to litigation is compelled, either by reason of a rule of court, or by reason of a specific order of the court, or otherwise, to disclose documents or information, the party obtaining the disclosure cannot, without the leave of the court, use it for any purpose other than that for which it was given unless it is received into evidence. The types of material disclosed to which this principle applies include documents inspected after discovery, answers to interrogatories, documents produced on subpoena, documents produced for the purposes of taxation of costs, documents produced pursuant to a direction from an arbitrator, documents seized pursuant to an Anton Piller order, witness statements served pursuant to a judicial direction and affidavits.

[29] There may be some controversy about the scope of "received into evidence". In this application the documents sought to be used by Northbuild have been exhibited to affidavits filed in the court and, submitted by Northbuild, in that manner, to have entered into evidence, and thereby into the public domain. It is the case that pursuant to r 981 of the *Uniform Civil Procedure Rules 1999* (Qld) a non-party may search a court file and, on payment of the prescribed fee, must be provided with the identified document which may then be inspected. But that process does not bring the document into the public domain so as to bring to an end a party's obligation not to use the documents for a purpose outside the proceedings in which it was produced. In any event, Mr Savage referred to observations by the Victorian Court of Appeal in *British American Tobacco Australia Services Ltd v Cowell (representing the estate of McCabe (deceased) No. 2)* [(2003) 8 VR 571] which strongly suggest that a party will always need leave to make collateral use of a document containing private or confidential material about another party even where the document has been tendered into evidence. That it has entered the public domain will be a factor in the exercise of the discretion to grant leave. It is unnecessary to enter into that interesting debate because Northbuild has proceeded on the basis that the mere attachment of these documents to affidavits does not absolve Northbuild of its obligation not to use them or any information or understanding arising from perusing them "for a collateral or ulterior purpose" [*Central Queensland Cement Pty Ltd v Hardy* [1989] 2 Qd R 509 per McPherson J at 510.] other than in the pursuit of the freezing order or the arbitration, without the leave of the court.

[30] The plurality in *Hearne v Street* noted: [at 107]

> The importance with which the courts have viewed the obligation under discussion is indicated by the fact that although it can be released or modified by the court, that

dispensing power is not freely exercised, and will only be exercised where special circumstances appear:

> 'Circumstances under which the relaxation would be allowed without the consent of the serving party are hard to visualise, particularly where there was any risk that the statement might be used directly or indirectly to the prejudice of the serving party' [footnote omitted].

[31] If a party wishes to be released from its obligation not to use material obtained from one proceeding in a different proceeding [the exception, generally, being to commence contempt proceedings against the offending party and within the proceedings themselves, *Crest Homes v Marks* [1987] 1 AC 829] what have been described as "special circumstances" must be shown. [*Crest Homes v Marks*] Lord Oliver in *Crest Homes* suggested that an order granting leave ought not occasion injustice to the disclosing party and whether granted will be dictated by the facts of each application.

[32] In *Springfield Nominees Pty Ltd v Bridgeland Securities* [(1992) 38 FCR 217] Wilcox J said that an applying party must identify "a special feature of the case" which is not usually present and which justifies the course proposed. He concluded, after mentioning several factors which may be relevant to the exercise of the court's discretion [at 225]:

> ... and, perhaps most important of all, the likely contribution of the document in achieving justice in the second proceeding.

[33] There is an overall public interest in insolvent companies not trading which Mr Savage urged would cause the court to exercise its discretion to grant leave in this case. Mr McCartney has deposed [footnote omitted] that the only action in which Discovery Beach is engaged is the holding and selling of lots it owns in the development at Marcoola, the costs associated with which are payable out of sale proceeds. There are no outstanding demands from Capital Finance in respect of the finance facility it has provided Discovery Beach; there are no creditors pressing for payment of any amounts alleged to be owing to them apart from Northbuild; there are no outstanding statutory demands against Discovery Beach. Furthermore, Mr McCartney deposes that Discovery Beach has paid all amounts which it has been ordered to pay to Northbuild by the interim determinations. Whilst Northbuild characterises itself as a substantial creditor of Discovery Beach, that is denied by Mr McCartney and, over payment to $5 million is asserted. Those very issues are the subject matter of the arbitration and expert determinations.

[34] Mr McCartney deposed that Discovery Beach's only continuing financial commitment is its legal costs in the proceedings involving Northbuild and that Moonbrook, a company of which he is director and which is a 50% shareholder in Discovery Beach, has supported and will continue to support by capital contributions Discovery Beach in those proceedings.

[35] A company is required to pay all of its debts as they fall due [Section 95A Corporations Act 2001] but not necessarily from its own money. As a matter of commercial reality, Moonbrook and Mr McCartney's close involvement, will continue to support Discovery Beach financially. As an aspect of leave to be relieved of the undertaking I conclude that Discovery Beach is not insolvent.

[36] As the many authorities to which counsel have referred make plain, where a party acting under the compulsion of a curial regime discloses private documents, it must be confident that [it] will not thereby be unfairly disadvantaged. [Excluding the special case of criminal (particularly serious) conduct revealed by the documents, *Bailey v Australian Broadcasting*

Corporation [1995] 1 Qd R 476 and the discussion by Lee J at 484–490]. If leave were given to Northbuild to use the documents in an application for leave to commence winding up proceedings against Discovery Beach it would, in effect, pre-empt the arbitration outcome. A winding up on the just and equitable ground will involve complex issues of the solvency of Discovery Beach when the impugned undervalue transactions occurred. If there is anything in that claim it, too, should await the outcome of the arbitration which will decided [sic] what, if anything, is owing to Northbuild by Discovery Beach and when that entitlement arose.

[37] In conclusion, Northbuild has not advanced any circumstance which would cause the court to grant leave to use the documents identified or any others for the purpose of commencing winding up proceedings. Northbuild's application is refused.

[See also *Barnes v Forty-Two International Pty Ltd* [2010] FCAFC 87.]

13.1.52   The rules in the Federal Court and New South Wales effect a change in the common law position. In the Federal Court (r 20.03), the rules provide that if a document is read or referred to in open court in a way that discloses its contents, any express or implied undertaking not to use a document except in relation to a particular proceeding no longer applies, unless the court otherwise orders. In New South Wales (r 21.7), a party cannot disclose or use a copy document, or information from a document, obtained on discovery for any purpose other than the conduct of the proceedings, without the leave of the court, but documents which have been received into evidence in open court are excluded from the prohibition. The release of the implied undertaking in New South Wales is therefore not as extensive as in the Federal Court, where the reading of or reference to the document in open court (as opposed to the receipt of the document in open court) is sufficient to put an end to the implied undertaking.

In the Australian Capital Territory (r 673), the rules make it clear that the fact that a document has been filed, received in evidence or read out in court does not remove the obligation to use the document only for the proper purposes of the action, but it does permit the court to take that fact into account in determining any penalty that should be imposed for breach.

Default

13.1.53   The court has inherent jurisdiction to enforce compliance with the rules, including power to strike out a proceeding and enter judgment. The rules also contain sanctions clearly intended to ensure that the interests of justice and the proper conduct of litigation are not defeated by the failure or refusal of parties to comply with procedural requirements. In most jurisdictions, they stipulate that if a party fails to serve any list or affidavit or to produce any document as required by the rules relating to discovery, or by a court order, the court may make such order as it thinks fit, including an order dismissing the proceedings where the plaintiff is in default, or striking out the defence if the defendant is in default: FCR rr 5.22, 5.23; ACT r 671; NT rr 24.02, 29.14; SA rr 12, 228; Tas r 372; Vic r 29.12.1 (a default notice must first be served on the party in default, that party then having seven days to comply with the notice); WA O 26 r 15. In New South Wales, the court's power to deal with default in relation to disclosure obligations falls within its general power to give directions and its powers to make a wide range of orders in default of compliance with those directions: Civil Procedure Act 2005 (NSW) s 61.

The rules in most jurisdictions provide that a party who fails to comply with an order relating to discovery or inspection of documents may be dealt with for contempt of court (ACT r 670; Qld r 225; NT r 29.14; Tas r 393; Vic r 29.14; WA O 26 r 15), or alternatively make it clear that the other specified consequences of default are not intended to limit the powers of the court to punish for contempt: FCR r 5.24; Civil Procedure Act 2005 (NSW) s 131.

In Queensland (r 225), a party who has not complied with disclosure obligations in respect of a document cannot tender the document, or adduce evidence of its contents, without the leave of the court. Similarly, in Tasmania (r 396), a document which has not been duly disclosed (either under Pt 13, or in a certificate of readiness filed under r 544, or joint letter of readiness filed under r 545) cannot be put into evidence. In New South Wales (Civil Procedure Act 2005 (NSW) s 61), the powers which may be exercised by the court specifically include a power to strike out, disallow or reject any evidence which that party has adduced or seeks to adduce.

In the Australian Capital Territory (r 674), documents not produced for inspection of another party in accordance with a notice in that regard cannot be put into evidence without the leave of the court. In deciding whether to give that leave, the court must act in accordance with the Commonwealth Evidence Act 1995 Pt 3.11 (Discretions to exclude evidence).

The rules in the other jurisdictions do not generally prevent the use at trial of documents which have not been properly discovered, but the omission may justify an adjournment, with costs ordered against the party in default: *State of Victoria v Davies* (2003) 6 VR 245.

13.1.54 It may be that a party has failed to make proper discovery of material documents, but this situation does not come to light until after the proceedings have concluded. In *Commonwealth Bank of Australia v Quade* (1991) 102 ALR 487, this failure was found to be sufficient to justify the court in ordering a new trial. The High Court made it clear that the primary consideration in determining whether a new trial should be ordered was whether this would best serve the interests of justice. Relevant factors included: the degree of culpability of the successful party, any lack of diligence on the part of the unsuccessful party, and the extent of any likelihood that the result would have been different if the order had been complied with and the non-disclosed material had been made available.

For recent applications of the decision in *Quade*, see: *Clarence City Council v Howlin (No 2)* [2010] TASFC 10; *Wiltshire v Amos* [2010] QCA 294.

13.1.55 Notes and questions

1. *In Sunland Waterfront (BVI) Ltd v Prudentia Investments Pty Ltd (No 4)* [2010] FCA 863, Logan J considers the origins of the practice of discovery of documents and the rationale for the change in approach which has been necessitated. His Honour said (at 5–6):

   However, by the latter part of the 20th century the advent in rapid succession of telex, photocopier, facsimile, email and electronic databases and the labour intensive quality of the task made the process of complying with general discovery applying the "train of inquiry" test an increasingly and at times inordinately expensive one to which the law of diminishing returns applied.

6. The practice was also one open to abuse by a well resourced party disposed to find controversy in relation to the extent of its discovery obligation or compliance by an adversary with its own such obligation. In this fashion, a less well-resourced adversary might be oppressed and a trial on the merits postponed or even avoided. Even in the absence of such abuses these same results with respect to adequacy of discovery, both Bench and Bar forgot that the practice was meant to be a handmaiden of justice, not its master.

See also: Australian Law Reform Commission, *Managing Justice: A Review of the Federal Civil Justice System*, ALRC 89, 2000, Ch 6; *Central Queensland Mining Supplies Pty Ltd v Columbia Steel Casting Co Ltd* [2011] QSC 183.

2. It has been observed that the rules in Tasmania (r 383(8)) specify that a party requiring discovery may choose not to require verification, in which case a list in appropriate form is sufficient. Similarly, in Western Australia (O 26 r 1), a party requiring discovery may decide to require only a list of documents attested by the party giving discovery or by a person authorised by the court to take affidavits. If the party requiring discovery does not agree to accept the list in that form, then the list must be verified by affidavit. In the Northern Territory (r 29.03), a party is only required to verify a list of documents if the party entitled to that list, by notice, requires it to be verified by affidavit. Under what circumstances would a party requiring discovery be best served by not requiring an affidavit? Certainly when the credibility of a party is in issue, discovery on affidavit is important. If the party fails to make complete discovery, this may assist in damaging that party's credit at the trial.

3. It has been seen that the rules generally provided that parties may inspect documents subject of the obligation to disclose, but in some circumstances an inspection is omitted and copies of documents provided upon request. In what circumstances would you envisage it to be important to inspect original documents rather than to simply rely on photocopies? What matters of potential significance may not be revealed by a photocopy, but would be apparent on inspection of an original document? Consider also whether a party complies with the discovery obligation by producing paper copies of emails or other documents created electronically. In what circumstances would you insist upon production of the document in its native electronic form?

4. It has been seen that the Queensland Rules allow for discovery by inspection when it is not convenient for a party to deliver documents because of the number, size, quantity or volume of the documents or some of them (r 216): see 13.1.6. Atkinson J held in *Shannon v Park Equipment Pty Ltd* [2006] QSC 284 that a party effecting disclosure under r 216 cannot be required to produce a list of documents. What practical problems follow from this conclusion about the effect of the Queensland rule?

5. 'Is discovery such a delicate flower that it will wilt if exposed to the full glare of the principles of free expression and open justice'? (I Eagles, 'Disclosure of Material Obtained on Discovery' (1984) 47 *MLR* 284 at 293.) Is the community able to judge the quality of justice administered in its courts if, though the proceedings are public, documentary evidence in those proceedings is not? In his article, Eagles

critically analyses the breadth of the restrictions which are imposed upon the use of discovered documents and the arguments supporting such restrictions. He also contrasts the very different judicial attitudes taken to this issue in America. For a more recent analysis of the implied undertaking, see M Groves, 'The Implied Undertaking Restricting the Use of Material Obtained During Legal Proceedings' (2003) 23 *Aust Bar Rev* 314. The author argues that criticisms that the undertaking interferes with 'open justice' are misdirected. He concludes the implied undertaking should be retained for pragmatic reasons and also because it provides a limited but useful form of protection of privacy.

6. There is authority that the implied undertaking about use of documents obtained on discovery will be overridden if a party in possession of such documents is served with a valid statutory demand to produce the documents to a regulatory body such as the Australian Competition and Consumer Commission or the Commissioner of Taxation: *Australian Securities Commission v Ampolex Ltd* (1995) 38 NSWLR 504. More conservative views were expressed in *Green v FP Special Assets Ltd* [1992] 1 Qd R 1. The conflict is considered by Paul Riethmuller in his paper: 'Confidentiality Agreements: How Useful are They' [1998] *AMPLA Yearbook* 118.

7. Differing views have been expressed about the extent of the obligation to particularise documents over which privilege is claimed. The issue seems to depend to some extent not only on the Rules of Court but also practices which have developed in each jurisdiction. In *Interchase Corporation (in liq) v Grosvenor Hill (Qld) Pty Ltd* [1997] 1 Qd R 163, the Queensland Court of Appeal concluded that the identification will be sufficient if it will facilitate production of a particular document for which privilege has been claimed if the privilege ceases or the court should order that privilege does not attach. In *Cape Wools SA v KPMG Corporate Finance (Vic) Pty Ltd* [2002] VSC 571, Habersberger J said (at [24]):

    > The decision in *Halliday* [*Halliday v ACN 003 075 394 Pty Ltd,* unrep, Sup Ct of Vic, app Div 11.4.94] makes it clear … that the ground or grounds of the privilege have to be related to each document. In the words of Ormiston J as his Honour then was 'the basis of which the privilege is claimed' in respect of each document has to be 'identified'. It is not sufficient as is commonly done, and was done, by the plaintiff in this case, to state a number of grounds at the start of the affidavit, without identifying which of them apply to which document. However, this does not mean, in my opinion, that a number of documents cannot in some way be grouped together under one or more grounds of privilege. The form is not important so long as it is clear in respect of each document the basis or bases on which privilege is claimed.

8. Although the general rule is that documents may only be used in the litigation in which they are discovered, the court may permit the use for another purpose if persuaded the use is proper. See 13.1.49–13.1.52. Would the 'public interest' be an appropriate justification for a departure from the general rule? An interesting discussion of this is contained in the judgment of Talbot J in *Distillers Co (Biochemicals) Ltd v Times Newspapers Ltd* [1975] 1 QB 613. In that case, the plaintiff successfully obtained an injunction restraining the defendants from using or disclosing documents which had been discovered by the plaintiff in an action brought against it for personal injury by users of the drug thalidomide, which

the plaintiff had marketed. His Honour noted the great interest of the public in the thalidomide story, but was not persuaded that the use which the defendants proposed to make of the documents (which included publication of a series of articles or a book based on information contained in them) was of greater advantage to the public than the public's interest in the need for the proper administration of justice, to protect the confidentiality of discovery of documents.

9. Another legal process which may entitle a party to access documents in the possession of a government agency is that created under freedom of information legislation. In *Johnson Tiles Pty Ltd v Esso Australia Ltd (No 3)* (2000) 98 FCR 311; (2000) 174 ALR 701, Merkel J concluded that a party's rights to seek and obtain information under freedom of information legislation are separate to the rights and obligations of disclosure under the Rules of Court, and there is generally no reason why they cannot be invoked concurrently with court processes. He held this was subject to the qualification that freedom of information legislation does not authorise any right or power conferred under the Act to be exercised in a manner that is vexatious or oppressive in the sense that it interferes with or undermines the integrity of the processes of the court.

10. What would you expect to be the position if documents have been destroyed *before* proceedings have commenced? That issue arose for consideration in the widely publicised decision of Eames J in *McCabe v British American Tobacco Australia Services Ltd* [2002] VSC 73, where his Honour had struck out the defence of British American Tobacco Services Ltd on the basis that it had systematically destroyed documents that might have been relevant to the plaintiff's case. The Court of Appeal reversed the decision. It concluded, in essence, that where one party alleges the destruction of documents before the commencement of the proceeding to the prejudice of the party complaining, the criterion for the court's intervention to strike out the pleading is whether that conduct of the other party amounted to an attempt to pervert the course of justice, or contempt of court before the litigation was on foot: *British American Tobacco Australia Services Ltd v Cowell* (2002) 7 VR 524. The plaintiff's application for leave to appeal to the High Court was refused.

In their article 'Destruction of Documents Before Proceedings Commence: What is a Court to Do?' [2003] *MULR* 12, Cameron and Liberman argue that the criminal test of attempting to pervert the course of justice (or contempt of court) as laid down by the Victorian Court of Appeal in *British American Tobacco Australia Services Ltd v Cowell* [2002] VSCA 197 is not the appropriate test, because it focuses on the lawfulness of the destruction rather than on the other party's ability to obtain a fair trial. The authors argue that the proper test should be whether the destruction of the documents has made a fair trial impossible, and they identify the factors they argue should influence a trial judge's exercise of discretion in a case where documents have been destroyed. See also: M Harvey and S LeMire, 'Playing for Keeps? Tobacco Litigation, Document Retention, Corporate Culture and Legal Ethics' (2008) 34(1) *Mon ULR* 163. This article also considers the decision in *McCabe*, the legislative responses to the decision, and the implications for legal ethics.

13.1.56 Further reading

H Austin, 'Protection of Confidential Information in Litigation' (2003) 77(1–2) *Law Inst J* 46 (discussion of various methods which can be used to protect commercially sensitive documentation).

The Hon M E J Black AC, 'New Technology Developments in the Courts: Usages, Trends and Recent Developments in Australia', *Seventh Worldwide Common Law Judiciary Conference*, London, May 2007.

D Coram and A Seskis, 'Litigation Support Systems' *Lawyers Weekly*, 31 May 2002.

M Groves, 'The Implied Undertaking Restricting the Use of Material Obtained During Legal Proceedings' (2003) 23 *Aust Bar Rev* 314.

S Jackson, 'New Challenges for Litigation in the Electronic Age' (2007) 1 *Deakin Law Review* 81.

S Le Mere, 'Document Destruction and Corporate Culture: A Victorian Initiative' (2006) 19 *AJCL* 304.

S Potter and P Farrelly, 'Managing E-files in Discovery in Civil Litigation Matters' (2003) 77(7) *LIJ* 38.

J Sher, 'Unmasking Masking: Covering Up Parts of Discoverable Documents' (2010) 10 *Aust Bar Rev* 35.

A Stanfield, *Computer Forensics: Electronic Discovery and Electronic Evidence*, LexisNexis Butterworths, Australia, 2009.

A Stanfield, *E-Litigation*, Thompson Legal & Regulatory Group, Australia, 2003.

S White, 'Comment: Discovery of Electronic Documents' [2000] *Digital Technology Law Journal* 1.

R Williams, 'Implied Undertaking: Express Reform Required', (2008) 34(1) *Mon LR* 147.

DISCOVERY FROM NON-PARTIES AND POTENTIAL PARTIES

13.2.1   Preliminary discovery is available in equity to assist in identifying a wrongdoer. There are also provisions in the Rules of Court for two forms of preliminary discovery: identity discovery, which is available to assist in identifying a prospective defendant; and information discovery, which is discovery from a defendant who has already been identified for the purpose of obtaining information or documents in order to decide whether to commence proceedings. The equitable procedure is particularly important for Queensland as (subject to a limited exception relating to interrogation of a non-party: see **13.3.4**) that jurisdiction does not have Rules of Court providing for preliminary discovery.

The Rules of Court also contain varying procedures which enable a party to obtain discovery by a person who is not a party to the existing proceeding.

Preliminary discovery in equity

13.2.2   It is possible in equity to obtain an order for discovery before a proceeding for substantive relief is commenced. The procedure is intended to facilitate the commencement of such a proceeding. The equitable procedure originated in the bill of discovery in equity to ascertain the identity of a wrongdoer. In its original form, the procedure was available only against persons who were themselves wrongdoers, compelling them to disclose the identity of other prospective defendants.

The procedure had ceased to be used in England after the introduction of the Judicature Act system. The decision of the House of Lords in *Norwich Pharmacal Co v Customs and Excise Commissioners* [1974] AC 133, however, made it clear that the procedure was still available. The House of Lords in this decision extended the scope of the procedure so as to permit an order against a person who was involved, even if innocently, in the wrongdoing. The plaintiff there obtained preliminary discovery from the Customs and Excise Commissioners to determine the identity of the importers of a chemical preparation into England in breach of the plaintiff's patent. The order was made on the basis that the Commissioners had unknowingly participated in the wrong by issuing a customs clearance to the importers.

Though initially permitting discovery to identify a wrongdoer, the principle has been extended in subsequent cases. In *Computershare Ltd v Perpetual Registrars Ltd* [2000] VSC 139, for example, it was used to order a party to an existing proceeding to give discovery not only of persons to whom confidential information had been wrongfully conveyed, but also the actual information that had been disclosed and accessed. For detailed consideration of the authorities in relation to the modern scope of the procedure, see *Idoport Pty Ltd v National Australia Bank Ltd* [2004] NSWSC 695 at [107]–[109].

Identifying a prospective defendant

13.2.3E   **Court Procedure Rules 2006 (ACT)**
Division 2.8.6 — Preliminary discovery

Discovery to identify potential defendant
650 (1) This rule applies if —
    (a)   a person (the applicant) has, or is likely to have, a cause of action against someone (the potential defendant); and
    (b)   either —
        (i)   the applicant wants to start a proceeding in the court against the potential defendant for the cause of action; or
        (ii)   the following provisions apply:
            (A)   the applicant is a party to a proceeding in the court;
            (B)   the potential defendant is not a party to the proceeding;
            (C)   the applicant wants to make a claim for relief in the proceeding against the potential defendant for the cause of action;
            (D)   the claim for relief could properly have been made in the proceeding against the potential defendant if the potential defendant were a party.
    (c)   the applicant, after making reasonable inquiries, cannot ascertain the identity or whereabouts of the potential defendant sufficiently to start the proceeding, or make the claim for relief, against the potential defendant; and

(d) someone else (the other person) may have information, or may have had possession of a document or thing, that tends to assist in ascertaining the identity or whereabouts of the potential defendant.

...

(5) The court may order the other person —

(a) to attend before the court to be examined in relation to the identity or whereabouts of the potential defendant; or

(b) to produce to the court any document or thing that is, or has been, in the other person's possession relating to the identity or whereabouts of the potential defendant; or

(c) to make and serve on the applicant a list of the documents or things that are, or have been, in the other person's possession relating to the identity or whereabouts of the potential defendant; or

(d) to produce for inspection by the applicant any document or thing that is, or has been, in the other person's possession relating to the identity or whereabouts of the potential defendant.

...

13.2.4 As in the Australian Capital Territory, the rules in most jurisdictions now provide specific procedures which enable a person to ascertain the identity of the proper defendant: FCR r 7.22; NSW r 5.2; NT r 32.03; SA r 32; Tas r 403C; Vic r 32.03; WA O 26A. The orders made by the court may require the respondent to give discovery, or to attend court to be orally examined and produce documents. Some of the rules specifically extend to a party to a proceeding who wishes to make a claim in the proceeding against a person who is not a party, although (except in New South Wales and Western Australia) they provide that the claim to be made must be one which could have been made in the proceeding if the unidentified person had been an original party: ACT r 650(1); NSW r 5.2(9); NT r 32.04; Tas r 403D; Vic r 32.04; WA O 26A r 3.

13.2.5 The procedures under the rules are free from the limitations of the procedure in equity, and mean that an order may be obtained against a person with the relevant information, whether that person obtained the information as a party to the transaction in question or simply as a mere witness. In *Hooper v Kirella Pty Ltd* (1999) 96 FCR 1; (1999) 167 ALR 358 at [31]–[34], the Full Court of the Federal Court summarised the considerations to be taken into account in determining whether to make an order for preliminary discovery under the rule as:

(a) An applicant must show that, after having made reasonable inquiries, he or she is unable to ascertain the description of a person sufficiently for the purpose of commencing a proceeding against that person;

(b) The applicant must show that 'some person' has or is likely to have knowledge of facts, or the possession of documents, tending to assist in identifying the prospective respondent. Unlike the equitable bill of discovery, there is no need for the person against whom relief is sought to be in any way implicated in the conduct of which the applicant complains;

(c) The applicant is not required to demonstrate a prima facie case against the prospective respondent. Nonetheless the power is not to be used where the proposed proceedings would be merely speculative and the prospect of the applicant succeeding in proceedings against the person he or she wishes to sue is a material factor; and

(d) As emphasised by the High Court in *John Fairfax & Sons Ltd v Cojuangco* (1988) 165 CLR 346 at 357, the order must be necessary in the interests of justice.

The rules in the Australian Capital Territory and New South Wales permit discovery of the whereabouts of the prospective defendant. Elsewhere the procedure is not available if the identity of the defendant is known and the applicant wishes to ascertain his or her whereabouts for the purpose of service: *Survival & Industrial Equipment (Newcastle) Pty Ltd v Owners of the Vessel 'Alley Cat'* (1992) 36 FCR 129.

Orders to assist in identifying a defendant do not override the ordinary position in relation to privilege: see under 'Privilege' at **13.5.1ff**. In several jurisdictions, this is expressly stated in the rules: FCR r 7.26; ACT r 652; NT r 32.02; Tas r 403B; Vic r 32.02.

Discovery from prospective defendant

13.2.6E   **Uniform Civil Procedure Rules 2005 (NSW)**
Discovery of documents from prospective defendant

5.3 (1) If it appears to the court that:
     (a) the applicant may be entitled to make a claim for relief from the court against a person ("the prospective defendant") but, having made reasonable inquiries, is unable to obtain sufficient information to decide whether or not to commence proceedings against the prospective defendant, and
     (b) the prospective defendant may have or have had possession of a document or thing that can assist in determining whether or not the applicant is entitled to make such a claim for relief, and
     (c) inspection of such a document would assist the applicant to make the decision concerned,
the court may order that the prospective defendant must give discovery to the applicant of all documents that are or have been in the person's possession and that relate to the question of whether or not the applicant is entitled to make a claim for relief.

     (2) An order under this rule with respect to any document held by a corporation may be addressed to any officer or former officer of the corporation.

     (3) Unless the court orders otherwise, an application for an order under this rule:
        (a) must be supported by an affidavit stating the facts on which the applicant relies and specifying the kinds of documents in respect of which the order is sought, and
        (b) must, together with a copy of the supporting affidavit, be served personally on the person to whom it is addressed.

     (4) This rule applies, with any necessary modification, where the applicant, being a party to proceedings, wishes to decide whether or not to claim or cross-claim against a person who is not a party to the proceedings.

13.2.7 The rules in the Federal Court (r 7.23), the Australian Capital Territory (r 651), the Northern Territory (r 32.05), Tas r 403E, Victoria (r 32.05) and Western Australia (O 26A r 4) each contain a rule similar to NSW r 5.3, which permits discovery from a prospective defendant in order for the plaintiff to decide whether to proceed. As in New South Wales, the procedure in each jurisdiction other than the Federal Court is specifically extended to cover the position of a party to a proceeding who has reason to believe that he or she has a right to relief from a person who is not a party: ACT r 651; NT r 32.06; Tas r 403F; Vic r 32.06; WA O 26A r 4.

In South Australia (r 32), the rule is wider. The same rule permitting a range of orders to assist in identifying a prospective defendant, including attendance by a person for cross-examination, also applies to assist a person who requires further information to determine whether a cause of action exists or to formulate a claim properly.

Discovery from non-party

<table><tr><td>**13.2.8E**</td><td>**Supreme Court (General Civil Procedure) Rules 2005 (Vic)**
Order 32 — Preliminary discovery and discovery from non-party</td></tr></table>

Discovery from non-party
32.07 On the application of any party to a proceeding the Court may order that a person who is not a party and in respect of whom it appears that that person has or is likely to have or has had or is likely to have had in that person's possession any document which relates to any question in the proceeding shall make discovery to the applicant of any such document.

13.2.9 The Federal Court (r 20.23), New South Wales (r 5.4), the Northern Territory (r 32.07), Tasmania (r 403FA) and Western Australia (O 26A r 5) have equivalent rules which allow for discovery against strangers to the proceedings. Under these rules, if the application is successful, the party against whom the order is made is required to serve an affidavit (or list) of documents and then give inspection in the usual way for documents not subject of a claim to privilege: see 'Discovery and inspection of documents' at **13.1.1Eff**.

There is a similar procedure in South Australia (r 146), where the person who is not a party to the proceedings (the respondent) may be ordered to disclose to the court whether or not the respondent is or has been in possession of evidentiary material relevant to a question in issue in the proceedings. The respondent may also be ordered to produce to the court any relevant evidentiary material still in the possession of the respondent, and also to give the court any information in the respondent's possession about the present whereabouts of relevant evidentiary material that has been but is no longer in the respondent's possession.

The rules under consideration require the party seeking discovery or disclosure by a non-party to make an application to the court, supported by affidavit evidence that it is likely the non-party has or had in his or her possession (which is defined to include 'custody or power') documents or classes of documents which relate to a question in the proceeding: FCR r 20.23 (the documents sought must be directly relevant to an issue raised on the pleadings or affidavits, and the affidavit must identify as precisely as possible the documents or categories of documents to which the application relates); NSW r 5.4(2) (the affidavit must specify the kinds of documents sought); NT r 32.08; SA r 146; Tas r 403FA(1); Vic r 32.08; WA O 26A r 5. Despite the apparent wide scope of most of these rules, the courts have demonstrated a reluctance to make orders for discovery by a non-party, and have tended to restrict the operation of the rule to cases 'outside the ordinary' where it is satisfied that such an intrusion into the affairs of a stranger to the litigation is necessary in the circumstances.

13.2.10E   **Richardson Pacific Ltd v Fielding**
                                         (1990) 26 FCR 188
                                      Federal Court of Australia

[The applicant sought an order for third party discovery under FCR O 15A. (See now FCR r 20.23.)]

Burchett J (at 188–90): Order 15A of the Federal Court Rules 1979 (Cth) expands the court's armoury to deal with cases which the previous law could not adequately reach. It is intended to overcome the limitation on the use of a subpoena *duces tecum* to obtain access to documents bearing upon litigation, which are not held by a party to the litigation but by some third party. In *Small's* case (*Commissioner for Railways v Small* (1938) 38 SR (NSW) 564), it was pointed out that a subpoena *duces tecum* could not be used as a substitute for discovery from a party or to obtain discovery from a third party. The new provisions contained in O 15A, by permitting discovery to be obtained from a third party, overcome that difficulty, and also provide a more practical and convenient means by which a party may obtain an opportunity to examine documents in advance of the hearing and with sufficient time to take such further steps as a perusal of them may suggest ...

[189] It is said that the court has traditionally adopted a policy of not burdening unduly a non-party to litigation in a manner comparable with the burden which is necessarily assumed by a party. As a generalisation this is true. It is then said that this policy would bar a general order for discovery by a third party not containing a quite precise specification of the documents to be discovered. While, in many situations, I accept that this represents a correct view of the approach which should be taken, indications to the contrary being absent, it should be pointed out that a purpose of O 15A is, quite expressly, to enable discovery to be obtained in some cases where anything less than the broad obligations imposed by an order for discovery would simply not meet the case.

The real question is whether the circumstances are sufficiently special to justify the use of the Order, for in my opinion the Order is intended, not for the general run of case, but for cases which do have about them something outside the ordinary. I do not agree that the court cannot go beyond what could be done upon a subpoena *duces tecum* issued in advance. I think in my discussion of *Small's* case, I have already made that plain. One limitation upon the use of O 15A, which has been suggested, is contained in *Williams Aviation Pty Ltd v Santos Ltd* (1985) 40 SASR 272, where it was held that, normally, an order for disclosure of documents by a stranger to proceedings should be made only when the stranger to the proceedings has the only copies of the particular documents, disclosure of which is sought, and the party to the proceedings, who is seeking disclosure, has exhausted his rights with respect to discovery against the other party to the proceedings. This is the kind of general proposition which highlights the exceptional nature of O 15A. I accept the general proposition, but at the same time I do not think that it would be at all appropriate to read down the language of O 15A by making such a general proposition into a fetter, restricting the applicability of the Order in cases where the evidence suggests that it would provide an appropriate and reasonable solution to real problems ...

[190] I agree with the view expressed by Kaye J in the apparently unreported decision of *Keviris Pty Ltd v Capital Building Society* (unreported, Supreme Court, Vic, 9 February 1988), which was cited to me by Mr Ireland, that the new jurisdiction which is exercised, when rules such as those contained in O 15A are implemented, should be exercised with caution. However, with respect, I do not think that the exercise of that jurisdiction should be fettered by any precise rules not suggested by the terms of O 15A itself. Rules, such as those which have been suggested in the cases, should, I think, be taken rather as general guides, as indeed it is plain was the approach adopted by O'Loughlin J in the *Williams Aviation* case (supra) to which I have already referred.

[See also *Rossi v Ballymore Tower* [1984] 2 Qd R 167; *Schutz DSL (Australia) Pty Ltd v VIP Plastic Packaging Pty Ltd (No 8)* [2010] FCA 1108.]

13.2.11 Queensland and the Australian Capital Territory now have streamlined procedures avoiding the necessity to apply for a court order. In Queensland (r 242), the procedure is termed 'non-party disclosure'. This procedure enables a party seeking disclosure of documents ('the applicant') to require a non-party ('the respondent') to produce documents that are directly relevant to an allegation in issue in the pleadings, that are in the possession or under the control of the respondent, and which are documents the respondent could be required to produce at the trial. There is a further restriction in that non-party disclosure cannot be used for the production of a document if there is available to the applicant another reasonably simple and inexpensive way of proving the matter to be proved by the document.

The procedure is initiated by the service of a 'notice of non-party disclosure' in the approved form: Form 21. The notice requires the production of the documents specified within 14 days after service of the notice on the respondent. The respondent must comply with the notice, but not before the end of seven days after service of the notice on the respondent: r 242. The notice is to state the allegation in issue in the pleadings to which the document sought is directly relevant, and must include a certificate signed by the applicant's solicitor (or the applicant, if acting personally) stating that there is not available to the applicant another reasonably simple and inexpensive way of proving the matter sought to be proved by the document. This requirement for certification reflects the view that non-party disclosure necessarily involves an infringement of the rights of non-parties and so far as possible those rights should not be infringed to any greater extent than is necessary to ensure the due conduct of the litigation. The notice is issued in the same way as a claim and is to be served within the same way as a claim, within three months of issue: r 243.

The uniform rules contain measures designed to protect persons who may in some way be affected by the production of the documents sought by the notice. They require that the applicant must serve a copy of the notice on any person, other than a party, about whom information is sought by the notice. If the applicant knows that the respondent does not own the document required to be produced, a copy of the notice must also be served on the owner of the document unless, after reasonable inquiries, the applicant cannot identify the owner of the document. The applicant must write the name and address of anyone who must be served with the notice on the notice itself, and on all copies. There are exceptions to the notice requirements if the applicant's solicitor believes, on reasonable grounds, that a person who would otherwise be required to be served is likely to fabricate evidence or perpetrate fraud if that person becomes aware of the notice. In that event, the notice requirements will not apply if the applicant's solicitor has completed a certificate in the approved form (Form 20), stating that the solicitor has that belief and that the interests of justice are likely to be jeopardised if the person were served with the notice. That certificate is to be tendered to the court after the close of the applicant's case: r 244.

The respondent, or a person who has been served with a notice of non-party disclosure, has a right to object to the production of some or all of the documents mentioned in the notice. The objection is to be taken within seven days after the notice is served or, with the court's leave, at a later time. There is also a right for another person who would be affected by the notice, but has not been served with it, to object to the production of some or all of the documents mentioned in the notice. This can be done at any time, but only with the leave of the court. The rules require that the objection be written and served on the applicant. If the person objecting is not the respondent, the objection must also be served on the respondent. The reasons for the objection must be clearly stated. The rules provide a list of a number of grounds which may be included in the reasons for objection, but the list is not in any way exhaustive: r 245. The service of an objection in the manner described operates as a stay of a notice of non-party disclosure: r 246.

Once an objection has been duly served, the applicant has seven days in which to apply to the court for a decision about the objection. The court has power to make any order it considers appropriate. This includes, but is not limited to, an order lifting the stay, an order varying the notice of non-party disclosure, or an order setting aside the notice. The parties to an application to decide an objection are to pay their own costs of the application, unless the court otherwise orders. The court is empowered to make such an order if, having regard to the merit of the objector's objections, the public interest in the efficient and informed conduct of litigation, and the public interest in not discouraging objections in good faith by those not party to the litigation, the court considers the circumstances justify it: r 247.

Unless the operation of a notice of non-party disclosure is stayed, and subject to any court order relating to an objection, the respondent must produce the document specified in the notice for inspection by the applicant at the place of business of the respondent, or the respondent's solicitor, within ordinary business hours, or at some other place and time agreed to by the applicant and respondent. If the respondent is in default, the court may, on application by the applicant, order compliance or make another order the court considers appropriate. The applicant is entitled to copy any document produced pursuant to a notice of non-party disclosure: r 248.

The applicant is required to pay the respondent's reasonable costs and expenses of producing a document (excluding those relating to an application to decide an objection). The respondent must give the applicant written notice of those costs and expenses within one month after producing a document. The applicant may, however, apply to the registrar for assessment of the costs and expenses, provided that application is made within one month after receiving the respondent's written notice: r 249.

13.2.12 A similar procedure to the Queensland procedure is available in the Australian Capital Territory, where the procedure is termed 'non-party production'. Consistent with the obligation in that jurisdiction to make discovery between parties, the procedure may be used to obtain production of any document that relates to a matter in question in the action, which is in the possession or under the control of the respondent, and which the respondent could be required to produce at the trial of the action: rr 660–667. Further procedural requirements related to the manner in which documents are to be produced, and directed towards ensuring a party has adequate opportunity to make a claim for legal professional privilege or to raise other grounds of objection are contained in Practice Direction No 2 of 2002: Non-party Production of Documents pursuant to Order 34B.

13.2.13 Further reading

B Kremer and R Davies, 'Preliminary Discovery in the Federal Court: Order 15A of the Federal Court Rules' (2004) 24 *Aust Bar Rev* 235.

N Suzor, 'Privacy v Intellectual Property Litigation: Preliminary Third Party Discovery on the Internet' (2004) 25 *Aust Bar Rev* 227.

INTERROGATORIES

What are interrogatories?

13.3.1 Interrogatories are a series of questions delivered by one party to the other which the party under interrogation is required to answer, usually on oath. The questions are designed to obtain admissions to assist in proving the case of the interrogating party, or to damage the case of the party under interrogation. As with other forms of discovery, they may also assist in narrowing the issues in dispute and in ensuring the interrogating party is apprised of the case to be met at trial. The rules in South Australia now describe the procedure as 'pre–trial examination by written questions'.

When are interrogatories permitted?

13.3.2E	Supreme Court (General Civil Procedure) Rules 2005 (Vic)

Order 30 — Interrogatories

When interrogatories allowed

30.02 (1) Subject to the other paragraphs of this Rule, any party may serve interrogatories on another party relating to any question between them in the proceeding.
   (2)   Where the pleadings between any parties are closed, interrogatories may be served without leave of the Court by any of those parties on any other of them.
   (3)   Where paragraph (2) does not apply, the Court may order that any party may serve interrogatories on any other party.
   (4)   By leave of the court an interrogating party may serve further interrogatories.
   …

13.3.3   As in Victoria, all jurisdictions have rules permitting the service of interrogatories on another party to the proceeding: FCR r 21.01; ACT r 630; NSW r 22.1; NT r 30.02; Qld Ch 7 Pt 1 Div 2; SA r 150; Tas r 405; WA O 27 r 1. These rules differ significantly, however, in relation to the nature of the proceedings and other circumstances in which interrogatories may be delivered. In the Australian Capital Territory (r 630), interrogatories may be served in any action without the leave of the court, although the court may order that interrogatories not be served in the action, or not be served by or on a particular party to the action, except to the extent (if any) stated in the order. In Victoria, interrogatories are allowed without the court's leave where the pleadings between the parties are closed, but otherwise leave is required. As in Victoria, the rules in the Australian Capital Territory (r 630(4)) limit the administration of interrogatories as of right to one set, with further interrogatories permitted only with leave.

In Tasmania (r 405), interrogatories may be delivered at any time before the certificate of readiness or joint letter of readiness is filed, or before an order is made that the proceeding be set down for trial, whichever occurs first. Rule 408A then sets out a procedure by which a party interrogated may give notice to the party interrogating that some or all of the interrogatories will not be answered, unless administered with the leave of the court or a judge. In that event, the party is under no obligation to answer the interrogatories specified, unless they are administered pursuant to the grant of leave. The party interrogating may apply for the necessary leave and this may only be granted if the court is satisfied that the interrogatory is necessary or that special reasons justify its administration.

13.3.4   Although at one time interrogatories were delivered as a matter of course, the rules in the Federal Court, New South Wales, the Northern Territory, Queensland, South Australia and Western Australia now require the court's leave for the delivery of interrogatories in all cases. The judgment of Greenwood J in *Australian Competition and Consumer Commission v ANZ Banking Group Ltd* [2010] FCA 230, extracted below at **13.3.6C**, includes a useful discussion of the background to the requirement for leave, and makes it clear that leave will not be granted as a matter of general practice.

Under the rules in the Federal Court, New South Wales, Queensland and South Australia, the application for leave to deliver interrogatories must be accompanied by a draft of the proposed interrogatories. Although this is not prescribed by the rules in the Northern Territory and Western Australia, the judgment in *Australian Competition and Consumer Commission v ANZ Banking Group Ltd* suggests that this is good practice in those jurisdictions as well.

In New South Wales (r 22.1(3)), the court may not make an order requiring any party to answer interrogatories in a personal injuries or fatal accident proceeding, unless it is satisfied that special reasons exist that justify the making of the order. In Queensland (rr 229, 230), the number of interrogatories is limited to 30, unless the court allows a greater number, and subject to an order of the court, leave is only to be granted where there is not likely to be available at the trial any other reasonably simple and inexpensive way of proving the matter sought to be elicited by interrogatory. (The Queensland rules are also unique, in that they authorise the court to grant leave for the delivery of interrogatories to a person, who is not a party to a proceeding, to help decide whether a person is an appropriate party to the proceeding, or would be an appropriate party to a proposed proceeding.) In South Australia (r 150), an application for the pre-trial examination by written questions must be made after the close of pleadings, but not more than 28 days after all parties have made disclosure of documents. A party will not be able to obtain a further order for pre-trial examination of the same party, unless the court is satisfied there are special reasons for the further order.

Scope of interrogatories

13.3.5 Interrogatories must relate to a question between the parties in the proceeding: *Buxton & Lysaught Pty Ltd v Buxton* [1977] NSWLR 285. They cannot be directed purely to ascertaining the names of witnesses, unless those names are themselves material facts, nor to the evidence which the party under interrogation intends to call. Similarly they may not be directed only to credit, or indeed to any fact which, if proved, will not establish anything material on the pleadings. The object of interrogatories and their permissible scope were discussed by Greenwood J in *Australian Competition and Consumer Commission v ANZ Banking Group Ltd* [2010] FCA 230, extracted below.

The Tasmanian rules set out more specifically than do those of the other jurisdictions the matters which may be the subject of interrogatories. Rule 406(1) permits interrogatories to obtain:

2. an admission of any fact which the party interrogating is required to prove on an issue against the opposite party;

3. an answer as to any fact directly in issue, or the existence or non-existence of which is relevant to the existence or non-existence of any fact directly in issue between the parties;

4. any fact, knowledge of which would inform the party interrogating of evidence of any fact directly in issue between the parties;

5. the name and address of any person who would be a necessary or proper party to the proceeding, if that information is required to make that person a party to the proceeding; or

6. any other fact as to which discovery may have been obtained in a suit in equity before the commencement of the Supreme Court Civil Procedure Act 1932 (Tas).

Rule 406(4) of the Tasmanian rules makes it clear that a party does not have the right to interrogate an opposite party with a view to finding out:

(a) a case for the party interrogating;

(b) the name of any person intended to be called or who might be called by the opposite party as a witness and whose name is not a material fact in the proceeding;

(c) the evidence of the opposite party;

(d) the manner in which the opposite party intends to establish their case;

(e) the line of facts, not being facts directly in issue, on which the opposite party intends to rely in support of their case; or

(f) the manner in which the opposite party intends to conduct the case at the trial.

The fact that a party who is otherwise bound to answer an interrogatory is not able to do so without disclosing the evidence or name of a person who might be called as a witness does not excuse the party from answering the interrogatory: r 406(5).

13.3.6C   Australian Competition and Consumer Commission v ANZ Banking Group Ltd
[2010] FCA 230
Federal Court of Australia

[The respondent (ANZ) sought a direction that it was not obliged to provide verified answers to interrogatories in response to a notice administered by the applicant (the ACCC) pursuant to an order granting leave under O 16 r 1 of the then Federal Court Rules to file and serve a notice requiring answers to interrogatories directed to matters described in the order. (See now FCR r 21.01. Under the new rule an application for an order requiring answers to interrogatories must be accompanied by an affidavit annexing the proposed interrogatories.) The judgment is extracted only so far as it considers the circumstances in which leave may be granted for the delivery of interrogatories and the scope of permissible interrogatories.]

Greenwood J (at 9, 14–15, 91–101):
[9] On 7 March 2009, his Honour, as Chief Justice of Australia, delivered an address to the annual conference of the Bar Association of Queensland on the topic *The Future of Litigation: Dispute Resolution in Jurassic Park?* In that address, on the topic of interrogatories, the Chief Justice at p 7, point 2, said this:

> *Interrogatories.* The Federal Court Rules required leave to interrogate. Experience with interrogatories over a period of time persuaded me of their extremely limited utility, if not total uselessness. Parties had to be reminded that interrogatories were not a form of pre-trial cross-examination. Applicants for leave were urged to agree all facts of which they sought admissions and to do so without resort to interrogatories unless there was a fact on which agreement could not be reached and the Court could be persuaded that it was appropriate to grant leave. Today interrogatories are something of a rarity.

...

Preferred practice
[14] As a matter of general practice, I am satisfied that no good purpose is served either in a case management sense or as a vehicle for serving the public interest by granting general leave to administer interrogatories. Notwithstanding that every case turns on its own circumstances, I find it difficult to identify a class of case where best practice does not require the applicant for leave to first formulate the precise questions for which leave is sought and serve those questions in draft on the other party or parties before seeking leave, irrespective of whether a party to be interrogated supports or consents to an order granting general leave to the interrogating party. The questions, formulated in a way which is consistent with the Federal Court Rules and the authorities, should be filed in Court supported by a short affidavit. The proposed interrogatories to be the subject of a leave application can then sensibly be discussed between the parties and when the question first comes before the Court, in controversy, steps might be taken at a directions hearing to attempt to resolve that controversy before a contested hearing occurs. There is no substitute for the discipline of reducing the proposed questions to writing (electronic or otherwise) before leave is sought. I would add this observation to the remarks of the Chief Justice quoted at [9]. Leaving aside the question of interrogatories directed to economic loss whether a claim for loss of profits or diminution in the value of a capital asset, which in any event, is invariably the subject of an expert's report, interrogatories in my experience in the conduct of commercial litigation

over approximately 30 years have rarely resulted in a party tendering an answer. More rarely has such an answer shortened the trial or reduced costs and even more rarely has the answer proved to be decisive on any central question of fact or issue in the litigation. The time, energy, effort and cost dedicated to addressing interrogatories and the inevitable challenge to them, is the true measure of the limited utility and lack of usefulness of interrogatories, the subject of the Chief Justice's remarks. I would however add one qualification. Properly formulated interrogatories directed to assertions of fact or perhaps facts from which inferences might be drawn about a pleaded fact in issue which elicit admissions, may possibly have the benefit of narrowing the issues and thus narrowing the scope of discovery, although that advantage may be more theoretical than real.

[15] For all the reasons mentioned by the Chief Justice of Australia in his 2009 address, the practice of first drafting the interrogatories and circulating the proposed interrogatories to the relevant parties and the Court, is to be preferred.

...

General approach

[91] I propose to deal with the question of whether each and every interrogatory is a proper interrogatory by asking these questions. First, is the interrogatory directed to a matter pleaded in the amended statement of claim but not admitted in the defence? That, fundamentally, was the proposition put in support of leave initially. Secondly, if the interrogatory is not directed to that question, is each interrogatory otherwise directed to a denial or non-admission which is said to be unclear? If so, on either basis, the third question is whether the interrogatory is vexatious or oppressive in the sense that those terms are understood in the authorities.

[92] Those questions seem to me to address the essential objective of interrogatories identified by Simpson J in *Green v Green* (1912) 13 SR (NSW) 126 at pp 132 and 133 (a view also adopted by Lockhart J in *WA Pines Pty Ltd v Bannerman* (1980) 30 ALR 559 at 574 (Bowen CJ agreeing at 562)) that interrogatories are characterised as questions in the nature of a demand for further and better particulars; questions directed to obtaining admissions as to facts which support the case of the interrogating party (here, the ACCC); questions directed to obtaining admissions as to facts which will destroy or damage the case of the interrogated party (here, ANZ); and, where the interrogated party is a fiduciary with an obligation to keep accounts, interrogatories may seek those accounts or a summary of them. Simpson J at p 133 also said this:

> I do not think the Court acts on hard and fast lines. If, for instance, the admission intended to be elicited will only afford a meagre or unsubstantial support to the plaintiff's case, while answering the interrogatory will involve the defendant in great labour and expense, I think the Court may exercise a discretion whether it will enforce an answer or not.

[93] Street J (with whom Cullen CJ agreed) said (at 138):

> I think the true rule on the subject is as stated in The Laws of England (Vol II, p 98), that 'where an account is claimed as part of the claim in an action, or questions of account arise in the action, interrogatories as to the details of the accounts may be allowed, *provided they are of sufficient importance to the party interrogating*, eg, enabling him to obtain an immediate decree or order at the trial, and *cause comparatively little trouble* to the party interrogated, *but not where the interrogatory would be oppressive*.' So stated, the rule seems to me to be in complete accordance with what was said by Collins MR in *White*

& *Co v Credit Reform Association and Credit Index Limited* [1905] 1 KB 653 at 659 that 'there is one general principle underlying the whole law as to interrogatories, namely, that *they must not be of such a nature as to be oppressive, and to exceed the legitimate requirements of the particular occasion.*' [emphasis added]

[94] In principle, an interrogatory ought only to be allowed if the end sought to be achieved by administering the question is reasonably proportionate to the effort required in answering the question.

[95] The first three classes of interrogatories identified by Simpson J were discussed by the Full Court of the Supreme Court of Victoria in *Adams v Dickeson* [1974] VR 77. At p 79, the Court (Winneke CJ, Gillard and Nelson JJ) said this:

The prime object of interrogation is to enable a party to litigation to obtain discovery of material facts in order either to *support or establish proof of his own case*, or to *find out what case (but not the evidence) he has to meet; or to destroy or damage the case brought by his opposition.* ...

...

The prime purpose is to obtain admissions from the respective parties so as to narrow the necessary proof of the issues raised in the pleadings. In jurisdictions where there are no pleadings, their main purpose lies in *obtaining particulars of the material facts* being alleged against the litigant interrogating. Above all, by such method, necessary proof of material facts which may be beyond doubt, can be facilitated by admission in answers to interrogatories, thereby removing proof of such facts from the arena of dispute at the trial, so saving time and expense of the parties, and permitting the court and the parties to get immediately to the vital issue or issues requiring determination by the court. [emphasis added]

[96] These passages were cited with approval by White J in *Bullivant's Natural Health Products v CF Planners* [1999] QSC 35 at [17] (unreported, Supreme Court of Queensland, 4 March 1999); by McDonald J *in CEO of Customs v Amron* [2001] VSC 373 at [52]; and by Duggan J in *State of South Australia v White* [2008] SASC 32 at [15].

[97] The ultimate aim of the process of discovery of information by interrogatories is to shorten the trial and save costs. Interrogatories are not a de facto written cross-examination of the interrogated party. The interrogatories must be relevant in the sense that they relate to a matter in question framed by the pleadings (including particulars contained in the pleading). In *Ring-Grip (Australasia) Pty Ltd v H.P.M. Industries Pty Ltd* [1971] NSWLR 798 at 800, the New South Wales Court of Appeal observed that it is not permissible to interrogate as to matters beyond the issues as disclosed by the pleadings and the particulars. In *Seidler v John Fairfax & Sons Ltd* [1983] 2 NSWLR 390, the phrase "relating to any matter in question" was understood to mean that the right to interrogate is not confined to the facts directly in issue but extends to any facts the existence or non-existence of which is relevant to the existence or non-existence of the facts directly in issue. See also *American Flange & Manufacturing Co. Inc. v Rheem (Australia) Pty Ltd (No. 2)* [1965] NSWR 193 per Myers J at 195; and *Marriott v Chamberlain* (1886) 17 QBD 154 per Lord Esher MR at 163.

[98] In *Potter's Sulphide Ore Treatment Ltd v Sulphide Corporation* Ltd (1911) 13 CLR 101, Griffiths CJ, at pp 109 and 110, considered that questions the answers to which might help, together with other facts, in establishing a body of facts from which an inference would be

drawn confirmatory of an element of the cause of action was the "very object of interrogatories" and that the degree of connection between the issues in the proceeding and the subject matter of the interrogatory must not be "remote or speculative". In *Tiver v Tiver* [1969] SASR 40 at 50, the Full Court of the Supreme Court of South Australia considered that the paramount consideration in determining whether an interrogatory is proper must be the relevance of the inquiry to the question in dispute and whether the information sought is strictly relevant and materially important in establishing the interrogating party's case. However, the two further objectives mentioned above are also important considerations. Generally, the ACCC supports the interrogatories on the basis that they go to matters pleaded but not admitted or a lack of clarity in the basis for a non-admission or denial. Other categories are identified at [87] of these reasons. The interrogatories must be "expressed in language of the most rigorous precision" and there is no place in interrogatories for "reading between the lines": *Kupresak v Clifton Bricks (Canberra) Pty Ltd* 57 ACTR 32 at p 34 per Blackburn CJ. Thus interrogatories must not be too uncertain or wide. Nor should the interrogated party or the Court be put in the position where it is required to go through the interrogatories and pick out, from a large number, those that are allowable discarding those that might be prolix, oppressive or unnecessary so as to ascertain which of them are admissible. The mere obligation to do so is itself unreasonable and can itself constitute oppression: *American Flange & Manufacturing Co. Inc. v Rheem (Australia) Pty Ltd (No. 2)* (supra) per Myers J.

[99] As to the question of whether an interrogatory is irrelevant, fishing, vexatious or oppressive or reflects ambiguity, I adopt the brief observations of Woodward J in *Aspar Autobarn Cooperative Society and Others v Dovala Pty Ltd & Others* (1987) 16 FCR 284 at 287–288 in these terms:

> ... I believe that 'vexatious' is used in the sense illustrated by *the Shorter Oxford Dictionary* when it says 'Of legal actions: Instituted without sufficient grounds for the purpose of causing trouble or annoyance to the defendant'.
>
> Thus an interrogatory administered for a purpose foreign to the proceeding would be vexatious, as would the traditional 'fishing' interrogatory, which seeks information on which to base claims not yet made. ...
>
> The word 'oppressive' ... means, I think, unfair, or unreasonable, in the sense that a good deal too much is expected of the party questioned. It may be that the details sought would take many hours to extract from records and would only be relevant to some side issue in the case. Or the question may be so ambiguous that it would be unfair to expect the party questioned to make assumptions about its meaning. Or the question may cover a wider geographic area or a longer period of time than is reasonably necessary in readying the case for trial. There are many questions which might be admissible in cross-examination, but are by their very nature inappropriate, and thus oppressive, in interrogatories. Questions going to credit or to motive are obvious examples.
>
> Thus it can be seen that the types of question which may properly be objected to as 'oppressive' are many and varied. Each contested instance will have to be resolved on the basis of the court's general impression as to what is reasonable.

[100] This passage was cited with approval by French J in *Nella v Kingia* [1987] FCA 299 at [12]–[18] and by Cox CJ in *Lowe v Marriott* [1998] TASSC 111.

[101] In *American Flange v Rheem* (supra), Myers J considered the following matters in ascertaining whether a set of interrogatories was oppressive:

- The number of individual interrogatories;
- The extent to which the providing an answer imposes an unreasonably onerous burden on the interrogated party;
- Whether the interrogatory required the interrogated party to form opinions, exercise judgment or draw conclusions;
- The repetitiveness of the questions;
- Whether the questions were in truth asked for the purpose of discovering trade secrets.

[His Honour then examined each of the 98 questions which had been put by the ACCC to ANZ. Leave was ultimately granted to the ACCC to issue and serve 18 questions as formulated and a further 16 questions as reformulated in the judgment. Leave to issue and serve 64 of the questions was refused. Following submissions as to costs, Greenwood J concluded that ANZ was successful in the main on matters of substance, and ordered that the ACCC pay 80% of the costs of ANZ: *Australian Competition and Consumer Commission v ANZ Banking Group Ltd (No 2)* [2010] FCA 567.]

Answers to interrogatories

13.3.7   In most jurisdictions answers to interrogatories are to be verified by affidavit: FCR r 21.03; ACT r 635; NSW r 22.3 (to the extent to which and in the manner in which the order giving leave for the interrogatories so requires); NT r 30.04; Qld r 231; Tas r 409; Vic r 30.04; WA O 27 r 1. In Western Australia, the rule provides that the party interrogating may elect to permit unsworn answers, but it is difficult to envisage circumstances in which it would be prudent to do so.

Subject to the rules permitting objections to answering interrogatories (see **13.3.15–13.3.17**), or in Tasmania to the rule permitting a party interrogated to give notice that some or all of the interrogatories will not be answered unless administered with the leave of the court (see **13.3.3**), a party served with interrogatories must answer to the best of his or her knowledge, information and belief. It may be that a party has no knowledge of the fact or matter inquired after, but has an enforceable right to information held by employees or agents who may have obtained the requisite knowledge in that capacity. In such event, the party is obliged to make all reasonable inquiries of such persons for the purpose (so far as possible) of forming a belief as to the fact or matter inquired after, and to answer the interrogatories in the light of the information obtained.

13.3.8C	**Sharpe v Smail**
	(1975) 5 ALR 377
	High Court of Australia

[The first defendant in the proceedings was the trustee of the estates of two bankrupts who had formerly carried on business in partnership as stockbrokers. The plaintiff claimed relief which included a declaration that she was entitled as against the first defendant as trustee, to a transfer of certain shares and to payment of sums representing capital monies and dividends paid in respect of those shares. Her claim was founded on allegations that the firm of stockbrokers received instructions to purchase particular shares and did purchase such shares on her behalf. However, instead of registering the shares in her name as they were bound to do, they transferred them to a private company controlled by them and of which, at the time of the proceedings, they were directors.

In setting out the basis of her claim the plaintiff had made certain allegations in relation to the conduct of one Pethard, who had been employed by the partners as a clerk. The defendants had commenced third party proceedings against Pethard. The plaintiff delivered interrogatories to be answered by the first defendant. In respect of one group of interrogatories, some but not all of which referred to Pethard, the first defendant answered:

> I have no personal knowledge of the matters enquired after. I have certain information about the said matters but I am unable to swear as to a belief in the truth of such information.

In respect of these (and other) answers given by the first defendant, the plaintiff brought an application for further and better answers to interrogatories.]

Gibbs J (at 378–80): The submission on behalf of the first defendant is that he cannot answer these interrogatories of his own knowledge and is not bound to answer from information supplied by Pethard unless he believes it to be true.

[379] The answer given to these interrogatories is insufficient. It does not state that proper — or indeed any — enquiries have been made and it is quite consistent with the answer given that if the defendant had made enquiries he could have obtained further information which he might have believed to be true. It is well established that a party interrogated must answer to the best of his knowledge, information and belief (unless he objects to answer) and that, to use the words of Bankes LJ in *Douglas v Morning Post Ltd* (1923), 39 TLR 402, at p 403, if he affirms as to one of these elements he must affirm as to all three. It is not enough to say that he has no knowledge, because he is bound also to answer according to information acquired from servants or agents who have gained it in that capacity, and where appropriate his answer must show that he has made all proper inquiries and that having made them he has no information enabling him to answer further: cf *Bank of Russian Trade Ltd v British Screen Productions Ltd*, [1930] 2 KB 90; *Ormond v Gunnersen*, [1920] VLR 402. A trustee in bankruptcy stands in the shoes of the bankrupt, and when he is sued to enforce an obligation owed by the bankrupt is under the same obligation to make discovery as the bankrupt would have been. No doubt those who were the servants of the bankrupt are not his servants, but in view of the special powers available to assist trustees administering bankrupt estates it does not follow that the trustee is absolved from making inquiries from the former servants of the bankrupt, although it might in some circumstances be oppressive to require him to do so. In argument it was submitted that it would be oppressive to compel the first defendant to make inquiries from Pethard, having regard to the fact that his interests are adverse to those of the first defendant. It does not follow, from the fact that Pethard has an adverse interest, that it would be oppressive to force the first defendant to make any inquiry of him — some inquiries might be quite innocuous and might relate to matters on which Pethard and the first defendant stood on common ground. However, the objections do not raise this matter, and the answers indeed suggest, not that the first defendant has not made inquiry of Pethard because it would be oppressive to require him to do so, but that he has obtained information from Pethard, and is unable to swear to a belief in its truth.

The answer to these interrogatories is insufficient; it does not show that the first defendant has made all proper enquiries and is answering to the best of his knowledge, information and belief. This would be enough to dispose of the matter so far as these interrogatories are concerned, but it is desirable to advert to the further submission made on behalf of the defendant, that he is not bound to given an answer based on information which he does not believe. In support of this submission reference was made to the decision of Lush J in *Gilchrist v R Wallace Mitchell Pty Ltd* [1972] VLR 481. Put shortly, the question discussed in that case was whether an employer need answer interrogatories upon the basis of information given to him by a servant who happens to be the opposing party in the action, or by a servant with an interest opposed to the employer's interests. Lush J [380] answered this question by saying that a defendant is bound to answer from information so supplied if he believes the information to be true but not otherwise. He accepted as the starting point of his discussion that a party, or a deponent answering on behalf of a corporation, must answer to the best of his knowledge, information and belief after making inquiries of his or its servants; that, as I have already indicated, is trite law. He went on to hold that a party cannot be compelled to admit a fact which he does not believe to be true or a fact in the truth of which he has no belief, and that a deponent cannot be required to swear that he has a belief in the truth of information when he has not. He then said (at p 483): 'If these principles are correct, they dispose of the present case. The deponent must answer after considering the information supplied by the plaintiff and the second defendant. If he has a belief based on this information there is no reason why he should not state it and he must state it. But if he has none, then he is not obliged to say that he has. I do not think that he is obliged to act on the basis that, the information which he has from these two parties being the only information he has, he must find the truth within it.' In my judgment this reasoning of Lush J is logically compelling and I regard it as correct. But the limits of the principles which he stated should be understood. Belief is not the same as knowledge and a party cannot truthfully swear that he has no belief based on information in his possession simply because he does not know that the information is true. Although he is not bound to say that he believes what he does not, he is not entitled to treat any information that he may receive with baseless suspicion, refusing to entertain belief unless it has ripened into certain knowledge. He cannot by refusing to believe information when there is no reason to doubt its truth escape from his obligation to answer to the best of his knowledge, information and belief. Moreover, the fact that information comes from a suspect source will not always be enough to render it worthy of disbelief; for example, it may be supported by other credible material.

[See also *Spedley Securities Ltd (in liq) v Yuill (No 4)* (1991) 5 ASCR 758 (NSW); *Spedley Securities (in liq) v Bank of New Zealand* (1991) 6 ASCR 416; *The Corporation of the Trustees of the Roman Catholic Archdiocese of Brisbane v Discovery Bay Developments Pty Ltd* [1995] Qd R 121.]

13.3.9 The obligation to make inquiries of servants and agents, or fellow officers, or servants or agents of a body corporate is now specified in the rules in the Australian Capital Territory: rr 633, 634.

13.3.10 In Victoria and the Northern Territory, the rules identify in more detail the sources from which a party is to answer interrogatories.

Source for answers to interrogatories

30.05 (1) A party interrogated shall answer each interrogatory insofar as it is not objectionable in accordance with the following provisions —

(a) the party shall answer from the party's own knowledge of the fact or matter which is inquired after by the interrogatory, and, if the party has no such knowledge, from any belief the party has as to that fact or matter;

(b) a party who has no knowledge of the fact or matter inquired after shall be taken not to have a belief as to the fact or matter where the party has no information relating to the fact or matter on which to form a belief or where, if the party has such information, for reasonable cause the party has no belief that the information is true;

(c) except as provided by paragraph (d), the party shall answer from any belief the party has as to the fact or matter inquired after irrespective of the source of the information on which the belief is formed;

(d) the party shall not be required to answer from the party's belief as to any fact or matter where the belief is formed on information that was given to the party in a communication the contents of which the party could not, on the ground of privilege, be compelled to disclose;

(e) where the party has no personal knowledge of the fact or matter inquired after, the party shall, for the purpose of enabling the party to form a belief as to the fact or matter (so far as the party can), make all reasonable inquiries to determine —

(i) whether any person has knowledge of the fact or matter which was acquired by that person in the capacity of his servant or agent; and

(ii) if that is the case, what that knowledge is;

(f) the party shall make the inquiries referred to in paragraph (e) notwithstanding that at the time the party is required to answer the interrogatory any person having the relevant knowledge has ceased to be that person's servant or agent;

(g) where the party is a corporation, this Rule shall apply, with any necessary modification, as if —

(i) the person who answers the interrogatories on behalf of the corporation were that party; and,

(ii) in particular, as if the reference in paragraph (e) to a servant or agent of the party were a reference to a servant or agent of the corporation.

(2) Where an interrogatory relates to a fact or matter alleged in the pleading of the party interrogated, nothing in paragraph (1)(d) shall affect the right of the interrogating party to obtain information as to that fact or matter pursuant to an application of the kind referred to in Rule 13.11.

13.3.12 The corresponding rule in the Northern Territory (r 30.05) is in almost identical terms. For the most part, these rules codify the established law and practice. Rule 30.05(1)(c), however, reflects a change in practice. It overcomes *Hawkes v Schuback* [1953] VLR 468, where it was decided that it was not necessary for a party to answer interrogatories from a belief which was based on information provided by a person who had personal knowledge of the fact inquired after, but was not the servant or agent of the party under interrogation.

13.3.13   Any one or more of the answers to interrogatories or any part of them may be tendered in evidence: FCR r 21.06; ACT r 636; NSW r 22.6; NT r 30.11; Qld r 238; SA r 152; Tas r 413; Vic r 30.11; WA O 27 r 9. However, in the same way that documents obtained on discovery may only be used in relation to the litigation in which they are obtained (see **13.1.49–13.1.52**), an implied undertaking arises in relation to answers to interrogatories to use them only in relation to the litigation in which they are given, although the liability in contempt for the later use of the answers will cease once the answers are tendered or read in open court: *Ainsworth v Hanrahan* (1991) 25 NSWLR 155 at 167–8 per Kirby P.

Default

13.3.14   In all jurisdictions, there are rules which allow the court to order a party who has failed to answer an interrogatory sufficiently, to answer, or to give a further answer, to the interrogatory: FCR r 21.05; ACT r 632; NSW r 22.4; NT r 30.09; Qld r 236; SA r 151; Tas r 410; Vic r 30.09; WA O 27 r 7. In most jurisdictions, the relevant rules also specifically permit an order requiring the person in default to attend for oral examination. The exceptions are the Northern Territory, South Australia and Victoria. In the Northern Territory and Victoria, there are separate procedures for oral discovery: see 'Oral discovery: Northern Territory and Victoria' at **13.4.1ff**. If a party defaults in complying with the order, the court may make such order as it thinks just, including an order that the action be stayed or dismissed, or that the defence be struck out and judgment entered accordingly: FCR r 5.23; ACT r 671; NSW r 22.5; Qld r 237; SA rr 12, 228 (these are general rules applying where there are procedural irregularities); Tas r 372; Vic r 30.09.1 (a default notice must first be served on the party in default; that party then having seven days to comply with the notice); WA O 27 r 8.

Objecting to answering interrogatories

13.3.15   The court has an inherent jurisdiction to strike out interrogatories which are oppressive or an abuse of process, or are otherwise generally inadmissible: *American Flange & Manufacturing Co Inc v Rheem (Aust) Pty Ltd (No 2)* [1965] NSWR 193. As is considered under 'Privilege', the court will also recognise several grounds upon which a party may claim privilege from answering an interrogatory. In several jurisdictions, a party may rely on the court's inherent jurisdiction in raising any objection to answering an interrogatory. The position is now different in the Federal Court, the Australian Capital Territory, New South Wales, Queensland and Victoria, where the rules restrict objections to the matters specifically covered by the relevant rules: see **13.3.17**. In each of these jurisdictions, however, the stipulated grounds for objection include both privilege and oppression.

13.3.16E   **Rules of the Supreme Court 1971 (WA)**
                                    Order 27 — Interrogatories

Grounds for objecting to answer

27.5 (1) A party may object in his statement in answer to interrogatories to answer any interrogatory on one or more of the following grounds —

   (a)   that it is scandalous or irrelevant, not bona fide for the purpose of the proceeding, unreasonable, prolix, oppressive or unnecessary;

   (b)   that the matters inquired into are not sufficiently material at that stage;

   (c)   privilege;

   (d)   any other ground on which objection may be taken.

13.3.17   As in Western Australia, the Rules of Court in most jurisdictions specify a number of grounds which justify a party's refusal to answer an interrogatory: FCR r 21.03; ACT r 631; NSW r 22.2; NT r 30.07; Qld r 233; Vic r 30.07. The rules in Tasmania (r 409(1)) permit a party to object to answering an interrogatory and provide a concise statement of the reasons for the objection, though they do not specify the grounds on which the objection may be based.

The specified grounds common to all jurisdictions where the grounds for objection are specified are that the interrogatory does not relate to any matter in question (or in Queensland, likely to be in question) between the party under interrogation and the party requiring the answer, and that the interrogatory is oppressive.

In most jurisdictions (FCR, ACT, NSW, NT, Qld, Vic, WA), the stated grounds also include privilege: see further under 'Privilege' at 13.5.1ff. Other grounds for objection specifically permitted in some jurisdictions include: that the interrogatory is vexatious (FCR, ACT, NSW, Qld); that it is unclear or vague or too wide (ACT, NT, Vic); that it requires the party under interrogation to express an opinion which he or she is not qualified to give (NT, Vic); that it is scandalous (ACT, WA); not bona fide for the purpose of the proceeding (WA); unreasonable (WA); prolix (ACT, WA); and unnecessary (ACT, Qld, WA); and that the matters inquired into are not sufficiently material at that stage (WA).

The Queensland rule also permits objection to answering an interrogatory on the ground that there is likely to be available to the interrogating party at the trial another reasonably simple and inexpensive way of proving the matter sought to be elicited by interrogatory. In this way, the rule reflects the requirement ordinarily to be satisfied in Queensland before leave will be granted for the delivery of interrogatories: see 13.3.4.

In the Northern Territory and Western Australia, the rules also permit objection on 'any other grounds' to be taken in a party's answers to interrogatories.

In Queensland (r 234), a rule headed 'unnecessary interrogatories' permits the court upon application to order that a person is not required to answer an interrogatory, or to limit the extent to which the person is required to answer an interrogatory.

In South Australia (r 151), a person who is required to supply written answers to written questions before trial may object to answering a question on any ground on which an objection might properly be made if the question were asked in the course of the trial, and in that event the respondent must set out in the response the text of the question and the grounds of the objection.

13.3.18   A number of the grounds which may justify objection to interrogatories were considered by Greenwood J in *Australian Competition and Consumer Commission v ANZ Banking Group Ltd* [2010] FCA 230, extracted above at **13.3.6C**. Another useful outline of some common objections to answering interrogatories is provided by A J H Morris in the extract below. Morris also provides some helpful suggestions for forestalling these objections by careful draftsmanship.

13.3.19E   **Drafting Interrogatories Made Simple**
                                           A J H Morris
                                    (1990) 20 *QLSJ* 445 at 450–1

Objections to Interrogatories

It is beyond the scope of this present paper, which is intended merely as a practical guide to the drafting of interrogatories, to examine in detail the technical grounds upon which interrogatories may be objected to.

Some of the available grounds of objection — particularly those involving recognized heads of 'privilege' — involve substantive legal problems which cannot be side-stepped however carefully the interrogatories are drafted: for example, privilege against self-incrimination, legal professional privilege, or crown ('public interest') privilege. Such grounds of objection do not, in any event, commonly arise in practice.

Many of the other grounds of objection, however, are capable of being forestalled by careful draftsmanship. I have already referred briefly to the objection that interrogatories assume matters of fact which are not admitted by the parties; and that is an objection which can fairly easily be anticipated and prevented, provided that the process of drafting interrogatories commences (as it must always commence) with an examination of the pleadings to see what matters are in issue.

The other major consideration in drafting unobjectionable interrogatories is the question of relevance. This question is often clouded, because the objection that interrogatories are irrelevant to the issues which appear from the pleadings may be taken in a number of forms: it may be said that the interrogatories are 'fishing', or that they relate to matters of credit or amount to cross-examination, or that they seek disclosure of the identity of witnesses, or that they are 'oppressive', 'vexatious' or 'scandalous'.

Broadly speaking, if an interrogatory is clearly directed to an issue which arises on the pleadings, none of those objections can be sustained: and this again makes it imperative that any attempt to draft interrogatories must commence with a critical review of the pleadings. Interrogatories are 'fishing' if their purpose is to 'fish' for evidence which may or may not exist; but it cannot be said that an interrogatory is 'fishing' if it is directed to issues of fact which have been [451] squarely raised on the pleadings and put in issue by the opposing party. Likewise, if an interrogatory goes to an issue of fact raised on the pleadings, it cannot be said to go *merely* to credit, or to involve cross-examination. An interrogatory which calls for the identification of witnesses is not objectionable per se: for example, if an interrogatory enquires as to the identity of a natural person who, on behalf of the opposing party, performed relevant acts, possessed relevant knowledge or a relevant intention, or participated in relevant communications, the interrogatory cannot be objected to because it will incidentally result in the identification of a potential witness. Again, the real question is whether the interrogatory is relevant to the issues on the pleadings.

There are some cases in which an interrogatory might be said to be 'oppressive', even though it relates directly to an issue in the pleadings; for example, where the information sought is very voluminous, and can more conveniently be obtained by another means. But, except in very unusual cases, it is unlikely that the objection that an interrogatory is 'oppressive' or 'vexatious' or 'scandalous' will be upheld, if it is apparent that the factual inquiry relates to a matter which is clearly in issue on the pleadings.

The point is, I trust, obvious: whilst it may be impossible to draw interrogatories which are guaranteed to be unobjectionable, the risk of objections successfully being taken will be minimised if the interrogatories are clearly confined to issues of fact which arise on the pleadings.

13.3.20 Notes

1. When administered on oath, as is usually the case, answers to interrogatories may be useful in cross-examination of the deponent, particularly if the deponent gives oral testimony inconsistent with the answers to interrogatories.

2. It has been seen that the obligation to answer interrogatories includes an obligation in some circumstances to make reasonable inquiries for the purpose of forming a belief about the fact or matter inquired after, and to answer in the light of the information obtained. From a practical perspective, however, if the person swearing the answer relies on information and belief, little can be done if the answer turns out to be incorrect. There is also very limited scope for challenging the truth of answers even if it is highly unlikely that they could be true.

3. In answering interrogatories, it is usual to incorporate the text of each interrogatory, followed by the relevant answer. This facilitates the reading and use of the answers. In some jurisdictions, the requirement to format answers to interrogatories in this way is explicit. See, eg, Supreme Court of Tasmania, Practice Direction No 4 of 2011 (9 September 2011). This practice direction also aids parties to adopt this practice by requiring that where those involved have email, upon the filing of interrogatories the party administering interrogatories is to email an electronic copy of the text of the interrogatories to the legal representative of the receiving party or, if unrepresented, the receiving party.

ORAL DISCOVERY: NORTHERN TERRITORY AND VICTORIA

13.4.1 The rules in the Northern Territory (O 31) and Victoria (O 31) provide a procedure for the conduct of an oral examination in lieu of interrogatories. The procedure appears to be rarely used, probably because it is available only if the party to be examined consents to this course. Under this procedure an examiner, who is appointed by agreement between the parties, fixes the time and place for the examination. In the event that a party fails to attend, he or she may then be compelled to do so by court order.

In the case of a corporation, the rules generally require that an officer of the corporation be examined, but any other person may be examined if the parties agree.

The principles in relation to the requirement to answer questions, objections to answering, the need to make reasonable inquiries, and the entitlement to tender answers at the trial are, in general terms, the same as those which apply to the interrogatory process.

The costs of an oral examination become a cost in the proceeding, unless the court otherwise orders.

13.4.2   Question

1. What advantages does the oral examination procedure offer when compared with interrogatories? What are the disadvantages? In what circumstances would a client be well-advised to agree to be orally examined?

13.4.3   Further reading

A Bates, 'Should Discovery by Oral Examination be Adopted in Queensland?' (1995) 16 *Queensland Lawyer* 92.

PRIVILEGE

Introduction

13.5.1   A common ground upon which a party may object to making documents available for inspection or to answering an interrogatory is that the document is privileged from production or that the party is privileged from answering the interrogatory, as the case may be. The common law has long recognised a number of grounds upon which such privilege may be claimed. In respect of each recognised ground of privilege, it is possible to identify a principle or relationship valued to such an extent that the law will protect or encourage it even if this results in the exclusion of evidence which would, or may, assist the court in determining where the truth lies. A valid claim to privilege means that documents to which the privilege applies need not be produced for inspection (though they must still be mentioned in the affidavit or list of documents), and that a party may refuse to answer interrogatories directed to privileged information. This section will consider the most important of the privileges recognised by the common law.

13.5.2   There are now also a number of significant statutory provisions which provide the source of a claim to privilege. The Evidence Act 1995 (Cth) (applying in the High Court, the Federal Court and the Australian Capital Territory), the Evidence Act 1995 (NSW), the Evidence Act 2001 (Tas), and the Evidence Act 2008 (Vic), contain largely uniform provisions which, where they apply, preserve, modify or extend the common law position. The Evidence (National Uniform Legislation) Act 2011 has also been passed in the Northern Territory, but at the time of writing that legislation has not yet commenced.

The provisions of the Evidence Acts are generally stated to apply to the *adducing of evidence*, rather than to ancillary non–hearing processes such as discovery, interrogatories and subpoenas. Some decisions initially interpreted the Acts so broadly as to apply their provisions in relation to privilege to pre-trial evidence-gathering processes (see eg, *Adelaide Steamship Pty Ltd v Spalvins* (1998) 81 FCR 360), but the High Court subsequently confirmed that the Acts clearly applied only to the adducing of evidence and not in non-hearing contexts: *Mann v Carnell* (1999) 201 CLR 1; *Esso Australia Resources Ltd v Federal Commissioner of Taxation* (1999) 201 CLR 49. However, several of the relevant provisions of the New South Wales, Tasmanian and the Victorian Evidence Acts are now stated to apply to pre-trial processes. Further, in the Federal Court, the Australian Capital Territory and New South Wales, the Rules of Court have been amended to apply to varying extents the privilege provisions of the applicable Evidence Act to pre-trial processes.

This section will note key statutory provisions relating to privilege as it applies to pre-trial processes. For more detailed analysis of the statutory provisions, reference should be made to specialist works relating to the law of evidence.

Legal professional privilege

Scope and rationale

13.5.3 To ensure that clients can feel free to engage in honest and complete communications with their legal practitioners, the law protects from disclosure communications between a client and a legal adviser to obtain confidential legal advice, as well as communications which are made for the purpose of existing or anticipated litigation. This privilege is known as legal professional privilege. The nature and scope of, and the rationale for, legal professional privilege were considered by the High Court in *Baker v Campbell* (1983) 153 CLR 52, extracted below.

13.5.4C   **Baker v Campbell**
                              (1983) 153 CLR 52
                           High Court of Australia

[The defendant, a member of the Australian Federal Police, in the exercise of a search warrant issued to him under the Crimes Act 1914 (Cth) s 10, attempted to seize documents held by a firm of solicitors. All of the documents had been brought into existence for the purpose of obtaining or giving legal advice, and in particular, advice concerning certain aspects of a scheme which the plaintiff had devised to minimise liability for sales tax. Some of the documents were created solely for that purpose and not in relation to any civil or criminal proceedings then in contemplation. The plaintiff sued the defendant in the High Court to restrain him from seizing the documents. **Wilson J** stated a case pursuant to the Judiciary Act 1903 (Cth) s 18, referring the following question to the Full Court:

> In the event that legal professional privilege attaches to and is maintained in respect of the documents held by the firm, can those documents be properly made the subject of a search warrant issued under s 10 of the Crimes Act?]

Dawson J (at 128–32): Whilst legal professional privilege was originally confined to the maintenance of confidence pursuant to a contractual duty which arises out of a professional relationship, it is now established that its justification is to be found in the fact that the

---

proper functioning of our legal system depends upon a freedom of communication between legal advisers and their clients which would not exist if either could be compelled to disclose what passed between them for the purpose of giving or receiving advice. This is why the privilege does not extend to communications arising out of other confidential relationships such as those of doctor and patient, priest and penitent or accountant and client. See *D v NSPCC* [1978] AC 171, at pp 238–239. The restriction of the privilege to the legal profession serves to emphasize that the relationship between a client and his legal adviser has a special significance because it is part of the functioning of the law itself. Communications which establish and arise out of that relationship are of their very nature of legal significance, something which would be coincidental in the case of other confidential relationships. It has been found necessary that professional guidance in the complex processes of the law should be uninhibited by the possibility that what is said to enable advice to be sought or given might later be used against the person seeking the advice. See *Greenough v Gaskell* (1833) 1 My & K 98, at p 105 [39 ER 618, at p 621].

As was pointed out by Lord Selborne LC in *Minet v Morgan* (1873) 8 Ch App 361, at p 366, the law did not at once 'reach a broad and reasonable footing, but reached it by successive steps, founded upon that respect for principle which usually leads the Court aright'. The cover of legal professional privilege was extended from communications relating to actual litigation to communications in anticipation of litigation and it is now 'sufficient if they pass as professional communications in a professional capacity'. See *Lawrence v Campbell* (1859) 4 Drew 485, at p 490 [62 E R 186, at p 188]; *Minet v Morgan* (1873) 8 Ch App, at p 368.

The conflict between the principle that all relevant evidence [129] should be disclosed and the principle that communications between lawyer and client should be confidential has been resolved in favour of the confidentiality of those communications. It has been determined that in this way the public interest is better served because the operation of the adversary system, upon which we depend for the attainment of justice in our society, would otherwise be impaired. See *Waugh v British Railways Board* [1980] AC 521, at pp 535–536. Even if it were otherwise possible (and I do not think that it is), it is too late now to suggest that the public interest would have been better served by restricting legal professional privilege to communications relating to actual or even anticipated litigation.

The privilege extends beyond communications made for the purpose of litigation to all communications made for the purpose of giving or receiving advice and this extension of the principle makes it inappropriate to regard the doctrine as a mere rule of evidence. It is a doctrine which is based upon the view that confidentiality is necessary for proper functioning of the legal system and not merely the proper conduct of particular litigation. It is inconsistent with that view to conclude that the compulsory disclosure of communications between legal adviser and client is in the public interest merely because the compulsion is for administrative rather than judicial purposes.

No doubt there are exceptions to the principle that confidentiality should prevail in relation to professional communications in the law. For example, the privilege may be waived and it has no application if the communications are in furtherance of a crime or fraud. Moreover, there is authority for the proposition that the privilege may be lost if a document to which it attaches comes into the hands of someone other than the legal adviser or his client, even dishonestly, so that secondary evidence of it may be given. See *Lloyd v Mostyn* (1842) 10 M&W 478 at p 482 [152 ER 558, at pp 560–561]; *Calcraft v Guest* [1898] 1 QB 759; *Waugh v British Railways Board* [1980] AC at p 536. But see *Ashburton (Lord) v Pape* [1913] 2 Ch 469; *ITC Ltd v Video Exchange Ltd* [1982] Ch 431; *Reg v Uljee* [1982] 1 NZLR 561. The exceptions do no more, however, than demonstrate that the basic principle is not absolute; they do not justify any general conclusion that the principle of confidentiality should yield to the principle that all relevant evidence should be disclosed ...

[131] The legislature may, of course, if it sees fit to do so, cut across the doctrine of legal professional privilege on occasions when it considers that it is more important to obtain information than to preserve the privilege and no doubt the inclination to do so will be greater in administrative proceedings where the principle has not been seen to operate as it has in judicial proceedings. The legislative imposition of an obligation to disclose professional confidences to the executive is relatively recent, although of increasingly frequent occurrence. But it does not seem to me that the law should ease the way for the legislature to expand the practice nor should it disguise the fact that a principle which the law regards as fundamental is involved.

It is necessary only to add a few words about one justification which is put forward for restricting the application of the doctrine of legal professional privilege to judicial or quasi-judicial proceedings. It is said that there is no appropriate means by which a question of privilege might be tested in a context other than that of judicial or quasi-judicial proceedings and that this is a factor indicating that the privilege should be limited to those proceedings. See, eg, *O'Reilly's Case* [(1983) 153 CLR 1] pp 25–26. I am bound to say, with respect, that in my view this would be an entirely inadequate reason, even if it existed, for [132] restricting the application of a fundamental principle. However, it does not seem to me that there is any real difficulty. In the first place, the doctrine of legal professional privilege is not ordinarily difficult to apply and there is no reason to suppose that its application in a non-judicial context is any less appropriate than the application of the many other rules of law which must frequently be applied in proceedings other than judicial proceedings. Moreover, should any dispute arise, the means exist whereby a judicial determination of the dispute may be obtained as is indicated by this and the other cases in which such a dispute has arisen. Such a reason was not thought to justify the exclusion of the privilege against self-incrimination from extra-judicial proceedings (see *Sorby v The Commonwealth* (1983) 152 CLR 281), nor should it do so in the case of legal professional privilege.

To view legal professional privilege as being no more than a rule of evidence would, in my view, be to inhibit the policy which supports the doctrine. Indeed, now that there appears to be a tendency to compel the disclosure of evidence as an adjunct to modern administrative procedure (see, eg, *Commissioners of Customs and Excise v Harz* [1967] 1 AC 760, at pp 809–810), it may well be necessary to emphasize the policy lest it be effectively undermined. For there can be no doubt that freedom of communication between a legal adviser and his client may be greatly diminished by a requirement that the instructions or the advice be disclosed with the consequence that the information might eventually be used in some action against the client, whether in administrative or judicial proceedings.

In my view, the doctrine of legal professional privilege is, in the absence of some legislative provision restricting its application, applicable to all forms of compulsory disclosure of evidence. Section 10 of the *Crimes Act* does not expressly or by necessary implication restrict the application of the doctrine and the section should, therefore, be construed as being not intended to affect it. The only relevant paragraph of s 10 would appear to be par (b), but nothing which appears in the section as a whole would lead to any different conclusion. The conclusion makes it unnecessary to consider the other submissions in this case, including the submission that the evidence to which s 10(b) refers is confined to evidence admissible in judicial proceedings.

I would answer the question in the negative.

> [**Murphy, Deane** and **Wilson JJ** delivered separate judgments to similar effect. **Gibbs CJ, Mason** and **Brennan JJ** dissented. In the view of the dissenting judges, the doctrine of legal professional privilege should be confined to judicial and quasi-judicial proceedings.]

The 'dominant purpose' test: common law

13.5.5   In Australia, and in the absence of any legislative provisions governing the scope of legal professional privilege (see **13.5.12E, 13.5.14E**), the High Court had chosen a narrow approach to legal professional privilege, confining the privilege to communications which are made *solely* for the use of a legal practitioner for the giving of advice, or for use in existing or anticipated litigation: *Grant v Downs* (1976) 135 CLR 674; *Waterford v Commonwealth of Australia* (1987) 163 CLR 54; 71 ALR 673. A broader test was adopted in England, extending legal professional privilege to a communication which is *dominantly* for the use of a legal practitioner: *Alfred Crompton Amusement Machines Ltd v Customs and Excise Commissioners (No 2)* [1974] AC 405; applied in *Waugh v British Railways Board* [1980] AC 521. The same approach is adopted in New Zealand: *Guardian Royal Assurance v Stuart* [1985] 1 NZLR 596.

In its decision in *Esso Australia Resources Ltd v The Commissioner of Taxation* (1999) 74 ALJR 339, however, the High Court re-examined the issue for Australia, and ultimately preferred the 'dominant purpose' test.

13.5.6C   **Esso Australia Resources Ltd v The Commissioner of Taxation**
                          (1999) 201 CLR 49; 168 ALR 123
                                High Court of Australia

[In 1996 the appellant had commenced proceedings in the Federal Court of Australia — appealing against amended assessments of income tax in respect of several earlier years. General orders for discovery were made. In June 1997 the appellant filed and served a list of documents verified by affidavit. Privilege was claimed in respect of a large number of documents. Ultimately there remained a dispute in relation to many of these documents, in that the appellant contended that 'their disclosure would result in disclosure of a confidential communication made between [the appellant] and a lawyer for the dominant purpose of the lawyer … providing legal advice to [the appellant]'. The descriptions of the purposes of the communications varied slightly, but in all cases where the claim was disputed it was based on an assertion of 'dominant purpose'. The respondents sought an order for the production of these documents.

Foster J ordered that two questions of law be decided separately. The first of those was whether the correct test for claiming legal professional privilege in relation to the production of discovered documents was the 'sole purpose' test formulated by the High Court in *Grant v Downs* (1976) 135 CLR 674 or the 'dominant purpose' test as set out in ss 118 and 119 of the Evidence Act 1995 (Cth). The other question related to the applicability in the circumstances of ss 118 and 119 of the Evidence Act 1995 (Cth).

Both **Foster J** and, on appeal, the Full Federal Court (by majority) answered the first question by finding that the correct test for claiming legal professional privilege in relation to the production of discovered documents is the 'sole purpose' test, as formulated by the High Court in *Grant v Downs*.

On the second question **Foster J** concluded that the court did not have power under O 15 r 15 of the then Federal Court Rules (see now r 20.11) to make an order excluding from production discovered documents on the basis that such documents meet the 'dominant purpose' test as set out in ss 118 and 119 of the Evidence Act 1995 (Cth). That answer was varied by the Full Federal Court, which held the court did have the requisite power under the Rules of Court, but that to exclude from production discovered documents for the sole reason that they meet the 'dominant purpose' test in ss 118 and 119 would not be a proper exercise of the power. The appellant appealed to the High Court.]

Gleeson CJ, Gaudron and Gummow JJ (at 138–9):

[138] The search is for a test which strikes an appropriate balance between two competing considerations: the public policy reflected in the privilege itself, and the public policy that, in the administration of justice and investigative procedures, there should be unfettered access to relevant information. Additionally, whatever test is adopted must be capable of being applied in practice with reasonable certainty and without undue delay and expense in resolving disputed claims.

At first sight, sole purpose appears to be a bright-line test, easily understood and capable of ready application. Many disputes as to its application could be resolved simply by examining the documents in question. However, there is reason to believe that the position is not quite as it appears. The main objection to the test is what was described in the Court of Appeal in New Zealand as its extraordinary narrowness. If it is to be taken literally, one other purpose in addition to the legal purpose, regardless of how relatively unimportant it may be, and even though, without the legal purpose, the document would never have come into existence, will defeat the privilege. This has led some judges to apply the *Grant v Downs* test in a manner which might suggest that it is not to be taken [139] literally. For example, in *Waterford v The Commonwealth* ((1987) 163 CLR 54 at 85), Deane J said the test of whether a document is to be protected is whether 'the cause of its existence, in the sense of both causans and *sine qua non*, must be the seeking or provision of professional legal advice'. That may be closer to 'dominant purpose' than 'sole purpose'. At the least, it seems to involve a reformulation aimed at avoiding the use of 'purpose' and also at avoiding the conclusion that the existence of any purpose in addition to the legal purpose, albeit minor and subsidiary, will mean that no privilege attaches. In argument in the present case, counsel for the respondent endeavoured to explain the meaning of the sole purpose test in a manner that equated it with the test expounded by Jacobs J in *Grant v Downs*. Whilst seeking to uphold a sole purpose test, they submitted that 'if a document is created for the purpose of seeking legal advice, but the maker has in mind to use it also for a subsidiary purpose which would not, by itself, have been sufficient to give rise to the creation of the document, the existence of that subsidiary purpose will not result in the loss of privilege'. That appears close to a 'dominant purpose' test. If the only way to avoid the apparently extreme consequences of the sole purpose test is to say that it should not be taken literally, then it loses its supposed virtue of clarity.

One of the considerations prompting rejection of the pre-existing test was that it was unduly protective of written communications within corporations and bureaucracies. The sole purpose test goes to the other extreme. Such organisations necessarily conduct a large proportion of their internal communications in writing. If the circumstance that a document primarily directed to lawyers is incidentally directed to someone else as well means that privilege does not attach, the result seems to alter the balance too far the other way. This may be the kind of result Deane J was intending to avoid in his reformulation of the privilege, but it seems to follow unless one puts a gloss upon the sole purpose test.

A 'dominant purpose' test was sufficient to defeat the claims for privilege in *Grant v Downs*, and *Waugh* [*Waugh v British Railways Board* [1980] AC 521]. The reason why Barwick CJ, the House of Lords, and the New Zealand Court of Appeal preferred that test was that they were unable to accept, as either necessary or desirable, the apparent absoluteness and rigidity of a sole purpose test. If the only way to avoid that absoluteness and rigidity is to water down the sole purpose test so that, in its practical application, it becomes more like the 'dominant purpose' test, then it should be abandoned. Either the test is too strict, or it lacks the clarity which the respondent claims for it.

It would be possible to seek to formulate a new test, such as that adopted by Jacobs J in *Grant v Downs*, or Deane J in *Waterford*, in a further attempt to adjust the necessary balance of competing policies. To do so, however, would produce only confusion. As a practical matter, the choice presently confronting this Court is between sole purpose and 'dominant purpose'. The 'dominant purpose' test should be preferred. It strikes a just balance, it suffices to rule out claims of the kind considered in *Grant v Downs* and *Waugh*, and it brings the common law of Australia into conformity with other common law jurisdictions.

[As to the applicability of the Evidence Act 1995 (Cth), **Gleeson CJ, Gaudron** and **Gummow JJ** determined that the Full Court of the Federal Court was correct in holding that the Act does not apply to the discovery and inspection of documents, either directly or by a derivative modification of the common law, and that O 15 r 15 of the then Federal Court Rules (see now r 20.11) should not be used to exclude documents from production solely because they meet the 'dominant purpose' test in ss 118 and 119 of the Evidence Act.

Callinan J delivered a separate judgment in which he also concluded that the appropriate test for claiming legal professional privilege at common law is the 'dominant purpose' test.

Both **Callinan** and **McHugh JJ** agreed with **Gleeson CJ, Gaudron** and **Gummow JJ** as to the applicability of ss 118 and 119 of the Evidence Act 1995 (Cth).

As to the appropriate common law test for a claim of legal professional privilege, both **McHugh** and **Kirby JJ** dissented. In separate judgments, both judges indicated that they were not persuaded that the court should overrule the 'sole purpose' test of *Grant v Downs*. **McHugh J** summarised his reasons for his conclusion in the following terms:]

McHugh J (at 140) However, I am unable to accept the proposition that the Court should now overrule the ratio decidendi of *Grant v Downs* ((1976) 135 CLR 674) and substitute a dominant purpose test of privilege for the sole purpose test laid down in that case. Two reasons lead me to that conclusion. First, it would extend the area of privilege with the result that a party to litigation, and the court, would have less access to relevant material. Second, it would impose a test that is not easy of application and which seems inconsistent with the rationale of legal professional privilege. Furthermore, a dominant purpose test is one that must lead to extensive interlocutory litigation because there seems to be a growing acceptance, contrary to earlier authority and former practice, that the person claiming privilege can be cross-examined on the affidavit claiming privilege [footnote omitted].

[The appeal was allowed.]

Confidential communications

13.5.7 The first limb of legal professional privilege applies to confidential communications between a legal adviser and client. It does not apply to a communication with a solicitor acting outside their professional capacity or to a communication which does not relate to any confidential advice.

13.5.8C	**Packer v Deputy Commissioner of Taxation**
	[1985] 1 Qd R 275
	Supreme Court of Queensland, Full Court

[A notice was issued by the Deputy Commissioner of Taxation under the Income Tax Assessment Act 1936 (Cth) s 264 requiring production of all trust account ledgers in the custody or under the control of the appellants' solicitors relating to the appellants' income from 1 July 1976 to 30 July 1983. The appellants were unsuccessful at first instance on an application for a declaration that legal professional privilege attached to the documents, and they appealed that decision to the Full Court.]

Andrews SPJ (at 278–9): It is now clear that, if legal professional privilege attaches to the ledgers at all it may be availed of here to prevent disclosure to the Deputy Commissioner of Taxation requiring such disclosure in the exercise of statutory and administrative powers.

Whether it attaches depends upon whether the documents disclose communications made or brought into existence for the sole purpose of seeking or giving advice or for the sole purpose of use in existing or anticipated litigation.

In *Baker v Campbell* [(1983) 57 ALJR 749] at p 778 Dawson J said, consistently with the majority view:

> There is no privilege for physical objects other than documents and there is no privilege for documents which are the means of carrying out, or are evidence of, transactions which are not themselves the giving or receiving of advice or part of the conduct of actual or anticipated litigation. Communications which would otherwise be privileged lose their immunity from disclosure if they amount to participation in a crime or a fraud. The compass within which the doctrine of legal professional privilege operates is, therefore, narrow having regard to the principle which it protects.

The above statement is relevant to two matters raised here which touch ultimately upon the same question. The first is what may amount to disclosure and the second concerns a submission for the applicants to the effect that, prima facie, trust account ledgers are privileged. As I understood that submission, it encompassed a contention that entries to form a proper record must refer to particular matters and to services provided in relation to them and thus tend to reveal, or towards revelation of legal advice sought by or given to one or more of the applicants. As I have pointed out above, the evidence relied upon was to that sole effect. Ordinarily one might regard 'disclose' or 'disclosure' [279] to relate to a direct revelation, but the matter is not nearly so simply disposed of. The importance of preserving the public interest involved in legal professional privilege has been stressed in the cases mentioned above and it calls for protection of confidentiality of communication between solicitor and client in the giving and seeking of advice etc. Disclosure is no less disclosure if it occurs 'by little and little'. If it is in that latter sense that the word 'tend' is used by the applicants then what they really say is that the ledgers do disclose privileged communications between solicitor and client.

I would say that, prima facie, trust account ledgers generally do not make such disclosure. If 'tend to reveal' means no more than 'may reveal' in the sense that something recorded in the ledger may, conjecturally, tend to contribute to eventual knowledge by the Deputy Commissioner to the disadvantage of the applicants, then in my view that does not amount to disclosure of privileged matter.

Some discussion occurred during argument as to the possibility that ledgers may be so compiled as plainly to contain privileged information beyond what might reasonably be expected in books of account. I would observe that if books kept according to usual procedures contain or refer directly to confidential matters, so as to disclose the subject of a communication for the purposes discussed, then to that extent they are privileged; but that if they are plainly laden with such information so as to demonstrate an intention to contrive a privileged situation, to that extent they are not related to the giving or seeking of legal advice and are not privileged. This is consistent with the view expressed by Deane J in *Baker v Campbell* (supra) at p 774 that legal professional privilege does not extend to protect things lodged with a legal adviser for the purpose of obtaining immunity from production.

[**McPherson** and **Shepherdson JJ** delivered separate judgments to like effect. The appeal was dismissed. See also (to similar effect): *Allen Allen and Hemsley v Deputy Commissioner of Taxation* (1989) 20 FCR 576.]

Existing or anticipated litigation

13.5.9   The second limb of legal professional privilege relates to communications with a solicitor for the purpose of existing or anticipated litigation. It is not necessary that litigation has actually commenced, provided there is a reasonable apprehension of such litigation. In *Mitsubishi Electric Australia Pty Ltd v Victorian WorkCover Authority* (2002) 4 VR 332, Batt JA noted that a variety of expressions has been used in the cases to describe the prospective litigation and said (at [19]):

> In summary then, as a general rule at least, there must be a real prospect of litigation, as distinct from a mere possibility, but it does not have to be more likely than not.

The privilege will generally protect communications between a solicitor and a third party or between a party and some other person, provided the communication is for the purposes of the litigation. This is subject, however, to an increasing number of statutory exceptions which compel exchange of medical reports and disclosure of other expert reports as part of caseflow management schemes: see **14.3.1** and **14.3.2**.

Copies of unprivileged documents

13.5.10   An important issue which has been the subject of a great deal of conflicting authority relates to the position of copies of unprivileged documents in the possession of a lawyer, where the copies have been made solely for the purpose of obtaining or giving legal advice or solely for use in legal proceedings. The High Court has held that under the common law test the copies will attract legal professional privilege.

13.5.11C   Commissioner, Australian Federal Police v Propend Finance Pty Ltd
(1997) 188 CLR 501; 141 ALR 545
High Court of Australia

[The proceedings involved various challenges in respect of the issue, validity, and execution of several search warrants. One of the questions before the court was whether a copy of a document may be privileged even if the original is not the subject of legal professional privilege. The judgments included (not extracted here) extensive examination of prior authorities on the issue.]

McHugh J (at 582–6): In Australia, a similar division of judicial opinion on the question has emerged [references omitted]. However, the balance of authority in this country favours the view that, if the original is not privileged, [583] neither is a copy, even if it was made for *the* sole purpose of advice or use in litigation. Because the precedents and their reasoning are so inconsistent, this Court can only decide the present case by reference to the fundamental principles and the rationale behind the doctrine of legal professional privilege.

The rationale for legal professional privilege
The court has stated the rationale for legal professional privilege [references omitted] in the following terms [*Grant* (1976) 135 CLR 674 at 685. More recently see, *Baker v Campbell* (1983) 153 CLR 52 at 79, 93–94; *Maurice* (1986) 161 CLR 475 at 487, per Mason and Brennan JJ; *Carter* (1995) 183 CLR 121 at 126–128, 132–133, 144–147, 160–161]:

> The rationale of this head of privilege, according to traditional doctrine, is that it promotes the [356] public interest because it assists and enhances the administration of justice by facilitating the representation of clients by legal advisers, the law being a complex and complicated discipline. This it does by keeping secret their communications, thereby inducing the client to retain the solicitor and seek his advice, and encouraging the client to make a full and frank disclosure of the relevant circumstances to the solicitor. The existence of the privilege reflects, to the extent to which it is accorded, the paramountcy of this public interest over a more general public interest, that which requires that in the interests of a fair trial litigation should be conducted on the footing that all relevant documentary evidence is available. As a head of privilege legal professional privilege is so firmly entrenched in the law that it is not to be exorcised by judicial decision.

Three important points emerge from this statement. First, the statement properly identifies the inherent tension in the doctrine of legal professional privilege: on the one hand, there is the need to protect the confidences of the client and, on the other, there is the public interest in parties to litigation having access to all relevant evidence [see dicta to this effect in *Waterford* (1987) 163 CLR 54 at 64–65].

Secondly, the statement correctly identifies the subject matter of the privilege — *communications*. This point, however trite it may seem, is fundamental to the determination of the present appeal. Much of the confusion present in the case law arises from a failure to apply it. Legal professional privilege is concerned with communications, either oral, written or recorded, and not with documents per se.

Thirdly, the statement emphasises the paramountcy of the principle of legal professional privilege in our legal system. In this country, legal professional privilege is more than a mere rule of evidence; it 'is a substantive general principle which plays an important role in the effective and efficient [584] administration of justice by the courts', [*Goldberg v Ng* (1995) 185 CLR 83 at

93–94. See also *Carter* (1995) 183 CLR 121 at 161; *R v Derby Magistrates' Court; Ex parte B* [1995] 3 WLR 681 at 695; [1995] 4 All ER 526 at 540–541, per Lord Taylor CJ] the best explanation of which is that it is a 'practical guarantee of fundamental, constitutional or human rights' [*Carter* (1995) 183 CLR 121 at 161]. See also *Maurice* (1986) 161 CLR 475 at 490, per Deane J, where his Honour described privilege as 'a bulwark against tyranny and oppression'. A similar sentiment was expressed by McEachern CJBC in the leading Canadian authority on point, *Hodgkinson v Simms* (1988) 55 DLR (4th) 577 at 581] I pointed out that:

> By protecting the confidentiality of communications between lawyer and client, the doctrine protects the rights and privacy of persons including corporations by ensuring unreserved freedom of communication with professional lawyers who can advise them of their rights under the law and, where necessary, take action on their behalf to defend or enforce those rights. The doctrine is a natural, if not necessary, corollary of the rule of law and a potent force for ensuring that the equal protection of the law is a reality.

No doubt it seems contrary to commonsense that the law should give privilege to the copy of a document when it does not give it to the original. But in this area of the law, as in other areas of law and life, commonsense turns out to be a misleading guide. This is because legal professional privilege turns on purpose, and no argument is needed to show that the purpose of a client or lawyer in making a copy document may be very different from the purpose of the person who created the original.

To concentrate on the similarity between the original and the copy or on how the copy came to be made is to miss the whole point of legal professional privilege. The privilege attaches whenever the communication or material is made or recorded for the purpose of confidential use in litigation or the obtaining of confidential legal advice. The protected communication or material may be a telephone conversation between a solicitor and client, a research memo of the legal adviser on an issue pertinent to the client's affairs or, as in the present case, the collection and collation of material and documents for the purpose of litigation or obtaining legal advice. As long as the communication was made or the material recorded for the sole purpose of legal advice or pending litigation and was intended to be confidential, the actual form of the communication or recording is irrelevant ...

[585] It follows that, if a solicitor makes a copy of a document that was not privileged, the copy will be privileged if it was created for the sole purpose of obtaining or giving confidential legal advice or for the confidential use of legal advisers in pending litigation. Similarly, if the client makes a copy of a document solely for that purpose or use, the copy will be privileged. If this were not so, inspection of the copied material could expressly or inferentially reveal information that would destroy the confidentiality of the communication between the legal representative and the client. Either in their assembly or their selection, disclosure of the documents could reveal a line of reasoning as to the relevant issues in the case or their relative merit. Moreover, once the privilege attaches, it remains until the client waives it. The copy document constitutes and records part of the communication between the lawyer and the client and was created solely for the purpose of obtaining legal advice. In these circumstances, the copy is always privileged. Even if it is sought for use in subsequent and unrelated proceedings, it is privileged from production [*McCaskill* [1984] 1 NSWLR 66 at 68] ...

[586] But the question of privilege for a copy document has no bearing on litigation where the original non-privileged document is in the hands of the party required to make discovery. That party must produce the original, whether or not any copy of it is privileged. Moreover,

if a party copied a non-privileged document with the intention of destroying the original, the copy would not be privileged even if it was also made for the sole purpose of obtaining legal advice or for confidential use in litigation. In that situation, the conclusion is inevitable that one of the purposes of making the copy was to ensure that the maker could safely destroy the original yet at the same time retain a record of the underlying transaction. Similarly, if a party copied a document and placed the non-privileged original in the custody of a lawyer, there would probably be no privilege for either document.

[**Brennan CJ, Gaudron, Gummow** and **Kirby JJ** also concluded, in separate judgments, that legal professional privilege applied to copy documents in the possession of a lawyer if they were made solely for the purpose of obtaining or giving legal advice, or solely for use in legal proceedings, even where the originals were not privileged. (The reference by all of the judges to the 'sole' purpose for which the copies were made must now be considered in light of the subsequent adoption by the High Court of the 'dominant' purpose test: see 13.5.5.) Toohey and Dawson JJ dissented on this point, only allowing privilege to attach to a copy of an unprivileged document in limited circumstances, such as where the copy was annotated or integrated with privileged material, or where the selection of copies would reveal the lawyer's line of thinking.]

'Client legal privilege' under legislation

13.5.12E   **Evidence Act 1995 (Cth)**

Legal advice
118 Evidence is not to be adduced if, on objection by a client, the court finds that adducing the evidence would result in disclosure of:
  (a)   a confidential communication made between the client and a lawyer; or
  (b)   a confidential communication made between 2 or more lawyers acting for the client; or
  (c)   the contents of a confidential document (whether delivered or not) prepared by the client, a lawyer or another person
for the dominant purpose of the lawyer, or one or more of the lawyers, providing legal advice to the client.

Litigation
119 Evidence is not to be adduced if, on objection by a client, the court finds that adducing the evidence would result in disclosure of:
  (a)   a confidential communication between the client and another person, or between a lawyer acting for the client and another person, that was made; or
  (b)   the contents of a confidential document (whether delivered or not) that was prepared;

for the dominant purpose of the client being provided with professional legal services relating to an Australian or overseas proceeding (including the proceeding before the court), or an anticipated or pending Australian or overseas proceeding, in which the client is or may be, or was or might have been, a party.

13.5.13   Under the provisions of the Evidence Act 1995 (Cth) (applicable to proceedings in the Australian Capital Territory, the Federal Court and the High Court), and under the corresponding provisions of the Evidence Act 1995 (NSW), the Evidence Act 2001 (Tas), and the Evidence Act 2008 (Vic), evidence is not to be 'adduced' of a confidential communication with a lawyer (s 118) or a communication in the course of existing or anticipated litigation (s 119), if the client objects. Several of the terms used in these sections are defined in s 117. Section 120 specifically extends the privilege to unrepresented parties.

These provisions introduce a legislatively defined concept, 'client legal privilege', which broadly corresponds to legal professional privilege at common law.

As originally enacted, the legislation of the Commonwealth, New South Wales and Tasmania applied only to the 'adducing' of evidence and did not of itself govern the discovery, production and inspection of documents in situations other than the adducing of evidence: *Esso Australia Resources Ltd v The Commissioner of Taxation*: see **13.5.6C**.

This position was modified by the Rules of Court in the Australian Capital Territory (r 601), which define privilege in the context of production of documents by reference to whether a document could be adduced under the operation of Pt 3.10 (which includes ss 118, 119) of the Evidence Act 1995 (Cth). Rule 605(3) also excludes specified confidential documents and communications involving legal practitioners from the discovery obligation. The position was also altered by the Rules of Court in New South Wales, which refer to various provisions of the Evidence Act 1995 (NSW) (including Pt 3.10 Div 1) for the purpose of defining privilege both in respect of discovery and inspection of documents and in specifying the grounds upon which a party may object to answering an interrogatory: rr 21.3, 21.4, 22.2, Dictionary.

Section 131A of the Evidence Acts of New South Wales and Tasmania have both been amended so as to extend the application of several provisions of the Act relating to privilege, including those relating to client legal privilege, to any compulsory process of disclosure. Section 131A of the Evidence Act 2008 (Vic) also extends the application of the provisions in relation to client legal privilege to pre-trial processes.

13.5.14E   **Evidence Act 2008 (Vic)**

Application of Division to preliminary proceedings of courts
131A (1) If:
  (a)   a person is required by a disclosure requirement to give information, or to produce a document, which would result in the disclosure of a communication, a document or its contents or other information of a kind referred to in Division 1 or 3; and
  (b)   the person objects to giving that information or providing that document —

the court must determine the objection by applying the provisions of this part (other than sections 123 and 128) with any necessary modifications as if the objection to giving information or producing the document were an objection to the giving or adducing of evidence.
(2) In this section, disclosure requirement means a court process or court order that requires the disclosure of information or a document and includes the following —

> (a)   a summons or subpoena to produce documents or give evidence;
> (b)   pre-trial discovery;
> (c)   non-party discovery;
> (d)   interrogatories;
> (e)   a notice to produce;
> (f)   a request to produce a document under Division 1 of Part 4.6;

Statutory removal of privilege for expert reports

13.5.15   Expert reports obtained by a party or their legal advisers for use in existing or anticipated litigation are protected by legal professional privilege, unless the privilege is removed or modified by statute. There are now a number of rules and practice directions which regulate the production of expert evidence to the court and ensure parties have access well in advance of trial to expert evidence to be called by another party. Most of the rules do not abrogate the right of a party to refuse to produce documents on the ground of privilege. Rather, they impose the obligation to disclose the report, or in some jurisdictions to disclose the substance of expert evidence, if the party intends to adduce the evidence as expert evidence at the trial. These rules are discussed in **Chapter 14**: see **14.3.1**.

The rules in Queensland and South Australia go further and remove the privilege which might otherwise apply. In South Australia, the rule in relation to pre-trial disclosure (r 160) applies whether or not a party intends to rely on the report at trial: see further **14.3.7**.

In Queensland, r 212 (2) provides: 'A document consisting of a statement or report of an expert is not privileged from disclosure.' In *Interchase Corporation Ltd (in liq) v Grosvenor Hill (Queensland) Pty Ltd (No 1)* [1999] 1 Qd R 141, the Queensland Court of Appeal concluded that the Queensland subrule was valid, but that it did not remove any privilege which might otherwise attach to ancillary documents relating to the production of an expert report, including correspondence between a party's solicitors and the experts, drafts and working papers, source materials and documents collated and copied by the expert in the course of preparing an expert report. It was also held that there is no waiver of any privilege attached to ancillary documents by the production of the expert report. Accordingly the question whether legal professional privilege attached to ancillary documents fell to be determined on general principles. In light of the Court of Appeal's analysis on that issue, legal professional privilege attaches to communications passing between an expert and a party's solicitor for the dominant purpose of giving legal advice in relation to, or obtaining evidence to be used in litigation, but such privilege does not protect other documents relating to the production of an expert report, such as drafts and working papers, source materials and documents collated and copied by the expert in order to prepare a report.

Self-incrimination, penalties and forfeiture

Scope and rationale of the privilege against self-incrimination

13.5.16   A party is not obliged to produce an incriminating document for inspection, nor to answer an interrogatory which would involve the provision of incriminating information. The common law long took the view that the privilege against self-incrimination applied to corporations as well as to individuals. The issue was the subject of detailed consideration by the

High Court in *Environment Protection Authority v Caltex Refining Co Pty Ltd* (1993) 178 CLR 477; the High Court concluding (by a bare majority of 4:3) that the privilege is not available to corporations. This position is now reflected in each of the Uniform Evidence Acts: Evidence Act 1995 (Cth) s 187; Evidence Act 1995 (NSW) s 187; Evidence Act 2001 (Tas) s 187; Evidence Act 2008 (Vic) s 187.

13.5.17 The privilege against self-incrimination is a rule of substantive law. In *Reid v Howard* (1995) 184 CLR 1; 131 ALR 609, extracted below, the High Court considered the rationale for the privilege. The High Court also made it clear that in Australia the privilege cannot be abrogated or modified unless clearly authorised by statute.

13.5.18C
Reid v Howard
(1995) 184 CLR 1; 131 ALR 609
High Court of Australia

[The plaintiffs brought proceedings against their former accountant, alleging that he had misappropriated monies they entrusted to him. They sought an interlocutory order requiring disclosure of his assets and the source of the funds with which they were acquired. The defendant consented to summary judgment in the action but resisted the interlocutory orders for disclosure, claiming privilege against self-incrimination. The disclosure orders were made at first instance, the court holding that the privilege did not apply because the defendant had made a statement to the police and would not be placed in greater jeopardy if required to comply with the disclosure orders sought. Upon appeal to the Court of Appeal, it was held that the particular disclosure orders made at first instance did expose the defendant to greater jeopardy than would otherwise be the case. The court rejected an argument raised by the plaintiffs that a trustee or fiduciary cannot claim privilege against self-incrimination in civil proceedings brought by a beneficiary, and concluded that the defendant was entitled to make and maintain the claim for privilege. However, the Court of Appeal then substituted orders which required disclosure in a more limited form and which imposed various conditions designed to safeguard the position of the defendant in respect of any criminal prosecution. The defendant brought a further appeal to the High Court, supported by the Attorney-General for the State of New South Wales, who was granted leave to intervene. There was no appearance for the plaintiffs.]

Toohey, Gaudron, McHugh and Gummow JJ (at 11–17): As there was no appearance for the respondents, it is appropriate to state that the Court of Appeal was correct in its conclusion that the appellant is entitled to make and maintain his claim of privilege and to indicate why that is so. The privilege, which has been described as a 'fundamental ... bulwark of liberty' [*Pyneboard Pty Ltd v Trade Practices Commission* (1983) 152 CLR 328 at 340] is not simply a rule of evidence, but a basic and substantive common law right. It developed after the abolition of the Star Chamber by the Long Parliament in 1641, [Holdsworth, *A History of English Law* (7th ed, 1956), vol 1 at pp 514–515] and, by 1737, it was said that 'there [was] no rule more established in equity' [*Smith v Read* (1737) 1 Atk 526 at 527 per Lord Hardwicke LC; 26 ER 332 at 332. And see the discussion of the recognition of the privilege in Chancery in *Environment Protection Authority v Caltex Refining Co Pty Ltd* (1993) 178 CLR 477 at 528]. More recently, the privilege has been [12] described as 'deeply ingrained in the common law' [*Sorby v The Commonwealth* (1983) 152 CLR 281 at 309. See also

Hammon v The Commonwealth (1982) 152 CLR 188 at 200; *Pyneboard Pty Ltd v Trade Practices Commission* (1983) 152 CLR 328 at 341, 347; *In re O (Restraint Order)* [1991] 2 QB 520 at 529; *Istel Ltd v Tully* [1993] AC 45 at 57, per Lord Griffiths, at 67, per Lord Lowry; cf *Cross on Evidence* (7th ed, 1990) at p 427]. It operates so that a person cannot be compelled 'to answer any question, or to produce any document or thing, if to do so "may tend to bring him into the peril and possibility of being convicted as a criminal"' [See *Sorby v The Commonwealth* (1983) 152 CLR 281 at 288, per Gibbs CJ, quoting *Lamb v Munster* (1882) 10 QBD 110 at 111].

As already indicated, the appellant's statement to the police has not resulted in the laying of criminal charges. Almost certainly, that is because it lacks detailed particulars of his misappropriations. There can be no doubt that disclosure of the assets upon which the appellant 'applied ... moneys or property entrusted to him' by the respondents and, in respect of each of those assets, 'the amount of any moneys and the identity of any property' applied in its acquisition, as required by the various orders which have been made against him, would place him in greater 'peril ... of being convicted as a criminal' than the perfectly general admission of fraudulent misappropriation contained in his statement to police. Thus, he is entitled to claim the privilege unless he falls within an exception of the kind contended for by the respondents in the Court of Appeal ...

[14] There is simply no scope for an exception to the privilege, other than by statute. At common law, it is necessarily of general application — a universal right which, as Murphy J pointed out in *Pyneboard Pty Ltd v Trade Practices Commission* [(1983) 152 CLR 328 at 346], protects the innocent and the guilty. There is no basis for excepting any class or category of person whether by reference to legal status, legal relationship or, even, the offence in which he or she might be incriminated because, as already indicated, its purpose is the completely general purpose of protecting against 'the peril and possibility of being convicted as a criminal' [*Lamb v Munster* (1882) 10 QBD 110 at 111]. For the same reason, there can be no exception in civil proceedings, whether generally or of one kind or another. Moreover, it would be anomalous to allow that a person could refuse to answer questions in criminal proceedings or before investigative bodies where the privilege has not been abrogated if that person could be compelled to answer interrogatories or otherwise make disclosure with respect to the same matter in civil proceedings ...

[15] As already indicated, the protection intended by the orders of the Court of Appeal is more limited than that afforded by the privilege. In particular, the orders do not operate, of their own force, to prevent the material disclosed in the affidavits from being used as the basis for investigations which might, in turn, provide evidence to support criminal charges — a possibility against which the privilege protects [*Busby v Thorn EMI Video Programmes Ltd* [1984] 1 NZLR 461]. However, it is clear that the Court of Appeal intended to provide protection against evidentiary use of the material in subsequent criminal proceedings. And it thought that this could be achieved by requiring undertakings from the respondents' solicitors and by tying the hands of prosecution authorities. ...

[16] The Court of Appeal proceeded on the basis either that it had inherent power to make the orders in question or that they could be made in the exercise of the jurisdiction conferred by s 23 of the *Supreme Court Act* 1970 (NSW). That section provides:

The Court shall have all jurisdiction which may be necessary for the administration of justice in New South Wales.

Although it has been said that the inherent power of a superior court cannot be restricted to defined and closed categories [*Tringali v Stewardson Stubbs & Collett Ltd* (1966) 66 SR (NSW) 335 at 344. See also *Jackson v Sterling Industries Ltd* (1987) 162 CLR 612 at 639; *Hamilton v Oades* (1989) 166 CLR 486 at 502; *Jago v District Court (NSW)* (1989) 168 CLR 23 at 25–26, 74; *Dietrich v The Queen* (1992) 177 CLR 292 at 364], the power is not at large. Nor is the jurisdiction conferred by s 23 of the Supreme Court Act. Neither the inherent power nor the completely general terms of s 23 can authorise the making of orders excusing compliance with obligations or preventing the exercise of authority deriving from statute ...

[17] Moreover and of more importance, the inherent power and the jurisdiction conferred by s 23 of the *Supreme Court Act* are to be exercised only as necessary for the administration of justice. Quite apart from the difficulties which the orders of the Supreme Court present for the administration of justice, to which reference has already been made, it is inimical to the administration of justice for a civil court to compel self-incriminatory disclosures, while fashioning orders to prevent the use of the information thus obtained in a court vested with criminal jurisdiction with respect to the matters disclosed. Nor is justice served by the ad hoc modification or abrogation of a right of general application, particularly not one as fundamental and as important as the privilege against self-incrimination.

[Their Honours ordered that the appeal be allowed and that, so far as they concerned orders for disclosure, the plaintiff's applications to the Supreme Court should be dismissed. **Deane J** delivered a separate judgment agreeing with the orders proposed. See also: *Korp v Egg & Egg Pulp Marketing Board* [1964] VR 563; *Rio Tinto Zinc Corp v Westinghouse Electric Corp* [1978] AC 847; *Rank Film Distributors Ltd v Video Information Centre (a firm)* [1982] AC 380.]

Penalties and forfeiture

13.5.19 The privilege against exposure to penalties and forfeiture is distinct from the privilege against self-incrimination (*Re Intercontinental Development Corp Pty Ltd* (1975) 1 ACLR 253 at 259), but they both reflect the underlying principle that persons alleging that a crime has been committed or a penalty incurred should not be able to compel the defendant to provide the proof of the allegations made.

If the object of a proceeding is the recovery of a statutory penalty, then the defendant will not be required to provide discovery or answer interrogatories, without any need for the defendant to claim the privilege: *R v Associated Northern Collieries* (1910) 111 CLR 738 at 742. If the exposure to a penalty or forfeiture would be an incidental consequence of the discovery of particular documents or answering of particular interrogatories in a civil proceeding, then appropriate objection should be taken in the affidavit of documents or answers to interrogatories.

The privilege against exposure to penalties and forfeiture is not available to a corporation: *Trade Practices Commission v CC (NSW) Pty Ltd (No 4)* (1995) 131 ALR 581; *Trade Practices Commission v Abbco Ice Works Pty Ltd* (1994) 123 ALR 503 at 534, 549–50. For the Australian Capital Territory, the Federal Court, the High Court, New South Wales, Tasmania, and Victoria, the provisions noted at 13.5.16 in respect of incrimination also apply to civil penalties, confirming the common law position that the privilege is not available to a body corporate.

Statutory recognition and modification

13.5.20 In most jurisdictions, the privileges against self-incrimination and exposure to a penalty are given some form of statutory recognition and/or modification.

In all jurisdictions except South Australia, there are statutory provisions which apply to the giving of evidence and which recognise privilege either in respect of both self-incrimination and exposure to civil penalty (Evidence Act 1995 (Cth) s 128 (Australian Capital Territory, Federal Court, High Court)); Evidence Act 1995 (NSW) s 128; Evidence Act 2001 (Tas) s 128; Evidence Act 2008 (Vic) s 128, or in respect of incrimination only: Evidence Act 1939 s 10 (NT); Evidence Act 1977 (Qld) s 10; Evidence Act 1906 (WA) ss 11, 24. Except in the Northern Territory and Queensland, the privilege is then modified in that the court may, if satisfied that the justice of the case requires the party to disclose the information, grant an indemnity certificate in respect of that information. In this event the party must answer, but the information cannot be used in subsequent proceedings, except in a criminal proceeding for perjury in respect of the evidence.

However, as these provisions relate only to the giving of evidence, it seems they will not modify the common law position in respect of self-incrimination or penalties in relation to the discovery of documents unless incorporated through the relevant Rules of Court. The rules in the Australian Capital Territory (r 601) and New South Wales (rr 21.3, 21.4, Dictionary) specifically recognise (in the case of a natural person) privilege in respect of both self-incrimination (extending to incrimination under foreign law) and liability to a statutory penalty, within the meaning of the applicable Evidence Act 1995.

It would appear the terms of the statutory provisions are wide enough to encompass the answering of interrogatories. This is clearly the case in Western Australia, where the provisions specifically extend to the answering of interrogatories, and in New South Wales (r 22.2, Dictionary) where the rules permit a natural person to object to answering an interrogatory on the basis of self-incrimination (extending to incrimination under foreign law) or exposure to a civil penalty, within the meaning of the Evidence Act 1995 (NSW).

Public interest

Scope and rationale

13.5.21 Public interest privilege, once known as Crown privilege, applies where the Crown is a party to litigation or where Crown documents have been subpoenaed. It has been extended to cover other information which has been collected in the course of public duties or public administration. The privilege protects from disclosure information, such as criminal intelligence or as to the inner workings of government which, in the public interest, should remain confidential. In *Sankey v Whitlam* (1978) 142 CLR 1 the High Court confirmed that it is for the court to determine for itself, whether the information in question is protected by public interest privilege. The judgments in that case include detailed analyses of the scope and application of, and the rationale for, public interest privilege.

[In complex proceedings brought against a former Prime Minister of Australia and three others who had recently ceased to be the members of his Ministry, one of the issues ultimately before the High Court was whether certain documents which had been sought by subpoena belonged to a class of documents which the public interest required should not be disclosed.]

Gibbs ACJ (at 38–47): The principles which I am about to discuss apply in relation to oral as well as to *documentary* evidence, but since in the present case it has been agreed that it would be premature to deal with the objections taken to oral evidence, I may confine my remarks to the application of the principles to documentary evidence.

The general rule is that the court will not order the production of a document, although relevant and otherwise admissible, if it would be injurious to the public interest to disclose it. However the public interest has two aspects which may conflict. These were described by Lord Reid in *Conway v Rimmer* [1968] AC, at p 940, as follows:

> There is the public interest that harm shall not be done to the nation or the public service by disclosure of certain documents, and there is the public interest that the administration of justice shall not be frustrated by the withholding of documents which must be produced if justice is to be done.

It is in all cases the duty of the court, and not the privilege of the executive government, to decide whether a document will be produced or may be withheld. The court must decide which aspect of the public interest predominates, or in other words whether the public interest which requires that the document [39] should not be produced outweighs the public interest that a court of justice in performing its functions should not be denied access to relevant evidence. In some cases, therefore, the court must weigh the one competing aspect of the public interest against the other, and decide where the balance lies. In other cases, however, as Lord Reid said in *Conway v Rimmer* [1968] AC, at p 940, 'the nature of the injury which would or might be done to the nation or the public service is of so grave a character that no other interest, public or private, can be allowed to prevail over it'. In such cases once the court has decided that to order production of the document in evidence would put the interest of the state in jeopardy, it must decline to order production.

An objection may be made to the production of a document because it would be against the public interest to disclose its contents, or because it belongs to a class of documents which in the public interest ought not to be produced, whether or not it would be harmful to disclose the contents of the particular document. In the present case no suggestion has been made that the contents of any particular documents are such that their disclosure would harm the national interest. The claim is to withhold the documents because of the class to which they belong. Speaking generally, such a claim will be upheld only if it is really necessary for the proper functioning of the public service to withhold documents of that class from production. However it has been repeatedly asserted that there are certain documents which by their nature fall in a class which ought not to be disclosed no matter what the documents individually contain; in other words that the law recognises that there is a class of documents which in the public interest should be immune from disclosure. The class includes cabinet minutes and minutes of discussions between heads of departments (*Conway v Rimmer* [1968]

AC, at pp 952, 973, 979, 987, 993; *Reg v Lewes Justices; Ex parte Home Secretary* [1973] AC, at p 412; *Australian National Airlines Commission v The Commonwealth* (1975) 132 CLR 582, at p 591), papers brought into existence for the purpose of preparing a submission to cabinet (*Lanyon Pty Ltd v The Commonwealth* (1974) 129 CLR 650), and indeed any documents which relate to the framing of government policy at a high level (cf *In re Grosvenor Hotel, London (No 2)* [1965] Ch 1210, at pp 1247, 1255). According to Lord Reid, the class would extend to 'all documents concerned with policy making within departments including, it may be, minutes and the like by quite junior officials [40] and correspondence with outside bodies': *Conway v Rimmer* [1968] AC, at p 952 ...

[I]t is inherent in the nature of things that government at a high level cannot function without some degree of secrecy. No Minister, or senior public servant, could effectively discharge the responsibilities of his office if every document prepared to enable policies to be formulated was liable to be made public. The public interest therefore requires that some protection be afforded by the law to documents of that kind. It does not follow that all such documents should be absolutely protected from disclosure, irrespective of the subject matter with which they deal ...

[43] I consider that although there is a class of documents whose members are entitled to protection from disclosure irrespective of their contents, the protection is not absolute, and it does not endure forever. The fundamental and governing principle is that documents in the class may be withheld from production only when this is necessary in the public interest. In a particular case the court must balance the general desirability that documents of that kind should not be disclosed against the need to produce them in the interests of justice. The court will of course examine the question with especial care, giving full weight to the reasons for preserving the secrecy of documents of this class, but it will not treat all such documents as entitled to the same measure of protection — the extent of protection required will depend to some extent on the general subject matter with which the documents are concerned. If a strong case has been made out for the production of the documents, and the court concludes that their disclosure would not really be detrimental to the public interest, an order for production will be made. In view of the danger to which the indiscriminate disclosure of documents of this class might give rise, it is desirable that the government concerned, Commonwealth or State, should have an opportunity to intervene and be heard before any order for disclosure is made. Moreover no such order should be enforced until the government concerned has had an opportunity to appeal against it, or test its correctness by some other process, if it wishes to do so (cf *Conway v Rimmer* [1968] AC, at p 953) ...

[44] Although an affidavit sworn by a Minister or departmental head is no longer conclusive, it appears to me to be still highly desirable that the person who swears the affidavit should himself have seen the documents in question. Where the claim is that it would be contrary to the public interest to publish the contents of a particular document, it is obviously essential that the person asserting the claim should himself have seen the documents in question. Even where the claim is that the document belongs to a class which should be withheld, the court is still required to give proper respect to the assertion by the Minister or departmental head that production would be contrary to the public interest, and the weight that would be given to an affidavit making an assertion of this kind would necessarily be reduced if the person swearing it had not himself seen the document.

It is however clear that the court should prevent the disclosure of a document whose production would be contrary to the public interest even if no claim is made by a Minister or other high official that its production should be withheld ...

[45] [I]t may be necessary for the proper functioning of the public service to keep secret a document of a particular class, but once the document has been published to the world there no longer exists any reason to deny to the court access to that document, if it provides evidence that is relevant and otherwise admissible. It was further submitted that if one document forming part of a series of cabinet papers has been published, but others have not, it would be unfair and unjust to produce one document and withhold the rest. That may indeed be so, and where one such document has been published it becomes necessary for the court to consider whether that circumstance strengthens the case for the disclosure of the connected documents. However, even if other related documents should not be produced, it seems to me that once a document has been published it becomes impossible, and indeed absurd, to say that the public interest requires that it should not be produced or given in evidence ...

[46] Finally, the power of the court to inspect the document privately is clear, and once a court has decided, notwithstanding the opposition of a Minister, that on balance the document should probably be produced, it will sometimes be desirable, or indeed essential, to examine the document before making an order for production: see *Conway v* Rimmer [1968] AC, at pp 953, 979, 981–2, 995; cf p 971. However, where the objection is to the disclosure of a document because it belongs to a class, and the Minister, being represented, does not suggest that there is anything in its contents that ought to be withheld from production, there will not always be the same need to examine the document before ordering its production if the objection is overruled ...

The documents in categories 1, 2 and 3 are all 'state papers' within the meaning I have given to that expression. They belong to a class of documents which may be protected from disclosure irrespective of their contents. Full respect must be paid to the objections taken to their production, even though the Ministers did not swear that they had personally seen the documents. On the other hand the documents relate to a proposal which was never put into effect, has been abandoned and is of no continuing significance from the point of view of the national interest. The matters to which they refer occurred over three years ago. Their disclosure cannot affect any present activity of government. Moreover, if the documents can be withheld, the informant will be unable to present to the court his case that the defendants committed criminal offences while [47] carrying out their duties as Ministers. If the defendants did engage in criminal conduct, and the documents are excluded, a rule of evidence designed to serve the public interest will instead have become a shield to protect wrongdoing by Ministers in the execution of their office ...

For these reasons I conclude that the public interest in the administration of justice outweighs any public interests in withholding documents of this class, and that the public interest does not render it necessary that the document in categories 1, 2 and 3 should be withheld from production.

[Separate judgments reflecting similar views were delivered by **Stephen, Mason** and **Aickin JJ. Jacobs J** found it unnecessary for other reasons to consider this issue.]

13.5.23 Despite an earlier view in England that the court would accept a Minister's affidavit to the effect that disclosure was contrary to the public interest, English courts now adopt a similar approach as in Australia and, where necessary, will examine a document to determine whether public interest privilege should extend to it: *Conway v Rimmer* [1968] AC 910. See also: *Attorney-General for New South Wales v Stuart* (1994) 34 NSWLR 667; *Western Australia v Minister for Aboriginal and Torres Strait Islander Affairs* (1994) 54 FCR 114.

Statutory recognition

13.5.24 Part 3.10 Div 3 of the Evidence Act 1995 (Cth), the Evidence Act 1995 (NSW), the Evidence Act 2001 (Tas), and the Evidence Act 2008 (Vic), contain provisions permitting the exclusion of certain evidence in the public interest. This includes information or documents evidencing the reasons for judicial decisions (s 129) and information or documents relating to matters of state: s 130. The legislation in New South Wales, Tasmania and Victoria extends the application of the public interest privileges to pre-trial processes: Evidence Act 1995 (NSW) s 131A; Evidence Act 2001 (Tas) s 131A; Evidence Act 2008 (Vic) s 131A.

The Rules of Court in the Australian Capital Territory (r 601) have the effect of restricting public interest privilege as it applies to the discovery process to documents falling within s 129 or s 130 of the Evidence Act 1995 (Cth).

In the Federal Court (r 20.01), Queensland (r 239) and Western Australia (O 26 r 14), the Rules of Court specify that requirements in relation to production of documents do not affect any rule of law which authorises or requires the withholding of any document, on the ground that its disclosure would be injurious to the public interest. The Federal Court has a similar rule relating to the answering of interrogatories: r 21.07.

Without prejudice communications

Scope and rationale

13.5.25 If parties have brought documents into existence in an attempt to settle a dispute, those documents are privileged from production on discovery: *Rush & Tompkins Ltd v Greater London Council* [1989] AC 1290 at 1305; *Austotel Management Pty Ltd v Jamieson* (1995) 57 FCR 411 at 416–19, and see **17.3.2**. Objection may similarly be taken to answering interrogatories which relate to settlement negotiations and associated documents. Any admissions which may be contained in any settlement negotiations are also inadmissible in evidence. Commonly negotiations will be in relation to existing litigation, but it is clear that it applies even if litigation had not commenced in relation to the dispute.

The High Court discussed the rationale of the privilege which applies to without prejudice communications in *Field v Commissioner for Railways for New South Wales*, extracted below.

13.5.26C   **Field v Commissioner for Railways for New South Wales**
(1957) 99 CLR 285
High Court of Australia

[The plaintiff brought proceedings against the Commissioner for Railways for New South Wales, seeking damages for personal injury. He alleged that the train in which he was a passenger had started while he was alighting and that he was thrown onto the platform, being injured as a result. The solicitors for the Commissioner opened negotiations for settlement of the action on a compromise basis in a letter which was marked 'without prejudice' and which sought a medical examination of the plaintiff by a medical specialist. Further correspondence followed, also marked 'without prejudice' through which an appointment was made for the medical examination. At the trial, the specialist was asked to recount the circumstances of the accident as told to him by the plaintiff. The plaintiff's counsel objected to this evidence on the basis that the interview with the specialist was privileged as being 'without prejudice'. The objection was overruled and the specialist gave evidence that the plaintiff had told him at the medical examination that he had stepped out of a slowly moving train as it had overrun the platform. The plaintiff applied to the Full Court of the Supreme Court for a new trial on grounds which included wrongful admission of evidence and misdirection. The application was refused and the plaintiff appealed to the High Court.]

Dixon CJ, Webb, Kitto and Taylor JJ (at 291–3): The law relating to communications without prejudice is of course familiar. As a matter of policy the law has long excluded from evidence admissions by words or conduct made by parties in the course of negotiations to settle litigation. The purpose is to enable parties engaged in an attempt to compromise litigation to communicate with one another freely and without the embarrassment which the liability of their communications to be put in evidence subsequently might *impose* upon them. The law relieves them of this embarrassment so that their negotiations to avoid litigation or to settle it may go on unhampered. This form of privilege, however, is directed against the admission in evidence of express or implied admissions. It covers admissions by words or conduct. For example, neither party can use the readiness of the other to negotiate as an implied admission. It is not concerned with objective facts which may be ascertained during the course of negotiations. These may be proved by direct evidence. But it is concerned with the use of the negotiations or what is said in the course of them as evidence by [292] way of admission. For some centuries almost it has been recognised that parties may properly give definition to the occasions when they are communicating in this manner by the use of the words 'without prejudice' and to some extent the area of protection may be enlarged by the tacit acceptance by one side of the use by the other side of these words: see *Thomas v Austen* (1823) 1 LJ (OS) KB 99; *Kurtz & Co v Spence & Sons* (1888) 58 LT 438 at p 441; *Paddock v Forrester* (1842) 3 Man & G 903, at p 919 [133 ER 1404 at p 1411]; *Hoghton v Hoghton* (1852) 15 Beav 278 at pp 314; *In re River Steamer Co*; *Mitchell's Claim* (1871) LR 6 Ch App 822 at pp 831, 832; *Walker v Wilsher* (1889) 23 QBD 335, at pp 337–338. Needless to say, the privilege is a matter to be raised by objection to the admissibility of the evidence. For the purpose of deciding such an objection the judge may take evidence on the *voir dire*. [The problem in the present case is whether what according to Dr Teece the plaintiff said to him as to the manner in which the accident occurred is within the protection of the privilege]. Looked at antecedently the question may be stated as being whether what he might unexpectedly say to Dr Teece should be regarded as within the area of protection. In the first place as a matter of ordinary knowledge it must have been within the contemplation of the parties that some statement would be made by the plaintiff to Dr Teece concerning the nature of his injuries. It could hardly be expected that an orthopaedic surgeon would not ask questions about symptoms, pain, capacity to move and so forth, and such matters must have formed part of the material upon which Dr Teece would form his opinion. Clearly enough, these were not matters which were considered by the parties to fall within the protection of without prejudice negotiations. For it is plain that Dr Teece was expected to give evidence of the opinion he formed should the negotiations for settlement break down. The question, however, does not depend altogether upon the expectations of the parties. It depends upon what formed part of the negotiations for the settlement of the action and what was reasonably incidental thereto. On the one hand it is contended that it was reasonably incidental to the negotiations to place the plaintiff without reserve in the hands of Dr Teece and allow him to talk freely. On the other hand it is pointed out that Dr Teece's function was wholly medical, that no one anticipated the plaintiff discussing the cause of action with him, that he had no function to perform in relation to the settlement except to report his medical judgment of the [293] plaintiff's condition, past, present and future, and that he was not a general agent of the defendant but was appointed only ad hoc to make a medical examination. Further, for purposes of the medical examination it was not necessary or reasonable that the plaintiff should state anything touching his cause of action.

The question really is whether it was fairly incidental to the purposes of the negotiations to which the medical examination was subsidiary or ancillary that the plaintiff should communicate to the surgeon appointed by the Railway Commissioner the manner in which the accident was caused. To answer this question in the affirmative stretches the notion of incidental protection very far. The defendant's contention that it was outside the scope of the purpose of the plaintiff's visit to the doctor to enter upon such a question seems clearly right. On the whole the conclusion of the Supreme Court that the plaintiff's admission fell outside the area of protection must command assent as correct. It was not reasonably incidental to the negotiations that such an admission should be protected. It was made without any proper connexion with any purpose connected with the settlement of the action. In these circumstances it appears that the evidence of Dr Teece on this subject was admissible.

[**McTiernan J**, dissenting, took the view that the 'without prejudice' privilege applied to the evidence in question. The appeal was dismissed.]

Statutory recognition and modification

13.5.27 Section 131(1) of the Evidence Act 1995 (Cth), the Evidence Act 1995 (NSW), the Evidence Act 2001 (Tas), and the Evidence Act 2008 (Vic) provides, in general terms, that evidence may not be 'adduced' in respect of settlement negotiations. The broad terms of subs (1) are qualified by s 131(2), which sets out 11 instances in which the privilege will not apply.

The legislation in New South Wales, Tasmania and Victoria extends the application of this privilege to pre-trial processes: Evidence Act 1995 (NSW) s 131A; Evidence Act 2001 (Tas) s 131A; Evidence Act 2008 (Vic) s 131A. In the Australian Capital Territory, the provisions of the Evidence Act 1995 (Cth) are specifically incorporated into the discovery rules: r 601.

Privilege for professional confidential relationships

13.5.28 The legislation in New South Wales and Tasmania provides a privilege for 'professional confidential relationships': Evidence Act 1995 (NSW) Pt 3.10 Div 1A; Evidence Act 2001 (Tas) Pt 3.10. Section 126A of the Acts in each of these jurisdictions defines a 'protected confidence' for the purpose of the Division as meaning a communication made by a person in confidence to another person (the confidant) in the course of a relationship in which the confidant was acting in a professional capacity, and when the confidant was under an express or implied obligation not to disclose its contents, whether or not the obligation arises under law or can be inferred from the nature of the relationship between the person and the confidant. The confidential relationships may include, for example, doctor and patient, psychotherapist and patient, social worker and client, or journalist and source.

The privilege is qualified, and allows the court to balance the likely harm to the confider if the evidence is adduced and the desirability of the evidence being given: Evidence Act 1995

(NSW) s 126B; Evidence Act 2001 (Tas) s 126B. The privilege extends to pre-trial processes: Evidence Act 1995 (NSW) s 131A; Evidence Act 2001 (Tas) s 131A.

In Tasmania, the Evidence Act 2001 (Tas) provides a separate privilege in civil proceedings for medical communications: s 127A. This provision is broad enough to extend to pre-trial processes, but in any event s 131A now specifically applies this privilege to pre-trial processes. In the Northern Territory, there is also statutory privilege in civil proceedings for medical communications: Evidence Act 1939 (NT) s 12(2).

Division 1A of Pt 3.10 of the Evidence Act 1995 (Cth) provides protection only to confidential communications between journalists and their sources. Section 131A of the Commonwealth Act extends this privilege to pre-trial processes.

The Evidence Act 2008 (Vic) does not provide a privilege for professional confidential relationships.

Priest and penitent

13.5.29   Though the weight of common law authority does not support the existence of any special privilege arising out of the priest–penitent relationship, there is now a statutory recognition in most jurisdictions of privilege in respect of religious confessions that is sufficiently broad to extend to civil proceedings: ACT r 601 (production); NSW rr 21.3, 21.4, Dictionary (production); Evidence Act 1995 (Cth) s 127 (Australian Capital Territory, the Federal Court and the High Court); Evidence Act 1995 (NSW), s 127; Evidence Act 1939 (NT) s 12(1); Evidence Act 2001 (Tas) s 127; Evidence Act 2008 (Vic) s 127.

Spousal privilege

13.5.30   *In Australian Crime Commission v Stoddart* [2011] HCA 47, the High Court found by a majority that communications between spouses are not privileged at common law.

In Western Australia, s 18 of the Evidence Act 1906 exempts spouses from being compelled in any proceeding to disclose the content of any communications between them during their marriage.

Waiver of privilege

13.5.31   Privilege may be waived. The waiver may be deliberate as by voluntary disclosure without claiming the privilege. It may also be the unintended consequence of mistaken disclosure or partial disclosure of related documents. An unintended disclosure, however, will only result in an implied waiver if it would be unfair to withhold other related privileged material, as, for example, if the undisclosed material puts a different light on the meaning of privileged material that has been disclosed: *Attorney-General for the Northern Territory v Maurice* (1986) 161 CLR 475. The High Court explained in *Mann v Carnell* (1999) 201 CLR 1 at 13 (per Gleeson CJ, Gaudron, Gummow and Callinan JJ):

> What brings about the waiver is the inconsistency which the courts, where necessary informed by considerations of fairness, perceive, between the conduct of the client and maintenance of the confidentiality; not some overriding principle of fairness operating at large.

In those jurisdictions, and in those circumstances, in which the Evidence Act 1995 (Cth), the Evidence Act 1995 (NSW), the Evidence Act 2001 (Tas), or the Evidence Act 2008 (Vic) apply, the manner in which client legal privilege may be lost is not quite as flexible as the common law 'fairness' approach. The effect of s 122 on each of these Acts is that client legal privilege provided by the legislation is waived if a disclosure is made 'knowingly or voluntarily' by the client or with the express or implied consent of the client or party. The section also identifies specific circumstances, such as disclosures made in confidence, as a result of duress or deception, or under compulsion of law, in which a voluntary and knowing disclosure will not cause the privilege to be lost.

13.5.32 Notes and questions

1. The benefit of legal professional privilege may be waived by the client: *Great Atlantic Insurance Co v Home Insurance Co* [1981] 1 WLR 529. Can it be waived by the legal advisers? See *Baker v Campbell* (1983) 153 CLR 52 at 67 where Gibbs CJ made it clear that the privilege is that of the client and cannot be waived by the solicitor. This position is also reflected in the provisions of Evidence Act 1995 (Cth), Evidence Act 1995 (NSW), Evidence Act 2001 (Tas), and Evidence Act 2008 (Vic) ss 118, 119.

2. There is a well-established principle that there is no property in a witness: *Harmony Shipping Co v Saudi Europe Line* (CA) [1979] 1 WLR 1380. The interaction between this principle and legal profession privilege was considered by the New South Wales Court of Appeal in *Fagan v New South Wales* [2004] NSWCA 182. In that case, a police officer brought proceedings against the New South Wales Police Service for damages for failure to provide a safe system of work. His solicitor tried to examine serving police officers but was informed that senior police officers had directed all police officers that they would have to provide copies of any written statements they signed, and if there were no written statements they would have to give a report about the contents of the interview. The plaintiff challenged the orders on various grounds, including that compliance with them would involve a breach of legal professional privilege. One of the grounds relied on by the employer was that the orders were consistent with the principle that there is no property in a witness. The plaintiff's challenge to the orders was rejected at first instance but upheld by the Court of Appeal. The Court of Appeal concluded that the principle that there is no property in a witness had to operate with other principles, including legal professional privilege. In its view, the directions given by the senior officers, if complied with, would involve a breach of legal professional privilege.

3. Consider the position of a former client who brings proceedings against his or her former solicitor for professional negligence or breach of contract. Are documents which were brought into existence for the purpose of giving or receiving advice privileged? See *Lillicrap v Nalder & Son* [1993] 1 All ER 724 where it was held that in these circumstances the client impliedly waives legal professional privilege for all documents which are relevant to the claim. See also *Benecke v National Australia Bank* (1993) 35 NSWLR 110 where the plaintiff alleged that in earlier proceedings between her and the bank, her solicitor and barrister entered into a compromise which she had not authorised. It was held that the plaintiff's allegations effected a waiver of the privilege which would otherwise attach to confidential legal advice.

4. An interesting issue as to imputed waiver of legal professional privilege came before the High Court in *Goldberg v Ng* (1995) 132 ALR 57. The case involved equity proceedings brought against a solicitor by former clients. The High Court held by a bare majority of 3:2 that there had been an imputed waiver of the legal professional privilege which otherwise applied to certain documents in the solicitor's possession. This was found to result from the voluntary production of the documents by the solicitor to the Law Society for the purpose of answering a complaint made against him by the former clients to the Law Society. It is noteworthy that the Law Society enjoyed certain statutory powers in dealing with complaints by clients, which included the right to cancel or suspend a practising certificate of a solicitor who failed to give a satisfactory explanation of specified conduct, but the court found that these powers had not been invoked, and that the solicitor's disclosure had been voluntary. It has been suggested as a result of this case (see T Middleton, 'Legal Professional Privilege Lost by Disclosure to the Law Society — *Harold John Goldberg v Bernard Ng*' (1996) 26 *QLSJ* 197 at 202) that a litigant may be in a better position for the purpose of retaining the protection of the privilege in other proceedings, if the litigant produces documents under compulsion rather than by voluntary disclosure.

5. In cases where a party wishes to claim privilege for a communication between a lawyer or the client and a third party as being for the dominant purpose of use in anticipated litigation, the nature of the affidavit and other evidence presented to the court will be of great importance. In *Mitsubishi Electric Australia Pty Ltd v Victorian WorkCover Authority* (2002) 4 VR 332, the WorkCover Authority claimed an indemnity from the manufacturer of a machine which had exploded and injured a worker, making the authority liable to pay the worker benefits. In its affidavit of documents, the manufacturer discovered five reports by a loss adjuster, commissioned by solicitors acting for the manufacturer on the instructions of the manufacturer's insurer to conduct investigations into the circumstances of the accident, and to identify the circuit breaker involved in the accident.

It also discovered two related reports from consulting and forensic engineers. One of these reports was commissioned by the solicitors and the other by the loss adjuster on instructions from the solicitors. When the reports were commissioned, no proceedings had been issued in respect of the explosion, but the solicitors had been instructed to advise the insurer on questions of liability, indemnity and quantum. A County Court judge refused to accept the manufacturer's claim that the reports were privileged. The Court of Appeal reversed the decision. It was satisfied on the evidence presented that, at the time the reports were commissioned, there was a real prospect of litigation because the explosion was inherently likely to lead to litigation, solicitors had been instructed early and the manufacturer had resorted to its insurer. The decision may be contrasted with that of the New South Wales Court of Appeal in *Sydney Airports Corp Ltd v Singapore Airlines Ltd* [2004] NSWCA 380, though in relation to an expert report into the accident under examination in that case. The Court of Appeal confirmed the view of the judge at first instance, who had considered closely the nature of the evidence presented and concluded that the claimant had not put sufficient evidence before the court to discharge the onus of establishing what the dominant purpose for preparation of the document was.

6. It is a common misconception that privilege attaches to any communications which are marked 'without prejudice'. Communications genuinely made as part of settlement negotiations are privileged, even if they are not so marked: *Rodgers v Rodgers* (1964) 114 CLR 608 at 614. The marking 'without prejudice' is certainly advisable if a party wants the privilege to apply, as it makes that intent and the nature of the communication clear, but such a notation on communications which are not part of negotiations in an attempt to settle a dispute will have no effect, and hence the communications will not be privileged (unless on some other recognised ground): *J A McBeath Nominees Pty Ltd v Jenkins Development Corp Pty Ltd* [1992] 2 Qd R 121 at 128–9.

Further reading

13.5.33   Articles

T Allan, 'Abuse of Power and Public Interest Immunity: Justice, Rights and Truth' (1985) 101 *LQR* 200.

D Bailey, 'Are Interrogatories Necessary?' [1995] *LIJ* 522.

A Bruce, 'The Trade Practices Act 1974 (Cth) and the Demise of Legal Professional Privilege' (2002) 30 *Fed LR* 373.

B C Cairns, 'A Review of Some Innovations in Queensland Civil Procedure' (2005) 26 *Aust Bar Rev* 158.

B C Cairns, 'An Evaluation of the Function and Practice of Discovery' [1987] 61 *ALJ* 79.

B Cairns, *The Law of Discovery in Australia*, Law Book Co, Sydney, 1984.

L David, 'Is there a Common Law Privilege against Spouse Incrimination?' (2004) 27(1) *UNSWLJ* 1.

The Hon Justice G L Davies and S Sheldon, 'Some Proposed Changes in Civil Procedure: Their Practical Benefits and Ethical Rationale' (1993) 3 *JJA* 111.

The Hon Justice D A Ipp, 'Reforms to the Adversarial Process in Civil Litigation — Part II' (1995) 69 *ALJ* 790 at 793–7.

R Fisher, 'Preserving Professional Privilege: Implications for Tax Investigatory Powers' (2003) 32 *ATR* 7.

N Francey, 'Legal Professional Privilege Under the New Statutory Regime' (1996–97) 15 *Aust Bar Rev* 73.

W Harris, 'Privilege and the Unrepresented Litigant' (1993) 23 *QLSJ* 7.

The Hon Justice J P Hamilton, 'Thirty Years of Civil Procedural Reform in Australia: A Personal Reminiscence' (2005) 26 *Aust Bar Rev* 258.

A Jones, 'Uniform Civil Procedure Rules, r 212 and Expert Reports: For Your Eyes Only?' (2003) 24(1) *Qd L* 25.

K Kendall, 'Prospects for a Tax Advisor's Privilege in Australia' [2005] *JATTA* 28.

S McNicol, 'Client Legal Privilege and Legal Professional Privilege: Considered, Compared and Contrasted' (1999) 18 *Aust Bar Rev* 189.

P Mendelow, 'Expert Evidence: Legal Professional Privilege and Experts' Reports', (2001) 75 *ALJ* 258.

V Morfuni, 'Legal Professional Privilege and the Government's Right to Access Information and Documents' (2004) 33(2) *Aust Tax Rev* 89.

A Newbold, 'Inadvertent Disclosure in Civil Proceedings' (1991) 107 *LQR* 99.

A Pomerenke, 'The Expert Witness and Legal Professional Privilege' (1998) 19 *Qd L* 18.

R Sackville, 'Lawyer/Client Privilege' (1999) 18 *Aust Bar Rev* 104.

K Smark, 'Privilege under the Evidence Acts' (1995) 18 *UNSWLJ* 95.

B Tamberlin and L Bastin, 'In-house Counsel and Privilege: "The Client's Man of Business"' (2008) 31 *Aust Bar Rev* 104.

B Tamberlin and L Bastin, 'In-house Counsel, Legal Professional Privilege and "Independence"' (2009) 85 *ALJ* 193.

G Watson and F Anu, 'Solicitor–Client Privilege and Litigation Privilege in Civil Litigation' (1998) 77 *CBR* 315.

K Willcock, 'Legal Professional Privilege and the In-house Lawyer — Principles and Practice' (1999) 27 *ABLR* 364.

T Wilson, 'Defining the Dominant Purpose' (2004) 31(7) *Brief* 20.

13.5.34　Texts

Australian Institute of Judicial Administration, *The Use of Discovery and Interrogatories in Civil Litigation*, AIJA, Melbourne, 1990.

B Cairns, *Australian Civil Procedure*, 8th ed, Lawbook Co, Sydney, 2009, Ch 10.

J D Heydon, *Cross on Evidence*, LexisNexis Butterworths, Australia, 2006, vol 1 (looseleaf).

S Odgers SC, *Uniform Evidence Law*, 9th ed, Lawbook Co, Australia, 2010.

Further Means of Obtaining Evidence

OVERVIEW

In addition to the processes of discovery of documents and interrogatories, as considered in **Chapter 13**, there are several other procedures available to parties to assist them in assessing the other party's case and in gathering evidence for the trial.

This chapter will consider procedures for the inspection and testing of property and procedures entitling a party to require another party to undergo a medical examination. Each of these processes resembles discovery, but is not a discovery procedure in the strict sense of the term. The chapter also considers rules which require the provision of particulars in personal injury litigation, rules which facilitate the obtaining and tendering of medical and other expert evidence, procedures which assist a party to obtain admissions from an opposing party prior to trial and the use of the subpoena process to compel the attendance of persons to give evidence at the trial or to produce documents either pre-trial or at the trial.

INSPECTION AND TESTING OF PROPERTY

Introduction

14.1.1   In all jurisdictions, except the High Court, the court has a specific power under the rules to order inspection and testing of property. As with other discovery processes there are no longer any specific rules in the High Court in this respect, and it is necessary should the need arise to obtain appropriate orders at a directions hearing.

The court also has an inherent jurisdiction which may provide assistance where the Rules of Court do not provide adequate relief. This inherent jurisdiction is considered at **16.4.1**ff. Although at one time the scope of the rules was restricted in a number of significant respects, the rules in most jurisdictions are now quite broad and far-reaching.

[*NOTE*: in this chapter a reference, such as WA O 9 r 2, is a reference to the relevant Rules of Court. All other legislation will be specified.]

14.1.2E **Supreme Court (General Civil Procedure) Rules 2005 (Vic)**

Order 37 — Inspection, Detention and Preservation of Property

Inspection detention, etc of property

37.01 (1) In any proceeding the Court may make an order for the inspection, detention, custody or preservation of any property, whether or not in the possession custody or power of a party.

(2) An order under paragraph (1) may authorise any person to —

    (a)   enter any land or do any other thing for the purpose of obtaining access to the property;

    (b)   take samples of the property;

    (c)   make observations (including the photographing) of the property;

    (d)   conduct any experiments on or with the property;

    (e)   observe any process.

14.1.3 There are similar rules in the Federal Court (Federal Court Rules 2011 r 14.01), the Australian Capital Territory (Court Procedures Rules 2006 rr 715–719), the Northern Territory (Supreme Court Rules r 37.01), New South Wales (Uniform Civil Procedure Rules 2005 r 23.8), Queensland (Uniform Civil Procedure Rules 1999 (Qld) r 250(1)), South Australia (Supreme Court Civil Rules 2006 r 147), Tasmania (Supreme Court Rules 2000 r 437) and Western Australia (Rules of the Supreme Court 1971 O 56 rr 2, 3). In the Australian Capital Territory the court may not make an order under r 715 unless it is satisfied that sufficient relief is not available under the Evidence Act 1995 (Cth), s 169. Similarly, in New South Wales an order is not to be made under r 23.8, unless the court is satisfied that sufficient relief is not available under Evidence Act 1995 (NSW) s 169 (r 23.8(4)).

The rules extend to property not in the possession, custody or power of a party, and they authorise a broad range of orders as to what may be done with the property.

Except in Tasmania and Western Australia there is no requirement to show that the property is related to the proceeding in any particular way. The rules in Tasmania and Western Australia extend only to property that is the subject matter of the proceeding, or as to which any question may arise in the proceeding. The appropriate interpretation of this restriction is not finally settled. Some authorities have suggested that it is necessary that there be a dispute over the property itself, whether in respect of its ownership, use or control: *Johnson v Tobacco Leaf Marketing Board* [1967] VR 427; *Nicholls v McLeay and Herald-Sun TV Pty Ltd* [1971] 1 SASR 442. Other authority has taken a less restrictive view, extending to property which could be of evidential value only: *Vowell v Shire of Hastings* [1970] VR 746.

14.1.4 The rules in the Northern Territory (r 37.02) and Victoria (r 37.02) also establish a procedure which enables a person to obtain an order for the inspection, detention, custody or preservation of property in the possession, custody or power of another, in order to determine whether to bring a proceeding against that person. The procedure and preconditions to be satisfied correspond with the equivalent rules for those jurisdictions in respect of discovery of documents before action: see **13.2.4**. The rules in the Australian Capital Territory (r 715) allow the making of an order for the inspection, custody or preservation of property before a proceeding starts as if the proceeding had started when the court has made an order under Div 2.8.6 (preliminary discovery) in relation to the proceeding. In Queensland (r 254) the court may, in urgent circumstances, make orders for the inspection, detention, custody or preservation of property (or for the sale or other disposal of perishable property) before the proceeding starts, as if the proceeding had started. Such an order may include conditions about starting the proceeding.

14.1.5 Notes and questions

1. Consider the wording of the rules relating to the inspection and testing of property. Do they, or should they, extend to an order for the delivery of a sample if the proposed testing would result in the destruction of the sample? See *Rutile Mining Development v Australian Oil Exploration* [1960] Qd R 480 where the Full Court of the Supreme Court of Queensland held the power did extend to such an order, although in the circumstances the court determined that the judge's decision at first instance not to exercise any discretion he may have had to make the order sought should not be interfered with.

2. Is human tissue of a deceased person 'property' for the purpose of the rules governing inspection and testing of property? See *Roche v Douglas* (2000) 22 WAR 331 where it was held that tissue samples were property and the court accordingly had power to make an order allowing for DNA testing of tissue specimens. See also *Bazley v Wesley Monash IVF Pty Ltd* [2010] QSC 118, where an order was made under r 250 of the Uniform Civil Procedure Rules 1999 (Qld) requiring the respondent to continue to hold and maintain straws of semen belonging to the applicant's deceased husband. White J held that the sperm extracted and stored could be described as 'property' and that the court had jurisdiction to make an order under r 250 for the temporary retention and preservation of the applicant's late husband's sperm and ultimate return to her or another storage facility. The decision includes a useful analysis of the development of the common law regarding property rights in human bodies and body parts.

3. In *Atwell v Roberts* [2006] WASC 269 an application was made under O 52 of the Rules of the Supreme Court 1971 (WA) (Detention etc of Property) for an order that the first defendant permit the plaintiffs or their agent to inspect the books of account of the partnership known as the Atwell Family Agency. The Case Management Registrar had dismissed the application on the basis that O 52 r 2(1) did not apply in the circumstances, and that any application for inspection of the documents should have been brought under O 26 r 6 (Order for Information as to Particular Documents). The appeal against that decision was dismissed. Master Newnes examined the distinction between O 52 r 2 and the procedure for disclosure and inspection of documents under O 26, concluding (at [16]) that 'except where the question concerns the document as a physical object, issues as to inspection of any document are normally to be determined under the discovery and inspection rules set out in O 26'.

PERSONAL INJURY PROCEEDINGS: MEDICAL EXAMINATIONS, PARTICULARS AND DOCUMENTS RELATING TO LOSS AND DAMAGE

Medical examinations

Rules of Court

14.2.1E   **Supreme Court (General Civil Procedure) Rules 2005 (Vic)**
Order 33 — Medical Examination and Service of Hospital and Medical Reports

Notice for examination

33.04 (1) The defendant may request the plaintiff in writing to submit to appropriate examinations by a medical expert or experts at specified times and places.

(2) Where a plaintiff refuses or neglects without reasonable cause to comply with a request under paragraph (1), the Court may, if the request was on reasonable terms, stay the proceeding.

14.2.2   Similar provision is now made by the rules of some courts for the defendant, by notice to the plaintiff, to require the plaintiff to be medically examined: NSW Pt 23; NT O 33; SA rr 153, 4 (interpretation); WA O 28. As these rules vary significantly, the applicable rule must be consulted on matters of detail. For example, except in Western Australia, all of the relevant definitions in the rules make it clear that the 'medical' examination extends to examinations by dentists and psychologists as well as medical practitioners. In New South Wales, occupational therapists, optometrists and physiotherapists are also specifically included. The South Australian rules specifically include physiotherapists, chiropodists, chiropractors and 'any other professional person qualified to diagnose or treat illness or injury'. Although the rules in the Northern Territory and Victoria apply only to the medical examination of plaintiffs, the rules in New South Wales, South Australia and Western Australia are broader, extending to the medical examination of any party to a proceeding. The remedies available against a party in default also vary, but may involve a stay of the proceedings, the striking out of a pleading, or the dismissal of proceedings in whole or part.

    The rules in the Northern Territory (r 33.06), Victoria (r 33.06) and Western Australia (O 28 r 1) require that the defendant must obtain a medical report following the examination and must serve a copy upon the person who has been examined. In South Australia (r 153), the party requesting the examination must give every other party a copy of the written report made by the examining medical practitioner. The South Australian rule further stipulates that if the party undergoing the examination does not receive a copy of the written report within 14 days after the date of the medical examination, the party examined may ask the medical practitioner for a report on the examination.

Statutory provisions

14.2.3   In addition to the provisions contained in the rules, there are statutory provisions in several jurisdictions applying either:

- generally to personal injury actions: Civil Law (Wrongs) Act 2002 (ACT) s 67 (excludes industrial accident claims); Personal Injuries Proceedings Act 2002 (Qld) s 25 (excludes motor vehicle and industrial accident cases) s 46A; Evidence Act 2001 (Tas) s 196A; or

- more specifically to motor vehicle personal injury actions: Road Transport (Third-Party Insurance) Act 2008 (ACT) s 120; Motor Accidents Compensation Act 1999 (NSW) s 86; Motor Accident Insurance Act 1994 (Qld) s 46A; Motor Vehicles Act 1959 (SA) s 127; Transport Accident Act 1986 (Vic) s 71; Motor Vehicle (Third Party Insurance) Act 1943 (WA) s 30; and

- industrial accident proceedings: Workplace Injury Management and Workers Compensation Act 1998 (NSW) s 119; Workers Compensation and Rehabilitation Act 2003 (Qld) s 282; Workers Rehabilitation and Compensation Act 1986 (SA) s 108; Accident Compensation Act 1985 (Vic) s 112; Workers Compensation and Injury Management Act 1981 (WA) s 64,

which require the plaintiff to comply with a request to undergo a medical examination.

Inherent jurisdiction

14.2.4 In addition to the power under the Rules of Court and in statutory provisions, the court also has inherent jurisdiction in personal injury litigation to require the plaintiff to also undergo a reasonable medical examination, and it may stay the action if the plaintiff refuses: *Starr v National Coal Board* [1977] 1 All ER 242. If the court orders the plaintiff to be medically examined for the defendant, it may also order an exchange of medical reports: *Clarke v Martlew* [1973] 1 QB 58.

Examination must be reasonable

14.2.5 Both the inherent jurisdiction and the jurisdiction under the rules or statutory provisions can only be used to require a medical examination that is reasonable. The question as to what is reasonable is one of fact requiring a balancing of the reasonableness and value of the examination against the reasonableness of the party's objections to undergoing it: *Stace v Commonwealth* (1989) 51 SASR 391. Surgery or dangerous medical procedures are not encompassed: *Pucci v Humes Ltd* (1970) 92 WN (NSW) 326. See also *Starr v National Coal Board* [1977] 1 All ER 242; *Vakauta v Kelly* (1989) 167 CLR 568.

Particulars and documents relating to loss and damage

14.2.6 The rules in most jurisdictions now require the provision of fairly detailed particulars in proceedings for damages for personal injuries. They also require the provision to varying degrees of supporting documents such as hospital and medical reports. In some jurisdictions the requirements in relation to these documents are included in the rules applying only to personal injury proceedings, while in others they are part of the broader rules relating to expert evidence: see **14.3.1ff**.

Australian Capital Territory

14.2.7 In the Australian Capital Territory the Rules of Court specify details that must be included in a statement of claim for damages arising out of the negligent use of a motor vehicle (r 52) or the negligence or breach of statutory duty by an employer: r 53. In addition to details relevant to liability, the statement of claim must include details of the nature and extent of the injuries and disabilities resulting from the accident sufficient for the defendant to nominate an appropriate expert to examine the plaintiff, the name of any health professional who treated the plaintiff for the injuries suffered, and for any condition exacerbated by those injuries, and the nature of any claim for past and future economic loss, including the name and address of each employer of the plaintiff during a reasonable period before and since the accident.

New South Wales

14.2.8 In New South Wales (Pt 15 Div 2) plaintiffs in personal injury cases are to serve a statement on the defendant, or on the defendant's insurer or solicitor, on or as soon as practicable after serving the statement of claim. The statement is to contain detailed information about the plaintiff's injuries and any continuing disabilities, special damages, particulars of any claim in respect of domestic assistance and particulars in respect of any claim for loss of income and earning capacity. The statement must be accompanied by documents available to the plaintiff in support of the claims, and a wide variety of document types are specified. An obligation is placed on the plaintiff to update any advice in a statement or document provided under these rules, as soon as practicable after becoming aware that information contained in it is no longer accurate and complete. Unless the court otherwise orders, the plaintiff is to file a copy of the final statement of particulars at least 42 days before the hearing date. The court may dismiss the proceedings or make such other order as it thinks fit if it is satisfied the plaintiff has not sufficiently complied with these obligations.

Queensland

14.2.9 The requirements in Queensland (Ch 14 Pt 2) are especially extensive. The pleadings and particulars are governed by the ordinary rules, but there are requirements for the delivery of separate 'statements of loss and damage' and 'statements of expert and economic evidence' which are additional to the pleadings; do not become part of the pleadings; and are not governed by the rules of pleading. Rule 547 requires the plaintiff to serve a statement of loss and damage on the defendant within 28 days after the close of pleadings. The statement must disclose:

(a)   details of any amount claimed for out-of-pocket expenses, and documents in the possession or under the control of the plaintiff about the expenses;

(b)   if there is a claim for economic loss, the name and address of each of the plaintiff's employers over the three years immediately before the injury, and since the injury, specifying in each case the period of employment, the capacity in which the plaintiff was employed, and the plaintiff's net earnings. Particulars are also to be provided as to any amount claimed by the plaintiff to the date of the statement for loss of income, as to any disability resulting in a loss of earning capacity and of the amount claimed for future economic loss. If the plaintiff is self-employed, such additional or other particulars must be provided as will substantiate the claim for economic loss;

(c)   particulars of the plaintiff's pain and suffering and loss of amenities caused by the injuries, including the physical, social and recreational consequences of the injuries;

(d)   particulars of any other amount sought as damages;

(e)   the names and addresses of all hospitals, doctors and experts who have examined the plaintiff or provided reports on the plaintiff's injury, loss or treatment. This includes reports as to economic loss;

(f)   all documents in the plaintiff's possession or control relating to the plaintiff's injury, loss (including economic loss) or treatment; and

(g)   details of any accident, injury or illness suffered by the plaintiff in the three years immediately before the injury, and since the injury.

The documents which must be identified include hospital and medical reports and accounts, documents about the refund of workers' compensation payments, social security benefits or similar payments, and various documents relating to the plaintiff's income and taxation position. Any of the documents identified must be made available to the defendant on request. If the plaintiff proposes to rely at the trial on expert evidence not contained in a report mentioned in the statement of loss and damage, a report or proof of the evidence must be served on the defendant before the request for trial date is filed. Any expert evidence which has not been disclosed to the defendant as required by the rule cannot be called or tendered at the trial (except by consent or in cross-examination) unless the court, for special reason, gives leave: r 548.

The plaintiff's statement is to be accurate when served. If there is a significant change in information given in the statement after service but before a trial date is set, the plaintiff must serve a supplement to the statement. After a trial date is set the plaintiff is to give any further documents of the nature of those to be identified in the statement to the defendant as soon as practicable or, if they are voluminous, must make them available for inspection by the defendant: r 549.

The defendant must serve a similar statement, referred to as a 'statement of expert and economic evidence', within 28 days after being served with the plaintiff's statement and before a request for a trial date is filed. It must disclose the names and addresses of all hospitals, doctors and experts who have provided reports on the plaintiff's injury, loss (including economic loss) or treatment: r 550. The defendant is required to provide to the plaintiff on request a copy of any report mentioned in the statement: r 551.

The defendant is subject to the same requirement as the plaintiff in respect of the service of a proof of evidence in respect of any expert evidence sought to be adduced at the trial, but not disclosed through the statement. The defendant may call expert evidence not disclosed or supplied to the plaintiff as required by the rule only if the court, for special reasons, gives leave: r 551. The defendant has the same obligations as the plaintiff in respect of the supplementing of the statement: r 552.

South Australia

14.2.10   In South Australia (r 106) plaintiffs are to file a 'statement of loss' within 28 days after service of the defence. The statement of loss must be in the form of an affidavit. If more than six months have elapsed since the last statement was filed and the defendant files a request for a further statement, an update is to be filed within 28 days after the request. The statement is to contain a wide variety of information relating to the plaintiff's injuries and any resulting disability, special damages, and loss of earnings and earning capacity. In recognition that this detailed information will follow the statement of claim, only the general nature of these matters is to be pleaded in the statement of claim: r 99(3).

Tasmania

14.2.11   In Tasmania (r 253A) the plaintiff in an action for damages for personal injuries is required to give the defendant written advice about the following matters:

(a)   the nature of the plaintiff's injuries;

(b)   the nature of any secondary illnesses suffered by the plaintiff;

(c)   the name of each hospital attended by the plaintiff in consequence of the injuries;

(d)   the name and address of each medical practitioner who has treated the plaintiff for the injuries, other than as part of his or her hospital treatment;

(e)   any expenses incurred as a result of the injuries;

(f)   the nature of employment or self-employment that the plaintiff claims he or she would have been likely to engage in had it not been for the injuries;

(g)   the estimated gross annual income for each category of employment or self-employment referred to in paragraph (f); and

(h)   whether the plaintiff's claim is that the injuries sustained impact totally or partially on that earning capacity.

This advice is to be given within 50 days after the close of pleadings or within such other time as the parties may agree or the court or a judge may order.

Victoria; Northern Territory

14.2.12   In Victoria (r 13.10(4)) and the Northern Territory (r 13.10(4)) detailed particulars in relation to economic loss must be included in a party's pleading: see **11.7.13E–11.7.14**. There is then a separate requirement for the exchange of medical reports: NT O 33; Vic O 33. The plaintiff must serve on each other party who has an address for service a copy of a medical or hospital report the plaintiff intends to tender or the substance of which is intended to be adduced in evidence at the trial. The defendant similarly serves copies of medical reports on the plaintiff. The reports have to be served within the times set by the rules. If the action is for damages for injury sustained because of medical treatment or advice, any report served under these rules may exclude an expression of opinion as to liability. In Victoria any statement about facts that relate only to liability may also be excluded.

In a trial by a judge alone, a report that has been duly served is admissible as evidence of the expert's opinion and, if the expert's oral evidence of a fact on which the evidence was based would be admissible, the report is evidence of that fact. The expert witness need attend only if the opposite party gives a notice to attend for cross-examination. If the expert fails to comply with a notice to attend for cross-examination, the court may order that the report not be received into evidence.

Medical evidence which has not been disclosed by serving a report under these rules cannot be given at the trial, except with the leave of the court, by consent of the parties, or in cross-examination.

DISCLOSING EXPERT EVIDENCE

14.3.1   Most jurisdictions now require that parties exchange expert reports or provide proofs of expert evidence as a condition of admitting expert testimony at the trial. These rules are consistent with the increased move towards case management and the 'cards on the table' approach to litigation. They assist in ensuring that parties are not taken by surprise at trial and that each party has the opportunity of considering, investigating and responding to expert evidence to be adduced by another party.

In most jurisdictions the rules do not have the effect of abrogating legal professional privilege which would otherwise apply to reports obtained by parties for use in existing or anticipated litigation, but rather apply only to require disclosure of the reports or proofs as to the substance of evidence to be given, if a party wishes to adduce the evidence at trial. It has been seen, however, that the rules in South Australia and Queensland do abrogate the privilege, and require pre-trial disclosure of expert reports, whether or not the party in possession of the report intends to rely on the report at trial: see 13.5.15.

Practice in each jurisdiction

Federal Court

14.3.2   In the Federal Court, Div 23.2 deals with parties' expert witnesses and expert reports. A party is only permitted to call an expert to give evidence at the trial if the party has delivered an expert report that complies with r 23.13 to all other parties. Rule 23.13 sets out detailed requirements about the content of expert reports. The party wishing to call the expert must also have otherwise complied with the requirements of Div 23.2: r 23.11.

Rule 23.12 requires that any party intending to retain an expert to give an expert report or to give expert evidence must first give the expert any practice note dealing with applicable guidelines for expert witnesses. The relevant Practice Note is Practice Note CM 7: Expert Witnesses in Proceedings in the Federal Court of Australia (1 August 2011). This Practice Note contains clear statements about the general duty experts owe to the court. It also sets out the requirements as to content as also expressed in r 23.11, and imposes a range of other obligations relating to the statements to be contained in an expert report and documents that must be included in, or attached to, the report.

A party may apply to the court for an order that another party provide copies of that other party's expert report: r 23.14.

If two or more parties intend to call experts to give opinion evidence about a similar question, r 23.15 permits any of the parties to apply to the court for relevant orders. A wide range of orders are potentially available, such as: orders requiring the experts to confer, orders limiting the expert's evidence to the content of the expert's report, orders requiring that all factual evidence relevant to any expert's opinions be adduced before the expert is called to give evidence, and orders that each expert gives an opinion about the other expert's opinion.

Australian Capital Territory

14.3.3   In the Australian Capital Territory, Pt 2.12 deals with expert evidence. Rule 1241 requires the active parties to exchange copies of all expert reports obtained. The plaintiff's expert reports are to be served at least 28 days before the certificate of readiness is filed. The defendant's reports are to be served within a further 14 days. An expert report is not admissible unless it has been served in accordance with the rule, except with the leave of the court or the agreement of all active parties, and that leave is not to be given unless there are exceptional circumstances or the expert report merely updates an earlier report which was duly served.

If an expert materially changes an opinion, a supplementary expert report must be served: r 1242. Except with the court's leave or the agreement of all the active parties, oral expert evidence is not admissible unless an expert report served in accordance with r 1241 contains the substance of the matters sought to be adduced in evidence: r 1243.

New South Wales

14.3.4 In New South Wales, r 31.28 governs the disclosure of experts' reports and hospital reports. Each party must serve experts' reports and hospital reports on each other active party. If a time is fixed by court order or practice note, the reports must be served accordingly. If no time is otherwise fixed, the reports must be served not later than 28 days before the date of the hearing at which the reports are to be used. An expert's report or hospital report is not admissible if the report has not been served as required by this rule, and oral expert evidence–in-chief is not admissible unless the substance of the evidence is contained in an expert's report or hospital report served under the rule. The evidence may, however, be given if the parties consent. The court may also make an order to permit tendering of the report or giving of the oral evidence, but such leave is only to be given if the court is satisfied this is warranted because of exceptional circumstances, or that the report concerned is merely an update of a report served in accordance with the rule.

Rule 31.29 provides that except in proceedings on a trial with a jury, an expert's report which has been served as required by the rules or an order under the rules is, without further evidence, admissible as evidence of the expert's opinion. If the expert's direct oral evidence of a fact on which the opinion was formed would be admissible the report is also, without further evidence, admissible as evidence of that fact. However, the rule also provides a procedure by which a party may require any expert whose report has been served by another party to attend for cross-examination.

Northern Territory

14.3.5 In the Northern Territory O 44 governs expert evidence, although it does not apply to medical and similar evidence in personal injury claims, which are dealt with separately: see 14.2.12. The rules in relation to expert evidence generally apply only to proceedings commenced by writ. A party who intends to adduce expert evidence must — within the time fixed by the rules — serve every other party with a statement giving the substance of the evidence. If the plaintiff's claim is for damages for death resulting from medical treatment or advice, the statement may exclude expressions of opinion about liability and statements about facts on which the opinion is based and which relate only to the question of liability. If expert evidence has not been disclosed under this procedure a party is not permitted to adduce the evidence except by consent of the parties, or with the leave of the court, or as part of cross-examination. A party who is served by another party with a statement of expert evidence may put it in evidence.

Queensland

14.3.6 In Queensland, extensive new rules about expert evidence were introduced in 2004: Ch 11 Pt 5. The rules do not apply to a witness who is giving evidence in a proceeding as a party, or to a person whose conduct is in issue in the proceeding. They also do not apply to a person who has given treatment or advice to an injured person, if the evidence is only about particular limited matters set out in the rules.

The rules make it express that the expert's overriding duty is to assist the court. There are detailed requirements in relation to the contents of any expert report. Rule 429 sets out the requirements for disclosure of expert reports. A party who intends to rely on an expert report must, unless the court otherwise orders, disclose the report within the time limits set out in the rules. For plaintiffs, the reports are to be disclosed within 90 days of the close of pleadings and for defendants, disclosure is to be made within 120 days of the close of pleadings. Other parties are to disclose within 90 days after the close of pleadings for the party. If an expert changes in a material way an opinion in a report that has been disclosed, the expert must provide a supplementary report stating the change and the reason for it, and this report must be disclosed as soon as practicable: r 429A. A party may tender an expert report only if it has been disclosed as required by the rules, unless the court gives leave. A party who has disclosed an expert report as required by the rules may tender the report as evidence-in-chief of the expert. Unless the court gives leave, oral evidence-in-chief may only be given by an expert if the evidence is in response to the report of another expert, or if it is directed to issues that first emerged in the course of the trial: r 427.

South Australia

14.3.7 In South Australia there is a separate rule requiring pre-trial disclosure of expert reports, whether or not a party intends to rely on the report at trial: r 160.

Within 60 days after the time limited for making an initial disclosure of documents, a party is to obtain all the expert reports that the party intends to obtain for the trial, and serve on every other party a copy of every expert report in the party's possession relevant to the subject matter of the action. The rule contains detailed requirements about the contents of the report.

A party who has disclosed an expert report, and proposes to rely on evidence from the expert at the trial, is required to comply with requests from another party for the provision of particular categories of documents and information relevant to the report. This includes documentary material (including computer data) on which the expert has relied, details of fees or benefits the expert has or will receive for preparing the report or giving evidence, and details of communications involving the expert relevant to the preparation of the report. There is provision enabling the court, on application by a party, to relieve the party of the obligation to disclose a report or provide requested information relating to it.

Rule 161 contains an exception to the disclosure obligation in the case of a 'shadow expert'. A shadow expert is an expert who is engaged to assist with the preparation or presentation of a party's case but not on the basis that he or she will, or may, give evidence at the trial. The expert must not have been previously engaged in some other capacity to give advice or an opinion in relation to the party's case or any aspect of it. To be regarded as a shadow expert, the expert must have given a certificate in the approved form at or before the time the expert is engaged. The rule imposes obligations on a party engaging a shadow expert to notify other parties of various details of the engagement. Evidence of a shadow expert is not admissible at the trial, unless the court determines there are special reasons to admit the evidence.

Unless the court otherwise orders, a party may not call a witness to give expert evidence at the trial of the action unless the evidence to be adduced has been disclosed to the other parties, either in the form of an expert report or an affidavit (or the court has relieved the party from the obligation of disclosure): r 214(2). An order permitting evidence which has not been disclosed will normally require the party in breach, or the party's lawyer, to pay costs associated with the non-disclosure: r 214(3).

With the court's permission, an expert report may be tendered at the trial and become in effect the evidence-in-chief of the expert: r 169.

Tasmania

14.3.8 In Tasmania r 515 prevents a party from adducing expert evidence at trial, unless the party has served on every other party a statement signed by the expert witness and containing a range of matters specified in r 516. These include the substance of the evidence, the facts and assumptions on which each opinion expressed in the statement is based, the reasons for each opinion expressed in the statement, references to any literature or other materials relied on in support of opinions expressed, and any qualifications of any opinions expressed. The statement is to be served within the time fixed by any order, or otherwise within a reasonable time before the commencement of the trial. A party who is served by another party with a statement of expert evidence may put it in evidence: r 517.

Victoria

14.3.9   In Victoria, O 44 governs expert evidence. This order applies to a proceeding however commenced. The order does not apply to medical reports in proceedings for damages for personal injuries, which are dealt with separately: see 14.2.12. This does not, however, exclude the application of the order to opinion evidence of medical practitioners as relevant to the question of liability, rather than to the medical condition of the plaintiff. The order excludes from its operation the evidence of a party who would, if called as a witness at the trial, be qualified to give evidence as an expert in respect of any question in a proceeding.

A party intending at trial to adduce the evidence of a person as an expert must provide the expert with a copy of the expert witness code of conduct in Form 44A as soon as practicable after the expert is engaged and before the expert makes a report. The expert's report must be served on each other party and a copy delivered for the use of the court not later than 30 days before the day fixed for trial. The rules contain detailed requirements in relation to the contents of the report and documents which accompany it. These requirements include an acknowledgment by the expert of having read the expert witness code of conduct and agreeing to be bound by it. The code includes statements that an expert witness has an overriding duty to assist the court impartially on matters relevant to the area of expertise of the witness, and that the witness is not an advocate for a party. If expert evidence has not been disclosed under this procedure, a party is not permitted to adduce the evidence, except by consent of the parties, or with the leave of the court, or as part of cross-examination. A party who is served by another party with a statement of expert evidence may put it in evidence.

The court may direct expert witnesses to confer and to provide the court with a joint report specifying matters agreed and matters not agreed and the reasons for non-agreement. The court may specify the matters on which the experts are to confer and make orders as to whether or not the legal representatives for the parties are to attend the conference. An agreement reached during the conference does not bind a party, except to the extent the party agrees in writing.

Western Australia

14.3.10   In Western Australia, O 36A r 2 applies to medical evidence in actions for personal injuries. It requires a party, within the times set out in the rule, to serve other parties with copies of all medical reports the substance of which the party intends to rely on at the trial. The court may relieve a party of this obligation and may direct that, instead of serving a copy of any medical report, the substance of all or any medical evidence that a party intends to rely on at the trial or hearing be disclosed in writing. Expert medical evidence not disclosed in a report, or otherwise in writing as directed by the court, can only be given at the trial if the court gives leave, or pursuant to a direction of the court, or where all parties agree. If a medical report contains statements by the party against whose interest the evidence is to be led or hearsay evidence as to the manner in which the personal injuries were sustained, or other evidence that would not be admissible at the trial, the court may regard this as sufficient reason for directing that the substance of the evidence be disclosed instead of the report, or for permitting the giving of evidence which has not been disclosed. There does not need to be disclosure to a defendant who did not enter an appearance.

A party who proposes to call other expert evidence must apply before trial for a direction as to whether the evidence or the substance of the evidence ought to be disclosed to the other parties: O 36A r 3. In the absence of an application for these directions, expert evidence cannot be given unless the court gives leave or the other parties agree.

Uniform Evidence Acts

14.3.11 Section 177 of the Evidence Act 1995 (Cth) (applying in the Australian Capital Territory, the Federal Court and the High Court), and the corresponding provision of the Evidence Act 1995 (NSW), the Evidence Act 2001 (Tas) and the Evidence Act 2008 (Vic) establish a procedure enabling the admission into evidence of expert opinions without calling the expert to give evidence. A party who intends to prove the opinion may provide a copy of the opinion to the other side, along with notice that the opinion will be tendered at the trial. This is to be done at least 21 days before the hearing. If the opposite party requires the expert to be called as a witness, the written opinion is not admissible, but otherwise, the party wishing to give the opinion as evidence may then tender a certificate setting out that opinion. Section 177 also involves a costs sanction, in that a party requiring the expert to be called may be ordered to pay the assessed costs if the court considers that the party had no reasonable cause for doing so. A similar position will apply in the Northern Territory when the Evidence (National Uniform Legislation) Act (NT) comes into force: see further 13.5.2.

14.3.12 Notes and questions

1. For an interesting and in-depth analysis of the notion of *objective* expert evidence, and whether this is 'possible or even desirable', and a challenge to many of the notions underlying procedural reforms in relation to expert evidence, see G Edmond, 'After Objectivity: Expert Evidence and Procedural Reform' (2003) 25 *Syd L Rev* 131.

2. Is it necessary to provide documents used by an expert in compiling a report to the opposing party with the report? This may require careful consideration of the wording of the rules in each jurisdiction. In *Wilson v Porter* (1988) 46 SASR 547, the court held that the term 'report' in r 38 of the then South Australian rules did not extend to material which was relied on by the expert in compiling the report, but was not included in the report. In the Northern Territory, r 33.03 defines a medical report to include any document intended to be read with the report. In *Coles Myer Ltd v Bailey* (1991) 105 FLR 465, it was held that a surgeon's report made it clear that questions posed in a letter from a solicitor to the surgeon requesting a medical report were intended to be read as part of the report and were therefore required by that rule to be disclosed.

14.3.13 Further reading

G L Davies and J Lieboff, 'Reforming the Litigation System' (1994) 14 *Proctor* 18.

G L Davies and S A Sheldon, 'Some Proposed Changes in Civil Procedural Reform: Their Practical Benefits and Ethical Rationale' (1993) 3 *JJA* 111.

Chief Justice Paul de Jersey AC, 'Experts and Adversarialism, a Non-partisan Solution: Queensland's Draft Rules', Queensland Law Society Continuing Legal Education Personal Injuries Conference, Stamford Plaza Hotel, Brisbane, 20 June 2003.

I Freckelton, P Reddy and H Selby, 'Australian Judicial Perspectives on Expert Evidence: An Empirical Study', Australian Institute of Judicial Administration Incorporated, Melbourne, 1999.

I Freckelton, P Reddy and H Selby, 'The Australian Magistrates' Perspectives on Expert Evidence: An Empirical Study', Australian Institute of Judicial Administration, Melbourne, 1999.

Justice Glass, 'Expert Evidence' (1987) 3 *Aust Bar Rev* 43.

J McMullan, 'Expert Witnesses: Who Plays the Saxophones?' (1999) 9(2) *JJA* 94.

H D Sperling, 'Commentary on Lord Justice May's Paper: "The English High Court and Expert Evidence"', *Supreme Court of New South Wales Annual Conference*, 22–24 August 2003.

Lord Woolf, 'Medics, Lawyers and the Courts' (1997) 16 *CJQ* 302.

NOTICES TO ADMIT

Introduction

14.4.1   In all jurisdictions, except the High Court, there are rules which specifically enable a party to request another party to admit, for the purpose of the proceedings, certain facts, or the authenticity of stipulated documents: FCR r 22.01; ACT r 491; NSW rr 17.3, 17.4; NT rr 35.03, 35.05; Qld r 189; Tas rr 399, 401; Vic rr 35.03, 35.05; WA O 30 rr 2, 5. In South Australia (r 156) the relevant rule is broader, extending to a notice to admit a particular 'assertion' that the party makes for the purposes of the action. The assertion may be as to a fact or the authenticity of a particular document. The assertion also may be that a particular document is, for stated reasons, either relevant to the subject matter of the action or admissible in evidence at the trial of the action. In South Australia such a notice cannot be given more than 28 days after the last party to the action has filed a list of documents, except by leave of the court. The main purpose of these provisions is to reduce the time and expense involved in the trial by allowing the trial to be restricted to the determination of questions genuinely in dispute between the parties.

The rules in the Federal Court, the Australian Capital Territory, New South Wales, the Northern Territory, Queensland and Victoria stipulate that a fact or document specified in a notice to admit is taken to be admitted, unless the party who is served with the notice gives a notice that the fact or document is not admitted. A similar consequence follows in Tasmania and Western Australia in relation only to a failure to admit documents, unless the court otherwise orders.

The equivalent rule in South Australia (r 156) is particularly extensive. A respondent who fails to respond in the manner required by the rule to an assertion in a notice to admit is taken to have admitted the assertion. This rule includes a procedure by which the court may order the respondent to give further and better notice of response within the time allowed by the court; or if satisfied the respondent has denied or failed to admit an assertion without adequate reasons for doing so, to determine the issue raised by the assertion in advance of the trial.

In circumstances where one party has made sufficient admissions, whether in response to notices to admit or in pleadings or otherwise, another party may apply to the court for judgment or any other order which the admissions may be found to justify: FCR r 22.07; ACT r 493; NSW r 17.7; NT r 35.04; Qld r 190; SA r 235; Tas r 403; Vic r 35.04; WA O 30 r 3.

Cost consequences

14.4.2   The Rules of Court include cost consequences which provide the incentive to use, and to respond to, a notice to admit. In the Australian Capital Territory (r 491(3)), New South Wales (rr 42.8, 42.9 (costs to be assessed on an indemnity basis)), the Northern Territory (r 63.16), Queensland (r 189), Victoria (rr 35.06, 63.18) and Western Australia (O 66 r 3), a party who has disputed a fact (or in Western Australia has failed to admit a fact) or the authenticity of a document the subject of a notice to admit, is required to bear the cost of proving the fact or document, unless the court otherwise orders. The corresponding provision in the Federal Court (r 22.03) does not include a specific power for the court to order otherwise.

A similar position prevails in Tasmania (r 401(2)), where a party who has failed to admit a fact in response to a notice to admit is to pay the other party's costs of proving the fact or document regardless of the outcome of the proceeding, unless the court certifies that the failure to admit was reasonable, or the court otherwise orders.

In South Australia (r 156(10)), the court is required to order a party who 'unreasonably' denies or fails to admit an assertion to pay costs arising from the denial or failure, unless there are good reasons for not doing so. These rules also contain a unique provision which acts as a disincentive to parties to serve inappropriate notices to admit. If a party 'unreasonably' asks another party for an admission, the court will, unless there are good reasons for not doing so, order that party to pay the costs arising from the request: r 156(11).

Practical observations

14.4.3   Some useful practical observations as to the advantages of skilful use of the notice to admit procedure, either instead of or in conjunction with interrogatories, are contained in the following extract.

14.4.4E   **Drafting Interrogatories Made Simple**
A J H Morris
(1990) 20 *QLSJ* 445 at 446–7

Notices to Admit

Litigators often lose sight of the potential advantages of a 'Notice to Admit Facts' and/ or a 'Notice to Admit Documents', either as an alternative to interrogatories, or as a step which might be taken prior to interrogating.

A 'Notice to Admit' has no compulsive force: you cannot require the opposing party to admit facts or documents, even if you suspect that those facts or documents are not seriously disputed. However, a potential costs penalty exists where a party refuses to make admissions sought by such a notice; and there is also, in my experience, a psychological benefit in delivering such notice, because for reasons which I do not really understand people seem reluctant to join issue in relation to matters set out in a Notice to Admit which are not seriously disputed, although no such reluctance is exhibited when the same matters are put in issue on the pleadings.

Notices to Admit are not subject to the same technical rules and grounds of objection which apply to interrogatories; and it is therefore considerably easier to draft an effective Notice to Admit than to draft interrogatories in a form which [447] is not susceptible to objection. If admissions are obtained, it becomes unnecessary to interrogate. If, on the other hand, admissions are not obtained by a Notice to Admit, there is nothing to prevent interrogatories subsequently being delivered in relation to the same issues.

Apart from affording one's client some protection in relation to costs (including the costs of interrogating), and apart from the fact that Notices to Admit are easier to draw than interrogatories but may achieve the same purpose, they have one other possible advantage. In those jurisdictions where interrogation is not available without leave ... [see **13.3.3**], leave will be more readily obtained if it can be shown that appropriate admissions have been sought and refused.

My point is simply that, when one is considering interrogation, it is often worthwhile considering whether the same benefits could or might be achieved by Notices to Admit. I should add that a Notice to Admit is often more effective in achieving its purpose if it is accompanied by a letter, explaining that the factual issues raised in the Notice will be expensive and time-consuming ones to prove at the trial: for example, if an admission is sought concerning a signature on a document which appears to be that of the opposing party, and no such admission is made, it may be necessary to obtain the expert advice of a forensic document examiner, and to call him as a witness at the trial. The covering letter should make it clear that, in the event that appropriate admissions are not forthcoming, the opposing party will be held responsible for the costs of proving the disputed facts at the trial 'whatever the result of the [trial] may be' ... Such a letter might also contain a warning that, if appropriate admissions are not made, interrogatories will be delivered (or leave will be sought to deliver interrogatories) in relation to those issues; and in that event, the opposing party will be held responsible for the costs thereby incurred.

Withdrawal of admissions

14.4.5 The court is specifically empowered to give leave to a party who has made an admission of fact to withdraw or amend the admission: FCR r 22.06; ACT r 492 (this rule extends to any admission); NSW rr 17.3, 17.4; NT rr 35.02(2), 35.03(3), 35.05(3); Qld rr 188, 189(3); SA r 158 (this rule extends to any admission); Tas r 401(4); Vic rr 35.02(2), 35.03(3), 35.05(3); WA O 30 r 2.

In *Coopers Brewery Ltd v Panfida Foods Ltd* (1992) 26 NSWLR 738 at 750, Rogers CJ (Comm D) noted that it was appropriate to balance the need to ensure that the procedure is not made meaningless by permitting withdrawal too readily, and the need to ensure parties are not discouraged from making admissions out of fear that they cannot be withdrawn.

In *Ridolfi v Rigato Farms Pty Ltd* [2001] 2 Qd R 455, the Queensland Court of Appeal dismissed an appeal against a refusal of an application for leave to withdraw a deemed admission. De Jersey CJ (with whom the other judges agreed) stated (at 458–9) that a court asked to exercise the discretion to permit withdrawal would ordinarily expect sworn verification of the circumstances justifying a grant of leave. Those circumstances may include why no response to the notice to admit was made as required, the response the party would belatedly seek to make, and confirmation that the response would accord with evidence available to be led at a trial. His Honour indicated further that issues of prejudice may also call for consideration on the hearing of such an application.

14.4.6 Notes and questions

1. Does an admission of the authenticity of a document involve an admission of the correctness of the contents of the document? In *Rapid Metal Developments (Australia) Pty Ltd v Griffiths* [2005] QDC 048, McGill DCJ explained that the term 'authenticity' in this context meant the document was what it purported to be, and this may provide a convenient way to prove that a document is 'authentic' in that way, if it would otherwise be necessary to call a witness simply for that purpose. He proceeded:

    > However it does not provide any additional significance to the contents of the document. In particular, a failure to respond to a notice to admit a document, or indeed a response admitting the authenticity of a document, says nothing as to the truth or accuracy of the contents of the document.

    The rules in the Federal Court (Sch 1 Dictionary), the Northern Territory (r 35.01) and Victoria (r 35.01) provide a definition of 'authenticity of a document' which is consistent with McGill DCJ's interpretation.

2. A party proposing to rely at trial on a deemed admission should give reasonable notice of that intention to the other party. Though not a requirement of the rules, this is good practice because it avoids the wasting of time and costs that might otherwise result. See the observations in this respect in *Rapid Metal Developments (Australia) Pty Ltd v Griffiths* [2005] QDC 048.

SUBPOENAS

Introduction

14.5.1 The service of a subpoena is the appropriate process to compel a person to attend a trial as a witness or to produce documents to the court. In most jurisdictions a subpoena may be issued for trial proceedings by any party as of right. The subpoena is an order in writing issued administratively by the court through the court registry. In the High Court (r 24.02.1) and Federal Court (r 24.01) it is necessary to first obtain the leave of the court or a judge, which may be given generally or for a particular subpoena or subpoenas. In New South Wales (r 33.2) a subpoena may generally be issued as of right by a party represented in the proceedings by a solicitor, but litigants in person are required to seek leave of the court to issue subpoenas: r 7.3. For proceedings commenced by originating claim, the rules in the Australian Capital Territory (r 6601A) limit the time at which a subpoena to produce may be issued without the court's leave.

Once a party has determined, in the course of preparation for trial, who he or she requires to give evidence at the trial, and what documents must be tendered in evidence, it will be necessary to determine whether to subpoena the witnesses required.

Normally, it will not be necessary or appropriate to subpoena expert witnesses who have been engaged for the purpose of giving evidence. Some witnesses will require a subpoena before they will attend. Police officers and public servants are examples. Other witnesses may wish to be served with a subpoena so that it is clear that they have been compelled to attend and give evidence and that they are not attending because of any partisan views. Similarly, an employee may require a subpoena so that he or she does not have a problem obtaining the necessary leave from work.

In most circumstances other witnesses should be subpoenaed, unless it is absolutely certain that they will attend the trial. Even a witness who has been extraordinarily cooperative can have a change in attitude as the prospect of coming under cross-examination approaches. If a subpoena has been served and the witness does not attend, then it is likely the party issuing the subpoena will be able to obtain an adjournment if this is necessary to get the witness to court. If a subpoena has not been issued, the party seeking an adjournment will certainly have to bear the costs of any adjournment and may not get the adjournment at all.

Harmonised rules

14.5.2 In October 2000, the Australian Council of Chief Justices appointed a committee of judges to develop a set of harmonised rules and forms relating to subpoenas. That committee produced a set of harmonised subpoena rules over a period from February 2001 to September 2003. This step was taken as part of a project to explore harmonisation of court rules in a range of subject areas.

The harmonised rules, with minor variations to meet local circumstances, have since been adopted by the Federal Court and the Supreme Courts of the Australian Capital Territory, New South Wales, the Northern Territory, South Australia, Tasmania, Victoria and Western Australia. Queensland has declined to adopt the harmonised rules.

Form

14.5.3   There are two forms of subpoena. One form commands the attendance of a witness to give oral testimony. It was historically referred to as a *subpoena ad testificandum*. The second form commands the production of documents to the court. It was referred to as a *subpoena duces tecum*. The rules now use the simpler terms 'subpoena to attend to give evidence' (ACT, NSW, NT, SA, Tas, Vic, WA) or 'subpoena to give evidence' (HC, Fed Ct, Qld) and 'subpoena to produce' (HC, Fed Ct, ACT, NSW, NT, SA, Tas, Vic, WA) or 'subpoena for production' (Qld) respectively.

The rules prescribe the appropriate forms of subpoena, and the particulars which should be contained in them: HCR r 24.02; FCR r 24.13; ACT r 6602; NSW r 33.3; NT r 42.03; Qld rr 414, 415; SA r 173; Tas r 496; Vic r 42.03; WA O 36B r 3. In general terms the required particulars include: identification of the addressee by name or by description of office or position; identification of the document or thing to be produced under a subpoena to produce and the date, time and place for production; and specification of the date, time and place for attendance required by a subpoena to attend to give evidence.

The approved forms in Queensland also include a form for request for the issue of the subpoena, which stays on the court file.

Subpoena to employer, company

14.5.4   A subpoena to give evidence should be directed specifically to the witness whose attendance is required. A subpoena for production of documents should usually be directed to the witness who has possession of the documents, although if that person has custody of the documents on behalf of another, it is in most instances preferable to address the subpoena to the person who has ultimate control over them. Accordingly, a subpoena for production of documents should usually be addressed to the employer, rather than to the employee responsible for their immediate custody.

A subpoena to give evidence requires the person served to attend court and give evidence on oath. As an oath cannot meaningfully be administered to a corporation, a subpoena to give evidence cannot validly be served on a corporation: *McDonald v Australian Securities Commission (No 2)* (1994) 48 FCR 210; 120 ALR 515 at 519. However, a corporation can be required to produce documents. It is usually the appropriate course to direct the subpoena to the corporation itself, requiring it, by 'its proper officer', to produce the documents: *Rochfort v Trade Practices Commission* (1983) 153 CLR 134 (extracted below).

The rules in the Federal Court, New South Wales, the Northern Territory, South Australia, Tasmania and Western Australia state explicitly that if a subpoena is addressed to a corporation, the corporation must comply with the subpoena by its appropriate or proper officer.

14.5.5C	**Rochfort v Trade Practices Commission**	
	(1983) 153 CLR 134; 43 ALR 659	
	High Court of Australia	

[An unincorporated trade association employed the appellant as an executive director whose duties included the provision of secretarial services for one of the members, which member was itself an unincorporated association. The appellant also had the title of executive director of the member association. The Trade Practices Commission brought proceedings in the Federal Court against nine companies, several of which belonged to the member association. On the application of the Commission, a *subpoena duces tecum* was issued and served on the appellant requiring him to produce certain documents of which he had custody and which had been prepared while he performed duties relating to the member. On the return of the subpoena, the appellant appeared and stated that the documents were in counsel's chambers but he objected to producing them on the basis that they were not in his personal possession but in the possession of the member association, its own members and its executive and he had no authority to produce them. The appellant had not sought any authority to produce to the court the documents mentioned in the subpoena.

Bowen CJ at first instance held that the appellant was employed by the unincorporated trade association and not the particular member association and that, in those circumstances, he was obliged to produce documents owned by the member association but in the appellant's possession and control. The Full Court of the Federal Court, though for slightly different reasons, dismissed the appellant's appeal, and by special leave he appealed from that decision to the High Court.]

Mason J (at 143-7): A special problem has arisen with respect to documents held by an employee in the course of his employment. In *Amey v Long* (1808) 9 East 473, at p 482 [103 ER 653, at p 657], Lord Ellenborough CJ, speaking for the Court, said that the sheriff's bailiff when served with a subpoena was bound to produce a warrant which he had 'an immediate physical ability' to produce. However, subsequently in *Crowther v Appelby* (1873) LR 9 CP 23 it was decided that an employee was not bound to produce a document which he held for his employer when the latter had forbidden its production. And later *Eccles* [*Eccles & Co v Louisville and Nashville Railroad Co* [1912] 1 KB 135] held that an employee was not bound to produce a document in response to an order made under the Foreign Tribunals Evidence Act 1856 (UK) when he had no authority from his [144] employer so to do. The fact that *Eccles* related to an order made under a statute does not distinguish the case from production under a subpoena. The reasoning of the majority applies with equal force to production pursuant to a subpoena. That certainly has been the view taken by Lord Denning MR in *Penn-Texas Corporation v Murat Anstalt (No 2)* [1964] 2 QB 647, at pp 661–664.

It is commonly said that the reason underlying the *Eccles* principle [is] that the employee's 'possession' is not his, but that of his master (*Earl of Falmouth v Moss* (1822) 11 Price 455 [147 ER 530]). This reason is sometimes coupled with another — that the employee, in the absence of the employer's consent, lacks authority to bring the documents and produce them to the court (see eg, the comments in *Eccles* of Vaughan Williams LJ [1912] 1 KB at p 145 and Buckley LJ [1912] 1 KB at pp 147–148). The correctness of this view was challenged by Kennedy LJ (dissenting) in *Eccles* [1912] 1 KB at pp 151–152. Like the majority, he thought that a person could be required to produce only such documents as were in his possession, custody or control. However, he considered that the authority of a number of employees amounted to a large degree of control and discretion to act independently, in which event they were at liberty to act, without express orders from their employer. They could then be regarded as having possession, custody or control of documents which they held for their employer and were bound to produce the documents, unless instructed by the employer not to do so ...

There is, accordingly, every reason for thinking that the court can compel a person to produce documents which he is physically able [145] to produce. But there are factors which need to be taken into account before deciding that the court will insist on production by an employee of his employer's documents.

The obligation to produce documents pursuant to a *subpoena duces tecum* is a qualification upon, or an intrusion into, the citizen's right to keep his documents to himself (*Penn-Texas (No 2)* [1964] 2 QB at p 667). In the absence of some compelling reason it is right that the owner of the documents should decide in the first instance whether any of them are caught by the subpoena and that he should bear the responsibility for not producing such of them as are ultimately held to be covered by the subpoena. To acknowledge that the employee's possession is sufficient in itself to sustain an obligation to produce, without reference to his employer, would be to disregard the employer's rights with respect to his documents. What is more, it would deprive him of the privilege of objecting to produce a document on the ground that it has a tendency to incriminate him. The privilege against self-incrimination is that of the witness who is called to produce. He cannot claim the privilege on the ground that the document tends to incriminate another (*Reg v Kinglake* (1870) 11 Cox CC 499, at p 501; *R v Adey* (1831) 1 M & R 94 [174 ER 32]; *Rio Tinto Zinc Corporation v Westinghouse Electric Corporation* [1978] AC 547, at pp 637–638).

Recognition of these interests of the employer suggests that in general it is he, not his employee, who should be required to produce the documents. Of course, the protection of the employer's interests must give way to the public interest in the efficient administration of justice in case of collision between the two. So, if it is impracticable to serve a subpoena on the employer, eg, by reason of absence overseas, incapacity or his whereabouts, being unknown, the court will insist on production of the documents by his employee or agent who holds them. In these circumstances the prompt dispatch of court business must prevail over the protection of the employer's interests.

And there are other situations, quite apart from that of the unincorporated association to be discussed later, where the employee has express or implied authority to deal with the employer's documents, viz the circumstances contemplated by Kennedy LJ, in which it is proper for the court to overrule an objection to produce made on the ground that the employee merely holds the document for his employer. However, these exceptions or qualifications should not obscure the general rule that a party should [146] subpoena the documents of an employer from the employer himself, not from his employee.

The production of documents by a corporation stands in a special position. In the past it seems to have been thought that a problem arose by reason of the corporation's inability to give evidence. This problem can be avoided by serving a subpoena on the corporation itself, requiring it, by its proper officer, to give evidence and produce the documents. As Lord Denning MR pointed out in *Penn-Texas (No 2)* [1964] 2 QB, at p 663, this is what was done in *R v Daye* [1908] 2 KB 333. The view which I have expressed is that stated by Lord Denning MR in *Penn-Texas (No 2)* and subsequently in *Senior v Holdsworth; Ex parte Independent Television News Ltd* [1976] 1 QB 23, at p 32. It is to be preferred to the contrary view of Harman LJ in *Penn-Texas Corporation v Murat Anstalt (No 1)* [1964] 1 QB 40, at p 69.

The production of the documents of unincorporated associations is necessarily governed by the principles applicable to individuals, rather than the rule relating to corporations. In applying these principles account has to be taken of the nature of the unincorporated association, and of the objects which it pursues. The variety of unincorporated associations is infinite. Generally speaking, such associations are formed for particular purposes with the result that their activities often reflect, not the purely private or personal elements of its constituent membership, but their common or group interests only. The assets, books and records of such associations are quite distinct from those of their individual members. The business of an unincorporated association is generally conducted by an executive officer, subject to directions given by an executive committee. See the discussion in *United States v White* (1944) 322 US 694, at pp 701–703 [88 Law Ed 1542, at pp 1547–1548] and the annotation in 152 ALR 1208.

The books and records of an association will often be entrusted to an executive officer who attends to the conduct of the association's business or affairs on a daily or continuous basis. Subject to such resolutions as may be passed by the executive committee or by the members of the association in general meeting that person has express or implied authority to deal with the association's books and documents in the course of conducting its business and affairs. He is the person who has possession, custody or control of the books and documents. Consequently, he is the person to be served with a *subpoena duces tecum* to produce them. It is obvious that possession, custody or control does not rest in the members of the [147] association who may in some cases be counted in hundreds and thousands. It is equally obvious that the executive committee does not have possession, custody and control to the exclusion of the executive officer. And it would be patently absurd to say that the production of the books and records of an association can only be compelled from the members, however numerous they may be. In many cases it would be a labour of Herakles to establish the identity and whereabouts of the members of an association and of the members of its executive committee. The business of the courts would grind to a halt if a party to litigation was expected to serve a subpoena on all the members of an association or even all the members of its executive committee.

[**Gibbs CJ, Murphy** and **Wilson JJ** delivered separate judgments. Each concluded that, on the facts, the appellant had such possession, custody or control of the documents that he was obliged to produce them in answer to the subpoena.]

Payment to witnesses

14.5.6   A witness is entitled to receive a sum of money or its equivalent, such as pre-paid travel, sufficient to meet their reasonable expenses of attending court as required by the subpoena, and returning after attending. This is referred to as 'conduct money'. The conduct money must be tendered to the witness at the time of service of the subpoena or a reasonable time before the date that attendance under the subpoena is required. In most jurisdictions this requirement is now stipulated by the Rules of Court: HCR r 24.02; FCR r 24.17; ACT r 6606(1); NSW rr 33.1, 33.6; NT r 42.06 (the issuing party must make, or attempt to make, appropriate arrangements under s 21 of the Evidence Act to meet the addressee's reasonable expenses for travel and accommodation for complying with the subpoena); Qld r 419; SA rr 171(1), rr 176(1); Vic r 42.06; WA O 36B rr 1, 6.

This right relates to the expenses required to enable the person served to come to court, as distinct from expenses incurred before the person served actually comes to court. This was confirmed by Sheppard J in the Federal Court in *Bank of New South Wales v Withers* (1981) 35 ALR 21. In that case the Bank of New South Wales had complied with subpoenas to produce documents at the hearing of proceedings between the respondents and other parties. It subsequently moved the court for an order that the respondent, on whose behalf the subpoenas had been served, pay its expenses in relation to searching for, collating and copying the documents. The bank was unsuccessful. Sheppard J held that there was no provision in the

Rules of Court dealing with the matter and that there was an established principle that there could be no recovery of expenses incurred before the person served actually comes to court, unless their payment was provided for in the rules.

Except in the High Court, the rules now overcome the problem revealed by *Bank of New South Wales v Withers* by enabling the court to order the issuing party to pay the amount of any reasonable loss or expense incurred in complying with the subpoena: FCR r 27.22; ACT r 6611; NSW r 33.11, NT r 42.11; Qld rr 417, 418; SA r 181; Tas r 500D; Vic r 42.11; WA O 36B r 11. These rules correspond to the Service and Execution of Process Act 1992 (Cth) s 35 (see **14.5.8**) and mean that the same expenses will be recoverable whether the subpoena is served under that Act or under the Rules of Court. In a practical sense the witness should negotiate with the issuing party about the costs of compliance, and apply to court only if those negotiations are unsuccessful.

Non-party witnesses will not normally require legal advice as to their general rights and responsibilities in answering a subpoena, but these rules will allow recovery of legal expenses reasonably incurred to comply with a subpoena in cases where it is proper that the interests of the witness should be protected by legal representation: *Pyramid Building Society (in liq) v Farrow Finance Corp Ltd (in liq)* [1995] 1 VR 464 at 468.

At common law witnesses, other than doctors and legal practitioners, are not entitled to payment for loss of time or income in attending court: *Collins v Godefroy* [1831] 109 ER 1040. This position is modified in most jurisdictions by scales of fees for witnesses which entitle them, according to the appropriate scale, to payment for loss of time as well as for payment of expenses of travelling to and from, and remaining at court: *Bank of New South Wales v Withers*, at 27.

Service

14.5.7   In general terms, most of the rules require that the subpoena be served personally on the addressee: HCR r 24.02; FCR r 24.16; ACT r 6605 (the requirement for personal service is qualified by rr 6481 and 6482 in relation to service on a party to the proceeding who is represented by a solicitor, and service on medical experts respectively); NSW r 33.5 (the requirement for personal service is qualified by r 31.32 in relation to service on a medical expert); NT r 42.05; SA r 175; Tas r 498; Vic r 42.05; WA O 36B r 5. In the Federal Court, the Australian Capital Territory, New South Wales, the Northern Territory, South Australia, Tasmania, Victoria and Western Australia, the issuing party must serve a copy of a subpoena to produce on each other party as soon as practicable after the subpoena has been served on the addressee.

In Queensland, service may now be effected in any manner permitted under Ch 4, Pts 2, 3, 4 and 5 of the Uniform Civil Procedure Rules 1999 (Qld). This includes personal and ordinary service. As a practical matter, however, it will usually be wise to arrange personal service. This is because the relevant rule also stipulates that compliance with a subpoena may only be enforced, and proceedings taken for non-compliance with a subpoena, if it is proved that the subpoena has been received by the person to whom it is addressed or the person has actual knowledge of it: r 421.

The rules in the Federal Court (rr 24.13, 24.17), the Australian Capital Territory (rr 6602, 6603; these rules are qualified by r 6482 in relation to service on a medical expert), New South Wales (rr 33.3, 33.6), the Northern Territory (rr 42.03, 42.06), South Australia (rr 173, 176), Victoria (rr 42.03, 42.06) and Western Australia (O 36B rr 3, 6) state that the last date of

service of the subpoena must be specified in the subpoena, and is to be five days before the
addressee is required to comply with the subpoena or an earlier or later date fixed by the court.
An addressee is not generally required to comply with a subpoena if it is not served before the
last date specified for service. In these jurisdictions there is a qualification that an addressee
must comply with a subpoena even if it has not been served personally on that addressee if the
addressee has, by the last date for service of the subpoena, actual knowledge of the subpoena
and its requirements.

The rules in the Federal Court (r 24.14), the Australian Capital Territory (r 6603A), the
Northern Territory (r 42.03A), South Australia (r 173A), Victoria (r 42.03.1) and Western
Australia (O 36B r 3A) permit the party issuing the subpoena to give notice to the addressee of
a date or time later than that specified in the subpoena as the time for compliance and, if such
notice is given, the subpoena has effect as if the date or time notified appears in the subpoena
instead of the date or time specified in the subpoena.

In the High Court and Queensland, the Rules of Court do not prescribe a specific time
before the trial or hearing for service to be effected, although in the High Court (r 24.02) a
subpoena must be served within 12 weeks of issue. The general position, however, is that there
must be a reasonable time allowed to the witness, taking into account the occupation and
location of the witness and any preparation to be done, such as locating documents.

Service out of the jurisdiction

Interstate service (state and territory Supreme Courts)

14.5.8 A subpoena may be served outside the jurisdiction and in another state or territory
of Australia under the Service and Execution of Process Act 1992 (Cth) (the Act). In the
same way that this Act removed the requirement that leave be obtained to serve an originating
proceeding interstate (see **8.9.3**), it also removed the requirement under the former Service
and Execution of Process Act 1901 (Cth) (s 16(1)) that leave be obtained to serve a subpoena
interstate. Section 29(1) of the Act provides that a subpoena issued in a state by a court or
authority may be served in another state (which term extends to the Australian Capital
Territory and the Northern Territory: s 5). By s 29(2) of the Act, the service is to be effected
in the same way as service of a subpoena in the place of issue. There are, however, some special
requirements under the Act which apply to the issue and service of a subpoena when service is
to be effected interstate:

- Under s 29(3), service of a subpoena is only effective if the subpoena contains an address for
  service of the person (if any) at whose request the subpoena was issued.

- The subpoena must be served not less than 14 days before the day on which the person
  subpoenaed is to comply with the subpoena, unless the court issuing the subpoena allows
  a shorter period: s 30(1). The issuing court may only allow a shorter period if satisfied of a
  number of things specified in s 30(2), namely:
  - the giving of the evidence likely to be given by the person to whom the subpoena
    is addressed, or the production of a document or thing specified in the subpoena, is
    necessary in the interests of justice;
  - there will be enough time for the person:
    - to comply with the subpoena without hardship or serious inconvenience, and
    - to make an application for relief from the subpoena (as specified in s 33).

In granting an application the court or authority is to impose a condition that the subpoena not be served after a specified day, and may impose other conditions.

- Copies of such notices as are prescribed must be attached to the subpoena or copy of the subpoena to be served: s 31. The appropriate notice is prescribed by the Service and Execution of Process Regulations 1993 (Cth) (for ordinary service, reg 4(1)(b), Form 2; for service upon a person in prison, reg 4(1)(c), Form 3). If an application has been granted for a shorter period of notice than 14 days to be given, then a copy of the order granting the application must also be attached.

- Section 32 requires that at the time of service, or at some other reasonable time before the person to whom the subpoena is addressed is required to comply with it, allowances and travelling expenses sufficient to meet the person's reasonable expenses of complying with the subpoena are paid or tendered to the person. This is supplemented by s 35, which provides that a person served with a subpoena is entitled to payment of an amount equal to the reasonable expenses incurred by that person in complying with the subpoena. This is to be paid by the person at whose request the subpoena was issued (if there was one), or in any other case by the state in which the subpoena was issued. The court issuing the subpoena may make orders to ensure this.

14.5.9 Section 33 of the Act applies where the person served with the subpoena has a right in the place of issue to apply to the court to set aside or obtain other relief in respect of the subpoena. There is such a right in all jurisdictions, although in the High Court this is based upon the inherent jurisdiction of the court rather than any specific Rule of Court: see 14.5.14–14.5.16C. Section 33 provides certain additional modes by which such application may be made, allowing it to be done by transmitting the application to the court by fax, and permitting service of a copy of the application on the person at whose request the subpoena was issued by fax transmission to the address of the person in the subpoena. The court may determine the application without a hearing, unless the applicant or the person issuing the subpoena objects. There are special procedures available for the hearing of the application by video link or telephone.

Section 34 relates to subpoenas which only require production of documents. As applies in the ordinary case in most jurisdictions (see 14.5.11), such a subpoena may be complied with by delivering the document or thing to the Registrar or clerk of the court, without any attendance by the person to whom the subpoena is addressed.

There are detailed provisions in s 36 of the Act relating to the service of subpoenas on persons under restraint. Part 3 Div 2 of the Act deals with the service of subpoenas on persons in prison.

International service

14.5.10 There is authority indicating that the rules authorising international service of an initiating process (see 8.9.10) do not extend to subpoenas: *Ward v Interag Pty Ltd* [1985] 2 Qd R 552 at 559. The courts have also taken the view that if there is power to give leave to issue a subpoena to a party outside Australia, the power should only be exercised in the most exceptional circumstances: *Stemcor (A/sia) Pty Ltd v Oceanwave Line SA* [2004] FCA 391; *Ives v Lim* [2010] WASC 136. This means it is generally not possible to subpoena witnesses who are outside Australia.

The position in relation to a witness in New Zealand is exceptional. That position is currently governed by the Evidence and Procedure (New Zealand) Act 1994 (Cth). It should be noted, however, that Trans-Tasman Proceedings Act 2010 (Cth) and the Trans-Tasman Proceedings (Transitional and Consequential Provisions) Act 2010 were both assented to on 13 April 2010. The substantive provisions of these Acts are yet to commence. However, on commencement the Transitional Act will repeal the Evidence and Procedure (New Zealand) Act. The provisions of the Trans-Tasman Proceedings Act will then govern the service of a subpoena in New Zealand.

The Evidence and Procedure (New Zealand) Act provides machinery for service of subpoenas issued by a federal court or prescribed courts of a state or territory. Under the Evidence and Procedure (New Zealand) Regulations 1995 (Cth), the prescribed courts include the Supreme Courts of the Australian Capital Territory, New South Wales, the Northern Territory, Queensland, South Australia, Tasmania, and Western Australia.

The Act permits the court to grant leave for service in New Zealand of a subpoena, which may require the person named to attend to give evidence or produce documents at a place in Australia or a place in New Zealand. The court's discretion as to whether it will grant leave is wide, but it is directed to consider the significance of the evidence sought, and whether it could be obtained by other means with less inconvenience to the person named. Service of the subpoena is to be effected in the same way as in the place of issue, must be accompanied by tender of expenses of complying with the subpoena, and must also comply with any conditions imposed by the court in granting the necessary leave. A subpoena requiring the production of a document or thing may be sufficiently complied with by delivery of the document or thing at a registry of the High Court of New Zealand.

A person served in New Zealand with a subpoena may apply to the court which issued the subpoena to set it aside. The court has a general discretion to set aside the subpoena but there are also a number of grounds specified in s 14 which, if they apply, require that it must do so. The Rules of Court in several jurisdiction include various procedural requirements governing an application for leave to serve a subpoena in New Zealand or for an order setting aside such a subpoena (with some of these jurisdictions having passed amendments to take effect when the substantive provisions of the Trans-Tasman Proceedings Act (Cth) commence): FCR O 69A (under Div 34.5A of the Federal Court Rules 2011 this order and all forms prescribed for it continue to apply to proceedings which commence before the substantive provisions of the Trans-Tasman Proceedings Act 2010 take effect); ACT Div 6.8.10; NSW Pt 32 (under Uniform Civil Procedure Rules (Amendment No 51) 2011 a new Pt 32 will commence when the substantive provisions of the Trans-Tasman Proceedings Act (Cth) commence); SA r 315; WA O 39A.

Production

14.5.11   Most jurisdictions now have rules, which reduce the obligations otherwise imposed on a person served with a subpoena for production. These rules permit compliance with the subpoena by producing the document or thing at the registry from which the subpoena is issued; a stipulated time before attendance to produce is otherwise required: FCR r 24.17; ACT r 6606(4); NSW r 33.6(4); NT r 42.06; Qld r 420; SA r 176(4); Tas r 499, Vic 42.06; WA O 36B r 6(4). The specified period is generally two clear days before the date specified in the subpoena for attendance and production, but in Queensland the subpoena must permit production by the day before the first day on which attendance is required. In Queensland the early compliance procedure is only available when the person named in the subpoena is not a party to the proceeding. In most jurisdictions the rules include detailed procedures for the inspection of, and dealing with, documents produced, otherwise than on attendance: FCR r 24.20; NSW r 33.9; NT r 42.09; SA r 179; Tas rr 500A, 500B; Vic r 42.09; WA O 36B r 9.

Subpoena for production before trial

14.5.12   Subpoenas were once regarded as appropriate only for obtaining evidence for the trial, and were not available for the purpose of obtaining inspection of documents before trial. In the Federal Court (r 24.13), the Australian Capital Territory (r 6602(5)), New South Wales (r 33.3(6)), the Northern Territory (r 42.03(6)), Tasmania (r 496), Victoria (r 42.03(6)) and Western Australia (O 36B r 3(6)), the rules now envisage that the court may allow the date specified to be before trial. They stipulate that the date specified in a subpoena must be the date of trial *or any other date as permitted by the court*. The rules in South Australia (r 172) contemplate that a subpoena may issue for the purposes of interlocutory proceedings, but only if a judge or master authorises the issue of the subpoena. It has also been recognised that, even apart from any special rules, the court has an inherent power to make a subpoena for documents returnable prior to the commencement of the trial: *Khanna v Lovell* [1994] 4 All ER 267.

Whether acting under its inherent power or under the authority in the Rules of Court, the court is unlikely to give leave for the issue of a subpoena returnable ahead of the date for substantial hearing, if the purpose of the party issuing the subpoena is to bypass the procedures for obtaining discovery from a non-party: see **13.2.8E–13.2.12**. There may, however, be considerations which persuade the court that the justice of the case requires the leave be granted. It may be, for example, that production of documents is needed to enable the party to prepare material which the court has directed be filed and served within a particular time: see *Temwell Pty Ltd v DKGR Holdings Pty Ltd* [2002] FCA 741. In that event, it would appear the court has adequate discretionary power to impose conditions on its grant of leave, so as to ensure that the non-party is not deprived of the protections granted under the rules for non-party disclosure: see *Tipperary Developments Pty Ltd v Western Australia* (1999) 21 WAR 250.

A more restrictive approach has been taken in Queensland, where the court has preferred the view that parties seeking documents of a non-party before trial should use the procedures for obtaining discovery from a non-party, as the following case illustrates:

14.5.13C   **Leighton Contractors Pty Ltd v Western Metals Resources Ltd**
[2001] 1 Qd R 261
Supreme Court of Queensland

[The plaintiff had sought documents from a non-party prior to any trial or hearing by use of a subpoena for production. The documents were produced to the court and the plaintiff made application for access to and permission to copy all documents to which a claim for legal professional privilege did not apply.]

McKenzie J (at 265): The rules relating to non-party disclosure are designed to provide safeguards to a non-party upon whom a notice is served and to more remote persons who might be affected. Where a deliberately prescriptive regime is provided for the obtaining of

---

documents from a non-party the question presents itself whether the intention was that those safeguards might be avoided by using a different procedure with requirements which are different but which have some common features ...

In my opinion there is no indication in the rules that it is intended that what is really non-party disclosure in the pre-trial phase may be obtained by issuing a subpoena to produce. In my opinion the rules do not effect a change from the philosophy in that regard under the repealed rules.

While it is not incumbent on the Registry to make specific inquiries in this regard, if it is apparent that a request for a subpoena is being made where it is unconnected with a trial or hearing, it would be appropriate for the discretion in r 414(4) to be exercised against using it. There can now be no misapprehension about the scope of the respective rules and any attempt henceforth to use a subpoena for the purpose of obtaining disclosure would be an abuse of process. If a subpoena were issued for that purpose, it would be liable to be set aside on that ground.

Setting a subpoena aside

14.5.14   The court has inherent jurisdiction to intervene to prevent an abuse of its process. The rules in all jurisdictions, except the High Court, also give the court specific power to set aside a subpoena, either wholly or in part: FCR r 24.15; ACT r 6604; NSW r 33.4; NT r 42.04; Qld r 416; SA r 174; Tas r 497; Vic r 42.04; WA O 36B r 4. A witness who has been served with a subpoena believed to be an abuse of process in that it is unnecessary, is being used for an improper purpose, or is oppressive, should apply to the court to have it set aside.

14.5.15C	**Commissioner for Railways v Small**
	(1938) 38 SR (NSW) 564
	Court of Appeal (NSW)

[One of the grounds for appeal by the defendant against a verdict in favour of the plaintiff following a trial of an action under the Compensation to Relatives Act 1897 (NSW), related to the use made by the plaintiff of a *subpoena duces tecum*. The judgment includes a consideration of the form of a subpoena requiring the production of documents and the nature of rights and obligations of the addressee.]

Jordan CJ (at 573–5): A writ of *subpoena duces tecum* may be addressed to a stranger to the cause or to a party. If it be addressed to a stranger, it must specify with reasonable particularity the documents which are required to be produced. A *subpoena duces tecum* ought not to be issued to such a person requiring him to search for and produce all such documents as he may have in his possession or power relating to a particular subject matter. It is not legitimate to use a subpoena for the purpose of endeavouring to obtain what would be in effect discovery of documents against a person who, being a stranger, is not liable to make discovery. A stranger to the cause ought not to be required to go to trouble and perhaps to expense in ransacking his records and endeavouring to form a judgment as to whether any of his papers throw light on a dispute which is to be litigated upon issues of which he is presumably ignorant: *Lee v Angas* LR 2 Eq 59; *Burchard v Macfarlane* [1891] 2 QB 241 at 247; *A-G v Wilson* 9 Sim

526; *Newland v Steer* 13 LT 111: 13 WR 1014. And if a *subpoena duces tecum* is issued to such a person in an objectionable form, the witness may apply to the Court to have it set aside.

If duly served with such a writ and provided with the proper conduct money, the person served must obey it and bring to the Court the documents mentioned in the subpoena if he has them, unless he procures the writ to be set aside as oppressive; and he must produce to the Court the documents which he has [574] brought unless he satisfies the Court that some good reason exists why they should not be produced: this he is always at liberty to do if he can: *In re Smith; Williams v Frere* [1891] 1 Ch 323 at 332; *R v Greenaway* 7 QB 126 at 135. A witness called on *subpoena duces tecum* may be asked, without being sworn, whether he has brought the documents, and if so, whether he produces them to the Court. If he states that he objects to produce them, he should be sworn and the grounds of his objection stated on oath so that the Court may judge of their sufficiency: eg, that they constitute his title deeds, or would incriminate him. The Court may allow a stranger who is a witness to be represented by counsel for this purpose if it thinks that the circumstances warrant it: *Wilkinson v Wilkinson* 1 SR Eq 285; *McLeod v Phillips* 5 SR 503; 22 WN 163; *Rowell v Pratt* [1938] AC 101 at 110. If the witness produces the documents, he produces them to the Court and not to the parties. He may, if he choose, state that he objects to their being handed to the parties for inspection. If so, it is for the Judge to make such examination of them as he thinks proper, and he may order such of them as he considers relevant to be read, or handed to the parties for inspection, as he may think desirable, with a view to their being tendered in evidence: *Burchard v Macfarlane* [1891] 2 QB 241 at 247–8.

Where the subpoena is addressed to a party, it is still necessary that it should state with reasonable particularity the documents which are to be produced: *A-G v Wilson* 9 Sim 526 at 529; *Earl of Powis v Negus* [1923] 1 Ch 186 at 190. It is true that a party, unlike a stranger, can be required to give discovery; but it is not legitimate to use a writ of *subpoena duces tecum* as a substitute for an application for discovery of documents, or as an alternative to an application for further and better discovery. Discovery applications should be made at the proper time and place. It would greatly impede the trial of actions at *nisi prius*, and impose an intolerable burden upon the presiding judge, if he were required from time to time to suspend proceedings and wade for himself through masses of documents for the purpose of endeavouring to determine whether any of them are relevant. Especially is this so when the documents [575] may be called for whilst the case is still at the stage when it is difficult or perhaps impossible for the Judge to know what may become relevant and what may not. In the absence of special circumstances, eg, *Griebart v Morris* [1920] 1 KB 659, a party is no more entitled to use a *subpoena duces tecum* than he is a summons for interrogatories, for the purpose of 'fishing', ie, endeavouring, not to obtain evidence to support his case, but to discover whether he has a case at all: *Hennessy v Wright* 24 QBD 445 at 448, or to discover the nature of the other side's evidence: *Griebart v Morris* [1920] 1 KB 659 at 666. Even if the documents are specified, a subpoena to a party will be set aside as abusive if great numbers of documents are called for and it appears that they are not sufficiently relevant: *Steele v Savory* [1891] WN 195.

In the present case, the subpoena required the production of (inter alia) (1) all documents already produced for inspection, (2) records, papers, books, memoranda, reports, recommendations, letters, estimates, plans, diagrams, sketches and other documents relating directly or indirectly to the installation of automatic or self-closing safety doors or similar safety devices for electric trains in NSW and/or any other places, (3) all documents, papers, reports and correspondence relating directly or indirectly to this action, (4) all documents, papers, reports and correspondence relating directly or indirectly to falls from electric trains, (5) all documents, papers, reports and correspondence relating directly or indirectly to complaints about the running and control of electric trains.

It is unnecessary to proceed further; but it may be mentioned that the subpoena appears actually to demand also the production of various public statutory rules and regulations. Now, if the first group of papers called for is intended to refer to the documents disclosed and inspected on discovery, no exception can be taken to it; but it is evident, having regard to the principles which have just been examined, that those marked (2) to (5) inclusive are quite improper, and that it was a serious abuse of the process of the Court that the issue of a subpoena in this form should have been procured.

[**Davidson** and **Owen JJ** agreed with the **Chief Justice**.]

14.5.16C   **Pasini v Vanstone**
                                      [1999] FCA 1271
                              Federal Court of Australia

[The applicants were the subjects of extradition requests made by the United Mexican States. The applicants brought separate proceedings for judicial review under s 39(B)(1) and (1A) of the Judiciary Act 1903 (Cth) challenging the validity of the s 16 notices on various grounds. They each issued a subpoena directed to the first respondent who was the Federal Government Minister who had issued notices under s 16 of the Extradition Act. The subpoena sought production of various categories of documents which were claimed to be relevant to the Minister's decision. In each proceeding the Minister applied to have the subpoena set aside in part.]

Finn J:
Subpoena as discovery
[29] The primary submission for the Minister is that the subpoenae seek material that would normally be obtained if at all pursuant to an order of discovery and that it is an abuse of process so to use a subpoena: *Commissioner for Railways v Small* (1938) 38 SR (NSW) 564. This submission needs to be considered both against the background of the evolving practice of this Court in relation to discovery and in relation to the use that properly can be made of a subpoena particularly against a party.

[30] *First*, discovery. (i) A party does not have an unqualified right to discovery under the Federal Court Rules: see *Cameron v Rural Press Ltd* (Burchett, Gummow and Hill JJ, 20 July 1990, unreported); Federal Court Rules O 10 r 2. (ii) As Practice Note 14 makes plain, general discovery will not be ordered as of course, discovery commonly being ordered only in relation to particular issues or defined categories of documents. (iii) 'The rules of court do not place on judges the responsibility of determining for the parties which of their respective documents are required to be discovered. Judges have not traditionally assumed such a role': *Diddams v Commonwealth Bank of Australia* [1998] FCA 497, Branson J. (iv) Where a proceeding is one for judicial review, discovery in that proceeding is not to be treated otherwise than according to the normal principles applicable in civil proceedings: *Australian Securities Commission*

v Somerville (1994) 51 FCR 38 at 53. Nonetheless, the nature of judicial review proceedings is commonly such either that the occasion for making an order will not arise or that discovery will only be ordered in relation to a particular issue or issues. (v) Whether or when discovery will be ordered 'depends upon the nature of the case and the stage of the proceedings at which the discovery is sought': *Australian Securities Commission v Somerville*, above, 50. (vi) With the rules of court having prescribed the method by which parties can obtain discovery or further discovery, and having regard to the constraints imposed on discovery, it is impermissible to attempt to achieve discovery through resort to the subpoena process: *Australian Competition and Consumer Commission v Shell Co of Australia Ltd* (1999) 161 ALR 686; *Kizon v Palmer* (1997) 75 FCR 261.

[31] Secondly, subpoenae. I need only note a number of matters of relevance to the present application. (i) A *subpoena duces tecum* can properly be used to obtain access to a document in the possession, custody or power of a party to a proceeding: *Trade Practices Commission v Arnotts Ltd* (1989) 88 ALR 90. (ii) Objection can be taken to such a subpoena on the grounds that (a) it is oppressive and vexatious: see *Southern Pacific Hotel Services Inc v Southern Pacific Hotel Corporation Ltd* [1984] 1 NSWLR 710; *Australian Competition and Consumer Commission v Shell Co of Australia Ltd*, above, 696; (b) its object in whole or in part is not to obtain evidence to support a case but to discover whether there is a case at all: *Commissioner for Railways v Small*, above, 575; or (c) it is an abuse of process in that 'it is not legitimate to use a writ of subpoena duces tecum as a substitute for an application for discovery of documents': *Commissioner for Railways v Small*, above, 574. (iii) The documents required to be produced must not only be sufficiently described, they must also be 'sufficiently relevant' in the sense of having apparent relevance to the issues in the proceedings: *Trade Practices Commission v Arnotts*, above; *Spencer Motors Pty Ltd v LNC Industries Ltd* [1982] 2 NSWLR 921. (iv) Where documents are produced into the control of the court the issue is then one of inspection. Inspection is not a matter of right but a matter for the exercise of judicial discretion: *National Employers' Mutual General Association Ltd v Waind* [1978] 1 NSWLR 372. (v) When inspection is sought, the party seeking it must be able to show the legitimate forensic purpose for which the access is sought: *R v Saleam* (1989) 16 NSWLR 14.

[32] Turning now to the subpoenae in issue in this matter, they are, in my view, objectionable. I would be slow to set the subpoenae aside if no more was shown than that as a matter of form they were used as a substitute for the discovery procedures prescribed in this Court's rules but in circumstances where the two procedures would produce the same result in substance. The ground of objection in the present case, though, is more than a formal one.

...

[34] Considering the subpoenae in isolation, I am prepared to assume for present purposes that the method used to identify and classify the documents sought is itself unobjectionable notwithstanding that the questions used to identify the five categories of documents could require the exercise of judgment in answering the questions for the purpose of determining whether documents fell within a particular category. Such difficulty as answering those questions may pose is undercut in the present case when one has regard to the nature of the administrative decision to which the subpoenaed documents relate in their various ways and to the fact that the subpoena is addressed to the decision maker.

[35] Where the objections lie, in my view, are in the width of the documentation sought and in the manner of its seeking, these objections being interrelated. First, it is not at all

apparent to me why the ordinary processes of this Court could not have been followed and discovery sought. Had that course been taken I am by no means satisfied that discovery of any magnitude, if at all, would have been ordered on this application as it is presently framed and particularised. I would add that there well may be a question whether the nature and purpose of a s 16 decision are such in the administrative process leading to a final decision under s 22 of the Act as would influence the preparedness of the court in any event to embark on the discovery process in relation to a s 16 challenge save in a demonstrably clear and obvious case which this does not appear to be: cf the fragmentation principle referred to in *Harris*'s case, above, at 412–413.

...

[38] Notwithstanding the 'particulars' given for the unreasonableness ground, for example, it is difficult to resist the conclusion on the material before me that the subpoenae in the terms in which they are cast are being used merely for the purpose of finding out whether or not there is evidence upon which to base their unreasonableness challenge to both the Minister's opinions and her decision. It is not apparent to me that the applicants have any knowledge or reason to believe or to suspect at all that any such information existed in the hands of the Minister and her departmental officers other than as a matter of speculation from what may be suggested from the language of the departmental memoranda that were actually before the Minister and were provided to the applicants respectively. I am far from satisfied that the subpoenae in the main involve other than fishing: see *Australian Securities Commission v Dalleagles Pty Ltd* (French J, 27 February 1992, unreported); and see *Somerville*'s case, above.

[39] Distinctly, while I have indicated that the method used to describe the categories of documents sought will be assumed not to be objectionable as such in the circumstances, I am nonetheless satisfied that the descriptions so given in relation at least to categories 1 and 2 in the subpoenae — if category 1 on its face can be ascribed intelligible meaning and legitimate forensic purpose — go well beyond the matters that are said to be 'in issue' (eg, the fact and consequence of the Amparo stays etc) in any event assuming that these matters can properly be said to be 'in issue'. They do so furthermore in a way that could well cast upon the judge into whose custody the documents in those categories and particularly category 2 came, the burden of inspecting the documents for 'apparent relevance' before allowing access to them (even assuming there was not, as here, any issue of privilege). That burden, as Branson J indicated in *Diddam*'s case, above, is not imposed on judges by the discovery process.

[40] The present use made by the applicants of subpoenae is a scarce disguised attempt to secure discovery by more favourable means. The fact that the respondent has been forced to make the present application to set aside the subpoenae and the rather tortured course of argument this has entailed only reinforces the view I take that no encouragement should be offered parties so to bypass the processes prescribed in this Court's rules for obtaining discovery. In so doing, the applicants have removed at the outset that form of judicial control over the discovery process that the rules and practices of this Court envisage. They have substituted a process that, in the event of an application to set aside the subpoena, places both judge and party in receipt of the subpoenae in positions that are the converse of what is contemplated by the rules where discovery is sought. I consider that the stance taken by the judges of this Court in *Diddam*'s case and the *Shell* case, above, ought likewise be taken in the present circumstances. I should add that the judicial control to which I referred is the more necessary in cases of judicial review for the very reason that discovery in such cases is often

enough unnecessary at all or save in relation to a narrow issue or issues. It is made the more so where, as here, the same group of 'issues' is used to inform a number of alleged grounds of review before being repackaged in an omnibus Wednesbury unreasonableness claim.

[Except in respect of one paragraph which had been complied with by the Minister and was not challenged by her on the application, the subpoena in each of the proceedings was set aside.

See also *In the Marriage of Epstein* (1993) 16 FamLR 588; *Yunghanns v Candoora No 19 Pty Ltd (No 5)* [2000] VSC 505; *South Sydney District Rugby League Football Club Ltd v News Ltd* [2000] FCA 519; *Hudson v Branir Pty Ltd* [2005] NTCA 5.]

Admitting into evidence documents produced on subpoena

14.5.17   The service of a subpoena for the production of documents does not necessarily get the documents into evidence. The production of documents upon subpoena, and their subsequent admission into evidence, is a three-stage process as explained by the Court of Appeal decision in *National Employers' Mutual General Association v Waind* [1978] 1 NSWLR 372, extracted below:

14.5.18C   **National Employers' Mutual General Association v Waind**
[1978] 1 NSWLR 372
Court of Appeal (NSW)

[The principal proceeding involved a claim by the plaintiff for damages for personal injuries suffered as a result of a road accident. The plaintiff appealed in respect of an order made upon the application of the defendant that the defendant's legal representatives be permitted to inspect certain documents. The documents had been produced to the court by the insurance company (subsequently joined as a respondent to the appeal) which carried the workers' compensation insurance applicable to the plaintiff, and in particular in relation to the road accident in question, pursuant to a subpoena for production. A claim by the insurance company for privilege had been rejected immediately prior to the making of the order permitting inspection.]

Moffitt P (at 381–6): As Jordan CJ pointed out in *Small's* case (1938) 38 SR (NSW) 564 at p 574; 55 WN 215 and, as appeared in *Burchard's* case [1891] 2 QB 241, at pp 247, 248 there are at least two steps in the procedure of having a third party bring documents to court, and in their use thereafter. Indeed, on a correct view, there are three steps.

The first is obeying the subpoena, by the witness bringing the documents to the court and handing them to the judge. This step involves the determination of any objections of the witness to the subpoena, or to the production of the documents to the court pursuant to the subpoena. The second step is the decision of the judge concerning the preliminary use of the documents, which includes whether or not permission should be given to a party or parties to inspect the documents. The third step is the admission into evidence of the document in whole or in part; or the use of it in the process of evidence being put before the court by cross-examination or otherwise. It is the third step which alone provides material upon which ultimate decision in the case rests. In these three steps the stranger and the parties have different rights, and the function of the judge differs.

Upon the first step the person to whom the subpoena is addressed may seek to, and have, the subpoena set aside on the ground that it was improperly issued and an abuse of the power to compel the production of documents in any one of a number of ways. Such a case is where the [382] subpoena is used for the purpose of discovery. The essential feature of discovery in this connection, as appears from *Burchard's* case [1891] 2 QB 241, at pp 247, 248 and *Small's* case (1938) 38 SR (NSW) 564, p 574; 55 WN 215 is that the person to whom the subpoena is addressed will have to make a judgment as to which of his documents relate to issues between the parties. It is oppressive to place upon a stranger the obligation to form a judgment as to what is relevant to the issue joining in a proceeding, to which he is not a party. Hence it is an abuse of the use of a subpoena to impose this obligation. It follows that it is an abuse to use any subpoena, ie, even to a party to obtain discovery. This was the reasoning in *Small's* case (1938) 38 SR (NSW) 564, at p 575; 55 WN 215, at p 218. Of course, discovery as such is otherwise available to a party. It follows that a subpoena can only properly be used for the production of documents described in particular or general terms which does not involve the making of such a judgement. It does not follow, however, that because the party who issues a subpoena is unaware of the precise description of a particular document, or whether a particular document or documents is in the possession of the witness, or even whether it exists, or is unaware of its contents, that the subpoena, or even a subpoena in general terms, amounts to the use of the subpoena for the purpose of 'discovery'. To state it does involve a misconception of the different functions of discovery and of a subpoena for production. Of course, it may be that the terms of a subpoena are so wide that it is oppressive, but this is not because it is used for 'discovery' in the sense used in *Small's* case (1938) 38 SR (NSW) 564, at p 574; 55 WN 215 and *Burchard's* case [1891] 2 QB 241, but because it imposes an onerous task on a stranger to collect and produce documents many of which can have no relevance to the litigation. To require the branch of a bank to produce all cheques received by it in a particular year in order to find, if it exists, a cheque of the opponent in a false name would be oppressive, whereas, to require a hospital to produce its file in respect of the medical treatment of the opposing party would not. It is a misuse of terms to say the person who inspects the latter is using it for the purposes of discovery, because he is unaware of the contents of the documents or some of them. It is not in point to seek to define the excessive use of the subpoena. The documents in this case are not such, and the witness itself does not so claim.

The issue of a subpoena may involve an abuse of the power in other ways and, as stated in *Small's* case (1938) 38 SR (NSW) 564, at p 574; 55 WN 215 objection to production to the court may be on other grounds. Thus, it would be an improper use of the subpoena if it were not sought for the purpose of the litigation, but for some spurious purpose, such as to inspect the documents in connection with other proceedings, or for some private purpose, or in collusive proceedings to give them publicity. A witness might argue the documents must be sought for some undefined spurious reason, as they have no conceivable relation to the proceedings. The court would jealously consider any of such submissions having regard to the invasion of the private rights of the stranger occasioned by the operation of the subpoena.

The second step is when the documents are produced to the court by the witness, the subpoena not having been set aside, and any other objection to their production, such as on the ground they were privileged, having [383] been rejected. At this point documents are in the control of the court, pursuant to the valid order of the subpoena. As pointed out in *Small's* case (1938) 38 SR (NSW) 564, at p 574; 55 WN 215 at this time the witness may state he objects to their being handed to the parties for inspection. If he states he does not object to the parties inspecting the documents, or by lack of objection is taken to have no objection, no doubt normally there would be little reason not to permit inspection by either party. However, the documents are under the control of the judge and, even if the witness has not objected, there may be good reason in the elucidation of the truth why the judge may eg, defer inspection by one party or the other. Indeed, no doubt, he will normally defer inspection by a party who has not issued a subpoena until his opponent has an opportunity to use the documents in cross-examination. There may be good reason why he may, or indeed should, refuse inspection of irrelevant material of a private nature, concerning a party to the litigation, or, concerning some other person who is neither a party nor the witness. It may well be that the documents are the property of some institution, but relate to private matters concerning some person and the officers of the institution do not take objection on the basis that the responsibility for disclosure rests with the court. The documents are in its control and are used on its responsibility so far as properly required for the purpose of the proceedings.

The critical question for present purposes, however, arises in relation to this second step, as to the exercise of the power of the judge to permit inspection ... [385] The crucial question in relation to the exercise of the discretion to permit inspection in the second step is whether the documents have apparent relevance to the issues. It is at the third step that questions between the parties of relevance in fact and admissibility are ruled upon. The judge is in some difficulty in determining whether documents are relevant prior to the presentation of the evidence or at the commencement of the case. If there is particular objection from the witness, or questions of privacy are involved, no doubt procedures can be adopted to ensure that only relevant documents are inspected. In other cases, it would appear appropriate to proceed to exercise the discretion, provided the documents are apparently relevant or are on the subject matter of the litigation. However, the limitation on the exercise of the judge's discretion to allow inspection is that the document contains information of apparent relevance to the issues. Once the judge has that opinion, inspection will normally be allowed, notwithstanding that the document is not admissible as it stands, and notwithstanding that the party seeking inspection has not given any undertaking to tender it, or use it in cross-examination.

The discretion is one concerning the invasion by the subpoena procedure of the rights of a stranger by the party who seeks inspection in aid of the presentation of his case to the court. No right of the opposing party is involved in making an order permitting inspection of a stranger's documents. It is difficult to see on what basis he can object. His right is to have only admissible evidence adduced. The exercise of the discretion does not involve the determination of an issue between the parties as to the relevance or admissibility of the document. It may well be, however, [386] that the judge may hear, or indeed invite, comment from an opposing party, if the documents are such that elucidation of the truth may best be served by delaying inspection, or because the documents reveal matter private to such party or his associates and is irrelevant to the proceedings. This may well be the case where the documents are produced as earlier indicated by some public authority and contain private matter, but the authority raises no specific objection on the presumed basis that it is the court's responsibility to permit or refuse inspection. It follows that a party, in this case the plaintiff, has no right to object to the judge allowing the other party, in this case the first defendant, to inspect a stranger's documents, or to appeal if the judge allows inspection.

However, I prefer to base my decision in this appeal, in the first instance, on the question argued by the appellant, and supported by the respondent insurance company, namely that the judge had no power to permit inspection. I have adopted this course because it is clear that the interests of the insurance company, and the plaintiff to prevent inspection of the documents by the defendant coincide, so that when the case before Carmichael J is resumed, it is likely that any deficiency arising from the circumstances that it is the plaintiff who objects will be remedied by like objection from the insurance company.

It seems that the order for inspection was premature in that it was ordered before the witness or the plaintiff had an opportunity to make an objection separate from the objection based on privilege. There is some ground to set aside the inspection order to allow the discretion to be exercised, after the judge inspects the documents. However, for the reasons I have indicated, I do not think such an order can be made on the application of the plaintiff. No doubt this could be procedurally adjusted, by giving the respondent insurance company an opportunity to become an appellant. However, I do not think in any practical sense that this is necessary. The order for inspection has not yet been carried into effect, it is interlocutory and hence is open to review by Carmichael J who can, and no doubt will, review the order as to exercise of the discretion when he has seen the documents.

The appeal should be dismissed with costs.

[**Hutley** and **Glass JJA** agreed with the **President.**]

14.5.19   As to the grounds of privilege which may be raised as objections to the production of documents, see **Chapter 13** under the heading **'Privilege'** at **13.5.1ff**.

Failing to attend on a subpoena

14.5.20   In the Federal Court (r 24.23), the Australian Capital Territory (r 6612); New South Wales (r 33.12), the Northern Territory (r 42.12), South Australia (r 182), Tasmania (r 500E), Victoria (r 42.12), and Western Australia (O 36B r 12), the rules expressly state that failure to comply with a subpoena without lawful excuse is a contempt of court and that the addressee may be dealt with accordingly. Even in the absence of a specific rule, however, a witness who fails to attend on a subpoena which has been properly served with appropriate conduct money, is liable to be punished for contempt of court: *R v Daye* [1908] 2 KB 333. It may also be a contempt of court to fail to produce documents in response to a subpoena.

There is some authority that, as well as being liable to punishment for contempt, a witness who disobeys a subpoena may be liable for damages to the party on whose behalf the subpoena was issued. This will only be the case, however, if it is established that the person served is a material witness, that he or she was served, and that the person could have appeared: *Roberts v J and F Stone Lighting and Radio Ltd* (1945) 172 LT 240 at 241. In New South Wales (r 42.27) the rules now provide that the court may order the person in default in these circumstances to pay costs occasioned by the default.

For a subpoena served interstate under the Service and Execution of Process Act 1992 (Cth), s 37(1) confirms that if the person served with the subpoena fails to comply with it, a court or authority of the place of issue may issue such warrant as it may have issued had the subpoena been served in the place of issue.

Notice to produce

14.5.21 Most rules include a procedure by which a party may serve on another party a notice to produce specified documents at the trial: FCR r 30.28; ACT r 623 (the rule applies to documents which have been disclosed); NSW Pt 34; NT r 35.08; Qld r 227 (the rule applies to documents which have been disclosed); SA r 215; Tas r 400, Vic r 35.08; WA O 30 r 4 (this rule deems a party who has served a list of documents under the obligation to make discovery of documents to have been served on the same date with a notice requiring production at trial of all of the documents in the list within the party's possession, custody or power.) The relevant rules in the Federal Court and New South Wales extend to 'things' as well as documents.

In New South Wales, the Northern Territory, Queensland, South Australia and Victoria these rules require that the documents be produced in response to the notice, subject to court order to the contrary. In these jurisdictions the notice to produce procedure has the same coercive effect as a subpoena. In the other jurisdictions, the rules are not expressed in mandatory terms, but merely facilitate the tendering of secondary evidence of the contents of documents by the party giving the notice if the other party fails to comply with the notice: *Morgan v Babcock & Wilcox Ltd* (1929) 43 CLR 163 at 172.

14.5.22 Notes and questions

1. Under what circumstances may it be necessary for a subpoena to issue on behalf of a party to litigation to compel the attendance of that party? The realities of the situation may be that a named party and an insurance company behind that party are different persons with different interests. See *Mulligan v Lancaster* [1969] 2 NSWR 284, where a subpoena was issued in these circumstances by the respondent's solicitors against the respondent himself.

2. It has been noted that a witness who fails to attend on a subpoena may be punished for contempt of court: see 14.5.20. What factors must be established before a witness may be dealt with for disobedience to a subpoena for the production of documents? See *O'Born v Commissioner for Government Transport* [1960] 77 WN (NSW) 80, in which the Court of Appeal of New South Wales indicated that it would not be possible to deal with a witness for disobedience to a subpoena for production unless some proof is given, both that the document existed at the time production is sought, and that it was in the possession and control of the witness. See also *Lane v Registrar of the Supreme Court of New South Wales* (1981) 35 ALR 322. In this case the Full High Court made it clear that a person may only be liable for contempt where it is established that the documents in question are within the terms of the subpoena, regardless of the motive for declining to produce them.

   It was the established position that if a subpoena has not been correctly served (see 14.5.7–14.5.8) the witness will not be guilty of contempt of court by failure to attend to give evidence, although that witness may be guilty of contempt of court if he or she has refused to be properly served with the subpoena, and has impeded the process server in the execution of his or her duty: see *Re Barnes* [1968] 87 WN (Pt 1) (NSW) 479. The position in this respect has changed in most jurisdictions, with the rules now stating that the addressee of a subpoena may be dealt with for contempt of court as if they had been properly served if it is proved that the addressee had, by the last date for service of the subpoena, actual knowledge of the subpoena and of its requirements: FCR r 24.23(2); ACT r 6612 (2); NSW r 33.12(2); NT r 42.12(2); SA r 182; Tas r 500E(2); Vic r 42.12(2); WA O 36B r 12.

3. The Rules of Court in several jurisdictions now entitle a party to obtain a court order for the payment of any 'loss or expense' incurred in complying with a subpoena: see **14.5.6**. Would this rule entitle a non-party witness served with a subpoena to give evidence to recover the costs incurred in obtaining legal advice and assistance to prepare to give oral evidence? In *Australian Prudential Regulation Authority v Rural and General Insurance Ltd* [2004] FCA 933, a solicitor instructed by the witness had prepared a draft affidavit which dealt with questions and issues which had been raised in correspondence from the defendant's solicitors. The affidavit was intended to serve as preparation for giving evidence in court. The witness was ultimately informed that she would not be required to give evidence. She applied under the then applicable rule in the Federal Court for an order for recovery of the costs. Gyles J accepted that the rule was not to be given a narrow interpretation, particularly where a witness not party to the litigation is involved, but he noted that a witness who is subpoenaed has no obligation to produce such a statement or to be prepared to give evidence in that way. He concluded the rule could not be stretched far enough to cover solicitor and client costs for preparation of a statement of evidence.

Further reading

14.6.1   Looseleaf

B C Cairns, 'Practice and Procedure', *Halsbury's Laws of Australia*, Butterworths, Sydney, 1995, vol 20.

Ritchie's Uniform Civil Procedure (New South Wales), LexisNexis, Sydney, looseleaf, [33.3.35]–[33.3.45] (a summary of regulations, internal directives and fee schedules applicable to various government departments in relation to service of a subpoena in New South Wales).

14.6.2   Articles

P Butt, 'Contempt of Court in Relation to Subpoenas Further Considered' (1982) 13 *CLA Bulletin* 105.

P Matthews, 'Truth, Justice and the American Way' [1994] *NLJ Practitioner* 1317 (comment upon *Khanna v Lovell* and the use of the *subpoena duces tecum* against a third party returnable prior to the actual trial date).

P Wood, 'Challenging *Subpoenas Duces Tecum*: Is there a Third Party View?' (1982–85) 10 *Syd L Rev* 379.

M Yorston, 'Subpoenas: Strict Rules Apply' (2003) 77(10) *Law Inst J* 66.

Affidavits

## CHAPTER 15

OVERVIEW

An affidavit is a sworn statement used in support of or against an application in court. Affidavits, like oral evidence, are subject to the rule against hearsay. However, the hearsay rule does not apply to affidavits used in interlocutory proceedings (which are accepted on information and belief, provided the source of the information and the grounds of belief are stated).

The Rules of Court contain detailed requirements as to the form and structure of affidavits. There are complicated rules concerning the form of the jurat and the procedures for swearing or affirming the contents of an affidavit. A jurat (meaning 'he or she swears') is a statement at the end of an affidavit setting out the name of the deponent, his or her signature, where and when the affidavit was made, the name of the person who took (witnessed) the affidavit, and the signature and title (or description) of the person who took the affidavit. Affidavits may annex or exhibit documents to which they refer, depending on the jurisdiction.

Affidavits are required to be filed and served before they can be used in proceedings. The maker of the affidavit may also be required to attend the court for cross-examination. The courts have power to prevent scandalous and irrelevant affidavit material making its way onto the court file. Alterations or erasures to affidavits must be authenticated by appropriate procedures. Non-compliance with the rules governing affidavits can be sanctioned with leave of the court.

Effective affidavits are built upon the exercise of drafting skills. Brevity, style and attention to detail should be the hallmarks of an affidavit. Affidavits are always a reflection of your ability to gather and present evidence in written form. But never forget that an affidavit is that of the deponent, not his or her lawyer.

INTRODUCTION

15.1.1   An affidavit is a written statement intended for use in litigation sworn to or affirmed, before a person having lawful authority to administer an oath: *Daniell's Chancery Practice*, 7th ed, Stephens and Sons Ltd, London, 1901, p 527. Affidavits are fundamentally different from pleadings (see *In Re Thom* (1918) 18 SR (NSW) 70 at 73) in the sense that affidavits:

(a)   anticipate defences;

(b)   state the evidence relied upon;

(c)   refrain from referring to the name of counsel; and

(d)   in opposition, do not have to address every issue in contention.

Some affidavits are of standard form, for example, an affidavit of service. However, most are tailored to the case in point. Affidavits can be used at either interlocutory stages or at trial. Affidavits for use in interlocutory applications may be based upon information and belief: see 15.3.1. Generally the grounds for the information and belief will be required to be set out in the affidavit. Interlocutory affidavits are received only as an exception to the general hearsay rule that a deponent depose to facts he or she is able to prove of his or her own knowledge or of his or her own direct perception. In trial affidavits, hearsay is not permitted, hence the affidavit is confined to facts a deponent can establish from his or her own knowledge: see 15.3.1. Precedents should be used with caution when drafting affidavits. Remember that the same rules of evidence apply to the admissibility of affidavits at trial as to oral testimony.

Documents brought into evidence by the deponent in an affidavit are either exhibited or annexed (see 15.7.1) depending on the jurisdiction and are customarily marked with the initials of the deponent and then the number of the document.

There is a modern trend towards enlarging the use of affidavit evidence: for example, Evidence Act 1995 (Cth) s 170. The argument justifying this trend is that time can be saved by avoiding oral testimony. Does the length and complexity of affidavit material compensate for the absence of cross-examination of the witnesses' oral testimony? See P Young and C Curtis, 'Oral or Written Evidence?' (1997) 71 *ALJ* 459.

[*Note:* in this chapter a reference, such as WA O 9 r 2, is a reference to the relevant Rules of Court. All other legislation will be specified.]

AFFIDAVITS AND ORAL EVIDENCE

15.2.1   At common law the general rule is that witnesses are examined orally in open court or by deposition. The common law rule is sometimes reflected in the Rules of Court: Court Procedures Rules 2006 (ACT) r 6700; Uniform Civil Procedure Rules 2005 (NSW) r 31.1 with exceptions; Rules of the Supreme Court of the Northern Territory of Australia (NT) r 40.02; Supreme Court Civil Rules 2006 (SA) rr 165, 166, 168; Supreme Court Rules 2000 (Tas) r 458; Supreme Court (General Civil Procedure) Rules 1996 (Vic) r 40.02; Rules of the Supreme Court 1971 (WA) O 36 r 1, O 38. The Uniform Civil Procedure Rules 1999 (Qld) r 390 makes a distinction between claims and applications. Evidence at the trial of a proceeding started by claim may only be given orally, but evidence in a proceeding started by application may only be given by affidavit. The Civil Proceedings Act 2011 (Qld) s 146 amends the Evidence Act 1977 (Qld) ss 129A, 129B by providing a fact in issue such as proof of handwriting, documents, identity of parties or proof of authority, in cases where the fact is not seriously in dispute or strict proof may cause unnecessary or unreasonable expense, delay or inconvenience, may be given at trial, or at any other stage of the proceeding, in anyway the court directs. This includes a statement on oath of information and belief, production of documents or of entries in records or copies.

Affidavits are an equitable exception to the general common law rule: *McDonald v Page* [1923] SASR 167. Originally affidavits were witness statements taken down before a chancery official for use by the Lord Chancellor. Affidavits are now prepared by the profession.

A court may at any time, for sufficient reason, order that any particular fact or facts be proved by affidavit, or that the affidavit of any witness may be read at a hearing or trial. The public may be afforded access to an affidavit: *Hammond v Scheinberg* (2001) 52 NSWLR 49.

However, where a party *bona fide* desires production of a witness for cross-examination and the witness is available, the witness must generally give oral evidence: see 15.11.1. If the witness fails to attend, the affidavit cannot be used without leave: FCR r 29.09(3); Evidence Act 1995 (Cth) s 173; ACT r 6721; NSW r 35.2; NT r 40.04(3) (the court may order that the affidavit not be received into evidence); Qld r 439 (the court may refuse to receive the affidavit into evidence); SA r 165 (the court may exclude an affidavit from evidence); Tas rr 463, 466; Vic r 40.04(3) (the court may order that the affidavit not be received into evidence); WA O 36 r 2.

Similarly, in all interlocutory court and chamber applications, evidence is usually adduced by affidavit but the court retains a discretion on application of either party to order attendance of a deponent for cross-examination: see 15.11.1; NSW r 31.2.

Reasonable notice of a new affidavit is required to be given to the other side before it can be used. Failure to provide adequate notice may result in an adjournment: see 15.9.1.

INTERLOCUTORY AND TRIAL AFFIDAVITS

15.3.1   Except in New South Wales, an affidavit designed for use in interlocutory proceedings may contain statements of information and belief (hearsay) provided that the sources and grounds of that information and belief are clearly identified in the affidavit: HCR r 24.01.6; FCR r 5.04; Evidence Act 1995 (Cth) s 172; ACT r 6711; NT 43.03(2); Qld r 430(2); SA r 162 (the court may dispense with this exception); Tas r 502(1) with exceptions listed in r 502(2), eg, applications to extend or waive time limits to start or continue proceedings imposed by statute, set aside a judgment, dismiss proceedings for want of prosecution, or final disposition of parties rights; Vic r 43.03(2); WA O 37 r 6(2), (3A); *Atherton v Jackson's Corio Meat Packing (1965) Pty Ltd* [1967] VR 850; *Re O'Brien* [1923] SASR 411 at 418.

Interlocutory affidavits failing to state the source of the information or belief are regarded as inadmissible (*Re J L Young Manufacturing Co* [1900] 2 Ch 753; *Hartwell Trent (Aust) Pty Ltd v Tefal Société Anonyme* [1968] VR 3) or of little weight: *Hardie Rubber Co Ltd v General Tyre and Rubber Co (*1973) 47 ALJR 462.

The source disclosed need not be the original source; it may be an intermediate source of lesser weight (*Deutsche Ruckversicherung AG v Walbrook Insurance Co Ltd* [1994] 4 All ER 181), for example, 'second-hand' hearsay, where the deponent states that he or she was informed by another person who was told by yet another person who saw the relevant event occurring. If the hearsay rule were to apply, only the person who actually saw the event could give the evidence.

In New South Wales no distinction is drawn between interlocutory and trial affidavits. Hearsay should be avoided in both interlocutory and trial affidavits.

In South Australia, Practice Direction No 3.1 — Contents of Affidavits (r 162) provides that a final paragraph in an affidavit that says 'I know the facts deposed to in this my affidavit from my own knowledge, except where otherwise appears', or similar, standing alone, may lead to the rejection of the affidavit. Affidavits based on information and belief though admissible may have little weight in contested interlocutory applications. A solicitor swearing an affidavit based on instructions from the client is a prime example. There is no equivalent rule of court or practice note or direction in the other jurisdictions.

Hearsay is permissible in interlocutory affidavits, but not in trial affidavits unless permitted by an exception to the hearsay rule. Trial affidavits are confined to matters that the witness knows of his or her own knowledge. The conditions for the admissibility of hearsay or interlocutory matters are strictly observed: *Community Development Pty Ltd v Engwirda Construction Co* [1968] Qd R 541. An affidavit or a portion of a trial affidavit containing hearsay material not authorised by the rules may be struck out: *Rossage v Rossage* [1960] 1 All ER 600; *Cowie v State Electricity Commission of Victoria* [1964] VR 788. This rule is strictly applied: *Community Developments Pty Ltd v Engwirda Construction Co* [1968] Qd R 541.

Typically affidavits arise at trial where a witness is unable to attend the trial or as part of a case management process. In all cases an affidavit should specifically address matters in issue in the trial.

It can be difficult to distinguish interlocutory from final proceedings. In *Gilbert v Endean* (1878) 9 Ch D 259, Cotton LJ said (at 268–9):

> I am not now adverting to the question as to whether or no [sic] the evidence ought to have been given *viva voce* or by affidavit, but to the question whether the rule that on interlocutory applications the Court may act upon evidence given on the witness's information and belief applies to the present case. But for the purpose of this rule those applications only are [269] considered interlocutory which do not decide the rights of parties, but are made for the purpose of keeping things in *status quo* until the rights can be decided, or for the purpose of obtaining some direction of the court as to how the cause is to be conducted, as to what is to be done in the progress of the cause for the purpose of enabling the Court ultimately to decide upon the rights of the parties. Now many of the cases which are brought before the Court on motions and on petitions, and which are therefore interlocutory in form, are not interlocutory within the meaning of that rule as regards evidence. They are to decide the rights of the parties, and whatever the form may be in which such questions are brought before the Court, in my opinion the evidence must be regulated by the ordinary rules, and must be such as would be admissible at the hearing of the cause.

In *Ex parte Britt* [1987] 1 Qd R 221, an application for an extension of time pursuant to s 4F of the Motor Vehicles Insurance Act 1936 (Qld) was held to be an interlocutory application upon which evidence by way of information and belief was admissible. McPherson J held that the test as to whether an application is interlocutory or final was whether the decision of the application would finally dispose of the rights of the parties, not merely as to the subject matter of the particular application in question, but also as to the ultimate dispute between the parties. See also G Jameson, 'Interlocutory Orders: Or are They Final' (1987) 17 *Qld Law Soc J* 39.

The following are examples of what may be classified as interlocutory:

(a)   contempt proceedings relating to breach of an interlocutory order (*Savings & Investment Bank Ltd v Gasco Investments (Netherlands) BV No 2* [1988] 1 All ER 975);

(b)   security for costs applications; and

(c)   applications for interim or interlocutory injunctions.

The following are examples of what is not classified as interlocutory:

(a)   summary judgment applications (*Settlement Wine Co Pty Ltd v National & General Insurance Co Ltd* (1988) 146 LSJS 150);

(b)   striking out for want of prosecution or abuse of process: *Lewandowski v Lovell* (1991) WAR 311; and

(c)   application for removal of a caveat.

15.3.2   Notes and questions

1.   Care should be taken with interlocutory affidavits as they:

(a) can be used in subsequent interlocutory proceedings or at trial;

(b) may afford an opponent the right to inspect documents mentioned; and

(c) can open the deponent to cross-examination.

2. What may be interlocutory for the purposes of determining whether there is an appeal as of right (see **19.3.7**) is not necessarily the same as 'interlocutory' for the purposes of the affidavit rules: *Re J* [1960] 1 All ER 603; *Ex parte Britt* [1987] Qd R 221. The right of appeal is governed by the terms of the statute.

3. Is 'second-hand' hearsay permissible in an interlocutory affidavit? See *Savings and Investment Bank Ltd v Gasco Investments BV* [1984] 1 WLR 271.

4. If 'second-hand' hearsay is permissible in an interlocutory affidavit, what evidentiary weight would it have?

FORM

15.4.1 The Rules of Court contain specific instructions concerning the construction of documents including affidavits: HCR r 1.07.3; FCR r 29.02, Pt 2 Div 2.2, r 29.02(1), Form 59; ACT r 6710, Form 6.11; NSW rr 4.2, 35.4; NT rr 27.01–27.07, 43.01; Qld rr 431, 960–4; Tas Pt 7 Div 1 — Documents, r 501; Vic rr 27.01–43.09, 43.01; WA O 37 r 2. Failure to comply with the instructions may result in the registrar refusing to file the affidavit and the taxing officer disallowing the costs of the affidavit, or part of it, upon taxation. In South Australia this is dealt with as a procedural irregularity: r 13. Some jurisdictions specify that the affidavit must be in the approved form: Federal Court Form 59; NSW Form 40; Qld r 431(1), Form 46; SA r 162, Practice Direction 3.1 — Contents of affidavits (Rule 162), Form 14. In Queensland, there are numerous prescribed forms of limited application.

In some jurisdictions, costs are not allowable for affidavits or parts of affidavits that unnecessarily contain hearsay, argumentative matter or copies or extracts from documents on the court file. Such costs may be required to be paid by the party filing the affidavit or in a proper case his or her solicitor: Qld r 430(3) (costs may be disallowed); WA O 37 r 6(3). In South Australia such material is caught by r 164. There are no equivalent rules in the other jurisdictions.

15.4.2E	**High Court Rules 2004**

1.08 Documents

1.08.1 Unless the Rules provide to the contrary, all documents filed in the Court shall be printed:

(a) in clear, sharp, legible and permanent type of at least 12 point size;

(b) on only one side of durable white paper of A4 size;

(c) with margins of at least 2.5 cm at the top, 2.5 cm at the bottom and 2.5 cm on each side of each sheet;

(d) with each page numbered and every tenth line on each page numbered in the margin; and

(e) without erasure or alteration that causes material disfigurement.

1.08.2 Unless the Rules provide to the contrary, the first page of every document filed in the Court shall be indorsed:

    (a)   first, with the title of the proceeding or proposed proceeding in which it is filed;

    (b)   next, with a short description of the document including, in the case of an affidavit, the name of the deponent;

    (c)   at the foot of the page with:

        (i)   the date of the document;

        (ii)   the party or other persons on whose behalf it is filed; and

        (iii)   if a solicitor prepares the document, the particulars referred to in rule 1.08.3; or

        (iv)   if the party or person on whose behalf it is filed is acting without a solicitor, the particulars referred to in rule 1.08.4.

1.08.3 If a solicitor prepares a document to be filed in the Court, the particulars which are to be indorsed at the foot of the first page of the document are the firm name, address, document exchange box number, telephone number and facsimile number of the solicitor, and the name of an individual in the firm to whom reference can be made in respect of the matter.

1.08.4 If the party or person on whose behalf a document to be filed in the Court is acting without a solicitor, the particulars which are to be indorsed at the foot of the first page of the document are the name, address, telephone number, and any facsimile number of that party or person.

1.08.5 Where a fee is payable in respect of the filing, issuing, sealing or dealing with any document, a Registrar shall, immediately upon payment of that fee, mark upon the document the amount of the fee paid and the date of payment.

1.09   Forms

    A form prescribed by these Rules must be used, with any variations that are necessary or as the Registrar directs.

15.4.3   Every affidavit intended to be filed is to be legibly and clearly written or printed, without blotting, erasure, and without any such alteration as to cause material disfigurement: see 'Alterations, erasure and withdrawal' at 15.14.1. Court forms prescribe the general form of an affidavit.

15.4.4E   **Uniform Civil Procedure Rules 2005 (NSW)**

Form 40 (version 1)
UCPR 35.1
AFFIDAVIT OF [NAME] [DATE]

COURT DETAILS
Court
#Division
#List
Registry
Case number

TITLE OF PROCEEDINGS
[First] plaintiff   **[name]**

#Second plaintiff
#Number of plaintiffs (if more than two)
[First] defendant   **[name]**
#Second defendant
#Number of defendants
(if more than two)

FILING DETAILS

    Filed for   **[name]** [role of party eg
                                                    plaintiff]

    #Filed in relation to   [eg plaintiff's claim,
                                                    (number)
                                                    cross-claim]
                                                    [include only if form to be
                                                    eFiled]

    #Legal representative   [solicitor on record] [firm]
    #Legal representative reference   [reference number]
    Contact name and telephone   [name] [telephone]
    [on separate page]

AFFIDAVIT

Name
Address
Occupation
Date
I [#say on oath #affirm]:
#I am [role of deponent].
[state information to be included in the affidavit in numbered paragraphs].
#SWORN #AFFIRMED at
Signature of deponent
Signature of witness
Name of witness
Address of witness
Capacity of witness   [#Justice of the peace
                                                                     #Solicitor #Barrister
                                                                     #Commissioner for affidavits
                                                                     #Notary public]

Note: The deponent and witness must sign each page of the affidavit. See UCPR 35.7B.

Use of facsimiles

15.4.5   The Rules of Court do not provide for a facsimile copy of an affidavit to be filed. The proper course is for a solicitor to exhibit the facsimile to his or her own affidavit. In South Australia, Practice Direction 1.3 — Facsimile Copies of Affidavits — provides that in cases of urgency a facsimile with original signatures may be accepted. The lawyer is permitted to swear an affidavit exhibiting a copy of the affidavit bearing the facsimile signatures. There are no equivalent provisions in the other jurisdictions.

STRUCTURE

Heading and title

15.5.1 Affidavits are entitled in the proceeding and bear the number, if any, of that proceeding. Where there are multiple parties, the title is the name of the first party followed by 'and others'. Where there are multiple matters, the title is by the name of the first matter followed by 'and other matters'. The costs of any unnecessary prolixity are usually disallowed at taxation. An affidavit may be sworn for use in proceedings, which are yet to be commenced and are entitled in the intended cause or matter.

Drafting

15.5.2 Affidavits are expressed in the first person and state:

- the title of the proceedings in which it is sworn;
- the name of the deponent;
- the address or place of residence of the deponent, or if none, a description of the deponent;
- the occupation of the deponent (vague descriptions should be avoided);
- whether the deponent is, or is employed by, a party to the proceeding in which the affidavit is used;
- the date on which and place at which it was taken or sworn; and
- the party on whose behalf it was filed.

    See generally HCR rr 24.01.1–24.01.3; FCR r 29.02; ACT r 6710; NSW Form 40; NT r 43.01; Qld r 431; SA r 162; Tas r 501; Vic rr 27.03, 43.01; WA O 37 rr 2, 13.

    Use of the passive voice is prohibited. Use of the first person requires the deponent to swear to the contents of the affidavit from his or her own knowledge, except with respect to affidavits based on information and belief: see **15.5.4E**. Affidavits should be unique, hence care should be taken before using boilerplate precedents.

    In the Northern Territory (r 43.01(3)) and Victoria (r 43.01(3)), where a deponent makes an affidavit in a professional or other occupational capacity the affidavit may state the address of the deponent's business, the position he or she holds, and the name of his or her firm or employer, if any. In Queensland (r 431(4)), an affidavit must describe the person making it and state the person's residential or business address or place of employment. There are no equivalent provisions in the other jurisdictions.

    Affidavits are divided into paragraphs, pages and paragraphs numbered consecutively, each paragraph being so far as possible confined to a distinct portion of the subject matter: HCR r 24.01.4. Sums of money, numbers and references in dates to days, months or years are expressed in figures not words. In Western Australia (O 37 r 2(6)) each page of an affidavit and annexures must be numbered consecutively in the upper right hand corner.

    The outside or side column of the affidavit should identify:

- the party on whose behalf the affidavit is filed;
- the name of the deponent; and
- the date of swearing.

It is possible for multiple deponents to make an affidavit jointly. A special jurat is required and must be severally sworn or affirmed: see **15.6.7**.

Objections may be taken to the form of an affidavit that contains:

- hearsay (if the affidavit is used at trial);

- indirect speech in conversations;

- incorrect use of adverbs; and

- argumentative material (material drawing legal inferences).

Leeway is given with respect to urgent interlocutory proceedings. In theory, affidavits should contain only evidential facts, not arguments or legal conclusions.

CONTENTS

15.5.3 Affidavits should be written in plain English. See Lord Justice Staughton, 'Courtly Language', (1988) Summer *Bar News* 34. Trial affidavits are confined to facts which the deponent is able of his or her own knowledge to prove: HCR r 24.01.5; ACT r 6711; NT r 43.03; Qld r 430(1) (evidence the person making it could give if giving evidence orally); SA Practice Direction 3.1 — Contents of Affidavits Rule 162; Tas r 502(1); Vic r 43.03; WA O 37 r 6. Interlocutory affidavits are discussed at **15.3.1**.

The contents of the affidavit should be governed by the evidence required to prove the issue addressed by the affidavit. It is necessary to analyse the order, section or rule which gives the court power to make the order sought, in addition to case law relevant to the exercise of the discretion. Practice directions detailing court policies should also be examined. All facts which are to be relied upon should be included, as evidence cannot be given from the bar table.

The affidavit should be that of the deponent, in the deponent's plain language, yet precise and concise, being a complete narration of relevant facts. The affidavit should be drafted in a style enabling the witness to regard it as his or her own words, not those of the solicitor. The witness is stating the facts on oath, and if knowingly false may be committing perjury. Practitioners should avoid creating legalistic affidavits in the practitioner's own style, as the affidavit may ultimately be disowned by the witness in the witness box. The witness should be interviewed before drafting an affidavit and should not be led, thus ensuring that he or she tells his or her own story. The deponent should have the consequences of making a false affidavit explained to them. Never blindly accept what a deponent tells you. Be conscious of the highly improbable and matters which the deponent could not possibly have knowledge of. Seek clarification and verify information to be included in an affidavit. The deponent should read and confirm all aspects of the affidavit. Affidavits should be readily understood by the reader without additional information.

Direct speech should be used for conversations identifying the place, date, who was present (that is, 'I said') and the evidential rules of admissibility should be adhered to: that is, hearsay, proof of the contents of a document and so on.

15.5.4E	**How to Draft an Affidavit**
	J P Bryson QC
	(1985) 1 *Aust Bar Rev* 250

Most litigation is solved when the relevant facts are ascertained and stated in chronological order. It is a large part of advocacy to see that the evidence which the client has available reaches the court in a form which is complete and can be readily comprehended. The object of counsel adducing evidence, orally or by affidavit, is to put before the court the admissible evidence of the witness about the relevant facts in issue. So far as possible the evidence should be put in chronological order. The principal contribution to an affidavit is what the witness can say. Counsel contributes to drafting an affidavit:

- knowledge of the law of evidence and of the practice about the form in which evidence is received;
- understanding the issues, relevance;
- capacity to marshal facts in order, and with circumstances, as to produce what the reader can regard as a complete narration;
- command of the English language: grammar, spelling and punctuation;
- knowledge of the rules and practices of the court about form of affidavits.

The use of affidavits saves time for the court. The evidence in chief emerges quickly. This advantage is only worth having if the evidence is clear and readily comprehensible, and is admissible. Many affidavits are formal; they put before the court facts which could not be disputed, and collect the history of the litigation, or of dealings in a trust, or they show what has happened in a long correspondence, or prove the results of searches; things that could be proved orally, with additional time and trouble, without an advantage to be gained by observing the witness's demeanour forming a view on his credit. On the other hand, affidavits may deal with the substance of the party's case and with matters which can be expected to be disputed.

An affidavit is the sworn evidence of a witness. What is taking place is a communication between the witness and the court. An affidavit is not an opportunity for counsel to open his mind to the court.

But they usually sound like a barrister talking. In a formal affidavit this is not important. Where there is to be an issue about the facts deposed to, the affidavit is much more use if the witness comes through. The witness bears the primary responsibility; he is putting his oath to the document and (if it is false) perjuring himself. Counsel's many responsibilities include responsibility to the witness for what counsel leads him into swearing. When challenged about passages in their affidavits witnesses sometimes resort to saying:

'I did not notice that when I read it';
'My lawyer put that in'; or
'I don't understand that part'.

A witness is not likely to say any of these about his oral evidence.

If the witness takes any of these lines, not much credit will be given to him or his affidavit. He will not take these lines if he really participated in the preparation of his affidavit.

Except for formal affidavits, it is not possible to draft an affidavit properly without seeing the witness. When you see him, do not do all the talking — get him to talk. If this takes time, you must use time. The document you produce must be something which the witness will regard as his own document. He may be drifting along in the belief that because you are drafting the affidavit, all will be well and he need not think about it. Do not let this happen. Put on him the task of reading through the draft and telling you it is correct, or where it should be corrected.

It is important to draw from the witness, and to get down in his affidavit, his relevant evidence, complete, as understood by him, and unembellished by anyone else's interpretation. He will only forget the embellishment and disavow it later.

The court will soon compare or contrast the comprehension and powers of expression shown in cross-examination with the language of the affidavit.

While the witness should come through, and his affidavit should be his expression, not yours, an affidavit should not sound like ordinary speech, because ordinary speech will not serve the purpose. A spoken stream of consciousness leaves the critical hearer with an accumulation of further questions to ask; matters left incomplete and impressions not based on the speaker's words but on other forms of expression; tones of voice, significant pauses, nudges and winks. Few people have the self-discipline to pursue a statement of one matter completely before turning to [252] another. Almost everybody finds it very difficult to do what the courts require, and relate the terms of a statement or conversation rather than its effect produced on their own minds. Counsel must get the witness to face up to what took place, and say what took place; and then get that down, with clear expression, in words.

The witness's story must be told with circumstances so as to give the reader an impression that there has been a complete narration of the relevant facts. If the evidence is of a conversation, it must say when it took place, where it took place, and who was there. It must say what each of those present said, or whether they said nothing. It must say what they said, and not give the results in indirect speech. If the witness has an exact recollection he should set it out, but if he is speaking to the best of his recollection without a precise memory of the words used, he should say so. If he says he sent a letter, he should say how.

It will be obvious that counsel cannot take part in the preparation of an affidavit which is known to be untrue. The ethical considerations are sufficiently pressing, and there are also practical advantages of frankness in affidavits. A witness giving oral evidence is sworn to tell the truth, the whole truth and nothing else, and is then taken through his evidence without being asked questions which suggest the answer desired. Leading questions are disallowed for the purpose of improving the court's opportunity to assess the credibility of the evidence. By receiving affidavit evidence, the court loses this advantage. Those so minded would find omission and suppression of relevant parts of the narration easier in an affidavit, but the effect of revelations in cross-examination is amplified by this. The results are adverse not only to the witness, but also to the professional advisers associated with the affidavit. It is just as important to be frank as it is in any other communication to the court. A cynical proverb said 'Truth will out, even in an affidavit'. It would be very unfortunate to have this said of one's own draft.

But further, advocacy founded on evasion or concealment is poor policy; even if it wins one or two cases, you cannot build a career on it. You should bring your own difficulties forward before somebody else does; otherwise unmasking them will come to seem the real issue in the case. By mentioning them first you may even create disbelief in their importance.

If counsel needs to prove some further facts to meet an objection and make part of an affidavit admissible, he is in a far worse position than when leading oral evidence. One or two questions of the witness may clear it up, but the witness may not be there; and if he is called to give evidence about some small circumstances in the middle of a long narration, he will have [253] trouble bringing his mind to the point. The affidavit should contain all the facts needed to show the admissibility of matter in it, or they should have been proved earlier.

Evidence must show the witness's means of knowledge if it is to be any use. Affidavits often attempt to relate facts in terms which show that the facts result from, or are conclusions based on, a further body of facts or events. The manager of a company, who has given his address at an office in Sydney, says, 'On the first day of January 1983 the plaintiff company sold a black horse to the defendant for the agreed price of $500 and delivered the same to the defendant at his station property at Bourke'. This is more or less what the witness will tell you at the beginning of the conference, and he will want to say it in his affidavit, and he will believe that he knows it and can swear to it. It is inadmissible in evidence for a series of reasons. The means of knowledge are not shown; the statement that there was a sale is a conclusion (involving the application of legal rules) from a series of events, probably consisting of conversations which can only be proved by someone who participated in or heard the conversations. Similarly delivery is an event to be proved by the evidence of someone who saw it happen, or did it. Three or four witnesses might be required to give admissible evidence from which the above statement could be concluded. The evidence might be admitted without objection; if all the underlying facts are correct the opponent might accept the inadmissible evidence. In preparing the evidence, counsel must make some judgment about the need to pursue everything. It is unwise to object to all inadmissible evidence just because it is inadmissible; if the court later finds that time and trouble have been given to proving strictly something which is correct on anybody's view, the court will think its time has been wasted and this cannot help the objector.

Generally, the whole law of evidence applies to affidavits, but there is an important exception for hearsay in interlocutory applications. This exception is restated and extended by Part 36 r 4 of the Supreme Court Rules [New South Wales]. Evidence may be given on information and belief where the deponent states the source and ground of the information. This rule applies where undue delay and hardship would otherwise be caused (r 4(1)). It does not apply to evidence on an issue at a trial, in proceedings commenced by statement of claim; see r 4(4) and r 1. This rule is useful and necessary, for example, where an urgent application is made for an injunction. Otherwise it should be relied on with discretion. There is no rule that says that the court is bound to accept and act on evidence of information and belief, and there is not much point [254] in dodging the witness box by getting the solicitor to tell the client's story on information and belief. Reliance on this exception is best confined to cases of urgency and to evidence of matters which are most unlikely to be contentious.

Each court has its own rules affecting the form of affidavits. These seem unimportant until you get them wrong, so you should study the applicable Rules and Forms, and you should not assume that they are the same as those you know best. In the Supreme Court of the Australian Capital Territory, the date of an affidavit appears in the jurat, at the end. Similar forms were once in use in New South Wales. In the past affidavits were sometimes made in the third person. You should observe the requirements in Supreme Court Rules Parts 38 and 65 and Form 49. An affidavit is in the first person (Part 38 r 2(1)). It is divided into paragraphs numbered consecutively, each paragraph being as far as possible confined to a distinct portion of the subject (r 2(2)). Each page is to be signed by the deponent and by the person before whom he swears the affidavit (r 2(5)). Notice the second form under Form 49, with two deponents. This form has its uses, but they are rather limited. It is usually used where two executors are setting out the formal history of their having obtained probate, or having been appointed trustees and proving their accounts, or stating non-contentious facts about action they have both taken. In such an affidavit, if the point is reached where one of them speaks for himself and the other does not know the matter dealt with, a paragraph can commence: '16. I Richard Roe for myself say etc ...'. Then the next paragraph must commence: 'We John Doe and Richard Roe further say etc', or in some other way indicate that they are both speaking again. Obviously if there is to be much of this, it is better that each make an affidavit of his own.

Sometimes affidavits are drafted so as to adopt and affirm other affidavits. The witness says, 'I have read a copy of the affidavit of Richard Roe sworn herein on 1 January 1985 and I say that the facts set out therein are true and correct'. This is poor practice. The witness should give his own evidence, even if it involves typing out the same story again. Oath-helping and compurgation should stay in the past. On a strict view, what the witness says about whether another witness's evidence is true is irrelevant.

Where the witness refers to a document, the law of evidence about proof of the contents of a document applies. But in practice Part 36 r 4(3) and xerox copying greatly simplify matters. Original documents, or bulky bundles of copies should not be annexed; you will have trouble getting them back and the court does not want the whole bundle in its file. As far as possible, the convenient thing to do is to annex a photocopy of each relevant [255] document to the affidavit. In interlocutory proceedings, Part 36 r 4 will probably make the copy admissible. Annexures are usually marked in alphabetical series — A to Z and so on. Exhibits are usually marked numerically. But if you have six witnesses on affidavit you can end up with six documents marked 'Exhibit 1', so it is useful to include the witness's initials in the exhibit reference, and mark Richard Roe's exhibits 'RR1', 'RR2' etc. If he has sworn an earlier affidavit in the same case pick up the series where the last affidavit left off.

A few flowers of speech recur in affidavits. The court itself is referred to as 'this Honourable Court' although there would probably be no harm in dropping back to 'this Court' after the first time. A judge is referred to as 'the Honourable Mr Justice Doe'; 'the Honourable Justice Roe'; 'His Honour Judge Doe' or 'Her Honour Judge Roe', although once again 'Mr Justice Doe' will probably do after the first reference. The affidavit of a party in support of an application often concludes 'I respectfully ask that the Court make the following orders' (setting them out) and some flourish like this is probably worth leaving in. Also seen is a concluding paragraph, usually in the solicitor's affidavit: 'I respectfully submit that etc' followed by a series of propositions in support of the application. The evidence is not the right place for this kind of material, but it is a customary inclusion and it can be convenient.

An affidavit is not a pleading. Nor is it an opportunity to present an argument. Some traces of pleadings are often seen in affidavits, and they may be useful; for example, 'In answer to paragraph 99 of the plaintiff's affidavit I say etc ...'. It is useful to have something of this kind for cross-reference, but it does not change the nature of the document. Just because this form has been adopted does not mean that the deponent must deal with everything in the affidavit being replied to and say, for example, 'In answer to paragraph 98 of the said affidavit I do not know and cannot admit the facts there deposed'. It might be a relevant fact that the deponent did not know those facts but otherwise there is no need to tell the court about his ignorance; the use the court will make of the first affidavit will not be influenced by knowledge that the deponent to the second affidavit did not know the fact, so leave it out. Another trace of pleading which sometimes appears in affidavits is in the form of denials; for example, 'In answer to paragraph 97 of the said affidavit I deny that Richard Roe was present at the time of the conversation there referred to'. The meaning of this evidence would be clearer if the traces of pleading were not there, and the witness, instead of proceeding by a series of answers to another affidavit, had stated the relevant events, [256] including who was present, and at the conclusion had gone on to state, 'Richard Roe was not present during any part of this conversation'. By looking like a pleading, an affidavit may lose clarity. It can go further and become a disaster if it starts to say that facts in another affidavit are not admitted.

A common objection is that an affidavit is argumentative. This usually means that as well as stating the facts which are the foundation for an inference, the affidavit goes on to draw the inference, a process which should be left to the court.

Correct spelling and grammar are of great importance, because they concentrate the reader's attention on the substance, whereas errors create distractions. Sweet disorder delighted a whole flower-generation of English teachers, but it is rebarbative to classicists. You want the reader's mind to stay on the evidence and not go off to unspoken reflections on the decline in literacy of the junior bar, so adhere to precision and Fowler, and spare the Bench your gender neutrality.

The best way to learn the subject is to read many affidavits, and then to sit in court while affidavits with which you are familiar are read in evidence, objected to and ruled on. The same is true for pleadings, interrogatories, for briefs and the whole work of the Bar. It is not for nothing that pupil barristers are called Readers; reading your Master's briefs and following the cases in court is the heart of the matter.

15.5.5E   Affidavits

Justice John Bryson
(1999) 18 *Aust Bar Rev* 166

I tune my lyre to no noble theme, but to very ordinary requirements of the Rules of Court. I will take you to practical concerns for the good lawyer. I will not deal with any important principles or with anything the mastery of which is very flattering to the self. Some characteristics of the good lawyer are involved. The good lawyer will be altogether in command of the English language and the art of communication. Communication, persuasion and ready use of written and spoken language are at the heart of our profession, which is concerned to avoid and if need be adjust with skill the conflicts which arise from the social nature of humanity. You cannot be a lawyer on your own, and you must bring a ready grasp of language to bear on the process of communication if you are to achieve any result. Written communications which you produce should be fully and readily comprehensible, and should not present their recipients with difficulties or inefficiencies of understanding. A document produced by a lawyer ought to evince a full participation in the culture of literacy. It is not usually the place for slang, colourful idiom or technical language which is not in general use, although these may be required, and may have to be explained if used.

The good lawyer is economical with time, busy and assiduous, and governs behaviour with appropriate regard to the needs of others also to be busy and efficient with their time. Preparing affidavits offers opportunities to use and demonstrate your facility in communication and your efficiency, or alternatively an opportunity to demonstrate in a clear way and in a humiliatingly public way that you lack those qualities. The advocate in the court room and the office lawyer preparing the advocacy material are both engaged in the art of persuasion, and as part of that art in communicating the witness' evidence to the judge in a manner which is clear, authentic to the witness and readily absorbed by the judge, so as to attain the efficiency of adducing the evidence in chief quickly. The art of persuasion requires that art should conceal art; the information communicated should seem to be all that is involved; the process of communicating it should not claim attention. If your documents are inartistic the judge will be distracted from the process you wish to engage the judge in, that is, absorbing the relevant evidence, and the judge's mind will be led to pathways where you do not wish it to go, and to doubts, hesitations and impediments to comprehension produced by the crudity of the attempt to give information.

Although this is not my main theme, I will say that you should approach the preparation of an affidavit imbued with literary culture, with legal culture, and with a love of language. If you do not do a lot of general reading, and if you do not have a feeling for language well used, and for a well printed well bound book, your failings may come through in a document which you [167] produce. If you read nothing but newspapers and racebooks this will show up. If all your reading is hurried and careless you will not notice misprints and basic errors of grammar. If you have not troubled to find out what are basic errors of grammar and spelling, or have not troubled to learn how to compose a clear sentence, the documents you draft will be hard to follow. They will present the careful reader with incidental disruptions and uncertainties.

You are not however left to your own resources and literary culture unaided. You should absorb the legal culture around you, and be free of stilted and archaic expressions, and use language and style which have ready currency. You should recognise what is excessively formal, and what has become out of date legalese. You have access to many examples of other people's work and the affidavits they prepare. It would be a great advantage to you to read many, reflect on how comprehensible they are, and on what it is that any difficulties of comprehension arise from, and try to place yourself in the position of the reader who has not seen the document before, and who is proceeding, in some haste, to collect information from it. With illustrations from other people's mistakes, or it may be their successes, you will assist yourself to a style which is clear and complete and can be convincing. Experience in conducting litigation should show you how much of a subject needs to be stated, and in how much detail, where it would be incomplete to break off and where it would be excessive to go on. It is very poor advocacy to give part of a narration and engage the reader's attention with something that seems to be developing into a useful piece of evidence, and then to break off without completing it.

In this line of study it would be as well to observe other people conducting hearings in which they have to read out affidavits, and get a sense of the process of communication which takes place, the troubles that can arise if things are not well expressed, and how things go wrong. A pupil barrister should have opportunities over many months to see other people conducting cases with briefs which the pupil has already read, so that the material is quite familiar. Most people will find it difficult to create an opportunity like this, but observation of other people conducting hearings well and badly is always a useful form of self instruction.

I want to spend my time today however on less lofty themes.

If you want success as an advocate a very good start is to look and sound like an advocate, prepared and in charge of the material. This extends to the appearance of your written material, which should be and also should look like documents which are important enough to have a claim to attention. I will direct myself to the Rules of the Supreme Court dealing with affidavits, as that court is my own concern, but you must study the rules of the particular court or tribunal where you have business. Do not worry about whether they have been right in their choices: you must conform with whatever they have chosen. There are many minor variations in the rules as you go from court to court, and these seem irrelevant or ridiculous until you get them wrong. So check what you are about. The most minor detail and the least apparent infelicity can turn out to be wrong somewhere, and it is better not to be wrong. (*Some references to Federal Court Rules are in italics, and they may not be identical with the Supreme Court Rules on the same subject*).

The Supreme Court Rules say a great deal of the obvious on the subject of [168] affidavits. I will repeat much of the obvious. Much of it can be made to seem trivial, but it is not; it is important because it is the rule. If you affect a fine disregard of rules on small matters you may seem a very hollow advocate.

At the very beginning, an affidavit is on paper. The rules have something to tell you about the paper (Pt 65 r 2): of durable quality, capable of receiving ink writing, and measuring about 297 mm long and 210 mm wide (FC O 41 r 2). (The rules do not say that the paper is to be white, but it always is. Do not branch out.) Simple as this requirement is, from time to time it is neglected. People produce affidavits on flimsy paper, or on photographic paper from a facsimile machine; not durable because the imprint fades, and not capable of receiving ink writing because it spreads. There are some more elementary and obvious things in Pt 65 r 2. Although there are choices, for convenience the writing should be on one face of the paper only: r 2(3)(a). There should be a margin at least 25 mm on the left: r 2(3)(c). The annexures should have margins. All the pages should be consecutively numbered: r 2(3)(d). The document should be securely fastened: r 2(3)(b).

More obvious requirements would be hard to imagine, yet they are disregarded everyday, so it seems to me from my experience in court. Anyone who has ever read a book or studied anything should need no persuasion of the need to number the pages of an affidavit, and to carry the numbering system through all the annexures in one consecutive series. Yet every day affidavits appear in which this has not been done. Elementary acquaintance with the process of reading an affidavit in court, where several parties take part, several advocates have to follow the document, and the judge has to be referred to parts of it, shows how essential numbering is. I find myself being told that a letter is Annexure Q, that it is about 12 pages from the back of the affidavit, and sometimes it emerges that the copy of the affidavit given to the judge has page numbers on it, but that no one else in court has a copy with page numbers; or they have different numbers, and the numbering has no real utility. Another recurring failure is that an annexure itself has numbered pages within it, a contract with say 10 numbered pages, and an advocate causes exasperation by slipping from one series to the other. The advocate causes infuriation by referring to both.

Part 65 rule 2(5) requires 'The writing shall be clear, sharp, legible and permanent'. By r 2(6) a carbon copy shall not be filed, and r 2(7) forbids blotting, erasure and material disfigurement.

Obvious though these requirements may seem, they are often disregarded. The fast fading fax copy is not permanent. A fax impression is not clear and sharp nor is a Xeroxed affidavit. Faxed copies become festooned with inscriptions of their transmission, and the presence of one or several of these, top and bottom, some upside down, injures the impression the document produces. The inscriptions are not part of the affidavit, and they should not appear on its face. Give the court the best print, not a fax print, and not a fuzzy Xerox. An annexure (typically it is an annexure) which is a product of several successive photocopyings of copies may not be legible. If this has happened the remedy is not to apologise, nor is it to offer an extra piece of paper with a transcription, to complicate the file when it is lost; the remedy is to produce a legible annexure in the first place, perhaps by re-typing, perhaps by [169] bothering to find and copy the original. It is no great sacrifice to make this effort.

There is also a provision about the minimum space of 3 mm between the lines of writing: r 2(3).

Then there is an exception to r 2 where the nature of a document renders compliance impracticable: r 2(1).

The crown of my complaints on Pt 65 r 2 is the requirement that the document shall be securely fastened. What could be more obvious than that if an affidavit is to appear convincing it should appear to be in the form which it took when it was sworn. An affidavit held together by a bulldog clip or a slide fastener, or by the fingers, will immediately raise doubts as to its integrity. How can the reader be sure that this is the bundle of papers, and in this order, that the witness gave his oath to? Anyone with any acquaintance with literacy, or facility in the use of written material, or experience in handling paper must know that an important record which is to remain in the court file for an indefinite number of years cannot be clipped together with a bulldog clip, but for those who cannot perceive this the rules of court prescribe that it must be securely fastened.

By now I have made quite a burden of complaints but I have not gone further than one of the rules of court. There are many more. I make these observations with a strong sense of entitlement to be presented with documents which do comply with these careful but simple requirements, and can readily be employed in the trial, and in the incidental processes of maintaining permanent records.

Part 65 has more to tell and should be read. At the moment I note r 4 (*FCO 41 r 4*) (dates sums and other numbers shall be expressed in figures and not in words) and r 1 which states a lot of grossly obvious matters which must be set out on the first page of any document (*FCO 41 r 1, r 3*). This must be taken with Form 1 (*FCO F1 and F2*) which illustrates the identifying information in the left hand margin of the first page of each document. For a court and its registry where cases are commenced in thousands and documents are filed in hundreds of thousands, ready identification of a document is essential. Form 1 shows that for an affidavit the name of the deponent and the date of swearing appear in the left hand margin. Many people find this difficult, as the same information can be read on the right-hand side of the page. That does not mean that it is unimportant to put the accurate information in the left-hand margin where people will look for it when they use the file. It is frequent to omit the name of the deponent, and even more frequent to omit the date of swearing it. There are variations on the last failing, and these include to omit it in the body of the affidavit as well, and to give different dates at different places. Another variation is to leave the date unstated in the affidavit but to show it in an annexure note. Form 49 is a general form of affidavit and shows that the date is to appear at the beginning, that is on the first page (*FCO F 20*). Form 49 also includes some forms of jurats: the date does not appear there. Other courts have other practices with the date at the end, but we wish you to follow our practice.

In Form 1 the names of each and every party both to the claim and to all cross-claims appear in the left-hand margin. This can lead to ridiculous results where there are many parties, and also where there are many cross-claims.

I [170] have seen affidavits in which the left-hand margin of the first page filled two pages; every name was set out and then they were all set out again in different arrangements again and again to refer to several cross-claims. For an affidavit this should be avoided by following Pt 65 r 1(4), which for many documents including affidavits authorises an abbreviated title (*FCO 41 r 1(4)*). For example, if there are 35 plaintiffs they can be referred to as 'JOHN LEE and others' and there is no need to set out the names of each and every one of them in each and every affidavit. Similarly with defendants, and the fact that there are many cross-claims need not be recited all over again in every affidavit.

Part 38 deals with other requirements for affidavits. These include division into paragraphs for distinct portions of the subject: see r 2(2) (*FCO 14 r 2(2)*). A paragraph which extends over many pages, or is divided into a great number of subparagraphs, does not comply, and it is of no use for finding passages in the affidavit. An affidavit should be signed on each page, by the deponent and the person before whom it is sworn: r 2(5) (*FCO 14 r 2(6)*). There is a detailed prescription for attesting alterations and interlineations in r 2(3) (*FC O 14 r 3, O 14 r 4*). In a word processing age it is better not to have any.

Part 38 rule 4 deals with annexures and exhibits (*FCO 14 r 4*). The governing consideration is that the affidavit must be of manageable size, not over 50 pages (r 4(2)) so that unduly bulky documents do not find their way into a court file (*not in FCR*). An annexure to an affidavit stays with the affidavit permanently. We have a reasonably complete archive from 1823 to the present. If you ever wish to have your document back again it must be an exhibit. This is true of most original documents, including conveyances and letters, birth certificates or whatever else they are. Broadly speaking, originals are exhibits and annexures are copies (*FCO 14 r 4(1)*). The law of evidence limits the circumstances in which copies are admissible. Those circumstances must be in your mind as you prepare an affidavit, and I am speaking at too elementary a level to attend to them now.

Overall your affidavit including annexures must be of no more than 50 pages: Pt 38 r 4(2). A disadvantage of numerous annexures is that two persons must sign each page. The annexures must be included in the numbering sequence. Annexures must also be identified by a certificate on the annexure (and not on a separate page: see r 4(3)). A sheet containing nothing but a certificate about some document other than the sheet is of no value, generates costs and is forbidden: r 4(3). It is the practice to distinguish annexures by letters, but I see no reason for having more than one means of identification, and no reason for not identifying them by their page numbers (*FCO 14 r 2(2B)*). An exhibit however must be identified by an attached certificate: r 4(4) (*FCO 14 r 4(2)*). An exhibit does not form part of the affidavit and must not be filed, although it must be produced for inspection or a copy made available to the opponent: r 4(5) and (6). The solicitor not the court staff is responsible for the production of the exhibit at the hearing and for its safekeeping unless and until it is admitted in evidence.

Affidavits of service can be a grievous cause of useless bulk in files, as copies of the documents served are annexed to them, and if there are several almost all the rest of the file may appear three or four times over in annexures with more bulk than the papers which claim attention and at great expense of paper and money. It is not necessary, but wrong to annex a copy of each [171] affidavit served, with all its annexures, at a cost of so much a page, to each affidavit of service; a description of the affidavit is enough: see Pt 38 r 7A.

An affidavit must be made in the first person (r 2(1)) and it follows that it is in direct speech; oratio recta and not as in other times and in other States in oratio obliqua (*FCO 14 r 2(1)*). The true substance of what is going on is that the witness is giving evidence to the court: the lawyer is not doing so, and the lawyer is not reporting the witness's evidence. The use of hearsay is regulated by evidence law, restated at least in part by Pt 36 r 4 and Pt 3.2 of the Evidence Act 1995. It would seem that both these provisions remain in force and that either can be relied on to admit hearsay material: I have made rulings on this basis. Hearsay and affidavit evidence are different subjects: there is no special exception for hearsay if you prove it by affidavit.

There are provisions in r 2 about jurats, illiterate and blind persons and incidental matters. Care is needed with jurats for foreign language speakers (*FCO 14 r 2(3) to (5)*).

When you have prepared your affidavit you are not to keep it to yourself. You should file it and serve copies, and do these things in a timely way: rr 6, 7 (*FCO 14 rr 6, 7*). An affidavit is filed in the registry so that it will be available for the judge to read. Surprisingly often I am told that copies were served, but the affidavit was not filed. Then I am told it has been lost. The copy is served on the opponent so that the opponent may know in advance what evidence is to be given, whether it is to be objected to, cross-examined on or met by other evidence. By filing and serving timeously you minimize possible troubles for yourself which might arise from your opponent's right to do these things. Filing means filing in the registry. Filing documents in court is not what the judge and the advocate are in court to do: it takes time which should be used for activities of more value. The judge will find using time in this way very distasteful, whether or not any remark is made. Affidavits should be filed not less than two days before the hearing day, or if that is not practicable they may be filed in court: see Pt 38 r 6 (*FCO 14 r 6*). An added inconvenience of filing documents in court is the departure from the regular course in which the filing is duly recorded in the court's computer system. It is best to avoid creating these problems. When grudgingly given leave to file an affidavit in court hand up the affidavit itself, not a copy, and not three copies. It is a very sour moment when you give the judge something superfluous, which the judge will have to assess, recognise as superfluous and hand back, while time passes. Refer to an affidavit by its own date, not by its filing date: the judge does not want to know the filing date, and does not want to know both dates.

Of course copies must be served. There may be a number of parties with more or less interest in the evidence. Do not leave out some relatively less important opponents and concentrate only on the main source of difficulties. It is prudent, when you have the time, to check with your opponents several weeks before the hearing, see whether you are all working with the same list of affidavits and confirm which of them will be read. It is also wise to check who is required for cross-examination. A party is not obliged to produce a witness for cross-examination unless reasonable notice is given, and it is prudent that these notices should be confirmed in writing: r 9 (*FCO 14 r 9*).

If anything is persistent in the observations I have made it is the steady note of complaint. I suggest that you notice the sense of grievance which this [172] subject can create, and do your best not to incur the disadvantages of it. Make a small inner resolution that the next time someone appears in court with an affidavit on a torn and irregular piece of fax paper, lacking a date, unnumbered, not filed in the registry and not acceptable to the clerks there, and its date identifiable only by a fax inscription upside down at the top of the first page, that person is not yourself. Avoid follies. Find a middle way between loftily ignoring the rules of court and the form and appearance of things, and appearing to be obsessed with them. The flow of events should be that everything is in good order so good order does not have to be mentioned. Perhaps I am telling you to be obsessed with the rules of court but not to let it show, and that is the note on which I end.

TAKING AN AFFIDAVIT

15.6.1 Practitioners should ensure the appropriate oath is administered or affirmation made. A deponent is at liberty to take either an oath or an affirmation as they choose.

When swearing an affidavit, the person administering an oath should:

(a) ask the deponent 'are you AB?' if the deponent is not known to the person administering the oath;

(b) ensure AB has read and fully understood the contents of the affidavit; and

(c) inquire whether AB considers an oath to be binding on their conscience. The oath must bind the conscience of the deponent according to their religion: *English v Legal Practitioners Complaints Committee* (1986) 41 SASR 217 at 221. If uncertain have the affidavit affirmed;

(d) hand the Bible to AB and say 'Do you swear that the contents of this your affidavit are true and correct to the best of your knowledge and belief?'. AB should reply 'So help me God';

(e)   sign each page of the affidavit and annexures/exhibits together with the deponent; sign the jurat and date the affidavit and exhibits. Both should initial any alterations or interlineations. Erasures should be rewritten in the margin and initialled by both.

When affirming an affidavit, the person administering an affirmation should:

(a)   repeat the steps outlined above except that the deponent is not given anything;

(b)   say to AB: 'Is the affirmation that you are about to give binding on your conscience?'. AB answers: 'Yes';

(c)   say to AB: 'Do you solemnly, sincerely and truly declare and affirm that the contents of this your affidavit are true and correct to the best of your knowledge and belief?'. AB answers: 'Yes'.

In South Australia the appropriate words for an affirmation are 'do solemnly and truly declare and affirm': Evidence Act 1929 (SA) ss 6–9, r 162(11). South Australian r 162(3) additionally requires that the person making the statement certify to the authorised witness his or her honest belief in the truth of the contents of the statement. For the position in New South Wales, see ss 21–25 of the Evidence Act 1995 (NSW) and the Department of Attorney General and Justice, *Handbook for Justices of the Peace in New South Wales*, 4th ed, 2011, p 16.

In Western Australia, s 4 of the Oaths, Affidavits and Statutory Declarations Act 2005 (WA) states that the form of oath should begin with one of the following, according to the person's preference: (a) I swear by Almighty God ...; (b) I swear by [*name of a deity recognised by his or her religion*] ... ; (c) I swear, according to the religion and the beliefs I profess, ... Other variations are possible and the validity of the oath is unaffected if the person at the time of taking the oath has no religious belief. Section 5 provides for an affirmation as an alternative to an oath: I sincerely declare and affirm... . Section 7 specifies in detail how the oath or affirmation is administered.

Generally the word 'affirmed' should be used instead of 'sworn' where a deponent is making an affirmation. Other jurisdictions do not make the distinction; for example, s 36 of the Acts Interpretation Act 1954 (Qld) defines 'swear' to include 'affirm, declare, and promise'. In the Australian Capital Territory, r 6715 suggests the form of jurat be varied to conform with the solemn affirmation of the deponent.

A practitioner who witnesses an affidavit knowing it not to have been sworn or affirmed may be guilty of unprofessional conduct: see *English v Legal Practitioners Complaints Committee* (1986) 41 SASR 217. The requirement for the use of the Bible is lessening in some jurisdictions: see *McShane v Higgins* [1997] 2 Qd R 373, where it was held that it was unnecessary to physically touch the Bible when swearing an affidavit. All that was required was that the form of oath employed should be considered by the oath-taker as binding upon his or her conscience to speak the truth.

15.6.2C   **English v Legal Practitioners Complaints Committee**
(1986) 41 SASR 217
Supreme Court of South Australia

[A solicitor witnessed an affidavit by signing his name in the jurat that purportedly stated that the affidavit had been sworn before him, when in fact no oath had been administered.]

Johnston J (at 224): I should mention that the appellant's solicitor placed before the Tribunal evidence which if accepted suggested that it was not uncommon for other solicitors to 'take' affidavits in a way which at best could only be described as extremely sloppy and at worst as not resulting in the oath ever being administered by the person supposedly administering it, or the taking of it by the deponent. The making and taking of affidavits is a very frequent event and as we all know familiarity can breed contempt.

15.6.3   Johnston J drew attention to three important matters, which must be stressed:

(1)   if the oath is not properly administered, the swearers of affidavits will inevitably become slack in the checking of their affidavits and their veracity;

(2)   in order to make out a case of perjury in relation to an affidavit, the prosecution must establish that the oath was properly administered. If this is not done the charge fails, no matter how deliberately false the statement may have been;

(3)   an affidavit purporting to have been sworn but not in fact sworn is not evidence. See also A Wawn, 'Administering Oaths: There but for the Grace of God ...' (1989) 27(3) *LSJ* 28.

Jurat and signatures

15.6.4   A jurat is a section at the end of the affidavit that states:

(a)   the full name of the person making the affidavit (the deponent);

(b)   the place where the affidavit was taken;

(c)   the date that it was sworn or affirmed;

(d)   the name and title of the person before whom it was taken; and

(e)   in the event the deponent does not take an oath, a solemn affirmation or declaration.

High Court r 24.01.8 limits the jurat to (b), (c) and (d). Victoria (r 43.01(7)) and Queensland (r 432(3)(e)) also require a statement of the capacity in which the witness has authority to take the affidavit.

Corporations can only act through their agents. Affidavits may be sworn by a director, secretary, or other person duly authorised by the body corporate to make an affidavit on its behalf. There is no equivalent provision in the other jurisdictions, though the practice is the same. The form of the jurat varies according to whether the affidavit is sworn or affirmed, made by multiple deponents, by illiterate or blind deponents, or by deponents unable to understand English.

15.6.5   New South Wales r 35.3 has very detailed rules concerning affidavits made by parties in different capacities:

35.3 Persons who may make affidavit
(cf. SCR Part 24, rule 2; DCR Part 22A, rule 7)

(1)   If a party is required by these rules to file an affidavit or to verify any matter by affidavit, such an affidavit may be made by the party or:

     (a)   if the party is a person under legal incapacity, by the party's tutor, or

     (b)   if the party is a corporation, by a member or officer of the corporation or (if it is in liquidation) by its liquidator, or

     (c)   if the party is a body of persons lawfully suing or being sued:

         (i)   in the name of the body, or

         (ii)   in the name of any member or officer of the body, or

         (iii)   in the name of any other person associated with the body, by a member or officer of the body, or

     (d)   if the party is the Crown or an officer of the Crown suing or being sued in his or her official capacity, by an officer of the Crown, or

     (e)   if the proceedings are being brought in the plaintiff's name by some other person pursuant to a right of subrogation:

         (i)   by that other person, or

         (ii)   if that other person is a corporation, by a member or officer of the corporation or (if it is in liquidation) by its liquidator.

Section 3(1) of the Civil Procedure Act 2005 (NSW) defines a 'person under legal capacity'.

15.6.6E   **Queensland Standard Jurat***

At the end of the body of the affidavit:
Sworn [or Affirmed] by (full name) on (date) at (place) in the presence of:

    (Signed by deponent)   (Signed by person taking affidavit)
    Deponent   (Statement of capacity to take affidavit)

who certifies that the affidavit was read in the presence of the deponent who seemed to understand it, and signified that that person made the affidavit. (If required: See R 433(1)) [who certifies that the affidavit was read or otherwise communicated in the presence of the deponent who seemed to understand it, and signified that that person made the affidavit, but was physically incapable of signing it. (If required: see R 433(2))

[*Reproduced from A West, 'Affidavits', *Court Form Precedents and Pleadings Queensland*, LexisNexis, Sydney, looseleaf.]

15.6.7   The jurat should contain the full details of multiple deponents. Where all deponents swear, affirm, or declare the affidavit before the same person instead of repeating the standard jurat, it is permissible to state sworn by 'both of the above-named deponents', 'all the above-named' deponents, or 'each of the above-named deponents'. See generally ACT r 6715; NT r 43.04; Qld r 432(4); Tas r 504; Vic r 43.04; WA O 37 r 3. Irregularities in the jurat cannot be waived: *Pilkington v Himsworth* (1835) 5 LJ Ex Eq 47.

15.6.8   Where a deponent is illiterate or blind, the person before whom the affidavit is made is required to certify in or below the jurat that:

(a) the affidavit was read in the deponent's presence;

(b) that the deponent seemed to understand, comprehend and approve it;

(c) the deponent made his or her mark in the presence of that person; and

(d) where the deponent is incapable of signing, there is an additional requirement that the deponent signify he or she swore the affidavit.

All these requirements are necessary before the affidavit can be used in evidence. See generally: HCR r 24.01.12 (attest); FCR r 29.04; ACT r 6716; NSW r 35.7; NT r 43.02; Qld r 433; SA r 162(7); Tas r 503(1); Vic r 43.02; Oaths, Affidavits and Statutory Declarations Act 2005 (WA) s 13.

15.6.9 Where it appears to the person before whom an affidavit is taken (the taker) that the deponent is unable to understand the affidavit when read in English the taker certifies in or below the jurat that an interpreter, whose name and address is stated in the certificate, swore, affirmed or declared before him or her that:

(a) he or she in the presence of the taker interpreted to the deponent the contents of the affidavit;

(b) the deponent seemed to understand it;

(c) he or she had interpreted to the deponent the oath, affirmation or declaration; and

(d) the deponent had sworn, affirmed or declared that the contents of the affidavit so interpreted to him or her were true.

See ACT r 6716; SA r 162(8), (where the interpreter's qualifications must also be set out in a certificate attached to the affidavit); and Oaths, Affidavits and Statutory Declarations Act 2005 (WA) s 14. A similar practice has developed in the other jurisdictions, despite the fact that there is no equivalent rule.

Courts have a discretion as to whether to allow a witness to give evidence through an interpreter. When a witness is more fluent in a language other than English the discretion to allow the affidavit in a foreign language will more likely be exercised: *Filios v Morland* [1963] SR(NSW) 331; *Dairy Farmers Co-operative Milk Co Ltd v Acquilina* (1963) 109 CLR 458. Affidavits can either be in a foreign language under various Evidence Acts (for example, Evidence Act 1929 (SA) s 14(2) (extracted below)) or in English after being sworn to via an interpreter: ACT r 6716; SA r 162(8) (accompanying certificate); Oaths, Affidavits and Statutory Declarations Act 2005 (WA) s 14.

Courts have a discretion as to whether to allow an affidavit in a foreign language. In the event that such an affidavit is allowed, it should be accompanied by a translation verified on oath by an interpreter: *Re Pakuza* [1975] Qd R 141 at 144–5. In South Australia, s 14(2) of the Evidence Act 1929 (SA) provides:

An affidavit or other written deposition in a language other than English shall be received in evidence in the same circumstances as an affidavit or other written deposition in English if it has annexed to it —

(a) a translation of its contents into English; and

(b) an affidavit by the translator to the effect that the translation accurately reproduces in English the contents of the original.

15.6.10 Affidavits require several signatures. Affidavits:

(a) are signed by the person making it (the deponent) in the presence of the person taking the affidavit, unless the deponent is incapable of signing;

　　(b)　have the jurat completed and signed by the person before whom the affidavit was taken; and

　　(c)　have each page signed by the deponent and the person before whom it is sworn: FCR r 29.02(7); Qld r 432(1); SA Practice Direction 3.1 — Contents of Affidavits 3.1.3.

In the High Court (r 24.01.11), Tasmania (r 501(g)) and Victoria (r 43.01(6)), the deponent's signature is not required on each separate sheet. South Australia (Practice Direction 3.1.3 — Contents of Affidavits 3) additionally requires each page to bear the date upon which it was sworn. In Western Australia, s 15 of the Oaths, Affidavits and Statutory Declarations Act 2005 (WA) prohibits the use of rubber stamps to make the person's signature or personal mark in an affidavit. Such affidavits are inadmissible.

Witness

15.6.11　The person witnessing an affidavit should not permit it to be sworn or affirmed if he or she has reason to believe that the deponent:

　　(a)　has insufficient mental capacity to understand the contents of the affidavit;

　　(b)　has insufficient mental capacity to understand the nature of an oath or affirmation;

　　(c)　has not properly acquainted himself or herself with the contents of the affidavit; or

　　(d)　has created an affidavit illegal in any part.

See generally *Bourke v Davis* (1889) 44 Ch D 110 at 126.

15.6.12　The categories of persons having authority to administer an oath or affirmation and to take and receive an affidavit vary between the jurisdictions. The statutory authority in each case is typically found in that jurisdiction's Evidence Act, Oaths Act or, sometimes, Rules of Court: for example, HCR r 24.01.7 (Note: Judicial notice of seal or signature: r 24.01.9); Evidence Act 1995 (Cth) s 186; Oaths Act 1867 (Qld) s 41(1); SA r 163(1); Tas rr 511, 512; Evidence Act 1958 (Vic) s 123C; Oaths Affidavits and Statutory Declarations Act 2005 (WA), Practice Direction No 1 of 2006. Categories of persons commonly permitted include court officers: judges, registrars, notaries, justices of the peace and lawyers. Other persons may also be approved by statute. For example, ss 2 and 2 A of the Evidence (Affidavits) Act 1928 (SA) empower justices of the peace and police officers. The statutes also prescribe the persons who may attest affidavits sworn outside the jurisdiction. Typically this would include Australian consular officers and any person having authority to administer an oath in that foreign place. In Western Australia only 'authorised witnesses' can witness an affidavit, see s 9 of the Oaths, Affidavits and Statutory Declarations Act 2005 (WA) and Supreme Court WA Practice Direction 1.2.4 Taking Affidavits. Authorised witnesses include a justice of the peace, an experienced lawyer, a notary public, registrar or clerk of a court.

In some jurisdictions there are limitations upon whether a party's solicitor may take an affidavit. The English rule that an affidavit sworn before the party (including the party's solicitors, agents, correspondents or employees including those of the solicitor but excluding the Crown and its employees) on whose behalf it is to be used cannot be used without leave applies in the Northern Territory: r 43.10. In South Australia (r 163(2)) and Tasmania (r 511(1)(k)), the English rule applies except that an affidavit may be taken by a party's solicitor.

In Queensland the court may not receive and a party may not file, an affidavit taken by a party personally: r 441.

High Court r 24.01.10 is very restrictive:

An affidavit sworn before:
(a) a party;
(b) a partner in a firm which is a party; or
(c) an employee of a party other than a body politic;
shall not be used in evidence by or on behalf of the party.

15.6.13 Affidavits sworn in a foreign country may generally be sworn before any person having authority to administer oaths in that country. See also Oaths Act 1900 (NSW) s 26; Australian Consular Officers' Notarial Powers and Evidence Act 1946 (Qld); Evidence Act 1929 (SA) s 66; Tas r 512(1)(b); Evidence Act 1958 (Vic) s 124; Evidence Act 1906 (WA) s 62 (documents admissible in Her Majesty's dominions), s 104A. There are no equivalent provisions in the other jurisdictions.

ANNEXURES, SCHEDULES AND EXHIBITS

15.7.1   An exhibit is a document received in evidence when tendered by one of the parties to a case. An annexure is an additional document attached or appended to an affidavit. A schedule is an additional document attached or appended to an affidavit containing matters subsidiary to the main purpose of the affidavit but which can more conveniently be set out in tabular form: see *Butterworths Australian Legal Dictionary*, Sydney, 1997.

In Queensland, the distinctions have become blurred — r 435(1) provides that a document to be used with and mentioned in an affidavit is an exhibit.

15.7.2   In some jurisdictions documents should be annexed to the affidavit where convenient or otherwise made an exhibit: ACT r 6712; NT 43.06(1), (2), PD No 3 of 2009; WA O 37 rr 3, 9. In these jurisdictions exhibits are referred to but not filed with nor affixed to the affidavit. Original documents are generally exhibited; copies are annexed. Annexures are affixed to and form part of an affidavit. They are filed and served with the affidavit. In other jurisdictions documents and other objects and things are exhibited, not annexed: HCR r 24.01.13; FCR r 29.02; Qld r 435(2); SA r 162(5); Tas r 501; Vic r 43.06(1). In New South Wales (r 35.6), a document used in conjunction with an affidavit may be either an annexure or exhibit. In practice, bulky documents are exhibited, not annexed.

As an alternative to making a document an annexure or exhibit, the relevant portion of the document may be included in the body of the affidavit provided the document is available for production.

Exhibits are identified by a certificate of the person before whom the affidavit is taken and the certificate is generally titled in the same manner as the affidavit: HCR r 24.01.14; FCR r 29.02(8); ACT r 6712; NSW r 35.6; NT r 43.06; Qld r 435(5)–(7); SA r 162(5) (the exhibit is marked in a way that clearly identifies it as the exhibit referred to in the affidavit); Tas r 501(h); Vic r 43.06(2), (3); WA O 37 r 9. Exhibits are filed with the affidavit, but not actually affixed to it: HCR r 24.01.13; Qld r 435(8).

Copies of exhibits or annexures are generally served with the affidavit (FCR r 29.05; elsewhere this is the practice), omission of which may create an irregularity: *Elder's Trustee and Executor Co Ltd v Sach* [1944] SASR 65; see also **15.9.1**. In the event that an exhibit cannot be copied it may be inspected: *Re Hinchcliffe* [1895] 1 Ch 117 at 120. In Western Australia,

O 37 r 2(7) requires that an index listing the affidavit, annexures and respective page numbers must be bound with the affidavit. Queensland r 435(10) requires documents to be presented in a way that will facilitate the courts' efficient and expeditious reference to them. There are no equivalent rules in the other jurisdictions.

In South Australia, r 162(6) provides that the registrar may on application of the party filing an affidavit direct a solicitor to hold an exhibit too large to be filed. There are no equivalent provisions in other jurisdictions.

15.7.3   Exhibits are numbered consecutively in the sequence determined by the body of the affidavit. A convenient practice is to number exhibits with the initials of the deponent followed by a number: 'SEC1', 'SEC2' and so on. Subsequent affidavits by the same deponent continue the exhibit numbering, that is, 'SEC3' and so on.
High Court r 24.01.15 provides:

> The certificate attached to each exhibit to an affidavit shall bear a distinguishing mark for the exhibit and a brief and specific description of the exhibit.

Federal Court r 29.02(6)–(11) provides:

(6)   Each page, including any annexure, must be clearly and consecutively numbered starting with page '1'.
(7)   Each page of the affidavit (but not any annexure) must be signed by the deponent (other than a deponent who is unable to sign the affidavit because of a physical disability) and by the person before whom it is sworn.
(8)   Each annexure and exhibit must be identified on its first page by a certificate entitled in the same manner as the affidavit and by the deponent's initials followed by a number (starting with '1' for the first annexure or exhibit).
(9)   The annexures and exhibits must be numbered sequentially.
(10)   No subsequent annexure or exhibit in any later affidavit sworn by the same deponent may duplicate the number of a previous annexure or exhibit.
(11)   Each exhibit to an affidavit must be signed on the first page of the exhibit by the person before whom the affidavit is sworn.

15.7.4   It is necessary to produce the original document if requested. Should an affidavit contain a reference to any other document, the opponent is entitled to require production of the document and is permitted to take a copy. Failure to comply with this request prevents the affidavit being used as evidence without leave. It is permissible to exhibit foreign language documents and translations: *Re Pakuza* [1975] Qd R 141 at 145.

FILING

15.8.1   Original affidavits are required to be filed, otherwise they may not be used without leave of the court: HCR rr 1.07.3, 2.02; FCR r 29.07; ACT r 6718; NSW r 35.9; NT r 43.09; Qld r 437; SA r 167 (interlocutory); Tas r 510; Vic r 43.09; WA O 37 r 13. Affidavits may be filed notwithstanding any irregularity as to their form: see **15.16.1**. Courts have complete jurisdiction over their own records, and may order affidavits to be taken off the file and destroyed or retained on file but not open to inspection without an order: *R v Collins* [1954] VLR 46. The general rule is that an affidavit remains on the court file until ordered to be removed.

Some jurisdictions have specialised rules relating to filing affidavits. Where a special time is limited for filing affidavits, an affidavit filed after that time shall not be used except with leave of the court: WA O 37 r 14. In Sydney, where practicable, an affidavit should be filed in the registry not less than two days before the court hearing (the date the matter is to be heard and the name of the judge, if known, should be indorsed). If less than the two days, the affidavit should be filed in court: NSW r 35.9. Practice Note No SC Gen 4 2005 (17 August 2005, NSW) states that affidavits may not be filed without leave of the court. Further, where a matter is for hearing, the party seeking to rely upon documents at the hearing must deliver not later than 48 hours prior to the hearing date a 'tender bundle' to the chambers of the presiding judicial officer. In South Australia, r 167 requires affidavits to be filed and delivered to all other parties two clear days before the occasion for using it arises. In the Federal Court r 5.04 enables directions to be given as to the filing of affidavits.

In Tasmania, r 510 specifies a period of at least 48 hours. There are no equivalent provisions elsewhere. In Tasmania, r 507 requires an affidavit to be filed in the registry in which the relevant proceeding is pending or is to be instituted.

Filing and service of affidavits and associated annexures or exhibits are conditions precedent to their becoming evidence, subject to rulings on admissibility or any order of dispensation. 'An affidavit which has been placed on the file does not become part of the proceedings until it is opened to the court': *Barristers' Board of Western Australia v Tranter Corp Pty Ltd* [1976] WAR 65 at 67; *Manson v Ponninghaus* [1911] VLR 239.

In Queensland, r 435(12) provides that if a document or thing has been filed, subsequent affidavits are to refer to and identify the document or thing, but not make it an exhibit to the affidavit.

SERVICE

15.9.1 A party intending to use an affidavit must serve or deliver a copy on the other party within a reasonable time before the hearing: FCR r 29.08; Evidence Act 1995 (Cth) s 173(1); ACT r 6718; NSW r 10.2; NT r 46.05; SA r 167 (two days); Tas r 510 (48 hours); Vic r 46.05; WA O 58 r 19(2) (14 days). Exceptions arise with respect to:

(a) *ex parte* applications;

(b) where a court otherwise directs;

(c) particular applications where set times are fixed: see **15.8.1**;

(d) previously read affidavits; and

(e) urgency.

Reasonable time is not defined but would be considered in the context of the urgency of the application, the date the affidavit was served, the length of the affidavit, the contents of the affidavit, and the extent of knowledge of the party required to respond to the affidavit.

In Tasmania (r 510(3), (4)), there is a special provision under which an adjournment may be granted where a party has not had the opportunity or sufficient time to file and serve an answering affidavit or an affidavit in reply. The opposite party should be given enough time to answer on affidavit a contested matter raised in an opponent's affidavit prior to the hearing.

In Queensland, r 438 gives the court discretion to grant leave to use an affidavit that has not been served, or served later than the time specified in the rules.

Rule 35.8 of the New South Wales Rules of Court provides simplified procedures to prove service of an affidavit. There are no equivalent provisions in the other jurisdictions.

TIMING

15.10.1 An affidavit for use in a proceeding may be taken before or after commencement of the proceeding: FCR r 29.01; ACT r 6714; NT r 43.07 (before — with leave); SA r 162(10); Tas r 507; Vic r 43.07. This rule was created to overcome the historical position that prosecutions for perjury could only be brought if proceedings were on foot in the court. There is no equivalent provision in the other jurisdictions.

CROSS-EXAMINATION

15.11.1 A party may require the attendance for cross-examination of a person making an affidavit on behalf of another party, by service of a notice: FCR r 29.09(1), (2); ACT r 6721; NSW r 35.2; NT r 40.04; Qld r 439(2); SA r 165(1) (court order required); Tas r 463; Vic r 40.04; WA O 36 r 2 (court order required); Evidence Act 1995 (Cth) s 173(2) (request). The deponent is not served. Service is effected on the party on whose behalf the affidavit was filed.

Courts have a discretion as to whether or not to allow cross-examination: *Southern Cross Commodities Ltd v Martin* (1985) 123 LSJS 480, (1986) 126 LSJS 306 (FC). Cross-examination as to any matter in issue or relevant to the issues and as to credit may be allowed: *Muir v Harper* (1900) 25 VLR 534; *Keogh v Dalgety & Co Ltd* (1917) 17 SR (NSW) 573; (1992) 66 *ALJ* 299; *Saunders v Hammond* (1965) QWN 39. Tactically it is necessary to consider whether the witness can give evidence concerning the deposed facts and whether they are capable of handling cross-examination.

It is rare for a court to exercise its discretion to allow cross-examination on an interlocutory application, particularly where the delay and expense of cross-examination may be unwarranted and prevent justice being done: *Scanlon v American Cigarette Co (Overseas) Pty Ltd (No 1)* [1987] VR 261.

In the event that cross-examination is permitted, failure by the deponent to attend for cross-examination prevents the affidavit being used without leave of the court: FCR r 29.09; ACT r 6721; NSW r 35.2 (or if the deponent is dead); NT r 40.04(3) (the court may order that an affidavit not be received into evidence); Qld r 439(4) (the court may refuse to receive the affidavit into evidence); SA r 165(2); Tas rr 463, 466 (the court may also exempt a deponent from attending); Vic r 40.04(3) (the court may order that an affidavit not be received into evidence); WA O 36 r 2. In some jurisdictions, the Rules of Court specifically provide that the court may compel a person to attend for cross-examination on an affidavit: ACT r 6721; Qld r 439(1); SA r 165(1). There are no equivalent provisions in the other jurisdictions. South Australia and Tasmania have provisions enabling the court to order that a person who refuses to make an affidavit be examined: SA r 166; Tas rr 472–473. In the Federal Court (r 29.09(4)), the Australian Capital Territory (r 6721), New South Wales (r 35.2) and South Australia (r 165(3)), a deponent who has been cross-examined may be re-examined by the party using the affidavit.

The court in the exercise of its discretion may reject the affidavit, admit it, or give limited weight to it: *Re O'Brien* [1923] 1 SASR 411; *Re Constantine* [1947] SASR 415. With respect to deceased or mentally ill deponents, the issue is one of weight: *Curley v Duff* (1985) 2 NSWLR 716.

In Re *O'Neil (dec'd)* [1972] VR 327 at 333 it was held:

> In cases where affidavits are challenged ... and the deponent is not available for cross-examination, the affidavit may either be rejected, or, if it is received, only slight weight may be given to its contents. ...

In principle, there seems to be no difference between the non-availability of a deponent for cross-examination due to wilful absence and non-availability due to death or illness. It will depend on the particular circumstances including the nature of the proceedings whether such an affidavit will be rejected or if admitted the weight to be given to it.

SCANDALOUS AND IRRELEVANT

15.12.1 Superior courts possess both inherent jurisdiction (*Rossage v Rossage* [1960] 1 All ER 600) and statutory power to strike out scandalous and irrelevant materials on their own motion, on application of a party, or on application of any person with a sufficient interest: see *Cayron v Russell* (1897) 23 VLR 399.

In *Legal Practice Board v Said* (unreported, SC (WA), Seaman J, No 2656 of 1991, 12 January 1994, BC9401499) it was said:

> Scandal consists in the allegation of anything which is unbecoming to the dignity of the court to hear or is contrary to good manners or which charges some person with a crime not necessary to be shown in the cause: to which may be added that any unnecessary (not relevant to the subject) allegation bearing cruelly upon the moral character of an individual is also scandalous.

As to public interest immunity, see *R v Governor of Brixton Prison; ex parte Osmon (No 1)* [1992] 1 All ER 108.

In New South Wales (r 4.15), the Northern Territory (r 27.07), Queensland (r 440); South Australia (r 164), Victoria (r 27.07), and Western Australia (O 37 r 7), a scandalous, irrelevant or oppressive affidavit may be taken off the court file, and in Queensland destroyed, or the offending portion struck out. In South Australia 'oppressive' has been replaced with the phrase 'an abuse of the process of the court'. In the Australian Capital Territory, r 6720 is as broad as the former jurisdictions except that the term 'offensive' is used in addition. The High Court (r 6.05) provision is restricted to scandalous matter, which may be struck out; in the Federal Court (rr 6.01, 29.03) only scandalous or oppressive affidavits may be taken off the court file. In Tasmania (r 508) the rule is limited to scandalous material, which may be struck out or removed from the file.

A relevant matter will not usually be struck out because it is also scandalous. It needs to be both scandalous and irrelevant to be struck out: see *Cayron v Russell* (1897) 23 VLR 399; *Rossage v Rossage* [1960] 1 All ER 600. Clearly irrelevant material is inadmissible in any case. A high proportion of scandalous and irrelevant matter may result in an order removing the affidavit from the court file: *Rossage v Rossage* [1960] 1 All ER 600. Affidavits containing matters, which would tend to prejudice, embarrass or delay a fair trial of an action may also amount to an abuse of process.

In South Australia (r 13) the rules provide that the solicitor filing an affidavit offending against the above rules may be liable for the costs. The costs of an affidavit containing scandalous and irrelevant matter will be disallowed on taxation: see *Slack v Burt* (1862) 1 QSCR 50; *Raven v Cleveland Divisional Board* (1894) 6 *QLJ* 67; *Whyte v Whyte* (1906) 23 WN (NSW) 85. In Tasmania, the costs of an application to strike out scandalous material are allowed on a higher costs scale: Tas r 508(2) (practitioner and client).

What then is the effect of striking out material from an affidavit? Courts have complete control over their own records and may order affidavits to be taken off the file and copies of them destroyed and restrain the parties' use of the contents of the affidavit: see *R v Collins* [1954] VLR 46. On one view, striking out affidavit material maintains the court record eliminating the necessity for responsive affidavits and overburdening the judge with irrelevancies: *Savings & Investment Bank Ltd v Gasco Investments (Netherlands) BV* [1984] 1 WLR 271 at 278; *Avery v Worldwide Testing Services Pty Ltd* (1990) 2 ACSR 834 at 839. On the other hand, in *Jones v Trinder, Capron & Co* (1918) 2 Ch 7 at 11 it was said:

> I think that an order taking affidavits off the file for the purposes of destruction has the effect of destroying a public record of certain statements, and I think that it goes further and renders those statements no longer privileged. But I do not think that it extends to making it an illegal act to repeat or disseminate copies of the affidavits that have been removed from the file.

15.12.2   Questions

1. Are the following scandalous or irrelevant?
   (a) the director of a plaintiff company making unfounded assertions (*Re A Pty Ltd v B* [1962] QWN 35, where such an affidavit was ordered to be taken off the court file);
   (b) in a claim for breach of promise, a statement that the plaintiff had 'permitted the defendant to debauch and carnally know her, whereby the defendant infected her with venereal disease': see *Millington v Loring* (1880) 6 QBD 190 (CA), where the facts were properly pleadable and were not scandalous nor tending to prejudice or embarrass the fair trial of the action.

2. Do you think a court file should remain complete despite the presence of scandalous material in affidavits?

USE OF AFFIDAVITS

Use of an earlier affidavit

15.13.1   Affidavits on file may be used subsequently in the same proceeding, though for a different purpose: NT r 40.11; Tas r 471; Vic r 40.11. In some jurisdictions, affidavits filed in one proceeding may be used in other proceedings with notice: ACT r 6702; WA O 36 r 10. In these jurisdictions leave is required if the second proceeding is an *ex parte* application. In the Federal Court (r 30.25), New South Wales (r 31.9), and Queensland (r 395) leave is required for use of an affidavit in another proceeding or use of an earlier affidavit in the same proceeding. There are no equivalent provisions in the other jurisdictions.

Evidential use of an affidavit

15.13.2 'Evidence is led by affidavit, not merely by filing the affidavit, but by reading it to the court': *Barristers' Board of Western Australia v Tranter Corp Pty Ltd* [1976] WAR 65 at 67 per Brinsden J; *Manson v Ponninghaus* [1911] VLR 239; FC Practice Note No 5, 1994. See also 15.2.1.

Use of an opponent's affidavit

15.13.3 The filing of an affidavit makes it available for use by an opponent, even if it was not read by the opponent or is used in another application in the same proceedings: *Muirfield Properties Pty Ltd v Kolle* [1988] VR 167. See also Shaw J, 'The Use of One Party's Affidavit by an Opponent' [1985] ACLD 36055. Extracts of an opponent's affidavit may be used, without putting the whole of the affidavit into evidence: see *Barristers' Board of Western Australia v Tranter Corp Pty Ltd* [1976] WAR 65 at 67; T Mehigan 'Practice Note Using an Opponent's Affidavit' (1986) 2 *Aust Bar Rev* 279. It is essential that an affidavit is confined to the points in issue and that the affidavit contains no inconsistencies or inaccuracies. The affidavit should be consistent with the overall case, for otherwise that deponent/witness will lose credibility.

In drafting an affidavit in reply, it should be stated that reference is being made to the opponent's affidavit, together with the paragraph in that affidavit which is being addressed. Each item that is being contested should be dealt with: for example, 'I refer to the affidavit of ABC dated …'.

15.13.4   Notes and questions

1. Can an affidavit filed in one action be admitted in another proceeding where one or both parties appear in both proceedings? See 15.13.1.
2. Affidavits are either filed in the court registry or by leave with the judge in court. An affidavit is 'read' to the court by stating the words: 'I read the affidavit of Smith.' This process signifies reliance on the evidence contained in the affidavit in support of an argument. On occasion, both processes are combined, for example: 'I seek leave to read and file the affidavit of Smith.'

ALTERATIONS, ERASURES AND WITHDRAWAL

15.14.1   An affidavit which has in the jurat or its body an interlineation, erasure or other alteration, may be filed but cannot be used without leave except where the alteration is authenticated by the signature or initials of the person taking the affidavit prior to the affidavit being sworn: FCR r 29.07; ACT rr 6107, 6717; NSW r 35.5; NT 43.05; Qld r 434; Tas r 505; Vic r 43.05. The rationale of the rule is to prevent alteration to sworn affidavits. Where there is no reason to expect impropriety, alterations which are not initialled may be accepted by the court: *Jansen v Beaney* (1878) 4 VLR (L) 167 (FC) (which dealt with uninitialled interlineations made before the affidavit was sworn. An affidavit may be filed where the interlineation was made after the affidavit was sworn); see also *In the Estate of Robert Orr-Edwards (dec'd)* (1900)

25 VLR 612. The rules apply to all interlineations, erasures or alterations whether material or otherwise.

In New South Wales (r 35.5) and Tasmanian (r 505) courts, a distinction is drawn between an erasure and an interlineation or alteration. In the case of an erasure, the person before whom the affidavit is sworn is required to rewrite in the margin of the affidavit any words or figures written on the erasure and sign or initial them.

Alterations to a sworn affidavit will require the affidavit to be resworn or reaffirmed: *Re a Barrister and Solicitor* (1984) 58 ACTR 1. While the oath or affirmation remains the same, a new jurat will be required:

Re-sworn/re-affirmed by the deponent at this day of 20 before me.

The re-swearing does not have to occur in the presence of the person before whom the affidavit was originally sworn. It is not necessary for the deponent to sign the affidavit again for re-swearing. The alteration should be initialled by the person before whom the re-swearing occurs: *Jansen v Beaney* (1878) 4 VLR (L) 167 (FC).

Once an affidavit is filed, errors can only be corrected by filing a further affidavit explaining and correcting the error.

In South Australia, r 162(4) provides that the contents of an affidavit cannot be altered after it has been certified. This does not prevent the making of a later affidavit drawing attention to the error contained in the earlier affidavit. The provisions in the Western Australian rules were repealed without replacement in 2006.

15.14.2   Question

1. Is it necessary for the person making, as distinct from taking, the affidavit, to initial an alteration or erasure?

TRIAL BY AFFIDAVIT

15.15.1   In all jurisdictions, except the High Court, there are specific rules permitting trial by affidavit. Trial by affidavit is a convenient procedural method where evidence is not contested or a witness is unavailable. Trial in this manner is inconvenient where there are substantial issues of credit: *Bonhote v Henderson* [1895] 1 Ch 742. Hearsay is inadmissible in trial affidavits unless permitted by an exception to the hearsay rule: see 15.3.1.

In South Australia, the parties may agree, or the court on its own initiative or on application by a party, may order that a trial proceed on the basis of affidavits rather than oral evidence: r 168. The South Australian rules specifically provide for reception of certain evidence at trial by way of affidavit or expert report: rr 169, 216. Cross-examination is permitted on notice: r 170.

In the Australian Capital Territory, unless the court otherwise orders, the parties to an originating claim may agree that evidence at the trial be given by affidavit: r 6701.

In Victoria and the Northern Territory, subject to an Act, the Rules or an agreement between the parties to the contrary, a trial of a proceeding commenced by originating motion is by affidavit (rr 40.02(c), 45.02(1)), whereas trial of a proceeding commenced by writ is by oral testimony: r 40.02(b). However, notwithstanding r 40.02, a court may order that evidence be given by affidavit at the trial of a proceeding commenced by writ. The court can order a deponent to attend for examination: rr 40.03(3), 40.04. Another party can also by notice require attendance of a deponent at trial for examination: r 40.04(2). If the deponent fails to comply with the order or notice and does not attend for examination, the court may order that the affidavit not be received into evidence: r 40.04(3).

The Federal Court may order, or the parties may agree, that evidence of particular facts be given by affidavit: r 5.04. In New South Wales the court may order that all or any of a witness' evidence at trial must be given by affidavit or, in defined circumstances, a witness statement. Rule 31.1 (NSW) provides that evidence must be given by affidavit if the only matters in question are interest up to judgment in respect of a debt or liquidated claim, the assessment of damages or the value of goods under Pt 30, or costs.

In Tasmania, r 562 simply states that a proceeding tried on affidavit is to be tried by a judge sitting without a jury.

In Western Australia, O 36 r 2 permits the court to order evidence at trial to be given by affidavit, either in whole or in part. The court can impose conditions and may give directions as to filing and serving of affidavits and production of deponents for cross-examination.

In Queensland the court may give directions in the management of a proceeding, including that evidence be given by affidavit (r 367(3)(d)), requiring submissions to be made in writing (r 367(3)(g)), or limiting the length of a written submission or affidavit: r 367(3)(i). In each case the interests of justice remain paramount. If the parties agree, the court may hear and decide a proceeding on an application for directions: r 369.

Queensland Ch 13 Pt 6 provides for a decision on the papers without oral hearing. The rules apply to the District Court and the Trial Division of the Supreme Court: r 488. In response to a party proposing that an application be decided without an oral hearing, the court will so proceed unless the court considers it inappropriate to do so (r 491), the respondent requires an oral hearing (r 494), or the applicant abandons the request for a decision without an oral hearing: r 495. See generally r 489.

The applicant provides a notice in the approved form, draft order, and written submissions. The registrar sets a return date at least ten days after the application is expected to be served on the respondent: r 490(1), (2). *Ex parte* applications are possible: r 490(3). If all or part of an application is resolved before the return date, written notice is to be given to the court by both parties. A respondent must file and serve on the applicant their written submission or evidence at least three business days before the return date: r 492(1). The applicant's reply, if any, must be filed and served at least one business day before the return date: r 493.

Any written submissions must be concise (r 496) and the court may obtain further information, including evidence by telephone, fax, email, or in another way: r 497. In this event the court must inform all parties to the application as to the substance of the inquiry, and provide an opportunity to be heard: r 497. The registrar sends to each party to the application a copy of the order by post, fax or email together with the court's reasons: r 498.

IRREGULARITIES AND DEFECTIVE AFFIDAVITS

15.16.1   Affidavits defective in title, jurat or form, or with any other irregularity (for example, mode of execution or swearing) may be used in evidence with leave: HCR r 2.02; FCR rr 29.06. 29.07; ACT r 6719; NSW r 35.1; NT r 43.08 (form irregularities); Qld r 436(2);

SA r 162(9); Tas r 506; Vic r 43.08; WA O 37 r 5(1), see also Oaths, Affidavits and Statutory Declarations Act 2005 (WA) s 16; *Atherton v Jackson's Corio Meat Packing (1965) Pty Ltd* (1967) VR 850. Where leave is granted to make use of an irregular or defective affidavit, the court may direct a memorandum or note to that effect be made on the affidavit: ACT r 6719; Qld r 436(2). Common defects include omitting the title, incorrect interlineations, incorrect exhibit markings, or incorrect positioning of the jurat.

Queensland r 436 provides that an affidavit may, unless the court orders otherwise, be filed despite an irregularity in form, including a failure to use the approved form.

15.16.2   Questions

1. What is an affidavit? There is generally no definition of 'affidavit'. The rules and legislation list formalities, such as the making of an oath or affirmation. In *Fastlink Calling Pty Ltd v Macquarie Telecom Pty Ltd* (2008) 217 FLR 366; [2008] NSWSC 299, the signatory used the words 'solemnly declare' instead of 'swear' or 'affirm'. There was no witness signature or date. The court concluded that the Oaths Act 1900 (NSW) contemplates the use of 'swear' or 'affirm' only, and that 'declare' is not interchangeable with either word. Regardless of this, the court found the use of the words 'Sworn at Greenacre' in the jurat resolved any ambiguity and represented that the deponent had made her statements on oath. The court then considered the fact that the solicitor before whom the document was sworn had not signed the document. It decided that resort could be had to extrinsic evidence to prove due swearing. It therefore had regard to an affidavit subsequently sworn by the solicitor, which said:

   2. I filed an Originating Process in [the matter the subject of the proceedings] dated 21 November [sic] 2008 together with an Affidavit of Ana Jebril a copy annexed herewith and marked with the letter 'A'.

   3. Ana Jebril swore the Affidavit and placed her signature on the Affidavit before me at Greenacre. I unintentionally and due to oversight at the time did not place my signature in the 'Signature of Witness' part of the Affidavit.

   As the court noted, the case 'illustrates the high price that may have to be paid for lack of attention to simple matters of detail'.

2. Are the following defective?

   (a) Omission of 'before me' in the jurat (see *Eddowes v Argentine Loan and Agency Co* (1890) 59 LJ Ch 392, where the affidavit was received in circumstances where it was sworn before the person who signed the jurat, though it was not so stated in it);

   (b) date of jurat altered but not initialled: see *In The Estate of Robert Orr-Edwards (dec'd)* (1900) 25 VLR 612, which held this is a matter of practice and where there is no ground for suspecting an impropriety, the court will allow the omission to pass.

15.16.3   Swearing a false affidavit may amount to perjury and carry substantial penalties: eg, Oaths Act 1900 (NSW) ss 29–31, 33. A false affidavit must be removed from the court file by the solicitor filing it: *Myers v Ellman* [1940] AC 482. Misleading the court is also an ethical breach: see **15.18.1**.

OBJECTIONS TO AFFIDAVITS

15.17.1 There may be great disadvantage in failing to take proper objection to inadmissible affidavit material when it is read because the court may act upon it, giving such weight as it merits. It is too late to take the objection on an appeal: *Gilbert v Endean* (1878) 9 Ch D 259 at 269. Objections must be taken orally before the whole or portion of an affidavit is read or relied upon. It may be necessary to seek further orders, for example, for material to be struck out, or the affidavit taken off the file.

A SOLICITOR'S DUTY WHEN PREPARING AFFIDAVITS

15.18.1 A solicitor is under an ethical duty to ensure that an affidavit accurately and truthfully presents a statement of the relevant facts for the information of the court in which it is filed; for example, Professional Conduct and Practice Rules 1995 (NSW) r 17 (based on Legal Profession Act 1987 (NSW)). Breach of this duty is capable of being professional misconduct (Legal Profession Act 2006 (ACT) s 386; Legal Profession Act 2004 (NSW) s 496; Legal Profession Act 2006 (NT) s 464; Legal Profession Act 2007 (Qld) s 418; Legal Profession Act 2004 (Tas) s 420; Legal Profession Act 2004 (Vic) s 4.4.2; Legal Profession Act 2008 (WA) s 402) or unsatisfactory unprofessional conduct: Legal Profession Act 2006 (ACT) s 387; Legal Profession Act 2004 (NSW) s 497; Legal Profession Act 2006 (NT) s 465; Legal Profession Act 2007 (Qld) s 419; Legal Profession Act (Tas) s 421; Legal Profession Act 2004 (Vic) s 4.4.3; Legal Profession Act 2008 (WA) s 403.

A solicitor must, having given reasonable notice, terminate the retainer and withdraw in circumstances where a client:

(a) will not provide necessary or accurate information; or

(b) informs the solicitor that a filed affidavit of that client is false in a material particular and refuses to allow the solicitor to correct the false affidavit.

A solicitor should never knowingly prepare a false affidavit, whether directly or indirectly or through omission. Such an approach may breach professional conduct rules and amount to unprofessional conduct or even professional misconduct. Independently verify information in affidavits where possible. In *Myers v Elman* [1940] AC 282 at 293, Viscount Maugham said:

> The swearing of an untrue affidavit of documents is perhaps the most obvious example of conduct which [his] solicitor cannot knowingly permit. He must assist and advise his client as to the latter's bounden duty in that matter; and if the client should persist in omitting relevant documents from his affidavit, it seems to me plain that the solicitor should decline to act for him any further. He cannot properly, still less can he consistently with his duty to the Court, prepare and place a perjured affidavit upon the file.

A solicitor who prepares affidavits in defiance of the rules may be ordered to personally bear the costs of the affidavit: see *Re J L Young Manufacturing Co Ltd* [1900] 2 Ch 753.

Further reading

15.19.1   Articles

A Apps, 'Rules on Affidavits' (1992) 66(3) *ALJ* 163.

A Dickey, 'Can a Party Withdraw a Filed Affidavit?' (1996) 70(3) *ALJ* 184.

K Downes, 'Drawing an Affidavit' (2000) 5 *Proctor* 20.

K Downes, 'Drawing an Affidavit: Part 2' (2000) 5 *Proctor* 20.

A Emmett, 'Practical Litigation in the Federal Court of Australia: Affidavits' (2000) 20 *Aust Bar Rev* 28.

A J Morris, 'Drafting Affidavits Made Simple' (1989) 6 *Qld Law Soc J* 247.

S Palga, 'Strategies for Producing Straightforward Pity Pleadings and Affidavits' (1998) 20(4) *Bulletin* (Law Society of South Australia) 14.

P W Young, 'Affidavits — Part 1' (1992) 66(3) *ALJ* 163.

P W Young, 'Affidavits — Part II' (1992) 66(5) *ALJ* 298.

P W Young and C Curtis, 'Oral or Written Evidence?' (1997) 71 *ALJ* 459.

15.19.2   Looseleaf

G Davis (updated, M Sevadalis), 'Affidavits', *Court Forms Precedents and Pleadings Victoria*, LexisNexis Butterworths, Sydney, vol 1.

P Donohoe QC, 'Affidavits', *Court Forms Precedents and Pleadings New South Wales*, LexisNexis, Sydney, vol 1.

A West, 'Affidavits', *Court Forms Precedents and Pleadings Queensland*, LexisNexis, Sydney, vol 1.

15.19.3   Texts

D Boniface, M Kumar, M Legg, *Principles of Civil Procedure New South Wales*, 2nd ed, Thomson Reuters, Pyrmont, 2012, Ch 12.

W Strunk and E White, *The Elements of Style*, 4th ed, Allyn & Bacon, New York, 2000.

N Williams, *Supreme Court Civil Procedure*, Butterworths, 1987, Ch 17.

Interlocutory Procedures

OVERVIEW

This chapter is concerned with summary applications made to judges, masters, associate judges, or registrars in chambers during the course of a proceeding, which do not finally determine the rights of the parties. These are known generically as interlocutory procedures or proceedings. The chamber jurisdiction replaced the historical practice of such applications being heard in a judge's chambers rather than in open court. Factual disputes and substantive issues that involve a final determination of the matters in dispute are heard and resolved by a trial court presided over by a judge.

In some jursdictions the roles of master, associate judge, and registrar are created by statute: Supreme Court Act 1933 (ACT) s 38; Supreme Court Act 1970 (NSW) s 118; Supreme Court Act (NT) s 11; Supreme Court Act 1935 (SA) s 7; Charter of Justice and Supreme Court Act 1959 (Tas) s 3; Constitution Act 1975 (Vic) s 75; Supreme Court Act 1935 (WA) s 7. Section 27A of the Supreme Court of Queensland Act 1991 (Qld) created the office of judicial registrar, which has never been used.

The distinction between court and chambers is retained in the Federal Court, Tasmania and Western Australia. The remaining jurisdictions do not retain the distinction and interlocutory procedures are determined in court: HCR r 6.04.4; Supreme Court Act 1933 (ACT) s 21; Supreme Court Act 1970 (NSW) s 11; Supreme Court Act (NT) s 9A; Supreme Court of Queensland Act 1991 (Qld) s 128; Supreme Court Act 1986 (Vic) s 4.

Interlocutory procedures may be broadly split into two types:

(1) The first type of interlocutory procedures seeks orders that do not make a final determination in respect of the rights of the parties, but are consequential to the management of the litigation. Examples of these procedures have been discussed throughout this book, including applications for abridgment of time, substituted service, amendment of pleadings, variation of parties, discovery and interrogatories etc. Medical examinations are a further example discussed in this chapter.

(2) The second type of interlocutory procedures are designed to preserve the status quo pending the hearing and final determination of a proceeding. The court is concerned with ensuring that steps, which might be taken by the parties prior to trial, do not thwart the final orders made in the proceeding. The court is concerned to ensure that its process is not abused and, to the extent possible, that any judgment or order

made at trial is enforceable. Examples of the second type of procedures include injunctions (final and interim), Anton Piller (search orders), Mareva (freezing orders), interim preservation, management and custody of property orders, security for costs, receivership and provisional liquidation, and accounts and inquiries.

JURISDICTION OF MASTERS, ASSOCIATE JUDGES AND JUDICIAL REGISTRARS

16.1.1   Masters exist in the ACT (r 6200), NT (r 77.01), SA (r 15) and WA (O 60 r 1). Associate judges exist in NSW (Pt 60 r 1A), Tas (r 962 — though applications are usually directed to a judge in chambers, r 524), and Vic (r 77.01). The jurisdiction of these offices is limited by the terms of the statutes that create them (*Excell v Excell* [1984] VR 1), hence they are unable to exercise the inherent jurisdiction of the court unless provided for by the rules. The ACT (r 6200), NT (r 77.01), SA (r 15), WA (O 60 r 1) and Qld (by Practice Direction) enable exercise of the inherent jurisdiction by these officers.

Judges generally exercise the jurisdiction of the court unless court practice or procedures under the rules permit otherwise: *Commonwealth v Hospital Contribution Fund of Australia* (1982) 150 CLR 49. In the NT (r 77.03), Vic (r 77.03) and WA (O 60 r 2), the officer may refer an application to a judge or a judge may grant leave requiring this.

Appeals from a non-final decision of a master, associate judge or registrar are to a judge: Supreme Court Act 1933 (ACT) s 9; NSW r 49.4; NT r 77.05; Qld r 795; SA r 17.

Appeals from final decisions of a master, associate judge or registrar are to the Court of Appeal: Supreme Court Act 1933 (ACT) s 9; NSW Pt 60 r 17; Supreme Court Civil Procedure Act 1935 (Tas) s 191B; Vic r 77.05.

In Western Australian all appeals from a master are to the Court of Appeal: Supreme Court Act 1935 (WA) s 58.

[NOTE: in this chapter a reference, such as Qld r 31, is a reference to the relevant Rules of Court. All other legislation will be specified.]

16.1.2   Judicial registrars exist in the Federal Court and potentially in Qld: r 451. The Federal Court Registrar may, at the direction of a court or judge, exercise the broad powers under the Federal Court of Australia Act 1976 (Cth) s 35A. The Federal Court or a state Supreme Court exercising federal jurisdiction (Federal Court of Australia Act 1976 (Cth) s 32A) may on its own motion review a registrar's decision, or the registrar may on application by a party, or on his or her own volition refer a matter to a judge for determination.

16.1.3   In other jurisdictions, registrars (as distinct from judicial registrars) have more limited powers specified by the rules of court: HCR r 7.02; FCR r 3.01, Federal Court of Australia Act 1976 (Cth) s 35A; ACT r 6250; NSW Civil Procedure Act 2005 (NSW) s 13; Qld r 452; SA r 19; Vic r 77.08; and WA O 60A r 1. There are no equivalent rules in the NT. Like the other subordinate judicial roles described above, registrars' decisions are subject to appeal (ACT r 6256; Vic r 77.08; WA O 60A r 4) or review (Federal Court of Australia Act 1976 (Cth) s 35A; NSW r 49.19; Qld r 791; SA (r 21)) to a court. A registrar may refer an application to a court (ACT r 6255; NSW r 49.16; Qld r 455; SA r 20; WA O 60A r 3) or a court may direct that the matter be determined by a court instead of a registrar: ACT r 6254; Federal Court of Australia Act 1976 (Cth) s 35A; NSW r 49.17; Qld r 456; SA r 20. In Qld, r 982 enables a party to require a registrar to refer a matter to a judge and to comply with that judge's direction.

The rules may also authorise registrars to exercise incidental or inherent jurisdiction: *Pyoja Pty Ltd v 284 Bronte Road Developments Pty Ltd* (2006) 67 NSWLR 1, *Cory v Registrar of the Federal Court of Australia* [2010] FCA 1215.

In Queensland, r 666 enables the parties to consent in writing to an order or judgment that a registrar considers appropriate as if made or given in court.

THE NATURE OF INTERLOCUTORY ORDERS

Distinguishing interlocutory from final orders

16.2.1 An interlocutory order is one that does not finally determine the rights, duties, obligations or the ultimate question between the parties — that is the role of a final order.

Interlocutory orders are a matter of procedure not substantive law. The distinction was explained in *Adam P Brown Male Fashions Pty Ltd v Philip Morris Inc* (1981) 148 CLR 170 at 176–7:

> ... substantive law is concerned with the ends which the administration of justice seeks; procedural law deals with the means and instruments by which those ends are to be attained. The latter regulate the conduct and relations of courts and litigants in respect of the litigation itself; the former determines their conduct and relations in respect of the matters litigated.

The distinction between interlocutory and final orders is explained in *Kowalski v NMAL Staff Superannuation Fund Pty Ltd* [2009] FCAFC 117. See **19.3.7**.

16.2.2C	**Kowalski v MMAL Staff Superannuation Fund Pty Ltd**
	[2009] FCAFC 117
	Full Court Federal Court of Australia

[The court had to consider whether an application for an appeal could be brought from an order for summary judgment.]

Spender, Graham, Gilmour JJ: [32] The question of whether or not the judgment of the primary judge of 5 February 2009 was interlocutory or not is an important one for consideration in this case. If the judgment was interlocutory, an appeal could not be brought from it 'unless the Court or a Judge gives leave to appeal' under s 24(1A) of the Federal Court Act.

[33] The usual test for determining whether an order is final or interlocutory is whether the order, as made, finally determines the rights of the parties in a principal cause pending between them. That question is answered by determining whether the legal effect of the judgment is final or not. If the *legal* effect of the judgment is final, it is a final order; otherwise it is an interlocutory order (see per McHugh ACJ, Gummow and Heydon JJ in *Re Luck* [2003] HCA 70; (2003) 78 ALJR 177; 203 ALR 1 at [4]; see also *Port of Melbourne Authority v Anshun Proprietary Limited [No. 1]* (1980) 147 CLR 35 ('*Anshun No. 1*') at 38).

[34] It may be that the practical effect of an order will be such as to render a further application fruitless unless supported by additional relevant facts, but that does not make an order one which finally determines the rights of the parties in a principal cause pending between them

(per Taylor J, Owen J agreeing in *Hall v The Nominal Defendant* [1966] HCA 36; (1966) 117 CLR 423 ('*Hall v The Nominal Defendant*') at 440–441 and 447; see also per Windeyer J at 444; per Gibbs CJ in *Carr v Finance Corporation of Australia Limited [No. 1]* [1981] HCA 20; (1981) 147 CLR 246 ('*Carr v FCA*') at 248 and, per Mason J, as his Honour then was, at 256–257).

[35] *Re Luck* was an appeal from a decision of Gleeson CJ, exercising the original jurisdiction of the High Court to control its own processes. Ms Luck had sought to issue a Writ of Summons in the High Court naming 32 defendants including judges of the High Court, the Supreme Court of Victoria and the Federal Court of Australia, the Attorney-General of the Commonwealth, medical officers and an unnamed telephonist employed by the Federal Police.

[36] McHugh ACJ, Gummow and Heydon JJ summarised the position in that case at [2] of their reasons for judgment as follows:

> [2] ... Chief Justice Gleeson held that the statement of claim disclosed no cause of action against any defendant, a holding with which we entirely agree. Not only does the writ and statement of claim fail to disclose any recognisable cause of action against any individual defendant, but they seek to join as defendants in one action many people who have nothing in common except that the applicant claims that each of them has tortured her.

[37] The High Court pointed out that it was not necessary to discuss the merits of Ms Luck's claims in any detail because she was seeking to appeal against an interlocutory order, a class of order that required the grant of leave to appeal, and none had been granted. The High Court ordered that Ms Luck's appeal be struck out as incompetent. At [12]–[13], McHugh ACJ, Gummow and Heydon JJ said:

> [12] Even if Ms Luck had sought leave to appeal against the decision of Gleeson CJ, we would have refused her application. An application for leave should establish both that the decision, the subject of the proposed appeal, is sufficiently doubtful to warrant a grant of leave and that it is in the interests of the administration of justice for this court to hear it. [13] The writ of summons that Ms Luck attempted to file does not disclose a cause of action against any of the 32 defendants listed. A grant of leave would be futile because an appeal would have no prospect of success.

[38] An order is an interlocutory order when it stays or dismisses an action or refuses leave to commence or proceed with an action because the action is frivolous, vexatious, an abuse of the process of the Court or does not disclose a reasonable cause of action (per McHugh ACJ, Gummow and Heydon JJ in *Re Luck* at [9].

[39] There have been numerous cases in the High Court which illustrate orders that are interlocutory and orders that are final applying the test as stated above:

- Orders dismissing applications for interlocutory injunctions and for orders striking out matter within a statement of claim, which it was said tended to prejudice and embarrass a defendant and to delay the fair hearing of the suit, are interlocutory (per Dixon, Williams, Webb, Fullagar and Kitto JJ in *Pye v Renshaw* [1951] HCA 8; (1951) 84 CLR 58 ('*Pye v Renshaw*') at 64, 77).
- Orders upholding a demurrer *ore tenus* to a statement of claim and granting a plaintiff liberty to amend a statement of claim are interlocutory (per Dixon, Williams, Webb, Fullagar and Kitto JJ in *Pye v Renshaw* at 64, 77).

- An order refusing an application for an extension of time within which to institute proceedings against the Nominal Defendant under s 65A(3) of the Traffic Act 1925 (Tas) is interlocutory (per Taylor, Windeyer and Owen JJ in *Hall v The Nominal Defendant* at 441, 445 and 447).
- Orders setting aside an order for substituted service and setting aside orders relating to the deemed validity of service of process are interlocutory (see *Licul v Corney* [1976] HCA 6; (1976) 180 CLR 213. See in particular, per Gibbs J, as his Honour then was, at 225).
- An order refusing to set aside a default judgment is interlocutory. It does not, as a matter of law, finally dispose of the rights of the parties, whatever its practical effect may be (see *Carr v FCA* at 248, 257 and 258).
- An order dismissing an application for removal of Family Court proceedings into the High Court is interlocutory (see *Bienstein v Bienstein* [2003] HCA 7; (2003) 195 ALR 225 at 231).
- An order staying an action as an abuse of process on the ground that the matters in question which it was sought to raise could and should have been litigated in earlier proceedings was a final one (per Gibbs J, as his Honour then was, Mason and Murphy JJ agreeing, in *Anshun No. 1* at 38).

[40] In our opinion, a case where summary judgment is given for a respondent in the absence of the full and complete factual matrix and full argument thereon, the Court being satisfied that the moving party has no reasonable prospect of successfully prosecuting the proceeding is no different from a case where an order is made dismissing an action because it is frivolous, vexatious, an abuse of the process of the Court or does not disclose a reasonable cause of action (see *Re Luck*) or one dismissing an appeal from an order of a Master refusing to set aside a default judgment (see *Carr v FCA*) (see *Zoia v Commonwealth Ombudsmen Department* [2007] FCAFC 143; (2007) 240 ALR 624 ('Zoia') per Spender J, Gilmour J concurring, at [14] and [19] and per French J as his Honour then was at [26]).

16.2.3 The following table sets out some further examples of interlocutory orders. See 15.3.1.

Extension of time to give notice	*Ex parte Britt* [1987] 1 Qd R 221
Order refusing an extension of time to comply with a self-executing order	*Southern Cross Exploration NL v Fire and All Risks Insurance Co Ltd (No 2)* (1990) 21 NSWLR 200
An application for extension of time under a Limitation Act	*Border Auto Wreckers (Wodonga) Pty Ltd v Strathdee* [1997] 2 VLR 49; *D A Christie Pty Ltd v Baker* [1996] 2 VR 582 (particularly the judgment of Brooking JA.
A decision refusing to set aside a statutory demand under the Corporations Act 2001 (Cth)	*Hardel Pty Ltd v Burrell & Family Pty Ltd* (2009) 103 SASR 408
An order dismissing a matter as frivolous, vexatious or without a reasonable cause of action disclosed	*In the matter of an appeal by Gaye Alexander Mary Luck* (2003) 78 ALJR 177
Default judgment subject to an application at first instance rather than on appeal	*Allmark v Mossero (a firm)* (2006) WASCA 127

A judgment upholding an interim award for workers' compensation	*GK Sandford Pty Ltd v Jansen* (1992) 36 FCR 83
Injunctions granted against infringement of copyright	*Computer Edge Pty Ltd v Apple Computer Inc* (1984) 54 ALR 767
Where judgment is given on some issues but others are left for determination	*Gold Peg International Pty Ltd v Korean Engineering (Aust) Pty Ltd* [2005] FCA 1794

Making an interlocutory application

16.2.4   The application will be made either by motion, summons or application: HCR rr 13.01, 13.02; FCR r 17.01; Court Procedures Rules 2006 (ACT) rr 728, 6007; Uniform Civil Procedure Rules 2005 (NSW) rr 18.1, 18.3; Supreme Court Rules (NT) r 46.02; Uniform Rules of Civil Procedure 1999 (Qld) rr 31, 32; Supreme Court Civil Rules 2006 (SA) r 131; Supreme Court Rules 2000 (Tas) r 525; Supreme Court (General Rules of Procedure in Civil Proceedings) Rules 2005 (Vic) r 46.02; Rules of the Supreme Court 1971 (WA) O 4 r 2, O 59 r 3. An application to a judge is made in chambers by summons or application. An application in court is by way of motion. The rule enabling the application determines whether the application is made in court or chambers.

An application for an interlocutory order will normally be heard on the basis of an affidavit or affidavits filed in respect of that application: see **Chapter 15**; HCR 13.02; FCR 17.01; ACT r 6007; NSW r 31.2; NT r 40.02; Vic r 40.02; WA O 36 r 2. The interlocutory application and affidavit(s) will be served on the respondent to the application: see **7.3.1–7.3.10E**. The affidavits may include statements based on information and belief, contrary to the rule against hearsay, provided the grounds of the belief and the sources of information are stated: see **15.3.1**.

The rules also prescribe the form of the application: HCR 13.02, Form 21; FCR r 17.01, Form 35; ACT r 6007, Form 6.2; NSW rr 18.1, 18.3, Form 20; NT 46.04, Form 46A; Qld r 31(2), Form 9; SA r 131, Form 16; Tas Supreme Court Forms Rules 2000 r 525(1)(a), Form 41; Vic r 46.04, Form 46A; WA O 59 r 4, Form 77.

The court may make interlocutory orders in the conduct of caseflow management, through directions hearings, without the filing of a formal application: see **1.10.1E–1.10.20**.

Service of interlocutory applications

16.2.5   Generally any party affected by the relief sought should be served with notice of the interlocutory application: HCR r 13.02; FCR r 17.03; ACT r 6008; NSW r 18.4; Qld r 32; SA r 133; Tas r 529; WA O 59 r 5, O 54 r 4. In the Northern Territory (r 46.03) and Victoria (r 46.03), only persons with a sufficient interest need be served. Service may be dispensed with in cases of urgency or where service may give rise to irreparable damage — such applications by their very nature are made *ex parte* (in the absence of the other party). In most jurisdictions, an application for a consent order need not be served: ACT r 6016; NSW r 18.4; Qld r 27; SA rr 131, 133; Tas r 530; WA O 54 r 3. Interlocutory applications usually involve ordinary service: FCR r 10.31; ACT r 6420; NSW r 10.5; NT r 6.06; Qld r 112; SA r 68; Tas r 144; Vic r 6.07; WA O 72 r 5. See **8.3.1**. The rules will specify exceptions where personal service is required.

Ex parte applications

16.2.6 Courts are cautious in making orders in circumstances where the respondent has no notice of the application. In *National Australia Bank Ltd v Bond Brewing Holdings Ltd* [1991] 1 VR 529, 538–539, the Full Court of the Supreme Court of Victoria suggested the following non-exhaustive guidelines in considering whether to grant *ex parte* relief:

- How urgent is it?
- When could notice first have been given?
- Would irreparable damage flow from making an ex parte order?
- Should undertakings be exacted?
- How long should the order run?
- How is the opposite party to be notified of the order?
- Should there be liberty to apply to set aside the order?
- How ought costs be resolved?

An application may be made *ex parte*, for example, where there is no respondent to the application (examples are applications to extend the time within which originating process is to be served: see **7.6.5**) or in applications for substituted service: see **8.8.14**; where there is a particular urgency about the application such as to warrant a dispensation from the provision of notice to the other party; or in cases where notice might thwart the making of the application (an example is an application for an Anton Piller (Search) order (see **16.4.1–16.4.15C**) where notice might allow the defendant to destroy evidence before the application is heard). The applicant in such cases is under a duty of absolute candour; the applicant must disclose all matters relevant to the application whether advantageous to the applicant or not: see **16.4.4 n 1**. In all other cases, the interlocutory applications will be *inter partes* (between parties on notice) rather than *ex parte* (in the absence of a party without notice).

16.2.7 *Ex parte* orders may be reviewed and set aside by a court under both the inherent jurisdiction and the rules of court: FCR r 39.05; ACT r 1613; NSW r 36.16; NT r 46.08; Qld r 27; SA rr 4, 242; Tas r 537; Vic r 46.08; WA O 58 r 23, O 59 r 7. The party seeking to set aside an *ex parte* order that has been perfected (entered in the Registry) will need to produce additional material in support of their case. Both the balance of hardship and material non-disclosure are relevant considerations in the exercise of the discretion. *Ex parte* orders can also be set aside or varied by consent of the parties.

Ex parte orders that have not been perfected may be recalled rather than being the subject of an appeal, at any time prior to becoming perfected: *Harvey v Phillips* (1956) 95 CLR 235; FCR r 39.04; NSW Pt 40 r 9. An order is meant to be final and is only set aside in the interests of justice, rather than simply permit a party to reopen a case: *Re Australian Meat Industry Employees' Union (WA Branch); Ex parte Ferguson* (1986) 67 ALR 491.

Interlocutory applications in the absence of an oral hearing

16.2.8 Certain interlocutory applications may be determined without an oral hearing in the Federal Court, Queensland and South Australia. Federal Court of Australia Act 1976 (Cth) s 20(3) provides for leave to institute or extend time, amend an application or stay a tribunal decision. The Federal Court Rules do not require an oral hearing for extending time to appeal, joining or removing a party to an appeal, leave to amend the grounds of appeal, dismissing an appeal for failure to comply with a direction, failing to attend, want of prosecution or disposal by consent, summary judgment and an application for directions (r 36.41). In Queensland, informal procedures arise in respect of matters listed in r 443 — an application for further and better particulars of a pleading (r 161), an application for directions under Ch 10, Pt 1, failure to comply with the rules or an order (Ch 10, Pt 2) or more generally. In South Australia r 132 enables a party to request written submissions or avoid oral submissions in non-contentious matters.

Medical examinations

16.2.9   In personal injuries litigation, the court has both inherent and statutory jurisdiction to order a plaintiff to undergo reasonable medical examinations. What is reasonable is a question of fact, but does not require the imposition of painful or dangerous procedures: *Stace v Commonwealth* (1989) 51 SASR 492. If the plaintiff refuses a reasonable request the proceeding may be stayed, or in NSW dismissed. Statutes require medical examinations in cases of:

- motor vehicle accidents: eg, Road Transport (General) Act 1999 (ACT) s 194; Motor Accidents Act 1988 (NSW) s 49; Motor Accident Insurance Act 1994 (Qld) s 45; Motor Vehicles Act 1959 (SA) s 127; Motor Vehicle (Third Party Insurance) Act 1943 (WA) s 30.
- industrial accidents: eg, Workers Rehabilitation and Compensation Act 1986 (SA) s 108.
- personal injuries claims: NSW r 23.1; NT r 33.03; SA r 153; Vic r 33.07; WA O 28 r 1.

Appeals from interlocutory orders

16.2.10   Appellate courts are generally reluctant to interfere with decisions made by a judge at first instance in relation to matters which involve the exercise of discretion on a matter of practice and procedure: see 19.3.7. Their reluctance stems from the recognition that litigation may become unduly protracted by appeals from interlocutory orders where the exercise of discretion is in issue and may unduly advantage 'the litigant with a long purse or a litigious disposition': *In re the Will of F B Gilbert (dec'd)* (1946) 46 SR (NSW) 318 at 323 per Jordan CJ. In that case, his Honour said (at 323):

> The disposal of cases could be delayed interminably, and costs heaped up indefinitely, [if such a litigant] could, at will, in effect transfer all exercise of discretion in interlocutory applications from a Judge to a Court of Appeal.

The passage was quoted with approval by the High Court in *Adam P Brown Male Fashions Pty Ltd v Philip Morris Inc* (1981) 148 CLR 170 at 177. The High Court provided an indication of the types of considerations, which will permit an appellate court to review an exercise of discretion in interlocutory proceedings. The court said (at 177):

> Nor is there any serious dispute between the parties that appellate courts exercise particular caution in reviewing decisions pertaining to practice and procedure. Counsel for [the appellant]

urged that specific cumulative bars operate to guide appellate courts in the discharge of that task. Not only must there be error principle, but the decision appealed from must work a substantial injustice to one of the parties. The opposing view is that such criteria are to be expressed disjunctively. Cases can be cited in support of both views; for example, on the one hand, *Niemann v Electronic Industries Ltd.* (1978) VR 431, at p 440; on the other hand, *De Mestre v A D Hunter Pty Ltd* (1952) 77 WN (NSW) 143, at p 146. For ourselves, we believe it to be unnecessary and indeed unwise to lay down rigid and exhaustive criteria. The circumstances of different cases are infinitely various.

The rules generally limit an appeal from an order in interlocutory proceedings to cases where leave of the appellate court or the court at first instance has been obtained. This is reflected in provisions such as Federal Court of Australia Act 1976 (Cth) ss 24(1), (1A) and 25(2); Supreme Court Act 1970 (NSW) s 101(2)(e); Supreme Court Act (NT) s 53; Supreme Court Act 1935 (SA) s 50(4), cf s 50(5)(c); Supreme Court Act 1986 (Vic) s 17A(4)(b); Supreme Court Act 1935 (WA) s 60(1)(f). There is no similar limitation in other jurisdictions: see **19.6.5**. Exceptions to the general rule, where leave is not required, arise in situations where the liberty of the subject or the custody of infants is concerned, or where an injunction or the appointment of a receiver is granted or refused, or in respect of final decisions: see Federal Court of Australia Act 1976 (Cth) s 24 (1C) — liberty, (1E) — final judgment; Supreme Court Act 1970 (NSW) s 101(3); Supreme Court Act 1935 (SA) s 50(5); Supreme Court Act 1986 (Vic) s 17A(4)(b); Supreme Court Act 1935 (WA) s 60(1)(f)(i), (ii), (iv).

Let us now consider the second type of interlocutory procedures, namely, procedures designed to preserve the status quo.

INJUNCTIONS

16.3.1 An injunction is 'a court order of an equitable nature requiring a person to do, or refrain from doing, a particular action. Injunctions may be classified as final or interlocutory; mandatory or prohibitory; *ex parte* or *inter partes* …': *Butterworths Legal Dictionary*, 1997, p 600. An injunction extends to activities beyond mere preservation or detention of property. An interim injunction may be granted for a short period of time in an emergency to preserve an applicant's rights or status quo. The interim injunction may be on notice (*inter partes*), but often is *ex parte* (in the absence of a party). At the return date of the interim injunction, the court will consider whether to grant an interlocutory injunction preserving the status quo pending determination at trial of a perpetual injunction that finally determines the rights of the parties. The opposite party must be provided with notice of the determination of both an interlocutory and perpetual injunction.

Injunctions are useful in preserving the status quo pending trial. For example, an injunction may prevent mixing of funds, operating bank accounts, and can be used to maintain goods and property.

Any party may apply for an injunction. However, an application made by a defendant must be related to the original claim brought by the plaintiff. Alternatively, a defendant may counter-claim and base their application for an injunction on the relief sought in the counter-claim.

To obtain an injunction, an applicant must establish two things:

(1)   that there is a serious question to be tried; and

(2)   that the balance of convenience favours the granting of an interlocutory injunction.

Serious question to be tried

16.3.2   In relation to a serious question to be tried, the High Court in *Beecham Group Ltd v Bristol Laboratories Pty Ltd* (1968) 118 CLR 618 at 622 referred to the fact that the plaintiff must make out a *prima facie* case.

> It is as well to begin consideration of the appeal by recalling the principles to be observed in dealing with applications for interlocutory injunctions in patent cases. The jurisdiction is discretionary, being a part of the jurisdiction under s 31 of the Judiciary Act 1903–1965 (Cth) to make all such orders as are necessary for doing complete justice in the cause. The court addresses itself in all cases, patent as well as other, to two main inquiries. The first is whether the plaintiff has made out a prima facie case, in the sense that if the evidence remains as it is there is a probability that at the trial of the action the plaintiff will be held entitled to relief: *Preston v Luck* (1884) 27 Ch D 497, at 506; *Challender v Royle* (1887) 36 Ch D 425, at 436. How strong the probability needs to be depends, no doubt, upon the nature of the rights he asserts and the practical consequences likely to flow from the order he seeks. Thus, if merely pecuniary interests are involved, 'some' probability of success is enough: *Attorney-General v Wigan Corporation* (1854) 5 De GM & G 52, at 53, 54 (43 ER 789) and in general it is right to say, as Roper CJ in Eq said in *Linfield Linen Pty Ltd v Nejain* (1951) 51 SR (NSW) 280, at 281:
>
> > There are disputes of fact as to a number of matters ... but this being an application for an interlocutory injunction I look at the facts simply to ascertain whether the plaintiff has established a fair prima facie case and a fair probability of being able to succeed in that case at the hearing.

Where the defendant goes into evidence on the interlocutory application the court does not undertake a preliminary trial, and give or withhold interlocutory relief upon a forecast as to the ultimate result of the case. The plaintiff must establish that if the evidence before the court on the hearing of the application for an interlocutory injunction were to remain as it is at trial, there is a probability that the plaintiff would be entitled to relief.

In *Australian Broadcasting Commission v Lenah Game Meats Pty Ltd* (2001) 208 CLR 199, the High Court affirmed that there must be a legal or equitable right to be determined at trial in order to base an interlocutory injunction.

Compare the approach of the High Court with that of the House of Lords in *American Cyanamid v Ethicon Ltd* [1975] AC 396 at 407–8 where Lord Diplock said:

> The use of such expressions as 'a probability', a 'prima facie case,' or 'a strong prima facie case' in the context of an exercise of a discretionary power to grant an interlocutory injunction leads to confusion as to the object sought to be achieved by this form of temporary relief. The court no doubt must be satisfied that the claim is not frivolous or vexatious; in other words, that there is a serious question to be tried.
>
> It is no part of the court's function at this stage of the litigation to try to resolve conflicts of evidence on affidavit as to facts on which the claims of either party may ultimately depend nor to decide difficult questions of law which call for detailed argument and mature considerations. These are matters to be dealt with at the trial. One of the reasons for the introduction of the practice of requiring an undertaking as to damages upon the grant of an interlocutory injunction was that 'it aided the court in doing that which was its great object, viz abstaining from expressing any opinion upon the merits of the case until the hearing': *Wakefield v Duke of Buccleugh* (1865) 12 LT 628, 629. So unless the material available to the court at the hearing of the application for

an interlocutory injunction fails to disclose that the plaintiff has any real prospect of succeeding in his claim for a permanent injunction at the trial, the court should go on to consider whether the balance of convenience lies in favour of granting or refusing the interlocutory relief that is sought.

As to that, the governing principle is that the court should first consider whether, if the plaintiff were to succeed at the trial in establishing his right to a permanent injunction, he would be adequately compensated by an award of damages for the loss he would have sustained as a result of the defendant's continuing to do what was sought to be enjoined between the time of the application and the time of the trial ...

It is where there is doubt as to the adequacy of the respective remedies in damages available to either party or to both, that the question of balance of convenience arises. It would be unwise to even attempt to list all the various matters which may need to be taken into consideration in deciding where the balance lies, let alone to suggest the relative weight to be attached to them. This will vary from case to case.

16.3.3 Recent cases tend to focus on being satisfied that there is a serious question to be tried: *Nicholas John Holdings Pty Ltd v Australia and New Zealand Banking Group Ltd* [1992] 2 VR 715. The two requirements listed in **16.3.1** must be examined together: [1992] 2 VR 715 at 723. The stronger the serious question to be tried, the less emphasis need be placed on the balance of convenience favouring the plaintiff over the defendant.

16.3.4 Where the interlocutory injunction sought by the plaintiff is of a mandatory nature, the injunction will not normally be granted, unless the court is satisfied with a high degree of assurance that at trial it will appear that the injunction was properly granted: *Queensland v Australian Telecommunications Commission* (1985) 59 ALJR 562. But see and compare the approach taken by Maxwell P and Charles JA in *Bradto Pty Ltd v State of Victoria* [2006] 15 VR 65 at 73:

In our view, it is desirable that a single test be applied in all cases where an interlocutory injunction is sought. There is nothing in the body of authority to which we have referred, nor any consideration of principle, which requires a special test to be applied to one sub-category of such injunction applications, namely, those where mandatory relief is sought. On the contrary, as pointed out convincingly by Hoffman J in *Films Rover* ([1987] 1 WLR 670), the grant of a mandatory interlocutory injunction may be justified in a particular case notwithstanding that the court does not feel the requisite 'high degree of assurance'.

An example of such an injunction is the Anton Piller (Search) order: see **16.4.1–16.4.15C**.

Balance of convenience

16.3.5 In relation to the balance of convenience favouring the granting of an interlocutory injunction, several issues are considered:

- a threat of damage is insufficient, the applicant must establish the respondent's intention to carry out the threat;

- the court will balance the relative damage to both parties if the injunction were granted;

- the possibility that the plaintiff may suffer irreparable damage if an injunction is not granted: *Aristoc Industries Pty Ltd v R A Wenham (Builders) Pty Ltd* [1965] NSWR 581;

- an injunction is unlikely to be granted where other forms of relief, such as damages, are an adequate remedy; and

- an applicant's failure to promptly make an application or a respondent's acquiescence may result in a court refusing to grant an injunction.

The High Court in *Beecham Group Ltd v Bristol Laboratories Pty Ltd* (1968) 118 CLR 618 at 623 confirmed that balance of convenience is an important discretionary factor. This involved consideration of the question, 'whether the inconvenience or injury which the plaintiff would be likely to suffer if an injunction were refused outweighs or is outweighed by the injury which the defendant would suffer if an injunction were granted' at 623.

Lord Diplock in *American Cyanamid Co v Ethicon Ltd* [1975] AC 396 at 406 explained balance of convenience in these terms:

> My Lords, when an application for an interlocutory injunction to restrain a defendant from doing acts alleged to be in violation of the plaintiff's legal right is made upon contested facts, the decision whether or not to grant an interlocutory injunction has to be taken at a time when *ex hypothesi* the existence of the right or the violation of it, or both, is uncertain and will remain uncertain until final judgment is given in the action. It was to mitigate the risk of injustice to the plaintiff during the period before that uncertainty could be resolved that the practice arose of granting him relief by way of interlocutory injunction; but since the middle of the nineteenth century this has been made subject to his undertaking to pay damages to the defendant for any loss sustained by reason of the injunction if it should be held at the trial that the plaintiff had not been entitled to restrain the defendant from doing what he was threatening to do. The object of the interlocutory injunction is to protect the plaintiff against injury by violation of his right for which he could not be adequately compensated in damages recoverable in the action if the uncertainty were resolved in his favour at the trial; but the plaintiff's need for such protection must be weighed against the corresponding need of the defendant to be protected against injury resulting from his having been prevented from exercising his own legal rights for which he could not be adequately compensated under the plaintiff's undertaking in damages if the uncertainty were resolved in the defendant's favour at the trial. The Court must weigh one need against another and determine where "the balance of convenience" lies.
>
> In those cases where the legal rights of the parties depend upon facts that are in dispute between them, the evidence available to the court at the hearing of the application for an interlocutory injunction is incomplete. It is given on affidavit and has not been tested by oral cross-examination.

In terms of what factors to take into account, Lord Diplock observed at 408:

> It would be unwise to attempt even to list all the various matters which may need to be taken into consideration in deciding where the balance lies, let alone to suggest the relative weight to be attached to them. These will vary from case to case.
>
> Where other factors appear to be evenly balanced it is a counsel of prudence to take such measures as are calculated to preserve the status quo. Where other factors appear to be evenly balanced it is a counsel of prudence to take such measures as are calculated to preserve the status quo. If the defendant is enjoined temporarily from doing something that he has not done before, the only effect of the interlocutory injunction in the event of his succeeding at the trial is to postpone the date at which he is able to embark upon a course of action which he has not previously found it necessary to undertake; whereas to interrupt him in the conduct of an

established enterprise would cause much greater inconvenience to him since he would have to start again to establish it in the event of his succeeding at the trial.

Save in the simplest cases, the decision to grant or to refuse an interlocutory injunction will cause to whichever party is unsuccessful on the application some disadvantages which his ultimate success at the trial may show he ought to have been spared and the disadvantages may be such that the recovery of damages to which he would then be entitled either in the action or under the plaintiff's undertaking would not be sufficient to compensate him fully for all of them. The extent to which the disadvantages to each party would be incapable of being compensated in damages in the event of his succeeding at the trial is always a significant factor in assessing where the balance of convenience lies; and if the extent of the uncompensatable disadvantage to each party would not differ widely, it may not be improper to take into account in tipping the balance the relative strength of each party's case as revealed by the affidavit evidence adduced on the hearing of the application. This, however, should be done only where it is apparent upon the facts disclosed by evidence as to which there is no credible dispute that the strength of one party's case is disproportionate to that of the other party. The court is not justified in embarking upon anything resembling a trial of the action upon conflicting affidavits in order to evaluate the strength of either party's case.

Courts will also take into consideration the impact of the granting of the injunction with respect to third parties not before the court: *Patrick Stevedores Operations No 2 Pty Ltd v Maritime Union of Australia* (1998) 195 CLR 1 at 41–3.

16.3.6 All superior courts have an inherent jurisdiction to grant interlocutory injunctions to preserve the status quo pending trial or earlier order of the court. In many jurisdictions there is provision for the court to grant interlocutory injunctions: HCR rr 8.07.1, 8.07.2; FCR r 7.01; ACT rr 726–733; NSW Pt 25; NT r 38.01; Civil Proceedings Act 2011 (Qld) s 9; Qld Ch 8 Pt 2; SA r 246; Tas r 443; Vic r 38.01; WA O 52 r 1; Federal Court of Australia Act 1976 (Cth) s 23; Supreme Court Act 1933 (ACT) s 26; Supreme Court Act 1970 (NSW) s 66(4); Supreme Court Act (NT) s 69; Supreme Court Act 1935 (SA) s 29; Supreme Court Act 1986 (Vic) s 37(1); Supreme Court Act 1935 (WA) s 25(9). In addition, the Civil Proceedings Act 2011 (Qld) s 9 provides for the court at any stage of a proceeding, by injunction, to restrain a threatened or apprehended breach of contract or other wrongful conduct.

16.3.7E	**Supreme Court Civil Rules 2006 (SA)** Part 12 — Injunctions

246 — Court's power to grant injunction

(1) The Court may, on application by a party, grant an injunction before, at or after the hearing and determination of proceedings in the Court.

(2) In a case of urgency, an application may be made without notice to other parties but the Court may, if it thinks fit, require the applicant to give notice of the application to other parties.

(3) If an injunction is granted on an application made without notice to other parties: —

   (a) the Court must fix a time for a hearing (a ***confirmation hearing***) either at the time of making the injunction or on the later application of a party affected by the injunction; and

   (b) if the Court decides at a confirmation hearing not to confirm the injunction — it then lapses.

(4) 'The usual undertaking as to damages', if given to the Court in connection with any interlocutory order or undertaking, is an undertaking to the Court to:

(a) submit to such order (if any) as the Court may consider to be just for the payment of compensation, to be assessed by the Court or as it may direct, to any person (whether or not a party) affected by the operation of the interlocutory order or undertaking or any continuation (with or without variation) of the order or undertaking; and

(b) pay the compensation referred to in (a) to the person or persons referred to in the order.

16.3.8 The power given by statute or rule to grant interlocutory injunctions does not limit the inherent power of superior courts to grant interlocutory injunctions: *National Australia Bank Ltd v Dessau* [1988] VR 521.

16.3.9 The court will not grant an interlocutory injunction in relation to a dispute over which it has no jurisdiction. A court cannot make an order of an interlocutory nature in support of a cause of action which is not justiciable within the jurisdiction of the court: *The Siskina* [1979] AC 210; compare *Channel Tunnel Group Ltd v Balfour Beatty Construction Ltd* [1993] AC 334. For example, if the court has no jurisdiction under its rules which permit service of process out of the jurisdiction (as to which see **Chapter 4**), it cannot grant interlocutory relief to restrain the defendant from dealing with assets within the jurisdiction. Similarly, the court cannot grant interlocutory relief in relation to a cause of action which remains incomplete or anticipated: *Vera Cruz Transportation Co Inc v VC Shipping Co Inc ('the Vera Cruz')* [1992] 1 Lloyd's Rep 353 at 357, 358–9; *Glamagard Pty Ltd v Enderslea Productions Pty Ltd* (1985) 1 NSWLR 138. But see and compare *Riley McKay Pty Ltd v McKay* [1982] 1 NSWLR 264 where Rogers J granted Mareva relief in relation to an anticipated claim, and where the New South Wales Court of Appeal on appeal in an unreported decision appears to have agreed that this was appropriate. The decision of the High Court in *Cardile v LED Builders Pty Ltd* (1999) 198 CLR 230; **16.5.6C** supports the view that an injunction should only be given in relation to a substantive right and against a person party to the action. A Mareva order (**16.5.1–16.5.11**) ought to be regarded as a particular type of remedy: 198 CLR 230 at 399 [40].

16.3.10C **Australian Broadcasting Corporation v O'Neill**
(2006) 227 CLR 27; 229 ALR 457; [2006] HCA 46
High Court of Australia

[In 1966, three children, aged nine, seven and four, members of the Beaumont family in South Australia, disappeared. The police suspect that the children were murdered, but investigations were inconclusive. It is one of Australia's most notorious unsolved crimes. In November 1975 the respondent was convicted of the murder, in Tasmania, in February 1975, of a young boy whom he had abducted. He was sentenced to imprisonment for life. The appellant prepared a documentary entitled 'The Fisherman' linking the respondent to missing children including the Beaumont family, which it intended to broadcast. The respondent brought an action for defamation and claimed damages, and permanent injunctive relief. The respondent also applied for interlocutory relief to prevent the appellant from broadcasting the documentary pending the hearing of the action. An interlocutory injunction was ordered that restrained the ABC from publishing any part of 'The Fisherman' that imputed or implied that O'Neill was responsible for the disappearance of the Beaumont children.]

Gleeson CJ and Crennan J:

[34] The primary judge, and the majority in the Full Court, erred in principle in two respects in their approach to the exercise of the discretionary power to grant an interlocutory injunction in the special circumstances of a defamation case. They failed to take proper account of the significance of the value of free speech in considering the question of prior restraint of publication, and they failed to take proper account of the possibility that, if publication occurred and was found to involve actionable defamation, only nominal damages might be awarded. The appeal should be allowed.

Gummow and Hayne JJ:

...

Interlocutory injunctions

[65] The relevant principles in Australia are those explained in *Beecham Group Ltd v Bristol Laboratories Pty Ltd*. This Court (Kitto, Taylor, Menzies and Owen JJ) said that on such applications the court addresses itself to two main inquiries and continued:

> The first is whether the plaintiff has made out a prima facie case, in the sense that if the evidence remains as it is there is a probability that at the trial of the action the plaintiff will be held entitled to relief ... The second inquiry is ... whether the inconvenience or injury which the plaintiff would be likely to suffer if an injunction were refused outweighs or is outweighed by the injury which the defendant would suffer if an injunction were granted.

By using the phrase 'prima facie case', their Honours did not mean that the plaintiff must show that it is more probable than not that at trial the plaintiff will succeed; it is sufficient that the plaintiff show a sufficient likelihood of success to justify in the circumstances the preservation of the status quo pending the trial. That this was the sense in which the Court was referring to the notion of a prima facie case is apparent from an observation to that effect made by Kitto J in the course of argument. With reference to the first inquiry, the Court continued, in a statement of central importance for this appeal:

> How strong the probability needs to be depends, no doubt, upon the nature of the rights [the plaintiff] asserts and the practical consequences likely to flow from the order he seeks.

[66] For example, special considerations apply where injunctive relief is sought to interfere with the decision of the executive branch of government to prosecute offences. Again, in *Castlemaine Tooheys Ltd v South Australia*, Mason ACJ, in the original jurisdiction of this Court, said that '[i]n the absence of compelling grounds' it is the duty of the judicial branch to defer to the enactment of the legislature until that enactment is adjudged *ultra vires*, and dismissed applications for interlocutory injunctions to restrain enforcement of the law under challenge.

[67] Various views have been expressed and assumptions made respecting the relationship between the judgment of this Court in *Beecham* and the speech of Lord Diplock in the subsequent decision, *American Cyanamid Co v Ethicon Ltd*. It should be noted that both were cases of patent infringement and the outcome on each appeal was the grant of an interlocutory injunction to restrain infringement. Each of the judgments appealed from had placed too high the bar for the obtaining of interlocutory injunctive relief.

[68] Lord Diplock was at pains to dispel the notion, which apparently had persuaded the Court of Appeal to refuse interlocutory relief, that to establish a prima facie case of infringement it was necessary for the plaintiff to demonstrate more than a 50 per cent chance of ultimate success. Thus Lord Diplock remarked:

> The purpose sought to be achieved by giving to the court discretion to grant such injunctions would be stultified if the discretion were clogged by a technical rule forbidding its exercise if upon that incomplete untested evidence the court evaluated the chances of the plaintiff's ultimate success in the action at 50 per cent or less, but permitting its exercise if the court evaluated his chances at more than 50 per cent.

[69] In *Beecham*, the primary judge, McTiernan J, had refused interlocutory relief on the footing that, while he could not dismiss the possibility that the defendant might not fail at trial, the plaintiff had not made out a strong enough case on the question of infringement. Hence the statement by Kitto J in the course of argument in the Full Court that it was not necessary for the plaintiff to show that it was more probable than not that the plaintiff would succeed at trial.

[70] When *Beecham* and *American Cyanamid* are read with an understanding of the issues for determination and an appreciation of the similarity in outcome, much of the assumed disparity in principle between them loses its force. There is then no objection to the use of the phrase 'serious question' if it is understood as conveying the notion that the seriousness of the question, like the strength of the probability referred to in *Beecham*, depends upon the considerations emphasised in *Beecham*.

[71] However, a difference between this Court in *Beecham* and the House of Lords in *Cyanamid* lies in the apparent statement by Lord Diplock that provided the court is satisfied that the plaintiff's claim is not frivolous or vexatious, then there will be a serious question to be tried and this will be sufficient. The critical statement by his Lordship is '[t]he court no doubt must be satisfied that the claim is not frivolous or vexatious; in other words, that there is a serious question to be tried'. That was followed by a proposition which appears to reverse matters of onus:

> So *unless* the material available to the court at the hearing of the application for an interlocutory injunction *fails to disclose* that the plaintiff has any real prospect of succeeding in his claim for a permanent injunction at the trial, the court should go on to consider whether the balance of convenience lies in favour of granting or refusing the interlocutory relief that is sought. (emphasis added)

Those statements do not accord with the doctrine in this Court as established by *Beecham* and should not be followed. They obscure the governing consideration that the requisite strength of the probability of ultimate success depends upon the nature of the rights asserted and the practical consequences likely to flow from the interlocutory order sought.

The second of these matters, the reference to practical consequences, is illustrated by the particular considerations which arise where the grant or refusal of an interlocutory injunction in effect would dispose of the action finally in favour of whichever party succeeded on that application. The first consideration mentioned in *Beecham*, the nature of the rights asserted by the plaintiff, redirects attention to the present appeal.

[The balance of convenience favoured the denial of the interlocutory relief.]

Interim injunctions

16.3.11   Courts may grant an interim injunction that continues for a short period of time, perhaps two or three days, in circumstances where delay may cause irreparable damage: ACT r 729; FCR r 7.01; NSW r 25.2; NT r 38.02; Qld r 259; SA r 246; Tas r 444; Vic r 38.02; WA O 52 r 1. An interim injunction is a sub-specie of an interlocutory injunction.

An application for an interim injunction will normally be made *ex parte* where there is an urgent need to protect the status quo, and notice of the application for relief might provide the defendant with an opportunity to thwart the application. The plaintiff will have to satisfy the court before the order expires that the injunction should continue until the trial of the proceeding, or some earlier date. The defendant will be given an opportunity to set aside the order. An illustration of an interim injunction is that obtained by Apple from the Federal Court (exercising jurisdiction under the Federal Court of Australia Act 1976 (Cth) s 23) seeking to restrain Samsung from releasing its tablet device in Australia: *Apple Inc v Samsung Electronics Co Ltd v Apple Inc* [2011] FCAFC 156. See generally I C F Spry, *Equitable Remedies*, 8th ed, Thomson Reuters, 2010, pp 505–14.

In making an application for an *ex parte* injunction the applicant must disclose all relevant facts, both for and against their case. An injunction may be dissolved if a misleading application has been presented: see *Grant Medich & Co Pty Ltd v Toyo Menka Kaisha Ltd* (1978) 3 ACLR 375.

Status quo

16.3.12   In *Liquorland (Aust) Pty Ltd v Anghie* (2001) 20 ACLC 58, [2001] VSC 362, Warren J made the following observations concerning the meaning of status quo:

[72] Ultimately, the plaintiffs' argument was one that relied upon retention of the status quo in support of the assertion that the balance of convenience weighed in their favour. Preservation of the status quo will depend always upon a variety of considerations in any particular case. Thus, although the most usual basis for the grant of an interlocutory injunction is to preserve the circumstances that exist at the time of the application until trial it is nevertheless a factor to be weighed very carefully. The discretion as to that which constitutes the status quo and its need for protection will often warrant the exercise of a very general discretion. As Spry observes in *Equitable Remedies* (6th ed.) (at 454) [See I C F Spry, *Equitable Remedies*, 8th ed, Thomson Reuters, 2010, pp 453–6)]:

It is clear that in exercising this very general discretion the Court is concerned primarily with such matters as the degree of probability that the material rights of the plaintiff exist, the degree of probability the defendant will act as the plaintiff alleges, the inadequacy of other remedies or forms of protection that are available and any other matters which bear on hardship as between the parties or which affect third persons and which render it more just to grant, or not to grant, as the case may be, the interlocutory injunction that is sought.

[73] Meagher, Gummow and Lehane, op cit, (at [2168]) defined the status quo as meaning '… the state of affairs in the period immediately before issue of the writ' (citing *Garden Cottage Foods Limited v Milk Marketing Board* (1984) AC 130).

Undertaking as to damages

16.3.13   On any application for an interim or interlocutory injunction, the court will require the plaintiff to provide 'the usual undertaking as to damages'. That is an undertaking given by the plaintiff personally, or by counsel appearing on behalf of the plaintiff, normally in the following terms:

> The plaintiff, by its counsel, undertakes to the court that it will abide by any order, which the court may make as to damages, should the court determine that the defendant has suffered any damage by reason of this order, which the plaintiff ought to pay.

In New South Wales (r 25.8), the form of undertaking is prescribed. See also Qld r 264(5).

In *National Australia Bank Ltd v Bond Brewing Holdings Ltd* [1991] 1 VR 386, the Victorian Appeal Division dealt with a case in which the usual undertaking as to damages had not been given, and noted with disapproval that the undertaking had not been so offered. In some jurisdictions there is provision for the giving of an undertaking as to damages: Qld r 264; Tas r 445.

In the event that at trial it is established that the interlocutory injunction should not have been granted, the court will conduct an inquiry as to damages. The onus is on the defendant to prove the damage sustained as a result of the injunction. In *Air Express Ltd v Ansett Transport Industries (Operations) Pty Ltd* (1979) 146 CLR 249, 268, Aickin J said:

> It is important in all cases, and particularly in the present case, to bear in mind the distinction adverted to in many of the cases (eg, per Myers CJ in *Newman Bros Ltd v Allum; SOS Motors Ltd (in liq) (No 2)* (1935) NZLR Suppl, at p 18) between damages flowing from the injunction and damages flowing from the litigation itself. There may not in every case be any difference between the two but, where there is a difference, it is essential that the damage flowing from the litigation should not be confused with the damage flowing from the interlocutory injunction. This is necessarily required by the form of the undertaking itself.

Aickin J's judgment was upheld on appeal: see *Air Express Ltd v Ansett Transport Industries (Operations) Pty Ltd* (1981) 146 CLR 309. For a recent application, see *Monty Financial Services Ltd v Cash Resources Australia Pty Ltd* [2001] VSC 84, per McDonald J. Payment of damages is enforced in the same way as a judgment.

16.3.14   Notes and questions

1.   In circumstances where a plaintiff would be required to provide security for costs (see **16.7.1**), the court might require the plaintiff to provide security for the undertaking as to damages. Where security is necessary, that security ought to reflect the value of loss flowing from the restraint imposed by the injunction and

not loss and damage said to have already occurred: *First Telecom Pty Ltd v Telstra Corporation* (2000) 101 FCR 77 at [22]–[24] and *Wells Fargo Bank Northwest v Victoria Aircraft Leasing Ltd* [2004] VSC 70, Habersberger J (defendant obtaining injunction to prevent lessor of aircraft from seizing the aircraft in circumstances where lease payments are ongoing).

2. Why do the courts insist on an undertaking as to damages?

3. Can a non-party injured by the 'wrongful' grant of an interlocutory injunction obtain damages? See Phipps AJ, 'Non-party Compensation for Wrongful Interim Injunctions: *Smithkline Beecham Plc v Apotex Europe Ltd* [2006] EWCA 685' (2007) 26 *CJQ* 10.

4. Can an injunction be granted against the world? See *Maritime Union of Australia v Patrick Stevedores Operations Pty Ltd* [1998] 4 VR 143 (Victorian Court of Appeal). In that case a judge had granted an injunction against all persons associated with a union picket line and all persons in the vicinity of certain premises where the picket was taking place. The Court of Appeal said that an injunction should not be granted against a person who is not a party to the proceeding. An injunction cannot be directed against the world at large, but should be directed to an identified person or persons. Where it is sought to obtain an injunction against a large group of people, it may be possible to obtain a representative order against one or more persons as representative of the group: see **10.9.2**. The two exceptions to this are wardship cases and those exceptional cases in which it is necessary to preserve the subject matter of the proceeding. Those exceptions are referred to in the judgment of Balcombe LJ in *Attorney-General v Newspaper Publishing plc* [1988] Ch 333 at 338–9.

5. Is it possible for a court to accept an undertaking by a defendant to do or not to do certain conduct rather than granting an injunction? See *Attorney-General (ex rel Lumley) v TS Gill & Son Pty Ltd* [1926] VLR 414; I C F Spry, *The Principles of Equitable Remedies*, 8th ed, 2010, pp 479–81.

6. A *quia timet* injunction may be grated to prevent a defendant in committing a wrong. See *CSL Ltd v GlaxoSmithKline Australia Pty Ltd* (2006) 70 IPR 128.

Service of order

16.3.15 In some jurisdictions it is necessary for the plaintiff to give notice to the defendant of the fact that an interlocutory injunction has been granted if the order is to be enforced. This will normally be achieved by ordinary service of the order on the defendant: FCR r 41.07; NT r 59.03; SA r 260(1); Vic r 59.03; WA O 42 r 3.

In other jurisdictions, a judgment or order takes effect on the date it was given or made, or if a court orders that it does not take effect until entered, the date on which it is entered. Service is not required: HCR r 8.02; NSW r 36.4; Qld rr 660, 661(4); Tas r 142.

The Victorian Court of Appeal in *Maritime Union of Australia v Patrick Stevedores Operations Pty Ltd* [1998] 4 VR 143 (see **16.3.14**, **n 4**) emphasised the importance of notice in the enforcement of an injunction and the need for a person enjoined to be heard in relation to the injunction. The court will need to be satisfied that the defendant was aware of the consequences of failure to comply with the order; *Miller v Eurovox Pty Ltd* [2004] VSCA 211. This will mean that the order should generally be endorsed with a notice warning the defendant of the consequences of failure to comply.

ANTON PILLER (SEARCH) ORDERS

16.4.1 The rules in relation to inspection of property are inadequate when dealing with potentially dishonest litigants. An alternative procedure is necessary in such cases. Anton Piller orders are *ex parte* orders authorising the search, preservation and seizure of documents and other evidence, if there are strong grounds for thinking that the defendant will otherwise destroy or remove such evidence. In its widest form the order may require a defendant to answer questions and produce documents. The court's power to grant such mandatory relief stems from its inherent power to award an injunction and to prevent an abuse of process. The rules of court also provide a basis for such orders. Anton Piller orders are not search warrants and do not permit forceable entry to premises. The order operates personally on the defendant, whose refusal to comply may amount to contempt of court. Secrecy is an essential element to be established when seeking an Anton Piller order.

At common law, the power to grant such relief was first recognised in the United Kingdom in *Anton Piller KG v Manufacturing Processes Ltd* [1976] Ch 55.

16.4.2C   **Anton Piller KG v Manufacturing Processes Ltd**
[1976] Ch 55
Court of Appeal (UK)

[The plaintiffs sought to restrain the defendants, their English agents, from infringing their copyright. They were concerned that the defendants, if notified of any application for interlocutory relief, would seek to destroy documents of a confidential nature in their possession or remove them from the jurisdiction. They sought authorisation, on an *ex parte* basis, for entry on to the defendants' premises in order to inspect, remove or make copies of documents belonging to the plaintiffs.]

Lord Denning MR (at 58): During the last 18 months the judges of the Chancery Division have been making orders of a kind not known before. They have some resemblance to search warrants. Under these orders the plaintiff and his solicitors are authorized to enter the defendant's premises so as to inspect papers, provided the defendant gives permission.

Now this is the important point: the court orders the defendant to give them permission. The judges have been making these orders on *ex parte* applications without prior notice to the defendant. None of the cases has been reported except *EMI Ltd v Pandit* [[1975] 1 All ER 418; [1975] 1 WLR 302] before Templeman J on 5th December 1974. But in the present case Brightman J refused to make such an order.

On appeal to us, Mr Laddie appears for the plaintiffs. He has appeared in most of these cases, and can claim the credit — or the responsibility — for them. He represented to us that in this case it was in the interests of justice that the application should not be made public at the time it was made. So we heard it in camera. It was last Tuesday, 2nd December. After hearing his submissions, we made the order. We now come to give our reasons in public. But at the outset I must state the facts, for it is obvious that such an order can only be justified in the most exceptional circumstances.

The plaintiffs are German manufacturers of high repute. They make electric motors and generators. They play an important part in the big new computer industry. They supply equipment for it. They have recently designed a frequency converter specially for supplying the computers of International Business Machines.

Since 1972 the plaintiffs have had, as their agents in the United Kingdom, a company here called Manufacturing Processes Ltd, which is run by Mr A H S Baker and Mr B P Wallace. These agents are dealers who get machines from the plaintiffs in Germany and sell them to customers in England. The plaintiffs supply the English company with much confidential information about the machines, including a manual showing how they work, and drawings which are the subject of copyright.

Very recently the plaintiffs have found out — so they say — that these English agents have been in secret communication with other German companies called Ferrostaal and Lechmotoren. The object of these communications is that the English company should supply these other German companies with drawings and materials and other confidential information so that they [59] can manufacture power units like the plaintiffs. The plaintiffs got to know of these communications through two 'defectors', if I may call them so. One was the commercial manager of the English company, Mr Brian Firth; the other was the sales manager, Mr William Raymond Knight. These two were so upset by what was going on in the English company that on their own initiative, without any approach by the plaintiffs whatever, on 2nd October 1975 one or both flew to Germany. They told the plaintiffs what they knew about the arrangements with Ferrostaal and Lechmotoren. They disclosed also that the English company were negotiating with Canadian and United States firms. In making these disclosures, both Mr Firth and Mr Knight were putting themselves in a perilous position, but the plaintiffs assured them that they would safeguard their future employment.

The disclosures — coming from defectors — might have been considered untrustworthy. But they were supported by documents which emanated from both Ferrostaal and Lechmotoren. They showed that the English company were in regular communication with those German companies. They were sending them drawings and arranging for inspection of the plaintiffs' machine, for the express purpose that the Lechmotoren company might manufacture a prototype machine copied from the plaintiffs. One of the most telling communications was a telex from Lechmotoren to Mr Wallace saying:

> It is the opinion of Mr S (of Lechmotoren) that the best way to find a final solution for the … prototype is to send Mr Beck to you as soon as the … latest design of [the plaintiffs] has arrived in your factory. In this case it is guaranteed that the Lech prototype will have exactly the same features as the [the plaintiffs'] type. We hope you will agree to this proposal and we ask you to let us have your telex in order to arrange Mr Beck's visit accordingly.

On getting this information, the plaintiffs were extremely worried. They were about to produce a fine new frequency converter called 'the silent block'. They feared that the English company, in co-operation with the German manufacturers, would make a copy of their 'silent block' and ruin their market. They determined to apply to the court for an injunction to restrain the English company from infringing their copyright or using confidential information or making copies of their machines. But they were fearful that if the English company were given notice of this application, they would take steps to destroy the documents or send them to Germany or elsewhere, so that there would be none in existence by the time that discovery was had in the action.

So, on Wednesday, 26th November 1975 the plaintiffs' solicitor prepared a draft writ of summons and, with an affidavit, they went before Brightman J and asked, first, for an interim injunction to restrain infringement etc, and, secondly, for an order that they might be permitted to enter the premises of the English company so as to inspect the documents of the plaintiffs and remove them, or copies of them. Brightman J granted an interim injunction, but refused to order inspection or removal of documents. He said:

> There is strong prima facie evidence that the defendant company is now engaged in seeking to copy the plaintiffs' components for its own financial profit to the great detriment of the plaintiffs and in breach of the plaintiffs' rights.

[60] He realised that the defendants might suppress evidence or misuse documentary material, but he thought that that was a risk which must be accepted in civil matters save in extreme cases. 'Otherwise', he said —

> it seems to me that an order on the lines sought might become on instrument of oppression, particularly in a case where a plaintiff of big standing and deep pocket is ranged against a small man who is alleged on the evidence of one side only to have infringed the plaintiff's rights.

Let me say at once that no court in this land has any power to issue a search warrant to enter a man's house so as to see if there are papers or documents there which are of an incriminating nature, whether libels or infringements of copyright or anything else of the kind. No constable or bailiff can knock at the door and demand entry so as to inspect papers or documents. The householder can shut the door in his face and say, 'Get out'. That was established in the leading case of *Entick v Carrington* [(1765) 2 Wils 275, [1558–1774] All ER Rep 41]. None of us would wish to whittle down that principle in the slightest. But the order sought in this case is not a search warrant. It does not authorise the plaintiffs' solicitors or anyone else to enter the defendants' premises against their will. It does not authorise the breaking down of any doors, nor the slipping in by a back door, nor getting in by an open door or window. It only authorizes entry and inspection by the permission of the defendants. The plaintiffs must get the defendants' permission. But it does do this: it brings pressure on the defendants to give permission. It does more. It actually orders them to give permission — with, I suppose, the result that if they do not give permission, they are guilty of contempt of court.

This may seem to be a search warrant in disguise. But it was fully considered in the House of Lords 150 years ago and found to be legitimate. The case is *United Company of Merchants of England, Trading to the East Indies v Kynaston* (1821) 3 Bli (OS) 153. Lord Redesdale said, at pp 163–4:

> The arguments urged for the appellants at the Bar are founded upon the supposition, that the Court has directed a forcible inspection. This is an erroneous view of the case. The order is to permit; and if the East India Company should refuse to permit inspection, they will be guilty of a contempt of the Court ... It is an order operating on the person requiring the defendants to permit inspection, not giving authority of force, or to break open the doors of their warehouse.

That case was not, however, concerned with papers or things. It was only as to the value of a warehouse; and that could not be obtained without an inspection. But the distinction drawn by Lord Redesdale affords ground for thinking that there is jurisdiction to make an order that the defendants 'do permit' when it is necessary in the interests of justice.

Accepting such to be the case, the question is in what circumstances ought such an order be made. If the defendant is given notice beforehand and is able to argue the pros and cons, it is warranted by that case in the House of Lords and by RSC Ord 29, r 2(1) and (5). But it is a far stronger thing to make such an order *ex parte* without giving him [61] notice. This is not covered by the rules of court and must be based on the inherent jurisdiction of the court. There are one or two old precedents which give some colour for it, *Hennessey v Bohmann Osborne & Co* [[1877] WN 14], and *Morris v Howell* [(1888) 22 LR Ir 77], an Irish case. But they do not go very far. So it falls to us to consider it on principle. It seems to me that such an order can be made by a judge *ex parte*, but it should only be made where it is essential that the plaintiff should have inspection so that justice can be done between the parties; and when, if the defendant were forewarned, there is a grave danger that vital evidence will be destroyed, that papers will be burnt or lost or hidden, or taken beyond the jurisdiction, and so the ends of justice be defeated; and when the inspection would do no real harm to the defendant or his case.

Nevertheless, in the enforcement of this order, the plaintiffs must act with due circumspection. On the service of it, the plaintiffs should be attended by their solicitor, who is an officer of the court. They should give the defendants an opportunity of considering it and of consulting their own solicitor. If the defendants wish to apply to discharge the order as having been improperly obtained, they must be allowed to do so. If the defendants refused permission to enter or to inspect, the plaintiffs must not force their way in. They must accept that refusal, and bring it to the notice of the court afterwards, if need be on application to commit.

One might think that with all these safeguards against abuse, it would be of little use to make such an order. But it can be effective in this way: it serves to tell the defendant that, on the evidence put before it, the court is of opinion that he ought to permit inspection — nay, it orders him to permit — and that he refuses at his peril. It puts him in peril not only of proceedings for contempt, but also of adverse inferences being drawn against him; so much so that his own solicitor may often advise him to comply. We are told that in two at least of the cases such an order has been effective. We are prepared, therefore, to sanction its continuance, but only in an extreme case where there is grave danger of property being smuggled away or of vital evidence being destroyed.

On the evidence in this case, we decided on 2nd December that there was sufficient justification to make an order. We did it on the precedent framed by Templeman J. [See *EMI Ltd v Pandit* [1975] 1 All ER 418, at 424, [1975] 1 WLR 302 at 308.] It contains an undertaking in damages which is to be supported (as the plaintiffs are overseas) by a bond for £10,000. It gives an interim injunction to restrain the infringement of copyright and breach of confidential information etc. It orders that the defendants do permit one or two of the plaintiffs and one or two of their solicitors to enter the defendants' premises for the purpose of inspecting documents, files or things, and removing those which belong to the plaintiffs. This was, of course, only an interim order pending the return of the summons. It is to be heard, we believe, tomorrow by the judge.

Ormrod LJ (at 61): I agree with all that Lord Denning MR has said. The proposed order is at the extremity of this court's powers. Such orders, therefore, will rarely be made, and only when there is no alternative way of ensuring that justice is done to the applicant.

[62] There are three essential pre-conditions for the making of such an order, in my judgment. First, there must be an extremely strong prima facie case. Secondly, the damage, potential

or actual, must be very serious for the plaintiff. Thirdly, there must be clear evidence that the defendants have in their possession incriminating documents or things, and that there is a real possibility that they may destroy such material before any application *inter partes* can be made.

The form of the order makes it plain that the court is not ordering or granting anything equivalent to a search warrant. The order is an order on the defendant *in personam* to permit inspection. It is therefore open to him to refuse to comply with such an order, but at his peril either of further proceedings for contempt of court — in which case, of course, the court will have the widest discretion as to how to deal with it, and if it turns out that the order was made improperly in the first place, the contempt will be dealt with accordingly — but more important, of course, the refusal to comply may be the most damning evidence against the defendant at the subsequent trial. Great responsibility clearly rests on the solicitors for the plaintiff to ensure that the carrying out of such an order is meticulously carefully done with the fullest respect for the defendant's rights, as Lord Denning MR has said, of applying to the court, should he feel it necessary to do so, before permitting the inspection.

In the circumstances of the present case, all those conditions to my mind are satisfied, and this order is essential in the interests of justice. I agree, therefore, that the appeal should be allowed.

[Shaw LJ concurred with the judgments of Lord Denning MR and Ormrod LJ.]

16.4.3 For an example of the form of an Anton Piller order, see *Miller v Eurovox Pty Ltd* [2004] VSCA 211:

TAKE NOTICE PAUL ANTHONY MILLER AND YVONNE MILLER

1. This Order orders you to allow the persons mentioned below to enter the premises described in the Order and to search for, examine and remove or copy the articles specified in the Order. The persons mentioned will have no right to enter the premises or, having entered, to remain at the premises, unless you give your consent to their doing so. If, however, you withhold your consent you will be in breach of this Order and may be held to be in Contempt of Court. The Order also requires you to hand over any of such articles which are under your control and to provide information to the Plaintiffs' solicitors, and prohibits you from doing certain acts. This part of the Order is subject to restrictions.

2. You should read the terms of the Order very carefully. You are advised to consult a Solicitor as soon as possible.

3. Before you, a Defendant or the person appearing to be in control of the premises, allow anybody onto the premises to carry out this Order, you are entitled to have the solicitor who serves you with this Order explain to you what it means in everyday language.

4. You are entitled to insist that there is nobody present who could gain commercially from anything they might read or see on your premises.

5. You are entitled to refuse to permit entry before 8:00am or after 6:00pm on any day.

6. You are entitled to refuse to permit disclosure of any documents which may tend to incriminate you ('incriminating documents') or to answer any questions if to do so may tend to incriminate you. It may be prudent to take advice because, if you so refuse, your refusal may be taken into account by the Court at a later stage.

7. You are entitled to refuse to permit disclosure of any documents passing between you and your Solicitors for the purpose of obtaining advice ('privileged documents').

8. You are entitled to seek legal advice, and to ask the Court to vary or discharge this order, provided you do so at once, and provided that meanwhile you permit the independent solicitor (who is a solicitor acting independently of the Plaintiff) and two of the Plaintiff's representatives, to enter but not start to search.

9. If you, a Defendant, disobey this Order you may be found guilty of Contempt of Court.

10. If any person with knowledge of this Order procures, encourages or assists in its breach, that person will also be guilty of Contempt of Court.

16.4.4   Notes

1. As an application for an Anton Piller order is necessarily made *ex parte*, the plaintiff is under an obligation to ensure that all relevant evidence, whether advantageous or detrimental to its case, is placed before the court. See, in this regard, *Columbia Pictures Industries Inc v Robinson* [1987] Ch 38. A more recent example in the case of a Mareva order is *Westpac Banking Corporation v Hilliard* [2001] VSC 187 (McDonald J) (non-disclosure of material facts on an application for a Mareva order — order discharged).

2. A practice has developed where the Anton Piller order has been extended to require a defendant, and in the case of a corporate defendant, its proper officer or officers, to answer questions (interrogatories) on oath, in relation to such matters as the supply of goods made in apparent breach of the plaintiff's intellectual property rights. See *EMI Ltd v Sarwar* [1977] FSR 146. A question arises in such cases regarding the extent to which the defendant can be required to answer questions which might incriminate them and the protection which might be given to the defendant in that regard.

3. The Uniform Civil Procedure Rules in Queensland attempted to partially codify Anton Piller orders: Qld Ch 8 Pt 2 Div 3.

16.4.5C	Rank Film Distributors Ltd v Video Information Centre (a firm)
	[1982] AC 380
	House of Lords

[The plaintiffs were owners of copyright in certain cinematograph films. There was evidence that the defendants were making and selling video cassette copies of the films. Orders were made permitting the plaintiffs to enter the defendants' premises to seize the offending copies. The orders required the defendants to answer interrogatories relating to the supply and sale of the copies. The defendants objected to discovery of the copies and to the interrogatories, on the basis that compliance with the orders would breach their privilege against self-incrimination.]

Lord Wilberforce (at 439): [His Lordship referred to the facts, to the decision at first instance and the decision of the Court of Appeal, before continuing:] The main question before this House is whether Mr Lee and Ms Gomberg can avail themselves of the privilege against self-incrimination in order to deprive the appellants of an important part of the relief which they seek. It may seem to be a strange paradox that the worse, ie, the more criminal, their activities can be made to appear, the less effective is the civil remedy that can be granted but that, prima facie, is what the privilege achieves. The orders under appeal are elaborate.

[His Lordship then referred to the orders and continued (at 440):]
Thus, for present purposes, the orders fall under three heads:

(1) Requiring the respondents to supply information.
(2) Requiring the respondents to allow access to premises for the purpose of looking for illicit copy films and to allow their being removed to safe custody. [441]
(3) Requiring the respondents to disclose and produce documents.

The orders under (2) were upheld by the Court of Appeal, and this part of the court's decision was not seriously contested in this House. In any event I am satisfied that there was jurisdiction to make these orders and that the privilege against self-incrimination has no application to them. The privilege against self-incrimination is invoked as regards (1) and (3). The essential question being whether the provision of the information or production of the documents may tend to incriminate the respondents, it is necessary to see what possible heads of criminal liability there may be. There are three: (1) Section 21 of the Copyright Act 1956 creates summary offences under a number of headings, some of which would have potential applicability to the respondents. For a first offence there is a maximum fine of £50 however many infringing articles are involved. (2) Conspiracy to commit a breach of section 21 of the Act. By virtue of the Criminal Law Act 1977 no greater punishment can be imposed for such a conspiracy than for the substantive offence under section 21. (3) Conspiracy to defraud — an offence at common law left unaffected by the Act of 1977.

As to (1) and (2), I think that a substantial argument could be raised that these should not be taken account of in connection with a claim for privilege. The criminal offences created by section 21 cover almost precisely the same ground as the bases for civil liability under the Copyright Act 1956. I would be reluctant to hold that in civil proceedings for infringement based on specified acts the defendants could claim privilege against discovery on the ground that those same acts establish a possible liability for a petty offence. In practice, as one would suppose, section 21 is very rarely invoked: only one case came to our knowledge, namely of one prosecution in 1913 under the Copyright Act 1911, and potential liability under it might well be disregarded as totally insubstantial. The same argument would apply as regard conspiracy to breach it.

However, it is only too clear (and I deliberately use the language of reluctance) that supply of the information and production of the documents sought would tend to expose the respondents to a charge of conspiracy to defraud. In the very nature of this activity, a number of persons are certain to be involved in it — in printing the master tapes, copying from the master tapes, seeking and accepting orders, and distributing the illicit copies. A charge of conspiracy to defraud, so far from being as it sometimes is, a contrived addition to other charges, is here an appropriate and exact description of what is being done. So far from it being contrived, fanciful, or imagined, it is the charge on which Mr Dawson, who appears on the existing evidence to be closely connected with Mr Lee and Ms Gomberg, is to stand trial. It cannot be said that charges under this head would be nothing but charges under section 21 of the Act of 1956 under another name. An essential ingredient in them is dishonesty, which may exist in cases brought under section 21, but which may not. The much heavier penalties also make it more likely that charges would be brought of conspiracy to defraud. Unless some escape can be devised from this conclusion, the privilege must inevitably attach.

[442] Mr Nicholls, for the appellants, courageously attempted to suggest an escape route on the following lines. The courts, he submitted, must in all cases try to reconcile protection of a defendant from possible self-incrimination with doing justice to a plaintiff. Whatever may have been the position when the privilege was first worked out by the judges, modern procedure is now more flexible, and makes it possible to do justice without denying protection. It is all the more necessary to find a flexible approach, because so many actions which formerly involved civil liability only are now, by modern trends in legislation, made criminal offences. Thus many ordinary cases of 'passing off' are now offences under the Trade Descriptions Act 1968. If full scope is given to the privilege against self-incrimination, potential plaintiffs, in this area of industrial property, will fail to get a remedy in the civil courts. Mr Nicholls was at pains to make clear that he was not, in these submissions, attempting to negate or undermine the privilege against self-incrimination. This has been too long established in our law as a basic liberty of the subject — in other countries it has constitutional status — to be denied. It has received modern recognition in section 14 of the Civil Evidence Act 1968 and in this House.

It is certainly correct to say, that existing law and practice to some extent prevent matter disclosed on discovery in civil proceedings from being used to the prejudice of the disclosing party. The protection is described with different words: the matter must not be used for an 'improper' purpose: *Alterskye v Scott* [1948] 1 All ER 469, or a 'collateral object' (*Bray on Discovery*, 1st ed (1885), 238) or, most strongly, 'otherwise than in the action in which they are disclosed': *Distillers Co (Biochemicals) Ltd v Times Newspapers Ltd* [1975] QB 613 at 621 per Talbot J.

In the most recent case, *Riddick v Thames Board Mills Ltd* [1977] QB 881, 896, Lord Denning MR used the words 'for any ulterior or alien purpose.' But it has never been held that these expressions, however wide, extend to criminal proceedings: if they did there would be no need for the privilege. Mr Nicholls was therefore obliged to suggest that even granting this, the courts had power positively to decide in a particular case, as the counterpart of the obligation to disclose, that any matter which is compulsorily disclosed as the result of the court's process should be inadmissible in evidence. But I cannot accept that a civil court has any power to decide in a manner which would bind a criminal court that evidence of any kind is admissible or inadmissible in that court. Certainly a criminal court always has a discretion to exclude evidence improperly obtained if to admit it would unfairly prejudice a defendant. But to substitute for a privilege a dependence on the court's discretion would substantially be to the defendant's detriment. That the civil court has not the power to declare evidence inadmissible is strikingly shown by section 31 of the Theft Act 1968 which contains an express provision by which a person is obliged to answer questions put in proceedings for the recovery of property and to comply with orders made in such proceedings and which states that no statement or admission so made shall be admissible in evidence against the person concerned in [443] proceedings for an offence under the Act. Infringement of copyright is not theft, so this section cannot be invoked.

The appellants' submission amounts to a request to the courts, by judicial decision, to extend this statutory provision to civil proceedings generally, or at least to these proceedings. But this, in my opinion, the courts cannot do. I should add that *Riddick's case* is no support for the proposition that answers or documents extracted in civil proceedings are inadmissible in criminal proceedings: the remark of Lord Denning MR in the Court of Appeal [1980] 3 WLR 487, 507G is made with reference to an argument for applying section 31 of the Theft Act by analogy (which I cannot accept) and clearly does not represent Lord Denning's view as to *Riddick's case*. That is accurately stated at 504.

There are some further points on this aspect of the case. First, I do not think that adequate protection can be given by extracting from the plaintiffs, as a term of being granted an Anton Piller order, an undertaking not to use the information obtained in criminal proceedings. Even if such an undertaking were binding (see to the contrary *Triplex Safety Glass Co Ltd v Lancegaye Safety Glass (1934) Ltd* [1939] 2 KB 395) the protection is only partial, viz against prosecution by the plaintiff himself. Moreover whatever direct use may or may not be made of information given, or material disclosed, under the compulsory process of the court, it must not be overlooked that, quite apart from that, its provision or disclosure may set in train a process which may lead to incrimination or may lead to the discovery of real evidence of an incriminating character. In the present case, this cannot be discounted as unlikely: it is not only a possible but probably the intended result. The party from whom disclosure is asked is entitled, on established law, to be protected from these consequences. Secondly, and this was very much an argument of last resort, Mr Nicholls suggested that protection could be given by a hearing, wholly or in part, in camera. But such procedure is totally alien, except in the most exceptional cases, to our procedure and I do not think that so wide an extension of it as the submission involves ought to be contemplated. Thirdly, there are some procedural considerations. The appellants argued that even, if, in principle, the privilege against self-incrimination is capable of attaching in cases such as the present, that should not prevent the order for information and production being made: the defendant should be left to raise the question of privilege, if he wishes, and if necessary the court should rule upon it. The difficulty is, however, that the orders are intended to take effect immediately upon the arrival of the plaintiff's representatives (including, under existing practice, a solicitor) at the defendant's premises, and if the defendant were to refuse to comply, even in reliance on the privilege, he might, at least technically, be liable in contempt. I do not think that this problem is for this House to resolve. Attention can merely be drawn to it, and in due course, no doubt, forms of order will be worked out which will enable the orders to be as effective as practicable while preserving the defendant's essential rights. All that this House can do is to decide that the privilege against self-incrimination is capable of being invoked. I would so decide.

[444] Some other points were taken by the respondents as to the orders made in this case. Some were said to be too widely expressed, in particular one which required each defendant to disclose the whereabouts of all illicit copy films or masters (ie, master copies) for making the same known to that defendant. I can see that they may have force, but the proper forum for them to be raised and debated is in the Chancery Division before judges particularly experienced in the framing and controlling of interlocutory orders. The record shows that they are fully sensitive to the need for keeping these orders within due limits.

I would dismiss the present appeal.

Lord Fraser of Tullybelton (at 445): [His Lordship referred to the facts and continued:] The respondents assert that if they are compelled to disclose the information mentioned in the parts of the orders to which they object, they will run a real risk of providing evidence tending to show that they have been guilty of criminal offences. Three offences are particularly suggested, namely (1) contravention of section 21 of the Copyright Act 1956, (2) the common law offence of conspiracy to defraud and possibly (3) an offence against section 18 of the Theft Act 1968. The risk of prosecution under the Theft Act may, I think, be disregarded as remote, because that Act applies to theft of 'property' which is defined in a way that does not appear to include copyright, but only, so far as this appeal is concerned, to the physical objects such as tapes and cassettes which are of small value by themselves. The risk of prosecution under section 21 of the Copyright Act 1956 is theoretically greater because acts which are infringements of copyright, including the making of unauthorised copies (section 13(5)) and knowingly importing, or selling infringing copies (section 16(2) and (3)(a)) are very likely also to be offences under section 21(1). But the offences created by section 21 are only ancillary remedies for breach of copyright, as appears from the cross-heading to Part III of the Act, and they are treated as comparatively trivial with a maximum penalty (as amended) of £50. It would, in my opinion, be unreasonable to allow the possibility of incrimination of such offences to obstruct disclosure of information which would be of much more value to the owners of the infringed copyright than any protection they obtain from section 21.

But conspiracy to defraud is a different matter. It is a serious offence. The risk of those who deal in or manufacture illicit films being prosecuted [446] for it is by no means remote or fanciful. Indeed the sixth respondent is now facing prosecution on that ground for the matters with which this appeal is concerned. Subject to a point, to be noticed hereafter, with regard to an offence of conspiracy, the possibility of prosecution on this ground does therefore raise the question whether the defendant can rely on the privilege against being compelled to incriminate himself. The privilege itself is well established in English law. It is impliedly recognised by section 14(1) of the Civil Evidence Act 1968, and authority for its existence is to be found in *Triplex Safety Glass Co Ltd v Lancegaye Safety Glass (1934) Ltd* [1939] 2 KB 395 and *In re Westinghouse Electric Corporation Uranium Contract Litigation M D L Docket No 235 (No 2)* [1978] AC 547. The appellants do not dispute the existence of a privilege against compulsory self-incrimination by discovery or by answering interrogatories. But their counsel presented a powerful argument to the effect that the privilege ought not to be upheld in its simple form, to the serious prejudice of the appellants, when the object of the privilege could be attained in a way that would not prejudice the interests of parties such as the appellants. It could be attained, according to the argument, by compelling the discovery and answers, while relying on a restriction, express or implied, against the use of information thereby disclosed in any prosecution of the party making the discovery.

At one stage, the argument seemed to depend on the possibility that the court which ordered the discovery might place an express restriction on the use of any information disclosed. In my opinion, any argument on that basis must be rejected. A restriction by the court making the order would, no doubt, be effective to bind the party who obtained the order, but it can hardly be suggested that it would be effective to prevent a prosecutor in the public interest from using, or an English criminal court (*a fortiori* a Scottish criminal court if a conspiracy were prosecuted in Scotland) from admitting the information in evidence at a trial. All evidence which is relevant is prima facie admissible in a criminal trial, although the trial judge has a discretion to exclude evidence which, though admissible, has been obtained by unfair means from the accused after commission of the offence: *Reg v Sang* [1980] AC 402. But it is obvious that a person who has to rely on an exercise of judicial discretion is in a less secure position than one who, by relying on the privilege, can avoid providing the information in the first place. We were referred to some old cases where the court had considered the restrictions on the use of documents which it ordered to be disclosed. In one case the court required an undertaking by the party in whose favour the order was made not to use answers for the purpose of enforcing penalties (*Jackson v Benson* (1826) 1 Y & J 32) and in *Reynolds v Godlee* (1858) 4 K & J 88, 92 Page-Wood VC said that the court had a right to say to the person who has obtained the production of documents: 'Those documents shall never be used by *you* except with the authority of the court' (emphasis added). Such qualified restrictions are clearly of much less value to the party making discovery than the privilege itself would have been.

The main basis of the argument was an implied rule, said to be derived from the case of *Riddick v Thames Board Mills Ltd* [1977] QB 881, to the effect that evidence which has been disclosed under compulsion in a [447] civil action cannot be used against a person who has disclosed it for the purposes of another civil action or of a criminal prosecution. It was argued that any incriminating information disclosed by a person making discovery or answering interrogatories would enjoy complete protection by reason of that rule, because the information would have been given under compulsion, in respect that refusal to give it would be contempt of court. I would make one preliminary observation on that argument. It seems to me to go much too far. If it is well-founded, it means that the established practice whereby judges warn witnesses that they need not answer questions addressed to them in oral examination in court, if the answers might tend to incriminate them, is unnecessary, because refusal to answer would, in the absence of the warning, be contempt of court and any incriminating evidence having been given under compulsion would not be admissible against them in criminal proceedings. I approach a proposition leading to that result with some scepticism. In any event, the case of *Riddick* was concerned only with the question of the use to which documents recovered on discovery could be put by the party who had obtained discovery. Lord Denning MR at 896H, stated the principle in a sentence thus: 'A party who seeks discovery of documents gets it on condition that *he* will make use of them only for the purposes of that action, and for no other purpose' (emphasis added). That statement of principle would have to be extended to include cases such as *Norwich Pharmacal Co v Customs and Excise Commissioners* [1974] AC 133, where an order was made for discovery of information for the purpose of its being used in another action. The principle is, I think, that information is not to be used by the party who gets discovery for purposes other than that for which production was ordered. But the case of *Riddick* had nothing to do with the use of information for prosecution in the public interest. On the contrary, both Lord Denning MR at 896 and Stephenson LJ at 901, referred with approval to the observations of Talbot J in *Distillers Co (Biochemicals) Ltd v Times Newspapers* [1975] QB 613, 621, recognising that there might be a public interest in favour of disclosure which would override the public interest in the administration of justice which goes to preserve the confidentiality of documents disclosed on discovery. That is clearly correct. If a defendant's answers to interrogatories tend to show that he has been guilty of a serious offence I cannot think that there would be anything improper in his opponent reporting the matter to the criminal authorities with a view to prosecution, certainly if he had first obtained leave from the court which ordered the interrogatories, and probably without such leave. If that is right the object of the privilege against self-incrimination would not be completely achieved by relying on any rule which can be derived from *Riddick v Thames Board Mills Ltd* [1977] QB 881.

Moreover, if the incriminating information given on discovery or in answer to interrogatories were disclosed subsequently in open court in the civil action, it might be heard and might then be used in a criminal prosecution against the defendant. In an attempt to meet this difficulty Mr Nicholls submitted that the defendant's interests could be protected by the courts sitting in camera whenever incriminating information disclosed on discovery was to be referred to. Such procedure would raise considerable practical difficulties and it would also be objectionable on principle. There [448] are cases where in order that justice may be done the court has to sit in camera (*Scott v Scott* [1913] AC 417) but it is important that such cases should be limited to those where proceedings in private are absolutely necessary in the interests of justice. If the procedure for which the appellants are contending would lead to more frequent hearings in camera, as I think it would, then that is an additional argument against adopting it. Accordingly I reach the conclusion, with some regret, that the respondents' objection based upon the fear of self-incrimination is well-founded and ought to be upheld.

An alternative and narrower contention was advanced by counsel for the appellants to cover the event of his being unsuccessful on the main contention. This narrower contention raises the point about a charge of conspiracy to which I have already referred. It was said that there is a special exception to the privilege against self incrimination where the incrimination relates to the offence of conspiracy, because of the wide range of facts that might be included in that offence. There is some support for this argument in observations by judges in cases to which we were referred (see *Mayor, Commonalty and Citizens of London v Levy* (1803) 8 Ves Jun 398, *Attorney- General v Conroy* (1838) 2 Jo Ex Ir 791 and *Chadwick v Chadwick* (1852) 22 LJ Ch 329) but in my opinion they do not provide any clear principle on which an exception to the general rule against compulsory self-incrimination could be based. They do not appear to have been followed in recent years. Accordingly I would not accept the narrower submission on this point.

The order of July 2 was criticised as being too wide, particularly in so far as it called on the defendants to disclose the names of all persons who are engaged in the production, distribution and sale of illicit films, and not merely those persons with whom the defendants have had business dealings. In my opinion that criticism was justified and the order ought to have been restricted in that way. For these reasons I would dismiss the appeal.

[Lord Diplock agreed with the speech of Lord Wilberforce. Lord Russell of Killowen and Lord Roskill agreed with the speeches of both Lords Wilberforce and Fraser of Tullybelton.]

Privilege against self-incrimination

16.4.6   A party need not answer questions or produce documents thereby creating a risk of self-incrimination or criminal prosecution: *Rank Film Distributors Ltd v Video Information Centre (a firm)* [1982] AC 380; Uniform Evidence Acts, s 128 (the Evidence Act 1995 (Cth), Evidence Act 1995 (NSW) and Evidence Act 2001 (Tas)) extracted below. Legal professional privilege may also prevent inspection of documents: *Metso Minerals (Australia) Ltd v Kalra (No 3)* [2008] FCA 1201 at [14].

16.4.7   In *Ross v Internet Wines Pty Ltd* (2004) 60 NSWLR 436, a case of a Mareva order (see 16.5.1–16.5.11), Austin J had made an order in the following terms:

3.   Subject to the provision below, an order that by 4.00 pm on Monday 25 August 2003, David Martin Ross swear and serve an affidavit in which he:
  (a)   gives details of all of his assets, both real and personal and all bank and other accounts maintained or controlled by him together with details of amounts held in those accounts; and
  (b)   identifies all funds removed by him from the bank account or any other account maintained by the fifth defendant or the sixth defendant since 1 January 2003, and —
  the circumstances under which those amounts were removed; to whom the amounts were paid; and identifying any part of the funds so removed remaining in his possession or control and the whereabouts of those funds. Provided that should David Martin Ross decide to make a claim for privilege against self incrimination, then the sworn affidavit be delivered to his Honour, Justice Austin's associate on or before 4.00pm on Monday 25

August 2003 in a sealed envelope, together with a notice of motion in which the claim for privilege against self-incrimination is made and any affidavit in support of that claim.

4. An order that any such notice of motion in which a claim for privilege against self-incrimination is made and supporting affidavit be served on the solicitors for the 1st Defendant, the 2nd Defendant, the 3rd Defendant and the 4th Defendant by 6.00 pm on Monday 25 August 2003.

The Court of Appeal held that this procedure infringed the defendant's privilege against self-incrimination.

16.4.8 In response to the Australian Law Reform Commission, *Discussion Paper 69 Review of the Uniform Evidence Acts*, s 128A was enacted.

16.4.9 **Evidence Act 1995 (Cth)**

128A Privilege in respect of self-incrimination — exception for certain orders etc

(1) In this section:

"disclosure order" means an order made by a federal court or an ACT court in a civil proceeding requiring a person to disclose information, as part of, or in connection with a freezing or search order, but does not include an order made by a court under the *Proceeds of Crime Act 2002*.

"relevant person" means a person to whom a disclosure order is directed.

(2) If a relevant person objects to complying with a disclosure order on the grounds that some or all of the information required to be disclosed may tend to prove that the person:

    (a) has committed an offence against or arising under an Australian law or a law of a foreign country; or

    (b) is liable to a civil penalty;

    the person must:

    (c) disclose so much of the information required to be disclosed to which no objection is taken; and

    (d) prepare an affidavit containing so much of the information required to be disclosed to which objection is taken (the *privilege affidavit*) and deliver it to the court in a sealed envelope; and

    (e) file and serve on each other party a separate affidavit setting out the basis of the objection.

(3) The sealed envelope containing the privilege affidavit must not be opened except as directed by the court.

(4) The court must determine whether or not there are reasonable grounds for the objection.

(5) Subject to subsection (6), if the court finds that there are reasonable grounds for the objection, the court must not require the information contained in the privilege affidavit to be disclosed and must return it to the relevant person.

(6) If the court is satisfied that:

    (a) any information disclosed in the privilege affidavit may tend to prove that the relevant person has committed an offence against or arising under, or is liable to a civil penalty under, an Australian law; and

---

(b) the information does not tend to prove that the relevant person has committed an offence against or arising under, or is liable to a civil penalty under, a law of a foreign country; and

(c) the interests of justice require the information to be disclosed;

the court may make an order requiring the whole or any part of the privilege affidavit containing information of the kind referred to in paragraph (a) to be filed and served on the parties.

(7) If the whole or any part of the privilege affidavit is disclosed (including by order under subsection (6)), the court must cause the relevant person to be given a certificate in respect of the information as referred to in paragraph (6)(a).

(8) In any proceeding in an Australian court:

(a) evidence of information disclosed by a relevant person in respect of which a certificate has been given under this section; and

(b) evidence of any information, document or thing obtained as a direct result or indirect consequence of the relevant person having disclosed that information;

cannot be used against the person. However, this does not apply to a criminal proceeding in respect of the falsity of the evidence concerned.

(9) Subsection (8) does not prevent the use against the relevant person of any information disclosed by a document:

(a) that is an annexure or exhibit to a privilege affidavit prepared by the person in response to a disclosure order; and

(b) that was in existence before the order was made.

(10) Subsection (8) has effect despite any challenge, review, quashing or calling into question on any ground of the decision to give, or the validity of, the certificate concerned.

16.4.10 The effect of this provision is to preclude a natural person from relying on the privilege against self-incrimination where he or she is simply asked to permit access to premises for the purpose of a search, to produce documents or disclose assets. The privilege against self-incrimination does not extend to corporations: see *Environment Protection Authority v Caltex Refining Co Pty Ltd* (1993) 178 CLR 477; 68 ALJR 127.

16.4.11 Notes and questions

1. Does s 128A require a defendant to answer interrogatories? See *A T & T Istel Ltd v Tully* [1993] AC 45 on the privilege against self-incrimination, as it affects interrogatories forming part of an Anton Piller order.

2. It will be noted from the *Rank Distributors* case that the court has power to prevent the defendant giving notice to a third party of the existence of the Anton Piller order.

3. How is an Anton Piller order to be executed? *Universal Thermosensors Ltd v Hibben* [1992] 1 WLR 840, 860–861; [1992] 3 All ER 257 at 275–6 (Nicholls VC) sets down guidelines for the execution of Anton Piller orders, which may be summarised as follows:

(a) Not only must the form of order state that before complying with the order the defendant may obtain legal advice, for such safeguard to be effective, Anton

Piller orders should generally be executed only on working days in office hours, when a solicitor can be expected to be available.

(b) If the order is to be executed at a private house, and it is likely that a woman may be in the house alone, the solicitor serving the order must be, or must be accompanied by, a woman.

(c) To minimise disputes, in general, Anton Piller orders should provide that, unless impracticable, a detailed list of the items removed should be prepared at the premises before they are removed, and that the defendant should be given an opportunity to check the list at this time.

(d) Anton Piller orders frequently contain an injunction restraining the respondent from informing others of the existence of the order for a limited period — an injunction for a whole week is too long.

(e) Anton Piller orders should provide that, unless there is a good reason for doing otherwise, the order should not be executed at business premises save in the presence of a responsible officer or representative of the company or trader in question.

(f) In cases where an Anton Piller order is taken out by a party against his or her competitor, there should be some means of preventing the applicant from executing the order himself or herself and taking the opportunity to carry out a thorough search of his or her competitor's business.

4.　The guidelines set out in the judgment of Nicholls V-C in the *Universal Thermosensors* case were referred to with approval by Powell JA in *Long v Specifier Publications Pty Ltd* (1998) 44 NSWLR 545 at 549. In that case a solicitor had given undertakings to the court in relation to the execution of an Anton Piller order. The order required the solicitor to make an inventory of items taken and to keep control of the items. The solicitor was found to have breached the undertakings and to be guilty of contempt. He appealed to the New South Wales Court of Appeal. The appeal was dismissed. Powell JA said (at p 548):

> Although, superficially, the primary order made in such cases might appear to be a search warrant, it must be emphasised that this is not so. On the contrary, the order is a mandatory order operating *in personam* on the defendant requiring him to permit a nominated person, either alone or accompanied by others, to enter, search, and, where appropriate, to take copies of, or remove, documents or other property. Two consequences flow from this, they being, first, that, if permission is refused, entry and search may not lawfully be had or made; and, secondly, that, if the defendant, having been duly served with an order, refuses permission, be liable to be dealt with for contempt.

Since such an order is an extraordinary remedy, and since an *ex parte* order should be no greater in extent than is necessary for the purpose, the primary order should, as a minimum, specify, or deal with, the following:

• the particular person or persons — whether by name or description — and the maximum number of such persons, to be permitted to enter;

• the premises to which entry is to be permitted;

- the times between which entry is to be permitted;
- the particular purposes, as for example:
  - to search for, inspect and copy, material alleged to infringe copyright or to constitute or to contain confidential information;
  - to remove identified material, it being noted that, as a general rule, removal should be permitted only where, under copyright law, or under the general law, the material in question is the property of the plaintiff, or the order provides, first, for the preparation of a detailed list of the items being removed — the defendant being given an adequate opportunity to check the list — for the return of documents the subject of the list once copies have been made and, when there is any dispute as to the title to the items removed, providing for the safe custody of the items not to be returned, pending the return of any originating process.

As well, the order should provide for the defendant to have an opportunity to consider and to take legal advice in respect of it before being obliged to comply and there should be, reserved to the defendant, liberty to apply on very short notice to discharge the order. Further, the originating process should, in any event, be made returnable on short notice consistent with the defendant having an adequate opportunity to obtain legal advice and to prepare to apply to discharge, or to oppose the continuation of the order and any associated relief.

And see 16.4.12–16.4.13 below on the harmonised rules and practice directions for search orders.

5. The difficulties inherent in executing an Anton Piller order are highlighted in Scott J's judgment in *Bhimji v Chatwani* [1991] 1 All ER 705:

> [Anton Piller orders] stand ... at the extremity of the court's jurisdiction. Some may think that they go beyond it. They involve the court in the hypocrisy of pretending that the entry and search are carried on because the owners of the premises have consented to it. They impose on the plaintiffs' solicitors the almost impossible task of describing fairly to non-lawyers the true effect and nature of the orders. They present respondents with orders of great complexity and jurisprudential sophistication and give little time for decisions to be taken as to the response to be made to them. They vest the plaintiffs, on one side of what is usually highly contentious litigation, with the trappings of apparent administrative authority to carry out the search. The usual presence of a policeman adds to this illusion.

These issues are explored in *J C Techforce and Adam Steinhardt v Wayne Pearce, Grant William Neville and Oke Industrial Pty Ltd* (1996) 138 ALR 522. In that case the respondents asserted that an Anton Piller order, which entitled the applicants to enter their premises and seize certain documents, had been oppressively executed, and that the applicants had seized documents which did not fall within the terms of the order.

The court rejected the assertions. In reaching this decision, Branson J stated (at 525) that '[t]he care with which Anton Piller orders are to be executed cannot, in my view, be over emphasised'. Her Honour referred to and approved Ormrod LJ's judgment in *Anton Piller KG v Manufacturing Processes* [1976] 1 Ch 55 at 61, finding that solicitors acting for an applicant on an Anton Piller order have a responsibility 'to ensure that the carrying out of such order is meticulously done and with the fullest respect for the defendant's rights in every regard' (at 525). Branson J emphasised that this responsibility is particularly relevant where the solicitor seeks to remove documents that fall outside the strict terms of the order. Her Honour stated (at 527):

> ... [e]ntry onto the premises of another gained by reason only of the compelling nature of an Anton Piller order is not, I consider, to be used for any purpose outside those fairly comprehended by the order itself. The only exception to this position which I am presently able to envisage is that which would arise were the respondents to the order to give a free consent to a departure from the strict terms of the order. Having regard to the exceptional nature of an Anton Piller order, the case will be rare, in my view, in which any consent to a course of conduct potentially adverse to it given by a respondent which has not first obtained legal advice of its own, will be regarded by a court as having been freely given.

6. Evidence which is obtained in breach of guidelines for the execution of Anton Piller orders — whether those guidelines have been attached as conditions to the granting of the order by the court or relate to the issue of consent as discussed above — may be deemed by the court to be inadmissible. See, for example, s 138 of the Uniform Evidence Acts, which invests the court with discretion to exclude evidence that has been obtained improperly or in contravention of an Australian law.

7. Courts will only allow documents obtained in the execution of an Anton Piller order to be used for the proper conduct of the action for which the interlocutory order was originally sought. Courts consider an applicant for an Anton Piller order to have given an implied undertaking to the court to refrain from using the documents for any collateral or ulterior purposes: *Home Office v Harman* [1983] 1 AC 280. In rare circumstances, however, the court may relieve a party of this implied undertaking. In *Dart Industries v Bryar* (1997) 38 IPR 389, Goldberg J held that the court would only relieve a party of such an undertaking if the party could establish the existence of a 'set of special circumstances'. Citing the judgment of Wilcox J in *Springfield Nominees Pty Ltd v Bridgelands Securities Ltd* (1992) 110 ALR 685, his Honour noted that any of the following circumstances could give rise to a 'special circumstance':

> ... the nature of the document, the circumstances under which it came into existence, the attitude of the author of the documents and any prejudice the author may sustain, whether the document pre-existed litigation or was created for that purpose and therefore expected to enter the public domain, the nature of the information in the document (in particular whether it contains personal data or commercially sensitive information), the circumstances in which the document came into the hands of the applicant for leave and, perhaps most important of all, the likely contribution of the document to achieving justice in the second proceeding.

Search orders under the rules of court

16.4.12 Most jurisdictions have now adopted harmonised rules and practice directions for Anton Piller orders based on the principles established at common law. These are known as search orders: FCR Div 7.5 Search Orders and Practice Note CM 11; ACT rr 750–755 and Court Procedures Practice Note (Search Orders) 2008 (No 2); NSW Pt 25 Div 3 and Search Orders Practice Note (SC Gen 13); NT O 37B and Search Orders Practice Direction (No 6 of 2006); Qld Ch 8 Pt 2 Div 3 and Search Orders Practice Direction (No 2 of 2007); SA r 148 and Search Orders Practice Direction (Direction 4.3); Tas Pt 36 Div 1B and Search Orders Practice Direction (No 4 of 2006); Vic O 37B and Search Orders Practice Note (No 6 of 2010); WA O 52B and Search Orders Practice Direction (No 6 of 2007, 9.6 Consolidated). These rules will be the primary focus for those seeking an Anton Piller/search order. There is no equivalent High Court rule.

The search order directs a person in charge of premises to permit an inspection, or provide information, things or service required by the order. The order may extend to premises beyond that of the defendant.

16.4.13 The relevant Australian Capital Territory provisions are set out below.

16.4.14E	Court Procedures Rules 2006 (ACT)

751 Search orders — General

(1) The Supreme Court may make an order (a **search order**) in any proceeding or in anticipation of any proceeding in the court for the purpose of securing or preserving evidence and requiring the respondent to allow people to enter premises for the purpose of securing the preservation of evidence that is or may be relevant to an issue in the proceeding or anticipated proceeding.

...

(3) The affidavits supporting an application for a search order must include the following information:

(a) a description of the things, or the categories of things, in relation to which the order is sought;

(b) the address of the premises in relation to which the order is sought and whether they are private or business premises;

(c) why the order is sought, including why the applicant believes that the things to be searched for will probably be destroyed or otherwise made unavailable for the purpose of evidence before the court unless the order is made;

(d) the prejudice, loss or damage likely to be suffered by the applicant if the order is not made;

(e) the name, address, firm and commercial litigation experience of an independent solicitor, who agrees to being appointed to serve the order, supervise its enforcement and do the other things the court directs;

(f) if the premises to be searched are or include residential premises — whether or not the applicant believes that the only occupants of the premises are likely to be young children or an unaccompanied female, or both;

(g)   if the application is made in the Supreme Court and the applicant claims that the applicant has an existing or prospective cause of action that is justiciable in Australia —

   (i)   the basis of the claim for principal relief; and

   (ii)   if the application is made without being served on the respondent — any possible defence or other response to the claim; ...

(4)   The court may amend or set aside the search order.

752 Search orders — requirements for making order

(1)   The Supreme Court may make a search order if satisfied that —

(a)   an applicant seeking the order has a strong prima facie case on an accrued cause of action; and

(b)   the potential or actual loss or damage to the applicant will be serious if the search order is not made; and

(c)   there is sufficient evidence in relation to a respondent that —

   (i)   the respondent possesses important evidentiary material; and

   (ii)   there is a real possibility that the respondent might destroy the material or cause it to be unavailable for use in evidence in a proceeding or anticipated proceeding before the court ...

753 Search orders — terms of order

(1)   A search order may direct everyone who is named or described in the order —

(a)   to allow, or arrange to allow, the other people named or described in the order —

   (i)   to enter premises stated in the order; and

   (ii)   to take any steps that are in accordance with the terms of the order; and

(b)   to provide, or arrange to provide, the other people named or described in the order with any information, thing or service described in the order; and

(c)   to allow the other people named or described in the order to take and keep in their custody anything described in the order; and

(d)   not to disclose any information about the order, for up to 3 days after the day the order is served, except for obtaining legal advice or legal representation; and

(e)   to do or not to do any act as the court considers appropriate.

(2)   Without limiting subrule (1) (a) (ii), the steps that may be taken in relation to a thing stated in a search order include —

(a)   searching for, inspecting or removing the thing; and

(b)   making or obtaining a record of the thing or any information it may contain.

(3)   A search order may contain other provisions that the court considers appropriate.

(4)   In this rule:

record includes a copy, photograph, film or sample.

754 Search orders — independent solicitors

(1)   If the court makes a search order, the court must appoint 1 or more solicitors (an *independent solicitor*), each of whom is independent of the applicant's solicitors, to supervise the execution of the order, and to do the other things in relation to the order that the court considers appropriate.

(2)   The court may appoint an independent solicitor to supervise execution of the order at any 1 or more premises, and a different independent solicitor or solicitors to supervise execution of the order at other premises, with each independent solicitor having power to do the other things in relation to the order that the court considers appropriate.

755 Search orders — costs

(1) The court may make any order about costs that it considers appropriate in relation to a search order.

(2) Without limiting subrule (1), an order about costs includes an order about the costs of anyone affected by a search order.

16.4.15C   **Austress Freyssinet Pty Ltd v Joseph**
                                    [2006] NSWSC 77
                          New South Wales Supreme Court, Equity

[The defendants sought to revoke or set aside an Anton Piller order on the basis of NSW r 36(16)(2)(b) and the inherent jurisdiction of the court. The defendant was formerly employed as the plaintiff's National Business Development Manager. The plaintiff's summons sought declarations against Joseph to the effect that he had received, used and distributed information, or documents in which the copyright is owned by the plaintiff, other than in the performance of his duties as an employee. There is an allegation that during the term of his employment he used confidential information of the plaintiff for the purpose of assisting in the establishment of a business in competition with the plaintiff, in breach of his duties of fidelity and good faith. The plaintiff sought a perpetual injunction against Joseph using or reproducing any of the confidential information or copyrighted material, and an injunction against inducing any current or former employee to breach their employment contract. Windeyer J, at first instance, made an Anton Piller order permitting Joseph's premises to be searched, and to disclose the whereabouts on his premises of documents relating to the business of the plaintiff. Due to the absence of Joseph, the Anton Piller order was unable to be exercised. Joseph applied to the duty judge for a stay of the order pending hearing of an application to have the orders discharged or varied. A temporary stay was granted.]

Campbell J:

[15] The principles of law which are relevant to the application were stated by Mr Moses, counsel for Mr Joseph, in the following terms, namely:

> There are four preconditions to the making of an Anton Piller order — none of which have been satisfied in this case:
>
> (a) There must be an extremely strong prima facie case;
> (b) The damage potential or actual, must be very serious for the Plaintiff;
> (c) There must be clear evidence that the Defendants have in their possession incriminating documents or things, and that there is a real possibility that they may destroy such material before any application *inter partes*; and
> (d) The harm likely to be caused by the Anton Piller order to the Defendants and their business affairs must not be excessive or out of proportion to the legitimate object of the order especially when it will allow the perusal of the Plaintiff of the Defendant's confidential commercial documents.

[16] The plaintiff did not quarrel with those principles of law. I shall accept them for the purpose of this judgment, without any further examination of whether they correctly state all the qualifications which there might be of any of the principles.

...

[25] The application which is made, to set the orders aside, is thus one made in circumstances where, unless reason is shown why the orders should be set aside, the orders will become operative once the stay expires. Thus, the situation in the present case is fundamentally different to the situation that ordinarily arises concerning *ex parte* applications for an injunction, where the injunction is granted for a very limited period of time, and when the matter returns to Court the onus is on the person who seeks the injunction to establish matters which show that it is appropriate that the injunction should be extended. In the present case, where an application is made to set aside the order, reason needs to be shown why that course should be taken. It is to be noted that Rule 36.16(2) says that the Court *may* set aside or vary a judgment after it has been entered if it is given or made in the absence of a party. It is not as though there is a right to automatically have such an order set-aside simply by asking. Nor is it correct that, on such an application, the person seeking to have the order set aside can require the person who has obtained the order to prove again the case in favour of making the order.

...

[97] In my view, there was sufficient evidence to justify a conclusion that, unless the order was made, there might be a destruction of documents, and indeed that the destruction of documents was likely if Mr Joseph became aware of the proceedings. The secrecy with which Mr Joseph proceeded, what appears on the present evidence to be his duplicity in setting up a rival business while still on the payroll of the plaintiff, his causing Mr La Hood to write a letter on 16 January 2006 stating that Mr Joseph had no idea what was meant by the suggestion that there might be a misuse of information which had been removed from the company files, his action in deleting from his laptop, immediately after his meeting with Mr Besset of 13 January 2006, the documents which were attachments to the emails, all lead, in my view, to a conclusion that there was a risk that documents might be destroyed.

...

[99] Significantly Mr Joseph, on this application, does not give any evidence himself which seeks to explain the apparent questions arising concerning his conduct, and in particular the question raised about just what the meetings were that he was attending which required him to have all of his files at home, or to give an explanation of what purpose he could have had e-mailing to himself at a hotmail account documents which were already on his laptop computer. That e-mailing occurred, it will be recalled, during Mr Joseph's vacation, when he had the laptop at home. It is not a case, of the kind which commonly enough happens, of an employee who is not on holidays sometimes sending work documents to his home computer address, so that he can work on them there. The failure of the defendant to provide that evidence leads to the conclusion that inferences otherwise available on the evidence against the defendant, and which the defendant might possibly have rebutted by giving evidence himself, can be drawn more strongly.

[100] I also take into account, on the present application, that the additional evidence of Mr Besset and Mr O'Dea has removed at least one of the levels of hearsay. However, I should make clear that if the hearsay information about Mr Joseph's activities was the only evidence, to the effect that he was proposing to enter into competition with the plaintiff, it may well be that that evidence would not be strong enough to justify an Anton Piller order. In the present case, however, the particularly hard and cogent evidence comes from the results of Deloittes reconstruction of the e-mail communications.

[101] That is not to say that, on an application like this, a judge is not entitled to take into account all of the evidence, even evidence which by itself is slight. Rather, the judge's task is to weigh all the evidence, and form a conclusion on the totality of it.

...

[103] Another attack which was made on the orders was to allege that there was a failure to disclose material information. It is well accepted that an applicant for *ex parte* relief has an obligation to make full disclosure of all material facts adverse to the applicant's case which are known to the applicant or would have been known if the applicant had made proper inquiries. See *Thomas A Edison Limited v Bullock* [1912] HCA 72; (1912) 15 CLR 679 at 682.

[Campbell J found no material failure to disclose.]

...

[106] Criticism is made of the way in which the order allowed officers of the plaintiff to enter the first defendant's home and potentially have unfettered access to commercially sensitive material relating to the new business which the first defendant had set up. It submits that this aspect of the orders was not brought to the attention of the Court on 1 February 2006. It is true that it was not specifically adverted to in the plaintiff's outline of submissions. However, it appears that the plaintiff went to Court on 1 February 2006 armed with draft orders. Those orders are ones which were initialled by Windeyer J on their first page. It is the first page of the orders which contains the permission for the officers of the plaintiff to be amongst those who were authorised to search. Windeyer J declined to make some of the orders which were included in the draft. The suggestion which, however it might be put, must be implicit in the submission, that his Honour made the orders without even glancing at the first page, to discover what the orders were which he was making, is one which does not bear serious examination.

...

[108] Another matter on which the plaintiff relies is delay in seeking the orders. It is true that a period of over two months elapsed from the first time that anyone on behalf of the plaintiff had even a hint that there might be something afoot concerning Mr Joseph engaging in competition which occurred on 25 November 2005, until the orders were applied for. However, the hearsay information which the plaintiff had prior to 9 January 2006 was nothing like material which would have justified it seeking orders of this kind. The discovery of 9 January 2006, that the first defendant had apparently cleaned out his office, raised suspicion, but likewise, the information known up to that date would probably not have been sufficient. It is really the obtaining of the information from Deloittes, concerning the sending of e-mails with significant documents attached, which provided the best evidence in support of the application. I do not regard there as having been undue delay in approaching the Court for the orders.

[109] In all these circumstances, I decline to set aside the orders. They will, however, be varied so that the representatives or agents of the plaintiff, who are corporate officers, may not attend at the execution of the orders. The way in which the orders gave that permission was by requiring Mr Joseph to permit the following people to enter:
   (a) not more than two partners or employees of then Plaintiff's solicitors, Mallesons Stephen Jaques; and
   (b) not more than three representatives or agents of the Plaintiff, not being a person described in paragraph (a) above; and (paragraphs (a) and (b) above are collectively the "Plaintiff's Representatives")
   (c) the Supervising Solicitor.

MAREVA (FREEZING) ORDERS

16.5.1   A Mareva order or freezing order is limited to preventing a defendant (or respondent to a counterclaim) from disposing of assets or removing them from the jurisdiction, so as to defeat any judgment, which the plaintiff may obtain against the defendant at trial. It derives from the court's equitable inherent power to prevent an abuse of process. The power to grant a Mareva injunction was first recognised in *Nippon Yusen Kaisha v Karageorgis* [1975] 2 Lloyd's Rep 137, and was first confirmed by the United Kingdom Court of Appeal in *Mareva Compania Naviera SA v International Bulkcarriers SA* [1975] 2 Lloyd's Rep 509.

The High Court in *Cardile v LED Builders Pty Ltd* (1999) 198 CLR 380, 393, 399–401 indicates it is now more appropriate to refer to a Mareva order rather than a Mareva injunction: see **16.5.6C**. The theoretical basis for a Mareva order is to prevent an abuse of process and to protect the administration of justice rather than being classed as a form of injunctive relief.

16.5.2C   **Mareva Compania Naviera SA v International Bulkcarriers SA**
[1975] 2 Lloyd's Rep 509
Court of Appeal (UK)

[The shipowner plaintiff sued the defendant charterers of a vessel for damages for breach of charter party. They issued a writ seeking $US30,800 for unpaid hire and damages. They sought an *ex parte* injunction to restrain the charterers from removing or disposing of any of the monies (which the charterers had received under the voyage charter) out of the jurisdiction.]

Lord Denning MR (at 509): This raises a very important point of practice. It follows on a case which we had the other day, *Nippon Yusen Kaisha v Karageorgis* [1975] 2 Lloyd's Rep 137. The plaintiffs, Mareva Compania Naviera SA, are shipowners who owned the vessel Mareva. They let it to the defendants, International Bulkcarriers SA, on a time charter for a trip out to the Far East and back. The vessel was to be put at the disposal of the defendants at Rotterdam. Hire was payable half monthly in advance and the rate was 3850 dollars a day from the time of delivery. The vessel was duly delivered to the defendants on May 12, 1975. The defendants subchartered it. They let it on a voyage charter to the President of India. Freight was payable under that voyage charter; 90 per cent was to be paid against the documents and the 10 per cent later.

[510] Under that voyage charter the vessel was loaded at Bordeaux on May 29, 1975, with a cargo of fertilizer consigned to India. The Indian High Commission, in accordance with the obligations under the voyage charter, paid 90 per cent of the freight but paid it to a bank in London. It was paid out to the Bank of Bilbao in London to the credit of the time charterers. The total sum which the India High Commission paid into the bank was £174,000. Out of that the time charterers paid to the shipowners, the plaintiffs, the first two instalments of the half monthly hire. They paid those instalments by credit transferred to the shipowners. The third was due on June 12, 1975; but the time charterers failed to pay it. They could easily have done it, of course, by making a credit transfer in favour of the shipowners. But they did not do it. Telexes passed which make it quite plain that the time charterers were unable to pay. They said they were not able to fulfil any part of their obligations under the charter, and

they had no alternative but to stop trading. Their efforts to obtain further financial support had been fruitless.

Whereupon the owners of the vessel treated the defendants' conduct as a repudiation of the charter. They issued a writ on June 20. They claimed the unpaid hire which comes to 30,800 US dollars and damages for the repudiation. The total will be very large. They have served the writ on agents here, and they have applied also for service out of the jurisdiction. But meanwhile they believe that there is a grave danger that these moneys in the bank in London will disappear. So they have applied for an injunction to restrain the disposal of those moneys which are now in the bank. They rely on the recent case of *Nippon Yusen Kaisha v Karageorgis* [1975] 2 Lloyd's Rep 137. Mr Justice Donaldson felt some doubt about that decision because we were not referred to *Lister v Stubbs* (1890) 45 Ch D 1. There are observations in that case to the effect that the Court has no jurisdiction to protect a creditor before he gets judgment. Lord Justice Cotton said:

> I know of no case where, because it was highly probable that if the action were brought to a hearing the plaintiff could establish that a debt was due to him from the defendant, the defendant has been ordered to give security until that has been established by the judgment or decree.

And Lord Justice Lindley said:

> ... we should be doing what I conceive to be very great mischief if we were to stretch a sound principle to the extent to which the appellants ask us to stretch it ...

Mr Justice Donaldson felt that he was bound by *Lister v Stubbs* and that he had no power to grant an injunction. But, in deference to the recent case, he did grant an injunction, but only until 17:00 today (June 23, 1975), on the understanding that by that time this Court would be able to reconsider the position.

Now Mr Rix has been very helpful. He has drawn our attention not only to *Lister v Stubbs* but also to s 45 of the Judicature Act, which repeats s 25(8) of the Judicature Act, 1875. It says:

> A mandamus or an injunction may be granted or a receiver appointed by an interlocutory order of the court in all cases in which it shall appear to the court to be just or convenient.

In *Beddow v Beddow* (1878) 9 Ch D 89, Sir George Jessel, the then Master of the Rolls, gave a very wide interpretation to that section. He said:

> I have unlimited power to grant an injunction in any case where it would be right or just to do so.

There is only one qualification to be made. The Court will not grant an injunction to protect a person who has no legal or equitable right whatever. That appears from *North London Railway Co v Great Northern Railway Co* (1883) 11 QBD 30. But, subject to that qualification, the statute gives a wide general power to the Courts. It is well summarized in Halsbury's Laws of England, vol 21, 3rd ed 348, par 729:

> ... now, therefore, whenever a right, which can be asserted either at law or in equity, does exist, then whatever the previous practice may have been, the Court is enabled by virtue of this provision, in a proper case to grant an injunction to protect that right.

In my opinion that principle applies to a creditor who has a right to be paid the debt owing to him, even before he has established his right by getting judgment for it. If it appears that the debt is due and owing — and there is a danger that the debtor may dispose of his assets so as to defeat it before judgment — the Court has jurisdiction in a proper case to grant an interlocutory judgment so as to prevent him disposing of those assets. It seems to me that this is a [511] proper case for the exercise of this jurisdiction. There is money in a bank in London which stands in the name of these time charterers. The time charterers have control of it. They may at any time dispose of it or remove it out of this country. If they do so, the shipowners may never get their charter hire. The ship is now on the high seas. It has passed Cape Town on its way to India. It will complete the voyage and the cargo discharged. And the shipowners may not get their charter hire at all. In face of this danger, I think this Court ought to grant an injunction to restrain the defendants from disposing of these moneys now in the bank in London until the trial or judgment in this action. If the defendants have any grievance about it when they hear of it, they can apply to discharge it. But meanwhile the plaintiffs should be protected. It is only just and right that this Court should grant an injunction. I would therefore continue the injunction.

[Roskill and Ormrod LJJ agreed with the judgment of Lord Denning MR.]

16.5.3 *Mareva Compania Naviera SA v International Bulkcarriers SA* [1975] 2 Lloyd's Rep 137 has been followed in Australia by the High Court in *Jackson v Sterling Industries Ltd* (1987) 162 CLR 612. In this case the High Court explained the jurisdictional foundation for a Mareva order.

16.5.4C	**Jackson v Sterling Industries Ltd** (1987) 162 CLR 612 High Court of Australia

[In this case, the court considered the circumstances in which a Mareva order might be granted.]

Deane J (at 622): Section 23 of the Federal Court of Australia Act 1976 (Cth) confers upon the Federal Court a broad power to make orders of such kinds, including interlocutory orders, as it 'thinks appropriate'. Wide though that power is, it is subject to both jurisdictional and other limits. It exists only 'in relation to matters' in respect of which jurisdiction has been conferred upon the Federal Court. Even in relation to such matters, the power is restricted to the making of the 'kinds' of order, whether final or interlocutory, which are capable of properly being seen as 'appropriate' to be made by the Federal Court in the exercise of its jurisdiction.

There may have been a time when it would have been strongly arguable that the making of an interlocutory order to preserve assets of a defendant pending the determination of proceedings against him could not properly have been seen as 'appropriate' to be made by a court in relation to the exercise of the jurisdiction to entertain the substantive proceedings. If that be so, that time has passed. Orders preventing a defendant from disposing of his assets so as to create a situation in which any judgment obtained against him would not be satisfied may be of comparatively recent development. They have, however, become an accepted incident of the jurisdiction of superior courts throughout most of the common law world. In this country, the jurisdiction to make such orders, commonly referred to as 'Mareva injunctions', has been progressively asserted and exercised by the Supreme Courts of Victoria, New South Wales, Western Australia, Queensland, the Australian Capital Territory and South Australia.

Initially, injunctive orders to preserve assets were made to prevent a non-resident defendant from removing assets from the territorial limits of a court's jurisdiction so as to frustrate the effectiveness of any judgment that might be obtained (see *Nippon Yusen Kaisha v Karageorgis* [1975] 1 WLR 1093; [1975] 3 All ER 282; *Mareva Compania Naviera SA v International Bulkcarriers SA* [1975] 2 Lloyd's Rep 509). In due course, it was perceived that a general interlocutory power to make orders preventing a defendant from disposing of his assets so as to defeat any judgment obtained in an action was an incident of the substantive jurisdiction to entertain the action and was not confined to the case where the defendant was a non-resident. That general power has been held to encompass an order requiring the disclosure by a defendant of his assets (see *Bekhor Ltd v Bilton* [1981] QB 923; *T D K Tape Distributor v Videochoice Ltd* [1986] 1 WLR 141; [1985] 3 All ER 345); an order for the delivery up (to a named solicitor) of [623] designated assets which were not specifically in issue in the proceedings (see *C B S United Kingdom Ltd v Lambert* [1983] Ch 37); and, an order restraining a local company from disposing of or dealing with assets which were outside the jurisdiction at least where they had been within the jurisdiction when the action commenced (see *Hospital Products v Ballabil Holdings* [1984] 2 NSWLR 662 and, on appeal, (1985) 1 NSWLR 155). Arguably, it extends to the making of an ancillary order after judgment to protect the efficacy of execution (see *Stewart Chartering v C & O Managements* [1980] 1 WLR 460; [1980] 1 All ER 718). As a general proposition, it should now be accepted in this country that 'a Mareva injunction can be granted … if the circumstances are such that there is a danger of (the defendant's) absconding, or a danger of the assets being removed out of the jurisdiction or disposed of within the jurisdiction, or otherwise dealt with so that there is a danger that the plaintiff, if he gets judgment, will not be able to get it satisfied' (per Lord Denning MR, *Rahman (Prince Abdul) v Abu-Taha* [1980] 1 WLR 1268, at 1273; [1980] 3 All ER 409, at 412 quoted with approval by Street CJ in *Ballabil Holdings*, (1985) 1 NSWLR 155, at 160).

To some extent, the general power of the English High Court of Justice to grant a Mareva injunction was initially seen as based on the provisions of s 45(1) of the Supreme Court of Judicature (Consolidation) Act 1925 (UK) (see also the Supreme Court Act 1981 (UK), s 37(3)). That general power should, however, now be accepted as an established part of the armoury of a court of law and equity to prevent the abuse or frustration of its process in relation to matters coming within its jurisdiction. That being so, the power to grant such relief in relation to a matter in which the Federal Court has jurisdiction is comprehended by the express grant to that court by s 23 of the Federal Court of Australia Act of power, in relation to such matters, 'to make orders of such kinds, including interlocutory orders, and to issue, or direct the issue of, writs of such kinds, as the Court thinks appropriate'. Indeed, even in the absence of the provisions of s 23, the Federal Court would have possessed power to make such orders in relation to matters properly before it, as an incident of the general grant to it as a superior court of law and equity of the jurisdiction to deal with such matters. In that regard, I agree with the following comments of Bowen CJ in his judgment in the present matter:

> In relation to a statutory court such as the Federal Court it is wise to avoid the use of the words 'inherent jurisdiction'. [624] Nevertheless a statutory court which is expressly given certain jurisdiction and powers must exercise that jurisdiction and those powers. In doing so it must be taken to be given by implication whatever jurisdiction or powers may be

necessary for the exercise of those expressly conferred. The implied power for example to prevent abuse of its process, is similar to, if not identical with, inherent power.

However, the present problem relates not so much to the existence in the Federal Court of a general incidental power to grant injunctive relief to prevent a defendant disposing of specific assets so as to render nugatory a judgment obtained against him in proceedings within the jurisdiction of the Federal Court. It relates rather to the extent of that general power and, in particular, to whether the actual orders which the Federal Court has purported to make in the present case come within it.

The orders of the Federal Court which are now challenged by the appellant are those requiring the appellant to 'provide security in the sum of $3,000,000'. Those orders fall in a different category to any interlocutory order for the preservation of assets which has previously been made, at least in a reported case in this country. The basis of the initial order made by Sheppard J was plainly adequate to warrant the grant of some relief in the nature of a Mareva injunction. That basis was that it appeared to his Honour that the present appellant, who was a respondent in the proceedings before him, remained in possession of assets representing the whole or most of an identified amount of $4.3m and that he was likely to dispose of those assets pursuant to an overall scheme to defeat any judgment which the present respondent, who was the applicant in those proceedings, might obtain against him. If the order had been restricted to injunctive relief preventing the appellant from disposing of so much of that $4.3m (or the assets representing that money) as remained in his possession, it would have clearly been within the powers of the Federal Court under s 23 of the Act. However, the order which his Honour made differed in nature from the mere grant of such restricted injunctive relief. In terms, it provided that the present appellant 'provide security in the sum of $3,000,000 in such manner and form as the parties may agree or, in default of agreement, the Court or its Registrar may approve.' In the absence of agreement between the parties, it was subsequently ordered by Burchett J that the 'manner and form of providing the security ordered' be the payment of $3m (in cash or by bank cheque or partly in cash and partly by bank cheque) 'to any Registrar' of the Federal Court or the '[p]rovision of security in the sum of $3,000,000 in such other manner and form as the Court or [625] its Registrar' may approve. Beyond specifying that the $3m should be paid or provided by way of 'security', the orders did not identify what, if anything, the money was to secure or what was subsequently to happen to it. Nor did they restrict the obligation of the appellant to pay the money by way of 'security' by reference to the extent of the appellant's assets. The combined effect of the mandatory orders was to impose an unqualified requirement that, in the absence of approval of some 'other manner and form', the appellant provide security by payment of the designated sum to a registrar of the Federal Court.

There are three related grounds upon which these combined orders are susceptible of attack. First, they required the appellant to pay into court not money identified as being within his possession but money which he was required to provide or obtain regardless of source. Second, they go beyond a mere order for the preservation of assets pending judgment or execution in that they specifically required that the money be paid into court as 'security'. Third, they failed to identify either what the money paid 'to any Registrar' was to secure or what the entitlement of the appellant (or any one else) was in relation to it after it has been so paid. Put in positive form, it appears to me that, when an order for the preservation of assets goes beyond simply restraining the defendant from disposing of specific assets until after judgment, it must be framed so as to come within the limits set by the purpose which it can properly be intended to serve. That purpose is not to create security for the plaintiff or to require a defendant to provide security as a condition of being allowed to defend the action against him. Nor is it to introduce, in effect, a new vulnerability to imprisonment for debt, or rather for alleged indebtedness, by requiring a defendant, under the duress of the threat of imprisonment for contempt of court, to find money, which he may or may not have (whether or not at some point of time it may have been available to him), to guarantee to a plaintiff that any judgment obtained will be satisfied. It is to prevent a defendant from disposing of his actual assets (including claims and expectancies) so as to frustrate the process of the court by depriving the plaintiff of the fruits of any judgment obtained in the action. It may be appropriate in a rare case that such an order requires the defendant actually to deliver assets to a named person or even to the court itself or (in 'a most exceptional case') extends to the appointment of a receiver of all or part of the assets of a defendant company (see the discussion in the judgment of Street CJ, *Ballabil* [626] *Holdings* (1985) 1 NSWLR 155, at 159ff.) Even in such cases however, the order must be confined to preserving assets until after judgment or, arguably, until there has been an opportunity to seek execution: it should not purport to create security over them in favour of the plaintiff and it should make clear that it goes no further than to deprive the defendant of possession of them for the purpose of precluding his disposal of them so as to defeat a judgment. That being so, any order requiring the delivery of assets should make clear that the assets will be held on behalf of the defendant until after judgment or further order and will then be re-delivered to the defendant unless they are made the subject of some other claim (eg, by a person entitled to claim under a writ of execution) on behalf of the plaintiff or some other creditor.

The conclusion which I have reached in the present case is that the combined orders made by the Federal Court went beyond any order which could properly be made by that court to the extent that they required the appellant to provide 'security' by paying the amount of $3m to 'any Registrar of the Court'. It is true that the general effect of those orders could have been procured by an express order requiring the appellant to pay $3m, being part of the identified sum of $4.3m or the proceeds thereof held by the appellant, to a designated person as receiver, to be held by that person on behalf of the appellant until a nominated time after judgment or until further order of the court with a proviso that that amount need not be paid to that person in the event that the appellant were to satisfy the Federal Court within a specified time that he had taken other steps (such as the provision of 'security') to ensure that his assets were not dissipated prior to any judgment. It is also true that it would seem apparent that the initial order was framed by Sheppard J on the basis that it represented a more favourable order from the appellant's point of view (by reason of the risk of self-incrimination) than would a simple order requiring the payment into court of $3m being part of the identified sum of $4.3m. Notwithstanding those considerations however, it seems to me that the express formal orders of the Federal Court to provide 'security' in the amount of $3m in the manner directed cannot properly be construed as not involving the creation of any security at all or as going no further than an order for the preservation of assets actually within the control of the appellant. That being so, the orders were not of a kind that it was within the power of the Federal Court to make as 'appropriate' in relation to [627] the proceedings before it or as an incident of its substantive jurisdiction to deal with those proceedings.

It follows that the appeal should be allowed. A question arises whether the relevant orders of the Federal Court were (at least formally) binding upon the appellant unless and until discharged or stayed (cf *Rubie v Rubie* (1911) 13 CLR 350, at pp 353–354) or were a nullity which the appellant was entitled to ignore (cf *Reg v Ross-Jones; Ex parte Green* (1984) 156 CLR 185, at 203). That question, which would be relevant to any contempt proceedings against the appellant by reason of his failure to comply with the terms of the mandatory injunction granted against him, was not canvassed in argument upon the hearing of the appeal to this Court. My tentative view upon it corresponds with that expressed by the Chief Justice in his judgment which I have had the benefit of reading subsequent to writing the foregoing. In the circumstances, and in the absence of further argument, no order should be made which might be construed as having the effect that the appellant is relieved from any consequences of his failure to comply with the requirements of the order of the Federal Court to provide security within the designated period.

Wilson and Dawson JJ (at 616): We agree with Deane J. Since the first appearance of the remedy, the power to grant a Mareva injunction has been a matter of debate. It was initially seen to be derived from the power of the English High Court to 'grant ... an injunction ... by an interlocutory order in all cases in which it appears to the court to be just or convenient so to do': s 45(1) Supreme Court of Judicature (Consolidation) Act 1925 (UK); *Nippon Yusen Kaisha v Karageorgis* [1975] 1 WLR 1093; [1975] 3 All ER 282; *Mareva Compania Naviera SA v International Bulkcarriers SA* [1975] 2 Lloyd's Rep 509. Section 23 of the Federal Court of Australia Act 1976 (Cth) gives to the Federal Court a comparable power, in relation to matters in which it has jurisdiction, 'to make orders of such kinds, including interlocutory orders ... as the Court thinks appropriate'.

[617] It is not without difficulty that reliance has been placed upon statutory provisions of this kind because, according to accepted doctrine, they permit interlocutory relief in relation to the disposition of property only in aid of some existing legal or equitable right, not a mere chose in action. See *Pivovaroff v Chernabaeff* (1978) 16 SASR 329; *Ex parte B P Exploration Co (Libya) Ltd; Re Hunt* [1979] 2 NSWLR 406. Initially the Mareva injunction was of limited scope being available only against a foreign defendant with moveable assets within the jurisdiction which, unless restrained, he was likely to remove. Some broader rationale was needed both to explain and fashion the eventual extension of the remedy to defendants resident within the jurisdiction and to the dissipation of assets within the jurisdiction for the purpose of defeating any judgment. See *Barclay-Johnson v Yuill* [1980] 1 WLR 1259, at 1264–1266; [1980] 3 All ER 190, at 194–195; *Rahman (Prince Abdul) bin Turki al Sudairy v Abu-Taha* [1980] 1 WLR 1268, at 1272; [1980] 3 All ER 409, at 411. It was to be found in the notion that the purpose of the Mareva injunction was to prevent the abuse of the process of the court by the frustration of its remedies: *Iraqi Ministry of Defence v Arcepey Shipping Co SA; The 'Angel Bell'* [1981] QB 65, at 72. The enactment in England of s 37(3) of the Supreme Court Act 1981 (UK), which confirmed the Mareva injunction in its extended form, rendered somewhat academic further debate in England upon the foundation of the remedy.

However, if the power of a court to grant injunctions of the Mareva type and associated relief is to be found in its capacity to prevent the abuse of its process, then it is as much to be found in its inherent power as in any statutory power to grant such relief as is 'just or convenient' or 'appropriate'. Thus it was that in *Riley McKay Pty Ltd v McKay* [1982] 1 NSWLR 264 the New South Wales Court of Appeal found the power to grant relief of the Mareva type in s 23 of the Supreme Court Act 1970 (NSW). Section 23 provides that the 'Court shall have all jurisdiction which may be necessary for the administration of justice in New South Wales'. No relevant distinction is to be drawn between the inherent power of the Court and that bestowed by the section although, as the Court of Appeal pointed out, the section confirms the inherent power without increasing it.

One important result of viewing the Mareva injunction in this way is to emphasize the limits of the remedy. Its use must be necessary to prevent the abuse of the process of the court. As [618] Ackner LJ pointed out in *A J Bekhor & Co Ltd v Bilton* [1981] QB 923, at

941–942, the Mareva injunction represents a limited exception to the general rule that a plaintiff must obtain his judgment and then enforce it. He cannot beforehand prevent the defendant from disposing of his assets merely because he fears that there will be nothing against which to enforce his judgment nor can he be given a secured position against other creditors. The remedy is not to be used to circumvent the insolvency laws.

In the Federal Court the power to grant a Mareva injunction may also be found in an inherent or, more correctly, implied power as well as in s 23 of the Federal Court of Australia Act. It is an implied power because of the statutory nature of the Court. Notwithstanding that the Federal Court is declared by s 5(2) of the Federal Court of Australia Act to be a superior court of record and a court of law and equity, there are limits upon its functions which differentiate it from other Australian superior courts. Ordinarily, a superior court of record is a court of general jurisdiction which means that, even if there are limits to its jurisdiction, it will be presumed to have acted within it. That is a presumption which is denied to inferior courts and is denied to a federal court such as the Federal Court. The consequence of the presumption is that prohibition does not, in general, go to a superior court, but prohibition is the means provided to keep such federal courts within the bounds of their jurisdictional limits: Commonwealth Constitution, s 75(v); Judiciary Act 1903 (Cth), s 33(1)(b). In those courts jurisdiction cannot be presumed so as to displace this remedy: *Reg v Ross-Jones; Ex parte Green* (1984) 156 CLR 185, at 207–221. In this respect, federal courts differ from the supreme courts of the states which, although of statutory origin, are truly designated superior courts because they are invested with general jurisdiction by reference to the jurisdiction of the courts at Westminster. Nor does s 32(1) of the Federal Court of Australia Act confer any general jurisdiction. That section, to the extent that the Constitution permits, confers jurisdiction on the Federal Court in respect of matters that are associated with matters in which the jurisdiction of the Court is invoked. Associated matters at common law or under state statute law form too wide a category to fall within any accrued or pendent jurisdiction which that Court may have and s 32(1) has been held to do no more than confer jurisdiction upon the Federal Court in associated matters which arise under Commonwealth laws but in respect of which jurisdiction has not otherwise been conferred [619] upon the Federal Court: *Philip Morris Inc v Adam P Brown Male Fashions Pty Ltd* (1981) 148 CLR 457, at 494, 502, 516 and 547.

However, the declaration of the Federal Court as a superior court is to be given effect as far as it can be and, as Aickin J remarked in *Philip Morris Inc v Adam P Brown Male Fashions Pty Ltd* at 535, the vesting of judicial power in the specific matters permitted by the Constitution (see ss 75, 76, 77) carries with it such implied power as is necessarily inherent in the nature of the judicial power itself. Having regard to the declaration of the Federal Court as a superior court and a court of law and equity, the implied power should be construed as being no less in relation to the jurisdiction vested in it than the inherent power of a court of unlimited, or general, jurisdiction.

Be that as it may, it cannot be suggested that either the power to grant relief under s 23 or an implied power to prevent an abuse of process extends to the creation and enforcement of rights in addition to those for the protection or enforcement of which the jurisdiction of the Court is invoked. The power given by s 23 is expressly limited to the making of orders in relation to matters in which the Court has jurisdiction and it does not extend the jurisdiction of the Federal Court. Nor could that Court's implied power be employed to create and enforce new rights. Whilst the implied power carries with it all that is necessary for the proper functioning of that Court, it does not extend its jurisdiction beyond that which is vested in it.

It has been a criticism of the Mareva doctrine that it constitutes an enlargement rather than the fulfilment of a court's function. See, for example, *Pivovaroff v Chernabaeff* per Bray CJ; Meagher, Gummow and Lehane, *Equity: Doctrines and Remedies*, 2nd ed (1984), pars 2183–2187. The criticism has not generally prevailed but it serves to emphasize the limited scope of the Mareva injunction. It exists not to create additional rights but to enable a court to protect its process from abuse in relation to the enforcement of its orders. It is neither a species of anticipatory execution nor does it give a form of security for any judgment which may ultimately be awarded. For the reasons given by Deane J, the orders made by the Federal Court went beyond the proper limits of the remedy and this appeal must be allowed.

Even though the orders ought not to have been made in the form in which they were, it does not appear to us that they were a nullity. The consequence is that the appellant was obliged to comply with them unless and until he obtained relief from them. It is not [620] necessary to decide the point now, but we are not persuaded that the Federal Court lacked jurisdiction in any sense which would deprive its orders of effect. It had jurisdiction to entertain the application for interlocutory relief and to determine that application judicially. It erred, not because it assumed a power which it did not have, but because it exercised an existing power in an impermissible way. It was an erroneous exercise of its jurisdiction to make the orders which it did, and not a wrongful assumption of jurisdiction. The distinction may at times be fine but it is a necessary one and not just a matter of semantics. In the same way, a court which is given power to determine the facts upon which its jurisdiction depends may, if it proceeds upon a wrongful determination, be said in one sense to exceed its jurisdiction, but its orders will be valid unless and until corrected on appeal. The position is otherwise where it is apparent on the face of a purported exercise of jurisdiction that there is no power or where the court's jurisdiction depends upon matters in dispute which cannot be conclusively determined by the court. See *R v Hickman; Ex parte Fox and Clinton* (1945) 70 CLR 598; *Reg v Ross-Jones; Ex parte Green; Reg v Gray; Ex parte Marsh* (1985) 157 CLR 351.

The orders made by the Federal Court are effective until set aside, discharged or stayed. The fact that they were erroneously made is something to be taken into account in any proceedings consequent upon their having been disobeyed. The principle remains, however, that the order of a competent court must be obeyed whilst it remains in force. See *Russell v East Anglian Railway Company* (1850) 3 Mac & G 104, at 124 (42 ER 201, at 208); *Partington v Booth* (1817) 3 Mer 148 (36 ER 57); *Hughes v Williams* (1847) 6 Hare 71 (67 ER 1087); *Rubie v Rubie* (1911) 13 CLR 350.

We would allow the appeal.

[Mason CJ and Brennan J delivered judgments in which they agreed with Deane J. Toohey and Gaudron JJ delivered dissenting judgments.]

16.5.5 Notes

1. A Mareva order may be granted in respect of the defendant's assets wherever they are situated: *National Australia Bank Ltd v Dessau* [1988] VR 521; *Yandil Holdings Pty Ltd v Insurance Co of North America* (1986) 7 NSWLR 571. The defendant must, of course, be subject to the court's jurisdiction: see Chapter 4.

2. The court may order, and normally will order, that the defendant give discovery of its assets in aid of the injunction: *Hospital Products Ltd v Ballabil Holdings Pty Ltd*

[1984] 2 NSWLR 662; *Ballabil Holdings Pty Ltd v Hospital Products Pty Ltd* (1985) 1 NSWLR 155. Discovery may give rise to questions of self-incrimination: see **16.4.6**.

3. The order will be limited so as to authorise the defendant to meet those expenses associated with the normal conduct of business (*Hortico (Aust) Pty Ltd v Energy Equipment Co (Aust) Pty Ltd* (1985) 1 NSWLR 545 at 558) and expenses associated with day-to-day living: *PCW (Underwriting Agencies) Ltd v Dixon* [1983] 2 Lloyd's Rep 197.

4. The generally accepted view is that the court cannot make an order in respect of property owned by a third party: *Bank of Queensland Ltd v Grant* [1984] 1 NSWLR 409. The High Court in *Cardile v LED Builders Pty Ltd* (1999) 198 CLR 380 allowed a Mareva order against a non-party to the litigation where it was necessary to protect the administration of justice.

16.5.6C   **Cardile v LED Builders Pty Ltd**
(1999) 198 CLR 380; 73 ALJR 657
High Court of Australia

[LED brought proceedings against Eagle Homes Pty Ltd. After the commencement of the proceedings, Eagle Homes paid a large dividend to its owners (the Cardiles) who set up another company, Ultra Modern Developments Pty Ltd. The business name 'Eagle Homes' was transferred to the new company which traded with that name. Neither the Cardiles, nor Ultra Modern, were parties to the proceeding between LED and Eagle Homes. Judgment was given in favour of LED for an account of profits. Pending the taking of accounts, LED sought a Mareva injunction against the Cardiles and Ultra Modern. In effect, it sought to freeze the proceeds of the dividend. This was an appeal to the High Court against an order of the Full Federal Court effectively freezing the proceeds of the dividend. The court examines in detail the legal basis for the order.]

Gaudron, McHugh, Gummow and Callinan JJ (at 198 CLR 385):

[1] This appeal raises a question whether an order identified as a *Mareva* injunction or order may be granted against a third party to proceedings in circumstances in which that party has not been shown to have an interest in the assets or funds (with one possible exception) of the potential judgment debtor.

[Their Honours recited the facts and the history of the litigation and continued:]

[20] Ultra Modern is entitled to dispose of assets that it owns or has lawfully acquired. To dispose of its own assets, without more and when no substantive proceedings have been taken against it, cannot be said to be an abuse or frustration of the court's process in respect of litigation between other parties.

[21] The only assets that have been shown to be in contention here are the dividends declared and paid by Eagle Homes which served temporarily to reduce, but not entirely eliminate, a

debt owed by Eagle Homes to Mr and Mrs Cardile, the business name 'Eagle Homes' and possibly goodwill attached to the business name 'Eagle Homes'.

[22] We will deal with the dividends first. There was no evidence that Mr and Mrs Cardile were mere conduits for the transmission to Ultra Modern of the funds, received by them by way of dividends, and accordingly no order on account of them should have been made in respect of Ultra Modern ...

[At 392:]

[24] Ultra Modern has not been shown to own or hold, or have the power of disposition over, any property of Eagle Homes nor in any way at all to owe any obligations or debts to that company (save perhaps for the business name 'Eagle Homes' which we set aside for separate consideration later). The evidence does not in our opinion go so far as to establish, even on a prima facie basis, that Ultra Modern is in possession of, or using, Eagle Homes' goodwill. It is not suggested that Eagle Homes, or a liquidator of it, or anyone else, would have any entitlement to set aside any transaction between Eagle Homes and Ultra Modern or to follow or trace any assets passing from the former to the latter. There have been no transactions between the companies and no assets have passed between them.

[25] None of the authorities cited to this Court went so far as to support an order of the width of that made in the Full Court. As the argument proceeded upon the grounds of appeal to which we have referred, several matters became apparent. One was that the English authorities appear to have developed to a stage where what is identified as the *Mareva* injunction or order lacks any firm doctrinal foundation and is best regarded as some special exception to the general law. Another was that, whilst it is undesirable that asset preservation orders of the *Mareva* variety be left as a *sui generis* remedy with no doctrinal roots, the term 'injunction' is an inappropriate identification of that area of legal discourse within which the *Mareva* order is to be placed. The third was the point encapsulated in the joint judgment of this Court in *CSR Ltd v Cigna Insurance Australia Ltd* (1997) 189 CLR 345 at 391.

The counterpart of a court's power to *prevent* its processes being abused is its power to *protect* the integrity of those processes once set in motion.

The integrity of those processes extends to preserving the efficacy of the execution which would lie against the actual or prospective judgment debtor: *Jackson v Sterling Industries Ltd* (1987) 162 CLR 612 at 623. The protection of the administration of justice which this involves may, in a proper case, extend to asset preservation orders against third parties to the principal litigation. This appeal concerns the identification of such proper cases.

[26] In *Jackson v Sterling Industries Ltd*, (162 CLR at 623) Deane J referred to the armoury of a court of law and equity to prevent the abuse or frustration of its process in relation to matters coming within its jurisdiction. By this means, the risk of the stultification of the administration of justice is diminished. Once the source of power is recognised, then, whatever may be the limitations with respect to inferior courts, in the case of the Federal Court the power will be seen to be comprehended by the express grant in s 23 of the Federal Court Act. In *National Australia Bank Ltd v Bond Brewing Holdings Ltd* (1990) 169 CLR 271 at 277, Mason CJ, Brennan and Deane JJ described as mistaken any proposition that *Mareva* relief could only be obtained against the defendant to an action if there were a positive intention to frustrate any judgment. However, the presence in s 23 of the expression 'as the Court thinks appropriate' points to the requirement to develop principles governing the exercise of the power in such a fashion as to avoid abuse. This need, as indicated above, is at the heart of the present appeal. Meeting that need is not facilitated, and may be impeded, by continued attempts to force

what has become known as the *Mareva* order into the mould of interlocutory injunctive relief as administered under that description by courts of equity ...

[Their Honours looked at the principles applicable to injunctions generally and the power of courts in Australia to grant them and continued (at 395):]

[31] However, in England, it is now settled by several decisions of the House of Lords that the power stated in Judicature legislation — that the court may grant an injunction in all cases in which it appears to the court to be just and convenient to do so — does not confer an unlimited power to grant injunctive relief. Regard must still be had to the existence of a legal or equitable right which the injunction protects against invasion or threatened invasion, or other unconscientious conduct or exercise of legal or equitable rights. The situation thus confirmed by these authorities reflects the point made by Ashburner that 'the power of the court to grant an injunction is limited by the nature of the act which it is sought to restrain'.

[32] Further, the injunction remains a discretionary remedy in a particular sense of that term. In *Bristol City Council v Lovell*, Lord Hoffmann observed ([1998] 1 WLR 446 at 453):

> The reason why an injunction is a discretionary remedy is because it formed part of the remedial jurisdiction of the Court of Chancery. If the Chancellor considered that the remedies available at law, such as damages, were inadequate, he could grant an injunction to give the plaintiff more effective relief. If he did not think that it was just or expedient to do so, he could leave the plaintiff to his rights at common law. The discretion is therefore as to the remedy which the court will provide for the invasion of the plaintiff's rights.

[33] Whilst s 23 of the Federal Court Act empowers the Federal Court to make 'orders of such kinds, including interlocutory orders ... as the Court thinks appropriate', the Federal Court is not thereby authorised to grant injunctive relief where jurisdiction is acquired under another statute which provides an exhaustive code of the available remedies and that code does not authorise the grant of an injunction. Nor does s 23 provide authority for the granting of an injunction where, whether under the general law or by statute, otherwise there is no case for injunctive relief. In *Patrick Stevedores Operations No 2 Pty Ltd v Maritime Union of Australia [No 3]* (1998) 72 ALJR 873 at 883, the Federal Court entertained the common law claims in conspiracy either in the accrued jurisdiction or as an associated matter within the meaning of s 32 of the Federal Court Act.

[34] In delivering the advice of the majority of their Lordships in *Mercedes Benz AG v Leiduck* [1996] AC 284, Lord Mustill outlined the development over 20 years of the remedy associated with the orders made in *Mareva Compania Naviera SA v International Bulkcarriers SA*. His Lordship observed that (at 299):

> [a]midst all the burdensome practicalities theory has been left behind.

Lord Mustill went on to outline three rationalisations which could be found in the English authorities, all of them unsatisfactory. One, later discredited by the House of Lords' decisions to which reference has already been made, was that the statutory power in Judicature systems to grant injunctive relief where just or convenient was relatively unlimited. Another was that, although framed as an injunction, the relief was a species of attachment, giving the claimant some rights of a proprietary nature in the assets in question and some advantage over other creditors of the defendant. Whilst not going that far in legal form, Mareva orders restricting dealings with assets do have characteristics of injunctive relief to enforce what are known in commerce as negative pledge agreements. However, the rationale of the Mareva order as a species of prejudgment attachment has been discredited by authorities which Lord Mustill collected. That left, in his Lordship's view, the Mareva injunction as 'a special exception to the general law'.

[35] In the Mareva case itself, Lord Denning MR had classified relief as injunctive on the footing that it went in aid of a legal right, namely the right of the plaintiff to be paid the debt owing, even before the establishment of that right by the getting of judgment for it. However, as Bray CJ observed in *Pivovaroff v Chernabaeff* (1978) 16 SASR 329 at 338–339, such a position was foreclosed by the long-standing decision of Lord Hatherley LC in *Mills v Northern Railway of Buenos Ayres Company* (1870) LR 5 Ch App 621. That decision had been taken as settled authority for the proposition, expressed by Joyce:

> A simple contract creditor of a company (having no mortgage or other security, and not having taken out execution) cannot sustain a bill to restrain the company from dealing with their assets as they please, on the ground that they are diminishing the fund for payment of his debt.

The remedies sought in Mills had included an injunction to restrain the payment of any dividend to shareholders until provision had been made for paying the creditor's debt. There had been prima facie evidence that the plaintiff was a creditor and had been unpaid for years. Thus, the plaintiff had made out, at least at the interlocutory level, the existence of his legal right. However, there being no security for the debt, the right was not, as then was considered important, proprietary in nature. Moreover, the contractual right itself would, on recovery of judgment, merge in the judgment. The substance of the relief sought by the plaintiff was anticipatory relief in aid of those rights that would at that later stage attach to the judgment debt.

[36] However, to deny injunctive relief in those circumstances did not mean that in comparable situations the court was powerless. In Australia, it has since been determined by the Appeal Division of the Supreme Court of Victoria and assumed by this Court [in *National Australia Bank Ltd v Bond Brewing Holdings Ltd*] that circumstances may arise in which the appointment of a receiver of the assets of a company which is not expressly alleged to be insolvent may be justified in pending litigation even on the application of a plaintiff who claims to be an unsecured creditor. Other examples were given by Emmett J [at first instance] ...

[40] The courts [have] developed doctrines and remedies, outside the injunction as understood in courts of equity, to protect the integrity of its processes once set in motion. The *Mareva* order for the preservation of assets should be seen as a further development. There is no harm in the use of the term *Mareva* to identify that development, provided the source of the remedy is kept in view when considering the form of the remedy in each particular case. An anterior question will be whether there is another interlocutory remedy among those considered above which will be suitable to meet the case in hand but be less extensive in scope.

[Their Honours then looked at the doctrinal basis of the Mareva order emphasizing the need to ensure the effective exercise of the court's jurisdiction and continued (at 401):]

[45] In this litigation, as has been mentioned, final judgment on LED's claim against Eagle Homes for a money sum is still pending. The appellants correctly submit that the statement of principle in *Patrick Stevedores* provides no basis for the making of an order against a non-party such as Ultra Modern which is not answerable or liable in some way to a party

(plaintiff or defendant) in a proceeding where judgment has not been obtained or execution recovered, or not holding, controlling or capable of disposing of the property of a party in that proceeding. This proposition, negative in character, should be accepted. ...

[48] LED's stance in this appeal is that it is not essential that the court's processes in support of which the *Mareva* relief is sought be confined to those set in motion upon a cause of action. That followed, it is submitted, from a passage in the speech of Lord Mustill in *Channel Tunnel Group Ltd v Balfour Beatty Construction Ltd,* [1993] AC 334 at 362 to which Hoffmann LJ referred in *Mercantile Group (Europe) AG v Aiyela* [1994] QB 366 at 375–6 in holding that the wife of the judgment debtor should be restrained from disposing of assets although no action had been brought against her. Lord Mustill said that the right to an interlocutory injunction which is incidental to, and dependent on, the enforcement of a substantive right usually, although not invariably, takes the shape of a cause of action. However, we do not think that his Lordship was suggesting that an order might be made against a non-party not amenable in some way ultimately to some coercive process requiring it to disgorge, or in some other way to participate in the satisfaction of, a judgment against a party.

[49] LED argues that its substantive rights are the final injunctive orders already made by Davies J against Eagle Homes following the determination of the issue of liability upon LED's actions for copyright infringement. Even if this be accepted for present purposes, LED still has the problem, which in our opinion the evidence does not resolve in its favour, of showing that recourse may be had to the appellants to satisfy LED's prospective money judgment against Eagle Homes.

[50] As LED submits, the development of this ancillary jurisdiction to grant *Mareva* orders has been an evolving process and the courts have approached the different factual situations as they have arisen 'flexibly'. There is a temptation to use the term 'flexible' to cloak a lack of analytical rigour and to escape the need to find a doctrinal and principled basis for orders that are made. There are significant differences between an order protective of the court's process set in train against a party to an action, including the efficacy of execution available to a judgment creditor, and an order extending to the property of persons who are not parties and who cannot be shown to have frustrated, actually or prospectively, the administration of justice. It has been truly said that a *Mareva* order does not deprive the party subject to its restraint either of title to or possession of the assets to which the order extends. Nor does the order improve the position of claimants in an insolvency of the judgment debtor. It operates *in personam* and not as an attachment. Nevertheless, those statements should not obscure the reality that the granting of a *Mareva* order is bound to have a significant impact on the property of the person against whom it is made: in a practical sense it operates as a very tight 'negative pledge' species of security over property, to which the contempt sanction is attached. It requires a high degree of caution on the part of a court invited to make an order of that kind. An order lightly or wrongly granted may have a capacity to impair or restrict commerce just as much as one appropriately granted may facilitate and ensure its due conduct ...

[At (404):]

[52] Another reason, unfortunately rarely adverted to in the cases, for care in exercising the power to grant a *Mareva* order is that there may be difficulties associated with the quantification and recovery of damages pursuant to the undertaking if it should turn out that the order should not have been granted. These matters were the subject of discussion by Aickin J in *Air Express Ltd v Ansett Transport Industries (Operations) Pty Ltd.* A further question to which a *Mareva*

order gives rise is the identification of the events to trigger its dissolution or an entitlement to damages. So far as this is possible, some attention to that question should be given at the time that the order is framed in the first instance.

[53] Discretionary considerations generally also should carefully be weighed before an order is made. Has the applicant proceeded diligently and expeditiously? Has a money judgment been recovered in the proceedings? Are proceedings (for example civil conspiracy proceedings) available against the third party? Why, if some proceedings are available, have they not been taken? Why, if proceedings are available against the third party and have not been taken and the court is still minded to make a *Mareva* order, should not the grant of the relief be conditioned upon an undertaking by the applicant to commence, and ensure so far as is possible the expedition of, such proceedings? It is difficult to conceive of cases where such an undertaking would not be required. Questions of this kind may be just as relevant to the decision to grant *Mareva* relief as they are to a decision to dissolve it. These are matters to which courts should be alive. As will appear, they are matters which should have been considered by the Full Court in this case.

[54] We have indicated our acceptance of a negative proposition put by the appellants. However, we consider that the general proposition for which the appellants contend — that the grant of Mareva relief against the third party should be limited to cases in which the third party holds or is about to hold or dissipate or further dissipate property beneficially owned by the defendant in the substantive proceedings — is too narrowly expressed. Nevertheless, it will be a rare case in which Mareva relief will be granted if such a situation does not exist ...

[At (405):]

[56] The matters referred to above show that the general power of superior courts which is comprehended by the express grant in s 23 of the Federal Court Act is a broad one. But, as the statements of Deane J in *Jackson v Sterling Industries Ltd* (1987) 162 CLR at 622, 625 make clear, orders made pursuant to that section (and under the general power) must be capable of properly being seen as appropriate to the case in hand.

[57] What then is the principle to guide the courts in determining whether to grant Mareva relief in a case such as the present where the activities of third parties are the object sought to be restrained? In our opinion such an order may, and we emphasise the word 'may', be appropriate, assuming the existence of other relevant criteria and discretionary factors, in circumstances in which:

(i) the third party holds, is using, or has exercised or is exercising a power of disposition over, or is otherwise in possession of, assets, including 'claims and expectancies', of the judgment debtor or potential judgment debtor; or

(ii) some process, ultimately enforceable by the courts, is or may be available to the judgment creditor as a consequence of a judgment against that actual or potential judgment debtor, pursuant to which, whether by appointment of a liquidator, trustee in bankruptcy, receiver or otherwise, the third party may be obliged to disgorge property or otherwise contribute to the funds or property of the judgment debtor to help satisfy the judgment against the judgment debtor.

[58] It is that principle which we would apply to this case. Its application is a matter of law, although discretionary elements are involved. [Footnotes generally omitted.] [It followed that the only asset which would satisfy these criteria was the business name 'Eagle Homes' and goodwill attached to that business name. Ultra Modern should be restrained from disposing

of the business name and goodwill attached to it. It was arguable that the dividend was an alienation of property within s 37A of the Conveyancing Act 1919 (NSW) and an order might be made against the Cardiles to the extent of the dividend only.]

[Kirby J delivered a separate judgment but agreed with the orders of the other members of the court, save in respect of costs.]

16.5.7 Notes and questions

1. See also L Aitken, 'Jurisdiction, Substantive Relief and the Asset Preservation Order' (2007) 81 *ALJ* 453.

2. Could a Mareva order have been made based on the former transaction provisions of the Corporations Act (ss 486A, 588FA–588ff, 598)? In this respect it will be noted that it was not suggested that a liquidator of Eagle Homes Pty Ltd would have any entitlement to set aside any transaction between Eagle Homes and Ultra Modern: 198 CLR at 393 [24].

3. Where a third party is in possession of assets which are the property of the defendant and it is put on notice of the existence of a Mareva order, the third party may be liable for contempt if it deals with such assets contrary to the injunction: *Z Ltd v A-Z* [1982] QB 588. The House of Lords has held that where a bank had notice of a Mareva order, it was not liable in damages for negligence for releasing funds contrary to the terms of the order; no duty of care arose and the only liability of the bank was for contempt: *Customs and Excise Commissioners v Barclays Bank plc* [2007] 1 AC 181.

4. The judgment of Gaudron, McHugh, Gummow and Callinan JJ in *Cardile v LED Builders Pty Ltd* recognises the power of the court to prevent a defendant from leaving the country without adequate bail or security: see 198 CLR 399 [39]:

   > … before judgment and in cases of an equitable debt or demand, courts of equity (and this Court in aid of its diversity jurisdiction) may, by order in the nature of a writ of *ne exeat colonia*, prevent a defendant quitting the country without giving adequate bail or security. Dixon J in *Glover v Walters* said that the order is made where:
   >> real ground appears for believing that the defendant is seeking to avoid the jurisdiction or for apprehending that if the defendant is allowed to depart the plaintiff will lose his debt or be prejudiced in his remedy.

5. See also *Pelechowski v Registrar, Court of Appeal* (1999) 162 ALR 336 (High Court) concerned with the power of the District Court of New South Wales to make a post-judgment order restraining judgment debtors from disposing or otherwise dealing with assets. While the court might have power to grant an asset preservation order in such a case, restraining the judgment debtor from dealing with property for such time as was necessary to enable execution to take place, the order before the court went much further and operated as security for the judgment debt: [52]–[54]. The judgment creditor is under an obligation to proceed expeditiously, as is the

plaintiff in pursuing proceedings in which such an order has been granted: *Cardile v LED Builders Pty Ltd* (1999) 198 CLR 380 at 404 [53].

6. On punishment for contempt of a Mareva order, see *Eurovox Pty Ltd v Miller* [2004] VSC 47, Hansen J and [2004] VSCA 21 where the Court of Appeal confirmed the order made of contempt, but set aside the term of imprisonment imposed by Hansen J on the basis that the defendant had not been made aware of the consequences of failure to comply with the order. Also see 16.3.15.

16.5.8 All jurisdictions, except the High Court, have now adopted harmonised rules for Mareva orders based on the principles established by the cases. These are known as freezing orders: FCR Div 7.4 Freezing orders and Freezing Orders Practice Note CM 9; ACT rr 740–745 and Court Procedures Practice Note (Freezing Orders) 2008 (No 1); NSW Pt 25 Div 2 and Freezing Orders Practice Note (SC Gen 14); NT O 37A and Freezing Orders Practice Direction (No 5 of 2006); Qld Ch 8 Pt 2 Div 2 and Freezing Orders Practice Direction (No 1 of 2007); SA r 247 and Freezing Orders Practice Direction (Direction 4.5); Tas Pt 36 Div 1A and Freezing Orders Practice Direction (No 3 of 2006); Vic O 37A and Freezing Orders Practice Note (No 5 of 2010; WA O 52 A and Freezing Orders Practice Direction (No 7 of 2007, 9.6 Consolidated). These rules will be the primary focus for those seeking a Mareva or freezing order. The rules expressly preserve the inherent jurisdiction as to Mareva orders: FCR r 7.36; ACT r 727; NSW r 25.15; NT r 36A.06; Qld r 260E; SA r 247; Tas r 937F; Vic r 37A.06; WA O 52 r 6. For a recent example of a freezing order, see *Pure Logistics Pty Ltd v Scott* [2007] NSWSC 595. The court may also make ancillary orders to elicit information concerning the assets the subject of a freezing order. Establishing and intention to fail to comply with a freezing order may amount to contempt of court: *Wexford v Doolub* [2008] NSWCSC 952.

16.5.9 The relevant Australian Capital Territory Rules are set out below.

16.5.10E **Court Procedures Rules 2006 (ACT)**

740 Definitions — Div 2.9.4.2

In this subdivision:

another court means a court outside Australia or a court in Australia other than the court.

applicant means a person who applies for a freezing order or ancillary order.

respondent means a person against whom a freezing order or ancillary order is sought or made.

741 Freezing orders — general

(1) The Supreme Court may make an order (a *freezing order*) for the purpose of preventing the frustration or inhibition of the court's process by ensuring that an order or prospective order of the court is not made valueless or diminished in value.

...

(3)   A freezing order may be an order restraining a respondent from removing any assets located in or outside Australia or from disposing of, dealing with, or diminishing the value of, those assets.

(4)   For the Supreme Court, a freezing order or ancillary order may be made whether or not the respondent is a party to an existing proceeding.

...

(6)   The affidavits supporting an application for a freezing order or ancillary order must include the following information:

(a)   information about —
(i)   the order mentioned in rule 743(1)(a) (Freezing orders — order against enforcement debtor or prospective enforcement debtor or third party); or
(ii)   if no order mentioned in rule 743(1)(a) has been obtained — the following information about the cause of action mentioned in rule 743(1)(b) or (c):
(A)   the basis of the claim for principal relief;
(B)   the amount of the claim;
(C)   if the application is made without being served on the respondent — any possible defence or other response to the claim;

(b)   the nature and value of the respondent's assets, as far as they are known to the applicant, in and outside Australia;

(c)   why the applicant believes —
(i)   the respondent's assets may be removed from Australia; or
(ii)   the dealing with the assets should be restrained by order;

(d)   why the applicant believes the order mentioned in rule 743(1)(a) may go unsatisfied if the removal or dealing mentioned in paragraph (c) happens;

(e)   the identity of anyone, other than the respondent, who the applicant knows may be affected by the order, and how the person may be affected.

(7)   The court may amend or set aside a freezing order or ancillary order.

742 Ancillary orders

(1)   The court may make an order (an *ancillary order*) ancillary to a freezing order or prospective freezing order as the court considers appropriate.

(2)   Without limiting subrule (1), an ancillary order may be made for either or both of the following purposes:
(a)   finding out information about assets relevant to the freezing order or prospective freezing order;
(b)   deciding whether the freezing order should be made.

(3)   On an application mentioned in rule 729(3) (Division 2.9.4 order without notice etc), the court may make an ancillary order if it considers it appropriate.

743 Freezing orders — order against enforcement debtor or prospective enforcement debtor or third party

(1)   This rule applies if —
(a)   an order has been given in favour of an applicant by —
(i)   the court; or
(ii)   for an order to which subrule (2) applies — another court; or
(b)   for the Supreme Court — an applicant has a good arguable case on an accrued or prospective cause of action that is justiciable in —
(i)   the court; or
(ii)   for a cause of action to which subrule (3) applies — another court

...

(2) This subrule applies to an order if there is a sufficient prospect that the order will be registered in or enforced by the court.

(3) This subrule applies to a cause of action if there is a sufficient prospect that —
    (a) the other court will make an order in favour of the applicant; and
    (b) the order will be registered in or enforced by the court.

(4) The court may make a freezing order or ancillary order (or both) against an enforcement debtor or prospective enforcement debtor if satisfied, having regard to all the circumstances, that there is a danger that an order or prospective order will be completely or partly unsatisfied because any of the following might happen:
    (a) the enforcement debtor, prospective enforcement debtor or someone else absconds;
    (b) the assets of the enforcement debtor, prospective enforcement debtor or someone else are —
        (i) removed from Australia or from somewhere in or outside Australia; or
        (ii) disposed of, dealt with or diminished in value.

(5) The court may make a freezing order or ancillary order (or both) against someone other than an enforcement debtor or prospective enforcement debtor (a *third party*) if satisfied, having regard to all the circumstances, that —
    (a) there is a danger that an order or prospective order will be completely or partly unsatisfied because —
        (i) the third party holds or is using, or has exercised or is exercising, a power of disposition over assets (including claims and expectancies) of the enforcement debtor or prospective enforcement debtor; or
        (ii) the third party is in possession of, or in a position of control or influence concerning, assets (including claims and expectancies) of the enforcement debtor or prospective enforcement debtor; or
    (b) a process in the court, is or may ultimately be, available to the applicant as a result of an order or prospective order, and, under the process, the third party may be obliged to disgorge assets or contribute toward satisfying the order or prospective order.

(6) This rule does not affect the court's power to make a freezing order or ancillary order if the court considers it is in the interests of justice to do so.

744 Freezing orders — service outside Australia of application for freezing order or ancillary order
An application for a freezing order or ancillary order may be served on someone who is outside Australia without the court's leave (whether or not the person is domiciled or resident in Australia) if any of the assets to which the order relates are in the ACT.

745 Freezing orders — costs
(1) The court may make any order about costs that it considers appropriate in relation to a freezing order or ancillary order.

(2) Without limiting subrule (1), an order about costs includes an order about the costs of anyone affected by a freezing order or ancillary order.

16.5.11 It is possible to discharge or vary injunctive orders. Collier J in *Bird v McComb (No 3)* [2011] FCA 697 outlined the following considerations for variation or discharge:

- The court's discretion to vary or set aside an order is to be exercised with great caution, having regard to the importance of the public interest in the finality of litigation.

- The discretionary power will ordinarily only be exercised in exceptional circumstances, including where an interlocutory order was obtained by fraud or non-disclosure of material facts, or through an accident or mistake that occurred without the fault of the parties.

- An order varying or setting aside the terms of an order can be made to correct an error or oversight or to give effect to a review of the contemplated order so that the orders made more adequately deal with the matter as it stands to be litigated.

- An application to discharge or vary interlocutory orders must not be used as an alternative to the appellate procedure in respect of the interlocutory judgment or used as an opportunity for a party to reargue its case for a second time.

- The failure of the party who has successfully applied for injunctive relief to diligently and promptly prosecute the primary proceedings will support an application for discharge of the order.

- An order may also be made to vary the relief where new facts come into existence or are discovered, such that it would be unjust to enforce the order.

Courts may set aside or vary interlocutory orders made by consent of the parties: *R D Werner & Co Inc v Bailey Aluminum Products Pty Ltd* (1988) 18 FCR 389.

INTERIM PRESERVATION, MANAGEMENT, CUSTODY OF PROPERTY

16.6.1 Each jurisdiction has provisions for the interim preservation and custody of property. In Western Australia O 52 r 2 provides:

(1) The Court may, on the application of any party to a cause or matter, make an order for the detention, custody, preservation or inspection of any property which is the subject-matter of a cause in action, or as to which any question may arise therein.

The equivalents to the Western Australian rule are: HCR r 8.07.2(d); FCR rr 7.01, 14.11; ACT r 715; NSW r 25.3; NT rr 37.01, 37.02; Qld r 250; SA r 248; Tas rr 436, 437; Vic rr 37.01, 37.02. The Victorian and Northern Territory provisions differentiate between the preservation of property of a party to the proceeding (r 37.01) and property (excluding documents) of a person not (yet) a party to the proceeding: r 37.02. The Victorian and Northern Territory r 37.02 is related to the preliminary discovery rules contained in r 32.05 of those rules.

16.6.2C	**Wentworth v Rogers (No 8)**
	(1986) 7 NSWLR 207
	Court of Appeal (NSW)

[The facts appear sufficiently in the judgment of Kirby P.]

Kirby P (at 207): Listed before the Court on 8 and 9 December 1986 is an appeal in proceedings between the claimant and her former husband.

Claim for return of funds by former solicitors:

The claimant wishes to have funds in order to be in a position to pay her solicitors so that they may retain counsel to represent her on the appeal. The claimant has recently changed her solicitors. Her new solicitors have told her that they must be put in funds to the extent of $10,000 by Thursday, 27 November 1986 in order to guarantee the fees of counsel. The Court has [208] been asked to draw the conclusion that, unless this step is taken, the solicitors will not retain counsel, thereby exposing the claimant to the peril that she would be unrepresented on the return of the appeal.

The claimant made an application which has been listed and is part-heard before Hodgson J. She has sought orders from his Honour that her former solicitors, who have been represented in this Court today, should return to her the funds which she has deposited with them. The precise amount of such deposited funds is in dispute. However, it seems that they have been in excess of $100,000.

Urgent relief in the Court of Appeal:

The rule upon which the claimant relies for relief in this Court is Supreme Court Rules 1970, Pt 51, r 5A. It provides, relevantly:

> Notwithstanding anything in these rules, where an application made under subr (2) of Pt 19 r 2 for any of the forms of relief specified in Pt 28, r 1, r 2 and r 3 has been refused, an application for a similar purpose may be made to the Court of Appeal within seven days of the refusal, or within such extended time as the Court of Appeal may within such seven days allow, without the filing or service of any notice of appeal, summons or notice of motion.

Two questions arise as to the standing of the claimant to have the relief of this Court under that rule. The first is whether Hodgson J has, at this stage, refused an application for the purposes of the rule. The Court has before it a judgment of his Honour dated 17 November 1986 on an application for the return of moneys. In the closing paragraphs of that judgment, his Honour states that, notwithstanding the difficulties of the applicant in relation to the hearing of her appeal, he did not think at the stage reached in the proceedings that he could or should make any interim order for the return of money to her. It would therefore appear that the judgment on the application for interim relief amounts to a refusal of an application and it is this refusal upon which the claimant relies. I will assume for the purposes of these reasons that the judgment in the claim for interim relief amounts to such a refusal as the rule contemplates.

Preservation of property — Is money property?

The second question is whether the claim made by the claimant before Hodgson J falls within the forms of relief specified in the Supreme Court Rules, Pt 28, r 1, that being a further pre-condition of the relief in this Court to which Pt 51, r 5A, is addressed. Most of the provisions of Pt 28, r 2 are plainly inapplicable to the present case. But the rule refers, in r 1(1)(c), to r 2 in Pt 28. This refers, in turn, to proceedings concerning any property or proceedings in which any question may arise as to any property. In such proceedings the Court may make orders for the detention, custody or preservation of the property.

The claimant says that the word 'property' includes the funds which she has deposited with her former solicitors. She argues that the rule thereby attracts the jurisdiction of the Court to make a preservation order in respect of such property.

There are three difficulties with this submission. The first is that, as a matter of fact, it cannot be seriously suggested that the funds deposited by the claimant with the solicitors amount to an actual separate fund of property [209] which has been separately kept by them. Indeed so much is not claimed. The contrary appears in par 5 of the statement of the nature of the case filed by the claimant under Pt 51, r 3(7) of the rules.

Secondly, it has been held in the Supreme Court of Victoria in *Pizzey Properties Pty Ltd v Edelstein* [1977] VR 161 that Supreme Court Rules, O 50, r 3, expressed in relevantly similar terms, does not apply where the specific property has been converted into money. That decision would appear to apply equally to the rule before us.

Thirdly, if the purpose of the rule is the preservation of the identity and integrity of specific property pending the disposition of the Court, Pt 28, r 2 has no application to a case such as the present. Here there is no need to preserve and protect particular identifiable property pending the disposal of the appeal.

The claimant submitted that upon this view Pt 28, r 2 would not sustain the 'Mareva' injunctions which are issued from time to time by the Court. However, such injunctions are ordered not under the rule referred to by the claimant.

They are probably based, ultimately, on the Supreme Court Act 1970, s 23. When this fact was pointed out, the claimant sought the relief of the Court as claimed in her summons under that section. However, that provision is an extraordinary one. It is not to be used as a vehicle for bypassing the normal procedures of the Court or the rules of the Court.

Refusal of leave to appeal:

It has not been shown in this case, by evidence admitted before us, that it is impossible for the claimant to solve the difficulties which she faces in other ways. One such way would be by the adjournment of the hearing of the appeal until after the completion of the proceedings before Hodgson J. Another would be by access to other funds that may be available to the claimant. It would not otherwise be appropriate to interfere in a decision of the kind which Hodgson J has made. That decision is an interlocutory one. His Honour has concluded the hearing of evidence and is considering argument before judgment.

There are serious differences as to the facts and differences as to their interpretation. The claimant primarily sought relief under Pt 51, r 5. However in the alternative, she sought leave to appeal from the order refusing interlocutory relief. Consistent with well-established principles which restrain the interference of appeal courts in interlocutory orders of this kind, to the extent that the summons seeks leave to appeal, I would refuse it.

Accordingly, the order which I propose is that the summons of the claimant be dismissed and the claimant pay the costs occasioned by the proceedings in the Court today.

Suggestion but no order to the trial judge:

In proposing this order, to which I am driven by the terms of the rules and the practice of the Court in interlocutory applications for leave to appeal, I do not wish to appear unmindful of the difficulty which the claimant faces in preparing for the hearing of the appeal before this Court. The case in which she is involved is one which has some extraordinary features. It is especially desirable that it should be heard with the assistance of counsel. With that consideration in mind I can do no more than to say to the parties, and through this judgment to Hodgson J, that if there were any way by which his [210] Honour's decision could properly be concluded before the hearing of the appeal and in such time as would allow the claimant to be put in any funds to which she is entitled from her former solicitors, that would further the interests of justice as I see them. However, so far as the orders sought by the claimant are concerned, I do not believe that any such orders should be made by this Court. That is why the orders I propose are that the summons be dismissed. The claimant must pay the costs.

Samuels JA (at 210): I would like to add a word or two for myself. The application before us is in form a summons for leave to appeal against, it seems, the refusal of Hodgson J to make some interim or interlocutory order in proceedings before him, the precise nature of which has not been established.

It is clear enough from his Honour's judgment that the proceedings relate to a fund once in the hands of Ms Wentworth's former solicitors, part of which or the whole of which ultimately she desires to recover back but which she says has now been paid away.

If the relief sought had been leave to appeal, it seems very clear to me that in the circumstances, and I have regard particularly to the interlocutory nature of the order made below which is in contest and the fact the judgment has been reserved and the timetable for resolution of the matter established, leave would not have been granted.

However, as an alternative it was put that these were proceedings governed by the Supreme Court Rules, 1970, Pt 51, r 5A, read in conjunction with Pt 28, it being unnecessary to notice Pt 19, r 2 which merely indicates the nature of the process. In order to invoke Pt 51, r 5A, which enables a first instance application to be made to this Court, it is necessary for the claimant not merely to establish that relief has been refused below but that what was refused was an application under Pt 28. Whether or not Pt 28 applies to the matters in contest, which I very much doubt, there is nothing before us to suggest that this rule was invoked in the proceedings before Hodgson J. Quite what, as I have said, the application before him was, I cannot say. However, there is no material to suggest that it was brought under Pt 28. For those reasons it seems to me the alternative application cannot succeed.

But further it seems to me also that whatever may be the general meaning of the word 'property', in the context of Pt 28, it means specific property or property in specie. As the President had pointed out, that is the construction accorded to a substantially identical rule of the Victorian Supreme Court.

Furthermore, the English Annual Practice dealing with O 29, r 2, which is the English equivalent, does not appear to contemplate that a chose in action of the kind in question here or a debt or an account is regarded as falling within the similar wording of that rule. I can see no case in the notes in the Annual Practice, which is all I have had time to read, which suggests to the contrary. It follows that in my opinion both the applications are misconceived.

There is one thing more. I appreciate that Ms Wentworth has the problem [211] to which the President has referred, but if it means that on 8 December the Court which sits to hear her appeal must hear it without the benefit of legal advice and advocacy on her side, then no doubt it will do its duty.

We must, I think, guard ourselves against temptations imposed upon us by our desire to save litigants in person from the adverse results of their professional illiteracy to exercise some kind of general benevolent direction over the proceedings in the courts. It would not have been appropriate in my view for us to offer any suggestion to Hodgson J as to how he should run his list or how he should conduct cases before him. We sit here only to correct him if he should turn out to be wrong. I agree with the order that has been proposed.

[Glass JA agreed with Kirby P.]

16.6.3 There is provision in each jurisdiction for the disposal of perishable property. In Western Australia O 52 r 4 provides:

(1)   The Court may on the application of a party make an order for the sale or other disposal by a person named in the order and in such manner and on such terms (if any) as the court thinks fit, of —
    (a)   any property of a perishable nature;
    (b)   any shares or securities which appear likely to depreciate in value; or
    (c)   any personal property which for any just and sufficient reason it is desirable to sell at once.
(2)   This rule applies to goods, wares, merchandise, shares, securities, and personal property which are the subject of a cause or matter or as to which a question arises in a cause or matter.

See also: FCR r 14.12; ACT r 716; NSW r 25.4; NT r 37.04; Qld r 251; SA r 248(3); Tas r 438; Vic r 37.04. There is no equivalent High Court Rule.

SECURITY FOR COSTS

Introduction

16.7.1 In each jurisdiction there is provision enabling the court to order that the plaintiff provide security for the defendant's costs in certain circumstances. The court is concerned to ensure that the defendant is able to enforce an order for costs made in its favour at trial in such cases. This question is discussed in S Colbran, *Security for Costs*, Longman Professional, Melbourne, 1993, Ch 1.

Security for costs is the security, which a defendant on application may require from a plaintiff for the payment of costs that may be awarded to the defendant in the event the plaintiff fails in their proceedings. The application may be founded on the court's inherent jurisdiction to prevent abuse of process or more commonly on the rules of court (see **16.7.2E** below) or specific legislation: see **16.7.3E** below. The main categories of cases in which orders for security for costs have been made include:

(a)   where the plaintiff is ordinarily resident outside the jurisdiction;
(b)   where a nominal plaintiff, not being a plaintiff suing in a representative capacity, is suing for the benefit of some other person and there is reason to believe the nominal plaintiff will be unable to pay the costs of the defendant if ordered to do so;
(c)   where the plaintiff's address is not stated or is incorrectly stated in the originating process, unless the court is satisfied that the failure was innocently made without the intention to deceive;
(d)   where the plaintiff changed their address during the course of the proceedings with a view to evading the consequences of the litigation;
(e)   arbitration proceedings; and
(f)   where the plaintiff is a limited liability company and there is reason to believe the company will be unable to pay the defendant's costs.

Whether security for costs is ordered is ultimately a discretionary matter in all the circumstances of the case. The following factors have been taken into account in exercising the discretion:

(a)   the means of persons who stand behind the litigation;

(b)   the prospects of success or merits of the litigation;

(c)   the bona fides of the litigation;

(d)   whether the plaintiff is an impecunious company;

(e)   whether the plaintiff's impecuniosity is attributable to the defendant's conduct;

(f)   whether the plaintiff is the party attacked and is in essence occupying the position of a defendant;

(g)   whether an order for security for costs would be oppressive;

(h)   whether an order for security for costs will stifle the litigation;

(i)   whether a pre-existing special relationship exists;

(j)   whether the litigation will involve a matter of public importance;

(k)   whether there has been an admission or payment into court;

(l)   whether there has been a delay in bringing the application;

(m) costs of enforcement procedures;

(n)   whether a loss-bearing, loss-sharing entity is involved;

(o)   the risk of dissipation of assets; and

(p)   costs.

See generally S Colbran, *Security for Costs*, Longman Professional, Melbourne, 1993.

Court rules

16.7.2E   Supreme Court (General Civil Procedures) Rules 2005 (Vic)
Order 62 — Security for Costs

62.01 Definitions
In this Order, unless the context or subject matter otherwise requires —
defendant includes any person against whom a claim is made in a proceeding;
plaintiff includes any person who makes a claim in a proceeding.

62.02 When security for costs may be ordered
(1) Where —
    (a) the plaintiff is ordinarily resident out of Victoria;
    (b) the plaintiff is a corporation or (not being a plaintiff who sues in a representative capacity) sues, not for his own benefit, but for the benefit of some other person, and there is reason to believe that the plaintiff has insufficient assets in Victoria to pay the costs of the defendant if ordered to do so;
    (c) a proceeding by the plaintiff in another court for the same claim is pending;
    (d) subject to paragraph (2), the address of the plaintiff is not stated or is not stated correctly in his originating process;
    (e) the plaintiff has changed his address after the commencement of the proceeding in order to avoid the consequences of the proceeding;
    (f) under any Act the Court may require security for any costs —
the Court may, on the application of a defendant, order that the plaintiff give security for the costs of the defendant of the proceeding and that the proceeding as against the defendant be stayed until the security is given.

(2) The Court shall not require a plaintiff to give security by reason only of paragraph 1(d) if in failing to state his address or to state his correct address the plaintiff acted innocently and without intention to deceive.

62.03 Manner of giving security
Where an order is made requiring the plaintiff to give security for costs, security shall be given in the manner and at the time the Court directs.

62.04 Failure to give security
Where a plaintiff fails to give the security required by an order, the Court may dismiss the plaintiff's claim.

62.05 Variation or setting aside
The Court may set aside or vary any order requiring a plaintiff to give security for costs.

[See also: HCR Pt 59; FCR r 19.01; ACT rr 1900–1906; NSW Pt 42, Div 6; NT O 62; Qld Ch 17; SA r 194; Tas rr 828–835; WA O 25.]

Other legislation

16.7.3E	**Corporations Act 2001 (Cth)**

Costs
1335 (1) Where a corporation is plaintiff in any action or other legal proceeding, the court having jurisdiction in the matter may, if it appears by credible testimony that there is reason to believe that the corporation will be unable to pay the costs of the defendant if successful in his, her or its defence, require sufficient security to be given for those costs and stay all proceedings until the security is given.

(2) The costs of any proceeding before a court under this Law shall be borne by such party to the proceeding as the court, in its discretion, directs ...

[For a summary of the principals applied to a s 1335 application, see *Acohs Pty Ltd v Ucorp Pty Ltd* [2006] FCA 1279 per Jessup J.]

Court's inherent power to make such orders

16.7.4 The court also has an inherent power to order security for costs: *Shannon v Australia and New Zealand Banking Group Ltd (No 2)* [1994] 2 Qd R 563. A defendant will not normally be required to give security for costs except in respect of any counterclaim or cross-claim or in those cases in which it is properly to be regarded as aggressor in the litigation: *Classic Ceramic Importers Pty Ltd v Ceramic Antiga SA* (1994) 12 ACLC 549.

16.7.5 Traditionally a court would not normally, in the case of an individual plaintiff, order that security for costs be given on the grounds of the plaintiff's impecuniosity: *Co-operative Farmers and Graziers' Direct Meat Supply Ltd v Smart* [1977] VR 386. However, the court has an inherent power to do so to prevent an abuse of process: see *Rajski v Computer Manufacture and Design Pty Ltd* [1982] 2 NSWLR 443 (Holland J) and [1983] 2 NSWLR 122 (Court of Appeal). Also see *Green (as liq of Arimco Mining Pty Ltd) v CGU Insurance Ltd* (2008) 67 ACSR 105 at [7]. Impecuniosity is but a factor in the exercise of discretion. An order can be made against a liquidator suing on behalf of a company in liquidation. In the *Arimco* case, there is discussion regarding the situation where a liquidator has litigation funding.

The court's discretion

16.7.6 It should be noted that the power to order security for costs is discretionary. This discretion is discussed in S Colbran, *Security for Costs*, Longman Professional, Melbourne, 1993, Ch 14.

There is a conflict of opinion as to whether the discretion should be ordinarily exercised so as to protect the defendant. In *Buckley v Bennell Design and Construction Pty Ltd* (1974) 1 ACLR 301 at 305, Street CJ said, having reviewed the authorities, that he preferred 'to regard the discretion conferred by [the predecessor to s 1335 of the Corporations Act] as being one which should be exercised merely with a predisposition in favour of the defendant party'. The Victorian Court of Appeal in *Ariss v Express Interiors Pty Ltd (in liq)* [1996] 2 VR 507 (application for security for costs against a company in liquidation) declined to follow Street CJ. And see also *Epping Plaza Fresh Fruit & Vegetables Pty Ltd v Bevendale Pty Ltd* [1999] 2 VR 191 and *Livingspring Pty Ltd v Kliger Partners* (2008) 66 ACSR 455, but compare the approach of the New South Wales Court of Appeal in *Jazabas Pty Ltd v Haddad* (2007) 65 ACSR 276.

16.7.7 Notes and questions

1. The extent to which the plaintiff corporation's impecuniosity has been caused by the defendant will be relevant to the exercise of the court's discretion in relation to an application for security for costs: *Jet Corp of Australia Pty Ltd v Petres Pty Ltd* (1983) 50 ALR 722 at 733. Conversely, the extent to which the plaintiff's financial difficulties have been caused by its own conduct will be relevant: *Newton's Travel Services Pty Ltd v Ansett Transport Industries (Operations) Pty Ltd* (1982) 44 ALR 163 at 166.

2. Delay by the defendant in applying for security for costs will be a relevant consideration: *Health & Life Care Ltd (recs and mgrs apptd) v Price Waterhouse* (1993) 11 ACSR 326.

3. Where the liquidator sues in the name of the company to enforce duties contained in the Corporations Act, should security for costs be required? See *Australian Quarry Holdings Pty Ltd (in liq) v Dougherty* (1992) 8 ACSR 569. Would the situation be any different if the liquidator was being funded under a litigation lending agreement? See C Einstein and S Krauss, 'Liquidators, Litigation Funding and Security for Costs: Echoes of Maintenance and Champerty in the Exercise of the Court's Discretion' (2008) 31 *Aust Bar Rev* 202; *Green (as liq of Arimco Mining Pty Ltd) v CGU Insurance Ltd* (2008) 67 ACSR 105; [2008] NSWCA 148.

4. The High Court in *Knight v F P Special Assets Ltd* (1992) 174 CLR 178, held that a court is able to order that costs be paid by a liquidator personally in the event that an action brought by the liquidator in the name of the company in liquidation is unsuccessful.

PROVISIONAL LIQUIDATION AND RECEIVERS

Provisional liquidation

16.8.1 Supreme Courts and the Federal Court have power to appoint a provisional liquidator under the Corporations Act 2001(Cth) s 472(2). The principles relevant to the appointment of a provisional liquidator were spelled out in *Re J N Taylor Holdings Ltd; Zempilas v J N Taylor Holdings Ltd* (1990) 3 ACSR 600 at 613–14 per Debelle J of the South Australian Supreme Court.

16.8.2C   **Re J N Taylor Holdings Ltd; Zempilas v J N Taylor Holdings Ltd**
(1990) 3 ACSR 600
Supreme Court of South Australia

Debelle J (at 613): The exercise of the power to appoint a provisional liquidator pursuant to [s 472] is a serious intrusion upon the company. From a commercial point of view, the practical effect of the appointment is to paralyse the company: *Re London, Hamburg & Continental Exchange Bank: Emmerson's Case* [1866] 2 Eq 231 at 237; *Re Capital Services Ltd* (1983) 1 ACLC 1270 ...

[614] Generally speaking, a provisional liquidator will be appointed only if the court is satisfied that there is a valid and duly authorised winding up application and there is a reasonable prospect that a winding up order will be made: *Re McLennan Holdings Pty Ltd* (1983) 7 ACLR 732; *Montgomery Windsor (NSW) Pty Ltd v Ilopa Pty Ltd* (1983) 2 ACLR 224. However, as Young J observed in *Alessi v The Original Australian Art Co Pty Ltd* (1989) 7 ACLC 595, this is not a rule of law and in the appropriate and extraordinary circumstances the court will appoint a provisional liquidator, not withstanding that it is unlikely that the company will finally be wound up ...

It is usually necessary to establish that the assets of the company are in some jeopardy: *Re Roadmakers Pty Ltd* (1985) 3 ACLC 591; *Re Adnot Pty Ltd* (1982) 7 ACLR 212; *Pitt v Bachmann; Re Lockyer Valley Fresh Foods Co-operative Assoc Ltd (Qld)* (1980) CLC 40671. In one sense, the need to demonstrate that the assets are in some jeopardy reflects the fact that the primary duty of a provisional liquidator is to preserve the status quo pending the hearing and determination of the application to wind up the company so that the assets of the company are preserved for the benefit of those who may ultimately be found entitled to them: *Re Carpark Industries Pty Ltd (in liq)* [1967] 1 NSWR 337; *Garden Mew-St Leonards Pty Ltd v Butler Pollnow Pty Ltd (No 4)* (1984) 2 ACLC 682; *Re Obie Pty Ltd* [1984] 1 Qd 371; *Re Rothwells Ltd* (1989) 15 ACLR 142 at 147.

16.8.3 A provisional liquidator may only be appointed once an application for the winding up of the company has been filed. It is usually necessary to show that the assets of the company are in some jeopardy: *Re Adnot Pty Ltd* (1982) 7 ACLR 212. The provisional liquidator preserves the assets of the company pending the final hearing of the application for winding up.

Receivers

16.8.4　Receivers may be appointed when a plaintiff establishes a prima facie right to property at risk of damage or loss unless the property is preserved pending trial of the proceeding. The court will provide safe custody for disputed property, prevent its destruction, or prevent its distribution to persons without adequate interest in the property. The Federal Court and the Supreme Courts of each state and territory have the power to appoint a receiver 'if it is just and convenient to do so'. For example, s 37(1) of the Supreme Court Act 1986 (Vic) provides that 'the Court may by order whether interlocutory or final ... appoint a receiver if it is just and convenient to do so'. See also Vic O 39. For similar provisions in other states and territories, see: Federal Court of Australia Act 1976 (Cth) s 57, FCR r 7.01, Div 14.3; Supreme Court Act 1933 (ACT) s 26, ACT Div 2.9.5; Supreme Court Act 1970 (NSW) s 67, NSW Pt 26; Supreme Court Act (NT) s 69, NT O 39; Qld Ch 8 Pt 3; Supreme Court Act (SA) s 29, SA Ch 11 Pt 15; Tas Pt 18; WA O 51. The power to appoint a receiver is discretionary. There is no equivalent High Court Rule. The application is usually upon notice: *Bond Brewing Holdings Ltd v Crawford* (1989) 1 WAR 154, but may be made ex parte in cases of emergency.

16.8.5C	**National Australia Bank Ltd v Bond Brewing Holdings Ltd**
	[1991] 1 VR 386
	Supreme Court of Victoria, Appeal Division

[The plaintiff applied *ex parte* for an order that a receiver be appointed to the assets and undertaking of the defendant companies. The defendants were unsecured creditors of the plaintiff. A judge ordered that a receiver be appointed. The order was subsequently confirmed by the judge on an application by the defendants to have the receiver removed. The defendants appealed. The Appeal Division set aside the order at first instance.]

Kaye, Murphy and Brooking JJ (at 539): The appointment of a receiver is one of the oldest remedies of the Court of Chancery, and a very useful remedy it is. But its very efficacy means that a corresponding caution must attend its employment. Where a receiver is sought to protect property of which no one is in actual possession, no one will be ousted by the appointment and probably no great harm will be done. But where the subject matter is in the defendant's hands he may suffer an irreparable wrong by being dispossessed and of course this danger will weigh with the judge from whom the remedy is sought. The appointment of a receiver is to be, so to speak, at the expense of the defendant's possession and without his consent is a step never to be taken without proper consideration of the defendant's position. ...

Where a receiver is sought, not merely of a particular asset of the defendant, but of all of his assets, particular caution is required and where, as in the present case, the receiver is to possess himself of and to manage the assets and undertaking of a collection of companies which, whether they are solvent or not, are in a very large way of business, very great circumspection is required. Of course in a strong enough case the Court might, without warning to a trading company, divest it of control of its undertaking and assets. But it must always be borne in mind that the appointment of a receiver in such a case authorises an irresistible invasion and that even if the army of occupation is withdrawn after only a short time things may never be the same again. Rights of property and the company's privacy are violated. Only the most pressing need can violate such an invasion without notice.

[The court noted that in this case no notice had been given to the defendants, and that in such a case (at 540):]

[I]t was necessary for the applicant to show a most powerful case of apprehended injury in order to induce a judge to make an order of such great consequence on the Friday afternoon as opposed to entertaining an application on notice during the long weekend or ... on the following Tuesday. ...

[553] The plaintiff, like the witch in Hansel and Gretel, may want a receiver to cage the defendant and fatten him up so he will make better eating, or at least to prevent him from wasting away. The Court might we suppose have taken a wide view and said that administration by a Court appointed officer, at all events if some criticism is made of the business abilities of those in control of the company, is likely to have the result that by the time the plaintiff obtains judgment for the debt the company still has assets with which to satisfy that judgment, and have said on this basis that there was no adequate legal remedy to protect the plaintiff as a creditor. But this wide view has not been taken ... The Court will not by injunction require a defendant to give security for the plaintiff's claim (*Lister & Co v Stubbs* (1900) 45 Ch D 1), nor will it by the appointment of a receiver achieve the same result. Some kind of interim administration of the affairs of a debtor in order to enhance the plaintiff's prospects of ultimately being paid if he obtains a judgment is objectionable in the same way as an injunction which requires the defendant to give security for the plaintiff's claim. Where there is danger that a defendant will dissipate his assets a Mareva injunction may be granted and in a strong enough case of that kind a receiver may be appointed.

16.8.6 A receiver is generally disinterested in the subject matter of the proceeding (*Re Lloyd; Allen v Lloyd* (1879) 12 Ch D 447) and acts as an officer of the court to hold and preserve the property, rather than carry on a business. If a receiver is also appointed as a manager, they are then permitted to carry on a business with a view to winding it up as a going concern over a short timeframe, whilst maximizing the value of the business.

ACCOUNTS AND INQUIRIES

16.9.1 A court may order an account where parties are in dispute over the balance of accounts, despite other outstanding issues: ACT r 2721; FCR r 30.51; NSW r 46.2; NT r 52.01; Qld r 527; SA r 251; Tas r 594; Vic r 52.01; WA O 45 r 2. An order for an account may be made at any stage of a proceeding. A court may give special directions concerning an account or inquiry: ACT r 2722; NSW r 46.4; NT r 52.02; Qld r 528; SA r 251; Tas r 575; Vic r 52.02; WA O 45 r 4.

Further reading

16.10.1   Articles

J Dine and J McEvoy, 'Are Mareva Injunctions Becoming Attachment Orders?' (1989) 8 *CJQ* 236.

M Dockray and H Laddie, 'Piller Problems' (1990) 106 *LQR* 601.

M Hetherington, 'Inherent Powers and the Mareva Injunction' (1983) 10 *SydLR* 76.

D Ong, 'Unsatisfactory Aspects of the Mareva Order and the Anton Piller Order' (2005) 17(1) *Bond LR* 92.

G Turner, 'Interlocutory Injunctions — Making Urgent Applications in the Equity Division of the Supreme Court' (2009) 47(6) *LSJ* 78.

P Venus, 'Shock and Awe — Obtaining Mareva Orders in Queensland Courts' (2004) 24(1) *Proctor* 15.

16.10.2   Texts

D Boniface, M Kumar and M Legg, *Principles of Civil Procedure New South Wales*, 2nd ed, Thomson Reuters, Pyrmont, 2012, Ch 5.

P Briscoe, *Freezing & Search Orders: Mareva & Anton Piller*, 2nd ed, LexisNexis, Butterworths, 2008.

B Cairns, *Australian Civil Procedure*, 9th ed, Law Book Co, Sydney, 2011, Chs 13, 14.

S Colbran, *Security for Costs*, Longman Professional, Melbourne, 1993.

S Gee, *Mareva Injunctions and Anton Piller Relief*, 4th ed, F T Law & Tax, London, 1998.

Settlement

## CHAPTER 17

OVERVIEW

The chapter begins by noting that the vast majority of cases are resolved without resort to trial. However, pre-trial resolution is by no means easy. Many cases are settled only on the eve of a scheduled trial, and settlement is complicated by the conflict between the parties' mutual interests in achieving settlement, and their individual interests in achieving the outcome which is in their best personal interests. Civil procedures seek to encourage settlement in two ways:

- by penalising parties who refuse to make or accept reasonable offers; and
- by providing support for institutions designed to ease negotiations.

   The 'stick' is the costs rules. Three types of costs rules are discussed:

- the traditional 'payment into court' system;
- the 'Calderbank' offer; and
- the more recent, and more flexible, offer of compromise rules.

   This chapter also examines processes for facilitating settlement, in particular mediation and neutral evaluation. It then discusses the status of settlements and the procedures for ensuring that they can be enforced if one party fails to do as it has promised. While many cases are terminated by settlement, some may be terminated by the plaintiff's unilateral decision to discontinue proceedings. While one would normally expect defendants to be grateful for such a decision, there are, as will become apparent, reasons why defendants might wish to oppose discontinuance. The chapter concludes with a discussion of the circumstances in which they might do so and when they might do so successfully.

INTRODUCTION

17.1.1   Litigation is best avoided, and generally is. Most disputes are resolved without the parties taking any legal steps at all. The aggrieved party may simply decide to do nothing. Alternatively, a complaint, request or demand may be met by a concession which is sufficient to satisfy the aggrieved party: R Miller and A Sarat, 'Grievances, Claims and Disputes: Assessing the Adversary Culture' (1980–81) 14 *L and Soc Rev* 525. Faced with an aggrieved client, it is good practice for a lawyer to explore the possibility of informal resolution. Sometimes this may be achieved by a delicate, non-confrontational approach, implying that one is sure that the failure to satisfy the client is all due to a terrible misunderstanding which can surely be resolved. In the absence of any threat (other than the threat implicit in the fact that it is a lawyer who is making the call) honour can be saved, and satisfaction achieved. Failing this, a written demand for the relief or remedy being sought may provoke a concession. The concession may not be the best possible concession, but it may be such as to make any further legal action unwise.

Litigation is a last resort and litigation is rarely pursued to the bitter end. American and Australian commentators suggest that as many as 95 per cent of cases filed never reach trial: R Banks, 'Alternative Dispute Resolution: A Return to Basics' (1987) 61 *ALJ* 569 at 572; M Pickering, 'The Art of Settlement and Negotiation' (1988) 10 *L Soc B* 197. Frustratingly, they cite no sources. However, the available evidence suggests that their estimates are only slight exaggerations. Williams et al estimated that only about seven per cent of intermediate court cases in Victoria and Queensland go to verdict: P Williams, R Williams, A Goldsmith and P Browne, *The Cost of Civil Litigation before Intermediate Courts in Australia*, Australian Institute of Judicial Affairs, Melbourne, 1992, p 9. A New South Wales study of cases from the 1992 Supreme Court Special Sittings reported that 65 per cent settled before trial, and another 27 per cent on the day of, or during, the trial: J Baker, *Who Settles and Why?*, Civil Justice Research Centre, Sydney, 1994, p 9. This probably underestimates the overall settlement rate: the sample consisted of cases which had already been in the system for many years. Conversely, settlement rates may have been inflated by the procedures used at the Special Sittings. However, settlement rates of this magnitude are not inevitable. A pilot study of Federal Court cases yielded a 31 per cent trial rate: ALRC, *Review of the Adversarial System of Litigation: Rethinking the Federal Litigation System*, Issues Paper 20, ALRC, Sydney, 1997, p 37. This may reflect the fact that 30 per cent of the cases in the sample were immigration disputes, a category of cases which does not lend itself to compromise. But this in turn points to the need to recognise that settlement rates may vary considerably according to the type of case handled by the court.

Recent court statistics throw little light on the role of settlement. Statistics published in Annual Reports of the Victorian Supreme Court in the 1990s suggested that fewer than 10 per cent of proceedings ended in trials. Data presented in successive Annual Reports suggested that between 2500 and 3000 writs, approximately 400 originating motions, 250 appeals and review applications, and 100 or so cases transferred from other jurisdictions were filed each year. Of these, approximately 1000 were listed for trial. Relating 'writ' statistics to 'listed for trial' statistics is complicated by the fact that the year in which a writ is filed is unlikely to be the year in which the case is listed, and this in turn may well not be the year in which a case is finalised. However, many of the relevant statistics were sufficiently stable from year to year to warrant a number of generalisations. The likelihood of settlement before the case was set down for trial was strongly related to the nature of the plaintiff's claim. Writs for possession accounted for almost half the writs filed each year, and of these only about five per cent were listed for trial. Writs for debt, which accounted for a considerable, but varying proportion of all writs, were likewise rarely listed for trial. The proportion of writs listed for trial was certainly less than 10 per cent and probably less than five per cent. One third of writs in which declarations were sought were subsequently listed for trial. In contrast, a majority of cases in which damages were sought proceeded to the point where they were listed.

Of 682 'known dispositions' of civil list cases finalised in 1998, 165 (24.2 per cent) were disposed of by verdict, 56 (8.2 per cent) were dismissed at trial, and 74 (10.9 per cent) were dismissed prior to trial. Settlement was only one of the reasons that cases do not go to trial. Most of the remainder were settled: 95 (13.9 per cent) at or before the pre-trial conference;

44 (6.5 per cent) at mediation; 103 (15.1 per cent) at call-over or before trial; 40 (5.9 per cent) on the date of the trial but prior to its commencement; and 50 (7.3 per cent) during the trial. Another 28 (4.1 per cent) were disposed of by consent judgments. The remaining cases included 20 disposed of by discontinuance, and seven by transfer to another court: Victorian Supreme Court *Annual Report 1998*. Subsequent changes to the jurisdiction of inferior courts mean that some of absolute settlement rates may have changed, but the different settlement rates for different types of claim highlight the need for caution when referring to global settlement rates, and suggest that the cases most likely to settle may be those which would be easiest to dispose of were they to go to trial.

Queensland statistics suggest somewhat similar conclusions. In each of the years 2004–05 and 2005–06, there were more than 2000 claims and more than 3000 originating applications. Notices of an intention to defend were filed in response to slightly more than half the claims. Over 300 cases were deemed resolved as a result of failure to file a default judgment, or failure to request a trial date. Fewer than 300 cases were placed on the civil list or given a trial date without a request being filed. Of these, a majority were disposed of other than by judgment. Aggregating the two years, 40 per cent were disposed of by judgment, 49.8 per cent were settled, 1.5 per cent were vacated, 1.3 per cent were discontinued, and 7.5 per cent were otherwise disposed of: Supreme Court of Queensland *Annual Report 2005–06*, Tables 18, 23, 25, 26. More recent statistics are less informative, but they confirm the conclusion that fewer than 10 per cent of initial filings are terminated by a judgment. In Western Australia, where there are more than 2000 lodgments per year, there were only 81 listings and 55 trials in 2005–06 and 120 listings and 78 trials in 2006–07: Supreme Court of Western Australia, *Annual Report 2006–07*, p 16.

As usual with statistics, these figures raise a number of questions. What was the basis for the Victorian dismissals? To what extent were they 'default' dismissals, as opposed to contested dismissals? What were the reasons for failure to file default judgments or requests for trial in Queensland? What was it that distinguished the cases that went to trial from those that did not? For instance, were damages cases which were listed for trial less likely to settle than other cases listed for trial? What was entailed in the 'settlements' — bargaining, or unilateral surrender? Nonetheless, the figures highlight the importance of formal and informal pre-trial procedures as the basis for the disposition of cases. The vast majority of cases are 'settled' by some means or other — possibly by agreement, possibly by unilateral default. Settlements are, however, more likely in some kinds of cases than others. While the overall settlement rate is in the 90–95 per cent range, possession and debt cases seem far more likely to settle than damages cases.

17.1.2 Modern legal systems are particularly anxious to promote settlement. Settlement is generally less corrosive of social bonds than litigation. Settlement probably leaves the parties less disillusioned with the legal system than they would be were they to pursue the matter to trial. Settlement may also reduce the pressures on the legal system, and may mean that contested cases can be brought to a conclusion more quickly than would otherwise be the case. However, the importance and persuasiveness of these considerations is far from self-evident. The very fact that litigation has been initiated suggests either that social bonds did not exist, or that if they once did they have already broken down. There is evidence which suggests that while parties tend to be happier with the results of settlement (and especially mediated settlement) than they are with the outcomes of trial, this may be because they are not always aware that they are settling for less than the 'objective' worth of their case. And while settlements certainly reduce pressures on the civil justice system, the relationship between settlement rates and pressures is complex. For instance, if settlement rates suddenly decreased, so that cases were resolved more quickly, some litigants, attracted by the improved efficiency of the system, might decide once more to opt for trial rather than settlement. Moreover there may be social costs associated with high settlement rates, and in particular, lack of information about 'going rates' and the greater inconsistency which characterises decision-making where decision-makers lack external cues and where decisions are basically unreviewable. Marc Galanter and Mia Cahill provide a good discussion of the possible downside of settlement in their article '"Most Cases Settle": Judicial Promotion and Regulation of Settlements' (1994) 46 *Stan LR* 1339.

Nonetheless, most legal systems have devised processes intended to encourage settlement. Some of these processes rely on threatened sanctions. Among the major devices for encouraging settlements are costs rules, the effect of which is to encourage parties to place realistic values on their cases, rather than pretending that their cases are worth far more than they really are. The trend has been to develop increasingly subtle costs rules. Threats are now more often supplemented by the development of institutions designed to facilitate settlement. These are discussed in **Chapter 2**. Modern case management strategies are oriented towards encouraging parties to make a full exchange of relevant material as early as possible in the proceedings, in order to maximise the scope for fully informed negotiation. Arbitration has long been an alternative to trial, although the attractiveness of traditional arbitral proceedings is often questionable: they may well prove to be no cheaper and no more expeditious than legal proceedings. Other procedures include mediation, which is becoming an important legal specialty. In some jurisdictions, there is provision for third party evaluation of cases.

COMPROMISE OF PROCEEDINGS

17.2.1   Settlement is complicated by the difficulties parties have in assigning a value to their respective cases, and by the fact that there is no single rational settlement for a given conflict. To begin with, note that at any given time, a party's case will have a value: VP (for plaintiffs) and VD (for defendants). The value will reflect both the value attached to possible outcomes, and their likelihood. If litigants were rational economic decision-makers, the value of their cases would equal their 'expected value', E_X, where $E_X = \Sigma p_i \times V_{iX}$ where p_i is the subjective probability of an outcome with value V_{iX} to party X. Σp_i always = 1. Thus if a party considered there was a 0.4 chance of total failure, and a 0.6 chance of winning $100,000, the 'expected value' of its case would be $60,000 ((0.4 x $0) + (0.6 x $100,000)). An offer to settle it for $70,000 would therefore be very attractive. An offer to settle for $50,000 would not. While V_X will bear a rough relationship to E_X, the two will not necessarily coincide; litigants and lawyers are not always particularly good at handling probabilities.

17.2.2   If parties are relatively well informed, and place similar value on the stakes at issue, V_P will be more or less equal to $-V_D$. However, except in routine suits for liquidated damages, these conditions are rarely satisfied. V_P and $-V_D$ will often be at considerable variance. There are several reasons for this. First, parties are likely to make different assessments as to the likelihood of the different possible outcomes. Each party will be better informed about the credibility and likely impact of their own witnesses than they will be about the credibility and impact of the other side's. Assessment may be further complicated by the tendency for parties to confuse what they would like to believe with what they are in fact justified in believing. Parties may come to assume that right is on their side and that being so, they must prevail:

L Babcock, G Loewenstein and S Issacharoff, 'Creating Convergence: De-biasing Biased Litigants' (1997) 22 *Law and Soc Inquiry* 913; L Babcock and G Pogarsky, 'Damage Caps and Settlement: A Behavioral Approach' (1998) 28 *J Leg Studies* 341. Lawyers will do their best to dampen such optimism: H Kritzer, 'Contingent-fee Lawyers and Their Clients: Settlement Expectations, Settlement Realities, and Issues of Control in the Lawyer–Client Relationship' (1998) 23 *Law and Soc Inquiry* 795. The client must, after all, be prepared for a loss which is explicable other than in terms of lawyerly incompetence or corruption. However, even lawyers are frequently overoptimistic.

Parties will also attach different values to particular outcomes. One reason for this is that parties and their lawyers may have little idea about the economic implications of a particular finding of fact. It will be a rare plaintiff who can know whether a lost eye is worth $40,000 or $400,000. Kritzer reports that media stories of massive payouts not infrequently lead plaintiffs to believe that even a trivial civil action is a foolproof path to untold riches. Consequently, a plaintiff will therefore rely on his or her lawyers for accurate information. Specialist personal injuries lawyers will probably be able to give a good indication of the value of the injury — experience will help. Specialists will also be familiar with sources which are likely to yield that kind of information. They will be willing to invest the time needed to acquire the information, which is likely to come in handy in subsequent cases. Non-specialists may be ill-informed, unaware of how to become informed, and even disinclined to conduct the research necessary to become informed.

The value attached to particular outcomes will also reflect discounting of the future, and risk aversion. Insurance companies are likely to carry their commitment to actuarialism into litigation. They will tend not to discount the future heavily and will tend not to be particularly risk averse. For insurance companies a 10 per cent probability of losing $100,000 is no more terrible than a 50 per cent chance of losing $20,000. Impecunious defendants will make different calculations. For a defendant with limited resources, damages of $1 million are no worse than losing $70 million. One-off plaintiffs are likely to discount the future relatively heavily ($80,000 today may well be more valuable than $120,000 in a year's time) and are also likely to be more risk averse. Most would prefer the certainty of $80,000 to a 90 per cent chance of $100,000, and a 10 per cent chance of nothing. That is why they take out insurance.

Private litigants, as opposed to corporations and governments, are also more likely to bring emotion into their litigation. Thus, a generous and apparently sincere apology may be valued far more highly by a private litigant than it will cost a corporation. On the other hand, private litigants may become obsessed with their litigation, or litigate because they are obsessed. The sheer joy of dragging others through the courts may be a source of satisfaction, albeit an expensive one. Hatred may mean that the subjective costs of compromise are far heavier than its objective costs.

Parties may also be influenced by the degree to which they care about the overall implications of the litigation. 'Repeat players' are likely to care about such matters as the impact of a settlement on their reputation as bargainers. They will also be aware that cases set precedents, and will be reluctant to proceed to trial if for legal or other reasons, a case could create an adverse precedent. One-off plaintiffs are likely to be indifferent to the precedential value of their case. Assessments of the precedential implications of a case may affect both whether parties settle before trial and whether they decide to cut their losses or appeal.

The classic study of different litigants' priorities and resources is: M Galanter, 'Why the "Have" Come Out Ahead: Speculations on Limits of Legal Change' (1974) 9 *Law and Soc Rev* 95. Subsequent research which has examined Galanter's hypotheses includes: D Songer, R Sheehan and S Haire, 'Do the "Haves" Come Out Ahead over Time? Applying Galanter's Framework to Decisions of the US Courts of Appeals, 1925–1988' (1999) 33 *Law and Soc*

Rev 811; C Albiston, 'The Rule of Law and the Litigation Process: The Paradox of Losing by Winning' (1999) 33 *Law and Soc Rev* 869; D Farole, 'Re-examining Litigant Success in State Supreme Courts' (1999) 33 *Law and Soc Rev* 1043.

Understanding settlement may also require attention to the interests of lawyers. Since many clients have little idea of what constitutes the worth of their case, they will rely heavily on advice from their legal advisers. Professionalism means that lawyers will normally be disinclined to mislead clients in order to achieve their own particular interests. However, Genn has pointed out that the difficulty of determining whether possible settlement terms actually constitute good terms means that lawyers' interests may cloud and influence their perceptions: H Genn, *Hard Bargaining: Out of Court Settlement in Personal Injury Actions*, Clarendon Press, Oxford, 1987, p 108. Moreover, the fact that lawyers must operate subject to various economic constraints means that lawyers must at least put their economic survival ahead of their clients' best interests in so far as the two are incompatible.

Asymmetrical values will sometimes increase the likelihood of settlement. Sometimes they reduce it. Where $V_P \leq -V_D$, settlement is possible. Remember that V_D is almost always negative, since defendants must almost always expect to have to make some sacrifice. The expected cost to D of the litigation is $-1 \times V_D$. There will be a range of possible settlement offers which each party will consider is superior to the expected value it attaches to the case. Where $V_P > -V_D$, settlement is not possible in the absence of such costs as are associated with litigation.

Much settlement takes place because $V_P \leq -V_D$. The asymmetrical valuations placed on the future and on risks by insurance companies and private individuals mean that there is a reasonable likelihood that there will be a mutually satisfactory range of possible settlements. Where emotions are involved, it may be possible for a settlement offer to take these into account and produce an outcome, which leaves each party better off. These are the 'win/win' solutions beloved of the more evangelical alternative dispute resolution practitioners, and familiar to the more cold-hearted game theorists. It should be noted that most of these 'win/win' solutions are possible only because plaintiffs accept less than the economic value of their claims.

However, what makes settlement even more likely is that litigation is expensive. While costs rules mean that winners may recover more than half their costs from losers (see below 20.3.1), expected costs must take account of the possibility of loss or of failure to do as well as might have been hoped. Moreover, regardless of the costs order, parties will not recover the full costs of their litigation. They will almost never recover the full legal costs of litigation, and costs awards do not cover the non-legal costs: time consumed by visits to lawyers, sleepless nights occasioned by fear of possible outcomes, and so on.

Genn (see Ch 2) also points out that litigation has differential costs for lawyers. For generalist lawyers, personal injuries litigation is likely to be scary. There are traps for the unwary: faced with these traps, non-specialists may be particularly anxious to avoid resort to trial. Specialists, on the other hand, may enjoy litigation. While the specialist will not go to trial when it is unwise to do so, they will not be unhappy about the possibility of running a moderately strong case should the other side not make an attractive offer.

17.2.3 P will have an incentive to accept an offer, O, from D so long as $O > V_P - C_P$, where C_P represents the additional costs likely to be incurred if the offer is not accepted. D has an incentive to make an offer, O, so long as $O < -V_D + C_D$. Thus, even if $V_P \geq -V_D$, the costs of litigation are likely to promote settlement. However, it is important to note that the costs which promote settlement will be those additional costs which a party anticipates incurring in the event that it does not settle at a particular time. Costs which have already been incurred will not encourage settlement, except in so far as they affect the offers parties are willing to make and accept. They may do so in several ways.

First, given the 'loser pays' rule, costs incurred will affect what each party is willing to accept or offer in total settlement of the claim. If, for instance, a defendant has an extremely good defence, there may come a time when the value of the defendant's expected award of costs, given the likelihood that the defence will succeed, exceeds its assessment of the value of the plaintiff's substantive case. In these circumstances, a defendant might be willing to settle only in exchange for an offer by the plaintiff to pay the difference between the defendant's costs and the value of the plaintiff's substantive claim.

The incurring of costs may also harden resolve. Parties which have made considerable financial investments in a case may be reluctant to accept that this is money thrown away. A plaintiff for whom V_p was initially positive, and who has incurred considerable legal expenses, is likely to resist suggestions that the only result of this is that the value of its case has now become negative, after allowing for the dangers of a costs award. Nor will the party's lawyers be eager to explain that the net result of their efforts is that their client would now be well advised to settle the claim and costs on the basis of payment of a small payment to the defendant. While ever mounting costs reduce the objective value of a party's case, they may at the same time increase its subjective value. R Fisher, *Basic Negotiating Strategy: International Conflict for Beginners*, Allen Lane, London, 1969, p 38, makes a similar point.

17.2.4   The relevant future costs will be those costs which a party anticipates possibly having to incur before the matter is settled or disposed of at trial. Since most cases are settled at some stage, expected future costs will almost invariably be less than the anticipated cost of trial. The costs of trial are likely to become salient only when the likelihood of settlement is perceived as small or when the likelihood of trial in the absence of immediate settlement is high. One reason why so many cases are settled on the eve, or even on the day of the trial, is that this is the point in the litigation process where even a brief postponement of settlement will prove extremely costly: see P Williams, R Williams, A Goldsmith and P Browne, *The Cost of Civil Litigation Before Intermediate Courts in Australia*, AIJA, Melbourne, 1992, Chs 4, 5.

The relevance of costs is likely to be greater for smaller claims, as while costs are strongly related to the amount at stake in a piece of litigation, the ratio of costs to amount at stake declines as stakes increase. The reason is that while cases with high stakes tend to be, and to be made, more complex, their complexity does not bear a linear relationship to the stakes. This is probably one reason why high stakes cases appear to be less likely to settle: see J Baker, *Who Settles and Why?*, Civil Justice Research Centre, Sydney, 1994, pp 22–3, 47.

17.2.5   Even where there are 'win/win' solutions, agreement will not always be possible as parties are sometimes greedy. While a given offer will leave a party better off than would going to trial, the party may believe that it can extract an even better offer. In many cases this will be true. There will be a range of theoretically possible 'win/win' solutions. Defendants will want to offer no more than $V_p - C_p$. Plaintiffs will want to extract offers close to $-V_D + C_D$. Winning the best possible outcome involves bluffing, and bluffing involves risks. There are two types of risk. First, each party may misestimate the value the other attaches to its case and the costs it anticipates. If a defendant underestimates V_p and overestimates C_p, then its offer may be so small that P quite rationally rejects it. Second, even if the parties accurately assess each other's expected values and costs, they may mistakenly assume that the other party will accept a borderline offer rather than risk the added costs associated with trial. So long as each party believes the other will make concessions rather than risk trial, each party may refuse to settle, and both, paradoxically, may therefore find themselves faced with the worst outcome. This phenomenon is well known to game theorists as the 'prisoner's dilemma': A Rapoport and A Chammah, *Prisoner's Dilemma*, University of Michigan Press, Ann Arbor, 1965.

The former kind of mistake is best avoided by pursuing a strategy of modified greed, and recognising that the risks associated with trying to extract the last dollar are too great to warrant trying to do so. The strategies for avoiding the latter kind of mistake are more complex. Game theorists suggest that it can sometimes help to have a reputation for irrationality and unreasonableness: T Schelling, *The Strategy of Conflict*, Oxford University Press, New York, 1960, pp 22–3. However, this is no help when each side has cultivated this image. Moreover, the reputation may have the effect of encouraging adversaries to assume that the irrationality of the 'madman' or 'madwoman' means that the 'madman's' or 'madwoman's' offers are not to be taken particularly seriously, even where they have been carefully calibrated to be acceptable, albeit barely so.

It may also be useful to distinguish between one-shot and regular encounters. There is some evidence to suggest that repeat players achieve the optimal aggregate results if they cooperatively dampen their ambitions and opt for satisfactory outcomes rather than aspiring to get the best possible outcomes: A Rapoport, *Fights, Games and Debates*, University of Michigan Press, Ann Arbor, 1961, pp 218–22.

The rules of civil procedure seek to encourage settlement in several ways. First, they seek to maximise the degree to which parties are accurately informed about the strength of each other's case. Second, they seek to impose costs on excessive greed. Their success in these respects is a matter which we shall examine later in this chapter.

17.2.6   Questions

1. Attitudes to risk vary according to whether there is a risk of missing out on a gain, or a risk of being subjected to a loss. In cases where people are asked to choose between the certainty of making a given gain, and a possibility of a considerably higher gain, most people opt for the former, even when the 'expected value' (probability of gain multiplied by size of gain) of the latter is somewhat greater than the former. When people have to choose between the certainty of a loss and a possible loss, people prefer the possible loss over the certain loss, even when the expected possible loss is somewhat greater than the 'certain' cost. These preferences are attenuated when people are offered the chance to take part in a series of similar gambles: see D Kahneman and Amos Tversky (eds), *Choices, Values and Frames*, Cambridge University Press, Cambridge, 2000, Chs 1, 3, 5–9. These effects cannot be explained by reference to the decreasing marginal utility of wealth (see Ch 11). What are the implications of this for the settlement of disputes between (a) plaintiffs and uninsured defendants; (b) repeat player plaintiffs and repeat player defendants?

2. A one-shot player has been given leave to appeal to the High Court against a repeat player defendant, who offers to settle. Is this a case where the one-shot player might be at an advantage?

3. Do lawyers' interests in their reputations as negotiators mean that their interests and their clients' interests are aligned?

FACILITATING SETTLEMENT

17.3.1 Settlement is generally regarded as highly desirable, and this is reflected in the law. A number of rules seek to encourage settlement. 'Without prejudice' rules are designed to encourage the kind of frank communication necessary to promote informed settlements. Costs rules, including the payment in and offer of compromise rules, are designed to place pressure on parties making unreasonable demands or being unreasonably inflexible.

Without prejudice

17.3.2 Frank negotiation often gives rise to, and requires, admissions. In order to encourage frankness, the law protects communications, which take place in the course of settlement negotiations by making them inadmissible as evidence. However, it is not always clear whether a given communication took place in the course of settlement negotiations: see also 13.5.28– 13.5.30. The common law presumption is reflected in rules which protect communications in the course of mediation: see 3.5.7–3.5.13E. Rules governing the making of offers of compromise also recognise the principle: details of an offer are to be communicated only after a verdict, and only for the purposes of decisions as to costs: see 17.3.35.

Formal offers to settle

17.3.3 The Rules of Court make provision for three types of formal offers to settle. South Australia makes provision for offers of settlement prior to the commencement of an action. Several jurisdictions maintain the traditional procedure, where a defendant could make a payment into court. If the plaintiff rejected the offer and if the offer turned out to be a reasonable one, this had costs implications. There are problems with this procedure. In particular, it fails to provide plaintiffs with an incentive to make offers, and it was inappropriate if the claim was for non-pecuniary relief. In order to overcome these, the rules in most jurisdictions now provide for the making of 'offers of compromise'. These can be made by either the plaintiff or the defendant. There are costs penalties for failure to accept a reasonable offer. In the Australian Capital Territory there is provision for payment into court, but not for offers of compromise. In the Northern Territory, South Australia and Tasmania, the rules enable both payments into court and offers of compromise.

Elsewhere, the rules provide for offers of compromise but not for payment into court (except for purposes largely unrelated to settlement). The offer of compromise rules vary slightly across jurisdictions. In particular, the Northern Territory and Victorian rules differentiate between personal injuries cases where damages are being sought, and other cases. No such distinction is made elsewhere. However, the application of the rules achieves similar results to those achieved under the Northern Territory and Victorian rules. South Australia uses a slightly different formula to achieve what other jurisdictions achieve by their offer of compromise rules.

Offers of settlement before action

17.3.4 The South Australian rules require would-be plaintiffs to make an offer of compromise before commencing an action based on a monetary claim. The rule does not apply where urgent relief is sought, where there is a danger of defendants removing assets from the jurisdiction (and where the plaintiff intends to seek appropriate interlocutory relief); or where courts give directions excluding the operation of the rule: r 33(1). If the rule applies, the plaintiff must give notice, and including an offer to settle on terms set out in the notice, enough details to ensure that the defendant can assess the offer and make an informed response to it, and any expert reports in the plaintiff's possession: r 33(2). The defendant has 60 days to respond by accepting, making a counter-offer, or by denying liability: r 33(4). If the plaintiff then commences an action, the court, in awarding costs, is to take account of whether the parties have complied with the rule, and the reasonableness of the terms of the offer and counter-offer, and any responses thereto: r 33(7). In some ways, this procedure resembles the offer of compromise system operating in other jurisdictions. However, it does not apply where non-pecuniary relief is sought, and its operation is unclear in relation to offers made subsequent to the commencement of proceedings. Where there have been pre-proceeding offers and counter-offers, post-proceeding offers and counter-offers may be treated as responses to the original offer and counter-offer, but would this cover a response to a response to an original offer or counter-offer? If a defendant makes a generous counter-offer, but only after the 60 days have elapsed, would this attract a favourable costs order? Probably: although it would not be an offer made under the rule, it would be a response to an offer made under the rule.

There is also statutory provision for early offers in relation to particular areas of litigation. One example is provided by the uniform defamation laws. These provide that publishers of allegedly defamatory statements may make 'an offer to make amends'. The deadline for making these offers is 28 days after service of a 'concerns notice' alleging and giving details of the alleged defamation. In the absence of a notice, offers may be made until a defence has been served in relation to any action brought by the person who claims to have been defamed. The publisher may offer to make an apology of a particular kind and in a particular form, and may offer to pay compensation or an amount to be determined in a specified way. Offers may be withdrawn and renewed. Acceptance of an offer precludes further litigation in relation to the matter, but a court may award compensation for the expenses incurred in accepting the offer, and may order that costs be assessed on an indemnity basis (as to which, see below, 20.3.1). Conversely, it is a defence to a defamation action that the offer was made expeditiously, was reasonable, and was one which the publisher was able and willing to carry out, if accepted. The practical effect of this is that a person who unreasonably turned down an offer to make amends could face an adverse costs award. To encourage apologies, the legislation provides that an apology is not to be taken as an admission of fault or liability: see generally Civil Law (Wrongs) Act 2002 (ACT) ss 124–132; Defamation Act 2005 (NSW) ss 12–20; Defamation Act 2006 (NT) ss 12–20; Defamation Act 2005 (Qld) ss 12–20; Defamation Act 2005 (SA) ss 12-20; Defamation Act 2005 (Tas) ss 12–20; Defamation Act 2005 (Vic) ss 12–20; Defamation Act 2005 (WA) ss 12–20.

Payment into court

17.3.5 The earliest device to encourage settlement was the provision of a procedure whereby a defendant could make a 'payment into court', which, if accepted by the plaintiff within a certain time, would constitute settlement of the case. The effect of making a payment into court was that, if the plaintiff refused the offer but ultimately was awarded less than the amount paid in, the defendant would normally be entitled to costs as from the time of making the offer. (On the origins and development of 'payment in' regimes, see M Ellis, 'The Cost of Compromising: Offers of Compromise and Calderbank Offers' (2008) 17 *J Jud Admin* 253 at

256–8). There is provision for this procedure in the Supreme Court Rules of the Australian Capital Territory, the Northern Territory, and Tasmania: Court Procedure Rules 2006 (ACT) Pt 2.10; Rules of the Supreme Court of the Northern Territory of Australia (NT) r 26.12; Supreme Court Rules 2000 (Tas) rr 268–76. There is no provision for a plaintiff to make an offer, except in relation to counterclaims. In South Australia, the 'payment in' rules have been assimilated to the offer of compromise rules, but in contrast to other offer of compromise regimes, South Australia expressly provides that a defendant who makes a monetary offer to settle a claim for a specified amount *may* pay that amount into court: Supreme Court Civil Rules 2006 (SA) r 187. References to South Australia relate to cases where defendants make offers of compromise and pay money into court. In addition, in defamation cases, under the uniform defamation legislation, there is provision for 'making amends'. The New South Wales rules contemplate that a defendant might offer to settle a case by making a payment into court, but are largely silent in relation to when such payments might be made, and whether and how offers might be accepted, or money withdrawn: r 42.22.

[*Note:* in this chapter a reference, such as WA O 9 r 2, is a reference to that jurisdiction's relevant Rules of Court. All other legislation will be specified.]

Deposit

17.3.6   In the Northern Territory, South Australia and Tasmania, the rules provide for the payment of a sum of money. In the Australian Capital Territory, a defendant may instead lodge a security or a bond: ACT rr 1002, 1003. Defendants may make several payments: ACT r 1000(6); NT r 26.21(2); SA r 187(6); Tas r 268.

In what kind of cases?

17.3.7   In the Northern Territory, payment into court is permitted where there is a claim or where interest on judgment is claimed: NT r 26.12. In the Australian Capital Territory (r 1000(1) (the rules vary depending on whether the claim is a wrongful death claim)), South Australia (r 187(1)), and Tasmania (r 268(1)), payment into court is permitted in relation to causes of action generally.

Offer

17.3.8   The defendant must serve on the plaintiff notice of having made a payment into court. The payment constitutes an offer to settle. It will be available for acceptance by the plaintiff within a prescribed period of the payment or if there are several payments, the last payment: ACT r 1006 r 6(3) (14 days); NT rr 26.17, 26.21 (14 days, two days when notice is given after trial has begun); SA r 187(1), (2) (21 days before date fixed for trial, four days prior to hearing on costs); Tas rr 268(2), (4), 269 (14 days, but not later than the commencement of trial). The notice must specify the cause or causes of action in relation to which the payment is made. In several jurisdictions it must also specify the apportionment of the sum among those causes (unless the court orders otherwise): ACT r 1000(2); NT rr 26.17, 26.18; SA r 187(3)(b). The defendant may not normally withdraw the money (or offer) within the prescribed period. However, defendants may be permitted to withdraw offers in exceptional circumstances.

17.3.9C	**Cumper v Pothecary** [1941] 2 KB 58 Court of Appeal, England and Wales

[After the payment in, the House of Lords gave a decision which altered the approach of the courts in England to the assessment of damages for loss of expectation of life. The defendant sought to reduce his payment in accordance with this decision.]

Scott and Goddard LJJ and Staple J (at 70): [I]t must not be thought that a defendant who has paid a sum into Court is entitled, as of right, to resile from that step. He must in our opinion, show that there are good reasons for his application — for instance, the discovery of further evidence, which puts a wholly different complexion on the case ... or a change in the legal outlook brought about by a new judicial decision, ... and there may be others. Having once put a valuation on the plaintiff's case, the defendant ought not to be allowed to alter it without good reason ... Apart from matters such as fraud or mistake affecting the original payment [the Court] should consider whether there is a sufficient change of circumstances since the money was paid in to make it just that the defendant should have an opportunity of withdrawing or reducing his payment.

Effect of acceptance

17.3.10 On payment, the cause in relation to which the payment is accepted is stayed: ACT r 1006(9); NT r 26.22; Tas r 269(4). On acceptance of an offer, the money is paid out to the plaintiff, who is entitled to costs incurred up to the time of the payment into court, along with costs incurred in relation to acceptance of the offer, and preparation of the bill of costs: ACT r 1007(3); Tas r 269(3), (6) (costs incurred until acceptance). In the Australian Capital Territory, where the defendant is not required to make an actual payment, there is provision for what is to happen if the defendant does not, on acceptance of the offer, make a prompt payment: r 1006(5).

What happens to the money if the plaintiff does not accept?

17.3.11 Once paid into court, the money may be withdrawn only by court order: ACT r 1009 (money not paid to plaintiff); NT r 26.20; Tas r 270(1). South Australia r 187(6) is similar, except that money may be withdrawn by consent and, after judgment, unless the court orders otherwise the money is to be returned to the defendant.

Multiple defendants

17.3.12 In some jurisdictions special provision is made in relation to cases involving multiple defendants: ACT r 1000(4)(b); NT r 26.21(8); Tas r 272. One or more defendants sued jointly or in the alternative may make a payment into court. They must give notice to the other defendants. If the plaintiff gives notice of acceptance, all further proceedings are stayed. The money is to be paid out only by court order dealing with the whole costs of the action.

Counterclaims

17.3.13 Plaintiffs may make payments in relation to counterclaims: ACT r 1005; SA r 187(3)(b); Tas r 274; compare NT r 26.14.

Parties under a legal disability

17.3.14   Where parties under a legal disability are suing, the court's approval is required before money paid in can be accepted: ACT r 1017; NT r 26.23(1)(f); SA r 257; Tas rr 269(3), 299(1). Approval is governed by the general rules which govern settlement of cases involving infants and persons under a legal disability: see 17.4.6–17.4.7C.

Acceptance of money paid in means there is no adjudication

17.3.15   There is no issue estoppel if the plaintiff were subsequently to seek to relitigate the matter or issues arising in relation to the matter: *A Martin French v Kingswood Hill Ltd* [1961] 1 QB 96 at 102 per Devlin LJ. Acceptance of an offer does, however, stay the action: *Cole v Austin Distributors Ltd* [1953] VLR 155.

Effect of failure to accept a generous offer

17.3.16   In exercising its discretion with respect to costs, the court is to take into account the fact that money has been paid into court, and the amount of that payment: ACT r 1011(4); NT r 26.26(5); Tas r 275(2). In South Australia, plaintiffs who fail to accept an offer equal to the judgment they receive must normally pay the defendant's costs as from 14 days after the offer: SA r 188(6A) (where payment in is accepted *after* 14 days), r 188(6)(b)(ii) (where payment is not accepted). The South Australian rules do not appear to place defendants who make payments into court in any better position than defendants who simply make an offer to settle for a pecuniary sum. Nonetheless, the greater security that payment in offers to plaintiffs might be a relevant consideration in relation to the exercise of discretion in relation to costs.

17.3.17   In *Westsub Discounts Pty Ltd v Idaps Australia Ltd (No 2)* (1990) 94 ALR 310; 17 IPR 251, Woodward J adopted as correctly stating the position in Australia the following statement from *Halsbury's Laws of England*, 4th ed, vol 37, [293]:

> In exercising its discretion as to costs the court must, to such extent as may be appropriate in the circumstances, take into account any payment of money into court and the amount of such payment. Since this discretion must be exercised judicially, if the plaintiff recovers in the action no more than the sum paid into court, the order for costs will give the plaintiff the costs of the action down to the date of payment in and the defendant his costs after that date. The modern practice is to look at the position of the parties at the end of the day to determine whether the amount paid is more or less than the total of the plaintiff's claim, and therefore not to make any special order with regard to the costs on the issue of liability after the date of payment. The underlying principle of the modern practice is that the court is applying the rule that costs follow the event, so that even though he may succeed on the issue of liability or on any other issue or question in the action, if the plaintiff recovers less than the amount paid in he has lost 'the event', and the defendant thereupon becomes entitled to the costs after the day of the payment in.

17.3.18   Payments in can create difficulties for plaintiffs, especially when they have been carefully calibrated so that they are ungenerous, but set at a level such that there is a real chance that the amount awarded might be even smaller. In such cases, judges have sometimes exercised their discretion not to apply the costs rules against plaintiffs. Some judges have regarded as relevant the degree to which an award has been on the conservative side: see *Mangan v Mendum*

(1970) 4 ACTR 44 (Smithers J). The justification for this approach is questionable. If judges consider that a particular award is conservative or not particularly generous, why did they make that award rather than a more appropriate award, which would presumably be neither conservative nor liberal? If a jury made the award, is it for a judge to evaluate its sufficiency? Moreover, is there to be allowance for defendants who have the misfortune to encounter a judge or jury on a day on which it is feeling generous?

17.3.19C	**Lauchlan v Hartley**
	[1979] Qd R 305
	Supreme Court of Queensland, Full Court

[The original claim was for $6000. This was amended at trial, but the amendment had been foreshadowed much earlier. An amendment to allege contributory negligence was also foreshadowed but not made until trial. The defendant paid into court $6000 and later a further $12,000, a total of $18,000. The trial judge awarded $16,875, but nonetheless ordered each party to bear his own costs from the date of the last payment, rather than awarding costs to the defendant. In his judgment, his Honour said (at 307):

> I point out that the defence originally delivered did not contain an allegation of contributory negligence. There was a purported delivery of an amended defence in October 1977 after the matter had been transferred to the Supreme Court and before the payment in of the amount of $12,000. In fact, under the Rules the purported amendment was not then effective and leave was eventually given part of the way through the trial. I mention that although, of course, what happened did at least give the plaintiff notice that during the trial, if it was necessary, there would be an application to amend the defence and allege contributory negligence. In addition to that the matter, although from some aspects simple enough, I think was very much one of impression and it was one in which different minds might have come to different conclusions on the questions of negligence and contributory negligence, on the question of apportionment and on the question of general damages and, if it matters, my mind fluctuated during the course of the trial and afterwards in relation to those matters. It is for those reasons that I propose to take the course which I have indicated.

The Full Court on appeal gave the defendant his costs, rejecting each of the matters considered by the trial judge.]

Connolly J (at 308–9): His Honour's second reason was that the result was one upon which different minds might come to different conclusions. Presumably the reasoning is that this successful plaintiff should not be called upon to pay any of the costs of an action the result of which was difficult to assess. If so, it confines attention solely to the position of the plaintiff. But the defendant also has rights under these rules. The defendant managed to make a very good assessment and it seems difficult to see why he should be deprived of the fruits of his payment in. The precise question came before the Court of Appeal in *Wagman v Vare Motors Ltd* [1959] 1 WLR 853. In that case the amount recovered was precisely the amount paid into court. One of the reasons which the learned judge gave for making exactly the order which was made in this case, namely that there should be no order as to costs from the date of payment in, was that he had been considering giving a somewhat larger sum, and that he had never thought of giving less than the amount of the ultimate award. The leading judgment was delivered by Morris LJ with whom Ormrod and Willmer LJJ agreed. At 861 the learned Lord Justice said:

> This shows the great care the judge devoted to the matter, but, with the utmost respect, I do not feel able to accept the view that that reason is any valid reason for the exercise of a discretion. The judge thought over the matter and he came to his conclusion to which he adhered, that £575 was the right amount. It cannot in my judgment be a good basis for any exercise of discretion to say that possibly a larger amount might have been awarded. It seems to me, therefore, that, on any showing such a consideration could not properly be a competent element of any exercise of discretion. In this case that appears to have been the operative reason for the exercise of discretion in the way in which it was exercised. That operative reason when analysed contains no substance.

[309] In my judgment therefore with all respect the second ground advanced by His Honour is not one which was relevant to the exercise of his discretion as to costs.

[The Appeal Division of the Victorian Supreme Court took a similar view: *Williams v Thomson* [1991] VR 355.]

17.3.20   In *Page v Incorporated Nominal Defendant* [1981] VR 170, Murphy J expressed the view that once special circumstances had been found to justify departing from the prima facie rule, the question of costs should be resolved on the basis of what was fair in the circumstances. Other judges, however, concluded that even where special circumstances were found to exist, discretion as to costs should be exercised in the light of the general policy underlying the rules relating to payment in. Allowance should be made for the fact that the plaintiff will need time to make a 'thoughtful decision', and for the fact that when a trial is imminent or in progress, expenses must inevitably be incurred while that time elapses. However, allowance should be made only for those expenses. While the practice of making very late offers complicates orderly case management, the rules permit it, and parties should not be penalised for exercising that right: *Berry v Coghill* [1982] VR 955. The latter view has prevailed: *Williams v Thomson* [1991] 1 VR 355.

In *Lauchlan v Hartley* [1979] Qd R 305, Connolly J rejected the argument based on the late amendment, for while the amendment was not made until the trial, the plaintiff had been given ample notice of the defendant's intention to apply for the amendment. This was a common and convenient practice, one which avoided unnecessary interlocutory applications. He continued (at 308):

> Where offers are made on the eve of a trial, rigid application of the rules could occasion unfairness. Evaluating the offer may require careful consideration, and it may not be feasible to give the offer thorough consideration prior to the commencement of the trial. Allowance is made for such considerations, and the lateness of the offer can constitute special cause for departing from the normal rule.

17.3.21   Where judgment is given in favour of both the plaintiff as claimant and the defendant as counterclaimant, costs are prima facie assessed on the relationship between the judgment in favour of each party and the amount paid in by each party. The fact that the net payment of a defendant to a plaintiff falls short of the amount paid in does not give the defendant a prima facie entitlement to costs in relation to the post-payment in period: *Gelonese v Blanken and Amler (Homes) Pty Ltd* (1977) 24 ACTR 30.

17.3.22 The rules relating to payment in represent one means of encouraging parties to settle. However, they are relatively crude.

First, their attractiveness to defendants is limited. Where payment in requires the actual deposit of money, the defendant must forgo access to the sum until the court orders otherwise. Even if the plaintiff does not accept it, it remains in court until the court orders otherwise. For financially strapped defendants (and financial difficulties may be one of the things that makes a person a defendant), this is a major disincentive to the making of payments in. Where the issue is one of liability rather than quantum, the procedure is even less attractive. There, if the defendant succeeds, the defendant gets costs anyway, regardless of any payment in. If the plaintiff succeeds, the plaintiff will get costs, except in the unlikely event of the defendant having paid in the full value of the claim, undiscounted for the possibility of failure, only to have this generous offer rejected by the plaintiff. Second, there is no corresponding means to enable plaintiffs to exert pressure on defendants to make realistic settlement offers. Third, there is no means to enable pressures to be placed on parties in cases where the issue is not one of debt or damages.

Genn, *Hard Bargaining: Out of Court Settlement in Personal Injury Actions*, Clarendon Press, Oxford, 2000 found that in English personal injury cases, insurers made little use of the rule: see pp 11–13. She considered that the money paid in could be used alternatively to earn higher returns.

Calderbank offers

17.3.23 An alternative to payment into court is the making of a formal offer to settle the case, coupled with a warning that this offer will be disclosed to the court in the context of the question of costs (in contrast to the normal 'without prejudice' offer). Such offers are usually known as 'Calderbank' offers, after the English family law case which sanctioned their use. (On the origins and development of Calderbank offers, see M Ellis, 'The Cost of Compromising: Offers of Compromise and Calderbank Offers' (2008) 17 *J Jud Admin* 253 at 262–5.) Calderbank offers have the potential to expand the capacity of parties to encourage their adversaries to settle. However, they raise a number of difficulties. Calderbank offers are easier to make than payments into court, but they offer plaintiffs rather less security than a payment into court. Is it right that those who make such offers should be able to achieve costs advantages if payment into court is also an available option? These issues are canvassed in *Messiter v Hutchinson* (1987) 10 NSWLR 525, extracted next.

17.3.24C	**Messiter v Hutchinson**
	(1987) 10 NSWLR 525
	Supreme Court of New South Wales

[Upon the death of a horse, its owner sought to recover under an insurance policy. There was dispute as to its value. To the evident relief of the trial judge, the question of value was referred by consent to an arbitrator. Prior to the hearing of evidence by the arbitrator, the defendant's solicitors wrote to the plaintiff's solicitors:

> Our client is concerned at the level of costs which might be incurred by the forthcoming hearing. For that reason and based upon the valuation reports which we have served upon you our client is

---

prepared to offer your client the sum of $120,000 inclusive of interest (plus agreed or taxed costs) to settle the claim provided that amount is accepted prior to 4.00 pm on Wednesday, 8 April 1987.

Please seek your client's instructions.

We also give you notice that our client intends to rely upon the making of this offer if and when the question of costs arises and intends to bring this letter to the attention of the Arbitrator or the Court in those circumstances.

There was apparently no response to the letter. The arbitrator valued the horse at $100,000. The defendant argued that it should therefore be entitled to costs as from 8 April.]

Rogers J (at 526–30): The Supreme Court Act, s 76, provides that, subject to the Act and the rules costs shall be in the discretion of the Court. Needless to say, the discretion so conferred has to be exercised judicially. Part 52 of the rules makes further provision with respect to costs. Rule 11 provides that, if the Court makes any order as to costs, then, subject to the provisions of Pt 52, costs shall follow the event 'except where it appears to the Court that some other order should be made as to the whole or any part of the costs'. Detailed provision is made by r 17 as to how costs are to be borne after a payment into Court has been made. The actual payment into Court is dealt with in Pt 22. Payment into Court is permissible only in respect of claims of debt or damages. In summary, a payment into court may be made, without leave of the Court, at any time up to twenty eight days prior to the date for hearing and after that date only with the leave of the Court. Rule 2(2) permits security to be filed in lieu of the actual deposit of money.

Part 72, in contrast to Pt 72A, makes no special provision with respect to payment into Court. This is no doubt due to the fact that a reference under [527] Pt 72 still leaves on foot the proceedings in Court and the provisions as to payment into court in Pt 22 may be fully utilised, notwithstanding the fact that a reference has been made to an arbitrator or referee. After receipt of the referee's report it is for the Court to decide questions of costs as part of the obligation under r 13 to direct the entry of judgment.

In the present case the defendant did not make a payment into Court and, indeed, it would have required the leave of the Court to make a payment on 3 April 1982. Nonetheless, the defendant submits that a special order should be made, by reason of the without prejudice offer that was made on that date and the outcome of the reference.

The offer made by the letter of 3 April is of a kind which in England has become known as a Calderbank letter, taking its name from the comments of Cairns LJ in *Calderbank v Calderbank* [1976] Fam 93; [1975] 3 WLR 586; [1975] 3 All ER 333. In *Cutts v Head* [1984] Ch 290 the Court of Appeal held that a Calderbank letter may be relied on in proceedings in any division of the Court, not just in family disputes. However, Oliver LJ, who delivered the principal judgment, repeatedly said (at 301, 309, 310, 312) that the procedure may be adopted only where the facility of a payment into Court is not available. His Lordship concluded, in a passage which had the explicit concurrence of Fox LJ (at 317), that (at 312):

I would add only one word of caution. The qualification imposed on the without prejudice nature of the *Calderbank* letter is, as I have held, sufficient to enable it to be taken into account on the question of costs; but it should not be thought that this involves the consequence that such a letter can now be used as a substitute for a payment into court, where a payment into court is appropriate. In the case of the simple money claim, a defendant who wishes to avail himself of the protection afforded by an offer must, in the ordinary way, back his offer with cash by making a payment in and, speaking for myself,

I should not, as at present advised, be disposed in such a case to treat a *Calderbank* offer as carrying the same consequences as payment in.

In the subsequent decision of the Court of Appeal in *Corby District Council v Holst & Co Ltd* [1985] 1 WLR 427; [1985] 1 All ER 321, where again the judgment of the Court was that of Oliver LJ, his Lordship said (at 433; 326):

> ... The costs of legal proceedings are by statute left to the discretion of the court, and that discretion is to be exercised in accordance with the rules. One of the matters which may be taken into account, and, indeed, ordinarily would be, is an open offer by the defendant of everything to which the plaintiff ultimately shows himself entitled. Whether, however, such an offer is to be treated for all purposes in the same way as a payment into court must itself be a matter on which the judge of trial will have to make up his own mind in the exercise of his discretion. So far as payment in is concerned, that is specifically dealt with in RSC Ord 62, r 5, which merely provides that such a payment shall to such extent, if any, as may be appropriate in the circumstances be taken into account. But whether what the judge has before him is an offer or a payment in, the effect of it is left to his discretion.

It is relevant to note that the Rule Committee in England has accepted the qualification laid down by Oliver LJ in *Cutts*. Although it has now, in O 22, [528] r 14, sanctioned the use of written offers endorsed 'without prejudice save as to costs' the proviso to subr (2) excludes from consideration on the question of costs such letters from a party who could have made a payment into Court.

There are good reasons why, generally speaking, in order to get the benefit of an offer of payment, a defendant should be required to comply with the provisions of Pt 72. It is no longer necessary that the defendant should actually be out of pocket by paying into Court the requisite sum of money; the provision of security is sufficient. However, the rules rightly take the view that, all other things being equal, a plaintiff who is desirous of accepting an offer should not be left to look for the actual amount from a possibly impecunious defendant. The fundamental difference between a Calderbank letter and a payment into Court is that the latter is backed either by a deposit of money in the Court or the bond of an authorised person (see Pt 22, r 14). Counsel for the plaintiff in the present case submitted that, as a matter of principle, for the reasons which prompted Oliver LJ and the Rule Committee in England, the Court should not have regard to a Calderbank letter in circumstances where payment into court can be effected under the rules.

I do not think it appropriate that the exercise of discretion under s 76 should be fettered in the way suggested. As the Court of Appeal pointed out in *Cutts,* there are in accepted practice, for example in Admiralty disputes, methods of making offers other than payment into Court and the Calderbank letter. In addition in New South Wales the rules themselves recognise offers of contribution (cf. Pt 6, r 11) as between tortfeasors. The public policy on which the judgments in *Cutts* rest argues against a hard and fast exclusion of the availability of this method for disposition of disputes by compromise. The purpose of a Calderbank letter is, after all, essentially the promotion of settlement of disputes. Although, historically, the Calderbank letter evolved in circumstances where the procedure of payment in, for one reason or another, was unavailable, there is to my mind no reason in principle why it must necessarily and invariably be so restricted. The discouragement to practitioners to the use of the Calderbank letter in instances where the procedure of payment in is available is that the consequences of payment in, prescribed by the rules, will not automatically be available. As Ormrod LJ pointed out in *McDonnell v McDonnell* [1977] 1 WLR 34 at 38; [1977] 1 All ER 766 at 770:

... It would be wrong, in my judgment, to equate an offer of compromise in proceedings such as these precisely to a payment into court. I see no advantage in the court surrendering its discretion in these matters as it has to all intents and purposes done where a payment into court has been made. A *Calderbank* offer should influence but not govern the exercise of discretion.

In my view, at least as a matter of principle, a Calderbank letter should be permitted to be taken into account by the Court in determining whether a special order displacing that which generally obtains of costs following the event should be made. Particularly should this be the case in New South Wales where, as I have pointed out, the rules permit security from an authorised person instead of the deposit of money. Why should the bond from an insurance company authorised by Pt 22 necessarily carry any more [529] weight than a Calderbank letter from BHP? In considering what weight should be given to an offer, the Court will no doubt pay regard to all relevant circumstances including the reason why no payment in was made, the security of payment available to the plaintiff and the time at which the Calderbank letter was received by the plaintiff.

So long as adequate consideration is given to the matters I have mentioned, it seems to me there is no reason why the Court should not foster all means whereby parties may properly attempt to dispose of their disputes prior to actual hearing, either in Court or by a referee or arbitrator. So long as it may fairly be done, the Court should do nothing which would dissuade or discourage a party from making bona fide offers of settlement, no matter how late. Delay in making an offer may, of course, entail consequences in the precise order made but should not automatically demand a complete disregard of the offer of settlement.

I feel greatly comforted in the view that I have taken by what fell from Oliver LJ in *Cutts* (ibid at 306):

... As a practical matter, a consciousness of a risk as to costs if reasonable offers are refused can only encourage settlement whilst, on the other hand, it is hard to imagine anything more calculated to encourage obstinacy and unreasonableness than the comfortable knowledge that a litigant can refuse with impunity whatever may be offered to him even if it is as much as or more than everything to which he is entitled in the action.

In the present case, the defendant, as I have said, is a solicitor of the Court representing a syndicate of Lloyd's underwriters. Whilst I appreciate the point made by counsel that the reliability and probity of Lloyd's underwriters has received setbacks in recent years, there is absolutely nothing before me to suggest that there was any likelihood of the plaintiff suffering detriment by accepting the Calderbank letter instead of actual payment into Court. Again, there is no doubt that the offer was made very late. Three April was a Friday. Going by the statement of claim, the plaintiff apparently lives in Sydney and there was no reason suggested why the offer could not have been evaluated on the Monday or Tuesday or even the Wednesday following. As against that the defendant indicated that it proposed to rely on reports and valuations received by it as long ago as April and May 1986 although there was also a valuation from a new valuer dated 23 March 1987. Under the rules, a plaintiff has fourteen days to accept a payment into Court. Here, the offer demanded acceptance by 4.00 pm on Wednesday.

The plaintiff did not suggest that she did not have sufficient time for a consideration of the defendant's offer or that in some other way she was prejudiced and unable to deal with the offer of settlement within the time limited. She made no effort to seek an extension of time for acceptance of the offer. On the other hand, the defendant gave no real explanation for letting five months go by without making an offer and forcing the plaintiff to consider one at the last minute. The fact that the matter proceeded before the referee indicates to me that, by implication at any rate, the plaintiff was unwilling to consider the offer of the defendant. In all the circumstances, including the fact that Calderbank letters have not previously been the subject of decision in New South Wales, I think justice will be done by an order that the defendant pay the plaintiff's costs, including counsel's brief fee, [530] up to and including 8 April and that there be no order for costs thereafter including the costs of this application.

17.3.25   There is some dispute as to whether Calderbank offers create a presumption in favour of costs on an indemnity basis, as opposed to constituting a matter to be taken into account in determining the nature of the costs order that the court should make. For a review of the case law, see *Pirotta v Citibank Ltd* (1998) 72 SASR 259; *Baulderstone Hornibrook Engineering Pty Ltd v Gordian Runoff Ltd (formerly GIO Insurance Ltd)* [2006] NSWSC 583.

   The importance of Calderbank offers in Australia is limited. The offer of compromise rules which operate in most Australian jurisdictions means that resorting to Calderbank is normally unnecessary: see **17.3.27–17.3.49**. Calderbank offers have been recognised in the Australian Capital Territory, which has not yet adopted a formal offer of compromise system; as to their operation, see *Whittle v Filaria Pty Ltd* [2004] ACTSC 131, BC200408767. There might also be a place for Calderbank offers in relation to High Court litigation, but the open-ended nature of the new High Court Rules, and the special attributes of High Court cases mean that they would rarely be likely to play a significant role in relation to High Court costs orders. They may also be appropriate in cases where the ordinary offer of compromise rules are inapplicable. In *R v Murfett (No 2)* [2004] VSC 181; BC200402988, Balmford J awarded indemnity costs in a case where the plaintiff had argued that the defendant was in contempt of court in that he had wilfully breached an undertaking, and had wilfully interfered with the administration of justice. One basis for the order was a finding that the charges were brought for ulterior purposes, and not for achieving compliance, but Her Honour also took into account a Calderbank offer whereby the defendant offered to settle on the basis that each party would bear its own costs.

   In Administrative Appeals Tribunal compensation cases, there is provision for the award of costs to successful applicants, but no provision for the making of offers of compromise. Nonetheless, Calderbank offers may be made by respondents, and are relevant to costs decisions even if the offer was to settle on terms not open to the tribunal: *Griffiths v Australian Postal Corporation* [2008] FCA 19.

17.3.26C	**Miwa Pty Ltd v Siantan Properties Pty Ltd (No 2)**
	[2011] NSWCA 344
	New South Wales Court of Appeal

[Six days before the trial, the plaintiff/appellant had made an offer to settle on terms which would, if accepted, have been extremely favourable to the plaintiff. (Success at trial was worth $45,000 to the defendant; the plaintiff offered $1000.) The appellant was unsuccessful at first instance, but succeeded on appeal. At issue was the question of whether the appellant should get its costs on an indemnity basis. The Court of Appeal stated the circumstances in an informal offer of compromise would warrant an award of indemnity, rather than 'party and party', costs.]

Basten J, with whom McColl and Campbell JJ agreed: [8] The approach frequently adopted in this jurisdiction has been to ask two questions, namely whether—

(a)   there was a genuine offer of compromise, and
(b)   it was unreasonable for the offeree not to accept it.

Genuine offer of compromise

[9] There is authority for the proposition that both an offer of compromise under the rules and an informal offer must involve 'a real and genuine element of compromise': *Anderson Group Pty Ltd v Tynan Motors Pty Ltd (No 2)* [2006] NSWCA 120; 67 NSWLR 706 at [8]. While this terminology is not entirely apposite, it has been described as 'serviceable': *Regency Media Pty Ltd v AAV Australia Pty Ltd* [2009] NSWCA 368 at [25] (Spigelman CJ, Beazley and McColl JJA). To characterise an offer by reference to epithets such as 'real' or 'genuine' adds little to the requirement of compromise, and may imply (wrongly) that the appropriate inquiry is as to the subjective intentions of the offeror: *Hancock v Arnold; Dodd v Arnold (No 2)* [2009] NSWCA 19 at [23] (Ipp, McColl and Basten JJA); *Evans of Robb Evans & Associates v European Bank Ltd (No 2)* [2009] NSWCA 170 at [17]–[18]. As explained by Giles J in *Hobartville Stud Pty Ltd v Union Insurance Co Ltd* (1991) 25 NSWLR 358 at 368:

> Compromise connotes that a party gives something away. A plaintiff with a strong case, or a plaintiff with a firm belief in the strength of its case, is perfectly entitled to discount its claim by only a dollar, but it does not in any real sense give anything away, and I do not think that it can claim to have placed itself in a more favourable position in relation to costs unless it does so.

Unreasonable refusal

[10] Most cases will turn on the second element, namely whether there has been an unreasonable refusal by the offeree. This in turn involves a number of considerations.

(a) timing

[11] It is not in doubt that the response of the offeree must be assessed at the time it was made, and not with the benefit of hindsight resulting from a known outcome, recorded in a judgment: *Regency Media* at [33]. However, that factor should not entail a detailed investigation into the state of preparation or knowledge of the offeree as at the date of the offer. The expense and use of resources which settlement is intended to avoid include those involved in the assessment and preparation of a case.

(b) relevant factors

[12] In *Hazeldene's Chicken Farm Pty Ltd v Victorian WorkCover Authority (No 2)* [2005] VSCA 298; 13 VR 435 the Court of Appeal (Warren CJ, Maxwell P and Harper AJA) identified the factors relevant to determining whether the rejection of an offer was unreasonable as including the following:

(a)   the stage of the proceeding at which the offer was received;
(b)   the time allowed to the offeree to consider the offer;
(c)   the extent of the compromise offered;
(d)   the offeree's prospects of success, assessed as at the date of the offer;
(e)   the clarity with which the terms of the offer were expressed;

(f)   whether the offer foreshadowed an application for indemnity costs in the event of the offeree's rejecting it.

[13] The court rejected the suggestion that an offer need set out with specificity the bases upon which it was said that the offeree should accept the compromise proffered. The relevance of such material would depend upon the extent to which the issues had already been canvassed, for example by way of pre-litigation correspondence, and whether there were circumstances with which the offeror might reasonably expect the offeree not to be conversant. In some circumstances greater leniency may be accorded to a defendant offeree at an early stage of proceedings, than to a plaintiff offeree.

[14] The extent of the compromise offered will always be a relevant factor in determining the reasonableness of the offeree's rejection. In *Robb Evans & Associates* an offer in compliance with the UCPR, r 20.26, involved an effective amount (after deducting a sum as to which there was no dispute) of less than $2,000 to settle a claim in excess of $800,000. The court stated:

> [20] ... If the offer were based on a legal assessment of the likelihood of success in an amount in excess of $800,000, the claim should have been struck out as frivolous and vexatious. It ultimately failed in this Court, but could not, on any view, be so categorized. It is implausible that the appellant so categorized it in quantifying his offer.
>
> [21] If the appellant had carried out a commercial evaluation, rather than a pure legal assessment of the likelihood of success, he would undoubtedly have concluded that, even if ultimately successful, he would be unlikely to recover many thousands of dollars of costs incurred if the litigation proceeded. A commercially based offer would have taken that matter into account. This offer clearly did not.
>
> ...
>
> [23] ... The amount offered, beyond that amount which was not in dispute, is properly characterized as trivial or contemptuous. It does not engage the costs consequences provided by r 42.15.

[15] A similar approach was applied in *Regency Media,* where an offer of $10,000 was made in response to a claim of approximately $600,000: at [16]. The court noted at [32]:

> If a derisory offer, of the kind made in these proceedings, could result in an order for indemnity costs, then it is likely that many, perhaps most, contract interpretation disputes would result in an indemnity costs order, if the formality of an offer in accordance with the rules had been made at an early stage. If the appellant were to succeed in the present case, it is quite likely that such an offer would accompany most statements of claim as a matter of commercial practice. The purpose of the special order — to encourage settlement — would no longer be served. An order for indemnity costs could, in our opinion, become the normal order in many commercial disputes.

(c) onus of proof

[16] The general rule is that costs payable under an order of the court are to be assessed on the ordinary basis: UCPR, r 42.2. The court may otherwise order, but the burden of persuading the court will lie with the offeror: *Black v Lipovac* [1998] FCA 699; 217 ALR 386 at [217] (Miles, Heerey and Madgwick JJ), which has been regularly followed in the Full Court — see, eg, *CGU Insurance Ltd v Corrections Corporation of Australia Staff Superannuation Pty Ltd* [2008] FCAFC 173 at [75] (Moore, Finn and Jessup JJ). Again, however, the reference to onus

of proof is not intended to suggest that an application for indemnity costs be turned into a mini-trial. Generally, such applications are dealt with on the papers, a practice which should be maintained. It is nevertheless correct, as a matter of principle, to say that it is the offeror which must persuade the court that the rejection of the offer was, in the circumstances at the relevant time, unreasonable.

[The court held that, given the outcome of the trial, and given that the offer did not include any provision for paying the defendant's costs, it was reasonable for the defendant to reject the offer. Nor should the respondent receive indemnity costs in connection with its successful appeal. Given its victory at trial, it would have been reasonable for the respondent to reject an offer in the terms offered by the appellant, and in any case, the appellant's offer could be treated as having expired following judgment at first instance.]

Offers of compromise and offers to settle

17.3.27   In the Federal Court, New South Wales, the Northern Territory, Queensland, South Australia, Tasmania, Victoria and Western Australia, the rules provide for a more flexible procedure: FCR Pt 25; Uniform Civil Procedure Rules (NSW) Pt 20 Div 4; NT rr 26.01–26.11; Uniform Civil Procedure Rules 1999 (Qld) Ch 9, Pt 5; SA rr 187–188; Tas Pt 9; Supreme Court (General Civil Procedure) Rules 2005 (Vic) O 26; Rules of the Supreme Court 1971 (WA) O 24A. These procedures enable either party to make an offer and this is the case whether the relief claimed is monetary or otherwise. In the Northern Territory (r 26.02(1)), however, a distinction is drawn between cases where there is a claim for damages for or arising out of death or bodily injury and other cases. In the former, either party may make an offer of compromise. In other cases, only the defendant may make an offer: r 26.02(2). However, r 26.11 provides a procedure whereby plaintiffs can make offers which, if open to be accepted by the defendant at the time of judgment, may be taken into account for costs purposes if they are not accepted by the defendant.

Parties, which fail to accept an offer and which subsequently receive a judgment less favourable than the offer, can be and usually are penalised by adverse costs awards. There are therefore rewards for making generous offers, and penalties for failure to accept such offers.

The key to the offer of compromise rules lies in their costs implications. Defendants' offers are treated similarly to defendants' offers under payment in schemes. If the judgment for the plaintiff is no more favourable than the offer, the plaintiff pays the defendant's post-offer costs, and the defendant pays the plaintiff's pre-offer costs. There are therefore rewards for making early offers, although the attractions of these rewards may be counterbalanced by the fact that in the early stages of proceedings, parties may lack sufficient information to be able to know with certainty whether an offer is generous or not.

The position of plaintiffs has no analogue under the payment in rules. If a plaintiff's offer is not accepted and if the judgment for the plaintiff is more favourable than the accepted offer would have been, the plaintiff is entitled to costs on an indemnity basis. Since costs on an indemnity basis are considerably higher than the party and party costs typically awarded, plaintiffs have an incentive to make moderately generous offers. (The difference between these two bases for awarding costs is discussed below: see **20.3.1–20.3.2C**.)

17.3.28C	**Maitland Hospital v Fisher (No 2)** (1992) 27 NSWLR 721 Court of Appeal (NSW)

Kirby P, Mahoney JA and Samuels AJA (at 724): It is clearly right that the rule should apply to this Court. It is just as much affected by the rapid increase in litigation as are the Divisions of the Supreme Court: see The Supreme Court of New South Wales, *Annual Review 1991* (at 23). Therefore, Pt 52, r 17 applies to proceedings in the Court of Appeal. The obvious purpose of providing Pt 52, r 17 is to facilitate the proper compromise of litigation. This has been attempted by the twin measures of a 'carrot' and 'stick'. Relevantly, the 'carrot' is the promise of indemnity costs to a plaintiff in the event that the defendant is found unreasonably to have refused an offer of compromise. The 'stick' is the threat of the penalty of the imposition of an indemnity costs order against a defendant in such circumstances. It is the obvious intention of the rule to oblige a defendant, which has received an offer of compromise, to give serious thought to the risk which it may run of losing the proceedings and then being ordered to pay costs on an indemnity basis.

The objects of the rule include:

1. To encourage the saving of private costs and the avoidance of the inherent risks, delays and uncertainties of litigation by promoting early offers of compromise by defendants which amount to a realistic assessment of the plaintiff's real claim which can be placed before its opponent without risk that its 'bottom line' will be revealed to the court;

2. To save the public costs which are necessarily incurred in litigation which events demonstrate to have been unnecessary, having regard to an earlier (and, as found, reasonable) offer of compromise made by a plaintiff to a defendant; and

3. To indemnify the plaintiff who has made the offer of compromise, later found to have been reasonable, against the costs thereafter incurred. This is deemed appropriate because, from the time of the rejection or deemed rejection of the compromise offer, notionally the real cause and occasion of the litigation is the attitude adopted by the defendant which has rejected the compromise. In such circumstances, that party should ordinarily bear the costs of litigation.

[See also *Hillier v Sheather* (1995) 36 NSWLR 414 at 422 per **Kirby P.**]

17.3.29 The differentiation between plaintiffs and defendants means that much can turn on whether one is a plaintiff or a defendant. This will rarely be problematic, however, there may be cases where a party described in the pleadings as a defendant is in substance a plaintiff.

17.3.30C	**Maitland Hospital v Fisher (No 2)** (1992) 27 NSWLR 721 Court of Appeal (NSW)

[This issue arose because the original plaintiff made an offer to the appellant who was the original defendant. Under the New South Wales rules (Pt 51 r 2(2)), a person who commences proceedings in the Court of Appeal is described as a plaintiff, and the respondent as a defendant. This raised the issue of whether a plaintiff for the purposes of the rules relating to appeals was a plaintiff for the purposes of the costs rules.]

Kirby P, Mahoney JA and Samuels AJA said (at 726–7): It is to be observed that the primary requirement in Pt 51, r 2(1) for the application of the rules governing the Divisions of the Supreme Court to the Court of Appeal envisages that those rules apply 'so far as applicable'. We take this to be a provision dealing not only with the matter of application and non-application but also with the manner in which a rule is to be applied. It is obviously sensible that the purpose of Pt 52, r 17 should be kept in mind in applying its provisions to the Court of Appeal. That purpose was to adopt a differential principle in respect of offers of compromise made by 'plaintiffs' in the Divisions of the Supreme Court and offers of compromise made by 'defendants'. The plaintiff is the person with the 'claim'. Part 52, r 17 refers to the costs of 'the claim'. Accordingly, the provisions of r 17 are applicable in the Court of Appeal only if the terms of Pt 51, r 2(2)(a) are modified to prevent a party who does not have a 'claim' from being regarded as a 'plaintiff' in the Court of Appeal, notwithstanding that such party is on the record as 'appellant'.

Normally, although not universally, 'plaintiffs' are ordinary individuals. 'Defendants' are frequently corporations and are often represented, upon subrogation, by their insurers. More importantly, if no differentiation were made between the plaintiff and the defendant, the only pressure on the defendant to settle would be the pressure which is inherent in litigating in [727] any event. The defendant is entitled, if the plaintiff fails at trial, ordinarily to recover its costs. Without differentiation an offer to settle would not of itself induce a defendant to settle: cf. letter [dated 28 April 1989] (1989) 19 *QLSJ* 257. This differentiation helps to explain the different rule adopted in the Divisions in respect of offers of compromise by, respectively, 'plaintiffs' and 'defendants'.

In these circumstances, to adopt the dictionary provided in Pt 51, r 2(2) would be to distort the clear purpose of the differential provision in respect of costs contained in Pt 52, r 17. Applying that rule in the Court of Appeal, in such a way as to achieve its obvious purpose, requires that 'plaintiff' and 'defendant' where appearing in subr (4) and subr (5) retain their ordinary meaning and not the special meaning provided under Pt 51, r 2(2). On that basis the offer of compromise in the Court of Appeal was made in this case by the 'plaintiff'. It therefore attracts in this Court the operation of Pt 51, r 17(4). It thus sustains the demand of the 'plaintiff' (respondent) in this Court for an indemnity costs order. No adequate reason has been advanced as to why such an order should not be made. The reasons of principle discussed above support the making of the order.

This conclusion relieves the Court of the necessity to determine whether otherwise the Court would, in this case, have ordered indemnity costs or made some other special costs order under its inherent power or under the general discretion given to it by s 76(1)(c) of the Supreme Court Act 1970: cf. *Doherty v Liverpool District Hospital* (1991) 22 NSWLR 284 at 289, *EMI Records Ltd v Ian Cameron Wallace Ltd* [1983] Ch 59 at 70ff, *Degmam Pty Ltd (In Liq) v Wright (No 2)* [1983] 2 NSWLR 354 at 359 and *Melouhowee Pty Ltd (Receiver and Manager Appointed) v Steenbhom* (unreported, SC(NSW) Equity, Waddell CJ, No 1190/1991, 6 February 1992, BC 9202095).

When may an offer be made?

17.3.31 The deadline for serving offers varies by jurisdiction: it is 21 days before the date fixed for trial in South Australia (r 187(1)); before the commencement of trial in Tasmania (r 280(6)); before judgment is given, in the Federal Court (r 25.05(1)), New South Wales (r 20.25) and Western Australia (O 24A r 3(8)), and before judgment or verdict in the remaining jurisdictions: NT r 26.03; Qld r 354(1); Vic r 26.03(1). Parties may make more than one offer: FCR r 25.05(2); NSW r 20.26(1); NT r 26.03; Qld r 353(2); Tas r 280(5)(a); Vic r 26.03;

WA O 24A r 3(2); compare *Halsbury's Laws of Australia*, 'Practice and Procedure', LexisNexis, Sydney, looseleaf, vol 20, [325–6800].

Withdrawal of offer

17.3.32 The offer must generally be open for acceptance for 14 days or, in some jurisdictions, 28 days unless the offer specifies a longer period: FCR r 25.05(3); NSW r 20.26(7) (28 days); NT r 26.03(3); Qld r 355(1); Tas r 280(7); Vic r 26.03(3); WA O 24A r 3(3) (28 days, or such time as is reasonable within two months of the trial date); compare NT r 26.11 (plaintiffs' offers in non-personal-injuries cases). The offer cannot be withdrawn during the period that it is open for acceptance, unless the court so orders or unless the offer is replaced by an offer which is more favourable to the offeree: FCR r 25.07; NSW r 20.26(1); NT r 26.03(5); Qld r 355(3); Tas r 283(2); Vic r 26.03(5); WA O 24A r 3(6). An abrupt change of circumstances might justify permitting a party to withdraw its offer in jurisdictions where leave is required: see *Cumper v Pothecary* [1941] 2 KB 58. In South Australia, an offer may be withdrawn at any time, in which case, subject to court order, it will be treated as if it had never been made: SA r 187(7).

Acceptance

17.3.33 An offer is accepted by written notice served on the offeror or the offeror's solicitor. In South Australia, it may be accepted up to seven days before the date fixed for trial: r 188(1)(a). Elsewhere it may be accepted within the time it remains open: FCR r 25.08; NSW r 20.27; NT rr 26.03(4), 358(1); Tas r 283(1); Vic r 26.03(4); WA O 24 r 3(5). This is the case notwithstanding that the offeree may have made a counter-offer: FCR O 23 r 5(6); NT r 26.03(6); Qld r 358(2); Tas r 283(3); Vic r 26.03(6); WA O 24A r 3(7). The New South Wales rules do not prescribe this, but they do not preclude it either. It should be noted that the effect of the offer on costs normally dates from the date of the offer, and not from the date of acceptance. Thus even if a defendant accepts an offer 13 days after it is made, the plaintiff will normally be entitled to its costs only until the date of the offer. After that, other rules determine liability for costs: *Malliaros v Moralis* [1991] 2 VR 501. In *Malliaros*, these rules would have produced an injustice. Since the plaintiff recovered less than half the County Court's jurisdictional limit, strict application of the rules would have meant that she would be subject to the considerable costs penalty involved in bringing a matter before the 'wrong' court. McGarvie J held that in the circumstances, the normal rule should not be applied. First, it was effectively the defendant who, following the offer, became responsible for the proceeding continuing in the 'wrong' court. Second, the effect of a strict application of the rules would be to discourage the making of offers of settlement by plaintiffs in circumstances such as this, since the making of an offer to settle for below half the relevant jurisdictional limit would expose a plaintiff to the risk of being severely out of pocket if the defendant chose to delay accepting the offer. This would give defendants considerable bargaining power.

Withdrawal of acceptance

17.3.34 In the Federal Court (r 25.09), New South Wales (r 20.28) and Western Australia (O 24A r 5), a party may withdraw its acceptance in exceptional circumstances. These include cases where the court gives leave to do so, and cases where the offer was to pay money and where the money was not paid within 28 days of acceptance, or within such other period as was provided in the offer.

Offers are without prejudice

17.3.35   An offer is without prejudice: FCR r 25.06 (but only if it states that it is without prejudice); NSW rr 20.30, 20.32; NT r 26.04 (does not expressly apply to r 26.11 offers); Qld r 356; SA r 187(4); Tas r 285 (unless the offer provides otherwise); Vic r 26.04; WA O 24A r 6. The terms of the offer should not be disclosed in pleadings or affidavits, and not communicated to the judge until all questions of liability and relief are determined: FCR r 25.06(2); NSW r 20.30; NT r 26.05; Qld r 357; SA r 187(4); Tas r 286; Vic r 26.05; WA O 24A r 7.

Incorporation into a judgment

17.3.36   In several jurisdictions, the court may incorporate any terms of an accepted offer into a judgment: NSW r 20.27; Qld r 358(4); SA r 188(5) (by consent only); Tas r 288(1); WA O 24A r 3(9).

Enforcement

17.3.37   The rules vary as to the position where a party fails to comply with the terms of an accepted offer. In South Australia (r 188(5)), judgment may be entered by consent, once the offer is accepted, and once judgment is signed or entered, is enforceable as a judgment. In Queensland (r 365), the other party may continue with the action as if the offer had not been accepted or apply to court for judgment in terms of the offer. The terms may already have been incorporated into a judgment. They could also be enforced on the basis that the offer and acceptance create a contract between the parties. In most other jurisdictions, the accepting party may elect either for judgment in terms of the offer, or alternatively for dismissal of a plaintiff's case, or an order that a defence be struck out (as appropriate): FCR r 25.10 (also allows stays); NSW r 20.29; NT r 26.07; Tas r 288 (but does not apply to offers to accept or concede a proportion of a claim, or where the court orders otherwise); Vic r 26.07; WA O 24A r 8. These are draconian consequences, the rationale for which lies in the desirability of discouraging offers in cases where the offeror cannot or does not intend to fulfill them. This is not a problem which arises in the context of money actually paid into court.

Specific parties

17.3.38   Actions involving parties under a disability may be compromised only with the approval of the court or, in Queensland, by the court or the Public Trustee: FCR rr 7.11, 9.70; Civil Procedure Act 2005 (NSW) s 76; NT r 26.06; Public Trustee Act 1978 (Qld) s 59, Qld r 359; SA r 257; Tas r 287; Vic r 26.06; WA O 70 r 10.

Multiple defendants

17.3.39   Where there are multiple defendants, an offer to or from any one of them may be made. However, where the defendants are jointly or jointly and severally liable, the plaintiff may only offer to settle with all and a defendant may offer to settle the action against all. If several defendants join in this offer, it must make them jointly or jointly and severally liable for the whole of the amount of the offer. Offers which do not comply with these conditions cannot be enforced in the event of default, and may not attract cost penalties if not accepted:

FCR r 25.11; NT r 26.09; Qld r 363; Tas r 290; Vic r 26.09; WA O 24A r 9. The New South Wales rules do not address this question directly, but they nonetheless appear to impose similar requirements. The South Australian rules are also silent, but the approved forms envisage the possibility of offers from multiple parties: Form 23.

Offers to contribute

17.3.40   In some jurisdictions the rules provide that where a defendant claims contribution or indemnity against a third party, either of them may offer to the other to contribute to the settlement of the claim made by the plaintiff. The court may take such an offer into account in determining costs to be paid between those parties and between either of them and the plaintiff: FCR r 25.13; NSW rr 20.32, 42.18; NT r 26.10; Qld r 364; Tas r 291; Vic r 26.10.

Interest

17.3.41   In determining the relationship between an offer and a judgment, the court must take account not only of damages, but also of the interest awarded on the judgment debt.

17.3.42C	**Hadzigeorgiou v O'Sullivan** [1983] Qd R 55 Supreme Court of Queensland

[The defendant had been awarded $3894.50 in general and special damages, an amount equal to the amount paid into court. He had not been awarded interest on the grounds that, in the opinion of the trial judge, it was impossible or difficult to determine the proportion of the damages which could be said to have accrued prior to judgment. The Common Law Practice Act 1867 s 72 permitted the awarding of interest.]

Andrews SPJ (at 57): Thus a defendant in deciding upon an amount to be paid in should, in his wisdom, have regard to interest which might be allowed by the Court. Interest, when ordered may properly be regarded as part of the damages awarded ...

In my view the proper approach to an exercise of discretion as to the granting of interest is that it ought to be granted unless there are proper reasons for withholding it ...

[58] A plaintiff should not be forced to compromise his claim by accepting an amount which makes no allowance for interest.

17.3.43   The Federal Court Rules (r 25.03) require that if a sum of money is offered and is inclusive of costs and/or interest, it may specify the amount attributable to the costs and/or interest. (See too SA r 187(3)(c), which is similar regarding costs.) Rules in some jurisdictions provide that for the purposes of determining the relationship between a judgment and an offer, interest awarded is taken into account only until and including the day of the offer: NSW r 42.16; NT r 26.08(5); Qld r 362(2); Tas r 289(4); Vic r 26.08(5); WA O 24A r 10(7). Thus, consider the cases where the defendant offers $50,000 which the plaintiff rejects. The plaintiff is awarded $45,000 and $12,000 interest. If $4000 of that interest related to the period up to the date of service of the offer, the defendant's offer would be more favourable than the ultimate judgment ($49,000). If $6000 of the interest related to the period up to the date of service, the defendant's offer would be less favourable than the judgment for the plaintiff ($51,000). The reason for this apportionment is that it is the plaintiff's failure to accept the offer which has caused the additional interest to accrue.

Costs implications

17.3.44 The relevant costs rules are complex. However, broadly they are as follows:

- If either party accepts an offer of compromise, the plaintiff is normally entitled to its costs on a 'party and party' basis up to the date of service of the offer (NT r 26.03(7); Tas rr 284(1), 289(2); Vic r 26.03(7)), or acceptance of the offer: NSW r 42.13A; WA O 24A r 10(1). In the Federal Court (r 25.03) and South Australia (rr 187(3), 188(1)(b)), the offer may either be a global figure or for principal relief and/or costs, and acceptance of the offer involves accepting it on its terms. If an accepted Federal Court offer does not include the offeree's costs, the offeree may tax costs on a 'party and party' basis up to 14 days after and including the date of the offer: r 25.12. In Queensland (r 358(5)), an offer of compromise may (but need not) include an offer to pay assessed costs, in which case the registrar must assess costs on the filing of a notice of acceptance.

- If a defendant does not accept a plaintiff's offer, the consequences vary depending on whether the plaintiff receives a judgment at least as good as the offer. If it is, it is the defendant's unreasonableness which has prolonged the trial; the plaintiff is therefore normally entitled to some compensation. In New South Wales, Victoria (other than in personal injuries cases) and Western Australia, the court in such cases should normally award costs on an indemnity basis from the day of the offer, and in the Federal Court the transition to indemnity costs begins at 11 am on the second business day after service of the notice. In the Northern Territory, Queensland, South Australia, Tasmania and Victoria (in personal injuries cases), indemnity costs date from commencement of proceedings. Otherwise, the defendant's refusal to accept does not attract any penalty: FCR r 25.14(3); NSW r 42.14; NT r 26.08(2); Qld r 360; SA r 188(6)(b)(ii); Tas r 289; Vic 26.08(2); WA O 24A r 10(4). The rules differ slightly where the relevant offer was made on the eve of, or during, a trial. If the plaintiff makes several rejected offers to settle and receives a judgment at least as favourable as two or more of them, the first of these offers is taken to be the only offer for the purposes of calculating costs under the Queensland rules: r 360(2). It is submitted that similar results would follow in other jurisdictions (in so far as the date of the plaintiff's offer is relevant). In the Northern Territory (r 26.11), where the plaintiff makes an offer other than in relation to a claim for damages in a personal injury matter, the presumptive rules do not operate as strongly. The court, in determining its costs award, is merely required to take account of the offer and the time for which it was open. This is also the case in Victoria, in relation to offers made in relation to appeals: r 26.12.

- If a plaintiff does not accept a defendant's offer, the consequences depend on whether the plaintiff receives a judgment better than the offer. If not, it is the plaintiff who has prolonged the trial, and the plaintiff must normally pay the defendant's costs on a 'party and party' basis for a period after the making of the offer. Typically the period begins on the day after the making of the offer: NT r 26.08(3); Qld r 361; SA r 188(6) (b)(i) (14 days after offer); Tas r 289(2); Vic r 26.08(3); WA O 24A r 10(5). If judgment is given for the defendant, the normal cost rules prevail, and the defendant gets its costs on a 'party and party' basis. The Federal Court rules are similar, but make provision for defendants to receive indemnity costs. If the applicant receives a judgment no more favourable than the respondent's offer, the applicant is normally entitled to 'party and party' costs incurred up to 11 am on the second business day after service of the offer, and the respondent to indemnity costs thereafter: r 25.14(1). Where the applicant's proceeding is dismissed, the respondent is normally entitled to 'party and party' costs, but if the applicant's refusal of the offer was unreasonable, the respondent is entitled to indemnity costs for the period starting after 11 am on the second business day after service of the offer. In New South Wales, there is also provision for indemnity costs where the judgment is no more favourable than a defendant's offer, but the test for entitlement to indemnity costs is not dependent on whether the success relates to quantum or liability: r 42.15. Victoria's provision for offers of compromise in relation to appeals permit the Court of Appeal to take account of offers of compromise in relation to the appeal and to award costs other than on a 'party and party' basis: r 26.12. In most jurisdictions, special provisions apply to offers made on the eve of trial or later: NSW r 42.15(2)(b)(ii) (on or after first day of the trial); Qld r 361(3); WA O 24A r 10(6); and see NT r 26.08(4); Vic r 26.08(4) (first or later trial day). If the defendant makes several rejected offers to settle and the plaintiff receives a judgment no more favourable than two or more of the offers, the first of them is taken to be the only offer for the purposes of calculating costs under the Queensland rules: r 360(2). It is submitted that similar results would follow in other jurisdictions.

- In most jurisdictions, a defendant is not entitled to costs under the rules unless the defendant was at relevant times able and willing to fulfil its offer: NSW r 42.17; NT r 26.08(7); Qld rr 360(1)(b), 361(1)(b); Tas r 289(3); Vic r 26.08(7); WA O 24A r 10(9). In South Australia, where there is not an express provision to this effect, this consideration might nonetheless be relevant to the court's discretion in relation to the award of costs.

- The court may exercise its discretion to depart from the presumptions created by the rules: FCR r 1.35 (general power to dispense with operation of the rules); NSW rr 42.14, 42.15; NT r 26.08; Qld rr 360(1), 361(2); SA r 188(6); Tas r 289(1); Vic r 26.08; WA O 24A r 10. This means that parties which make 'generous' offers do not necessarily receive the presumptive benefit, but it also means that such parties may receive more than the presumptive benefit. There is Victorian authority to the effect that a defendant who has made an offer of settlement, but who is completely successful may, in the exercise of the court's discretion, be awarded costs on a solicitor and client basis from the time of service of the offer: see *Stipanov v Mier (No 2)* [2006] VSC 424 at [2].

Dichotomous decisions

17.3.45 The rules work best where quantum rather than liability is in dispute. If liability is in dispute, the rules can sometimes produce injustice, especially where quantum is an all or nothing affair. Consider a case where a plaintiff sues for $50,000 damage done by the defendant to her BMW, as a consequence of the defendant having fire-bombed it. The defendant denies the bombing. The plaintiff might offer to settle for $49,500, knowing that, if successful, she would be entitled to $50,000 (assuming that BMWs are fungibles with easily ascertainable values). The defendant's cost position is unaffected by when or whether he makes an offer. If the defendant wins, he gets costs, regardless of any offer he might have made, and regardless of the generosity of such offer. The defendant's sole incentive to make an offer lies in the unattractiveness of litigation per se. On the other hand, in jurisdictions where there is provision for defendants to receive indemnity costs, a defendant might offer to settle for $50. If the evidence is ambiguous, the presumptive rules might work badly in favour of a successful defendant.

Different systems tackle this problem in different ways. In the Northern Territory, a distinction is drawn between personal injuries cases where there is a damages claim and other cases. In the former category of case, liability may be at issue, but quantum is almost certain to be at issue. In other cases, liability may be the principal matter at issue. The Federal Court rules recognise the problem by differentiating between cases where the applicant has had some success, and cases where it has had none. In the latter case, the defendant's entitlement to indemnity costs is predicated on the reasonableness of the offer. Even if the respondent won on liability, an offer to settle the BMW claim for $50 would probably be unreasonable if there was some evidence pointing to the defendant's liability. Under the Northern Territory rule (r 26.11), in such cases, the court is to take account of offers in determining costs. The court is invited to consider the whole range of possible options, including solicitor and client costs from the start of the proceedings; solicitor and client costs from the time of the offer; and such costs from such other time as it sees fit. In Victoria (r 26.08(9)) where an identical rule once operated, the rules now provide that where liability but not quantum is in dispute, the plaintiff is entitled to solicitor and client costs only if its offer is of a 'genuine compromise'. Victoria's rule in relation to appeals (r 26.12) gives the court a very broad discretion to take into account the reasonableness of offers.

Elsewhere, a somewhat similar result has sometimes been achieved by requiring that an offer of compromise involves a real compromise. In *Tickell v Trifleska Pty Ltd* (1991) 25 NSWLR 353, the plaintiff's offer was to settle for the whole of the amount claimed, with interest. The plaintiff had subsequently been awarded precisely that. Rogers CJ (Comm D) said (at 355):

> Unless circumstances are wholly exceptional a demand for payment to the plaintiff of everything, to which it may possibly be entitled, hardly falls in the category of the compromise. It is true, as Mr Campbell pointed out, that there are difficulties in cases of a claim for liquidated damages when one is called upon to formulate an offer of compromise. He suggested that it was inconceivable that a court should be required, in the circumstances of Pt 52, r 17(4), to have to decide in each and every case whether an offer represented a bona fide compromise. With respect I do not think it is inconceivable at all. What the court is invited to do is to determine whether in the totality of the circumstances, the offer by the plaintiff represented any element of compromise or whether it was merely, yet another formally stated demand for payment designed simply to trigger the entitlement to payment of costs on an indemnity basis.
>
> It was never in the minds of the draftsmen of the rule, or the members of the Rule Committee responsible for the passing of this rule, that Pt 22 should be utilised simply as a statutory demand which, other circumstances being equal, will automatically entail the payment of costs on an indemnity basis.

See also *Hobartville Stud Pty Ltd v Union Insurance Co Ltd* (1991) 25 NSWLR 358, where the plaintiff successfully claimed $500,000 allegedly due to it under a horse insurance policy. Having initially offered to settle for $500,000 with 15 per cent interest to the date of the offer, it subsequently softened its stance and offered to accept $499,999 in settlement of all the elements of its claim, except for those for interests and costs. This too was held not to amount to an offer of compromise.

However, if a party's case is a strong one, the party may be justified in making an offer close to the best outcome the party could hope for, as illustrated by the following extract:

17.3.46C	**Maitland Hospital v Fisher (No 2)** (1992) 27 NSWLR 721 Court of Appeal (NSW)

[A plaintiff (Fisher) had been awarded $206,090 damages. The defendant appealed. The plaintiff made an offer of compromise of $200,000. Upon the appeal failing, she sought costs from the date of service of the offer on an indemnity basis. The Court of Appeal so ordered.]

Kirby P, Mahoney JA and Samuels AJA (at 724–6): In the present case, the amount by which the respondent offered to compromise her claim, on the appeal, did not fall far short of the judgment entered by Lee AJ. Indeed, it was only $6,090 less than his Honour's judgment. It might have been slightly more if the offer to accept 'costs' of the trial were to be taken as ordinary party and party costs, because no [725] reference was made to the special provision for 'indemnity costs' ordered by Lee AJ.

Although the amount of the deficit is small being only 2.5 per cent of the judgment sum, it is real and not trivial or contemptuous. For a person in the position of the respondent, who was a kitchenmaid when injured in the service of the appellant, $6,090 is a real sum. Furthermore, the respondent would have been advised (correctly in the event) that she stood very little chance of losing her judgment in the appeal. Lee AJ's reasons were careful. On liability they provided two possible bases for recovery, although only one was considered in this Court. Most of the elements in the damages claim were either conceded or uncontested. The amount awarded for past general damages was regarded as 'modest'. Thus, even if a reassessment had been required, it was extremely unlikely that a judgment of much less than that recovered would have been entered. All of this the respondent was probably told. In such circumstances, the offer of compromise was one which realistically assessed the chances of success in the appeal. It offered an inducement (admittedly small) to the appellant against the risks which are inherent in any litigation. Events have borne out the justification of the actual offer made and the wisdom of making it. It is important to stress, however, that a 2.5 per cent compromise is not to be taken as having general precedental significance.

The decision to award or withhold indemnity costs where a plaintiff's settlement offer has been made but not accepted, involves a discretion to be exercised by reference to all of the circumstances of the case, not by applying a fixed mathematical formula.

Professional obligations in the context of the Rules:
Subject to what appears below concerning the operation of the Rules of Court, the respondent is therefore entitled to the order for indemnity costs which she sought. The lesson of this case is that (at least in proceedings of this character) legal practitioners advising parties to proceedings in the Supreme Court will themselves be well advised to consider, including in appeals, the application of Pt 52, r 17 of the Rules.

Saying this does not lend the weight of the Court's authority to the conduct of litigation, any more than it is, as a form of litigious lottery in which a litigant (and those advising it) are subjected unreasonably to an added peril: that of a special costs order. The rule does no more than to oblige litigants, and those advising them, to consider realistically, upon the best information available to them, the prospects of success and the likely outcome of the litigation. Where, in the particular circumstances, the litigant or its advisers misjudge the prospects of success or miscalculate the outcome, their mistake may be warranted on the material which they had available. Alternatively, it may be no more than a miscalculation in a case with large imponderables where the course they took was nonetheless perfectly reasonable. Litigation is inescapably chancy. The purpose of the rule is to put a premium on realistic assessment of cases. It is not to demand perfect foresight which is denied even to the judges. That is why a discretion is retained, under the rule, for the Court to order otherwise than as the rule provides. But the ordinary provision is expected to apply in the ordinary case. It has added a new duty to the functions of legal practitioners advising litigants. It is a duty which is both protective of the interests of litigants and [726] of the public interest in the prompt and economical disposal of litigation. It is the duty of courts, allowing for exceptions in particular cases, to give effect to the purpose of the rule: cf. *Larkin McDonald & Associates v Mahoney* (unreported, QCA, McPherson, Derrington JJ, No 43 of 1991, 24 June 1992, BC9202508).

17.3.47   What is the position where there are several successive offers, such that even early offers are 'better' than the final judgment? This was discussed in *Hillier v Sheather* (1995) 36 NSWLR 414 where a majority of the New South Wales Court of Appeal (Kirby P and Cole J; Mahoney J dissented) held that the date at which a plaintiff becomes liable for a defendant's costs is the date of service of the first offer to be more generous than the subsequent judgment.

In *Ettingshausen v Australian Consolidated Press Ltd* (1995) 38 NSWLR 404, the New South Wales Court of Appeal considered the position where there had been a retrial in which a plaintiff received more than an offer of compromise which he had made prior to the earlier trial.

17.3.48C	**Ettingshausen v Australian Consolidated Press Ltd**
	(1995) 38 NSWLR 404
	Court of Appeal (NSW)

[The plaintiff, who sued for defamation, made an offer of compromise of $85,000 in December 1991, and received an award of $350,000 from a jury in February 1993. On appeal, the matter was sent for retrial. The plaintiff did not renew his offer. The defendant offered $60,000, but the jury subsequently awarded the plaintiff damages of $100,000. The trial judge at the second trial ruled that the plaintiff was not entitled to his costs of the second trial on an indemnity basis, either under the rules, or in the exercise of the court's discretion.]

Gleeson CJ and Priestley JA (at 408–10): The following features of the rules are significant.

First, the subject of an offer of compromise is a claim in proceedings (Pt 22, r 2). In the present case, the claim was for damages for defamation. In accordance with the rules, the appellant's offer to compromise was expressed as an offer to compromise that claim for a certain sum of money plus costs. The concept of the relevant compromise being the compromise of a claim is basic to the rules in question: see Pt 22, rr 2, 3. It is not a compromise of a hearing, or of one round in a bout of litigation. The appellant had only one claim, and it was that which he offered to compromise. The same claim was litigated at the second trial. That claim was only finally heard and determined at the conclusion of the second trial (and, still then, subject to the appeal process).

Secondly, in the present case, the offer, following one of the paths contemplated by the rules, and one frequently used in practice, was open for acceptance for only twenty-eight days after it was made. In the present case, again as frequently happens, the period of twenty-eight days expired a substantial time before the commencement of the first trial. This is of some importance, because Badgery-Parker J was influenced by what he described as: '... the absurd and unjust consequence that a party would be adversely affected by an offer which it was no longer open to that party to accept.'

This consequence, far from being absurd and unjust, is one the Rules quite deliberately contemplate. The fact is that, pursuant to the Rules, it is possible for offers of compromise to be open for acceptance only for a limited period [409] which may expire long before the trial commenced. This is perfectly consistent with the scheme of the Rules, one evident purpose of which is to require parties to litigation to give prompt consideration either to settling, or to taking the various risks of not settling, which now include the costs risks created by the Rules. A great many parties adversely affected by an offer of compromise are adversely affected by an offer no longer open to them to accept.

Thirdly, either party may make more than one offer. As it happens, in the present case the respondent, after the Court of Appeal made its orders, made a fresh offer of compromise, although at a figure substantially below the verdict given for the appellant in the second trial. The ability of the parties to make more than one offer is important, because the forensic situation in a case could change from time to time, and for a variety of reasons. Witnesses might disappear, points of law might be argued and won or lost, or, as in the present case, an appellate court might set aside a judgment entered at first instance.

As was noted above, there is nothing unusual about what happened in the present case. Nor, so far as the operation of the Rules is concerned, would it seem to make any difference that what was involved was a second trial, rather than a reassessment of damages by the Court of Appeal. (Obviously, Badgery-Parker J did not think it would have made any difference.) It is not easy to accept that the drafters of the Rules overlooked these possibilities. They are routine contingencies of litigation.

Badgery-Parker J said:

> It appears to me that (there) are powerful indications that once a trial is had, which, being before a jury continues at least to the point where the judge begins to sum up, the consequences in terms of costs which flow from the making of that offer and the non-acceptance of it are exhausted once that trial comes to an end, whether by verdict or by discharge of the jury without verdict.

The indications to which his Honour was referring are to be found in subr (8) and subr (3) of Pt 22, r 3.

It is important also to note the provisions of Pt 22, r 3(5).

[Offers must be expressed to be open for at least 28 days: Pt 22 subr 3(3). Subrule 3(5) provides that they may be accepted within 28 days unless an event prescribed by subr 3(8) has occurred. The effect of subr (8) is that an offer cannot be accepted once the judge has begun to sum up to a jury or once a judge or Master gives a decision or begins to give reasons for a decision on a judgment.]

The provisions in question are part of a scheme which imposes a strict limit upon the time within which an offer is to be open for acceptance. Subrule (5) identifies certain alternative possibilities, and concludes by providing that an offer may be accepted within whichever is sooner amongst those possibilities.

In that context, it was clearly necessary for the Rules to fix a latest time by which an offer might be accepted. Obviously, it would be absurd to permit an offer to be accepted after a decision had been given in the case in question, even though the offer might only have been made shortly before the decision was given. Accordingly, subr (8) addresses a series of different circumstances, and makes commonsense provision concerning the latest time at which an offer may be accepted.

There is nothing in that which either requires or justifies the conclusion that the consequences of an offer are 'exhausted' once the trial, prior to which the offer was made, comes to an end. As was noted, the offer is made, not in respect of a trial, but in respect of a claim. Depending upon the circumstances of a case, a claim may not be finally heard and determined until after there have been a number of appeals, and, perhaps, a number of trials. Furthermore, as the language of his reasons makes clear, if the point which Badgery-Parker J took from subr (8) is valid, then it must necessarily apply equally to a case where an [410] appellate court reassesses damages as to a case where an appeal is allowed and a new trial is ordered. In truth, this Court routinely reassesses damages on appeal, and is frequently asked to make, and makes, orders for indemnity costs based upon offers of compromise that were made before the original trial.

Kirby P (at 418): [T]hree considerations tell against the construction of the relevant rules urged for the appellant. They argue in favour of the construction adopted by the primary judge.

1. First and most important, is the fact that Pt 52, r 17(4) of the Supreme Court Rules, being meant to operate (as Pt 52, r 17(1) of the Supreme Court [419] Rules indicates) upon an offer of compromise 'in accordance with Pt 22, r 3(5)' incorporates the scheme which Pt 22, r 3 of the Supreme Court Rules establishes. That scheme contemplates a particular kind of offer of compromise, subject to particular time constraints. The time constraints which define the character of the offer of compromise in question are to be found in Pt 22, r 3(8) of the Supreme Court Rules. The particular offer which is contemplated is one which has an ultimate terminating effectiveness as defined by that subrule. But that subrule operates, and is only intended to operate, upon a single trial or proceeding as there defined. In the case of a trial before a jury (as this case was) the time prescribed runs out, at the latest, 'after the Judge begins to sum up to the jury'. Likewise, in the case of an arbitration, it runs out, at the latest, at the 'conclusion of the arbitration hearing'. In another case it terminates where the judicial officer 'gives his decision or begins to give his reasons for decision'. Thus, the scheme of the Rules contemplates that, at the latest, an offer will expire at the point of the conclusion of the particular trial to which the offer is directed. This is consistent with the focus of Pt 52, r 2 of the Supreme Court Rules upon the 'proceedings', as there stated.

The notion that, notwithstanding subr (8), the offer made under Pt 22 of the Supreme Court Rules will endure beyond a first trial to a second trial simply cannot stand with the express terminus listed in Pt 22, r 3(8) of the Supreme Court Rules for the final conclusion of the time within which the offeree may accept the offer. By providing, as was done in subr (7), the drafter made it clear that the offer was intended to operate upon a particular trial or arbitration proceedings and *in no case* beyond the points defined. It could expire earlier. But it could never expire later. The final date of the expiry of the offer thus fixes its character as being an offer which related to the particular trial or proceeding. Badgery-Parker J so held. He was correct;

2. If, from this attention to the language of the Rules, the Court lifts its eyes to their purpose, it is clear that the purpose supports the construction to which the primary judge came. The object of an offer of compromise is to encourage the settlement of 'any claim in the proceeding'. The making of the offer is therefore directed to that objective. The sanctions as to costs, including relevantly indemnity costs, are designed to promote early settlement and to impose consequences upon what is later revealed as an unreasonable refusal to accept a compromise offer. But once a second trial is ordered, the litigious goalposts have changed. It

would take an otherworldly ignorance of the realities of litigation to pretend that an offer of settlement, made before judgment in a first trial, is unaffected by the outcome of that trial. That outcome inevitably becomes a major consideration in any settlement of the claim at or before a second trial. Even where set aside (as the judgment following the jury's verdict in the first trial here was), the outcome cannot be ignored in the practical business of negotiation and settlement of claims. To deny this is to defy the realities of litigation, as it is conducted. The Rules of this Court are designed to work in the real world of such litigation. They do not have a disembodied life which is to be given meaning apart from that reality. Therefore, stretching the language of Pt 22 of the Supreme Court Rules to apply to a case such as the present requires this Court (as it did the primary judge) to interpret the phrase in Pt 52, r 17(4) of the Supreme Court Rules 'obtains ... judgment on the claim to which the offer relates', as meaning no more than 'obtains [for the first time] judgment on the claim to which the offer relates'.

[420] The addition of these words does no violence to the meaning of the subrule. It merely carries into effect the achievement of the purpose of the rule being that of promoting compromised settlement, but upon a given set of premises which have not been altered. A supervening appellate judgment necessarily changes the equation. When these practical considerations as to the intended operation of the rule are borne in mind, the impact of Pt 22, r 3(2) of the Supreme Court Rules becomes all the more potent. To hold a party forever to an offer which has terminated and is no longer available for acceptance, but which continues to hang over the party's head through the meandering vicissitudes of litigation, does not promote the compromised settlement of cases. It may indeed inhibit the making of further offers. Yet further offers are specifically contemplated by Pt 22, r 3(2) of the Supreme Court Rules. I do not believe that the rule makers intended such a capricious operation of the offer of compromise rules. This Court should hold back from giving the rules that construction for there is no requirement to do so and the primary judge rightly rejected it;

3. If there is ambiguity in the meaning of the rules, the Court should favour that construction which best promotes the achievement or the objective of promoting realistic assessments of cases, based upon the changing circumstances which arise from time to time in the course of protracted litigation. Because a party may make more than one offer, the appellant could certainly, following the first jury's verdict, have made a further offer to reflect the changed circumstances. If his offer, before the first verdict, were to accept judgment in the sum of $85,000, can it seriously be thought that he would have offered to accept the same sum after that verdict? If he would not, why should the peril of the litigation continue for ever to rest upon the initial assessment made before a major event occurred in the litigation which altered radically the equation reflecting the perceived worth of the case? The respondent increased its offer. As events proved, it did not do so by a sufficient sum. But it doubled the original offer which it had made before the first verdict. Clearly, it did so out of recognition of the alteration of the prospects which that verdict introduced. The proper operation of the Rules, in such a way as to reflect the real marketplace of litigious bargaining (as distinct from a disembodied, capricious operation of the Rules not to be ascribed to the rulemakers) would require, for a second trial, that parties should be obliged to make new assessments reflecting those changed circumstances and directed to the ultimate objective of this Part of the Rules. This is the sensible compromise of the 'claim in the proceedings' as it then looked — not as it had originally been assessed.

Thus, the proper construction of the Rules, the achievement of their purpose and the avoidance of capricious results frustrating that purpose all point in the direction which Badgery-Parker J took.

I see no inconsistency between this construction of the rules and the practice of this Court, before now, in providing costs on an indemnity basis following the outcome of an appeal. This is because the Court is conducting, not a completely new trial, but a rehearing of the first trial on the papers. If it were to substitute a different judgment for that obtained at the first trial, it is, in effect, specifying the judgment which ought to have been entered in *that* trial.

But that is not the case for the second trial which has its own integrity and purpose. This is illustrated by the present case. The second trial was entirely different from the first. By order of this Court, liability was no longer in issue. [421] The trial was much shorter. It was conducted in a substantially different way. Indeed, for the appellant, it was complained that much of the prejudicial value of the conduct of the *first* trial was lost, inevitably, by the constraints of the *second*. What was involved was not a substitution for the proper judgment of the first trial, but the achievement of an entirely new judgment in the second.

17.3.49   Notes and questions

1. What are the advantages of a rule which entitles a plaintiff to indemnity costs regardless of when the offer is made? How far is this rule to be understood in terms of other aspects of the relevant jurisdiction's rules on offers of compromise?

2. What kinds of factors would you expect a Northern Territory court to take into account in exercising its discretion in relation to plaintiffs' offers under r 26.11 (offers other than in personal injuries cases)? Should courts attempt to evaluate retrospectively the 'worth' of the case, and how might they do it? What, if any, would be the problems if a court were to say that in its opinion, the unsuccessful defendant might reasonably have thought that it had a 35 per cent chance of winning?

3. Suppose you were charged with redrafting the New South Wales rules in the wake of *Ettingshausen*. What, if anything, would you do? What did the court do?

4. The defendant offers $250,000 to settle. The plaintiff rejects the offer. Later, after the offer has expired, the plaintiff realises that the offer was an attractive one as does the defendant. The plaintiff offers to settle for $250,000 and when this offer is rejected, offers $240,000 which is also rejected. The case goes to trial and the plaintiff receives $247,000. Assuming the rules were applied strictly, what costs order would be made in: (a) New South Wales; and (b) Victoria? How likely is it that the presumptive order would be made?

The relationship between the offer of compromise rules and Calderbank offers

17.3.50C	**Pirrotta v Citibank Ltd** (1998) 72 SASR 259 Supreme Court of South Australia (Full Court)

[The plaintiffs sued Citibank, a firm of solicitors, and an employee of the firm in relation to a dispute about securities. The action against Citibank failed and a counterclaim by Citibank succeeded, but the plaintiffs succeeded in their claims against the solicitors. Prior to the trial, they had made a Calderbank offer which, if accepted by the three defendants, would have resulted in the case being disposed of on terms less favourable to the plaintiffs than the terms of the eventual judgment. Accordingly, they sought costs against the solicitors on an indemnity basis. The trial judge awarded costs on a 'party and party' basis and the plaintiffs appealed from this decision. In the course of his judgment, Debelle J discussed the relationship between Calderbank offers and r 41 (which has been superseded by rr 187–188).]

Debelle J (with whom Milhouse and Olsson JJ agreed) (at 266–7): First, although r 41 provides a regime for the making of offers by plaintiffs to compromise actions, it should not be regarded as the only means by which plaintiffs might make such offers. There will obviously be situations which do [267] not fall precisely within the rule. Rule 41 is in terms addressed to litigation between one party and another and thus might not always apply in multi-party litigation or where the litigation is otherwise complex. Thus, regard should, in appropriate circumstances, be had to a *Calderbank* letter for the purpose of determining whether an order for indemnity costs should be made.

Secondly, it is undesirable to permit a regime which differs in important respects from that contemplated by the Rules of Court and imposes more onerous obligations. Thus, while recognising that the Rules do not provide for every occasion and that there are circumstances which justify the writing of a *Calderbank* letter, the terms in which such a letter are couched should, as a general rule and so far as is reasonably practicable, conform to the regime in r 41. ...

Thirdly, given the terms of r 41.04, a *Calderbank* letter might result in an order as to costs on a basis similar to that provided in r 41.04. One question to be determined is whether a plaintiff should have his costs on a solicitor and client basis for the whole of the action or only from a reasonable time after the offer has been made. There is much to be said for the latter view but I do not express a concluded opinion. Another question is whether any presumption should operate in favour of a plaintiff who made a *Calderbank* offer. The effect of r 41.04 is that costs will be ordered on a solicitor and client basis unless the court thinks it proper to order otherwise. To that extent, the rule expresses a prima facie presumption that it will operate in favour of a plaintiff who has been awarded a monetary sum higher than he had been prepared to accept.

17.3.51   Notes and questions

1. One reason why the Full Court dismissed the appeal in *Pirrotta* was that the offer allowed less time for acceptance than the time prescribed by the rules.

2. Courts in other jurisdictions have also accepted that account can be taken of a Calderbank offer, notwithstanding that the relevant rules enable the making of offers of compromise. Recent examples include: *Aircraft Technicians of Australia Pty Ltd v St Clair; St Clair v Timtalla Pty Ltd* [2011] QCA 188; *Miwa Pty Ltd v Siantan Properties Pty Ltd (No 2)* [2011] NSWCA 344; *Australian Executor Trustees Ltd v Propell National Valuers (WA) Pty Ltd (No 2)* [2011] FCA 966. Moreover, even when the offer of compromise rules make no provision for the awarding of indemnity costs to a defendant, such costs may be awarded in a case where a Calderbank offer has been made: *Stipanov v Mier (No 2)* [2006] VSC

424. (What is the justification for this?) In *Miwa Pty Ltd v Siantan Properties Pty Ltd (No 2)* [2011] NSWCA 344, at [22]–[23], Basten J, with whom McColl and Campbell JJ agreed, noted that courts had accepted the possibility that the Court of Appeal might take account of a Calderbank offer in a case where the offeror was unsuccessful at first instance but successful on appeal. But he also noted that counsel had cited no cases where courts had made a more favourable costs order in such a case, and declined to do so in the instant case.

3. What are the gaps in the offer of compromise rules where Calderbank offers might be appropriate? See M Ellis, 'The Cost of Compromising: Offers of Compromise and Calderbank offers' (2008) 17 *J Jud Admin* 253 at 267–9 who discusses the relative attractions of the two kinds of offers to plaintiffs and defendants, noting that Calderbank offers may provide a basis for defendants to win indemnity costs in cases where they had an obviously strong case.

4. What is the effect of offer of compromise rules on the type of settlement reached, and on the likelihood of settlement? L Bebchuk and H Chang have discussed this in relation to the relatively unsophisticated offer of compromise scheme which applies in the United States Federal Courts: 'The Effect of Offer-of-Settlement Rules on the Terms of Settlement' (1998) 28 *J Leg Studies* 461. Do the refinements to be found in the Australian rules make any difference to their analysis? As to the rules' effect on the likelihood of settlement, see A Farmer and P Pecorino, 'Bargaining with Informative Offers: An Analysis of Final-Offer Arbitration' (1998) 27 *Leg Studies* 415. Is it a relevant difference that they are discussing final offer arbitration rather than offers made prior to trial?

17.3.52 Worked example

1. P sues D for breach of conflict, claiming $1.5m. In its defence, D pleaded that it did not admit that there was a contract in the terms alleged by the plaintiff, and further said that if P suffered loss (which was denied), the loss was far less than claimed. After discovery, P wrote to D offering to settle if D paid it $1.3m and its costs to date, as assessed. D rejected the offer, and made a counter-offer of $300,000, and P's costs to date as assessed. P rejected this offer. The trial judge found in favour of the defendant on the liability issue, noting that her decision reflected a recent High Court decision that had strengthened the defendant's legal case, and observing that her decision in relation to the facts had not been an easy one. The judge also observed that even if the alleged breach had been made out, she doubted whether damages would have been more than a fraction of what P had claimed. What costs order would the judge probably make if the offer was (a) an offer of compromise which formally complied with the rules, and (b) a Calderbank offer?

D has been completely successful, and even in the absence of an offer of compromise, would be presumptively entitled to its costs on a 'party and party' basis or equivalent. The question is whether it would be presumptively entitled to its costs on a more generous basis. Under the offer of compromise rules of most jurisdictions, it would not. The exceptions are New South Wales and the Federal Court, which contemplate the awarding of costs on an indemnity basis to D. Under the New South Wales rules, the offer appears to satisfy r 42.15(1). But it must be an offer of compromise. On the facts given, it may constitute such an offer. It makes some allowance for the possibility that P could have won, and for the possibility that, if successful, P would have been awarded considerable damages. It might, however, be an offer which is not worth as much as the 'expected value' a dispassionate observer would attach to P's case. This would not be decisive against D. *Maitland Hospital v Fisher (No 2)* (see **17.3.28C** and **17.3.46C**) turned on its own facts, but it suggests judicial receptivity to the use of indemnity costs orders to encourage settlement, and to the principle that the presumption prevails 'in the ordinary case' which, subject to one qualification, this seems to be. Complicating the picture is the reference to the recent High Court decision. If it preceded the offer, it would be irrelevant. If it post-dated the offer, the offer would be correspondingly less generous. Assuming the offer can be treated as an offer of compromise, P gets its costs on an indemnity basis from the beginning of the day following the offer, and on the ordinary basis until then: r 42.15(2).

Under the Federal Court rules, the question is whether the applicant unreasonably failed to accept the offer: r 25.14(b). This appears to be a more demanding test than the New South Wales test, and is correspondingly less likely to be satisfied. It is not necessarily unreasonable to refuse a reasonable offer. Assuming the non-acceptance was found to be unreasonable, D would get its costs on a 'party and party' basis until 11 am on the second business day after service of the offer, and on an indemnity basis thereafter.

2.   Claims, defences and offers are as in question 1, but P is awarded $1.38m damages. What costs orders would be made (a) under offer of compromise rules, and (b) following a Calderbank offer?

P has been awarded damages, and is therefore presumptively entitled to its costs on at least a 'party and party' basis. It is also presumptively entitled to indemnity costs since it has received an award more favourable to itself than the offer it made to D: FCR 25.14(3); NSW r 42.14; NT r 26.08(2); Qld r 360; Tas r 289; Vic r 26.08(2)(b); WA O 24A r 10(4). (Except under the FCR, it suffices that the award is *as* favourable, but this is not material here). The rule is presumptive only, and it is arguable that the offer was not particularly generous, once allowance is made for the possibility that D might have succeeded on liability. But the excess of the award over the offer suggests that the offer can be treated as involving genuine compromise. If so, P gets its costs on an indemnity basis from the day beginning after the offer (NSW, Vic, WA) or 11 am on the second business day after the offer (FC), and on an ordinary or 'party and party' basis until then. In the Northern Territory, Queensland and Tasmania, P presumptively gets all its costs on an indemnity basis.

It is unlikely that P would be entitled to costs on an indemnity basis in the event of having made a Calderbank offer. First, albeit to an unknown extent, it would have been reasonable to reject the offer, if D had some basis for believing that it might succeed on the liability issue. Second, given that P was awarded an amount not much greater than the amount it offered to accept, it was not unreasonable for D not to accept the offer.

FORMALISING SETTLEMENT AGREEMENTS

Consequences of formalising settlement

17.4.1   Settlements can be formalised in various ways with various consequences. These are discussed in *Green v Rozen* [1955] 1 WLR 741, a case which highlights the complexities of this issue, but which has in some respects been rejected by Australian courts.

17.4.2C   **Green v Rozen**
                                    [1955] 1 WLR 741
                    High Court of England and Wales, Queen's Bench Division

---

[The parties had agreed to dispose of a matter in a particular way. The terms were entered on the lawyers' briefs: 'By consent, all proceedings stayed on terms indorsed on briefs. Liberty to apply.' No court order had been sought. When the defendant defaulted on payments, the plaintiff sought an order that the defendant pay the amount owing.]

Slade J (at 743–6): There are various ways in which an action can be disposed of when terms of settlement are arrived at when the action comes on for trial, or in the course of the hearing. I have had experience of at least five methods of disposing of an action in such circumstances. They are not exhaustive. One can in an appropriate case, as was done in one of the cases to which Mr Frankenburg referred, get the terms of the compromise made a rule of court provided it appears that one of the terms of the compromise is that the terms shall be made an order of the court. But I am dealing with methods of disposing of an action of a less formal character than that. The first method which I have found to be very useful where the terms of compromise consist of an agreement by the defendant to pay a specified sum [744] of money by specified instalments on specified dates is to give judgment for the total amount agreed to be paid coupled with a stay of execution so long as the instalments are paid in accordance with the terms agreed. I am sometimes asked to give judgment by consent and sometimes by the defendants submitting to it, and I have pointed out when invited to give judgment by consent that section 27 of the Debtors Act 1869, (it also appears in the Annual Practice, 1955, 2007) requires that a consent judgment shall be registered at the Central Office within 21 days and if it is not so registered it will be void against the defendant's creditors. In the result, therefore, the form usually adopted is for the defendant to submit to judgment in open court.

The second method, which is no doubt more appropriate when the terms of settlement are not so straightforward as the mere payment of an agreed sum of money by specified instalments, is to secure an order of the court made by consent that the plaintiff and the defendant shall do the things which they have respectively engaged themselves to do by the terms of settlement. In such a case the order would take this form. There would be the title and the preamble, and then the order would recite, the terms having been agreed between the parties: 'It is ordered that (a) the defendant do,' etc, 'the plaintiff do,' etc, making each of the agreed terms an order of the court that it shall be carried out.

The third method I have known is what has become known as the Tomlin form of order, a form suggested by Tomlin J: [1927] WN 290. The Annual Practice, 1965 at page 2007 says: 'Where an action is stayed by consent on terms scheduled, the terms cannot be enforced on an application to commit or attach, but an injunction or an order for specific performance must first be obtained;' and it cites for the authority of that statement of practice: *Dashwood v Dashwood* (1927) 64 LJNC 131. Then it says (ibid) 'After this decision Tomlin J stated that in future when an action was proposed to be stayed on agreed terms to be scheduled to the order, the order should be as follows' — this is the Tomlin form of order — 'And the plaintiff and defendant having agreed to the terms set forth in the schedule hereto, it is ordered that all further proceedings in this action be stayed' — now these are the important words — 'except for the purpose of carrying such terms into effect. Liberty to apply as to carrying such terms into effect.' I understand from the chief associate that some doubt exists as to how far the Tomlin form of order will enable the terms set out in the order to be enforced by the court ...

[745] The fourth method I have come across is an order of the court made by consent staying all further proceedings in the action upon the terms agreed and indorsed on counsels' briefs. In that method there is an order of the court staying all further proceedings, but in the fifth method, that adopted in the present case, there is no order of the court at all, the court merely being told by counsel that the case has been settled upon the terms indorsed on counsels' briefs. That method I have known to be supplemented by a request for leave to withdraw the record, and I think in the case of a trial by jury a request for the withdrawal of a juror, although I believe that in the latter case the action can be set down and reheard if the terms are not complied with.

It will perhaps emphasize which is the easiest method of disposing of an action to consider what steps can be taken in each case to enforce the terms if they are not complied with. The first one seems to be simplicity itself. The court has already given judgment and the stay of execution lasts only so long as the agreed terms are complied with. If there is a failure to comply with them the party who suffers merely has to proceed to levy execution.

In the second case, the court has made an order in the terms I have indicated, that the plaintiff do so and so, the defendant do so and so, and if the plaintiff or the defendant, as the case may be, fails to carry out the court's order it is only necessary for application to be made to the court and the court will enforce it, what each party is to do or refrain from doing being part of the order itself.

The third case is the Tomlin form of order with which I have already dealt, and parties who choose that form of order may, if the terms are not complied with, find contentions raised against the enforcement of it, the nature of which I have already indicated.

In the fourth case the court, at the request of the parties, has made an absolute and unqualified order for a stay of all further [746] proceedings. I say 'absolute and unqualified' in contradiction to the form of order where it is qualified by the words 'save for the purpose of carrying the terms into effect.' Parties who wish to adopt the fourth method would be wise before doing so to read the note which appears at the top of page 3182 of the Annual Practice, 1955. Under the rubric 'Effect of a stay of proceedings' it says: 'Two views may be taken: first, that it is a discontinuance, and therefore cannot be removed. Secondly, that it is not equivalent to a discontinuance, but may be removed if proper grounds shown.' If you are anxious to resolve an interesting point of law as to which of those two schools of thought is correct, you could not do better than adopt the fourth method.

The fifth method, which is the only one I propose to decide, is the one adopted in the present case. The court has made no order of any kind whatsoever, and having considered such authorities as I have been able to find, I arrive at the conclusion that in those circumstances the court has no further jurisdiction in respect of the original cause of action, because it has been superseded by the new agreement between the parties to the action, and if the terms of the new agreement are not complied with the injured party must seek his remedy upon the new agreement.

17.4.3   Tomlin orders are discussed in *Horizon Technologies International v Lucky Wealth Consultants Ltd* [1992] 1 WLR 25. In that case, a dispute was settled by deed. By agreement, a Tomlin order was made, with those provisions relating to the defendant's obligations to make payments to the plaintiff being incorporated in the schedule. The defendant failed to make a payment, and the plaintiff applied for final judgment on the amount owing. The defendant sought to rely on a clause in the deed which was not referred to in the schedule. At first instance, he was held entitled to rely on the clause (assuming the requisite facts could be established). On appeal, the Privy Council reversed the appeal court's decision, Sir Maurice Casey saying (at [29]):

> Counsel informed their Lordships that there is no direct authority in England or Hong Kong for the proposition that a party to a Tomlin order, faced with a claim to enforce the schedule, may rely as a defence on contractual rights not included in that schedule. It is, of course, a feature of such orders that the schedule forming the basis of the stay of proceedings is not part of the order: it is simply a record of the compromise reached between the parties.

The present nature and scope of the Tomlin order is fully set out in the following passage from *Atkin's Court Forms*, 2nd ed,1988, vol 23, p 197:

> A form of consent order commonly found in the Chancery Division where the parties are sui juris is the Tomlin order, in which the terms agreed between the parties are set out in a schedule and all further proceedings in the action are stayed except for the purpose of giving effect to the terms, for which purpose liberty to apply is given. The terms are not part of the order, and if a term is not observed by a party, application under the liberty to apply will usually be necessary to give effect to it: *Dashwood v Dashwood* [1927] WN 276, per Tomlin J. If by a term a party is to pay a [30] sum of money to another party and does not carry it out, application must be made for an order for payment to enable judgment to be entered and execution to issue. It should be particularly noted that if by one of the terms a party gives an undertaking to do, or to refrain from doing, something, the undertaking is not an undertaking given to the court: it is merely an agreement between the parties. Terms scheduled to a Tomlin order represent an arrangement between the parties, and the court is not concerned with approving them although it may properly offer suggestions upon them if it appears to the court that they may cause some difficulty: *Noel v Becker* [1971] 1 WLR 355. The terms need not be within the ambit of the original dispute but the court will refuse to enforce terms which are too vague or insufficiently precise.
>
> Accordingly it will be appreciated that the defendant's attempt to invoke the terms of the deed cannot be rejected on the simple ground that the schedule is to be treated as the final order of the court. However, it is clear that as a record of the parties' agreement it is unambiguous and self-contained; the only reference to the deed is in paragraph (iv) which provides that any breach of its terms will accelerate payment of the total. The schedule does not incorporate or refer to any other provisions of the deed and this was regarded as a powerful factor by the Court of Appeal in support of its view that they were separate and independent documents.

He then turned to the construction of the deed, noting the provision that the 'terms set out herein are interdependent on each other', and finding that this was intended to apply both to those clauses which appeared in the Tomlin order and to those which did not. He continued (at [31]):

> Counsel rightly accepted that the deed has not been superseded by the Tomlin order and is still effective among the parties. They also accepted (as did the Court of Appeal) that a party

could seek a remedy by independent action in respect of any default thereunder, a declaration and injunction being mentioned as appropriate in this case. The existence of such independent remedies under the deed which might enable the defendant to resist the plaintiff's claim suggests a degree of artificiality in the proposition that the terms of that document cannot be used directly as a defence, in the way the defendant now seeks to do.

The parties entered into this deed to resolve the complex situation which had developed among them. As part of that settlement the defendant was to pay the amounts set out in the schedule. That schedule is clearly an integral part of the deed, but put, as it were, in parenthesis to take advantage of the Tomlin order procedure for summary judgment, so that the payments could be quickly and cheaply enforced. In their Lordships' opinion, the segregation of those items for that purpose does not remove them from the operation and effect of the rest of the deed. The whole of that document could have been incorporated in the schedule, but to do so would have been unwieldy and unnecessary. Sensibly, the parties' advisors put in only those terms which were most appropriate for summary enforcement. Nevertheless, as part of the deed, they remain subject to all its provisions. Accordingly it is open to the defendant to raise an allegation of default under clause 7 as a possible defence to the plaintiff's claim to enforce the order.

17.4.4C   Roberts v Gippsland Agricultural and Earthmoving Contracting Co Pty Ltd
[1956] VLR 555
Supreme Court of Victoria, Full Court

[Roberts had been involved in three separate actions with the respondent (the company) and two other parties. These disputes had been settled by an agreement between all the parties. All the parties to the agreement but Roberts had done what they had agreed to do. After the multi-partite agreement, Roberts and the company agreed to vary the terms of the agreement as it applied as between them. Roberts subsequently defaulted. The company then applied for judgment in accordance with the agreement. It was successful, and Roberts appealed to the Full Court. At issue was the question of whether the court could hear the matter as a motion in the original proceeding, or whether new proceedings were required.]

Smith J (at 564–6): [His Honour discussed the jurisdiction to make orders in these circumstances, noting that there were circumstances in which, prior to the Judicature Act, Chancery had been willing to make orders enforcing settlements. He concluded that the Judicature Act 1873 s 24(7) and Supreme Court Act 1928 (Vic) s 61(7) (which embodied it) 'should be construed liberally'. He continued:]

It is necessary, however, for the sake of clarity, to consider separately what has been the effect of the introduction of the new [post-Judicature Act] system in relation to actions in respect of matters formerly within the jurisdiction of the Court of Chancery, and what has been its effect in relation to common law actions.

In relation to the former class of actions the resulting position would appear to be as follows —

(i)   The Court will now enforce the agreement of compromise upon motion in the action whenever the circumstances are such that it would have been enforced in a corresponding manner in the old Court of Chancery.

(ii)   In addition, the agreement may be so enforced notwithstanding the fact that it involves matters extraneous to the action, and notwithstanding that there is a substantial question raised as to the terms or validity or enforceability of the agreement, provided that the Court is clearly satisfied that justice can be done under the summary procedure. At least this is so where all that the Court needs to order for the purpose of enforcing performance upon just terms is a stay of proceedings or a dismissal of the action or some relief claimed in the action.

In deciding whether justice can be done under the summary procedure the Court, of course, needs to consider a variety of matters involving questions of degree. These, I think, must include the extent to which extraneous matters are involved, how substantial are the questions to be determined, to what extent questions of credibility are likely to arise, and whether pleadings and discovery may be desirable.

The view that the jurisdiction may now be more freely exercised to the extent I have indicated is supported, I consider, by the provisions of sec 61(7), coupled with two further considerations. One is that [565] under the Judicature Act system the right to relief is not ordinarily affected by the absence of parties interested, so long as justice can be done without joining them. The other is that the force of the view that trial on affidavit is unsatisfactory is greatly reduced when cross-examination of the deponents is freely allowed, as it now is: cf. *Dawson v Newsome* (1860) 2 Giff 272 and in relation generally to the views which have been stated reference may be made to the following cases in addition to authorities already referred to: *Johnston v Boyd* (1885) 6 ALT 236; *Baker v Blaker* (1886) 55 LT 723; *Vale v Vale* (1899) 5 ALR (CN) 65; *Swain v Reynolds* (1895) 21 VLR 150; *Aiken v Aiken* [1941] VLR 124.

Two further points may be mentioned. First, if the action has been stayed or struck out, then it is necessary that the stay should be lifted, or the action reinstated as an action for trial, before the agreement is enforced on motion in the action; cf. *Re Hearn* (1913) 108 LT 452; *Practice Note* [1927] WN 290; *Aiken v Aiken* (supra). And once an action has been stayed without qualification there may be difficulty in having the stay removed: see *Green v Rozen* [1955] 2 All ER 797; but see also *MacCabe v Joynt* [1901] 2 IR 115. Secondly, though the fact that the agreement expressly stipulates that it shall be made a rule of Court, or that it shall be enforced by order in the action, is still, I think, an important consideration in determining whether the summary procedure should be adopted, the Court is not bound to give effect to such an agreement. It has a discretion as to whether it will do so, which appears to be wide enough to enable it to give effect to any matter of such a nature as would afford a defence in an action for specific performance: see *Neale v Lennox* [1902] AC 465; *Lewis v Lewis* (1890) 45 Ch D 281; *Shepherd v Robinson* [1919] 1 KB 474.

The next question to be considered is whether the introduction of the Judicature Act system has had the effect of making the principles that have been stated applicable in common law actions.

The answer to this question must, I think, depend primarily upon the effect to be given to sec 61(7) of the Supreme Court Act 1928. I have already indicated that in my view that provision should be liberally construed with a view to effectuating the purpose to which it is directed of avoiding multiplicity of legal proceedings, and it seems clear that to construe it as having no application in relation to the summary enforcement of compromises in common law actions would involve restricting its operation to an extent for which considerations of justice could provide no warrant. The better view appears to me, therefore, to be that a claim for summary enforcement cannot be excluded from the category of claims for relief 'properly brought forward' in the 'cause or matter' merely because the claim is made in a common law action. But if that view be once accepted, then some principles must be found or devised to determine the limits within which summary enforcement ought to be granted in such actions. And it appears to me that the natural and proper course to adopt is to apply, so far as they can be applied, the same principles that are applicable to the summary enforcement of compromises in actions of an equitable nature. In support of this view it may be observed that the principles to be found in the authorities relating to actions and suits of an equitable nature appear to have been treated as applicable to the summary enforcement of compromises in winding-up proceedings: see *In re Gaudet Frères Steamship Co* (1879) 12 Ch D 882; in a probate suit: see *Graves v Graves* (1893) 69 LT 420; and possibly in a suit for judicial separation: see *Smythe v Smythe* (1887) 18 QBD 544; *Howard v Howard* (1897) 77 LT 140. And it may be that support is provided, too, by the provision in sec 62(6) of the Supreme Court Act 1928 that in cases of conflict the rules of equity shall prevail.

[566] For these reasons I think that the true view is that where an application for the summary enforcement of a compromise is made in a common law action the Court should apply, so far as they are capable of application, the same principles as would be applied if the action were of an equitable nature.

[His Honour then considered some authority which appeared to be inconsistent with his analysis, and concluded that the circumstances of this case were such that it was appropriate that the agreement be summarily enforced. **Lowe CJ** and **O'Bryan J** agreed.]

17.4.5C   General Credits (Finance) Pty Ltd v Fenton Lake Pty Ltd
[1985] 2 Qd R 6
Supreme Court of Queensland

[The plaintiff sought an injunction restraining the dealing with a ship and rectification of the register of ships. The parties negotiated a settlement of the matter and agreed by deed that certain things be done and orders be made by consent. Most of the terms were carried out but a disagreement as to payment of stamp duty led to delay in completion of the terms and the defendants claimed the deed had been terminated due to the plaintiff's repudiation by conduct. By notice of motion the plaintiff sought an order that the register be rectified.]

McPherson J (at 9): [I]t was at one time correct to say that an agreement of compromise embodying matters going beyond the scope of the action was enforceable only in separate proceedings and not in the original action itself. By requiring that, in every cause pending before it, the court should grant all such remedies as the parties appeared entitled to, so that as far as possible all matters in controversy between them might be finally determined and multiplicity of legal proceedings avoided, s 4(8) of the Judicature Act of 1876 (Qld) enlarged the circumstances in which a compromise might be enforced by order in the action ... The decision in *Green v Rozen* may represent a reversion to earlier doctrine ... But the wider view ... seems likely to prevail in Australia.

... Even though it may involve matters extraneous to the action, an agreement compromising the action may be summarily enforced by application in the action provided that the court is 'clearly satisfied' that justice can be done under the summary procedure ... Whether justice can be done requires consideration of a variety of matters involving ... 'Questions of degree', and including the extent to which extraneous matters are involved, how substantial are the questions to be determined, to what extent questions of credibility are likely to arise, and whether pleadings and discovery may be desirable.

[His Honour considered that this was a case in which it was appropriate to enforce the terms of the compromise summarily on motion in the action. The question to be decided depended entirely upon proper inferences to be drawn from documents and correspondence. The compromise agreement dealt with matters beyond the scope of the action, but all those matters had already been attended to. The motion therefore sought only orders which had been claimed in the original action.]

Infants and people under a legal disability

17.4.6 Where a person under a disability brings an action claiming money or damages, no settlement or compromise is valid unless sanctioned by a judge or, in Queensland, the Public Trustee: FCR r 9.70; ACT r 282; Civil Procedure Act 2005 (NSW) s 76; NT r 15.08; Public Trustee Act 1978 (Qld) s 59; SA r 257; Tas r 299(1) (subject to the Guardianship and Administration Act 1995); Vic r 15.08; WA O 70 r 10(1).

17.4.7C	**Fowler v Gray**
	[1982] Qd R 334
	Supreme Court of Queensland

[This case dealt with a request that the Master sanction a compromise of an action for damages on behalf of the plaintiff, who had suffered spastic quadriplegia and brain damage following a severe injury.]

Master Lee QC (at 349–51): [T]he court has a special responsibility for the welfare of persons under a legal disability. They lack full legal capacity, they are incapable of waiving their rights, and they cannot give a discharge to the defendant under the 'agreement' unless it is sanctioned by the court ... The court is, in reality, a *persona designata*, vested with responsibility of protecting the interests of the person under a legal disability. If the compromise is sanctioned, agreement entered into between the parties has legal effect insofar as that person is concerned, and binds him. The court is not determining a *lis inter partes*. It does not try issues in dispute nor does it arrive at a decision as at a trial. It is only concerned whether, in all of the circumstances of a particular case as presented, the settlement is reasonable and for the benefit of the person under the disability. If that opinion is formed the compromise takes effect as in any other case between persons of full legal capacity. This shows that care should be taken when a sanction is sought. The next question concerns the material to be produced. The nature of the material to be placed before the Court when a sanction of a compromise of an infant's claim for damages is sought when the action comes before the Court was clearly laid down by WB Campbell J in *Madden v Hough* [1969] QWN 7. In my opinion, such considerations are equally applicable to all persons under a legal disability, and in [350] respect of whom a sanction is sought. That term in s 59 of the Act includes persons not of full age as well as those not of full mental capacity or having the status of an incapacitated person under the Act: *Karvelas v Chikirou* (1976) 26 FLR 381 at 382.

In *Madden v Hough* (supra) His Honour referred to the 'long established practice' which should always be followed. There should be informed assent by the next friend or guardian by affidavit; and affidavit by the solicitor who, after considering all relevant aspects of the case and counsel's advices, is able to state that with respect to liability and quantum he believes the compromise to be beneficial for the person under a disability; counsel's opinion should be to the like effect. Facts and circumstances as to liability, if any, should be clearly stated: *Karvelas v Chikirou (supra)* at 383; there should also be up-to-date medical and other relevant opinions; as to quantum, Cairns, *Australian Civil Procedure* (1981) at 389 states:

> Once the Court is satisfied that questions of liability have been properly disposed of, it turns its attention to quantum. The nature of the injury, and the loss and damage, both present and prospective, must be fully explained. From the information the Court must be able to assess whether the amount offered is adequate for recompense for the alleged loss and damage. Particular attention is given to settlements — where there is a discrepancy between what is offered and the loss suffered. There are many perfectly adequate reasons for such a discrepancy. What must be explained to the Court is that reason. In addition, the Court must be able to measure the risk of proceeding against the certainty of accepting settlement. If the risk of proceeding outweighs the apparent disadvantage of accepting what appears to be an inadequate offer, then acceptance of a compromise is a preferable course.

> It is appropriate for the parties to a compromise to take into account interest which a Court might award under s 72 of the Common Law Practice Act 1867–1978, if the action was tried and a judgment given. All heads of damages past and future should be properly investigated and considered. This of course includes past economic loss including, if applicable, medical and nursing care and the like, including any sums properly claimable under the principle in *Griffiths v Kerkemeyer* (1976–7) 139 CLR 161, as well as future economic loss, if any, pain, suffering and loss of amenities, and needs which would not otherwise have existed: *Teubner v Humble* (1962–3) 108 CLR 491 at 505, which of course includes, if applicable, future nursing care, future hospitalisation and the like, as well as needs for his comfort and his well being. In a particular case, unless it is readily apparent to the Court that proper consideration has been given to all likely heads of damage appropriate to the particular plaintiff, the Court is not in a position to [351] say whether the settlement proposed is reasonable or not in the circumstances.

Entering consent judgments

17.4.8   All jurisdictions provide procedures for embodying an agreement in a judgment or order. Procedures vary slightly from jurisdiction to jurisdiction: HCR r 8.04; FCR r 39.11; (ACT) rr 1611–12; (NSW) Pt 20 Div 5; (NT) r 59.06; (Qld) r 666; (SA) r 227; (Tas) rr 340, 341; (Vic) rr 59.06, 59.07; (WA) O 42 rr 7, 8.

DISCONTINUANCE AND WITHDRAWAL

17.5.1   Plaintiffs who wish to cease prosecuting their case are normally permitted to discontinue. One might wonder why there should be any limits on their right to do so, and in particular, why defendants should ever be concerned about a plaintiff's decision to discontinue. In general, defendants will have no objections to discontinuance, subject, perhaps, to recompense for costs incurred up to the time of the discontinuance. However, there may be some circumstances in which a defendant's interests would have been better served by the action continuing as the cases extracted below show.

The rules

17.5.2 The rules with respect to discontinuance vary slightly with respect to when cases can be discontinued. In the High Court, the Australian Capital Territory, Queensland, Tasmania and Western Australia, where there are pleadings, the plaintiff may discontinue the whole or any part of the action before receipt of a defence. Even after receipt of the defence, so long as the plaintiff has taken no other step in the proceedings (other than making any interlocutory application), the plaintiff may discontinue in Tasmania. Otherwise, discontinuance is by leave of the court (HCR r 27.10.2 (before filing of defence); Qld r 304; Tas r 376; WA O 23 rr 1, 2) or with the consent of the other parties: HCR r 27.10.2; Qld r 304(2). Even in the absence of such provisions, there is nothing the courts could do if parties agreed to treat an action as discontinued. The Queensland rules (r 304(3)) also require consent where there was more than one plaintiff or where there was a counterclaim against the plaintiff. The Queensland rules (r 304(1)(b)) apply in a similar way to applications, with the cut-off point being the first affidavit in reply. The Tasmanian rules (r 377) provide that proceedings not commenced by writ may be discontinued by consent or by leave of the court.

In the Federal Court (r 26.12(2)(a)), Northern Territory (NT rr 25.02, 25.03) and Victoria (rr 25.02, 25.03), a person making a claim can discontinue a claim at any time prior to the return date fixed in the originating application (Federal Court) or the close of pleadings (if there are pleadings): Northern Territory, Victoria. In Federal Court cases with no pleadings, plaintiffs can discontinue without leave until the first directions hearing. Otherwise, plaintiffs may discontinue with the consent of the other parties or by leave of the court. Where discontinuance is by consent, the notice of discontinuance must bear the other parties' consent: FCR r 26.12(3); NT r 25.04; Vic r 25.04. On when pleadings close, see *Packer v Meagher* [1984] 3 NSWLR 486. In New South Wales (rr 12.1, 12.2), a plaintiff may discontinue at any time before trial with consent or by leave of the court. In the Australian Capital Territory, discontinuance is permitted until the time when the court sets a hearing date (in cases where there is no requirement that a certificate of readiness be filed), and until either the filing of the certificate or a direction that a proceeding be given a listing hearing. Otherwise, discontinuance is by permission of the court or agreement of the other parties: r 1160. In South Australia (r 107(3)), a plaintiff may discontinue at any time before the court has ordered that the matter proceed to trial, after which discontinuance is permitted by consent or with the permission of the court.

17.5.3 One co-plaintiff to a joint cause of action cannot withdraw as of course: *Henty v Henty* (1899) 25 VLR 151 (and see ACT r 1160(3); Qld r 304(3)). In that case, three plaintiffs instituted an action against a number of defendants. In the case of one of them, the decision to institute proceedings had been taken on her behalf by her attorney. She subsequently refused to have anything to do with the action, either by withdrawing or by assisting the other plaintiffs. They sought to have her struck out as a plaintiff and made a defendant. In the course of his judgment, Holroyd J said (at 153):

> There is no rule in my opinion in our Judicature Rules which is applicable to a case of this kind. Order XXVI r 1 which has been referred to, does not touch the difficulty that arises here at all. As far as I can see, that rule, permitting the plaintiff to discontinue, means the plaintiff, or the

plaintiffs in a case together, however many there may be, if they act unitedly. If more than one or one alone, they or he may discontinue in the manner stated. Under that rule one of plaintiff only out of several plaintiffs cannot discontinue the action on his own account.

His Honour made the order requested. The parties were represented by six barristers (one with a junior) and five firms of solicitors. Costs of six guineas were awarded.

17.5.4C   **In Re Mathews; Oates v Mooney**
[1905] 2 Ch 460
High Court of England and Wales, Chancery Division

[A defendant reached an agreement with a co-plaintiff whereby her claims against him were to be settled (for a dubiously inadequate consideration). He and his co-defendant sought to have the action stayed as between the co-plaintiff and them or, alternatively, an order that her name be removed from the record.]

Swinfen Eady J (at 463–4): It has been pointed out in several cases that it is not a matter of course to allow a co-plaintiff to withdraw and have his name struck out at any time. The general rule is that where co-plaintiffs disagree the name of one is struck out as plaintiff and added as defendant. But it is stated in *Daniell's Chancery Practice*, 7th ed vol i, p 224, that 'An order to strike out a name of a co-plaintiff will not be made as a matter of course even on the terms of giving security for costs.' In *Attorney-General v Cooper* (1837) 3 My & Cr 258 information was filed at the instance of several relators, and on their application an order [464] of course was obtained for amending the information by striking out the names of all the relators except one ...

[The Lord Chancellor] discussed the question whether there was any ground for the application that the names of some of the relators should be struck out. He said that the relators must shew 'that justice will not be done, or that the suit cannot be so conveniently prosecuted unless the alteration is made.' He then examined the circumstances, and refused the application. Another case to the same effect is *Brown v Sawer* (1841) 3 Beav 598 which shews that where there are two co-plaintiffs one cannot sever as of right. There the two co-plaintiffs had duly authorized the institution of the suit. One of them by a written notice to his solicitor withdrew from the suit, and forbade his taking any further steps therein. The other co-plaintiff moved for liberty to amend by striking out the name of the co-plaintiff who had revoked his authority as plaintiff, and adding it as defendant. That was objected to. The Master of the Rolls said: 'I think I must make the order ... The plaintiff who had, in this case, given written instructions to his solicitor, afterwards revokes the authority, and prevents the other plaintiff going on with the suit. The case is within the words of the case of *Attorney-General v Cooper* 3 My & Cr 258, 261: the suit cannot be prosecuted unless the alteration is made, and therefore justice "will not be done unless the alteration is made"'. The Master of the Rolls made the order asked for on the terms of security being given for the original defendant's costs.

17.5.5   Even where plaintiffs appear to have a right to discontinue, purported discontinuances may be disallowed if the case amounts to an abuse of process, and discontinuance would deprive a defendant of an opportunity which would otherwise be open to it.

17.5.6C   **Castanho v Brown & Root (UK) Ltd**
[1981] AC 557
House of Lords

[The plaintiff was injured in an accident and sued. The defendants made two interim payments. At this point some entrepreneurial Texan lawyers suggested to the plaintiff that he might do better if he sued in Texas and he sought to discontinue his action in order to avail himself of this opportunity. At first instance, the notice was struck out as an abuse of process. An appeal to the Court of Appeal was successful, and on appeal to the House of Lords was dismissed.]

Lord Scarman (at 571–2): [On the question of whether the trial judge erred in finding that he had jurisdiction to strike out a discontinuance on the grounds that it amounted to an abuse of process, his Lordship said:] Unless, therefore, it is possible to treat a notice or discontinuance without leave which complies with the Rules of the Supreme Court as an abuse of process (which is what Parker J did), the notice cannot be struck out.

In the Court of Appeal, Lord Denning MR was prepared so to hold (p 855). Brandon LJ expressed no opinion. Shaw LJ, however, held that it was not possible. It seemed to him 'an inversion of logic to speak of an act which purports to terminate a process as being an abuse of that process.' (p 864D). I am not sensitive to the logical difficulty. Even if it be illogical (and I do not think it is) to treat the termination of legal process as an act which can be an abuse of that process, principle requires that the illogicality be overridden, if justice requires. The court has inherent power to prevent a party from obtaining by the use of its process a collateral advantage which it would be unjust for him to retain; and termination of process can, like any other step in the process, be so used. I agree, therefore, with Parker J and Lord Denning MR that service of a notice of discontinuance without leave, though it complies with the rules, can be an abuse of the process of the court.

[572] Was it, then, in the circumstances of this case, an abuse? In my judgment, it was. A sensible test is that which both the judge and Lord Denning MR applied. Suppose leave had been required (as it would have been, if the notice had been served 24 hours later), would the court have granted unconditional leave? It is inconceivable that the court would have allowed a plaintiff, who had secured interim payments and an admission of liability by proceeding in the English court, to discontinue his action in order to improve his chances in a foreign suit without being put upon terms, which could well include not only repayment of the moneys received but an undertaking not to issue a second writ in England.

The notice being an abuse of process, Parker J was right, in my judgment, to strike it out. It does not, however, follow that the court may not thereafter give the plaintiff leave upon terms to discontinue. Because he reached the conclusion that he should restrain the respondent from proceeding with his claim in America, the judge, logically and appropriately, made no order staying or discontinuing the English action. But, had he refused the injunction, it would have been necessary for him to consider what he ought to do with the English action upon the basis that the American action was proceeding. This he never did; for the situation did not, on his judgment, arise.

17.5.7C   **Packer v Meagher**
[1984] 3 NSWLR 486
Supreme Court of New South Wales

[Packer initiated a libel action against Meagher and subsequently sought leave to discontinue the action. Meagher sought to have the notice struck out and sought the dismissal of the proceedings as an abuse of process. Subsequently, in the course of the hearing, Packer's counsel sought to withdraw his notice of discontinuance. Hunt J found that the notice of discontinuance had been filed prior to the close of pleadings. Leave to file was not therefore required. For reasons set out in his judgment, Hunt found that the proceedings amounted to an abuse of process.]

Hunt J (at 500): All of these circumstances suggest to me very strongly that there may indeed have been a vindictive desire on the part of the plaintiff to make the defendant as uncomfortable as possible, for as long as possible, by having these proceedings hanging over his head in order to punish him for his part in assisting in the compilation of the report of the Royal Commission. Whether or not such a vindictive desire existed, I am nevertheless satisfied that the plaintiff's proceedings were brought for the dominant ulterior and collateral purpose of investigating the conduct of Mr Costigan's Royal Commission, and not to vindicate the plaintiff's own reputation. I am satisfied that such a purpose is not one for which defamation proceedings are properly designed and exist. I am satisfied also that the defendant has succeeded in the task of establishing, upon strong evidence, that the plaintiff's proceedings are an abuse of process. Finally, I am satisfied that the notice of discontinuance was filed in order to deny to the defendant his chance of obtaining a public vindication by demonstrating that the plaintiff was unable properly to plead a verified case against him that he was guilty of the act of grave impropriety alleged against him and that the proceedings were an abuse of process. The defendant should now have that public vindication. He has successfully and publicly called the plaintiff's bluff.

Lord Denning, in *Goldsmith v Sperrings Ltd* [1977] 1 WLR 478; 2 All ER 556, said that the court should act to stay or to dismiss proceedings as an abuse of process only in exceptional cases. I am satisfied that the present is such an exceptional case. Indeed, it is to be hoped that that which has happened in this case will remain exceptional, and that it will never be repeated.

I refuse the plaintiff's application to withdraw his notice of discontinuance. I strike out that notice as an abuse of process. I dismiss the proceedings themselves as an abuse of process.

17.5.8C   **Ernst & Young v Butte Mining Plc**
[1996] 1 WLR 1605
High Court of England and Wales, Chancery Division

[In connection with an application to have set aside a judgment given in default of a defence, the defendant provided affidavit evidence including an affidavit exhibiting a draft defence and a counterclaim for more than £100,000,000. The plaintiffs (whose claim had been for a mere £315,000) were aware that it was too late for the defendants to assert the matters set out in the counterclaim other than in a counterclaim. Accordingly they decided that the best course of action was to discontinue their claim before a counterclaim could be filed in response to it. To ensure this, they agreed to a consent order setting aside the default judgment and giving the defendant seven days to file and serve a defence and counterclaim. They arranged that it should be the plaintiff's solicitors who would be responsible for the sealing of the consent order.

Their solicitors obtained the sealed order soon after midday. At 1.20 pm, they faxed a notice of discontinuance to the defendant's solicitors. At 1.50 pm they faxed a copy of the perfected order. At 2.20 pm they served or re-served the order and the notice of discontinuance. At 3.45 pm the defendant's solicitors served the defence and counterclaim. Robert Walker J found that the counterclaim had not been served in time, and that there was no agreement that there would be no discontinuance prior to the expiry of seven days. Immediately the order was sealed, the plaintiff served a notice of discontinuance. The defendant had had no time to serve a counterclaim, and was not otherwise in a position to assert the relevant rights, since the claim had become statute barred.]

Robert Walker J (at 1619–22): It is therefore necessary to consider the third issue, abuse of process. The proposition that a notice of discontinuance may be an abuse of process was novel in *Castanho v Brown & Root (UK) Ltd* [1981] AC 557, as appears from the difference of judicial opinion and the paucity of authority cited (on that point) in different courts. Moreover, apart from the *Fakih Brothers* case [1994] 1 Lloyd's Rep 103 there seems to have been little authority since. In the *Fakih Brothers* case the third of Hobhouse J's five points at 109, was that in considering whether or not the service of the notice was an abuse of process it is necessary to have regard to the overall position of the parties, and what the plaintiff is trying to achieve by discontinuance. Looking at the overall position cannot in my view exclude looking at any allegation that one side has [1620] misled the other and has thereby put itself in a position to serve a notice of discontinuance which it might not otherwise have been able to serve. ...

[1621] The practice as to which solicitor has carriage of an order is a procedural nicety on which I was not referred to any authority (it is touched on, but not fully explained, in the Chancery Division practice directions in *The Supreme Court Practice 1995*, vol 2, 165, para 810, subpara (d)). But Mr Hirst did not dispute Mr Boyle's submission that in having carriage of an order a solicitor would be acting as an officer of [1622] the court and should not use that responsibility in order to secure some partisan advantage. But that is, as I must conclude, what Miss Canning tried to achieve in this case. The fact that Miss Bassett readily agreed to Miss Canning having carriage of the consent order is to my mind the clearest indication that she had come to believe that Ernst & Young were not going to discontinue in the near future. I must also regretfully conclude that misleading conduct on the part of Miss Canning was the major cause of Miss Bassett's mistaken belief. It is to Miss Canning's credit that she was so candid on these matters in her oral evidence.

In deciding whether the service of the notice of discontinuance in these circumstances amounted to an abuse of process and if so what should be done about it I have well in mind Mr Hirst's submission (put colloquially but then developed) that Ernst & Young did not owe Butte any favours. I have well in mind that Butte's initiation and conduct of the Montana action has been characterised by Rix J and Miss Dohmann QC as oppressive and that that is why Ernst & Young were successful in the anti-suit action. But it is a commonplace that two wrongs do not make a right.

Heavy hostile commercial litigation is a serious business. It is not a form of indoor sport and litigation solicitors do not owe each other duties to be friendly (so far as that goes beyond politeness) or to be chivalrous or sportsmanlike (so far as that goes beyond being fair). Nevertheless, even in the most hostile litigation (indeed especially in the most hostile litigation) solicitors must be scrupulously fair and not take unfair advantage of obvious mistakes: see the decision of the Court of Appeal in *Derby & Co Ltd v Weldon (No 8)* [1991] 1 WLR 73 (this was not cited by counsel but the general principle is I think uncontroversial). The duty not to take unfair advantage of an obvious mistake is intensified if the solicitor in question has been a major contributing cause of the mistake.

For these reasons I conclude that the service of the notice of discontinuance was in all the circumstances an abuse of process.

17.5.9 The mere fact that a plaintiff will gain an advantage by discontinuing does not mean that discontinuance is an abuse of process. *Brown v Parker* [1961] WAR 194 provides an example. The plaintiff had brought an action under the Fatal Accidents Act 1846 (UK) following the death of her husband in an accident. Her damages were considerably reduced once account had been taken of her widows' pension. After the trial judge had announced the damages he would be awarding, but before judgment was entered, the plaintiff sought leave to discontinue. The law had been amended so that in actions brought subsequent to the passage of the law, widows' pensions were no longer to be taken into account. Woolf CJ granted leave to discontinue, considering that this was what the justice of the case demanded.

Nor is it an abuse of process for a plaintiff to discontinue an action after having decided that its financial position is likely to improve and that it will be able to conduct its case more effectively if the case is delayed until it is able to finance a more effective presentation of its case: *Running Pigmy* [sic] *Pty Ltd v AMP General Insurance Co Ltd* [2001] NSWSC 431 (Palmer J).

On discontinuance, the plaintiff normally becomes liable for the defendant's costs: HCR r 27.10.6; FCR r 26.12(17) (where discontinuance is as of right); ACT r 1163; NSW r 42.19; NT r 63.15; Qld r 307; SA r 107(4); Tas r 378; Vic r 63.15; WA O 23 r 2(1). For an example of circumstances where discontinuance was permitted without an order as to costs, see *Tasmanian Conservation Trust Inc v Minister for Environment and Heritage* [2004] FCA 883, BC200404660. There litigation had been initiated on the basis of a misapprehension as to a relevant fact. Six weeks after the respondent had informed the applicant of the misapprehension, the applicant sought to discontinue. It was held (per Jacobson J) that the circumstances surrounding the discontinuance warranted a departure from the normal rule, and that the six weeks delay in making the decision to discontinue was not excessive.

Discontinuance does not give rise to issue estoppel and does not preclude a plaintiff from bringing fresh proceedings (FCR r 26.14; ACT r 1167; NSW r 12.3; NT r 25.06; Qld r 310; SA r 108; Vic r 25.06; WA O 23 r 2(2)); and see *The Kronprinz* (1887) 12 AC 256. However, this will not be possible if the claim has become statute barred. Moreover, if fresh proceedings are brought before the costs of the earlier proceedings have been paid, the court may stay those further proceedings pending payment of the costs: FCR r 26.15; ACT r 1169; NSW r 12.4; NT r 25.07; Qld r 312; SA r 108; Tas r 380; Vic r 25.07; WA O 23 r 4. In the Tasmanian Conservation Trust case, however, the order granting leave stated that this was on the basis that discontinuance was to be a defence against any attempt to canvass the same issues again.

Defendants can withdraw their appearance at any time by leave of the court and they may withdraw their defence or matters pleaded in their defence, but if this would prejudice other parties, only with the consent of other parties or the court. Wording varies slightly: HCR r 27.10.1 (appearance only); FCR r 26.11 (may withdraw plea); ACT rr 1162, 1164;

NSW rr 12.5, 12.6; NT rr 25.01, 25.02; Qld rr 306, 308; SA r 107(2)(a) (may withdraw any matter in a defence); Tas r 375 (withdraw appearance only); Vic rr 25.01, 25.02; WA O 23, rr 1, 2(4) (withdrawal of defence or part thereof requires consent or leave).

Further reading

17.6.1　Journals

Australian Dispute Resolution Journal, Thomson Reuters, Sydney.

Commercial Dispute Resolution Journal, LexisNexis Butterworths, Sydney.

17.6.2　Looseleaf and online

A Archer, 'Compromise of Proceedings', in *Court Forms, Precedents and Pleadings Victoria,* LexisNexis, Sydney.

M Dempsey and J Steele, 'Compromise and Settlement', in *Court Forms, Precedents and Pleadings New South Wales,* LexisNexis, Sydney.

Halsbury's Laws of Australia, LexisNexis Butterworths, Sydney, vol 20, Title 325 Practice and Procedure, 'Ch V Settlement', [325–6700]–[325–6840].

Laws of Australia, Thomson Reuters, Sydney, vol 5, section 5.5, Ch 3.

G Thompson et al, 'Compromise of Proceedings', in *Court Forms, Precedents and Pleadings Queensland,* LexisNexis, Sydney.

17.6.3　Texts

H Astor and C Chinkin, *Dispute Resolution in Australia,* 2nd ed, LexisNexis Butterworths, Sydney, 2002.

L Boulle, *Mediation: Skills and Techniques,* Butterworths, Sydney, 2001.

H Brown and A Marriott, *ADR Principles and Practice,* Sweet & Maxwell, London, 1993.

B Cairns, *Australian Civil Procedure,* 9th ed, Thomson Reuters, Sydney, 2011, Ch 11.

R Charlton and M Dewdney, *The Mediator's Handbook: Skills and Strategies for Practitioners,* 2nd ed, Lawbook Co, Sydney, 2004.

T Sourdin, *Alternative Dispute Resolution,* 3rd ed, Lawbook Co, Sydney, 2008.

## CHAPTER 18

Trial

OVERVIEW

This chapter examines the progress of a case from its being set down for trial to judgment. It begins by outlining the procedures for setting cases down for trial. It then discusses the three major modes of trial:

- trial by judge (the norm);
- trial by jury (which is largely extinct in most jurisdictions); and
- the hearing of cases and issues by referees and arbitrators.

The presentation of the case is then discussed. This will involve a consideration of:

- when cases can be 'split';
- the order in which addresses are given and evidence presented;
- the effect of failure of a party to attend;
- no case submissions;
- when cases can be re-opened; and
- when cases can be adjourned.

Procedures in cases conducted by referees are also discussed. The chapter then examines the status of jury verdicts and referees' reports, and the relationship between these and judgments. The chapter concludes by considering the circumstances in which a court may amend or set aside its judgments.

INTRODUCTION

18.1.1   As noted at **17.1.1**, civil cases are overwhelmingly resolved by procedures other than trial. However, trials are not unimportant. Settlement takes place in the shadow of those cases that have gone to trial. Trials also provide information to non-participants. They indicate what the law is in areas where the law has previously been unclear or, not uncommonly, that law which was once regarded as clear is no longer so. They provide information about change and lack of change in the standards being applied by judges and juries. They communicate details about the degree to which lawyers have been able to make accurate assessment of the 'value' of their cases, and these will affect a lawyer's reputation in the eyes of their clients and other lawyers. They stand as cautionary tales to be cited to recalcitrant clients. Trials will normally reflect failed negotiations. At the same time, trials facilitate successful negotiation by clarifying ambiguities, and by the threat they pose to all who inadvisably become involved in them.

SETTING DOWN FOR TRIAL

18.2.1   Cases do not come on for trial automatically, even after pleadings have closed. Case management has meant that parties enjoy less control over this process than was once the case. Case management does not, however, mean that non-settled cases proceed inexorably to trial on a nominated date. Procedure and terminology vary considerably across jurisdictions, as well as according to whether or not the matter has been initiated by writ. Matters initiated other than by writ rarely involve questions of fact. The consequent simplification of the dispute means that it can be scheduled for trial relatively expeditiously.

Cases initiated by writ or by statement of claim can be far more complex and the procedure for setting down for trial is more formal. Traditionally, the progress of cases was largely left to the parties. Case management systems mean that courts now exercise greater control over the progress of cases. Readiness for trial continues to be a necessary condition for the allocation of a trial date, but courts are increasingly concerned to ensure that parties' assurances that cases are ready are in fact well-grounded. The procedure for allocating trial dates varies across and within jurisdictions. The diversity in procedure for setting cases down for trial means that they are best described jurisdiction by jurisdiction.

Federal Court

18.2.2   In the Federal Court (FCR r 5.04(3), item 33), a trial date may be fixed at a directions hearing.

[*NOTE:* in this chapter a reference, such as WA O 9 r 2, is a reference to the relevant jurisdiction's Rules of Court. All other legislation will be specified.]

Australian Capital Territory

18.2.3   Before a case can be set down for trial, the parties must file a Certificate of Readiness, and a listing hearing must be held. The process for filing a Certificate of Readiness is commenced when a party completes and signs one as prescribed in Form 2.38, and serves copies on each other active party to the proceeding: Court Procedure Rules 2006 (ACT) r 1306(1). The other parties must either complete and sign the form and return it to the party who served it, or tell the party who served it what it thinks must be done before it is ready for trial, and the amount of time this will require: ACT r 1306(2). If all the active parties sign the certificate of readiness, and if relevant statements of particulars have been filed, the signed certificate may be filed: ACT r 1306(3). A date is then fixed for a listing hearing. If one or more of the served parties do not sign, the party which served the certificate may apply for a directions hearing at which the court may give directions that the proceeding be given a listing hearing. It may also give directions in relation to having the matter made ready for trial, or it may adjourn the hearing: r 1308(6). The purpose of the listing hearing is to canvass possibilities of settlement, and ways in which any trial that might take place can be streamlined. The court must also decide, however, whether the case is ready for trial. If it decides that it is not ready, its options include setting aside the Certificate of Readiness, giving directions as to how the case might be made ready for trial, and adjourning the listing hearing: r 1309(4). If it decides the case is ready for trial, it must set a date for the trial: r 1309(3). Special procedures may govern trials which are estimated to last more than five days (or three days if tried in the Magistrates Court), and there is provision for application for expedited trial: rr 1301, 1311. Two weeks prior to the date set for trial, the plaintiff must file a 'court book', including the originating process, pleadings, particulars, third party notices, contribution or indemnity notices, orders, affidavits to be used; and relevant statements of particulars: r 1312.

New South Wales

18.2.4   In the Common Law Division of the New South Wales Supreme Court, cases are handled according to a complex case management scheme. Common Law Division cases initiated by statement of claim are divided into default and other cases. The former are cases which 'may be wholly determined by way of the entry of a default judgment'. These cases are handled administratively until and unless a defence is filed, at which point the case would continue as a defended General or Possession List case.

Cases other than default cases are allocated a Directions Hearing before a Registrar. Parties must give explanations if they fail to comply with a direction, and adjournments are granted sparingly, and only for short periods. When a matter is ready for hearing, it is listed before the 'List Judge' for call-up: Practice Note SC CL 1. Procedures also depend on the list to which the case belongs: see Practice Notes SC CL 5 (General Case Management List), SC CL 6 (Possession List), SC CL 3 (Administrative Law List), SC CL 4 (Defamation List) and SC CL 7 (Professional Negligence List).

Cases filed in the Equity Division are assigned either to a specialist list, or allocated to particular lists according to their urgency and likely duration: Practice Note SC Eq 1. As in the Common Law Division, adjournments are discouraged. Procedures in most specialist lists are further governed by practice notes: SC Eq 2 (Admiralty), SC Eq 3 (Commercial List and Technology and Construction List), SC Eq 4 (Corporations List), SC Eq 7 (Family Provision), SC Eq 9 (Commercial Arbitration) and SC Eq 10 (Revenue).

Northern Territory

18.2.5   The Northern Territory procedures are similar to those which operate in the Australian Capital Territory, but are governed by detailed rules rather than by practice direction: Rules of the Supreme Court of the Northern Territory of Australia (NT) O 48. The rules require the filing of a Certificate of Readiness for trial, signed by all parties to the proceeding, and make provision for what is to happen if a party refuses to sign the certificate. They provide for a listing hearing which considers similar matters to those considered in Australian Capital Territory listing hearings. If the judge or Master conducting the hearing is satisfied that these matters have been satisfactorily resolved and that the matter is ready for trial, the proceeding is placed in a list for trial. Otherwise the matter is normally adjourned for further hearing.

However, in certain circumstances, less complicated cases may nonetheless be listed as ready for trial. Alternatively, the listing hearing may be treated as concluded. There is also provision for a matter to be placed in the list of proceedings ready for trial, even if no Certificate of

Readiness has been filed, if, at a *directions* hearing, the judge or master is satisfied that the matter is ready for, or should proceed to, trial. Trial dates for less complicated cases are allocated at a callover. Dates are normally to be allocated on the basis of priority on the relevant list. In more complicated cases, dates are allocated at a pre-trial Directions Hearing. If counsel for a party does not attend the callover, the party's counsel must file a certificate from its counsel stating, among other things, that the proceeding is ready for trial. Earlier certificates to this effect are evidently (and probably justifiably) to be treated with a grain of salt. The procedure for cases commenced by originating motion is governed by O 45.

Queensland

18.2.6   On the filing of an originating or other application, the Registrar determines a return date for its hearing. The hearing may, however, be adjourned to a particular date, or to a date to be fixed. In the latter case, either party may ask that it be relisted, in which case the party must give notice of the new date to other parties. Parties may also agree to a new date, in which case it may be listed for that date or the next available date thereafter: Uniform Civil Procedure Rules 1999 (Qld) rr 462–464. Other cases can be set down for trial only if all parties sign a request for a trial date or if the court dispenses with that requirement: r 467. A party who wants a trial date set prepares and signs the prescribed form, and submits it to other parties who may sign it. The form is filed once all parties have signed. A condition for signing is that the party is ready for trial. Readiness presupposes that pleadings are finalised, that there are no further particulars required, that discovery processes are complete, that all the party's necessary witnesses are available, and that the matter is otherwise ready for trial. There is provision for dispensing with the requirement that all parties sign the request for a trial date: r 469. A party who signs the form may not without leave amend pleadings, seek particulars or make applications in the proceedings: r 470. A trial date may then be set at callover or by or at the direction of a judge: r 466.

South Australia

18.2.7   In South Australia, actions may proceed to trial only by court order: Supreme Court Civil Rules 2006 (SA) r 120(1). Such orders may not ordinarily be made unless a Certificate of Readiness (draft form 25), has been signed by representatives of all the parties: r 120(3). A judge or Master may also order that an action proceed if satisfied that one or more parties is or are not ready for trial through their own default: r 120(6).

Tasmania

18.2.8   Before an action can be listed for trial, there must be a 'compulsory conference', and the filing of a Certificate of Readiness: Supreme Court Rules 2000 (Tas) rr 541, 544. Similar requirements operate in connection with proceedings commenced by originating motion. A party may require the holding of a 'compulsory conference' once pleadings have been closed for 21 days, and where there are no pleadings, when the party is ready to proceed to a hearing: r 543. The purpose of this conference is to discuss the possibility of settlement, whether agreement can be reached on any issues, and possible dates for trial: rr 541, 542. The holding of a conference, the finalisation of pleadings and the completion of discovery and interrogation are conditions precedent to the filing of a joint Certificate of Readiness: r 544 (and see r 545 in relation to proceedings initiated by originating motion). Where a party is unwilling to sign a Certificate of Readiness, the other party may apply to the court for directions or for an order dispensing with the requirement of a certificate: r 546. This may be followed by a further pre-trial conference. Alternatively, a judge may order that the matter be listed for trial without the need for a conference: r 547. Once a judge has ordered that a proceeding be listed for trial, the Registrar is to do so, after consulting the parties as to a convenient date and time: r 548.

Victoria

18.2.9   Victorian Supreme Court procedures vary according to the list to which a case is allocated. The Supreme Court (General Civil Procedure) Rules 2005 O 48 governs the determination of dates for trial except for cases in the following lists: Admiralty; Technology, Engineering and Construction; Commercial; Corporations; Intellectual Property; and Valuation, Compensation and Planning: r 48.01(2). The court may fix a date for trial either following the filing and service of a notice for trial, or subject to the plaintiff's doing so: r 48.02. The following procedures were introduced by Practice Note No 4 of 2006 as from January 2007 following the court's 'concern about the inconvenience to the Court, the parties and lawyers that may result from the vacation of trial dates at a late stage'. This, the Note observed, 'has very often been the result of the case not being ready for trial'. The procedures apply to civil cases other than those which fall into the following three classes: (a) cases in lists where the managing judge is also the trial judge; (b) cases where the managing judge has caused the case to be set down for trial early; and (c) cases in the nature of appeals or reviews. In other civil cases, the process of listing for trial begins when lawyers for the parties inform the Master or the judge that the matter is ready for trial. The matter is then referred to the Listing Master who allocates a Directions Hearing date within the following two to four weeks. Prerequisites must be met before a case is given a trial date. Mediation must have taken place. If witness statements and a court book have been ordered, the statements must have been delivered, and the book prepared. A second mediation may then be ordered, in which cases, it will take place 'well in advance' of the trial date. Counsel, and in the absence of counsel, solicitors with primary responsibility for the case, must have signed a statement giving an estimate of the length of the trial, and stating that pleadings and discovery are complete, and that statements have been delivered and the court book prepared. Practitioners who believe the information has ceased to be accurate are obliged to notify the Listing Master. Applications to vacate a hearing date will be viewed with disfavour, if based on an inaccuracy which has not been drawn to the court's attention, and if the date is allowed, there may be an order for costs thrown away. Trials are to stop at the expiry of the estimated time for trial, to resume at a later date. Costs orders may deal with the consequent costs thrown away.

Other practice notes govern cases in specialised lists.

Western Australia

18.2.10   In Western Australia, a Certificate of Readiness must be filed before a matter can be entered for trial: Rules of the Supreme Court 1971 (WA) O 33 r 8. It is normally the plaintiff who enters a matter for trial by filing and serving an entry for trial: O 33 r 1. Should the plaintiff fail to do so within four weeks of the end of pleadings (or equivalent), the defendant has the option of filing an entry or, alternatively, seeking to have the action struck out for want of prosecution: O 33 r 2.

A party on whom an entry for trial is served may seek to have the entry countermanded: O 33 r 9. One reason why a party might want to do this is that entry for trial precludes the making of a range of interlocutory applications in relation to pleadings, parties, discovery and evidence: O 33 r 10. After an entry is filed, a trial date is allocated according to the practice of the court: O 33 r 12. After that, adjournments and withdrawals from the list are permitted only by leave of the court: O 33 r 11(2). The party entering the case for trial is obliged to provide two copies of the pleadings (or equivalent), particulars and requests for particulars, and relevant orders: O 33 r 14.

These rules coexist with case management rules whereby the requirement of a Certificate of Readiness can be dispensed with: O 4A r 2(m). The management rules provide for a series of conferences for cases other than those in the Commercial and Managed Cases List: a status conference, within three weeks of the first appearance; a case evaluation conference, which is normally within 28 weeks of the status conference; and a listing conference: O 4A rr 18–20. The rules envisage that the case evaluation conference will canvass whether, at the time of the listing conference, the case will be ready for trial: O 4A r 7(4)(d). The listing conference is to be held as soon as possible after the case is entered for trial. At the conference, the judge may fix a trial date: O 4A r 8(6).

18.2.11 Questions

1. Rules sometimes provide that entry for trial can take place at any time after the close of pleadings, and that defendants can apply to have a case struck out for want of prosecution if there is no entry for trial within a short period of the close of pleadings. Is this realistic? When, for example, do the Western Australian case management rules envisage that entry for trial is likely to take place? How long after the close of pleadings is this likely to be? If the relevant period is unduly short, is there any point in having such a rule?

2. The Victorian Supreme Court Practice Note No 3 of 1995 notes:

   > Experience has ... shown that many cases that have been certified as ready for trial and entered in the list of cases waiting trial are not in fact ready at all, or require further significant interlocutory steps before trial can be arranged.

   Why might this be so?

18.2.12 Further reading

K Downes, 'Preparing for Trial' (2007) June *Proctor* 43 (a practical account of what's involved in being ready for trial).

See also **Chapter 1**, in particular 1.7.1, 1.10.20, 1.11.1–1.11.11E.

MODE OF TRIAL

18.3.1 The normal mode of trial is trial by judge alone. (In exceptional cases, the trial can be by two or more judges.) Except in the Australian Capital Territory and South Australia, there is also provision for trial by jury. The rules further provide for questions arising in a proceeding to be referred to arbitrators or referees. There is also provision for decisions to be made by courts consisting of both a judge and assessors. The rules also make provision for the use of different modes of trial in relation to different issues.

Trial by judge alone

18.3.2 Trial by judge alone is the normal mode of trial in civil cases. In cases where parties have a right to opt for trial by jury (see **18.3.3**), cases are normally tried by judge alone unless a party takes the necessary steps to entitle it to a jury trial. In other cases, trial by jury is restricted to cases where judges, either on their own motion, or on application from a party, make an order for jury trial. Such orders are rarely sought and rarely made.

In a small minority of cases, questions of fact are referred to referees or arbitrators (see **18.3.20ff**). While provision exists for courts consisting of a judge and assessors, courts are rarely if ever constituted in this way. While the rules in several jurisdictions envisage that the trial court may consist of more than one judge, it is exceptional for trial courts to be constituted other than by a single judge.

Juries

18.3.3 The use of juries is regulated by a complex mixture of Acts, rules and practices. In the Australian Capital Territory and South Australia, jury trials in civil cases have been abolished by legislation: Supreme Court Act 1933 (ACT) s 22; Juries Act 1927 (SA) s 5. In Queensland, personal injuries cases must be tried by a judge sitting without a jury: Civil Liability Act 2003 (Qld) s 73. But except where legislation provides otherwise, parties may elect for jury trial: Qld r 472. In some of the other states, legislation and/or the Rules of Court provide for a prima facie right to jury trial in certain circumstances, provided one or more parties opts for jury trial: Tas r 557; Vic r 47.02(1). This right is a qualified one. Courts may order trial by judge alone if the case is complex: Qld r 474; Tas r 558; Vic r 47.03.

In the federal courts, the territories, New South Wales and Western Australia, there is no general prima facie right to jury trial. Rather, the court has the power to order one: Judiciary Act 1903 (Cth) ss 77A, 77B; Federal Court of Australia Act 1976 (Cth) ss 39, 40; Supreme Court Act 1933 (ACT) s 22; Supreme Court Rules 1937 (ACT) O 33 r 1(2)(k); Supreme Court Act 1970 (NSW) s 85; WA O 32 r 2(3). In several of these jurisdictions, there is, however, a presumptive right to jury trial in defamation cases: Defamation Act 2005 (NSW) s 21 (but only in relation to the question of liability); Juries Act (NT) s 7; Supreme Court Act 1935 (WA) s 42. In Queensland, Tasmania and Victoria, courts may order jury trial in relation to some categories of case where parties do not possess a prima facie right to opt for trial by jury: Qld r 475; Tas r 558; Vic r 47.03.

When is there a prima facie right to a jury trial?

18.3.4 In general the prima facie right to jury trial is largely restricted to common law cases. Indeed, the prima facie right to jury trial is generally restricted to a subset of such cases. In

Tasmania (r 557), the right to jury trial exists in relation to common law matters. In Victoria (r 47.02(1)), jury trial is, prima facie, available in claims based on contract or tort. In Western Australia, the right exists only in relation to defamation and to a number of intentional and morally charged torts: Supreme Court Act 1935 (WA) s 42. In New South Wales, there is a presumptive right to a jury trial in defamation cases where there are issues of fact to be tried: Defamation Act 2005 (NSW) s 25. In Queensland, it does not extend to personal injuries cases, but it is formally available in other common law actions, and there is even a prima facie right to jury trial of questions of fact arising in equity matters: r 472. Elsewhere, there is no such right, a state of affairs which reflects the pre-Judicature Act position and the difficulties involved in the use of juries in equity cases where the issues to be tried lend themselves far less readily than common law cases to division between questions of fact and questions of law. These problems are noted in *Jenyns v Public Curator (Queensland)* (1953) 90 CLR 113 at 118 per Dixon CJ, McTiernan and Kitto JJ. Judges' views of the appropriateness of the use of juries in cases smacking of equity are epitomised by Barton CJ's observation in *Hay v Dalgety & Co Ltd* (1907) 4 CLR 913 at 919, a case involving a claim arising out of an alleged breach of a mortgage covenant:

> One cannot help feeling glad that a jury need not be summoned to try a case of this kind.

The jurisdictional issues which bedevilled pre-Judicature Act civil procedure continue to have the capacity to haunt. However, with juries, in practice (and, in New South Wales and Western Australia, in law) largely restricted to actions in tort, it is rarely necessary to decide whether a matter is an equitable rather than a common law matter, as evidenced by the lack of recent cases on the subject.

18.3.5   In determining whether a matter is a common law matter, courts look to the substance rather than the form of the claim: *Hay v Dalgety & Co Ltd* (1907) 4 CLR 913; *Kerrison v Lowell* [1915] VLR 145; *Walker v Walbran* [1917] VLR 231; *Dayton v Western Australian Insurance Co Ltd* [1924] VLR 153.

18.3.6   In contrast to the pre-Judicature Act position, parties enjoy a right to a jury trial only if one or the other so opts, and usually within a prescribed period: NSW r 29.2A (defamation cases only: only if notification of intent to elect for jury trial has been filed prior to date fixed for trial); Qld r 472 (jury trial to be sought in claim, defence, or reply to counterclaim); Vic r 47.02(1) (plaintiff in writ; defendant within 10 days of appearance); WA O 32 r 2 (seven days of entry for trial). Tasmania appears to place no limits on when a jury may be sought. A jury trial may also be conditioned upon the payment of jury fees prior to the trial: Defamation Act 2005 (NSW) s 21(2)(b) (payment on filing of election for jury trial); Juries Act (NT) s 8; Vic rr 47.02(1)(b), 47.03; Juries Act (WA) s 44(1)(a). It does not matter who pays the fees: *Pezzimenti v Seamer* [1995] 2 VR 32, where the plaintiff refused to pay jury fees after the first day, but a defendant subsequently agreed to do so.

18.3.7   The right to jury trial has also been qualified by particular statutes. Admiralty cases are to be tried without a jury: Admiralty Act 1988 (Cth) s 38. Queensland statutory provisions which restrict the right to jury trial include a host of 2001 Acts providing for occupational licensing. These make it a tort to take reprisals against witnesses and providers of relevant adverse information. Actions for damages under these Acts are to be heard by a judge sitting without a jury. A typical provision is to be found in the Occupational Therapists Registration

Act 2000 s 135. Analogous provisions are to be found in other pieces of legislation aimed at protecting information providers: Commission for Children and Young People and Child Guardian Act 2000 (Qld) s 389(3); Health Practitioners (Professional Standards) Act 1999 (Qld) s 390(3); Health Quality and Complaints Commission Act 1991 (Qld) s 195(3); Public Interest Disclosure Act 2010 s 42(3) (Qld); Residential Services (Accreditation) Act 2002 (Qld) s 175(3); Transplantation and Anatomy Act 1979 (Qld) s 49C(3). There are also several enactments which preclude jury trials for specified damages actions: State Development and Public Works Organisation Act 1971 (Qld) s 168; Workers Compensation and Rehabilitation Act 2003 (Qld) s 301. In Tasmania, the (virtually never exercised) right is restricted by the Motor Accidents (Liabilities and Compensation) Act 1973 (Tas) s 22 and, rather unnecessarily, by the Electoral Act 2004 (Tas) s 212 (disputed elections). Jury trials are also excluded by and in connection with the Petroleum (Submerged Lands) Acts 1982 in New South Wales (s 73); Northern Territory; Queensland; Victoria and Western Australia (s 72); and South Australia and Tasmania: s 71.

Rebutting the prima facie presumption

18.3.8   In New South Wales (defamation cases), Western Australia (defamation and morally charged torts cases), Queensland and Tasmania, the court may order trial by judge alone if it is of the opinion that the case involves a cause, matter or issue requiring 'any prolonged examination of documents or accounts, or any scientific or local examination which cannot conveniently be made with a jury': Defamation Act 2005 (NSW) s 21(3) (defamation cases); Qld r 474; Tas r 558; Supreme Court Act 1935 (WA) s 42. In Victoria, the court enjoys a broader discretion: Vic r 47.02(3). What matters in the context of an examination of documents is whether it is the jury which will have to examine the documents. If there are complex documents which only the judge must examine, this does not justify ordering trial by judge alone: see *Hay v Dalgety & Co Ltd* (1907) 4 CLR 913.

The fact that a case satisfies one or more of the conditions is a necessary but not a sufficient condition for exercising the discretion to dispense with a jury. A jury trial should not be dispensed with unless there are aspects of the case which make a jury trial undesirable. Matters which are 'universal to all jury trials' may not be taken into account in determining this, since the existence of a prima facie right to a jury trial is inconsistent with these matters being relevant to the quality of justice. The relative length and expense of a jury trial as compared with a non-jury trial is therefore irrelevant: *Pambula District Hospital v Harriman* (1988) 14 NSWLR 387; *Smit v Chan* [2003] 2 Qd R 431; [2001] QSC 493; *Trevor Roller Shutter Services Pty Ltd v Crowe* [2011] VSCA 16.

When will jury trials be ordered in the absence of a prima facie right?

18.3.9   Where parties have lost, or do not have, a right to a jury trial, jury trials may nonetheless be ordered: Federal Court of Australia Act 1976 (Cth) s 40; Supreme Court Act 1970 (NSW) s 85(1); Qld r 475; Tas r 556; Vic r 47.02(2); Supreme Court Act 1935 (WA) s 42. Applications may have to be made within a prescribed period: NSW r 29.2 (by motion, within varying periods, depending on whether P or D is applying); WA O 32 r 2 (within seven days of entry for trial) and jury fees must be paid: Supreme Court Act 1970 (NSW) s 85(2)(a)(ii); Juries Act (NT) s 8; Vic r 47.03; Juries Act (WA) s 44(1)(a). The following extract outlines the considerations taken into account.

18.3.10C   Darrell Lea (Vic) Pty Ltd v Union Assurance Society of Australia Ltd
[1969] VR 401
Supreme Court of Victoria

Lush J (at 405–6): ... I think that in exercising my discretion under O XXXVI, r 7(a), I must consider the state of the pleadings at the time when the application under that rule comes before me, and I think I am entitled to regard as a consideration relevant to the exercise of my discretion that issues have developed which the plaintiff had no reason to expect. In the present case, using such knowledge as I have of similar cases, I accept that the plaintiff had, when the writ was issued, reason for thinking that the only issue was amount and that the nondisclosure issue, raised in fact after discovery was not then expected by it. But this is only one of the matters to be taken into account in exercising the discretion.

The discretion given by r 7(a) is absolute, so far as a judicial discretion can be so described. Examples of its use are to be found in *Hoare v Norton* [1913] VLR 192; 19 ALR 175 and *Borg v Australian Consolidated Press Ltd* [1964] VR 129.

There is an onus involved in the rule. In a case where a party, as distinct from the Court acting *suo moto* (see *Wragge v Downard* [1938] VLR 353; [1938] ALR 511) seeks an order for trial by jury under r 7(a) it is for that party to persuade the Court or the judge that the trial should be so held.

In the present case I take into consideration as a relevant matter the development in the pleadings to which I have referred. I also take into consideration that there will be extensive evidence on the issue of amount involving the advancing not only of conflicting valuations but of several different theories of valuation; that there will be evidence going to the true issues involved in the nondisclosure plea, the only difficult one of which is materiality, on which technical evidence of insurers may well be called. I take into consideration the undoubted hope of the plaintiff of deriving some advantage from having a jury as the tribunal before which to sue an insurance company, and the possibility that a jury [406] might, even after careful instruction, find difficulty in giving proper effect to the nondisclosure of a fact not proved to be relevant to the loss. I do not take into consideration two matters pressed on me by Mr Stephen [for the defendant], the possible length of the trial and the volume of accounts discovered by the plaintiff. The fact that a trial may be long is not a reason for refusing a jury: and in the present case I see no reason why either judge or jury should be obliged to give direct consideration to the accounts. The contents and significance of these should be a matter for expert explanation and opinion.

Upon all these consideration I am unable to come to the conclusion that this is a case in which an order for trial by jury should be made. Indeed, on the contrary, it seems to me to be a case in which justice is more likely to be done, and certainly more likely to appear to be done, by a judge sitting alone.

[The Full Court dismissed the appeal on the grounds that Lush J had not clearly erred in the exercise of his discretion.]

18.3.11C   **Borg v Australian Consolidated Press Ltd**
                                            [1964] VR 129
                                        Supreme Court of Victoria

[The plaintiff sued the defendant for libel. Neither the plaintiff nor the defendant sought a jury trial within the prescribed period. Subsequently, however, the defendant sought a jury trial.]

Sholl J (at 132–3): [On an appeal from a decision by the Master ordering a jury trial:] I think the onus, as a matter of law, rests on the party who seeks to change the method of trial which the rules have now prima facie fixed ... But the defendant's counsel is right in saying that prima facie, where the plaintiff's complaint is of libel, the Court will regard that as a proper case for trial by jury. Defamation is peculiarly a matter which the courts have thought fit to entrust to the determination of a jury, since usually the cause of action involves a consideration of the reputation of the plaintiff and the determination of disputed issues of fact, or the construction of ordinary language, usually in some popular journal.

[This case was complicated by two considerations. First, the plaintiff had been involved in a group of companies which had collapsed in circumstances affecting large numbers of people. There had been about 10,000 Victorian shareholders and 20,000 debenture holders. There were also approximately 5000 resident Victorian creditors of the group and 150,000 group debtors. There was therefore, 'a distinct risk that in a jury of citizens there may be one or more persons financially affected by the failure, or that there may be one or more persons related to or closely acquainted with someone else who has been financially affected' (at 133). In addition, there had been considerable press coverage of matters which might prejudice the plaintiff's case. In particular there had been a vigorous denunciation of the group in the Victorian parliament.]

Sholl J (at 133): When one adds together the two factors which I have been discussing, the possibility of a juror being personally affected or closely acquainted with someone who is, and the possibility of a juror being disposed to prejudge the matter by reason of prior publicity, one is driven to the conclusion that it is a safer method of trial to have trial by a judge alone than to entrust the plaintiff's case and the defendant's defences to the determination of a jury, the views of which are likely to be the subject of so much uncertainty. It was said by Hodges, J, in *Hoare v Norton* [1913] VLR 192, that a judge might be just as prejudiced as a jury about a matter of religion. That kind of comment cannot be made about an action of the present type. If it should be the fact that the trial judge was in any way personally affected by the Reid Murray failure, no doubt he would refuse to sit. A judge on the whole is less likely to be prejudiced in the light of various public discussions and newspaper publicity than the average juror. At any rate, it can be predicated with more confidence of a judge that he will remain unaffected than it can be predicated of six or twelve unknown jurymen.

18.3.12   Question

1. The above two cases are examples of where the parties would have had a prima facie right to jury trial had they exercised that right in time. Both are Victorian cases. In Queensland, r 475 governs applications for jury trials where neither party seeks a jury trial within the time prescribed by r 472. In *Nielsen v State of Queensland* [2001] 1 Qd R 500, a personal injuries case, Byrne J held that a belated applicant for a jury trial did not have to show that a jury trial was more appropriate, only that it was not inappropriate. Was this a different approach to that taken by the Victorian Supreme Court?

Rebutting the presumption in favour of trial by judge alone: the Commonwealth and the territories

18.3.13   Federal and territory courts appear to be even more reluctant to order jury trial. Almost the only case in which they are countenanced is in defamation actions, and even then jury trials will not necessarily be ordered. In *McDermott v Collien* (1953) 87 CLR 154, Fullagar J refused to order a High Court jury trial in an action for damages arising out of the supply of an allegedly defective motor car. It is inconceivable that the court would even contemplate this possibility today. Relevant Federal Court cases include *Insurance Commissioner v Australian Associated Motor Insurers Ltd (No 2)* (1982) 49 ALR 714, where a trade practices action had been combined with a defamation action. Refusing jury trial, Northrop J noted that the facts which brought the case within the Federal Court's jurisdiction were not those which were the basis for the libel action, and that in any case, the concept of a jury of one's peers made questionable sense in the context of a dispute between two corporations. In *Construction Industry Long Service Leave Board v Odco Pty Ltd* (No 1) (1988) ATPR 40–886, Jenkinson J considered that a jury trial could be appropriate in a libel case, but considered that given the lack of facilities for such a trial in Melbourne, the appropriate course of action was to make an order transferring the matter to the Supreme Court of Victoria, unless all the parties declared themselves willing to have the matter tried by judge alone. A jury trial was ordered in *Ra v Nationwide News Pty Ltd* (2009) 182 FCR 148; [2009] FCA 1308 (which involved defamation), but this is the only case in which a jury trial has been ordered, and was settled before trial: *Comcare v John Holland* (2010) 189 FCR 173; [2010] FCA 981 at [17].

For the position in the Australian Capital Territory, see *Civil Procedure Australian Capital Territory*, LexisNexis Butterworths, Sydney, looseleaf, [9301.25]. See too *Snell v Sanders* (1994) 122 ALR 520 where Wilcox J's judgment implies that trial by jury will almost never be more appropriate than trial by judge alone (if only on the grounds that it costs more), and that it was particularly inappropriate in Norfolk Island.

Can trial by judge alone be ordered after a jury trial has begun?

18.3.14   There may be situations in which it becomes apparent, after a jury trial has begun, that the matter is one which would be better handled by a judge alone. In such cases, what are the powers of the judge? Can the judge discharge the jury and order a new trial? Can the judge discharge the jury, but continue to hear the matter?

Authority differs. In *G & J Shopfittings & Refrigeration Pty Ltd (in liq) v Lombard Insurance Co (Aust) Ltd* (1989) 16 NSWLR 363, the New South Wales Court of Appeal considered the position where a trial judge discharged a jury prior to the end of a trial and continued the trial as one by judge alone. The court held that the statutory provisions relating to jury trial precluded this course of action. In the course of his judgment, Kirby P said (at 371):

> Typically, the presentation of a case before a jury, as the tribunal of fact, is different from the presentation of evidence in the same case before a judge, sitting alone. Not only will the presentation of witnesses and style of advocacy be different. Different decisions may be taken as to the calling of witnesses, the examination and cross-examination of witnesses and the tender of documentary material. In these circumstances, a trial conducted upon the footing that the tribunal of fact is a jury may result in evidence being adduced which is different from that which would have been adduced at a trial by a judge sitting alone. Of course, the issues for trial remain the same. The substance of the evidence will therefore usually be the same. In some cases the differences in the evidence that would be called would be slight or insignificant. But in other cases it would be substantial. That is why, had it been intended that a judge under s 89(2) should have power, notwithstanding the commencement of a trial, to dispense with the jury and thereafter to proceed on the basis of the evidence which had been placed before the jury, it is reasonable to contemplate that Parliament would have specifically so provided and in terms which would address the risk of injustice that could arise from such a change of tribunal. Parliament did not so do. No other authority for doing so could be identified by the respondent, save for the remarks of Sholl J [in *Wilson v Burridge* [1955] VLR 433 at 435] to which I have referred. But as I have said, his Honour's remarks are obiter, they are addressed to rules which are in relevantly different terms and they specifically leave open whether, once the jury is discharged, the trial must start de novo.
>
> For the saving of time, which was an understandable concern of Smart J [the trial judge], the Supreme Court Act 1970 should perhaps be amended to permit a judge in particular circumstances and on particular conditions to dispense with a jury once a trial has started and thereafter to proceed to try the case on the same evidence as the tribunal of fact. But the Act does not presently so provide. In my opinion it is not legitimate, in the context in which it appears, to attempt to derive such a power from s 89(2).

18.3.15 Questions

1. Section 89(2) of the Supreme Court Act 1970 (NSW) provided:

> In any proceedings to which section 88 applies, the Court may order, despite that section, that all or any issues of fact be tried without a jury where —
> a) any prolonged examination of documents or scientific or local investigation is required and cannot conveniently be made with a jury ...

Smart J had found that the condition had been satisfied. The Victorian rule considered in *Wilson v Burridge* [1955] VLR 433 (O XXXVI r 5) provided:

> Notwithstanding anything contained in Rule 2, the court or a judge may direct the trial without a jury of any cause or issue requiring any prolonged examination of documents or accounts, or any scientific or local investigation which cannot in their or his opinion conveniently be made with a jury.

Is there a material difference between these two provisions?

2. The current Victorian rule (r 47.02(3)) provides:

> (3) Notwithstanding any signification under paragraph (1) the Court may direct a trial without a jury if in its opinion the proceeding should not in all the circumstances be tried before a jury.

In *Altmann v Dunning* [1995] 2 VR 1, the Appeal Division of the Victorian Supreme Court considered whether this rule empowered a judge to dispense with a jury mid-trial. The court held that the rule conferred on a judge the power to dispense with a jury at any point in a trial. Marks J doubted whether *G & J Shopfittings & Refrigeration Pty Ltd (in liq) v Lombard Insurance Co (Aust) Ltd* (1989) 16 NSWLR 363 could be distinguished from *Wilson v Burridge*. Hedigan J considered that the New South Wales decision was inapplicable to Victoria, given the breadth of the Victorian rule. None of the judges considered that parties might be inconvenienced through the changed composition of the court. If the parties were inconvenienced, would this be reason for persisting with a jury trial?

3. How might the interest of justice be adversely affected by a mid-term change of mode of trial? In *Messade v Baires Contracting Pty Ltd (Rulings No 2, 3 & 4)* [2011] VSC 75, [43], Forest J pointed out that one problem would be that if the case were to proceed without a jury, he would 'be asked to retrospectively evaluate the plaintiff's credit. This was not my role during the course of the trial'.

The use of juries

18.3.16 The state rules generally appear to allow parties to opt for jury trial in a broad range of cases. The federal and territory rules envisage a presumption against jury trial, but do not preclude it. In practice, however, parties tend not to avail themselves of the opportunity to elect or seek trial by jury, especially at Supreme Court level. Statistics on the use of juries are difficult to find, and are not always particularly helpful. The High Court has conducted several jury trials, notably *Cunningham v Ryan* (1919) 27 CLR 294: see **18.6.8C**.

Data relating to the use of juries elsewhere is sparse. It is a long time since the Annual Reviews of the New South Wales Supreme Court last gave any statistics about the use of juries. Figures from the Victorian Supreme Court indicate that jury trials were still a favoured mode of trial in personal injuries cases, but that they were rarely used otherwise. Forty-five per cent of writs for trial in the Common Law Division sought jury trial. Of personal injury cases pending in the Civil List as at 31 December 2002, two motor vehicle, 27 industrial and 19 'others' were listed for trial. The corresponding non-jury figures were five, zero and 16. There were also 11 other damages cases listed for jury trial, and 31 listed for trial by judge alone: Supreme Court of Victoria, *Annual Report 2002*, pp 14, 16. Its 2005–06 Annual Report was less helpful, but revealed that 8 per cent of writs were for trial by jury: p 10.

The 2009–10 Annual Report of the Supreme Court of Queensland stated that 'civil matters are almost always determined by a judge': p 19. The Western Australian Supreme Court's recent Annual Reviews have made no reference to civil juries.

Does the jury still have a role to play?

Gerlach v Clifton Bricks Pty Ltd
(2000) 209 CLR 478; 188 ALR 353; [2002] HCA 22
High Court of Australia

[The appellant sued the respondent in the New South Wales District Court. The respondent/ defendant exercised its then right to seek trial by jury. A few days before the date fixed for trial, the plaintiff applied for an order dispensing with the jury.

The defendant did not immediately appeal against the order, and in the trial (before a different judge to the one who had made the order), it lost. On appeal from both the interlocutory order and the judgment, the Court of Appeal held that the application ought not have been granted, and set aside the judgment in the plaintiff's favour. The plaintiff appealed to the High Court. The majority dismissed the appeal. The Court of Appeal's power to direct a new trial was conditioned on 'some substantial wrong or miscarriage'. Even if the decision to order trial by judge alone was flawed, it would be a 'startling proposition' to contend that trial by judge alone could of itself be said to constitute a miscarriage of justice.]

Kirby and Callinan JJ dissenting: [32] The meaning, and intended operation, of the provisions of the Act governing the powers of a judge of the District Court to dispense with trial by jury, where a jury has been summoned to try an action, can be understood best after a reminder of the history of jury trials of civil proceedings.

[33] In England, for more than five hundred years, jury trial was commonly observed in civil cases. There were some exceptions, principally in the "very limited classes of cases assigned to the Chancery Court": *Ford v Blurton* (1922) 38 TLR 801 at 805 per Atkin LJ; cf *Ward v James* [1966] 1 QB 273 at 290. Such cases apart, trials before juries were very common, indeed standard. This fact, like other features of English legal practice, is reflected in the Constitution of the United States which still provides for such jury trials: United States Constitution, VIIth Amendment: "In Suits at common law, where the value in controversy shall exceed twenty dollars, the right of trial by jury shall be preserved ..."

[34] Following a report of the common law commissioners in England in 1853, and notwithstanding the passage in the 1870s of the Judicature Acts, the right to jury trial was substantially maintained for contested issues of fact in civil causes. Only the manpower shortage due to the First World War led, in 1918, to a temporary interruption: *Ford v Blurton* (1922) 38 TLR 801 at 805. When in 1933 the right to jury trial of civil causes was substantially restored in England (Administration of Justice (Miscellaneous Provisions) Act 1933 (UK)) provision was made, nonetheless, for a general discretion in a judge to determine whether the trial is to be "with or without a jury": ibid s 6. It was because the legislation was so stated that the judicial power to dispense with the jury in England was sometimes inaccurately described as an absolute one: *Ward v James* [1966] 1 QB 273 at 291–293 referring to *Hope v Great Western Railway Co* [1937] 2 KB 130. Certain exceptions were preserved for trial by jury in so-called "reputational" cases. Moreover, the judge was empowered to order that any matter requiring prolonged examination of documents and so forth might be tried by judge alone: Administration of Justice (Miscellaneous Provisions) Act 1933 (UK), s 6.

[35] Partly because of the language of the legislation under which civil juries were revived in England and partly because of attitudes that had developed during the interregnum following

their abolition in that country, judicial elaborations of the applicable legislation introduced in England notions that an applicant for jury trial had to show "special circumstances". This was so although such requirements were not, as such, part of the legislative prescription: See *Watts v Manning* [1964] 1 WLR 623; [1964] 2 All ER 267; *Hennell v Ranaboldo* [1963] 1 WLR 1391; [1963] 3 All ER 684; *Sims v William Howard & Son Ltd* [1964] 2 QB 409. The judicial approach in England also appears to have been influenced by judicial policy. Until very recently juries were commonly thought to be unfavourable to defendants and insurers; if judges decided damages actions, there was a greater potential for consistency than if juries did so: cf *Pambula* (1988) 14 NSWLR 387 at 396. In this way, following the interruption to longstanding practice, judicial attitudes to jury trials of civil causes in England began to change.

[36] With the establishment of the Australian colonies, it was natural for the free settlers from England to desire jury trial both for criminal and civil cases. The delay in introducing that mode of trial was a major source of friction with the colonial governors. The first provisions for trial by jury in civil causes, both in New South Wales and Van Diemen's Land, have been described elsewhere: *Caledonian Collieries Ltd v Fenwick* (1959) 76 WN (NSW) 482 at 488–490; Henchman, "The New South Wales Jury of Four Persons", (1959) 33 *Australian Law Journal* 235. Once juries were introduced, at least so far as New South Wales was concerned, they became the ordinary mode of trial. Thus "all actions at law and civil issues of fact ... and all damages and sums of money recoverable" were to be assessed by jury: Jury Act 1912 (NSW), s 29.

[37] Provision was eventually made for the parties to agree to dispense with a jury in proceedings before the Supreme Court of the colony: Supreme Court Procedure Act 1900 (NSW), s 3(1). Even then, a judge might at any time order that all or any of the issues of fact be tried with a jury "if it appears to him to be expedient": Supreme Court Procedure Act 1900 (NSW), s 3(2).

[38] In the District Court of New South Wales it was long provided that in actions where the amount claimed exceeded a specified sum, the plaintiff or defendant could require that a jury be summoned to try the claim ... Indeed, provision was made for the judge to so order although the parties had not made such a requisition: District Courts Act 1912 (NSW), s 90(1). Such provisions reflected the practice that was observed in New South Wales before the enactment of the comprehensive legislation of the 1970s governing the Supreme Court and the District Court. That legislation can only be fully understood if viewed against the background of the law that preceded it.

[39] As to the District Court, provision was made in the Act of 1973 for the summoning of a jury. Relevantly, the provision read:

> **78**(1) In any action (other than an action to which section 79 applies), where the amount claimed exceeds $100, any party may, within the prescribed time, by filing a requisition for trial with a jury and paying the fee prescribed by the regulations made under section 150 require that a jury be summoned to try the action, and a jury shall be so summoned.

[40] Section 79 of the Act, to which reference is there made, made special provision in relation to what are described in the marginal notes as "running down cases". However, even then, relevantly to the proceedings such as the present, s 79(4) made it clear that the section did not apply to an action for damages in respect of bodily injury to any person where

the action "is based upon an act, neglect or default of the defendant for which, if proved, he would, as the employer of that person and not otherwise, incur liability to the plaintiff".

[41] In short, as originally enacted in 1973, the Act substantially continued in the District Court of New South Wales the facility of jury trial inherited from the predecessor legislation governing District Courts in that State. Where a special exception was intended, it was provided for in terms: see the history as described in *Pambula* (1988) 14 NSWLR 387 at 397. Similar provisions were made in the Supreme Court Act 1970 (NSW): s 87.

[42] In 1987, a suggestion was made by a judge of the Supreme Court of New South Wales that a power to dispense with jury trial was needed wider than that provided under the Supreme Court Act 1970 (NSW). The judge was concerned with a case where the parties could not agree to dispensing with the jury but the plaintiff was dying of an asbestos-related condition. The judge called for the conferral of "an unfettered discretion to order trial by judge alone ... to accommodate cases in need of an urgent hearing", except in the limited classes of case where jury trial was specifically prescribed: *Peck v Email Ltd* (1987) 8 NSWLR 430 at 435. See Supreme Court Act 1970 (NSW), s 88 (since repealed by the Courts Legislation Amendment (Civil Juries) Act 2001 (NSW) Sched 2 item 1). As to defamation in New South Wales see now Defamation Act 1974 (NSW), s 7A. This suggestion was picked up by the Parliament of New South Wales. It enacted Bills to amend the legislation governing both the Supreme Court and the District Court: Supreme Court (Amendment) Act 1987 (NSW); District Court (Amendment) Act 1987 (NSW). Introducing the amendments, the State Attorney-General described the decline in the use of civil juries in most parts of Australia (although not Victoria): New South Wales, Legislative Assembly, Parliamentary Debates (Hansard), 16 September 1987 at 13657. He referred to the judicial proposal for law reform. And he described the new provision in the Bill as one designed to confer a discretion on a judge of each court "to order that a trial proceed without a jury": ibid at 13659. However, the Attorney-General emphasised that "The right of a party to a common law action to elect ... to have a matter tried by a jury will continue, but subject to this new discretion which will allow a court to direct otherwise ... In exercising this discretion, the court will be able to have regard to all relevant circumstances and be able to make a decision consistent with the needs of justice in each particular case": ibid at 13658. With respect to the District Court, the new provision, s 79A of the Act, was enacted: District Court (Amendment) Act 1987 (NSW). It read:

> In any action, the Court may order, despite sections 77, 78 and 79, that all or any questions of fact be tried without a jury.

[Their Honours then considered whether an objection to an interlocutory order could be made on appeal from a subsequent substantive decision, and concluded that it could. Nor should it be assumed that where a person who has a right to have a case heard by a jury is wrongly deprived of that right, that no injustice has thereby been occasioned.]

[63] In earlier times it was plaintiffs who pressed for jury trial and defendants who resisted them: *Darrell Lea* [1969] VR 401 at 405 referring to O XXXVI r 7(a) Rules of the Supreme Court of Victoria. The wheel has turned full circle. Yet in each case, it is the parties who seek to advance their perceived interests. Judges should not ignore their perceptions. It can be assumed that the legal advisers have much greater experience in the outcomes of District Court trials today than the Justices of this Court do. As this Court has repeatedly described it, the jury is the "constitutional" mode of trial for questions of fact: *David Syme & Co v Canavan*

(1918) 25 CLR 234 at 240; *Hocking v Bell* (1945) 71 CLR 430 at 440; cf *Mechanical and General Inventions Co Ltd v Austin* [1935] AC 346 at 373 per Lord Wright. Where, by law, it is a party's right, relevant reasons are needed for dispensing with it.

[64] With the decline of the number of civil jury trials, the congestion of court lists and pressures of court management (*Sali v SPC Ltd* (1993) 67 ALJR 841 at 849; 116 ALR 625 at 636; *Queensland v J L Holdings Pty Ltd* (1997) 189 CLR 146 and 153), it is not surprising that some judges, in jurisdictions where civil juries remain, would be sympathetic to motions to dispense with the jury. It may equally be expected that appellate courts would then have a function to protect from unlawful deprivation of a jury those who have requisitioned jury trials and who maintain their legal entitlement. A State Parliament could abolish completely any entitlement to a civil jury trial (as occurred in South Australia: Juries Act 1927 (SA), s 5). Or Parliament could confine that entitlement to limited cases so as to exempt cases such as the present. Following the hearing of the present appeal the New South Wales Parliament enacted a Bill designed to curtail civil jury trials both in the Supreme Court and the District Court: Courts Legislation Amendment (Civil Juries) Act 2001 (NSW). The amending Act commenced operation on 18 January 2002 ... It provides some evidence of an acceptance by that Parliament of the law applied by the Court of Appeal in the present case. If the law were as the appellant suggested, the amending Act would have been unnecessary.

[65] Unless the Court of Appeal intervened in a case such as the present, effectively, the interlocutory order dispensing with the jury would be final. A party dissatisfied with the judge's order would be faced in every case with the supposed *Darrell Lea* principle. There would then be no effective sanction against inappropriate and unlawful deprivation of the right to jury trial for which the law provides. We cannot accept such a withdrawal of judicial protection of established legal rights.

[Their Honours then discussed the authorities which should guide the exercise of the relevant discretion, concluding that *Pambula* was good law. In applying those principles, they said:]

[81] The strong language in which, during argument, Christie DCJ expressed his opposition to jury trial of civil proceedings would naturally make an appellate court examine his Honour's decision in this case with added vigilance. It is true that Christie DCJ reserved his decision. The interval for reflection was only a matter of hours. It is true that his Honour stated that he had merely expressed a "personal view" about civil juries and that it had not influenced his decision in this case. But even then, he went on to refer to the "enormous cost of litigation", thereby suggesting that jury trial contributed unreasonably to such cost. It is true that there are some in efficiencies in civil jury trials. But there are also countervailing advantages. Precisely because their verdicts are unpredictable, juries tend to promote settlement. Jury verdicts in civil actions also tend to promote finality: cf *Naxakis v Western General Hospital* (1999) 197 CLR 269 at 286–287 [52]–[53]. The practical necessities of jury trials also tend to discourage undue length of proceedings which has lately become a feature of much civil litigation. The remarks of Christie DCJ are therefore disputable. Despite his Honour's denial, they tend, with respect, to suggest that his Honour remained unrepentant and adhered to the strong opinions that he had stated when the motion had been before him earlier in the day.

[82] Because Christie DCJ rejected as irrelevant the way that a jury might treat the appellant's criminal convictions, the ultimate ground for his Honour's order was the simple fact that a medical witness had to come from interstate. Some other lay witnesses also had to come from the country. These were, in a sense, matters special to the particular case before the

court. But they were completely unconvincing considerations for the order that followed. The respondent had made it clear that the interstate medical witness would be required to attend, whatever the mode of trial. For simple forensic reasons the lay witnesses would also probably be required. With every respect, the notion that conducting the trial before a jury would render appropriate arrangements for such witnesses difficult or impossible, lacks all conviction. One is therefore left with no reason for the order but Christie DCJ's dislike of civil jury trial.

[83] As this consideration was incompatible with the provisions of the Act that continued to provide for jury trial and the right of parties to summon juries to try their cases in defined cases in the New South Wales District Court, it was a consideration incompatible with the law as stated in *Pambula*. More to the point, it was incompatible with the scheme of the Act as it then stood. The Court of Appeal was right to intervene to correct the erroneous order that Christie DCJ had made. It was correct to set aside the judgment which followed a trial before a tribunal other than that to which the respondent was entitled in terms of the Act.

18.3.18   Even in the United States, where the civil jury enjoys constitutional protection at federal level and in many states, litigants rarely opt for jury trial: estimates suggest that as few as 2 per cent of trials are jury trials. In England, they are, effectively, no longer available in personal injuries cases. In British Columbia, use of juries has declined to the point where only 1–2 per cent of Supreme Court civil trials are jury trials. (By contrast, the Ontario Supreme Court uses juries relatively frequently, and between 1988–89 and 1994–95, their use increased from 15 per cent to 22 per cent of civil trials.) See J Bouck, 'Civil Jury Trials — Assessing Non-pecuniary Damages — Civil Jury Reform' (2002) 81 *Canadian Bar Review* 493. This, combined with the Australian trends, suggests either that the Supreme Court's faith in the civil jury is not generally shared, or alternatively, that many doubt whether the fact-finding capacity of the civil jury justifies the extra costs occasioned by jury trial.

There has been some research into jury decision-making. Empirical studies of jurors have taken a variety of forms, some of which would be illegal in Australia, without the approval of the Attorneys-General. Judges have been surveyed to assess the degree to which they agreed with jury verdicts. Jurors have been interviewed after trials. Arrangements have been made to observe how 'shadow juries' handle actual cases being decided by real juries. On the basis of archival research, multivariate analyses have been conducted with a view to assessing the impact of various legal and extra-legal variables on outcomes. In addition, researchers have conducted a host of 'simulations' of varying degrees of similitude. An early piece of research envisaged bugging jury rooms but was nipped in the bud before it yielded fruit.

Space does not permit a detailed summary of the sizeable research literature. However, a lucid, well-documented summary of the relevant literature (as at 1989) is provided by E Greene 'On Juries and Damage Awards: the Process of Decision-making' (1989) 52 *L & CP* 225. Another good, comprehensive (and more up-to-date) summary of the evidence is provided by N Vidmar, 'The American Civil Jury for Ausländer (Foreigners)' (2003) 13 *Duke J Comp & Int'l L* 95. (The reason for the bizarre title is that the article appears in an edition of the journal honouring a German.) L Noah, 'Civil Jury Nullification' (2001) 86 *Iowa L Rev* 1601 includes a discussion of evidence bearing on the extent to which American civil juries disregard law.

There is support for the following generalisations, and, encouragingly, this support often comes from studies using a variety of research methods.

- Juries tend to agree with judges. When they do not, criminal juries tend to find for defendants; civil juries tend to find for plaintiffs and be about 20 per cent more generous in their damages awards.

- There is method to judge–jury differences. In general, judges are able to understand why juries have disagreed with them. The explanations judges give for such disagreements are consistent with findings which emerge from empirical research into jury decision-making practices.

- Juries sometimes take account of extra-legal variables. In civil cases, this means implementing de facto contributory negligence regimes even when the legal system makes no such provision; basing damages on the defendant's perceived capacity to pay; and awarding pre-judgment interest even in jurisdictions which make no provision for such an award. Juries take account of the possibility that defendants are insured. They not infrequently take account of lawyers' fees and are familiar with the usual contingency fee arrangements that operate in the United States.

- Damages awards vary directly with the strength of the plaintiff's case relative to the defendant's, and directly with the defendant's perceived blameworthiness.

- Juries take their role seriously. In routine cases — and, arguably — more complex cases as well, they appear to handle evidence well and their deliberations tend to improve the quality of their decisions. Their capacity to apply the law appears to be markedly inferior to their capacity to weigh up facts. Their deliberations in this connection are as likely to lead them astray as towards a correct understanding of the law.

Cecil, Hans and Wiggins have reviewed the literature on the capacity of juries to handle complex civil cases, an issue which arises in the United States by virtue of the fact that the United States Constitution entrenches the right to trial by jury in civil cases where more than $20 is at stake: J Cecil, V Hans and E Wiggins, 'Citizen Comprehension of Difficult Issues: Lessons from Civil Jury Trials' [1991] *Am ULR* 727. They argue that juries are capable of handling complex cases. They note that judges are evenly divided as to the merits of juries as compared with panels of experts (not quite a ringing indorsement of juries). While jurors vary in competence, the more knowledgeable guide the less knowledgeable. While juries have difficulty understanding economic arguments, Cecil et al note that the same might be said of judges. They concede that juries have particular problems with statistical evidence but, oddly, do not raise the possibility that the same might be said for at least some judges. They report studies which indicate juries are particularly resistant to experts' risk assessments, but suggest that this may well be justified. They conclude by arguing that jurors' performance could be improved if issues were more clearly delineated, if more use were to be made of special verdicts, and if juries were to be allowed to take notes.

These findings should be treated with care. The composition of juries varies over time and place. There are institutional differences too. However, the United States findings suggest that the arguments for the case for the civil jury are heavily dependent on whether one is seeking to rebut a presumption in its favour or against it. There is no evidence to suggest that it performs *better* than judges, except in so far as some scholars regard disregarding the law in the interests of justice as a virtue. It is scarcely an efficient means of fact finding, although against the added costs it entails must be offset the fact that — unlike judges — juries are not obliged to give reasons. They can therefore give their verdict shortly after having heard all the evidence, and they save the judge the time that would otherwise be consumed by the writing of reasons to justify his or her findings of fact. (But by this logic, it would be desirable to exempt judges from having to give reasons for their findings of fact.)

The case for the civil jury must therefore largely lie elsewhere. Where dispensing with jury trial would require amendment to a Bill of Rights, it is understandable that it would be resisted: it requires little imagination to recognise that once a precedent is created for curbing constitutional rights, other constitutionally entrenched rights might also be in danger. It is also arguable that it is desirable that citizens participate in the judicial process and that a judicial system is the better for its regulars having to pitch their arguments to ordinary citizens rather than to each other. If one's concern is with the legitimacy of judicial decisions, it may be as well that decisions reflect the interpretation placed on the evidence by semi-randomly selected members of the public rather than by professionals. And poll data suggest that, at least in the United States and Ontario, there is widespread support for civil juries. However, it is clear that these considerations carry relatively little weight with lawmakers or litigants. For a recent discussion of the issue see J Horan, 'The Law and Lore of the Australian Civil Jury and Civil Justice System' (2006) 9 *FJLR* 29. This article highlights the degree to which beliefs about civil juries are based on anecdote rather than systematic research, and presents some useful data which go a small way towards filling the evidentiary void. In particular, on the basis of a survey of Victorian civil jurors, she demonstrates that contrary to a common stereotype, juries are better educated than the overall Victorian demographically representative; more heavily drawn from the middle-aged, and less from the over 65s; indistinguishable in gender distribution to the general population, and only slightly less likely to be non-English speaking: at 47. Jurors, civil court judges and court staff indicated that they would prefer jury trial if they were plaintiffs, but not to the same extent if they were defendants. Of 18 judges interviewed, two indicated that they would always opt for trial by judge alone, four would always opt for jury trial, and fourteen would opt for a jury if they were plaintiffs and a judge if they were defendants: at 48. Interpreting these figures is complicated by the discrepancy between the number of respondents and the number of responses, but it suggests that judges regard either juries or judges as biased.

18.3.19 Further reading

R Boubjerg, F Sloan, A Dor and C Hsieh, 'Juries and Justice: Are Malpractice and Other Personal Injuries Created Equal?' (1991) 54 *L & CP* 5 (archival research).

P Carrington, 'The Civil Jury and American Democracy' (2003) 13 *Duke J Comp and Int'l L* 79 (arguments for, and acknowledgment of the problems with, civil juries).

J Cooper, E Bennett and H Sukel, 'Complex Scientific Testimony: How do Jurors Make Decisions?' (1996) 20 *Law and Human Behavior* 379 (experimental, using members of a middle-class community).

V Hans and W Lofquist, 'Jurors' Judgments of Business Liability in Tort Cases: Implications for the Litigation Explosion Debate' (1992) 12 *Law and Soc'y Rev* 85 (interviews of former jurors).

R MacCoun, 'Differential Treatment of Corporate Defendants by Juries: an Examination of the "Deep Pockets" Hypothesis' (1996) 30 *Law and Soc'y Rev* 121 (experimental, using jurors from jury pool).

A Reifman, S Gusick and P Ellsworth, 'Real Jurors' Understanding of the Law in Real Cases' (1992) 16 *Law and Human Behavior* 539 (survey of citizens who had been called for jury duty).

N Vidmar, 'Making Inferences about Jury Behavior from Jury Verdict Statistics' (1994) 18 *Law and Human Behavior* 599 (critique of archival research).

(All readings cited are American.)

Arbitration and referees

18.3.20   Rules and legislation provide for proceedings or parts of proceedings to be referred to arbitrators and referees: Federal Court of Australia Act 1976 (Cth) ss 53A–54B; FCR Div 28.6; ACT r 1532; Civil Procedure Act 2005 (NSW) ss 35–55; NSW Pt 20, Div 3; Supreme Court Act (NT) 1979 ss 26, 27, 30; Qld r 501; Supreme Court Act 1935 (SA) ss 66, 67; SA rr 208(2)(c), 221; Tas r 574; Vic rr 50.01, 50.08; Supreme Court Act 1935 (WA) s 50; WA O 32 r 5. The powers of arbitrators and referees vary somewhat from jurisdiction to jurisdiction and some confusion is occasioned by the nomenclature employed in the rules: *Astor Properties Pty Ltd v L'Union des Assurance de Paris* (1989) 17 NSWLR 483.

The traditional Australian arrangements have their origin in nineteenth-century English provisions. They distinguished between reference of a question arising in a case to a referee or court official who was to make a report, and ordering the trial of a proceeding or a question arising in a proceeding by an official, an arbitrator or referee whose award or report would, unless set aside, enjoy the status of a jury verdict. References for the making of a report did not require the consent of the parties. Orders that a case or question be tried by an arbitrator or referee could be made with the consent of the parties. Orders could be made without consent if:

(a) the issue required prolonged examination of documents, or scientific or local investigation which could not be conveniently done by a jury or judge; or

(b) the matter involved the taking of accounts.

However, if the case or question was to be *tried* by an arbitrator or referee, the arbitrator or referee had to be a person on whom the parties could agree.

Most jurisdictions maintain a distinction between references for reports and references to an arbitrator for a determination. For the sake of convenience, the term 'referee' will be used to denote the person responsible for making a report, and the term 'arbitrator' to denote the person responsible for making a determination or award.

All state and territory courts are empowered to refer a matter to a referee for the making of a report. The consent of the parties is not required. In general, a question arising in a proceeding may be referred, but not (except in the Federal Court, the Australian Capital Territory, New South Wales and South Australia) the whole proceeding: FCR r 28.61(1); ACT r 1531(1); NSW r 20.14; Supreme Court Act 1979 (NT) ss 25, 26; Qld r 501; Supreme Court Act 1935 (SA) s 67; SA r 208(2)(c); Tas r 574; Vic r 50.01; Supreme Court Act 1935 (WA) s 50; WA O 4A, r 3(2), O 32 r 3.

In most jurisdictions, there is provision for reference of a proceeding or a question arising in a proceeding to an 'arbitrator' for determination: Federal Court of Australia Act 1976 (Cth) s 53A(1)(a), FCR Divs 28.1, 28.2; Civil Procedure Act 2005 (NSW) ss 35–55; Supreme Court

Act 1979 (NT) ss 27, 30; Supreme Court Act 1935 (SA) s 66; SA r 221; Vic r 50.08; Supreme Court Act 1935 (WA) ss 51–2. In the Northern Territory, Victoria and South Australia, the parties' consent is required: Supreme Court Act (NT) s 27(1)(a); Vic r 50.08; Supreme Court Act 1935 (WA) s 51(1).

In New South Wales, the court, of its own motion or on application, may refer proceedings for determination by an arbitrator if the matter involves a claim to recover damages or money or for equitable relief ancillary to such a claim: Civil Procedure Act 2005 (NSW) s 38. However, changes to the jurisdiction of the District Court have meant that it is now rare for arbitrations to be conducted in the Supreme Court. In the Supreme Court's Annual Review for 2009, the court reported that:

> The use of arbitration declined primarily because the District Court's jurisdiction expanded to include most of the work that had typically been arbitrated in the Supreme Court. During the past five years, the Court has referred only one case to arbitration: [at 28]

The history of the relevant provisions has been set out in a number of decisions. Cole J provided a lucid history of the New South Wales provisions in *Astor Properties Pty Ltd v L'Union des Assurance de Paris* (1989) 17 NSWLR 483.

18.3.21C **Super Pty Ltd (formerly known as Leda Constructions Pty Ltd) v S J P Formwork (Aust) Pty Ltd**
(1992) 29 NSWLR 549
Court of Appeal (NSW)

[Questions arising in a building dispute were referred to a referee. The trial judge adopted the referee's report, having rejected an attempt by the unsuccessful party to reagitate the factual issues which had been canvassed before the referee. The appeal raised the question of what principles should be adopted by a court in deciding whether and to what extent to adopt a referee's report. In the course of his judgment, Gleeson CJ discussed the background to the relevant provisions. Pt 72 regulated references to referees under the now repealed rules.]

Gleeson CJ (at 558–60): The historical background to the provisions of Pt 72 can be seen from an examination of the judgments of Stephen J and Jacobs J in *Buckley v Bennell Design & Constructions Pty Ltd* (1978) 140 CLR 1 and Cole J in *Astor Properties Pty Ltd v L'Union des Assurance de Paris* (1989) 17 NSWLR 483.

The former case was concerned with the provisions of the Arbitration Act 1902 in so far as they applied to references to arbitration under an order of the court. Under that Act the court had the power to order that proceedings, or any question or issue of fact arising therein, be tried before an arbitrator agreed on by the parties or before a referee appointed by the court for the purpose. The referee or arbitrator was deemed to be an officer of the court and was obliged to conduct the reference in accordance with the rules of court and subject to any directions of the court. The report or award of a referee or arbitrator on such a reference was, unless set aside by the court, equivalent to the verdict of a jury given in proceedings triable by a jury.

The same Act also provided for extracurial submissions to arbitration, and the question in the case was whether the grounds upon which the court might set aside or remit an award by an arbitrator or referee agreed or appointed under the provisions dealing with reference pursuant to an order of the court were the same rather narrow grounds as those upon which a court might set aside an award of an arbitrator operating pursuant to an extracurial submission. The High Court answered that question in the negative, overruling a decision of the Supreme Court that had stood since 1896.

Stephen J pointed out that a reference under an order of the court to an [559] arbitrator or referee, as distinct from extracurial or conventional arbitration, was simply a special form of trial. This was emphasised by the provisions that the arbitrator or referee was deemed to be an officer of the court, and the award was equivalent to the verdict of a jury. His Honour pointed out that there was a long history, in England, of special methods of trial of a like character. The Court of Chancery had been accustomed to refer disputed issues of fact for report by a master or chief clerk, or for trial at Common Law before a judge and jury or to be awarded upon by experts specially selected for the purpose. The courts of Common Law had power to refer matters of account to arbitrators or to court officers or, in country cases, to county court judges. These were procedures with a history quite separate and distinct from that of conventional arbitration resulting from submission to arbitration out of court.

The majority of the High Court concluded that an award of an arbitrator or referee, under the provisions of the Arbitration Act 1902 concerning references pursuant to an order of the court, could be set aside on grounds similar to those upon which the verdict of a jury could be set aside, that is to say, for error of law, or where the decision was against the evidence and the weight of evidence. Jacobs J said (at 36):

> ... The authority of the referee or arbitrator is only that given by Rules of Court or directions of the Court. If a referee or arbitrator is given express or implied authority to determine questions of law, including the admissibility of evidence it cannot be implied that he has authority to determine those questions against the law. If he decides contrary to law or acts perversely or unreasonably, as he would do if he decided against the evidence and weight of evidence, he exceeds his authority and the report or award may be set aside, or remitted.

It is not without significance that the High Court decision in *Buckley* was deliberately made with a view to encouraging greater use of the available procedures for references by the court to arbitrators or referees. The members of the majority thought that those procedures had been stultified by the approach that had previously been taken of limiting the scope for review to that applicable to conventional arbitration out of court. Jacobs J expressed the hope that new rules of court would be promulgated which contained a clearer definition of the authority of referees and arbitrators and of the power of the court to review what they did. This, it was expected, would encourage more use by judges of the procedure of reference to an arbitrator or a referee.

By the time the High Court, in *Buckley*, came to reconsider the established law concerning review of the awards of arbitrators or referees made under an order of the court pursuant to the Arbitration Act 1902, the Supreme Court Act 1970 had been enacted, and the rules of court included Pt 72, which dealt with arbitrators and referees. The Arbitration Act 1902 was repealed with the introduction of the Commercial Arbitration Act 1984. The latter Act dealt only with conventional arbitration, that is to say, arbitration pursuant to submissions out of court. The rules of the Supreme Court were then amended and Pt 72A was inserted to deal with arbitrations that were the subject of the Commercial Arbitration Act 1984. Part 72 remained to deal with references to arbitrators or referees under order of the court. The Supreme Court Act was amended to insert s 124(2), which empowered the [560] making of rules to make provision for the Court to refer the whole of proceedings, or any question or issue arising in any proceedings, to an arbitrator or referee and for the consequences of a determination or report by an arbitrator or referee, the manner in which such a determination or report may be called in question, and whether or not, or to what extent, a determination or report may be called in question on a matter of fact or law. Obviously, the rulemaking power thus conferred is very wide, and that itself tends to undermine the contention that all litigants have a right to have all issues in any case determined by a judge. ...

In *Astor Properties Pty Ltd*, Cole J pointed to certain anomalies and uncertainties resulting from the continued use in Pt 72 of the terms 'arbitrator' and 'referee', and of the differences in some of the provisions of Pt 72 relating to the effect of a decision of an arbitrator or referee, and the procedure for review of that decision. He said that, in the light of the history, the references in Pt 72 to arbitrators were probably intended to apply to persons who were selected or agreed on by the parties, in contrast to referees, who were nominated or appointed by the judge. He thought the distinction served no continuing purpose. His Honour pointed out (at 490) that one thing, however, was clear. Whether one was dealing with an arbitrator or a referee, the decision contained in the report only had legal effect as the result of an order of the court made pursuant to Pt 72, r 13. The recommendations for further change were taken up, and Pt 72 was amended in September 1989. The relevant provisions of Pt 72 as thus amended have been referred to above.

18.3.22 For the analogous pre-Commercial Arbitration Act provisions in Victoria, see Brooking J's judgment in *Nichols v Stamer* [1980] VR 479. For the pre-1996 South Australian provisions, see Debell J's discussion in *Leighton Contractors (SA) Pty Ltd v Hazama Corp (Aust) Pty Ltd* (1991) 56 SASR 47.

18.3.23 Private arbitrations are not discussed here. However, note *Aerospatiale Holdings Australia Pty Ltd v Elspan International Ltd* (1992) 28 NSWLR 321, where the contractual arrangements between a number of the parties (but not all) to a dispute provided that the dispute was to be resolved by arbitration. Cole J ruled that the arbitrator should also act as a referee and report in relation to the dispute in so far as it involved parties not party to the private arbitration. His judgment includes a careful discussion of why this course was appropriate.

Courts vary in their attitude to arbitration and references. Compare the views expressed in *Honeywell Pty Ltd v Austral Motors Holdings Ltd* and *Park Rail Developments Pty Ltd v R J Pearce Associates Pty Ltd* (extracts below).

18.3.24C **Honeywell Pty Ltd v Austral Motors Holdings Ltd**
[1980] Qd R 355
Supreme Court of Queensland

[The plaintiff sued for money allegedly due under a lease of a computer. The defendant argued that the computer had turned out to be totally useless and counterclaimed for money already paid to the plaintiff. The plaintiff sought a trial of the issues of fact by an arbitrator appointed by the court. The defendant sought trial by jury.]

Campbell J (at 359–61): Order 97, r 1 gives to the court a discretion to order that any matter in dispute be referred to arbitration. In my opinion that discretion should rarely be exercised in the absence of consent of both parties. I think that there is much force in the argument for the defendant that every person is as a general rule entitled to have his civil disputes tried and determined in a court of law and that the discretion to refer to arbitration should in the absence of consent, be exercised only in cases of an exceptional nature. The attitude of the parties to litigation towards the mode of trial is a relevant consideration. In *Silk v Eberhardt* [1959] QWN 29, Philp J expressed the view that, except in special cases, building contracts should not be sent to arbitration because of the great cost to the parties. His Honour said:

> If one party objects, my feeling is that we should not impose that expense — that the judges should do the work.

I am not persuaded that I should make an order that the trial of the issues of fact in this case be determined by an arbitrator. The issues [360] will involve undoubtedly a great deal of scientific and technical evidence of a complex nature but it seems to me that a judge with the help of experts in the relevant fields should be able to come to a proper decision. This is a case, like so many others which come before the courts these days, where expert witnesses will give material evidence but it is not they who decide the issues. Similarly, when assessors are appointed it is for them to advise and for the judge to decide.

The defendant wishes to have the decision of a judicial tribunal and not the decision merely of a person skilled in the appropriate scientific field. It is very likely in this case that the fact finding process will be a difficult one and it is likely that there will be conflicting views and opinions of expert witnesses. In my opinion the fact finding process will be more satisfactorily handled by a judicial officer than by a person who lacks the training, experience and skills of a trial court judge. In a complex case of this sort there will be problems arising as to the admissibility of evidence and a person lacking legal training will find such matters very difficult to decide.

After the lengthy process of discovery is completed and further particulars relating to the behaviour of the computer are provided it is probable that the issues will become more clearly defined; even during the course of the trial itself there may be a redefinition and reclarification of the matters in dispute. It may be that the pleadings will have to be amended at a later stage, particularly after the inspection of the relevant documents is completed, and the action may take a different shape.

There are often advantages in having the facts of building and engineering disputes and of some relating to trade and commerce decided by arbitration, for such a procedure may well be quicker and cheaper than submitting the issues to the ordinary processes of the law. Moreover, building disputes frequently involve the tribunal in a detailed examination of a large number of separate or unrelated items analogous to the taking of accounts. The arbitrator selected by the parties is generally a person well acquainted with the particular trade or area of commerce; he is chosen because of his knowledge and experience and the calling of numerous expert witnesses therefore becomes unnecessary. The arbitrator brings to the issues his own judgment and is not merely concerned with weighing expert evidence. Although here there are allegations of numerous breakdowns and failures by the computer they are all subsidiary to the major questions, namely, whether it was inherently defective and incapable of functioning and whether it was in accordance with the terms (express or implied) of the written contract of supply.

In short, it is my opinion that this case is concerned with the sort of disputes which normally call for judicial determination and which should, if one of the parties so wishes, be tried by a judicial tribunal in accordance with the proper rules of evidence and procedure in an open public forum. The parties will have available to them persons with the relevant [361] experience and specialised knowledge who will be able to impart the necessary knowledge not only to counsel but also to the trial judge. I do not consider that the factual issues are so technical or complex as to warrant my taking them away from a judge. Of course, the trial judge may, in certain events and in relation to specific issues, determine to seek assistance from scientifically qualified assessors or to obtain the report of a special referee, but at this juncture a court is not in a position to make up its mind as to whether any issues should be so dealt with, or to make any proper adjudication as to whether any and which issues should be referred to arbitration.

[Summons dismissed.]

18.3.25C   Park Rail Developments Pty Ltd v R J Pearce Associates Pty Ltd
(1987) 8 NSWLR 123
Supreme Court of New South Wales

[The plaintiff applied to have a matter referred to an arbitrator pursuant to NSW Pt 72.]

Smart J (at 126–30): There has been a change in the attitude of the courts as to the value of arbitrations and references and the desirability of people of suitable standing, experience and qualifications dealing with, inter alia, technical matters and contract administration. In part, this has been due to the training provided for arbitrators by bodies such as the National Institute of Arbitrators. Delay, costs, and their effect, have been important. With the heavy loads on the court lists it has often not been possible, despite the best will of the courts in organising lists and trying to streamline the hearing and the profession in preparing matters, to provide for the early hearing desired, especially when the increasing complexity of construction cases often results in a two to four weeks hearing and sometimes longer. Many contractors, subcontractors and small consultants have limited financial resources and need the money claimed to survive financially or to carry on and develop their business in the normal way. As arbitrations and references usually take place promptly the parties are not encumbered with the costs of proceedings extending over several years awaiting a hearing. Because of the technical knowledge of the arbitrators or referees, the hearing may be quicker. It is sometimes submitted that the hearing before an arbitrator or referee will be more expensive because of the need to pay the arbitrator, the increased transcript costs and room hire. In the overall context of the legal fees, those of the expert consultants, and the costs of the lost executive time, this extra expense is usually not significant. It is often offset by the factors mentioned earlier, and if, as is often the case, the amount at issue is large, it loses any importance.

To shorten the hearing and to crystallise the issues the parties have, at the direction of the Court, filed affidavit evidence. It is expected that the hearing [127] time will occupy from one to two weeks. Having regard to the other matters ahead of this one in both the Building and Engineering List and the Long Causes List, this matter is unlikely to be heard before the end of 1988, notwithstanding that the Court on 22 October 1986 expedited the hearing in view of the plaintiffs' financial position. A hearing date in late 1988 will leave the Plaintiffs in a difficult position ...

[129] Both *Honeywell* and *A T & N R Taylor & Sons Pty Ltd v Brival Pty Ltd* were decided prior to the Commercial Arbitration Act 1984 and the insertion of subs (2) into s 124 of the Supreme Court Act of this State. Whatever be the position in other States, in New South Wales there are a number of referees well-known to the Court in its Building and Engineering List with extensive experience in handling a variety of large complex building and engineering matters. They are used to having junior and senior counsel appear before them, ruling on evidence, controlling proceedings and resolving difficult factual and contractual issues. They are familiar with the standards required of professional engineers and architects. In appropriate cases retired judges of this Court, with experience in building and engineering matters, are appointed as referees. This Court does not make an order for a reference unless the parties agree on a referee — and this often happens even where there has been a dispute whether there should be a reference — or a suitable referee is available. As a matter of practice, if during a hearing an issue arises on which the referee feels the court should rule in the first instance he tells the parties and the matter comes back before the court and is dealt with promptly. It is not uncommon for the court to deal with the matter at 9.30 am and for the reference to resume later in the morning. The parties and the referee know that during a reference the court is available to assist on short notice.

As a general rule defendants are often not as dismayed by a delay of two to three years in a hearing date as plaintiffs. While interest is payable on a verdict, it is no substitute for having the money promptly and being able to carry on one's business in the normal way. Further, in an industry as fluid as the construction industry, witnesses move interstate to other jobs and over the years the various jobs tend to merge and memories become less distinct and reliable.

In New South Wales the court has no predisposition to making or refusing an order for a reference depending on the wishes of one party. It has power to appoint a referee against the wishes of both parties although it is understandably cautious in doing so. Each opposed application for the appointment of an arbitrator or referee has to be considered on its own merits in the light of all the prevailing circumstances. In some cases no reference will be appropriate whereas in others it will be appropriate to refer the whole of the proceedings or some issues. On occasions the reference will be to [130] determine the issues and on others to inquire and report. The matters which will generally require consideration include:

(a) the suitability of the issues for determination by a referee and the availability of a suitable referee;

(b) the delay before the court can hear and determine the matter and how quickly a suitable referee can do so. Building and engineering matters, because of their length and complexity, often require either the judge or the referee to devote extensive time after the hearing to considering and resolving the issues;

(c) the prejudice the parties will suffer by any delay;

(d) whether the reference will occasion additional costs of significance or is likely to save costs;

(e) the terms of any reference including the issues and whether they should be referred for determination or inquiry or report.

In this case I am satisfied that the issues are suitable for determination by a referee and that there are a number of suitable referees used by the Court who could hear and determine the matter, that the delay in the Court being able to hear the matter is too long and that the plaintiffs will suffer serious financial prejudice by such a delay. I do not think that the extra expense is likely to be significant overall. It will be offset by the matter being resolved promptly rather than in two years time. Witnesses' memories and their availability are likely to be better now than after the lapse of another two years.

18.3.26   Question

1. To what extent do the differences between *Honeywell* and *Park Rail* reflect: (a) the role and powers of arbitrators under different rules; (b) assessments of the quality of available arbitrators; (c) assessments of the relative costs of trial by judge as opposed to 'trial by arbitrator/referee'; (d) the pressures operating on the relevant courts; and (e) familiarity with use of references? See *Bold Park Senior Citizens Centre & Homes Inc v Bollig Abbott & Partners (Gulf) Pty Ltd* (1997) 19 WAR 281 where Ipp J endorsed the *Honeywell* approach and discussed why the New South Wales courts took a different approach. In *Abigroup Contractors Pty Ltd v BPB Pty Ltd* [2000] VSC 261, Byrne J concluded (at [15]) that an order 'for reference out would be made over the objections of a party only in exceptional circumstances'.

18.3.27   For a rare example of a successful appeal against the terms of appointment of a referee, see *Rankine v Rankine* (1995) 18 ACSR 725; 14 ACLC 116. There Thomas J at ACSR 732; at ACLC 123, said:

Issues such as the propriety of the company's actions; the commission of breaches of a duty by the respondents, and the manner in which the valuation should be varied so as to eliminate the effects of the oppression in the granting of the ultimate relief are not matters that an accountant or valuer can decide ...

However, Thomas J considered that referees could be appointed before a trial had begun, and displayed a generally sympathetic attitude to the use of referees.

18.3.28   Official statistics about the use made of the reference power are elusive and possibly non-existent. Use of referees seems not to be particularly common, especially outside New South Wales. A survey of Austlii yielded 557 decisions and orders given by the New South Wales Supreme Court in 2011. The word 'referee' appears in 40 of these decisions, but of those only 22 were given in relation to cases in which an order had been made referring the matter to a referee. These related to 16 cases. (The other 18 decisions were cases where 'referee' was used in a different sense, where a citation made reference to referees, where the court made reference to the possibility that an issue could usefully be dealt with by a referee, or where an application for reference was refused.) Use of referees seems even rarer elsewhere. Similar Austlii searches indicate that referees were used in three Federal Court cases; one in a Queensland case, and none in the other jurisdictions.

These figures could be expected to yield underestimates of the use of referees, since there are likely to be cases where referees are appointed without leaving traces in Austlii's collections, and a comparison between the total Austlii figures and normal filings (around 13,000 for the Common Law and Equity lists, per annum) highlights the degree to which this is the fate of most cases. Observations by Allsop J suggest that references play a more important role than the statistics might suggest:

> The success of this procedure in the Supreme Court of New South Wales can be measured by the huge extent of the building, technology and construction list. Any perusal of the newspapers, generally on a Friday, will indicate a huge number of matters in the list. However, there has not been a judge hear the factual basis of a building case in the Supreme Court for some years. The court effectively acts as a clearing house for such disputes with careful supervision of directions and references to a wide variety of referees. An enormous body of work is dealt with to the general satisfaction of the commercial community, which brings disputes from all over Australia to be dealt with in this fashion: 'The judicial disposition of cases: dealing with complex and specialised factual material' (2009–10) Summer *Bar News* 75 at 80.

This would be consistent with use of the procedure nonetheless being an atypical procedure for the resolution of cases in general, especially given that annual filings in the Construction and Technology List have not exceeded 120 in recent years. However, the Austlii referee decisions highlight the fact that a majority of reference cases seem to involve non-construction issues, and — in particular — accounting. But whatever the position might be in New South Wales, the Austlii statistics and Allsop J's observations suggest that other jurisdictions make considerably less use of the procedure than does New South Wales.

SPLITTING TRIALS

18.4.1   There are obvious potential advantages in courts being able to make conclusive findings in relation to some issues in a proceeding before considering others. If a plaintiff's success is dependent upon a particular finding in relation to a legal issue, it may well be more convenient for all concerned that the legal issue be resolved before the court considers evidence whose importance is dependent on the outcome of the legal issue. Likewise, if a decision on the question of liability can be made relatively quickly, it may be convenient that this issue be resolved before consideration of the question of damages. Conversely, however, it is usually more efficient to hear a case in *toto*. Doing so wards off duplication in the delivery of evidence and averts the delays that could arise if witnesses, counsel and a trial judge had to be gathered together on several occasions.

To some extent, the procedures for seeking summary judgment enable parties to avoid an unnecessarily prolonged trial. However, these procedures are not always satisfactory. The summary judgment procedures are largely designed for disposing of 'hopeless' cases: see 12.3.1E–12.5.1. It is therefore not appropriate in those cases where a preliminary legal issue is relatively complex and its solution by no means straightforward. Nor are the preliminary judgment procedures appropriate where a decision in relation to a preliminary issue involves arguable questions of fact. Accordingly, the rules provide procedures for splitting cases so that a court may hear and decide some of the questions arising in a given matter before proceeding (if this be necessary) to a consideration of other issues: FCR r 30.01; ACT r 1521; NSW r 28.2; NT r 47.04; Qld r 483(1); SA r 211; Tas r 559; Vic r 47.04; WA O 32 r 5.

The High Court Rules no longer make express provision for splitting trials, but they allow for the making of directions: r 27.06. Parties can respond to pleadings by demurrer, in which case further proceedings are governed by directions: r 27.07. There is also provision for the hearing (by consent) of one or more questions of law: r 27.08.

There is a presumption against splitting a trial. Determination of separate questions is to be ordered only when it is 'just and convenient' to do so. It is inappropriate to consider a question of law in circumstances where the facts are in dispute. In such a case, the answer to the question does: no more than declare that the law dictates a particular result when certain facts in the material or pleadings are established. ... Such a result cannot assist the efficient administration of justice. It does not finally resolve the dispute or quell the controversy. Nor does it constitute a step that will in the course of the proceedings necessarily dictate the result of those proceedings: *Bass v Permanent Trustee Co Ltd* (1999) 198 CLR 334 at 357 [49] per Gleeson CJ, Gaudron, McHugh, Gummow, Hayne and Callinan JJ.

It would not be appropriate to canvass liability and damages separately if the same evidence was likely to bear on both. This would mean a danger that much evidence would have to be examined twice. Moreover, even in cases where the 'sub-cases' might seem relatively discrete, courts might well be worried about the danger that splitting the case would occasion delay. Assembling the *dramatis personae* for a case can be a logistic nightmare. Doing this on several discrete occasions may be even more difficult. In complex cases, these problems might well produce anomalous situations. Different bodies of available evidence might mean that in relation to some factual issues, the outcome might differ according to the stage of the proceedings. Courts will therefore be inclined to split a case into 'sub-cases' only if it is clear that there are good grounds for doing so, and no good reason for not doing so.

The following extract is an example of where the court decided against splitting the trial:

18.4.2C	**Evans Deakin Industries Ltd v Commonwealth**
	[1983] 1 Qd R 40
	Supreme Court of Queensland, Full Court

[The plaintiff contracted to provide an oil carrier to the defendant. It did not do so by the prescribed time, but claimed that a number of unexpected events which had interfered with its fulfilment of the contract constituted frustration, and that it was entitled to be paid on a *quantum meruit* basis. The defendant denied that there had been frustration, and sought to split the trial, arguing that a decision favourable to it on the frustration issue would obviate the need to consider the *quantum meruit* issue. It argued that the *quantum meruit* issue would involve 'a very laborious and detailed investigation of very numerous and significant items claimed as expenses incurred in a proper course of work on which it is based'. The plaintiff resisted this proposed course, arguing that it would not be possible to separate the frustration and the *quantum meruit* issues, and that, in consequence, some questions would need to be canvassed in two different trials. At first instance, Wanstall CJ dismissed the Commonwealth's application that the issue of liability be tried separately from the issue of quantum.]

Andrews SPJ (at 44–5): I think the circumstances will rarely arise to justify this kind of an order and that great care must be taken before a decision to make one. I think the rarity of such an order does not really reflect a principle, but rather establishes that the circumstances rarely arise to justify it.

Difficulties which may arise where there is no clear demarcation between issues are probably numerous. I have referred to the mustering of witnesses. As well it is apparent that there would be two sets of cross-examination upon evidence touching upon the same sets of facts and two separate decisions as to credibility bearing on overlapping issues of fact. It is by no means certain that the trials would occur before the same judge. There will I think in such a situation be a duplication of costs and, unless it is fairly plain that the resolution of one will ensure a considerable reduction in time and expense involved in the investigation of the balance of the issues, there is no real justification for making an order of this kind, assuming that to be the only relevant consideration.

It should be borne in mind here, that the only assurance in this behalf which has been given by the plaintiff, is that there is a 'serious possibility' that a resolution of the frustration issue would get rid of the case.

I think it is relevant to have a view even though not a definitive view at this stage as to the prospects of success of the plaintiff on the [45] frustration issues. ... I think it is also proper to be influenced to some extent by such a view in coming to a decision on an application of this kind and it seems to me as to those matters that the plaintiff has quite significant difficulties. The learned judge below has said that, although the frustration issue in this case is a major one, its decision would still leave a number of other 'big issues arising on the pleadings'. That is consistent with the view that I have of the matter.

[Thomas J agreed with Andrews J; Campbell J delivered a judgment to the same effect.]

18.4.3   Notes

1. See *TAG Pacific Ltd v McSweeney* (1991) 34 FCR 438; 106 ALR 651 for an example of a split case. Liability had been determined before quantum. The issue was whether the decision on liability (which had been favourable to the applicant) was an interlocutory decision, in which case, leave to appeal would have been required. In *O'Neill v Mann* (1994) 49 FCR 370; 121 ALR 524, the defendant asserted absolute privilege in response to a defamation action. The Federal Court tried the privilege issue separately. Its finding in favour of the defendant effectively disposed of the case. In *AWB v Cole* [2006] FCA 913, Young J reviewed the law relating to trying issues separately and refused an application for a separate trial of legal questions.

2. Trial of preliminary issues under r 47.04 has been found useful in the Victorian Supreme Court's Building Cases List: *Annual Report 1995*, p 29.

PRESENTING THE CASE

18.5.1   All jurisdictions have striven for more efficient trials. Courts are increasingly concerned with discouraging the canvassing of unnecessary issues. Pleadings are now treated as only one of the means whereby the issues are to be defined: see Chapter 11. As noted above, courts have developed other means of confining the issues. Notices to admit represent one such means, albeit one which appears not to be used as often as many commentators would wish (The Honourable Justice M Moynihan, 'Towards a More Efficient Trial Process', paper presented at the *Tenth Annual AIJA Conference*, 1992, p 15; B Lander, 'Commentary', paper presented at the *Tenth Annual AIJA Conference*, p 27), as do the creative use of costs rules to penalise ultimately successful parties who fail on particular issues: see **Chapter 20**. For trial by affadavit, see **15.15**. More important, however, has been the establishment of structures within which parties can better explore the possibility of agreement over some of the issues arising in a proceeding: see **Chapters 3** and **16**. In all jurisdictions there is provision for conferences to explore the degree to which it is possible to confine the issues arising in a particular dispute. Parties are encouraged to facilitate the trial process by agreeing on the evidence that may be admitted, and without requiring proof according to the full rigours of evidence law. Parties are encouraged to identify the issues as sharply as possible. In one sense, parties should be able to do this without needing formal structures.

However, there are several respects in which formal conferences can contribute. They overcome the problem posed by the fear that the first to seek to initiate negotiations may be seen as weak. They take place in the presence of a third party whose presence may serve to discourage unreasonableness. They appear to be effective: The Honourable Justice M Moynihan, 'Towards a More Efficient Trial Process', paper presented at the *Tenth Annual AIJA Conference*, 1992 at pp 8–9, 15–16.

Attempts to achieve greater efficiency appear to coexist with developments which are making for increasingly complex cases. This is not surprising. It is the apparently increasing complexity of trials which is making the achievement of efficiency all the more urgent. Moreover, a system's success in achieving settlement is likely to be reflected in the degree to which its remaining case load is characterised by particularly difficult cases.

Order of evidence and addresses

18.5.2 In most jurisdictions the rules specify the order in which the parties shall normally present their cases: ACT r 1508; NSW r 29.6; NT r 49.01; Tas r 569; Vic r 49.01; WA O 34 r 5. Normally the plaintiff begins, provided that the burden of proof on at least one issue lies with the plaintiff. In the unlikely event of the burden of proof on all issues lying on the defendant, the defendant begins. The party which opens the proceedings (usually the plaintiff) begins with a summary of what its case is to be, followed by evidence from its witnesses. At the end of the opener's case, the opposite party has the option of deciding whether to call witnesses. If that party decides to call witnesses, it sets out the nature of its case and calls its witnesses. At the end of its case, it addresses the court. The opening party then replies. If, however, the opposite party calls no evidence, it is the opener who addresses the court and the other party who replies. In jury trials, having the 'last word' is regarded as an advantage. 'Opposite parties' (in effect, defendants) may therefore prefer to rely on the possibility that the opener's witnesses will not be believed rather than to call evidence in rebuttal. However, this option is not open when opposite parties are relying on a 'positive' defence which they must prove.

In trials before a judge alone, having the last word is likely to be less important. The value attached to having the last word can encourage defendants to seek to define the case in such a way that it is they who open. However, this is not easily done.

18.5.3C   **Portelli v Port Waratah Stevedoring Co Pty Ltd**
[1959] VR 195
Supreme Court of Victoria

[In an action for negligence, the defendant admitted negligence in its amended defence, but alleged contributory negligence. This raised the question: Who should open the case?]

Lowe J (at 195–6): The plaintiff's claim is a claim for damages for negligence and there was in the first instance a denial of negligence and the issue of contributory negligence was raised by the defendant. In an amended pleading, however, the defendant has admitted that the accident was contributed to by negligence on its part or that of its servants of agents, so that the issues of negligence and damage are no longer contested before the jury. The way in which the matter arises now is an application by Mr Laurie [for the plaintiff] for a ruling as to who should open the facts and whether he should have any rebutting case upon evidence in relation to contributory negligence led by the defendant. I think in order to understand the position one has to bear in mind what are the elements of the action brought by the plaintiff. He must allege and prove negligence on the part of the defendant which was a cause of the injury to him and he must also prove the damage which he has suffered from that negligence. In addition, where the issue of contributory negligence is raised and established, he must persuade the jury of the apportionment which has to be made as between the plaintiff and the defendant, having regard to his own share in the responsibility for the damage which has occurred to him. Now under those circumstances I have come to the conclusion that there still remains upon the plaintiff the obligation to show the extent of the damage which he has suffered and how damages should be apportioned to the satisfaction of the jury and in order to do that it seems to me that he ought to bring before the jury in the first instance the facts upon which he relies to establish those issues. It is true enough that the issue of contributory negligence is one as to which the onus lies upon the [196] defendant and if there were nothing more in the case than that, it might be proper to direct that the defendant should take the labouring oar and should open to the jury, a course which would entail that he would ordinarily have the final word to the jury, but here I think the case is not quite so simple as that, and, having regard to the issues which still remain upon the plaintiff, I think the proper course, and most convenient course, is for the plaintiff to open to the jury the facts upon which he relies. There remains, of course, the question, whether the plaintiff should have any rebutting case in regard to the evidence which is led by the defendant.

As the case stands at present I think he should not have a rebutting case. I think to allow it would really be to allow him to split the case which he is putting to the jury. That of course does not finally conclude any matter which may arise *ex improviso*, as it is put — something which cannot be foreseen — and as to which it might be in the interests of justice to permit him to call further evidence. Short of an exceptional case of that kind, I think the plaintiff must put his whole case to the jury.

18.5.4   There are several exceptions to these general rules. In particular, these rules cover only those cases where there is a plaintiff and a defendant. The position is obviously more complicated where there are several parties. In these cases, the court may give directions. However, in the absence of directions, where there are multiple defendants and they all adduce evidence, the order of the addresses will be their order on the record: *Merrett v Merrett* [1933] VLR 177; *Field v Field* [1948] VLR 400; *Hole v Robinson Bros & Co Pty Ltd* [1956] VLR 13. Where there are multiple defendants but only one adduces evidence, the plaintiff will nonetheless have the last word: *Powell v Begg* (1898) 9 QLJ 110.

The content of addresses

18.5.5 The addresses to the court should contain references to the facts that the party intends to prove. Addresses should not include reference to facts which are irrelevant but prejudicial, and should not be 'inflammatory'. Relevance is determined by pleadings and particulars. Among facts which may be legally irrelevant, but prejudicial, is the fact that a defendant is insured, although, as the Supreme Court noted in *King v Wilkinson* (1957) 57 SR (NSW) 444 at 448:

> Common sense suggests that at the present day few, if any, juries would not be aware of the fact that the defendant on the record is insured.

The amount of damages claimed is not to be mentioned. However, counsel may present a figure or a range of figures in relation to claims for pain and suffering and loss of enjoyment of life: *Marsh v Suleyman* [1983] 1 VR 483, where the court considered that it might well be strategically unwise to do so. *Wellington v Lake George Mines Pty Ltd* (1962) 62 SR (NSW) 326; [1962] NSWR 627 provides an example of an 'inflammatory' address. There the plaintiff had been injured in a mining accident. In his address to the jury, plaintiff's counsel had said that he would show that the accident was caused by a practice designed to maximise the volume of ore extracted, even if this reduced the stability of the mining area.

The legal consequence of a breach of these requirements will depend upon the degree to which the breach has prejudiced the other party's right to a fair hearing and on the kind of measures necessary to compensate for such prejudice. In extreme cases, the judge may deal with a breach by discharging a jury and ordering the offending party to pay the costs. In non-jury cases, a judge could terminate the trial and make a similar costs order. However, this power is a discretionary power, to be used only where there is no satisfactory alternative. Alternatives include doing nothing, reprimanding counsel, permitting the other party to take steps to overcome any detriment it has suffered in consequence of a breach of the requirements, and advising a jury to disregard a particular piece of data. Some of the research into jury behaviour suggests that this may backfire. Juries may become particularly likely to attach weight to the prohibited piece of information. However, other studies suggest that the effect of inadmissible evidence may be strongly context-based: see W Thompson, G Fong and D Rosenhan, 'Inadmissible Evidence and Juror Verdicts' (1981) 40 *J Personality & Social Psychology* 457, and the works cited there.

In trials by judge alone, it will be rare for a judge to admit to being so prejudiced by an inadmissible statement as to leave him or her with no alternative but to terminate the case. In jury trials, judges are more willing to assume that the prospects of a fair trial have been irretrievably prejudiced. However, appeal courts have warned against lightly discharging juries. In *Wellington v Lake George Mines Pty Ltd* (1962) 62 SR (NSW) 326 at 327–8, Evatt CJ and Wallace J held (Ferguson J dissenting) that the trial judge had erred in discharging the jury:

> We wish to say at once that in our opinion the discharge of a jury is, by reason of the attendant consequences of frustration and delay in the administration of justice, such a serious step that it should only be taken where real injustice cannot otherwise be avoided. Thus to discharge a jury in an accident case in these days of practically universal insurance because a reference to

insurance is inadvertently made during the hearing is in our opinion, an outmoded and wrong procedure. The judgment of this Court in *King v Wilkinson* (1957) 57 SR (NSW) 444; 74 WN (NSW) 222 makes an appropriate reference to this subject. We mention this matter because the first trial in the instant case was aborted on the third day of the hearing because a medical witness referred to insurance. It was in this setting that the second trial began and a different trial judge on this occasion was prevailed upon by the defendant's counsel to discharge the jury because of the nature and content of the opening address of the plaintiff's counsel. His Honour appears to have had two reasons for taking this action namely (1) because the address was inflammatory and prejudicial to the defendant, (2) because counsel opened up material which went beyond the particulars which had been given of the two counts in the declaration.

It is a commonplace occurrence for material of a more or less inflammatory nature to be placed before a jury. Sometimes (and most effectively) it is done with a measure of subtlety or restraint, but on many occasions more direct methods are used. Challenging and critical language is not confined to jury actions and is used — perhaps not always with efficacy — in other jurisdictions. Prima facie therefore it would appear to be a somewhat startling proposition that a third trial should be necessary [328] because of an inflammatory opening address at a second hearing. There are, of course, recorded instances where grossly improper and unfair questions or statements have made a new trial quite imperative and an example is *Croll v McRae* (1930) 30 SR (NSW) 137; 47 WN (NSW) 50. Furthermore it is conceived that an appellate court would only with reluctance and anxiety intervene in a case where a trial judge has exercised his discretion on a matter of practice and procedure especially where the immediate subject of appeal relates in an objective sense to a question of costs only. But in the instant case we are of opinion, with the utmost respect to the learned trial judge, that we should state our reasons why we think his Honour erred in discharging the jury — if only to avoid the possible catastrophe of a fourth trial.

The effects of non-attendance

18.5.6   The discussion to date has assumed that both sides attend the trial. They normally do so. However, the rules provide for the eventuality of parties not attending the trial. In some jurisdictions, the relevant rules explicitly provide that in that event, a trial may be adjourned: FCR r 30.21(1)(a)(ii), (1)(b)(ii); NSW r 29.7(2)(b); NT r 49.02(1)(c); Vic r 49.02(1)(c). Elsewhere it would be open to a court to exercise its general powers of adjournment in such a case: see **18.5.16C**. If the court decides to proceed, and if the plaintiff attends and the defendant does not, the position varies somewhat by jurisdiction. In New South Wales, if the amount claimed is a liquidated sum, the court can give judgment for the plaintiff without proceeding to trial, upon the plaintiff giving evidence of the sum due at the time of the claim and of the amount (if any) by which that sum has subsequently been reduced: r 29.7(3). In the Northern Territory (r 49.02), the court may strike out the defence and enter judgment accordingly. In South Australia (r 234(2)), the plaintiff is entitled to such judgment as it would have been entitled to in default of filing of a defence. If it would not have been entitled to judgment in default of a defence, it must prove its case.

In the Australian Capital Territory (r 1505(1)), Queensland (r 476(1)) and Tasmania (r 570(1)(a)), the plaintiff must prove its case, even if the defendant does not attend. Elsewhere the rules do not make express provision for this to happen: FCR r 30.21(1)(b); NSW r 29.7 (claims other than for liquidated damages); Vic r 49.02; WA O 34 r 2. But non-attendance in these jurisdictions does not operate in the same way as failure to appear or failure to serve and file a defence. It is therefore for the plaintiff to prove its case. For example, in *MY Distributors*

Pty Ltd v Omaq Pty Ltd (1992) 36 FCR 578, the applicant sought damages under the Trade Practices Act 1974 (Cth). The respondent failed to file and serve a defence. While this would have entitled the applicant to move for judgment by default, the plaintiff chose instead to proceed with the trial. The court found that the applicant had not proved its case, and dismissed the application. The applicant appealed against this decision on the grounds that under the Federal Court Rules, failure to deny an allegation in a defence is to be taken as an admission of it. This argument was rejected on the grounds that the operation of the rule was predicated upon a defence having been filed and served.

If the defendant appears and the plaintiff does not appear, the defendant may apply to have the plaintiff's claim dismissed. This is expressly stated in some jurisdictions: ACT r 1505(2); NT r 49.02; Qld r 476(2); SA r 234(1); Tas r 570(1)(b). Elsewhere it is implicit. It is beside the point that the defence to a claim is a 'confess and avoid' defence, capable of being sustained in a normal trial only if the defendant proves the facts it alleges. On application, judgment should still be entered for the defendant: *Armour v Bate* [1891] 2 QB 234. If the defendant has a counterclaim, the defendant's position is the same as a plaintiff's in relation to a non-attending defendant.

If neither party attends, the court may strike the case out of the list: ACT r 1505(4); NT r 49.02; Tas r 570(1)(c); Vic 49.02(1)(a); WA O 34 r 1. In the Federal Court and South Australia, the court may dismiss the action: FCR r 30.22(b) (the court may also adjourn); SA r 234(1).

No case submissions and the requirement to elect not to call evidence

18.5.7   At the end of the plaintiff's case, the defendant may consider that the plaintiff has failed to make out its case. It may believe that even placing as favourable construction as possible upon the evidence, the plaintiff cannot succeed. Alternatively, it may believe that the plaintiff's witnesses have been so unpersuasive that the plaintiff has not discharged its burden of proof. In such cases, the defendant may elect not to call evidence and, if its assessment of the case is justified, it will succeed. However, there are obvious risks inherent in this procedure. The following case discusses whether and in what circumstances it is possible for a defendant to seek to have the claim struck out, while reserving its right to proceed if the application is unsuccessful.

18.5.8C   **J Corp Pty Ltd v Australian Builders Labourers Federated Union of Workers (Western Australian Branch) (No 2)**
(1992) 38 FCR 458
Federal Court of Australia

[After the applicants had closed their case, the second respondent, the Building Trades Association of Workers (BTA), sought to make a no case submission and to do so without being required to elect to call no evidence.]

French J (at 460–5): In considering the three questions which arise on the BTA's application to be heard on a no case submission without being required to elect, it is convenient to begin by examining the way in which no case submissions have been dealt with generally in the authorities. I begin with the simple case of civil proceedings involving a single defendant. There is ample authority for the proposition that as a general rule a defendant will not be permitted to advance a submission at the close of the plaintiff's case that there is no case to answer unless an election is first made to call no evidence. Where that course is taken, the judge's decision is made on the basis of all the evidence that is to be called. Whichever way the judge decides, the decision is dispositive of the issues being tried between plaintiff and defendant in that action. Where a defendant is permitted to submit that there is no case to answer without being required to elect to call no evidence, then the judge's decision is dispositive of the case only if the submission is upheld. If the submission is not upheld then it is an interim decision that there is a prima [461] facie case. The final decision must then await consideration of all the evidence including the evidence (if any) which may be adduced by the defendant.

The question whether a defendant should be required to elect before a no case submission is entertained falls for determination as a matter of judicial case management. Under that characterisation which reflects the general approach adopted by Australian courts, there is an irreducible element of discretion for the judge confronted with a no case submission. That discretion is informed by the long experience of the courts which indicates strongly that the better course in most cases is to hear all the evidence before making any decision on its effect. There have been some cases when the accumulated experience of the law in this respect has been expressed as a somewhat inflexible direction to trial judges. But the cases taken overall do not support inflexibility in the resolution of these essentially procedural questions.

[French J then discussed the relevant case law and continued (at 463)]:

It is necessary now to consider the case where there are two or more respondents, not all of whom seek to submit that there is no case to answer ...

[His Honour discussed the judgment of Toohey J in *James v ANZ Banking Group Ltd* (1986) 64 ALR 347 and continued:]

In my respectful view, which I hope is not inconsistent with what his Honour [464] said in that case, the question whether or not to entertain a no case submission by one of several respondents is, like the simple case of one respondent, a matter of proper case management having regard to the interests of justice, including the convenience and economy in time and money that might be achieved in an appropriate case. His Honour's observations would not seem to preclude the possibility, for example, that the court might entertain a no case submission based upon a proposition of law rather than one which goes to the adequacy of the evidence adduced against the party seeking to make the submission.

[His Honour then referred to *Hummerstone v Leary* [1921] 2 KB 664, *Menzies v Australian Iron and Steel Ltd* (1952) 52 SR (NSW) 62, and *Trade Practices Commission v Allied Mills Industries Pty Ltd* (1981) ATPR 40–252, and continued:]

[465] The question is in essence one of practice within the general discretion of the court to regulate the conduct of the trial: O 32, r 4(1). The discretion is necessarily to be regulated by the powerful practical considerations to which the authorities cited refer. But that is not to say that circumstances may not arise in which one respondent may without inconvenience be dismissed out of a case notwithstanding that the case proceeds against another. One example might be on a question of jurisdictional fact. It may be that at the close of an applicant's case in proceedings under the Trade Practices Act a respondent whose liability depends upon whether it can be characterised as a trading or financial corporation within the meaning of the Act, may submit that the evidence is not capable of establishing that characterisation. Such a submission can conceivably be made without involving any of the practical inconveniences

referred to in the cases mentioned above. And in the contemporary climate where judicial time is limited and the costs of legal services are high, it is my opinion that courts should not be slow to consider the possibility of entertaining a submission of no case to answer from one of a number of respondents where the interests of justice are not compromised and economies may be effected thereby.

18.5.9 Note and questions

1. See *Residues Treatment & Trading Co Ltd v Southern Resources Ltd* (1989) 52 SASR 54, which discusses the exceptional circumstances in which South Australian courts permit no case submissions without requiring election.

2. In New South Wales, a defendant can apply for an order dismissing the proceedings or part of the proceedings on the grounds that on the evidence a judgment for the plaintiff could not be supported: r 29.9. A plaintiff may also apply to have proceedings dismissed: r 29.8. Why would it want this? Rule 29.10 allows a defendant to apply for judgment. Are there circumstances in which a defendant's application could succeed under one rule but not the other? What are the advantages and disadvantages of applying under r 29.9 as compared with r 29.10?

No case submissions after the defendant has given evidence

18.5.10 Occasionally, a party will want to make a kind of 'no case' submission *after* the defendant has given evidence. If the trial is before a judge sitting alone, there will be no point in doing so. Why? However, in the case of a jury trial, a party might fear an adverse verdict, notwithstanding the lack of any evidence to support such a verdict. It is clear that judges can direct juries to find in favour of a particular party if the evidence does not permit any other verdict, but it is also clear that a jury may disregard such a direction. The following case discusses whether a judge can simply bypass the jury in a 'no evidence' case.

18.5.11C   **Humphrey v Collier**
[1946] VLR 391
Supreme Court of Victoria, Full Court

[At the conclusion of the plaintiff's case, the defence submitted that there was no evidence on which a jury could make a finding of negligence. The trial judge (Martin J) withdrew the matter from the jury and entered judgment for the defendant. On appeal, the Full Court held that there was evidence on the basis of which a jury could have made a finding for the plaintiff.]

Macfarlan J (at 402): [On the question of whether a judge was warranted in withdrawing a matter from the jury, his Honour said if the judge came to the conclusion that there was no case to answer:] ... his strictly proper course, in my opinion, is to direct the jury to return a verdict for the defendant before entering judgment, but my recollection is that that practice has on occasions not been followed obviously being a mere formality.

In the present case, as no objection was taken to the course followed at the trial, I should not favour allowance of the appeal and the granting of a new trial on this ground.

Gavan Duffy J (at 408): In our Courts it has been the practice of some Judges, at any rate, to enter judgment without taking a verdict or to give leave to move after verdict for judgment when either course was thought desirable, irrespective of any consent, and I think such a practice is justified by the Supreme Court Act 1928 and the Supreme Court Rules, and in the absence of any authority binding on us to the contrary should be followed.

[See also *Prestinenzi v Steel Tank and Pipe Consolidated Pty Ltd* [1981] VR 421 (**18.7.8C** below).]

18.5.12   Question

1. In *Bernard v Seltsam Pty Ltd* (2010) 28 VR 46; [2010] VSC 305, Bell J found that the defendant had succeeded in its 'no case' submission and concluded that it would be open to him to enter judgment without taking a verdict. However, he adopted the 'strictly proper' course of directing a verdict, followed by the entry of judgment, setting out his reasons for doing so at [33]–[34], and outlining the procedure he adopted at [35]–[39]. The jury gave a verdict as directed, but what would have happened if the jury has returned a verdict in favour of the plaintiff? See below 18.7.7–18.7.8C.

Reopening cases

18.5.13   In general, a party may not reopen its case. However, there may be circumstances in which justice is served by permitting a case to be reopened, and in which the other party is not prejudiced nor the court inconvenienced. For example, see *Watson v Metropolitan (Perth) Passenger Transport Trust* [1965] WAR 88, where the plaintiff claimed damages on the basis of injuries sustained when attempting to board a trolley bus. The case received publicity as a result of which a witness came forward to say that the plaintiff had in fact tried to jump on the bus as it was moving off. The defence case had been closed, but judgment had not been delivered. The witness could not reasonably have been discovered earlier. Woolf CJ said at 89:

> I consider that a court should be cautious in [re-opening the evidence] ... and should admit fresh evidence of this nature only when it is so material that the interests of justice require it, and the evidence, if believed would most probably affect the result, and further that the evidence could not by reasonable diligence have been discovered before.

18.5.14C   **Margiotta v Michielan**
                                         (1981) 26 SASR 356
                                    Supreme Court of South Australia

[In a personal injury case, the plaintiff sought to reopen his case to call evidence bearing on developments since the trial.]

Walters J (at 358–9): While judgment remained reserved, there developed in relation to the plaintiff's medical condition signs and symptoms which had not become clearly manifest at the time of trial. In consequence of the signs and symptoms which newly appeared, the plaintiff consulted Mr Lind, who referred him for physiotherapy treatment. There was no successful response to that treatment, and Mr Lind arranged for a myelogram to be performed on the plaintiff on 9th July, 1980. The results of the myelogram indicated to Mr Lind that there existed a degeneration of a lumbosacral junction of the plaintiff's spine, and Mr Lind decided that surgical intervention was necessary. On 21st July, 1980, Mr Lind performed a laminectomy at the L–5–S1 level of the plaintiff's spine.

Next, there followed an application by the plaintiff by summons in Chambers, seeking leave to reopen his case. The application was supported by his own affidavit, as well as by an affidavit of Mr Lind, in which the fresh evidence sought to be adduced was foreshadowed. As it happened, the defendants' counsel did not oppose the application to reopen the case. Even though this was the attitude of the defendants' [359] counsel, it seemed to me that because of the fresh matters put forward by affidavit and, more particularly, because of the conflicting state of the medical evidence given at the trial, the interests of justice warranted the granting of leave to the plaintiff to reopen his case, and I made an order accordingly. In acceding to the application, I had in mind the dicta of Napier CJ in *Betts v Whittingslowe (No 1)* [1944] SASR 163 at 165 'that until the issues of fact and law have been finally determined by verdict or judgment (as the case may be) the trial Judge must have an inherent right, analogous to "The inherent right", formerly exercised by the court *in banco*, "to set aside the verdict for any purpose of justice"'. Moreover, I think that my decision to allow the plaintiff leave to reopen the case accords, in a general way, with the course of proceedings in *Lim v Camden Health Authority* [1980] AC 174 where, both in the Court of Appeal and in their Lordships' House, the parties were granted leave to adduce fresh evidence, even at the appellate stage of the litigation. As Lord Scarman pointed out (at 183), leave to adduce fresh evidence can 'mitigate the injustice of a lump sum system by enabling the appellate courts to bring the award into line with what has happened since trial'. As it seems to me, his Lordship's remarks apply a *fortiori* in a case where, since trial and before judgment, a new factual basis has developed which will assist the court in reaching a conclusion on conflicting medical evidence and where, otherwise, the court would be left to choose between the diagnoses and prognoses of expert medical witnesses, or to make a finding of fact intermediate between the two opinions.

18.5.15   Question

1. Would and should the plaintiff in this case have been able to reopen his case if there had been a jury trial?

18.5.16C	**Hanlon v Wadlow Ltd** [1961] SASR 94 Supreme Court of South Australia

[At trial, counsel for the defendant had elected not to call evidence. After judgment had been reserved, the defendant learned of the whereabouts of a potential defence witness whom it had not been able to track down in time for the trial, and sought to reopen its case to adduce that evidence.]

Reed J (at 98–9): It seemed to me, however, that as the defendant had intimated through its counsel that it would call no evidence, it could not subsequently be permitted to call evidence, even though the evidence might not have been discovered by the exercise of due diligence at the time of the trial. That appears to be the correct view of the law, as appears from the decision in *Darby v Ouseley* (1857) 1 H & N 1; 156 ER 1093. ... [99] The position appears to me to be the same whether a case is tried with or without a jury. If counsel for a defendant announces that he calls no evidence, the intimation means that the defendant is content to have the case decided upon the evidence called by the other party, and by it the defendant abandons any right he might have to place evidence before the Court, either at that stage or later. Consequently, the election made by counsel for the defendant Wadlow Limited is binding upon that party and no evidence may be adduced by it, whether the evidence was or was not available at the time of the trial.

Adjournments

18.5.17 The rules in most jurisdictions provide for adjournments at any stage before or during a trial: FCR O 19 r 6 (adjournment of motions); ACT r 1506; Civil Procedure Act 2005 (NSW) s 66; NT r 49.03; Qld r 477; Supreme Court Act 1935 (SA) s 46; Tas r 571; Vic r 49.03; WA O 34 r 4. In any case, the court has an inherent power to adjourn a trial: *Hinckley and South Leicester Shire Permanent Benefit Building Society v Freeman* [1941] Ch 32. Whether adjournments are granted is a matter for the court's discretion. In *Myers v Myers* [1969] WAR 19 at 21, Jackson J said:

> ... [to] grant or refuse an adjournment is a matter for the discretion of the court to whom the application is made. But where the refusal of an adjournment would result in serious injustice to one party, an adjournment should be granted unless in turn this would mean serious injustice to the other party.

In determining where the 'balance of justice' lies, the court should take account of orders which it could make which would minimise the inconvenience caused by the adjournment. In *Myers* (a custody dispute), the husband had sought an adjournment so that he could attend to urgent business affairs in London. This was refused by the magistrate. Jackson J considered that the wife's interests could have been met by an interim custody order, and orders to compensate the wife for the expenses that the adjournment would involve. Normally, too, the grant of an adjournment would be accompanied by a costs order.

Courts have traditionally been extremely reluctant to deny requests for adjournments, especially when doing so would effectively deny a party a chance to present its case adequately. However, this reluctance has been tempered by recognition that the immediate parties to a dispute are not the only people with relevant interests. Courts are also doubting whether costs awards are sufficient compensation for the inconvenience occasioned by adjournments. In *Sali v SPC Ltd* (1993) 116 ALR 625, the High Court considered an appeal against the refusal by a Full Court of the Victorian Supreme Court of a half-day adjournment sought by a party which claimed not to have been able to brief a suitably qualified barrister in time for its appeal. The Full Court recognised that its refusal was unique, but based its decision on a finding that the excuse was simply an attempt to buy time. In the High Court, Brennan, Deane and McHugh JJ said (at 629):

> In determining whether to grant an adjournment, the judge of a busy court is entitled to consider the effect of an adjournment on court resources and the competing claims by litigants in other cases awaiting hearing in the courts as well as the interests of the parties.

Toohey and Gaudron JJ agreed (at 636), but considered that the court had erred in its findings in relation to the applicant's *bona fides*.

See *Newjur Pty Ltd v Pangas* (1997) 140 FLR 196 for an example of refusal of an application for an adjournment. This coexisted with an assessment by Bryson J that other delaying tactics pursued by the defendants were such that 'It would soil justice if I allowed this kind of procedural contrivance to succeed'.

Doubts about the adequacy of costs awards as compensation have been expressed in several courts. In *G S A Industries Pty Ltd v N T Gas Ltd* (1990) 24 NSWLR 710, Samuels JA said (at 716):

> ... [I]n that more leisured age an order for costs was generally regarded as complete compensation for delay occasioned either by the grant of an amendment or the grant of an adjournment. However the emollient effect of an order for costs as a panacea must now be consigned to the Aladdin's cave which Lord Reid rejected as one of the fairy tales in which we no longer believe.

French J in *Bomanite Pty Ltd v Slatex Corp Australia Pty Ltd* (1991) 32 FCR 379 at 392 expressed similar views:

> Non-compensable inconvenience and stress on individuals are significant elements of modern litigation. Costs recoverable even on an indemnity basis will not compensate for time lost and duplication incurred where litigation is delayed or corrective orders necessary. The public interest also has become an increasingly significant element in the application of judicial resources. Inefficiencies in their use arising from lost and wasted time can never be compensated by costs.

However, even in *Bomanite*, Pincus J considered that the adjournment should have been granted. The full report deserves attention as an example of the problems faced by case flow managers. The dissents in *Sali* point to the problems that can arise where tactical delay is suspected, but not clearly proved or provable.

Procedures in hearings by special referees

18.5.18 Referees generally enjoy considerable flexibility in the conduct of their inquiries. In Tasmania and Western Australia, the procedures are to be those used in actions tried by juries, and the rules relating to the taking of evidence, securing the attendance of witnesses, and conducting the inquiry, are those for a trial conducted by judge alone. The Queensland position is similar, except that the procedures are also those applying to a trial conducted by judge alone. These rules are, however, subject to the court ordering otherwise: Qld r 502(3) (procedure as for trial by judge alone); Tas r 577 (procedure as for trial conducted in the court); WA O 35 rr 2, 3 (but note the provision for directions in referee cases: O 4A r 9). Elsewhere, procedures are more flexible. In the Australian Capital Territory, procedures are those which would apply to an arbitration under the Commercial Arbitration Act 1986: r 1534(3). Elsewhere, subject to court directions, referees are to conduct proceedings and to inform themselves in such manner as they think fit: FCR r 28.65(1)–(3); NSW r 20.20; Supreme Court Act 1979 (NT) s 28; NT r 50.02; Vic r 50.02. The New South Wales rules expressly provide that the referee is not bound by the formal rules of evidence. For examples of Victorian directions to similar effect, see N J Williams, *Civil Procedure Victoria*, LexisNexis, Sydney, looseleaf, [I50.02.10]. Arbitrations under the rules are typically governed by the same rules as references for reports. However, in Victoria (r 50.08), there is express provision that they are to be conducted in accordance with the procedures under the relevant Commercial Arbitration Act. In South Australia, arbitrations are to be conducted as the court directs: r 222(1). The Federal Court Rules place no limits on the procedures, but provide for applications for orders specifying how the arbitration is to be conducted: r 28.11(1)(b).

18.5.19C | **Xuereb v Viola**
(1988) 18 NSWLR 453
Supreme Court of New South Wales

[The plaintiffs complained that they had suffered loss as a result of work done on the defendants' dam. Questions relating to the work were referred to a referee whose report was adverse to the defendant, who argued that the court should decline to adopt the report. Among her arguments was that the referee had denied her procedural fairness. Part 72, rr 1–10 now appear as NSW rr 20.13–20.22 and r 13 is now r 20.44. Former rr 11 and 12 are reflected in r 20.23.]

Cole J (at 465–72): Part 72, as substituted on 22 November 1985, were the rules of the court contemplated to be made under s 124(2) of the Supreme Court Act 1970 as inserted by the Supreme Court (Commercial Arbitration) Amendment Act No 166 of 1984, s 4(b). Thus they regulate the circumstances in which questions may be referred to a referee, the powers of such referees, and the manner in which such references are to be conducted. As I have said, it is clear from s 124(2)(b) that referees are not, by virtue of that position, officers of the Court (see also Pt 72, r 3(1)). Part 72 makes no reference to a trial by the referee. Rule 8 specifies the manner in which proceedings under the reference are to be conducted. The Court may give specific directions as to such manner of conduct (r 8(1)). Subject to that, the referee may conduct the proceedings under the reference in such manner as he thinks fit (r 8(2)(a)). Nor is he bound by the rules of evidence and may 'inform [466] himself ... in relation to any matter in such manner as the referee thinks fit'(r 8(2)(b)). The referee may himself take the examination of any person (r 8(4)) and the parties are obliged 'to do all things which the referee requires to enable a just opinion to be reached' (r 8(6) as amended 22 September 1989).

The power to conduct proceedings as he sees fit (subject to order of the Court), to examine witnesses himself, to set aside the rules of evidence, and to inform himself otherwise than by hearing evidence from witnesses called by the parties, together with the power to require parties to do such acts as he regards as necessary to permit the formation of a just opinion, rather than to base his opinion upon material submitted by parties, is the very antithesis of the obligation which Powell J found upon a referee to 'generally conduct his inquiry as if it were a trial of that question by a Judge'. The clear purpose of Pt 72 as substituted in 1985, and as amended on 22 September 1989, is to enable the Court to have the facility to obtain a report from a referee, which report may be obtained in the most efficient, expeditious and least expensive method available. This is particularly so where technical or accounting issues are involved and where it may be considered inappropriate or unnecessary for the processes normally adopted in the conduct of a trial to be availed of to obtain a just opinion upon the question referred. It is for those reasons that r 8(6) stresses the prohibition upon a party wilfully delaying or preventing a just opinion being reached.

The purpose of r 8(1) is to permit the Court to mould such directions as it considers appropriate to obtain the expression from the referee of a just opinion upon a question referred. That question may be one of fact or law.

Further, there is no longer any provision which equates the opinion of a referee to the finding of a jury. Pursuant to Pt 72, r 13, the Court must consider whether to adopt, vary or reject the report in whole or in part. The report is of no legal consequence unless and until it is adopted. It is the Court which makes findings of fact or law either explicitly, or implicitly, by adopting a report.

In my judgment it is not correct, in the face of Pt 72, r 8, to hold that a referee should conduct his inquiry as if it were a trial by a judge.

The question immediately arises, in consequence, of what is required of a referee in the conduct of proceedings under a reference. Clearly the referee must conduct the reference in accordance with any directions given pursuant to Pt 72, r 8(1). In the absence of such directions, the referee may conduct proceedings in such manner as he thinks fit, not being bound by the rules of evidence and being permitted to inform himself in such manner as he thinks fit (r 8(2)(a) and r 8(2)(b)). He may require the parties to do things to assist him in reaching his opinion (r 8(6)). But this statement of the Rules masks the difficulties inherent in the referee's task for it does not give the referee any clear direction as to procedure which he must follow to ensure that the opinion reached by him is a 'just opinion' (r 8(6)). By 'just opinion' is meant an opinion which is just between the parties. Implicitly that means that in reaching his opinion concepts of natural justice must have been adhered to by the referee. The recent amendment to Pt 72, r 8, by the insertion of a new subr (5) provides:

> Each party shall, within a time fixed by the referee but in any event before the conclusion of evidence on the inquiry, give to the referee and [467] each other party a brief statement of the findings of fact and law for which the party contends.

This ensures that each party is given the opportunity to place before the referee its submissions on fact and law. Of course, if parties breach their obligation under r 8(5) by failing to comply with it, they cannot complain of a failure of natural justice.

Rule 8(5) is but an explicit instance of the implicit requirement that the parties receive natural justice. What may be required by natural justice may vary with the particular circumstances of the particular question upon which the referee is asked to report. I will return to this. However, it is clear, in my judgment, that concepts of natural justice must be observed in the conduct of a reference. This is so notwithstanding that the referee is not an officer of the Court, a delegate of the Court, is not conducting a trial, is not making a finding of fact or law and is not determining any issue.

[468] It should not be thought that in all instances natural justice requires similar procedures to be followed. For instance, the legislature has enacted that in certain circumstances the Court may dispense with rules of evidence: Supreme Court Act, s 82 and Commercial Arbitration Act, s 19(3). A similar provision is found in Pt 72, r 8(2)(b). The legislature has thus recognised that non-compliance with the rules of evidence does not result in a denial of natural justice.

Equally, in my judgment, it can be said that non-compliance with procedures normally applied in court proceedings does not, of necessity, result in denial of natural justice. Were an inquiry to be directed by a court as to what monetary indebtedness of a party was shown by a set of books of account (as distinct from determining the indebtedness generally), there may be no denial of natural justice to either party by a judge directing a competent accountant, as referee, to report on that matter without reference to the parties. In contrast, if a referee were asked to report upon the indebtedness of A to B having regard to the set of books of account and any other circumstances, it may well constitute a denial of natural justice not to permit each party to advance to the referee such factual circumstances relating to indebtedness, or falsity of such books, as may be relevant. Equally it may constitute a denial of natural justice not to permit a party to respond to an allegation of indebtedness made against him.

The example I have given is an endeavour to illustrate that what is required by concepts of natural justice will vary with particular circumstances.

In considering pursuant to Pt 72, r 13, whether to adopt a referee's report, the Court will be vigilant to ensure that in reaching his 'just opinion', the referee has engaged and implemented any relevant concepts of natural justice. I discussed the matters which will attend the mind of a judge considering a report pursuant to Pt 72, r 13, in *Chloride Batteries Australia Ltd v Glendale Chemical Products Pty Ltd* (1988) 17 NSWLR 60 at 166–9. As Marks J said in *Integer Computing Pty Ltd v Facom Australia Ltd* (Marks J, Supreme Court of Victoria, 10 April 1987, unreported): 'The fundamental objective of the Court is to satisfy itself that the ends of justice are satisfied.'

Referees, no doubt, look to the courts for elucidation upon what is meant by 'natural justice'. Its absence is readily recognised but its constituents are difficult to define. In essence it means fairness between the parties. If an allegation is put by one party against the other, the other should have the chance to respond. Yet the process of responding is not indeterminable. For once a party is aware of the case or argument or fact asserted against him, natural justice is usually satisfied by giving to his opponent the opportunity to respond. The response may, of course, throw up material not adverted to by the first party. It is usual, in the courts, for the first party to be given a limited right of reply to deal with any such new material, whether factual, argumentative or a matter of legal concept. But it is not always essential that such a right be given. If issues are clearly defined, particularly if they be of a technical nature, and if each party is given a full opportunity to place before the referee that which it wishes in relation to those issues, it does not necessarily follow that there is a denial of natural justice by not permitting each then to respond to any new material advanced by the other. Particularly [469] is that so where the referee is a person of technical competence able to understand and evaluate the material placed before him by each party.

Quite apart from Pt 72, r 11(c), natural justice requires that a referee give reasons for his opinion. This is not just to permit the court better to exercise its functions under Pt 72, r 13. The deeper reason is that it enables the parties and the disinterested observer to know that the opinion of the referee is not arbitrary, or influenced by improper considerations but is the result of a process of logic and the application of a considered mind to factual circumstance.

I adopt, with respect, the passage in the judgment of Samuels JA in *Strbak v Newton* (Court of Appeal, 18 July 1989, unreported), in speaking of the requirements for reasons in the judgment of a District Court judge, as being an appropriate statement of principle applicable to the statement of reasons required by a referee:

> ... it is going too far to suggest that in every case a judge must submit the material before him or her to the most meticulous analysis and carry into judgment a detailed exposition of every aspect of the evidence and the arguments. What is necessary, it seems to me, is a basic explanation of the fundamental reasons which led the judge to his conclusion. There is no requirement, however, that the reasons must incorporate an extended intellectual dissertation upon the chain of reasoning which authorises the judgment which is given.
>
> In the present case, the reasons are certainly succinct, but that is often to be regarded as a judicial virtue. Trial Judges must always endeavour to balance their duty to explain with their duty to the brief.

Another aspect of natural justice is that the referee must be actually impartial, and must be perceived by a disinterested bystander to be so. Accordingly he must not hear evidence or receive representations from one side behind the back of or in the absence of the other.

[470] How are such principles to be reconciled with Pt 72, r 8, and in particular r 8(2)(b) which permits the referee to 'inform himself ... in relation to any matter in such manner as the referee thinks fit'. Further, it has become common for orders made pursuant to Pt 72, r 8(1), to permit a referee 'to communicate with experts retained on behalf of the parties or any of them'. The utility of such a direction is obvious for it enables a person technically qualified who does not understand a particular technical aspect of the report of an expert retained by a party to inquire of that expert what he meant. But such an order is not to be understood as permitting a referee to have a private conversation with one expert. He may call the experts for opposing parties together to seek clarification, or he may arrange a conference telephone discussion with the experts for competing parties. Pursuant to r 8(2), the referee may be permitted to carry out his own tests. But if he does so, prior to preparing his 'just opinion' he must give, in most cases, the information so derived to the competing parties to permit them to express their views upon it to him. There is nothing in Pt 72, r 8, or in the usual order made by the Court pursuant to r 8 (1) which permits private discussions between the referee and only one party or his expert. Similarly, normally if communications are received by a referee from a party they should be provided to the other party, unless it has previously been arranged that the party providing a document to the referee will also provide it to his opponent.

As I have said, the referee makes no decision: he expresses an opinion to the court. But if it appears to the court that the parties have had a fair opportunity to place their evidence and arguments before the referee, and if his opinion discloses the application of reason to the material before him, even if the court may have been disposed to come to a contrary conclusion, there will be a disposition in the court to adopt and rely upon the report. In this manner, the referee is, although himself not making any decision, potentially caught up in the decision making processes of the court. It follows that he must observe concepts of natural justice in preparing his opinion. For if he does not do so, the court, being obliged to apply concepts of natural justice, must reject his report. The utility of the reference will be lost and time and expense would have been unnecessarily wasted and incurred. To adapt the words of Mason J, in *Kioa* [(1985) 159 CLR 550], the parties to a reference have a legitimate expectation that their rights or interests may be potentially affected by the opinion of the referee delivered to the court for its review, adoption or rejection. The potentiality of adoption of a referee's report, notwithstanding that it involves the court applying its mind to an examination of the report, is sufficient to give rise to that expectation, and thus to require the referee to engage the principles of natural justice in forming his 'just opinion'.

Referees in each instance must consider what is required to achieve fairness between the parties in the particular circumstances of their reference.

18.5.20   Notes and questions

1. This case is also of socio-legal interest. The report includes samples of dialogue between the referee and counsel which make it clear that engineers' concepts of proof and probability are sometimes radically different to those of lawyers: see especially at 458–9. In so far as such concepts have different meanings to referees and judges, what implications does this have for the use of referees in the decision-making process?

2. What was Cole J's rationale for rejecting the report? (a) denial of natural justice; (b) the referee's failure to comply with a mandatory condition; or (c) some other ground? If (c), what other ground? If (a), how can this be reconciled with *Public Service Board (New South Wales) v Osmond* (1986) 159 CLR 656; 63 ALR 559? Is *North Sydney Council v Ligon 302 Pty Ltd* (1995) 87 LGERA 435 applicable?

18.5.21   The rules of natural justice and procedural fairness include the bias rule. A person is disqualified from serving as a referee if that person is biased against a party or if a reasonable bystander might conclude that they were so biased. For instance, *Najjar v Haines* (1991) 25 NSWLR 224 arose from a building dispute between a builder and a government department. The referee failed to disclose that his company had been negotiating with the department for a substantial government contract. The New South Wales Court of Appeal held that the builder had established a case for a reasonable apprehension of bias. The referee had therefore not been eligible to report. The decision adopting the report was therefore a nullity. It had not been 'cured' by acquiescence; the builder had sought to challenge it promptly upon discovering the referee's links with the department.

VERDICTS AND REPORTS

18.6.1   The task of a jury is to reach (or to decide it cannot reach) a verdict. Arbitrators make a determination. Referees make reports. Jury verdicts normally resolve the factual issues in a case. Arbitrators' awards or determinations (nomenclature varies) enjoy the status of jury verdicts in some jurisdictions; that of private arbitrators' awards in others; and yet other statuses in yet other jurisdictions. In New South Wales, an arbitrator's award 'is final and conclusive and is taken to be a judgment of the referring court': Civil Procedure Act 2005 (NSW) s 40. Referees' reports have less legal force, although they nonetheless usually carry considerable weight.

Verdicts

18.6.2 At law, a jury may deliver either a special or a general verdict. The difference between these two types of verdicts is discussed in *Otis Elevators Pty Ltd v Zitis* (1986) 5 NSWLR 171. (The law in New South Wales has now been changed by legislation (Supreme Court Act 1970 s 90), but the law set out in this case still reflects the common law.) It is also a widespread practice of judges to put particular questions to the jury. While juries are not obliged to answer these questions, they are often not told that this is the case. Nor, in practice, are they always asked to record a formal general or special verdict. The implications of this are discussed in *Anderson v Ntzounas* [1988] VR 748: see 18.6.5C.

18.6.3C	**Otis Elevators Pty Ltd v Zitis**
	(1986) 5 NSWLR 171
	Court of Appeal (NSW)

[At trial, the judge put seven questions to the jury. The first two went to the general verdict. The last five related to particular factual issues. The appellant claimed that there was an inconsistency between the general verdict and the answers to two of the other questions. The majority (Priestley and McHugh JJA; Kirby P dissenting) held that the answers to the two questions were not inconsistent with the general verdict.]

McHugh J (at 197–201):

General verdicts and special verdicts:

At common law no judgment could be entered without the verdict of a jury: *Phillips v Ellinson Brothers Pty Ltd* (1941) 65 CLR 221 at 228–229.

The verdict of the jury could be a general verdict, a special verdict, or a notional general verdict subject to the decision of the Court on a special case. No power existed at common law for the judge to enter judgment on answers to questions submitted to the jury without the express or implied consent of the parties: *McDonnell & East Ltd v McGregor* (1936) 56 CLR 50 at 55–6. Moreover, the judgment of Dixon J in that case shows that, without the express or implied consent of the parties, there is no power to do so under the Supreme Court Act, s 91 which provides that the Court shall direct judgment to be entered 'as it thinks fit'. Nor as the decision in *Mourani* [(1983) 50 ALR 519] makes plain is there any such power under s 90.

A general verdict in a civil proceeding is a statement by the jury as to the party for whom it finds together with the amount of damages assessed if the finding is for the plaintiff or as to the sum awarded if the issue is one of assessment only: *Halsbury's Laws of England*, 4th ed, vol 26, par 642 at 333; *Russell v Victorian Railways Commissioners* [1948] VLR 118 at 130 per O'Bryan J. A general verdict involves a compound of law, fact, and the application of law to fact: Starkie, *Practical Treatise of the Law of Evidence* (1823) at 765, 768; Sunderland, 'Verdicts, General and Special' (1920) 29 *Yale LJ* 253 at 258; *Phillips v Ellinson Brothers Pty Ltd* at 239 per McTiernan J. Since a general verdict may conceal error by the jury in its understanding of the trial judge's directions, in its finding of the facts, or in its application of the law to the facts, it has often encountered criticism: eg, Sunderland (at 259); Frank, *Courts on Trial* (1950) at 111–18. It also has many powerful supporters: Thayer, *A Preliminary Treatise on Evidence* (1898) at 218–219; Wigmore, *A Program for the Trial of a Jury Trial* (1929) 12 *J Am Jud Society* 166 at 170 cited Dudnik, 'Special Verdicts: Rule 49 of the Federal Rules of Civil Procedure' (1965) 74 *Yale LJ* 483 at 496–7. It was because of the possibility that the general verdict concealed error that, from the 17th century onwards, the judges encouraged the giving of special verdicts so that they could apply the law and give judgment on the facts. At an earlier point of time, for reasons I will give, they had demanded general verdicts.

A special verdict in a civil proceeding is a statement by the jury of all the facts which it finds and which are relevant to the outstanding issues on the record. The statement of the jury must contain the specific facts found and not merely recite the evidence from which the facts are to be inferred: *Starkie* (at 11); Tidd's *Practice*, 9th ed (1828) vol II at 897; *Encyclopaedia of the Laws of England*, 2nd ed, vol XIV at 478; Wicker, 'Special Interrogatories to Juries in Civil Cases' (1926) 35 *Yale LJ 296* at 301; *Fryer v Roe* (1852) 12 CB 437; 138 ER 977; *Russell v Victorian Railways Commissioners* (at 121, 130); *R v Brown* [1949] VLR 177 at 183. The minutes for a special verdict intended to be found are approved by the judge and delivered to the jury before its finding. They are usually signed by one counsel for each party: *Bacon's Abridgement*, 7th ed (1832) vol VIII at 99. At common law the jury's findings were entered on the *nisi prius* record: Tidd (at 900). The special verdict contained no definite finding for the plaintiff or defendant. It ended with a recital of the jury's ignorance of the law and sought the advice of the [198] Court as to how it should find on the facts: *Mowatt v Lord Londesborough* (1854) 4 El & Bl 1; 119 ER 1; *R v Wardens and Assistants of the Saddlers' Co* (1861) 30 LJ (NS) 186 at 200; *Russell v Victorian Railways Commissioners* (at 121, 130). A standard form of the conclusion to a special verdict is found in Sutton, *Personal Actions at Common Law* (1929) at 128:

> That they are ignorant in point of law on which side they ought upon those facts to find the issue, but if upon the whole matter the Court shall be of opinion that the issue is proved for the Plaintiff, they find for the Plaintiff accordingly, and assess the damages at such and such a sum, but if the Court are of an opposite opinion then they find for the Defendant.

The *nisi prius* record was then brought before the Court *in banc*. The Court gave judgment for the party who, in point of law, was entitled to judgment on the findings of fact. No further inferences of fact could be drawn by the Court from any of the jury's findings: *Hubbard v Johnstone* (1810) 3 Taunt 177 at 209; 128 ER 71 at 83. If the special verdict did not find all necessary facts or the verdict was uncertain or ambiguous, a *venire de novo* was awarded upon which a further trial was heard: *Fryer v Roe* at 444; 980 per Jervis CJ; *Bacon's Abridgement* (at 100, 102–103); *Brown v Lizars* (1905) 2 CLR 837 at 847. Frequently, the findings of the jury in a special verdict were extensive and required a lengthy statement. In *Lickbarrow v Mason* (1794) 5 TR 683; 101 ER 380, the facts constituting the special verdict occupy three pages of the original report. The better opinion seems to be that the Court had no power without consent to amend a special verdict concerning any question of fact: *Bacon* (at 101). Accordingly, as Lord Blackburn said in *Dublin, Wicklow and Wexford Railway Co v Slattery* (1878) 3 App Cas 1155 at 1204–1205, there was so much technical nicety required in framing a special verdict that it required some good fortune to be able to raise the real question in the case.

General and special verdicts at common law are to be contrasted with a notional general verdict subject to a special case. The jury found a general verdict for one of the parties but subject to the opinion of the Court on a special case stated by both counsel with regard to a matter of law. The postea 'stayed in the hands of the officer of nisi prius' till the question was determined: *Tidd* (at 898). A verdict was then entered for the plaintiff or defendant in accordance with the finding on the case. This procedure had the disadvantage that the judgment of the Court *in banc* on the special case was final. No appeal lay to the Court of error: *Sutton* (at 128). Frequently, however, the parties reserved the right to turn the special case into a special verdict, so that a writ of error would lie against the judgment: see, eg, *Lord Londesborough v Mowatt*.

The jury's right to bring in a general or special verdict:

Until the enactment of s 90 [Supreme Court Act 1970], a jury in any civil or criminal trial, at its will, could bring in either a general or a special verdict and nothing else: *Cunningham v Ryan* (1919) 27 CLR 294 at 297 per Isaacs J; *Panel v Moor* (1553) 1 Plowd 91; 75 ER 145; *Dowman's Case* (1586) 9 Co Rep 7b; 77 ER 743; Morgan 'A Brief History of Special Verdicts and Special Interrogatories' (1923) 32 *Yale LJ* 575 at 588, 591. The right was not established without a struggle.

[McHugh JA then discussed the development of this right.]

[199] The right of the jury at common law to refuse to answer questions:

A special verdict at common law is not to be confused with a jury's answers to questions. During the period when the justices were liable to be [200] attainted, they questioned jurors, giving special verdicts, to ensure that all relevant facts were ascertained. In the early stages of the common law, the justices may well have had the right to require an answer to their questions when a special verdict was given: Pollock and Maitland, the *History of English Law*, 2nd ed (1895) vol II at 631.

But certainly by the 19th century, the common law accepted that, while a judge might put certain questions to the jury, he could not require their answer. This was the logical consequence of the jury's right at its option to bring in a general verdict instead of a special verdict. ...

[I]n *Walton v Potter* (1841) 3 Man & G 411; 133 ER 1203, the Court of Common Pleas went even further. They said that the judge had no right to put questions without the consent of the parties.

In *Brown v Lizars* (1905) 2 CLR 837, however, the High Court expressly recognised the right to ask questions of the jury — at least to the extent that the answers might be regarded as enabling a *general* verdict to be entered (see at 847, 869).

In *Mack v Elvy* (1916) 16 SR (NSW) 313; 33 WN 99, the Full Court of this Court also recognised a general right in the trial judge to put questions to the jury concerning 'issues of fact left to them in the course of summing up': see (at 319–320, 321 and 322; 100) Sir William Cullen CJ (with whose judgment Street J concurred) said, however, that it was improper beyond all question to ask a jury for the reason for its decision. All members of the Court accepted that the jury was not required to answer any questions of fact put to them (at 319, 321 and 322; 100). In *Cunningham v Ryan*, Isaacs J, when hearing a defamation action in the High Court with a jury, took the view that he was entitled to put a series of questions to the jury without informing them of their right to give a general verdict (see at 298–300). His Honour also thought that he was entitled to ask further questions based on the answers to the [201] questions already obtained. In *Russell v Victorian Railways Commissioners* (at 132) O'Bryan J regarded *Cunningham v Ryan* as authority for the judge asking the jury questions and then directing them what the general verdict should be having regard to their answers even if the parties had not consented. I cannot accept the statement (at 123–124) of Gavan Duffy J in the same case, however:

... that a Judge may ask a jury questions at his own discretion, without anyone's consent and without telling them that they may return a general verdict, and having received their answers, may enter whatever verdict is appropriate.

This seems quite contrary to what Dixon J said in *McDonnell & East Ltd v McGregor*. In *Morosi v Mirror Newspapers Ltd* ([1977] 2 NSWLR 749 at 759) this Court also thought that, quite apart from s 90, it had 'always been a permissible procedure for the presiding judge to ask the jury to answer questions'.

I think therefore that it should now be taken as settled that, notwithstanding the statements in *Walton v Potter*, a trial judge has a discretion to leave to the jury questions concerning any issues of fact which are left to them in the general summing up. But, in the absence of a legislative provision such as s 90, the jury cannot be required to answer a question.

One class of question, however, always seems to have been regarded as outside the judge's power: he cannot ask a question for the purpose of ascertaining the basis of a general verdict once it has been given.

18.6.4   For a similar discussion, albeit one which, in a minor respect, McHugh JA considered to be incorrect, see the judgment of O'Bryan J in *Russell v Victorian Railways Commissioners* [1948] VLR 118 at 130.

18.6.5C	**Anderson v Ntzounas**
	[1988] VR 748
	Supreme Court of Victoria, Full Court

[A County Court jury had been asked to answer four standard questions. It had done so, but, in accordance with normal practice, had been discharged without giving a formal verdict. In this case the jury had found that the defendant had not been negligent and the trial judge, on the basis of its answers, ordered a new trial. If the jury's findings could have been treated as a verdict, the trial judge would have had no power to order a new trial: County Court Act 1958 (Vic) s 73(3), (3A).]

Brooking J (at 750–1): What happened in this case, up to and including the time when the jury was finally discharged, was in no way different from what happens daily in trials by jury in the County Court or this Court. Contributory negligence having been raised, questions are, at least without objection from the parties, put to the jury and answered by it, and the jury is then discharged and judgment entered in accordance with the answers. The formal step of obtaining a general verdict consistent with the answers is, I suspect, never now taken, although judges may often, as indeed I still do myself, take the precaution of asking counsel, before the jury is discharged, whether there is any reason why the jury should be detained, thereby inviting counsel by implication to insist, if he desires, on the formality of a general verdict. But I cannot accept that the omission of this precaution makes any difference: if counsel does not intervene to prevent the discharge of the jury before a general verdict is taken, then by his silence he dispenses with that step. We do not know whether in this case the trial Judge murmured the usual enquiry before discharging the jury, but, as I have said, in my view this makes no difference. All that we know is that the jury were discharged without objection, and this is enough.

I am not prepared to hold that the answer to the first question itself constituted a verdict within the meaning of s 73(3A), although Mr Dove was able to assemble a considerable number of instances where members of the High Court or this Court had spoken of the verdict that had been given where the jury had done no more than answer questions of the present kind. Nor do I think that the solution lies in the view that by implication subs (3A) extends to the case in which, a trial by jury having been had and the jury having answered the questions put to it, the parties have dispensed with the giving of a verdict. The answer to the problem lies, not in the extension of the scope of subs (3A) as a matter of implication in the course of construction, but simply in the adoption of the view that in a case like the present the jury has 'given a verdict' within the meaning of the subsection. I say this, not on the footing that the jury gives a verdict by answering the questions put to it, but on the basis that, where neither party insists on the formality of the actual giving of a general verdict and the jury is simply discharged after answering the questions, the jury does by implication give, and the judge accepts, a general verdict, which serves as the foundation of his judgment. This verdict, not express but implied, is a verdict within the meaning of the new subsection.

This is not the occasion for a long review of the cases dealing with the distinction between special verdicts and mere answers to questions. It will suffice to refer to the following authorities: *Edmond Weil Incorporated v Russell* (1936) 56 CLR 34, at 46–7 per Dixon and Evatt JJ; *McDonnell & East Ltd v McGregor* (1936) 56 CLR 50, at 55–6 per Dixon J; *Russell v Victorian Railways Commissioners* [1948] VLR 118, at 130–3 per O'Bryan J; *R v Brown and Brian* [1949] VLR 177, at 178–9; *Vlahos v Easywear (Aust) Pty Ltd* [1974] VR 155, at 157–8 and *Prestinenzi v Steel Tank and Pipe Consolidated Pty Ltd* [1981] VR 421, at 422 per Young CJ, at 430–1 per Kaye J and at 440 per McGarvie J. These authorities show that where, as in this case, questions are put to the jury without objection and answers given in a form which warrants their acceptance by the court, and the jury is then discharged without objection, the jury is taken to have authorised the [751] general verdict which is appropriate in the light of the answers to the questions and the parties are taken to have irrevocably consented to the acceptance by the trial Judge of that general verdict and the entry of judgment accordingly. (If leave has been reserved to a party to move for judgment notwithstanding the verdict, then, as *Prestinenzi's Case* shows, that party will not be taken to have authorised the entry of judgment, but even in such a case the irrevocable consent to the taking of the tacit general verdict still remains.) It should be emphasised, although the question does not arise on this appeal, that consent to the taking of the general verdict is irrevocable once the questions have been answered in a form which warrants their acceptance by the Judge; this was the view of O'Bryan J in *Russell's Case*, at 132 in a passage which may be said to have been generally approved by the Full Court in *R v Brown and Brian*. I mean by this that, once the questions have been answered in an acceptable form, the parties (by whose express or implied consent those questions were asked) are precluded from resisting the taking of the appropriate general verdict.

[Young CJ and Nicholson J concurred.]

18.6.6   Questions

1. What would be the position if the aggrieved party had been unrepresented at the County Court hearing?
2. The Supreme Court Act 1970 (NSW) s 90 provides: 'It shall be the duty of a jury to answer any question of fact that may be left to the jury by the presiding Judge at the trial.' What are the advantages and disadvantages of such a rule?

When is a verdict final?

18.6.7   Examples of juries changing their minds are rare. Normally they have little time for this. Indeed, once a jury has announced its verdict, it is typically discharged: *Anderson v Ntzounas* [1988] VR 748 at 750 per Brooking J.

18.6.8C	**Cunningham v Ryan**
	(1919) 27 CLR 294
	High Court of Australia

[Ryan, a Labor Premier, had sued the editor, a proprietor, the printer, publisher, and the lead writer of the Melbourne *Argus* in relation to a libel alleged to have been published in that paper. The trial judge, Isaacs J, had asked the jury to answer a set of questions. The jury was unable to achieve unanimity, but gradually reached the stage where nine of its 12 members were able to agree on the answers to some of the questions, and the foreman reported these conclusions to Isaacs J. The defendant suspected that at least nine jurors had agreed that the plaintiff had suffered no damage. However, after deliberating late into the night the jury was not able to reach that level of agreement on all the questions. By next morning, the fragile semi-consensus had fallen apart. The jury was hopelessly divided, and after having been unable to reach the prescribed level of agreement (nine out of 12) on any verdict, was discharged.

Isaacs J refused to enter either a verdict or a judgment for the defendant. One reason was his conclusion that the jury had not in fact agreed on a verdict or on answers which could lay the basis for a verdict. He also considered the question of whether, assuming they had reached a verdict, they could change their minds.]

Isaacs J (at 307–13): ... [E]ven if a jury hand in a verdict ever so clear and distinct and perfect, yet until the verdict is definitely accepted by the Court and recorded the jury are at liberty to change their minds and so declare. A verdict recorded must be at that moment the real existing verdict of the jury, and not an abandoned opinion. Once the two things, the offer of a verdict and its acceptance by record, synchronize, it is final; but not before. And even then it is final subject to correction of a mistake.

... But as to the reason in point of law I shall assume for the sake of argument that there were handed in, at 9.32 or 10.30 on Thursday evening, answers as final, and complete answers so far as they went. I referred counsel to some decided cases, and in addition to those cited at the Bar Mr Knox has been [308] good enough to send me a further case — *R v Crisp* 28 TLR 296. I had already read that case in the Criminal Appeal Reports 7 Cr App R 173 and will come to it later. There can be no doubt that the language used by the learned Judges in the two English cases I cited (*Napier v Daniel* 3 Bing N C 77 and *R v Meany* Le & Ca, 213) is clear, and, if correct as it stands, completely covers, and more than covers, this case. But it was very strenuously contended by Mr Knox that the language used is more comprehensive than it needed to be, and that the instances of verdicts retired from were cases of, so to speak, impossible verdicts in law. I have carefully traced the authorities so far as I can reach them, and am convinced that the judgments in those cases are correctly phrased, and are to be understood as they are expressed. The meaning of the word 'verdict' (Latin *veredictum*) is, in plain English, 'The saying of the truth.' It is simply having, as expressed in *Dowman's Case* 9 Rep, at 13a 'The truth of the case found.' I shall quote some of the authorities, early ones, though not strictly in order of date.

[He then reviewed the authorities and concluded that they:] far more than cover this case. The request in this case for reconsideration came not from me; for I not only did not originate it, but told the jury expressly that I did not ask them to do it.

On the grounds, therefore, both of technical law and broad justice the defendants' motion to enter a verdict must be refused.

As to the application for judgment, that of necessity falls if the first falls. But, further, there are additional reasons why it should fail.

[An appeal to the Full Court was dismissed.]

18.6.9   Note and question

1. The outcome satisfied no one. Ryan would have been satisfied to have his name cleared. The defendants would have been happy not to have to pay damages. In the retrial before Rich J, both got their wish. The jury awarded a farthing's damages, but Ryan was given his costs: see D Murphy, *TJ Ryan: A Political Biography*, University of Queensland Press, St Lucia, Qld, 1975, pp 339, 443–4, 474 (for the background see Ch 13 generally). Ryan also sued the Hobart *Mercury*, unsuccessfully, dying before his appeal could be heard. The Public Curator, acting on behalf of his estate, was held entitled to continue the appeal: *Ryan v Davies Bros Ltd* (1921) 29 CLR 527. The matter was settled: Murphy, pp 508–10, 515.

2. This is a rare example of a High Court jury trial. Why was the High Court the forum for the trial?

18.6.10C   **Bradbury v NZ Loan and Mercantile Agency Co Ltd**
(1926) 26 SR (NSW) 15
Supreme Court of New South Wales, Full Court

[The plaintiff was an assignee of a debt allegedly owed by the defendant to one Chambers. The defendant denied that there had been a debt, contending that the sum represented by the debt had been used to discharge a promissory note which had been assigned to the defendant by Furner & Co, to whom Chambers had given the note.]

Street CJ (at 17–8): [His Honour set out the history of the case and continued:] The jury after deliberation brought in a verdict for the plaintiff for the full amount claimed, and then, after a request had been made by counsel for the company that they might be asked to answer certain specific questions, but before any questions had been put to them by the Judge, the foreman said 'We would like to add a rider that that note comes back to life again.' The Judge said 'You thought, gentlemen, there was a mistake of fact?' and the answer was 'We think so, yes.' On that the Judge told them that they should find that there was a setoff of the amount claimed, and that they should return a verdict for the defendant company. They deliberated again, and after that returned to Court and asked whether, if they gave a verdict for the plaintiff, Furner or the defendant company could proceed against Chambers for the amount of the note. The Judge answered that in the negative, and again directed them to find a verdict for the defendant company on the ground that on what they had said there was a setoff which balanced the plaintiff's claim. They went back again to their room, and again returned and asked whether they might eliminate their rider. The Judge declined to allow them to do this, and again directed them to return a verdict for the defendant company. They again returned a verdict for the plaintiff, which the Judge refused to accept. The foreman said 'We find a verdict for the plaintiff.' the Judge said 'I cannot accept that verdict.' The foreman said 'Not with the rider added?' [18] and the Judge replied to that 'If you like to leave it like that, I shall then have to ask you to find a verdict for the defendant.' They again retired, and on returning refused to find a verdict for the defendant company by direction, and the Judge, after telling them that if they did not do so he would direct a verdict to be entered for the defendant company, suggested that they should retire again. Later on they returned, and, after asking the Judge if they were bound to give a decision according to his direction, and after being told that they were, and that they were in contempt for not doing so, they returned a verdict for the defendant company. The plaintiff now seeks to set this verdict aside.

It is clear, I think, that a Judge is not bound to receive the first verdict that a jury may give and that he may direct them to reconsider it, giving them such further direction and assistance as he may think proper. It is clear, too, that a jury may alter their verdict if they wish to do so before it is recorded; but I do not think that, in a case, the determination of which depends upon disputed facts, a Judge is entitled to force a jury to give a verdict which they do not wish to give. If they insist on their right to return a general verdict for one party or the other, the presiding judge must receive it and leave the miscarriage of justice, if any miscarriage has taken place, to be rectified on appeal. I think therefore that in the present case when the jury showed by their persistence their wish to adhere to the general verdict for the plaintiff which they first returned, the Judge should have received it, and I think that the verdict that he forced them to return must be set aside, unless in the interest of justice it is seen that no useful purpose would be served by doing so, and that, on the facts disclosed in the case, a new trial could only have the same result as that reached in the first.

Special referees' and arbitrators' reports

18.6.11 The rules are clear as to the status of referees' reports. The court may do with them as it sees fit; it may adopt the report in full or in part or it may choose not to adopt the report at all. It may require a further explanation; it may remit any part of the report for further consideration; it may decide the matter on the evidence taken by the referee; and it may enter such judgment or order as it sees fit: FCR r 28.67; ACT r 1537; NSW r 20.24; NT r 50.03; Qld r 505; Tas r 575(2)–(6); Vic r 50.04; WA O 35 r 6. A referee's report, if adopted wholly or in part, may be enforceable as a judgment of the court. This, effectively, is the position in other jurisdictions: see *Plumley v Adgauge Pty Ltd & McLoud* (1998) 29 ACSR 315 at [11] per Buchanan JA with whom Brooking and Phillips JJA agree.

Where matters are referred for determination of the proceedings or a question arising in the proceedings, the status of the report or the determination varies by jurisdiction. In two jurisdictions, the determination, unless set aside, enjoys the status of a jury verdict: Supreme Court Act 1979 (NT) s 30; Supreme Court Act 1935 (WA) s 52. In New South Wales, an arbitrator's award is to be taken as a judgment of the court which referred the matter: Civil Procedure Act 2005 (NSW) s 40. In South Australia, the determination will normally be adopted as a judgment: Supreme Court Act 1935 (SA) s 66; r 222(4). In Victoria, r 50.01 distinguishes between references for a report and references to decide the question. It is not clear whether anything turns on this distinction, and if so, what: see *Plumley v Adgauge Pty Ltd & McLoud* (1998) 29 ACSR 315 at [5] per Buchanan JA with whom Brooking and Phillips JJA agreed. In Victoria, determinations by arbitrators, unless set aside, enjoy the status of decisions under the Commercial Arbitration Act 1984 (Vic): r 50.08. The Federal Court may make an order for the registration of the award, whereupon the award has the effect of a court order: Federal Court of Australia Act 1976 (Cth) s 54; FCR r 28.13 (orders made under a r 28.02 arbitration). For a discussion of the criteria taken into account by a court in determining whether to accept a report by a referee charged with making a report, the following cases are illustrative.

18.6.12C	**Nicholls v Stamer**
	[1980] VR 479
	Supreme Court of Victoria

[A referee in a building case was required to produce a report within a specified time. He failed to do so, and no extension of time was sought. Brooking J held that the time for making the report could be retrospectively enlarged. In his judgment, he discussed the status of a referee's report, and the circumstances relating to its adoption by a judge.]

Brooking J (at 495–6): One looks in vain for any general statement of the principles on which the court acts in exercising the discretion to adopt a report wholly or partially or to decline to do so. Having regard to the obvious breadth of the discretion, this is perhaps not surprising, and it is perhaps undesirable that any such general statement should be essayed. A brief report may show, as in *Birmingham Corp v Allen* [1877] WN 190, no more than that the court reduced the damages as assessed by the referee. *Rust v Victoria Graving Dock Co and London & St Katherine Dock Co* (1887) 36 Ch D 113 affords an example of a successful attack upon a referee's report under s 56 of the Judicature Act 1873 which resulted in the disallowance by the Court of Appeal of a number of items allowed by the referee in his assessment of the damages, the Court of Appeal being of opinion that those items were as a matter of law not recoverable.

I am not aware of any case in which the reference was for inquiry and report and an attack was made on the report based upon something which occurred during the reference, such as the admission or rejection of evidence or the refusal of an adjournment. *In Re Maplin Sands* (1894) 71 LT 56; on appeal (1894) 71 LT 594, an unsuccessful attack was made based on the rejection of evidence by the referee, but the case appears to have been one of reference of the whole matter for trial pursuant to s 14 of the Arbitration Act 1889.

In Re *Taylor; Turpin v Pain* (1890) 44 Ch D 128 an order was made under s 56 of the Judicature Act 1873 requiring an official referee to take certain accounts and report thereon. The report failed [496] to disclose which items or sets of items the Official Referee had allowed or partially allowed, or disallowed or partially disallowed, and the plaintiffs sought an order remitting the report to him, their complaint being that the report was in such a form that they could not put their finger on anything and bring it before the court as a matter with regard to which they could say that the Official Referee had erred. The Official Referee made a supplementary report, and Chitty J refused the plaintiffs' motion, on the ground that the plaintiffs had available to them all the materials which they needed to attack the report, if there were any grounds of substance for attacking it. At (44 Ch D) 139 his Lordship said: 'No doubt counsel would find it a very great labour to read through all the Official Referee's notes to understand them and to put the items together; but the parties who were before the Official Referee will be able, if there is really any ground for saying that substantial justice has not been done, by reference to these notes to pick out the material points and bring them before the Court.'

This mention of the doing of substantial justice illustrates to my mind the breadth of the discretion conferred by s 14(2).

18.6.13C   **Super Pty Ltd (formerly known as Leda Constructions Pty Ltd) v SJP Formwork (Aust) Pty Ltd**
(1992) 29 NSWLR 549
New South Wales Court of Appeal

Gleeson CJ (at 562–4): [On the question of the approach a trial judge should take to parties' attempts to reagitate matters considered by a referee:]

The applicable principles:
I am unable to accept, either as an absolute rule, or as a prima facie rule subject to defined or definable exceptions, that a party who is dissatisfied with a referee's report is entitled as of right to require the judge acting under Pt 72, r 13, to reconsider and determine afresh all issues, whether of fact or law, which that party desires to contest before the judge.

My reasons are as follows:

1.   Such a conclusion finds no support in the language of Pt 72 and is inconsistent with the discretionary powers conferred by Pt 72, r 13.
2.   The history of the rule tends against such an approach. The present rules replaced provisions dealing with decisions of arbitrators and referees to whom matters were referred by order of the court. Those decisions were given the effect of a verdict of a jury. The provisions were interpreted by the High Court as meaning that such decisions could be reviewed for error of law, perversity or manifest unreasonableness. There was no general right of [563] review or appeal by way of rehearing. The modern rules are expressed in language which provides wider discretionary flexibility, but it would be a radical departure from the history of the rules to treat them as giving a dissatisfied party an automatic right to a hearing *de novo*.
3.   If one were constrained, by weight of authority or practical necessity, to admit exceptions to such a rule, then it becomes difficult to identify the principle underlying

the exceptions and to reconcile that principle with the rule. However, unless one can identify such a principle, it is impossible to decide, other than on pragmatic grounds, whether a new case is to be treated as an exception.

4.   It would be inconsistent with the object and purpose of the rules, and potentially productive of delay, expense, and hardship, that the practical effect of appointing a referee should be simply to add an extra level to the hierarchy of decision makers in a given case.

5.   That consequence would also be inconsistent with the modern trend towards encouragement of alternative dispute resolution, as reflected, for example, in the provisions of the Commercial Arbitration Act 1984: see the discussion by Sheller JA of developments in relation to minimising judicial intervention in commercial arbitration in *Promenade Investments Pty Ltd v State of New South Wales* (1992) 26 NSWLR 203.

What is involved in an application under Pt 72, r 13 is not an appeal, whether by way of a hearing *de novo* or a more limited rehearing. This is consistent with the right of the referee to conduct the reference as the referee thinks fit and unconstrained by the rules of evidence. Rather, the judge, in reviewing the report and deciding whether to adopt, vary or reject it, has a judicial discretion to exercise in a manner that is consistent both with the object and purpose of the rules and with the wider setting in which they take their place.

That wider setting is a system for the administration of justice according to law. In so far as the subject matter of dissatisfaction with a referee's report is a question of law, or the application of legal standards to established facts, then a proper exercise of discretion would require a judge to consider and determine that matter afresh. That was decided by this Court in *Homebush Abattoir Corporation v Bemria Pty Ltd* (1991) 22 NSWLR 605: see also, *Cape v Maidment* (1991) 98 ACTR 1 at 4. That conclusion is entirely consistent with the history of the rules and the reasoning of the High Court in *Buckley* which, although the case related to different provisions is also instructive as to the present provisions.

Subject to what has just been said, it is undesirable to attempt closely to confine the manner in which the discretion is to be exercised: cf *Nicholls v Stamer* [1980] VR 479 at 495 per Brooking J. The nature of the complaints made about the report, the type of litigation involved, and the length and complexity of the proceedings before the referee, may all be relevant considerations. The purpose of Pt 72 is to provide, where the interests of justice so dictate, a form of partial resolution of disputes alternative to orthodox litigation, and it would frustrate that purpose to allow the reference to be treated as some kind of warm-up for the real contest. On the other hand, if the referee's report reveals some error of principle, some absence or excess of jurisdiction, or some patent misapprehension of the evidence, that would ordinarily be a reason for rejecting it: cf *Jordan v McKenzie* (1987) 26 [564] CPC (2d) 193. So also would perversity or manifest unreasonableness in fact finding. As to the last-mentioned matters, I refer again to the history of the rules and to *Buckley*.

On the particular question, relevant to the present case, of the approach to be taken to disputed findings of fact, where there is shown to be evidence available to support such findings, or the issue involves a choice as between conflicting evidence, I agree with the views of Giles J as expressed in the extracts from his reasons for judgment quoted earlier. I also agree with what was said by Cole J in *Chloride Batteries Australia Ltd v Glendale Chemical Products Pty Ltd*. In that case Cole J made extensive reference to, and relied upon, what was said by Marks J in *Integer Computing Pty Ltd v Facom Australia Ltd* (Marks J, Supreme Court of Victoria, 10 April 1987, unreported). Those two last-mentioned judgments are of particular relevance to reports involving technical (non-legal) expertise.

18.6.14   Notes

1. See *Cape v Maidment* (1991) 98 ACTR 1 (reference, by consent to Sir Laurence Street, for taking of accounts). It was held by Miles CJ that although, at the time, there was no Australian Capital Territory counterpart to the then NSW Pt 72, the same principles should be applied in decisions as to whether to accept a report. There being evidence for the conclusions of fact, and no evidence of legal error in the reasons, the report should be accepted. For applications of the *Super Pty Ltd* principles, see *E S Gordon v Idameneo (No 123) Pty Ltd* (1994) 14 ACSR 536 and *Foxman Holdings Pty Ltd v NMBE Pty Ltd* (1995) 38 NSWLR 615; see *Plumley v Adgauge Pty Ltd & McLoud* (1998) 29 ACSR 315; *Wenco Industrial v W W Industries* (2009) 25 VR 119 at 126–7; [2009] VSCA 191 at [17] (stating the principles to be taken into account in determining whether to adopt a report).

2. The broad powers conferred on the court mean that it can choose to accept the answers given in a report, while not holding itself bound by the reasoning in the report. The importance of (and rationale for) this distinction is illustrated by *Astor Properties Pty Ltd v L'Union des Assurance de Paris* (1989) 17 NSWLR 483. There a referee provided answers to questions which the defendant was willing to accept. The answers were based in part on the referee's assessment of the integrity of relevant witnesses. Cole J rejected the plaintiff's argument that he should regard himself as bound by this assessment.

3. In *Multicon Engineering Pty Ltd v Federal Airports Corporation* (1997) 47 NSWLR 631, the appellant argued that when courts exercised federal jurisdiction, parties who disagreed with a referee's report were entitled to a re-hearing in relation to matters with which they were dissatisfied. The appeal failed, but on the grounds that, having itself sought the reference, and not having taken the constitutional point at a time when it might have affected the conduct of the trial, it would be contrary to the interests of justice to allow the appellant to rely on it as an appeal point. The Court of Appeal did, however, suggest that if it had had to decide the matter, the appellant would also have failed on the constitutional issue.

JUDGMENT

18.7.1 There is a distinction between verdict and judgment. The verdict consists of the jury's finding of facts. The judgment is the orders made by the court in consequence of those facts. This distinction is apparent and material in cases tried by juries. It is less apparent in cases tried by judge alone. In practice, judges pronounce their findings of fact at the same time as they make such orders as the case calls for. The orders and the finding of fact are almost invariably accompanied by a statement of reasons justifying the judge's conclusions. While the term 'judgment' is normally used to describe the orders, the finding of facts and the reasoning, 'judgment' is also used in a narrower sense to mean the orders given by the judge. When, for instance, judgment is 'entered', it is the judge's orders that are entered. The findings of fact and the reasoning are usually relevant only in so far as they constitute the basis for argument in a subsequent appeal, although a minority of cases will have a life after death as ammunition in legal arguments, and perhaps even as authority for subsequent judgments. In most jurisdictions, a judge may give judgment without any motion or application to this effect from any party: FCR r 1.41; ACT r 1605; NSW r 36.1; NT r 59.01; Qld rr 658–660; Tas r 573; Vic r 59.01; WA O 34 r 8. In several jurisdictions there is express provision for applications to be made for judgment; cf ACT r 1600; SA r 240(1); Tas r 573(1)(c) (with leave); WA O 34 r 8 (judge may leave a party to move for judgment).

18.7.2   There is a distinction between the pronouncement of judgment and entry of judgment. A judgment is pronounced when it is delivered. It is entered when embodied in a formal, sealed record and recorded in the court's records. Judgments normally take effect from their pronouncement. However, a condition for appealing from, or enforcing, a judgment is that it be entered on the court record.

Jury trials

18.7.3   Once a jury has given its verdict and been discharged, its role in the proceedings is done. However, its verdict cannot take effect unless or until and in so far as it is embodied in a judgment. The judge may give judgment without formally being asked to do so. If the judge does not give judgment, any party may move for one. Normally it will be the successful party which will move for judgment (in its favour). However, there are several circumstances in which this may not happen. First, there may be some cases where the successful party does not wish to move for judgment. Second, there are cases where the unsuccessful party may be able to move for judgment in its favour, notwithstanding the jury's verdict. The following case extract provides an example of a case where the 'successful' party was reluctant to move for judgment.

18.7.4C	**Turner v Manier (No 1)**
	[1958] VR 350
	Supreme Court of Victoria

[The plaintiff, who had been injured in an industrial accident, sued in negligence, but received an award reduced by two-thirds on the basis of the plaintiff's contributory negligence. The plaintiff was not anxious to have judgment entered, since this would mean that he would not be able to pursue a workers' compensation claim, a claim which would yield more than the limited damages he had been awarded by the jury. However, the defendant moved that judgment for the plaintiff be entered in accordance with the verdict.

Sholl J adjourned the motion until after the plaintiff had made his application for workers' compensation, holding that it would be unjust to deprive the plaintiff of his full workers' compensation benefits, especially since, by virtue of the operation of the relevant legislation, the defendant's liability would actually be reduced if the plaintiff were successful. There was, however, no reason in principle why the defendant should not be able to move that judgment be entered for the plaintiff.]

Sholl J (at 355): Though Mr O'Driscoll [for the plaintiff] indicated that he might desire hereafter to submit that the defendant could not or should not be allowed to have judgment entered for the plaintiff, I entertain no doubt that this Court has in a proper case jurisdiction to accede to a motion by a defendant to have judgment entered for the plaintiff if the plaintiff does not move to that effect himself. At one time it seems to have been thought that the plaintiff might delay the entry of judgment as long as he liked, but during the 19th century a different view was taken see *Tidd's Practice* (9th ed), (1828), vol II, 931; Chitty's *Archbold*, 12th ed, (1866) vol 1, pp 524–5; *Taylor v Nesfield* (1855) 4 El & Bl 462; *Baker v Saunders* (1860) 7 CB NS 858. I see no such difference in the relevant legislation and rules as would make those authorities inapplicable in Victoria today, and I agree, if I may respectfully say so, with the Court of Queen's Bench in thinking that it is a very useful and salutary power for the Court to have. To the instances of its use mentioned in those cases might be added the case given in argument here of the defendant paying into Court more than the amount ultimately awarded to the plaintiff. There the plaintiff might seek to avoid indefinitely, if he thought the result as to costs would be to his disadvantage, the entry of the judgment; but of course he could not be allowed to do so. Even after the receipt by the plaintiff of workers compensation, the Court, in my opinion, could, and in a proper case should, enter judgment for the plaintiff in an action such as this at the instance of the defendant, if such judgment would constitute a record useful to the defendant, though no longer enforceable according to its terms against the defendant.

18.7.5   Question

1. What is the relevance of post-verdict events? How does one prove them?

18.7.6C   Turner v Manier (No 2)
[1958] VR 358
Supreme Court of Victoria

[The plaintiff subsequently sought a workers' compensation award and was successful. The plaintiff then moved that judgment be entered in his favour. The defendant sought leave to withdraw its motion. It sought by affidavit to prove the award.]

Sholl J (at 359): It cannot be right to say, as Mr O'Driscoll [counsel for the plaintiff] said, that the occurrence after verdict and before judgment of facts going in bar of the plaintiff's right can in no case be established except by the verdict of a jury. I have myself already held earlier in this year, in *Francis v T R & L Cockram Pty Ltd* [1957] VR 538 that the fact of the making of [360] weekly payments of workers compensation, deductible from common law damages under s 14 of the Workers Compensation Act 1953, is a matter for the attention of the judge and not of the jury. It will be observed that in that kind of case some of the weekly payments might follow the verdict and precede the judgment, and it will be further observed that the total of such weekly payments might actually exceed the amount of a common law verdict for damages. In such a case, therefore, the judge might have to investigate for himself facts occurring both before and after verdict, and if it were established that the total of the weekly payments exceeded the amount of the verdict for common law damages, the judge, in my view, would not be justified in entering judgment for the plaintiff. The proper course in such a case would be, I think, to enter judgment for the defendant, reciting the verdict and the facts as subsequently ascertained by the judge himself in pursuance of his function under the 1953 Act. Again, the death of a plaintiff after verdict and before judgment abated an action at common law, and if judgment were entered notwithstanding the death, that was 'error' for which a writ of error would lie. By the statute 16 & 17 Car II c 5, that position was relieved against if the judgment was entered within two terms after the verdict, but *contra* if it was not and questions of fact in relation to the operation of that statute were decided by the judges and not by juries see *Tidd's Practice*, 9th ed (1828) vol II, pp 933, 1116–7; *Copley v Day* (1812) 4 Taunt 702; and *Lawrence v Hodgson* (1827) 1 Y and J 368. Furthermore, in Victoria today the only right to a jury is, generally speaking, that given by the Rules of Court and those Rules say nothing expressly about such a case as this, nor do I think that by implication they confer on the plaintiff the right to have a matter of this kind determined by a jury. Another example which might be given is the case of a statute passed after verdict and before judgment, and so expressed as to apply to the action and to bar the plaintiff's right to judgment. It seems to me that in such a case it clearly would be the function of the judge to determine the matter of the applicability of the statute to that proceeding, even though that determination might involve investigation of some facts, and in that case again, his proper duty would be to enter judgment for the defendant, reciting however, the initial verdict in favour of the plaintiff and the subsequent matters operating to bar the entry of judgment thereon.

Even, however, if (contrary to my view) it were right to say that, if the fact of the receipt of workers compensation by the plaintiff were in this case disputed, the matter would be determined by a jury, this is a case in which no possible dispute or issue about the point has been or can, I think, be suggested. There is, in short, no issue about the matter for any jury to try. The material fact is not really denied by the plaintiff at all; he has simply succeeded in doing what all along he sought an adjournment for the purpose of attempting to do. I think it is my function to determine the matter, and accordingly I receive the affidavit and hold that the plaintiff has since verdict received workers compensation within the meaning of the Workers Compensation Acts; that he should not now have judgment at all; and that judgment should be entered for the defendant, reciting the verdict of the jury and the subsequent recovery by the plaintiff of workers compensation.

Cases where there is no evidence to support a verdict

18.7.7   Cases where there is no evidence to support a particular verdict may be disposed of by a successful 'no case' submission, or by the entry of judgment without the taking of a verdict (notwithstanding that this may be questionable). Alternatively, if directed to give a particular verdict, the jury will normally give that verdict. But what happens if a jury gives a verdict which cannot be supported by the evidence? In some cases, the unsuccessful party may, prior to the verdict, have reserved the right to move for a verdict in its favour, notwithstanding a jury verdict otherwise. If the other party has agreed to this reservation, the judge may enter a judgment which is inconsistent with the jury's verdict, in the event of there being no evidence to support that verdict. If leave has not been reserved, or if the other party has refused to agree to it, the position is more complicated.

The pre-Judicature Act position was clear: the jury's verdict prevailed. However, the subsequent position is less clear. In England, the rules appear to permit judges to enter judgments inconsistent with the jury's verdict. Australian rules have been interpreted as allowing less scope for this. However, Australian courts have nonetheless been prepared to enter judgments inconsistent with jury verdicts, and courts have sometimes endorsed this practice. Cases which appear to endorse the practice should be handled with care. If they are English cases, they may turn on the English rules. Regardless of jurisdiction, they may in fact have been cases where leave to move has been reserved, or where it has been treated as having been reserved. Even when neither of these conditions applies, cases may be flawed by virtue of undue reliance on cases which can be so explained.

Conversely, there is now specific provision in the New South Wales rules to the effect that if a jury gives its verdict, '[t]he court may give judgment as it thinks fit despite the verdict, finding or assessment': r 29.11. Cases based on earlier rules may therefore no longer be relevant in New South Wales.

In *Phillips v Ellinson Bros Pty Ltd* (1941) 65 CLR 221, the High Court divided 2–2 on the issue. Rich and McTiernan JJ ruled that in the absence of reservation, trial judges lacked the power to enter judgments inconsistent with juries' verdicts. Starke and Williams JJ held otherwise. Starke J in particular relied on *Skeate v Slaters Ltd* [1914] 2 KB 429, a decision based on the English rules, and one whose relevance and authority had earlier been questioned by Dixon and McTiernan JJ in *McDonnell & East Ltd v McGregor* (1936) 56 CLR 50 on the grounds that: (a) the relevant statement was obiter; and (b) it was inconsistent even with the English rules.

18.7.8C   **Prestinenzi v Steel Tank and Pipe Consolidated Pty Ltd**
[1981] VR 421
Supreme Court of Victoria, Full Court

[In an action for negligence, the jury found that the defendant had been negligent, but reduced the plaintiff's damages by two-thirds on the grounds of contributory negligence. After this verdict, the trial judge accepted the plaintiff's submission that there was no evidence of contributory negligence and that he should therefore enter judgment for the plaintiff for the total damages assessed. On appeal, the court considered both the question of whether the judge had this power, and whether there was indeed no evidence to support the finding of contributory negligence.

Kaye J's judgment includes a detailed discussion of the relevant case law. While recognising that there was authority for the proposition that judges could enter judgments inconsistent with juries' verdicts, regardless of whether leave had been reserved, he argued that this authority was not persuasive. Some cases were based on the English rules which, on their face, appeared to allow broader powers to trial judges than did the Victorian rules. In so far as Australian decisions were based on those English authorities, their conclusions were correspondingly suspect. Further, there was considerable authority to support the proposition that judges' powers to disregard jury verdicts were limited to cases where a party had, before verdict, moved for judgment notwithstanding the jury's verdict.]

McGarvie J (at 438–41): At a common law trial where the plaintiff does not make out a case on the evidence, it was open to the judge to *non suit* the plaintiff or to direct the jury to find a verdict for the defendant. If he were non suited the plaintiff could bring another action. A judgment of *non suit* could be entered on the application of either the plaintiff or the defendant. It could be entered at the close of the plaintiff's case or at the end of all the evidence: *Jones v Dunkel* (1959) 101 CLR 298, at 322–4 and 329–30.

In ordinary circumstances, where the plaintiff appeared in court at all times, the trial judge could exercise the power to *non suit* the plaintiff only with his consent: *Jones v Dunkel* (1959) 101 CLR 298, at 324–5; *Humphrey v Collier* [1946] VLR 391, at 404. If the trial judge, without dissent from the plaintiff, heard an application by the defendant for a *non suit* the plaintiff was taken by implication to have consented and was bound by the decision if it was against him: *Jones v Dunkel*, supra, at 325. If the plaintiff did not consent the trial judge directed a verdict for the defendant: *Jones v Dunkel*, supra, at 325–9; *Humphrey v Collier*, supra, at 404.

At common law, after verdict, judgment was entered only upon a motion to the court *in banc*: *Phillips v Ellinson Bros Pty Ltd* (1941) 65 CLR 221, at 228. After verdict for the plaintiff the court *in banc* could enter a *non suit* or verdict and judgment for the defendant but its power to do so was based on the consent of the parties and jury: *Edmond Weil Incorporated v Russell* (1936) 56 CLR 34, at 46–7. If the trial judge, before verdict and without dissent from the plaintiff, heard an application by the defendant for leave to move for *non suit* or for a verdict for the defendant notwithstanding the verdict of the jury, the plaintiff would be taken impliedly to have consented to the exercise of the appropriate power: *Edmond Weil Incorporated v Russell*, supra, at 45–7; *Phillips v Ellinson Bros Pty Ltd,* supra, at 229; *Jones v Dunkel*, supra, at 324–5. In the absence of consent the court *in banc* would order a new trial: *Heydon v Lillis* (1907) 4 CLR (Pt 2) 1223 at 1227–8.

Under the system of the Judicature Acts the practices of the common law continue to be followed unless abolished or modified by the new system: *Phillips v Ellinson Bros Pty Ltd,* supra, at 229. Two changes made by the judicature system were that *non suit* was abolished and power to give judgment after verdict went from the court *in banc* to the trial judge: *Phillips v Ellinson Bros Pty Ltd,* [440] supra, at 228; *Humphrey v Collier*, supra, at 402 per Macfarlan J, and pp. 404–6; *Jones v Dunkel*, supra, at 330–1, Rules of the Supreme Court of Victoria O 36, r 32.

The trial judge may give judgment for the defendant after the close of the plaintiff's evidence or at the end of all the evidence: *Humphrey v Collier*, supra, at 402–3 and 408; *Jones v Dunkel*, supra, at 330–1. In *Humphrey v Collier*, supra, at 403–8, Gavan Duffy, J, with whose reasons Herring, CJ agreed, expressed the view that power to do this does not depend on consent: it is a permissible shortening of procedure, by which the formality of directing and obtaining a verdict is omitted. Other views have been expressed which indicate that the power to give judgment without obtaining a verdict must depend on consent. *Humphrey v Collier,* supra, at 402, per Macfarlan, J; *Thompson v Amos* (1949) 23 ALJ 98, at 103–4. On either view the giving of judgment is the equivalent of directing and obtaining a verdict and then giving judgment.

In this Court, after a trial judge has accepted a general or special verdict, or the jury has answered questions submitted to it and been discharged, there is no power in the judge to give judgment inconsistent with the verdict or findings of the jury. No power remains to give judgment directly instead of directing and obtaining a verdict and giving judgment, because the jury has finally given its verdict or finally authorized only the entry of a verdict consistent with its findings: *Edmond Weil Incorporated v Russell*, supra, at 45–7; *McDonnell and East Ltd v McGregor* (1936) 56 CLR 50, at 56–7. An English rule providing that the trial judge shall 'direct judgment to be entered as he shall think right' has been held to give the judge power to direct entry of a judgment which is inconsistent with the verdict of a jury: *Skeate v Slaters Ltd* [1914] 2 KB 429, at 438–9. In Victoria, O 36 r 32 providing that the judge shall 'give judgment for any party' does not confer such a power: *Phillips v Ellinson Bros Pty Ltd*, supra, at 230.

The trial judge may, however, by the consent of the parties, disregard the jury's verdict or findings and give a contrary judgment: *Edmond Weil Incorporated v Russell*, supra, at 46, *Phillips v Ellinson Bros Pty Ltd*, supra, at 229 and 239. By a practice which corresponds with that at common law, if the trial judge before verdict and without dissent, hears an application by the defendant for leave to move for judgment notwithstanding verdict, or himself raises and considers the grant of such leave, the parties are treated as impliedly consenting to that course and are bound if the leave is given: *Edmond Weil Incorporated v Russell*, supra, at 46; *Phillips v Ellinson Bros. Pty Ltd*, supra, at 229–32.

In *Humphrey v Collier* [1946] VLR 391 at 407–8 in the reasons of Gavan Duffy, J, there are expressions indicating that consent is not necessary to enable a trial judge to give a judgment which is inconsistent with the jury's verdict. I do not consider that his Honour was saying that such a judgment could be given where no leave had been granted to move for judgment notwithstanding verdict. When he said at 408 that it had been the practice of some judges to give leave to move after verdict for judgment irrespective of any consent, I think he was referring to express consent, because almost always when leave is given, consent [441] is implied. If a plaintiff objected to the judge considering the grant of leave to the defendant to move for judgment after verdict, his consent could not be implied. Then, if the judge decided that the plaintiff had not made out a case on the evidence he would give judgment for the defendant (or direct a verdict for the defendant). The plaintiff would then have lost his chance of a favourable verdict in that trial. Such a situation will seldom occur and we were referred to no case where it had. The common case in which liberty is reserved to a defendant to move for judgment notwithstanding verdict, occurs where, upon a submission at the close of the evidence, the judge is of the view that the plaintiff has not made out a case on the evidence, or doubts whether he has but desires to give the plaintiff the opportunity of obtaining a verdict and arguing on appeal that he had made out a case. Then if the plaintiff succeeds on appeal no new trial is necessary. In any event, if anything said in *Humphrey v Collier*, supra, implies that a defendant without the express or implied consent of the plaintiff can move for judgment notwithstanding verdict, that was not essential to the decision in that case.

I have discussed the position where it is a plaintiff who fails to make out a case on the evidence. I consider that similar principles apply where a defendant fails on the evidence to make out a case upon an issue on which he bears the onus of proof. That was the approach of Lowe, J in *Mannu v Ford Motor Co of Australia Pty Ltd* [1962] VR 464.

I conclude that it was not open to the trial judge in this case to give a judgment which was inconsistent with the findings on contributory negligence. The defendant had not expressly or by implication consented to the judge deciding after verdict (or after the jury answered questions and was discharged) whether there was evidence of contributory negligence and giving judgment on the basis of that decision.

If the defendant in a jury trial desires to submit that the plaintiff has not made out a case on the evidence, it is desirable that the plaintiff and the judge be informed of this not later than the close of all the evidence. It may be fair to permit the plaintiff to reopen his case to mend his hand, cf: *Hampton Court Ltd v Crooks* (1957) 97 CLR 367, at 372. The judge should be aware of the defendant's submission when he prepares his charge and prepares any questions he may submit to the jury, cf: *Grinstead v Hadrill* [1953] 1 WLR 696, at 698–9. It is not desirable that a defendant should be entitled to leave it until after the jury's verdict or answers to questions to submit that some element of the plaintiff's case has not been made out. Little or no attention may have been given to that aspect of the case by the plaintiff, judge or jury. Similar considerations apply when the submission is that of the plaintiff upon an issue on which the defendant has the onus of proof. Under the present practice, a trial judge in deciding whether to grant leave to move for judgment notwithstanding verdict and in hearing any application to call further evidence, can consider the position of any party who may be prejudiced by being taken by surprise.

[Young CJ agreed with Kaye and McGarvie JJ and all agreed that there was no evidence to support the contributory negligence finding. The defendant was ordered to pay the costs of the trial and the appeal.]

18.7.9 Questions

1. In the light of the matters raised in McGarvie J's judgment, are the powers of a trial judge to set aside verdicts adequate? Or, are they too broad?

2. Suppose that there was no evidence to support a jury's answers to a number of questions put to it by the trial judge and it handed down a misconceived verdict. In view of the decision in *Altmann v Dunning* [1995] 2 VR 1, would a Victorian trial judge be entitled to discharge the jury and give judgment in the face of the jury's answers? See *Rigg v State of New South Wales* (1993) Aust Torts Reports 81–230; *Pezzimenti v Seamer* [1995] 2 VR 32.

18.7.10C	**Sayers v Perrin (No 2)**
	[1966] Qd R 74
	Supreme Court of Queensland

[While employed as a welder, the plaintiff suffered an electric shock and subsequently was affected by poliomyelitis. This caused paralysis to his right arm. He argued that the paralysis would not have ensued but for the electric shock. He received a favourable verdict from the jury, notwithstanding that there was no evidence that the shock had caused the paralysis. Counsel for the defendant had applied to have the matter withdrawn from the jury, but the trial judge (Wanstall J) made no decision on this. Counsel then moved for judgment *non obstante veredicto*.]

Wanstall J (at 86–7): I apply the long established practice of this court which acknowledges that a trial judge has statutory power, not dependent upon consent of parties, and notwithstanding a jury's findings, to enter judgment 'consistently with them', in cases in which upon the evidence the other party is, as a matter of law, entitled to the verdict. Such a situation arises when, assuming acceptance of all the evidence adduced in support of the claim, it falls short of establishing any cause of action, so that there was never any case in law to go to the jury. Again it may occur [87] when the party favoured by the findings bore the onus of establishing an issue of fact but failed to adduce evidence sufficient in law to establish it, the insufficiency of evidence to support an issue being a question of law. Again the outcome of an issue or of the action may turn upon the interpretation to be put upon documents or uncontroverted facts, which remains a matter for the judge although he has elected to ask the jury for its conclusions or inferences therefrom. In my view, neither the existence of the power nor its exercise to the extent indicated depends upon reservation of leave to move for judgment, or the postponement of decision on an application for a directed verdict, since the Judicature Act and rules. The constitutional necessity for such a reservation at common law is explained by Dixon J in *Shepherd v Felt and Textiles of Australia Ltd* (1931) 45 CLR 359 at 379, and in *Edmond Weil Incorporated v Russell* (1936) 56 CLR 34 by Dixon J and Evatt J at 46. In this case I exercise the powers on motion for judgment conferred by the Rules of Court as long construed by its judges. In the exercise of those powers I enter verdict and consequent judgment for the defendants on the issue involved in the eighth question, they being entitled thereto as a matter of law in consequence of the failure of the plaintiff to adduce evidence sufficient in law to establish a causal connection between his receiving an electric shock and suffering paralysis of his arm.

But for my belief that I have that power under the Rules of Court, and my concurrence with the school of thought which recognises the advantages of ascertaining the views of the jury in any event, I would, at the end of the plaintiff's case, have adopted the course favoured by Starke J in the following *dicta* from *Shepherd v Felt and Textiles of Australia Ltd* at 373: 'Where on the uncontroverted facts the action or an issue must be determined in favour of one party, then, as a matter of law, that party is entitled to the verdict in the action or upon the issue. And it is necessarily wrong to leave any conclusion or inference in such circumstances as a question of fact to the jury. In such a case a direction should be given to the jury that as a matter of law the verdict must be for the party entitled to succeed. ...' If a judge in this court cannot do what I have done, but is constrained to take the case, or an issue, from the jury, on his view of the law, before getting their answers, as Starke J advises, there will be much unnecessary waste of costs. As I understand the law in this State our Court has, from the beginning, favoured a construction of its Rules which avoids such costly frustration of litigants.

18.7.11   Question

1.   It is tempting to conclude that the issue will never matter. In particular, it is hard to see how it can affect the outcome of an appeal. If there was no evidence, and the judge wrongly entered judgment for the unsuccessful party, the result of the appeal will be a pyrrhic victory for the appellant. If there was in fact evidence, then the appeal will be successful because the trial judge will have erred in finding otherwise. Given these considerations, are there any circumstances in which the issue is of practical importance?

Entry of judgment

18.7.12   The rules make provision for the formal entry of judgments on the court's records. This normally requires no more than the performance of routine clerical functions: HCR Pt 8; FCR Div 39.4; ACT r 1606; NSW r 36.11; NT O 60; Qld r 661(2)–(3); SA r 241; Tas Pt 33; Vic O 60; WA O 43. In some jurisdictions, judgments may be enforced or appealed from only after they have been entered: FCR r 39.31(1)(b); NT r 60.01(1); Qld r 661(4); Tas 812(1); Vic r 60.01. Until judgment is entered, courts have the jurisdiction to reconsider their judgments. Having given judgment, they are not obliged to reconsider their judgment on the application of a disgruntled party and ordinarily the public interest in the finality of litigation will mean that the court will decline to reconsider its judgment: *Smith v New South Wales Bar Association* (1992) 176 CLR 256; *Autodesk Inc v Dyason* (1993) 176 CLR 300. If an application is made for a reconsideration of a judgment, the application should be made to the judge or judges who made the decision whose reconsideration is being sought, and it should normally be that judge or those judges who reconsider the application. However, the matter may be reconsidered by a differently constituted court, and should be reconsidered by a differently constituted court in the event if there is an arguable case that the court as originally constituted was biased. The mere fact that a court has already pronounced judgment does not of itself mean that it is biased: see *McAdam v Robertson* (1999) 73 SASR 360.

Setting aside and 'correcting' judgments

18.7.13 The legal system's interest in finality means that judgments are not lightly set aside. Parties aggrieved by a judgment will normally have only two alternatives: to grin and bear it, or to appeal. However, there are circumstances in which judgments may be set aside. Judgments made in default of a party's attendance at trial may be set aside. In this respect, they are similar to other default judgments. In addition, judgments may be set aside on the grounds of fraud or new evidence. This discretion is sparingly exercised.

There is also provision for correcting minor errors in judgments. This process assumes the general correctness of the judgment, but recognises that through mistakes on the part of parties or the judge, the judgment may either not embody the judge's intentions, or that it might not reflect what the judge's intentions would have been had the judge's attention been drawn to a particular matter.

Judgments in default

18.7.14 There is a general power to set aside judgments made in default of a party's attendance at trial: FCR r 39.05(a); ACT r 1613(2)(a); NSW r 36.16(2)(b); NT r 49.02(2); Qld r 476(4); SA r 230; Tas r 570(2); Vic r 49.02(2); WA O 34 r 3. So long as the non-appearing party had notice of the hearing, it is not grounds for setting aside a default judgment that the successful party failed to present to the court material in its possession which would have been favourable to the non-appearing party: *Elder v Cameron (No 2)* [2007] NSWSC 984. In most jurisdictions, applications to set aside judgment must be made expeditiously: within six days of the verdict in Tasmania; within seven days of the verdict or judgment in the Australian Capital Territory, New South Wales and South Australia; and within 14 days of the trial in the Northern Territory, Victoria and Western Australia. The power is a discretionary one.

18.7.15C   **Surfers Paradise International Convention Centre Pty Ltd v National Mutual Life Association of Australasia Ltd**
[1984] 2 Qd R 447
Supreme Court of Queensland

[The applicants, not having appeared at the trial of an action brought against them by National Mutual, subsequently sought to have judgment against them set aside.]

Andrews SPJ (at 453–9): [His Honour outlined the history of the litigation, and turned to the matters relevant to the exercise of his discretion to set aside the judgments, saying:] Before considering the merits in detail I propose referring to O 39, r 33 of the Rules of the Supreme Court and to some of the cases.

Order 39, r 33 provides that a judgment obtained where one party does not appear at the trial may be set aside by the Court or a Judge upon such terms as may be just.

In *Aboyne Pty Ltd v Dixon Homes Pty Ltd* [1980] Qd R 142 Kelly J had to consider an application under O 18A, r 7 of the Supreme [454] Court Rules to set aside a summary judgment for specific performance obtained after default of appearance by the defendant. The headnote there says that the defendant must show that:

(i)   it has a satisfactory explanation for the failure to appear;

(ii)   any delay in bringing the application is not such as to preclude it from obtaining relief; and

(iii)   had it appeared at the hearing of the application for summary judgment, it should have been granted leave to defend.

In fact, Kelly J did not rule that the defendant must so show but in his judgment, with which I agree, makes it plain that these are relevant matters. The facts there are quite different from those here. It was in fact found that the defendant in that case failed to appear as a result of an oversight on the part of its solicitor, whereby neither the defendant nor its solicitor was aware that the matter had been set down on the return date.

... In *Watt v Barnett* (1878) 3 QBD 363 ... [i]t was held that as the order for substituted service had been properly made and service effected under it the judgment was regular; that the defendant could not therefore, *ex debito justitiae*, claim to be let in to defend; but that the Court in the exercise of its discretion could allow him to do so if it were shown that he had no knowledge of the proceedings and had a defence on the merits. The Court there held that the giving of security in a sum equal to the sum claimed to be owing was appropriate.

In *Atwood v Chichester* (1878) 3 QBD 722 the Court of Appeal was concerned with a case in which it was thought that no irreparable wrong would be done to the plaintiff by setting aside a judgment by default ...

[455] Thus far, subject to statements in latter cases as to the relative significance of other relevant matters, it is established that a person with merits may be let in to defend if no irreparable wrong will be done to a plaintiff who has obtained judgment by default, but that good faith on the part of the applicant is a matter to be considered.

In *Evans v Bartlam* [1937] AC 473 in the House of Lords it was held that, while the Court of Appeal will not normally interfere except on grounds of law with the exercise of a judge's discretion, if it is seen that on other grounds his decision would result in injustice being done the Court of Appeal has both the power and duty to remedy it. In coming to his decision Lord Atkin speaking of a discretionary power given to a Judge in Chambers to set aside a default judgment said at 480:

> The discretion is in terms unconditional. The Courts, however, have laid down for themselves rules to guide them in the normal exercise of their discretion. One is that where the judgment was obtained regularly there must be an affidavit of merits, meaning that the applicant must produce to the Court evidence that he has a prima facie defence. It was suggested in argument that there is another rule that the applicant must satisfy the Court that there is [456] a reasonable explanation why judgment was allowed to go by default, such as mistake, accident, fraud or the like. I do not think that any such rule exists, though obviously the reason, if any, for allowing judgment and thereafter applying to set it aside is one of the matters to which the court will have regard in exercising its discretion. If there were a rigid rule that no one could have a default judgment set aside

who knew at the time and intended that there should be a judgment signed, the two rules would be deprived of most of their efficacy. The principle obviously is that unless and until the Court has pronounced a judgment upon the merits or by consent, it is to have the power to revoke the expression of its coercive power where that has only been obtained by a failure to follow any of the rules of procedure.

But in any case in my opinion the Court does not, and I doubt whether it can, lay down rigid rules which deprive it of jurisdiction. Even the first rule as to affidavit of merits could, in no doubt rare but appropriate cases, be departed from. The proposed second rule does not in my opinion exist.

Lord Russell of Killowen expressed himself in similar terms. He went on to say at 482 that 'from the nature of the case no judge could, in exercising the discretion conferred upon him by the rule, fail to consider both (a) whether any useful purpose could be served by setting aside the judgment, and obviously no useful purpose would be served if there were no possible defence to the action, and (b) how it came about that the applicant found himself bound by a judgment regularly obtained, to which he could have set up some serious defence'.

I was referred, as to the exercise of the discretion generally and to the particular question of delay, to *Grimshaw v Dunbar* [1953] 1 QB 408 a decision of the Court of Appeal with particular reference to statements made at 414 and 415 by Jenkins LJ. The observations there made which do not really carry the matter further depend very much on the facts of the case. ...

[457] In *Rosing v Ben Shemesh* [1960] VR 173 the Victorian Full Court came to a decision expressed in the headnote in terms similar to those used in *Evans v Bartlam* and *Grimshaw v Dunbar* (supra). In that case the learned County Court Judge had regarded conduct by a defendant as humbug and was suspicious that the defendant in his behaviour was merely seeking to delay the day when he would have to meet the plaintiff's claim. The Full Court there commented upon the fact that suspicions can only be established as well or ill founded upon proper examination of the defendant, including cross-examination, which had not taken place. The defendant there in affidavit material categorically and specifically denied the plaintiff's claims and was regarded as having been denied an opportunity to have an issue tried in a proceeding in which he was said to be entitled to be heard. ...

I found particular assistance from the statements in *Vacuum Oil Co Pty Ltd v Stockdale* (1942) 42 SR (NSW) 239 a decision of the Full Court of New South Wales. ... [458] At 243 Jordan CJ said:

> The present is not a case in which judgment was signed by default through some procedural omission on the part of the defendant or his legal advisers. The action followed the ordinary course, except that its coming on for trial was delayed through dilatoriness on the part of the defendant. It is one in which, the action coming on for trial in its ordinary place in the list, no one was present in Court to conduct it for the defendant, and it therefore proceeded in his absence. In such a case, when the plaintiff is in no respect in default, a new trial will not be granted save in very special circumstances: *Chitty's Archbold*, 10th ed, 1457; 12th ed, 1526. In every such case the Court has an inherent and unfettered though judicial, discretion, in the exercise of which it will however, necessarily consider (a) whether any useful purpose would be served by setting aside the judgment, and (b) how it came about that the applicant found himself bound by a judgment regularly obtained: *Evans v Bartlam* [1937] AC 473 at 482. As a general rule

(although not necessarily in every case, if some reason exists for departing from it: *Collins' Book Depot Pty Ltd v Bretherton* [1938] VLR 40; Austn Digest (1934–1939) 1859), the Court requires an affidavit showing prima facie that the defendant has a good defence on the merits: *Evans v Bartlam* [1937] AC 473 at 480, 488–9, and also an explanation of his absence which shows that justice requires that in the circumstances it should be excused. And if there has been gross negligence on the defendant's part, the Court will be the more disposed to require at least a reasonably clear case of merits to be shown, to incline it to interfere: *Nash v Swinburne* 3 M & G 630 at 632; *Weitzel v Eriedenreich* 14 WN 7; 1 Austn Digest 376.

It is obvious that decisions on other sets of facts are of no assistance in arriving at a decision as to how it would be proper to exercise the Court's discretion in the present case. The question is whether, upon the material that has been placed before us, there is a real likelihood that it would be unjust to the defendant to allow the judgment to stand. If so, it should be set aside on such terms as will minimise the possibility of injustice to the plaintiff. If not, we should not interfere. I have come to the conclusion that, although we undoubtedly possess a discretion, we should not be justified in exercising it in the defendant's favour.

The Court there considered the material on which the defendant would base his case. The plaintiff's claim was to recover the equivalent of a sum of $960 which was not really disputed except for the equivalent of a sum of about $20. A further claim by the plaintiff related to recovery [459] of the cost of some 10,000 gallons of petrol which had been held in stock by the defendant which was missing but unaccounted for. The defendant denied that it would have been possible for so much petrol to have disappeared in a relevant period. His reasons were expressed as based upon sales of fuel which might have occurred during a certain period of six weeks and also upon the dimensions of the fuel depot. This might be argued to constitute sufficient defence to call upon the plaintiff to prove its case but was not thought sufficient to justify setting aside the judgment.

I have been referred as well to *Midland Bank Trust Co Ltd v Green* [1979] 2 All ER 193 in which the applicant was successful. That case confirms that circumstances in which the discretion is called upon vary greatly and highlights the practical efficacy of statements such as were made in *Evans v Bartlam* (supra) as to the unfettered nature of the discretion. The facts in *Midland Bank Trust Co Ltd v Green* were altogether different from those with which we are here concerned and were described by Oliver J as exceptional. ...

In my view in the circumstances under consideration, Gray is required to show that there is substance in the case he would reply upon. It is therefore appropriate to consider the alleged merits in some detail.

[His Honour then considered the merits of the applicant's cases, and concluded:]

In my view the points relied upon by Gray are insubstantial, even though they might be thought to be faintly arguable.

The other circumstances considered are, however, overwhelmingly against him.

In each case I order that the application be dismissed and that the applicant pay the respondent's costs of the application to be taxed.

Setting aside on the grounds of fraud or new evidence

18.7.16   The Federal Court (r 39.05(b)), ACT (r 1613(2)(b)) and Queensland (r 667(2)(b)) rules expressly provide that judgments may be set aside on the grounds of fraud. In New South Wales judgments may be set aside if made irregularly, illegally or against good faith: r 36.15. See too SA r 242 (where justice of a case so requires).

18.7.17C   Monroe Schneider Associates (Inc) v No 1 Raberem Pty Ltd (No 2)
(1992) 37 FCR 234
Federal Court of Australia, Full Court

[On an application to set aside a judgment, the trial judge considered, as a preliminary issue, whether it was open to the applicants to raise a particular issue in their statement of claim. He held that it was not. The applicants appealed from this decision.]

Gummow, Spender and Lee JJ (at 238–40): The jurisdiction invoked in an original action to impeach the earlier judgment for fraud, is, as was pointed out in *Wentworth v Rogers (No 5)* (1986) 6 NSWLR 534 at 538, 'equitable in origin and nature'. The position at common law is discussed by Mr D M Gordon QC in his article 'Fraud or New Evidence as Grounds for Actions to set Aside Judgments' (1961) *77 LQR* 358 (Pt 1) 533 (Pt 2). Once judgment had been entered after trial before a jury, the common law courts entertained no fresh action to set aside the judgment. But entry of judgment was delayed until the term after the trial. In the meantime, the disaffected party might present a motion for a [239] new trial. An order for such a new trial would be an interlocutory remedy because until the new trial was concluded there would be no formal judgment, but an order refusing a new trial would be final: *Hall v Nominal Defendant* (1966) 117 CLR 423 at 443, per Windeyer J. The grounds relied upon might include fraud or the discovery of new evidence. But the efficacy of the new trial procedure was inhibited by the absence of a record of the evidence called before the jury (Gordon QC at 366). Evidence might be led on the motion that witnesses had been suborned: see *Fabrilius v Cock* (1765) 3 Burr 1771; 97 ER 1090, discussed by Dixon CJ, Fullagar, Kitto, Taylor JJ in *McCann v Parsons* (1954) 93 CLR 418 at 426–7. Their Honours referred to that case as denying the proposition that in the Supreme Court of New South Wales, before the introduction of the Judicature system, an application to impeach a jury verdict for fraud might be brought only as an equity suit and not, as had been done in that case, on a motion for a new trial brought before the Full Court. But in *McDonald v McDonald* ((1965) 113 CLR 529) at 532 Barwick CJ indicated that a separate proceeding was the preferable course as did Handley JA in *Spies v Commonwealth Bank of Australia* (1991) 24 NSWLR 691 at 699 (a case involving a consent order).

The procedure in Chancery by way of a bill of review for a rehearing by the Lord Chancellor is described by Cozens Hardy LJ in *Charles Bright & Co Ltd v Sellar* [1904] 1 KB 6 at 10–1. The equitable jurisdiction in addition to allowing rehearing of final decrees before entry, extended to bills of review to set aside Chancery decrees even after entry. The 'equity' was based on the presence of fraud or the discovery of new evidence. Where fraud was alleged the bill of review could be presented without leave. Otherwise a preliminary petition for leave was necessary. Further, the authority exercised in Chancery extended to restraining, on the grounds of fraud and discovery of new material evidence, enforcement of final judgments which had been entered by a common law court: *Re Barrell Enterprises* [1973] 1 WLR 19 at 24–7; [1972] 3 All ER 631 at 636–40.

But whilst Chancery might set aside its own decrees, it had to be more circumspect in dealing with the record as it stood in a common law court and it would not declare the common law judgment void. Rather Chancery acted *in personam* against the party having the benefit of the judgment, so as to prevent it taking any advantage from it: see *Hazel Atlas Glass Co v Hartford Empire Co* 322 US 238 at 245 (1944); Gordon QC at 367–8. It might enjoin (by a species of common injunction) the fraudulent judgment holder from enforcing the judgment, send issues to a common law court for trial by a new jury, or oblige the judgment holder to enter satisfaction of it upon the judgment roll of the common law court. Within courts operating under the Judicature system the common injunction is abolished. There is no longer any occasion for the exercise of such indirect methods, because in respect of a conflict between rules of law and equity with reference to the same matter, equity prevails: Judicature Act 1873 (UK), s 25(11). Hence there has been no difficulty in treating all judgments impeached for fraud in a Judicature system court in the same way as previously Chancery treated its own decrees on a bill of review: cf Gordon QC at 369–70.

But what of the jurisdiction in respect of new material evidence where fraud is not alleged? In *Re Barrell Enterprises* (supra) at 24–7; 636–40, Russell LJ pointed out in that case, there were no examples of such an action to set aside a judgment on the ground of fresh evidence having [240] succeeded in England since the introduction of the Judicature system and the creation of the modern appellate structure.

[Their Honours then analysed the circumstances under which a judgment might be set aside on the grounds of fraud, and on the basis of this analysis, dismissed the appeal.]

18.7.18C Wentworth v Rogers (No 5)
(1986) 6 NSWLR 534
New South Wales Court of Appeal

[Young J struck out a statement of claim in which the plaintiff sought to have a judgment set aside. His grounds were that the claim and the supporting documentation failed to constitute a basis on which he could find that there was a reasonable chance that she would succeed in the proceedings. He also concluded that some references to persons not parties to the litigation were 'scandalous'.]

Kirby P (at 538–9): It is useful to state a number of principles which are established by law and which govern proceedings of the kind which the appellant wishes to bring.

First, the essence of the action is fraud. As in all actions based on fraud, particulars of the fraud claimed must be exactly given and the allegations must be established by the strict proof which such a charge requires: *Jonesco v Beard* [1930] AC 298 at 301; *McHarg v Woods Radio Pty Ltd* [[1948] VR 496] (at 497).

Secondly, it must be shown, by the party asserting that a judgment was procured by fraud, that there has been a new discovery of something material, in the sense that fresh facts have been found which, by themselves or in combination with previously known facts, would provide a reason for setting aside the judgment: see Lord Selborne LC in *Boswell v Coaks (No 2)* (1894) 6 R 167 at 170, 174; 86 LT 365 at 366, 368; *Cabassi v Vila* (1940) 64 CLR 130 at 147; *McDonald v McDonald* (1965) 113 CLR 529 at 533; *Everett v Ribbands* (1946) 175 LT 143 at 145, 146; *Birch v Birch* [1902] P 130 at 136, 137–138; *Ronald v Harper* [1913] LR 311 at 318. This rule has an ancient lineage: see, eg, *Shedden v Patrick* (1854) 1 Macq

535 at 615, 622; *Halsbury's Laws of England*, 4th ed, vol 26, par 560 at 285. It is based upon a number of grounds. There is a public interest in finality of litigation. Parties ought not, by proceeding to impugn a judgment, to be permitted to re-litigate matters which were the subject of the earlier proceedings which gave rise to the judgment. Especially should they not be so permitted, if they move on nothing more than the evidence upon which they have previously failed. If they have evidence of fraud which may taint a judgment of the courts, they should not collude in such a consequence by refraining from raising their objection at the trial, thereby keeping the complaint in reserve. It is their responsibility to ensure that the taint of fraud is avoided and the integrity of the court's process preserved.

Thirdly, mere suspicion of fraud, raised by fresh facts later discovered, will not be sufficient to secure relief: *Birch v Birch* (at 136, 139); *McHarg v* [539] *Woods Radio Pty Ltd* (at 498); *Ronald v Harper* (at 318). The claimant must establish that the new facts are so evidenced and so material that it is reasonably probable that the action will succeed. This rule is founded squarely in the public interest in finality of public litigation and in upholding judgments duly entered at the termination of proceedings in the courts.

Fourthly, although perjury by the successful party or a witness or witnesses may, if later discovered, warrant the setting aside of a judgment on the ground that it was procured by fraud, and although there may be exceptional cases where such proof of perjury could suffice, without more, to warrant relief of this kind, the mere allegation, or even the proof, of perjury will not normally be sufficient to attract such drastic and exceptional relief as the setting aside of a judgment: *Cabassi v Vila* (at 147, 148); *Baker v Wadsworth* (1898) 67 LJQB 301; *Everett v Ribbands* (at 145, 146). The other requirements must be fulfilled. In hard fought litigation, it is not at all uncommon for there to be a conflict of testimony which has to be resolved by a judge or jury. In many cases of contradictory evidence, one party must be mistaken. He or she may even be deceiving the court. The unsuccessful party in the litigation will often consider that failure in the litigation has been procured by false evidence on the part of the opponent and the witnesses called by the opponent. If every case in which such an opinion was held gave rise to proceedings of this kind, the courts would be even more burdened with the review of first instance decisions than they are. For this reason, and in defence of finality of judgments, a more stringent requirement than alleged perjury alone is required.

Fifthly, it must be shown by admissible evidence that the successful party was responsible for the fraud which taints the judgment under challenge. The evidence in support of the charge ought to be extrinsic: cf *Perry v Meddowcroft* (1846) 10 Beav 122 at 136–9; 50 ER 529 at 534, 535. It is not sufficient to show that an agent of the successful party was convicted of giving perjured evidence in the former proceeding, the result of which it is sought to impeach. It must be shown that the agent, in so acting, was in concert with the party who derived the benefit of the judgment: *Ronald v Harper* (at 318); *Sheddon v Patrick* (at 643).

Sixthly, the burden of establishing the components necessary to warrant the drastic step of setting aside a judgment, allegedly affected by fraud or other relevant taint, lies on the party impugning the judgment. It is for that party to establish the fraud and to do so clearly. In summary, he or she must establish that the case is based on newly discovered facts; that the facts are material and such as to make it reasonably probable that the case will succeed; that they go beyond mere allegations of perjury on the part of witnesses at the trial; and that the opposing party who took advantage of the judgment is shown, by admissible evidence, to have been responsible for the fraud in such a way as to render it inequitable that such party should take the benefit of the judgment.

[Kirby P, Hope and Samuels JJA dismissed the appeal.]

Correcting minor errors: the 'slip rule'

18.7.19   While errors in judgments may be dealt with on appeal, there are some errors too trivial to warrant the necessity to appeal. The rules provide for the correction of such errors: HCR r 3.01.2; FCR r 39.05(e), (g), (h); ACT r 1613(2)(d); NSW r 36.17; NT r 36.07; Qld r 667(2)(d); SA r 242(1); Tas r 435; Vic r 36.07; WA O 21 r 10.

These rules have been interpreted liberally. These errors will include transcription errors, as when the judgment does not accurately reflect the judge's intention when delivering judgment. They also include errors which, upon their being drawn to the judge's attention, will immediately be recognised as such. Distinguishing between cases where the 'slip rule' has been applied and cases where the court has refused to apply it is not always easy.

18.7.20C	**Arnett v Holloway** [1960] VR 22 Supreme Court of Victoria, Full Court

[On 1 February 1959, the Victorian costs rules changed so that a plaintiff suing in the Supreme Court who recovered less than half of the County Court's jurisdictional limit was entitled only to County Court costs unless the Supreme Court ordered otherwise. Previously the fraction had been one-fifth. On 6 February 1959, the trial judge, Adam J, awarded £465 in damages to the plaintiff, and made an order for costs. The County Court's jurisdictional limit was £1000. Counsel for the plaintiff was unaware of the change in the costs rules, as was the trial judge, who would have awarded costs on the Supreme Court scale had his attention been drawn to the new rule. Counsel for the plaintiff subsequently applied for an order amending the judgment. Adam J dismissed the summons.]

Lowe, O'Bryan and Pape JJ (at 33–5): [Their Honours first considered whether the new rule had immediate application to judgments made after its making and, on the basis that it was a procedural rule, found that it did. On whether amendment was possible, their Honours said:]

We, therefore, turn to the grounds of appeal as set out in the notice of appeal as originally drawn. Order XXVIII, rule 11 provides that 'clerical mistakes in judgments or orders or errors arising therein from any accidental slip or omission may at any time be corrected by the Court or a judge on motion or summons without an appeal'. Counsel on each side presented us with a very full argument upon the correct interpretation of this rule, and we know of no relevant authority, either in Great Britain or Australia, which was not cited and discussed. The rival propositions for which counsel contended may be broadly stated thus: Mr McInerney, for the plaintiff, contended that the rule distinguished between clerical mistakes and errors arising from any accidental slip or omission and, therefore, was not limited to the correction of mistakes in drawing up judgments or orders and, therefore, is not limited to cases in which the judgment or orders as recorded differ from the judgment or order as pronounced or as was intended by the Court or the judge. His contention was that it extended to any case where the judgment as passed and entered omits through an antecedent slip or [34] omission to deal with a matter which the Court would have dealt with in a particular manner if its attention had been drawn thereto, where the failure to draw the Court's attention to the matter arose by an accidental slip or error on the part of counsel, or the solicitors, or the parties. In such a case, he said, you had an accidental slip on the part of the Court arising from an accidental slip by the parties or their legal advisers. Mr McInerney did not contend that under this rule a judgment or order could be corrected so as to rescind, vary or vacate an order deliberately made and to substitute another order in its place: *Preston Banking Co v Allsup*, [1895] 1 Ch 141; *Chessum & Sons v Gordon* [1901] 1 KB 694, at 698. On the other hand, Mr Bradshaw, for the defendant, contended that such a construction was too wide, and that the rule should be confined to cases where the judgment or order as drawn up and entered has failed to express the intention of the Court when pronouncing the judgment or order. The difference between the two arguments relevant to this appeal would appear to be this, that Mr Bradshaw contended that what is relevant is the intention which the Court had in fact, when it pronounced the order, whereas Mr McInerney contended that the intention which the Court *would* have had but for its failure, by reason of an accidental slip or omission on the part of counsel, to advert to a relevant consideration, was the criterion.

The cases to which we were referred are by no means consistent, and judges have taken different views regarding the scope of the rule and what the intention of the Court pronouncing the order or judgment was. We think that this appeal may be decided without embarking upon an examination of those cases. It is apparent from the very careful judgment of Adam J, that his Honour did not advert in any way to the question of whether the costs he awarded would be on the County Court scale. He says, at 23, ante: 'No application was made to me at the trial for any special order for costs and I did not, at the time, consider whether a special order would have been proper. The order for costs as pronounced by me and as recorded in the judgment as drawn up means such costs as were allowable under the Rules of the court, and that was costs on the County Court scale'. Later on his Honour said, at 24 ante: 'It is well settled by authority that an error rectifiable under the slip rule appears in a recorded judgment when the judgment as passed and entered does not accord with the real intention of the court when pronouncing judgment. ... I consider that there was no error in this sense in the judgment recorded in this action. My intention in giving judgment, so far as *I had any specific intention* [the italics are ours] was none other than to award to the plaintiff the costs to which he was entitled under the Rules and the judgment so passed and entered did accurately record that intention'.

Later on, again, his Honour said, at 24–5, ante:

Although in the absence of any application I did not advert, when giving judgment, to the question whether the circumstances warranted the making of a special order for costs on the Supreme Court scale, I now feel no doubt, after hearing argument, that it would have been proper for me to have done so. Under the Rules in force when the action commenced in the Supreme Court in 1957 a plaintiff was entitled to Supreme Court costs if he recovered one fifth or more of the limit in point of amount to which the jurisdiction of the County Court was limited. This together with difficulties arising from the nature of the action and the duration of the trial have persuaded me that such an order would have been proper, and I feel sure that I would have acceded to an application by the plaintiff for costs on the Supreme Court scale.

[35] His Honour dismissed the summons because he regarded the judgment as passed and entered as expressing the intention he had when he pronounced the order for costs.

In so doing, he, in our opinion, took an unduly narrow and artificial view of what his real intention was. The action was begun in the Supreme Court, and had been litigated in the Supreme Court. Neither counsel nor the learned judge ever adverted to the question of whether the costs were to be taxed on the County Court scale, probably because they all assumed that as more than £200 had been recovered, the order would carry Supreme Court costs. When an action is commenced and tried to a conclusion in the Supreme Court and an order for costs *simpliciter* is made, if the judge does not for some reason advert to taxation under some special scale, such an order would, we think, be intended by him to mean costs taxed on the Supreme Court scale. That appears to be this case. In addition, the learned trial judge here added to his order for costs a Certificate for pleadings which in the circumstances of this case points more strongly to a general taxation on the Supreme Court scale than a like Certificate did in the circumstances of *Dowden v Shire of Cranbourne* [1933] VLR 255; 39 ALR 360.

In these circumstances, even if the learned judge's view that O XXVIII, rule 11 is confined to cases where the judgment as recorded has failed to express the intention of the Court be correct (and upon this we express no views), we think that he should have decided that this judgment did not express his intention which, we think, was to give costs on the Supreme Court scale. The fact that in the circumstances as now known he could only give effect to that intention by specifically 'otherwise ordering' does not, we think, affect the question.

We think that this was a case in which the learned judge, having regard to what he has said, should have made the order sought, and that justice required that the judgment be amended accordingly. Similar orders have been made in Victoria in other cases: see *Dougherty v Dougherty* (1889) 15 VLR 294; *Melbourne Harbour Trust Commissioners v Cuming Smith & Co Pty Ltd* [1906] VLR 192; 12 ALR 142; and *McKenzie v Fyander* [1927] VLR 569; 33 ALR 412.

It is true that there are other cases in Victoria to a contrary effect, but we cite these cases merely to show that many judges have thought it desirable that the slip rule should be so construed that relatively minor matters should be capable of being put right without subjecting the parties to the costs of an appeal. Whatever view be taken of the precise application of O XXVIII, rule 11, we think that an unduly narrow approach to it on facts similar to the facts in this case should not be taken. The appeal will therefore be allowed.

18.7.21 Notes and questions

1. See, eg, *Australia & New Zealand Banking Group Ltd v Luck* (1995) 4 Tas R 328. Judgment in default of delivery of a defence was given for a sum which, through the plaintiff's solicitor's miscalculation, included an additional day's interest. It was held that this error could be corrected under the slip rule. The plaintiff sought the amendment. For its reasons, see the full report of the case. See also: *Westpac Banking Corporation v E&W Jury Pty Ltd* (1998) 16 ACLC 547. Westpac had failed to seek an extension of time for the determination of winding up proceedings. It was clear that had it done so, the application would have been granted, and an order retrospectively supplementing earlier orders was made accordingly, thereby overcoming what would otherwise have been a statutory time limit.

2. How does one determine what a judge's 'real' intention would have been? *Snell v Pryce (No 2)* (1992) 109 FLR 328 was an application by a successful appellant in a criminal case to have the judgment amended to include an order for costs, no such order having been sought at the time. The application was made 18 months after the judgment. Angel J dismissed the application on the grounds that the case

was one of 'afterthought rather than an oversight'. What is the difference, and how might one assess how to classify a particular case?

3. The 'slip' must be such that had it been drawn to the court's attention, its relevance and implications would have been immediately apparent: *Sands & McDougall (Wholesaler) Pty Ltd (in liq) v Commissioner of Taxation* [1999] 2 VR 114 (the court's ignorance of an offer of compromise in circumstances not provided for under the rules is not a 'slip' since the implications of the offer for the award of costs are not self-evident).

4. The slip rule is not available as a basis for setting aside a judgment simply because the court lacked jurisdiction in the matter: *Rothmore Farms v Belgravia Pty Ltd (No 2)* (1999) 17 ACLC 1676.

Supplemental judgments

18.7.22 A distinction has been drawn between orders which would involve varying a judgment (which may not normally be made) and orders supplementary to a judgment (against which the presumption is weaker). Even after judgment has been given as to the rights of the parties, an order may be made requiring that a non-party pay the costs of a party against whom a costs order has been made: *Caboolture Park Shopping Centre Pty Ltd v White Industries (Qld) Pty Ltd* (1993) 43 FCR 224; *UTSA Pty Ltd v Ultra Tune Australia Pty Ltd* (1998) 28 ACSR 444; *Akedian Co Ltd v Royal Insurance Ltd* [1999] 1 VR 80. Compare, however, *Ken Morgan Motors Pty Ltd v Toyota Motor Corporation Australia Ltd* (unreported, SC (Vic), Hayne J, No 2164 of 1993, 23 November 1993, BC9304156). In *Akedian*, this case was distinguished on the ground that the judgment already included a costs order against a third party and, it seems, on the ground that it had involved an application to a single judge to make an order supplemental to a decision of the Full Court. It might also have been distinguished on the grounds that in contrast to the orders in *Caboolture and Akedian*, the proposed order would have affected the rights and duties of those parties in favour of, or against whom, orders had already been made.

Further reading

18.8.1 Looseleaf and online

C Eagle and M Flynn, updated by M Rozner, 'Trial', in *Court Forms, Precedents and Pleadings Victoria*, LexisNexis, Sydney, vol 4.

C Ecob, updated by R Wyld, 'Trial', in *Court Forms, Precedents and Pleadings New South Wales*, LexisNexis, Sydney, vol 1.

Halsbury's Laws of Australia, LexisNexis, Sydney, vol 20, Title 325, Practice and Procedure, 'Ch VI Trial' [325–8000]–[325,8535]; 'Ch VII Judgment and Execution', [325–9000]–[325–9040].

J Harrison, updated by M Walker, 'Judgments and Orders', in *Court Forms, Precedents and Pleadings New South Wales*, LexisNexis, Sydney, vol 1.

P Hodson, 'Judgments and Orders', in *Court Forms, Precedents and Pleadings Victoria*, LexisNexis, Sydney, vol 2.

E Kempin, 'Judgments and Orders', in *Court Forms, Precedents and Pleadings Queensland*, LexisNexis, Sydney, vol 2.

Laws of Australia, LBC Information Services, Sydney, vol 5, section 5.7, Ch 2.

18.8.2 Texts

B Cairns, *Australian Civil Procedure*, 9th ed, LBC Information Services, Sydney, 2011, Chs 2, 15.

Appeal and New Trial

## CHAPTER 19

OVERVIEW

An appeal is a substantive right created by statute enabling a party to seek to set aside or vary an order. The conferring statute determines the nature of an appeal, which typically falls into one of three types: appeals by way of rehearing, appeals by way of hearing *de novo* and strict appeals (*stricto sensu*).

Australian court systems have multiple levels of jurisdiction. Each level, with the exception of the High Court, generally has an avenue of appeal. The scope and nature of the appeal depends upon the terms of the statute creating the right of appeal. Appellate courts have wide powers to affirm, vary, or reverse judgments under appeal. Other powers include sending a case back for a retrial, setting aside jury verdicts, and granting a retrial.

Appeals are commenced by a notice of appeal, which briefly states the grounds of the appeal. In some cases leave to appeal is required. The appeal court will require the appellant to prepare an appeal book or record, including pleadings, affidavits, orders and transcripts of evidence. Appeals may also have related applications. Examples include seeking a stay of execution pending an appeal, security for costs, leave to appeal and an application for an extension of time in which to file or serve a notice of appeal.

There are many substantive bases upon which appeals are brought. The most common include errors of law, errors in the exercise of a discretion, incorrect findings of fact, incorrect inferences drawn from facts, excessive or insufficient assessments of damages and misdirection of a jury by a trial judge.

Considerable difficulty arises in relation to the admission of fresh evidence available at trial, and to a lesser extent where a new point arises after judgment. New points and objections may also arise before judgment.

Appellate courts have the power to grant a new trial where there has been a substantial wrong or miscarriage of justice. New trials tend to be avoided due to the duplication of costs incurred in rehearing the evidence.

Appeals are an essential process for ensuring consistency and maintaining the high quality of the Australian judicial system.

INTRODUCTION

19.1.1   Appeal is 'the formal procedure by which an unsuccessful party seeks to have the formal order of a court set aside or varied in his favour by an appellate court': *Commonwealth of Australia v Bank of New South Wales* (1949) 79 CLR 497 at 625. See also *Jeray v Blue Mountains City Council* [2010] NSWCA 281. The appellant is the party who brings the appeal; the respondent opposes it. All interested persons should be made parties to an appeal, whether they were involved at first instance or not. However, a person must consent before becoming an appellant. Failure to consent will render that person a respondent. As to standing to bring an appeal, see N J Williams, *Civil Procedure Victoria*, LexisNexis Butterworths, Sydney, looseleaf, vol 1, [I64.01.95]–[I64.01.115]. The rationale for an appeal is to correct errors of law or fact, or the miscarriage of discretion, to conduct a review removed from the drama of the trial, to encourage better judicial performance at first instance, and develop the law by resolving previously unresolved issues. The appellate court has power to set aside, vary, discharge, or substitute the judgment of the court below. The downside of an appeal relates to the cost, delay and uncertainty associated with further proceedings.

The right of appeal is derived from legislation. There is no common law right to an appeal: *Lacey v Attorney-General of Queensland* [2011] HCA 10 at [8]. It is a substantive right, not a matter of procedure. The scope of the appeal depends upon the statutory provision that creates the right of appeal. The time limit for an appeal is set by the Rules of Court, though in some instances, this may be varied by the statute creating the right of appeal. The mode and content of the appeal are governed by the Rules of Court in each jurisdiction. The general appeal rules are found in the following provisions: Federal Court of Australia Act 1976 (Cth); HCR Pt 42; FCR Ch 4 Appellate Jurisdiction; Court Procedures Rules 2006 (ACT) Ch 5; Supreme Court Act 1970 (NSW); Uniform Civil Procedure Rules 2005 (NSW) Pt 51; Rules of the Supreme Court of the Northern Territory of Australia (NT) O 82–87; Civil Proceedings Act 2011 (Qld) s 193; Supreme Court of Queensland Act 1991 (Qld) ss 69A and 69B; Uniform Civil Procedure Rules 1999 (Qld) Ch 18, Civil Proceedings Act 2011 (Qld) s 193, Supreme Court of Queensland Act 1991 (Qld) ss 69A and 69B; Supreme Court Civil Rules 2006 (SA) Ch 13; Supreme Court Civil Procedure Act 1932 (Tas); Rules of the Supreme Court 2000 (Tas) Pt 27; Supreme Court (General Civil Procedure) Rules 2005 (Vic) O 64; Rules of the Supreme Court 1971 (WA) O 65. New South Wales, Victoria and Queensland have dedicated courts of appeal. The appellate division is headed by the President of the Court of Appeal and staffed by full-time appellate judges. Supreme Court judges in these jurisdictions also sit on the Court of Appeal. Elsewhere the Court of Appeal is comprised of three Supreme Court judges in rotational sittings. The appellate court usually comprises the Chief Justice, the President of the Court of Appeal and appeal judges. Supreme Court judges may be invited to sit as appeal judges. A sitting appellate court ordinarily consists of three judges of appeal, presided over by the most senior judge present. When hearing criminal matters, the court is known as 'The Court of Criminal Appeal'.

[*Note*: in this chapter a reference, such as WA O 65 r 2, is a reference to the relevant Rules of Court. All other legislation will be specified.]

TYPES OF APPEAL

19.2.1   The term 'appeal' is used in three broad senses: strict appeal, *de novo* appeal and a rehearing. In each case the nature of the right is determined by the applicable statutory provision.

A strict appeal occurs when the court is required to confine its consideration to whether the judgment appealed from was correct when it was given. New circumstances cannot be taken into account. Only the law and circumstances that existed when the judgment was given can be considered. If the court concludes that the judgment was correct when it was given, then it cannot be set aside or varied by an appeal. The rights of the parties are considered as at the date of the judgment under appeal, rather than at the date of the hearing of the appeal. Federal Court appeals are by way of rehearing: *Western Australia v Ward* (2002) 213 CLR 1 at 87, Federal Court of Australia Act 1976 (Cth) s 24, cf *White v Minister for Immigration and Multicultural Affairs* (2000) 96 FCR 511. However, s 27 allows further evidence on appeal, hence it may not matter whether an appeal is strict or by way of rehearing: *Lai-Ha v McCusker* (2000) AIPC 91-554.

A *de novo* appeal involves recording of the evidence again; in effect a retrial before an appellate court. The witnesses are called again and the appellate court forms its own independent view as to the truth of testimony and the inferences that can be drawn. Such an appeal may also enable the admission of fresh evidence.

A rehearing is the most common form of appeal: Supreme Court Act 1970 (NSW) s 75A(5); Qld r 765, PD No 2 of 2010; SA r 286; Supreme Court Civil Procedure Act 1932 (Tas) s 46, r 657; WA O 63 r 8. A rehearing determines the rights and obligations of the parties as at the date of the rehearing on the record of evidence before the trial judge. Under this procedure, the court has an exceptional power to consider new circumstances and may (rarely) admit new evidence if it thinks it is proper to do so. It reviews the evidence before the trial judge via the transcript and reaches its own conclusion. The appeal court will review the findings of fact and assessments made by the trial judge. The court is not confined to the determination of whether a trial judge was right or wrong, on the evidence before it, or limited to the correction of any errors found. The rehearing is a new determination of the rights and liabilities of the parties rather than the correction of errors in the determination of the court below. In addition, a rehearing is conducted on the basis of the law as at the date of the rehearing. See *Fox v Percy* (2003) 214 CLR 118 at 120 and 132. If a decision is to be reviewed by way of rehearing, the statutory provisions creating the rights usually stipulate that such is to be the case. The appellant must demonstrate, 'that, having regard to all the evidence now before the appellate court, the order that is the subject of the appeal is the result of some legal, factual or discretionary error': *Kostas v HIA Insurance Services Pty Ltd* [2010] HCA 32 at 27; *Allesch v Maunz* (2003) 203 CLR 172 at 180.

19.2.2C   **Builders' Licensing Board v Sperway Constructions (Syd) Pty Ltd**
(1976) 135 CLR 616
High Court of Australia

[An issue arose whether an appeal from a licensing board established by the Builders Licensing Act 1971 (NSW) was a *de novo* appeal or otherwise.]

Mason J (at 619–20): An appeal is not a common law proceeding. It is a remedy given by statute: *Victorian Stevedoring and General Contracting Co Pty Ltd and Meakes v Dignan* (1931) 46 CLR 73 at 108; *Commissioner for Railways (NSW) v Cavanough* (1935) 53 CLR 220 at 225. Upon an appeal *stricto sensu* the question considered is whether the judgment complained of was right when given (*Ponnamma v Arumogam* [1905] AC 383 at 388), that is whether the order appealed from was right on the material which the lower court had before it.

An appeal *stricto sensu* is to be distinguished from an appeal by way of rehearing of which the most notable example has been the appeal to the English Court of Appeal provided for by the *Supreme Court of Judicature Act* 1873, ss 18–19 and the Rules of Procedure contained in the Schedule to the Act of 1875. It was provided that the appeal should be by way of re-hearing and that the court should have power to take fresh evidence and draw inferences of fact (see O 58 rr 1, 4). The appeal had its origin in the jurisdiction of the Court of Appeal in Chancery established by 14 & 15 Vict c 83 to rehear cases determined in Chancery. This appeal by way of re-hearing involves re-hearing of the cause at the date of the appeal, that is 'by trial over again [620] on the evidence used in the Court below; but there is special power to receive further evidence': *In re Chennell; Jones v Chennell* (1878) 8 Ch D 492 at 505. On such an appeal the rights of the parties must be determined by reference to the circumstances as they then exist and by reference to the law as it then exists; the appellate court may give such judgment as ought to be given if the case at that time came before the court of first instance. But this appeal by way of rehearing did not call for a fresh hearing or hearing *de novo*; the court does not hear the witnesses again. See generally the *Victorian Stevedoring Case* (1931) 46 CLR at 107–9; *Da Costa v Cockburn Salvage & Trading Pty Ltd* (1970) 124 CLR 192 at 208.

[**Barwick CJ** and **Stephens J** agreed with **Mason J**.]

19.2.3C   **Coal and Allied Operations Pty Ltd v Australian Industrial Relations Commission**
(2000) 203 CLR 194
High Court of Australia

[The case concerns the nature of an appeal that lies from the Full Bench of the Australian Industrial Relations Commission under the Workplace Relations Act 1996 (Cth) s 45.]

Gleeson CJ, Gaudron and Hayne JJ (at 202–3): It was pointed out in *Brideson [No 2]* that "the nature of [an] appeal must ultimately depend on the terms of the statute conferring [203] the right [of appeal]" [*Brideson [No 2]* (1990) 170 CLR 267 at 273–274. See also *Builders' Licensing Board v Sperway Constructions (Syd) Pty Ltd* (1976) 135 CLR 616 at 621–622, per Mason J; *CDJ v VAJ* (1998) 197 CLR 172 at 185–186 [53], per Gaudron J.] The statute in question may confer limited or large powers on an appellate body; it may confer powers that are unique to the tribunal concerned or powers that are common to other appellate bodies. There is, thus, no definitive classification of appeals, merely descriptive phrases by which an appeal to one body may sometimes be conveniently distinguished from an appeal to another. [See *Turnbull v NSW Medical Board* [1976] 2 NSWLR 281 at 297–298, per Glass JA.]

It is common and often convenient to describe an appeal to a court or tribunal whose function is simply to determine whether the decision in question was right or wrong on the evidence and the law as it stood when that decision was given as an appeal in the strict sense. An appeal to this Court under s 73 of the Constitution is an appeal of that kind. [See *Mickelberg v The Queen* (1989) 167 CLR 259; *Eastman v The Queen* (2000) 203 CLR 1.] In the case of an appeal in the strict sense, an appellate court or tribunal cannot receive further evidence [see *Mickelberg v The Queen* (1989) 167 CLR 259; *Eastman v The Queen* (2000) 203 CLR 1] and its powers are limited to setting aside the decision under appeal and, if it be appropriate, to substituting the decision that should have been made at first instance [see *Allesch v Maunz* (2000) 203 CLR 172].

If an appellate tribunal can receive further evidence and its powers are not restricted to making the decision that should have been made at first instance, the appeal is usually and conveniently described as an appeal by way of rehearing. Although further evidence may be admitted on an appeal of that kind, the appeal is usually conducted by reference to the evidence given at first instance and is to be contrasted with an appeal by way of hearing *de novo*, the matter is heard afresh and a decision is given on the evidence presented at that hearing [See *Allesch v Maunz* (2000) 203 CLR 172].

Ordinarily, if there has been no further evidence admitted and if there has been no relevant change in the law [*Victorian Stevedoring and General Contracting Co Pty Ltd v Dignan* (1931) 46 CLR 73 at 106–108, per Dixon J], a court or tribunal entertaining an appeal by way of rehearing can exercise its appellate powers only if satisfied that there was error on the part of the primary decision-maker [*Allesch v Maunz* (2000) 203 CLR 172. see also *CDJ v VAJ* (1998) 197 CLR 172 at 201–202 [111], per McHugh, Gummow and Callinan JJ]. That is because statutory provisions conferring appellate powers, even in the case of an appeal by way of rehearing, are construed on the basis that, unless there is something to indicate [204] otherwise, the power is to be exercised for the correction of error [see *CDJ v VAJ* (1998) 197 CLR 172 at 201–202 [111], per McHugh, Gummow and Callinan JJ]. However, the conferral of a right of appeal by way of a hearing *de novo* is construed as a proceeding in which the appellate body is required to exercise its powers whether or not there was error at first instance [*R v Pilgrim* (1870) LR 6 QB 89 at 95, per Lush J; *Sweeney v Fitzhardinge* (1906) 4 CLR 716; *Turnbull v NSW Medical Board* [1976] 2 NSWLR 281 at 297–298, per Glass JA; *Southwell v Specialised Engineering Services Pty Ltd* (1990) 70 NTR 6 at 7–8, per Kearney J].

Kirby J (at 222–4): Appeal, as such, was unknown to the common law. It is a creature of statute. It is not possible to adopt any hard and fast or universal approach to the process called 'appeal' in a particular statute. The word encompasses 'different litigious processes which have few unifying characteristics'. No fewer than six forms of a procedure loosely called an 'appeal' have been identified. Within these broad categories are various subcategories reflecting the particular nature of the 'appeal' in question, the issues which the appeal presents and the purpose for which it exists, derived from the language in which it is expressed.

In every case where the issue is that of the duty and function of an appellate court or tribunal, the only safe starting point is a careful examination of the language and context of the statutory provisions affording the appellate right, together with a consideration of the powers enjoyed by, and duties imposed on, the body to which the appeal lies.

The range and variety of decisions that may, with leave, be the subject of an appeal under the Act is such as to suggest that generalities will be dangerous. So different are the various decisions amenable to appeal that it will only be of limited help to catalogue the process within the broad class of an 'appeal in the strict sense' or an 'appeal by way of rehearing', as if, without much more, such classification dictates the way in which the particular appeal must be approached. True, such broad categories will offer a limited measure of guidance. But it remains for the appellate body in every case to discharge its functions in a way apt for all of the statutory provisions that are brought into play.

It is necessary to make this point because some of the discussion of the nature of the appeal to the Full Bench of the Commission, both within the Commission and in the reasons of the Full Court, might on superficial reading, be taken to suggest that there is a particular classification of appeals generally, being 'appeals against discretionary decisions', which is in some way to be distinguished from 'appeals by way of rehearing'. This is a false dichotomy. Many appeals by way of rehearing involve appeals from discretionary decisions. The rehearing identifies the materials upon which the appellate body acts. It will have relevance for any supervening changes in the facts or applicable law.

On the other hand, the character of the decision under appeal (as discretionary, interlocutory, final or otherwise) will govern the approach to be taken by the appellate body in discharging its function. In the case of discretionary decisions, that approach in the case of appeal is one of caution and restraint. This is because of the primary assignment of decision-making to a specific repository of the power and the fact that minds can so readily differ over most discretionary or similar questions. It is rare that there will only be one admissible point of view. Disputation and litigation are expensive, distracting and time-consuming. Therefore, the law, for policy reasons, recognises these features of discretionary decisions. Except in appeals involving a complete hearing *de novo*, all other appeals will approach with restraint the reconsideration of discretionary decisions which are based on the same material that was before the primary decision-maker.

Because of the necessity to ascertain the ambit of the appellate function in a particular case by reference to the legislation in question, it is obviously useful where the task of classification has already occurred to accept the guidance of a previous decision.

19.2.4C	**Fox v Percy**
	(2003) 214 CLR 118, [2003] HCA 22
	High Court of Australia

[The case concerns an appellant seriously injured when her horse collided with the respondent's motor vehicle. Both gave evidence they were on the correct side of the road. The trial judge accepted a police officer's record that the respondent was on the correct side of the road where skid marks appeared, nevertheless entered judgment for the appellant on the basis that the accident happened on the appellant's correct side of the road. The Court of Appeal overturned the trial judge and held the police officer's record fell into the category of inconsistent facts 'incontrovertibly established by the evidence'. The appellant was granted special leave to the High Court on whether the Court of Appeal erred in disturbing the trial judge's findings of fact, and if the Court of Appeal was correct, whether the correct order should have been a new trial, rather than a judgment in the respondent's favour. The appeal was dismissed.]

Gleeson CJ, Gummow and Kirby JJ:

The powers and functions of the Court of Appeal

[20] Appeal is not, as such, a common law procedure. It is a creature of statute (*Attorney-General v Sillem* (1864) 10 HLC 704 at 720–721 [11 ER 1200 at 1207–1208]; *South Australian Land Mortgage and Agency Co Ltd v The King* [1922] HCA 17; (1922) 30 CLR 523 at 552–553; *CDJ v VAJ* [1998] HCA 76; (1998) 197 CLR 172 at 196–197 [91]–[95], 230 [184]; *SRA* [1999] HCA 3; (1999) 73 ALJR 306 at 322 [72]; [1999] HCA 3; 160 ALR 588 at 609; *DJL v Central Authority* [2000] HCA 17; (2000) 201 CLR 226 at 245–246 [40]; *Allesch v Maunz* [2000] HCA 40; (2000) 203 CLR 172 at 179–180 [20]–[22], 187 [44].). In *Builders Licensing Board v Sperway Constructions (Syd) Pty Ltd* ((1976) 135 CLR 616 at 619–22; 14 ALR 174 at 176–9. See also *Eastman v R* (2000) 203 CLR 1 at 40–1 [130]; 172 ALR 39 at 65.), Mason J distinguished between (i) an appeal *stricto sensu*, where the issue is whether the judgment below was right on the material before the trial court; (ii) an appeal by rehearing on the evidence before the trial court; (iii) an appeal by way of rehearing on that evidence supplemented by such further evidence as the

appellate court admits under a statutory power to do so; and (iv) an appeal by way of a hearing *de novo*. There are different meanings to be attached to the word "rehearing" (*Builders Licensing Board v Sperway Constructions (Syd) Pty Ltd* [1976] HCA 62; (1976) 135 CLR 616 at 620–621.). The distinction between an appeal by way of rehearing and a hearing *de novo* was further considered in *Allesch v Maunz* ((2000) 203 CLR 172 at 180–1 [23], 187 [44]; 172 ALR 39 at 44, 47). Which of the meanings is that borne by the term "appeal", or whether there is some other meaning, is, in the absence of an express statement in the particular provision, a matter of statutory construction in each case.

[21] In New South Wales a right of appeal from a judgment of the District Court lies to the Supreme Court pursuant to the *District Court Act 1973* (NSW), s 127(1). In the present case such appeal lay as of right (*District Court Act 1973* (NSW), s 127(3). See also s 127(2)(c)(i).). Within the Supreme Court such an appeal is assigned to the Court of Appeal (*Supreme Court Act 1970* (NSW), ss 48(1)(a)(iv) and 48(2)(f).). The character and features of the appeal are governed by the *Supreme Court Act 1970* (NSW). Section 75A of that Act provides, relevantly:

> (5) Where the decision or other matter under appeal has been given after a hearing, the appeal shall be by way of rehearing.
> (6) The Court shall have the powers and duties of the court ... from whom the appeal is brought, including powers and duties concerning:
>   (a) ...
>   (b) the drawing of inferences and the making of findings of fact, and
>   (c) the assessment of damages and other money sums.
> (7) The Court may receive further evidence.
> (8) Notwithstanding subsection (7), where the appeal is from a judgment after a trial or hearing on the merits, the Court shall not receive further evidence except on special grounds.
> (9) ...
> (10) The Court may make any finding or assessment, give any judgment, make any order or give any direction which ought to have been given or made or which the nature of the case requires.

[22] The nature of the "rehearing" provided in these and like provisions has been described in many cases. To some extent, its character is indicated by the provisions of the sub-sections quoted. The "rehearing" does not involve a completely fresh hearing by the appellate court of all the evidence. That court proceeds on the basis of the record and any fresh evidence that, exceptionally, it admits. No such fresh evidence was admitted in the present appeal.

[23] The foregoing procedure shapes the requirements, and limitations, of such an appeal. On the one hand, the appellate court is obliged to "give the judgment which in its opinion ought to have been given in the first instance" (*Dearman v Dearman* (1908) 7 CLR 549 at 561. The court there was concerned with s 82 of the Matrimonial Causes Act 1899 (NSW) which provided that "on appeal every decree or order may be reversed or varied as the Full Court thinks proper": see (1908) 7 CLR 549 at 558.). On the other, it must, of necessity, observe the "natural limitations" that exist in the case of any appellate court proceeding wholly or substantially on the record (*Dearman v Dearman* (1908) 7 CLR 549 at 561. See also *Scott v Pauly* (1917) 24 CLR 274 at 278–81.). These limitations include the disadvantage that the appellate court has when compared with the trial judge in respect of the evaluation of witnesses' credibility and of the "feeling" of a case which an appellate court, reading the transcript, cannot always

fully share (*Maynard v West Midlands Regional Health Authority* [1984] 1 WLR 634 at 637; [1985] 1 All ER 635 at 637 per Lord Scarman with reference to *Joyce v Yeomans* [1981] 1 WLR 549 at 556; [1981] 2 All ER 21 at 26. See also *Chambers v Jobling* (1986) 7 NSWLR 1 at 25.). Furthermore, the appellate court does not typically get taken to, or read, all of the evidence taken at the trial. Commonly, the trial judge therefore has advantages that derive from the obligation at trial to receive and consider the entirety of the evidence and the opportunity, normally over a longer interval, to reflect upon that evidence and to draw conclusions from it, viewed as a whole (*SRA* (1999) 160 ALR 588 at 619–20 [89]–[91]; 73 ALJR 306 at 330 citing *Lend Lease Development Pty Ltd v Zemlicka* (1985) 3 NSWLR 207 at 209–10; *Jones v R* (1997) 191 CLR 439 at 466–7; 149 ALR 598 at 619–20.).

[24] Nevertheless, mistakes, including serious mistakes, can occur at trial in the comprehension, recollection and evaluation of evidence. In part, it was to prevent and cure the miscarriages of justice that can arise from such mistakes that, in the nineteenth century, the general facility of appeal was introduced in England, and later in its colonies (*Builders Licensing Board v Sperway Constructions (Syd) Pty Ltd* (1976) 135 CLR 616 at 619–20; 14 ALR 174 at 176–9; *SRA* (1999) 160 ALR 588 at 609–13 [72]–[80]; 73 ALJR 306 at 322–5.). Some time after this development came the gradual reduction in the number, and even the elimination, of civil trials by jury and the increase in trials by judge alone at the end of which the judge, who is subject to appeal, is obliged to give reasons for the decision (*Public Service Board (NSW) v Osmond* (1986) 159 CLR 656 at 666–7; 63 ALR 559 at 656–6 citing *Housing Commission (NSW) v Tatmar Pastoral Co Pty Ltd* [1983] 3 NSWLR 378 at 386; *Soulemezis v Dudley (Holdings) Pty Ltd* (1987) 10 NSWLR 247 at 257–8, 268–73, 277–81.). Such reasons are, at once, necessitated by the right of appeal and enhance its utility. Care must be exercised in applying to appellate review of the reasoned decisions of judges, sitting without juries, all of the judicial remarks made concerning the proper approach of appellate courts to appeals against judgments giving effect to jury verdicts (eg, *Hocking v Bell* (1945) 71 CLR 430; (1947) 75 CLR 125 at 131–2; cf *Naxakis v Western General Hospital* (1999) 197 CLR 269 at 271–2 [2], 274–5 [16], 282–3 [41]–[42], 288–90 [57]–[58], 310–11 [119]–[123]; 162 ALR 540 at 541, 544, 550–1, 555–6, 572–3.). A jury gives no reasons and this necessitates assumptions that are not appropriate to, and need modification for, appellate review of a judge's detailed reasons.

[25] Within the constraints marked out by the nature of the appellate process, the appellate court is obliged to conduct a real review of the trial and, in cases where the trial was conducted before a judge sitting alone, of that judge's reasons. Appellate courts are not excused from the task of "weighing conflicting evidence and drawing [their] own inferences and conclusions, though [they] should always bear in mind that [they have] neither seen nor heard the witnesses, and should make due allowance in this respect" (*Dearman v Dearman* (1908) 7 CLR 549 at 564 citing *The Glannibanta* (1876) 1 PD 283 at 287.). In *Warren v Coombes* ((1979) 142 CLR 531 at 551; 23 ALR 405 at 423.), the majority of this Court reiterated the rule that:

> [I]n general an appellate court is in as good a position as the trial judge to decide on the proper inference to be drawn from facts which are undisputed or which, having been disputed, are established by the findings of the trial judge. In deciding what is the proper inference to be drawn, the appellate court will give respect and weight to the conclusion of the trial judge but, once having reached its own conclusion, will not shrink from giving effect to it.

As this Court there said, that approach was "not only sound in law, but beneficial in ... operation" ((1979) 142 CLR 531 at 551; 23 ALR 405 at 423. See also *Taylor v Johnson* (1983) 151 CLR 422 at 426; 45 ALR 265 at 267; *Jovanovic v Rossi* (1985) 58 ALR 519 at 522; cf *Moran v McMahon* (1985) 3 NSWLR 700 at 715–16 per Priestley JA.).

[26] After *Warren v Coombes*, a series of cases was decided in which this Court reiterated its earlier statements concerning the need for appellate respect for the advantages of trial judges, and especially where their decisions might be affected by their impression about the credibility of witnesses whom the trial judge sees but the appellate court does not. Three important decisions in this regard were *Jones v Hyde* ((1989) 85 ALR 23 at 27–8; 63 ALJR 349 at 351–2.), *Abalos v Australian Postal Commission* ((1993) 177 CLR 472 at 479, 482–3; 112 ALR 641 at 645–6, 648–9.) and *Devries v Australian National Railways Commission* ((1990) 171 CLR 167 at 179; 96 ALR 354 at 363.). This trilogy of cases did not constitute a departure from established doctrine. The decisions were simply a reminder of the limits under which appellate judges typically operate when compared with trial judges.

[27] The continuing application of the corrective expressed in the trilogy of cases was not questioned in this appeal. The cases mentioned remain the instruction of this Court to appellate decision-making throughout Australia. However, that instruction did not, and could not, derogate from the obligation of courts of appeal, in accordance with legislation such as the *Supreme Court Act* applicable in this case, to perform the appellate function as established by Parliament. Such courts must conduct the appeal by way of rehearing. If, making proper allowance for the advantages of the trial judge, they conclude that an error has been shown, they are authorised, and obliged, to discharge their appellate duties in accordance with the statute.

[28] Over more than a century, this Court, and courts like it, have given instruction on how to resolve the dichotomy between the foregoing appellate obligations and appellate restraint. From time to time, by reference to considerations particular to each case, different emphasis appears in such reasons (See discussion in *SRA* (1999) 160 ALR 588 at 606–7 [61]–[64], 613–22 [81]–[93], 629–30 [132]–[137]; 73 ALJR 306 at 321, 325–31, 337–8.). However, the mere fact that a trial judge necessarily reached a conclusion favouring the witnesses of one party over those of another does not, and cannot, prevent the performance by a court of appeal of the functions imposed on it by statute. In particular cases incontrovertible facts or uncontested testimony will demonstrate that the trial judge's conclusions are erroneous, even when they appear to be, or are stated to be, based on credibility findings (eg, *Voulis v Kozary* (1975) 180 CLR 177; 7 ALR 126; *SRA* (1999) 160 ALR 588; 73 ALJR 306; cf *Trawl Industries of Australia Pty Ltd v Effem Foods Pty Ltd* (1992) 27 NSWLR 326 at 349–51.).

[29] That this is so is demonstrated in several recent decisions of this Court (eg, *Effem Foods Pty Ltd v Lake Cumbeline Pty Ltd* (1999) 161 ALR 599 at 603 [15]–[16]. See also *SRA* (1999) 160 ALR 588; 73 ALJR 306.). In some, quite rare, cases, although the facts fall short of being "incontrovertible", an appellate conclusion may be reached that the decision at trial is "glaringly improbable"(*Chambers v Jobling* (1986) 7 NSWLR 1 at 10.) or "contrary to compelling inferences" in the case (*Brunskill v Sovereign Marine & General Insurance Co Ltd* (1985) 62 ALR 53 at 57; 59 ALJR 842 at 844.). In such circumstances, the appellate court is not relieved of its statutory functions by the fact that the trial judge has, expressly or implicitly, reached a conclusion influenced by an opinion concerning the credibility of witnesses. In such a case, making all due allowances for the advantages available to the trial judge, the appellate court must "not shrink from giving effect to" its own conclusion. Finality in litigation is highly desirable. Litigation beyond a trial is costly and usually upsetting. But in every appeal by way

of rehearing, a judgment of the appellate court is required both on the facts and the law. It is not forbidden (nor in the face of the statutory requirement could it be) by ritual incantation about witness credibility, nor by judicial reference to the desirability of finality in litigation or reminders of the general advantages of the trial over the appellate process.

[30] It is true, as McHugh J has pointed out, that for a very long time judges in appellate courts have given as a reason for appellate deference to the decision of a trial judge, the assessment of the appearance of witnesses as they give their testimony that is possible at trial and normally impossible in an appellate court. However, it is equally true that, for almost as long, other judges have cautioned against the dangers of too readily drawing conclusions about truthfulness and reliability solely or mainly from the appearance of witnesses (eg, *Trawl Industries of Australia Pty Ltd v Effem Foods Pty Ltd* (1992) 27 NSWLR 326 at 348 per Samuels JA). Thus, in 1924 Atkin LJ observed in *Société d'Avances Commerciales (Société Anonyme Egyptienne) v Merchants' Marine Insurance Co (The "Palitana")*((1924) 20 LI L Rep 140 at 152. See also *Coghlan v Cumberland* [1898] 1 Ch 704 at 705.):

> ... I think that an ounce of intrinsic merit or demerit in the evidence, that is to say, the value of the comparison of evidence with known facts, is worth pounds of demeanour.

[31] Further, in recent years, judges have become more aware of scientific research that has cast doubt on the ability of judges (or anyone else) to tell truth from falsehood accurately on the basis of such appearances (see material cited by Samuels JA in *Trawl Industries of Australia Pty Ltd v Effem Foods Pty Ltd* (1992) 27 NSWLR 326 at 348 and noted in *SRA* (1999) 160 ALR 588 at 617–18 [88]; 73 ALJR 306 at 329). Considerations such as these have encouraged judges, both at trial and on appeal, to limit their reliance on the appearances of witnesses and to reason to their conclusions, as far as possible, on the basis of contemporary materials, objectively established facts and the apparent logic of events. This does not eliminate the established principles about witness credibility; but it tends to reduce the occasions where those principles are seen as critical.

19.2.5   Questions

1. Is a right of appeal a limitation of the first court's jurisdiction? See *Attorney-General v Sillem* (1864) 10 HL Cas 704 at 720; *The Commonwealth v The Limerick Steamship Co Ltd* (1924) 35 CLR 69 at 92 per Issacs and Rich JJ, who said:

   > ... a right of appeal from any Court is a limitation of that Court's jurisdiction. It lessens or may destroy the obligatory force of its orders; it delays or prevents execution of its orders. It necessarily follows that the jurisdiction of a Court to decide and enforce finally and free from appeal is a larger jurisdiction than the jurisdiction to decide and enforce subject to an appeal.

2. Is the judgment of a court the same as the reasons for judgment? See *Driclad Pty Ltd v FCT* (1968) 121 CLR 45 at 64. An appeal may lie from the formal judgment or order but no appeal lies from the reasons, which, while having precedential value, are not the judgment of the court.

3. Compare and contrast the differences between a strict appeal and a rehearing. Note in particular the power to consider new circumstances and admit new evidence under the latter procedure: see *Quilter v Mapleson* (1882) 9 QBD 672 at 676 per Jessel MR, who said:

> On an appeal strictly so called, such a judgment can only be given as ought to have been given at the orginal hearing; but on a rehearing such a judgement may be given as ought to be given if the case came at that time before the Court at first instance.

AVENUES OF APPEAL

19.3.1 Judicial systems in Australia involve multiple levels of jurisdiction. Generally each level, with the exception of the High Court, has an avenue of appeal. The scope and nature of the avenue of appeal depends upon the terms of the statute creating the right of appeal.

High Court

19.3.2 Where the High Court grants special leave, the court hears appeals from judgments, whether final or interlocutory, from the state Courts of Appeal, state Supreme Court Trial Divisions, the Northern Territory Court of Appeal, and the Full Federal Court: Federal Court of Australia Act 1976 (Cth) s 33; Judiciary Act 1903 (Cth) ss 35, 35AA. It is irrelevant whether the lower court judgment was pronounced in the exercise of federal jurisdiction or otherwise. Appeals from the ACT Supreme Court go to the Federal Court (Federal Court of Australia Act 1976 (Cth) s 24), then ultimately the High Court. If the Northern Territory Court of Appeal is the court of first instance, an appeal lies to the Full Federal Court, then the High Court. An appeal lies as of right from a single High Court judge except with respect to an interlocutory application, where leave is required: Judiciary Act 1903 (Cth) s 34.

The High Court filters the matters that it considers by requiring special leave as prescribed by HCR Pt 41. See D Jackson QC, 'The Lawmaking Role of the High Court' (1994) 11 *ABR* 197; D O'Brien, *Special Leave to Appeal: The Law and Practice of Applications for Special Leave to Appeal to the High Court of Australia*, LBC Information Services, Sydney, 1996. The principles applicable to an application for special leave are contained in the Judiciary Act 1903 (Cth) s 35A.

19.3.3E   **Judiciary Act 1903 (Cth)**
Criteria for granting special leave to appeal

35A In considering whether to grant an application for special leave to appeal to the High Court under this Act or under any other Act, the High Court may have regard to any matters that it considers relevant but shall have regard to —

    (a) whether the proceedings in which the judgment to which the application relates was pronounced involve a question of law —

        (i) that is of public importance, whether because of its general application or otherwise; or

(ii) in respect of which a decision of the High Court, as the final appellate court, is required to resolve differences of opinion between different courts, or within the one court, as to the state of the law; and

(iii) whether the interests of the administration of justice, either generally or in the particular case, require consideration by the High Court of the judgment to which the application relates.

[For further detail see B Darbyshire, B Fry and N Moshinsky QC, 'Appeal', *Court Forms, Precedents and Pleadings Victoria*, LexisNexis, Sydney, vol 1, [900]ff.]

19.3.4C   **Morris v R**
                                      (1987) 163 CLR 454
                                   High Court of Australia

Dawson J (at 475): All too often in applications before this Court insufficient attention is given to the distinction between leave to appeal and special leave to appeal. Leave to appeal may be given where an applicant makes out a prima facie case of error. That is not enough to attract special leave to appeal, which should only be given where, in addition, there is some special feature of the case which warrants the attention of this Court. It would be wrong to attempt to formulate rules which would confine the exercise of the jurisdiction to grant special leave. It remains a discretionary jurisdiction. Sufficient has, however, been established in the decided cases to provide a clear guide to those occasions when it is appropriate to grant special leave and those when it is not.

Section 35A of the Judiciary Act 1903 (Cth) allows the Court to have regard to any matters that it considers relevant, which confirms the discretionary nature of the jurisdiction to grant special leave. The section goes on to provide that, in exercising that jurisdiction, the Court shall have regard to the public importance of any question of law and the need to resolve judicial differences of opinion concerning the state of the law. In addition the Court shall, under the section, consider whether the administration of justice, either generally or in the particular case, requires an application for special leave to be granted. Those criteria are to be found in previous decisions of the Court and the section, as far as it goes, is declaratory.

In exercising its wide discretion to grant special leave to appeal, it is proper that the Court should be influenced by the function which it performs as the final appellate court in the judicial hierarchy. The number of applications for special leave increases year by year, particularly in the criminal law. Since the number of cases with which the Court can properly deal in any one year is limited, it is inevitable that a careful choice must be made having regard to the duty which the Court has to develop and clarify the law and to maintain procedural regularity in the courts below. The Court must necessarily place greater emphasis upon its public role in the evolution of the law than upon the private rights of the litigants before it. Whilst procedurally and otherwise this Court performs in many ways a truly appellate function, more significantly it operates as a court of review and this must ultimately be the most important factor in the selection of those cases in which special leave to appeal is to be granted: see generally Jolowicz, 'Appeal and Review in Comparative Law: Similarities, Differences and Purposes', *Melbourne University Law Review*, vol 15 (1986), at p 618.

19.3.5 It is rare to obtain special leave to appeal in the following circumstances: (i) where the inferior court judgment is plainly right; (ii) where only a question of fact is involved; (iii) on interlocutory matters involving matters or questions of practice and procedure points; (iv) from decisions based on the exercise of discretions as to costs; or (v) involving questions of leave.

Once successful on an application for special leave, HCR Pt 42 governs High Court procedures on appeal.

State, Federal Court and Northern Territory appellate courts

19.3.6 Appeals lie from single trial judges to appellate courts within the same jurisdiction. Leave is generally not required. An appeal does not automatically result in a stay of proceedings in the action. For example, execution may proceed based on the judgment of the inferior court. Appeals also lie from inferior courts and decisions of various officers of the court, eg, registrars, to single Supreme Court judges. For example, in Queensland appeals lie from magistrates, District Courts, registrars and chamber judges. In the Australian Capital Territory, appeals lie from masters, registrars, tribunals and magistrates.

Interlocutory judgments and orders

19.3.7 An appeal lies from a final judgment or order concerning the substantive question in the proceeding. The distinction between final and interlocutory orders is vexed, being dependent upon the nature of the application and its legal effect. The test is: does the order made finally dispose of the rights of the parties in the action? See *Hall v Nominal Defendant* (1966) 117 CLR 423; *Carr v Finance Corporation of Australia Ltd* (1981) 147 CLR 246. In *Salter Rex & Co v Ghosh* [1971] 2 QB 597 at 601, Lord Denning MR suggested:

> This question of 'final' or 'interlocutory' is so uncertain that the only thing for practitioners to do is to look up the practice books and see what has been decided on the point. Most orders have been the subject of decision. If a new case should arise, we must do the best we can with it. There is no other way.

The applicant will need to establish the first instance decision was wrong or doubtful and that a substantial injustice will arise by allowing the decision to stand: *Australian Dairy Corporation v Murray Goulburn Co-op Co Ltd* [1990] VR 355.

Leave to appeal is generally required in appeals from interlocutory orders, particularly those made by consent or discretionary cost orders: see **19.6.5**. Similarly, appellate courts will not hear hypothetical cases, give opinions on points of law and equivalents, or hear an appeal to confirm a favourable judgment.

The failure to appeal from an interlocutory order does not prevent the Court of Appeal from giving such decision as may be just: ACT r 5052; NSW r 51.52; Qld r 766(4); SA r 286(2); Tas r 672(8); Vic r 64.22; WA O 65 r 4; Federal Court of Australia Act 1976 (Cth) s 28(4). There is no equivalent provision in the Northern Territory.

19.3.8C	**Meddings v The Council of the City of Gold Coast**
	[1988] 1 Qd R 528
	Supreme Court of Queensland, Full Court

[Mrs Meddings, a resident of Victoria, was injured in a fall at a rest room on the Gold Coast during 1980. The address of the rest room was not identified until 1985, though was capable of being so identified at an earlier date. A District Court plaint was issued in 1986 together with an application for extension of time which was refused. The appeal was dismissed on the basis that the District Court's refusal to extend time was interlocutory, not final, therefore there was no appeal to the Supreme Court as of right. The case is useful in distinguishing between final and interlocutory orders.]

Macrossan J (at 529): Characterisation of a judgment or order as being either final or interlocutory is frequently a difficult process but there is now substantial authority at hand when the question involves an appeal rule cast in the form of s 92 or some similar form. The test which results from the decisions of the High Court in *Hall v Nominal Defendant* (1966) 117 CLR 423, *Licul v Corney* (1976) 50 ALJR 439 and *Carr v Finance Corporation of Australia Ltd* (1981) 147 CLR 246 should be applied here. Where there remains a right to make some further application of the kind which has been dealt with, it cannot be held that the order which has been made finally determines the rights of the parties. Also where an order made does not directly deal with the rights in contest in an action, it cannot be regarded as one finally determining those rights. An enquiry into the practical effect of an order which has been made should not be undertaken as the appropriate way of deciding whether the order is final or interlocutory: see *Carr v Finance Corporation of Australia Ltd* (above) at 248 per Gibbs CJ and at 256 per Mason J.

McPherson J (at 534–5): In any event the question was raised whether an appeal such as this lies by right. Under s 92 of the District Courts Act 1967–1985 a party dissatisfied with a 'final judgment' of a District Court may, subject to certain qualifications, appeal to the Full Court of the Supreme Court. In other cases leave is required. An application under s 31(2) of the Limitation of Actions Act for an extension of time within which to bring an action seems to me to be one that concludes with an order, which, whether the application is granted or refused, is necessarily interlocutory. If procedural form were decisive, the present application would be interlocutory because it was made in the matter of an action already instituted in the District Court by Mrs Meddings against the Council. But in Australia the decisive factor is not procedural but whether the judgment or order finally disposes of the rights of the parties. The principal authorities in support of this approach are *Licul v Corney* (1976) 50 ALJR 439, 444; *Port of Melbourne Authority v Anshun Proprietary Ltd (No 1)* (1980) 147 CLR 35; and *Carr v Finance Corporation of Australia Ltd* (1981) 147 CLR 246, which, with other decisions, are referred to in *Ex parte Britt* [1987] 1 Qd R 221, 224. Many of the relevant decisions on the point are helpfully reviewed and analysed in an article by Mrs G Jameson in (1987) 17 *Qld Law Socy Jnl* 39.

In the present case the practical effect of refusing the application was to deprive Mrs Meddings of her right to prosecute her action against the Council. It would have been different if the limitation period had been extended. But a determination of whether an application is final or interlocutory cannot depend on the actual outcome of the application itself. If it did, it would be impossible to know until the decision was given whether the proceedings were final or interlocutory. It would also mean that in all cases like this, there would be a right of appeal if the application to extend time was refused, but not if it was granted; and that would be so whether, viewed objectively, the decision was right or wrong.

The point is, I think, concluded for us by what was said by Gibbs J in *Licul v Corney* (1976) 50 ALJR 439, 444. His Honour there posed the question —

Does the judgment or order, as made, finally dispose of the rights of the parties?

The order in that case was one made by the Full Court of Victoria setting aside an order made by a county court judge extending the time for service of proceedings commenced by summons in that court. Having posed the question, his Honour answered it by holding that the Full Court judgment was not a final order. He said —

It does not have the effect of finally disposing of the rights of the parties. It leaves open — at least in theory — to the applicant to make a further application ... for an extension of time for service [535] of each summons, and if that extension is granted, and the summonses are served, to proceed with the actions.

It will be seen that his Honour regarded as the decisive criterion whether or not it would be open to the applicant to make and prosecute a fresh application notwithstanding the failure of the earlier application. As Gibbs CJ, his Honour pursued the same line of inquiry in *Carr v Finance Corporation Ltd* (1981) 147 CLR 246, 248, holding that an order refusing an application to set aside a default judgment was not final but interlocutory because it did not preclude a second or subsequent such application. That was so even though such an application might be 'doomed to failure because the issues of substance which it raised would have been decided adversely to the defendant in the first application'. The learned Chief Justice concluded by saying (147 CLR 246, at 248) —

In my opinion the test in *Licul v Corney* requires the Court to have regard to the legal rather than the practical effect of the judgment. If this were not so, the question whether a judgment is final or interlocutory would be even more uncertain than it is at present. In some cases it would be necessary for the Court, for the purpose of determining the practical effect of an order refusing to set aside a default judgment, to embark on a detailed inquiry as to the facts of the matter and the course of the proceedings already taken — an inquiry quite inappropriate when the only issue is whether a right of appeal exists. As will be seen, it would be necessary to make an inquiry of that kind in the present case if the practical test were to be adopted. The rigour of the rule that the legal effect of the judgment is decisive may of course be mitigated by the exercise of the Court's power to grant special leave to appeal.

To like effect were the remarks of Mason J in the same case (147 CLR 246, at 256) —

The question remains whether the refusal of an application amounts to a final order, when the practical effect of that order is to preclude the defendant from making another application to set aside the judgment, although in strict law the defendant is free to bring his application, knowing that it will inevitably fail. The present case is a striking example. Naturally the Court of Appeal could not be expected to depart from its earlier decision. Consequently a further application to set aside the judgment is of no value to the appellants. In *Hewitt* [1977] 17 ACTR 1 it was very different.

The choice for the Court is whether it should continue to adopt the traditional classification of orders of this kind as interlocutory because there is the right to make another application and because the order does not deal directly with the rights in contest in the action or whether it should now classify such orders as final when their practical effect is to shut out the defendant from contesting the default judgment.

Although the second alternative has some attractions, it has the disadvantage that the character of the order (whether it be final or interlocutory) could not be determined on its face, but could only be ascertained after an explanation of the grounds on which the application to set aside was made, the grounds on which it was refused and the formation of a judgment as to the impact of the grounds of refusal on the prospects of bringing a second application. The adoption of this approach would bring yet a further complication to the complexities which already bedevil the existence of appeals as of right to this court.

19.3.9C   **Carr v Finance Corporation of Australia Ltd**
(1981) 147 CLR 246
High Court of Australia

[The issue was whether a decision of the New South Wales Court of Appeal in upholding an order by a master, who refused to set aside a default judgment, was final or interlocutory.]

Gibbs CJ (at 248): The respondent submits that the appeal is incompetent because the judgment appealed from is not a final judgment within s 35 of the *Judiciary Act*. The question whether a judgment is final or interlocutory for the purpose of the rules relating to appeals is one productive of much difficulty. The test now applied in this Court for determining whether a judgment is final or not is whether the judgment or order appealed from, as made, finally determines the rights of the parties: *Licul v Corney* (1976) 50 ALJR 439 at 444. An order refusing to set aside a default judgment does not as a matter of law finally dispose of the rights of the parties, for it is open to the disappointed defendant to apply again to have the judgment set aside: *Hall v Nominal Defendant* (1966) 117 CLR 423 at 440. In practice, in some cases a second application of that kind might be successful, for example, when the first application had been dismissed on a technicality. In other cases, however, the second application would be doomed to failure because the issues of substance which it raised would have been decided adversely to the defendant in the first application. The appellants here submit that their right to make a further application is purely theoretical, since any such application must necessarily fail, and urge that in these circumstances the judgment should be regarded as a final one.

In my opinion the test in *Licul v Corney* requires the Court to have regard to the legal rather than the practical effect of the judgment. If this were not so, the question whether a judgment is final or interlocutory would be even more uncertain than it is at present. In some cases it would be necessary for the Court, for the purpose of determining the practical effect of an order refusing to set aside a default judgment, to embark on a detailed inquiry as to the facts of the matter and the course of the proceedings already taken — an inquiry quite inappropriate when the only issue is whether a right of appeal exists. As will be seen, it would be necessary to make an inquiry of that kind in the present case if the practical test were to be adopted. The rigour of the rule that the legal effect of the judgment is decisive may of course be mitigated by the exercise of the Court's power to grant special leave to appeal.

I therefore hold that the judgment appealed from is not a final judgment and that the appeal is incompetent.

Mason J (at 253): The objection to competency is that the order of the Court of Appeal is not a final order. The respondent contends that an order dismissing an application to set aside a default judgment is not a final order because it does not prevent the defendant from making another and later application to set aside the judgment.

In *Licul v Corney* (1976) 50 ALJR 439 at 444, Gibbs J, after noting that there had been disagreement as to the test for determining whether a judgment is final or interlocutory, said:

> One view — which was preferred by the Court of Appeal in *Salter Rex & Co v Ghosh* [1971] 2 QB 597 — is that the test depends on the nature of the application made to the court. The other view which, since *Hall v Nominal Defendant* (1966) 117 CLR 423, should, I think, be regarded as established in Australia, depends on the nature of the order made; the test is: Does the judgment or order, as made, finally dispose of the rights of the parties? Within either of those tests the judgment of the Full Court in the present case is not a final judgment. It does not have the effect of finally disposing of the rights of the parties. It leaves it open — at least in theory — to the [254] applicants to make a further application, upon prior notice served on the respondent himself, for an extension of time for service of each summons, and if that extension is granted, and the summonses are served, to proceed with the actions.

19.3.10   Questions

1. Why is a distinction drawn between interlocutory and final decisions? See *Gilbert v Endean* (1878) 9 Ch D 259 at 268–9 per Cotton LJ.

2. Would no restrictions on interlocutory appeals delay litigation, favour the wealthy, or promote unfavourable settlements? See *Re Will of Gilbert* (1946) 46 SR (NSW) 318 at 323 per Jordan CJ.

3. Is the test of whether the judgment or order finally disposes of the rights of the parties satisfactory? See *Hall v The Nominal Defendant* (1966) 117 CLR 423 at 440, 443.

4. Would a distinction between interlocutory and final decisions based on procedural form be more decisive? For example, is the application made in the matter of an action already instituted? See **19.3.8C** per McPherson J.

JURISDICTION

19.4.1   The diverse jurisdiction of appellate courts is found in the statutes, which create the right of appeal. Appellate courts are superior courts of record and have appellate, original and inherent jurisdiction: see, eg, Commonwealth Constitution s 73; Federal Court of Australia Act 1976 (Cth) s 24; Supreme Court Act 1933 (ACT) s 20; Supreme Court Act 1970 (NSW) ss 44, 75A, 101, 102, 107, 108, NSW r 51.52; Supreme Court Act (NT) s 55; Supreme Court of Queensland Act 1991 (Qld) ss 29, 69; Supreme Court Act 1935 (SA) s 50; Supreme Court Act 1986 (Vic) s 10; Supreme Court Civil Procedure Act 1932 (Tas) s 40, r 693; Supreme Court Act 1935 (WA) ss 58, 60, O 65 r 4. A full discussion of jurisdiction can be found in **Chapter 4.**

POWERS OF THE APPELLATE COURT

19.5.1   The powers of appellate courts are defined by statute and the Rules of Court. Courts of Appeal generally have the power to:

(a)   draw inferences of fact not inconsistent with jury findings;

(b)   make any order that ought to have been made or further orders, notwithstanding:

    (i)   limitations in the notice of appeal; or

    (ii)   effect on non-parties to the appeal; and

(c)   to make any order as to the costs of the appeal as may be just.

For example, the powers exercisable by the Full Federal Court on appeal in civil matters are prescribed in the Federal Court of Australia Act 1976 (Cth) s 28 (extracted below).

19.5.2E   **Federal Court of Australia Act 1976 (Cth)**

28 (1) Subject to any other Act, the Court may, in the exercise of its appellate jurisdiction:

(a)   affirm, reverse or vary the judgment appealed from;

(b)   give such judgment, or make such order, as, in all the circumstances, it thinks fit, or refuse to make an order;

(c)   set aside the judgment appealed from, in whole or in part, and remit the proceeding to the court from which the appeal was brought for further hearing and determination, subject to such directions as the Court thinks fit;

(d)   set aside a verdict or finding of a jury in a civil proceeding, and enter judgment notwithstanding any such verdict or finding;

(f)   grant a new trial in any case in which there has been a trial, either with or without a jury, on any ground upon which it is appropriate to grant a new trial; or

(g)   award execution from the Court or, in the case of an appeal from another court, award execution from the Court or remit the cause to that other court, or to a court from which a previous appeal was brought, for the execution of the judgment of the Court.

19.5.3   The procedure regulating the institution and conduct of appeals in the Federal Court is prescribed by FCR Ch 4 Appellate jurisdiction.

See also the legislation mentioned in 19.4.1.

PROCESS

19.6.1   The process of appeal involves determining the parties, satisfying any requirements for leave, filing a notice of appeal and preparing the necessary court materials. Appeals are generally conducted by an oral hearing, though some jurisdictions allow certain applications on the papers alone: eg, FCR rr 36.41–36.43.

Institution of an appeal

19.6.2 To institute an appeal three things are needed: service, filing and security. The judgment or order appealed from must be taken out and entered prior to the appeal: *Tannous v Mercantile Mutual Insurance Co Ltd* [1978] 2 NSWLR 331; *Commonwealth v Bank of New South Wales* (1949) 79 CLR 497; [1950] AC 235 at 294.

19.6.3 An appeal must be brought within the time fixed by the Rules of Court or statute. The period of time varies. In the Federal Court (r 36.03, r 35.13 — leave to appeal), Western Australia (O 65 r 9) (notice of motion), South Australia (r 281) and Tasmania (r 659) the period is 21 days from the date of the judgment being appealed. In the Australian Capital Territory, the period is governed by the relevant Act, court order or 21 days after the date of the decision appealed from (r 5405). In the High Court (r 41.02 — special leave application), New South Wales (r 51.8, PN SC CA 1 of 2009), the Northern Territory (r 85.02(2)) and Queensland (r 748) the period is 28 days. In Victoria (r 64.03) the period is 14 days. The appeal commences with the notice of appeal. Appeals brought by leave, eg, from interlocutory rather than final decisions, generally have shorter time periods: 14 days. An appeal will be dismissed if leave to appeal has not been granted: eg, Vic r 64.03.

The court has an unfettered discretion to extend the time for instituting an appeal or service: *Hughes v National Trustees Executors & Agency Co of Australasia Ltd* [1978] VR 257. Delay is a significant factor operating against the exercise of the discretion. Other relevant factors include the chances of the appeal being successful, cost, efficiency, fairness, and any degree of prejudice or injustice arising in the circumstances. See generally: FCR r 36.05, Form 67, r 35.14(1), Form 118; ACT r 5405; NSW rr 51.9(1)(b), 51.10(2), 51.16(2); NT rr 85.02, 85.03; Qld r 748; SA rr 289, 291, 292, cf 281; Tas inherent; Vic r 64.03; WA O 65 r 10. The court may impose conditions, such as adverse costs orders. In the High Court, delay in filing an appeal will result in having to reapply for special leave to appeal. Courts also have a wide discretion to extend or abridge the time for filing and lodgment of documents: eg, Qld PD No 2 of 2010.

Parties to an appeal

19.6.4 The appellant should ensure each person who is affected by the relief sought in the appeal, or who is interested in maintaining the decision of the court below, is joined as a respondent to the appeal: FCR r 36.31; ACT r 5404; NSW r 51.4; NT r 85.11; Qld r 749; SA r 283; Tas r 672; Vic r 64.04. In Western Australia, O 65 r 10(6) merely requires service on the respondent. All interested parties should be served: *Gillooly v Gillooly* [1950] 1 All ER 118. The rules provide for persons to intervene in an appeal: eg, FCR r 36.32.

Leave to appeal

19.6.5 Leave to appeal is a procedural control device to promote efficiency in the use of limited judicial resources. In *Coulter v R* (1988) 164 CLR 350, 359 Deane and Gaudron JJ stated:

> The requirement that leave or special leave be obtained before an appeal will lie as a necessary control device in certain areas of the administration of justice (eg, appeals to a second appellate court) in this country. As a filter of the work which comes before some appellate courts, it

promotes the availability, the speed and the efficiency of justice in those appeals which are, in all the circumstances, appropriate to proceed to a full hearing before the particular court. It also represents a constraint upon the overall cost of litigation by protecting parties, particularly respondents, from the costs of a full hearing of appeals which should not properly be entertained by the relevant court either because they are hopeless or, in the case of a civil appeal to a second appellate court, because they do not possess special features which outweigh the prima facie validity of the ordinary perception that the availability of cumulative appellate processes can, of itself, constitute a source of injustice.

Except in the High Court (see 19.3.2) and Federal Court (r 35.12(1), Form 117 — where an Act requires obtaining leave), the general rule is that an appeal can be brought as of right without leave: FCR r 36.01; Federal Court of Australia Act 1976 (Cth) s 24; Supreme Court Act 1970 (NSW) s 101; Supreme Court Act 1979 (NT) s 51; Supreme Court of Queensland Act 1991 (Qld) s 69; Supreme Court Act 1935 (SA) s 50; Supreme Court Civil Procedure Act 1932 (Tas) s 40; Supreme Court Act 1986 (Vic) s 10; Supreme Court Act 1935 (WA) s 58. There are exceptions to the general rule, as follows:

- specific matters for which there is no right of appeal: Federal Court of Australia Act 1976 (Cth) s 24 (limited list); Supreme Court Act 1970 (NSW) s 101 (extensive list except by leave); Supreme Court Act 1935 (SA) s 50(1) (limited list); Supreme Court Civil Procedure Act 1932 (Tas) s 43 (extensive list), r 679; Supreme Court Act 1986 (Vic) s 17A(4) (limited list); Supreme Court Act 1935 (WA) s 60(1) (extensive list); there are no equivalent provisions in the other jurisdictions;

- interlocutory orders generally: FCR r 35.01; Federal Court of Australia Act 1976 (Cth) s 24 (with exceptions); Supreme Court Act 1970 (NSW) s 101; Supreme Court Act (NT) s 53; Supreme Court Act 1935 (SA) s 50 (with exceptions), r 288; Supreme Court Civil Procedure Act 1932 (Tas) s 43; Supreme Court Act 1986 (Vic) s 17A(4); Supreme Court Act 1935 (WA) s 60(1)(f); there are no equivalent provisions in the other jurisdictions. The test for distinguishing final orders from interlocutory orders is discussed at 19.3.7;

- consent orders and discretionary costs orders: Judiciary Act 1903 (Cth) s 27; Supreme Court Act 1970 (NSW) s 101; Supreme Court Act 1935 (SA) s 50, r 288 (costs); Supreme Court Civil Procedure Act 1932 (Tas) ss 43, 44; Supreme Court Act 1986 (Vic) s 17A; Supreme Court Act 1935 (WA) s 60(1)(e); WA O 65 rr 15, 18; there are no equivalent provisions elsewhere.

In New South Wales, r 51.6 enables a party to file a notice of intention to appeal, or if necessary, a summons seeking leave to appeal within three months of the initial judgment or other period the court may order — see Form 103. The notice preserves an entitlement to appeal notwithstanding the subsequent expiry of the normal 28-day appeal period — r 51.16.

Notice of appeal

19.6.6   An appeal is usually commenced by a notice of appeal, the contents of which are prescribed by the Rules of Court: HCR r 42.01, Form 24; FCR rr 36.01, 36.02, Form 122; ACT r 5402, Form 5.11; NSW rr 51.16, 51.18, 51.19, Form 105; NT r 85.10(2); Qld rr 746, 747, Form 064; SA r 282, Form 29; Tas r 657; Vic r 64.05; WA O 65 r 10 (Appeal notice), Form 2. The notice of appeal should briefly and specifically state and particularise the grounds in support of the appeal: *Caldwell v Spratt* [1966] 1 NSWR 295; *Tame v New South Wales*

(2002) 211 CLR 317. It should state whether the appeal is from the whole or part only, and what part of the decision in the court below; and what judgment, order, verdict or determination the appellant seeks in place of the decision in the court below, and specify a return day. For example, WA O 65 r 10(2) states that the grounds of appeal must not merely allege that the primary court erred in fact or law, or that the primary court's decision is against the evidence or the weight of evidence or is unreasonable and cannot be supported having regard to the evidence, or that the primary court's decision is unsafe or unsatisfactory.

New South Wales Practice Note SCCA 1 of 2008 specifically states all rights of appeal arise under statute. The notice of appeal should identify the provision under which the right of appeal arises.

The appellant's argument is limited to the grounds of appeal, though this can be readily amended. The appellant's action at first instance further limits the arguments available on appeal, unless leave is granted, typically to overcome irregularities or to clarify issues in contention: *Suttor v Gundowda Pty Ltd* (1950) 81 CLR 418 at 438; *Green v Sommerville* (1979) 141 CLR 594 at 607–8. It is not permissible, eg, to raise a ground available but not taken at first instance; nor to raise objections abandoned at first instance. The respondent's arguments are at large. A respondent may rely on any ground to maintain the judgment at first instance. Grounds not previously argued require notice.

19.6.7   Notes and question

1. The rules discussed above also apply to matters of law.
2. Appeals can be conducted electronically: eg, Qld PD No 2 of 2010; WA PD 1.25.
3. Why is an appellant's notice of appeal limited to points raised at trial while a respondent may support a judgment on any ground appearing on the evidence, even if the point was not taken below? See *Osborne & Co v Anderson* [1905] VLR 427 at 436; *Suttor v Gundowda Pty Ltd* (1950) 81 CLR 418 at 438.

19.6.8E	**Supreme Court Civil Rules 2006 (SA)**

282. How to commence appeal

(1)   An appeal is commenced by filing a notice of appeal.

(2)   A notice of appeal —

    (a)   must be in an approved form; and

    (b)   must identify the judgment, order or decision subject to the appeal; and

    (c)   must state in detail the grounds of the appeal; and

    (d)   must state the orders sought by the appellant on the appeal; and

    (e)   if the appeal is of a kind for which permission to appeal is necessary —

        (i)   must include a request for the necessary permission; or

        (ii)   if permission has been obtained already, must state when, and from which court, permission to appeal was obtained; and

    (f)   if an extension of time for commencing the appeal is necessary — must include an application for the necessary extension of time.

(3)   Unless the Court otherwise directs, an appellant may not rely on grounds that are not stated in the notice of appeal.

FORM 29 Rule 282

NOTICE OF APPEAL

The [*Party/Parties*][*Name(s)*] appeal [(s)] to the [*Full Court/a single Judge*] of the Supreme Court of South Australia against the [*judgment/order*] of a [*single Judge/ Master*] of the [*Court*] dated [*date*][*month*][*year*].

Date of [*judgment/order*]:

[*If applicable*] Date of grant of permission:

Judicial Officer appealed from:

File No of Court appealed against:

Respondent[(s)] address[es]:

[*Judgment/order*] appealed against:

[*Set out text of relevant judgment/order*]

The appeal is against [*the whole of /the following portion of*] the [*judgment/order*].

[*If applicable specify that portion appealed against*]

[*If applicable*] The appellant seeks permission for the appeal on the following grounds:

[*Specify grounds in successively marked paragraphs*]

[*If applicable*] The appellant[s] seek[s] an extension of time within which to appeal, upon the following grounds:

[*Specify grounds in successively numbered paragraphs*]

The grounds of appeal are:

[*Specify grounds in successively numbered paragraphs*]

The appellant[s] seek[s] the following orders:

[*Set out relief sought in successively numbered paragraphs*]

[*If applicable*] The Registrar of the [*Court*] is requested:

(1)   to advise the Registrar of the Supreme Court of the existence of the appeal and afford that Court access to any electronic file relating to this matter; and

(2)   to forward to the Registrar all hard copy material relevant to the appeal, which is not contained in such electronic file.

[*Signed*] ....

[*Solicitor for the Appellant (s)*]

[*OR*]

[*Appellant(s)*]

NOTES:

1   This notice is to be accompanied by Form 1, duly completed.

2   The party or parties appealing must serve a copy of the notice of appeal on the Registrar or other proper officer of any other Court appealed from and the respondent(s) forthwith, as required by Rule 284.

3   If this document is filed electronically, the initials and name(s) of the issuing Solicitor or Party/Parties should be typed in, in lieu of a signature.

19.6.9E   **Appeals**
The Honourable Mr Justice J A Dowsett
Bar Practice Centre, Queensland, 1985

Drafting the Notice of Appeal

With the general decline in the quality of pleading in our courts has come a belief that a notice of appeal is rather like a writ — it does not serve any other useful purpose than to initiate the proceedings in question. This is an erroneous view of the nature of a notice of appeal. A judge rarely looks at a writ for the purpose of determining the nature of the action to be tried (unless it is a specially endorsed writ). However, judges in appellate courts will usually look at the notice of appeal perhaps before looking at any other part of the record. Hence a notice of appeal which clearly defines the issues between the parties and the issues to be argued on appeal will put a judge reading it into an appropriate frame of mind to consider your argument and the rest of the record. Thus the notice of appeal which states very broad grounds without relating them to the evidence or issues at the trial will not assist the judge in finding out what the appeal is about at an early stage.

Before drafting the notice of appeal, it is desirable that you identify clearly in your own mind the issue or issues to be stated. Again, you should select your points in order of strength so that the first ground stated is your primary ground or at least one of your primary grounds. It should be very specific and related to the case. It should not be a mere allegation that 'the learned trial judge erred in fact and/or in law and the finding was against the evidence and/or the weight of the evidence'. If a feeling of insecurity moves you to include such broad grounds in your notice of appeal (and many of us must plead 'guilty' to that charge) put it at the end of your notice of appeal rather than at the beginning.

Where possible, the grounds should be expressed in short discrete paragraphs which can be read quickly and easily understood. Although they must relate to the case under appeal, try to avoid extensive references to the facts of the case which will not make sense to the judge unless he has read the record. One way of doing this is to try to summarize the issue and the finding and then to identify the ground of appeal in relation to that issue and finding. The use of sub-paragraphs within each paragraph may assist in this regard.

Finally, where the form of notice of appeal requires you to state the orders that you claim ought to have been made below, use the same precision in drafting those orders as you would in drawing a draft order for a judge in chambers. Although an appellate court is unlikely to dismiss a meritorious appeal merely because the orders sought are not clearly spelled out, good drafting in this area will again assist in explaining to the Court what it is you say is wrong with the judgment and how it can be fixed up.

Obviously, many of the observations made above are counsels of perfection. You will always be faced with the problem of compromising between brevity on the one side and sufficient clarity of explanation on the other. You must try to find the middle ground, identifying the critical issues to be communicated in the notice of appeal and then expressing them in the most economical way. Always remember that the Judges of the appellate court do not know what happened at the trial, and so detailed reliance upon such knowledge is inappropriate in the notice of appeal.

Sample grounds

19.6.10E   **Appeals**
R V Hanson QC
in *Court Forms Precedents and Pleadings Queensland*
LexisNexis, Sydney, looseleaf, vol 1
Precedents 80.40, 80.45, 80.50 (not reproduced in current service)

Precedent 80.40
Sample grounds of appeal on question of law

1. the learned trial judge was wrong in law in holding that section [8] of the [Judicature] Act means [*insert details*];
2. the learned trial judge was wrong in law in holding that the plaintiff and the defendant had reached a concluded agreement;
3. the learned trial judge was wrong in law in holding that the defendant's conduct in [*insert details*] amounted to a repudiation of the agreement;
4. the learned trial judge was wrong in law in holding that by reason [*insert details*] the contract had been discharged by frustration;
5. the learned trial judge was wrong in law in holding that there was no consideration for the contract, in that [*insert details*] amounted to good consideration;
6. the learned trial judge was wrong in law in finding that the guarantee was discharged by [*insert details*];
7. the learned trial judge erred in law in admitting (or failing to admit) evidence of [*insert details*];
8. the learned trial judge was wrong in law in holding that clause [8] of the lease entitled the lessor to [*insert details*];
9. the learned trial judge was wrong in law in holding that there was a fiduciary relationship between the plaintiff and the defendant;
10. the learned trial judge was wrong in law in holding that the defendant was stopped from denying there was a contract between the plaintiff and the defendant.

Precedent 80.45
Sample grounds in an appeal on questions of fact

1. the learned trial judge erred in fact in finding that the defendant had been negligent;
2. the learned trial judge erred in fact in finding that the plaintiff had been guilty of contributory negligence;
3. the learned trial judge erred in fact in finding [*insert details*] in that the evidence of [*name*] was inconsistent with undisputed facts, [*or,* the evidence of (*name*) was glaringly improbable];
4. the learned trial judge erred in fact in finding [*insert details*] in that [*insert details*] could not reasonably be inferred from the undisputed facts [*or,* the facts found by his Honour].

Precedent 80.50
Sample grounds of appeal from discretionary order

1. The learned trial judge erred in granting leave in that his Honour had regard to irrelevant matters, namely [*insert details*] [*or,* gave no consideration to material factors, namely, (*insert details*) *or,* gave undue weight to (*insert details*)].

Service

19.6.11   The notice of appeal should be served on all parties directly affected by the terms of the appeal. The court may also direct service on other parties and non-parties: HCR r 42.05; FCR r 36.04; ACT r 5409; NSW r 51.4, Practice Note SCCA 1 of 2008; NT r 85.12; Qld r 752; SA rr 283, 284; Tas r 672; Vic r 64.04(1), (3); WA O 65 r 4. The method of service is prescribed by the Rules of Court for service of ordinary documents (see **Chapter 8** under 'Ordinary Service'). In the Federal Court (r 36.06) and Tasmania (r 661), service of the notice may be effected personally or at the address for service given in the proceedings at first instance. In the Federal Court (r 36.07), the respondent must file a notice of address for service before taking a step in the proceeding. A copy of the notice of appeal must be filed in some jurisdictions: Vic r 64.07; WA O 65 r 10. In South Australia notification of an appeal is given by serving a copy of the notice of appeal, within two days of filing, on all parties to the appeal. Filing and service are required within the time prescribed for commencing an appeal.

Amendment

19.6.12   In many jurisdictions, the notice of appeal may be amended at any time by leave of the appellate court in accordance with the Rules of Court: HCR r 3.01; FCR rr 36.10, 36.11; NT r 84.05; Qld r 751; SA r 294; Tas r 672(3); Vic r 64.06(1); WA O 65 r 4. Amendment may be necessary because formal reasons for judgment may not have been available prior to expiry of the time limited for appeal, resulting in a very scant notice of appeal. Appellate courts have all the powers and duties (including amendment) of the court appealed from.

In the Australian Capital Territory (r 5412), New South Wales (r 51.23), the Northern Territory (rr 83.15, 84.05), Queensland (r 751), South Australia (r 294) and Victoria (r 64.06(2)), leave to amend by the court is not required if an amended notice is filed and served early in the appeal proceedings, typically prior to preparation of the appeal book, or, in New South Wales, before the date of the callover, in Queensland, within the time limited for starting an appeal and in the Australian Capital Territory, before the date appointed for starting the appeal papers. In Victoria, leave of the Registrar is required. Where leave to amend is required, relevant factors in the exercise of the discretion include:

(a)   the significance of the amendment sought;

(b)   oppression or prejudice; and

(c)   whether the point could have been raised at first instance: see **19.8.22E**.

The appellate court has power to amend, to determine the real question or issue raised on appeal: Judiciary Act 1903 (Cth) s 77; FCR rr 8.21, 15.15 (on application of a claimant or cross-claimant); Supreme Court Act 1970 (NSW) s 75A(6)(a); Supreme Court Act (NT) s 80; NT r 36.01; Qld r 750 (parties); SA r 295(1)(b); Supreme Court Civil Procedure Act 1932 (Tas) s 47(1); Vic r 64.22; WA O 65 r 4. Examples include adding parties and amending proceedings generally. It is good practice for oral and written submissions to match the grounds of appeal.

Callover (setting the appeal down for hearing)

19.6.13   Notices of appeal have a return date and are listed on an appellate court callover list: Federal Court Practice Note APP 1 — Appeals to a Full Court; NSW r 51.20; Supreme Court of South Australia Practice Direction 6.21. The list is called over prior to the commencement of the sittings. In New South Wales, appeals are to be called over and assigned to special lists.

Cross-appeals, notices of contention and objections to competency

Cross-appeals

19.6.14   A respondent may seek a cross-appeal where he or she wishes to:

(a)   challenge or appeal the actual order, ruling or judgment (or part of the judgment) which the appellant appeals; or

(b)   vary part of the judgment at first instance.

The requirements of a notice of appeal apply equally to cross-appeals: HCR r 42.08; FCR r 36.21, Form 123, rr 36.22, 36.23; ACT r 5413; NSW rr 51.3, 51.17; NT r 84.06; Qld rr 754–756, Form 065; SA r 285 (14 day cross-appeal period); Tas r 664; Vic r 64.17; WA O 65 r 12. The cost consequences must be weighed up before cross-appealing. If the appeal and cross-appeal both succeed or fail, each party may be ordered to bear its own costs or a portion of those costs.

Notices of contention

19.6.15   Where a respondent to an appeal wishes to contend that the decision at first instance should be affirmed on grounds other than those relied on by the court below, but does not seek to discharge or vary any part of the decision of the court below, he or she may, in some jurisdictions, file and serve a notice of contention instead of filing a notice of cross-appeal: FCR r 36.24, Form 124; ACT r 5416; NSW r 51.40, Form 106; Qld r 757, Form 066; SA r 285; *Penrith Whitewater Stadium Ltd v Lesvos Enterprises Pty Ltd* [2007] NSW CA 131. Such respondents will be taken to have entered an appearance.

Objections to competency

19.6.16   A respondent who objects to the competency of an appeal must apply to the court for an order dismissing the appeal as incompetent or otherwise risk entitlement to costs: NSW r 51.41. An example is where opponents to a needless application for leave to appeal will not be entitled to all of their costs should they fail to point out that the appeal lies as of right: *Gillard v Hunter Wire Products Pty Ltd* [2001] NSWCA 450.

Court materials

Appeal record

19.6.17   The appellant also carries the burden of adducing material to prove the grounds of appeal in the form of an appeal book or record. Typically the appeal record will include:

(a)   originating documents and pleadings from the action;

(b)   affidavits from the action which depose to matters in issue;

(c)   transcripts of evidence below which are relevant to the grounds of appeal;

(d)   exhibits; answers to interrogatories;

(e)   formal judgment or order, and reasons for judgment at first instance; and

(f)   notice of appeal, cross-appeal or contention.

In jury trials the appeal record will also include the transcript of summing up, the verdict of the jury, or the jury's answers to specific questions.

The appeal record is prepared by the appellant under the supervision of a court officer in accordance with the Rules of Court: HCR rr 42.10–42.13; FCR Div 36.5, Federal Court Practice Notes APP 1 — Appeals to a Full Court; ACT rr 5130–5134; NSW r 51.24. Under NSW rr 51.25, 51.26, the appeal book must be divided into different coloured sections to distinguish between formal documents, transcripts, affidavits and exhibits; ACT r 5134; NT rr 84.03, 84.07– 84.10; Supreme Court of Queensland Practice Direction No 26 of 1999; Qld rr 758, 759 (Registry preparation of appeal book), PD No 2 of 2010; South Australia Practice Directions 6.8–6.18; SA r 298; Tas rr 665–669; Vic rr 64.08, 64.09; WA O 65 rr 10, 11 — the primary obligation is on the appellant to file the relevant documents, cf O 65 r 16. A detailed index to the appeal book is also prepared.

If further documents are to be included, or any of those listed excluded, then the registrar must settle the contents of the appeal record.

Notices

19.6.18 See 19.6.6 for the notice of appeal.

Outlines of argument, written submissions, lists of authorities and chronologies

19.6.19 Most jurisdictions require written synopses or outlines of argument to be filed and served on the other party prior to the hearing of an appeal: HCR rr 44.01–44.08; FCR r 36.55, Federal Court Practice Notes APP 1 — Appeals to a Full Court, CM 2 — List of authorities, citation of cases and legislation for proceedings generally; ACT rr 5438, 5439; NSW rr 51.34– 51.38; NT rr 85.14–85.17; SA rr 295(1)(f), 297 (summary of argument), SA PD 6.28–6.34; Supreme Court of Tasmania Practice Directions No 1 and No 6 of 2005; Supreme Court of Victoria, Court of Appeal Practice Statement No 1 and No 2 of 1995, No 1 of 2008; Supreme Court of Western Australia Practice Directions No 2.1. Some jurisdictions require the outline to be delivered at the beginning of oral argument: Supreme Court of Queensland Practice Direction No 2 of 2010, No 26 of 1999, Nos 10, 11 of 2000, No 9 of 2001, No 6 of 2002 (preparation of material to be relied upon at a hearing).

19.6.20E   **Uniform Civil Procedure Rules 2005 (NSW)**

Content of written submissions (c.f. SCR Part 51, rules 46 and 46A)
51.36 (1) Written submissions filed in an appeal must:
   (a) be divided into paragraphs numbered consecutively; and
   (b) so far as practicable, refer to matter in the Appeal Book by section name, volume number (if any), page number and letter, and not extract that matter, and
   (c) so far as practicable, not extract matter in a judicial authority, and
   (d) be signed by the barrister or solicitor who prepares it or, where the party is not represented by a barrister or solicitor, by the party, and

   (e)   have the following typed or printed in a neat and legible manner under the
         signature referred to in paragraph (d):
         (i)   the name of the signatory,
         (ii)   a telephone number at which the signatory can be contacted,
         (iii) if available, the signatory's facsimile number,
         (iv)   if available, the signatory's email address, and
   (f)   not exceed 20 pages (not counting the pages of any statement included in the
         submissions for the purposes of subrule (2)).
(2) Submissions raising substantial challenges to findings of fact must include a statement
     in narrative form (not exceeding 20 pages) setting out:
   (a)   the findings challenged, and
   (b)   the findings contended for and the reasons why the Court should substitute those
         findings, and
   (c)   supporting references to the transcript and other evidence.
(3) If damages for death or bodily injury are in issue:
   (a)   the appellant's written submissions must state:
         (i)   the manner in which the damages were assessed, or in the case of trial by
                jury, may be supposed to have been assessed, and
         (ii)   the heads of damages that are in issue in the appeal, and
         (iii) briefly but specifically, the basis of the challenge, and
         (iv)   where applicable — the alternative assessment contended for, and
   (b)   the respondent's written submissions must state:
         (i)   the extent to which the assessment will be challenged or supported by
                cross-appeal or contention, and
         (ii)   any alternative assessment sought, and briefly but specifically, the basis for it.
(4) The written submissions must address:
   (a)   any claim for an order for reinstatement or restitution and the form of the order
         sought, and
   (b)   where restitution is sought with interest that is at a rate other than the relevant
         rate set out in rule 36.7(1) — the rate of interest that should be applied.

19.6.21   The parties are required to provide a list of case and statutory authorities,
which they intend to rely on. Photocopies may be required in some jurisdictions:
HCR rr 26.03.2, 26.04.2, 41.05.2, 41.06.2, 41.10.3, Forms 18, 19; Federal Court Practice
Note No 1 (14 August 2003); South Australia Practice Direction 6.29; Supreme Court of
Victoria, Court of Appeal Practice Statement No 1 of 1995. Lists of authorities should
include authorised reports.

Extrinsic materials

19.6.22   Some jurisdictions require a party proposing to rely on extrinsic material to give
notice to the other parties and the registrar, otherwise leave will be required: Supreme Court of
Queensland PD No 23 of 91; Supreme Court of Victoria, Court of Appeal Practice Statement
No 1 of 1995. There are no equivalent provisions elsewhere.

RELATED APPLICATIONS

19.7.1 Applications to an appellate court may be made for many reasons. Common examples include an application for:

- a stay of execution pending an appeal: see **19.7.3**;
- security for costs: see **19.7.7**;
- leave to appeal: see **19.6.5**;
- dismissal for want of prosecution: see **19.12.1**;
- an extension of time in which to file or serve a notice of appeal: see **19.6.3**;
- consent orders;
- competency of appeals;
- non-compliance with directions;
- injunctions; and
- expedition of a hearing without consent.

Applications can be brought in very short time frames — eg, Supreme Court of Victoria, Court of Appeal Practice Statement No 1 of 2002.

19.7.2   Question

1. Should a Court of Appeal deal with related applications or refer the matter to others to determine? See New South Wales Practice Note SCCA 1 of 2008, which enables a Registrar to determine many of these applications.

Stay of execution pending appeal

19.7.3 An appeal does not operate as a stay of proceedings unless so ordered. An application for a stay is a separate proceeding. Such an order may be made as to whole or part of the proceedings. The court or a judge at first instance, may, at or after the time of giving judgment or order, stay execution until such time as he or she may think fit, eg, on the basis that a party intends to appeal. The length of any stay granted before the trial judge will usually correspond to the time limited for appeal. See generally: FCR r 41.11; NSW r 51.44; NT r 84.14; Qld r 761(1); Enforcement of Judgments Act 1991 (SA) s 17, SA r 300; Tas r 676; Vic r 66.16; WA O 31 r 6(2), O 65 r 1 (interim order). An appellant is entitled to execute on judgment and costs pending an appeal by him or her as to the inadequacy of the judgment amount, without fear of an estoppel, release, or election barring the right of appeal: *Karabotsos v Plastex Industries Ltd* [1981] VR 675.

Once an appeal is instituted an appellate court or judge has sole jurisdiction to grant a stay: Federal Court of Australia Act 1976 (Cth) s 29; HCR r 42.09; ACT r 5301; Qld r 761(2); Tas r 672(5); WA O 65 r 4. In the Federal Court (r 36.08), Northern Territory (r 84.14), New South Wales (r 51.44) and Victoria (r 64.25), concurrent jurisdiction with the inferior court remains.

The appellant seeking a stay carries the burden of satisfying the discretionary requirements and identifying circumstances that warrant a departure from the general rule that the judgment below should be presumed to be correct and is appropriate to be enforced. A party successful at first instance is entitled to the fruits of its judgment, unless the applicant for a stay establishes sound reasons or an appropriate case for the exercise of the discretion: *Klinker Knitting Mills Pty Ltd v L'Union Fire and Accident General Insurance Co Ltd* [1937] VLR 142; *Tolj v O'Connor* (1988) 13 ACLR 653. For example, where refusal would render the appeal futile; where to refuse a stay would deprive the appellant of the means of prosecuting the appeal; where new evidence gives rise to a complete defence (*Ellis v Scott* [1964] 2 All ER 987); where it is necessary to preserve the subject matter of the litigation from destruction; where irreparable loss may arise to the respondent; or where the balance of convenience favours the granting of a stay: *Jennings Construction Ltd v Burgundy Royale Investment Pty Ltd (No 1)* (1986) 161 CLR 681. The overriding principle is to uphold the interests of justice in the particular circumstances: *New South Wales Bar Association v Stevens* (2003) 52 ATR 602. In New South Wales, the applicant need only demonstrate a reason or an appropriate case to invoke the exercise of the discretion in his or her favour: *Alexander v Cambridge Credit Corp Ltd* (1985) 10 ACLR 42.

19.7.4C	**Alexander v Cambridge Credit Corp Ltd (recs apptd)** (1985) 2 NSWLR 685 Court of Appeal (NSW)

[At first instance, Rogers J in the Commercial Division concluded that Alexander, an auditor, was negligent in failing to require a provision to be made in the annual accounts of Cambridge for a debt owed to it by a third party. Judgment was entered in the sum of $145 million. Alexander sought a stay of judgment pending appeal. Cambridge argued that the stay should not be granted and that they should be protected with respect to Alexander's assets and professional indemnity insurance entitlements.]

Kirby P, Hope, McHugh JJA (at 692, 694–5): These arguments are not accepted. This Court has its own jurisdiction, upon motion, to determine whether or not a stay will be granted, regardless of orders made by the court below.

The rule (Pt 51 r 10) is in ample terms. It does not purport to limit the circumstances in which the Court of Appeal may direct a stay to cases where the trial judge has refused it. The language of the rule is perfectly general. The English rule upon which the decision in *J Lucas (Batteries) Ltd* [[1978] FSR 159; [1978] RPC 389] is based does not contain the words which appear in the local rule ('except so far as the Court of Appeal may direct'). These words are designed to assure and preserve the jurisdiction of the Court of Appeal. In any event, the decision in *J Lucas (Batteries) Ltd* is not binding on this Court. In so far as it expresses a different conclusion of principle, it should not be followed. Matters of practice, such as the issue of a stay of execution of a judgment depend very much upon the language of the rules, the view taken concerning the inherent jurisdiction of the court (cf *Ellis v Scott* [1964] 1 WLR 976; [1964] 2 All ER 987(n)) and the view of the court concerning the efficient and just dispatch of its business. In our view it would not only be incompatible with the broad language of Pt 51, r 10, and the normal practice of the court to adopt the approach urged by the opponents. It would also be wrong in principle and inconvenient in practice. It would limit this Court in the adjustment of the position of the parties in appeals pending before the Court. It would control the Court in at least those cases where a stay had been granted, by reference to what the judge below had fixed as the conditions upon which the party came before the Court, even during the course of the proceeding on appeal. It would involve a one-sided limitation, permitting only appellants who failed to secure a stay to approach the Court as of right. It would reduce the Court's supervision of the cases before it. If new circumstances arose after a stay was granted by the court below, this Court would, upon this view, be powerless, except by way of appeal, to review the matter, laying down its own condition for a stay, as appeared just to it. Such a limitation upon the powers of the Court should not be introduced without a clear requirement in the rule or a decision, binding on the Court, which drives it to that conclusion. In the present case, the rule does not require such a conclusion. And no authority binds the Court to reach it. ...

[694] Thirdly, recent decisions of this Court, reflecting the language of the rules and the frequency and nature of appeals, have expressed the approach to be taken without reference to the need for 'special' or 'exceptional' circumstances to justify a stay. Thus in *Waller v Todorovic* (at 3) the court merely pointed to the need for the party seeking a stay to establish a reason therefor. To like effect is the judgment of Mahoney JA (with whom Moffitt P and Glass JA agreed) in *Re Middle Harbour Investments Ltd (In Liq)* (Court of Appeal, 15 December 1976, unreported). In that case, Mahoney JA said this (at 2):

> Where an application is made for a stay of proceedings, it is necessary that the applicant demonstrate an appropriate case. Prima facie, a successful party is entitled to the benefit of the judgment obtained by him and is entitled to commence with the presumption that the judgment is correct. These are not matters of rigid principle and a court asked to grant a stay will consider each case upon its merits, but where an applicant for a stay has not demonstrated an appropriate case but has left the situation in the state of speculation or of mere argument, weight must be given to the fact that the judgment below has been in favour of the other party.

Although it is true that, in a number of more recent decisions of the Court, reference has been made to the requirement of 'exceptional' and 'special' circumstances, and although the same requirement appears still to be observed in Victoria, the general practice of the Court conforms more closely to that stated by Mahoney JA. In our opinion it is not necessary for the grant of a stay that special or exceptional circumstances should be made out. It is sufficient that the applicant for the stay demonstrates a reason or an appropriate case to warrant the exercise of discretion in his favour.

There are other principles to be kept in mind. The onus is upon the applicant to demonstrate a proper basis for a stay that will be fair to all parties: *Trlin*. The mere filing of an appeal will not, of itself, provide a reason or demonstrate an appropriate case, nor will it discharge the onus which the applicant bears: see Supreme Court Rules, Pt 51, r 10; *Waller v Todorovic*. The Court has a discretion whether or not to grant the stay and, if so, as to the terms that would be fair. In the exercise of its discretion, the Court will weigh considerations such as the balance of convenience and the competing rights of the parties before it: *Attorney-General v Emerson* (1889) 24 QBD 56. Where there is a risk that if a stay is granted, the assets of the applicant will be disposed of, the Court may, in the exercise of its discretion, refuse to grant a stay: cf *Clyne v Deputy Commissioner of Taxation* (1982) 56 ALJR 857. Sometimes as a condition of the grant of a stay, where funds are [695] available, a court will impose on the applicant the payment of the whole, or part, to the judgment creditor: *Andrews v John Fairfax & Sons Ltd* [1979] 2 NSWLR 184. Even where no order is made for the payment of part of a verdict, it is not at all unusual for the Court, in the exercise of its discretion, to grant a stay on terms that the appellant give to the judgment creditor security in terms defined by the Court as appropriate to the fair adjustment of the rights of the parties. This is what was done in *Trlin v Marac Finance Australia Ltd.* In the case, as a condition of the continuance of a stay of execution of judgment, the Court ordered the applicant to pay into a joint trust account, jointly administered by the solicitors for the parties, a sum equivalent to the interest payable under the mortgage, the subject of dispute, such sum (and the further payments falling due under a disputed mortgage pending the determination of the appeal) to be held on trust and thus available to disposition by order of the Court on the conclusion of the appeal. The object of this order was clearly in recognition of the fact that the stay would deprive the judgment creditor of the fruits of the judgment, to protect it and, by the accumulation of interest, to compensate it for the delays in recovery.

Two further principles can be mentioned. The first is that where there is a risk that the appeal will prove abortive if the appellant succeeds and a stay is not granted, courts will normally exercise their discretion in favour of granting a stay: *Scarborough v Lew's Junction Stores Pty Ltd* (at 130); applied in *Sun Alliance Insurance Ltd v Steiger* (Full Court, Supreme Court of Victoria, 22 March, 1985, unreported). Thus, where it is apparent that unless a stay is granted an appeal will be rendered nugatory, this will be a substantial factor in favour of the grant of a stay: *Wilson v Church (No 2)* (1879) 12 Ch D 454; *Re Middle Harbour Investments Ltd (In Liq)* (at 2). Secondly, although courts approaching applications for a stay will not generally speculate about the appellant's prospects of success, given that argument concerning the substance of the appeal is typically and necessarily attenuated, this does not prevent them considering the specific terms of a stay that will be appropriate fairly to adjust the interest of the parties, from making some preliminary assessment about whether the appellant has an arguable case. This consideration is protective of the position of a judgment creditor where it may be plain that an appeal, which does not require leave, has been lodged without any real prospect of success and simply in the hope of gaining a respite against immediate execution upon the judgment. Where, in the present case, Rogers J specifically contemplated in his judgment that an appeal would be lodged; where commentators on the judgment predicted a certain appeal (see eg, R Baxt, Comment (1985) 13 *ABLR* 154 at 160); where the size of the verdict and the novelty of the issues raised suggested the likelihood of an appeal; and where it is properly conceded by the claimant that the appeal is arguable, no question arises relevant to the stay or to the terms upon which it should be granted, that the appeal has been filed simply to gain time for the opponents.

19.7.5   Questions

1. Can *Klinker Knitting Mills Pty Ltd v L'Union Fire Accident and General Insurance Co Ltd* [1937] VLR 142 be reconciled with *Alexander v Cambridge Credit Corp Ltd* (1985) 10 ACLR 42 (extracted above)?

2. In what circumstances will an injunction be a preferable remedy to a stay? See *Jesasu Pty Ltd v Minister for Mineral Resources* (1987) 11 NSWLR 110.

19.7.6   Factors relevant to the exercise of the discretion include:

(a)   the balance of convenience between the parties;

(b)   competing rights of the parties;

(c)   the risk that execution of the judgment at first instant will render the appeal nugatory; and

(d)   arguable grounds of appeal.

Stays may be granted on terms, eg, the provision of security: *Rosengrens Ltd v Safe Deposit Centres Ltd* [1984] 3 All ER 198. Costs of a stay application are paid by the applicant. Injunctions may also be granted retaining the status quo pending an appeal: *Jesasu Pty Ltd v Minister for Mineral Resources* (1987) 11 NSWLR 110.

Security for costs

19.7.7   An appellant may be ordered by the appellate court to provide security for the respondent's costs of an appeal. Jurisdiction is founded on the Rules of Court and the inherent jurisdiction of the court: Federal Court of Australia Act 1976 (Cth) s 56; HCR Pt 59; FCR r 36.09; ACT r 5302; NSW r 51.50; NT r 85.13 (none required unless court directs); Qld rr 772–774, inherent jurisdiction (*Harpur v Ariadne Australia Ltd* [1984] 2 Qd R 523); SA (inherent); Tas r 671 (none required unless ordered); Vic r 64.24(2); WA O 65 r 13 (interim order).

The respondent must ask the appellant to provide security for costs (known as a prior demand) before seeking a court order for security for costs: *Aspendale Pastoral Co Pty Ltd v W J Drever Pty Ltd* (1983) 7 ACLR 937. Security for costs may be ordered in the exercise of the appellate court's unfettered discretion on the following basis:

(a)   the appeal is an abuse of process or is vexatious;

(b)   the appellant is an impecunious corporation: Corporations Act 2001 (Cth) s 1335; or

(c)   the appellant is ordinarily resident outside the jurisdiction except where there is sufficient property within the jurisdiction.

Discretionary factors include, but are not limited to:

(a)   whether the appellant is an impecunious natural person;

(b)   the merits of the appeal;

(c)   whether public interest or liberty of the appellant is involved;

(d)   poverty of the appellant arose from the actions of the respondent;

(e)   delay (a prompt application is required); and

(f)   failure to pay costs at first instance.

The amount of security for costs is also subject to the discretion of the court. A reasonable amount will be required: see S Colbran, *Security for Costs*, Longman Professional, Melbourne, 1993, Ch 16.

SUBSTANTIVE BASIS UPON WHICH APPEALS ARE BROUGHT

19.8.1   Judges exclusively make decisions on questions of law and exercise judicial discretion. A judge decides questions of fact, except in rare civil cases, where a jury decides the facts. The grounds of appeal associated with juries are outlined at 19.8.28. This section examines the substantive bases upon which appeals are brought.

The principles governing the determination of an appeal from a decision on a point of practice and procedure may be gathered from the joint judgment of Gibbs CJ, Aicken, Wilson and Brennan JJ in *Adam P Brown Male Fashions Pty Ltd v Philip Morris Inc* (1981) 148 CLR 170 at 176–7 (extracted below). Such a decision is discretionary in character.

19.8.2C   **Adam P Brown Male Fashions Pty Ltd v Philip Morris Inc**
(1981) 148 CLR 170
High Court of Australia

[Both the appellant (men's clothing) and the respondent (cigarettes) marketed their respective products using a 'red rooftop' design. The respondent sought an injunction and damages under the Trade Practices Act 1976 (Cth) and in respect of the tort of passing off. An undertaking was given by Brown not to sell any of the contentious products pending determination of the matter. It was later sought to vary the undertaking to allow sales of such products 'for the purposes of the conduct of a professional market and/or public opinion survey to be carried out in aid of the defence' which Smithers J of the Federal Court permitted. Philip Morris Inc appealed to the Full Court, which allowed the appeal. On further appeal to the High Court, the order of the Full Court was overturned. It was held that the Full Court was not justified in thinking Smithers J had failed to give adequate consideration to the question whether Brown should be released from its original undertaking. The High Court held that the Full Court had not been justified in the circumstances in assuming the responsibility of exercising for itself the discretion in a matter of practice and procedure.]

Gibbs CJ, Aickin, Wilson and Brennan JJ (at 176–7): The appellant Brown argues that their Honours CA Sweeney J and Northrop J approached the problem in the wrong way. They each dealt with it as if the decision of Smithers J was no more than a discretionary judgment to the review of which it was sufficient to apply the principles so well established by this Court in many cases, including *House v The King* (1936) 55 CLR 499, *Lovell v Lovell* (1950) 81 CLR 513 and *Mace v Murray* (1955) 92 CLR 370.

These principles are, of course, applicable. The decision was a discretionary judgment. But Brown's complaint is that in the application of the general principles their Honours failed to exercise that added restraint which an appellate court should exercise in reviewing a decision made in relation to a matter of practice and procedure. Had they done so, it is said, they would not have disturbed the decision.

On the other hand, the respondent Philip Morris submits that however stringent may be the tests governing the appellate review of a decision such as that in question here, the Full Court of the Federal Court was fully justified in setting aside the order of Smithers J because it was a decision that was not only infected by error but occasioned substantial injustice to it. The error was said to lie in the fact that his Honour failed to recognize the heavy onus resting on Brown to show cause why it should be released from the original undertaking. The learned judge was content to consider, as if he was considering *ab initio* an application for an interlocutory injunction, the effect of the proposed variation on the respective interests of the parties by reference to what he called the balance of convenience. In the course of this exercise he neglected to pay due regard to the interests of Philip Morris, thereby occasioning the injustice of which complaint is made.

There is no reason to doubt that the disputed decision of Smithers J concerned a matter of practice and procedure. The essence of such a matter is described in terms which are sufficient for present purposes in *Salmond on Jurisprudence* 10th ed (1947), p 476:

> Substantive law is concerned with the ends which the administration of justice seeks; procedural law deals with the means and instruments by which those ends are to be attained. The latter regulates the conduct and relations of courts and litigants in respect of the litigation itself; the [177] former determines their conduct and relations in respect of the matters litigated.

An interlocutory order for an injunction is a matter of practice and procedure. See *McHarg v Universal Stock Exchange Ltd* [1895] 2 QB 81, at p 82; *Minister for the Army v Parbury Henty and Co Pty Ltd* (1945) 70 CLR 459, at p 489; *White v White* [1947] VLR 434, at p 438.

Nor is there any serious dispute between the parties that appellate courts exercise particular caution in reviewing decisions pertaining to practice and procedure. Counsel for Brown urged that specific cumulative bars operate to guide appellate courts in the discharge of that task. Not only must there be error of principle, but the decision appealed from must work a substantial injustice to one of the parties. The opposing view is that such criteria are to be expressed disjunctively. Cases can be cited in support of both views: eg, on the one hand, *Niemann v Electronic Industries Ltd* [1978] VR 431, at p 440; on the other hand, *De Mestre v A D Hunter Pty Ltd* (1952) 77 WN (NSW) 143, at p 146. For ourselves, we believe it to be unnecessary and indeed unwise to lay down rigid and exhaustive criteria. The circumstances of different cases are infinitely various. We would merely repeat, with approval, the oft-cited statement of Sir Frederick Jordan in *In re the Will of F B Gilbert (dec)* (1946) 46 SR (NSW) 318, at 323:

> ... I am of opinion that, ... there is a material difference between an exercise of discretion on a point of practice or procedure and an exercise of discretion which determines substantive rights. In the former class of case, if a tight rein were not kept upon interference with the orders of Judges of first instance, the result would be disastrous to the proper administration of justice. The disposal of cases could be delayed interminably, and costs heaped up indefinitely, if a litigant with a long purse or a litigious disposition could, at will, in effect transfer all exercises of discretion in interlocutory applications from a Judge in Chambers to a Court of Appeal.

[See also *Brambles Holdings Ltd v Trade Practices Commission* (1979) 40 FLR 364 at 365; 28 ALR 191 at 193; *Dougherty v Chandler* (1946) 46 SR (NSW) 370 at 374. It is safe to say that the question of injustice flowing from the order appealed from will generally be a relevant and necessary consideration.]

Error of law

19.8.3   The application of wrong principles of law to the facts (including wrongful admission or rejection of evidence) may amount to an error of law. However, a finding of fact which is perverse, contrary to the weight of evidence, or displays demonstrably unsound reasoning, such that no reasonable person could have made, it is not an error of law, it is an error of fact: see 19.8.8C. But law, correctly stated, when applied to the facts found producing a conclusion which is not reasonably open, may amount to an error of law: *Azzopardi v Tasman UEB Industries Ltd* [1985] 4 NSWLR 139. It is necessary to show the outcome at trial would have been different had the correct principles been applied: *Norbis v Norbis* (1986) 161 CLR 513 at 518–19. There are no difficulties for an appeal court in substituting its decision on the law for an erroneous decision by a trial judge.

Other examples of an appeal based on a question of law include:

- denial of natural justice or procedural fairness: *Escobar v Spindaleri* (1986) 7 NSWLR 51 (where counsel refused an opportunity to address the court resulting in a denial of natural justice); see also *Stead v State Government Insurance Commission* (1986) 60 ALJR 662; *Mahon v Air New Zealand Ltd* [1984] AC 808; and

- a trial judge's failure to state adequate reasons for his or her decision. Reasons should be given to establish the basis for the decision so as not to nullify any right of appeal: *Housing Commission of New South Wales v Tatmar Pastoral Co Pty Ltd* [1983] 3 NSWLR 378; *Pettitt v Dunkley* [1971] 1 NSWLR 376.

For sample grounds of appeal based on a question of law, see 19.6.10E.

Judge wrongly exercised discretion

19.8.4   An appellate court will only interfere with the exercise of a discretion if the judge at first instance has acted on a wrong principle or upon incorrect facts, has allowed extraneous or irrelevant matters to guide or affect him or her, has wrongfully admitted or rejected evidence, has mistaken the facts, has failed to take into account some material consideration, or has not given enough weight to relevant matters. The appellant must show that the primary judge was clearly wrong. For a sample ground of appeal based on a discretionary order, see 19.6.10E.

Sholl J in *Russo v Russo* [1953] VLR 57 in considering the nature of a discretionary determination said (at 62):

What is a discretionary determination? … At least the concept involves a considerable latitude of individual choice of a conclusion — a right in the tribunal, adhering to certain general principles, and taking into account relevant factors, to decide nevertheless according to its individual opinion. It involves further that the tribunal, instead of merely ascertaining and declaring existing rights, formulates for the first time, and declares, new rights according to its own opinion — the only pre-existing right having been to have the tribunal's discretion exercised on the correct materials.

19.8.5C	**House v R**
	(1936) 55 CLR 499
	High Court of Australia

[House, who was bankrupt, admitted to having pawned property he had obtained on credit. House was sentenced to three months' imprisonment with hard labour. He appealed against the sentence to the High Court on the basis that it was excessive in the circumstances. The appeal was dismissed on the ground that the trial judge properly exercised the discretion.]

Dixon, Evatt, McTiernan JJ (at 504–5): But the judgment complained of, namely, sentence to a term of imprisonment, depends upon the exercise of a judicial discretion by the court imposing it. The manner in which an appeal against an exercise of discretion should be determined is governed by established principles. It is not enough that the judges composing [505] the appellate court consider that, if they had been in the position of the primary judge, they would have taken a different course. It must appear that some error has been made in exercising the discretion. If the judge acts upon a wrong principle, if he allows extraneous or irrelevant matters to guide or affect him, if he mistakes the facts, if he does not take into account some material consideration, then his determination should be reviewed and the appellate court may exercise its own discretion in substitution for his if it has the materials for doing so. It may not appear how the primary judge has reached the result embodied in his order, but, if upon the facts it is unreasonable or plainly unjust, the appellate court may infer that in some way there has been a failure properly to exercise the discretion which the law reposes in the court of first instance. In such a case, although the nature of the error may not be discoverable, the exercise of the discretion is reviewed on the ground that a substantial wrong has in fact occurred.

19.8.6C   **Australian Coal and Shale Employees' Federation v The Commonwealth**
(1953) 96 CLR 621
High Court of Australia

[The plaintiffs applied for a review of the taxation of a bill of costs brought under an order of Dixon J.]

Kitto J (at 627–8): I shall not repeat the references I made in *Lovell v Lovell* (1950) 81 CLR 513, at pp 532–534 to cases of the highest authority which appear to me to establish that the true principle limiting the manner in which appellate jurisdiction is exercised in respect of decisions involving discretionary judgment is that there is a strong presumption in favour of the correctness of the decision appealed from, and that that decision should therefore be affirmed unless the court of appeal is satisfied that it is clearly wrong. A degree of satisfaction sufficient to overcome the strength of the presumption may exist where there has been an error which consists in acting upon a wrong principle, or giving weight to extraneous or irrelevant matters, or failing to give weight or sufficient weight to relevant considerations, or making a mistake as to the facts. Again, the nature of the error may not be discoverable, but even so it is sufficient that the result is so unreasonable or plainly unjust that the appellate court may infer that there has been a failure properly to exercise the discretion which the law reposes in the court of first instance: *House v The King* (1936) 55 CLR 499, at pp 504, 505. So, too, in my opinion, the exercise of the jurisdiction to review a taxation of costs is subject to no narrower limitation than that which was stated by Bovill CJ and Brett J in *Hill v Peel* (1870) LR 5 CP 172: — 'A very wide discretion must necessarily be left to the taxing officer, which must be exercised by him after a careful consideration of the particular circumstances of each case; and where, after properly considering the matter, the master has arrived at a decision, it lies upon those who impeach his decision to satisfy the Court that he is wrong. Where a principle is involved, the Court will always entertain the question, and, if necessary, give directions to the master; but, where it is a question [628] of whether the master has exercised his discretion properly, or it is only a question as to the amount to be allowed, the Court is generally unwilling to interfere with the judgment of its officer, whose peculiar province it is to investigate and to judge of such matters, unless there are very strong grounds to shew that the officer is wrong in the judgment which he has formed' (1870) LR 5 CP, at pp 180, 181.

I take it to be true that the decision of the taxing officer as to *quantum* is generally speaking final, and that it must be a very exceptional case in which the Court will even listen to an application to review such a decision: *In the Estate of Ogilvie* [1910] P at 245. But the authorities as a whole (not omitting to notice *White v Altrincham UDC* [1936] 2 KB 138), do not establish as an absolute proposition that a judge will never review a taxing officer's decision on a question of *quantum* only.

19.8.7   Questions

1. With respect to an appeal based on the exercise of a discretion, will appellate courts be more willing to intervene concerning substantive rights as distinct from matters of practice and procedure? See *Adam P Brown Male Fashions Pty Ltd v Philip Morris Inc* (1981) 148 CLR 170 at 177: see **19.8.2C**.

2. Which of the following discretions affect substantive rights?
   (a) dismissal for want of prosecution;
   (b) dismissal for breaching a limitation period;
   (c) extension of time to serve; or
   (d) an adjournment.

3. Is the distinction between discretions affecting substantive versus procedural issues similar to the distinction between final and interlocutory orders?

Judge's findings of fact were wrong

19.8.8C	**Da Costa v Cockburn Salvage & Trading Pty Ltd**
	(1970) 124 CLR 192
	High Court of Australia

[Da Costa was employed by Cockburn Salvage & Trading Pty Ltd as a labourer for a building demolition. Da Costa was injured when unfastened roofing iron gave way. Da Costa sued his employer. The trial judge found both equally negligent. The plaintiff appealed, and the defendant cross-appealed to the Full Court of the Supreme Court of Western Australia. The appeal was dismissed and the cross-appeal allowed. The further appeal to the High Court was allowed, where the verdict and judgment of the trial judge was restored.]

Windeyer J (at 201–2, 206–10, 214): Lord Denning once said, 'we must not condemn as negligence that which is only a misadventure': *Roe v Minister of Health* [1954] 2 QB 66, at p 87. If I had had to try this case at first instance, I would have reminded myself of that; and, had I found the facts as they are now put before us, I feel fairly sure that my decision would have been in favour of the defendant. But I was not the trial judge. Nevile J was. And, strictly, the question for us in this Court is not was his conclusion right. It is, was the Full Court right in saying that it was wrong, and in setting his judgment aside?

An appeal has been described by the Privy Council as 'the formal proceeding by which an unsuccessful party seeks to have the formal order of a court set aside or varied in his favour by an appellate court': *Commonwealth of Australia v Bank of New South Wales* [1950] AC 235, at p 294; (1949) 79 CLR 497, at p 625. Lord Westbury has said in 1864 that 'an appeal is [202] the right of entering a superior court, and invoking its aid and interposition to redress the error of the court below': *Attorney-General v Sillem* (1864) 10 HLC 704, at p 724 (11 ER 1200, at p 1209). Appeals are creatures of statute. They were not known to common law as distinct from Chancery procedure: *Grierson v The King* (1938) 60 CLR 431, at p 436. The common law process to correct a mistake of law made by a judge at *nisi prius* was writ of error. After attaints had disappeared there was, practically speaking, no process to remedy mistakes of fact by a jury until the advent of new trials in the second half of the seventeenth century. Appeal being a remedy given by statute, it is necessary to observe what powers are conferred upon the appeal court by the relevant statute, for all such courts are not in the same position. And the word 'appeal' has itself more than one sense for modern law: eg, *Ex parte Australian Sporting Club Ltd; Re Dash* (1947) 47 SR (NSW) 283. The origin of this Court's jurisdiction to hear appeals from the Supreme Court of the States is s 73 of the Constitution. The manner of its exercise is regulated by the *Judiciary Act* 1903–1959 (Cth), ss 36 and 37. The latter provides that 'The High Court in the exercise of its appellate jurisdiction may affirm reverse or modify the judgment appealed from, and may give such judgment as ought to have been given in the first instance ...'. That, as I understand it, involves our considering the judgment of the learned trial judge in this case, not so much to determine whether we would have come to the same conclusion on the facts, but rather to determine whether or not the Full Court should have disturbed it. ...

[206] The case, as I see it, thus raises again what this Court has called 'the everrecurring question how far a court of appeal is justified in going in reviewing a finding of fact made on oral evidence': *Riebe v Riebe* (1957) 98 CLR 212, at p 222. A brief formulation by this Court of the answer to that question is as follows:

> On an appeal from a judge of fact it is the duty of an appellate court to examine the evidence itself, due regard being had in weighing that evidence to any opinion formed by the trial judge of the credibility of the witnesses and to those advantages he derives from the general atmosphere of the trial: *Committee of Direction of Fruit Marketing v Spence* (1953) 27 ALJ 427, at p 428.

There are more elaborate statements of the same principle in many cases which are collected and analyzed in the judgment of Dixon CJ and Kitto J in *Paterson v Paterson* (1953) 89 CLR 212, at pp 219–24. When the decision of a judge sitting without a jury is open to appeal on both [207] law and fact, an appellate court must have regard to the evidence, and its effect so far as the written transcript reveals it. Lord Halsbury said in *Riekmann v Thierry* (1896) 14 RPC 105, at p 116 — in a passage quoted by Isaacs J in *Dearman v Dearman* (1908) 7 CLR 549, at p 560, and more recently by Lord Reid in *Benmax v Austin Motor Co Ltd* [1955] AC 370, at p 376 — that on an appeal there is no presumption that the judgment in the court below is right. But ambiguity lurks there in the word 'presumption'. For Lord Esher MR had said sixty years before that where a case came before the Court of Appeal on appeal from the decision of a judge without a jury the Court would presume that the judge's decision on the facts was right and would not disturb his judgment unless the appellant satisfactorily made out that it was wrong: *Colonial Securities Trust Co Ltd v Massey* [1896] 1 QB 38. That case is cited in *Halsbury's Laws of England*, 3rd ed, vol 30, p 471, for a statement that 'the presumption is that the decision appealed against is right'. In the article, now in *The Law Quarterly Review*, vol 71, p 402 — to which Lord Simonds acknowledged his indebtedness in the *Benmax Case* [1955] AC 370 — Professor Goodhart, expressly preferring the word 'presupposition' to 'presumption', said that it had become accepted doctrine that 'the appellant, in seeking for the reversal of the judgment below, must establish his case, and that there is a presupposition that the trial judge was correct in his conclusion'. It has been said many times that the decision of a judge of fact ought not to be set aside on appeal unless the appellate court, duly considering the advantages the judge had had in hearing the evidence, is satisfied that his conclusion was wrong. In *Powell v Streatham Manor Nursing Home* [1935] AC 243, at p 250, Lord Sankey said it must be 'plainly wrong'. There have been differences in emphasis in judicial affirmations of this doctrine. At one extreme are the statements that the judge of the facts must have been 'plainly wrong' or 'clearly wrong' before his judgment will be set aside. At the other end is Lord Cave's insistence that it is 'the duty of the Court of Appeal to make up its own mind, not disregarding the judgment appealed from and giving special weight to that judgment in cases where the credibility of witnesses comes into question, but with full liberty to draw its own inference from the facts proved or admitted, and to decide accordingly': *Mersey Docks and Harbour Board v Procter* [1923] AC 253, at pp 258–9. Whatever words be used, I think that it must appear convincingly that the judge of fact came to a wrong conclusion before it is reversed. I consider [208] that the statement by the Chief Justice in *Whiteley Muir and Zwanenberg Ltd v Kerr* (1966) 39 ALJR 505 points the approach for this Court to take.

There is a technical distinction between a simple right of appeal and an appeal expressed to be by way of re-hearing: see *Attorney-General v Vernazza* [1960] AC 965, at pp 974–5, 978, 982. This was considered historically in its bearing on the jurisdiction of this Court, and the relevant authorities were collected, by Dixon J in *Victorian Stevedoring and General Contracting Co Pty Ltd and Meakes v Dignan* (1931) 46 CLR 73, at pp 107–10. His Honour's observations there shew that, in the exercise of its appellate jurisdiction, this Court has full authority to decide whether a judgment of the court below ought or ought not to have been given on the evidence before it seen in the light of the law as it then stood. Such an appeal, on both fact and law, although limited to the material before the court below, may be conveniently called a re-hearing, provided it is not thought that the use of this term without statutory authority enlarges the powers of the court. But, strictly speaking, it may not be appropriate to call an appeal to this Court from the Supreme Court of a State a re-hearing, as Isaacs J pointed out in the course of his dissenting judgment in *Werribee Council v Kerr* (1928) 42 CLR 1, at pp 20–1.

I turn now to the position of the Full Court of the Supreme Court of Western Australia on an appeal from a judgment of a judge of that Court sitting without a jury. This, as I understand it, depends upon ss 58 and 59 of the *Supreme Court Act*, 1935–1967 (WA). The origin and history of these provisions in the form they had in 1957 appears from the judgment in *Riebe v Riebe* (1957) 98 CLR 212, at pp 217–21. It suffices here to say that, in the form these sections now have, s 58(1)(a) confers appellate jurisdiction upon the Full Court in any cause or matter tried or heard by a judge or before a judge and jury: and s 59(6) provides that in any cause or matter where there has been a trial by a judge sitting without a jury every application to set aside his verdict, finding or judgment is to be made in accordance with the relevant Rule of Court. The rule referred to appears to be O 58 r 1 which provides that all appeals shall be 'by way of re-hearing'. This does not mean that the appeal is a complete re-hearing as a new trial is. It means that the case is to be determined by the Full Court, its members considering for themselves the issues the trial judge had to determine and the effect of the evidence he heard as appearing in the record of the proceedings before [209] him, but applying the law as it is when the appeal is heard not as it was when the trial occurred: see *Attorney-General v Birmingham Tame and Rea District Drainage Board* [1912] AC 788, at pp 801–2, and *Attorney-General v Vernazza*, [1960] AC 965. Order 58 provides too that the Full Court shall have power to draw inferences of fact and to give any judgment and to make any order that ought to have been made. This is more or less standard form. It confers a wide power. But it does not I think curtail the recognition or respect that an appeal court should accord to the decision of a trial judge. That has been recognized in many cases, among them in the judgment of Jordan CJ in *Carberry v Gardiner* (1936) 36 SR (NSW) 559. Whether the express authority to draw inferences of fact be necessary may be doubted, for it would seem to be necessarily implicit in a power to hear appeals on a question of fact. Nevertheless it is a significant provision for it leads on to the matter discussed by the House of Lords in the *Benmax Case* [1955] AC 370.

I take one sentence from the judgment of Lord Reid in that case as a statement of the relevant principle. His Lordship said [1955] AC, at p 376:

> But in cases where there is no question of the credibility or reliability of any witness, and in cases where the point in dispute is the proper inference to be drawn from proved facts, an appeal court is generally in as good a position to evaluate the evidence as the trial judge, and ought not to shrink from that task, though it ought, of course, to give weight to his opinion.

The distinction thus made between primary facts and inferences of fact is a sound one; and its bearing upon the way in which an appeal court should approach its task has long been appreciated. For example in 1905, quite early in the history of this Court, Griffith CJ, in *Luke v Waite* (1905) 2 CLR 252, at p 265 said:

> It was pressed upon us that this Court ought not to disturb the conclusions of the Court appealed from on a mere question of fact. This is, no doubt, the general rule, but it has no application when, as in this case, there is no conflict of testimony, and the only question of fact is as to the effect of the facts proved in raising further inferences of fact: *Thurburn v Steward* (1871) LR 3 PC 478.

More recent recognitions of this in this Court, in addition to *Paterson v Paterson* (1953) 89 CLR 212 and cases there collected, may be found in the judgments in *Jones v Capaldi* (1956) 98 CLR 615; *Mann v Mann* (1957) 97 CLR 433. But this [210] doctrine ought not, I consider, to be taken by judges in courts of appeal as a grant of an uninhibited liberty to review all conclusions of ultimate fact of a judge of first instance. An appeal court is, it is said, in the circumstances envisaged in as good a position to evaluate the evidence as the trial judge. This does not necessarily mean that its members are in a better position to do so than he was. Moreover it is a rule easier to state than to apply: and in *Salmond on Torts*, 14th ed (1965), p 318, it is said of the *Benmax Case* [1955] AC 370 that:

> While it is useful to have such clear and authoritative guidance, it may perhaps be regretted that the law should have been laid down in such very wide terms. The reports contain many cases in which judges of the greatest eminence have differed as to the evaluation of

admitted facts and if appellate tribunals are to make full use of the powers given to them by *Benmax v Austin Motor Co Ltd* the uncertainty of the law will greatly increase.

That is a salutary warning. ...

[214] In short, in a case of this kind, the primary facts not being in question, I would treat the decision of the trial judge as the equivalent in all respects of the verdict of a jury, unless from his reasons it appeared that he had in some way misdirected himself. It seems to me that — adopting the words of Lord Esher, then Brett J, in *Bridges v North London Railway Company* (1874) LR 7 HL 213, at p 235 concerning the verdict of a jury — the question in the end is still whether the finding is 'such as reasonable and fair men might not unfairly arrive at'. I expect that some will say that this view is a departure from orthodoxy as now declared, and that I am obdurate in heresy. Some may say too that I evade the duty of a member of a court of appeal; for in *London Bank of Australia Ltd v Kendall* (1920) 28 CLR 401, at p 407, Isaacs and Rich JJ, holding that the finding of a judge should not be treated as equivalent to the verdict of a jury, said:

> Where the law says that the court, and not a jury, is to determine the facts, and also says that an appellate court can be asked to reconsider them, and therefore should reconsider them, it is the duty of the appellate tribunal (and it is the statutory right of the litigant who invokes it to require of it the performance of that duty) to determine for itself the true effect of the evidence so far as the circumstances enable it to deal with the evidence as it appeared in the court of first instance.

19.8.9C   Edwards v Noble
(1971) 125 CLR 296
High Court of Australia

[One evening Edwards' car collided with Noble's motorcycle which was stationary on the road. The trial judge did not find Edwards negligent. The Full Court of the Supreme Court of South Australia set aside the judgment and found Edwards one-third liable. In allowing Edwards' appeal, the High Court held that the trial judge's conclusion was one that was open to him on the facts. His verdict and judgment should not have been set aside by the Full Court.]

Barwick CJ (at 303–4): Here as I have said, the primary judge is not shown to have made any error of law or to have misapprehended or failed to take account of any material fact. It was not suggested either in argument or in the reasons for judgment by any of the members of the Full Court that his finding of no causative negligence was so unreasonably erroneous that it must have sprung from some unexpressed error of law. It is therefore appropriate to consider the principles which an appellate court ought to observe in considering whether or not to disturb a finding of fact untainted by error of law or misapprehension or oversight of fact ...

I do not understand anything said in the reported cases and in particular in such cases as *Powell v Streatham Manor Nursing Home* [1935] AC 243 and in *Benmax v Austin Motor Co Ltd* [1955] AC 370 to deny the [304] proposition that an appellant to succeed in an appeal against a finding of fact made by a judge sitting alone must convince the appellate court that the primary judge was wrong in his conclusion. That the appeal may be by way of re-hearing does not, in my opinion, really bear on this question. The consequence of that description of the appeal is that the appeal is one on fact as well as on law and that the appellate court in deciding it may apply the law as it may then exist: further, where additional evidence has been received it may do so in the light of that evidence along with what had been adduced before the court from which the appeal is brought. A rehearing is not however a retrial of the issues. The question is not whether the appellate court can substitute its view of the facts which, of course, it is empowered to do: but whether it should do so. In any appeal against a finding of fact, whether or not by way of rehearing, however much the appellate court may be in an equal position with the trial judge as to the drawing of inferences, in my opinion, the appellate court ought not to reverse the finding of fact unless it is convinced that it is wrong. If that finding is a view reasonably open on the evidence, it is not enough in my opinion to warrant its reversal that the appellate court would not have been prepared on that evidence to make the same finding. Merely differing views do not establish that either view is wrong. But in deciding that its own view is right and that of the primary judge wrong, the nature of the 'fact' found by the primary judge is a matter for consideration. Many of the 'facts' within the province of the jury involved elements of judgment, some evaluative aspects akin to an exercise of discretion. Perhaps the 'fact' of negligence or no negligence is of this kind. Others of such facts are mere inferences from other facts or combinations of facts, though even in that case there is an element of judgment in the decision to draw or not to draw an inference or to prefer one where more than one inference is reasonably open. But, in any case, the appellate court in my opinion is not bound to reverse a primary judge's finding of fact merely because it held a different opinion to that of the primary judge. Where the members of the appellate court are themselves not of a unanimous view, there would seem to be good reason to doubt the propriety of reversing the primary judge if his finding was reasonably open on the material before him.

Walsh J (at 318): It may be said, in my opinion, that in whatever form of words the principle is expressed, it requires, even in a case in which the credibility of witnesses is not involved and in which the contest is as to the inference or conclusion that should be drawn from a set of primary facts, that if a choice has to be made between two conclusions both of which are open on the evidence and which are fairly evenly balanced, then the decision of the trial judge should stand. The appellate court should not deal with the case as if it were trying it at first instance. But, as has often been stated on high authority, the court has a duty to make up its own mind. It will do this taking into account the judgment of the primary judge and recognizing that it ought not to be set aside merely because of a slight preference for a different view upon a question upon which two views are open and as to which there is no definite preponderance of one view over the other. Subject to that limitation and subject to the well-recognized limitations concerning conflicting testimony and the credibility of witnesses, the appellate court should give effect to its own conclusion.

Incorrect inferences drawn

19.8.10C	**Warren v Coombes**
	(1979) 142 CLR 531
	High Court of Australia

[Warren, a thirteen-year-old boy, was injured when his bicycle was hit by a car driven by Coombes. Warren sought damages in the Supreme Court of New South Wales for Coombes' alleged negligent driving. The trial judge did not find Coombes negligent, a conclusion which was upheld by the Court of Appeal. The High Court allowed the appeal and held the decision of the trial judge could not stand. Several inferences could properly be drawn from undisputed facts or facts found by the trial judge that Coombes had been negligent and that this had contributed to the accident; both parties had been negligent.]

Gibbs ACJ, Jacobs and Murphy JJ (at 551–3): There is in our respectful opinion no authority that entitles us to depart from the doctrine expounded in this Court in cases before and including *Paterson v Paterson* (1953) 89 CLR 212 and in the House of Lords in *Benmax v Austin Motor Co Ltd* [1955] AC 370. The balance of opinion in cases since *Edwards v Noble* inclines in favour of adherence to that doctrine. Shortly expressed, the established principles are, we think, that in general an appellate court is in as good a position as the trial judge to decide on the proper inference to be drawn from facts which are undisputed or which, having been disputed, are established by the findings of the trial judge. In deciding what is the proper inference to be drawn, the appellate court will give respect and weight to the conclusion of the trial judge, but, once having reached its own conclusion, will not shrink from giving effect to it. These principles, we venture to think, are not only sound in law, but beneficial in their operation.

With the very greatest respect for the opinion of Windeyer J, we can see no reason to favour the suggestion, which he himself [552] recognizes as heretical, that in a case of negligence, where the primary facts are not in question, the decision of the trial judge should be treated as the equivalent of the verdict of a jury. That suggestion has not found favour with any other member of this Court and we need say no more about it than that the traditional and practical reasons for the reluctance of an appellate court to interfere with the verdict of a jury do not exist where the judgment is that of a judge sitting alone; for one thing, the judge gives reasons, whereas the verdict of the jury is, as Lord Denning MR has said, 'as inscrutable as the sphinx': *Ward v James* [1966] 1 QB 273, at p 301. Again with the greatest respect, we can see no justification for holding that an appellate court, which, after having carefully considered the judgment of the trial judge, has decided that he was wrong in drawing inferences from established facts, should nevertheless uphold his erroneous decision. To perpetuate error which has been demonstrated would seem to us a complete denial of the purpose of the appellate process. The duty of the appellate court is to decide the case — the facts as well as the law — for itself. In so doing it must recognize the advantages enjoyed by the judge who conducted the trial. But if the judges of appeal consider that in the circumstances the trial judge was in no better position to decide the particular question than they are themselves, or if, after giving full weight to his decision, they consider that it was wrong, they must discharge their duty and give effect to their own judgment. Further there is, in our opinion, no reason in logic or policy to regard the question whether the facts found do or do not give rise to the inference that a party was negligent as one which should be treated as peculiarly within the province of the trial judge. On the contrary we should have thought that the trial judge can enjoy no significant advantage in deciding such a question. The only arguments that can be advanced in favour of the view that an appellate court should defer to the decision of the trial judge on such a question are that opinions on these matters very frequently differ, and that it is in the public interest that there should be finality in litigation. The fact that judges differ often and markedly as to what would in particular circumstances be expected of a reasonable man seems to us in itself to be a reason why no narrow view should be taken of the appellate function. The resolution of these questions by courts of appeal should lead ultimately not to uncertainty but to consistency and predictability, besides being more likely to result in the attainment of justice in individual cases. The interest of the community in the speedy termination of litigation might, no doubt, be an [553] argument in favour of the complete abolition of appeals, although that would be far too high a price to pay merely for finality. However, if the law confers a right of appeal, the appeal should be a reality, not an illusion; if the judges of an appellate court hold the decision of the trial judge to be wrong, they should correct it.

19.8.11   Appellate courts can overturn jury findings and substitute their own findings if they think it just and there was only one decision open on the evidence.

In *Conrad v The Chermside Hospitals Board* [1982] Qd R 242 it was held that the Full Court of the Supreme Court of Queensland has power to set aside a finding of a jury against the party carrying the burden of proof and to substitute an alternative finding where the evidence is such that only one verdict could reasonably have been given on the evidence. The court also has power to draw inferences of fact not inconsistent with findings of the jury.

In *Baird v Magripilis* (1925) 37 CLR 321 at 334 Starke J commented:

Under the Judicature Rules, an appellate Court, where all the facts are before it, and it is satisfied that the evidence is such that only one possible verdict could reasonably be given, is not bound to order a new trial, but has jurisdiction to give any judgment and make any order which ought to have been made, notwithstanding the verdict of a jury: *Miller v Toulmin* (1886) 17 QBD 603; *Allcock v Hall* [1891] 1 QB 444; *Skeate v Slaters Ltd* [1914] 2 KB 429, at p 441; *Winterbotham, Gurney & Co v Sibthorp and Cox* [1918] 1 KB 625; *Clouston & Co v Corry* [1906] AC 122; *Paquin Ltd v Beauclerk* [1906] AC 148; *Everell v Griffiths* [1921] 1 AC 631; and cf *Toulmin v Millar* (1887) 12 App Cas 746. The *Rules of the Supreme Court* of Queensland are not precisely the same as the Judicature Rules (cf Order LXX rr 11 and 26). They allow 'any inferences of fact not inconsistent with the findings of the jury, if any.' It is not disputed that the Supreme Court has always exerted the same power under its Rules as the Court of Appeal has exerted under the *Judicature Act*. And I think this practice can be supported as a matter of law. The Court clearly has jurisdiction to set aside the verdict of a jury which is unreasonable or perverse, and if a finding is set aside and no longer exists, then it seems to me that the authority to draw inferences of fact under the Rules may be exercised (cf *United States v Motor Trucks Ltd* [1924] AC 196). But that authority will only be exercised where the evidence is such that only one possible verdict could reasonably be given upon the evidence: it is a strong power and must be exercised with considerable caution.

For a sample ground of appeal based on a question of fact see **19.6.10E**.

Judge's view taken of conflicting testimony

19.8.12   The appeal court has not seen the witnesses and will not interfere, unless the trial judgment is clearly wrong on grounds which do not depend merely on credibility, eg, glaring improbability, or inconsistency with established facts: *Da Costa v Cockburn Salvage & Trading Pty Ltd* (1970) 124 CLR 192 at 212–14 per Windeyer J.

19.8.13C	**Paterson v Paterson**
	(1953) 89 CLR 212
	High Court of Australia

[A wife was accused of adultery. The husband seized an unopened letter from his wife's lover. The issues were whether the trial judge, Barry J, was correct in allowing cross-examination of the respondent upon the contents of the letter she had not seen and the consequences upon Barry J's judgment if that cross-examination ought not to have been allowed. The High Court disallowed the cross-examination but thought it held no consequences for the trial judge's judgment. The appeal was dismissed.]

Dixon CJ and Kitto J (at 219–24): Soon after the *Judicature Act* came into operation a full exposition of the duty of a court of appeal in rehearing questions of fact was made by Baggallay JA. The case was *The Glannibanta* (1876) 1 PD 283, at pp 287–288, and the Court consisted of James LJ, Baggallay JA, and Lush J. After referring to the language of the Privy Council in admiralty cases to the effect that, if there was conflicting evidence and the judge, having had the opportunity of seeing the witnesses and observing their demeanour, had come on the balance of testimony to a clear and decisive conclusion, the Privy Council would not be disposed to reverse such a decision except in cases of extreme and overwhelming pressure, his Lordship said that they felt just as strongly the great weight that is due to the decision of a judge of first instance whenever in a conflict of testimony the demeanour and manner of the witnesses who have been seen and heard by him are material elements in the consideration of the truthfulness of their statements; but — (1695) *Skinner* 517 [90 ER 231] the parties are entitled to demand the decision of the court of appeal on questions of fact as well as of law; (1695) *Skinner*, at p 523 [90 ER, at p 235]; the court cannot excuse itself from weighing conflicting evidence and drawing its own inferences and conclusions, though it should bear in mind [220] that it has neither seen nor heard the witnesses and should make due allowance in that respect (1898) 1 Ch 704, at p 705; in the case in hand there was no reason to suppose that the judge at all proceeded upon the manner or demeanour of the witnesses. The decision below was reversed. In the same year in *Bigsby v Dickinson* (1876) 4 Ch D 24, at pp 28–29, James LJ, Baggallay and Bramwell JJA followed *The Glannibanta* (1876) 1 PD 283 and reversed a Vice-Chancellor's decision on facts in a case of nuisance. Their Lordships emphasized that an appeal on questions of fact existed. Then came the often cited case of *Coghlan v Cumberland* (1898) 1 Ch 704, at p 705. Lindley MR sitting with Rigby and Collins LJJ said in substance that the court of appeal must (1) rehear and reconsider the materials, (2) make up its own mind taking the judgment of the primary judge into account, (3) be guided by his impression when the question which witness is to be believed turns on demeanour, (4) be warranted in differing even on credibility when other circumstances show whether the evidence is credible or not. It will be seen that so far the tendency of the decisions was to formulate and concede the restrictive considerations or rules but, at the same time, to emphasize and act on the power to review findings of fact. This tendency may be seen in *Montgomerie & Co Ltd v Wallace James* [1904] AC 73. The House of Lords reversed concurrent findings of fact that there had been a user of a way by the public of forty years duration. Lord Halsbury LC proceeded on the ground that there was no question of truthfulness of testimony but the question was what were the proper inferences; [1934] AC, at p 75. Lord Shand conceded the importance to be attached to the primary judge's opportunity of seeing the witnesses and to the fact of the finding being unanimously sustained, but said that the case was a special one; [1904] AC, at p 79. Lord Davey dealt with both topics extensively in reasons which should be read though this is not the place to set them out; [1904] AC, at p 83. Lord Lindley said that there was no rule preventing the reversal of concurrent findings; [1904] AC, at p 92. The earliest occasion on which this Court dealt with the matter was probably in *Dearman v Dearman* (1908) 7 CLR 549. The Court restored the decision of a primary judge who refused to act on the evidence of persons who said they were eyewitnesses of adultery. The position of a court of appeal was examined at length by Isaacs J (1908) 7 CLR, at p 561. Four years later in *Khoo Sit Hoh v Lim Thean Tong* [1912] AC 323, at p 325 Lord Robson for the Judicial Committee restated the [221] considerations. The substance of what his Lordship said was that (1) the court of appeal should be influenced by the opinion of the primary judge because he can estimate the intelligence position and character of the witnesses; (2) it should remember that many points are elucidated at the trial which may be represented ambiguously or imperfectly by the notes and the elucidation may be through counsel; (3) but it may turn out (a) that the judge has failed to take something into account, or (b) that he has given credence to evidence afterwards shown to be self-inconsistent or contrary to indisputable fact; (4) except in rare cases such as those which are capable of being dealt with wholly by argument a court of appeal will hesitate to interfere. In the same year in this Court in *Craine v Australian Deposit & Mortgage Bank Ltd* (1912) 15 CLR 389, Griffith CJ and Isaacs J reversed a finding by Madden CJ as to the date when a fence was erected, basing themselves on the authority of Lord Robson [1912] AC, at p 325. Barton J dissented, placing his dissent on the authority of Isaacs J in *Dearman v Dearman* (1908) 7 CLR, at p 561. An interesting contribution to the topic was made in *MacBean v Trustees Executors & Agency Co Ltd* (1916) VLR 425, at pp 441–3 by Cussen J, who (a) commented on the judicial tendency to distinguish between the findings of judges and those of juries (b) pointed out that in order LVIII, r 1, of the then Rules of the Supreme Court of Victoria the words 'by way of re-hearing' were not reproduced and that the two classes of findings were assimilated, and (c) depreciated the court of appeal acting upon its own opinion upon a question of *quantum*. Next an example occurred of the connection which may exist between logical inference from observed facts and the impression created by witnesses. In *Perpetual Executors & Trustees Association of Australia Ltd v Wright* (1917) 23 LR 185, this Court refused to disturb a finding that a document of an unusual nature was genuine because, although made on a comparison of handwriting, the demeanour and credibility of a witness who said that he had found the document must have entered into the question. The principles in question and the differences that exist between primary and appellate courts were discussed again by Barton ACJ (1917) 23 CLR, at pp 190–1, by Isaacs, Gavan, Duffy and Rich JJ (1917) 23 CLR, at p 195. Shortly afterwards in *Scott v Pauly* (1917) 24 CLR 274, where a decision of the Supreme Court upsetting the finding of the primary judge (Northmore J) was affirmed, Isaacs J took occasion to discuss the authorities and their effect (1917) 24 CLR, at pp 278–81. [222] Then once more the distinction was emphasised by the Judicial Committee between cases where the result depends upon a view taken of conflicting testimony and cases where it depends upon inferences from uncontroverted facts: *Dominion Trust Co v New York Life Insurance Co* [1919] AC 254. In *Mersey Docks & Harbour Board v Procter* [1923] AC 253, at pp 258–9, Viscount Cave referred again to the subject and said that it was the duty of a court of appeal to make up its own mind, not disregarding the judgment appealed from and giving special weight to that judgment in cases where the credibility of witnesses comes in question but with full liberty to draw its own inferences from the facts proved or admitted. The distinction between inferences from fixed facts and findings based on testimony frequently recurs. In *Cooper v General Accident, Fire,*

& *Life Assurance Corporation Ltd* (1922) 128 LT 481 Lord Cave said: 'The question is, not what are the facts, but what is the proper inference to be drawn from the facts proved, and upon that point, as has been often said, the appellate tribunal is not less competent to judge than the judge who actually hears the case'; (1922) 128 LT, at p 483. In *SS Hontestroom v SS Sagaporack* [1927] AC 37 Lord Sumner gave an important summary of the competing considerations. His Lordship said: 'Of course, there is jurisdiction to retry the case on the shorthand note ... None the less, not to have seen the witnesses puts appellate judges in a permanent position of disadvantage as against the trial judge, and, unless it can be shown that he has failed to use or has palpably misused his advantage, the higher Court ought not to take the responsibility of reversing conclusions so arrived at, merely on the result of their own comparisons and criticisms of the witnesses and of their own view of the probabilities of the case. The course of the trial and the whole substance of the judgment must be looked at, and the matter does not depend on the question whether a witness has been crossexamined to credit or has been pronounced by the judge in terms to be unworthy of it. If his estimate of the man forms any substantial part of his reasons for his judgment the trial judge's conclusions of fact should, as I understand the decisions, be let alone'; [1927] AC, at p 47. These cautions did not prevent this Court reversing Mann J on a pure question of fact depending on testimony in *Federal Commissioner of Taxation v Clarke* (1927) 40 CLR 246. Discussions of the principles will be found per Isaacs ACJ (1927) 40 CLR, at pp 262–6 and by Rich J [223] dissenting (1927) 40 CLR, at pp 292–3. In the same way in *Webb v Bloch* (1928) 41 CLR 331, Knox CJ (1928) 41 CLR, at p 356 and Isaacs J (1928) 41 CLR, at pp 359–60 reversed a finding of Starke J that there was an absence of malice in the publication of a libel by various persons called as witnesses before him. They did so on the ground that his finding was not based on credibility. Isaacs J referred to the existence of 'a constitutional and statutory duty upon this appellate Court to form its own independent opinion as to the proper construction of documents and the proper inferences from the evidentiary facts'; (1928) 41 CLR, at p 360. Some of these actual decisions may seem to impair the value in practice of the rules which govern the duty of the court of appeal in dealing with questions of fact, but from the very nature of such questions it is impossible for a report to reproduce the evidence which influenced the court except in outline and in many of the cases the strength of the considerations against the findings of the primary judges was very great. Any tendency to relax the rules was checked by the House of Lords in *Powell v Streatham Manor Nursing Home* [1935] AC 243, at pp 263–8. Lord Wright made the following points: 1. An appellant's counsel opens as he chooses. (It is to be hoped that in making this point his Lordship did more than justice to counsel and less than justice to appellate courts.) 2. There is an antinomy in a duty to re-hear and a restriction to recorded material. 3. Before a court of appeal upsets a finding into which credibility enters it should be convinced that the primary judge is wrong. 4. The court of appeal is not entitled to ignore findings based on credibility and to consider probabilities on the written material. 5. His Lordship repeats the questions put by Lord Sumner in *SS Hontestroom v SS Sagaporack* [1927] AC, at p 50. Finally Lord Wright discusses the modes of assessing the value of oral testimony. Another kind of finding was brought more decisively under the protection of the rules in *Owen v Sykes* [1936] 1 KB 192, where the court of appeal refused to review an award by Greaves LJ of 10,000 pounds for personal injuries and discussed the grounds on which an appellate court should interfere with an estimate of damages by a trial judge. In *Yuill v Yuill* [1945] P 15, at pp 20–22, Lord Greene MR restates the standards and refers to *Hvalfangerselskapet Polaris A/S v Unilever Ltd* (1933) 46 LIL Rep, 29 as an illustration of the jurisdiction of the court of appeal to set aside a finding based in part on credibility because on carefully checking the whole evidence by a critical examination the primary judge's impression on the subject of demeanour was [224] found to be mistaken. In *Watt* or *Thomas v Thomas* [1947] AC 484, Lord Thankerton described the principle as a simple one and stated it thus: 'I. Where a question of fact has been tried by a judge without a jury, and there is no question of misdirection of himself by the judge, an appellate court which is disposed to come to a different conclusion on the printed evidence, should not do so unless it is satisfied that any advantage enjoyed by the trial judge by reason of having seen and heard the witnesses, could not be sufficient to explain or justify the trial judge's conclusion; II. The appellate court may take the view that, without having seen or heard the witnesses, it is not in a position to come to any satisfactory conclusion on the printed evidence; III. The appellate court, either because the reasons given by the trial judge are not satisfactory, or because it unmistakably so appears from the evidence, may be satisfied that he has not taken proper advantage of his having seen and heard the witnesses, and the matter will then become at large for the appellate court. It is obvious that the value and importance of having seen and heard the witnesses will vary according to the class of case, and, it may be, the individual case in question. It will hardly be disputed that consistorial cases form a class in which it is generally most important to see and hear the witnesses, and particularly the spouses themselves'; [1947] AC, at pp 487–488. Lord Simonds said: 'I suppose that if ever there was a class of case, in which an overwhelming advantage lies with the judge who has the witnesses before him, it is in the arena of connubial infelicity and discord'; [1947] AC, at p 492.

When the rules, which are formulated in the foregoing cases with such variety of detailed expression but with such identity of substance, are applied to the present case they lead almost inevitably to the conclusion that this Court must abide by the finding of Barry J, that is unless it is vitiated by the erroneous admission of the evidence to which the respondent and corespondent objected. The learned judge's estimate of the respondent and co-respondent was of first importance. His assessment not only of the general credibility of the witnesses for the petitioner but of the reliability of their detailed observation could hardly but be decisive. These are matters in which his opinion could not be reversed by a court of appeal notwithstanding its undoubted jurisdiction to re-examine the whole case.

Inferences from uncontroverted facts

19.8.14 The appeal court is in as good a position as the trial judge to decide on the proper inference to be drawn from facts which are undisputed or which, having been disputed, are established by the findings of the trial judge: *Brunskill v Sovereign Marine* (1985) 62 ALR 53 at 56.

19.8.15C   **Brunskill v Sovereign Marine & General Insurance Co Ltd**
                          (1985) 62 ALR 53
                          High Court of Australia

[Brunskill insured his truck with Sovereign Marine. The truck was damaged in a collision. The policy contained an endorsement, which rendered it inoperative at the time the damage occurred. Brunskill's insurance broker Mr Wardrop gave evidence that the endorsement was deleted prior to the collision by agreement with an agent of Sovereign Marine, Mr Manicom. Brunskill succeeded at trial before Rogers J. The New South Wales Court of Appeal overturned that decision. The High Court allowed the appeal from the Court of Appeal as the trial judge's decision resulted from his view of conflicting testimony. The decision was consistent with established fact, not glaringly improbable, nor clearly wrong on grounds not dependent merely on credibility. There was no error shown.]

Gibbs CJ, Wilson, Brennan, Deane and Dawson JJ (at 56–7): The authorities have made clear the distinction which exists between an appeal on a question of fact which depends upon a view taken of conflicting testimony, and an appeal which depends on inferences from uncontroverted facts. In the former case, to use the well-known words of Lord Sumner in *SS Hontestroom v SS Sagaporack* [1927] AC 37 at p 47, which was cited in *Paterson v Paterson* (1953) 89 CLR 212 at 222: '... not to have seen the witnesses puts appellate judges in a permanent position of [57] disadvantage against the trial judge, and, unless it can be shown that he has failed to use or has palpably misused his advantage, the higher court ought not to take the responsibility of reversing conclusions so arrived at, merely on the result of their own comparisons and criticisms of the witnesses and of their own view of the probabilities of the case': see also *Warren v Coombes* (1979) 23 ALR 405 at 412; 142 CLR 531 at 537, and following.

Although Rogers J did not expressly say that his decision was based on the view which he had formed of Mr Wardrop's credibility, it sufficiently appears from the passage from his judgment which has been cited that the conclusion which he reached was so based. Samuels JA said that the assessment made by the learned trial judge of Mr Wardrop, as being neither forceful nor self-evidently competent, was merely advanced as an explanation why, after the event, Mr Wardrop failed to act consistently with the agreement to which he had deposed. It was no doubt correct to say that this explanation is not capable of supporting Mr Wardrop's credibility, but it does seem to have been advanced as a reason why the judge accepted Mr Wardrop as a witness worthy of belief, notwithstanding the events that had occurred after the date of the collision. Rogers J could have been satisfied that the arrangement to which Mr Wardrop had deposed was made only if his Honour had believed Mr Wardrop.

The question that then arises is whether the decision of the learned trial judge can be seen to be clearly wrong on grounds which do not depend merely on credibility; for example, on the ground that the evidence which was accepted was inconsistent with established facts or was glaringly improbable. The evidence given by Mr Wardrop, which the learned trial judge accepted, cannot be said to be inconsistent with facts incontrovertibly established by the evidence or to be glaringly improbable. Mr Wardrop's conduct can be explained as Rogers J explained it. It was not quite right to say, as Samuels JA said, that there were two antagonists in the evidentiary contest, since Mr Manicom's inability to recollect the conversation can be explained by the fact that no record of it appeared in the files, but if there had been a contest it could have been resolved by a decision whether or not the evidence of Mr Wardrop should be believed, and the learned trial judge disposed of the case by believing Mr Wardrop. His conclusion has not been shown to have been affected by error and should not have been disturbed. The appeal should be allowed.

19.8.16   In *Warren v Coombes* (1979) 142 CLR 531, it was observed that in deciding what is the proper inference to be drawn, the appellate court will give respect and weight to the conclusion of the trial judge, but, once having reached its own conclusion, will not shrink from giving effect to it.

Fresh evidence sought to be tendered on an appeal

19.8.17   State appellate courts have power to admit further evidence, in appeals by way of rehearing in the form of oral evidence, affidavit, or deposition as directed: ACT r 5052; Supreme Court Act 1970 (NSW) s 75A(7)–(9), NSW r 51.51; Supreme Court Act (NT) s 54; NT r 84.23; Qld r 766, PD No 2 of 2010; SA r 286(3); Supreme Court Civil Procedure Act 1932 (Tas) s 48; Vic r 64.22; WA O 65 r 4. The discretionary powers are used very sparingly and are limited to questions of fact (after all, the evidence should have been called at trial) and in some jurisdictions, special grounds are required. Regard is also had to the general undesirability of admitting further evidence, the essentially appellate function of the appeal court (*Doherty v Liverpool District Hospital* (1991) 22 NSWLR 284), and the public interest in finality of litigation: *Mulholland v Mitchell* [1971] AC 666. An appeal to the High Court is strict and not by way of rehearing, hence further evidence cannot be received: *Coal and Allied Operations Pty Ltd v Australian Industrial Relations Commission* (2000) 203 CLR 194. Gleeson CJ, Gaudron and Hayne JJ said at 202–3:

> [12] It is common and often convenient to describe an appeal to a court or tribunal whose function is simply to determine whether the decision in question was right or wrong on the evidence and the law as it stood when that decision was given as an appeal in the strict sense. An appeal to this court under s 73 of the Constitution is an appeal of that kind. In the case of an appeal in the strict sense, an appellate court or tribunal cannot receive further evidence and its powers are limited to setting aside the decision under appeal and, if it be appropriate, to substituting the decision that should have been made at first instance. [Footnotes omitted]

An appeal to the Federal Court is hybrid in the sense that it can receive additional evidence, provided the evidence does not relate to matters occurring after the judgment at first instance: FCR rr 33.29, 36.57; Federal Court of Australia Act 1976 s 27; *Petreski v Cargill* (1987) 18 FCR 68.

Further evidence arising after judgment: appeals by way of rehearing

19.8.18   The Rules of Court in all state jurisdictions, except South Australia and Western Australia where it is the practice, refer to further evidence arising after the date of judgment. The discretion to admit evidence of facts arising after the trial is broader than the pre-trial discretion mentioned above. Evidence of matters occurring before judgment relates to the question whether a new trial is appropriate: see 19.11.1.

Byrne J in 'Practice and Procedure', *Halsbury's Laws of Australia*, vol 20, [325–11965], suggests:

> It is not possible to lay down any precise formula by which the discretion to admit further evidence should be exercised. However, some indications as to the manner of exercise of discretion are:
>
> (1)   fresh evidence ought not to be admitted when it bears upon matters falling within the field or area of uncertainty, in which the trial judge's estimate has previously been made;
>
> (2)   it may be admitted if some basic assumptions, common to both sides, have clearly been falsified by subsequent events, particularly if this has happened by the act of the respondent; and
>
> (3)   it may be expected that courts will allow fresh evidence when to refuse it would affront common sense or a sense of justice.

In *Mulholland v Mitchell* [1971] AC 666 Lord Wilberforce, when referring to the admission of evidence of events after the trial, said (at 679–80):

> Negatively, fresh evidence ought not to be admitted when it bears on matters falling within the field or area of uncertainty, in which the trial judge's estimate has previously been made. Positively, it may be admitted if some basic assumptions, common to both sides, have clearly [680] been falsified by subsequent events, particularly if this has happened by the act of the defendant. Positively, too, it may be expected that courts will allow the fresh evidence when to refuse it would affront common sense, or a sense of justice. All these cases are only non-exhaustive indications; the application of them, and their like, must be left to the Court of Appeal. The exceptional character of cases in which fresh evidence is allowed is fully recognised by that court.

19.8.19   Note and questions

1. Further evidence may be received on an appeal from grant of an injunction, to determine whether the injunction is still necessary: see *The Attorney-General v Birmingham, Tame and Rea District Drainage Board* [1912] AC 788 at 801.

2. Are the rules concerning admission of fresh evidence consistent with the public policy that litigation is final? See *Brown v Dean* [1910] AC 373 at 374.

3. Would fresh evidence of the death of a plaintiff be admitted, where life expectancy was an issue in the case? See *Doherty v Liverpool District Hospital* (1991) 22 NSWLR 284, where the Supreme Court of New South Wales exercised its discretion so as not to receive evidence of the death of the plaintiff which would have had the effect of reducing damages.

4. Would fresh evidence relating to remarriage of a plaintiff be admitted, where the prospect of remarriage was an issue in the case? See *Sinclair v Graham* [1984] 2 NSWLR 253.

5. Would fresh evidence relating to the accuracy or otherwise of a medical prognosis be admitted? See *Radnedge v Government Insurance Office of NSW* (1987) 9 NSWLR 235.

19.8.20C   Clarke v Japan Machines (Australia) Pty Ltd
[1984] 1 Qd R 404
Supreme Court Queensland, Full Court

[Japan Machines supplied machinery to Clarke. Citicorp acquired title to the machinery and leased it to Clarke. Clarke's company supplied collateral security; namely, a mortgage over certain property. Clarke defaulted in lease repayments. Citicorp required Japan Machines to repurchase the equipment at a fixed price pursuant to an agreement. Citicorp then gave notice of exercise of power of sale of Clarke's mortgaged property. The chamber judge granted Clarke's company an interlocutory injunction restraining Japan Machines and Citicorp from exercising power of sale. On the appeal the appellants sought to present new evidence that prior to the grant of the injunction Clarke had transferred the business to a trustee company of which Clarke was a director, shareholder and primary beneficiary. The issue was whether this further evidence could be received on an appeal from an interlocutory matter.]

Thomas J (at 408–9): It was contended that the Clarkes were no longer carrying on the business when the injunction was granted, and that His Honour relied heavily on the Clarkes' interest in the continuance of that business as a reason for granting the injunction.

Order 70 r 10 of the Rules of the Supreme Court gives this Court 'full discretionary power to receive further evidence upon questions of fact'. The last sentence of the rule provides that upon an appeal from a judgment 'after ... hearing of a cause or matter upon the merits, such further evidence ... shall not be admitted except on special grounds'. The definition of 'cause' includes subsidiary proceedings such as proceedings for an interlocutory injunction. The question arises whether the hearing of this motion was 'on the merits'. The position was canvassed by Hunt J, in *Martin v Abbott Australasia Pty Ltd* [1981] 2 NSWLR 430 at 435–6, where His Honour construed a similar provision in New South Wales as referring to 'the hearing of any interlocutory matter in which both parties appeared and in which the issue between them in that interlocutory matter (whether of fact and/or law) was investigated by the relevant tribunal'. His Honour further said:

> There is no need for the issues between the parties in the proceedings as a whole to be investigated or determined for the hearing to be one 'On the merits'. The issue to be investigated or determined is that which arises between the parties in that particular interlocutory proceedings in question.

Counsel for the appellants did not suggest to the contrary. It follows that special grounds are needed before the evidence should be received.

The classic statement of what amounts to 'special grounds' for reception of further evidence upon an appeal was approved recently by Lord Bridge in *Langdale v Danby* [1982] 3 All ER 129 at 137–8. Three conditions must be fulfilled. 'First it must be shown that the evidence could not have been obtained with reasonable diligence for use at the trial; second, the evidence must be such that, if given, it would probably have an important influence on the result of the case, although it need not be decisive; third, the evidence must be such as is presumably to be believed, or in other words, it must be apparently credible, though it need not be incontrovertible.'

The evidence could not have been obtained by the appellants at the time of the original hearing. It is also credible, in as much as the respondents have conditionally filed affidavits in reply and swear that it is true. Thus the first and third criteria are established. There is less certainty as to the importance which His Honour attributed to this particular aspect of the case. Certainly it was not the decisive point. Its relevance appears to be confined to the exercise commonly known as [409] determining 'the balance of convenience'. Nevertheless it was mentioned at two stages in His Honour's judgment, and prima facie it was a fact of sufficient influence to make it desirable that the true position be understood in the determination of the injunction.

Accordingly, I think that the criteria are satisfied, and that it is proper that the evidence be received. Its effect in the ultimate decision will be considered later.

[**Campbell CJ** and **Andrews SPJ** agreed with **Thomas J**.]

New point arising after judgment: appeals by way of rehearing

19.8.21   Generally a new point cannot be raised on appeal unless expedient or in the interests of justice. In *Water Board v Moustakas* (1988) 180 CLR 491, 497 Mason CJ, Brennan and Dawson JJ observed:

> More than once it has been held by this Court that a point cannot be raised for the first time upon appeal when it could possibly have been met by calling evidence below. Where all the facts have been established beyond controversy or where the point is one of construction or of law, then a court of appeal may find it expedient and in the interests of justice to entertain the point, but otherwise the rule is strictly applied. [Authorities omitted].

See also *O'Brien v Komesaroff* (1982) 150 CLR 310 at 319 per Mason J; *Multicon Engineering Pty Ltd v Federal Airports Corporation* (1997) 47 NSWLR 631 at 645 per Mason P; and *Banque Commerciale SA, En Liquidation v Akhil Holdings Ltd* (1990) CLR 279 at 290 per Brennan J.

New points and objections arising before judgment

19.8.22E   **Appeals to the New South Wales Court of Appeal**
Bernard Gross QC
paper presented for the
Continuing Legal Education Department of the College of Law
23 October 1993, pp 17–19

A frequent source of appellate failure is that the point sought to be argued on appeal was not made or a relevant objection not made in the court below. To allow a party to raise in an appellate court a matter which was not litigated in the trial court not only undermines the respective functions of the trial and appellate courts and the policy of the law but also deprives the appellate court of the benefit of the views of the trial court: *Holcombe v Coulton* (NSWCA 22.12.1988 per McHugh JA).

Two bases for refusing to entertain a new question of law not taken at trial are that the point will involve the Court ordering a new trial (*Coulton v Holcombe* 162 CLR 1) or that the point might have been answered by evidence given at the trial: *Suttor v Gundowda Pty Ltd* (1950) 81 CLR 418, 438. A party can only raise a new point of law in the Court of Appeal if on the evidence before the Court below, the point was not curable by evidence: [18] *George Hudson Ltd v Australian Timber Workers Union* CLR 413, 426. In *MWSDB v Moustakas* (1988) 62 ALJR 209 the High Court confirmed that a point cannot be raised for the first time on appeal when it could possibly have been met by the other party calling evidence at the trial. However, the High Court accepted that where all the facts are established beyond any controversy or the point is one of construction or of law, a Court of Appeal may find it expedient and in the interests of justice to entertain the point. Indeed many cases hold that points not argued down below can be raised for the first time in the appellate Court where those points involve pure questions of law, or of construction of the terms of documents.

In *Hoover (Australia) Pty Ltd v Combatti* (1989) 18 NSWLR 235 the appellant succeeded on a ground which was not pressed before the trial judge, which was not mentioned in the original notice of appeal, nor alluded to (except obliquely) in the written submissions which preceded the hearing. The respondent complained that to allow the new ground of appeal was forbidden by principles governing procedural fairness in respect of issues raised for the first time on appeal. However the Court of Appeal allowed the ground of appeal to be relied on, for the question ultimately argued 'concerns the application of the law to agreed or uncontested facts' where the court was in as good a position as the trial judge to reach its conclusion. The Court protected the respondent against surprise by permitting supplementary written submissions to be filed and the appeal was then twice relisted for further oral submissions. The appellant then succeeded on the fresh legal point argued.

Some cases suggest that the making of concessions at trial may create an estoppels which precludes the appellant taking a contrary position on appeal by seeking to argue a ground not relied upon or pressed in the court below: *Randall v Tuxford* (1875) 9 SALR 1; *Costalos v Button* (1941) 16 SALR 192; *Helidon Spa Water Co Ltd v Campbell* (1900) 10 QLR 1; *Garfath v Garfath* (1959) 59 SR (NSW) 362. Further, the role played by an opponent in inducing or contributing to a particular error may be relevant on the question of whether a matter can be raised for the first time: [19] *Mapley v Radial Industries* (1982) 61 FLR 189; *Bright v Sampson & Duncan Enterprises Pty Ltd* [1985] 1 NSWLR 346.

The difficulty of getting leave to argue points not taken down below greatly increases if it is necessary before doing so, to obtain the leave of the Court on the hearing to amend the grounds of appeal. There is a great advantage in carefully drafting the grounds of appeal in the original notice of appeal, or at least seeking (by consent or otherwise) amendment of the notice of appeal long before the hearing of the appeal to include all necessary grounds of appeal, including grounds not relied on at trial, and thereby avoid a situation that prior to doing so it is necessary on the hearing of the appeal itself to get the leave of the Court to amend the notice of appeal. Nevertheless in *Clayton Robard Management Ltd v Siu* (1987) 6 ACLC 57 the Court of Appeal held that the principle that Courts should, subject to the question of prejudice to the other party, permit all necessary amendments to ensure that matters in dispute between parties are adjudicated according to law, is not confined to trial judges but applies to the Court of Appeal itself.

Excessive or insufficient assessment of damages

19.8.23 The appellate court will determine excessive or insufficient assessment of damages as a ground of appeal in the same way as if asked to interfere with the exercise of discretion by a trial judge: *Moran v McMahon* [1985] 3 NSWLR 700. See also **19.8.4**.

19.8.24C	**Gamser v The Nominal Defendant**
	(1977) 136 CLR 145; 13 ALR 387
	High Court of Australia

[Gamser was injured when struck by a negligently driven uninsured motor vehicle. The trial judge awarded $150,000 general damages and $10,000 agreed special damages; there was no allocation to the main heads of damage. The Court of Appeal reduced damages to $125,000. The appellant then suffered a seizure, which diminished his future earning capacity. The appellant having already appealed to the High Court, sought to add a new ground of appeal relating to the fact of the seizure. The High Court proceedings were adjourned pending relief from the Court of Appeal. The appellant appealed the refusal by the Court of Appeal to grant new relief. All appeals were heard together. The appeal concerning the Court of Appeal's reduction of damages was allowed.]

Aickin J (at 158–60): The critical question however is not whether the sum which the Court of Appeal arrived at is one which could be supported in the circumstances but whether any basis is shown for interfering with the award made by the trial judge. The occasion for the Court of Appeal to arrive at its own view as to the proper amount of damages arises only if the case is one in which it is proper to interfere because the verdict is 'out of all reason' or 'unreasonably disproportionate to the circumstances of the injury'. If it is thought proper for that purpose to consider one individual factor, and to quantify that, it is necessary that some explanation should be given as to how such quantification has been arrived at before one can confidently proceed to the next step of saying that the balance over and above the figure, eg, for economic loss, is one which could not be regarded as proper for the remaining components. In the present case this Court has the difficulty which arises from the fact that the sum of $25,000 is stated as a [159] maximum for economic loss without explanation as to how it is arrived at or what exactly has been classified as economic loss.

For myself I can see no rational basis upon which one could choose a figure of $25,000 as the maximum which 'could reasonably be justified' in respect of economic loss. The causes, the extent and the duration of economic loss to a man in the condition of this appellant are even more imponderable than such factors often are in physical injury cases. They are all in the future and to seek to quantify them separately as a total sum to cover all such losses at this stage in this case seems to me to be a difficult, if not an impossible, task. What is certain is that there is a substantial loss of earning capacity in the sense that prospects of promotion in his present job are reduced, and the range of alternative jobs which he could perform and which he might obtain is greatly diminished but no means of calculation is available.

The problems arising when a challenge is made to a trial judge's assessment of damages have been examined in this Court in two recent cases, *Precision Plastics Pty Ltd v Demir* (1975) 132 CLR 362 and *Wilson v Peisley* (1975) 50 ALJR 207. The judgments in those cases demonstrate the difficulties involved in the application of settled principles in this branch of the law to particular facts. I do not think that the present case depends on any matter where any difference of principle has arisen. It is sufficient to say that I regard the following observations of Barwick CJ in the latter case as apposite in the present case (1975) 50 ALJR, at p 209:

> The setting aside of an award of damages in a trial which has not been irregular or unfair, and where there is neither challenge to the findings of fact made by the trial judge nor any demonstrated misconception of the evidence should, in my opinion, be a most unusual event, to occur only in circumstances where the disproportion between injury and award of damages is so great as to make the award quite unreasonable, indeed outrageous, in the circumstances, whether by being too great or too small: and therefore of itself a demonstration of error present though otherwise undisclosed. The less ponderable the elements of the damages under consideration, the less likely will there be a case for setting aside an award by a judge who has not overlooked any significant fact at the end of a trial not blemished by error or irregularity.

In my opinion the proper approach to this case is to look at the total sum awarded as general damages and at all the circumstances, the pain and suffering, past, present and future, the [160] physical disabilities, the medical and psychological problems which are inevitable for the future, the effect on earning capacity and the kinds of additional costs which the appellant will necessarily incur, and to ask oneself whether the sum of $150,000 is 'out of all reason' or 'wholly disproportionate to the circumstances'. No doubt every case is in some sense 'special', but there is no question that here the injuries and disabilities are unusually severe. I do not myself think that the figure is wholly disproportionate to these circumstances and I do not think that any basis has been shown for that conclusion.

I am therefore of opinion that this appeal should be allowed, the order of the Court of Appeal set aside, and the order of the trial judge restored.

Order

Appeal No 148 of 1976 dismissed with costs. Appeal No 98 of 1975 allowed with costs. Order of the Supreme Court of New South Wales (Court of Appeal Division) set aside and in lieu thereof order that the appeal to that Court be dismissed with costs.

[Barwick CJ, Gibbs and Stephen JJ agreed with Aikin J.]

19.8.25 Questions

1. How excessive must an award of damages be in a trial free from error or irregularity before an appeal court will intervene? See *Wilson v Peisley* (1976) 50 ALJR 207.
2. Should minor errors, which can be corrected without disadvantage, be corrected?

Non-grounds

19.8.26 A ground to the effect that 'the learned trial judge misdirected himself or herself or the jury in law and/or in fact' is an insufficient ground of appeal: *Cataldo v Clark* [1936] St R Qd 283. As to an intervening superior court decision changing the law pending hearing of an appeal as a ground, see *Eggins v Brooms Head Bowling and Recreational Club Ltd* (1986) 5 NSWLR 521 (extract below).

19.8.27C   **Eggins v Brooms Head Bowling and Recreational Club Ltd**
(1986) 5 NSWLR 521
Court of Appeal (NSW)

[An unsuccessful party to an action sought to have an unfavourable verdict set aside on the basis that prior to hearing the appeal a superior court held that the previously accepted state of the law was invalid.]

Samuels JA (at 522-3): It is quite clear in my view that the decision in *Piening v Wanless* (1968) 117 CLR 498 disposes of this submission. The headnote in that case states the following holding, amongst others:

> A verdict given after a trial cannot be set aside and a new trial ordered merely because a decision binding upon the trial judge and upon which counsel presumably relied in determining the conduct of the case has been subsequently overruled.

McHugh JA has referred to particular dicta in the judgments which I need not repeat. But I think that it may be useful to point out that the decision in *Piening* addresses circumstances different from those considered in cases such as *Burchett v Kane* (1980) 2 NSWLR 266(n) and the others to which I referred in *Bright v Sampson and Duncan Enterprises Pty Ltd* (1985) 1 NSWLR 346 at 360–1. As the author of the judgment in question I add my own voice to that of McHugh JA in observing that holding (10) in the [523] headnote to the report of *Bright* is incorrect. I did not (at 357) adopt the submission, but merely referred to it.

I concur in the reasons expressed by McHugh JA.

McHugh JA (at 524–5): The issues at a trial are decided on the basis of the 'law' which applies to them at the date of the trial. If a party believes that the current state of the law is erroneous, he must object to its application to his case or be bound by it. If he fails to raise the point at the trial, he cannot be allowed to raise it on appeal because of the accident that he has lodged an appeal and that, before the hearing of the appeal, a superior court has decided that the law is different from what it was conceived to be at the date of the trial. If the unsuccessful party succeeds in obtaining a new trial for a reason unconnected with any change in the law, then he may apply to amend his pleadings, if necessary, so that the new trial can be governed by the changed state of the law. But in my opinion he cannot seek to have a verdict, based on an accepted state of law, set aside on the ground that the law is later held to be different from what the parties accepted it to be. No one suggests that, where appellate proceedings are concluded or no appeal has been lodged, a party is entitled to have a verdict set aside on the ground that the law is later declared to be different from what it was at the date of the trial or the appeal. The accident of filing an appeal cannot alter this situation. *Ex hypothesi* the unsuccessful party, who cannot point to an error in the trial conducted in accordance with an accepted state of the law, has no appeal. It would be extraordinary if an unsuccessful party who had filed an appeal could have a verdict set aside because of a subsequent change in the state of the law while a party who recognised that he had no right of appeal could not get a new trial because he had failed to lodge a notice of appeal.

As the courts have often pointed out, new trials are 'an enormous evil': *Scott v Scott* (1863) Sw & Tr 319 at 322; 164 ER 1298 at 1299; *Bonette v Woolworths Ltd* (1937) 37 SR (NSW) 142 at 156; 54 WN 57 at 60. In an era where solicitor and client costs greatly exceed that which is recoverable on a party and party taxation basis, a new trial means that substantial costs are always incurred which are irrecoverable even by the successful party. If a party suffers an 'injustice' by reason of the failure of his legal advisers to take a point, he must seek his remedy, if any, against his legal advisers and not by depriving the successful party of his verdict.

With great respect to the statement in *Mears v Coal and Allied Industries Ltd, Piening v Wanless* (1968) 117 CLR 498 decides that a litigant cannot obtain a new trial because of a change in the law after the trial unless he has [525] taken objection to the application of the old law at the trial. Barwick CJ said in that case (at 506):

> ... the remedy for the erroneous decision is by way of such a challenge and not, as the majority of the Supreme Court seems to have thought, in the prolongation of litigation by affording a litigant a second opportunity after the error has been put right in other proceedings by other litigants.

McTiernan and Kitto JJ agreed with the judgment of the Chief Justice. Menzies J said (at 509–10) that it was for counsel to determine whether or not he would challenge or accept a decision which stands in his way and having accepted it, his mistaken acceptance cannot be made the basis for setting aside any verdict which is returned by the jury upon the case submitted to them. Windeyer J said (at 511) that the proposition was quite remarkable 'if it means that the verdict of a jury on an issue of fact, submitted to them without objection by either side, is to be set aside because one party might have put his case differently from the way he chose to do'. It may be that, notwithstanding the statements in *Piening v Wanless*, in some very exceptional circumstances a change in the law might entitle a court to order a new trial although the point was not raised at the trial. But if any exception exists, it is not applicable here.

It was for the foregoing reasons that I joined in the order that the plaintiff's application for leave to amend the pleadings in the course of the appeal should be rejected.

Jury grounds

19.8.28   An appeal following a jury trial will arise with respect to either:

(a)   the verdict;
(b)   the judgment; or
(c)   both.

An appeal with respect to the judgment involves a question of law, that is: Did the court apply the wrong legal rule to the facts found by the jury? An appeal based on the verdict revolves around the contention that:

(a)   a trial irregularity led the jury into error (eg, misdirection to the jury, wrongful admission or rejection of evidence); or
(b)   the verdict was against the evidence or the weight of evidence.

In *Hocking v Bell* (1945) 71 CLR 430 Dixon J (at 499) said:

A distinction has always existed between cases on the one hand in which the verdict is vitiated by some legal error, such as a material misdirection or misreception of evidence, or was perverse in the sense that the jury disregarded a judge's direction and, on the other hand, cases where, on conflicting evidence, a verdict is found which is said to be against the weight of the evidence. In the former case, apart from the modern rule about substantial miscarriage, a new trial was granted *ex debito justitiae*. In the latter it was matter depending on a more general discretion.

19.8.29   Note and question

1.   A successful appeal based on any of the above jury grounds may result in a new trial: see **19.11.1–19.11.5**.
2.   What is the distinction between a verdict against the evidence and a verdict against the weight of evidence? See *Mount Bischoff Tin Mining Co Registered v Mount Bischoff Extended Tin Mining Co NL* (1931) 15 CLR 549 at 559.

PREPARING AN APPEAL

19.9.1E	**Appeals** The Honourable Mr Justice J A Dowsett Bar Practice Centre, Queensland, 1985

Preparation for the Appeal

'With the best will in the world, you will regularly find that your preparation is left to the last minute. This seems inevitable in the sort of profession that we have. Nonetheless, it is obvious that the earlier you attend to your preparation the better prepared you will be. Again, it is necessary that you identify the real issues. Your preparation time will probably be short, and you must use it as economically as possible. Hence you should not waste time on matters that are not really going to be in issue or which are not really relevant. If a point has not been contested below then it is probable that it will not be contested on appeal. Hence you should not spend a lot of time preparing an argument in respect of that point, although it may be that occasionally you will be caught out because your opponent makes an issue of something that was only faintly argued below. You must make a judgment as to the likelihood of this happening. Similarly, you should not waste time on points which are obvious, for example there is little point in citing authority for the proposition that a contract requires consideration. Again, points which appear not to require authority to Counsel are not always as obvious to judges. It is important that you acquire the ability to identify those points which are sufficiently obvious to require only their assertion and those which acquire authority to support them.

When looking at the authorities to support your principal propositions, remember that an appellate court will rightly consider itself to be the arbiter of the law. Hence, although references to text books or digests may be of some value at first instance, an appellate court is less inclined to look at those references and more inclined to look at the cases. There is little point, for example, in citing *Halsbury* to the High Court because the High Court will point out that *Halsbury* only really records the decisions of courts. Similarly, although in some areas the opinions of text book writers are thought to be of value, in general appellate courts will take the view that such opinions are nothing more than just that.

You must also identify the level of the appellate court in which you are to appear, and then choose your authorities appropriately. For example, the Full Court may well be interested in decisions of the Court of Appeal in England and of other state appellate courts. The High Court, on the other hand, is unlikely to be particularly interested in decisions other than its own or perhaps decisions of the House of Lords or Privy Council. Hence in preparing an appeal to the Full Court you might well make extensive reference to decisions in a variety of jurisdictions, but in conducting the same appeal in the High Court you may well limit your references to decisions of the ultimate courts of appeal in the various common law jurisdictions, for example the House of Lords or the High Court.

The above observations should not be taken as meaning that you should limit your researches to the decisions of the Australian and English courts. New Zealand decisions are often received with favour in Australia, as in some areas American decisions are also of value, as are some Canadian and Irish decisions. However, it is always important to estimate the value of the decision to your case. This involves an assessment of the authority of the court and the judge or judges comprising it at the time of the decision and the similarity or otherwise of the law which then prevailed to the law in issue in your appeal. For example, if you are referring to a 19th century decision in support of a point which relates to pleading and practice, it would be as well to ascertain whether or not the 'Judicature Act' system had been adopted at the time of the decision.

Finally, particularly in the early stages of your career, do not be afraid of writing out your argument on appeal in full. Indeed, many very successful appellate advocates in this State have adopted the practice of having their submissions typed out in full. By forcing yourself to express your submissions in a way in which you will express them in court you will be more able to assess firstly, their correctness as propositions of law and secondly, whether or not you are communicating them in an effective way.

Once you have written out your submissions, you should not be afraid to read them out aloud. This will give you an idea of how they sound, as you will pick up any errors or inconsistencies in grammar and also any terms that you may have misused or used loosely. You will be surprised at the number of errors you pick up by so reading the submissions that you propose to make.'

CONDUCTING AN APPEAL

19.10.1E

Appeals
M Oakes and A Ashe
Court Forms Precedents and Pleadings New South Wales
LexisNexis Butterworths, Sydney, looseleaf, vol 1, [960], [963]

Approaches to appellate presentation
[960] Sir Harry Gibbs has commented [(1986) 60 *ALJ* 496 'Appellate Advocacy'] that advocacy is an art or a skill not achieved by study or instruction. The purpose of this paragraph is merely to note the different approaches so that practitioners may consider them in selecting appellate advocates against the type of case. The approaches are:

The builder approach: This advocate carefully presents the evidence and law so as to build a more powerful case than that of the respondent. It changes the emphasis of the case from that perceived by the trial judge.

The destroyer approach: This advocate attacks the judgment at first instance head on in an attempt to leave the court wondering how the trial judge could ever have come to the conclusions that he did.

The flexible approach: [Sir Anthony Mason, 'The Role of the Advocate and Appellate Advocacy' (1984) 58 *ALJ* 537 at 541.] This advocate seeks to keep all issues fluid, until the court's attitude has begun to manifest itself during the hearing. The points favoured by the court are then taken up and emphasised. This approach was more favoured when appellate courts conducted hearings on the 'Socratic dialogue' [Sir Anthony Mason (1984) 58 *ALJ* 537 at 539] method, but is now less used since appellate courts have moved away from that approach ...

Common complaints of appellate judges
[963] As an aid on what to avoid, common complaints of appellate judges include:

(a)   the appellant failing to take advantage of the opening to encapsulate the case;

(b)   late written submissions;

(c)   written submissions not settled by senior counsel;

(d)   oral presentation completely departing from the written submissions;

(e)   case authorities not being read so as to elucidate the ratio decidendi of the case;

(f)   extracts from judgments being read without indicating whether the judge was in the majority or whether other members of the court expounded on the same point;

(g)   points of argument not being developed separately so that (for example) the argument wanders back and forth over duty, breach and damage without direction; and

(h)   the respondent's argument being commenced with an anti-climax (such as correction of some minor statement of the appellant's counsel) rather than advantage being taken of presenting the respondent's main point in a dramatic way. [See Sir Anthony Mason (1984) 58 ALJ at 542 for an illustration to the contrary.]

Counsel should assume that the court has read the appeal book and in particular the reasons for judgment of the trial judge (or the summing up as the case may be).

19.10.2E   **Appeals**

The Honourable Mr Justice J A Dowsett
Bar Practice Centre, Queensland 1985

Conduct of the Appeal

Most of the considerations relating to preparation of the notice of appeal and the summary of argument could be repeated here. Your presentation must aim at communicating the issues to the judges in the shortest possible time and also your submissions concerning those issues. You must strike a balance between spending a lot of time referring to the transcript so that the judges know what happened below on the one hand, and keeping your presentation as short as possible on the other. In some cases, extensive references to the record will be necessary. It is suggested that you try to make all the appropriate references at the one time. This avoids the judges going in and out of the appeal book at odd times throughout the hearing. This is obviously inconvenient to them. If you can have your page references in sequence and go to the appropriate references by page and line number so that they understand the parts of the evidence which you say are relevant, you can then proceed to develop your legal arguments without interrupting them by having to go back to the record, which is always an inconvenient and clumsy operation.

Although I have counselled you to write out your submissions in full, at least in your early years, do not fall into the trap of thinking that you will be able to read them out verbatim. As a method of presentation that would be unsatisfactory in any event, but given that you are going to be cross-examined with varying degrees of ferocity by the Court, you will find it impossible to keep to your argument. Hence your submissions will be largely based on what you have written but should not be read out from them.

You must be responsive to the judges. If a judge shows an interest in a particular area you must respond to that interest. Very often the interest will relate to a point that you wish to deal with at a later stage in your presentation. A judge will usually permit you to respond in that way to an enquiry and allow you to come to the point in your own time, however sometimes his opinion as to the importance of a particular point will be so firm that he will want you to go to that point immediately, because he is of the view that if you are right or wrong on that point you will win or lose, everything else being irrelevant. If a judge evidences such a strong interest in a particular point you should consider breaking from your prepared sequence to go to that point. If you deal with it successfully early, you may find the rest of your submission much easier. On the other hand, if you refuse to respond to his interest he may make the rest of the day quite difficult for you. It is important to answer questions from judges rather than try to avoid them. If the question is quite beyond the scope of your preparation (through your fault or the judge's) it is probably best to say so and offer your opinion as the answer rather than to pretend that you have fully researched the question but haven't got the authorities with you. If the appeal is likely to extend past a long break such as luncheon or overnight, see if it is possible to put the point off so that you can prepare it during the break and make your submissions afterwards.

Finally, as with everything else keep your submissions as simple as possible. Make the statements clear and precise, using language appropriate to the legal submissions. Do not make broad generalizations that cannot be supported either by the authorities or the evidence.

NEW TRIAL

19.11.1   Appellate courts have the power to grant a new trial, whether trial at first instance was before a jury or otherwise, where there has been a substantial wrong or miscarriage of justice: Federal Court of Australia Act 1976 (Cth) s 28(1)(f); Judiciary Act 1903 (Cth) s 36; Supreme Court Act 1970 (NSW) s 102; NSW r 51.53; Supreme Court Act (NT) s 56; Qld r 770; Supreme Court Act 1935 (SA) s 48; Supreme Court Civil Procedure Act 1932 (Tas) s 39; Supreme Court Act 1986 (Vic) s 10(1)(b); Vic r 64.23; Supreme Court Act 1935 (WA) s 59(1). Alternatively, in some jurisdictions the appellate court may determine the matter without recourse to a new trial: Supreme Court Act 1970 (NSW) ss 102, 105, 107; Supreme Court Act 1986 (Vic) s 14; Supreme Court Act 1935 (WA) s 59(5). Such an approach is not feasible where the issue turns on evidence not available to the appellate court, or turns on issues of credibility.

The appellate court may limit the nature of a new trial rather than let a new trial proceed generally. A new trial places an oppressive burden on a successful party. In *Dakhyl v Labauchere* [1908] 2 KB 325 at 325, Lord Loreburn lamented:

In all cases it is a most deplorable result, not to be entertained upon any but the most solid grounds, as the only means of redressing a clear miscarriage of justice.

Common grounds for a new trial are:

(a) some mistake or misdirection by the judge in summing up to the jury: eg, where a trial judge explains the law generally, but fails to explain to a jury how the law is applied to the facts: *Afford v Magee* (1952) 85 CLR 437 at 466; see also *Balenzuela v Degrail*, extracted below. The misdirection may be on a matter of law or fact: *Bright v Sampson and Duncan Enterprises Pty Ltd* (1985) 1 NSWLR 346;

(b) some fault of the jury: eg, a verdict against the weight of evidence: *Hocking v Bell* (1945) 71 CLR 430;

(c) misbehaviour by the jury resulting in an unfair trial. While evidence of jury deliberations is inadmissible (*David Syme & Co v Swinburne* (1910) 10 CLR 43), evidence of impropriety is admissible — eg, jurors communicating with witnesses: *Perdrian v Moore* (1888) 9 LR (NSW) 143, or non-jurors: *Trewartha v Confidence Extended Co (NL)* [1906] VLR 285;

(d) excessive or inadequate award of damages: *Australian Iron & Steel Ltd v Greenwood* (1962) 107 CLR 308 at 317;

(e) misconduct of counsel: *R v Birks* (1990) 19 NSWLR 677;

(f) perjury of witnesses: *McCann v Parsons* (1954) 93 CLR 418;

(g) surprise at trial;

(h) judgment obtained by fraud: *Boughen v Abel* [1987] 1 Qd R 138;

(i) discovery of fresh evidence: evidence freshly discovered of matters occurring before judgment at first instance can base an application for a new trial. In relation to fresh evidence a new trial will not be ordered, unless there has clearly been a miscarriage of justice. The fresh evidence must be likely to have produced a different result at trial and that failure to adduce the evidence at trial was not due to any lack of due diligence by the party seeking to rely on it;

(j) by reason of a judge's conduct: *Stead v State Government Insurance Commission* (1986) 60 ALJR 662 (denial of natural justice on the basis that counsel was not given proper opportunity to develop arguments on a critical issue); *Carryer v Kelly* (1969) 90 WN (PT 1) (NSW) 566 (refusal of an adjournment) (extremely limited); *Jones v National Coal Board* [1957] 2 QB 55 (failure to stay neutral); *R v Watson; Ex parte Armstrong* (1976) 136 CLR 248; *Vakauta v Kelly* (1989) 167 CLR 568 (reasonable apprehension of bias);

(k) wrongful rejection or admission of evidence: *Bray v Ford* [1896] AC 44, 49. Parties are entitled to have their cases dealt with on the basis the court or jury has considered only relevant and properly admissible evidence;

(l) erroneous exercise of a discretion;

(m) perverse verdicts against evidence, or the weight of evidence: *Hocking v Bell* (1947) 75 CLR 125; and

(n) raising points not taken at trial.

The affidavit material in support of the application for a new trial must establish the credibility of the evidence, its highly probative or decisive nature (see *CDJ v VAJ* (1998) 197 CLR 172) and how the evidence could not have been obtained with reasonable diligence for use at first instance: see *Sheddon v Patrick* (1869) LR 1 CL 470, 545. If successful, fresh evidence in this context will be dealt with by way of a new trial.

The following case, *Orr v Holmes* (1948) 76 CLR 632, deals with the rationale for a new trial.

19.11.2C　　　　　　　　**Orr v Holmes**
(1948) 76 CLR 632
High Court of Australia

[Orr claimed a share of a lottery prize, the ticket in which he alleged was purchased jointly with the defendant on 12 August. The defendant produced highly probable but inconclusive and incomplete evidence that the ticket could not have been issued before 13 August. The plaintiff succeeded before a jury. Publicity of the result gave rise to further evidence for the defendant, which in turn gave rise to a practical certainty the ticket could not have been issued on 12 August. The Full Court of the Supreme Court of Queensland ordered a new trial. The plaintiff appealed to the High Court, which allowed the appeal on the grounds that the evidence:

(a)　was available at trial had the defendant exercised reasonable diligence; and

(b)　went to the credibility of the plaintiff and did not give rise to a different complexion on the case nor a reversal of the former result.]

Dixon J (at 640–2): If a trial has been regularly conducted and the party against whom the verdict has passed cannot complain that evidence has been wrongly received or rejected or that there has been a misdirection or that he has not been fully heard or has been taken by surprise or that the result is not warranted by the evidence, the successful party is not to be deprived of the verdict he has obtained except to fulfil an imperative demand of justice. The discovery of fresh evidence makes no such demand upon justice unless it is almost certain that, if the evidence had been available and had been adduced, an opposite result would have been reached and unless no reasonable diligence upon the part of the defeated party would have enabled him to procure the evidence. In *Scott v Scott* (1863) 3 Sw & Tr 319, at pp 322, 326 (164 ER 1298, at pp 1299, 1300) the Judge Ordinary (Lord Penzance) observes upon the enormous evil that new trials are in themselves, though justice [641] sometimes demands them: 'No element in the administration of justice is so destructive of its efficiency as uncertainty; and no grievance more sorely felt by suitors than that which snatches success away at the moment of its accomplishment, and sets all abroad and in doubt again after one complete hearing and decision. Nothing shakes so much that confidence in the law which it is the first duty of all tribunals to uphold.' Afterwards his Lordship speaks of the practice at common law with reference to new trials because of the discovery of fresh evidence. 'It has never been the habit in Westminster Hall to grant new trials on the simple ground that the party could make the same case stronger by corroborating testimony (even though newly discovered) if another trial were allowed. And if it were otherwise, there are few cases that would not be tried a second time.' The rule stated in *Chitty's Practice* was that if new evidence discovered after the trial is such as to satisfy the court that if the party had had it at the trial he must have had a verdict, the court will grant a new trial on the payment of costs in order to do justice between the parties. Variations of phraseology occur in later cases but however it is expressed the sense of the rule remains that the new evidence must have so high a probative value with reference to an issue essential to the cause of action or defence as the case may be that it cannot reasonably be supposed that had the evidence been adduced the issue would not have been found for the party seeking the new trial. In *Brown v Dean* [1910] AC 373, at p 374, Lord Loreburn LC says: 'When a litigant has obtained a judgment in a court of justice ... he is by law entitled not to be deprived of that judgment without very solid grounds; and where (as in this case) the ground is the alleged discovery of new evidence, it must at least be such as is presumably to be believed, and if believed, would be conclusive.' Lord Shaw [1910] AC, at p 376 says that he cannot go the whole length of the proposition that it must be conclusive. 'It is possible to figure cases in which it might be so gravely material and so clearly relevant as to entitle the court to say that that material and relevant fact should have been before the jury in giving its decision.' In *Hip Foong Hong v Neotia & Co* [1918] AC 888, at p 894, Lord Buckmaster, speaking for the Judicial Committee, says: 'In all applications for a new trial the fundamental ground must be that there has been a miscarriage of justice. If no charge of fraud or surprise is brought forward, it is not sufficient to show that there was further evidence that could have been adduced to support the claim of the losing parties; the applicant must go [642] further and show that the evidence was of such a character that it would, so far as can be foreseen, have formed a determining factor in the result.' The language of Collins LJ in *Young v Kershaw* (1899) 81 LT 531, at p 532 is 'practically conclusive — that is, evidence of such a class as to render it probable almost beyond doubt that the verdict would be different.' That of *Williams* J in *Kennedy v Jones* (1887) 6 NZLR 81, at p 85 is that 'it ought to be clearly established that the effect of the suggested evidence would be not only to render it possible that a different conclusion might be arrived at, but that it would be the duty of the jury to come to a different conclusion.' The test proposed by Scrutton LJ in *Guest v Ibbotson* (1922) 126 LT 738, at p 740 is that the evidence is so material that its absence will cause or has caused a miscarriage of justice. In *R v Copestake; Ex parte Wilkinson* (1927) 1 KB, at p 477 his Lordship said that the Court of Appeal had clearly decided that the evidence must be of such weight, as if believed, would probably have an important influence on the result but had not gone so far as the full extent of Lord Loreburn's statement. This language was adopted by the Supreme Court of New South Wales in *Meredith v Innes* (1930) 31 SR (NSW) 104, at p 108. In *Preston v Green* (1944) 61 WN (NSW) 204, Jordan CJ no doubt has this in mind when, in framing the questions to be considered in determining whether a new trial should be directed, he expresses the two that are material to the strength of the evidence thus — (1) Is the new evidence prima facie likely to be believed? (2) If believed, would it be likely to be a determining or at least a very important factor in the result of the trial? In Queensland a like test has been framed: *Boyd v Boyd* [1940] QSR 331; *Stiffler v Stiffler* [1944] QSR 81.

No doubt some of the foregoing expressions are susceptible of a weaker application than others of them. But the evident purpose of all of them is to ensure that new trials will not be granted because of fresh evidence unless it places such a different complexion upon the case that a reversal of the former result ought certainly to ensue. The fact which the new evidence tends to prove, if it does not itself form part of the issue, must be well nigh decisive of the state of facts upon which the issue depends. The evidence must be so persuasive of the existence of the fact it tends to prove that a finding to the contrary, if it had been given, would, upon the materials before the court, appear to have been improbable if not unreasonable.

19.11.3C   **Balenzuela v De Gail**
(1959) 101 CLR 226; 66 ALR 283
High Court of Australia

[In an action for damages for personal injury arising out of the negligent driving of a motor vehicle, the place where the accident occurred was in question. Evidence tending to identify the location of the accident referred to by a witness was erroneously rejected.]

Dixon CJ (at 235–7): But whether it be the rule at common law or under the judicature system a much more important restraint must be observed upon the discretion of the court to refuse a new trial. The court, where the determination of questions of fact is not entrusted to it, cannot substitute its judgment for that of the jury in purporting to decide whether a substantial wrong or miscarriage has occurred. Care must be taken lest in exercising an authority to decide whether an error of law occurring at the trial is likely to have influenced the result, what is really done is to examine the evidence as if the court were forming a conclusion of fact for itself. The basal distinction between the court's duty and the function of the jury cannot be confused in this way. The question whether an error of law made at a trial calls for a new trial depends on definite considerations involving a legal criterion. Cases may be put on one side where, although there has been some error of law committed at the trial, whether in the judge's direction to the [236] jury or in his rulings as to the reception or rejection of evidence, the verdict may be sustainable because the successful party in any case is entitled as a matter of law to such a verdict or because had a contrary verdict been returned it must have been set aside. Apart from such cases it is enough if it appears to the court deciding an application for a new trial that an error of law has been made at the trial which may operate to do any of the following three things — (a) improperly to limit or enlarge the evidentiary materials by which it is not an unreasonable hypothesis to suppose the judgment of the jury might be affected, even if illogically; or (b) in the case of misdirection touching standards or criteria of liability, wrongly to expose the party to a hazard that is appreciable and not illusory of a verdict for or against him that otherwise might not have been found; or (c) in matters of burden of proof, of the legal need of corroboration or of other like incidents of the jury's consideration of the case, to provide an erroneous guidance which it is not unreasonable to regard as capable of contributing to the result. These categories are probably not exhaustive but it is enough if a case falls within one of them; if it does it is necessary to treat it as involving a substantial wrong or miscarriage. What has been said relates entirely to misdirection, the erroneous reception or rejection of evidence and other errors of law. As to erroneous dealing with facts, for present purposes it is enough to refer to what Cussen J says as to the distinction in *Holford's Case* (1909) VLR, at p 527. But where the error is of law and is one of the foregoing description, it is not for the court to proceed to inquire into the facts of the case and form a conclusion as to what the jury would or should have done had the trial proceeded entirely in conformity with law and without any misdirection or misreception or erroneous rejection of evidence. That is what the decision of the House of Lords in *Bray v Ford* [1896] AC 44 means. See per Lord Greene MR in *Braddock v Bevins* [1948] 1 KB 580, at pp 599, 600.

In the present case, as it seems to me, it would be contrary to principle to refuse a new trial on the ground that there was no substantial wrong or miscarriage. The basal fact is that material evidence was erroneously excluded from the consideration of the jury, evidence that touched the question upon which the case turned. It was something the party was entitled to lay before the jury for its consideration. It lies outside the province of the Court to inquire into the effect which the evidence if admitted would produce upon the Court if the Court were the tribunal of fact, and it lies outside the province of the Court to speculate on the effect [237] which it would have produced on the jury. It is enough that evidence definitely material to the determination of the case was excluded at the instance of the defendants. That leaves the unsuccessful plaintiff entitled to a new trial.

In my opinion the appeal should be allowed, the order of the Full Court of the Supreme Court should be discharged and in lieu thereof it should be ordered that a new trial be had between the parties.

Windeyer J (at 242–4): Since *Crease v Barrett* (1835) 1 C M & r 919 (149 ER 1353) it has been generally accepted that, notwithstanding earlier decisions to the contrary, if admissible evidence which might have influenced the jury be rejected, there must be a new trial; unless, of course, the case was one in which any verdict other than that found by the jury would be so unreasonable that it would be set aside. Except in circumstances such as those referred to in *Chitty's Archbold's Practice*, 12th ed (1866), p 1506, and apart from the modern rule under the judicature system about substantial miscarriage, to which I shall refer later, a court of appeal has no discretion to overlook an improper rejection of evidence. The consequences of an improper admission of evidence are, generally speaking, similar. But, in my view, the rule is there, if anything, less strict. This is because evidence may be inadmissible by reason of irrelevancy and because it relates only to some matter remote from and immaterial to any matter in issue. Its reception in such circumstances might be only an immaterial error; and a new trial could properly be refused if its reception could not reasonably be supposed to have affected the jury's verdict. But the position is, I consider, logically rather different if evidence which ought to have been admitted be rejected. Such evidence can never be irrelevant. It must *ex hypothesi* be material to some issue. The very reason why it should be received is that it might assist the jury in arriving at a verdict. Its rejection, therefore, necessarily deprives the jury of knowledge of some testimony which the party [243] tendering it was entitled to have them know. Subject to this distinction, which in some circumstances may make wrongful rejection an *a fortiori* case, the general principles stated in *Piddington v Bennett and Wood Pty Ltd* (1940) 63 CLR 533 by Dixon J (as he then was) (1940) 63 CLR, at p 554 and discussed by Evatt J (1940) 63 CLR, at pp 560–4 are as applicable to improper rejection as to improper reception, which was there under consideration

We were pressed with the view that a new trial is always a most 'deplorable result'. But whenever there has been a significant error in law it is a necessity of justice, to be deplored but not refused. No doubt it is probable that the jury were aware, at all events after the rejected questions had been asked, that the house in the photograph was the house of which Adams spoke. The learned Chief Justice of New South Wales seems to have thought this to be so, for he said: 'the shutting out of what I am satisfied must have been common knowledge, namely, that this house shown in ex B (a photograph) was the house where the dogs were sold, could not have such an influence on the result of the trial as to require this court now to order a new trial for the purpose of redressing an injustice'. If I could feel sure that the jury did know what the rejected evidence would have established I would agree. But I cannot be sure; I think we are not justified in speculating as to what influence the rejected evidence might have had with the jury had it been admitted. General statements that new trials should not be lightly granted have been frequently made and are frequently quoted. The most eloquent is perhaps that of Lord Penzance in *Scott v Scott* (1863) 3 Sw & Tr 319, at p 322 (164 ER 1298, at p 1299) and see *Dakhyl v Labouchere* (1908) 2 KB 325, at p 327 and *Turnbull & Co v Duval* (1902) AC 429, at p 436. But such statements ought not to be read apart from the context in which they were made, or as meaning that an appeal court has in every case a complete discretion to grant or refuse a new trial. A new trial cannot be refused just because the court thinks the jury's verdict right, any more than a new trial can now be granted merely because the court thinks the verdict wrong. There is a clear distinction between, on the one hand, applications for a new trial on the ground that the verdict was against the weight of evidence or because of discovery of fresh evidence or because the judge's summing-up was, in relation to the facts, insufficient, and, on the other hand, complaints of misdirection of law or wrongful rejection and reception of evidence. In the former cases a new trial is, within limits, a discretionary remedy to be [244] applied only if the court thinks there has been a miscarriage of justice. But in the latter cases there has been an error in law; and the court must assume that it has, or may have, resulted in a miscarriage of justice, for a party has a right to have his case tried according to law. The distinction between the two classes of cases is referred to in, among other places, passages in the judgments of the present Chief Justice in *Hocking v Bell* (1945) 71 CLR 430, at p 499; *Orr v Holmes* (1948) 76 CLR 632, at pp 640–2 and *Wollongong Corporation v Cowan* (1955) 93 CLR 435, at p 444. Motions for new trials became common after the seventeenth century as a means of redressing perverse, corrupt or altogether unreasonable verdicts of juries at *nisi prius*. They were at one stage readily granted if the trial judge reported his dissatisfaction with the verdict. The courts *in banc* at different periods exercised different degrees of discretion in allowing or refusing new trials. Where the ground alleged was error in law, a motion to a court *in banc* for a new trial was, as the Chief Justice has pointed out, a substitute for a writ of error upon a bill of exceptions for a *venire de novo*; and this tended at one time to restrict the court's discretion. But when the complaint was not of error of law but of the jury's verdict, the courts *in banc* seem to have allowed themselves a wide discretion to grant or refuse a new trial: *Blackstone Commentaries* Bk III c 24; *Wilkinson v Payne* (1791) 4 TR 468 (100 ER 1123).

I agree too with the Chief Justice that the common law principles obtaining in New South Wales and the rules under the judicature system are, in relation to new trials, not so far apart as might appear. To deprive a jury of knowledge of a material fact which could influence them in arriving at their verdict must, in my view, ordinarily be a 'substantial wrong' within the meaning of the rule under the judicature system. That rule does not empower a court of appeal to usurp the function of the jury. It may make it necessary, in jurisdictions where it operates, for an appellant to satisfy the court that rejected evidence might, if it had been admitted, have influenced the jury. But the field is not one in which questions of where the onus lies can often be decisive. In *Lakeman v Finlay* (1959) SR (NSW)5; 75 WN 479 the Supreme Court of New South Wales recently recognised that where there has been an error in law there is no such general discretion to refuse a new trial or any so pronounced presumption against granting one as was contended for here. I think the Supreme Court was right in that view and that [245] error in law in the conduct of a trial, whether it be by misdirection or in relation to the reception of evidence, if proper objection were taken at the time, prima facie furnishes a ground for a new trial *ex debito justitiae*.

It was also argued for the respondent that the plaintiff's case must fail because of contributory negligence. But the trial judge was right in refusing to direct a verdict on that ground.

Appeal allowed with costs. Set aside the order of the Full Court of the Supreme Court of New South Wales. In lieu thereof order that the appeal to that Court be allowed with costs, the verdict of the jury set aside and a new trial ordered. Costs of the first trial to abide the event.

19.11.4C   Council of the City of Greater Wollongong Corporation v Cowan
(1955) 93 CLR 435
High Court of Australia

[The Supreme Court of New South Wales granted a new trial upon the ground of the discovery of new evidence. The respondent was injured when she slipped on polished linoleum and fell after paying her rates at the Town Hall. The new evidence related to previous incidents and subsequent injuries and precautions which were taken to make the floor safe. The High Court allowed the appeal as the standard of cogency of the fresh evidence and its likely effect was not sufficient.]

Dixon CJ, Williams, Webb, Kitto, Taylor JJ (at 444–5): The law which governs the grant of new trials on the ground of the discovery of fresh evidence is not in doubt. It has been discussed in this Court in different aspects recently on three occasions. We dealt with it at length in an aspect which affects this case in *Orr v Holmes* (1948) 76 CLR 632. We also dealt with it in an aspect where it touches the issue of damages in *Commissioner for Government Tram & Omnibus Services v Vickery* (1952) 85 CLR 635 and in a very unusual aspect as it governs the presentation of a false claim, we dealt with it in *McCann v Parsons* (1954) 93 CLR 418.

If cases are put aside where a trial has miscarried through misdirection, misreception of evidence, wrongful rejection of evidence or other error and if cases of surprise, malpractice or fraud are put on one side, it is essential to give effect to the rule that the verdict, regularly obtained, must not be disturbed without some insistent demand of justice. The discovery of fresh evidence in such circumstances could rarely, if ever be a ground for a new trial unless certain well-known conditions are fulfilled. It must be reasonably clear that if the evidence had been available at the first trial and had been adduced, an opposite result would have been produced or, if it is not reasonably clear that it would have been produced, it must have been so highly likely as to make it unreasonable to suppose the contrary. Again, reasonable diligence must have been exercised to procure the evidence which the defeated party failed to adduce at the first trial.

In *Orr v Holmes* (1948) 76 CLR, at pp 640–642 there are collected a number of different expressions which have been judicially used at various times. Their result is then summed up in these words: — 'No doubt some of the foregoing expressions are susceptible of a weaker application than others of them. But the evident purpose of all of them is to ensure that new trials will not be granted because of fresh evidence unless [445] it places such a different complexion upon the case that a reversal of the former result ought certainly to ensue. The fact which the new evidence tends to prove, if it does not itself form part of the issue, must be well nigh decisive of the state of facts upon which the issue depends. The evidence must be so persuasive of the existence of the fact it tends to prove that a finding to the contrary, if it had been given, would, upon the materials before the court, appear to have been improbable if not unreasonable' (1948) 76 CLR, at p 642.

19.11.5   Note particularly that a new trial may be ordered even when not specifically sought, and a judgment may be given by the appeal court although a new trial was sought. Care should be taken when reading the cases to determine what relief was sought, by what procedure, and what relief was granted and why. For a discussion of the history of an application for a new trial, refer to *Musgrove v McDonald* (1905) 3 CLR 132 at 147–9.

STRIKING OUT, WANT OF PROSECUTION AND DISCONTINUANCE

19.12.1   The appellate court's inherent jurisdiction enables a notice of appeal to be struck out where there is no right of appeal, the grounds of appeal are frivolous or vexatious, amount to an abuse of process, or the notice of appeal is irregular, eg, out of time.

It is possible for an appeal to be dismissed for want of prosecution if acts required by the rules of court are not prosecuted with due diligence: HCR r 42.16; FCR rr 36.74, 36.75, 33.33; ACT rr 5191, 5603; Supreme Court Act 1970 (NSW) s 46; NT r 84.13; Qld r 775, PD No 2 of 2010; SA r 295(h) (summary dismissal); Tas r 665; Vic (inherent power) r 64.16 (abandoned); cf Tas r 675 (not abandoned). Examples include failure to settle the appeal book and failure to comply with an order for security for costs. In the remaining jurisdictions, the inherent jurisdiction of the court to regulate its own process allows an appeal to be dismissed for want of prosecution: *Moto v Faul* [1980] VR 26. Generally there must be gross delay: *Birkett v James* [1978] AC 297.

An appellant may discontinue an appeal wholly or in part by filing and serving a notice of discontinuance and paying the respondent's costs so incurred: HCR rr 41.12, 42.14, Form 25; FCR r 36.73(1), Form 126; ACT r 5171; NSW r 51.56; NT r 84.15; Qld r 762, Form 068 (dismissal by consent); SA r 287; Tas r 675; Vic rr 64.14, 64.15; WA O 65 r 17 (discontinuance notice, Form No 16). It is possible for an appellate court to order an appeal not be discontinued.

COSTS

19.13.1   Costs are in the discretion of the appellate court, though usually costs follow the event. The successful appellant will receive the costs of appeal, the costs below, including any intervening appeals. With respect to a new trial, the costs of the first trial follow the outcome of the new trial. In respect of the wide discretion to award costs see generally: Federal Court of Australia Act 1976 (Cth) s 43; Judiciary Act 1903 (Cth) s 26; HCR Ch 5; Supreme Court Act 1933 (ACT) s 23; ACT rr 1721, 5473; NSW r 42.1, NT r 63.03; Qld r 771 (assessed by registrar); Supreme Court Act 1935 (SA) s 40; SA r 263; Supreme Court Act 1986 (Vic) s 24; Vic r 64.24; WA O 65 r 17(4); *Malpas v Malpas* (1885) 11 VLR 670 at 710–11. The High Court sometimes makes it a condition of leave to appeal that the appellant pays the respondent's costs of the High Court appeal in any event. For a general discussion of costs, refer to **Chapter 20**.

19.13.2   Questions

1.   Will a successful party be refused costs where the appeal succeeds on a ground not raised at trial? See *Drew v Moubray* (1890) 16 VLR 484, where the point upon which the Full Court decided to overrule the decision of the primary judge had not been raised below, the appeal was allowed without costs.

2.   Should each party to an appeal pay their own costs where both contend the decision at first instance is in error?

SETTLING AN APPEAL

19.14.1   In all jurisdictions the parties to an appeal may by consent settle the appeal. For example, see HCR rr 8.04, 26.10.2; ACT r 5174; NSW rr 51.47, 51.48; NT r 59.06; Qld r 788; WA O 65 r 18. Elsewhere the parties may rely on the rules concerning discontinuance of an appeal when included as part of the compromise.

INDEMNITY CERTIFICATES

19.15.1   In some jurisdictions a respondent whose appeal succeeds on a question of law or fact may, at the appellate court's discretion pursuant to statute, receive a certificate entitling them to a small indemnity out of a statutory fund for costs incurred in defending the appeal, up to a predetermined statutory limit: Suitors' Fund Act 1951 (NSW) s 6(1)(a) — $20,000 to the High Court, otherwise $10,000; SA rr 189–191; Appeal Costs Fund Act 1968 (Tas) s 8(1); Appeal Costs Act 1998 (Vic) s 4. In other jurisdictions the certificate is limited to questions of law: Appeal Costs Fund Act 1973 (Qld) s 15, PD No 2 of 2010; Suitors' Fund Act 1964 (WA) s 10. In relation to High Court appeals and Federal Court appeals generally, the appeal must succeed on a question of law: Federal Proceedings (Costs) Act 1981 (Cth) ss 3(1), 6; Suitors' Fund Act 1951 (NSW) s 6(1)(b). There is no equivalent legislation in the Australian Capital Territory or the Northern Territory.

The respondent seeks the appellate court to exercise its discretion to grant a certificate on an *ex parte* application for that purpose.

A certificate will only be granted where the appeal succeeds on a question of law; this is a necessary though not sufficient condition. The error, which occurred below, must result from an error in the administration of justice not occasioned by the party seeking the certificate. Such errors ought not to be paid for by the parties, but ought rightly to be paid from a fund contributed to by all litigants: *Acquilina v Dairy Farmers Co-op Milk Co Ltd (No 2)* [1965] NSWR 772 at 773.

19.15.2C   **Lauchlan v Hartley**
                              [1980] Qd R 149
                    Supreme Court of Queensland, Full Court

[The Full Court allowed an appeal from an order refusing the defendant appellant the costs of the action after the date of what was an adequate payment into court. The issue arose as to whether the respondent was entitled to an indemnity certificate from the appeal costs fund in circumstances where the defendant's counsel sought a departure from the settled practice in relation to orders for costs after payment into court.]

Connolly J (at 151–2): Where a decision is reversed on a point of law it will frequently be the case that both sides of the debate are fairly arguable. Thus a situation where the authorities are or appear to be in conflict provides an obvious instance in which a resort to the appellate process is justifiable although of course the limits to which it can properly be taken at the expense of the fund must depend on the particular circumstances. Again the proper construction of a particular instrument will often call for a nice balancing of competing considerations so that the opposing views may properly be regarded as fairly arguable. Again, appeals from the exercise of a judicial discretion will frequently turn on the weight to be given to one or more of the relevant considerations. Yet another instance is provided by the appeal from a value judgment such as those aspects of the assessment of damages which are at large.

A different category of case altogether however is that where the Full Court is of the view that there was no basis on which the judgment or order under appeal could properly have been made out. In such a case it is material to consider the part played by the successful respondent in leading the tribunal to the decision. Where the advocate, barrister or solicitor, invites a decision for which there is no legal warrant, or which is inconsistent in some respect with settled legal principle, the question arises whether his contentions were in truth fairly arguable. If, in the opinion of the Full Court, the legal warrant was arguably available or the [152] settled principle was arguably distinguishable, the respondent may still succeed in obtaining a certificate. If not he will ordinarily fail to obtain the certificate.

[It was held that there was no basis upon which the departure could have been made. The order which was sought and made was based upon propositions which were not fairly arguable. The certificate was refused.]

19.15.3C   **Vella v Larson**
[1982] Qd R 298
Supreme Court of Queensland, Full Court

Macrossan J (at 301–2): To obtain a certificate the obligation is upon the applicant to show some ground calling for the exercise of the discretion in his favour and he does not do this merely by showing that the appeal has succeeded on a question of law ...

It has also become well established that the conduct of the applicant below and his responsibility, if any, for the erroneous decision of law in question is of relevance when application is made for a certificate. ...

If a respondent was encouraged to take a particular line and advance the arguments that he did because of a lead thrown out or an attitude taken by a judge or a tribunal below then this may be of significance. In a particular case, if a strong line is taken by the judge below, with the result that the respondent is virtually carried along by the court's attitude, this may be a strong circumstance in the exercise of the discretion. If one were to devise a scale for the measurement of degrees of responsibility for an error of law which may have occurred below, then at one end of the scale would be those cases where the court has made its own erroneous pronouncement on a point not argued by the parties and perhaps not even adverted to by them. Close to such cases would be those where the court has, of its own motion, raised the point in question and adhered to it unswervingly, with only a passive acceptance or at most lukewarm support exhibited by the party who is favoured. ... [302] It needs no demonstrating that instances where error has been solely the tribunal's responsibility will provide stronger claims of entitlement to a certificate than cases where responsibility for the error is shared since then other factors relevant to the exercise of the discretion may be brought into greater prominence.

19.15.4   Note

1. For further information on the Suitors Fund Act 1951 (NSW) see V Musico, *The Suitor' Fund Act 1951*, NSW Government Crown Solicitor's Office <http://www. lawlink.nsw.gov.au>.

Further reading

19.16.1   Articles

R Barrett, 'Re-opening of Decisions by Appellate Courts' (2002) 76(7) *ALJ* 424.

C Barry, 'Appellate Review of Procedural and Factual Error' (1991) 65 *ALJ* 720.

M Kirby, The Hon Justice, 'Ten Rules of Appellate Advocacy' (1995) 69 *ALJ* 964.

K Malleson and S Roberts, 'Streamlining and Clarifying the Appellate Process' (2002) *CrimLR* 272.

The Rt Hon Lord Oliver of Aylemerton, 'The Appeal Process' (1992) 2 *JJA* 63.

G Santow and M Lemming, 'Refining Australia's Appellate System and Enhancing its Significance in Our Region' (1995) 69 *ALJ* 348.

19.16.2　Looseleaf

D Byrne, The Hon Justice, 'Appeals', 'Practice and Procedure', *Halsbury's Laws of Australia*, vol 20, LexisNexis Butterworths, Sydney.

B Darbyshire, B Fry and N Moshinsky QC, 'Appeal', *Court Forms Precedents and Pleadings Victoria*, LexisNexis, Sydney, vol 1.

Hamilton and Lindsay (Ed), *NSW Civil Practice and Procedure*, Law Book.

M Oakes and A Ashe, 'Appeals', *Court Forms Precedents and Pleadings New South Wales*, LexisNexis, Sydney, vol 1.

D Smith and R Hanson QC, 'Appeals', *Court Forms Precedents and Pleadings Queensland*, LexisNexis, Sydney, vol 1.

19.16.3　Texts

G Blank and H Selby (ed), *Appellate Practice*, Federation Press, 2008.

B Cairns, *Australian Civil Procedure*, 9th ed, Law Book Co, Sydney, 2011, Ch 18, 'Appeals and New Trial'.

S Colbran, *Security for Costs,* Longman Professional, Melbourne, 1993.

D O'Brien, *Special Leave to Appeal: The Law and Practice of Applications for Special Leave to Appeal to the High Court of Australia*, LBC Information Services, Sydney, 1996.

Costs

## CHAPTER 20

OVERVIEW

This chapter examines the circumstances in which one party may be ordered to pay another party's costs and the procedures for determining how those costs are to be calculated. It begins by noting the general rule that the loser pays the winner's costs and discusses the scope of this rule in relation to unrepresented parties and those parties whose litigation is funded by others. Costs can be awarded on several bases, notably the conservative 'standard' or 'party and party' basis, and the more generous 'indemnity' or 'solicitor and client' basis. These different criteria are discussed, together with the circumstances in which different awards are made. The chapter then goes on to discuss how costs are allocated in cases where it is not altogether clear who are the winners and who are the losers in a case. This is followed by an examination of circumstances in which courts exercise their discretion not to award costs to 'winners'. Procedures for determining costs entitlements are then discussed. The chapter concludes with a consideration of the circumstances in which a plaintiff will be required to give security for costs. There is also brief reference to appeal costs funds.

INTRODUCTION

20.1.1 Lurking behind all civil litigation is the question of costs. A study of New South Wales cases found that the median ratio of plaintiffs' costs to amount recovered was 27 per cent in the District Court and 20 per cent in the Supreme Court. For defendants, the figures were 28 per cent and 14 per cent. In Victoria, the median ratios for plaintiffs were 32 per cent in the County Court and 15 per cent in the Supreme Court; for defendants, the figures were 30 per cent and 14 per cent: see D Worthington and J Baker, *The Costs of Civil Litigation*, Civil Justice Research Centre, Sydney, 1993, pp 24–9, 48–53. Costs vary considerably. A study prepared for the Australian Law Reform Commission estimated that the median costs of proceedings in the Federal Court of Australia were $15,820 for applicants and $8463 for respondents. In cases which went through to a hearing, median applicants' professional fees were $7063 and median disbursements, $4748. (For respondents, the figures were $13,000 and $5475.) The somewhat odd fact that median costs were higher for Federal Court cases which were settled is attributable to the fact that commercial cases were more likely to settle than migration cases. In Family Court cases, median costs were $2209 for applicants and $2090 for respondents, increasing sharply for those cases listed and proceeding to trial. The number of such cases in the Family Court sample was too low to yield reliable estimates of the median cost of cases going to trial. These figures should be increased by about 15 per cent to adjust for inflation and GST: see ALRC Report No 89, [4.12]; T Matruglio, *Federal Court Empirical Report Part Two*, Table 4; T Matruglio, *Family Court Empirical Report Part Two*, viewed 8 February 2012, <http://www.alrc.gov.au>. These figures are now somewhat dated, but unfortunately, seem to be the most up to date figures available.

Rules which determine who pays whose costs will therefore play an important role in determining whether litigation is, or is likely to prove, worthwhile. In most United States systems, the rule is that each party bears its own costs. This was also the position at common law. This rule over-rewards those with weak cases, and under-rewards those with strong cases. In England the rule in Chancery was different. Chancery maintained that it had an inherent jurisdiction to order costs, and it was willing to use that discretion to order that the loser paid the winner's costs. Moreover, by statute, common law courts gradually acquired the power to award costs and — in exercise of this power — generally awarded costs to the successful party.

In Australia, the rule is now that, in general, the loser pays: costs are said to follow the event. This is also the position in Western Europe. The rationale of the rule is obvious: those who bring weak cases, and those who mount weak defences, should pay for the costs occasioned by their stubbornness. Those who are unjustly sued and whose claims are unjustly resisted should not have to pay the expenses of their defences or their claims.

20.1.2 However, the underlying principle, which is predicated on the assumption that losers deserve to lose, may prove difficult to apply in practice. It also implies that there are limits to the degree to which a winner should be rewarded. Winners who waste resources litigating should not be compensated for all they spend, and indeed should be made to compensate those whose time and resources they waste. We have already seen one example of this principle in operation: those who reject generous settlement offers are penalised for forcing the other side to fight on: see **17.3.16**, **17.3.23–17.3.29C**, **17.3.45**. Those who fail to comply with court directions may be penalised. There are other rules which embody this principle. There are formulae, which set upper limits on the costs which a successful party can claim and relate costs to the court in which the matter is being fought. The higher the court, the more generous the costs.

This principle could have perverse effects. It could encourage parties to litigate in inappropriate courts. To overcome this possibility, there is a second body of rules, which impose costs penalties on parties which sue in the wrong court. Further, there may be cases where it is not clear who the winner is. One rationale for the offer of compromise rules would be that the party, which gets damages less than a prior settlement offer, is in fact a loser. Moreover, in civil litigation, parties may win on some issues and lose on others. One would expect costs rules to take some account of this. Finally, there may be cases where the winner is not the innocent victim of the other party's intransigence. In these cases, one might expect the rigour of the prima facie costs rules to be relaxed.

THE GENERAL RULE

20.2.1   In *Knight v FP Special Assets Ltd* (1992) 174 CLR 178, Mason CJ and Deane J summarised the powers of the courts to award costs prior to its provision by statute as follows (at 182–3):

Historically, there were marked differences between the powers of the courts at common law and in equity to award costs: *Garnett v Bradley* (1878) 3 App Cas 944, at 953–4, 962. The courts at common law had no inherent jurisdiction to award costs. In *Garnett v Bradley*, Lord Blackburn summarised the position of the common law courts in this way at 962:

> Costs in Courts of Common Law were not by Common Law at all, they were entirely and absolutely creatures of statute. There had been statutes passed at different times giving costs some in one case and some in another, the earliest being the Statute of Gloucester, passed many centuries ago, which gave costs, if I recollect rightly, to demandants who recovered damages in a real action, which they had not had before. Subsequent statutes were passed at different times giving a Plaintiff a right to recover costs in any action, and there were other statutes passed at different times upon the subject of costs in the Common Law Courts. I think the first that gave costs to the Defendant was as late as James I, and there were several other statutes giving costs, but all those statutes went upon one principle throughout. The result was, that, as a general rule, in every case in Courts of Common Law the party who succeeded got his costs, whether he was Plaintiff or Defendant, whether he succeeded by a verdict or upon demurrer. I say the general rule established by all those numerous statutes (for there was no one statute which laid it [183] down) was that the successful party got his ordinary taxed costs; in other words, that the costs followed the event, and that the party who was successful had them as a matter of right.
>
> From that general rule, however, certain statutes made several exceptions in particular cases.
>
> On the other hand, in equity the giving of costs was entirely discretionary: *James v Coxeter* (1742) 2 Atk 400; [26 ER 642]. The Court of Chancery exercised a wide discretion not only as to the circumstances under which costs were awarded but also as to the measure and extent of the costs: *Andrews v Barnes* (1888) 39 Ch D 133 at 138.

Courts now possess a statutory power to award costs in all cases: Federal Court of Australia Act 1976 (Cth) s 43; Judiciary Act 1903 (Cth) s 26; Court Procedures Act 2004 (ACT) Sch 1, Pt 1.2, item 26i; Civil Procedure Act 2005 (NSW) s 98; Supreme Court Act (NT) s 86; Civil Proceedings Act 2011 (Qld) s 15; Supreme Court Act 1935 (SA) s 23; Supreme Court Civil Procedure Act 1932 (Tas) s 12; Supreme Court Act 1986 (Vic) s 24(1); Supreme Court Act 1935 (WA) s 37. In each jurisdiction, the rules contain extensive provisions relating to the determination of costs: High Court Rules 2004 Ch 5; Federal Court Rules Pt 40; Court Procedures Rules (ACT) Pt 2.17; Uniform Civil Procedure Rules 2005 (NSW) Pt 42; Supreme Court Rules (NT) O 63; Uniform Rules Civil Procedure 1999 (Qld) Ch 17, Pt 2; Supreme Court Civil Rules 2006 (SA) Ch 12; Supreme Court Rules 2000 (Tas) Pt 34; Supreme Court (General Civil Procedure) Rules 1996 (Vic) O 63; Rules of the Supreme Court 1971 (WA) O 66. The general rule is that the loser pays the costs necessarily incurred by the winner, but that courts may order otherwise. This rule is expressly stated in some of the rules: NSW r 42.1; Qld r 681; SA r 263(1); WA O 66 r 1. In some jurisdictions, the rules simply state that costs are at the court's discretion: HCR r 50.01; ACT r 1721(1); Civil Procedure Act 2005 (NSW) s 98(1); NT r 63.03(1); Supreme Court Civil Procedure Act 1932 (Tas) s 12(2); Supreme Court Act 1986 (Vic) s 24. The relationship between statute and rules can be complicated: *Knight v F P Special Asset Ltd* (1992) 174 CLR 178 at 183–5 per Mason CJ and Deane J.

The relevant orders are much more detailed than most other orders and parts. They include some provisions in relation to who is to pay costs; they set out the criteria to be taken into account in determining costs, and the processes by which costs are to be determined. They regulate the allocation of costs between parties. Typically they also help regulate the costs that may be charged by practitioners. These costs, however, are also regulated by other statutes.

In all jurisdictions except New South Wales, costs are determined by reference to scales of costs, set out as appendices to the rules. These set out what may be charged for particular legal tasks, both in the context of disputes between lawyers and clients (in circumstances where there has not been an agreement to charge according to a non-scale formula), and in the context of disputes as to the costs one party must pay to another. Their role in determining fees charged to clients seems to vary considerably across jurisdictions. Even when New South Wales provided for charging by scale, the vast majority of law firms charged on a time or work-value basis rather than the scale. In Victoria, however, scale-based charging was the usual basis for fees charged: see D Worthington and J Baker, *The Costs of Civil Litigation*, Civil Justice Research Centre, pp 9–11, 35–6.

Awards of costs are not intended to indemnify a party for all the expenses it has incurred in litigation. At most, costs are intended to indemnify a party against the legal expenses it has incurred and against payments necessarily made in relation to the prosecution or defence of the case. It follows therefore that unrepresented parties are not permitted to claim for the time they have taken to prepare their cases, although (perhaps anomalously) self-representing solicitors are entitled to their costs.

[*NOTE:* in this chapter a reference, such as WA O 9 r 2, is a reference to the relevant jurisdiction's Rules of Court. All other legislation will be specified.]

20.2.2C	**Cachia v Hanes**
	(1994) 179 CLR 403
	High Court of Australia

[The respondents had unsuccessfully sought an order requiring the appellant to restore structural support to their land. Costs were awarded in favour of the appellant who had self-represented. However, a claim for compensation for loss of time spent preparing and conducting the case was disallowed by the Master and, on appeal, by a majority of the Court of Appeal.]

Mason CJ, Brennan, Deane, Dawson and McHugh JJ (at 412): [Their Honours examined the New South Wales legislation and rules and concluded that '[t]o use the Rules to compensate a litigant in person for time lost would cut across their clear intent. Costs, within the meaning of the Rules, are reimbursement for work done or expenses incurred by a practitioner or a practitioner's employee'. They then discussed the 'somewhat anomalous exception' whereby solicitors who represented themselves were entitled to costs. They doubted the rationale for a rule whereby a solicitor who is successful 'not only receives the amount of the verdict but actually profits from the conduct of the litigation', but concluded:]

If the explanations for allowing the costs of a solicitor acting for himself are unconvincing, the logical answer may be to abandon the exception in favour of the general principle rather than the other way round. However, it is not necessary to go so far for the [413] purposes of the present case. It suffices to say that the existence of a limited and questionable exception provides no proper basis for overturning a general principle which has, as we have said, never been doubted and which has been affirmed in recent times.

[On the policy implications of the current rules, their Honours said (at 414):]

If costs were to be awarded otherwise than by way of indemnity there would be no logical reason for denying compensation to a litigant who was represented. That would in some cases dramatically increase the costs awarded to a successful litigant. In corporate litigation of complexity, for example, a litigant may expend considerable time and effort in preparing its case.

Whilst the restricted basis upon which party and party costs are awarded may be debated as a matter of policy, it is to be borne in mind that party and party costs have never been regarded as a total indemnity to a successful litigant for costs incurred, let alone total recompense for work done and time lost. Putting to one side the question posed by the relatively rare exception of a solicitor acting in person, there is no inequality involved: all litigants are treated in the same manner. And if only litigants in person were recompensed for lost time and trouble, there would be real inequality between litigants in person and litigants who were represented, many of [415] whom would have suffered considerable loss of time and trouble in addition to incurring professional costs. The partial indemnity which the law allows represents a compromise between the absence of any provision for costs (which prevails as a matter of policy in some jurisdictions) and full recompense. In these days of burgeoning costs, the risk of which is a real disincentive to litigation, the proper compromise is a matter of both difficulty and concern.

That choice has been made in New South Wales at least in the rules which govern the taxation of costs — rules which are in accordance with established law. The Rule Committee may or may not be able to use its statutory powers to change the basis upon which costs are awarded so that they become, not costs in the accepted sense of the word, but compensation of a more comprehensive kind. We express no view upon that. No doubt the Rule Committee, if it had such power, would wish to inform itself adequately of the reasons for and against such a change and no doubt it would be able to do so in a way in which a judge or court cannot.

Whilst the right of a litigant to appear in person is fundamental, it would be disregarding the obvious to fail to recognise that the presence of litigants in person in increasing numbers is creating a problem for the courts. The problem is well documented in the United States: see Mueller, 'Abusive Pro Se Plaintiffs in the Federal Courts: Proposals for Judicial Control', *Journal of Law Reform*, vol 18 (1984) 93, at 101; Rubin, 'The Civil *Pro Se* Litigant in the Legal System', *Loyola University Law Journal*, vol 20 (1989) 999; Gillies, 'Who's Afraid of the Sanction Wolf: Imposing Sanctions on Pro Se Litigants', *Cardozo Law Review*, vol 11 (1989) 173.

It would be mere pretence to regard the work done by most litigants in person in the preparation and conduct of their cases as the equivalent of work done by qualified legal representatives. All too frequently, the burden of ensuring that the necessary work of a litigant in person is done falls on the court administration or the court itself. Even so, litigation involving a litigant in person is usually less efficiently conducted and tends to be prolonged: see Powles, 'Litigant in Person — Discussion Paper' in Australian Institute of Judicial Administration, *The Litigant in Person* (1993) 7, at 10–11.

The costs of legal representation for the opposing litigant are increased and the drain upon court resources is considerable. On the other hand, there is no doubt that the inability of a litigant in person to obtain recompense for time spent in the conduct of successful litigation must on occasions be a significant deterrent to the exercise of his right to come to court in person. (cf British Columbia, Law Reform Commission, *Report on Civil Procedure: Pt 1 — Costs of Successful Unassisted Lay Litigants* (1975); South Australia, Law Reform Committee, *Report Relating to the Award of Costs to a Litigant Appearing in Person* (1974).)

[416] We mention these matters not to express any view, but merely to indicate that there are considerations which must be weighed before any reasoned conclusion can be reached. A court engaged in litigation between parties, even if it were not constrained by the legislation and rules, is plainly an inappropriate body to carry out that exercise or to act upon any conclusion by laying down the precise nature of any change required.

[Gaudron and **Toohey JJ** dissented.]

20.2.3   Notes and questions

1. While the award of costs of self-representing solicitors is anomalous, would it be in the interests of parties involved in disputes with solicitors that solicitors be entitled to costs only if they retained the services of another solicitor? See *Dobree v Hoffman* (1996) 18 WAR 36 at 42 per Parker J.

2. As to whether self-representing solicitors are entitled to their costs, authority is divided. In *Brott v Almatrah* [1998] 2 VR 83, Batt J considered that the state of High Court authority was such that solicitors were entitled to their costs (except for those which are unnecessary: they could not claim items based on the costs of obtaining instructions, nor those of attending on themselves). However, the Full Court in *Dobree v Hoffman* dismissed an appeal against a ruling that self-representing solicitors were not entitled to costs, ruling that solicitors were also not entitled to costs where represented by a firm of which they were partners. The decision was based both on an analysis of authority and an interpretation of the Western Australian costs rules.

3. The Australian Law Reform Commission's 1995 report into costs (*Costs Shifting — Who Pays for Litigation?,* Report No 75, AGPS, Canberra) recommended, among other things:

    Recommendation 57 — unrepresented parties may recover costs
    A party who does not have legal representation should be able to recover his or her costs in accordance with the relevant rules.
    Recommendation 58 — the costs an unrepresented party may recover
    An unrepresented party who is awarded costs may recover disbursements (including witness expenses and any reasonable legal costs) and his or her own costs for work reasonably necessary to prepare and conduct his or her case subject to the following conditions:

    *   The party's own costs should be limited to that allowed under a schedule setting out lump sum amounts according to the type and complexity of the matter. These amounts should not exceed the reasonable costs of a solicitor performing the same work.
    *   An unrepresented litigant should not be able to recover any costs in relation to the litigation that would not be recoverable by a represented litigant.
    *   A court may allow an unrepresented litigant to recover costs in excess of the relevant lump sum in appropriate circumstances, provided that it does not exceed the amount of costs actually incurred by the litigant.

Should these recommendations be given legal force, given that legal aid is likely to be severely rationed for the foreseeable future?

4. Why should successful parties not be compensated for all losses they suffer as a result of litigation, bearing in mind the considerable psychological and economic costs involved?

5. Should the purpose of costs rules be to discourage self-representation?

6. What is the impact on the likelihood of settlement and on aggregate expenditures on litigation, of the rule that the loser pays the winner's costs? American analyses suggest that there are theoretical grounds for believing that what they call the 'English rule' may have counter-intuitive results: see A Polinsky and D Rubinfeld 'Does the English Rule Discourage Low-Probability-Prevailing Plaintiffs' (1998) 27 *J Leg Studies* 141 and the references cited in it. They agree with the conventional wisdom in so far as it suggests that people with weak cases will be less likely to sue under the English than the United States rule. They argue, however, that the effect of the English rule is that as cases become weaker, defendants' offers to settle decline more rapidly than plaintiffs' expected values of going to trial. This relative difference means that while plaintiffs with weak cases stand to win less from trial under the English rule, their incentive to go to trial (given ungenerous settlement offers) is greater.

Costs awards where litigation has been funded by a third party

20.2.4. Litigation is not always funded by the parties on the record. Plaintiffs' litigation is sometimes funded by trade unions. In negligence actions, the defence is typically conducted by the defendant's insurer. Plaintiffs' litigation is sometimes run on a contingency basis, the plaintiff being charged by its legal representatives only in the event of success (but sometimes at a higher rate than would otherwise be the case). In these cases, parties may not be liable to pay for the legal expenses they incur. On the question of whether they are entitled to compensation, see the case below.

20.2.5C	**Johnson v Santa Teresa Housing Association**
	(1992) 107 FLR 441
	Northern Territory Supreme Court

[An employee was entitled to be indemnified by his employer in relation to a successful suit by the plaintiff. The employer argued that it was not required to indemnify the employee in relation to his legal costs since these were to be borne by the Territory Insurance Office.]

Mildren J (at 445–7): It is true that there are authorities to the effect that, if a party is not liable to pay any costs to his own solicitor, no costs can be recovered by the other side: see, eg, *Irving v Gagliardi; Ex parte Gagliardi (No 2)* (1895) 6 QLJ 200, per Griffith CJ. However, more recent authorities show that that principle cannot be taken too far. One well established exception is where a party is represented by a solicitor employed by the Crown, and the party really represented the Crown's interests: see, eg, *Lenthall v Hillson* [1933] SASR 31. In that case, the Full Court (Napier and Angas Parsons JJ) said (at 36):

We think that the principle that costs are given as an indemnity can be carried too far. It comes from the unwritten law, and depends upon considerations of public policy and convenience, and it follows that it must be reasonably understood and applied.

Later (at 37) their Honours concluded:

It is apparent that in these circumstances the rule that costs are an indemnity must have been understood, as it was understood in *Irving v Gagliardi,* ie, as applying to the liability of the real and not of the nominal plaintiff.

There is no reason why any distinction should be made between plaintiffs [446] and defendants. In the instant case, the 'real' defendants were the Territory Insurance Office and the first defendant's employer's indemnity insurer, as they ultimately will bear the losses.

In *Backhouse v Judd* [1925] SASR 395, the Society for the Prevention of Cruelty to Animals employed an inspector called Judd who was the complainant in certain proceedings against Backhouse which were successful. Judd was represented by solicitors and counsel employed by the society. Poole ACJ held that unless it was shown that Judd was under no liability to pay his solicitor's costs, an order for costs could be made against Backhouse, notwithstanding the indemnity for costs which was given by the society. This decision was upheld on appeal ([1925] SASR 400). In the Full Court, Angas Parsons J said (at 402–3):

The facts are similar to those which one would expect in a case where an insurance company undertakes the conduct of proceedings instituted by the assured or against him, nor do they differ, in my opinion, from those where an information is laid by a member of the police force for whom counsel is briefed by the Law Department. In such a case, although the police officer accepts the services of such counsel, and would not contemplate that in any event he would be left to pay the costs, yet the proper inference to be drawn is that liability therefor, in the absence of bargain to the contrary, is not to be taken to be negatived, and in everyday practice such an informant may be awarded costs if successful.

Each of the judges in *Backhouse v Judd* (supra) followed *Adams v London Improved Motor Coach Builders* [1921] 1 KB 495. That was a case where a trade union gave a plaintiff legal aid and instructed solicitors to act on his behalf. The solicitors issued proceedings and briefed counsel. The plaintiff succeeded at trial, and was held to be entitled to his costs. The Court of Appeal held that once it was established that there were solicitors acting on the plaintiff's behalf with his knowledge and approval, the plaintiff must become liable for his solicitor's costs, notwithstanding that the union also undertook to pay his costs. In order for the plaintiff's claim for costs to fail, the court held that it would be necessary to go further and show that there was a bargain to the effect that under no circumstances was the plaintiff to be liable for his solicitor's costs.

In *Blackall v Trotter (No 1)* [1969] VR 939, the Full Court of the Supreme Court of Victoria took the matter one step further. In that case, an employed solicitor of the Victorian Insurance Commissioner represented a defendant insured under a policy of the commissioner. The defendant was successful in the entitlement to a costs order even though the solicitor was employed by the Crown (the Insurance Commissioner being the Crown in another guise). It is true that that case depended in the end on the fact that the solicitor was an employee of the Crown, but it is pertinent to observe that their Honours said (at 942):

The present is a case involving a Crown employed solicitor, but we are not to be taken as deciding that the principle is limited to such a case. In *New Pinnacle Group Silver Mining Co v Luhrig Coal and Ore Dressing Appliances Co* (1902) 2 SR (NSW) 50, for instance, the Full Court of New South Wales held that a plaintiff company in civil proceedings represented by a private solicitor against whose costs it was legitimately indemnified was not disentitled to recover such costs (see in particular [447] per Walker J at 56, and also *Elborough v Ayres* (1870) LR 10 Eq 367 — referred to in *Lenthall v Hillson, supra*).

There is no evidence that the second defendant has an agreement with his solicitors that, come what may, only the Territory Insurance Office will be liable to meet his costs. Indeed, it would be surprising if that were the case, given that the office's obligation under s 40(1)(d) is to indemnify the second defendant against all costs and proceedings. If the second defendant's solicitors have agreed not to charge the second defendant under any circumstances, of what value would an indemnity be?

Costs awards against third parties

20.2.6 If costs rules mean that third parties may effectively be able to recover costs from unsuccessful litigants, are there circumstances in which litigants may be able to recover costs from third parties? See below, *Knight v F P Special Assets Ltd*.

20.2.7C	**Knight v F P Special Assets Ltd**
	(1992) 174 CLR 178
	High Court of Australia

[The Queensland Supreme Court made costs orders against the receivers of companies which had unsuccessfully litigated.]

Mason CJ and Deane J (at 189–90): [In their judgment, their Honours reviewed the pre-Judicature Act position in relation to the awarding of costs against non-parties, concluding:] Having regard to the variety and nature of the circumstances in which an order for costs was made against a person who was not a party according to the record, we cannot accept that there was [190] before the Judicature Acts a general rule that there was no jurisdiction to order costs against a non-party in the strict sense. It is plain enough that the courts from time to time awarded costs against a person who, not being a party on the record, was considered to be the 'real party'. It may be that these cases are capable of being explained on various grounds, including the ground that the non-party ordered to pay costs was guilty of abuse of process, taking a very broad view of what constitutes an abuse of process, but to say that does not deny that there was jurisdiction to make an order for costs against a non-party even if the jurisdiction was exercised in limited circumstances only.

Against this background, it is impossible to construe the wide and general words of O 54, r 1 and its successor O 91, r 1 as delimiting the jurisdiction to order payment of costs as one which was and is confined to parties to the proceedings. The language of the rule is quite inapt to give expression to the complex course of judicial decisions at common law and in equity before the Judicature Acts. Moreover, the extended concept of 'party', including as it does a variety of persons on whom notice of proceedings is served, makes it inappropriate to introduce a limitation which was applied at a time when the concept of 'party' related to a person on the record of the proceedings.

It is preferable to interpret the words of the rule according to their natural and ordinary meaning as conferring a grant of jurisdiction to order costs not limited to parties on the record and ensure that the jurisdiction is exercised responsibly.

[**Mason CJ** and **Deane J** considered and dismissed the argument that provisions providing for orders for security for costs could be used as a ground for concluding that jurisdiction to award costs against third parties was implicitly negatived. Their Honours referred to *Aiden Shipping Ltd v Interbulk Ltd* [1986] AC 965 as supporting their conclusions, and continued (at 192–3):]

The conclusion that the wide words of O 91, r 1 should not be read down so as to preclude jurisdiction to make an order for costs against a non-party does not, of course, mean that a judge has an unfettered discretion to make any order that he or she chooses. The wide jurisdiction conferred by the rule 'must be exercised judicially and in accordance with general legal principles pertaining to the law of costs', to take up the words of Lambert JA in *Oasis Hotel Ltd v Zurich Insurance Co* (1981) 124 DLR (3d) 455, at 462. (In that case, an order for costs as between solicitor and client was made against a director and principal shareholder of the insolvent plaintiff company, notwithstanding that he was a non-party, on the ground that he had instigated an action which sought to make the court an instrument of fraud.) Obviously, the prima facie general principle is that an order for costs is only made against a party to the litigation. As our discussion of the earlier authorities indicates, there are, however, a variety of circumstances in which considerations of justice may, in accordance with general principles relating to awards of costs, support an order for costs against a non-party. Thus, for example, there are several long established categories of case in which equity recognized that it may be appropriate for such an order to be made: see the discussion in *Oasis Hotel,* ibid, at 458–9.

For our part, we consider it appropriate to recognize a general category of case in which an order for costs should be made against a non-party and which would encompass the case of a receiver of a company who is not a party to the litigation. That category of case [193] consists of circumstances where the party to the litigation is an insolvent person or man of straw, where the non-party has played an active part in the conduct of the litigation and where the non-party, or some person on whose behalf he or she is acting or by whom he or she has been appointed, has an interest in the subject of the litigation. Where the circumstances of a case fall within that category, an order for costs should be made against the non-party if the interests of justice require that it be made.

20.2.8   For examples of the exercise of this power, see: *The Beach Retreat Pty Ltd v Mooloolaba Marina Ltd* [2009] 2 Qd R 356; [2009] QSC 84 (indemnity costs); *McMillan Investment Holdings Pty Ltd v North Coast Property Pty Ltd* [2011] NSWSC 1432; *Offstage Support Association Inc v Time of My Life Pty Ltd [No 2]* [2011] FCA 1183.

The ACT rules (rr 1703, 1704) expressly prohibit costs orders against non-parties except:

(a)   relators — that is, people without standing to sue, on whose behalf the Attorney-General has agreed to sue;

(b)   persons bound by judgments and orders of the court;

(c)   people who fail to comply with orders;

(d) people who commit contempt or court or abuse of process (insofar as their contempt or abuse has added to the costs of proceedings);

(e) people subject to a subpoena who fail to turn up;

(f) people who purport, without authority, to act on behalf of others; and

(g) practitioners.

These rules limit whatever discretion might exist pursuant to the court's inherent powers. In *Jeffery & Katauskas Pty Ltd v SST Consulting Pty Ltd* (2009) 239 CLR 57; [2009] HCA 43, in a case involving the interpretation of a similar New South Wales provision, which has been subsequently repealed, the High Court majority held that it was not an abuse of process for a non-party litigation funder to contribute to the plaintiff's legal expenses in exchange for a share of the proceeds (if any). Nor was it an abuse that the agreement did not include a provision whereby the funder agreed to indemnify the plaintiff against costs: [25]–[30]. It was relevant to an award of costs against funders that the rule precluded awards except in specified circumstances: [31]–[43].

Costs awards against practitioners

20.2.9   Courts may award costs against a party's legal advisers. The rules envisage this (HCR r 50.05; FCR r 40.07; ACT rr 1703(2)(g), 1753; NSW r 42.3(2)(g), Civil Procedure Act 2005 (NSW) s 99; NT r 63.21; Qld r 690; SA r 274(3)(d) (costs caused by unjustified adjournments); Tas r 840; Vic r 63.23; WA O 66 r 5), and in any case, the power to award costs against third parties implies a power to award costs against a party's legal representatives. The Legal Profession Act 2004 (NSW) s 348 provides for costs orders against practitioners and their firms when it appears to a court in which proceedings for damages have been taken that 'a law practice has provided legal services to a party without reasonable prospects of success'. Such orders are discretionary and may provide full or part indemnity to the winning party. As to what constitutes a proceeding 'without reasonable prospects of success', see *Degiorgio v Dunn (No 2)* (2005) 63 NSWLR 300, [2005] NSWSC 3, BC20050375; *Lemoto v Able Technical Pty Ltd* [2005] NSWCA 153, BC200502983 where the courts accepted that the effect of the legislation is to expand the range of circumstances in which practitioners can be held liable for costs. The latter case also includes a lengthy discussion of the courts' general jurisdiction to award costs against practitioners: at [84]–[115]. Section 348 overlaps with Civil Procedure Act 2005 (NSW) s 99, but in cases where it is alleged that services have been provided without reasonable prospects for success, s 348 imposes a more exacting standard on practitioners than does s 99: *Hickey v Fitzpatrick* [2010] NSWSC 1119, [125] (Barrett J).

20.2.10C   **De Sousa v Minister for Immigration, Local Government and Ethnic Affairs**
(1993) 41 FCR 544
Federal Court of Australia

[An application for an order of review failed. The trial judge found that the applicant had been ill-advised in relation to an application for entry permits and had applied for permits to which she and her child were clearly not entitled, rather than for permits to which they might have been entitled. As a result, they were out of time for making any applications for any permits for which they might have been eligible. They were therefore not entitled to stay in Australia and the Department had rightly decided that they had become 'illegal entrants'. They were therefore required to leave Australia or face deportation.]

French J (at 546): [His Honour discussed the jurisdiction to award costs. Order 62 r 9 FCR provided: 'The Court or a Judge may, after reference to and report by the taxing officer, order a solicitor to repay to his client costs ordered to be paid by the client to another party where those costs had been incurred by that party in consequence of delay or misconduct on the part of the solicitor.' In relation to this, French J said:]

That rule assumes the existence under the Act of power to make an order for costs against a solicitor. The mechanism it establishes for the exercise of that power however is facultative and not exhaustive. Were it exhaustive it would prevent the court or judge from exercising the power without first obtaining a report from the taxing officer. It would also prevent the court from making an order that a solicitor pay the costs of the successful party direct. I cannot accept that it was intended to so constrain the broad power conferred by s 43.

[An analogous rule had been interpreted as an exercise of the court's inherent jurisdiction over solicitors, and could also be seen as an exercise of the court's broader power to make costs orders against non-parties. **French J** continued (at 547–8):]

I accept the proposition that the jurisdiction is to be exercised with care and discretion and only in clear [548] cases. The mere fact that litigation fails is plainly no ground for its exercise. There has to be something which amounts to a serious dereliction of duty: *Edwards v Edwards* [1958] P 235 at 248. It is not necessary to ground the power to order costs against a solicitor in the existence of any duty to the opposing party and whether it can be so grounded is open to doubt: *Orchard v South Eastern Electricity Board* [1987] 1 QB 565 at 571 but cf Lord Denning MR in *Kelly v London Transport Executive* [1982] 1 WLR 1055 at 1064, 1065; [1982] 2 All ER 842 at 850–1. It is debatable whether the traditional immunity of counsel would extend to limit the statutory power of the court in this respect, but it is not necessary to decide that question in this case. Although practising in a fused profession the applicant's solicitor was acting in his capacity as a solicitor when he lodged the application for the permits and as a solicitor or solicitor and barrister when he instituted these proceedings. I note that Sir John Donaldson MR observed in *Orchard v South Eastern Electricity Board* (*supra*) that he could 'find no basis in logic or authority for holding that the essential public interest immunity affirmed in *Rondel v Worsley* [1969] AC 191 protects the bar in relation to claims by their own lay clients, leaving them unprotected in respect of the far greater risk of claims by disgruntled litigants on the other side'. It may be that one answer to that contention is that the power to award costs against counsel, if it is an element of the statutory power, would arise in the case of a breach of a duty to the court and not to counsel's client or any other party.

In the circumstances of this case which I have already outlined, I am satisfied that an order for costs is appropriate against the solicitor. The application lodged with the Department, in my opinion, reflected a serious failure to give reasonable attention to the relevant law and facts as did the proceedings instituted in this Court: cf *Broughton v Broughton* [1955] SASR 241 at 246–9. Worse, the applicants were exposed to the possibility of prejudice by being excluded from applying for an entry permit in some other category.

[His Honour found that some of the solicitor's mistakes in relation to the application were excusable, and ordered that the solicitor pay three-quarters of the Department's costs, with the applicant to pay the rest.]

20.2.11 The ALRC favours extending liability to pay costs to barristers: see Report No 75, [11.12]–[11.14]. The Commission recommended:

> *Recommendation* 36 — costs orders against legal and other representatives
> A *court* or tribunal should be able to:
>
> - disallow costs as between the representative and the party;
> - direct the representative to repay to the party any costs which the party has been ordered to repay to any other party;
> - direct the representative to pay to any other party the costs incurred by that party;
> - where, in the opinion of the court *or* tribunal, the representative was responsible for all or part of the costs being incurred improperly or without reasonable cause or being wasted by undue delay or by any other misconduct or default.

The ALRC noted at [11.12] in relation to existing rules that '[t]here have been concerns that these orders are rarely made and that as a result the parties often bear the costs of lawyers' poor conduct'. Why are such orders rarely made? Would the ALRC's recommendations overcome this problem?

In *In the Matter of a Notice of Motion Filed on Behalf of Colin George Dunstan* (2000) 155 FLR 189, Miles CJ ordered that a barrister pay costs occasioned as a result of his misconceived advice that a misconceived motion be brought using criminal procedures, to achieve an end that should have been pursued through alternative means. His Honour considered that courts may even have the jurisdiction to make costs orders against barristers in relation to their conduct of trials, but did not resolve this issue.

20.2.12 One situation which has arisen on a number of occasions is the case of solicitors purporting to act for parties by which they have not been retained. In this case, the appropriate order is that they be substituted for the party they purportedly represent, that proceedings be dismissed and that they be liable for the successful party's costs: *Harry S Bagg's Liquidation Warehouse Pty Ltd v Whittaker* (1982) 44 NSWLR 421. Another situation is where solicitors lend their assistance to a case which amounts to an abuse of process: *White v Flower & Hart* (1998) 156 ALR 169 where, at 229–53, Goldberg J provides a detailed analysis and application of the principles relevant to the making of such an order. The mere fact that a case is hopeless does not mean that it is an abuse of process, but if there is no rational basis on which legal arguments could succeed, this could suggest that the arguments are being raised for extrinsic purposes (such as delay): see *Levick v Deputy Commissioner of Taxation* [2000] FCA 674, where the Full Court canvassed the competing issues and posed the question of whether a costs order should be made against a solicitor. This is only one of many cases in which Levick and counsel briefed by him have relied on his patently untenable arguments. Others include *Poonan v Deputy Commissioner of Taxation* [1999] NSWSC 1121; *McKewins Hairdressing and Beauty Supplies Pty Ltd v Deputy Commissioner of Taxation* [2000] HCA 27; and *Buckingham Gate International Pty Ltd v ANZ Banking Group* [2000] NSWSC 946 (where Santow J at [19] suggested that the time was approaching when more effective sanctions than indemnity costs might be needed). Indemnity costs have also been awarded against a body called the Institute of Taxation Research Pty Ltd which encouraged and (for a fee) assisted would-be tax-non-payers to use similar arguments: *Money Tree Management Services Pty Ltd v Deputy Commissioner of Taxation (No 2)* [2000] SASC 63 (where the order was made notwithstanding that the Deputy Commissioner's costs would be paid even in the absence of such an order).

However, courts are reluctant to order solicitors to pay costs in cases that pass the threshold necessary to survive strike-out applications and applications for summary judgment: see *Hickey v Fitzpatrick* [2010] NSWSC 1119.

20.2.13   Section 1335(2) of the Corporations Act 2001 (Cth) provides that 'the costs of any proceeding before a Court under this Law shall be borne by such party to the proceeding as the Court, in its discretion, directs'. Does this mean that in litigation under the Corporations Act, courts may not make costs orders against third parties? See *Australian Forest Managers Pty Ltd (in liq) v Bramley, Simbert & Houston* (1996) 65 FCR 13; *Re Wridgemont Display Homes Pty Ltd* (1992) 39 FCR 193. Compare: *UTSA Pty Ltd (in liq) v Ultra Tune Australia Pty Ltd* [1999] 1 VR 204 (where Chernov J held that under s 24(1) of the Supreme Court Act 1986 (Vic), s 1335(2) did not preclude costs against non-parties (at [17]–[32]) and that the relevant proceedings were not in any case proceedings under the Act. See too: *Madeas Pty Ltd v Ashley* [2011] FCA 250, [148]–[149] (purported demands were out of time, or without authority, in each of which cases, they were not 'under the Act').

TYPES OF COSTS AWARD

20.3.1   Courts will normally order that the loser pays the winner's legal costs. However, costs awards do not and are not intended to compensate parties for unnecessary expenditure. Plaintiffs who ring their solicitor each day to ask about the progress of their case cannot expect the other side to pay for the daily 'telephone conferences'. Solicitors who intend to charge their clients for each 'telephone conference' should warn their clients of this. Better still, they should try to keep clients sufficiently informed of the progress of the case to induce a degree of client security. Aggressive defendants who use QCs to defend actions in debt brought by their newsagent in respect of unpaid paper bills cannot expect huge costs if they succeed in their defence. A distinction is therefore drawn between the costs which a solicitor is entitled to recover from the client, and the costs which may be awarded to a successful party. While an order might be made that costs be paid by the losing party, so as to provide coverage of all the costs of the winning party, this would be done only in extraordinary circumstances.

In general, costs orders usually order costs on a relatively conservative basis. In Victoria and most other jurisdictions, this is known as the 'party and party' basis. Nomenclature varies. In the Northern Territory and Queensland, party and party costs are referred to as 'standard' costs, and the term 'indemnity costs' is often used more or less synonymously with 'solicitor and client' costs. In the Victorian r 63.29, party and party costs are defined as follows:

> On a taxation on a party and party basis all costs necessary or proper for the attainment of justice or for enforcing or defending the rights of the party whose costs are being taxed shall be allowed.

Party and party costs are to be contrasted with solicitor and client costs. Victorian r 63.30 provides:

> On a taxation on a solicitor and client basis all costs reasonably incurred and of reasonable amount shall be allowed.

This is more generous than the 'party and party' or 'ordinary' basis, and in some jurisdictions is known as the 'indemnity' basis. Somewhat similar definitions apply to corresponding terms in the Australian Capital Territory (rr 1751(2), 1752(3)); Northern Territory (rr 63.29, 63.30) and Queensland (rr 702(2), 703(3)); and see South Australia r 264(2), (5)(a); and Tasmania rr 859, 862. In Queensland, the assessment of reasonableness is to take account, among other factors, of any costs agreement between the solicitor and the client. In *Casey v Quabba & Allianz Australia Insurance* [2006] 1 Qd R 297, the Court of Appeal held that the obligation was to take account of a valid costs agreement. An agreement which did not comply with the prescribed requirements was void, and therefore irrelevant to the assessment of reasonableness. For a critique of the decision, see P Garrett and R Quick, 'Assessment of Indemnity Costs Orders — A New Approach' (2006) 26(9) *Proctor* 19.

Just to complicate matters, the ACT, South Australia and Victoria now recognise a third basis for determining costs — the 'indemnity' basis: ACT r 1752(4); SA r 264(5)(b); Vic r 6.30.1:

(1)   Subject to paragraph (2), on a taxation on an indemnity basis all costs shall be allowed except in so far as they are of an unreasonable amount or have been unreasonably incurred.

(2)   Any doubt which the Taxing Master may have as to whether the costs were unreasonably incurred or were unreasonable in amount shall be resolved in favour of the party to whom the costs are payable.

The Federal Court distinguishes between a 'party and party' and an 'indemnity' basis, with the terms being defined in a similar manner to the Victorian terms (FCR Dictionary: 'costs as between party and party', 'costs on an indemnity basis'). New South Wales does not provide for a corresponding distinction between 'party and party', solicitor and client, and indemnity costs. Instead, costs are ordered either on an ordinary or an indemnity standard. The 'ordinary basis' means 'the basis of assessing costs set out in section 364(1) and (2) of the Legal Profession Act 2004': Civil Procedure Act 2005 s 3. These sections are reproduced below: **20.7.5E**. They appear more generous than the 'party and party' basis, but the extent to which this is so will obviously depend on how they are applied.

The indemnity standard is defined generously. Where a party acts as a trustee, executor, administrator, personal representative or in some other fiduciary capacity, and is entitled to costs out of property held or controlled in the relevant capacity, all costs are allowed, except those incurred in breach of the party's relevant duties: r 42.5(a). Otherwise, the standard is defined in terms similar to those which apply in the ACT, South Australia and Victoria: r 42.5(b).

It is not always clear what these definitions mean. In *W & A Gilbey Ltd v Continental Liqueurs Pty Ltd* [1964] NSWR 527, Asprey J, at 533–4, discussed the issue, making the point that the phrase 'necessary and proper' implies that a cost can be proper, notwithstanding that it is not necessary. More generally (at 534):

> A taxing officer in a party and party taxation should allow a successful litigant, in whose favour an order for costs has been made, a just and reasonable amount in respect of each item claimed in such litigant's bill of costs where such item was, in fact, incurred on behalf of the litigant by his solicitor in respect of some step in the matter in the litigation which either (1) was necessarily taken or performed for the attainment of justice or the maintaining or defending of the litigant's rights in the circumstances of the individual case, or, (2) although not necessarily taken or performed for such purposes, would reasonably have been taken or performed for any of those purposes without extravagance in conformity with the then situation of the case and not in conflict with the statutes and rules, the practice of the Court, and the usages of the legal profession appertaining to such a case.

And (at 535):

Allowance should be made for the parties' different positions, and in particular for the fact that the defendant may not be in a position to know the kind of case it will have to meet. Determinations of what is necessary and proper should not be made with the wisdom of hindsight.

But given this approach, how do 'party and party' costs differ from solicitor and client costs, given that each formula apparently allows for costs reasonably incurred? The answer seems to be that indemnity or solicitor and client costs differ from standard or 'party and party' costs in that items which are doubtful as 'party and party' costs can be claimed as solicitor and client costs. In determining whether an item is to form part of 'party and party' costs, the presumption in doubtful cases is in favour of the party which is to pay the costs. In determining solicitor and client or indemnity costs, the presumption is in favour of costs being allowed, unless they are unreasonable. In jurisdictions which provide for awards on both a 'solicitor and client' and an 'indemnity' basis, 'indemnity costs' are more generous, given the express presumption that costs incurred on an indemnity basis have been reasonably incurred.

In practice, 'party and party' costs normally amount to considerably less than the expenses actually incurred. Estimates are likely to be rather rubbery. However, one study reported (on the basis of a small sample of cases) that the median ratio of 'party and party' to total costs in New South Wales was 59 per cent for cases which went to verdict, and 72 per cent for cases which settled. In Victoria, the figures were 67 per cent and 69 per cent: D Worthington and J Baker, *The Costs of Civil Litigation*, Civil Justice Research Centre, Sydney, 1993, pp 19–20, 44–5. More recently, the Victorian Law Reform Commission reported that 'many experienced practitioners have suggested to the commission that only about 50 per cent of the total amount of the actual costs is likely to be recovered from the losing party in many instances': Victorian Law Reform Commission, *Civil Justice Review Report*, 2008, p 648. There are, therefore, obvious advantages in being awarded costs on an indemnity or a solicitor and client basis. However, special circumstances must be shown to justify such an award. Failure to accept a plaintiff's generous offer of settlement is one such circumstance: see 17.3.45–17.3.49. A dispute over a fund is another. Examples of such disputes include cases where there is a dispute about entitlements under a will. Indemnity costs may also be ordered in cases which are found to amount to an abuse of process: see *Packer v Meagher* [1984] 3 NSWLR 486.

20.3.2C   **Hurstville Municipal Council v Connor**
(1991) 24 NSWLR 724
Supreme Court of New South Wales

[This was an appeal from a decision by a magistrate to award costs on what appeared to be an indemnity basis.]

Loveday J (at 730): A useful starting case on a consideration of the subject of the extent of his discretion to award costs is *EMI Records Ltd v Ian Cameron Wallace Ltd* [1983] Ch 59, where Sir Robert Megarry VC sets out and discusses (at 63–4) [731] the 'main bases of taxation' of costs. The five bases noted by him in ascending order (except perhaps as to 4 and 5) are as follows:

1. The party and party basis.
2. The common fund basis.
3. The trustee basis.

4. The solicitor and own client basis.
5. The indemnity basis.

In a solicitor and own client taxation all costs should be allowed 'except in so far as they are of an unreasonable account or have been unreasonably incurred'. All costs incurred with the client's express or implied approval are 'conclusively presumed to have been reasonably incurred; and there is a rebuttable presumption that any costs which in the circumstances are of an unusual nature, and would not be allowed on a party and party taxation, have been unreasonably incurred, unless the solicitor expressly informed his client before they were incurred that they might not be allowed'.

Sir Robert Megarry VC also notes in *EMI Records* that the English rules contain no express mention of indemnity costs although for many years the courts have been making such orders particularly against contemnors (at 64).

From the cases referred to by him, it seems that there is a good deal of confusion of terms. In *Reed v Gray* [1952] Ch 337 at 347–8, reference is made to '… a solicitor and own client taxation — or in other words, an indemnity'. He cites a number of cases in which orders for indemnity costs or costs on an indemnity basis have been made. These cases include *Hoffman La Roche and Co AG v Sieczko* [1968] RPC 460 and *Faith Panton Property Plan Ltd v Hodgetts* [1981] 1 WLR 927; [1981] 2 All ER 877, in which orders were made following a breach of an undertaking given to the court and *Chanel v 3 Pears Wholesale Cash and Carry Co* [1979] FSR 393, where the person made to pay indemnity costs was in contempt of court.

In Australia the widening gap between party and party costs and the costs actually incurred has led to an increase in the number of cases in which special orders for costs have been sought and, in some cases, made. In *Degmam Pty Ltd (In Liq) v Wright (No 2)* [1983] 2 NSWLR 354, Holland J made an order for indemnity costs where the unsuccessful party had prolonged the trial by deliberately false defences and allegations of fact. At 358 of the judgment, he said:

> … the allegations of fact she [the party against whom he was making the order] made as the basis of her defences and causes of action were in my opinion false and deliberately concocted by her in an attempt to deny the plaintiff its rights and to shift all blame and legal liability to the plaintiff from herself to the second crossdefendant. As well as that, she so conducted herself in the proceedings, by multiplying allegation upon allegation, and by prevaricating in the witness box, as grossly to prolong the litigation, thereby to cause the other parties to incur liability for solicitor and client costs far beyond what they could reasonably have expected to incur in litigation of genuine issues.

His Honour in that case allowed as indemnity costs, all costs incurred with the exception only of costs of an unreasonable amount or unreasonably incurred. His Honour referred to an order made by Yeldham J on 16 December 1981 in *Barclays Australia Ltd v Dan* (Yeldham J, 15 December 1981, unreported), a commercial cause in which a defence of fraudulent [732] misrepresentation had been abandoned at the hearing after the plaintiff had come to the trial fully prepared to meet it. His Honour noted that counsel for the plaintiff in that case asked for a complete indemnity for the costs incurred in preparing to fight the abandoned issue and that Yeldham J held that it was a proper order in the circumstances.

[His Honour then referred to *Packer v Meagher* [1984] 3 NSWLR 486, *AGC v De Jager* [1984] VR 483, and *Wentworth v Rogers (No 5)* (1986) 6 NSWLR 534, before continuing:]

In *Qantas Airways Ltd v Dillingham Corporation* (Rogers J, 14 May 1987, unreported) Rogers J in examining orders for costs noted that cost orders have for a long time yielded unsatisfactory results from the point of view of successful litigants. At 4 of his judgment he said this:

> In the course of the last twenty or thirty years the incomplete indemnity provided by party and party costs came to satisfy less and less of the actual costs. There is now a yawning gap between costs recovered by a successful party from the other party on a party and party taxation of costs and the costs payable by the successful party to its own solicitors. In a paper delivered in June 1986 to a Colloquium on Alternative Dispute Resolution organized in Canberra by the Commonwealth Attorney General, two well-known and experienced Sydney solicitors said without contradiction that:
>
> > 'Taxed costs never compensate in full the party in whose favour the award has been made. The rule of thumb is that you recover one-half to two-thirds of your actual costs.'
>
> [733] The effects may be financially disastrous to a party successful in the outcome of the litigation. Ironically, the successful party may finish in penury whilst the financially better off opponent who actually lost the litigation continues to flourish. In a long case, as many cases are these days, the difference in costs may spell financial ruin.

In that case Rogers J made an order for costs on an 'indemnity basis' in similar terms to that ordered by Holland J in *Degmam* saying:

> Not only have the defendants to a large extent been unsuccessful, vis-à-vis the plaintiff but failed completely as against Sir Lennox Hewitt and Mr Yates. Furthermore, even this result was arrived at only after what seemed like an unending stream of amendments and adjournments on the application of the defendants/crossclaimants.

A little later he said:

> It is intolerable that persons, whatever their means may be, should be exposed to legal costs in resisting claims the subject of an unending stream of amendments and which are found to be totally lacking in foundation either in law or in fact.

Fountain Selected Meats (Sales) Pty Ltd v International Produce Merchants Pty Ltd (1988) 81 ALR 397 was a matter in the Federal Court and concerned an application made under the Trade Practices Act 1974 (Cth). The presiding judge, Woodward J, stated that in his view special circumstances must necessarily be shown to exist before any order for costs other than party and party costs should be made. He thought that:

> ... It is appropriate to consider awarding ... 'indemnity' costs, whenever it appears that an action has been commenced or continued in circumstances where the applicant, properly advised, should have known that he had no chance of success. In such cases the action must be presumed to have been commenced or continued for some ulterior motive, or because of some willful disregard of the known facts or the clearly established law. Such cases are, fortunately, rare.

In the result he ordered that [a] portion of the costs be paid in that case on a party and party basis and [a] portion being those costs incurred after publication of a High Court decision, on an indemnity basis, adopting the form of order used by Holland J in *Degmam*. The indemnity costs were awarded for the period during which the action was maintained 'without sufficient grounds for the purpose of causing trouble or annoyance to the defendant' (the definition of 'vexatious' in the *Shorter Oxford Dictionary*.)

Fountain was recently followed and an order for indemnity costs made in favour of the plaintiff by Hunt J in *Blackburn v State of New South Wales* (Hunt J, 9 August 1991, unreported) in respect of a crossclaim which the defendant *should have known* had no chance of success. In that case however the defendant had been warned by the plaintiff that there was no basis for the crossclaim and that indemnity costs would be sought. Notwithstanding this warning and notwithstanding views expressed by Hunt J the defendant had continued to press the crossclaim.

[734] Two recent cases demonstrate that a special order for costs may be made without the necessity for showing that the party against whom the order is made had been guilty of some inappropriate conduct.

In *Baltic Shipping Co v Dillon* 'Mikhail Lermontov' (1991) 22 NSWLR 1 the plaintiff at the trial had sought an order for costs on an indemnity basis. Carruthers J, the trial judge, in light of the doubt cast on such orders by *Premier Woodworking Co Pty Ltd v Siganisucu* (Court of Appeal, 30 November 1989, unreported) treated the application as one for costs on a solicitor and client basis.

His Honour refused the application holding that there was no 'lack of merit on the part of the defendant in the way in which the case was conducted'. On appeal the Court held (Gleeson CJ and Kirby P agreeing, Mahoney JA not deciding) that the test applied by his Honour was too narrow and that there were other bases upon which a special order for costs could be made. In the result costs on a solicitor and client basis were awarded in relation to the costs of that part of the proceeding that related to the issue of liability, since the action so far as it related to liability, was fought as a test case to apply to a number of other prospective plaintiffs, passengers on the same ship who had similar claims for damages.

In *Australian Federation of Consumer Organisations Inc v Tobacco Institute of Australia Ltd* (1991) 100 ALR 568, the applicant for costs on an indemnity basis was a public interest group that had brought proceedings for the purpose of restraining the respondent from making misleading or deceptive statements on matters of public health. Morling J considered that the aspect of public interest together with the fact that the proceedings were in the nature of a test case on the issue of whether passive smoking is a hazard to the health of non-smokers justified him in making an order for indemnity costs.

[His Honour allowed the appeal.]

20.3.3 See also *Huntsman Chemical Co Australia Ltd v International Pools Australia Ltd* (1995) 36 NSWLR 242. In that case, two parties to an appeal abandoned the appeal at the last minute. The respondent sought costs against them on an indemnity basis. Kirby P was sympathetic to this submission on the following grounds: 'party and party' costs would not fully compensate the respondent; from a commercial point of view there was much to be said for shifting the full costs of the appeal to those who had withdrawn; an indemnity costs award would discourage parties from pursuing futile appeals; and it was possible (but pure speculation) that the appeal had been brought to bring pressure to bear on the respondent to settle on favourable terms. Countervailing considerations included:

(a) the rarity of indemnity awards; the undesirability of perversely encouraging parties with hopeless appeals to persist in those appeals;

(b) the possibility that realisation of the hopelessness of the appeal reflected characteristic lawyerly procrastination;

(c) the undesirability of the courts unilaterally creating a special rule in relation to commercial litigation;

(d) the utility of the party/party rule as a disincentive to over-expenditure; and

(e) the undesirability of imposing what would effectively be retrospective liability.

Kirby P found the reasons advanced by the respondents compelling, and ruled that costs should be awarded on a 'party and party' basis. (Mahoney JA agreed; Rolfe AJA dissented.)

Costs on an indemnity basis may be awarded when 'the proceeding, and in particular the timing and circumstances in which it was brought, amounted to a misuse and abuse of the litigation process': *Bollag v Attorney-General (Commonwealth)* (1997) 149 ALR 355 at [375] per Merkel J. However, indemnity costs may be awarded even where there has not been an abuse of process, but where the course taken by a party has unreasonably prolonged a trial: *Rosniak v GIO* (1997) 41 NSWLR 608.

20.3.4 In *Verna Trading v New India Assurance* [1991] 1 VR 129, 'solicitor and own client' costs were awarded against a *successful* defendant on the grounds that it was not until the last day of the trial that the defendant revealed to the plaintiff a meritorious ground for refusing its claim. Had there been adequate disclosure of this defence at an earlier stage, unnecessary litigation might have been avoided. This seems extremely generous in the circumstances; the fact that the decision was upheld on appeal seems better explained in terms of the broad discretion conferred on a trial judge than in terms of the merits of the decision.

20.3.5 Indemnity costs were awarded on 'public interest' grounds in *Australian Electoral Commission v Towney (No 2)* (1994) 54 FCR 383. This case arose out of a dispute surrounding the conduct of an election. Due to errors by the Electoral Commission (AEC), it seemed that a fresh election would have to be called. The applicants were able to present the Court of Disputed Returns with details of a forensic scientific process whereby envelopes containing voting papers could be matched with voter identification slips. This meant that votes which otherwise could not have been counted now could be counted. The AEC argued that this was not a test case, since the proceeding would not establish any binding precedent. Foster J said (at 391):

> Whilst these proceedings cannot be described as a 'test case' in the true sense of that phrase they, nevertheless, 'have a wider effect than merely inter parties'. They introduced into electoral law the concept of using forensic scientific expertise to overcome the effects of human error in the electoral process. It was at least a path-finding or trial-blazing approach, more than a mere one-off practical solution.

Indemnity costs were awarded. (The form of the order is to be found at 392.)

Another ground for seeking indemnity costs in this case had been the financial disadvantages to Aboriginals or Aboriginal communities if costs were awarded on a 'party and party basis' only. Further, it was argued, if 'party and party' costs were ordered, a considerable proportion of the costs would have to be borne by the Aboriginal and Torres Strait Island Commission, or the applicants' legal representatives, since the applicants themselves would not be able to pay those costs. On the basis of earlier decisions (*Colgate Palmolive Co v Cussons Pty Ltd* (1993) 46 FCR 225, 118 ALR 248 and *AFCO v Tobacco Institute* (1991) 100 ALR 568), Foster J did not consider that these constituted grounds for awarding indemnity costs.

20.3.6   '[A]s a general rule a court will be more reluctant to make an order for indemnity costs against a litigant in person than against a represented litigant': *Macedon Ranges Shire Council v Thompson* [2009] VSCA 209 at [19] and see at [18]–[27], per Redlich JA and Beach AJA.

20.3.7   Question

1. The Victorian Law Reform Commission favours liberalisation of the basis for awarding costs in standard cases, so that the 'solicitor and client' basis would be the norm: Victorian Law Reform Commission, *Civil Justice Review Report*, 2008, p 581. The Law Institute of Victoria had advocated this change (although it 'had not seen the research to support the proposal'). The Australian Corporate Law Association, Telstra and IMF also favoured reform of the 'party and party' formula. The Insurance Council of Australia did not support the proposal. Can one make sense of these different stances? What are the advantages and disadvantages of the proposed reform?

PROBLEMATIC WINNERS

20.4.1   Sometimes the winner is clear. However, there are other circumstances in which this is not the case, such as where a party gets less than the amount offered in an offer of compromise. As already noted, such parties are at a costs disadvantage. A related problem arises where parties are successful on the question of liability but where their damages are such that the action could and should have been brought in a lower court. A party may be successful on some issues but not on others. In the same vein, the party may win on one of the several arguments it raised in support of the relief claimed, but lose on all the others.

Party wins in the wrong court

20.4.2   Jurisdictional limits mean that large claims may not be brought in lower courts, but they do not preclude the bringing of small claims in higher courts. In theory, a person who objected to the arbitration procedures operating in the Magistrates' Court could opt for trial in the Supreme Court or (in some cases) in the Federal Court. This would not normally happen. The costs of running such a case in a higher court would deter most prospective litigants and in any case, the matter could then be transferred under legislation such as the Courts (Case Transfer) Act 1991 (Vic).

However, the costs rules provide for those who wish to litigate in courts of higher jurisdiction. The formulae vary by jurisdiction. In the Federal Court, there are penalties for recovering less than $100,000 or if the case could have been brought in some other court or tribunal. In that event, the successful party recovers only two-thirds of its costs: FCR r 40.08. In most state and territory courts, there may be penalties for recovering amounts which would have been within the jurisdiction of a lower court to award. In the Australian Capital Territory, plaintiffs awarded less than $175,000 in a case that would have been within the Magistrates Court's jurisdiction are entitled to a specified proportion of their Supreme Court costs, depending on the amount they are awarded: r 1725. See too in relation to plaintiff's costs: NT r 63.22 (Local Court costs if plaintiff gets award within Local Court jurisdiction; no costs if plaintiff gets < $2,000); Qld r 697 (if judgment obtained could have been given by a lower court, costs will be those which would have been awarded had the case been commenced in the lower court); SA r 263(2) (f)–(h) (no order for costs if plaintiff receives < $150,000 in a motor car case; < $25,000 for defamation; or < $75,000 otherwise); Vic r 63.24 (The County Court scale operates if, in a defamation action, the plaintiff wins no more than $50,000 (r 63.24(1.1) or if, in a case where the County Court does not have unlimited jurisdiction, the plaintiff receives an amount no more than half the sum representing the jurisdictional limit: r 63.24(1). Since the County Court jurisdiction no longer is limited by the damages being sought, r 63.24(1) is practically irrelevant); WA O 66 r 17 (costs at Magistrates' Court level). In Tasmania, the Scale of Costs provides for lower costs entitlements in certain low stakes cases: r 837, Sch 1, Pt 2, but see Supreme Court Civil Procedure Act 1932 (Tas) s 13 which gives the court discretion in relation to the scale on which costs are to be awarded in cases which could have been brought in an inferior court.

The rules are discretionary. There may be cases where a party will be entitled to costs notwithstanding the small stakes. More generous costs may be awarded if a claim for a small amount of money involves a complex question of law such that a higher court is the appropriate forum. The exercise of the court's discretion in this regard was discussed in *O'Doherty v McMahon* [1971] VR 625 extracted below. Departure from the general rule might also be warranted if the purpose of bringing the action in a higher court was to take advantage of a particular remedy available only in the higher court. In Queensland, for example, charging orders may be made only by the Supreme Court.

20.4.3C   **O'Doherty v McMahon**
                                          [1971] VR 625
                              Supreme Court of Victoria, Full Court

---

[Under the relevant rules, costs penalties for suing in the higher court came into effect when a party recovered less than half the jurisdictional limit of the court below. In this case, the plaintiff recovered less than a sixth of the relevant jurisdictional limit, but was nonetheless awarded costs by the trial judge.]

Winneke CJ, Gowans and **Menhennitt JJ (at 627–30):** In his reasons for so doing [the judge] acknowledged that it was for the plaintiff to persuade him to exercise his discretion in her favour, and that he must exercise his discretion judicially. He then continued:

> However, in my opinion it is wrong to consider only the verdict when exercising my discretion. To do otherwise is to place too harsh a burden on the plaintiff and her solicitor when a decision has to be made as to the court [628] in which the action should be brought. In my opinion, it is proper when exercising one's discretion to look not only at the amount recovered but also at the situation which confronted the plaintiff and her solicitor when the action was about to be launched. Looking at this case it seems to me that it would be reasonable to take the view that the plaintiff could recover an amount in the vicinity of $1,000.00. It is notorious that assessments by juries and judges as to scars vary enormously. No one looking at this case could say that plaintiff or her solicitor had acted rashly or without any real consideration of the evidence when bringing this action in this Court.

Accordingly, I exercise my discretion in favour of the plaintiff. I do not think that she should be limited to magistrates' court costs. ...

The object of the rule is to protect the defendant against the unnecessary expense of higher costs in a court which is not appropriate for the case. The plaintiff, however, is left free to select his court. If he fails, no protection of the defendant is necessary because he receives costs applicable in the court to which he is taken. If he succeeds, the defendant is liable for costs appropriate to the court to which he is taken, provided, however, that the plaintiff obtains more than half of the amount which the lower court has jurisdiction to award. If the plaintiff recovers less than that amount the defendant is liable only for costs applicable in the lower court, in the absence of a special order.

The purpose of conferring a discretion to make a special order is to enable the court to order greater costs where the case has about it some special characteristic justifying the ordering of greater costs ...

[629] It, therefore, appears to us that the question in the present appeal is whether such special circumstances are shown to exist by reason of a view being taken that the plaintiff and his or her solicitor might reasonably consider that the plaintiff would or might recover an amount in excess of that to which the jurisdiction of the lower court is limited.

In this connexion, the first thing that is pertinent is that the rule itself already has an inbuilt mechanism for the protection of both parties in relation to this matter on the basis that it is a matter recognized as incapable of accurate estimation. In providing that, unless the judge otherwise orders, the plaintiff is entitled only to such costs as are applicable in the lower court where he recovers not more than half of the amount to which the jurisdiction of the lower court is limited, the rule itself has provided a wide margin for differences of opinion and errors of judgment. It is only where the error has gone to the extent of anticipating twice or more than twice the amount actually recovered that it will operate. Accordingly, the provisions of the rule itself tend to point to the conclusion that what has already been taken into account specifically should not be again considered in the exercise of the discretion.

This conclusion is reinforced by the consideration that to consider this matter on any other basis than the pragmatic rule laid down would often be unworkable. This would be particularly so in personal injury claims. One common element of a personal injury claim is a question of whether the plaintiff has suffered and is suffering and is likely to continue to suffer any pain, and its particular nature and degree. Another is whether there is limitation of movement to any and what extent. Sometimes there is a question as to whether the plaintiff had a pre-existing condition which was aggravated by the accident and, if so, what was the nature and extent of that condition and the aggravation. In determining what a plaintiff would or might reasonably have expected to recover, it would, of course, be insufficient to rely upon what the plaintiff said about any of these matters which involve subjective elements because the plaintiff might be exaggerating or deliberately misstating the position. On the other hand, to determine what amount could reasonably have been expected if a plaintiff were reasonably and competently advised would often be difficult, and even impossible. Whether the matter was considered on an objective basis of what a reasonable legal adviser would consider, or on the basis of the information before the actual adviser, it would involve the impossible task of attempting to determine to what extent such a legal adviser should have disbelieved the plaintiff or discounted his claims.

It was argued that in considering what a plaintiff might reasonably have expected to recover, the trial judge was entitled to consider whether the jury should have awarded the plaintiff more than it did. But any such approach would involve the judge forming a view of the facts in conflict with the finding of the jury. We think that any such approach would be erroneous as it would involve one part of the tribunal adopting a view of the facts in conflict with that adopted by another part of the same tribunal (compare in respect to criminal proceedings *R v Harris* [1961] VR 236, at 237). It is pertinent to observe that in the present case, where the general damages were assessed by the jury at $150, it would have involved the trial judge concluding that the general damages should have been about six times that amount in order to bring the total damages (inclusive of the special damages of $114.80) over the limit of the jurisdiction in the magistrates' court. If the approach which we would have discussed were put on a more limited basis, namely, that it would at all events be appropriate to consider [630] whether the plaintiff and his adviser might reasonably have expected to recover more than half of the lower court jurisdiction, it is apparent that this approach, conceding as it does that all that could reasonably have been expected could have been recovered in the lower court, would never provide a justification for ordering the defendant to pay the costs appropriate to the higher court. Further it is apparent that what is then being attempted is to substitute for the actual recovery, to which the rule refers, an expectation of recovery, subjective to the plaintiff or his advisers. ...

It is unnecessary and undesirable to attempt in this case to define the kind of considerations or to set out illustrations of the considerations which would justify a favourable exercise of the discretion conferred by O 65 r 12, of the Supreme Court Rules or O 51 r 2, of the County Court Rules beyond saying that the complexity of the case or other like difficulties might be regarded as special circumstances justifying the resort to the higher court. We would not, however, wish to limit the class of such special circumstances further than is necessary for this decision.

20.4.4 A final victory may follow interlocutory skirmishing. Decisions in interlocutory disputes may include orders that a particular party pay the costs of the particular hearing, and may order that costs be paid immediately rather than later. Costs of interlocutory proceedings may be far from trivial: *Magna Alloys & Research Pty Ltd v Kevin Lindsay Coffee (No 2)* [1982] VR 97, where costs of $39,000 were awarded, along with the costs of the appeal in relation to those costs. Usually, however, the question of costs in interlocutory proceedings is deferred, pending a final decision in relation to the case. The rationale for this is that the justification for seeking interlocutory decisions may sometimes not be apparent until later in the proceeding. When decisions are deferred, the decision on costs can be framed in a number of ways, each with different implications:

- An order that a party pay *costs in any event* means that it must pay the costs of an application even if it is ultimately successful, but (subject to provisions in rules to the contrary) only at the conclusion of the litigation: *Bull Nominees Pty Ltd v McElwee* (1998) 7 Tas R 339. These are likely to be ordered where the party against whom the order has been made is in breach of the rules.

- An order for *costs in the cause* means that the costs of the application must be borne by the party which ultimately must bear the costs of the action. An order that costs be, for example, the plaintiff's costs in the cause, means that if the plaintiff is ultimately held entitled to costs, these costs will include the plaintiff's costs. If the defendant is successful, the defendant is not entitled to his or her costs in the application. This type of order would be normal where the application is made because the rules require it, rather than because there has been a procedural irregularity.

- Costs *of the proceeding* includes costs of trial as well as the costs of any interlocutory applications, and is to be contrasted with *costs of trial* which (on the basis of the *expressio unius est exclusio alterius* principle) include only the costs of the trial: see Qld r 679.

- *Costs thrown away* are the costs which have been incurred in connection with the taking of steps which have been rendered worthless as a result, for example, of a default judgment being set aside.

- *No order as to costs* means that each side must bear its own costs.

- If *an order is silent as to costs*, the following presumptions operate:
  - successful applicants and successful opponents of applicants are entitled to costs as costs in the cause. Unsuccessful parties are not entitled to their costs as costs in the cause; and
  - where there is an unopposed motion, the costs of both parties are costs in the cause.

- Where *costs are reserved*, the decision about who must bear the costs is deferred until the end of the trial. At that point, an order must be made in relation to the costs before a party can include those costs among the costs to be taxed: see Qld r 698.

In some jurisdictions (for example, FCR r 40.13; NSW r 42.7(2); NT r 63.04; SA r 265(2)(b), but cf ACT r 1701(1)(a); Qld r 682; Vic r 63.03; WA O 66 r 10), costs in interlocutory proceedings are not payable until the end of proceedings unless the court orders otherwise. The ALRC (Report No 89, [7.185]–[7.187]) has recommended that the rule should be amended to remove the presumption against orders that costs in interlocutory matters be paid immediately. Conversely, the Victorian Law Reform Commission has recommended that 'interlocutory costs orders should not be taxed prior to the determination of the case unless the court orders otherwise': Victorian Law Reform Commission, *Civil Justice Review Report*, 2008, p 680.

Party ultimately wins, but loses on several issues

20.4.5   Normally, the winner gets costs. If one of the issues has been the subject of a notice to admit (see 14.4.1–14.4.6), normally the party must pay the costs of proof of the fact in question. Otherwise, it is at the discretion of the court, although there are *dicta* and (in some jurisdictions) rules which suggest that, except in defined circumstances, successful parties are usually entitled to their costs. However, there are some cases in which costs will be apportioned by issue, which may involve difficult calculations. More usually, an order may be made that the loser pays only a proportion of the winner's costs. The proportion is likely to involve not much more than an intelligent guess, with errors tending to favour the successful party, especially if it is the defendant who is successful: see, for example, *Koninklijke Philips Electronics NV v Remington Products Australia Pty Ltd* (1999) 45 IPR 634; [1999] FCA 1225; *Fexuto Pty Ltd v Bosnjak Holdings Pty Ltd (No 3)* (1998) 29 ACSR 315; [1998] NSWSC 616; *Alborn v Stephens* [2010] QCA 58, [7]-[9], [12]; *Tomanovic v Global Mortgage Equity Corp Pty Ltd (No 2)* [2011] NSWCA 256, [81]–[117]. In *Rosniak v GIO* (1997) 41 NSWLR 608, the Court of Appeal upheld an order awarding the plaintiff costs on a standard basis, except in relation to one issue on which she lost, in relation to which it awarded costs to the defendant on an indemnity basis. In *McFadzenn v FMEU* (2007) 20 VR 250, [2007] VSCA 289, [148]–[168], where the plaintiffs had some success, the trial court had awarded the defendants 40 per cent of their costs, and the Court of Appeal refused leave to appeal.

Byrns v Davie
                                   [1991] 2 VR 568
                               Supreme Court of Victoria

Gobbo J (at 569–71): The plaintiffs have failed in their action on what was essentially a threshold matter, namely, the construction of the covenant. The plaintiffs succeeded in respect of other matters that occupied a large proportion of the hearing. I refer to the question as to whether, as the second and third named defendants both pleaded and contended, the plaintiffs consented to the breach of covenant. I also refer to the other question that occupied much time, namely, whether there was any effect on view, and, in particular, whether there was any damage by way of depreciation in value of the higher land owned by the plaintiffs.

The plaintiffs submitted that the proper order was that there be no order as to costs. The first defendant submitted that in no circumstances should the first defendant be deprived of her costs. The second and third-named defendants submitted that they should receive their full costs or, at worst, be deprived of only a small portion of their costs.

Only one authority was referred to me, namely, *Ritter v Godfrey* [1920] 2 KB 47. That decision was relied upon by Mr Johnston, who appeared for the second and third defendants, as supporting the proposition that a successful defendant should not be deprived of his costs except in the specific circumstances set out in the judgment of Atkin LJ in that case.

The matter of costs is first dealt with in s 24 of the Supreme Court Act which provides:

Unless otherwise expressly provided by this or any other Act or by the Rules, the costs of and incidental to all matters in the Court, including the administration of estates and trusts, is in the discretion of the Court and the Court has full power to determine by whom and to what extent the costs are to be paid.

There are also the Rules of Court and I refer in particular to O 63 of the Rules of the Supreme Court and in particular to rr 63.02 and 63.04. The present rules are in somewhat different form to the previous rules but I am of the view that there has not been any substantial change relevant to the present case.

The Act and the rules do not, in my view, support an argument that no apportionment according to issues can be made against a defendant that is ultimately successful, even though such defendant fails on particular issues or in respect of particular parts of the proceedings.

It is clear that an order may be made as to costs of part of a proceeding even if such part does not relate to a distinct issue in the action or a cause of action or a defence pleaded by any defendant. This was so decided by the High Court in relation to the relevant rule of the Supreme Court of Victoria in *Woolf v Burman* (1940) 13 ALJ 431.

Further, it has not been the practice to treat successful defendants as in a wholly different position to plaintiffs in deciding on an award of costs in cases where a party has only been partly successful. Thus the discussion in the Full Court decision, in particular, in the judgment of Cussen J in *Willis v Wilson & Mackinnon* [1922] VLR 453 illustrates this being a case where the costs of a partly successful defendant were in issue. These judgments in this case do not, in my view, support the kind of proposition that was sought to be made out before me.

I return to the decision in *Ritter v Godfrey,* and, in particular, to the passage that was relied upon in the judgment of Atkin LJ, at 60, where he said: 'In the case of a wholly successful defendant, in my opinion the [570] judge must give the defendant his costs unless there is evidence that the defendant (1) brought about the litigation, or (2) has done something connected with the institution or the conduct of the suit calculated to occasion unnecessary litigation and expense, or (3) has done some wrongful act in the course of the transaction of which the plaintiff complains.'

As the above passage indicates, the decision was directed to cases where the defendant was wholly successful. That alone suffices to distinguish its application here.

Moreover, I do not read the decision as confining the ambit of judicial discretion, at any rate, where there are separate issues that were litigated in respect of which the defendant failed. This is evident in the case of *Jackson v AngloAmerican Oil Co Ltd* [1923] 2 KB 601 where the decision in *Ritter v Godfrey* was explained and applied. Lush J said, at 605–6: 'If there had been a separate issue in the case on which the defendants failed, the county court judge could, no doubt, have ordered them to pay the costs of that issue, and to set these costs off against those of the issues on which they had succeeded. I do not say whether in such a case the judge could order each party to pay their own costs. In this case, however, there were not separate issues.'

I should point out that in that case the trial judge had deprived the defendants of their costs in circumstances where there was a claim for negligence and the defendant had pleaded contributory negligence which had been made out. This was, of course, a case in 1923 at a time when that defence was decisive as to liability. Accordingly, it was held that the defendant was wholly successful and had not failed on a separate issue.

[571] Finally, in relation to the costs of a successful defendant, I note the decision of the Court of Appeal in *Gold v Patman and Fotheringham Ltd* [1958] 2 All ER 497. In that case there had been a dispute over a building contract and the defendants raised a great many factual issues, on all of which they failed, but they succeeded on the construction of the contract. The Court of Appeal held that as the question of construction could have suitably been decided on a preliminary issue limited to that question, in the circumstances, though the contractors had succeeded in the appeal on the question of construction the appeal would be allowed with costs but they would be given only half their costs in the court below.

Sellers LJ says in the course of that decision, at 503: 'If a plaintiff makes unnecessary and unfounded claims, they can well be segregated and he may be penalised in costs; but a greater latitude is given to a defendant.' Then later on it was pointed out that a party in the position of the defendant could have taken the course of having the contractual issue brought forward, thus obviating considerable expense. In those circumstances only half the costs were allowed to the successful defendant.

I have come to the conclusion that the decision in *Ritter v Godfrey* is not applicable to the present circumstances, both because of its terms and the later comments on it, and also because of the particular rules of this court and its overriding discretion.

I am satisfied in the present case that some 70 per cent of the hearing time was taken up with those parts of the proceedings described by me in respect of which the plaintiffs were successful and in respect of which the second and third-named defendants failed.

In particular, I take into account the impact that this had on the costs of all parties in respect of the hearing. I also have regard to the fact that some portion of the rehearing costs would have related to the matters I have referred to, in particular, the valuation evidence that was led.

In my view, the general discretion as conferred by the Act and the rules enables me to make an order that is a single order, fixing what proportion of a party's costs should be paid by another party, thus obviating cross orders or particular orders as to particular items of costs.

It is not, in these circumstances, necessary to make a specific order under r 63.04(2) which is really directed to assisting the Taxing Master by indicating what portion of the costs is represented in time by a mere order as to a particular question or part of a proceeding.

> In my opinion, substantial justice will be done if I order as I do, that the second and the third-named defendants recover only 40 per cent of their taxed costs, including reserved costs.
>
> As to the first defendant, I do not see why she should be deprived of her costs. True it is that her counsel cross-examined on the two matters on which the plaintiffs succeeded, but she called no evidence on those matters and she added to the action, as a result, only by a matter of one or two hours.

COMPLEX CASES

20.5.1   Decisions on costs become more complicated when a case is more than a simple plaintiff and defendant action. Counterclaims raise questions about how costs decisions are to be made, when both claimant and counterclaimant succeed. Cases involving multiple parties raise the question of who should bear whose costs, especially in cases where some defendants succeed in their defence, while others fail.

20.5.2   Where there is a claim and a counterclaim, and the same party is successful on each, there are no problems. Where the plaintiff succeeds on the claim but loses on the counterclaim, it would be entitled to costs for the claim, and the defendant would be entitled to costs in relation to the counterclaim. Some costs will have been incurred in relation to both. These must somehow be apportioned. This will involve an element of guesswork. Each party's costs will depend on the size of their victory on the claim or counterclaim, and not on their net victory. Often this will not overly matter. However, it is easy to think of circumstances in which it may make a considerable difference:

- The plaintiff wins $400,000 on its claim but makes a net gain of only $20,000. The plaintiff's case was far more complicated than the defendant's and required a far greater outlay. If costs were determined on the basis of the net gain, the plaintiff would be severely disadvantaged.

- The plaintiff wins $400,000 on its claim, and makes a net gain of $100,000. The defendant's party and party costs in connection with the counterclaim exceeded the plaintiff's in relation to the claim. Under a net gain rule, the plaintiff would be better off. Under the rules as they stand, the defendant will be ahead.

20.5.3   Where the plaintiff succeeds against some defendants but not others, the court must decide who pays the costs of the successful defendants. It has several options:

- to order that the plaintiff pays the costs of the successful defendants, and that the unsuccessful defendants pay the plaintiff's costs, but not those costs incurred by the plaintiff in the action against the successful defendants;

- to order the plaintiff to pay the costs of the successful defendants, with the plaintiff being entitled to indemnity from the unsuccessful defendants; and

- to order that the unsuccessful defendants: (1) pay the costs of the plaintiff; and (2) that they pay the costs of the successful defendants.

All three orders are encountered, the last two being known as Bullock and Sanderson orders respectively. The former order takes its name from *Bullock v London General Omnibus Co*

[1907] 1 KB 264; the latter from *Sanderson v Blyth Theatre Co* [1903] 2 KB 533. Decisions as to costs in this situation involve two issues: first, whether the unsuccessful defendants should be directly or indirectly liable for the costs of the successful defendant; second, if so, whether the payment is to be direct or indirect.

20.5.4C	**Gould v Vaggelas** (1984) 58 ALJR 560 High Court of Australia

[The appellants and the respondents negotiated an agreement for the sale by the respondents of a business and the property on which it was conducted. The agreement was embodied in a series of contracts. The business did not prosper. The company created to run it went into liquidation. Since the company still owed money to the respondents at the time of liquidation, the respondents sued the appellants as guarantors of the company. The appellants counterclaimed for fraudulent misrepresentation. They also joined their accountants as respondents. They were awarded damages against the respondents, but their claim against the accountants was dismissed. A Bullock order was made against the respondents.

On appeal to the Full Court, the trial judge's decision was reversed, and the appellants appealed to the High Court. The appeal was allowed. Among the issues considered was the appropriate costs order.]

Gibbs CJ (at 565–6): It is sometimes said that the court may make ... a Bullock order — where it is reasonable in all the circumstances for the plaintiff to bring the action against two or more defendants: see the Supreme Court Practice (UK) 1982 par 62/2/39 and *Halsbury* (4th ed) vol 37 par 219. There are some statements in the authorities which appear to support that view, including the judgment of Latham CJ in *Johnson Tyne Foundry Pty Ltd v Maffra Corporation* (1948) 77 CLR 544 at 556. In my respectful [566] opinion, however, the mere fact that the joinder of two defendants was reasonable does not mean that the unsuccessful defendant should be ordered to pay, directly or indirectly, the costs of the successful defendant. Obviously a judge should make a Bullock order only if he considers it just that the costs of the successful defendant should be borne by the unsuccessful defendant, and, if nothing that the unsuccessful defendant has said or done has led the plaintiff to sue the other defendant, who ultimately was held not to be liable, it is difficult to see any reason why the unsuccessful defendant should be required to pay for the plaintiff's error or overcaution.

The ground on which a *Bullock* order may be made is, in my opinion, more accurately stated in a passage in *Sanderson v Blyth Theatre Co* [1903] 2 KB 533 at 539, which was cited with approval in *Bullock v London General Omnibus Co* [1907] 1 KB 264 at 272 and *Hong v A & R Brown Ltd* [1948] 1 KB 515 at 522, viz that the costs which the plaintiff has been ordered to pay to the defendant who succeeded, and which the plaintiff recovers from the defendant who has failed 'are ordered to be paid by the unsuccessful defendant, on the ground that ... those costs have been reasonably and properly incurred by the plaintiff as between him and the [unsuccessful] defendant'. In *Johnson Tyne Foundry v Maffra Corporation*, Williams J at 572–3 stated the principle in a similar way and Starke and Dixon JJ in giving their reasons for making a Bullock order, both relied on the circumstance that the attitude adopted by the successful defendant had induced the plaintiff to join the other defendant: see at 559–60, 566. In my respectful opinion the true position was clearly stated by Blackburn CJ in *Steppke v National Capital Development Commission* (1978) 21 ACTR 23 at 30–1, when he said that 'there is a condition for the making of a *Bullock* order, in addition to the question of whether the suing of the successful defendant was reasonable, and that the conduct of the unsuccessful defendant has been such as to make it fair to impose some liability on it for the costs of the successful defendant'.

The decision whether or not to make a Bullock order lay within the discretion of the judge. By s 9 of the Judicature Act 1876 (Q) no *order* made by a judge 'as to costs only which by law are left to the discretion of the judge' is subject to appeal except by leave of the judge making the order. The effect of the corresponding section in the United Kingdom has been held to be that 'when a judge, deliberately intending to exercise his discretionary powers, has acted on facts connected with or leading up to the litigation which have been proved before him or which he has himself observed during the progress of the case, then it seems to me that a Court of Appeal, although it may deem his reasons insufficient and may disagree with his conclusion, is prohibited by the statute from entertaining an appeal from it': *Donald Campbell & Co v Pollak* [1927] AC 732 at 812; *Jones v McKie* [1964] 1 WLR 960 at 966. I am not sure that this statement means any more than that it would not be enough to justify interference with an order for costs that the members of the Court of Appeal themselves took that view that if they had been in the position of the judge of first instance they would have taken a difference [sic] course. However, since no reliance was placed on s 9 of the Judicature Act in argument before us, I shall assume, in favour of the present respondents, that the rules applicable are no more stringent than those stated in *House v The King* (1936) 55 CLR 499 at 504–5, with regard to appeals against any discretionary decision.

It was pointed out on behalf of the respondents that the causes of action against Messrs Ingles and Tiffin [the accountant] on the one hand and Mr and Mrs Vaggelas and the vendor companies on the other were unrelated. Failure against one did not mean success against the other. The case against Messrs Ingles and Tiffin primarily depended on the evidence of the Goulds, and not on the evidence of Vaggelas. However Connolly J relied on the fact that Vaggelas contended that he had made available to Mrs Gould and to Mr Ingles his books and records so that they could form their own judgement, and that in consequence if Mrs Gould has relied on anyone it was on Mr Ingles. It does not appear to me that the learned judge has arred [sic] in law or mistaken the facts, or that he has taken into account any matter which he was not entitled to take into account or failed to consider anything which he should have taken into account. Although I am not sure that I would have taken the same view had I been called on to exercise my own discretion, it seems to me that the case was not one in which the full court should have interfered.

[**Murphy, Wilson** and **Brennan JJ** agreed.]

20.5.5 *Thorne v Doug Wade Consultants Pty Ltd* [1985] VR 433 arose out of an acrimonious neighbourhood dispute. The first three defendants were a company, which owned a house in Parkville, and Mr and Mrs Wade, who owned and controlled the company. The fourth defendant was the City of Melbourne, which had purportedly granted a permit to make modifications to the house. The plaintiffs objected to the alterations and sought their demolition. They contended that the permit under which the alteration had been approved was void, proper procedures not having been complied with. They also contended that the defendants knew this. Their action against the City succeeded in the sense that the court found that the council had indeed failed to comply with prescribed procedures. However, the action against the City was largely unsuccessful. Several plaintiffs were found to lack *locus standi*. The court found that it would be futile to make a declaration to the effect that the permit was void. It also found that the action against the first three defendants failed: they were not aware that the permit was void, and therefore it would not be fair to order the demolition of the offending alterations.

The plaintiffs argued that the City should bear their costs and those of the successful defendants.

O'Bryan J rejected the submission, saying (at 475):

> The City of Melbourne was joined as party some time after the action commenced to assist the plaintiffs to obtain injunctive relief against the Wades. Declaratory relief and not damages was sought from the City of Melbourne. The principal relief sought by the plaintiffs in the form of a mandatory injunction was against the Wades. The court determined that in all the circumstances it was not appropriate to grant equitable relief against the Wades. The reasons for not granting relief had nothing to do with the conduct of the City of Melbourne. As the Court has refused to grant the relief claimed by the plaintiffs, prima facie it would seem neither just nor reasonable to throw the burden of the plaintiffs' costs upon the City of Melbourne. Accordingly I must refuse the application for an order that the fourth defendant pay either the plaintiffs' costs or the costs which the plaintiff must pay to the Wades.

The effect of the decision was to threaten the residents with bankruptcy and the Wades with underpayment of their costs. Legislation was subsequently passed enabling the City of Melbourne to assume the burden of their costs, which it did. In the aftermath of the litigation, legislation was also passed limiting the Supreme Court's jurisdiction in planning matters, and permitting the Supreme Court to grant leave to appeal in costs matters. The Wades no longer live in Parkville.

20.5.6 In many cases, it will not matter whether a Bullock or a Sanderson order is made. The net gains and losses to the plaintiff, the successful defendants and the unsuccessful defendants are the same. Where it matters is where the unsuccessful defendants are impecunious. There, the first type of order will leave the successful defendants indemnified, and the plaintiff out of pocket. The second order will leave the successful defendants somewhat out of pocket. A Bullock order was made in *Barradine v Westworld* [1988] 1 Qd R 498. Barradine alleged breach of an agreement between itself and Westworld. Westworld argued that it had given no authority to its solicitors to negotiate the agreement in question. As a result, Barradine joined the solicitors, alleging breach of a warranty of authority. Andrews CJ found that Westworld had in fact given the authority in question. The solicitors were therefore entitled to costs, and Barradine was entitled to costs from Westworld. He ordered that Barradine pay the solicitors' costs and that Westworld (which was being wound up) indemnify Barradine. Barradine had brought the solicitors into the action. Their understanding of the facts was that Westworld had indeed given the authority in question. It was therefore appropriate that Barradine, rather than the solicitors, bear any loss occasioned by the unsuccessful defendant's inability to pay.

20.5.7 A Sanderson order would be appropriate if the successful defendants were joint contractors with the plaintiffs, but reluctant to join in the litigation. In that case, the plaintiffs could succeed only by joining the remaining contractors as defendants. In resisting the plaintiffs' claim, the defendant would have left it with no alternative but to do so. It would be appropriate that the defendant pay the successful defendants' costs.

COSTS WHICH DO NOT FOLLOW THE EVENT

20.6.1 The general rule that costs will be awarded to the successful party (subject to the partial exceptions set out above) is a strong presumption. However, the ALRC in Report No 75 recommended that there should be certain categories of case where losing parties are safe from costs awards and may even be awarded costs. These included public interest cases and cases where a party's circumstances were such that the risk of having to pay costs could adversely affect the party's capacity to negotiate a fair settlement, or present its case properly: ALRC Report No 75, p 63.

Public interest litigation

20.6.2C	**Oshlack v Richmond River Council**
	(1998) 193 CLR 72; [1998] HCA 11
	High Court of Australia

[The appellant challenged a proposed development in the New South Wales Land and Environment Court. His application failed, but Stein J declined to make a costs order against him. His grounds were as follows:

1. The traditional 'loser pays' principle was more appropriate in private law cases than in public law actions where application of the principle could defeat the purpose of the relevant legislation as evidenced by its broad standing rules.

2. Something more than the fact that the litigation was 'public interest' litigation was required to justify departure from the usual rule.

3. Oshlack was motivated not by personal interests but by a public-spirited desire to see environment law enforced, and by concern that the proposed development threatened a koala habitat.

4. Oshlack's concerns were widely shared.

5. The litigation resolved some significant issues in relation to the interpretation and administration of the provisions relating to endangered species and proposed developments.

6. Considerations (3)–(5) warranted departure from the 'usual rule'.

The developer did not appeal against this finding, but the Council did. The New South Wales Court of Appeal held that Stein J's exercise of discretion had miscarried. Oshlack appealed to the High Court which allowed the appeal in a 3:2 decision. **Gaudron** and **Gummow JJ** based their decision largely on the breadth of the court's jurisdiction in relation to costs, but considered that it was open to Stein J to take the public interest elements in the case into account, given the statutory scheme involved in the case. **Kirby J** considered that it was a relevant consideration that the litigation involved 'public interest' issues, given the legislative context in which the decision was made. **Brennan CJ** and **McHugh J** dissented on the grounds that the case was indistinguishable from *Latoudis v Casey* where the court had decided that the 'usual rule' applied to the awarding of costs to successful criminal defendants in the Victorian Magistrates' Courts, notwithstanding that prosecutions involved a strong 'public interest' element.]

Gaudron and Gummow JJ (at 91): [49] The primary judge reasoned from a starting point which favoured costs orders against the appellant as the unsuccessful party. However, he correctly drew a distinction earlier expressed as follows by Menzies J, with the concurrence of Kitto, Taylor and Windeyer JJ: *Cooney v Kuringgai Corporation* (1963) 114 CLR 582 at 605:

> Prohibitions and restrictions such as those under consideration are directed towards public health and comfort and the orderly arrangement of municipal areas and are imposed, not for the benefit of particular individuals, but for the benefit of the public or at least a section of the public, *viz* those living in the municipal area.

Having characterised the nature of the litigation as concerned with public rather than private rights, Stein J stated that 'something more' than the categorisation of proceedings as public interest litigation was needed before a successful defendant should be denied costs: (1994) 82 LGERA 236 at 244. Stein J then isolated the factors identified in pars (iii), (iv) and (v) [grounds 3–5, above] of the summary given earlier in these reasons as sufficient special circumstances. In proceeding to exercise in this fashion the discretion conferred by s 69, Stein J did not take into account considerations which can be said to have been definitely extraneous to any objects the legislature could have had in view in enacting s 69 and in relation to the operation of s 69 upon proceedings instituted under s 123 of the EPA Act. The contrary is the case.

McHugh J (at 100): [75] His Honour's judgment does not refer to any principle or criterion which would enable other courts to determine why the matters that he mentioned made the case 'public interest litigation'. Nor does he refer to any principle or criterion that would enable other courts to distinguish this case from prosecutions, and constitutional and administrative law matters that are matters of public controversy in which there is a public interest in the outcome of the litigation or which involve an analysis of statutory provisions which should prove helpful in other cases. Without an organising principle to apply or a set of criteria to guide, there is a real danger that, by invoking the 'public interest litigation' factor in cases that affect the public interest or involve a public authority, an award of costs will depend on nothing more than the social preferences of the judge, a dependence that will be masked by reliance on the protean concept of public interest litigation.

Kirby J (at 123–4): [136] The Council argued that the cost discretion had miscarried because of the reference to an indeterminate class of 'public interest' litigation. It was submitted that this concept introduced a nebulous consideration of a social, economic or political kind. It was unhelpful as a criterion authorising departure from the ordinary compensatory [124] principle. I agree that it is difficult to define with precision what is meant by 'public interest' litigation. Stein J acknowledged this. However, the series of cases to which his Honour referred illustrates, clearly enough, that in this country, as well as in England (*Donald Campbell & Co v Pollak* [1927] AC 732 at 811–812), New Zealand (*Ratepayers and Residents Action Association Inc v Auckland City Council* [1986] 1 NZLR 746; *Auckland Bulk Gas Users Group v Commerce Commission* [1990] 1 NZLR 448 at 472–473), Canada (*Mahar v Rogers Cablesystems Ltd* (1995) 25 OR (3d) 690 at 703–704; *Reese v Alberta* [1993] 1 WWR 450) and elsewhere (*Southeast Alaska Conservation Council Inc v State of Alaska* 665 P 2d 544 at 553–554 (1983)) a discrete approach has been taken to costs in circumstances where courts have concluded that a litigant has properly brought proceedings to advance a legitimate public interest, has contributed to the proper understanding of the law in question and has involved no private gain. In such cases the costs incurred have occasionally been described as incidental to the proper exercise of public administration (*R v Archbishop of Canterbury*

[1902] 2 KB 503 at 572; *Latoudis v Casey* (1990) 170 CLR 534 at 550, citing *Ex parte Hivis; Re Michaelis* (1933) 50 WN (NSW) 90 at 92). Upon that basis it has been considered that they ought not to be wholly a burden on the particular litigant.

[137] The approach just described is not entirely dissimilar to that long taken in courts of equity in cases in which trustees and other litigants in a special position, who have properly brought a matter before a court, are spared costs orders against themselves personally: Nevill and Ashe, *Equity Proceedings with Precedents (New South Wales)* (1981) at par [1412]. See also Dale et al, *The Practice of the Chancery Division ('Daniell's Chancery Practice')*, 7th ed (1982), vol 1 at 953. Nor is this approach dissimilar to the special orders which this Court quite frequently makes providing special leave to appeal upon condition that the appellant will pay the costs of a respondent whatever the outcome of the appeal: see for example the offer of the appellant in *Northern Sandblasting Pty Ltd v Harris* (1997) 188 CLR 313 at 417. Nor is it different from the principle long applied to that type of case recognised by the courts as a 'test case': *Attrill v Richmond River Shire Council* (1995) 38 NSWLR 545 at 556. Such orders could not be supported if the *sole* criterion for the exercise of the costs discretion were compensation to the successful party and if that were necessary to the word 'costs' itself.

20.6.3 Notes and questions

1. Could one argue that governments and councils are also concerned with the public interest, motivated by altruistic concerns, and capable, by their litigation, of contributing to clarification of the law? If 'no', why? If 'yes', should they be required to pay costs if they lose environmental cases?

2. In *Friends of Hinchinbrook Society Inc v Minister for Environment* (1998) 99 LGERA 140, the Full Federal Court held that the applicant should pay the respondents' costs. The fact that the litigation was 'public interest litigation' was immaterial. *Oshlack* was distinguished on the grounds that it turned (a) on the legislative provisions governing costs in the Land and Environment Court and (b) on the fact that the judge who had made the original costs order had been exercising a very wide discretion. How convincing are these grounds? How far can *Friends of Hinchinbrook* and *Oshlack* both be justified by reference to the same underlying principle? More recent cases include: *Bat Advocacy NSW Inc v Minister for Environment Protection, Heritage and the Arts (No 2)* (2011) 280 ALR 91; [2011] FCAFC 84 (normal costs order); *Roe v Director General, Department of Environment and Conservation* [2011] WASCA 57 (no order).

3. The Judicial Review Act 1991 (Qld) s 49(2) provides for exemption from costs in certain 'public interest' cases.

4. The ALRC in Report No 75 favoured special rules for costs in public interest litigation:

Recommendation 45 — public interest costs orders

A court or tribunal may, upon the application of a party, make a public interest costs order if the court or tribunal is satisfied that:

- the proceedings will determine, enforce or clarify an important right or obligation affecting the community or a significant sector of the community;
- the proceedings will affect the development of the law generally and may reduce the need for further litigation; and
- the proceedings otherwise have the character of public interest or test case proceedings.

A court or tribunal may make a public interest costs order notwithstanding that one or more of the parties to the proceedings has a personal interest in the matter.

Recommendation 46 — objects clause

The legislation establishing public interest costs orders should state that the object of such orders is to assist the initiation and conduct of litigation that affects the community, or a significant sector of the community, or will develop the law.

Recommendation 47 — terms of a public interest costs order

If the court or tribunal is satisfied that there are grounds for it to make a public interest costs order, it may make such orders as to costs as it considers appropriate having regard to:

- the resources of the parties;
- the likely cost of the proceedings to each party;
- the ability of each party to present his or her case properly or to negotiate a fair settlement; and
- the extent of any private or commercial interest each party may have in the litigation.

The orders the court or tribunal may make include an order that:

- costs follow the event;
- each party bear his or her own costs;
- the party applying for the public interest costs order, regardless of the outcome of the proceedings, shall:
  – not be liable for the other party's costs;
  – only be liable to pay a specified proportion of the other party's costs;
  – be able to recover all or part of his or her costs from the other party; or
- another person, group, body or fund, in relation to which the court or tribunal has power to make a costs order, is to pay all or part of the costs of one or more of the parties.

An order under this provision will be subject to the power of the courts or tribunal to make disciplinary and case management costs orders.

Recommendation 48 — determining the resources of the parties

When considering the 'resources of the parties' the court must have regard to the financial circumstances of each party and to whether the financial capacity of any of the parties to pay an adverse costs order is being affected in whole or part by legal aid, contingency fees, insurance, fighting funds, tax deductibility or any other factor.

The rationale for these recommendations is set out in ALRC Report No 75, Ch 13. The Victorian Law Reform Commission's recent report includes an extensive analysis of the public interest issue, and concludes:

> The commission believes there should be express provision for courts to make orders protecting public interest litigants from adverse costs in appropriate cases. This could include orders made at the outset of the litigation. The fact that a litigant may have a pecuniary or other personal interest in the outcome of the proceeding should not preclude the court from determining that the proceedings are in the public interest: Victorian Law Reform Commission, *Civil Justice Review Report* (2008), 676.

What would be the practical effect of the implementation of these recommendations? Suppose litigants were to seek an injunction restraining a development capable of generating 100 jobs in an area of high unemployment. The development will threaten the habitat of a rare species of Grevillea. The litigation would not proceed unless a favourable public interest costs order was made. The development will not proceed if the litigation goes ahead. There is a weak but arguable case that the body granting the approval made a procedural error in doing so. What order would probably be made in these circumstances? Would it be in the public interest? Should judicial determinations of what the public interest entails be based on the judge's values, the values of judges in general, evidence of public opinion, or the policies of elected governments and municipal councils? Or does 'public interest' really mean no more than an interest shared by a sizeable section of the public, in which case there is no reason why litigation should not involve plaintiffs and defendants, each of which is a public interest litigator?

5. The effect of permitting public interest orders would clearly be to increase the power of groups that find it difficult to mobilise resources, such as environmental and consumer protection groups. Corporate groups would be disadvantaged, but their cultural, economic and political power would nonetheless continue to be considerable. How would you expect them to respond in the event of public interest orders being introduced?

Impecunious parties

20.6.4   Costs awards can bankrupt unsuccessful parties of even moderate means, and this creates a powerful incentive for all except the wealthy to settle rather than run even a small risk of an adverse costs award. Risk aversion will mean settling cases for less than their value to a more affluent party. In the United States, where (as elsewhere) plaintiffs outnumber defendants, the solution to this problem is contingency fees, coupled with a rule that each party bears its own costs. Since gains forgone are usually less painful than assets stripped away, this is in some ways a satisfactory solution. Its downside is that it also facilitates the use of legal action as a form of extortion, and leads to undue reliance on the legal system to do what could probably be far better, efficiently and equitably done by an adequate social welfare system.

20.6.5   In its Report No 75, the ALRC recommended changes to the costs rules to make allowance for the 'chilling' effects of the threat of costs.

Recommendation 40 — alternative costs orders where a party's ability to litigate or negotiate is materially and adversely affected

A court may, at any stage of the proceedings, upon the application of a party, make an alternative costs order if it is satisfied that the risk of having to pay the other party's costs if unsuccessful will materially and adversely affect the ability of the party to:

- present his or her case properly; or
- negotiate a fair settlement.

Recommendation 41 — presumption that a party's ability will be materially affected

The court shall presume, unless satisfied otherwise, that a party's ability to present his or her case properly or to negotiate a fair settlement will be materially and adversely affected if the court is satisfied that the party would suffer substantial hardship if required to pay the other party's costs.

20.6.6   Questions

1. Is it fair that a party's entitlement to costs should depend on whether it has the misfortune to be sued by a relatively impecunious party?

2. Is it fair that a party's prospects of success in litigation should depend on whether it has the good fortune to have injured a relatively impecunious party?

3. Does it make sense to expect equality of access to justice in a society where access to wealth is unequally distributed?

Other exceptions

20.6.7C	**Verna Trading Pty Ltd v New India Assurance Co Ltd**
	[1991] 1 VR 129
	Supreme Court of Victoria, Appeal Division

[Verna had a policy of marine insurance with New India. This covered goods from the time at which they left the warehouse to the time they were delivered either to another warehouse, or to a place of storage which the assured elected to use for storage other than in the ordinary course of transit. Goods purchased by the assured were dispatched in a container and arrived by sea in Melbourne. They were then stored by the stevedore and subsequently taken to the stevedore's bond area where the container in which they arrived was stored for a month. On 7 January Verna took delivery of the container and opened it, and found that the goods had been stolen. On discovering this, Verna promptly notified New India, whose surveyor reported that they had been stolen before delivery to Verna's warehouse. New India inquired about what the goods were doing in the bond area and was told that Verna had not been able to accept delivery until the first week of January. New India made no reply to numerous requests for payment, and in September, Verna sued.

New India's defence denied that the goods were insured, did not admit that the goods were stolen, denied that Verna suffered loss, and denied that the alleged loss had occurred at a time or place covered by the alleged policy.

On the first day of the trial New India was granted leave to amend its defence to include a defence based on the contention that even conceding the facts as alleged by Verna, the policy did not cover Verna's loss. This defence was not developed until the second (and last) day of the trial. **Beach J** found that Verna's loss was not covered by the policy. However, in view of the fact that New India had steadfastly refused to inform Verna of why it was refusing to indemnify it, he held that New India could be found to be sufficiently responsible for the litigation to warrant a costs order against it. To rub salt into the wounds, he made this an order on a solicitor and own client basis. Verna appealed and New India sought leave to appeal on the costs issue. Verna's appeal failed.]

Kaye J (at 151–6): In support of its application, the respondent's counsel relied upon the High Court's decision in *Hally v Dennis* (1955) 95 CLR 661 refusing leave to appeal against an order imposing costs on the successful party to a proceeding. The application was against that part of the order of the Full Court of the Supreme Court of Queensland whereby the successful appellant was directed to pay part of the respondent's costs occasioned by the order of the judge of first instance. Dixon CJ, delivering the judgment of the court, referred to a passage from the judgment of Swift J in *London Welsh Estates Ltd v Phillip* (1931) 144 LT 643 to the effect that there is no power in a court to make a successful defendant pay the costs of an [152] unsuccessful plaintiff. Authority for the proposition was said by his Lordship to be found in the judgment of Brett LJ in *Foster v Great Western Railway Co* (1882) 8 QBD 515, to which Dixon CJ added the authority of *Dicks v Yates* (1881) 18 Ch D 76. Yet the Chief Justice did not comment upon the correctness or otherwise of Swift J's proposition. Special leave was refused because the application involved determination of fact and review of an order relating to costs depending on the exercise of discretion.

However, *Foster v Great Western Railway Co* and *Dicks v Yates* together with other cases decided before the *Judicature Act* 1890, were held by the Court of Appeal in *Knight v Clifton* [1971] Ch 700 to be no longer binding authorities in relation to the court's power to award costs of a proceeding against a successful defendant. It was so held for the reason that s 5 of the Judicature Act 1890 enlarged the jurisdiction of the court where before the enactment the court did not have jurisdiction in respect of costs: *Re Fisher* [1894] 1 Ch 450, at 453–4.

Beach J's order as to costs was made in the exercise of discretion conferred by s 24(1) of the Supreme Court Act 1986 which is in these terms:

> Unless otherwise expressly provided by this or any other Act or by the Rules, the costs of and incidental to all matters in the Court, including the administration of estates and trusts, is in the discretion of the Court and the Court has full power to determine by whom and to what extent the costs are to be paid.

The provisions of s 24(1) are substantially the same as those provided by s 5 of the Judicature Act 1890. It is obvious that detrimental consequences sustained by a successful defendant from an order requiring him to pay the unsuccessful plaintiff's costs outweigh those which a successful defendant suffers from being denied his costs. Nevertheless, basic to the exercise of discretion where an order is made against a successful defendant and where no order is made in his favour is the requirement that there must be proper material on which the discretion is exercised. In *Ritter v Godfrey* [1920] 2 KB 47, at 60 Atkin LJ stated 'principles upon which a judge is to discern whether the necessary materials exist' for the exercise of his discretion as to costs as follows: 'In the case of a wholly successful defendant, in my opinion the judge must give the defendant his costs unless there is evidence that the defendant (1) brought about the litigation, or (2) has done something connected with the institution or the conduct of the suit calculated to occasion unnecessary litigation and expense, or (3) has done some wrongful act in the course of the transaction of which the plaintiff complains.'

Eve J, at 66 said in connection with the same matter: 'I venture to suggest that in determining whether a good ground exists for the exercise of the judicial discretion, the judge must eliminate from consideration the conduct constituting the alleged cause of action, and must then inquire whether the defendant has so conducted himself *ante litem motam* (1) as to induce in the plaintiff's mind the reasonable belief that there is no valid defence to the claim, or (2) has so misconducted himself as to have goaded the plaintiff into a litigation on which he would never have embarked but for such misconduct. The judge, however much he may disapprove of the defendant's behaviour, is not entitled to refuse him his costs unless he has materials upon which he is prepared to hold judicially that the defendant [153] has thereby created a mistaken belief in the plaintiff's mind or that his misconduct was the real cause of the action being brought.'

The correctness of the guiding principles formulated by Atkin LJ and stated by Eve J expressing as imperative a requirement to grant costs to a successful defendant except in the enumerated circumstances was the subject of adverse criticism by Viscount Cave LC in *Donald Campbell & Co Ltd v Pollak* [1927] AC 732, at 811–12.

On the other hand the Lord Chancellor described as substantially the true view of the principles those stated by Lord Sterndale in *Ritter v Godfrey,* at 52–3 as follows:

> ... there is such a settled practice of the Courts that in the absence of special circumstances a successful litigant should receive his costs, that it is necessary to show some ground for exercising a discretion by refusing an order which would give them to him. The discretion must be judicially exercised, and therefore there must be some grounds for its exercise, for a discretion exercised on no grounds cannot be judicial. If, however, there be any grounds, the question of whether they are sufficient is entirely for the judge at the trial, and this Court cannot interfere with his discretion.
>
> On the authorities as they now stand the line between cases tried before a jury and cases tried by a judge is very fine.

His Lordship added:

> One other consideration applies to these cases. The principle as to the exercise of discretion is the same in the case of plaintiffs and defendants, but it is clear that considerations sufficient to justify a refusal of costs to a plaintiff are not necessarily sufficient in the case of a defendant, for the former initiates the litigation while the latter is brought into it against his will.

Lord Atkinson, at 814 in *Donald Campbell & Co v Pollak* adopted as a clear and accurate statement of law and of the prevailing practice the entire passage of Lord Sterndale's judgment which I have quoted. It is noteworthy that Lord Sterndale continued: 'Speaking generally, I think it may be said that, in order to justify an order refusing a defendant his costs, he must be shown to have been guilty of conduct which induced the plaintiff to bring the action, and without which it would probably not have been brought.'

I do not read in the speech of the Lord Chancellor in *Donald Campbell's Case* rejection that in an appropriate case any one of the three circumstances described by Atkin LJ in *Ritter v Godfrey* might not constitute a proper basis for the exercise of discretion adversely to a successful defendant. The substance of the Lord Chancellor's criticism of Atkin LJ's principles appears to have been that the same were too restricted ...

More compelling circumstances are required for the exercise of discretion as a result of which a successful defendant is not only denied his costs but also compelled to pay the whole or part of the plaintiff's costs of the proceedings. This is so for the reason that proceedings are initiated by the plaintiff and the plaintiff fails to gain the relief which he sought.

Evershed MR in *Ottway v Jones* [1955] 1 WLR 706, at 711, in the course of his judgment dismissing an appeal against an order directing the successful defendant to pay the whole costs of the action, said: 'I should like to say (what is indeed obvious) that, where a plaintiff in the end fails, it must be a very unusual thing to order the successful defendant to pay the costs; and it would only be in exceptional cases that a judge would think it right to make such an order. Still, this is a matter of discretion; and, unless it is shown here that the judge erred upon some matter of principle, we should not, according to the well-established rules applicable to such matters, vary the discretion of the judge or seek to substitute a discretion of our own.'

[156] ... [F]rom the time of service of its original defence until the second day of the hearing, the respondent relied upon grounds of defence which, in the circumstances, were unmeritorious. It was not until the first day of the hearing that the respondent disclosed its three reasons for not settling the claim and its defences to the action. Furthermore, it was not until the second day that it sought to rely on those three defences. In my view the combination of the circumstances leading up to the issue of the writ were very exceptional. Those circumstances could have been avoided had the respondent, acting responsibly, made proper and frank responses to the appellant's request for settlement by payment of its claim. In the event the respondent by its conduct after receiving the investigator's report brought about the litigation, which might have been rendered unnecessary had it disclosed its real reasons for withholding settlement.

[McGarvie J agreed with Kaye J.]

Ormiston J (at 175): The provisions in the statutes and the rules relating to costs and the authorities make it virtually impossible for the trial judge's discretion to be attacked, in an appeal from a trial of this kind. Those statutes and rules were originally drafted and the authorities, for the most part, decided at a time when the cost of litigation was far less than it is at present and when very few trials were as complicated as they are today. No doubt it is convenient and in many cases appropriate that the exercise of the trial judge's discretion should be difficult to impeach, for so often matters occur at the trial, and before it, which only a trial judge can appreciate. Nevertheless, I would see it as undesirable that a successful litigant, who was, on the merits, wrongly vexed with litigation, should be required to pay the three penalties I have referred to, without receiving a cent by way of costs in respect of its successful defence. It is no doubt difficult to draft sections and rules which might prevent this happening in future but, untrammelled by authority, I would have reached the conclusion that it should have suffered no more than being deprived of its own costs. This is no doubt a matter which will in due course be taken up by those enquiring into the costs of litigation, for it is imperative that a system be devised for the future which allocates costs more fairly.

20.6.8   See also *Capolingua v Phylum Pty Ltd* (1991) 5 WAR 137. In that case the defendants also succeeded. However, points which could have disposed of the case early, if taken as preliminary points, were not so taken. The defence was such that its real basis and the basis on which the defendant ultimately succeeded began to become apparent only on the second day, and did not become completely apparent until the fourth and last day of the trial. The defendant's solicitors did not cooperate in the mediation pursuant to WA O 31a. On this point, Ipp J said (at 140):

> In my view where, at a mediation conference, a party to an Expedited Proceeding under O 31A adopts an obstructive or uncooperative attitude in regard to attempts to narrow the issues, and where it is subsequently shown that, but for such conduct, the issues would probably have been reduced, the extent to which the trial is in consequence unnecessarily extended is a relevant factor when deciding upon an appropriate award of costs.

In the circumstances, he held that there should be no order as to costs.

20.6.9   Question

1.   Beach J said (*Verna Trading Pty Ltd v New India Assurance Co Ltd* [1991] VR 129 at 140): 'Had New India disclosed [its] reasons prior to the date of issue of the writ, it is possible Verna would not have launched the present litigation.' Given that it made an unsuccessful appeal to the Appeal Division in relation to the construction of the policy, is this likely? Should this consideration have affected the Appeal Division's decision?

DETERMINING THE QUANTUM OF COSTS

20.7.1   The fact that a party is entitled to costs does not resolve the question of quantum. It may be clear that the case was one in which it was appropriate that the successful party be represented by a relatively junior barrister. But does that mean that the other party is to be required to pay that barrister's fees if they are $450 per day? What is the position if the barrister had charged $1750 per day? If documents are to be copied, is the appropriate compensation 12 cents per page (the La Trobe University library); 50 cents per page (the Victorian Supreme Court library); $1.80 per page (a charge designed to cover the salary of an extremely well-paid photocopyist)? One solution to these issues would be to let the market handle them. Lawyers would be required to lodge fee agreements and bills with the court prior to the case as a condition for their being able to claim their fees from their clients. These would determine such matters as barristers' fees and photocopying charges.

No Australian jurisdiction has opted for a pure market-based system as a basis for determining costs. In some cases, courts may give lump sum costs orders, based on a sense of what seems reasonable in the circumstances. More usually, costs are assessed according to a relatively primitive piecework formula, dating from a time when it was regarded as appropriate to determine remuneration on the basis of whether particular things with particular ascertainable values were done, rather than on the basis of who performed them and on how much people were willing to pay them for it. Lawyers, according to the piecework model, will be paid more if they are efficient. They will not be paid more if they are otherwise better.

The piecework formulae are to be found in the scales of costs associated with most Rules of Court. These vary from court to court: HCR Sch 2; FCR Sch 3; ACT Sch 4; NT Appendix to O 63; Qld Sch 1; SA Sch 1; Tas Sch 1, Pt 1; Vic Appendix A. In Western Australia, O 66 r 11(1), (2) provides that recoverable costs are governed by determinations under the Legal Profession Act 2008 (WA) s 252. See Legal Practitioners (Supreme Court) Contentious Business) Determination 2010 (WA) Sch, for the determination. Under the determination, entitlements tend to time-based, rather than related to piecework, as is the case with more traditional scales, such as the example reproduced below, from the Supreme Court of Victoria. Other scales use different categories, and, in the lower and intermediate courts in particular, there is a tendency for items recoverable to vary according to the amount recovered.

20.7.2E   **Supreme Court (General Civil Procedure) Rules 2005 (Vic)**
Scale of Costs
Appendix A

Instructions

1.	To institute or defend any proceeding or appeal	$303.00
2.	To make or oppose any interlocutory application	$72.00
3.	For statement of claim whether indorsed on writ or third party notice or served separately, or counterclaim	$149.00
4	For any other pleading, particulars in lieu of pleading or amended pleading	$72.00
5	For counsel to advise or give an opinion	$72.00
6	For counsel to make an interlocutory application where no other brief	$72.00
7	For witness statements, summaries of evidence or like documents, interrogatories, answers to interrogatories, oral examination for discovery, affidavit or other document for filing on an interlocutory application other than a short, formal affidavit or other document	$149.00
8	For a necessary document not otherwise provided for, such fee as may be reasonable in the circumstances	
	No allowance for instructions shall be made under the above items where an allowance for the work is claimed in detail and allowed on that basis	
	Instead of the fees for instructions above, such larger sum may be allowed as the Costs Court thinks reasonable in the circumstances	
9	Instructions for brief on trial of proceedings, including an assessment of damages or value or a trial before special referee, or an appeal, such allowances as the Costs Court thinks reasonable in the circumstances	

Originating Process

10	Writ or originating motion or summons (where filed as originating process)	$175.00
11	If any of the above exceed three folios (when not drawn by counsel) for each extra folio	$32.00
	The above allowances include all indorsements of claim, copy for filing and one copy for service and attendance to file, but not Court fees	

Corporations Law Short Form Bill

11A	Costs of obtaining a winding-up order up to and including authentication, filing and service of the order under section 470 of the Corporations Law and the obtaining from the Costs Court of an order as to costs	$3488.00
	Additional costs are allowable in accordance with item 34 or 35 for any adjournment in respect of which costs have been reserved by the Court	

Interlocutory Process

12	Summons before Judge or Associate Judge	$149.00
13	Subpoena	$88.00
	If a subpoena exceeds three folios, for each extra folio	$12.00
	These allowances include preparation of document, copy for filing and one copy for service and attendance to file	

Execution Process

14	Warrant of execution	
	This allowance includes preparation of the warrant, copy for filing and one copy for service and attendance to file	$175.00

Notices and Memoranda

15	Notice to produce or any other necessary or proper notice or memorandum not otherwise provided for, or any demand	$60.00
	This allowance does not apply to a short notice or memorandum indorsed on another document, but an allowance may be made there for as part of the allowance for the document	
16	If the notice is special, or necessarily exceeds three folios, for each folio	$32.00
	The above allowances include preparation of the notice and one copy for filing or service	

Appearance

17	Preparing and attending filing notice of appearance (including one copy for service)	$105.00

Drawing Pleadings and Other Documents

18	(a) Pleadings, including petitions, indorsement constituting statement of claim on writ or third party notice, including particulars	$149.00
	(b) If exceeding three folios, for each extra folio	$32.00
19	Any other necessary document, per folio	$32.00

No allowance is to be made to a solicitor for drawing a document drawn by counsel, but a fee may be allowed for drawing matter necessary to instruct counsel

In allowing for drawing, the Costs Court may disallow anything which is a repetition or adaptation of matter for the drawing of which allowance has otherwise been made in the proceeding. The Costs Court may increase these allowances if in the circumstances the Costs Court thinks it reasonable to do so

20	For preparing each exhibit	$6.20

Engrossment and Copies

21	Engrossment of documents, per folio	$6.20
22	(a) Copy or photocopy of document, per page	$2.20
	(b) Reproduction of document from microfiche, microfilm or like process, per page, the actual cost or	$2.20
23	Where under the Rules or any order of the Court or for other sufficient cause any document is printed out and it would not have been reasonable to send the original to the printer, a copy for the printer shall be allowed, per page	$2.20
24	Where more than ten copies of the same document are required, the amount actually and properly paid to a printer (in addition to all necessary attendances on the printer), or, if reproduced by the solicitor, the equivalent amount or such lesser amount as the Costs Court considers fair and reasonable having regard to commercial rates for similar services, shall be allowed	

Where it is necessary to print any part of a document in a foreign language, or as a facsimile, or in any unusual or special manner, or where any alteration in the document printed becomes necessary after the first proof, such further allowance shall be made as the Costs Court thinks reasonable

Perusals

25	Of all pleadings, amendments of pleadings (which exceed three folios), third party notices, interrogatories, answers thereto, transcripts of discovery by oral examination, notices, affidavits, draft orders submitted for approval by another party, drafts of documents to be settled by an officer of the Court, orders (unless an allowance has been made previously for perusal of a draft), opinions or advices of counsel where requested, bills of costs necessarily perused by the solicitor for the party on whom it was served	$46.00
	Or per folio	$6.40

26	Of all other documents, including deeds, correspondence (including incoming correspondence), exhibits, per folio	$5.30

If the solicitor is or ought to be familiar with the contents of the document or if it is not necessary to read all of it carefully, the Costs Court shall allow such smaller amount as he thinks reasonable. No allowance shall be made for the solicitor perusing letters which he receives unless the Costs Court considers there are special circumstances for doing so

27	Alternatively, for examining a document or checking a proof or print or examining an appeal book	
	Solicitor, per quarter hour	$72.00
	Clerk, per quarter hour	$42.00

Service

28	Service of any document where necessary, and not able to be served by post	$71.00

Or such charge as is reasonable having regard to the number of necessary attendances, the time taken, the distance travelled and any expense incurred

29	Where by reason of the location of the person to be served it is proper to effect service through an agent, instead of an allowance for service	
	(a) for correspondence with the agent	$46.00
	(b) the amount actually and reasonably charged by the agent	

Where more than one attendance is necessary to effect service, or to ground an application for substituted service, the Costs Court may make such further allowance under items 28 and 29 as he thinks reasonable

For service out of Victoria, the Costs Court shall make such allowance as he thinks reasonable

30	Service of document on a party by filing or leaving at the office of the party's solicitor or other address for service, where that mode of service is necessary	$42.00
31	Service of document on a party by post or leaving at document exchange	$25.00

Only one fee for service shall be allowed where two or more documents are or could have been served together

Attendances

32	(a) On counsel with brief on trial of proceeding, including an assessment of damages or value or a trial before a special referee or on appeal	$89.00

	(b) On counsel with any other brief or papers or to appoint consultation or conference (including all attendances to settle counsel's fees)	$60.00
33	(a) On consultation or conference with counsel	$149.00
	(b) Where a consultation or conference occupies more than one half hour, if the Costs Court thinks it reasonable, for each subsequent half hour	$149.00
	(c) If the solicitor does not attend personally, the allowance shall be as the Costs Court thinks reasonable, but not exceeding, for—	
	the first half hour	$72.00
	each half hour thereafter	$72.00
34	On any application or attendance before a Judge, an Associate Judge, the Costs Court or Prothonotary, examination of a witness, discovery by oral examination, assessment of damages or value, trial or inquiry, trial of a proceeding or hearing of an appeal, where in list or likely to be heard	$149.00
35	(a) At trial or hearing, for each hour	$303.00
	But, according to circumstances, not to exceed per day of six hours (including luncheon and dinner adjournments)	$1453.00
	or,	
	If attended by clerk	$722.00
	(b) To hear reserved judgment, for each half hour	$149.00
	(c) By appointment or on short or formal application to a Judge or an Associate Judge, the Costs Court or Prothonotary	$149.00
36	Where in the opinion of the Costs Court the attendance of two principals or of a solicitor and clerk at trial is necessary, an additional allowance may be made not exceeding per day of six hours (including luncheon and dinner adjournments)	$1453.00
37	To settle judgment or order, per half hour	$149.00
38	In addition to reasonable expenses for travel and sustenance, allowance may be made for a solicitor travelling to a place more than 50 kilometres distant from his or her place of residence or business where	
	(a) the journey was necessary and proper for the purpose of the proceeding and what was done by the solicitor could not have been done satisfactorily by an agent; and	
	(b) the solicitor was necessarily absent from his or her office, and for that time no charge could otherwise be made, and having regard to what other allowances may be made to the solicitor in the proceeding	
	Not exceeding per day	$1453.00

If the journey is not undertaken solely for the purpose of the proceeding, the Costs Court may allow a proportion of the fee as he thinks reasonable.

39	To file or lodge any document, to obtain an appointment from an officer of the Court, or to insert an advertisement or other attendance of a similar nature capable of performance by a junior clerk.	$42.00
40	If the exercise of skill or legal knowledge is involved so as to require the personal attendance of the solicitor, per quarter hour	$72.00
	Or, if attendance by solicitor's clerk, per quarter hour	$42.00
	Or such larger amount as the Costs Court thinks reasonable having regard to the importance or difficulty of the subject matter of attendance.	
41	Making an appointment or similar attendance by telephone, at the discretion of the Costs Court	$13.00
42	Arranging attendance of a witness or any attendance for which no other provision is made, per quarter hour	$42.00
43	Sending or receiving telex, telegram or facsimile documents	$42.00
	Or such larger amount as is reasonable in the circumstances having regard to the length.	
44	Letter making an appointment or forwarding document without explanation or the like	$22.00
45	Letter, ordinary	$38.00
46	Letter, special	$50.00
	Or such amount as the Costs Court thinks reasonable	
47	Circular letter, after the first	$12.00
	For each additional page after the first page, the photocopying charge shall apply	
	The above allowances include the standard surface rate of postage, but, if any communication is necessarily made by telex, telegram or transmission of a facsimile, the appropriate statutory charges may be allowed as a disbursement	
48	Where any agent is employed, for correspondence with the agent which the Costs Court thinks reasonable, per quarter of the year	$72.00 to
	Or, if special or extensive, in the discretion of the Costs Court	$303.00

20.7.3 The scales cover work for which solicitors can seek remuneration. Solicitors also make disbursements. They may need to pay filing fees and for scientific tests, interpreters and expert witnesses. These represent a substantial percentage of total legal costs, especially for plaintiffs: D Worthington and J Baker, *The Costs of Civil Litigation*, Civil Justice Research Centre, Sydney, 1993, pp 15–18, 29, 40–3, 53. They may (and sometimes must) assume responsibility for the payment of barristers. The rules make express allowance for some of these expenses (for example, setting upper limits on witnesses' expenses). Even in the absence of express provision, claims may be made for disbursements, provided that these can be justified.

The scales often have a slightly musty air about them. Moreover, one might ask: Where do the figures come from? Why are perusals of other documents charged at $5.30 per folio? A partial answer is because this is what it is after successive costs of living adjustments. However, we assume someone must have once engaged in some sort of time and motion study to determine the relevant levels.

These questions are, however, beside the point. The fact is that the scales exist, and govern costing at least in relation to proceedings. Their role in relation to the determination of the fees that may be charged to clients is diminishing. This means that, in some respects, costing is a relatively mechanical process, although there will always be room for disputes about whether particular items of expenditure have been necessarily and reasonably incurred, and over the rate at which they should be costed.

20.7.4   Note and questions

1. Peruse the Victorian scale. Are there any important items of legal expenditure which are not encompassed by the scale of costs? What expenditures would you consider would be likely to give rise to difficulties?

2. Are there items which you consider to be: (a) over-rewarded; or (b) under-rewarded?

3. Following Professor P Williams et al, *Report of the Review of Scales of Legal Professional Fees in Federal Jurisdictions*, Attorney-General's Department, March 1998, the ALRC recommended the replacement of scale-based awards of costs with 'event-based' scales. The proposed scheme envisaged a judge deciding at an initial directions hearing the category of complexity for a particular case. For each category, costs would have been set and calculated by reference to stages in the process. For example, costs stages recommended by the Federal Court scale were (ALRC, *Managing Justice: A Review of the Federal Civil Justice System*, Report No 89, [4.89]):

   • instructions and close of pleadings;
   • close of pleadings and completion of discovery;
   • completion of discovery and fixing of date for trial;
   • fixing date and start of trial; and
   • during trial or at judgment.

   The Commission acknowledged criticisms of the Williams Report, and concluded that its estimates of the appropriate costs underestimated the costs likely to be reasonably incurred by litigants. However, it suggested that this problem could be overcome by recalculations to reflect current market rates for particular legal services. What are the advantages and disadvantages of event-based costs, and how far could they be set so as to encourage settlement? See ALRC report, [4.87]–[4.99].

The New South Wales position

20.7.5E   **Legal Profession Act 2004 (NSW)**

364 (1) In conducting an assessment of legal costs payable as a result of an order made by a court or tribunal, the costs assessor must consider:

    (a) whether or not it was reasonable to carry out the work to which the costs relate, and

    (b) whether or not the work was carried out in a reasonable manner, and

    (c) what is a fair and reasonable amount of costs for the work concerned.

  (2) In considering what is a fair and reasonable amount of legal costs, a costs assessor may have regard to any or all of the following matters:

    (a) the skill, labour and responsibility displayed on the part of the Australian legal practitioner or Australian-registered foreign lawyer responsible for the matter,

    (b) the complexity, novelty or difficulty of the matter,

    (c) the quality of the work done and whether the level of expertise was appropriate to the nature of the work done,

    (d) the place where and circumstances in which the legal services were provided,

    (e) the time within which the work was required to be done,

    (f) the outcome of the matter.

  (3) An assessment must be made in accordance with the operation of the rules of the relevant court or tribunal that made the order for costs and any relevant regulations.

  (4) If a court or a tribunal has ordered that costs are to be assessed on an indemnity basis, the costs assessor must assess the costs on that basis, having regard to any relevant rules of the court or tribunal and relevant regulations.

365 (1) A costs assessor may obtain a copy of, and may have regard to, a costs agreement.

  (2) However, a costs assessor must not apply the terms of a costs agreement for the purposes of determining appropriate fair and reasonable costs when assessing costs payable as a result of an order by a court or tribunal.

366 This Division does not limit any power of a court or a tribunal to determine in any particular case the amount of costs payable or that the amount of the costs is to be determined on an indemnity basis.

20.7.6 Question

1. What are the advantages and disadvantages of the New South Wales approach as compared with the approach adopted by other jurisdictions?

Resolving disputes over quantum

20.7.7 The determination of costs may be performed by the lawyers involved in the litigation. In the lower courts, this is typically the case. Following a decision, the lawyers are expected to confer, nominate an agreed figure for costs, and report back to the court which then makes an order for costs in the agreed sum. On the whole, the relevant scales are sufficiently unambiguous to enable the lawyers to reach agreement without too much difficulty. However, even there, disputes about costs can sometimes last as long as the original dispute. In the higher courts, costs calculations are normally more complicated, except in relation to some interlocutory applications. (Compare, however, *Magna Alloys & Research Pty Ltd v Kevin Lindsay Coffee (No 2)* [1982] VR 97 for an appeal on costs in relation to an interlocutory matter which lasted for six days and in which costs of almost $39,000 were awarded.) The difficulties of calculating costs are such that lawyers may prefer to hand this task to a specialist firm of cost consultants. (The Melbourne *Yellow Pages* lists one such business, and there are others which are not listed there.) Their reputation depends on their ability to make estimates of cost entitlements, which will hold up if questioned by the relevant court officials.

In relation to higher court matters, the parties may nonetheless be able to reach agreement. If they do not, someone else must quantify the costs award. Different systems handle the matter in different ways. In most systems, costs are determined by a 'taxing master' or 'taxing officer', who is a master or an officer of the court: HCR Pt 53; FCR Div 40.2; ACT Divs 2.17.4–2.17.6 (registrar); NT O 63 Pts 4, 5; Qld Ch 17A Pt 3 (costs assessed by an assessing registrar or a costs assessor) rr 706–707, 709–720, 724–776; SA Ch 12 Pt 3; Tas rr 845–866; Vic O 63 Pts 4, 5 (by a Costs Judge, or at the judge's direction, by a Costs Registrar or a Prothonotary or their deputy); WA O 66 Div 2.

The procedure is as follows (subject to non-material inter-jurisdictional variations). A party applies for an order that costs be taxed, and serves the summons on the other party. The party must also file and serve a 'bill of costs' on the party liable for costs, except when that party was a defendant who did not file an appearance. The bill of costs is a document which lists, in chronological order, each item of work done by the solicitor, and stating beside each item the amount claimed as remuneration for that work and the amount disbursed. (These items are listed in separate columns.) The party on whom the summons and bill are served may object, by notice. The notice must list each item to which the party objects, stating briefly the grounds for its objection and must be served on other parties.

If there has been no objection, the Master or officer may nonetheless disallow items in the bill. If there are objections, there is a hearing at which the costs are taxed. Items are usually considered individually, separately and in order. Disputes at such hearings may relate to whether a party is entitled to claim costs in relation to a particular item, to the level of costs which may properly be claimed and as to how discretions should be exercised. There may be disputes over questions of fact. Good record keeping is essential, so that the purpose of any claimed item of expenditure is clear, as is its necessity or reasonableness. An adequate costs statement can only be prepared from a well-organised and maintained file.

Following this hearing, an order is made which may include an order in relation to the costs of the taxation. There is normally provision for review by the Taxing Master of his or her original decision (the Federal and High Courts are exceptions). Applications must list the grounds of the objection, and may be supported by additional evidence. Parties may require reasons to be given for decisions regarding the disputed items.

Final decisions may be reviewed by a judge. Again, the notice must specify the items subject to the objection and the grounds for the objection. Unless the judge orders otherwise, no new evidence is received; otherwise the judge possesses all the powers and discretions of the Taxing Master or officer. Unless otherwise ordered, review does not stay execution or proceedings under the relevant order of the Taxing Master or officer.

In New South Wales, decisions on costs are made by costs assessors, who are not officers of the court. Applications may be made to the Manager, Costs Assessment, for a review of an assessment decision by a review panel. Appeals against assessment decisions lie as of right where there has been an error of law, and otherwise by leave. Where there has been an appeal on the grounds of error of law, the Supreme Court may affirm the decision, make the determination it considers the assessor should have made, or remit the decision to the assessor for redetermination. If the matter is remitted for redetermination, the assessor may take account of new evidence. If the appeal is by leave, it is by way of a rehearing and evidence additional to, or different from, that given at the original proceeding may be given. If an appeal by leave relates to a decision which has not been reconsidered by a panel, the court may refer the matter to a panel: Legal Profession Act 2004 (NSW) ss 373–390.

Rules in most jurisdictions include provisions for making offers of compromise or settlement or their equivalent in relation to the costs of a taxation: FCR r 40.33(2); ACT r 1811; NT r 63.34(3); Qld r 707 (parties may agree on costs); SA rr 187(3)(c), 188(2)(b); Tas r 850; Vic r 63.36(3). In Western Australia, *Calderbank* offers can achieve the same effect: R Quick, *Quick on Costs*, LBC, Sydney, looseleaf, [5.6560]. In addition, rules sometimes provide that a party is not normally entitled to the costs of a taxation unless it is awarded a substantial proportion of the amount claimed: HCR r 58.03 (83% and the solicitor responsible may be ordered to pay some or all of the other party's costs of the taxation); FCR r 40.33(1) (party objecting to a taxing officer's provisional estimate must pay the costs of the taxation unless the taxation is 15% more favourable than the estimate); ACT r 1834 (85%); NT r 63.34(5) (80%); Qld r 735 (85%); Tas r 865 (83%, in which case the other party may receive some of *its* costs of the taxation).

Victorian data suggest that compromise plays a considerable role in the settlement of costs disputes. A review of the 247 Supreme Court taxing summonses filed between July–December 2006 found that 54% (134) proceeded to a taxation, the remainder being dismissed, generally because they had been settled. In cases where costs were taxed, the party recovered, on average, 77% of its costs, recovery rates ranging from 28% to 99.66%. In cases resolved by consent, they recovered 74%: Victorian Law Reform Commission, *Civil Justice Review Report*, 2008, pp 650–1. Given the costs of taxations, the settlers seem to have fared better than the fighters, although at least one of the fighters was clearly vindicated by its decision. It is also striking that the average recovery rate in contested summonses was considerably less than the recovery rate at which, in most jurisdictions, the applicant becomes liable for some or all of the respondent's costs of the taxation.

20.7.8 The criteria to be applied by the reviewing judge were discussed by Fullagar J in *Magna Alloys & Research Pty Ltd v Kevin Lindsay Coffee (No 2)* [1982] VR 97 at 102–3:

> The general principles to be applied by the court on judicial review of a taxation by a taxing master of a bill of costs are, in my opinion, clear. In the case of *582 St Kilda Road v Campbell* (unreported, 5 September 1975), Lush, J said: 'The nature of the powers exercised by the judge on a review of the decision of the taxing master is identical with that exercised by any tribunal reviewing a discretionary decision. There are many authorities on which this subject has been considered, and it is thought by some that there are different lines followed in different authorities. However that may be, I think that for a considerable time past it has been unnecessary to go beyond the judgment of Kitto, J in *Australian Coal & Shale Employees Federation v The Commonwealth* (1953) 94 CLR 621.' Lush, J then cited the very well-known passage appearing at (94 CLR) 632, from the reference to *Lovell v Lovell* (1950) 81 CLR 513 down to the reference to *House v R*, and then added: 'That passage is cited so often and in so many contexts that it is worth recording again that the case is related to the review of a matter of costs taxation'. Lush, J also followed

and applied the observations of Kitto, J upon questions which relate to amount only, that is to say, upon the general approach of the court 'where the question is one of amount only', which is one of strong reluctance to interfere at all. The reluctance is, however, based on obvious reasons and not on any 'tyrannical rule' fettering the judicial discretion.

I shall accordingly apply the general principles indicated by Kitto, J and by Lush, J. The court must distinguish in its approach between, on the one hand, cases where a matter of principle is involved and, on the other hand, cases 'where it is a question whether the master has exercised his discretion properly, or it is only a question as to the amount to be allowed', in which latter cases 'the court is generally unwilling to interfere with the judgment of its officer, whose peculiar province it is to investigate and to [103] judge of such matters, unless there are very strong grounds to show that the officer is wrong in the judgment which he has formed'. It has thus been said that 'it is only in an extreme case' that the court will interfere with the master's decision on a matter involving nothing but quantum, though it must be remembered that such phrases are not the words of any statute or rule, but a very compendious judicial summary of the general approach to determinations of an officer whose peculiar province it is to investigate and judge of such matters, by judges whose special or particular province or training it certainly is not.

Needless to say, the court will correct any arithmetical errors it discovers. In *Magna Alloys* there were a number of these, some favouring the plaintiff and some the defendant. Overall, the result of the appeal (which had been brought by the plaintiff and in which there had been a cross-appeal by the defendants) was that the costs payable to the defendant were increased by $1609, an increase of 4.3%. The case warrants perusal on a number of grounds: as illustration of the ferocity with which commercial litigation is sometimes fought; as an example of the issues which arise in taxation; and as a warning to those naive enough to believe that barristers' high fees are obtained effortlessly.

SECURITY FOR COSTS

20.8.1   A problem of obvious concern to litigants is the possibility that the successful party will not be able to extract such costs as might be awarded against an unsuccessful party. This may be because the unsuccessful party is likely to lack the resources to pay any costs order. It may be because the unsuccessful party is likely to refuse to comply with any costs order. This will be of particular concern if the unsuccessful party's assets lie largely outside Australia.

In connection with this problem, the position of defendants is somewhat different from that of plaintiffs. Defendants do not choose to be defendants. Yet they may face the prospect of crippling legal costs, notwithstanding that they have successfully defended an action. However, plaintiffs can at least make calculations about the likely value of litigation before embarking on it. That said, plaintiffs face the possibility that defendants will arrange their assets so as to make it difficult for the successful plaintiff to recover not only costs, but any other relief the plaintiff might have been granted.

There are various ways in which this problem could be handled. Plaintiffs as a matter of course could be required to deposit bonds to cover defendants' costs. In the case of impecunious plaintiffs, specialist 'bondsmen' would evaluate the case and float the action, not unlike the American bail bondsmen who finance the freedom on bail of some of that country's numerous felons. Courts might have a right to exempt plaintiffs upon being convinced that a case has particular merit. However, in a 'laissez-faire' system, this assessment could, of course, be handled by the bondsmen. One effect of such a system would be to raise barriers against the impecunious, who already find litigation difficult.

Defendants are not so easily dealt with. However, the problems posed by non-paying defendants are typically not confined to the recovery of costs. There is therefore no obvious reason why plaintiffs' rights to costs should be treated differently to plaintiffs' rights to be able to recover whatever the court awards in the way of damages, interest and costs.

Australian jurisdictions have dealt with the problem by recognising that, in certain circumstances, defendants have a prima facie right to security for costs. However, plaintiffs have a prima facie right to be able to seek to enforce their legal rights, unencumbered by the need to make heavy initial investments.

20.8.2E   **Security for Costs**
Stephen Colbran
Longman Professional, Melbourne, 1993
(footnotes omitted)

[1.1] Security for costs may be defined as the security which a defendant in an action may require from the plaintiff for payment of the costs that may be awarded to the defendant. The procedure for seeking security for costs is one of a species of procedures founded upon the court's inherent jurisdiction to curtail abuse of process by ensuring payment of legal costs.

[1.2] Legal costs are of importance to all parties to litigation, though in practice the risk of an unfavourable costs order is not shared equally. While a plaintiff has a choice whether or not to litigate, a defendant is in a less advantageous position, for in order to avoid default judgment, the defendant is compelled to litigate or settle, whether the plaintiff has available assets sufficient to pay the costs of a successful defence or otherwise. Courts relying upon their inherent jurisdiction have sought to redress this imbalance, and any consequential abuse of process, by ordering security for costs, both at first instance and on appeal.

[1.3] The purpose of security for costs is twofold:
    (a) to provide protection for a defendant by ensuring an available fund to defray costs incurred by the defendant in defending a frivolous claim; and
    (b) to discourage the filing of unmeritorious and frivolous claims which may amount to vexatious harassment.

[1.4] The twin purposes of security for costs are reflected in the main categories of cases in which orders have traditionally been made. The categories include:
    (a) where the plaintiff is ordinarily resident out of the jurisdiction;
    (b) where a nominal plaintiff, not being a plaintiff who is suing in representative capacity, is suing for the benefit of some other person and there is reason to believe the nominal plaintiff will be unable to pay the costs of the defendant if ordered to do so;
    (c) where the plaintiff's address is not stated in the writ or other originating process or is incorrectly stated in such process, unless the court is satisfied that the failure to state the address or the misstatement was made innocently and without intention to deceive;
    (d) where the plaintiff changed their address during the course of the proceedings with a view to evading the consequences of the litigation;
    (e) arbitration proceedings; and
    (f) where the plaintiff is a limited liability company and there is reason to believe the company will be unable to pay the defendant's costs.

[1.5] Security for costs is designed to prevent abuse of process and is ultimately founded on the Court's inherent jurisdiction. The inherent jurisdiction has also been complemented by the growth of statutory jurisdiction, in the form of Rules of Court and specific legislation. Both sources of jurisdiction, inherent and statutory, provide a wide basis for the exercise of an unfettered discretion to order security for costs.

[1.6] Historically, courts have sought to fetter their discretion through attempts to define its breadth by categorising the types of cases in which orders may be made as is reflected in the main categories of case previously described.

[1.7] The rules of precedent also assisted the fettering of the discretion and the development of traditional categories of case in which to order security for costs. Judges bound by the limited exercise of discretion of superior courts perpetuated the process of fettering the discretion to order security for costs. Categories of case emerged where security for costs was never ordered, or conversely, was always ordered.

[1.8] It is important to realise that while the traditional categories of case in which security for costs was ordered tend to be reflected in the Rules of Court, these neither limit the extent of the jurisdiction nor fully characterise the factors relevant to the exercise of the discretion. It should not be forgotten that prevention of abuse of process is the primary consideration.

[1.9] Ultimately a balance needs to be struck enabling impecunious plaintiffs to prosecute their claims while protecting a party who is brought to court against the possibility that the plaintiff, if unsuccessful, will be unable to meet an order for costs. Such a fine balance can only be achieved through the exercise of an unfettered discretion based on all the circumstances of the case.

20.8.3   The inherent power is discussed in *Shannon v ANZ Banking Group Ltd (No 2)* [1994] 2 Qd R 563, where Williams J said (at [563]):

The application is made pursuant to the inherent power of the Court to order security for costs. Such a jurisdiction has been recognised at least since the decision in *J H Billington Limited v Billington* [1907] 2 KB 106. It is only necessary to refer briefly to the judgment of Lord Alverstone CJ at 109:

I have always understood that the power of the Supreme Courts of common law to order security for costs arose from the inherent jurisdiction of those Courts over their own procedure. It is true that [564] security was as a rule ordered only in a few exceptional cases which were subject to special considerations — for example, where the action was brought by a foreigner or merely nominal plaintiff, where it was obviously unjust that the action should be allowed to proceed unless payment of the costs were secured; but I am not aware of any statute conferring this power upon the Courts of common law.

Holland J recognised the jurisdiction in *Rajski v Computer Manufacture & Design* [1982] 2 NSWLR 443 at [447]:

I think that it is settled by modern authority that power to require security for costs is inherent in the Court whether functioning at Common Law or in equity.

I accept that the inherent jurisdiction is neither confined by nor replaced by the express power conferred on the Court by O 33 of the Supreme Court Rules. It has been recognised that one of the purposes of the Court's inherent power was to overcome or defeat any attempt to thwart or in any way hinder the Court's process. Recent illustrations are provided by the judgment of Lord Morris in *Connolly v Director of Public Prosecutions* [1964] AC 1254 at 1301 and Gaudron J in *Jackson v Sterling Industries Ltd* (1987) 162 CLR 612 at 638–9. The facts of *Rajski* are not dissimilar to the facts of this case and provide a good illustration of the circumstances in which the jurisdiction will be exercised.

The relevance of the inherent power arose because the application was for the court to order security for costs in relation to a matter for which there was no provision under the rules. In the words of Williams J (at 564):

> The applicant's case here is that the respondents have deliberately divested themselves of assets since commencing this litigation so as to make it difficult, if not impossible, for the applicant to recover any costs against the plaintiffs should they be unsuccessful in their action. Looked at in this light it is said that the plaintiffs are not impoverished natural persons; there is no suggestion in the material that they would be unable to provide security if it was in fact ordered. In that regard senior counsel for the applicant referred to *Rajski* at 455, *Bell Wholesale Co Pty Ltd v Gates Export Corporation* (1983) 8 ACLR 483, and *P S Chellaram & Co v China Ocean Shipping Co* (1991) 65 ALJR 642 at 643. To adopt terminology used in *Rajski* at 452, the plaintiffs' 'lack of assets and income is self-inflicted'.

Williams J found that assets had indeed been transferred in a way which would make it difficult for the bank to execute against the plaintiffs. He did not order that the plaintiffs provide security for the whole of the bank's estimated future costs. It was rare for courts to make orders to cover even the whole of a defendant's party and party costs. Also relevant was the fact that on the pleadings 'the plaintiffs may well have a strong case' (at 569) and the 'rather exceptional circumstances' in which security had been ordered. The final security represented about 40 per cent of the defendant's estimated costs.

In *Knight v F P Special Assets Ltd* (1992) 174 CLR 178, Mason CJ and Deane J said (obiter) at 192:

> Security cannot be ordered against a defendant or a plaintiff who is an individual and who resides in the jurisdiction.

Is this consistent with the decision in *Shannon v ANZ Banking Group Ltd (No 2)* [1994] 2 Qd R 563?

Rules

20.8.4   New South Wales Uniform Civil Procedure Rule 42.21 provides:

(1)   If, in any proceedings, it appears to the court on the application of a defendant:

    (a)   that a plaintiff is ordinarily resident outside New South Wales, or

    (b)   that the address of a plaintiff is not stated or is mis-stated in his or her originating process, and there is reason to believe that the failure to state an address or the mis-statement of the address was made with intention to deceive, or

    (c)   that, after the commencement of the proceedings, a plaintiff has changed his or her address, and there is reason to believe that the change was made by the plaintiff with a view to avoiding the consequences of the proceedings, or

    (d)   that there is reason to believe that a plaintiff, being a corporation, will be unable to pay the costs of the defendant if ordered to do so, or

(e) that a plaintiff is suing, not for his or her own benefit, but for the benefit of some other person and there is reason to believe that the plaintiff will be unable to pay the costs of the defendant if ordered to do so,

the court may order the plaintiff to give such security as the court thinks fit, in such manner as the court directs, for the defendant's costs of the proceedings and that the proceedings be stayed until the security is given.

Somewhat similar rules operate in other jurisdictions: HCR Pt 59 (general discretion); FCR r 19.02 (a)–(c), (e); ACT r 1901 (categories (a)–(e); also plaintiffs with limited resources who are about to leave Australia); Qld r 672 (categories (a)–(e); also plaintiffs with limited resources about to leave Australia); SA r 194 (categories (a), (e) and also where authorised by statute or where justice requires it, and where there are reasonable grounds for suspecting that the action may have been brought for an ulterior purpose); Tas r 828 (categories (a)–(e); also corporations, and where there is a pending proceeding in Tasmania for the same cause of action). In the Northern Territory and Victoria, the five standard categories are supplemented by two others: cases where proceedings are pending in another court in relation to the same claim; and cases where under any law the court may require security for costs: r 62.02. Western Australian grounds include (a) (and variants); or that the plaintiff is an undischarged bankrupt, a company in liquidation or receivership or under administration, or a relator: O 25 r 2.

The Corporations Act 2001 (Cth) s 1335(1) provides:

Where a corporation is plaintiff in any action or other legal proceeding, the court having jurisdiction in the matter may, if it appears by credible testimony that there is reason to believe that the corporation will be unable to pay the costs of a defendant if successful in his, her or its defence, require sufficient security to be given for those costs and stay all proceedings until the security is given.

20.8.5 While it has been argued that, once a plaintiff falls within a relevant category, the rules confer a discretion only as to the quantum of the security, this view is hard to reconcile with the wording of the rules and has not commended itself to Australian courts. The New South Wales and Federal Courts have both interpreted the rule as conferring discretion as to whether to order security, and if so, for what amount: *Connop v Varena Pty Ltd* [1984] 1 NSWLR 71; *Barton v Minister for Foreign Affairs* (1984) 2 FCR 463. In the latter case, Morling J noted that an Australian judgment could be enforced in the United Kingdom (where the applicant was resident) under the Foreign Judgments (Reciprocal Enforcement) Act 1933 (UK) s 2. The fact that the applicant was an undischarged bankrupt was not relevant (at 469):

It may well be the fact that he has no significant assets. If this is so (and there appeared to be a tacit agreement at the bar table that it probably was the case) the reality of the situation is that the respondent would not be able to enforce any judgment for costs against the applicant even if he was ordinarily resident in Australia. Counsel for the applicant submitted, correctly in my view, that it would be an odd result if an impecunious plaintiff was ordered to give security merely because he was ordinarily resident outside Australia, although his absence from Australia had little, if any, prejudicial effect on the respondent's prospects of recovering his costs.

He decided that the proper course was to order that the applicant give security for costs of $2000, this being an estimate of the cost of registering and enforcing a Federal Court judgment in the United Kingdom. A similar approach had also been taken by Rath J in *Connop v Varena Pty Ltd*. Because the respondent had not succeeded on his major argument, costs of the application were ordered to be costs in the substantive application.

20.8.6 The situation as to where a person is a nominal plaintiff was considered in *Coyle v Cassimatis* [1994] 2 Qd R 262. The plaintiffs had reached an agreement with their creditors whereby they were permitted to pursue a professional negligence action for $1,000,000 against their former solicitor. The respondent argued that, given his assets (and insurance), the plaintiffs were unlikely to recover more than $650,000, the amount owed by the plaintiffs to their creditors. This meant that the plaintiffs were in effect nominal plaintiffs, suing on behalf of their creditors. Ryan J rejected this argument. The fact that the defendant might not be able to meet the full claim was irrelevant (at 265):

> In the instant case, the plaintiffs have brought an action in their own names for the recovery of damages they claim are payable to them. They cannot be said to be nominal plaintiffs in the sense of being persons really put forward by some other person to bring an action on behalf of that person. See *Cook v Whellock* (1890) 24 QBD 658 at 661. I am not satisfied on the material before me that they are nominal plaintiffs in the sense that they are suing as bare trustees for the creditors. At least that is not the effect of the composition. But even if they are nominal plaintiffs, I consider that I should exercise my discretion so as not to make an order. The allegation by the plaintiffs is that they have lost their assets as a consequence of the defendant's negligence. That is, in my opinion, a matter to be taken into account in deciding whether to impose an order which would probably make it impossible for the plaintiffs who are both invalid pensioners to pursue their action. I have regard also to the terms of cl 8 of the Composition [between the plaintiffs and their creditors], by which it may be terminated if a stay of proceedings is ordered until security for costs is given. Costs of the application were reserved.

20.8.7 While security for costs may be sought in relation to a cross-claim or a counterclaim, the cross-claimant will not normally be required to provide security if the cross-claim does not go beyond matters raised in the cross-claimant's defence: *Federal Commissioner of Taxation v Macquarie Health Corporation* (1998) 39 ATR 389.

20.8.8E	**Security for Costs**
	Stephen Colbran
	Longman Professional, Melbourne, 1993
	(footnotes omitted)

[14.1] The making of an order for security for costs represents the exercise of an unfettered discretion, to be exercised judicially having regard to all the circumstances of the case, in order to achieve justice between litigants. A balance needs to be struck between the interests of a defendant in securing his position against the desirability of the plaintiff not being foreclosed from his action. Whilst no rules can be formulated in advance by any judge as to how the discretion shall be exercised, in any given case, numerous categories of discretionary factors have been identified by the courts.

[14.2] The discretionary factors relevant at first instance to applications for security for costs based on inherent or statutory jurisdiction involving corporate or natural persons, include, but are by no means limited to the following:

    (a)   the means of persons who stand behind the litigation;

    (b)   the prospects of success or merits of the litigation;

(c) the bona fides of the litigation;

(d) whether the plaintiff is an impecunious company;

(e) whether the plaintiff's impecuniosity is attributable to the defendant's conduct;

(f) whether the plaintiff is the party attacked and is in essence occupying the position of a defendant;

(g) whether an order for security for costs would be oppressive;

(h) whether an order for security for costs will stifle the litigation;

(i) whether a preexisting special relationship exists;

(j) whether the litigation will involve a matter of public importance;

(k) whether there has been an admission or payment into court;

(l) whether there has been delay in bringing the application;

(m) costs of enforcement procedures;

(n) whether a loss bearing, loss sharing entity is involved;

(o) dissipation of assets; and

(p) costs.

[Security for costs in the context of appeals is discussed above at 19.7.6.]

20.8.9 These criteria correspond closely to those prescribed by the Queensland rules: r 672.

APPEAL COSTS

20.9.1 While it is often reasonable that litigants should bear the risks associated with unsuccessful litigation, there is one circumstance in which this is arguably unfair. If a party succeeds before a court of first instance and loses on appeal, it cannot normally be said that its decision to litigate was not reasonable. Moreover, it will normally be reasonable for that party to contest the appeal. In recognition of this, jurisdictions have made provision for the costs ordered against unsuccessful respondents to be paid for out of a special fund: Federal Proceedings (Costs) Act 1981 (Cth); Suitors' Fund Act 1951 (NSW); Appeal Costs Fund Act 1973 (Qld); Appeal Costs Fund Act 1979 (SA); Appeal Costs Fund Act 1968 (Tas); Appeal Costs Act 1998 (Vic); Suitors' Fund Act 1964 (WA). See 19.14.1 above for a full discussion.

Further reading

20.10.1 Looseleaf and online

A Ashe, *Legal Costs Australian Capital Territory*, LexisNexis, Sydney.

A Ashe and J Grace, *Legal Costs New South Wales*, LexisNexis, Sydney.

J Grace, *Legal Costs Federal*, LexisNexis, Sydney.

J Grace, *Legal Costs Victoria*, LexisNexis, Sydney.

LexisNexis, *Halsbury's Laws of Australia*, Vol 20, Title 325, Practice and Procedure, 'Ch VII Judgment and Execution', [325–9500]–[325–9770].

P Norman, *Legal Costs South Australia*, LexisNexis, Sydney.

R Quick (assisted by D Garnsworthy), *Quick on Costs*, Thomson Reuters, Sydney.

20.10.2 Reports

ALRC, *Costs Shifting — Who Pays for Litigation*, Report No 75, 1995. (This report includes numerous recommendations for changes to the relevant law; references to the sources of support for, and opposition to, those changes; and an indication of the Commission's rationale for preferring some options to others.)

ALRC, *Managing Justice: A Review of the Federal Civil Justice System*, Report No 89, 2000, Ch 4. (This chapter presents empirical evidence of costs levels in federal courts and tribunals, discusses the rules relating to the determination of lawyers' fees, and assesses possible reforms.)

ALRC, *Who Should Pay? A Review of the Litigation Costs Rules*, Issues Paper No 13, 1994. (This includes a review of the rules and raises issues surrounding their possible reform.)

Victorian Law Reform Commission, *Civil Justice Review Report*, 2008, Ch 11. (This provides a comprehensive analysis of costs regimes in Australia and elsewhere, summaries of the arguments for and against different costs regimes, and insight into the difficulties of resolving costs issues.)

20.10.3 Texts

B Cairns, *Australian Civil Procedure*, 9th ed, Thomson Reuters, Sydney, 2011, Ch 16.

S Colbran, *Security for Costs*, Longman Professional, Melbourne, 1993.

Enforcement

OVERVIEW

This chapter examines the procedures for enforcing judgments. It begins with a discussion of the circumstances in which judgments can be enforced forthwith, and the circumstances in which execution may be stayed. It then examines the steps successful parties should take to preserve their interests and the means whereby they can acquire information about the defendant's resources. The chapter then discusses the various procedures available for the enforcement of judgments. These include: instalment orders; writs and warrants of execution; garnishee orders; charging and stop orders; and the use of receivers. It then examines procedures for enforcing 'non-money' judgments, including substituted performance, committal for contempt, and sequestration. The chapter concludes with a review of the procedures for the enforcement of interstate and foreign judgments, and a brief reference to bankruptcy and winding-up procedures.

INTRODUCTION

21.1.1 One of the reasons for civil procedure is that laws are not self-executing. Nor are judgments, other than those which leave the status quo completely unchanged. A successful party may be lucky; the unsuccessful party may do what it is required to do. Defendants may have indemnity insurance. This may explain why it was possible for the case to go all the way to trial. The defendant may be an affluent, bureaucratic organisation, basically accustomed to acting according to law. Defendants may simply be timid.

The defendant may also recognise the cost of failure to comply. Judgment debts carry interest. In relation to costs, interest accrues from the time of the taxation. Otherwise, it accrues from the date on which judgment was given. Rates vary by jurisdiction, but tend to be far higher than ordinary commercial rates, which is probably appropriate, since it compensates for the risks of non-payment.

Judgment debtors may be mindful of the fact that enforcement involves cost, and it is usually they who must bear such costs. Costs fall into two categories. There are the costs involved in applications for orders, and the costs incurred in executing orders. Where the sheriff is involved in the enforcement process, the sheriff's expenses must ultimately be borne by the judgment debtor, and when property is sold, the proceeds will go towards satisfying not only the original debt but the sheriff's expenses. In garnishee proceedings, the garnishee is entitled to be compensated for expenses incurred in paying the debt to the judgment creditor rather than to the debtor.

In addition, execution may involve economic losses. If property is taken and sold, it will usually realise a price well below its market price, or what it is worth to the debtor (cases reported below provide illustrations). This last consideration sometimes leads to brinkmanship, with debtors capitulating at the last moment. (This is also discussed below.)

21.1.2   Defendants are not always cooperative. Failure to pay promptly may mean that the money 'saved' can be used to ward off bankruptcy proceedings while assets are diverted or consumed; money not paid to judgment creditors may be used in an effort to save a business. Moreover, regardless of whether the judgment is for payment of money or for some other form of relief, parties may refuse to comply out of sheer bloody-mindedness, convinced that they are the victims of evil opponents and a corrupt and incompetent legal system. Procedures exist to deal with such people.

There are several courses of action open to a successful party faced with a recalcitrant opponent. Some of these exist quite apart from the Rules of Court. In particular, failure to pay a judgment debt may be a basis for proceedings in bankruptcy against an individual or proceedings for winding-up against a corporation. However, the rules also provide mechanisms for the enforcement of judgments. Many of these involve the sheriff, whose role is far more mundane than that of his or her counterpart in Nottingham or the Western United States. Under the Australian Capital Territory and Queensland rules, the relevant officials are called 'enforcement officers'. Here, 'sheriff' will be used as the generic term to describe such officials. Australian sheriffs are officers of the court and are responsible for enforcing judicial decisions. (For a useful historical analysis, see J M Bennett 'The Office of Sheriff: Historical Notes on its Evolution in New South Wales' (1976) 7 *Sydney LR* 360.) Sheriffs probably continue to annoy contemporary Robin Hoods (who are the kind of people to leave unpaid debts everywhere), but they do not conduct shoot-outs at high noon (or any other time), and creditors sometimes regard them as unduly averse to conflict.

21.1.3   Since non-compliance with judgments is a problem which dates back to the time judgments were first handed down, it is scarcely surprising that many of the enforcement procedures have a long history. The writ of *fieri facias* (the writ of *fi fa*), modern equivalents of which survive in all jurisdictions, dates back seven centuries. Holdsworth (*A History of English Law*, Sweet & Maxwell, London, 1973, vol 8, p 131) notes:

> It was enacted in 1285 (13 Edward I st 1c 18) that 'when a debt is recovered or acknowledged in the king's court, or damages awarded, it shall henceforth be in the election of him that sueth for such debt or damages to have a writ of *fieri facias* unto the sheriff for to levy the debt from the lands and goods; or that the sheriff shall deliver to him all the chattels of the debtor (saving only his oxen and the beasts of his plough) and the one half of his land upon a reasonable price or extent.' The creditor held the land till the debt was paid. [Footnotes omitted]

Until recently, evidence of the distant origins of civil enforcement procedures could still be found in Rules of Court, in which Latin terms abounded, and which used the time-honoured mode of address of the Queen to her sheriffs. Newer rules have abandoned the Latin and the florid addresses. Conceptually, however, the newer rules generally reflect their antecedents, and ancient cases continue to be cited as authority for propositions of continuing modern relevance. Of the 14 cases cited in Williams in relation to the seizure of property by sheriffs, six date from the seventeenth century or earlier and only one from the twentieth century: N Williams, *Supreme Court Civil Procedure Victoria*, Butterworths, Sydney, 1987, pp 341–2.

Until recently, there were no federal sheriffs. However, federal courts may mobilise state and territory enforcement procedures. High Court and Federal Court judgments can be enforced in a given state or territory in the same way as the local Supreme Court's judgments can be enforced. This is subject to any relevant Rules of Court: Judiciary Act 1903 (Cth) s 77M; Federal Court of Australia Act 1976 (Cth) s 53. The Federal Court Rules also provide that where there is to be enforcement in several jurisdictions, the procedures of any one of the relevant jurisdictions may be used in the other jurisdictions: Federal Court Rules r 41.10(3). The Federal Court now has a sheriff whose duties include enforcement and whose enforcement authority is similar to that of their state or territorial counterpart: r 41.10(1) in the jurisdiction in which enforcement is taking place.

In addition to procedures which depend on sheriffs, there exist enforcement procedures based on court orders requiring third parties with control over debtors' property, to transfer this to the judgment creditor or otherwise deal with it in such a way as to protect the judgment creditor's interests. In most jurisdictions, there is provision for enforcement by instalment orders. These are of relatively recent origin.

21.1.4   Complicating the rules with respect to enforcement is the fact that the types of enforcement procedures correspond only approximately to different types of judgment. While some types of judgment are enforceable only by certain types of procedure, most categories of judgment are enforceable by more than one procedure; some procedures are available for enforcing a number of types of judgment. Broadly, judgments can be divided into four classes: those requiring the payment of money; those entitling a successful party to possession of land; those requiring the delivery of goods; and those which involve mandatory or injunctive orders. This classification seems to lack conceptual elegance; like the remedies, it is rooted in the ad hoc nature of legal history.

It also reflects the fact that some kinds of judgments can be enforced more readily than others. Money judgments are relatively easily enforced, since they need not be satisfied by the transfer of particular items of property. The fact that most forms of property can be converted into money means that, so long as the judgment debtor owns property, there is something that can possibly be taken to satisfy the debt. Judgments for possession of land are, in practice, relatively easy to enforce, although this has not always been so, and is still sometimes fraught with difficulty. For instance, judgment debtors in rural districts, with strong emotional attachments to their land, are occasionally not above warding off adversaries with firearms. Judgments for the return of moveable property are less readily enforced, as the property may have been hidden or disposed of. And while property may be seized or transferred even when the debtor resists, it is far more difficult to prevent people from doing what is forbidden and from failing to do what is required.

21.1.5   Questions

1. If you were drafting a statute for the enforcement of judgments, blissfully ignorant of existing procedures, would you employ this four-fold classification?

2. Given modern electronic banking and finance, what are the arguments for and against retaining an execution system based on ancient precedents? Is reform necessary?

21.1.6   Remedies are various. Instalment orders are a relatively recent statutory innovation but are now generally available. Warrants or writs of seizure and sale, of delivery, or of possession are the classic common law remedies. Attachment of debts or, where possible, earnings, supplement the traditional common law remedies. Charging orders and the appointment of receivers have their origins as equitable remedies. Committal for contempt tends to be a remedy of last resort, as is use of sequestration orders. Substituted performance is sometimes available instead of specific performance. Generally, instalment orders will be sought by those required to make payments. The making of such an order normally trumps other enforcement procedures. Writs or warrants constitute the normal means of enforcing monetary judgments, given that they are easier to obtain than orders giving access to alternative procedures. Committals for contempt are not lightly made, but committal and sequestration constitute the only way in which recalcitrants can be dealt with should they not do as ordered, or in the event of their doing what they have been enjoined not to do.

21.1.7   The relationship between procedures and types of judgments is set out in the following table:

Procedure	Payment of money	Possession of land	Delivery of goods	Orders to do or not to do
Instalment order: Civil Procedure Rules 2006 (ACT) Div 2.18.4; Civil Procedure Act 2005 (NSW) s 107; Uniform Civil Procedure Rules (NSW) Pt 37; Uniform Civil Procedure Rules 1999 (Qld) Ch 19, Pt 7; Enforcement of Judgments Act 1991 (SA) s 5; Debtors Act 1870 (Tas); Judgment Debt Recovery Act 1984 (Vic); Supreme Court (General Civil Procedure) Rules 2005 (Vic) O 61; Supreme Court (General Rules of Procedure in Civil Proceedings) Rules 1996 (Vic); Civil Judgments Enforcement Act 2004 (WA) s 33.	Y			
Levy of property/order, warrant of seizure and sale: ACT Div 2.18.5; Civil Procedure Act 2005 (NSW) s 106(1)(a); Supreme Court Rules (NT) O 69; Civil Procedure Act 2011 (Qld) s 90(2)(a); Qld Ch 19 Pt 4; Enforcement of Judgments Act 1991 (SA) s 7; Tas Pt 35 Div 4; Vic O 69; Civil Judgments Enforcement Act 2004 (WA) Pt 4 Div 6.	Y			
Order, writ or warrant of possession: ACT Div 2.18.13; Civil Procedure Act 2005 (NSW) s 104 (also writ of restitution); Civil Procedure Act 2005 (NSW) s 106(1)(b); NT O 70; Civil Procedure Act 2011 (Qld) s 90(2)(d); Qld Ch 20 Pt 4 r 874; Enforcement of Judgments Act 1991 (SA) s 11; Tas r 874; Vic O 70; Civil Judgments Enforcement Act 2004 (WA) Pt 5 Div 1.		Y		

Procedure	Payment of money	Possession of land	Delivery of goods	Orders to do or not to do
Order, writ or warrant of delivery: ACT Div 2.18.14; Civil Procedure Act 2005 (NSW) s 105; Civil Procedure Act 2005 (NSW) s 105; NT Form 68C; Civil Procedure Act 2011 (Qld) ss 81(1), (2)(a), 90(2)(e); Qld r 897; Enforcement of Judgments Act 1991 (SA) s 11; Tas r 875; Vic Form 68C; Civil Judgments Enforcement Act 2004 (WA) Pt 5 Div 1.			Y	
Attachment of debts: ACT Divs 2.18.6, 2.18.7; Civil Procedure Act 2005 (NSW) ss 106(1)(b), 107; NT O 71; Civil Procedure Act 2011 (Qld) s 90(2)(b); Qld Ch 19 Pt 5; Enforcement of Judgments Act 1991 (SA) s 6; Tas Pt 35 Div 5; Vic O 71; Civil Judgments Enforcement Act 2004 (WA) Pt 4 Div 5.	Y			
Attachment of earnings: ACT Div 2.18.8; Civil Procedure Act 2005 (NSW) ss 106(1)(c), 119; NT O 72; Civil Procedure Act 2011 (Qld) s 90(2)(c); Qld Ch 19 Pt 6; Enforcement of Judgments Act 1991 (SA) s 6; Tas Pt 35 Div 6; Vic O 72; Civil Judgments Enforcement Act 2004 (WA) Pt 4 Div 4.	Y			
Charging orders/stop orders etc: ACT Divs 2.18.9, 2.18.10; Civil Procedure Act 2005 (NSW) ss 106(1)(c), 111; NT O 73; Civil Procedure Act 2011 (Qld) s 90(4),(5); Qld Ch 19 Pt 8; Enforcement of Judgments Act 1991 (SA) s 8; Tas Pt 36 Div 1; Vic O 73.	Y			
Appointment of receiver: ACT Div 2.18.11; NSW r 40.2(1)(a); NT O 74; Qld Ch 19 Pt 10; Enforcement of Judgments Act 1991 (SA) s 9; Tas Pt 36 Div 2; Vic O 74; Civil Judgments Enforcement Act 2004 (WA) Pt 4 Div 7; WA O 51.	Y			

Procedure	Payment of money	Possession of land	Delivery of goods	Orders to do or not to do
Contempt: HCR rr 10.02.4, 10.02.5, 11.02–11.04; FCR rr 41.04–41.06; ACT Div 2.18.16; NSW r 40.6(2); NT O 75; Civil Procedure Act 2011 (Qld) s 81(2)(a); Qld Ch 20 Pt 7; Enforcement of Judgments Act 1991 (SA) s 12; Tas Pt 36 Divs 3, 4; Vic O 75; Civil Judgments Enforcement Act 2004 (WA) s 98; WA O 46 r 3A.		Y	Y	Y†
Sequestration: HCR rr 11.02–11.04; FCR rr 41.04–41.06; ACT Div 2.18.15; NSW r 40.2(1); NT O 76; Civil Procedure Act 2011 (Qld) s 90(2)(f); Qld Ch 20 Pt 6; Tas Pt 36 Div 5; Vic O 76; Civil Judgments Enforcement Act 2004 (WA) s 98; WA O 46 r 3A.		Y	Y	Y†
Substituted performance: HCR r 10.02.2; FCR r 41.09; ACT r 2442(4); NSW r 40.8; NT r 66.11; Qld r 899; Enforcement of Judgments Act 1991 (SA) s 13; Tas r 877; Vic r 66.11; Civil Judgments Enforcement Act 2004 (WA) s 99.				Y (specific performance)

†   In New South Wales, the Northern Territory and Victoria, judgments for payment of money into court may be enforced by one of these means. The court may, however, authorise or direct a Master or the Prothonotary to enforce a judgment for payment of money into court by one or more of the means available for enforcing a judgment for payment of money. In New South Wales, sequestration is available to enforce all judgments to pay money (whether into court or otherwise); committal is not available: rr 40.2, 40.6(1). Elsewhere such a judgment would be enforced as if it were an order for the payment of money.

[*Note:* in this chapter a reference, such as WA O 9 r 2, is a reference to the relevant jurisdiction's Rules of Court. All other legislation will be specified.]

The Federal Court rules for the enforcement of monetary judgments are far less specific than those of the states and territories. However, the Federal Court may give directions about the enforcement or execution of an order: r 41.01.

21.1.8   In some jurisdictions, judgments and orders may normally be enforced only after a process known as authentication or perfection, and after filing the authenticated document. Authentication is an administrative process: In some jurisdictions, judgments may be enforced or appealed from only after they have been entered: FCR r 39.31(1)(b); NT r 60.01(1); Qld r 661(4); Tas 812(1); Vic r 60.01. As to authentication, see above 18.7.12. In South Australia a judgment must be served on any person against whom it is to be enforced: r 260.

WHEN IS THE JUDGMENT ENFORCEABLE?

21.2.1   Once the judgment is authenticated or perfected it is normally enforceable immediately. However, there are several exceptions.

Equitable relief is not enforceable immediately

21.2.2 If equitable relief is granted, the judgment must specify a time within which the party must comply with its terms. Only after that time has expired may action be taken against the recalcitrant party. In addition, before any action is taken, the party subject to the judgment must have been given notice of the judgment. The distinction between common law and equitable relief is sometimes a rather fine one. While it is customary to think of equitable relief as involving orders to do or not to do a specified act, common law orders are also effectively orders to do a specified act such as pay money, deliver goods or hand over possession of land. Traditionally, however, there were formal differences. The form of judgment did not order anyone to do anything. Judgments were for the recovery of damages or land etc. This meant, however, that whereas a judgment for the recovery of damages was a common law form of relief, an order that a defendant pay a sum of money to the plaintiff was an equitable order.

21.2.3C	**Finance Allotments Pty Ltd v Young**
	[1961] Qd R 452
	Supreme Court of Queensland

[A mortgagee sought possession of land following default by the mortgagor. The statement of claim was described as being 'to recover the possession of [the land]'. The relief claimed was, as required by the rule in question, 'delivery of possession of the said land by the defendant to the plaintiff'. Whether the summary judgment sought by the plaintiff could be delivered depended on whether the writ had been indorsed with a claim for 'delivery of possession'. Under the rules, a writ of possession could be used to enforce both a judgment for the recovery of land and a judgment for the delivery of possession of land.]

Gibbs J (at 455): An order to deliver up possession is an order to do an act within O 44 r 4, and must therefore state the time within which delivery of possession is to be made: *Savage v Bentley* (1904) 90 LT 641. On the other hand a judgment to recover possession need not state any time for such recovery. Although both a judgment for recovery of land and a judgment for the delivery of possession of land may be enforced by a writ of possession, where the judgment is to deliver up possession of land the writ of possession can only be sued out on filing an affidavit under O 51 r 2 showing that the judgment was served and that it had not been obeyed. In my opinion it is quite erroneous to regard 'recovery of possession' and 'delivery of possession' as interchangeable terms.

[His Honour held that the writ had not been indorsed with a claim for delivery of possession in view of the fact that it began with a claim for recovery of possession. He ruled, however, that it could be amended so as to rectify that deficiency.]

21.2.4 This artificial distinction disappears in the newer rules. These differentiate between judgments which specify time limits and those which do not. Those which do not specify a time by which an obligation is to be performed can be enforced only by the methods traditionally available for the enforcement of common law relief. Those which specify a time for performance may be enforced by 'equitable' enforcement procedures, including punishment for contempt. In practice, time limits are not set where a judgment is for payment of money, possession of land, or delivery of goods. This means that the practical effects of the modern rules differ little from those of the more traditional rules. However, if a party wants to mobilise a court's contempt powers to deal with a recalcitrant debtor, it can do so by applying to the court to specify a time limit by which the judgment is to be performed.

Conditional judgments

21.2.5 A person entitled to judgment only upon a particular condition being satisfied may do nothing in relation to the enforcement of that judgment until the condition is satisfied or unless and until the court dispenses with the condition: FCR r 41.02; ACT r 2014; NSW r 39.50; NT r 66.13; Qld r 796; Tas r 885; Vic r 66.13; Civil Judgments Enforcement Act 2004 (WA) s 13(1)(a).

STAYS

21.3.1 A party may apply for a stay of execution of judgment. Courts possess an inherent power to do this. In addition, the rules specify a range of circumstances in which parties may apply for a stay. These include:

- a general power to stay;
- stays pending an appeal;
- stays of execution of summary judgment pending trial of counterclaims;
- stays where summary judgment is for part only of a plaintiff's claim; and
- stays where facts arise after judgment which would justify a different judgment. Stays are at the discretion of the court.

21.3.2C   **J C Scott Constructions v Mermaid Waters Tavern Pty Ltd (No 2)**
[1983] 2 Qd R 255
Supreme Court of Queensland, Full Court

[Judgment had been given in favour of the plaintiff/respondent. The defendant had appealed. The defendant had also claimed a set-off equal to approximately half the amount awarded to the plaintiff. However, at the time of the initial trial, the defendant was not ready to proceed with the claim, and the trial of the set-off was ordered for a date subsequent to the trial. The defendant sought a stay of execution.]

Derrington J (at 258–9):
There are two grounds submitted here for a grant of relief to the applicant:

1. The entering of an appeal, which it is said raises serious and genuine questions of law and will, if successful, reduce the judgment to nil.
2. The existence of a counterclaim, which could not be heard at the trial allegedly because of the unavailability of the trial judge at the end of this already lengthy hearing. This reason will be seen to be incorrect.

As to the first, because of the way in which O 70 r 28 is framed, a stay being the exception, the applicant must show special circumstances: *Klinker Knitting Mills Pty Ltd v L'Union Fire General and Accident Insurance Co Ltd* [1937] VLR 142; *Amoco Australia Pty Ltd v Rocca Bros Motor Engineering Co Pty Ltd* (1972) 7 SASR 324 at 325; *Scarborough v Lew's Junction Stores Pty Ltd* [1963] VLR 129 at 130; *Cox v Mosman & Anor* [1908] QSR 210. It is argued that no fetter should be placed upon the Court's discretion, but where the construction of the rule endowing it implies a fetter, as in this case, there is no foundation for denying it. A discretion is not necessarily and naturally a creature born free. It is always a matter of construction of the source of the power.

A plaintiff, having succeeded in the court below, is entitled to the fruits of its judgment: *Annot v Lyle* [1886] 11 CPD 114 at 116 (CA); *McBryde v Sandland* (1918) 25 CLR 369 at 375. That is so unless good reason is shown to the contrary.

[259] The applicant claims that its grounds of appeal raise a serious question of law and not merely a dispute as to facts, which would be largely in the province of the trial judge. That alone is not enough to move this Court to exercise its discretion favourably to the applicant — *Atkins v Great Western Railway Co* [1886] 2 TLR 400; *Amoco v Rocca* (supra); *McBryde v Sandland* (supra at 375); *Halsbury's Laws of England*, 4th ed, vol 17, para 451.

While not providing any evidence that a stay would not harm the respondent by reason of any state of the applicant's own financial affairs the applicant claimed that the financial state of the respondent was such as to cause apprehension that a successful appeal would find the applicant bereft of any chance of recovering moneys paid under the judgment — a large amount of $567,982. This is said to be good reason for a stay: *Cox v Mosman & Anor* (supra); *Polini v Gray* [1879] 12 ChD 438, at 446; *McBryde v Sandland* (supra).

While agreeing with the principle, I can see no satisfactory evidence to provide the necessary factual base to apply it. The onus is on the applicant, who must come armed with material: *Barker v Lavery* [1885] 14 QBD 769 (CA). The financial stability of the respondent is not shown to be insecure and undertakings will be given as to retention of present ownership. In the absence of any other reason, the application must fail where it relies upon the existence of an appeal.

The second leg of the argument depends upon the existence of a counterclaim in the sum of $285,000, and is sought under both O 70 r 28 and O 47 r 18. This does not go to the whole of the judgment, but although the latter rule does not, as contrasted with the former refer to a stay explicitly as to part of the judgment as well as the whole, the Court can still use it to stay part of a judgment. Apart from the rule that the greater includes the less, a practical view would demand such a construction in these circumstances. There is a real question however as to whether this rule endows jurisdiction beyond the Court or judge who gave the judgment or made the order. It may be a valid construction so to confine it. However this Court has an inherent jurisdiction to stay proceedings: *Tringali v Stewardson Stubbs & Collett Ltd* 66 SR (NSW) 335, *Ferris v Lambton* [1905] 22 WN (NSW) 56; *Cox v Mosman* (supra) but the circumstances of this case do not invoke it.

Had there been diligent pursuit by the applicant of its counterclaim, and had it been merely fortuitous that the counterclaim was not heard and determined at the same time as the claim, in my view the Court would have seriously considered a stay *pro tanto* of the judgment upon the same principle as that applied where there is summary judgment under O 18 r 1 or a judgment on admissions under O 36 r 5, associated with a counterclaim and where judgment is given but stayed pending determination of the counterclaim. Cf *Logan v Lyons* [1955] QWN 78; *Caltex Oil (Aust) Pty Ltd* [1958] QWN 7; *Commonwealth* [260] *v Chesterfield & Jenkins (Qld) Pty Ltd* [1949] QWN 49; *Thwaites v Bank of Australasia* (1895) 1 ALR 21. (It is immaterial that O 18 r 1(2) expressly provides for a stay, because it is discretionary.) But, contrary to the submissions of the applicant, the facts of this case do not justify such action, for the failure to have both claims determined at once lies at its own door. Further, in the five months since the trial, it has taken no action to proceed. I do not accept the existence of any logical nexus between that claim and the appeal on the original judgment. Totally different questions are involved and the results are quite discrete. This dilatory conduct is consistent with the applicant's behaviour throughout the action, which is all very well for it while it is holding a large disputed sum. In my opinion this Court should clearly exercise its discretion against the applicant.

[Campbell CJ and Kelly J agreed. On stays pending appeals, see 19.7.3]

Limitation periods

21.3.3   The enforcement of judgments is subject to limitation periods. These are extremely generous: 12 years in most jurisdictions, 15 years in South Australia and Victoria: Limitation Act 1985 (ACT) s 14; Limitation Act 1969 (NSW) s 17; Limitation Act (NT) s 15; Limitation of Actions Act 1974 (Qld) s 10(4); Limitation of Actions Act 1936 (SA) s 34; Limitation Act 1974 (Tas) s 4(4); Limitation of Actions Act 1958 (Vic) s 5(4); Civil Judgments Enforcement Act 2004 (WA) s 12. Even prior to the expiry of the limitation period, leave is required to issue a writ or warrant to enforce a judgment if more than six years has elapsed since the judgment: see 21.7.4.

PRE-EMPTIVE STRIKES BY JUDGMENT CREDITORS

21.4.1   Parties can take a number of steps to protect their interests.

Mareva/Preservation of property orders

21.4.2   Even before judgment is given, a party may take action to ensure that success will not prove illusory, and at common law, courts had the power to issue an order restraining a party if there was a danger that a party would remove assets from the jurisdiction in order to frustrate execution. These were and are known as 'Mareva' orders in honour of the case which constituted authority for their use, *Mareva Compania Naviere SA v International Bulk Carriers SA* [1980] 1 All ER 213: see 16.4.1. Specific provision is now made for such orders in the rules of all jurisdictions other than the High Court — see above: FCR Div 14.2; ACT rr 740–745; NSW Pt 25 Div 1; NT O 37A; Qld rr 260–260G; SA r 247; Tas Pt 36 Div 1A; Vic O 37A; WA O 52A.

Attachment

21.4.3   Plaintiffs who fear that a defendant will abscond before they are able to enforce judgments in their favour may apply for orders protecting their interests. The legislation varies across jurisdictions. South Australia makes statutory provision for absconding debtors. If a plaintiff is seeking a monetary sum, and if there are grounds for believing that the defendant is about to leave the state and that the defendant's absence would seriously prejudice the plaintiff's prospects of enforcing any judgment that might be given or might have been given in the plaintiff's favour, the court may require the defendant to appear before the court for examination. Following this examination, it may require that the defendant give security for the satisfaction of the (possible) judgment: Enforcement of Judgments Act 1991 (SA) s 14.

An alternative is the defendant's arrest. In the Australian Capital Territory, Queensland, Tasmania, Victoria and Western Australia, there is provision for the pre-trial arrest of civil defendants in actions for debt and liquidated damages. In Queensland, the provisions cover civil defendants in general. This requires proof by affidavit of damage, of the defendant's being likely to leave the jurisdiction, and of the need for the defendant's apprehension if the action is not to be defeated. Upon such proof being given, the court may order the defendant's arrest. Once arrested, the person is to remain in custody until the court orders the person's release, or the person gives adequate security: Qld Ch 20 Pt 8; Debtors Act 1879 (Tas) s 5(2); Supreme Court Act (WA) 1935 ss 63–64; and see Court Procedures Act 2004 (ACT) ss 64–68; Supreme Court Act 1986 (Vic) ss 87–100. (The Queensland rules also make provision for the making of an order restraining a person from leaving Australia: r 259(2)(c).) In contrast to the provisions relating to the attachment of goods, there appears to be no requirement that the plaintiff give security to cover the eventuality that the claim for damages is not ultimately sustained. Why might this be? The power is strictly construed. It is not enough that the person to be attached has a long-term intention of leaving the jurisdiction, even if the person is making some preparations to give effect to these. Arrest will not be ordered unless the person's likely flight is imminent: *QB Investments Pty Ltd v Reed* [1979] Qd R 58. Arrest may be ordered only if the potential judgment debtor's flight will defeat the action. It is not enough that it will make enforcement more difficult or more expensive: *Moss & Co v Johnston* (1896) 22 VLR 530 at 531 per Hood J; *O'Connor v Pitcairn* (1901) 27 VLR 2 at 6 per Hood J; Qld r 942. It is, moreover, a discretionary power, which need not be exercised in favour of the plaintiff even if the conditions, precedent to its exercise, have been made out.

In all jurisdictions the rules provide that where a summons has been filed seeking a person's committal for contempt, and where that person appears likely to abscond or leave the jurisdiction, or has done so, the court may issue a warrant for the person's arrest: HCR r 11.02.3; FCR r 42.14; ACT r 2503; Supreme Court Rules 1970 (NSW) Pt 55 r 10; NT r 75.08; Qld r 927; Enforcement of Judgments Act 1991 (SA) s 12, Tas r 942(4); Vic r 75.08; WA O 55 r 6.

Do not delay

21.4.4 Parties that are in any doubt about whether judgment will be satisfied should also protect their interests by initiating enforcement procedures as quickly as possible. Judgments for sums of money are normally enforceable from the moment they are authenticated, and while procedures such as seizure and sale are sometimes brutal in their effect, perusal of the reports suggests that there is much to be said for the use of such procedures, provided, as always, that those resorting to them do not expect to resume good relations with the judgment debtor. Parties seeking to realise against real property should ensure that as soon as a writ or warrant is issued, steps are taken to ensure that details are entered on the title in the land titles registry.

Defendants who are concerned that plaintiffs might not have the resources to pay such costs as may be awarded against them should, if possible, have sought security for costs: see 20.8.1ff.

GATHERING RELEVANT INFORMATION

21.5.1 There are various legal ways in which judgment creditors may learn about the judgment debtor's assets. These include titles office searches, share and shipping registry searches, and searches of motor registration records and of motor vehicle security registers. Such searches should be conducted sufficiently early for plaintiffs to be able to be confident that the defendant will have sufficient resources to warrant the expense of litigating to the point of judgment. Following judgment, there are formal procedures available for judgment creditors who want information about the judgment debtor's assets: ACT Div 2.18.3; Civil Procedure Act 2005 (NSW) s 108; NSW Pt 38; NT r 67.02; Qld rr 803–812; Enforcement of Judgments Act 1991 (SA) s 4; Tas rr 888–890; Vic O 67; Civil Judgments Enforcement Act 2004 (WA) ss 26, 27, 29, 30. These procedures might be useful in cases where a debtor's readily identifiable assets are insufficient to satisfy a debt. These procedures are also available to assist parties seeking non-pecuniary relief.

On application from a person entitled to enforce a judgment, the court may order a person bound by the judgment to attend the court to be examined and to produce any relevant document or thing in his or her possession, custody or power. This procedure is known as an oral examination. The subject of the examination is any debt owed by the person bound, property which might be capable of satisfying the judgment, and any matters relating to the enforcement of the judgment which are specified in the order for examination or production. The application does not require notice, but the order must be served personally.

21.5.2 The scope of the examination is potentially wide-ranging. The person bound can be required to give all information which will assist in the location of relevant property. However, there are limits. In *Republic of Costa Rica v Strousberg* (1880) 16 QBD 8 at 9–10, Mallins VC said of the power to examine:

> Now, considering that that is a power which has been in force ever since 1854, it is certainly somewhat remarkable that no authority can be produced on either side as to how that examination ought to be conducted, or to what extent it can be justifiably carried.

Perhaps even more remarkably, there has been almost no authority since. In *Strousberg*, Mallins VC considered that the examination should not involve cross-examination and that it should be closely confined. This view was rejected in the Court of Appeal. Jessel MR said (at 12):

> Any question, therefore, fairly pertinent to the subject-matter of the inquiry, which means put with a view to ascertain so far as possible, by discovery from a reluctant defendant, what debts are owing to him, ought to be answered by the defendant.

James LJ said in a famous, short, sharp judgment (at 12–13):

> I am of the same opinion. The examination is not only intended to be an examination, but to be a cross-examination, and that of the severest kind.

Australian authority is sparse, but see *McCormack v National Australia Bank Ltd* (1992) 35 FCR 303. The bank, which had obtained judgment against McCormack, sought to question McCormack about a transfer of property to his wife, allegedly pursuant to a maintenance agreement under the Family Law Act 1975 (Cth). The object of the questions was to investigate whether the relevant deed and transactions carried out under it could be set aside. The court said (at 306):

We would not read the term 'means' as limited to pecuniary resources presently, in the sense of instantly or currently available. Order 43 r 31 uses no such description. The term 'means' of its very nature denotes not only existing property or assets but also resources or sources whereby assets or property may become available for satisfaction of the judgment debt. But, nevertheless, the rule allows only an examination as to the property and means which the judgment debtor has to satisfy the judgment.

Order 43, r 31 does not, as does s 81 of the Bankruptcy Act 1966 (Cth), allow for a general, wide-ranging inquiry into the financial transactions of the debtor. The purpose of the examination is to ascertain from what sources the debtor may satisfy the judgment debt. The term 'means' does not denote other possible methods by which the judgment creditor may obtain satisfaction of the debt. It is the means of the debtor which are the subject of the examination. Therefore we would not agree with Higgins J [from whom the appeal was brought] that 'the term is wide enough ... to enable the creditor to determine whether the alternative process of bankruptcy is worth taking or not'.

The process of the Supreme Court ought not be used as form of pre-trial discovery to aid a judgment creditor to institute proceedings under the Family Law Act or under the Bankruptcy Act.

21.5.3 New South Wales legislation specifically limits questions to 'material questions', these being, in relation to a person who is ordered to pay money:

(i) questions as to whether any and, if so, what debts are owing to that person, and (ii) questions as to whether that person has any and, if so, what other property or other means of satisfying the judgment or order ...

In relation to other judgments, they are confined to questions 'concerning or in aid of the enforcement or satisfaction of the judgment or order as may be specified in the order under this section': Civil Procedure Act 2005 (NSW) s 108(5).

21.5.4 The costs of such an examination may be awarded against the debtor, but normally are not: B C Cairns, 'Practice and Procedure', *Halsbury's Laws of Australia*, LexisNexis, Sydney, looseleaf, vol 20, [325-9930].

21.5.5 Information can also be obtained illegally, and sometimes is. Government databases may be mined for police records, taxation data, and social security information. Business databases may be used to supply information on banking transactions or phone records. Legal advisers use, recommend and turn a blind eye to such procedures at their professional peril.

INSTALMENT ORDERS

21.6.1 There is provision in most jurisdictions for ordering that a debt be paid by instalments: ACT Div 2.18.4; Civil Procedure Act 2005 (NSW) s 107; NSW Pt 37; Qld Ch 19 Pt 7; Enforcement of Judgments Act 1991 (SA) s 5; Debtors Act 1870 (Tas) s 4(5); Judgment Debt Recovery Act 1984 (Vic); Civil Judgments Enforcement Act 2004 (WA) ss 21, 28–31, 33. In the Northern Territory there is provision for instalment orders only in relation to proceedings in the Local Court: Local Court Act (NT) s 27. (Is there a reason why such orders should sometimes not be available in relation to Supreme Court litigation?) In some jurisdictions, an instalment order may be made at the instance of either party; in others, it may be made only at the request of the creditor.

The court may make an order only after an investigation of the defendant's means, or after a decision to dispense with an investigation. The decision is to be made after taking account of the debtor's means of satisfying the judgment, the necessary living expenses of the debtor and the debtor's dependants and the debtor's other liabilities. There is provision for the rescission, suspension or variation of an order, and this may be on application from either the creditor or the debtor. There is provision for default. In the event of default, the judgment debtor is to attend court to be examined. The court may then cancel or vary the order. However, in several jurisdictions there is also provision for more serious sanctions. Debtors who, 'without proper excuse' (Enforcement of Judgments Act 1991 (SA) s 5(7)) or 'persistently and wilfully and without an honest and reasonable excuse' (Judgment Debt Recovery Act 1984 (Vic) s 19(1)) or 'did not have a reasonable excuse' (Civil Judgments Enforcement Act 2004 (WA) s 90(1)(b)(ii)) default, and who have the means to pay instalments may be imprisoned for up to 40 days. However, on paying the instalments on which there has been default, the judgment debtor is to be discharged. The Australian Capital Territory, New South Wales and Queensland legislation contains no such provision.

In South Australia and Western Australia, it is only the creditor who can apply for an instalment order (Enforcement of Judgments Act 1991 (SA) s 5(1); Civil Judgments Enforcement Act 2004 (WA) s 31), although both debtors and creditors may apply for rescission and variation.

Under ACT rr 2151, 2153, Qld r 868 and the Judgment Debt Recovery Act 1984 (Vic), both creditors and debtors may apply. Where an instalment order is in effect and where it is being complied with, it acts as a stay on any other form of execution of the judgment debt: ACT r 2155 (first application stays enforcement), r 2159 (no other enforcement while order in force); NSW r 37.5(1); Qld r 870; Judgment Debt Recovery Act 1984 (Vic) s 9. This can constitute an extremely useful weapon for a party which is seeking to ward off judgment (and other) creditors. In Western Australia, an instalment order does not preclude other orders, but these may be made only by leave of the court and only if hardship would not result: Civil Judgments Enforcement Act 2004 (WA) ss 22, 33.

Before the cancellation or variation of an order, the debtor must be examined. If the debtor refuses to attend court, a warrant for his or her apprehension may be issued.

In Victoria, it has been held that instalment orders may be made only where the amount of the instalments is such that the payment of the instalments will reduce the amount owing, after making allowance for the interest accruing on the unpaid debt: *Cahill v Howe* [1986] VR 630.

Quite apart from any legislative provisions, parties may agree to payment by instalments, possibly on the basis of terms which compensate the creditor for loss of immediate payment and the risks of default. The Australian Capital Territory rules (r 2157) and the New South Wales rules (r 37.1A) make specific provision for this. Instalment payments may be attractive if the alternative is the debtor's bankruptcy. The obvious downside is the danger of default. Minor defaults may not justify the costs involved in attempting to enforce performance. Major defaults may leave the creditor worse off than it would have been had judgment been executed immediately.

WRITS OR WARRANTS OF EXECUTION

21.7.1   Most jurisdictions have provisions for what are variously called writs or warrants of execution. These typically represent directions to the sheriff or enforcement officer to do certain things. In other jurisdictions, such orders have been subsumed within a broader concept, enforcement orders, with the standard orders to the sheriff forming particular instances of the broader category.

The most usual order is that the sheriff should seize and sell property. Other orders of great antiquity include orders to take possession of land on the part of the successful plaintiff and to take delivery of goods to which the successful plaintiff is entitled. Historically, the general rules which applied to these orders also governed the procedures for requiring sheriffs to arrest recalcitrant defendants or to exclude them from access to their property. They differed, however, from those governing applications for other enforcement orders, such as orders for the redirection of debts, or orders imposing charges over the defendant's property. Over the last 20 years, the rules have diverged to the point where it is difficult to generalise about the procedures to be used for obtaining enforcement orders. In most jurisdictions, there are straightforward procedures for obtaining orders that the sheriff seize and sell property, take possession of land, or take delivery of goods. There are rather more elaborate procedures for obtaining orders which affect third parties. And there are special procedures for obtaining orders against defendants who refuse to obey orders to do or not do specified things.

This trichotomy describes the New South Wales, Northern Territory, Tasmania and Victorian regimes reasonably well, and broadly corresponds to the regime which operates in South Australia. Queensland, the Australian Capital Territory and Western Australia fit uneasily into this analysis. In Queensland, there are two sets of general provisions. The first set of rules relates to warrants for the enforcement of money orders. The second set of general rules relates to warrants for the enforcement of non-money orders. The Australian Capital Territory and Western Australia draw a similar distinction between money and on-money orders, but — in addition to general rules relating to the enforcement of money orders — the relevant legislation includes general rules relating to all types of order. While their rules provide for the functional equivalents of writs and warrants of execution, they do not generally recognise these as a special category of enforcement orders. This is of little substantive importance, but it is of some procedural significance. For the purposes of this section, the terms 'writ', 'warrant' and 'order' will be used interchangeably except in contexts where it is relevant that an order falls within the narrow 'writ of execution' category rather than the broader 'enforcement order' category.

The procedure for obtaining an order or warrant

21.7.2   In the Northern Territory, South Australia, Tasmania and Victoria, the person requesting an order or warrant for seizure or sale, delivery of chattels, or recovery of land produces a form of the order or warrant and evidence of the relevant judgment to the relevant official (the Registrar or the Prothonotary). In the Australian Capital Territory, New South Wales and Queensland, the procedure is similar, except that the rules expressly provide that the application must be supported by affidavit material: ACT rr 2201, 2451, 2460; NSW rr 39.2, 39.3. Applications are normally made to the court which delivered the relevant judgment. However in Queensland, the relevant court is the lowest court which would have had jurisdiction to give the judgment: r 801. Similar (but more flexible) rules now apply in the Australian Capital Territory: rr 2009, 2010.

21.7.3   Once the relevant officer is persuaded that the party requesting the order is entitled to it, the document is sealed. Most jurisdictions make provision for the issuing of separate orders for the judgment debt and for costs: ACT r 2005; Civil Procedure Act 2005 (NSW) s 137(1);

NT r 68.03; Qld r 798; Tas r 899; Vic r 68.03. (What is the rationale for this provision?) The process of issuing warrants and writs is normally a purely administrative one. However, there are some circumstances in which the leave of the court is a precondition for issue of a writ or warrant. In the Australian Capital Territory, these conditions apply in relation to any form of execution: r 2012. In South Australia, these conditions also apply where a person is to be arrested to be charged with contempt. In Queensland, the relevant preconditions apply to all enforcement orders sought in connection with payment of money, but they do not apply in relation to the enforcement of non-money orders. In Western Australia, these preconditions apply to all enforcement orders under the Act: Civil Judgments Enforcement Act 2004 (WA) s 13(1). In practice, little turns on this. In jurisdictions which do not expressly require leave as a condition precedent for particular enforcement procedures, there is typically provision for an *inter partes* hearing at which people affected by an order can raise grounds for objecting to its being made.

21.7.4 These typically involve non-routine situations. The special cases are:

- cases where more than six years have elapsed since the judgment took effect (12 years in New South Wales): HCR r 10.01.1; ACT r 2012(1)(a); Civil Procedure Act 2005 (NSW) s 134(2); NT r 68.02(1)(a); Qld r 799(2)(a); Tas r 897(1)(a); Vic r 68.02(1)(a); Civil Judgments Enforcement Act 2004 (WA) s 13(1)(a);

- cases where there are changes in the identity of the party entitled to or liable to execution through assignment, death or otherwise: HCR r 10.01.1; ACT r 2012(1)(d); NSW r 39.1(a); NT r 68.02(1)(b); Qld r 799(2)(b); Tas r 897(1)(b); Vic r 68.02(1)(b); Civil Judgments Enforcement Act 2004 (WA) s 13(1)(d), (e);

- cases in which execution is sought against assets of a deceased person coming into the hands of his or her executor or administrator after date of judgment: HCR r 10.01.1; ACT r 2012(1)(b); NSW r 39.1(1)(b); NT r 68.02(1)(c); Qld r 799(2)(b); Tas r 897(1)(c); Vic r 68.02(1)(c); Civil Judgments Enforcement Act 2004 (WA) s 13(1)(e);

- cases in which judgment is conditional: FCR r 41.02; ACT r 2012(1)(c); NSW r 39.1(1)(c); NT r 68.02(1)(c); Qld r 796(1)(b); Tas r 897(1)(d); Vic r 68.02(1)(d); Civil Judgments Enforcement Act 2004 (WA) s 13(1)(b);

- cases where the order or warrant is issued against property in the hands of a court-appointed receiver or a sequestrator: ACT r 2012(1)(g), (h); NSW r 39.1(1)(e), (f); NT r 68.02(1)(e); Tas r 897(1)(e); Vic r 68.02(1)(e); Civil Judgments Enforcement Act 2004 (WA) s 13(1)(c);

- cases in which the order or warrant is issued in aid of another warrant of execution: ACT r 2012(1)(j); NSW r 39.1(1)(g); NT r 68.02(2); Vic r 68.02(2); WA O 47 r 2;

- cases in which the judgment is for a sum in a foreign currency: NT r 68.02(1)(f); Tas r 897(1)(g); Vic r 68.02(1)(f);

- cases where legislation requires leave: NSW r 39.1(4); NT r 68.02(2); Qld r 799(2); Tas r 897(2); Vic r 68.02(2). This requirement would exist apart from the rules; the rule simply highlights the possibility that there may be relevant legislation;

- cases in which a party is entitled to execution upon a judgment of assets *in futuro* (in the future): ACT r 2012(1)(i); Tas r 897(1)(f);

- cases in which a party is entitled to execution against any of the shareholders of a company upon a judgment recorded against such company, or against a public officer or other person representing such company: ACT O 43 r 22(d); Civil Judgments Enforcement Act 2004 (WA) s 13(1)(h);

• if the writ is for possession of land: ACT r 2012(1)(f); NSW r 39.1(1)(d);

• where the judgment was given against a non-party: Civil Judgments Enforcement Act 2004 (WA) s 13(1)(d), (e); and

• some cases where judgment is given against partners or a partnership: Civil Judgments Enforcement Act 2004 (WA) s 13(1)(f), (g).

Applications for this leave need not be on notice unless the court orders otherwise: ACT r 2012(2); NSW rr 39.1(2), 39.2; NT r 68.02(3); Qld r 799(3); Tas r 897(3); Vic r 68.02(3); WA O 47 r 3; and see Civil Judgments Enforcement Act 2004 (WA) s 13(2). The Australian Capital Territory, New South Wales, Northern Territory, Tasmanian and Victorian rules provide that applications must be accompanied by affidavits providing details of:

(a)   the amount of money due, including interest, at the time of the application (where there is a claim for payment of money);

(b)   reasons for delay (where more than the prescribed period has elapsed);

(c)   details of any change of parties;

(d)   demands having been made (where there has been change of parties or conditional judgment);

(e)   the applicant's entitlement to the proceeds of execution; and

(f)   the liability of those subject to execution.

Queensland (r 799(4)) imposes similar requirements, but does not expressly require supporting affidavits. However, even apart from the rules, such affidavit material would be necessary. The grant of leave is discretionary. Circumstances relevant to the exercise of that discretion were considered in *World Square Pty Ltd v Taylor* [1990] 1 Qd R 583.

21.7.5C   **World Square Pty Ltd v Taylor**
                                                        [1990] 1 Qd R 583
                                              Supreme Court of Queensland

[The defendant had guaranteed loans made by the plaintiff to N Ltd. N Ltd defaulted and the plaintiff obtained a default judgment against the defendant. After the plaintiff had initiated winding-up proceedings against N Ltd and bankruptcy proceedings against the defendant, the parties agreed that for six months N Ltd would make payments by instalments. At the end of six months, N Ltd had not defaulted under the agreement. Nor had it repaid the loan. The plaintiff sought to execute against the defendant. Lee J held that the plaintiff was not entitled to issue execution as N Ltd was not in default of its obligations. The default on which the original judgment had been based was therefore extinguished. More than six years had elapsed since the judgment.]

Lee J (at 585, 588–9, 593–5): [In discussing the exercise of his discretion under the rules, his Honour said:] These rules remain in substantially the same form since 1901 and are similar in material respects to the former Victorian O 42 rr 22, 23 and the former English O 42 rr 22, 23. They do not specify whether an application may be made ex parte or upon notice. Nor do they specify what the affidavit of the plaintiff in support must contain. The current English

O 46 rr 2, 4 and the current Victorian O 68 r 2 however, require the affidavit in support to specify (inter alia) the reasons for the delay and as well, allow the application to be made ex parte unless the court otherwise orders. It appears that the amendment to the English Rule as to the explanation for delay merely gave effect to what was in fact the then prevailing practice. So also with the rule expressly allowing the application to be brought ex parte.

However, the practice in Victoria under the former rule and in Queensland differed. It was decided by Hood J in *Hammon v Kampfhenteel* (1895) 21 VLR 202, that when six years had elapsed since the judgment or where there had been a change of parties, a summons must be issued and served on the defendant. This decision along with the decision of the Irish Court of Appeal in *National Bank v Cullen* [1894] 2 IR 683 and that of Griffith CJ in *Queensland National Bank v Stewart* (1898) 9 QLJ (NC) 40 were applied by Gibbs J in *Litherland v Litherland and Randage* [1963] QWN 24. This practice was complied with in the present case. ...

It was conceded by counsel for the plaintiff (and adopted by senior counsel for the defendants) that the judge hearing the application had an unfettered discretion whether or not to grant the application, once the plaintiff shows that it was entitled to issue execution. This seems to be established: *Hulbert and Crowe v Cathcart* [1896] AC 470 (HL); *TV T Lamb & Sons v Rider* [1948] 2 KB 331 (CA); *Hine v Hine* [1969] QWN 38 (Hart J); *Arnold v Martyr* [1974] Qd R 206 (E S Williams J); *Halsbury* 4th ed vol 17 para 409 at 242. ...

[588] It seems to me that the foregoing authorities indicate that notwithstanding that the plaintiff establishes a legal right which the defendant has not negatived, the court has a general discretion under its rules of procedure whether or not to grant leave to the plaintiff to issue execution. Either party is entitled to place before the court matters which are relevant to the exercise of discretion. There is an evidentiary onus on the defendant to show some other arrangement or reason why it would be inequitable or unjust for the plaintiff to issue execution: per Hood J. Likewise, demonstrated prejudice may be a factor for the court to take into account in the exercise of its discretion. Even though the rule does not expressly require the plaintiff to explain the delay, it would seem to be a prudent practice (as is now regularised by the current Victorian and English Rules) for the plaintiff to provide an explanation for the delay, particularly where the indulgence of the court is sought to invoke its enforcement procedures after the cutoff point of six years has expired.

I accept the submissions by counsel for the plaintiff that a relevant consideration in the granting of leave is the fact that the plaintiff was still in time to sue by separate action upon the judgment itself. Section 10(4) of the Limitation of Actions Act 1974–1981 provides that an action [589] shall not be brought upon a judgment after the expiration of twelve years from the date on which the judgment becomes enforceable. ...

[593] In the alternative to the argument based upon a denial of the legal entitlement of the plaintiff to issue execution and if the above submissions failed, it was submitted that as a matter of the court's discretion, it would be unjust to allow the plaintiff to now execute on that judgment after such a lengthy unexplained delay and because the defendants would now have no prospect in successfully appealing from the decision of Weld M. ...

[594] The evidence is clear that the defendants did not prosecute the appeal from the decision of Master Weld after 21 January 1983. I accept the submission that this was simply because the defendants considered there was no necessity to do so. I also accept that the plaintiff [595] did not proceed further to issue bankruptcy petitions and that the defendants were entitled to assume that the plaintiff no longer proposed to take any such course. In the circumstances of this case, the delay alone is likely to cause prejudice.

21.7.6   Regardless of whether the issue of a writ requires the exercise of the court's discretion, there are limits to the number of writs that may be issued in relation to a judgment. In general, only one writ may be issued for the recovery of a sum of money, although a second writ may be issued for costs. Even where separate writs may be issued they must each be for the execution of the whole of the judgment (apart, if relevant, from costs). Thus, if a judgment creditor assigns part of a judgment debt, the creditor and the assignee may not execute independently for their share of the debt. Assignees of a judgment debt enjoy the same rights of enforcement as the judgment creditor.

21.7.7   Orders for sale and seizure, possession of land, and delivery of property are valid for one year and may be extended for up to one year: ACT r 2052(1) (also orders for detention of property); NSW r 39.20; NT r 68.05; Civil Proceedings Act 2011 (Qld) s 91 (unless warrant states that it ends earlier); Qld r 821; Tas r 901(1); Vic r 68.05; Civil Judgments Enforcement Act 2004 (WA) s 102(1). The other party need not be notified of applications to extend the time of a warrant, but a copy of the order granting the extension must be given to the sheriff by the party obtaining the order: ACT r 2052(2); NT r 68.05; Qld r 821(2); Tas 901(3)(b); Vic r 68.05. An alternative to making an application is simply to reissue. However, there are several situations in which this option is not attractive. First, in some circumstances (see 21.7.5), leave would be needed to reissue. Second, where enforcement depends on an auxiliary writ, reissuing will not be enough; the auxiliary writ having lapsed with the original writ, it must be taken out anew: *Finegan (Timber) Pty Ltd v Beechey* [1983] 2 VR 215. Third, if a writ is reissued, it loses such priority as the earlier writ may have had: *In re Broughton* (1916) 17 SR (NSW) 29 at 33 per Harvey J; *General Credits Ltd v Beattie* [1982] VR 551 at 555 per Young CJ.

21.7.8   Whether and when the court will renew a writ was discussed in *General Credits Ltd v Beattie* [1982] VR 551. The relevant facts are described by Young CJ (at 551):

> On 19 August 1980 the plaintiff entered judgment in default of appearance in this action for possession of the land described in the statement of claim. On 27 August 1980 a writ of possession was issued. It was forwarded to the Sheriff for execution on the same day. However, it was not immediately executed, for negotiations took place between the parties and the Sheriff was instructed not to proceed with the execution. The plaintiff evidently agreed to proposals by the defendants for the repayment of moneys owing to it by instalments but whenever default was made in the repayment proposals the plaintiff's solicitors instructed the Sheriff to proceed with the execution but each such instruction was followed by a further instruction to stay. In this way the writ of possession remained unexecuted for more than a year from its date of issue because of the readiness of the plaintiff to allow the defendants every opportunity to repay the moneys owing by them.

In due course, 12 months elapsed from the issue of the writ. It remained unexecuted, and the sheriff subsequently refused to execute it. One issue was whether the 12 months' limit applied to writs of possession, these not being expressly included under the rubric 'writs of execution'. Young CJ held that they were impliedly included and therefore subject to the 12 months' limit. On whether writs could be renewed, his Honour said (at 555):

> Next, the plaintiff applies after the writ has expired and r 20 speaks of a writ being renewed 'at any time before its expiration'. But I agree with Lush J, that the practice which has for many years applied to the application of O 64 r 6 to the renewal of writs of summons under O 8 r 1 should be applied to the renewal of writs of execution under O 42 r 20: see *Walker v Buksh*

1981 VR 1061 at 1062–3. The practice which his Honour traced back at least to *Stott v Smith* (1888) 10 ALT 159 perhaps began with the decision of Jessel, MR in *Re Jones* (1877) 25 WR 303; see *Licul v Corney* [1976] VR 177 at 180. Accordingly I think that I have power on the present application to grant the renewal sought.

In *Walker v Buksh, supra*, Lush J found a positive indication in O 42 justifying the issue of one or more writs of *fi fa*. His Honour held that the reference in O 42 r 17 to 'one or more writs of fieri facias' can only refer in Victoria to the suing out of successive writs, although the same words in the English rule appear to have been directed to the possibility of writs being simultaneously directed to the sheriffs of different counties. There is no similar indication in the case of writs of possession but I am nevertheless of the opinion that no reason appears why a second writ should not be issued out of the Prothonotary's office, provided of course that the first writ has been returned. The second writ should recite the first writ and the return to it. Rule 22 of O 42 provides that execution may issue at any time within six years from the recovery of the judgment and accordingly suggests that the mere expiry of the original writ of execution should not be regarded as an impediment to the issue of a second writ.

The question that therefore remains is whether I should grant the renewal sought by the plaintiff or leave it to issue a second writ of possession reciting the first and the return to it.

I have come to the conclusion, as Lush J did in *Walker v Buksh*, supra, that the preferable course is to leave the applicant to sue out a second writ. In the notes to O 46 r 8 of the current English rules contained in the *Supreme Court Practice*, 1979, vol 1, at [750], it is said that it is not the usual practice either in the Chancery Division or in the Queen's Bench Division to extend the validity of a writ of execution under the rule except in cases where priority of date is important. There is no relevant difference between renewing a writ of execution and extending its validity. No question of priorities arises on the material before me and no reason was suggested to me for preferring one course over the other. Further, I think, like Lush J that it is better not to involve the Court in making orders without a full knowledge of the possible consequences if that can be avoided and although it cannot help the present applicant, I think it is preferable not to put a litigant to the unnecessary expense of making a further application to the Court.

21.7.9 Question

1. In *General Credits Ltd v Beattie* [1982] VR 551, the relevant rule provided:

   A writ of execution, if unexecuted, shall remain in force for one year only from its issue, unless renewed in the manner hereinafter provided; but at any time before its expiration, any such writ may, by leave of the Court or a Judge, be renewed by the party suing it out for one year from the date of such renewal, and so on from time to time during the continuance of the renewed writ … and a writ of execution so renewed shall have effect, and shall be entitled to priority, according to the time of the original delivery thereof.

   On what basis, then, could a writ be extended after its expiry? The rules in the Northern Territory and Victoria are now explicit ('an order … shall not be made after the expiry of the warrant'): NT 68.05(2); Vic r 68.05(2). In Western Australia, the provisions of O 3 r 5(2) (which enable the retrospective extension of time limits) do not apply to an application to extend time: Civil Judgments Enforcement Act 2004 (WA) s 102(5).

Finegan (Timber) Pty Ltd v Beechey
                                    [1983] 2 VR 215
                            Supreme Court of Victoria, Full Court

[No sale having been effected, the sheriff made a return to that effect, and the judgment creditor sued out a writ of *venditioni exponas* (an order that the sheriff sell goods seized but not sold). No action had been taken under this writ when the original writ of *fi fa* (the equivalent of a warrant of seizure and sale) expired. The judgment creditor applied to have the writ of *fi fa* renewed.]

Young CJ (at 217–18): If the judgment creditor had applied for a renewal of the writ of *fi fa* under O 42 r 20 before it expired and had supported the application with evidence showing that it was important to maintain the priority of date under the original writ, it may be that no difficulty would have arisen. If the writ of *fi fa* had been renewed it would presumably have remained in force until May 1983 and the writ of *venditioni exponas* would have remained in force for one year from its issue. But the writ not having been renewed before its expiry, the question is what is now to be done? The judgment creditor may, as Gray J said, undoubtedly issue a new writ of *fi fa*, but that would almost certainly lead to the necessity for the issue of a writ of *venditioni exponas* in due course, and the judgment creditor seeks to avoid the delay and expense involved.

Mr Braun for the judgment debtor submitted that we should not take a course which would avoid that process because priorities of other interests might be affected. In *General Credits Ltd v Beattie* it was said, at 555, that it is not the usual practice in England to extend the validity of a writ of execution except in cases where priority of date is important. (See also *Williams' Supreme Court Practice*, 2nd ed, O 42 r 20 et seq.)

This might have been a case, if the Court had been given fuller information, for renewing the writ of *fi fa* and for the making of a special [218] order which would relieve the judgment creditor of his difficulties. But the material before the Court leaves many questions unanswered. It is not, for instance, stated whether the Sheriff retains possession of any of the judgment debtor's property. There is a reference in the affidavit in support of the summons to the judgment debtor's having an equitable interest in 'the said property' which appears to be his place of residence as it is said that he is a joint purchaser under a terms contract from the Housing Commission. It is also said that a memorandum of the particulars of the judgment was not filed pursuant to s 209 of the Property Law Act until 31 August 1981, whereas the writ of *fi fa* had been issued on 27 May 1981.

The affidavit in support of the summons states that the deponent has been informed by the Sheriff's officer that upon extension of the life of the original writ of *fi fa* the said property will be put to auction without reserve under the writ of *venditioni exponas* once a current search of the title has been conducted and consent for the sale of the property obtained by the Sheriff from the Crown Solicitor. The affidavit does not, however, state when this information was received by the deponent, nor does it explain the significance of the consent of the Crown Solicitor to the sale. Nor does it state why the application for renewal of the writ was made after it had expired. A much fuller explanation of the course of events would be necessary before the Court could decide that a renewal should be granted. There is an assertion in the final paragraph of the affidavit that the judgment creditor seeks to preserve the priority and sequence of the original writ of *fi fa*, but nothing upon which the Court can determine whether the legitimate interests of any other parties would be affected by any order made.

In these circumstances it is not appropriate for the Court to make an order renewing the writ of *fi fa* or to make a special order relieving the judgment creditor of his difficulties. He can, as Gray J indicated, issue a fresh writ of *fi fa* and accordingly the appeal should be dismissed.

[Anderson and McGarvie JJ agreed.]

21.7.11 In most jurisdictions the procedures for applying for orders for seizure and sale, possession of land, and delivery of goods are different from those for seeking other enforcement orders. This means that a person seeking to enforce a money order must make a separate application for a writ/warrant of seizure and sale, and for orders, such as an order for the redirection of debts, or for the appointment of a receiver. A judgment creditor who has taken out a writ/warrant of execution is not precluded from making an application for an additional order. In jurisdictions which provide a common procedure for seeking enforcement orders, an order may provide for several concurrent modes of enforcement: ACT r 2001(4); Civil Judgments Enforcement Act 2004 (WA) s 22. In Western Australia the legislation states that the court may make concurrent orders only if it is satisfied that doing so is justified given existing orders and that the additional order will not impose unreasonable obligations on the debtor: Civil Judgments Enforcement Act 2004 (WA) s 22. Even in the absence of such a requirement, the criteria for the making of orders other than those discussed here is such that courts will be required to take account of the reasonableness of the additional orders. The amount for which the warrant is issued shall, unless the court orders otherwise, include an amount representing the costs involved in the issuing of previous warrants: ACT r 2201(2)(f); Civil Procedure Act 2005 (NSW) s 137(2)(a) qualified by NSW r 39.47; NT r 68.06; Qld Form 74; Vic r 68.06.

21.7.12 Writs or warrants take the form of commands issued on behalf of the court to the sheriff, commanding that the sheriff take action of the kind specified. Writs must comply strictly with the rules. In *O'Neil v Hart* (No 2) [1905] VLR 259 at 266, Madden CJ said:

Now I think that the authorities go this length, at all events, that if a writ of *fieri facias* does not follow the judgment as it ought to, but departs from it in any particular — as to parties for instance — it must show on its face why it departs from the judgment — what is the real reason for the departure.

Execution is in the nature of a penal operation. A writ of execution warrants the seizure of the property of a person, and it must be shown to that person on the face of the writ that there is proper authority for what is being done.

There had also been an objection based on the fact that the writ had been issued on the first working day after the day on which costs had been taxed. His Honour rejected that argument, saying (at 268):

Now, if execution had been issued on the [date of the taxation], it would have been wrong, as an abuse of the process of the Court, on the reasonable ground that a man does not know what he has to pay until the costs have been taxed, and certainly it would be very unfair and very unreasonable to rush execution in, when to do so might prevent a person able and willing to pay from paying what he knew for the first time on that very day was payable. In the present case there is nothing of that kind. The day referred to in the case cited, being the day on which the costs were taxed, had passed, and a new day, a holiday, had intervened and gave really two days before execution was issued.

He ordered that proceedings by the judgment creditor be stayed until payment of the debtor's costs, and further, refused any set-off of those costs against the costs payable by the original judgment debtor.

21.7.13 The sheriff makes a 'return' to the writ or warrant. This is a written report stating what has been done pursuant to the writ. The return must report whether or not the debtor had any assets and if so, what was done in relation to them. For example, if there has been an auction, but no acceptable bid, this would be reported. A frequent return to a writ is that there were no relevant goods to be found. To avoid such a return (where the judgment debtor does in fact own property), a judgment creditor should direct the sheriff as to what assets might be seized and where they might be found. A return may be made before the writ has been fully executed: B C Cairns, at [325–9905].

Types of orders

Orders for the seizure and sale of property

21.7.14 This order of great antiquity rejoiced for about seven centuries in its Latin name, *fieri facias* (cause this to be done), or more usually, in its abbreviated form, *fi fa*. New South Wales uses the term 'levy of property', and the other jurisdictions provide for warrants or orders for the 'seizure and sale' of property: ACT r 2201, Form 2.59; Civil Procedure Act 2005 (NSW) s 106; NT O 69; Civil Proceedings Act 2011 (Qld) s 90(2)(a); Qld r 828; Enforcement of Judgments Act 1991 (SA) s 7; Tas r 906; Vic O 69; Civil Judgments Enforcement Act 2004 (WA) ss 59, 60.

21.7.15 Orders are addressed to the sheriff or enforcement officer, and forms are prescribed. Until recently, the Australian Capital Territory Supreme Court Rules included a splendidly archaic form, which was reproduced in earlier editions of this book. It has been replaced. The Victorian form reproduced below is typical.

21.7.16E   **Supreme Court (General Civil Procedure) Rules 2005 (Vic)**
Form 68A — Warrant of Seizure and Sale
Rule 68.08
[heading as in originating process]

TO THE SHERIFF:
In respect of the judgment [or order] dated [eg 20 June 20] by which it was adjudged [or ordered] that [*judgment debtor*] pay $ to [*judgment creditor*] together with costs, which have been taxed at $, [or by which it was ordered that] [*judgment debtor*] pay certain costs to [*judgment creditor*], which have been taxed at $, Levy On The Property of [judgment debtor] which is authorised by law to be taken in execution for —

(a) $, being $ now due and payable exclusive of taxed costs and $ for taxed costs; [or $ for *taxed* costs];

(b) $, being interest at the rate or rates fixed in accordance with law, on [*amount due and payable exclusive of taxed costs*] from the date of the judgment [or order];

(c) $, being interest at the rate or rates fixed in accordance with law, on [*amount of taxed costs*] from 19 [*date of taxation of costs*];

(d) $, being the costs of this [*and of any prior*] warrant and;

(e)   your fees and expenses for this [*and for any prior*] warrant,

And Pay the amount so levied other than your fees and expenses to [*judgment creditor*] or otherwise as the law requires. And Indorse on this warrant immediately after you have performed all your obligations under it a statement of the date, time and place at which you have executed or attempted to execute the warrant and the results of the execution and send a copy of the statement to [*judgment creditor*].

Issued,   20.

By the Court

Prothonotary

Issued at the request of [*judgment creditor*].

The last known address of [*judgment debtor*] is [*add if it is different*] and the address of the place where it is believed the property of [*judgment debtor*] may be found is [*addresses*].

21.7.17   Execution is to be parsimonious. If there appears to be more than enough property to satisfy the amount levied, the sheriff need not seize all the property listed in the order. Once the debtor's goods have been seized, the sheriff is entitled to fees and the costs involved in execution. The creditor thereupon becomes obliged to compensate the sheriff accordingly.

However, the debtor must indemnify the creditor. The sheriff may therefore seize and sell such property as is needed to pay the judgment debt and the sheriff's expenses: ACT r 2201(2)(f); Civil Procedure Act 2005 (NSW) s 106(2)(a); NT r 68.08, Form 68A; Qld r 797; Tas r 902, Sch 3; Vic r 68.08, Form 68A; Civil Judgments Enforcement Act 2004 (WA) s 65; WA O 47 r 8.

21.7.18   When there is a writ for seizure and sale, there are typically three crucial dates: the date the writ is delivered to the sheriff; the date of seizure of possession; and the date of the sale. From the date of delivery, the process is binding on the debtor. This is the case notwithstanding that the debtor is not aware of the delivery. The date of delivery determines priority among creditors. Thus, if several writs are to be executed against a debtor, but proceeds exceed judgment debts, earlier creditors are paid in full until there is not sufficient money to pay a creditor in full. That creditor is part paid. The remaining creditors receive nothing. They must wait for some subsequent sale of assets for payment, or pursue some other avenue for redress.

The position may be complicated in the case of Torrens title land. Judgment creditors may arrange for their writ to be notified on the title, and indeed must do so if they wish to protect their interests against purchasers of the land, and as a precondition for the seizure and sale of the land: Land Titles Act 1925 (ACT) s 170; Real Property Act 1900 (NSW) ss 105–105D; Land Title Act (NT) ss 105–7; Land Title Act 1994 (Qld) Div 7; Real Property Act 1886 (SA) ss 105–7; Land Titles Act 1980 (Tas) s 61; Transfer of Land Act 1958 (Vic) s 52; Transfer of Land Act 1893 (WA) s 133. The order in which they do so does not necessarily correspond to the order in which writs are delivered to the sheriff. There is authority to the effect that the priorities which count are those relating to delivery of writs (*Beath v Anderson* (1883) 9 VLR (L) 41), but there is also authority to the contrary: *Peace v Sheriff of Queensland* (1890) 4 QLJ 33. That case suggests that priority is according to the time of registration on the title. In Western Australia, the legislation makes the position clear. Priority goes to any creditors who have registered their orders in the order in which they did so, followed by creditors who did not register orders, according to the order in which the orders were received by the sheriff: Civil Judgments Enforcement Act 2004 (WA) s 72(7), (9). The lack of recent authority suggests that the question is not a pressing one. Why might this be so?

The Australian Capital Territory rules are slightly different: ACT r 2054. What matters is the precise time at which the application for the enforcement order is made to the court. This determines the order in which courts may make enforcement orders, and the order in which orders may be enforced. The fact that it is the court which transmits the order to the enforcement officer means that there is little danger that there will be any discrepancy between the relative times at which orders are sought, made and executed.

Seizure and sale

21.7.19   When an attempt is made to seize property, there may be some dispute as to whose property it is. Personal property located on premises occupied by judgment debtors has a remarkable tendency to belong to family, friends and nameless strangers who have simply left it there with the intention of later collecting it. More plausibly, it may belong to hire purchase companies. The rules provide procedures for resolving disputes between the sheriff and third parties as to the ownership of property. These are known as interpleader proceedings. On learning that someone other than the judgment debtor is asserting ownership of property which has been, or might be seized, the sheriff must notify the judgment creditor. If the creditor admits the claim, the creditor is liable for the sheriff's costs only for fees incurred prior to the notice. On the creditor making the admission, the sheriff withdraws, and may obtain an order providing protection against any action in relation to the seizure and possession. If the creditor does not admit the claim, the sheriff can apply to the court for a determination of whose property it is. If the court decides that the sheriff is entitled to the relief sought, it gives directions in relation to the hearing of the competing claims: FCR Div 18.2; ACT Pt 2.19; NSW Pt 43; NT O 12; Qld Ch 21; SA r 202; Tas Pt 7 Div 16; Vic O 12; Civil Judgments Enforcement Act 2004 (WA) ss 63, 83–84.

21.7.20   The powers of the sheriff in relation to seizure vary by jurisdiction. In South Australia, the sheriff may enter the land, using such force as is necessary: Enforcement of Judgments Act 1991 (SA) s 7(3)(a). In Western Australia, the sheriff may enter premises where property (or records of title to property) is reasonably believed to be present: Civil Judgments Enforcement Act 2004 (WA) s 76(1). In the Australian Capital Territory, an enforcement officer who is refused entry may apply for an order permitting the use of such force and assistance as is reasonably necessary to obtain entry: r 2203(2). More usually, the sheriff's powers of entry are limited. In seizing goods, the sheriff is subject to one important constraint: the sheriff may not break into the debtor's house. However, failure to grant the sheriff access constitutes contempt. Once inside, however, the sheriff may break down interior doors and may break into trunks in which property might be kept. The sheriff need not physically seize all the goods. It is enough that the sheriff seizes part of the goods in the name of all the goods. Indeed, a declaration by the sheriff that goods are seized will suffice as against the debtor even if no goods are physically seized. However, a declaration is not good against another person in possession nor against a person who claims a lien over them. In the Australian Capital Territory (r 2207), the Northern Territory (r 68.08) and Victoria (r 69.07), and also in Queensland (r 831) once in possession, the sheriff may remain in possession by leaving in a prominent place on the property a notice stating that goods have been seized and the items seized. It is not necessary for the sheriff to remain in occupation of the property. An alternative course of action is for the sheriff to take 'walking possession'. This involves an agreement between the sheriff and the debtor whereby the debtor agrees not to remove the goods. As a quid pro quo, the sheriff leaves the premises. In *Watson v Murray & Co* [1955] 2 QB 1, this arrangement was used to avert the need for the sheriff to have his officer on the premises.

21.7.21 The property that can be seized includes real and personal property, along with money and bills of exchange. However, not all goods may be seized. In particular, legislation in some jurisdictions protects basic possessions. The formula varies somewhat. In the Australian Capital Territory, Queensland, South Australia and Victoria, the protected property is that property which would be protected in the event of the debtor's bankruptcy: ACT rr 2000, 2200 (the court may also exempt additional property to avoid exceptional hardship to the debtor or the debtor's dependents: r 2202); Supreme Court Act 1991 (Qld) Sch 2; Qld r 828, Sch 4; Enforcement of Judgments Act 1991 (SA) s 7(2); Supreme Court Act 1958 (Vic) s 42. Under s 116 of the Bankruptcy Act 1966 (Cth), the following property is not divisible among a bankrupt's creditors:

• household property of a kind prescribed by the regulations, or which is identified by a resolution passed by the creditors before the trustee realises the property: s 116(2)(b);

• property used by the bankrupt for earning income which does not have a total value greater than the limit prescribed by the regulations; which is identified by a resolution passed by the creditors; or which is identified by an order made by the court on an application by the bankrupt: s 116(2)(c);

• property used by the bankrupt primarily as a means of transport and whose aggregate value does not exceed either a prescribed amount or a larger amount determined by a creditors' resolution passed before the trustee realises the property: s 116(2)(ca);

• certain life insurance policies; interests in superannuation funds, and payments from them: s 116(2)(d); and

• rights to recover damages and compensation arising out of personal injuries: s 116(2)(g).

Regulation 6.03 of the Bankruptcy Regulations specifies which items of household property are not divisible among the bankrupt's creditors and reg 6.03B determines the 'prescribed values' for tools of trade and means of transport: see **21.7.22E** below.

21.7.22E **Bankruptcy Regulations 1996 (Cth)**
regs 6.03 and 6.03B

Household property

6.03 (1) For the purposes of subparagraph 116(2)(b)(i) of the Act, household property of the bankrupt specified in this regulation is household property to which subsection 116(1) of the Act (which deals with property divisible among the creditors) does not extend.

(2) Subsection 116(1) of the Act does not extend to household property (including recreational and sports equipment) that is reasonably necessary for the domestic use of the bankrupt's household, having regard to current social standards.

---

(3) In particular (but without limiting by implication the generality of subregulation (2)), subsection 116(1) of the Act does not extend to property of the following kinds:

    (a) in the case of kitchen equipment, cutlery, crockery, foodstuffs, heating equipment, cooling equipment, telephone equipment, fire detectors and extinguishers, anti-burglar devices, bedding, linen, towels and other household effects — that property to the extent that it is reasonably appropriate for the household, having regard to the criteria mentioned in subregulation (4);

    (b) sufficient household furniture;

    (c) sufficient beds for the members of the household; and

    (d) educational, sporting or recreational items (including books) that are wholly or mainly for the use of children or students in the household;

    (e) television set;

    (f) 1 set of stereo equipment;

    (g) 1 radio;

    (h) either:

        (i) 1 washing machine and 1 clothes drier; or

        (ii) 1 combined washing machine and clothes drier;

    (i) either:

        (i) 1 refrigerator and 1 freezer; or

        (ii) 1 combination refrigerator/freezer;

    (j) 1 generator, if relied on to supply electrical power to the household;

    (k) 1 telephone appliance;

    (l) 1 video recorder.

(4) For the purposes of deciding whether property, other than property of a kind mentioned in paragraphs (3)(b) to (l) (both inclusive), is property to which subregulation (2) applies, regard must be had to the following criteria:

    (a) the number and ages of members of the bankrupt's household;

    (b) any special health or medical needs of any of those members;

    (c) any special climatic or other factors (including geographical isolation) of the place where the household residence is located;

    (d) whether the property is reasonably necessary for the functioning or servicing of the household as a viable and properly run household;

    (e) whether the costs of seizure, storage and sale of the property would be likely to exceed the sale price of the property;

    (f) if paragraph (e) does not apply — whether for any other reason (for example, costs of transport) the sale of the property would be likely to be uneconomical.

(5) The preceding provisions of this regulation do not prevent subsection 116(1) of the Act from extending to antique items.

(6) For the purposes of subregulation (5), an item is taken to be antique if, and only if, a substantial part of its market value is attributable to its age or historical significance.

Property divisible among creditors — prescribed amounts

6.03B (1) For the purposes of subparagraph 116(2)(c)(i) of the Act, the maximum total value of a bankrupt's property that is for use by the bankrupt in earning income by personal exertion is:

    (a) in the case of a bankruptcy occurring or continuing in the period commencing on the commencement date and ending at the end of 30 June 1997 — $2,600; or

    (b)   in the case of a bankruptcy occurring in a financial year commencing on 1 July 1997 or on 1 July of a subsequent year — the amount worked out in accordance with subregulation (2).

(2)   For the purposes of subparagraph (1)(b), the applicable amount is:

    (a)   in the case of the financial year commencing on 1 July 1997 — $2,600 increased in accordance with the CPI rate for the financial year that commenced on 1 July 1996 and rounded down to the nearest multiple of $50; and

    (b)   in the case of a subsequent financial year — the amount worked out in accordance with this subregulation for the immediately preceding financial year, increased in accordance with the CPI rate for that financial year and rounded down to the nearest multiple of $50.

(3)   For the purposes of paragraph 116(2)(ca) of the Act, the maximum aggregate value of property used by the bankrupt primarily as a means of transport is:

    (a)   in the case of a bankruptcy occurring or continuing in the period commencing on the commencement date and ending at the end of 30 June 1997 — $5,000; or

    (b)   in the case of a bankruptcy occurring in a financial year commencing on 1 July 1997 or on 1 July of a subsequent year — the amount worked out in accordance with subregulation (4).

(4)   For the purposes of subparagraph (3)(b), the applicable amount is:

    (a)   in the case of the financial year commencing on 1 July 1997 — $5,000 increased in accordance with the CPI rate for the financial year that commenced on 1 July 1996 and rounded down to the nearest multiple of $50; and

    (b)   in the case of a subsequent financial year — the amount worked out in accordance with this subregulation for the immediately preceding financial year, increased in accordance with the CPI rate for that financial year and rounded down to the nearest multiple of $50.

[In New South Wales, clothes, bedroom or kitchen furniture, and tools of trade are protected if used by the debtor or members of the debtor's family: Civil Procedure Act 2005 (NSW) s 106(3). In Western Australia, apparel, household equipment and tools of trade are protected: Civil Judgments Enforcement Act 2004 (WA) s 76, and see Civil Judgments Enforcement Regulations 2005, reg 35.

In most other jurisdictions, limits on seizure apply only to lower court judgments: Magistrates Court (Civil Division) Rules 1998 (Tas) r 131(1).]

21.7.23   In several jurisdictions, the rules provide for the criteria to be used in determining which property gets sold when. In selling the property, the sheriff should, if possible, sell moveable property first, then real property (unless the debtor directs otherwise). The precise provisions vary somewhat: ACT r 2212; NSW r 39.6(3); NT r 69.04(3); Enforcement of Judgments Act 1991 (SA) s 7(5)(b); Tas r 906(4); Vic r 69.04(3). In addition, in several jurisdictions, the sheriff is to be guided by additional principles. In New South Wales, the Northern Territory, Tasmania and Victoria (NSW r 39.6(2) (subject to r 39.6(3)); NT r 69.04(2) (subject to r 69.04(3)); Tas r 906(3) (subject to r 906(4)); Vic r 69.04(2) (subject to r 69.04(3))), the sheriff is to take account of three considerations, such that the first trumps the second, and each trump the third:

(a)   sell in the order which best ensures prompt and economical enforcement;

(b)   sell in the order the debtor directs; and

(c)   sell in the order which appears to the sheriff to minimise hardship to the debtor and others.

These directions may be subject to court orders otherwise: NT r 69.04(4); Tas r 906(5); Vic r 69.04(4). The position is similar in Queensland, except that there is no express provision for taking account of the debtor's wishes: r 829(1), (3). In addition, land which is the debtor's principal place of residence is to be sold only if all other property has been sold, or this is what the debtor directs: r 829(2). In the ACT, (c) trumps (b), which applies only in relation to cases where the debtor asks that real property be sold first: r 2212(1).

21.7.24   Sale is to be by auction at first instance, and by private sale only if the auction fails to attract any adequate bids: ACT r 2216; NSW r 39.7 (but court has a general power to order private sale); Sheriff Regulations (NT) reg 5; Qld r 832 (subject to order otherwise); Enforcement of Judgments Act 1991 (SA) s 7(5)(a); Civil Process Act 1870 (Tas) s 5; Tas r 907; Vic r 69.05(2) (land only). In Western Australia, the sale must not be for less than the fair value of the property, unless the court orders otherwise, after a hearing at which the debtor is entitled to be heard: Civil Judgments Enforcement Act 2004 (WA) s 69.

In seizing and selling goods, the sheriff is obliged to behave reasonably. This duty is a common law duty, which is as one would expect, given that seizing and selling property involves considerable interference with property rights. There is express provision to this effect in Queensland: r 830.

21.7.25   The sheriff's powers are conditional upon the validity of the writ or warrant which purportedly confers those powers. A sheriff who acts under an invalid warrant has committed trespass. A judgment creditor who causes a sheriff to act in this way may also be sued, as may solicitors who are responsible for the issuing of invalid warrants. Cautionary tales include *Morris v Salberg* (1889) 22 QBD 614. In that case, the writ was taken out by the judgment creditor's solicitor who indorsed it:

> Levy 1701 16s 11d on the goods of the defendant, &c: the defendant is a gentleman who resides at Sarnau Park, Llandyssil, Cardigan, South Wales.

In fact it was the judgment debtor's father who lived there, and whose goods were seized. The Court of Appeal held that if the indorsement was a direction to the sheriff, the judgment creditor had made the sheriff his servant and was therefore liable for such trespass as he committed. Whether an indorsement had that effect was a question of fact (which had been decided by the trial jury in the debtor's father's favour).

Once judgment is satisfied, there is no authority to levy execution.

21.7.26C   **Clissold v Cratchley**
[1910] 2 KB 244
High Court of England, Court of Appeal

[The creditor's solicitor had an office in London and a branch office in the country. Three hours before the solicitor took out a writ of *fi fa* against the debtor, the debtor paid the amount owing to a person authorised to receive such payments at the country office. The solicitor learned of that payment only after the writ had been executed.]

Vaughan Williams (at 249–50): But, as it has been argued that a want of execution is good so long as the judgment under which the moneys have been paid has not in law been set aside, it is convenient to shew the authority for the proposition that, when the total amount of a judgment debt has been paid, the judgment ceases to be of any avail. In *Tebbutt v Holt* (1844) 1 Car & K 280, at 289 Parke B said, 'The law also is that, if the debt and costs are paid or satisfied, the judgment is at an end.' This judgment is at an end. And in *Bullen and Leake's Precedents*, 3rd ed at 353, I find this statement: 'An action will not lie for an arrest on final process upon a subsisting unsatisfied judgment (*Blanchenay v Burt* (1843) 4 QB 707; *Huffer v Allen* 7 LR 2 Ex 15; 36 LJ Ex 17); but if the party arrested can get the judgment set aside for irregularity or on any other ground, or can shew that the judgment was satisfied by payment or otherwise before the arrest, he may then maintain an action: the arrest in such case would in general support an action of trespass.' Under the circumstances it seems unnecessary to add anything. The cases on which reliance has been placed on behalf of the defendants are all instances of actions on the case for maliciously issuing [250] process; not a single authority has been cited to justify the proposition that a satisfied judgment is nevertheless still an existing judgment for the purpose of issuing a writ of execution. If the judgment was not an existing judgment, it is manifest that the writ of execution issued under it was void ab initio, and that an entry has been made upon the plaintiff's premises under a writ void ab initio. The defendants are consequently liable in an action of trespass.

[Trespass on the case would not lie, in the absence of proof of malice. Fletcher Moulton and Farwell LJJ agreed.]

21.7.27   *Watson v Murray & Co* [1955] 2 QB 1 (extracted below), highlights the practical and legal pitfalls which await those charged with enforcing debts.

21.7.28C   **Watson v Murray & Co**
                                  [1955] 2 QB 1
                    High Court of England, Queen's Bench Division

[Creditors sought to execute against dresses in an upmarket but financially insecure dress shop. On several occasions a sheriff's officer entered the shop and announced that he was taking control of all the goods in the shop. By agreement, the plaintiff agreed to acknowledge possession, thereby obviating the need for the sheriff to maintain possession by keeping a person permanently on the premises. In exchange for this and an undertaking to make payments, she was allowed to stay in business. On one occasion, the officer took possession of 120 dresses. A sale was arranged but cancelled at the last minute when the debt was paid. Subsequently, yet further writs were issued but payments were not forthcoming. Unable to find auction rooms willing to provide a venue for the sale of stock, the defendant decided to hold an auction at the shop and put up posters announcing the intended auction. The defendant took exclusive possession of the shop, excluding the plaintiff from the premises. At the last minute, the debtor paid the amount owing, and the sale was cancelled.]

Hilbery J (at 11–12): That an excessive seizure gives such a cause of action was decided in *Gawler v Chaplin* (1848) 2 Exch 503. In that case the first alleged breach of duty on the part of the sheriffs was that they had wrongfully seized goods of the plaintiff of greater value than sufficient to pay the [12] debt, interest, poundage and expenses, although they well knew part would be sufficient. On motion in arrest of judgment after verdict the question was whether that alleged breach was good in law. It was held that it was. In giving the judgment of the court Parke B said at 12 '... in the first instance, the duty of the sheriff is confined to seizing goods that would be reasonably sufficient, if sold, to pay the sum indorsed on the writ — that is, the debt, interest upon the debt, poundage, and expenses; and if the sheriff seizes more, prima facie he is a wrongdoer.' There can be no doubt on the evidence that the stock in the plaintiff's shop was far more extensive than it was necessary to seize to satisfy the judgment debt in respect of which either of the writs of *fi fa* in hand in January and February was issued together with the other charges enumerated by Parke B.

There was, therefore, in my judgment a seizure on each occasion which was excessive. But it resulted in no damage to the plaintiff. She was allowed to carry on her business as before and did so until the sheriff was paid out. With regard to the alleged seizure in March on the *fi fa* issued in respect of the Portenay judgment for £235 and £13 costs, I am satisfied that when May called to execute the writ of *fi fa*, substantially the same course was followed, and that there was therefore what amounted in law to a seizure in the first place of all the plaintiff's stock at her shop, and this was an excessive seizure. Again, however, there was an exactly similar walking possession agreement signed by the plaintiff, and again she was allowed to carry on her business without interruption and with power to dispose of any of the items which formed part of the stock by way of sale until March 18.

On March 18, however, the defendants took actual possession of 120 dresses and removed them for sale, and it was conceded in the course of the case that this actual seizure and removal was not excessive. ...

[His Honour then turned to the events leading to the auction, continuing (at 14–19):]

On receipt of that letter Moon, by telephone, tried to [15] arrange as before with Reeves Ltd auction rooms for a sale of whatever articles he decided must be taken from the plaintiff's stock to satisfy the current executions and charges.

Reeves Ltd, however, refused facilities for the sale. On June 23, 1952, they wrote giving their reasons, saying: 'Our auction rooms are open for the reception of goods for absolute sale at any convenient time, but where goods have to be withdrawn after the sale has been advertised and prepared entails not only pecuniary loss as on the last occasion, but upsets the timing of the sale of other lots besides putting us in disfavour with the trade.'

Pursuant to his instructions, Moon attended to prepare for sale, deciding in his own mind that in the circumstances the sale must be held on the premises. I am satisfied that he decided he must hold the sale on the premises in good faith, and not with any malice towards the plaintiff. By the delays which the defendants had conceded, they were in danger so far as the several judgment creditors were concerned. It was urgently necessary that they should sell and satisfy the several writs and executions then in hand before what had occurred constituted an act of bankruptcy on the part of the plaintiff.

From experience they knew that it would be most difficult to find any auctioneer with an auction room which could accommodate the goods for sale who would be willing to hold the sale. From experience they knew that any such auctioneer would make the same objection as Reeves had made when refusing to undertake the sale, more especially as all auctioneers knew that the remuneration allowed them on a sheriff's sale was much less than that which they ordinarily charged and received. Any auctioneer would know that he might be allowed only 7 per cent if the sheriff's bill was taxed, as against his ordinary remuneration of 12 per cent.

The defendants had delayed selling the plaintiff's goods at the request of the plaintiff to give the plaintiff time to get in hand the moneys which her solicitor was saying were expected and which would enable her to pay out the executions. The consequence was that the selling of the goods had become a matter of extreme urgency. It was for these reasons that Moon decided to sell on the premises.

[16] The questions which have to be decided in connexion with these happenings in June and July are: first, did the defendants trespass by preparing for this sale on the premises and by using the premises for their preparations for the sale and by posting the bills announcing the sale on the plaintiff's premises without her permission and in spite of her objection, of which they knew?; and secondly, did the defendants on this occasion make an excessive seizure in taking for sale what appears in the catalogue?

On the second question there was much evidence on both sides. The plaintiff's contention that the seizure was excessive is mainly based on evidence that at such a sale one might ordinarily expect to realize a certain fraction or percentage of the retail prices of the articles, and on the fact that at a later date the fixtures which were included in the catalogue sold for a comparatively large sum, and the other articles realized, when sold by tender, about 25 per cent of their retail price. On the other hand, the defendants' evidence and contention was that it is in the highest degree uncertain what such goods will fetch under hammer, much depending on whether there is a good or a poor attendance at the sale; that a sale such as this held in the country will be likely to realize less than if held in a London auction room; that such a sale largely depends on the weather and on the trade buyers attending, and that the sheriff must always allow a margin, as he has a duty to the execution creditors to execute the writ so as to make of the goods sufficient to satisfy the executions.

I am satisfied that the defendants, in lotting and cataloguing what they did, acted in good faith; and I am not satisfied, having regard to the hazards attending such a sale, that there was an excessive seizure. It must be remembered that most of the goods in question were seasonal and fashion goods. Moreover, it by no means follows that anything like all the lots would necessarily have got a bid at all.

The serious question which remains is whether the defendants had any right in law to insist on using the plaintiff's premises as they did for the purposes connected with holding this sale there. It is clear that the writ of *fi fa* does not require [18] or authorize the sheriff to seize the land or premises of a debtor. It requires him to make of the goods of the debtor sufficient to satisfy the execution creditors' judgment debt. It gives the sheriff a right to remain on the debtor's premises for a reasonable time, and no longer (see *Ash v Dawnay* (1852) 8 Exch 237) and it empowers him to sell sufficient of the debtor's goods to satisfy the debt in respect of which the writ was issued.

Reed v Harrison (1778) 2 Wm Bl 1218 is authority for saying, as the headnote to that case expresses it, that 'on attachment of goods, the officer' cannot legally continue in possession of the defendant's house, 'or keep the goods therein for a long and unreasonable time,' but must remove them to a place of safe custody: else he is 'a trespasser ab initio.'...

[19] It may be that if the sheriff can show that it was not possible to sell the goods except on the debtor's premises, it would be lawful for him so to do. Part of his duty is to sell the goods so as to make of them sufficient to satisfy the debt which is the subject of the writ of *fi fa* which he has to execute, and the law will not require of him that which is impossible. But the defendants in this case have not established that it was impossible to remove and sell the goods away from the plaintiff's premises. They have shown that by the concessions they had made to the plaintiff it had become extremely difficult for them so to do before an act of bankruptcy by the plaintiff was committed, but their evidence does not amount to more than this.

There were, therefore, in my view trespasses on the plaintiff's property committed by them when they did those acts which were solely done for the purposes of and as incidental to the holding of the sale on the plaintiff's premises.

21.7.29C   **Anderson v Liddell**
                          (1968) 117 CLR 36
                          High Court of Australia

[Land was sold under a writ of *fi fa*. The judgment debtor (who had at and before the issue of the writ been in Papua New Guinea, with 'the apparent aim of avoiding his creditors' (at 40 per Barwick CJ)) argued (among other things) that the sale was void. The land had been sold for less than its value and more land had been sold than was necessary to realise the judgment debt. The land had been sold for $16,500. The purchasers had initially been willing to offer up to $24,500, subject to their obtaining finance, but had only been able to obtain $16,500 in cash prior to the date of the auction.]

Barwick CJ (at 44–6): The next attack on the sale is that the sheriff, being under an obligation to get a fair price, failed to do so. In my opinion, there is no substance in this submission. There was no evidence in this case upon which it could be concluded that the price obtained was other than a fair price for what was sold in the circumstances in which it was sold. The price at which the respondents earlier offered to treat did not itself indicate, in my opinion, that the price obtained at the sheriff's sale was unfair. It was said that the sheriff ought to have obtained a valuation by an expert as to the value — presumably the market value — of the land. No doubt the sheriff should know what he is selling to the point that he can decide whether or not a bid at the auction is illusory or unfair: but, in my opinion, he is not required to obtain a valuation of the market value of the land. Clearly he is not required to refuse to accept a bid which is less than the market value of the land. Provided the sale conforms to the statutory requirements, generally speaking the amount bid by members or a member of the public will indicate what the property will bring in the circumstances of such a sale. It seems to me that the sheriff is entitled to accept at the auction any bid which is genuinely made and which bears a fair relationship to what is being sold. It is in this connexion [45] that the sheriff must know what he is selling for it is rightly said, in my opinion, that he must obtain a reasonable price for what he sells: see *Keightley v Birch* (1814) 3 Camp 621; 170 ER 1467. It is to be reasonable having regard to what is offered, namely, a debtor's right title and interest, if any, and the circumstances of the sale. If there is no such bid, the sheriff is justified in returning, and he should return, a want of buyers. But in this case I can see no reason connected with the amount of the respondents' bid in relation to the property offered for sale which would have warranted the sheriff in refusing to accept it.

The appellant then made what appears to me to be his main submission. He said that the writ of *fieri facias* does not authorize the sheriff to sell land which has a value — by which I take it the appellant means is likely to realize in the sheriff's public auction a sum — greater than the amount of the levy to be raised under the writ. So soon as the sheriff appreciates that the land is of such a value, it is said that he should return to the writ the fact that the land has been taken but that there are no buyers, thus giving the judgment creditor the opportunity to obtain the further writ of *venditioni exponas*. This submission, in my opinion, is misconceived. Land is 'liable to be taken' under a writ of *fieri facias* in Queensland and, in my opinion, may be sold under the writ as any other item of property may be sold thereunder. In the case of chattels, the sheriff must not sell any further items of property once he has realized the levy under the writ. But, not having reached that sum, the sheriff may properly sell a further chattel though the amount which might reasonably be expected to be realized from that sale is greater than the unrealized balance of the levy: see *Wooddye v Coles Baily of Southw* (1595) Noy 59; 74 ER 1027; *Stead v Gascoigne* (1818) 8 Taunt 527; 129 ER 488. It seems to me the same principles apply in relation to the sale of land by the sheriff. The sheriff is entitled to sell a parcel of land no matter what sum its sale might reasonably be expected to bring. His duty to the judgment creditor requires so much. The judgment debtor may nominate the order of the sale of his assets and thus require chattels first to be sold; or other land of lesser value first to be sold. But, in default of such action on the judgment debtor's part, the sheriff is entitled, indeed, in my opinion, bound to sell the debtor's interest in the land, whatever sum it may bring so long as at the time of the sale he has not raised by other means the full amount of the levy. He is not required, in my opinion, to sell parcels of land in any order.

[46] Also the submission indicates a misunderstanding of the use of the writ of *venditioni exponas*. It may be conceded that with the extension of the writ of *fieri facias* to include land and interests therein, the writ of *venditioni exponas* also became available for use in connexion with execution of a judgment against land. But its issue depended upon a return by the sheriff to the writ of *fieri facias* to the effect that he had taken property of the judgment debtor for which he had received no bid: ie, that for that property he had no buyer. Such a return was open to the sheriff where, although he nominally had received a bid, the amount bid bore so little relation to the evident worth of the property offered that in reality it did not constitute a bid at all. Acceptance of such a bid, at least where the buyer could be involved in knowledge of its nature, would not result in a sale and any transfer of the property consequent thereon would be set aside: see *Edge v Kavanagh* (1888) 24 LR Ir 1 and *Owen v Daly* [1955] VLR 442. Placed on this ground I am able to agree with the result in this last mentioned case. Such a return would also be open to the sheriff where the bid though not illusory was unfair or unreasonable in the sense that it bore no fair or reasonable relation to that which was offered for sale.

But if the sheriff has taken land or any interest in land owned by the judgment debtor, he must in duty to his judgment creditor offer it for sale though thereby he will recover more than the amount of the levy and, he must accept any bid which is not illusory or unfair, in the sense of bearing no real relation to the evident worth of the land or interest offered. As I have said, the sheriff must know what he is offering but, in my opinion, is not required to have or to have obtained expert knowledge as to its market value. Having land to sell, though it be of an evident worth beyond the amount of the levy under the writ, the sheriff could not make such a return as would warrant the issue of a writ of *venditioni exponas* if he had received a bid which was neither illusory nor unfair. The bid in this case was such that, in my opinion, there was no occasion for resort to the writ of *venditioni exponas*. In my opinion, this submission of the appellant should be rejected.

[McTiernan and Kitto JJ agreed.]

21.7.30 Notes and questions

1. See *Owen v Daly* [1955] VLR 442, where, through an error on the part of the creditor's solicitors, the owner was not notified of the impending sale and where the land (subject to encumbrances) was sold for £10, a sum which inspection would have revealed to be well below its true unencumbered value of £1500. Dean J considered that this was not a real sale, and said (at 448):

   > The proper return was that the debtor's property remained in his hands for want of buyers. The creditor might then have obtained a writ of *venditioni exponas* — see *Chitty's Archbold* (14th ed), at 830–1. Such a writ would authorise a sale for whatever the property may bring. I think the plaintiff is entitled to some relief.

   He also considered that compliance by the sheriff with the statutory requirements in relation to the advertising of the sale was not sufficient. In this respect, Barwick CJ disagreed: *Anderson v Liddell* (1968) 117 CLR 36 at 43. The writ of *venditioni exponas* is available under the Tasmanian rules to compel sale of property at any price where the sheriff makes a return to the effect that it had not been possible to sell the property at a reasonable price: Tas r 909.

2. The rules of several jurisdictions now require that the debtor be given notice of an intended sale of land. Personal service of this notice is required prior to the sale, although except in the Australian Capital Territory the court may dispense with this requirement: for example, ACT r 2221(6); NSW r 39.22(1)(h); NT r 69.07(4); Vic r 69.06(4). In Queensland, the enforcement officer must send a copy of a notice of the intended sale of property to the judgment creditor at the debtor's last known address: r 828(6). Would this have assisted the judgment debtor in *Anderson v Liddle*?

21.7.31 In the Australian Capital Territory, property worth more than $500 must not be sold at auction for less than a reserve price, which must be an amount not less than a reasonable amount for the property. In determining this, the officer may engage a valuer: rr 2216(8), 2217. The New South Wales rules require that before selling property, the sheriff 'must fix the approximate market value of the property, having regard to all the circumstances of the case': r 39.10. In doing so, the sheriff may engage a suitably qualified and experienced valuer. 'Property must not be sold by public auction for a price substantially below its approximate market value, as fixed …': r 39.7(2).

> Other jurisdictions are less directive. Is the New South Wales requirement redundant given: (1) the requirement that the sheriff act reasonably; and (2) the requirement that sales be by publicised auction?

The Northern Territory (r 69.07) and Victorian (r 69.06) rules require that before putting land up for sale, the sheriff:

> …shall advertise the sale by giving notice of the time and place of sale and of particulars of the property in the manner which seems to him best to give publicity to the sale.

The Queensland rules (r 834) require notification at the relevant court registry, in a newspaper, or on the land to be sold or the place of sale. New South Wales (r 39.23) requires newspaper advertisements where land is being sold, and notice at the place of sale, and (if the circumstances warrant it) in a newspaper, if goods are to be sold: r 39.31.

In the event of the reserve price not being achieved, the sheriff may apply to the court for an order permitting sale without a reserve price. This course of action was taken in Victoria after an attempt to sell a debtor's house failed to attract a bid above the reserve price. An Associate Judge of the Supreme Court of Victoria made an order giving the sheriff leave to conduct the sale without a reserve price, subject to service on the judgment debtor and 'provided that such leave does not thereby derogate from, or relieve the sheriff of a duty at law to the owner of the land when exercising a power of sale': *Kousal v Suncorp-Metway* [2011] VSC 312, [11], Mukhtar AJ. Despite being given leave to apply to have the order discharged, the owner (whose English seems to have been limited) did not apply to have the order discharged. The house (which was located in Braybrook) was later auctioned at the Sheriff's office in Carlton, and attracted an initial bid of $100, a counter-bid of $200, and a final bid of $1000. The house had been valued at $630,000 but was subject to a mortgage of $440,000. Subsequently, the judgment debtor applied to have the relevant judgment set aside, but this made little progress, partly because of legal doubts as to whether the application had to be made to the Magistrates' Court of the Supreme Court (to which the judgment had been transferred for enforcement purposes), and partly because the judgment debtor could not afford representation.

In the meantime, the mortgagee had refused to hand over the certificate of title to the 'purchaser', who was unable to register the transfer. The purchaser sought an order that the mortgagee hand over the certificate. The court therefore had to consider whether it could or should issue the certificate on the grounds of 'manifest undervalue'. The Associate Judge held that it could be. First, even if the original judgment were to be set aside, that would not affect the validity of the orders for execution and the sheriff's right to sell. Second, the apparently poor return did not necessarily invalidate the sale: *Owen v Daly* could be distinguished: apart from the undervalue, there were irregularities surrounding the sale, and the judgment creditor had been closely involved in the transaction. Without argument from the judgment debtor, it was not possible to say that the auction price was a manifest undervalue. The Associate Judge therefore granted made orders whose effect was to give the judgment debtor a last opportunity to take steps to protect his interest.

The judgment debtor, Zhipping Zhou, then applied for an order setting the sale aside. Vickery J dismissed an argument to the effect that the purchaser was acting unconscionably in insisting on his legal right to have the sale registered and title transferred to him. The evidence did not support such a claim. However, he found that the sheriff had exceeded his powers and that the sale could and should be set aside: *Zhou v Sheriff for the State of Victoria* [2012] VSC 187. While the sheriff became an employee of the Department of Justice under the Sheriff Act 2009, he remained 'an officer of the court for the purpose of enforcing its warrants of seizure and sale and other such warrants issued out of the Court': at [110]. His duties included both those arising under the statute and those to which sheriffs were subject at common law:

> The accepted principles governing the duties of Sheriffs which have developed under the common law are important protections for both judgment debtors and judgment creditors alike. They should not be swept away except by clear words which abrogate the duties or which seek to protect the Sheriff from suit, provided he observes the statutory requirements: at [117].

This meant that:

[122] In terms of a sale, the Sheriff may only sell property seized:

(a)   if the transaction can in truth be regarded as a "sale" and not an illusory sale founded upon a price which is so low that it could be said that there was no sale at all, or that it was not a real sale or that it was in fact illusory;

(b)   if the sale is undertaken in accordance with the relevant court and enforcement legislation, or a warrant that authorises the seizure of property; and

(c)   if the sale in undertaken for the purpose of applying the proceeds of the sale to the payment of a payable amount.

[123] In my opinion, the Sheriff is also bound to apply the principles of the common law in the conduct of a valid sale under s 24.

[124] The principles of common law to be applied to a Sheriff's sale are these:

(a)   The Sheriff is bound to act reasonably in the interests of both the judgment creditor and the judgement debtor in order to obtain a fair price: *Owen v Daly*, ibid, per Dean J at 446;

(b)   A fair price is not necessarily the market value, for it is well recognised that compulsory sales under legal process rarely bring the full value of the property sold: *Owen v Daly*, ibid, per Dean J at 446. In making a determination as to the adequacy of the highest bid, the Sheriff is entitled to take into account that the sale, being a compulsory process, is usually one at which a full and fair market value for the property will not be expected and some allowance must be made for low prices being obtained at such sales: *Smith v Colles* (1871) 2 VLR 195, per Barry ACJ at 196;

(c)   In determining the fair price in all the circumstances, matters from the prospective buyer's perspective must be weighed. Such factors may include: the fact that buyers must be prepared to complete their purchases on the spot; the fact that buyers, particularly in the case of real estate, will not have usually have had the opportunity to inspect the property sold (at least internally); the fact that the title to the property may be encumbered or it may be physically occupied, giving rise to risks for the purchaser in acquiring clear title or rights of occupation without undue expense or delay; and other such risks which may be attendant for the purchaser on the purchase;

(d)   Another factor to be weighed in the balance will be the amount, if any, obtained for the judgment creditor after the expenses of the sale have been deducted;

(e)   If it is apparent to the Sheriff that in fact or in all probability the highest bid received is so far below the true value of the property offered for sale that he would be acting unreasonably if he was to accept it, the Sheriff should not accept the bid and pass in the property: *Owen v Daly*, ibid, per Dean J at 446; *Anderson v Liddell*, ibid, per Barwick CJ at 44–45, and per Kitto J at 49;

(f)   If the Sheriff breaches his common law duty and sells property at a price which, in all the circumstances is unfair, the following consequences may follow:

(i)   the transaction may be set aside: *Owen v Daly*, ibid, per Dean J at 446; *Anderson v Liddell*, (1968) 117 CLR 36, per Barwick CJ at 44–45. On setting the transaction aside, no damages would arise in the usual case for which the Sheriff could be liable: *Owen v Daly*, per Dean J at 446; or

(ii)   where the price obtained on the highest bid is so low that it could be said that there was no sale at all, or that it was not a real sale or that it was in fact illusory, *Owen v Daly*, per Dean J at 447, there would be no sale within s 24 of the *Sheriff Act*, and therefore no sale within Division 5 with the result that the immunity of the Sheriff from a suit in damages conferred by s 25 would be removed. There would not in truth be a "sale of property under this Division" for the purposes of s 25(2). In these circumstances, if the transaction is not set aside and loss and damage is in fact sustained, the Sheriff could be exposed to an award of damages at common law.

Applying these principles, Vickery J held that the sum paid bore no relation to Mr Zhou's equity, which amounted to about $165,000; that the sale was not in accordance with the order permitting a sale without reserve, since the sale was expressly conditioned on compliance by the sheriff with his duties at law; and that since the amount realised was less than the costs of conducting the auction, the sale was 'not for the purposes of applying the proceeds of the sale to the payment of a payable amount due to the judgement creditor' (at [134]) and therefore not a sale for the purpose of the Act.

Recovery of land

21.7.32 This writ or warrant is designed to deal with one of the oldest problems facing the common law courts: dealing with trespassers on land. In the Australian Capital Territory (r 2451), New South Wales (Civil Procedure Act 2005 (NSW) s 104), Northern Territory (r 66.03), Queensland (Civil Proceedings Act 2011 (Qld) s 90(2)(d); r 915), Tasmania (r 874(1)(a)), Victoria (r 66.03) and Western Australia (Civil Judgments Enforcement Act 2004 (WA) ss 94–96) the rules provide for writs, warrants, or orders of possession. These issue administratively in cases where there has been a judgment for possession of land. The contempt and sequestration procedures are also available, but subject to the usual conditions. In the Australian Capital Territory, the order must have been served on the defendant/occupier, and if the person in occupation is a person other than the defendant, execution requires leave of the court: r 2452(2). In Tasmania (r 874(1)(a)), an applicant for the writ must provide affidavit evidence of service of the order and of the defendant's failure to comply with it. In South Australia, a judgment for possession is enforced by a warrant of possession: Enforcement of Judgments Act 1991 (SA) s 11.

The Northern Territory and Victorian rules (r 70.01) also make it clear that the sheriff is not required to remove any goods found on the land. These continue to be the defendant's property.

Third parties on land who claim that they are in possession must comply with the warrant. If they wish to contest possession, they must seek to have judgment in favour of the obtainer of the warrant set aside.

An order for recovery of possession and for costs can be enforced either by one writ or warrant, or by separate writs for possession and for costs: ACT rr 2001(4), 2005; Civil Procedure Act 2005 (NSW) s 137; NT r 68.03; Qld Form 85; Tas r 874(2); Vic r 68.03; Civil Judgments Enforcement Act 2004 (WA) s 95(4).

For delivery

21.7.33 Where there are proceedings for the detention of goods, there are three possible outcomes. First, a successful plaintiff may obtain judgment for payment of the value of the goods. Second, the court may give judgment requiring that the defendant either deliver the goods or pay their assessed value. A third possibility is judgment for the delivery of goods alone. The first such judgment would be enforced by seizure and sale. Writs or warrants of delivery exist for the other two forms of judgment. These direct the sheriff to require delivery of the goods, and provide for such seizure and sale of property as may be necessary to cover damages, costs and interest. If the judgment is for delivery of goods, or for payment of their value, the writ or warrant provides for seizure and sale of property instead of delivery.

Writs or warrants may also include provisions whereby the sheriff may seize a person's property in the event of non-delivery. Damages, interest and costs may be sought in the same or a different writ or warrant: ACT r 2460(7); Civil Procedure Act 2005 (NSW) s 137; NT r 66.04(3); Civil Proceedings Act 2011 (Qld) s 90(2)(e); Qld Form 86; Tas r 875(4); Vic r 66.04(3); Civil Judgments Enforcement Act 2004 (WA) s 95(4).

21.7.34E   **Supreme Court Rules 2000 (Tas)**
                              Rule 900(3)
                Form 68 — Writ of Delivery or Assessed Value
       TO THE SHERIFF AND THE OFFICERS AND ASSISTANTS OF THE SHERIFF

Whereas by a judgement [*or order*] dated [*date*] it was adjudged [*or ordered*] —

1. that [*name of party against whom judgment entered or order made*] deliver the goods described in the Schedule to this writ to [*name of party in whose favour judgment entered or order made*] or pay [*amount*] their assessed value; and

2. that [*name of party against whom judgment entered or order made*] pay [*name of party in whose favour judgment entered or order made*] certain costs [*or certain damages and costs, or as the case may be*] the [*total*] amount of which appears in the Schedule to this writ.

You are commanded —

1. that you cause the goods to be delivered to [*name of party in whose favour judgment entered or order made*]; and

2. that, if the goods cannot be found in the State of Tasmania, of the lands, goods and chattels of [*name of party against whom judgment entered or order made*] you cause to be made the sum of [*insert amount of assessed value*]; and

3. that of lands, goods and chattels of [*name of party against whom judgment entered or order made*] you further cause to be made the sum appearing in the Schedule to this writ in accordance with the judgment [*or order*]; and

*4. that you pay any sum to me immediately after the execution of this writ to be paid to the [*name of party in whose favour judgment entered or order made*] in accordance with the judgment [*or order*]; and

5. that you inform the Registrar in what manner you have executed this writ immediately after its execution.

SCHEDULE

Description of goods —
[*Set out description of land as it appears in the judgment or order*]
*Particulars of amount to be levied —
$
*Judgment amount
*Costs ordered or taxed
*Less amount paid (if any) [*attach list of dates and amounts of payments*]
*Balance

*Add interest accrued on judgment amount [*attach particulars of calculations*]
*Balance due as at [*date*]
Add costs of execution
Add sheriff's poundage, officer's fees, costs of levying and all other incidental expenses
Total amount to be levied

TOGETHER WITH interest on [*set out total of judgment amount and ordered or taxed costs less any payments other than those appropriated to interest*] at the rate of [*insert percentage rate*] from [*insert date up to which interest had been calculated in the above schedule*] until payment.
[**delete if writ for delivery or assessed value only*]
Dated
Registrar [*or District Registrar*]

ORDERS AGAINST THIRD PARTIES

21.8.1 Judgment debts can sometimes be recovered from third parties. Since these procedures impose obligations on third parties, they require an application to the court which has the discretion to make a third party order. In this respect, they contrast with writs or warrants which affect only the judgment debtor. Slightly different regimes therefore apply to their issue. In some jurisdictions, writs against third parties are classed as writs of execution, but are subject to distinctive requirements. In others, they are treated separately. Little turns on these differences. More crucial are jurisdictional differences in the availability of garnishee orders against earnings.

Attachment of debts/enforcement warrants for redirection of debts/garnishee orders

21.8.2 The rules provide procedures whereby people who are indebted to the judgment debtor may be ordered to pay the amount owing to the judgment creditor: ACT Div 2.18.6; NSW Pt 39 Div 4; NT r 71.04; Civil Procedure Act 2011 (Qld) s 90(2)(b); Qld rr 839–854; Enforcement of Judgments Act 1991 (SA) s 6; Tas rr 910–914; Vic r 71.04; Civil Judgments Enforcement Act 2004 (WA) ss 45–58.

A precondition for the attachment of debts is the existence of a judgment for a specific sum of money. It is therefore not available when the judgment is for the assessment of damages. However, unlike the writs to the sheriff, attachment proceedings may be commenced before entry of judgment. The reason is that, unlike most writs to the sheriff, attachment is possible only by leave of the court and the court can dispense with the requirement that a judgment be entered.

21.8.3 A second condition is that there should be a debt to be attached. This is by no means a trivial condition. First, the debt must be owing or accruing and due. There is no attachment of 'future debts'. For instance, see *Fellow v Thornton* (1894) 14 QBD 335, where the order originally sought was that the garnishee pay, among other things, any sum of money then or thereafter to come into his hands as trustee under an ante-nuptial settlement. An order to this effect was granted by the registrar, but was set aside by Pollock B in Chambers, in a decision which was treated as self-evidently correct on appeal.

A less obvious context in which this issue arises is in relation to bank accounts. While common sense would suggest that a credit in a bank account is a debt owed by the bank to the depositor, common sense does not prevail. Credit balances in current accounts have generally been treated as simple debts owed by the bank to the customer: *Rogers v Whiteley* [1892] AC 118; *Rekstin v Severo Sibirsko etc and the Bank for Russian Trade* [1933] 1 KB 47; *Music Masters Pty Ltd v Minelle and the Bank of New South Wales Savings Bank Ltd* [1968] Qd R 326; compare *Re Australian and New Zealand Savings Bank Ltd; Mellas v Evriniadis* [1972] VR 69. Savings accounts have been treated as involving contracts whereby withdrawals will be permitted only if certain conditions are satisfied (such as the presentation of a passbook): *Music Masters* case [1968] Qd R 326; *Re Australian and New Zealand Savings Bank* case [1972] VR 69; *Bank of New South Wales v Fremantle Arts Centre Pty Ltd* [1973] WAR 161. The savings bank anomaly has now been dealt with in most jurisdictions: ACT r 2306; Civil Procedure Act 2005 (NSW) s 117(2); NT r 71.03; Enforcement of Judgments Act 1991 (SA) s 6; Vic r 71.03. However, even when funds in a bank account are chargeable, the only funds chargeable are those in the account at the time of the order *nisi*. Subsequently deposited funds do not constitute a debt 'owing or accruing' at the relevant time. The Australian Capital Territory and Queensland rules make provision for an order to be made to a financial institution to make regular transfers where a fourth party regularly deposits earnings into a judgment debtor's account: ACT Pt 2.18.7; Civil Proceedings Act 2011 (Qld) s 97; Qld rr 840, 847–857. Western Australia also makes provision for orders in relation to debts which subsequently become payable: Civil Judgments Enforcement Act 2004 (WA) s 51(5).

21.8.4   Attaching a debt typically involves a two-stage process. First, the creditor must apply to the court for an order *nisi* or for leave to serve notice on the person or body which owes the debt to the judgment debtor. This person is usually called the 'garnishee' or 'third party'. Second, the garnishee must be given an opportunity to show why an attachment order should not be made. In South Australia, the initial application is to the court for an order, and the proceedings are adjourned in order to give the debtor and the garnishee a chance to be heard: Enforcement of Judgments Act 1991 (SA) s 6(3)(b), (c).

The initial stage is *ex parte*: ACT r 2302(5); NSW r 39.34(2); NT rr 71.04, 71.05; Qld r 840 (debtor may also apply for order); Enforcement of Judgments Act 1991 (SA) s 6(3)(b), (c); Tas r 912; Vic rr 71.04, 71.05; Enforcement of Civil Judgments Act 2004 (WA) ss 19, 49. A prerequisite for the order is that there be affidavit evidence of such matters as the judgment; the unrecovered judgment debt (and of its value); and that the alleged garnishee is a debtor to the judgment debtor and is within the jurisdiction: ACT r 2302(2) (no express 'within jurisdiction' requirement); NSW r 39.35; NT r 71.05; Qld r 840(2); Tas Form 69; Vic r 71.05. Some rules (notably those of the Northern Territory and Victoria) require further details. The provisions for compulsory examination may well be helpful in this respect.

In Queensland (r 841) a similar result is produced by virtue of the court's power to order an enforcement hearing before issuing the redirection warrant. In the Australian Capital Territory and South Australia, the court is also to have regard to the debtor's means, expenses and other liabilities: ACT r 2303(3); Enforcement of Judgments Act 1991 (SA) s 6(4).

The decision to grant the order or to order the filing and serving of the notice or summons does not resolve the question of the garnishee's obligations. The notice does not have any legal effect until it is served. It must be personally served on both garnishee and debtor, and in some jurisdictions, it may be served only within the state: ACT r 2308(1) (service on third party only; may be served outside ACT); NT r 71.06; Qld r 842(1); Tas r 913; Vic r 71.07. Service temporarily freezes the nominated debts in the hands of the garnishee but only pending the outcome of the hearing of the summons or an objection to the order: ACT r 2308(2); NSW r 39.39; NT r 71.07; Qld r 842(2); Enforcement of Judgments Act 1991 (SA) s 6(3); Tas r 913(3); Vic r 71.08; Civil Judgments Enforcement Act 2004 (WA) s 51(1). In most jurisdictions, the judgment creditor must serve a summons requiring the garnishee's attendance at a hearing of the issues set out in the summons. In others, the order prevails, subject to an application by a person affected by the order to have the order set aside: ACT r 2051(3); Qld rr 819, 907.

21.8.5   Service does not conclusively resolve the question of whether the garnishee is required to make payments to the judgment creditor, but it does affect rights in relation to the debt so as to give the judgment creditor priority. See, for example, *Ex parte Joselyne; In re Watt* (1878) 8 Ch D 327 where Cotton LJ said (at 331):

> The question is whether the Respondents became, by virtue of the garnishee order *nisi*, creditors holding security upon the property of the liquidating debtor. I am of opinion that they did. It is called an order *nisi*, but, as against the judgment debtor, it was a final and complete order ... It was an order *nisi* only against the ... garnishee; for of course he was entitled to be heard upon the question whether any money was in fact due from him ...

See also *Galbraith v Grimshaw and Baxter* [1910] 1 KB 339 where Farwell LJ described the effect of the order *nisi* (at 344):

> ... [A]lthough there has been no actual transfer of the debt, there is such a charge on it that the garnishee could not safely hand over the money [to another person with claims on it] for if he did so he would still be liable to the defendants.

However, if, prior to service of a garnishee order *nisi* or its equivalent, a judgment debtor has assigned a debt, a garnishee order does not lie against the person who owes the assigned debt, notwithstanding that the assignor has not given notice to that person of the assignment: *Holt v Heatherfield Trust Ltd* [1942] 2 KB 1.

The order *nisi* (or its equivalent) operates in relation to the entire debt to which it relates. Even if the debt exceeds the judgment debt, judgment debtors are not entitled to require garnishees to pay the excess to them. In *Rogers and Riches v Whitleley* [1892] AC 118, the judgment debtor (Rogers and Riches) claimed damages for injuries to credit and reputation by virtue of the respondent as banker having refused to honour cheques drawn on it by the plaintiffs. The plaintiffs' credit balance exceeded £6800. The judgment creditor was owed £6000. The garnishee order was that 'all debts owing or accruing due' from the banker to Rogers be attached.

On the basis of the order, the banker refused to honour cheques drawn on the £800 difference between the original credit balance and the judgment debt. The House of Lords effortlessly and unanimously dismissed the plaintiffs' appeal. The banker had had no alternative but to comply with the order. There was some division on whether part of a debt could be attached. Lord Morris thought it could be; Lords Halsbury, Watson and Field declined to express a view. Lord McNaghten made no comment.

Once the garnishee has been served with the order, it has several options. It may pay the amount it owes the judgment debtor, or the amount payable under the judgment or order: ACT r 2310; Civil Procedure Act 2005 (NSW) s 123; Tas r 914(1)(b). Alternatively, (depending on the rules) it may choose not to appear in response to the provisional order, or not to object to the order. If it so chooses or, if having appeared, it does not dispute the existence of the debt, the garnishee may be levied for the debt: ACT r 2315 (on application); Civil Procedure Act 2005 (NSW) s 124; NT r 71.11; Tas r 914(1)(b); Vic r 71.11; Civil Judgments Enforcement Act 2004 (WA) s 56 (on application). In Queensland, this results from the fact that the enforcement warrant for redirection of debts operates from the time it is served on the garnishee, subject to an application by the garnishee or the debtor to have it set aside. If the garnishee disputes its liability, the court may order a trial of any question of fact which thereby arises: ACT r 2311; NSW r 39.40; NT r 71.10; Qld r 844; Tas r 914(2); Vic r 71.10; Civil Judgments Enforcement Act 2004 (WA) s 55. If the garnishee suggests (or if it otherwise appears) that a fourth party owns or has a lien over the debt, the court may require that the fourth party be notified of the garnishee application so it can give the court details of its entitlement: ACT r 2307; NSW r 39.41; NT r 71.11; Qld r 845; Tas r 914(5); Vic r 71.11; Civil Judgments Enforcement Act 2004 (WA) s 54(3)(c). After such hearings, the court makes a finding as to whether the objections by the garnishee or any third party are well-founded.

21.8.6 Normally, garnishee proceedings are matters as between the garnishee and the judgment creditor. There may, however, be circumstances where the debtor may be heard on the return of the order *nisi* or where it may be able to seek to have the order set aside.

21.8.7C	**Pioneer Concrete (Gold Coast) Pty Ltd v Cassidy**
	(Engwirda Construction Co garnishee)
	[1968] Qd R 81
	Supreme Court of Queensland

[On the return of the order *nisi*, the debtor sought to argue that the creditor was no longer entitled to enforce judgment in view of an agreement between counsel for the creditor and the debtor.]

Hoare J at (83–5): [Hoare J noted that while the English rules expressly provided that the debtor was to be served with notice of garnishee orders *nisi*, the Queensland rules made no such provision. However, he also noted that the change in the rules had been made in order to achieve uniformity of practice between the Chancery division which had required such notice, and King's Bench, which did not. His Honour continued:] The argument of Counsel for the Judgment Creditor that it is necessary for the Court to restrict itself to the express provisions of O 49 with the result that, as there is no provision for a Judgment Debtor to be served or to be heard, he has no right of audience on the return of the Order Nisi and therefore cannot be heard and accordingly, should be left to pursue whatever remedies the law allows, has a superficial attraction. I have no doubt that it would be persuasive to some legal minds. However ... I prefer to approach the problem in the following manner.

The provisions of The Common Law Practice Act and later the provisions of The Rules of the Supreme Court, have enabled a Judgment Creditor to enforce his judgment by a particular process of execution, namely attachment of debts. The provisions of O 49 provide inter alia for that procedure to be available when there has been a judgment duly obtained which is still unsatisfied in whole or in part.

O 49 r 1 requires the fact that the judgment is unsatisfied to be established by affidavit but it is important to remember that this is a mere machinery or procedural provision to inform the Court that the judgment is in fact unsatisfied in whole or in part. If, notwithstanding the Judgment Creditor's affidavit, the Court ascertains that in fact the judgment has been satisfied in some other way then the Court should not use its process to enforce that judgment. This is part of the inherent jurisdiction of the Court and does not depend upon the provisions of s 59 of The Common Law Practice Act. Under the provisions of the Queensland Rule the Judgment Debtor ordinarily has no opportunity of showing the Court that the Judgment was in fact satisfied. It is true that, as submitted by counsel for the Judgment Creditor, there could be practical difficulties created by debtors recklessly asserting that the judgment had been satisfied, a situation which apparently did not daunt Sir George Jessel nor the English Rule making authorities in 1905 and since. Thus, it seems to me that if the Court is in some way apprised of facts which indicate that the judgment has been satisfied, it should not enforce the judgment.

The alternative course would be for the Court to say, in effect, that it will proceed to enforce the judgment even though it knows it to be unenforceable. It is difficult to envisage a Judge of a superior Court adopting this narrow, restricted approach if he could possibly avoid it. He would surely say in effect 'Now that the Court knows that the judgment is not enforceable against the debtor, at the least, it will not take any steps to enforce it.'

[84] What should the Court do when it is apprised of facts which do not indisputably establish that the judgment is unenforceable but may well establish that fact? Should it take the narrow approach and point out that no machinery is expressly provided by the Rules to deal with the situation or should it take the broader view and try to ascertain the facts as to the enforceability of the judgment before enforcing it. Every case is governed by its own facts and if there is a somewhat shadowy case made out by a Judgment Debtor then in that case the Court may well proceed to enforce the judgment leaving the Judgment Debtor to his other remedies. However, if it appears that there is a real risk that the judgment may not be properly enforceable, it seem to me that, generally speaking, the Court should first determine that matter before proceeding to enforce execution on the judgment. That is the approach which I propose to take. I am fortified in this approach by observations of Brett LJ (as he then was) in *Roberts v Death* (1881) 8 QBD 319 at 323 where His Lordship observed 'The point of practice, however, which we hold is that where the money sought to be attached under the garnishee proceedings is trust money, or said to be such on any reasonable ground, the cestui que trust is not to be damaged because the garnishee will not act, but he has a right to come forward (not indeed under Rules 6 and 7, but apart from such rules) and to inform the Court that the money is trust money belonging to him, and therefore the garnishee order ought not to be made, provided, of course, he does so in due time.' The other members of the Court, Cotton LJ and Lindley LJ concurred and Lindley LJ at 325 observed 'I think he put too narrow construction on those rules in refusing to hear a suggestion from anyone but the garnishee.'

I desire to make it clear that I am not for one moment suggesting that a mere unsupported assertion by a Judgment Debtor would be sufficient to induce the Court to stay its hand. However in the present case, it appears from the correspondence which I permitted to be read that there is a clear claim of an express agreement made between counsel the effect of which could have rendered the judgment unenforceable except as to $2,500. In the circumstances I am satisfied that this matter should be further investigated before the Order Nisi is made absolute. I am not unmindful of the possibility of the Judgment Debtor becoming bankrupt and I have regard to the provisions of s 118 of the Bankruptcy Act 1966.

... So far as concerns the issues raised by the Judgment Debtor, he is in the position of a Plaintiff who is resident out of the jurisdiction and there is also some indication of insolvency. Accordingly, I accede to the request for counsel for the Judgment Creditor to order a limited security for costs.

21.8.8 In South Australia, the position is, in form, somewhat different. The Enforcement of Judgments Act 1991 (SA) s 6(4) envisages the making of an order based on the debtor's means, expenses and other liabilities. The decision to make a final order is not simply a matter as between the creditor and the garnishee.

21.8.9 The status of a 'final' garnishee order was considered by the Full Court of the Supreme Court of Victoria in *Tile Centre v Symons* [1972] VR 965. A garnishee order was made. Subsequent developments meant that rather than the garnishee owing money to the judgment debtor, the judgment debtor was likely to owe money to the garnishee. The question whether the court could set aside the order was referred to the Full Court (Winneke CJ, Little and Anderson JJ) (at 969–72):

> We think that the explanation for the absence of any authoritative statement to the effect that a garnishee order absolute is one which may not be so set aside derives from the nature of the order absolute itself. The order absolute, so called, is the order, so far as the present case is concerned, which the County Court judge makes under O 29 r 36, of the County Court Rules. That rule provides that upon the return of the garnishee order nisi, if the garnishee does not dispute his debt to the judgment debtor or if the garnishee does not appear to show cause, the judge may order execution to issue to levy the amount due from the garnishee or so much as may be sufficient to satisfy the judgment creditor's judgment or order. Order 29 of the County Court rules is the order dealing with execution of judgments and orders, and it is in that context that r 36 authorizes the issue of execution. It is in the context of "execution" that garnishee proceedings are generally discussed in the law books. In the 1945 *Annual Practice* (as well as the other editions) the note to O 45 r 1, is, we think, of significance. That note reads: "*Object of the Process*. It should always be borne in mind that the object and intention of the process is to render 'debts' as a form of property available in execution. This marks both the nature of the [970] process and its limitations." What the process is designed to do is to levy execution upon what in reality is the property of the judgment debtor, namely, the debt owing by the garnishee to the judgment debtor, which is to be taken to satisfy the judgment debt. The order is not one made in a "cause or action" (*Mason v Wirral Highway Board* (1879) 4 QBD 458) though it is, as its name indicates, a "proceeding" (*Llewellyn v Carrickford* [1970] 2 All ER 24); it is not "a judgment or order for the recovery or payment of money" (*McKenzie & Co v Walker* (1891) 17 VLR 221); it does not operate to transfer the debt or make the garnishee the debtor of the judgment creditor (*Re Combined Weighing and Advertising Machine Co* (1889) 43 Ch D 99; [1886–90] All ER Rep 1044).
>
> "There cannot be said to be any equitable debt. There is no assignment in equity, and I cannot see that there is any legal debt. There is an order of a Court of Common law that a sum equal to the original debt shall be paid by the garnishee to the judgment creditor, or as an alternative that execution may issue; but I think that the relation which is created by that section and the orders made under it does not create a debt at all; it creates an attachment of portion of a debt, and, in case of nonpayment confers the right of issuing execution and nothing more": per Bowen, LJ, at (Ch D) 105. A judgment creditor cannot take bankruptcy proceedings against the garnishee, (ibid), nor can he take garnishee proceedings against a debtor of the garnishee: *McKenzie v Walker*, supra.
>
> At least so far as proceedings under O 29 r 36, are concerned, there is no *lis* between the judgment creditor and the garnishee; it is only when the garnishee disputes his liability that the judge, under O 29 r 39, may order an issue to be tried. That there is no *lis* between the judgment creditor and the garnishee until an issue is ordered to be tried is emphasized by the decision in *Murdoch v Flexmore* (1906) 2 Tas LR 78, where the court set aside an order absolute which

had been made in the absence of the garnishee and directed that the appropriate issue be tried. There are so many things that a garnishee order is not, that it is very much *sui generis*. The garnishee procedure which is now in almost identical form in all jurisdictions owes its origin to the Common Law Procedure Act 1854, in England, and has constantly been referred to as a means of execution.

"It is impossible, as it seems to me, on any principle to distinguish this case of an execution against debts from an execution against goods and chattels. In this particular case the creditor is made his own sheriff, and he is allowed to make his own execution just as a landlord puts in a distress himself for rent": per James LJ, in *Re Stanhope Silkstone Collieries Co* (1879) 11 Ch D 160, at 162; see, too, Jessel, MR, at 161, 162.

Garnishee proceedings have been variously described as being in the nature of or a species or method of execution: per Vaughan Williams, LJ, in *Martin v Nadel* [1906] 2 ER 26, at 29; [1904–7] All ER Rep 827; per Montague Smith, J, in *Re Price* (1869) LR 4 CP 155, at 158; per Vaughan Williams, LJ, in *White, Son & Pill v Stenning* [1911] 2 ER 418, at 427, and per Kennedy LJ, at 431. In *White Son & Pill v Stenning*, supra, where a judgment debtor had been given time to pay, and the time had not expired when the judgment creditor commenced proceedings against the garnishee, Vaughan Williams LJ said at 427: "I think that garnishee proceedings are a species of execution, and that a judgment creditor ought not to be allowed to take out a garnishee summons, or get an order thereon, under Order XXVI, [971] r 1 if the state of things is such that he cannot issue execution against the judgment debtor's chattels."

We think, in light of the views expressed in the foregoing cases, that the evident reason why the principle exemplified in *Bailey v Marinoff* (1971) 125 CLR 529 has not been applied to the garnishee cases is because what is referred to as the garnishee order absolute is in effect no more than the granting of leave to issue execution upon the property of the judgment debtor which in the particular instance happens to be a debt owing by the garnishee to the judgment debtor. Just as the court may, in a case where chattels are seized under an execution and an adverse claim is made to them, adjudicate in interpleader proceedings and make such order as it deems proper, so where it appears that the order attaching the debt is about to be enforced in circumstances working an injustice, the court has an inherent power, in controlling its own process, to avoid that result. In other words, what flows from the operation of O 29 r 36, is not a judgment or order of the kind which when recorded is final or perfected and beyond recall or revision by the court making it; it is rather a direction or an authorization to satisfy a judgment of the court by means of a particular article of property of the judgment debtor. Even though the process may in some respects involve the exercise of judicial functions (see *Llewellyn v Carrickford, supra*), the execution of the court's judgment or order as the cases show, is essentially administrative capable of being supervised by the court, and liable to revocation.

Mr Fricke, however, advanced a further argument against the proposition that the County Court had jurisdiction to set aside a garnishee order absolute. He submitted that whatever may be the position in the case of a court of plenary jurisdiction, the County Court, being a court of limited jurisdiction, did not possess the power to do other than what was granted to it by statute and since the power to set aside a garnishee order absolute had not been given to it by the County Court Act 1958 or the Rules made under that Act, there was no basis for saying that there was such a power. He sought to strengthen his argument by pointing out that there was a paucity of decisions on the matter in relation to courts of limited jurisdiction. There is, however, a number of decisions which recognize such a power in courts of limited jurisdiction, including the Western Australian case of *Henderson v Johnson & Henderson* [1969] WAR 3, and we do not think that the paucity of reported cases on the subject really assists his argument. We think that the question whether the County Court has the power for which Mr Crossley contends is concluded by the provisions of s 49 of the County Court Act 1958 and the reasons of this Court in *Duncan v Lowenthal* [1969] VR 180, support this view. By s 49 of the County Court Act it is provided that the County Court "shall have power to make any order that could be made in regard to any action or matter ... in as full and ample a manner as might and ought to be done in the case by the Supreme Court or a Judge thereof ".

In our opinion, the County Court is amply empowered by s 49 to set aside for good cause a garnishee order absolute in the same manner as the Supreme Court or a judge thereof would do so; and we think, too, that the County Court has, as well, an inherent jurisdiction to do so.

"There is authority that the grant of jurisdiction to hear and determine actions of the kind specified in a statute in itself carries with it the grant of such incidental powers as are necessary for the exercise of the jurisdiction and to prevent abuses of process"; see *Duncan v Lowenthal* [1969] VR 180, at 182, and the cases there referred to. These observations which were made by the Full Court in relation to the County [972] Court's inherent jurisdiction to strike out an action for want of prosecution are, we consider, equally applicable to its jurisdiction to set aside a garnishee order absolute.

21.8.10   If the garnishee refuses to pay money as ordered to the judgment creditor, the judgment creditor may proceed against the garnishee using the standard procedures for recovering orders in relation to the payment of money: ACT r 2315; Civil Procedure Act 2005 (NSW) s 124(1)(b)(i); NT r 71.09(4); Enforcement of Judgments Act 1991 (SA) s 6; Tas r 914(1)(b); Vic r 71.09(4); Civil Judgments Enforcement Act 2004 (WA) s 56. In Queensland, failure to comply with a warrant for redirection of debts can constitute contempt of court: Form 76. Even if the garnishee refuses to pay the creditor, the garnishee does not become a debtor to the creditor. The creditor cannot deal with a recalcitrant garnishee by initiating bankruptcy proceedings.

21.8.11   Payment by the garnishee to the creditor operates to discharge the garnishee's liability to the judgment debtor: ACT rr 2312, 2315(4); Civil Procedure Act 2005 (NSW) s 123(4); NT r 71.12; Qld r 846; Tas r 917; Vic r 71.12; Civil Judgments Enforcement Act 2004 (WA) s 57.

Attachment of earnings

21.8.12   The rules, with respect to the attachment of earnings, vary across jurisdictions. First, it should be noted that, in the absence of express statutory provision, there is no power to garnishee an employee's wages or salary except when, at the time of the order *nisi*, these have become due for payment. This means that in the case of a debtor who is paid weekly, a new garnishee order would be needed each week. While a determined creditor could pursue this strategy, it would not be a satisfactory one, either from the standpoint of the creditor or from that of the debtor. The only point of such a regime would be that it would create a framework within which creditor and debtor could bargain with each other about terms of repayment.

There are further complications. Attempts to garnishee earnings tend to prejudice employers against employees. This may be because the garnisheeing of wages involves added administrative burdens for the employer. It may be because employers mistrust employees who incur, and fail to pay, debts. This mistrust may not be altogether without foundation. However, because in many cases it will not be justified, all jurisdictions recognise the need to protect employees. One way of doing so is to impose penalties on employers who dismiss employees in response to garnishee orders.

A second is to restrict the circumstances in which employees' income can be garnisheed. Quite apart from the need to protect employees from their employers, there are good reasons for limiting the degree to which wages can be garnisheed. Even the most hard-hearted policy makers would recognise that those who work should be allowed to enjoy some of the fruits of their labour: shelter, food and basic medical care. If creditors could garnishee a debtor's entire income, this would mean either that workers would cease to work (which would be a bad thing) or that they and their dependents might starve or fall ill (which would also be a bad thing). Provision is made accordingly.

21.8.13   All jurisdictions provide for the attachment of future earnings: ACT Div 2.18.8; Civil Procedure Act 2005 (NSW) ss 119–122; NT O 72; Qld Ch 19, Pt 6; Enforcement of Judgments Act 1991 (SA) s 6; Tas Pr 35 Div 6; Vic O 12; Civil Judgments Enforcement Act 2004 (WA) ss 34–44. In all jurisdictions, limits exist to the degree to which wages can be attached: Court Procedures Act 2004 (ACT) s 77; ACT r 2353; Civil Procedure Act 2005 (NSW) ss 119–122; NT r 72.05; Civil Procedure Act 2011 (Qld) s 90(2)(c); Qld r 856(3); Enforcement of Judgments Act 1991 (SA) s 6(4), (5); Tas r 923(7), Form 74, para 2; Vic r 72.05; Civil Judgments Enforcement Act 2004 (WA) ss 21, 22, 34. There are special provisions which permit the ordering of deductions from public servants' salaries to meet judgment debts: Public Service Act 1999 (Cth) s 75; Public Service Regulations 1999 (Cth) Pt 8A. (What is the justification for making special provisions for public servants?)

In the Australian Capital Territory, the judgment creditor makes an *ex parte* application for an earnings redirection order. Once made, it must be served on both the employer and the judgment debtor, and it does not come into force until seven days after service on the employer: r 2356. While in force it precludes the making of other enforcement orders, except by leave of the court: r 2359. This does not affect the operation or orders which have already been made, and does not preclude contemporaneous orders for redirection of debts: see, eg, r 2057. On application, the order may be set aside: r 2360.

In New South Wales, the procedures for obtaining an order garnisheeing wages are similar to those for obtaining an ordinary garnishee order: Pt 39 Div 4. The maximum amount payable under orders in relation to income is that which would reduce the garnishee's income (after compulsory deductions) to less than the standard workers' compensation benefit: Civil Procedure Act 2005 (NSW) s 122. In the Northern Territory (r 72.02) and Victoria (r 72.02), an application to garnishee wages involves an application initiated by summons, accompanied by affidavit material. Forms prescribe the nature of the summons and the affidavits. These and a notice (Form 72C) must be served on the judgment creditor at least 14 days before the date fixed for hearing of the application. In Victoria, an order for attachment earnings may not be made where a warrant has been issued under the Imprisonment of Fraudulent Debtors Act 1958. If the warrant has not been issued, the court may discharge the warrant with a view to making the attachment order.

The court may make the order if satisfied that:

(a)   the debtor is a person to whom earnings are payable or likely to become payable;

(b)   that the unpaid debt exceeds $20; and

(c)   that the debtor has persistently failed to comply with an order.

If satisfied, it may order a person who is apparently the debtor's employer to make payments out of the debtor's earnings.

The court may order the debtor to provide details about means, commitments, earnings and employment and this information shall be evidence in attachment proceedings. It may also act on evidence by or on behalf of the employer or the debtor's spouse. The rules prescribe forms for applications for means orders, and orders with respect to these.

The court may make orders of attachment even if the debtor and/or spouse do not attend. If so, and if there is relevant evidence, the court shall specify a protected income rate and a normal deduction rate. Otherwise, the court shall make such order as it thinks reasonable.

An upper limit on repayments is set by the protected earnings rate, which is determined by the earning rate which the court thinks is the minimum needed having regard to the resources and needs of the debtor and spouse. It is normally at least 80 per cent of the debtor's net earnings. The order is also to specify the rate at which the court thinks it reasonable to apply the debtor's earnings to the repayment of the debt.

Attachment of earnings orders must be served on the debtor and the employer. The employer is then bound to make payments to the creditor. The precise amount is determined by a complex formula: NT r 72.07; Vic r 72.07. No other enforcement proceedings are permitted without leave of the court once an order for attachment of earnings comes into force: NT r 72.09; Vic r 72.09.

In Queensland (rr 855, 856), creditors or debtors may apply for an enforcement warrant for redirection of earnings. In deciding whether to issue such a warrant, the court is to have regard to the debtor's employment status and employer, the debtor's capacity to pay, the impact of the order on the debtor, and (if the debtor seeks the order), whether its issue would be consistent with the efficient and expeditious enforcement of the order. A successful applicant must serve the warrant on the debtor and the debtor's employer: r 859(1). While the warrant is in force, other enforcement warrants may be issued in relation to a money order only by leave of the court: r 861. Warrants may be set aside, suspended or varied: r 862. Where two warrants are in force, the employer must comply with the first to be served: r 864. Persons served with warrants who are not, or cease to be, employers, must give notice: rr 865, 866.

The Queensland rules (rr 847–854) also provide for warrants to financial institutions requiring them to make regular payments from earnings paid into an account. These are governed by similar rules to those which apply to warrants for the redirection of earnings, except that they are directed to financial institutions. There are no equivalent provisions in other jurisdictions.

In Tasmania (rr 921–923), the procedure is initiated by an *ex parte* application. On the making of a provisional garnishee order, the garnishee and the debtor must be served with notice of the order. The garnishee and the debtor then have 21 days in which to reply. In the absence of any objections, the order becomes absolute and can be enforced accordingly. Otherwise there is a trial of the issues in dispute. Payments under a garnishee order are set at 20 per cent of net earnings after various deductions have been made.

In South Australia, salaries and wages may only be subjected to a garnishee order if the judgment debtor consents: Enforcement of Judgments Act 1991 (SA) s 6(2).

Western Australia allows 'earnings appropriation orders' but only after a means inquiry and only if an instalment order has previously been made, disobeyed and cancelled, and if there is no other appropriate order in effect. Orders take effect upon service on the third party, who may object: Civil Judgments Enforcement Act 2004 (WA) ss 21, 35(3), (4), 37(1), 40–41.

CHARGING ORDERS AND STOP ORDERS

21.9.1 Most jurisdictions have provisions for charging orders to be made, which generally may only be made against the beneficial interest of the judgment debtor in any securities:

ACT Div 2.18.9; Civil Procedure Act 2005 (NSW) ss 126–128; NT O 73; Civil Procedure Act 2011 (Qld) s 90(4), (5); Qld Ch 19 Pt 8, 9; Tas r 931; Vic O 73. In South Australia, they may be made against the debtor's property: Enforcement of Judgments Act 1991 (SA) s 8. Somewhat confusingly the Australian Capital Territory rules provide that the procedures for obtaining such orders are as provided by the Court Procedures Act 2004 (ACT) Div 7.6, which in fact makes no reference to these orders.

In general, an application involves a two-stage process or its equivalent. The first stage involves an *ex parte* application. If an order nisi or equivalent is granted, notice must be given to the judgment debtor and to anyone else who might be affected; they may make submissions at a subsequent hearing. However, there are cross-jurisdictional variations. In the Northern Territory (r 73.03) and Victoria (r 73.03), the creditor applies for an order that a charging summons be filed and served. The Victorian rules explicitly provide that the application is to be accompanied by an affidavit stating that a judgment debt has not been wholly satisfied, the securities in respect of which the order is sought, and that the judgment debtor has a beneficial interest of a stated nature in respect of the securities. If the application is successful, the debtor and the other parties affected by the order must be served with notice of the order. In the Australian Capital Territory, New South Wales, Queensland and South Australia, the judgment creditor makes an *ex parte* application for a charging order: ACT rr 2401, 2402; NSW r 39.44; Qld r 817. South Australian law is similar, but the legislation is silent as to whether applications may be made *ex parte*: Enforcement of Judgments Act 1991 (SA) s 8(1).

Service of the provisional order, enforcement warrant or the application (as appropriate) generally freezes the securities: ACT r 2403(1), (2); Judgment Creditors' Remedies Act 1901 (NSW) s 27(2); NT r 73.07; Supreme Court Act 1995 (Qld) s 39(1); Qld rr 877, 878; Supreme Court Civil Procedure Act 1932 (Tas) s 167, Tas r 932(2)(b); Vic r 73.06; cf Civil Procedure Act 2005 (NSW) s 126(3) (order takes effect when made). Anyone with notice who permits the transfer of charged property shall be liable to the judgment creditor for the value of the property or the debt (whichever is less). No disposition by the debtor is good as against the creditor.

21.9.2 In the Northern Territory, Tasmania and Victoria, the next stage is a hearing which the judgment debtor may attend. Under the Tasmanian rules, the debtor may show cause why the order should not be made absolute: Supreme Court (Civil Procedure) Act 1932 (Tas) s 167; Tas r 935. In the Northern Territory and Victoria, the court is simply empowered to make an order: NT r 73.08; Vic r 73.08. This is implicit in South Australia. Orders may, on the application of a debtor, be discharged or varied: NT r 73.10; Supreme Court Civil Procedure Act 1932 (Tas) s 167; Vic r 73.10.

In Queensland (r 819), there need not be a hearing, but a person served with the enforcement warrant may apply to have it set aside. In the Australian Capital Territory, New South Wales and Queensland, the orders stand unless there is an application to have them set aside, those affected by them having a right to apply for the setting aside of the initial order: ACT r 2051; NSW r 36.16(2)(b); Qld r 819.

The effect of a charging order is that the judgment creditor is treated as having a charge over the securities. In some jurisdictions, the order may be enforced against judgment debtors only after having been served on them: ACT r 2403(2); Civil Procedure Act 2005 (NSW) s 126; Qld r 876. The creditor can enforce the charge by having the securities sold and being paid from the proceeds. In some jurisdictions, no proceeding shall be taken to have the benefit of a charging order until the end of a prescribed period from the date of the order or when the service of it has elapsed: ACT r 2403(4) (one month after service on both the judgment debtor and the person who issued or administers the property); Civil Procedure Act 2005 (NSW) s 126(4) (three months from date of order); Qld r 876(3) (three months after service of order on debtor and person administering the property); Supreme Court Civil Procedure Act 1932 (Tas) s 166 (six months from date of order).

21.9.3   The fact that a charging order gives a judgment creditor priority over unsecured creditors is a factor, which may be taken into account in determining whether such an order should be made. In *Rainbow v Moorgate Properties* [1975] 1 WLR 788, the plaintiffs (Rainbow) had succeeded in actions against Moorgate. Moorgate was a subsidiary company in a large group of companies which were in financial difficulties and whose parent company had gone into voluntary liquidation. A meeting of creditors (to which Rainbow was not party) had unanimously resolved to agree to a moratorium on the enforcement of debts. Subsequently, Rainbow applied for charging orders *nisi* which were granted. Moorgate presented a petition for its winding-up. Rainbow then applied for and was granted a charging order absolute. Allowing an appeal against this decision, Buckley LJ (with whom Ormrod LJ agreed) said (at 793):

> ... I think it is wrong, when the court is aware of the fact that the [794] debtor is, or is likely to turn out to be, insolvent, that one creditor should be given an advantage over other creditors by an exercise of the discretion of the court ... It is not that the moratorium is binding upon the plaintiffs and that they are doing, or have done, anything wrong in seeking to obtain the charging orders; the moratorium is clearly not binding upon them because they were not party to the resolution setting it up. But the court has to be satisfied that it is proper for the court, in the exercise of its discretion, to place them at an advantage over other creditors. If there were no countervailing reasons the court would make charging orders in the present case but, in my judgment, there are countervailing reasons connected with the moratorium and the proposed scheme of arrangement which I have mentioned which in this case do make it improper to give the plaintiffs an advantage over other creditors. It is a misfortune for the plaintiffs, but there it is.

In *Roberts Petroleum Ltd v Kenny Ltd* [1983] 2 WLR 305, the House of Lords considered the position where voluntary liquidation of a company intervenes between the making of the order *nisi* and the date for showing cause why the order should not be made absolute. Their Lordships rejected the argument that *Rainbow* applied only to cases where there was the possibility that there had been set on foot a scheme of arrangement which had a reasonable prospect of success. Holding that 'the imposition on the assets of an insolvent company of the statutory scheme for the distribution of those assets among the unsecured creditors was a "sufficient cause" for not converting the order *nisi* into an order absolute' (at 320), Lord Brightman added that he reached the conclusion without regret:

> First, it may help to avert an unseemly scramble by creditors to achieve priority at the last moment. Secondly, it establishes a clear working rule, and avoids the uncertainties of an inquiry as to whether a scheme of arrangement "has been set of foot ... and has a reasonable prospect of succeeding".

Orders may also be made in relation to money, securities and bonds which have been paid into court and which stand to the judgment debtor's credit. In the Australian Capital Territory (r 2421), New South Wales (r 41.16), Queensland (r 882), Tasmania (r 937) and Victoria (r 72.12), judgment creditors (and others) may apply for an order preventing dealings in funds in court without notice. Applications must be served on anyone with an interest in the funds. In the Northern Territory (r 72.13) and Queensland (r 881), the court may order payments to the judgment creditor from payments by the debtor into court.

RECEIVERS

21.10.1   Among the procedures devised by Chancery for the enforcement of its orders was the appointment of receivers. The receivers' powers were extensive. All jurisdictions retain provisions for the appointment of receivers: Court Procedures Act 2004 (ACT) s 63; Supreme Court Act 1970 (NSW) s 67; Supreme Court Act 1979 (NT) s 69; Civil Proceedings Act 2011 (Qld) s 12; Supreme Court Act 1935 (SA) s 29(1); Supreme Court (Civil Procedure) Act 1932 (Tas) s 11(12); Supreme Court Act 1986 (Vic) s 37; Supreme Court Act 1935 (WA) s 25(9). There is express provision in most jurisdictions for the appointment of receivers to receive the income from the property of a judgment debtor: ACT Div 2.18.11; NSW r 40.2(1) (a); NT O 74; Qld rr 883–888; Enforcement of Judgments Act 1991 (SA) s 9; Tas rr 938, 939; Vic O 74; Civil Judgments Enforcement Act 2004 (WA) ss 86, 87. The appointment of receivers has sometimes been described as a form of 'equitable execution'. Use of this terminology has, however, been criticised as misleading.

21.10.2C	**Re Shephard; Atkins v Shephard**
	(1889) 43 QBD 131
	High Court of England, Chancery Division

[Shephard was entitled to a freehold subject to a mortgage. A judgment creditor applied for the appointment of a receiver. The application was adjourned on the grounds of Shephard's ill health. Shephard was indeed ill. He died (intestate) before the hearing could resume. An order was nonetheless made appointing a receiver. The action had not been revived, nor was the heir-at-law before the court. Subsequently a dispute arose as to whether the receiver had been properly appointed.]

Cotton LJ (at 135–6): It was urged that ... this was equitable enforcement and must follow the analogy of legal execution; that legal execution could be issued ex parte after the death of the judgment debtor, and that therefore there was no reason why equitable execution should not. But is this to be considered as equitable execution and as subject to the same objections only as legal execution, and, assuming that legal execution could be issued against the estate of a dead person without taking any intermediate step, a proposition to which I am not disposed to assent, does it follow that equitable execution can be so issued? In my opinion it does not. Confusion of ideas has arisen from the use of the term 'equitable enforcement.' The expression tends to error. It has often been used by judges, and occurs in some orders, as a short expression indicating that the person who obtains the order gets the same benefits as he would have got from legal execution. But what he gets by the appointment of a receiver is not execution, but equitable relief, which is granted on the ground that there is no remedy by execution at law; it is a taking out of the way a hindrance which [136] prevents execution at common law. Until recently nobody ever thought that an order for a receiver could be obtained in aid of a legal judgment unless there was a hindrance to obtaining execution at law. If any practice has grown up of granting such an order where there is no hindrance to obtaining execution at law it is a practice which has never been brought before the Court of Appeal, and which in my opinion is wrong. The obtaining of a receivership order is not taking out execution, it is obtaining equitable relief by a subsequent order, which must be made against some one against whom the Court has jurisdiction to make an order. It cannot be made against the estate which formerly belonged to a dead man, but which as he is dead is no longer his, it must be made against his heir or devisee, and under such circumstances that the Court has jurisdiction over the heir or devisee.

[Bowen and Fry LJJ agreed.]

21.10.3   The appointment of a receiver will involve considerable expense as the receiver must be paid. Moreover, it may involve considerable disruption to the debtor's affairs as, for instance, where a receiver is appointed over the debtor's business for the purposes of paying debts out of its earnings. Appointment of a receiver will therefore normally be a strategy of last resort. Receivers will not normally be appointed when ordinary modes of execution are available: *Goldschmidt v Oberrheinische Metallwerke* [1906] 1 KB 373; *Morgan v Hart* [1914] 2 KB 183. Normally, alternatives are available.

However, occasionally there will be circumstances where the debtor's property cannot be taken under the ordinary procedures. This will be the case only for relatively unusual property interests. Examples include: reversionary interests under wills (*Fuggle v Bland* (1883) 11 QBD 711); debtors' interests in property held on trust for sale (*Bank of Australasia v Whitehead* (1898) 24 VLR 308); shares of intestate estates where no administrator has been appointed (*Levermore v Levermore* [1979] 1 WLR 1277); situations where the debtor's and others' property are mingled; situations where debtors are not in possession of property but are entitled to receive income from it; and where goods are owned by the debtor but in the possession of a firm with a lien over them: *Levasseur v Mason & Barry* [1891] 2 QB 73.

There must be an application for the appointment of a receiver. In this respect, the procedures generally contrast with those relating to seizure and sale where, in general, the writs and warrants are generally available as of right. In Queensland, enforcement orders for the appointment of receivers are governed by the same rules as those governing the issuing of other warrants. The application of those rules would, however, involve the court following procedures similar to those followed in other jurisdictions in relation to the appointment of receivers. The application should be on notice. (Note, however, that an *ex parte* application was the basis for the appointment of the receiver in *Levasseur v Mason & Barry* [1891] 2 QB 73.) Some rules provide that the appointment is to be preceded by a kind of cost–benefit analysis. Account must be taken of the amount claimed, the amount likely to be obtained, and the costs of the appointment of the receiver: ACT r 2433(1); NT r 74.02; Qld r 886; Tas r 939(a); Vic r 74.02; Civil Judgments Enforcement Act 2004 (WA) s 87(1). There is also, implicitly, authority to this effect; receivers will not be appointed where the judgment debt is small (and where, presumably, its recovery by appointment of a receiver would be inefficient): *Sandford v King* (1900) 26 VLR 387; *J Walls v Legge* [1923] 2 KB 240 at [245] per Scrutton LJ.

Appointment of a receiver and priorities

21.10.4C	**Levasseur v Mason & Barry** [1891] 2 QB 73 High Court of England, Court of Appeal

[At the request of Mason & Barry, a receiver was appointed of property subject to a lien. A week later, the judgment debtor went into liquidation. The liquidators then sought to have the order set aside. The application was dismissed, although the order was varied to require the director not to pay out anything received without direction of the court. The liquidators then served notice on the receiver claiming to be entitled to the property which he had been authorised to receive.]

Lord Esher MR (at 80): The receivership order ... has the effect of giving to the judgment creditor a right to have the property in dispute handed to him after a certain difficulty has been got rid of. When the order is made and the receiver appointed, he has nothing to do but to get rid of the difficulty, and then to take possession of the goods, or receive the money. The order may be that he shall at once take possession of the goods or receive the money and hand over the goods or pay the money. But the court, although it makes the receivership order — which is a positive order that the receiver shall, the moment the difficulty is out of the way, hold the goods or money for the execution creditor and for him alone — may hold its hand and may say: 'You, the receiver, are to receive that property, or that money, into your possession. So far as you are concerned you are to hold it for, and will have to hand it over to me, the judgment creditor and nobody else. But, as it may be that some other person will come before us, or that some other point will be taken with respect to the right to the property or money, we will not at once make the order for you to hand or pay it over.' If no further difficulty arises which justifies the Court in interfering further, they are bound, the moment they are satisfied of that, to order that the goods be handed over, or the money be paid over to the execution creditor.

[Coleridge and Fry LJJ agreed.]

SUBSTITUTED SPECIFIC PERFORMANCE

21.11.1   Where a judgment requires a party to perform an act and where the party refuses to do so, the court may direct that the act be done by a person appointed by the court (and order that the refusing party pay costs and expenses): HCR r 10.02.2; FCR r 41.09; ACT r 2442(4); Civil Procedure Act 2005 (NSW) s 94; NSW r 40.8; NT r 66.11; Qld r 899; Enforcement of Judgments Act 1991 (SA) s 13; Tas r 877; Vic r 66.11; Civil Judgments Enforcement Act 2004 (WA) s 99. This power may be exercised in addition to the power to punish for contempt.

CONTEMPT AND SEQUESTRATION

21.12.1   All jurisdictions have provisions for the imposition of sanctions on those who fail to comply with orders. These sanctions are, in effect, punitive. However, their purpose is to encourage compliance rather than to punish past non-compliance. Sanctions, once imposed, may therefore be lifted in response to an indication by the sanctioned party that it is willing to comply. There are two powers which courts can use to deal with the recalcitrant: they can punish this form of contempt of court by fines and, in extreme cases, imprisonment; or they can 'sequestrate' the offending party's property. Sequestration is a sanction which has no obvious analogue in the criminal justice system (although it might usefully be used in relation to affluent offenders). It involves the non-compliant party being separated from its property.

21.12.2 Parties will not lightly be punished for failure to comply with court orders. First, if the judgment requires that a party do or stop doing something, the party must be given time to do or refrain from doing it: HCR r 8.05; FCR r 41.06; ACT r 2446(1)(b); NSW r 36.5(2); NT r 66.05; Qld r 904(1)(b); SA r 225(2); Tas r 883(1)(b); Vic r 66.05; WA O 42 r 3. Where a time is not fixed, the court may subsequently fix a time.

21.12.3 A condition for a finding of contempt or a sequestration order is that the party to be attached or committed be aware of the order with which it is failing to comply. Thus, proceedings may not be commenced unless a copy of the judgment has been served personally on the party required to comply with it: FCR r 41.07(1); ACT r 2446(1)(a); NSW r 40.7(1); NT r 66.10; Qld r 904(1)(a); SA r 225(3); Tas r 883(1)(a); Vic r 66.10; WA O 46 r 4. This requirement is dispensed with if the party was present when judgment was given, or if the party had been otherwise notified of the judgment: FCR O 37 r 2(5); ACT r 2446(2); NSW r 40.7(4); NT r 66.10(5); Qld r 904(2); Vic r 66.10(5).

Parties should also be aware that contempt proceedings have been initiated against them. Notice serves two functions. First, it is an essential ingredient of procedural fairness. Second, it puts the offending party on notice that continued failure to comply with a judgment or order may entail severe sanctions. Since the contempt and sequestration powers are to be used to encourage compliance rather than to punish non-compliance, this is of obvious importance. However, as we shall see, while notice is normally required, there are some cases where it is not.

Committal and sequestration will not be ordered lightly.

Contempt

21.12.4C	**Australian Consolidated Press Ltd v Morgan**
	(1965) 112 CLR 438
	High Court of Australia

[The respondents (Morgan) conducted public opinion polls, 'according to the Gallup method'. The results of these were published in selected newspapers which paid Morgan for the privilege. They were also published in newspapers owned by the appellants (ACP) who did not. This led to litigation which was 'settled' on the basis of an agreement whereby the defendant undertook '[t]hat it will not at any future time publish in any form whatsoever any Gallup Poll results in respect of which you the said Roy Edward Morgan and/or the said company has the copyright'. This was a contractual undertaking, not an undertaking to the court. Subsequently, alleging breach, Morgan sued for a restraining injunction in the Supreme Court.

The matter was stood over on ACP giving an undertaking (this time to the court) in the same terms as the contractual undertaking. Subsequently, ACP published an article based on, and reporting, some of what had appeared (by agreement with Morgan) in another

Sydney newspaper. (For full details, see Owen J at 510–14). Morgan sought liberty to issue a writ of sequestration against ACP.

At the hearing of the motion, Else-Mitchell J found that there had been a breach of undertaking and imposed a fine of £1500 on ACP for contempt. At issue had been the question of what the undertaking meant, given that there was some dispute over what constituted the poll results, and over what it was that Morgan had copyright. On appeal, one of the matters considered was whether the court had the power to fine in face of 'civil' contempt. On appeal to the High Court, the order was set aside.]

Barwick CJ (at 492): The appellant submitted that unless the language of the undertaking was unambiguous and certain, it should not be enforced by contempt proceedings: and sought support for the submission in *Redwing Ltd v Redwing Forest Products Ltd* (1947) 177 LT 387 and *Iberian Trust Ltd v Founders Trust and Investment Co* [1932] 2 KB 87. In my opinion, these authorities do not support this conclusion. If the order or undertaking is so expressed as to be meaningless, there is of course nothing which can be enforced. But, if it bears a meaning which the Court is satisfied is one which ought fairly to have been in the contemplation of the person to whom the order was directed or who gave the undertaking as a possible meaning, the fact that that meaning results from a process of construction and involves a choice of possible meanings does not, in my opinion, preclude the Court from enforcing the order or undertaking in the sense which the Court assigns to it. If the Court is satisfied that the party said to be in contempt bona fide believed himself bound only by a construction which the Court thinks to be erroneous, it may for that reason, in its discretion, refuse to make an order or, if it makes an order, refuse to make an order for costs against that party. But, even in such a case, the enforcement of the plaintiff's rights must not be left out of account. A party who has bona fide acted on an erroneous view of an order or undertaking may, according to the circumstances, none the less be justly adjudged guilty of contempt in procedure. In my opinion, this is equally so where, because of its terms or circumstances, the order or undertaking requires construction in order to determine its meaning and remove ambiguities patent or latent.

I now turn to the order which his Honour made. If there were no valid objections to this order, the criticisms which I have so far offered of the course taken by his Honour would not have led me for those reasons to intervene to set aside his order. I would have regarded what he had done as no more than an erroneous exercise of his discretion with which I should not in this case interfere. But, in my opinion, there is a serious objection to the order.

Windeyer J (at 497–501, 503): The undoubted power to fine for criminal contempt merely strengthens my misgivings about the fine in this case, for disobedience of an injunction or breach of an undertaking is not a criminal offence. If authority for that be wanted, the following will suffice. In *Scott v Scott* [1913] AC 417 Lord Atkinson, after referring to several cases, said: 'It was contended that these cases show that the disobedience of an order of Court constitutes in itself a crime, [498] a criminal contempt of Court. Unfortunately for this contention, however, they do something more than that; they show I think, conclusively, that if a person be expressly enjoined by injunction, a most solemn and authoritative form of order, from doing a particular thing, and he deliberately in breach of that injunction, does that thing, he is not guilty of any crime whatever, but only of a civil contempt of Court' [1913] AC at 456. And in New South Wales, more than sixty years ago Walker J spoke of 'the mistaken view that all the offences generically known as contempts stand on the same footing, and that all contempts are criminal and must be dealt with as though they were the subject of a criminal indictment'. 'This', he said, 'is not so.' Dealing with an application for the sequestration of the property of a trade union that had disobeyed an injunction he said 'This is not an application by the plaintiff that the Court should exercise its criminal jurisdiction, and punish the union for a criminal offence; it is a step in the suit by which the plaintiff endeavours, by the only means open to him, to enforce against the union the injunction of the Court': *Keogh v The Australian Workers' Union* (1902) 2 SR Eq (NSW) 265 at 281, 282.

Sequestration is an old weapon of the Chancery Court to compel a party's obedience to either mesne process or a decree: see the entertainingly expressed report of *Rowley v Ridley* (1784) Dick 622; 21 ER 413. Originally sequestration was the final weapon in the Chancery Court's armoury, used — when attachment, proclamation of attachment and commission of rebellion had been unavailing — to compel a recalcitrant defendant to appear and answer the plaintiff's bill. The old procedure for contempts of mesne process was substantially altered by the Chancery Contempts Act, 1830. But committal and sequestration continue today as means of enforcing compliance with the decrees of a court of equity. They are used primarily to compel obedience rather than to punish disobedience; for equity acts *in personam*, and historically the purpose of the processes of the Court of Chancery was to rectify and reform the conscience of the wrongdoer. The jurisdiction was, to use Professor Ashburner's phrase, 'a cathartic jurisdiction': *Ashburner on Equity*, 2nd ed (1933) at 38. When contempt lies in disobedience of a court's order to do something, the contemnor may be imprisoned, until by doing what was ordered he purges his contempt. When contempt lies in disobedience of an injunction not to do something, the contemnor is ordinarily permitted to purge his contempt by [499] an apology to the court, making reparation for the damage done by the forbidden act and paying the costs as between solicitor and client: see the article 'Contempt of Court' in the *Encyclopedia of the Laws of England*. I do not suggest that a person who contumaciously disobeys a decree may not in some cases be, sentenced to remain in custody for a fixed term by way of expiation. There are instances of that in the reports; and see s 93 of the Equity Act 1901–1957 (NSW). Nevertheless the processes that an equity court uses to enforce its orders are primarily coercive or remedial rather than punitive. In the absence of express statutory authority they do not, I think, include the essentially penal sanction of a fine.

It is true that in the sixteenth and seventeenth centuries, when the Chancellor's Court was with some difficulty asserting its authority, it sometimes made use of severe fines, in addition to other measures, to force recalcitrant persons to submit to its jurisdiction and to obey its decrees: see *Spence, Equitable Jurisdiction*, vol II, 392; *Ashburner on Equity*, 2nd ed (1933), 31; and *Strahan's Digest of Equity*, 6th ed (1939), 433. And I am aware that in Comyn's Digest, under 'Chancery' Y4, it is said that a defendant committed for disobeying a decree shall not be discharged until he performs the decree in all things presently to be performed and gives security for the performance of the parts to be performed in the future and that 'the Chancellor also may fine him for the contempt and estreat the fine'. The authority given for this is the *Practical Register in Chancery*. That work, first published in 1714 and in an enlarged form in 1800, has not been available to me. But, whatever the practice in times long past, I have not found in any modern textbook any support for the proposition that a fine can be imposed for a contempt not criminal. This is not, as far as I have noticed, suggested in *Daniell's Chancery Practice or in Seton on Decrees*, in either the edition before or those after the Judicature Acts, or in any other work that I have consulted. ...

[500] It is true that a fine may — depending upon its amount — be a less severe consequence of disobedience than attachment or committal in the case of an individual or sequestration in the case of [501] a company. But that does not, to my mind, show that a

power to fine is a legal or logical alternative to the other remedies. Moreover their severity can be exaggerated. A writ of sequestration may be ordered to issue without being immediately executed. It is often ordered to lie in the office until the contempt be cleared by submission, making reparation for past disobedience and payment of costs. And even when the property of a contemnor is actually sequestered and held under sequestration it is not confiscated. The contemnor is deprived of the enjoyment of his rents and profits for the duration of the sequestration; but he does not forfeit his property in them. When whatever is considered necessary to clear the contempt has been done, the sequestration is discharged by the order of the Court: and the sequestrators must then give up possession on having their costs and expenses. As it is put in *Bacon's Abridgment* under 'Sequestration', 'Then whatsoever hath been seized shall be accounted for and paid over to him (the party whose property was sequestered). However, the court have the whole under their power, and may do therein as they please and as shall be most agreeable to the justice and equity of the case'. Sometimes it may be appropriate that the proceeds of the sequestration, or part thereof, should be applied to the discharge of an equitable obligation, as for example by a direction that equitable debts, the nonpayment of which had led to the sequestration, be first paid out of the fund; or that the fund be applied so far as necessary in reparation of the damage caused by the contemnor's disobedience. But this only illustrates again that sequestration for a civil contempt is coercive and compensatory rather than punitive.

Decisions of courts in the United States accord with the view that I have expressed. It is recognized there that the line between civil and criminal contempt cannot always be sharply drawn, for conduct by a litigant may amount to both if he not only disobeys a court's order but does so in a deliberately defiant way. Mere breach of an injunction is, however, not criminal.

[His Honour then discussed some English cases which suggested otherwise, distinguished them, and continued (at 503):]

His Honour said that the appellants having acted on a mistaken construction of the undertaking did not mitigate the breach of it, construed as his Honour held it should be construed. But, with respect, I cannot altogether agree. This is not a case in which the extent of obligations undertaken is ascertainable simply by construing the undertaking according to ordinary grammatical rules. If that were so, I would agree that a mistake in construction could not excuse disobedience, although it might perhaps mitigate its consequences. Those who give undertakings to a court are bound by the language they use. If its true meaning, although not immediately plain, can be ascertained according to ordinary rules of construction, then the person giving the undertaking is bound by it in that sense. But the uncertainties that lurk in the words of this undertaking, and which were exposed during the argument, cannot be resolved in that way, for they do not arise from a debatable construction but from an uncertain denotation.

[Owen and Windeyer JJ agreed that 'breach' of an ambiguous undertaking ought not constitute contempt.]

Attachment and committal

21.12.5   Courts have broad powers, both by virtue of their inherent powers, and by virtue of the rules, to punish for contempt. Failure to comply with an order is only one of the many forms that contempt can take. If a party to a proceeding wants another party dealt with for contempt, it makes an application, on notice to the respondent, setting out details of the contempt: HCR r 11.02; FCR rr 42.12, 42.13; ACT r 2501; Supreme Court Rules 1970 (NSW) Pt 55 r 7; NT r 75.06; Qld r 926(1), (3); Enforcement of Judgments Act 1991 (SA) s 12; SA r 301(3) (may be *ex parte*, but court may require notice be given); Tas r 942(1); Vic r 75.06; Civil Judgments Enforcement Act 2004 (WA) s 98; WA O 55 r 4. There is provision for issuing a warrant for a party's arrest, prior to hearing, by leave of the court if there is a danger that the respondent will abscond or leave the jurisdiction (or if the respondent has done so): HCR r 11.02; FCR r 42.14; ACT r 2503; Supreme Court Rules 1970 (NSW) Pt 55 r 10; NT r 75.08; Qld r 927; SA r 303(6); Tas r 942(4); Vic r 75.08 (see also r 75.08.1); WA O 55 r 6. The warrant is addressed to the sheriff or enforcement officer. There is then a hearing into whether the allegations have been made out.

21.12.6   If contempt is shown, there is provision for post-hearing incarceration. There is also provision for fining an offending party: HCR r 11.01.2(d) ('make whatever order … is just'); FCR r 41.08(1)(a), (2)(a) (no provision for fines); ACT r 2506(2) (make an order that may be made under the Crimes (Sentencing) Act 2005); Supreme Court Rules 1970 (NSW) Pt 55 r 13(1); NT r 75.11(1); Qld r 930(2)(a) (also allows orders under the Penalties and Sentences Act 1992 (Qld)); SA r 304(1); Tas r 942(9)(b); Vic r 75.11(1). Western Australia also makes provision for punishment by fine: O 55 r 7(1). The seizure of corporate property can be ordered against a corporation: FCR r 41.08(2)(b); ACT r 2506(3); Supreme Court Rules 1970 (NSW) Pt 55 r 13(2); NT r 75.11(2); Qld r 930(3); Vic r 75.11(2). Punishment may be on terms: ACT r 2507; NT r 75.12; Qld r 930(4); Tas r 942(11); Vic r 75.12; WA O 55 r 8. Costs are at the discretion of the court, whether or not an order for committal is made: NT r 75.14; Qld r 932; SA r 306(3) (but only if guilt is made out); Tas r 942(9)(d); Vic r 75.14; and see HCR r 11.02.2(d). This enables courts in most jurisdictions to deal with cases where they decide that while an applicant has not made out a case for contempt, the respondent's behaviour has been sufficiently reprehensible to justify requiring the respondent to pay the costs of the proceedings.

Sequestration/Seizure of property

21.12.7   Sequestration is a rather unusual sanction. It involves a party being excluded from access to its property. Sequestration orders are provided for, but only minimally regulated, by the following rules: FCR r 41.08(1)(b), (2)(b); ACT rr 2470–2471; Supreme Court Rules 1979 (NSW) Pt 55 r 13; NSW rr 40.3, 40.7; NT r 66.05; Civil Procedure Act 2011 (Qld) s 90(2)(f); Tas r 945; Vic r 66.05; WA O 55 r 7(3). The circumstances in which such an order may be made are largely determined by common law. They may be made only when the court is convinced beyond reasonable doubt that a party is in contempt. They may therefore not be used as a form of punishment where a party has discharged its contempt. Nor can they be made in cases where contempt is merely likely.

When a sequestration order is made, the court appoints people as sequestrators: at least one in the Northern Territory (r 76.03); the enforcement officer in Queensland (r 917); the sheriff in Tasmania (Form 79) and at least four persons in Victoria (r 76.03). They, or some of them, are authorised and required to take possession of the sequestratee's real and personal property. They collect the rents and profits and retain them until the sequestratee complies with the judgment order, or until the sequestration order otherwise comes to an end, whereupon the property and the proceeds are returned to the sequestratee.

In contrast to warrants of execution, sequestration permits possession only. The sequestrators acquire no right of disposal over the property. They may not therefore use it to discharge judgment debts. Indeed, they are required to exercise care in their management of the property. Failure to do so can render them liable to a negligence suit, notwithstanding that they are officers of the court. The issue of a writ of sequestration to enforce an order that money be paid into court does not therefore make the judgment creditor a secured creditor for the purposes of bankruptcy proceedings: *In re Pollard; Ex parte Pollard* [1903] 2 KB 41. For these reasons, sequestration would almost never be used in cases where a party is seeking to recover a judgment debt, even where it might be available. Its use would normally be confined to cases where a party is seeking to enforce an equitable order.

Sequestration orders appear to be extremely rare. A search of law reports discloses few examples of such orders, and while this may reflect the inability of those who are subject to such orders to finance litigation, this does not explain why sequestration orders have generated so much less litigation than other enforcement procedures. However, there are exceptional circumstances in which leave has been granted to issue a writ of sequestration.

21.12.8C   **Webster v Southwark London Borough Council**
[1983] 1 QB 696
Divisional Court

[Webster was a parliamentary candidate for the National Front. Under the United Kingdom electoral legislation, he had a right to require that a hall be made available to him in order to propagate his views. The defendant council refused to make one available. Webster sued. In accordance with normal practice, a declaratory order was made to the effect that Webster was entitled to have a hall made available to him. The council nonetheless still refused to make a hall available. On Saturday 23 October, Webster made an *ex parte* application to the judge, at his home, for committal of the mayor and two councillors.

This was refused on the grounds that motions for committal must be made in open court. That afternoon, Webster made a further application for leave to issue a writ of sequestration. This application was granted. This had its intended effect. Forbes J said (at 705):

I understand that in consequence the court tipstaff, who was one of the commissioners named in the writ, was able to ensure that the plaintiff held his election meeting in the Warwick Hall, although considerably later than the hour of 4 o'clock when the meeting was supposed to start.

Further hearing of the case was adjourned. The defendants were given leave to apply to discharge the writ on 27 October or earlier. At the resumed hearing, Webster indicated that he did not want to proceed with any motion to commit the three named councillors. The issues which remained were whether the court should nonetheless proceed to commit and whether leave should have been granted to issue the writ of sequestration.]

Forbes J (at 706, 709–10): I propose to examine first Mr Turner-Samuels's main submission that proceedings for contempt only lie where what has been done, or not done, is a breach of a coercive order of the court. Without going into the authorities — and Mr Turner-Samuels was good enough to remind me of several — I readily accept the proposition that where a court makes only a declaratory order it is not contempt for the party affected by the order to refuse to abide by it. If he does so refuse no doubt the other party can go back to the court and seek an injunction to enforce the order; but mere refusal of one party to an action to abide by a declaratory order is not, as I understand it, contempt of court.

[His Honour discussed a number of cases which held that even if a party was not in contempt, non-parties could be in contempt if they encouraged the party in its disobedience. However, he considered that these cases did not apply where a corporate entity was not in contempt and where those charged were the corporation's agents:]

[709] The cases to which Mr Turner-Samuels has drawn my attention in which leave to issue the writ has in fact been given or, for that matter, refused are all cases in which the order disobeyed has been a coercive one. In my view this is not conclusive of the matter because the court has, I apprehend, an inherent jurisdiction to enforce its orders where justice demands that those orders should be enforced.

I turn, accordingly, to the evidence in this case at the time at which leave to issue the writ was sought, namely, at around 2.30 pm on Saturday, October 23. That evidence disclosed this state of affairs:

(1) This local authority, although it must have been advised that its attitude was illegal, chose to adopt a policy which, to its knowledge, inevitably resulted in denying the plaintiff his rights under the Representation of the People Act 1949; in other words, it flatly refused to discharge a duty laid on it in the clearest possible terms by a statute and thus deliberately flouted the sovereign will of Parliament.

(2) When the existence of the duty was made clear to it by this court it continued, by its duly authorised representatives, to treat both Parliament and this court with contempt.

(3) There had been much press interest in the proceedings, and part of the evidence before the court was a further affidavit from the plaintiff which contained this passage:
> 8. At 4.15 of Friday, October 22, 1982, I was interviewed by a reporter of the Press Association and he told me that 'councillors had queued up in order to be jailed,' and had otherwise expressed their desire to resist the order granted to me by the Rt [sic] Hon Mr Justice Forbes. The Press Association reporter told me that the council, or councillors, he did not specify which, had issued a press statement expressing their support for the decision not to grant me a hall.

This is, of course, only information and belief, but nevertheless appeared creditworthy. It is perhaps worth noting that although I have had affidavits sworn subsequently from councillors and an officer of the local authority there has been no challenge to the accuracy of that information. From this information it appeared at any rate probable that if a coercive order — for instance, a mandatory injunction — had been sought and made at that time, [710] councillors would choose rather to defy it and take the consequences than to give to the plaintiff what Parliament had decreed he should have, namely, a hall to hold an election meeting.

(4) That election meeting had been advertised to start at 4 o'clock in the afternoon and no other such meeting was planned or possible, as the plaintiff has told me, before polling day. It was then 2.30pm. It follows, it seems to me, from this evidence, that unless the court acted at once in some way which would result in a hall actually being available, the wrong doers would have succeeded in their wholly unjustifiable aim of preventing this parliamentary candidate from holding an election meeting before polling day.

As I indicated earlier, the court has, in my view, an inherent jurisdiction to see that its orders are carried out where the interests of justice demand this. It was improbable that a coercive order would, at that stage, result in a hall being made available on the Saturday afternoon because councillors might be happy to don the martyr's crown on Monday, the first day on which committal proceedings could have been heard, secure in the knowledge that their illegal act had succeeded. Sending councillors to jail may be a salutary lesson to them that the court's orders are meant to be obeyed, but it does not actually produce obedience to the court's orders. Mr Turner-Samuels has correctly pointed out that all the cases about leave to issue this writ have proceeded on the basis that there existed a coercive order which had been disobeyed. I accept that. But I do not think that that disposes of the matter. The circumstances here were exceptional, if not unique. The intermediate step of making a coercive order and waiting for it to be disobeyed before giving leave was, in the circumstances, shown to be supererogatory because the response of the council was almost inevitable. The time was exceptionally short, through no fault of the plaintiff.

In those exceptional circumstances I think that the court cannot just stand by and confess that it is powerless. In my view leave to issue the writ of sequestration was properly sought and properly given. As it has fulfilled its purpose it should now be discharged.

21.12.9   Sequestration can also be ordered against an officer of a corporation in order to encourage compliance by a corporation with a judgment: ACT r 2472; NT r 66.05; NSW r 40.6(2)(c)(ii); Qld r 919; Tas r 876(3)(c)(ii); Vic r 66.05; Cairns, [325–10035], note 3.

ENFORCEMENT OF INTERSTATE JUDGMENTS

21.13.1   The Service and Execution of Process Act 1992 (Cth) provides a simple procedure for enforcing in one state or territory the judgment of a court in another.

21.13.2E   **Service and Execution of Process Act 1992 (Cth)**
PART 6 — JUDGMENTS

Interpretation
104 In this Part:
'court of rendition' means:
   (a) in relation to a judgment of a court, the court in which the judgment was given, entered or made; or
   (b) in relation to a judgment that is an order of a tribunal:
      (i) if the law of the State in which the tribunal is established provides that the order is enforceable without registration or filing of the order in a court — the tribunal; or
      (ii) in any other case — the court of that State in which the order is registered or filed;
'enforcement', in relation to a judgment, includes execution of the judgment;
'place of rendition', in relation to a judgment, means the State in which is established the court of rendition of the judgment;

'sealed copy', in relation to a judgment, includes a copy of the judgment that is certified as a true copy by:

(a)   if the court of rendition is a tribunal — a member of the tribunal; or

(b)   in any other case — a judge, magistrate or registrar of the court of rendition.

Enforcement of proceedings

105(1) Upon lodgment of a sealed copy of a judgment, or a fax of such a sealed copy, the prothonotary, registrar or other proper officer of the appropriate court in a State other than the place of rendition must register the judgment in the court.

(2)   Subject to subsection (4), a registered judgment:

(a)   has the same force and effect; and

(b)   subject to sections 106 and 108, may give rise to the same proceedings by way of enforcement;

as if the judgment had been given, entered or made by the court in which it is registered.

(3)   If the copy lodged is a fax, a sealed copy of the judgment is to be lodged with the prothonotary, registrar or other proper officer of the court within 7 days (not including any day that is a Saturday, a Sunday or a public holiday or bank holiday in the place at which the fax was lodged) after the fax was lodged.

(4)   If the sealed copy of the judgment is not so lodged within the 7 day period, until the sealed copy is lodged with the prothonotary, registrar or other proper officer of the court, a proceeding to enforce the judgment is not to be commenced or continued without the leave of the court.

(5)   A judgment is capable of being enforced in or by a court of a State in which it is registered only if, and to the extent that, at the time when the proceeding for enforcement is or is to be taken, the judgment is capable of being enforced in or by:

(a)   the court of rendition; or

(b)   a court in the place of rendition.

(6)   In this section:

'appropriate court', in relation to a State other than the place of rendition of a judgment, means:

(a)   if the court of rendition is the Supreme Court of the place of rendition — the Supreme Court of the firstmentioned State; or

(b)   in any other case:

(i)   the court of the firstmentioned State (including, if applicable, the Supreme Court of that State) in or by which relief as given by the judgment could have been given; or

(ii)   if there is more than one such court — the court of more limited jurisdiction; or

(iii) if there is no such court — the Supreme Court of the firstmentioned State.

Stay may be granted

106(1) A court of a State in which a judgment has been registered under subsection 105(1) may, on application by a person against whom the judgment has been given, entered or made, order that proceedings in that court by way of enforcement of the judgment:

(a)   not be commenced until a specified time; or

(b)   be stayed for a specified period.

  (2) The order:

      (a) must be made subject to conditions that:

          (i) within the period specified in the order, the person make and prosecute an appropriate application for relief in respect of the judgment; and

          (ii) the application be prosecuted in an expeditious manner; and

      (b) may be made subject to such other conditions, including conditions as to the giving of security, as the court thinks fit.

  (3) For the purposes of paragraph (2)(a), an appropriate application for relief is an application to set aside, vary or appeal against the judgment, being an application made to a court or tribunal that has jurisdiction under the law in force in the place of rendition to grant the application.

Costs

107(1) The following are recoverable in proceedings by way of enforcement of a judgment that is registered under subsection 105(1):

      (a) the reasonable costs and expenses of, and incidental to, obtaining and lodging the copy of the judgment; and

      (b) the costs and expenses reasonably incurred in attempting to execute the judgment in the court of rendition or in another State.

  (2) The entitlement of a person to, and the liability of a person for, the costs or expenses of and incidental to such proceedings are the same as they are in proceedings by way of enforcement of:

      (a) a similar judgment given, entered or made by the court in which the judgment is registered under subsection 105(1); or

      (b) if there is no such similar judgment — the most closely analogous judgment given, entered or made by that court.

Interest

108 Interest on the amount of a judgment that is registered under subsection 105(1):

      (a) is payable at the same rate or rates and in respect of the same period or periods as would be applicable in the court of rendition; and

      (b) is recoverable to the extent that the judgment creditor satisfies the court in which proceedings by way of enforcement of the judgment are taken as to the amount of the interest.

Rules of private international law not to apply

109 If a judgment is registered in a court of a State under subsection 105(1), the courts of the State must not, merely because of the operation of a rule of private international law, refuse to permit proceedings by way of enforcement of the judgment to be taken or continued.

ENFORCEMENT OF JUDGMENTS OUTSIDE AUSTRALIA

21.14.1   In certain circumstances, Australian judgments can be enforced in other countries. Until 1991, foreign judgments were enforceable under state legislation and Rules of Court. They are now the subject of Commonwealth legislation, the Foreign Judgments Act 1991 (Cth). In some jurisdictions, this legislation is supplemented by Rules of Court.

Broadly, foreign judgments are enforceable under this legislation on the basis of reciprocity; that is, Australian courts enforce judgments which will be enforced in similar terms by the relevant foreign courts. This principle is made operational by provisions that if the Governor-General is satisfied that the relevant foreign courts afford substantial reciprocity to Australian judgments, regulations may provide that Pt 2 of the Act applies to those judgments. Regulations may so specify in connection with three classes of judgments: money judgments given in superior courts; money judgments given in inferior courts; and non-money judgments. To be enforceable, money judgments must be final and conclusive, but may be under or subject to appeal: s 5.

The regulations have steadily increased the number of countries whose courts have been prescribed under the Act (Foreign Judgments Regulations), starting with New Zealand (SR 1992 No 321), followed by a host of British Commonwealth courts, along with those of France, Germany, Israel, Italy and Japan (SR 1993 No 143); United Kingdom inferior courts (SR 1994 No 283); more British Commonwealth courts (SR 1995 No 35); Manitoba Provincial Courts; Swiss and Taiwanese superior and inferior courts (SR 1996 No 145); Hong Kong superior courts (SR 1997 No 205); Polish superior and inferior courts (SR 1998 No 16) and Korean courts (SR 1999 No 334). Notable omissions include the United States and its states; most Canadian jurisdictions (including Ontario and Quebec); Scandinavia; Indonesia; and mainland Asia (other than the Republic of Korea). There have been no regulations enabling the enforcement of non-money foreign judgments.

Judgment creditors wishing to enforce foreign judgments may apply within the usual six years to have a judgment registered in an 'appropriate court'. Broadly, superior courts are 'appropriate courts', except in relation to non-money judgments, which are registrable only in the Federal Court. The order must specify a period during which the judgment debtor may apply to have the registration set aside. If no application is made to have the registration set aside, the judgment can be generally enforced as if it were a judgment of the court in which it is registered. If an application to set aside has been made, enforcement must await dismissal of the application.

Applications to have a registration set aside may be based both on a number of grounds. A registration must be set aside if it relates to a judgment:

(a) made by a court which lacked jurisdiction to make it (s 7(2)(a)(iv)), the criteria for jurisdiction being the criteria set out in s 7(3)–(5) of the Act (rather than the relevant laws of the original forum);

(b) which has been set aside or reversed on appeal: s 7(2)(a)(vii);

(c) if the party against whom enforcement is sought had not been given notice of the relevant trial: s 7(2)(a)(v); or

(d) obtained by fraud: s 7(2)(a)(vi).

Registration must also be set aside if:

(a) enforcement of the judgment would be contrary to public policy: s 7(2)(a)(xi);

(b) rights under the judgment were not vested in the person applying for registration: s 7(2)(a)(viii);

(c) the judgment has been discharged or wholly satisfied: s 7(2)(a)(ix), (x); or

(d) there are irregularities in the registration, such as registration for a sum at variance with the original judgment; registration of a judgment to which Pt 2 does not apply; or registration otherwise in contravention of the Act (s 7(2)(a)(i)–(iii)). Judgments not enforceable in the country of judgment may not be registered: s 6(6).

Enforcement may also be stayed pending appeal in the foreign forum: s 8(1). A stay of enforcement may be subject to conditions including expeditious prosecution of the appeal and the giving of security for costs.

Judgments to which Pt 2 applies are enforceable only by proceedings by way of registration. They are, however, conclusive as between the parties in all proceedings founded on the same cause of action and may be relied upon by way of defence or counterclaim, except when registration has been (or would be) set aside on the grounds of lack of jurisdiction, denial of procedural fairness, fraud or public policy: s 12.

In times of currency fluctuations, one obvious issue in relation to the enforcement of judgments is how a foreign currency award is to be treated by local courts. The Act allows the judgment creditor to opt for registration of an amount expressed in foreign currency units. Otherwise, the amount is to be converted to Australian dollars at the rate prevailing on the day of the application: s 6(11).

21.14.2   Questions

1. In many ways these criteria are similar to those which bear on the validity and enforceability of judgments of local inferior courts. However, there are some differences: what are they?

2. The judgment creditor's right to choose the currency in terms of which the judgment is to be registered creates the possibility of windfall profits if (improbably) the foreign currency is depreciating against the Australian dollar. Is this fair? What could a judgment debtor do to minimise the adverse effects of their exposure to currency fluctuations?

Other foreign judgments

21.14.3   Judgments to which Pt 2 does not apply may be enforced at common law. However, a condition for this is that the foreign court had jurisdiction. Section 11 of the Act provides that a court is not to be taken as having had jurisdiction if the judgment debtor appeared or participated merely to:

(a) protect property seized, threatened with seizure, or under restraint;

(b) contest a court's jurisdiction; or

(c) invite a court not to exercise its jurisdiction in the proceedings.

The common law treats foreign money judgments as giving rise to a debt which can be sued on as if it were a simple contract debt: *Newland v Horseman* (1681) 1 Vern 21; 23 ER 275. Alternatively a new action can be brought, based on the original cause of action. In the subsequent litigation, parties are treated as estopped from asserting facts inconsistent with the foreign judgment. Commentators have noted the contradiction underlying this procedure. The new action can be brought only because the foreign judgment is not recognised, while estoppel is based on the fact that it is. Foreign judgments can also be raised as a defence, or as the basis for a counterclaim, again on the basis of estoppel. Nevertheless, common law claims can be met with a variety of defences, of which the most obvious is that the foreign judgment has already been satisfied. They can also be met by objections based on lack of jurisdiction, denial of natural justice, fraud and public policy.

In many ways, then, the Foreign Judgments Act 1991 (Cth) can be seen as a codification of the common law. It should be noted that the Commonwealth legislation clarifies the lack of jurisdiction defence, and narrows the scope of the 'natural justice' defence.

21.14.4 Notes and questions

1. See generally: P E Nygh, *Conflict of Laws in Australia*, 8th ed, LexisNexis Butterworths, Sydney, 2010, Ch 9. Articles on the enforcement of foreign judgments must be read in the light of legislative changes. However, older articles continue to be of value as analyses of the common law: for example, P Brereton, 'Refusing to Enforce Foreign Judgments on the Grounds of Fraud' (1993) 10 *Aust Bar Rev* 224 (where Brereton argues that the 'fraud defence' in relation to foreign judgments is broader than that applied in relation to the setting aside of local judgments); D J Fine, 'Defences against Recognition or Enforcement of Foreign Judgments' (1987) 61 *ALJ* 329 (a comprehensive but slightly dated general review).

2. In what cases might a Pt 2 foreign court's judgment be recognised notwithstanding that it had denied procedural fairness to the judgment debtor?

3. Under current Australian law, foreign non-monetary judgments are generally unenforceable by Australian courts. What are the rationales for limiting enforcement to monetary judgments? Should Australian courts be willing to enforce foreign non-money judgments? If the latter, are there any restrictions that should be imposed on their doing so, and what should they be? See K Pham, 'Enforcement of Non-Monetary Foreign Judgments in Australia' (2008) 30 *Syd LR* 663.

Enforceability of Australian judgments abroad

21.14.5 Implicit in the Foreign Judgments Act 1991 (Cth) and the regulations made under it is the enforceability of Australian judgments, in particular foreign courts, although presumably there will be cases where the Governor-General's satisfaction will turn out to be unfounded. Moreover, even when a jurisdiction is not a Pt 2 jurisdiction, its law may make provision for the enforcement of foreign judgments. There are, for example, important common law jurisdictions which have not been nominated in the regulations.

To assist foreign enforcement, s 15 provides that where a judgment creditor wishes to enforce an Australian judgment, the registrar of the court must issue a certified copy of the judgment, along with a certificate containing details of the causes of action to which the judgment relates, and the interest rate applicable to amounts payable under the judgment. For an example of the issues involved in foreign enforcement of Australian judgments see J Rosengarten, 'Recognition and Enforcement of Foreign Judgments in Germany: Acting for Australian Clients against German Defendants' (1992) 20 *Aust Bus L Rev* 230. This is also of interest for the light it throws on how other systems handle the problem of foreign judgments.

BANKRUPTCY AND WINDING-UP

21.15.1 In dealing with a recalcitrant judgment debtor, bankruptcy or its corporate equivalent, winding-up is always a possibility. These procedures present both opportunities and threats. Judgment creditors may use the threat of bankruptcy or winding-up to encourage debtors to disgorge. Service of a bankruptcy notice on the debtor means that he or she must pay the debt within 14 days. Failure to do so constitutes an 'act of bankruptcy' which entitles the creditor to take a second step, the presentation of a bankruptcy petition. If the debtor is then declared bankrupt, a trustee is appointed to realise the bankrupt's assets.

However, this may not avail the creditor. After the deduction of expenses to cover the petition and the trustee's administrative expenses, the remaining assets (if any) are distributed on a pro-rata basis among all those who can prove debts owing to them. The fruits may be better than nothing, but, if the bankrupt's economic position had been improving, it might prove a rather unsatisfactory outcome.

Bankruptcy also affects whether execution is possible and whether the fruits of recent, successful execution can continue to be enjoyed. Once notice is given to a sheriff of the presentation of a creditor's petition, he or she may not sell the debtor's property or attach the debtor's debts. Nor may sheriffs pay any proceeds of a sale or attachment to the creditor, pending the court's hearing of the petition: Bankruptcy Act 1966 (Cth) s 119(1), (2). Nor may any court officer pay to the creditor the proceeds of any sale or attachment which have been paid into court: s 119(4), (5). Creditors who have enjoyed the fruits of execution may also be in difficulty if they have received those fruits six months or less before the presentation of the petition.

If so, and if the debtor subsequently becomes bankrupt, they must repay the money received to the trustee in bankruptcy: s 118(1), (2). In the subsequent distribution, they are unlikely to recover much of it.

21.15.2   Question

1. In what circumstances might such a creditor be: (a) no worse off; or (b) better off, following a debtor's bankruptcy? How would bankruptcy affect a successful plaintiff's ability to enforce a judgment for possession of land?

21.15.3 Similar provisions apply in relation to the winding-up of an insolvent corporation. Once a judgment creditor has notice of a proposed winding-up resolution, its enforcement rights are frozen. Notice to the sheriff freezes the sheriff's power to sell corporate property. Proceeds held but not distributed must be paid to the liquidator: Corporations Act 2001 (Cth) s 570. Once a winding-up resolution has been passed, or once winding-up has been commenced by court order, enforcement proceedings become void: ss 468(4), 500. Execution creditors who recovered money within six months of the start of the winding-up must account for it to the liquidator, but costs of enforcement may be deducted from the amount to be reimbursed: s 569.

Further reading

21.16.1   Looseleaf

Halsbury's Laws of Australia, LexisNexis, Sydney, vol 20, Ch VII.

Laws of Australia, Thomson Reuters, Sydney, vol 5, s 5.7, Ch 3.

21.16.2   Texts

B C Cairns, *Australian Civil Procedure*, 9th ed, Thomson Reuters, Sydney, 2011, Ch 18.

P E Nygh and M Davies, *Conflict of Laws in Australia*, 7th ed, Butterworths, Sydney, 2002, Pt III.

Index

References are to paragraph numbers
Extracts are in bold

C

U

Undertakings by solicitors *see* **Solicitors**

Unincorporated associations
service on 8.4.9

Unrepresented litigants
costs **20.2.2C**, 20.2.3

V

Verdicts
arbitrator's awards as 18.6.1, 18.6.11
judgment inconsistent with 18.7.7–18.7.9
jury verdicts 17.6.6, 18.6.1, 18.6.2
    finality 18.6.7–**18.6.10C**
    special or general 18.6.2–**18.6.5C**
move for judgment 18.7.3, **18.7.4C,**
    18.7.6C
no evidence to support 18.7.7–18.7.9

Vexatious litigants
declaration of 12.8.4
    legal principles **12.8.5C**–12.8.7
definition 12.8.1
guidelines for determining 12.8.7
High Court **12.8.2E**
power to restrain 12.8.3
summary judgment **12.1.1E, 12.6.2E**

Vexatious pleadings
striking out **11.8.1E**, 11.8.2, 11.8.8,
    12.1.1E
    no reasonable cause of action
        .... 11.8.4–**11.8.6C**

Victoria
alternative dispute resolution 3.9.19
    referral of case to 2.4.22
amendment to add statute-barred claims
    .... **5.2.15E**, 5.2.16
associate judges 16.1.1
attachment of earnings 21.8.13
case management 2.4.13
costs, scale of **20.7.2E**
disclosure of documents 13.1.2, 13.1.3
    exempted documents 13.1.25
    non-parties **13.2.8E**
    oral discovery 13.3.14, 13.4.1
    particular discovery 13.1.36, **13.1.37E**
    relevance test 13.1.24
expert evidence disclosure 14.3.9
inspection and testing of property **14.1.2E,**
    14.1.4
interrogatories **13.3.2E**, 13.3.3
    sources for answers to 13.3.10, **13.3.11E**
joinder of parties **10.4.3E**
judicial resolution conference 2.4.22
ordinary service **8.3.2E**

originating process 7.4.4, 7.6.1
overarching obligations certification 7.4.9,
    7.4.10E
overriding purpose clause 2.5.5
particulars **11.7.1E**
    inadequate **11.7.11E**
    personal injuries **11.7.13E**, 14.2.12
personal injuries proceedings
    medical examinations **14.2.1E**
    particulars **11.7.13E**, 14.2.12
pleadings
    content **11.2.2E**
    defence **11.5.1E**
    formal requirements **11.2.20E**
    particulars **11.7.1E**
pre-action protocols 7.2.5
proper basis certification 7.4.9, **7.4.10E**
security for costs **16.7.2E**
setting down for trial 18.2.9
specialist lists 2.4.13
statement of claim **11.4.1E**, 11.4.2
    general relief **11.4.15E**
Supreme Court jurisdiction 4.1.25
    cross-vesting *see* **Cross-vesting of**
        jurisdiction
trial by affidavit 15.15.1
unconditional appearance, form **9.7.3E**
vexatious litigants **12.8.5C**, 12.8.6
warrant of seizure and sale **21.7.16E**

W

Waiver
appearance 9.11.2, 9.11.3
    unconditional, waiving irregularities 9.7.6
privilege 13.5.31, 13.5.32

Want of prosecution
appeal 19.12.1
dismissal of proceedings 5.3.1–5.3.6
    case management and 5.3.5
    criteria for 5.3.4, 5.3.5
    inherent jurisdiction, under 5.3.2, 5.3.3
    rules of court, under 5.3.4
    setting aside order for 5.3.6

Warrant of execution *see* **Writs/warrants of**
execution; Writs/warrants of seizure
and sale

Western Australia
alternative dispute resolution 3.9.20
amendment to add statute-barred claims
    .... 5.2.18
attachment of earnings 21.8.13
case management 2.4.6
consolidation of proceedings **10.8.2E**
default judgments **12.2.3E**